THE BRITISH OVERSEAS

THE
BRITISH OVERSEAS

Exploits of a Nation of Shopkeepers

BY

C. E. CARRINGTON, M.A.

The fault of our going was our own. What could
be thought fitting or necessary we had; but what we
should find or want we were all ignorant.
Such actions have ever since the World's beginning
been subject to accidents, and everything of worth is
found full of difficulties; but nothing so difficult as
to establish a Commonwealth so far remote from
men and means.
But to proceed... CAPTAIN JOHN SMITH

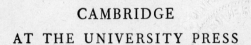
CAMBRIDGE
AT THE UNIVERSITY PRESS
1950

PUBLISHED BY
THE SYNDICS OF THE CAMBRIDGE UNIVERSITY PRESS

London Office: Bentley House, N.W. 1
American Branch: New York

Agents for Canada, India, and Pakistan: Macmillan

Printed in Great Britain at the University Press, Cambridge
(Brooke Crutchley, University Printer)

CONTENTS

CONTENTS

LIST OF ILLUSTRATIONS

PORTRAITS

Acknowledgements

Nos. 4 (a) and (b), 10, 16, 29 (a), 29 (b), 30 (a) and (b) are reproduced by courtesy of *Picture Post Library*; No. 3 by courtesy of the Walker Gallery, Baltimore, U.S.A.; Nos. 5 (a) and (b), 6 (a) and (b), 8, 9, 11, 17, 18, 19, 20 (a) and (b), 21, 22, 23, 24, 25, 27 (a) and (b), 28, and 32 by courtesy of the National Portrait Gallery; No. 12 (b) by courtesy of Australia House; No. 15 by courtesy of the Canterbury Museum, New Zealand; Nos. 24 (a) and (b), and 26 by courtesy of Messrs Elliott and Fry; No. 7 by courtesy of the National Maritime Museum.

MAPS

COLOURED MAPS

GRAPHS

PREFACE

TEN generations ago, in the age of Shakespeare and Ralegh, these small islands were inhabited by six or seven millions of people whom we may loosely call the British race. For the most part they were rustic, though they were showing signs of a change from a life of agriculture to a life of commerce. In the course of this change which transformed them, for a time, into the richest and strongest community (or rather group of communities) in history, two phenomena may be observed, each of them unique, so far as our meagre records show. In the first place the British, with whom for brevity of reference I include the Irish, increased in numbers from something less than 7,000,000 to something more than 140,000,000, a rate of multiplication unequalled by any other nation in Europe or Asia. In the second place the majority of the British race have abandoned the British Isles and made their homes elsewhere, a *diaspora* which in its effect upon the progress of mankind can be compared only with the Dispersion of the Jews.

It is hardly an exaggeration to say that the British have populated every temperate region in the whole world which was empty when their period of expansion began, if I may be allowed to describe as temperate every region having a climate like that of north-western Europe. In three instances only did the other colonising nations establish themselves in temperate regions, and all three settlements, French Acadie, Dutch Manhattan, and Dutch South Africa, were brought under British control. Elsewhere the expansion of France, Spain, Portugal, Holland, Belgium, and even of Russia has been into sub-arctic or sub-tropical lands. Even in the Argentine, if that is another exception, the development was largely due to British pioneers and British money. Much of the interest of early imperial history lies in the determination of the climatic frontier which limits white man's country; much of the history of the last fifty years depends upon the dietary and hygienic discoveries which have enabled the men from temperate climes to subdue the Arctic and the tropics.

Beyond the limits of white man's country the pioneers have usually found other races in possession. There the British, like the other imperial nations, have founded an empire of influence not of settlement. The one by its nature is temporary, the other permanent, though the distinction has often been overlooked. Hundreds of years hence, if the world endures, India will still retain traces of British influence in her law and philosophy, long after the British rulers have departed, as England still retains traces of Roman rule. But in Asia imperialism is in full retreat. Though there the white man is laying down his burden, it cannot be laid down in Australia, or in the United States, where it is the burden of life. Nor would the descendants of the pioneers be any less the British race overseas, if the inhabitants of the United Kingdom were caught up into the air by an atom-bomb in the twinkling of an eye.

The long process of British expansion has completed itself in ten generations. Between the two German Wars the Dominions reached maturity; the decision was taken to withdraw from Egypt and India; the new colonial policy based upon the significant word 'trusteeship'—a temporary relation—took shape. But these were the external signs of a far more fundamental change; the British race had ceased to expand. In the year of the Statute of Westminster (1931) the inward migration from the Dominions to Great Britain exceeded the outward migration towards them. Though there may be a redistribution of population between the different parts of the Commonwealth it does not seem possible that the expansion of England can be renewed within our time. The phase is ended and its history can now be written. I do not however imply that the mission of the British is concluded nor infer that the race is decadent. The next stage in their development will be qualitative, not quantitative. I believe that the nations of the Commonwealth, whatever their political future, will retain their moral unity and may retain the moral leadership of the world.

The permanent settlements of the British in the empty lands of the temperate zone have been the principal objects of my attention. To them I give a larger share of space than has been usual in books about the Empire. Such interesting topics as the histories of French Canada, Dutch South Africa, and Moslem India are subsidiary to my theme; my concern is with the British overseas, with pioneers and emigrants. Why and where did they go, and how did they behave in their new environment? It is sometimes said that the British acquired their Empire in a fit of absence of mind; but without justification. Much hard thinking and bold planning went into the making of the Empire, but it was done by men at the circumference, not by men at the centre. The impetus rarely came from Whitehall. It has been my task to search elsewhere for the motive force of Empire.

My original intention was to conclude the book at the Statute of Westminster and the Ottawa Agreements, which marked a complete period. The rapidity of political change in Asia has, however, obliged me to take cognisance of some later events, especially of the year 1947 which was so critical for the British Empire. Yet, generally speaking, I have drawn to a close in the 1930's and have used, mostly, statistics from the reference books for 1939. No account is attempted of the second World War.

The limits I have set myself forbade me to discuss adequately one theme which a comprehensive view of the Empire should have included; I mean the history of Ireland. Many crises in colonial affairs might have been elucidated by reference to the age-long struggle between the English and Irish nations; every stage in the constitutional progress of the Dominions had its counterpart in the Irish agitation for home rule; every wave of migration has ebbed or flowed on Erin's shore. But I must not digress further here upon a topic which I have touched upon but lightly in the body of my book.

It is not false modesty that prompts me to apologise for my deficiencies nor do I delude myself with the fancy that I can disarm the critics by appealing to their clemency. No one life is long enough to master the history of the British Empire in all its complexity and diversity. I rarely open a newspaper without noting some imperial problem that I ought to be better acquainted with, and never glance at a bibliography without marking down a standard work that I ought to have read. Few and small are the plots in this vast field of research that I have cultivated intensively. I must express my obligation to the *Cambridge History of the British Empire*, and especially its bibliographies, which I recommend to those who wish to check my references or study the topics I have touched upon. I have quoted references only when I owe a special debt to an individual author.

Foreign names are spelt in the way I thought most familiar to English readers, without submission to pseudo-scientific systems.

May I add that I should not have undertaken this task if I had not the good fortune to be born into one of those middle-class families whose members, for a hundred years, have moved freely about the Empire. An uncle or cousin in every Dominion is a great help to thinking imperially. I would particularly acknowledge the advice of my brothers, the Most Rev. Dr Philip Carrington, Archbishop of Quebec, and the late Major A. H. Carrington, the biographer of Captain Cook. A painting in water-colour by my wife (to whom I am also obliged for help with maps and diagrams) is reproduced on the jacket.

After the obligation to my family I acknowledge a debt to the Universities Bureau of the British Empire for enabling me, many years ago, to carry out some researches in Australia and New Zealand; to the Syndics of the Cambridge University Press for allowing me to draw upon the resources of the *Cambridge History of the British Empire*, and for providing me with the opportunity of travelling through several Dominions and colonies on their behalf; to my colleagues at the Cambridge University Press for their patience with a troublesome author; and to the following ladies and gentlemen who have helped me with information upon particular points. They are not, however, to be held responsible for my allegations or my opinions:

The Master of St John's College, Cambridge; Mr H. L. Beales; Mrs V. M. Beales; Miss K. Carrington; Mr H. J. Habakkuk; Mr E. H. Hallett (of the United Africa Company); Mr G. F. James; Dr E. D. Laborde; the Rev. D. B. MacGregor; Professor W. P. Morrell; Mr G. C. Morris; Dr C. N. Parkinson; Mr George Bernard Shaw; Dr W. L. Sperry; Dr R. E. P. Wastell; Professor E. A. Walker; Major R. M. Wood; the Librarian of the Royal Empire Society; and the staff of the University of London Library. I must also mention here the late Sir John Clapham and the late Mr Philip Guedalla.

For permission to quote from Professor Hancock's *Survey of British Commonwealth Affairs* and from J. A. Hobson's *Imperialism*, I am obliged to the Oxford University Press and to Messrs George Allen & Unwin respectively. For permission to use graphs from their journal I am obliged to the Royal Statistical Society.

C. E. C.

November 1949

'I DIRECT YOUR ATTENTION TO AFRICA'

(DAVID LIVINGSTONE, *in the Senate-house at Cambridge, 4 December 1857*)

Senate-house and crowded street
Ring, as Cambridge honours still
The grey old men whom young men greet
In crowds that press from Market Hill.
Old tardy Time, on King's Parade
Lurks in wait to kidnap youth;
There I too must ply my trade,
Sift his hour-glass sand for truth.

Turn the glass till the dark sands
Of ninety winters fall away,
Raise an old ghost. There he stands!
Crying, 'Look to Africa!'
Dream the old Scotch doctor's dream,
Hear the very words he spoke,
Where Zambesi's shining stream
Slips into the sounding smoke.

See again great Lambton ride
In state by Québec's cobbled steep,
Receive the word he spoke with pride,
'The North and West your future keep.'
Or watch (where Selkirk sowed a seed)
Wraiths of pioneers who pass,
Their bones bleached like tumble-weed
That flits along the prairie grass.

Wakefield, on your windy hill,
You rest beneath the southern pole,
Your saplings grow, and thus you still
Work i' the earth so fast, old mole.
Not so blind but you foresaw
Fruits the southern soil would nourish,
Where, beneath a kindly law,
Cities rise and farmlands flourish.

Farewell! The tree-trunks, pale and stripped,
The sparkling distance, silver-blue,
The parrots in the eucalypt
Above the city avenue!
They fade in sandy Leeuwin's haze
The southern landskip wheels away
Till, with the turning globe, my gaze
Dispels an age, restores to-day,

Where Senate-house and crowded street
Ring with Cambridge honours paid
To old men coming out to meet
The young men's cheers on King's Parade.
Tell me, Time, does youth no less
Respond with hope? Or calls in vain
A voice out of the wilderness:
'To Africa, look, look again'?

C. E. C.

December 1947

I

EARLY VENTURES OVERSEAS

Argument: Little is known of the earliest English voyages. Certainly in the fifteenth century and increasingly after the Reformation, English merchant-venturers visited the Atlantic Islands and West Africa, sometimes with the connivance of the Spanish and Portuguese, sometimes in spite of their hostility. Before 1583 the Newfoundland fisheries were frequented and regulated by customary law.

Settlement in North America was promoted by a group of political theorists who stimulated religious and philanthropic bodies to plant many systematic colonies between 1607 and 1733. Their record in treatment of the Indians shows an improvement throughout the period. The earlier ideological struggle of Dutch and English against the Spanish monopoly ended at the Treaty of Utrecht which virtually admitted the principle of spheres of influence in the New World. It left England supreme at sea on both sides of the North Atlantic.

1. INTRODUCTORY

THE tale begins with the migration of certain tribes known somewhat indiscriminately as Saxons or Angles from Angeln in Germany to that part of the island of Britain which they renamed England. The cause and the method of this migration and the number of persons who migrated are quite unknown. All that we know is that the English first appear in history as a wandering and colonising race. They had to fight hard for their foothold for more than three hundred years before driving away or subduing the native Britons and fixing the English as opposed to the British frontier. With their backs to the sea they had become and remained for many centuries a race of land-lubbers. We know no reason for the change. They were now woodmen, ploughmen, swineherds, shepherds; they cleared the forests, drained the fens, multiplied and replenished the land until, a thousand years after the first migration from Angeln to England, there was a stirring in the hearts of the English who turned again to the sea and before long were sending out their sons to found another New England, and after that many more.

During the thousand sedentary years, two new strains of blood were crossed with the Anglo-Saxons. First the Norsemen, a nation of sea-traders and buccaneers, invaded and overran England. It is perhaps not fanciful to ascribe to them the emergence of a taste for commerce. Then came the Normans who damped down national patriotism for some generations, but brought to England the spirit of chivalry. Though Knight-errantry and Crusading were an outlet for the adventure-seekers, the English were still land-bound. Their exploits at first hardly carried them farther than the opposite shores of the English and the Irish Channels. There were raids and conquests, and feudal lordships won and lost in Scotland, Ireland, Wales and France; there was between the eleventh and the sixteenth centuries only one clear example of permanent English colonisation, the planting of 'Little England' among the Welsh of Pembrokeshire.

In Tudor times there was much talk of Empire, but of Empire in a sense quite different from that which fascinated Disraeli in the reign of Queen Victoria. The Statute of Appeals, by which the Parliament of England threw off the jurisdiction of the Pope, began with a magniloquent declaration in the preamble that this realm of England is an Empire and is so described in 'divers sundry old authentic histories and chronicles'. But in that context, and when Milton wrote, a hundred years later, of 'this Britannick Empire with all her daughter-islands about her' the English were not thinking of the Dominion over palm and pine that later imperialists applauded; their eye was fixed upon the large island Britain, with its satellites, Ireland, the Hebrides, Jersey, Man and the others. According to the mythical histories of King Arthur, which in Elizabethan England were accepted as true, the British Isles had successfully asserted their independence of Rome and formed an imperial realm, a thousand years before King Henry VIII. Remote as the fictions of Geoffrey of Monmouth may seem to be from modern colonial expansion, they have this nominal connexion. To the Elizabethan adventurers the word Empire conveyed suggestions of Arthurian romance; to the constitutional lawyers it suggested the old relation of the Crown to the Estates of Jersey, to the dependent kingdom of Man, and to the Dominion of Ireland. It is this that should be called the First British Empire; the American colonies came second, when feudal gave way to commercial expansion.

England slowly became an exporting country, her staple product being wool. For this the first of English trading companies, the Merchants of the Staple, set up a depot at Calais. Later a rival company, the Merchant Adventurers, established themselves at Bruges and Antwerp. There was, so long as victories over the French allowed, an import trade from Bordeaux which made claret, for a time, as cheap as beer in England; but a more profitable import was fish. The English sailors were not yet as active as the Portuguese, the Normans, or the Biscainers, and for long their progress was less than that of the Dutch, but the English fisheries had begun in the North Sea and occasionally had reached as far as Iceland. This industry came to be regarded as the nursery of English naval power and the school of navigation. Other foreign trade was chiefly in the hands of German and Italian shippers.

Small as these English undertakings were, there is other evidence that the English had a taste for voyaging. When spring returned, wrote Chaucer:

> Then priketh them nature in hir corages
> Then longen folk to goon on pilgrimages
> And palmers for to seken strangë strandës
> And fernë halwes couth in sondry landës.

The knight in Chaucer's day might go to Prussia and to Tunis, the Squire to 'chivachye' in Artois and in Flanders, the shipman to Spain; nor was the wife of Bath the only one who had 'passëd many a strangë stream' on the tourists' road to the Holy Land.

2. EARLY ENGLISH VOYAGES

CHAUCER'S Dartmouth skipper knew all the 'creeks from Brittany to Spain', the natural direction of west-country commerce in the Middle Ages. The old alliances between the English and the Christian principalities of Portugal and Castile were long-established when John of Gaunt renewed them in Chaucer's day. English knights had fought in the twelfth-century crusades against the Moors and had assisted at the birth of the Portuguese kingdom. History records no time when English seamen did not frequent their seaports. Among the petty kingdoms of the Iberian Peninsula, as the Moors were driven southwards, Castile predominated, except over Portugal, which retained its independence with English help. John of Gaunt had interests in both camps; but, having designs of his own upon the Castilian throne, he led an army of English archers to help the Portuguese against the reigning king of Castile. He negotiated the Anglo-Portuguese Treaty of Windsor (1386), so often renewed and still, after 563 years, effective. Sturdy Portugal was England's ally, but diplomatic and commercial links with Castile were also strong. During the Age of Exploration, English seamen were associated with their fellows of both nations, but, when Spain and Portugal fell out, aligned themselves with the Portuguese.

According to an unconfirmed though quite credible tradition, it was an Englishman, Robert Machin (or Macham) of Bristol, who made the first advance into the Atlantic. The story is not as familiar as it should be:

In the year 1344 [Hakluyt quotes from a Portuguese chronicle] the island of Madeira was discovered by an Englishman, which was named Macham, who, sailing out of England into Spain, with a woman that he had stolen, [Anne D'Arcy according to another version] arrived by tempest in that island, and did cast anchor in that haven or bay which now is called Machico, after the name of Macham. And because his lover was seasick, he went on land with some of his company, and the ship with a good wind made sail away, and the woman died for thought. Macham, who loved her dearly, built a chapel or hermitage to bury her in, calling it by the name of Jesus and caused his name and hers to be written or graven upon the stone of her tomb, and the occasion of their arrival there. And afterwards, he ordained a boat made of one tree (for there be trees of a great compass about) and went to sea in it, with those men that he had and were left behind with him, and came upon the coast of Afrika without sail or oar. And when the Moors which saw it took it to be a marvellous thing, and presented him unto the king of that country for a wonder, that king also sent him and his companions for a miracle unto the king of Castile. In the year 1395 . . . the information which Macham gave of this island . . . moved many of France and Castile, to go and discover it, and also the great Canaria.

Had the general outline of the African coast ever been quite unknown to medieval seamen? Probably not, since Levantine merchants dealt with Arabs whose commerce ran right down the east coast of Africa from the Gulf of Aden to Madagascar; and, on the west coast, followed the trade wind from Morocco down to Cape Verde. But the Atlantic islands, though known and described in antiquity and marked on Ptolemy's map, can only have received the most casual of visits from travellers; or so it

appears from the state of their inhabitants when rediscovered in
the fifteenth century. The 'Guanches' of the Canaries were an
aboriginal white race, tall, fair-haired and blue-eyed, still living
in palaeolithic simplicity as cave-dwellers, dressed in skins, with
stones as their only weapons. The name Canaria was given to
the principal island because of the great dogs which 'served the
islanders instead of sheep for victual'. Perhaps Horace was right
in declaring that Phoenician traders had never reached these
islands:

> non huc Sidonii torserunt cornua nautae,
> Laboriosa nec cohors Ulixei.

A voyage to so primitive a land reads like a chapter from
Herodotus, or like one of the Labours of Hercules, who was
indeed renowned for having reached these 'fortunate isles'.
Under that name, the crown of the Fortunate Isles was conferred
upon a Castilian prince (1360) by a grant from Pope Clement VI,
the source of all later Spanish claims and papal arbitrations upon
the dominion of the New World. Thirty years later a Norman
knight, with some legal pretension to administer this 'crown',
led an expedition to explore and subjugate the Canaries. His
right eventually lapsed to the kings of Castile, who intermittently sent expeditions to the islands during the fifteenth century.
These Spaniards, says Hakluyt, 'had divers English gentlemen in
their company whose posterity at present lives in the islands'.

The English also took part in the early Portuguese voyages.
'English merchantes and Almains' helped the Portuguese at the
siege of Ceuta in 1415, their first foothold in Africa and 'the first
occasion of all Portuguese discoveries'. The alliance was, in that
generation, firmly knit, its pledge being the great Prince Henry
the Navigator, the son of John of Gaunt's daughter. But, during
the systematic exploration of West Africa which he organised,
though French interlopers challenged and sometimes preceded
the Portuguese expeditions, we have no record of English intervention until the end of the period. In 1481 King John of Portugal
appealed to his good ally Edward IV to restrain his English
subjects from encroaching on the Portuguese 'seigneurie of
Guinea' where the strong castle of Sao Jorge al Mina (known to
the English as Elmina) had just been founded. Edward IV willingly agreed to put a stop to an expedition which William
Fabian and John Tintam were fitting out under Spanish patronage,

by an embargo which seems to have deterred Englishmen from other than clandestine trade with West Africa for two generations.

What part was taken by English mariners in the Discovery of the New World cannot be stated precisely, but it was not spectacular. The Bristol voyages to Labrador and Newfoundland originated in the North Atlantic fisheries of which no written record exists. As well as the Danes and Norwegians who voyaged to Iceland and beyond, the Bretons, Normans and Biscainers, English and Irish worked the deep-sea fisheries perhaps as far as the Newfoundland Banks without publishing their logs. They knew, and Columbus probably knew, the tale of Eric the Red, of the Danish settlements in Greenland still surviving in the fifteenth century, and of the voyages thence southward to a land where vines grew wild and the savages had copper-coloured skins. The Atlantic seaboard rang with similar stories of islands discovered in the west by Welsh princes, Irish monks and Norman adventurers long before the celebrated Spanish voyages. But the rough north-western seas revealed no Gold Coast, no Mexico or Peru, to tempt the cupidity of the kings of Europe as did the voyages south-westward from Portugal and Spain.

One series of early explorations cnly, that of John Cabot, has been recorded, and scantily. He was an Italian resident in Bristol whose ships made a landfall on some part of North America in 1497. Little more is known but that the parsimonious King Henry VII gave him a gratuity ('to him that found the new isle, £10') and retained him and his son Sebastian on a pension. Many years later at the court of Henry VIII, Sebastian Cabot was reputed an expert in geography and navigation and may have exaggerated his own youthful exploits. Further voyages from Bristol, from one of which, in 1502 some Indians were brought to England, led to no settlement in America, but originated the Newfoundland fisheries. John Rut in a king's ship, in 1527, found Normans, Bretons and Portuguese fishing for cod off the Newfoundland Banks. The French and Portuguese were deep-sea fishermen who brought home their catch packed in salt, but the English, who had no abundance of salt, preferred to fish off-shore and to preserve their fish by drying it on the beach. At some date unknown, seasonal fishermen's settlements appeared at St John's and other Newfoundland anchorages. By the end of Queen Elizabeth's reign there were reckoned to be engaged in the fisheries 9,000 seamen, the main force of the Royal Navy in time of war.

Trading ventures in those days were usually carried out by chartered companies of merchants, organised as guilds, that is to say trading associations, not financial companies. Within the guild each adventurer traded on his own account, investing his own goods, a great or small stock according to his means. If he had nothing better, Whittington the apprentice might even venture out his cat.[1] The Crown, for a consideration, extended its protection to the guildsmen, endowing them with a monopoly and the right to exclude interlopers. The guildsmen made their own conditions of trade. The system, with variations, was world-wide. In all countries within and without Christendom merchants endeavoured to obtain, from the rulers of foreign countries to which they traded, 'capitulations', that is the right to establish depots in which their resident agents enjoyed self-government under their own laws. The capitulation often included the right to raise a guard of soldiers for the defence of the settlement. The system was very ancient, having its origin in Roman law; it had been common throughout the history of Islam; it was still flourishing in many parts of the world in the twentieth century, and relics still survive here and there. The British Capitulations in China were relinquished only in 1943. At the period of the exploration of the New World several companies of Merchant Adventurers traded from English ports in this way, and new ventures tended to take this form. In 1530, King Henry VIII chartered the English merchants in Spain, long-established family firms like the Thornes of Bristol and the Hawkinses of Plymouth, who had resident agents not only in Spain but in the Canaries and at least one, a certain T. Tison, in the Spanish West Indies (1526).

But the middle of the sixteenth century was a time of financial instability. The introduction of bullion from America, especially

---

[1] There was a market for cats in Africa. On John Lock's voyage (1554) an English sailor stole a 'muske cat' from the natives who were 'very wary people in the bargaining'. They declined to trade any more and when the ship made sail along the coast to another market, the sailors found that the story of the cat had preceded them. No trade could be done until the cat was restored or paid for (Hakluyt). Von Harff, a German pilgrim of the fifteenth century, also reported that cats were still held sacred in Moslem Egypt as they had been in the days of the Pharaohs.

of silver from Mexico in the fifteen-forties, produced a great expansion in the currency and a corresponding rise in prices. At the same time the seizure of Church lands in the Protestant countries unsettled agriculture, glutting the market with land at knock-down prices and with unemployed labourers. Finally, the wars of religion broke the commercial links between the farming and fishing communities of north-western Europe and the trading and commercial cities of Flanders and the Rhineland. The loss of Calais to the French and the occupation of Antwerp by the Spaniards seemed to spell ruin to the English sheep-farmer.

From all these changes the profit came to the moneyed man. This is the period of the emergence of capitalism, in continental Catholic countries as much as in the Protestant countries around the North Sea. Wealth now came to consist of money rather than of goods, and money was available for investment overseas. The English capitalists were at first small men compared with the financiers who backed the King of Spain and the Emperor, but they made their market in the end. The first recorded joint-stock enterprise in English history is the Muscovy Company, incorporated in 1553. Nicholas Thorne of Bristol, a wealthy man who had been to America in 1502, long resided in Seville and wrote from there, in 1527, a letter to Henry VIII urging the despatch of voyages to find the North-east and North-west Passages. During the reign of Edward VI, Sebastian Cabot, now an old man, was again in England stimulating interest in exploration. Rivalry with the Hanse merchants of the Baltic suggested a new direction for adventure. As Edward VI lay dying, the ships of Willoughby and Chancellor were putting down London River for the discovery of a North-east Passage to the riches of the East. The Portuguese had found the South-east Passage round the Cape of Good Hope; the Spaniards the South-west Passage through Magellan Strait, and in searching for that had stumbled across the mines of Mexico and Peru; it was now the dream of the English to find a way north-east or north-west about. Willoughby and his men were lost in the ice, but Chancellor reached the White Sea and the Court of Czar Ivan the Terrible at Moscow. Diplomatic relations and a sporadic trade followed, but these belong to the history of commerce rather than the history of empire, though groups of English merchants settled in Novgorod and Moscow and have descendants there to-day. The significance of the Muscovy Company is that it was a financial company, not a mere trading association. The adventurers pooled their capital in a 'joint-stock', risking it all and agreeing to share the profits.

The outburst of activity in 1553 seems to have been a symptom of Protestant enthusiasm. The Wars of Religion in France and Holland began with privateering against the Catholic and maritime powers of Spain and Portugal. The English voyages to the north were matched by voyages, at the same time, into the forbidden waters of our old ally Portugal. In August 1553, Captain Thomas Windham sailed from Portsmouth with the *Primrose* and *Lion*, under guidance of a renegade Portuguese pilot, on a 'voyage unto Guinea and Benin, at the charges of certain merchant adventurers of London,... before never enterprised by Englishmen, or at least so frequented as at this present they are and may be... if the same be not hindered by the ambition of such, as for the conquering of forty or fifty miles here or there, and erecting of certain fortresses, think to be lords of half the world'. Accordingly, the avoidance of these 'certain fortresses' and especially of the Castle of Elmina was necessary to the voyage. Not many miles away they made a landfall and bought from the natives eighty tons of pepper which should have made a trading profit for an otherwise unfortunate venture. Windham and the pilot quarrelled perpetually and both died of fevers before the ships came home.

Next year Captain John Lock made a voyage to the Coast in the *Trinity*, a London ship. A long account of his voyage was published by Hakluyt with a wealth of geographical and other information, containing many wonders and much useful knowledge. He noted that the Africans above all things coveted brass wire for anklets and 'manilios';[1] and expatiated on the trade in 'Oliphants' teeth'. According to rumour, he brought home 5000 ounces of gold dust, 'certain black slaves, whereof some were tall and strong men, and could well agree with our meats and drinks'.

[1] 'Manilios', now known as 'manillas', are metal bracelets which still pass for currency in South-eastern Nigeria. Two hundred years ago, the Bristol firm of R. and W. King (long since merged into the United Africa Company) was manufacturing hoops of bronze for export to the Coast, as Manilla currency.

William Towerson, who made two voyages to the Coast (1555 and 1556), was much impressed with the hard bargaining of the natives and already noted the influence of the European slave-trade. 'The Portugales were bad men,' said the natives, 'and made them slaves if they could take them.' Towerson preferred to make an effect with his panoply and then to barter 'manilios' for gold dust. He sent boats up some steamy African estuary, tricked out with Renaissance pageantry: twelve men 'with their morions and corslets; four trumpets, a drum and a fife; and a boat all hanged with streamers of silk'. He sent his men ashore with English longbows to shoot before an African king who 'with all his people wondered to see them shoot so far, and assayed to draw their bows and could not'. He also set out to hunt elephants with swords and longbows, but the elephants had the best of it.

The succession of voyages lapsed while Philip of Spain, as Queen Mary's husband, was England's ruler, and affronts to the Catholic powers were frowned on but, with the accession of the young Elizabeth, ventures to the Coast were soon renewed. In 1561 plans were set afoot for building a fort at Kormantin, a few miles from Elmina. William Rutter brought home 1750 lb. of ivory from thereabouts in 1562. There were tales of English merchants who had gone up-country farther to the east in the Bight of Benin. In 1566 George Fenner bought 'civet, musk, gold and grains' far to the west near Cape Verde, where he found the natives so suspicious of slave-raiders that they would not traffic without first exchanging hostages. A few years later Towerson was again on the Coast at Kormantin getting ivory and gold dust by the ounce, in exchange for basins and pots of tin, beads, blue coral, horse-tails, red cloth and kersey, brass basins and ewers, bells, gloves, and leather bags, but above all for 'manilios' of Brummagem wire. Every voyage found the Africans more suspicious and the Portuguese more active against these interlopers, until the voyages of John Hawkins led to diplomatic action. Three times between 1561 and 1564 embassies came from the court of Portugal to protest to Queen Elizabeth. In 1562 Hawkins picked up a cargo of 300 slaves off the African coast, by piracy the Portuguese alleged, from a Portuguese ship, and looked around for a market, which he found at Hispaniola in Spanish America. The trade, in our eyes infamous in itself, seems not to have been thought morally wrong; diplomatically it was audacious. The slave-traders broke the Portuguese law by exporting from Africa, and the Spanish law by importing to America, but the Spanish authorities at first turned a blind eye. Hawkins's third voyage (1567) ended in disaster, for there had arrived a new Spanish governor who treated the English interlopers as pirates. Their ship, crew and cargo were trapped at St Juan d'Ulua (near Vera Cruz in Mexico) and taken after a bloody fight, from which one of the few to escape was young Francis Drake, thereafter the lifelong enemy of Spain.

By the Papal Bull of 1493 and its later amendments, all the newly discovered lands west of a meridian in mid-Atlantic had been allotted to the King of Spain and those east of the line to the King of Portugal, but from the beginning the English never admitted the claim of Spain and Portugal to exclude all other nations from these territories and even from adjacent seas. They might have objected on the grounds that Free Trade had been established by treaty with both Portugal and Spain, or on the ground that Protestant Englishmen now rejected the international jurisdiction of the Pope. In fact they stood on other grounds. Queen Elizabeth never subscribed to the doctrine put forward by most other sovereigns, English and foreign, that there could be national dominion over the sea. 'The use of the sea and air', she said, is 'common to all.' As for the land, she and her advisers soon developed the useful principle that there could be no dominion without 'effective occupation'. Merely to proclaim the annexation of a territory was insufficient; a ruler who asserted his dominion should be in a position to enforce it. The Portuguese had a fine castle at Elmina on the Gold Coast. Very well, that and the region controlled by it were lawful territory of the Portuguese King. But if the English were gladly received a hundred miles away by a native prince who was anxious to exchange gold dust for trade goods the Portuguese King should not complain. His remedy was to forbid his subjects to trade with the English and to enforce his orders, if he could. Queen Elizabeth took shares in several African ventures and found them very profitable; she rather enjoyed the ensuing diplomatic exchanges with the Portuguese ambassador.

A new turn in the negotiations came in 1580 when King Philip of Spain asserted his right to the Portuguese throne on the death of the king, and proceeded to the conquest of Portugal. Then for sixty years the New Worlds in the east and west were united under one despotic ruler, in economic and religious enmity to the petty Protestant states of northern Europe. When the old alliance between England and Portugal parted after wearing thin in the preceding years, Elizabeth could harass Philip of Spain by cherishing Don Antonio, her pretender to the Portuguese throne, and could make trouble for Spain by stirring conspiracies in Portugal. As for the adventurers, they could now enrich themselves in the lands the Portuguese affected to call their dominion, treating that as they treated the dominions of Spain.

In 1585 letters-patent were issued to 'noblemen and merchants of London for a trade to Barbary' within the dominions of the Emperor of Morocco; and in 1588 a charter to merchants of Exeter and London for a trade to 'the river of Senega and of Gambia in Guinea'. The latter, for the first of the African Companies, was a stroke in Anglo-Portuguese politics. 'The traffique' would 'in time be very beneficial to these our realms and dominions,...also a great succour and relief unto...those Portugals who live here under our protection'. The merchants were to have a monopoly, which was justified on the grounds that the 'adventuring and enterprising of a new trade cannot be a matter of small charge and hazard to the adventurers in the beginning'.

English trade was spreading south and east. The Levant Company, whose merchants ran the gauntlet between Barbary rovers and Spanish galleys, was chartered in 1581 and soon made figs, dates and currants and muslin cloth from Mosul better known in England.

The first Englishman, so far as we know, to visit India was Father Thomas Stevens, a Jesuit, who was sent to the Portuguese establishment at Goa in 1579. He was a man of science, who wrote home to explain the method of finding the longitude by studying the variation of the compass, and became so proficient in Indian languages as to compose vernacular poems which are still admired. No doubt this good man welcomed the sight of a fellow-countryman's face when, in 1582, Ralph Fitch, with two other Englishmen, appeared at Goa and threw themselves on Stevens's mercy. Ralph Fitch was a merchant who had made earlier voyages in the Near East. In 1582 he set off for Aleppo in the *Tiger* (the ship cursed by the witches in *Macbeth*) with a party of merchants of the Turkey Company, carrying a letter from Queen Elizabeth to the Great Mogul Akbar, whom they addressed as the King of Cambay. John Newbery led the expedition, their intention being, it seems, to trade in gems with the help of William Leeds, a jeweller; but there were others in the party including James Story, a portrait-painter, who joined them on his own account as a private venture.

The party came to Goa by sea from Ormuz, having passed from one Portuguese post to another, often finding a friendly reception. But at Goa they were imprisoned and threatened with expulsion from the Portuguese dominions; and with worse treatment when King Philip, now King of Portugal as well as of Spain, came to hear of their arrival. However, with the good offices of Stevens, since all three professed to be papists, they were released on bail and allowed to escape over the frontier. In 1584 or 1585 they reached Akbar's court at Agra, though their letters say little of what they achieved there. It is not known whether they succeeded in delivering the Queen's letter to the Mogul. Leeds settled at the Mogul's court, where a jeweller would not lack business. Fitch went on alone to Bengal, Arakan, Bassein, and the kingdom of Pegu, where he was mightily impressed by the Shwe Dagon Pagoda, 'the fairest place, as I suppose, that is in the world'. He even reached the Portuguese station of Malacca and brought back news of the Chinese trade at Macao. He returned home in 1591 by the Portuguese sea-routes, after an absence of eight years. His companions vanished from the pages of history.

Fitch concluded his report by 'declaring some of the things which India and the country further eastward do bring forth': pepper, ginger, cloves, nutmegs, mace, sandalwood, camphor (which is sold 'dearer than golde') aloes, benjamin, long pepper, musk, ambergris, rubies, sapphires, 'spinelles', diamonds, pearls and many kinds of drugs. He described the places where they are found and the method of obtaining them like a tradesman, with accuracy, and no doubt expatiated on these subjects when, eight years later, he was summoned to advise the founders of the East India Company.

At least one private adventurer anticipated the East Indian merchants. A disreputable free-lance named John Mildenhall found his way to the court of Akbar in 1603, asserting that he had a commission from Queen Elizabeth. Later he reappeared in England saying that he had obtained concessions from the Mogul, for which he demanded large payments from the Company. His whole story lacked confirmation beyond the fact that he had been to Agra where he antagonised the Portuguese agents, and, apparently, had spoken with the great Akbar, the only Englishman who claimed to have done so. In 1611 he was again in India selling what was said to be stolen merchandise. He died in 1614 and was buried at Agra where his tomb is shown, the oldest existing relic of the British in India.

The outbreak of war with Spain led to an extension of the privateering war into the eastern seas. James Lancaster with three ships, *Penelope*, *Marchant Royal* and *Edward Bonaventure* led a commerce-raiding expedition into the Indian Ocean in 1591. He called at the Cape, not yet occupied by the Dutch, to buy cattle and fat-tailed sheep from 'very brutish black salvages', at the rate of a beast for a knife of Sheffield steel, and saw besides 'divers sorts of wild beasts unknown to us and great store of overgrown monkeys'. At Zanzibar he attempted negotiation with the Portuguese on the score that 'we were Englishmen come from Don Antonio [the Pretender] upon business to his men in the Indies', but met such plain evidence of hostility as to justify reprisals in the Indian Ocean.

All through 1592, after sending home one ship for lack of men and parting company with another, Lancaster cruised in the Indian Ocean, from Galle in Ceylon to Penang in Malaya, taking two large prizes and several smaller ones; but more valuable than his plunder, which he was not fated to bring home, was the news of the trade the Portuguese had tapped with 'the Maine of India': 'Pavilions for beds and wrought quilts' from 'Bangala', Calicut cloth, rice from Tenasserim, rubies and diamonds from Pegu. What prospects of wealth might not lie beyond since 'the Portugals have discovered the coast of China to the latitude of 59°, finding the sea still open to the northward and giving great hope of the Northeast and Northwest Passage'?

On his way home in 1593, Lancaster put in at the lonely island of St Helena to take up a maroon, John Segar of Bury, who had been left there fifteen months earlier by one of the other ships. The unfortunate man was found 'in good plight of body but half out of his wits...'. Whether in fright or of sudden joy at seeing Lancaster's ship he became 'idle-headed' and soon died.

Lancaster's voyage ended in disaster. His crew, turning mutinous, deserted him in the West Indies so that he arrived home empty-handed and almost alone, as a passenger in a French ship. The news he brought of the riches of the East opened prospects for trade on a vaster scale than Guinea, Barbary or Newfoundland afforded, and led to the foundation of the East India Company on the last day of the sixteenth century.

3. THE WEST-COUNTRY ADVENTURERS

THE group of west-countrymen who founded Virginia began their careers with the French and Dutch Protestant rebels. Such a mixture of motives is rarely to be found as that of the Gilberts, the Grenvilles and their kind, Devon and Cornwall squires, aristocrats by birth, scholars by breeding, pirates and wreckers by local tradition. A quixotic knight-errantry, exemplified in the last fight of the *Revenge*, was in their blood:

> Who seeks to wear the laurel crown
> Or hath the mind that would aspire,
> Let him his native land eschew,
> Let him go range and seek a new.

These were verses of the elder Richard Grenville, and this was the spirit in which Nicholas Thorne of Bristol said to Henry VIII, 'I judge there is no land unhabitable nor sea innavigable.'

Politically they were of the anti-Spanish party at a time when appeasement of Spain was the aim of Queen Elizabeth's government. They were Protestant leaders in the west country and opposed to the old religion which lingered there. They are largely responsible for the English prejudice against the Pope and the King of Spain, whom they most inaccurately represented as inseparable allies sworn to destroy the prosperity, the freedom, and the religion of England. The leader of this group was Humphrey Gilbert; young Walter Ralegh (1552–1618) was his half-brother. The Grenvilles, a dynasty of splendid adventurers, were headed in this generation by Sir Richard of the *Revenge*, one of Gilbert's associates. Richard Hakluyt (1552–1616) devoted a laborious life, as chronicler of the group, to recording *The*

*Principal Navigations, Voyages, Traffiques and Discoveries of the
English Nation made by sea or over Land to the Remote and farthest
Distant Quarters of the Earth at any time within the compass of
these 1600 years.* Francis Drake (1540–96), the curate's son from
Tavistock, the greatest sailor of them all, was an outlier, associated in some of their enterprises but hardly to be counted one
of their number.

Since about 1560 the French Huguenots had been attempting
to found colonies in America; again and again the settlers were
dispersed and massacred by the Spaniards. Thus the west-
country privateers, who were friends of the Huguenot leaders,
turned their attention to the Spanish Main. As early as 1574
Grenville had petitioned the Queen for a Charter to plant 'certain rich lands fatally and it seemeth by God's providence
reserved for England', in the direction of the River Plate.
Drake's voyage round the world (1577–80), the second such
voyage following the path taken by Magellan sixty years earlier,
was authorised by those members of the English government
who desired to limit the expanding frontiers of the Spanish Empire
and to encroach upon the Spanish power. Walsingham, the
Secretary of State, supported him; the Queen and Burleigh were
believed to favour, in public at least, the policy of appeasing
Spain. Hence some mysterious features in Drake's story; Drake
had his private wrongs to avenge upon the Spaniards. He was a
merciful man, most unlike his fellow-adventurers in being not at
all addicted to bloodshed, but he would take his reprisal for the
loss of his ship and cargo at St Juan d'Ulua. It was probably for
some political difference between the peace party and the war
party among his officers that he denounced his friend Doughty
as a traitor, and executed him after court-martial on the bare
coast of Patagonia.

Not till he had passed Magellan Strait and entered the Pacific
did Drake cease to be a peaceable free-trader and begin to wage
private war against the commerce of the King of Spain. The
treasure ship *Cacafuego* which, said Drake, should have been
named Spit-silver not Spit-fire, the pile of silver ingots quietly
removed from the care of a sleeping Spanish sentry at Valparaiso,
the mule-train of silver seized on the Isthmus of Panama, with
some smaller prizes, satisfied his cupidity and made the name of
El Draque, the dragon, renowned as the worst of all pirates in

Plate 1 A

SIR FRANCIS DRAKE
(1540?–96)

This and the following portraits
of Gilbert and Frobisher are taken
from *Heroologia*, an illustrated
series of biographies edited by
H. Holland, 1620. The engravings
are based upon contemporary
portraits. *See p. 16*.

Plate 1 B

SIR HUMPHREY GILBERT
(1539?–83)

Projector and pioneer of British
expansion overseas. *See p. 17*.

Plate 2A

CAPTAIN JOHN SMITH
(1580–1631)

Aged 37. The frontispiece to
description of New England.
p. 21.

Plate 2B

SIR MARTIN FROBISHER
(1535?–94)

'Very valiant but withal harsh
and violent.' *See p. 18.*

Spanish story. Later in the voyage came his work as empire-builder. He sailed north along the American coast as far as California, to latitude 38° N., landed and proclaimed 'New Albion' a dominion of Queen Elizabeth. No Englishman went there again for 200 years, but the doctrine of effective occupation, which we found so useful against Portugal and Spain, was now conveniently overlooked and, in the eighteenth century, the lands known later as California, Oregon and British Columbia were claimed for Britain by right of Drake's annexation.

This was for the future. More immediately valuable was his descent upon the Spice Islands across the Pacific from the East. It was no slight blow to Portuguese pretensions and no small advantage in Queen Elizabeth's eyes that in the Moluccas he made a treaty of friendship and commerce with the Sultan of Ternate. Drake returned westward about the Cape of Good Hope. The Queen's share in the profits of his voyage was £80,000, of which she invested half in the stock of the Levant Company.

Drake's later voyages against Spain and the Indies fall outside the scope of this book. His character was true English. An affable, short, stocky, bullet-headed man with reddish hair, he was practical, business-like, plain-spoken, and no theoriser; a good citizen and benefactor of Plymouth in the time of his prosperity. He had his pride, and dined alone at sea off silver to the sound of violins, but showed an honest contempt for idle gallants. He 'would have the gentlemen to pull and haul with the common sailors'. Drake's legendary drum sounded again in 1939, in Exeter Guildhall, to record another triumph for the men of Devon in action off the River Plate against a different foe. The old trade is still plying.

Sir Humphrey Gilbert (1539–83) was an indefatigable writer and projector. His *Discourse of a Discovery for a New Passage to Cataia* led to the founding of the abortive Company of Cathay and to at least fifteen voyages in search of the North-west Passage (Frobisher 1576, 1577, 1578; Davis 1585, 1587; Waymouth 1601; Knight 1606; Hudson 1610, 1611; Button 1612; Baffin 1615, 1616; Fox 1631; James 1631, 1632). Their little ships pried into the icy straits and sounds, searching for an ice-free route to the west, and searching also for the gold and silver mines that other voyagers to the Americas had found. The maps based upon

Baffin's charts showed a knowledge of the lie of the land that rather decayed during the next 200 years. Hudson Strait, Frobisher Bay, Davis Strait, James' Sound and, in the farthest north, Smith Sound named after Sir Thomas Smythe (or Smith), the patron of so many ventures, were charted by these early explorers, who contributed mightily to the literature of travel. James's voyages provided much of the local colour used by Coleridge's *Ancient Mariner*.

Sir Martin Frobisher (1535–94), who brought home accounts of the Red Indians of Newfoundland, was the first adventurer to proclaim the annexation of American ground to the English Crown, in 1576, on the frigid coast of Baffin Land. Entering Frobisher Bay, which he called Frobisher Strait, he supposed that the land on his right hand was a projection of North-east Asia and that his strait was the long-sought passage. His later voyages were treasure-hunts, since he was allured by the mineral wealth of the Arctic. Though he mistook pyrites for gold he pioneered better than he knew, by discovering the riches that lay unused in Northern Canada until our own age. Frobisher was 'very valiant', says Hakluyt, 'but withal harsh and violent (faults which may be dispensed with in one of his profession)'. Having commanded a Queen's ship against the Spanish Armada he was killed in one of the later battles of the war.

In 1578 Gilbert obtained from the Queen a charter authorising him 'to discover, find, search out and view such remote heathen and barbarous lands not actually possessed by a Christian prince or people...and the same to have, hold, occupy and enjoy for ever with all commodities, jurisdiction and royalties both by sea and by land', a generous donation, as extravagant as anything ever granted by the Pope to the King of Spain. But this comprehensive plan included something more than peaceful settlement. The colony was to be a base from which to harass the Spaniards without open declaration of war, and to stake out claims in the New World.

In 1583 Gilbert set out to found his colony, intending, as he wrote, to find a cure for unemployment by planting labourers in America where their needs would make a market for English manufactured goods. Trade with our own colonies would reduce the necessity of importing from foreign lands and thus adjust the balance of trade in our favour; such was the economic theory of the age. On his way to America, he put in at St John's Bay, Newfoundland, where he ceremoniously proclaimed its annexation 'two hundred leagues every way' before the crews of thirty-six English, French and Portuguese fishing craft. After a short stay he set off 'to annoy the Spaniards', promising to return next year with greater force. Bearing away southward in stormy weather, Gilbert proudly shifted his flag into the smaller of his two vessels, a mere fishing-smack of ten tons, which vanished in a squall. The last who saw him from the larger ship described him sitting in the stern-sheets, wrapped in a cloak, reading in More's *Utopia*, and crying out through a lull in the storm More's words: 'we are as near heaven by sea as by land'.

An earlier visitor to Newfoundland, Anthony Parkhurst, had told Hakluyt in 1578 that Spanish and Portuguese ships outnumbered English and French on the Banks, although the English who landed to dry their fish were 'commonly lords of the harbours'. He was for occupying and fortifying the island in order to monopolise the fisheries. Gilbert did not stay to carry out this project, which was not revived for another thirty years. But when war broke out with Spain in 1585, one of the opening moves was a raid upon the Spanish Newfoundland fleet by Sir Bernard Drake, a kinsman of the great Sir Francis. The Spanish ships were seized or scattered and did not again frequent the Newfoundland coast. The first permanent settlement of Newfoundland, in 1610, may be reserved for a later chapter.

On the death of Gilbert, his half-brother Ralegh took up the cause. He remains after a hundred criticisms an inexplicable and fascinating figure. 'He was a tall handsome bold man but...he was damnable proud.' His colony of Virginia was to have been no mere trading post or dependency but a new home for Englishmen. His colonists were to 'enjoy all the privileges of free denizens of England' and were conceived as substantial yeomen, 'the least that he hath granted being 500 acres'. But the first Virginia colony at Roanoke failed. The settlers were ill-chosen and lacked capital and the site on Chesapeake Bay was unlucky. The settlement was made in 1584; by 1587 all had disappeared, their fate being unknown.

Next year (1585) came the open breach with Spain and a host of other activities for Ralegh. His contemporary fame rested more on his Guiana voyage of 1595 and the rolling eloquence with which he wrote of it. Guiana, the land between the Orinoco and the Amazon, was a land of wonders and treasures which the Spaniards had not grasped. Ralegh's fatal search for the Golden City of Manoa was a more romantic quest than the Virginia expedition. Yet who need set limits to his imagination after reading what the Spaniards had already found in Mexico and Peru? There was sound sense as well as vision in the quest for Eldorado, even for the Amazonian women whom Ralegh hoped to bring under the protection of a Virgin Queen. There was gold, as he proved, but no gilded cacique, rich city or tribe of women-warriors so far as he could find, yet a country where the Spaniards might be forestalled. Even though his second voyage, twenty years later, did embroil him with a Spanish force, Guiana was never a Spanish Dominion. Many attempts to colonise it were made by English, French and Dutch during the next hundred years, the only lasting settlements being the Dutch colony at Essequibo (1616) and the French at Cayenne (1665).

The later years of Ralegh's active life before his disgrace and imprisonment were given to another colonising project, the 'plantation of Ireland'. From the days of Elizabeth to those of Cromwell the language of colonisation—'natives', 'settlers', 'plantations'—is habitually used by Englishmen of Ireland. The 'wild Irish' were to be subdued, expropriated in favour of English settlers and confined to certain districts; they were, in short, to be treated as the American Indians were treated, according to the social morality of the age. Not only the proud, fierce Ralegh but such mild humane men as the poet Spenser wrote in this strain. The organisation of the first American colonies owes something to experience gained in the plantation of Derry.

Ralegh is traditionally reputed to have introduced the potato from America to Ireland. He is also remembered as the man who made tobacco-smoking fashionable in England. These two homely results of his American undertakings would alone have made the name of a lesser man. After the accession of James I (who among many fads hated the smell of tobacco) Ralegh fell into disfavour. He was imprisoned and attainted and, largely to curry favour with the Spanish ambassador, was at last beheaded. Before his death a new Virginia colony had begun to flourish. 'I shall yet live to see it an English nation', he had prophesied in his dark days.

4. THE FIRST ENGLISH COLONIES

(1) VIRGINIA

WHEN in financial difficulties in 1589 Ralegh assigned his interests in Virginia to a group of adventurers among whom were Hakluyt, Sir Thomas Smythe a rich merchant, and two returned settlers named White and Dare. After the Peace with Spain in 1604 they revived the old schemes. Hakluyt's efforts brought in the political support of the Earl of Southampton, Shakespeare's patron, and Smythe aroused the interest of the city. In 1606, when Ralegh was a prisoner in the Tower, a Royal Council for Virginia was created in London, to administer the trade and plantation of the American coast between the thirty-fourth and forty-fifth parallels of latitude. Two colonies were to be established, a 'London' and a 'Plymouth' colony. Both were founded in Virginia in 1607, and both were financial failures. In the whole history of colonisation, then and for many generations thereafter, it was never appreciated that a steady continuous flow of capital and labour was required in the early years of a new settlement. The 'Plymouth' colony on the Kennebec River was abandoned; the 'London' colony at Jamestown was like to have been until the settlers were disciplined, organised and set to work by the redoubtable Captain John Smith (1580–1631).

Smith had been everywhere and claimed to have tried his hand at everything. The evidence about his adventures in the Turkish wars and about his experiences with the Red Indians depends solely upon his own sensational narratives; the facts are that he bullied and cajoled the Jamestown colonists through the critical winter of 1608–9, and set up friendly relations with the Indians, exchanging trade goods for food. Pocahontas, the Indian princess who, according to Smith's narrative, saved his life from her father Powhatan really lived and befriended the English. She married an Englishman named John Rolfe, the first settler to cultivate tobacco in Virginia, and died at Gravesend during a brief visit to England, where she was long remembered as 'la belle sauvage'.

In 1609 and again in 1612 the Virginia charter was remodelled. The general government was placed in the hands of the shareholders in London, with Sir Thomas Smythe as treasurer. Membership was extended to those who invested £12. 10s. in the common stock, and to the 'planters' whose contribution was their labour and that of their servants. In the colony there was no prosperity until the original communism was abandoned and individual holdings of twelve acres of land allotted. Labouring servants, who might eventually work out their indentures and join the class of free planters, were also imported. This system of indentured labour was used to rid the home country of undesirables and unemployables. As well as the few men of high blood whom the 'First Five Hundred Families' of Virginia now proudly claim as their ancestors there were also convicted felons and insolvent debtors. Gondomar, the Spanish ambassador, reported to his master a tale of three condemned felons who were offered the choice of Virginia or the gallows. Two seized the chance of life, but the third heartily preferred to be hanged and stood to his decision.

Rarely in colonial history has a satisfactory solution been found of the problem how and when to turn over the administration from the founders at home who provide the capital to the settlers abroad who employ it. Originally the intention had been for the settlers to elect a local council with authority to make grants of land in the name of the Crown and to prepare local by-laws which should be 'not repugnant to the laws of England'. The hardships and failures of the first few years made a sterner rule necessary. From 1609 to 1618 the colony was under the military rule of powerful governors sent out to represent the shareholders. In 1618 political changes at home led to an attack on the privileges of the Company and to the displacement of Smythe. The Company lingered on till 1632 but never paid a dividend. Meanwhile a new era of free trade began in Virginia where there were now 1000 white settlers. Instructions were sent out for the governor to summon a 'house of burgesses', the first offspring of the Mother of Parliaments, in 1619. Prosperity was now in sight. An export trade was at last established in tobacco, and already a cargo of negro slaves had been imported to work for the planters.

(2) CALIBAN'S ISLAND

One of the early governors of Virginia brought out in his train Sir George Somers who, in 1609, was cast ashore on a beautiful unknown island in mid-Atlantic, where his men lived for months on turtles and wild pigs. Somers's nephew, who succeeded to the command on his uncle's death, persuaded the Virginia Company to plant this isle, Bermuda, the third British colony after Virginia and Newfoundland. In 1612 they sent out a modest company of fifty settlers under Richard Moore, a ship's carpenter, who found, when they reached Bermuda, three maroons in residence, deserters from Somers's ship. Like most founders of colonies Moore met with mutiny and discontent at his settlement of St George's in the first years, until the plantation became self-supporting. A subsidiary company was formed in 1615, the 'London Company for the Somer Islands', which played the unpopular role of absentee proprietor until 1684 when, at the petition of the colonists, it was dissolved. Otherwise their life was of Arcadian simplicity. In 1629 their numbers had reached 2000 and in 1679, 8000, by which time they had been reinforced with political exiles and some negro slaves; but slavery in Bermuda was of a mild domestic character. Some puritan malcontents, under William Sayle (d. 1670), moved on from Bermuda in 1656 to found another island community at Eleuthera in the uninhabited Bahamas.

From 1684 Bermuda was a royal colony; its Assembly, elected since 1620 by representatives of the nine parishes, is second only to the Assembly of Virginia in seniority among the Parliaments overseas.

This delightful land, an isle
> full of noises
> Sounds and sweet airs that give delight and hurt not

caught the popular imagination. The English discoverer named the group the Somers Islands, but two great poems in the seventeenth century fixed upon the Islands their Spanish name, Bermuda, 'in the Ocean's bosom unespied', 'an isle far kinder than our own', as Andrew Marvell wrote. To the mature mind of Shakespeare the 'Bermoothes', the magic isle of Ariel and Caliban, gave the occasion for his last masterpiece, perhaps the most deeply philosophical and the most purely poetical of all his works, a closely constructed symphony on the subject of calm after storm and shipwreck. Among the strains that build up the harmony the themes of sea-adventure and discovery, the nobilities and the meannesses of empire-builders, the Utopian dreams of projectors, the well-intentioned paternal government that overreaches itself, the grossness of savagery with its sudden surprising gleams of grandeur, and the great design like to be marred by the beastliness of the drunken underlings, 'the poor whites', all occur and recur in the music till, 'like this insubstantial pageant faded', the projects and the projectors pass away leaving the sea-girt island to its aboriginal inhabitants.

The Tempest is not a treatise on the art of colonisation, but it contains a notable portrait of a savage. The first quite primitive, quite barbarous nation encountered by the English mariners were the Caribs of the West Indies, now almost extinct. They were fierce in defence of their liberties and untamable. Neither Spaniards nor English could make either slaves or converts of them. They stood condemned in Christian eyes because they occasionally practised the rite of sacrificing and eating human flesh, a custom which inspired our ancestors with superstitious horror. Caribs or Cannibals, the name is spelt either way, were beyond the bounds of pity. Shakespeare's monster, Caliban, offspring of the devil and a witch, whose name is but a poetic variant of 'cannibal', presents the savage as an Elizabethan audience expected to see him. He learns to speak intelligibly only from his white master, yet he will not

> ...fetch in firing
> At requiring,
> Nor scrape trencher,
> Nor wash dish.

In return for kindness he only plots to murder his master and ravish his master's daughter. But the universal sympathy of Shakespeare went deeper than that, and was exercised to draw a subtle parallel between the savage and the renegade white sailor. The savage was the better man.

The horror of barbarous rites lasted long even among Europeans who were themselves indifferent Christians. A hundred years later the writings of Defoe are full of violent denunciations of cannibalism. Crusoe on his island, for all his piety and all his natural tenderness towards Man Friday, could not refrain from slaying at sight those other Indians whom he believed guilty of eating human flesh. Other barbarisms might be eradicated and forgiven, but not that. This abomination, this European taboo on a practice which has been world-wide, remained in full force until the present age, and, no doubt, still exists, though the analysis of primitive customs by modern anthropologists has thrown a new light upon it.

Savages who practised these 'abhorred', 'inhuman' customs got no consideration at law. The scholastic philosophers had written and argued on the civil rights of pagans in conflict with Christians, but this did not become a practical problem until the age of colonisation. The early Spanish missionaries, especially Las Casas, in vain demanded legal protection for their actual and potential converts. Greed for land and contempt for the habits of the Indians alike swayed the settlers in the other direction. The common form of colonial charters was to allow the adventurers to occupy at will 'lands not actually possessed by any Christian prince or people': which suited the settlers very well when it was a question of expropriating a few naked barbarians, but which they did not see fit to attempt if they happened upon the shores of a monarch as powerful as the Sultan of Turkey or the Great Mogul.

Among the mixed motives of the English voyagers the impulse to extend the Christian religion was not wanting. It is very prominently given as a motive in the Virginia charter of 1606. One of the projectors was the celebrated pietist Nicholas Ferrar. 'In all places where I came,' wrote one of Ralegh's staff, 'I did my best to make God's immortal glory known.' 'Reducing heathen people to civility and true religion' is mentioned by Captain John Smith as a more important object than 'gaining provinces' for the King's crown. Drake's chaplain wrote that when the Californian Indians seemed to worship the voyagers as gods, 'we fell to prayers and singing of psalms whereby they were allured to forget their folly'. But these slight evidences of intention are poor indeed beside the heroic zeal of the Spanish Jesuits in America and Asia.

The English were not yet a missionary people. It was by ruder qualities that they were beginning to make their mark. 'The

English', wrote a Venetian ambassador, 'would never yield and though driven back and thrown into confusion they always return to the fight.' As with the men so with their ships: 'for strength, assurance, nimbleness and swiftness of sailing there are no vessels in the world to be compared with them', wrote another contemporary. A thousand lesser men like these are forgotten while a few great names are recorded. A commonplace of colonial history is the arrival of a chartered and renowned expedition at the goal to find some nameless squatter or interloper already in possession. To identify the first settler, even the first discoverer of a new island, is rarely an easy task. Especially in the West Indies, voyages of exploration overlap, charters regrant what has unknowingly been granted to another claimant, settlers with designs on one island plant another, claims are jumped, or schemes anticipated. Ralegh's Guiana voyage and first Virginia colony were followed by scores of English expeditions and projects. Soon the merchant adventurers were flocking to these islands which contained at least two British settlements before King James died.

Among obscurer men should not be forgotten those fore-runners of overseas expansion who sailed under foreign flags, such men as Chambers, the English sailor of whom we know nothing but that he sailed with Magellan; Henry Hudson who commanded a Dutch ship to the river and bay that bear his name; and William Adams of Gillingham who found his way to Japan, also in a Dutch ship, and ended his days there building ships for the Mikado.

(3) NEW ENGLAND

Captain John Smith first drew attention to the land he called New England. After leaving Virginia he went on several whaling voyages off the North American coast. 'Of all the four parts of the world that I have yet seen not inhabited,' he wrote in 1616, 'I would rather live [there] than anywhere....New England is great enough to make many kingdoms and countries, were it all inhabited.' The proprietary rights over New England were disputed between two authorities in London, the Virginia Company and a new 'Council for New England' over which presided the Duke of Buckingham. Against both of them the west-country fishing interests were arrayed since it was thought that access to the Newfoundland fisheries would be restricted by settlers on adjacent shores. These barren quarrels may now be forgotten, for a colonising influence of a new and stronger kind was at work.

For many years small groups of uncompromising English puritans had been settled in Holland, the only European state where there was complete religious toleration. In 1617, one such congregation determined to plant a new state in the New World far from all corrupting influences. Their agents were received favourably by the Virginia Company who made them a grant of land 500 miles to the north of the previous Virginian settlements. They obtained the permission of the Crown to go overseas, and had little difficulty in raising capital from a group of London merchants who saw possibilities in the New England fur trade and the fisheries.

Thus began the voyage of the *Mayflower* which left Plymouth on 6 September 1620, and anchored off Cape Cod two months later. Of the 102 passengers thirty-five were the original Puritan congregation; the remainder were casual emigrants including, as all companies of settlers included, a proportion of wastrels.

During the voyage the colonists, who were saddled with no Lord Proprietor and no governing council, drew up a 'social contract', one of the few actual examples of such a document in the history of the world. Admitting themselves to be already members of a civil society they formally constituted it a state. Forty-one signatures were appended, on 11 November 1620, to this declaration: 'In the name of God, amen. We whose names are underwritten, the loyal subjects of our dread sovereign King James, having undertaken, for the glory of God and advancement of the Christian faith and honour of our King and country, a voyage to plant the first colony in the northern parts of Virginia, do, by these presents, solemnly and mutually in the presence of God and of one another, covenant and combine ourselves together into a civil body politic, for our better ordering and preservation and furtherance of the ends aforesaid; and by virtue thereof to enact, constitute and frame such just and equal laws, ordinances, acts, constitutions, and offices, from time to time, as shall be thought more convenient for the general good of the colony, unto which we promise all due submission and obedience.'

This admirable document, the first written constitution in the history of the Anglo-Saxon peoples, did not imply that New England was to be a free state, but quite the contrary. The original Puritan settlers held themselves to be a chosen people who had withdrawn from the world and did not propose to allow its corruptions to seep in. Their little commonwealth was an exclusive oligarchy ruled by the elders of the Church with ferocious intolerance. They had not gone out into the wilderness to indulge freedom of thought but to ensure a rigid uniformity. Let us forgive them that. They starved in the snow of a New England winter, survived to sow and reap their first harvest and made for it a yearly festival of Thanksgiving to the God who sent Abraham and Moses by faith into the wilderness. In faith they built 'a city with foundations'.

The little colony of the Pilgrim Fathers drew small attention at the time. The second Puritan colony was a much larger affair. The Rev. John White of Dorchester was a coloniser on a great scale. His *General Considerations for Planting New England* appeared in 1629 when the dispute between King Charles I and the Puritans had reached its first crisis. He desired to make a city of refuge in America for the righteous, 'to raise a bulwark against the Kingdom of Antichrist which the Jesuits labour to build up in all parts of the world...to avoid the plague while it is foreseen and not to tarry'. When it came to the point, however, White did not find it necessary to go there, nor did the authorities of the Kingdom of Antichrist show hostility to the righteous. The process of plantation took the usual form. With the help of the Puritan Earl of Warwick a grant of land was got from the Council for New England, and the Massachusetts Company was formed under a charter from the Crown. It differed from the trading companies of earlier days in the essential feature that so soon as the legal forms were complete, and an advance party had prepared the ground, the whole Company, its members and their families with their patent from the Crown, transferred themselves in a body to New England. The advance party had consisted of 300 settlers; in 1630 John Winthrop led the main body of 1000 settlers to the new colony. Their numbers rapidly increased until, ten years later, they were 14,000. As among the Pilgrim Fathers, political power was strictly confined to Church members, who were not more than one in five of the adult males.

Religious orthodoxy was imposed with far more rigour than in royalist England. Religious persecution of minorities broke out almost at once.

Comfort, though not luxury, quickly came to New England. The English were in those days still a rustic agricultural people. The New Englanders came from a frugal, industrious and enterprising branch of that farming stock. Land was to be had for the taking in Massachusetts without the irksome restrictions of English customary tenure. Here there were no common fields to lower the standard of the best farmer to the standard of the worst, no surviving feudal dues and restrictions, no law of settlement to prevent an honest man from seeking to better himself. In New England began the outward drift to the frontier, the encroachment upon the wilderness by the most daring of the new settlers who left their original plantations near the coast to be eagerly taken up by newly-arrived settlers from London. Everywhere in New England farming paid its way. Within seven years from the landing at Cape Cod the Pilgrim Fathers had been able to buy out the stock-holders in London and to become the owners of the land they tilled.

The rigid form of Church government in Massachusetts soon enough produced rebels, who were treated with much greater harshness in New England than the original settlers had been in Old England. From Massachusetts there broke off, against the will of the rulers of the Church, colonies of a still more radical type. In 1636 Thomas Hooker led away to the Banks of the Connecticut River a body of settlers who formed there a completely democratic republic with religious toleration. The Constitution of Connecticut gave no recognition of the superior power either of the Massachusetts government or of the English King.

Another rebel in Massachusetts was Roger Williams, an extreme democrat, who asserted among other alarming propositions that grants of land made in the name of King Charles were invalid because they ignored the rights of the Indians, the true owners of the soil. Williams was tried for his heresies and was banished. He fled for refuge to the Indians of the district later called Rhode Island where he was joined by other malcontents. In 1637 the Pequot Indians, whose lands had been seized by Connecticut settlers, retaliated with war. The

Massachusetts preachers cried out for vengeance and massacre. Williams demanded peace and conciliation. Before these troubles were concluded the Long Parliament had assumed the executive power so that Rhode Island received its first charter[1] from a parliamentary commission. Another colony with a completely democratic form of government was founded at Newhaven, where even the common law was abandoned and the 'Word of God' was the only rule.

5. PROPRIETARY AND ROYAL COLONIES

(1) GENERAL PRINCIPLES

WHEN the New England colonies took root and flourished, there was one respect in which they proved disappointing to political theorists at Whitehall: they produced no staple, no product or crop for export which could not as easily be found or cultivated at home. They drew off men from Old England without providing any visible advantage to balance the account. Since the fear of over-population and unemployment vanished with the sixteenth century, the export of good citizens required some justification. From the earliest time the utility of planting Massachusetts was questioned. By some opinions such colonies were useful only because they eased the morbid humours of the commonwealth. Puritans with their republican fancies might be transported for the public good, as might popish recusants and, in later time, Quakers, Scottish and Irish rebels, and undesirables of all sorts. This sort of colonisation had been denounced by Francis Bacon, the most eminent follower of Gilbert and Hakluyt, as being no better than planting a field with thistles.

Bacon's essay, *Of Plantations*, reveals a change in the approach of enlightened men to the problem after a generation of painful experiment. Colonisation is now regarded as an affair of high policy, not a mere profit-making venture. He assumes that the settlers will first take measures to become self-supporting and then concentrate upon the 'maine business', the provision of staple for export to England, which must not be expected too

[1] Toleration was permitted in Rhode Island on the ground that the colony was too remote to make any breach in the 'unity and uniformity established in this nation'.

soon. 'The destruction of most plantations hath been the base and hasty drawing of profit in the first years.' From this wise lesson, which has proved its truth in every succeeding generation, Bacon derived the principle that the 'undertakers' of a new colony should be 'rather noblemen and gentlemen than merchants, for they [the merchants] look ever to the present gain'.

Accordingly attempts were made under the Stuart kings to frame a systematic colonial policy, bringing the Plantations more directly under control of the Crown. The settlers were to enjoy the rights and liberties of Englishmen living abroad, instead of being merely the resident agents of financiers in London. On the whole the new policy was surprisingly liberal, though here and there attempts were made to entail upon the New World the feudal notions that were already obsolescent in the Old. Virginia, under the constitution which became effective in 1624, with its Royal Governor, its Assembly elected by the freeholders, its established Anglican Church, and its use of English common law, was the model upon which fifty or sixty colonies have been based. Several British colonies to-day are governed much as the Old Dominion was governed 300 years ago. And Virginia could export tobacco.

As Bacon had recommended, 'noblemen and gentlemen' were engaged in the task of empire-building by devolving the royal prerogative upon certain lords of the Council and their associates as Lords Proprietor of new plantations. They were to exercise the functions of government, either in person or by deputy, and to reimburse themselves from the profit of unappropriated land which by common law was reputed the property of the Crown. It would be both the duty and the interest of the Lord Proprietor to bring in settlers, so that the 'maine business' of exporting some commodity required in England would follow in due course. The prerogative of the Lords Proprietor was described in some charters as being equivalent to that enjoyed by the Prince-Bishops of Durham in their palatinate, which sounded formidable but did not amount to much, since the guarantees of civil liberty under the common law were, in every case, in the hands of the colonists. Furthermore, a large part of the Lord Proprietor's revenues depended upon the votes of the assembly which soon came into existence in every colony. His real advantage lay in patronage and in control of the undeveloped land.

(2) NATIONAL RIVALRY AND THE LEEWARD ISLANDS

After 1618, the world was deeply divided by the widening struggle of the Thirty Years War. Beginning as a struggle between the Catholic and Protestant powers, the issues were confused by the intervention of Catholic France on the Protestant side. The original cause of quarrel was lost in the ruthless fight for world power between Richelieu and his Protestant allies on the one hand and the Hapsburg dynasties of Spain and Austria on the other. The part played by England was as insignificant as ignoble. At first intervening feebly on the Protestant side she then withdrew, and blundered into a separate and again a feeble campaign against France. In 1632 England retired from the war and was not a party to the negotiations which produced the Treaty of Westphalia, 1648, after the first general peace conference held by the European nations.

In the New World the hostilities were reflected by three-cornered fights between English, French and Spanish colonists. Plantations were made, and dispersed, and sometimes reformed at less conspicuous sites after long intervals, so that 'effective occupation' was indeed the only good title to dominion. Such murmurs of these little wars as reached the ear of European statesmen were much confused by ignorance of geography. No one in Whitehall knew where the islands really were. Barbados was frequently confused with Barbuda and sometimes even with Bermuda, a thousand miles away.

The adventurers who made free with the coasts and islands of the Spanish Empire found that the lure of gold had drawn the Spaniards on to the central group of the Greater Antilles (Porto Rico, Jamaica, San Domingo, Cuba) and to the Main, leaving the outer chain of smaller islands, the Lesser Antilles, unoccupied. Claims were staked out upon these islands by English, French, and Dutch men who abandoned their rivalry with one another only to combine occasionally against the overweening Spaniards. All the islands were fertile and beautiful; some were inhabited by hostile Caribs; the 'desert' islands, that is the uninhabited islands, were the first to be settled.

In 1623 Captain (afterwards Sir) Thomas Warner landed with a small party upon St Christopher, the island which Columbus had named after his own patron saint, built a fort and grew a crop

Plate 3

CECIL CALVERT, 2ND LORD BALTIMORE (1605–75)

Baltimore ('the wisest and most successful of English colonisers', according to Gibbon
Wakefield) passes a map of Maryland to his infant son Charles, afterwards 3rd Lord
Baltimore. From a painting by Gerard Soest, about 1640. *See p. 36.*

Plate 4A

GENERAL JAMES
OGLETHORPE
(1696–1785)

Founder of Georgia, soldier
and philanthropist. *See p. 80.*

Plate 4B

WILLIAM PENN
(1644–1718)

Founder of Pennsylvania, late in
life. After a portrait by Kneller.
See p. 52.

of tobacco. Next year he returned to England to engage the patronage of some courtier for a more ambitious colony. In 1625 he crossed the seas again with a commission as governor not only of St Christopher, which the English called St Kitts, but of a large group of West Indian islands which were very imperfectly known. On the very day of his landing, a party of French settlers came ashore in another part of the isle. With unusual good sense French and English came to terms, agreeing to divide the little realm, which is smaller than the Isle of Man.

Meanwhile, in England, great confusion had been caused by overlapping grants to rival colonising syndicates. After negotiation, an overriding charter was given to King James's favourite, the Earl of Carlisle (1627), as Governor of all the 'Caribbee Islands' with powers similar to those of the 'Bishop of Durham in his Palatinate'. The Carlisle grant, the first of the great proprietary charters, was treated as the foundation of English rights in the Lesser Antilles for many years.

St Kitts prospered exceedingly, receiving thousands of adventurous settlers who soon began to swarm off to neighbouring islands within the Carlisle concession: to Nevis in 1628, to Antigua and Montserrat in 1632, to the Virgin Islands in 1650. Yet there were still said to be 4000 Englishmen at St Kitts in 1640. Warner retained his post as governor through the Civil War until his death at St Kitts in 1649.

At about the same time the French settled in Guadeloupe and Martinique (1635) and the Dutch in St Eustatius (1632). The jewel of the group, St Thomas with its admirable harbour, fell to the Danes (1670) and stood neutral in the wars.

(3) BARBADOS

Outside the ring of islands, farther to windward—that is exposed to the first breath of the trade-wind—lies Barbados, a fertile healthy island as large as the Isle of Wight, not too mountainous for settlement, but unfortunately without a natural harbour. It was quite uninhabited when annexed in 1624 by a merchant captain named John Powell who called there on his way home from an unsuccessful voyage to Guiana. In the following year a London merchant of Flemish origin, Sir William Courten (1572–1636), invested £10,000 in a design of trading to the Dutch settlements in Guiana from Barbados, with his fleet of twenty ships. He sent out Captain H. Powell, a brother of the discoverer, with a band of forty settlers who founded Jamestown early in 1625 and attracted 1600 colonists in three years. Courten's highly profitable schemes provoked competition in London from other projectors, especially from Lord Carlisle, the Proprietor of 'the Caribees', who despatched a rival group of sixty-four settlers under a Captain Charles Wolferston, to found a colony which they called Bridgetown (1628).

After intricate negotiation the rival claims were put to arbitration which went in favour of Lord Carlisle. The two colonies coalesced and, by 1636, there were said to be 6000 Englishmen in Barbados. Some of them, in their first year, had gone farther afield to settle in Tobago, but that colony withered away.

The great age of Barbados was when Captain Philip Bell was governor (1641–50). The population was swollen by great numbers of political exiles who seemed to find in that equable island a refuge from the political animosities of England. Barbados was royalist but calm. By 1643 there were said to be 8000 English landholders in the island, making with their families a white population of 18,000 and employing no more than 6000 slaves. Their wealth at first lay in tobacco plantations until, after 1640, a glut on the London market led the settlers to look about for an alternative crop. In those years Bell introduced the sugar-cane from Brazil, a plant which was to multiply the financial wealth of the island while destroying its Utopian social system. Whereas tobacco was cultivated on small-holdings by working proprietors, sugar required large estates, capital, and gangs of slaves. Thirty years later there may have been 20,000 whites in Barbados—the figures sometimes quoted are unreliable—but 50,000 slaves, and thereafter the proportion of slaves to freemen steadily rose. The number of holdings had dropped, by 1676, from 8000 to 800. Yet Barbados was richer, better cultivated, more populous, more civilised, and socially more stable than any of the other islands. Philip Bell had given it a constitution which still (1949) survives, dividing it into nine parishes from each of which two representatives were elected to the Assembly. Before 1650, though the exact date is unknown, the first Assembly had met.

The proprietary government of Lord Carlisle had lapsed when he died, insolvent, in 1636. After long dispute his right passed to Francis, Lord Willoughby of Parham (1613?–66), whose career will be considered in a later chapter (see page 49).

(4) NOVA SCOTIA

An attempt to found a colony of a different sort was made to the northward of New England. From an early period in his reign King James I had given his countenance to Scottish plantations in Ulster. A somewhat shabby device for attracting capitalists had been the creation of a hereditary order of knighthood, the baronetcy, and the open sale of Ulster baronetcies to those who took up a plantation. In the same way, when a poetical courtier, Sir William Alexander, proposed an American plantation by Scotsmen, to be named Nova Scotia (1621), the King allowed capital to be raised by the sale of Nova Scotia baronetcies. The system was neither so corrupt nor so irregular as it seems to modern ears, since knighthood was in the seventeenth century a social duty rather than an award for honourable services. Rich men were occasionally fined for refusing to take up knighthood and the public responsibilities it implied. The proprietor of a large grant of land in a plantation might well be expected to take up knighthood and to pay the price. Rebellion against all such feudal inequalities was in the seventeenth century a new and tiny spark kindled in the breast of some few mutinous soldiers in Cromwell's army and of some Connecticut and Rhode Island farmers, and nowhere else.

Nevertheless the grant provoked the wits to draw comparisons between Sir William Alexander, a poet who wanted to be a king, and James I and VI, a king who wanted to be a poet. In effect, no more than one or two of Alexander's knights-errant visited their province. For, in spite of the grant, the French were already in possession. As early as 1605, before the foundation of Virginia or Quebec, a small French settlement had been formed at Port Royal in the Bay of Fundy and a claim established to the district which they loosely called Acadie. A piratical expedition from Virginia scattered the Acadians in 1613, but they re-assembled, the first of many such episodes. For 150 years the dispute dragged on, the Acadian French clinging to their land, the British colonials, by virtue of some paper charter or treaty, trying to evict them. A handful of Scottish settlers who landed in 1623 withdrew on finding themselves outnumbered by the French.

The Nova Scotia grant was renewed by Charles I and exploited, on Alexander's behalf, by Sir David Kirke, an adventurer who engaged in a long series of plots with Huguenots of uncertain allegiance, and in campaigns against the French-Canadians. In his time (1628) a Scottish colony was founded near the site of the modern town of Granville. In 1629 he captured Quebec, but, when Canada and Acadie were receded at the Peace Treaty of 1632, he withdrew with his settlers to Newfoundland.

But the Nova Scotia claim in the abstract was maintained by the New England colonies. Cromwell sent a force which seized Port Royal again in 1654, but did not colonise the country. Being empty and unprofitable—except to the handful of Acadian peasants—it was a second time receded to France in 1667.

(5) MARYLAND

The colony of Maryland was founded in 1632 as a place of refuge for English Roman Catholics. Sir George Calvert (1578–1632) was a hardworking civil servant and Secretary of State to James I, until he disagreed with the King over his decision to break relations with Spain. Calvert then declared himself a papist and was allowed to retire from the King's service with a pension and, a year or two later, a peerage. He took the Irish title of Lord Baltimore. While in office he had sent a relative, Captain Edward Wynne, with some Welsh settlers to found a colony at Ferryland in Newfoundland and in 1632 was given a charter for his new province which he called Avalon. He visited the colony in 1627 and returned with his family in 1629 intending to remain. A contemporary praises his stone house and his 'brood of horses, cows and other bestial'; he had done more 'for building and planting than was ever performed of any in so short time', at a cost of £25,000. But before long he was petitioning the King for a province in a better climate. He died while on a visit to England, in 1632, before the patent for his new 'palatinate' had passed the Great Seal.

Cecil Calvert, second Lord Baltimore, the traditional founder of Maryland, acted for the most part by deputy, sending his younger brother, Leonard Calvert, to represent him (1632). Leonard set sail with 'twenty gentlemen of very good fashion and three hundred labouring men', to the shore of Chesapeake Bay,

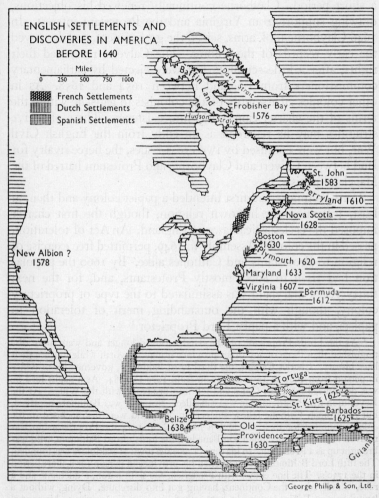

ENGLISH SETTLEMENTS AND
DISCOVERIES IN AMERICA
BEFORE 1640

Miles
0   250   500   750   1000

French Settlements
Dutch Settlements
Spanish Settlements

Baffin Land
Davis Strait
Frobisher Bay
1576
Hudson Strait

St. John
1583
Ferryland 1610
Nova Scotia
1628
Boston
1630
Plymouth 1620
Maryland 1633
Virginia 1607
Bermuda
1612

New Albion ?
1578

Tortuga
St. Kitts 1625
Barbados
1625
Belize ?
1638
Old
Providence
1630
Guiana

George Philip & Son, Ltd.

Map 1

which King Charles I named Maryland after his Queen; and from the beginning met trouble because settlers from Virginia, especially Richard Clayborne, claimed the land by right of earlier possession.

The struggle between Calvert and Clayborne lasted nearly

twenty years, the period of the Great Rebellion in England. Calvert drew help from his brother Lord Baltimore who, although a royalist, managed to maintain his chartered rights except for a short period. Clayborne continually renewed his objections, drawing support from Virginia and the Protestant interest. In 1646 Clayborne took arms, seized the government, and destroyed the early records of the colony. The Calverts reasserted their rights, after a little scuffling, but were ejected by parliamentary commissioners from England between 1654 and 1658. As in other colonies an assembly of the colonists to legislate within the terms of the charter came early into existence. These primitive struggles may be regarded as an eddy from the English Civil War, but were confused by two cross-issues, the fierce rivalry for land between Calvert and Clayborne, and Protestant hatred of the Maryland papists.

Lord Baltimore had first intended a papist colony and then, at least, toleration for his own religion, though the first charter imposed the ecclesiastical laws of England. An Act of toleration, passed in the colonial Assembly in 1649, permitted free exercise of religion to Protestants and Catholics alike. By 1660 the population had risen to 8000, mostly Protestants, and, for the next thirty years, Maryland was assimilated to the type of proprietary colony, though with the outstanding merit of toleration to papists, and with a papist Lord Proprietor.[1]

[1] As the Lords Proprietor of Maryland survived longer and were more distinguished than those of any other province it may be worth while to trace their later history. Charles Calvert, the third Lord Baltimore, governed his province in person from 1661 to 1676 and again from 1679 to 1684. As a papist lord he was denounced by Titus Oates and fell into disfavour with the Whigs. At the Revolution the Proprietorship was cancelled. Not only was Baltimore deprived, but his Roman Catholic fellow-subjects in Maryland were disfranchised in the colony founded for their relief. On his death in 1714 the Proprietorship was revived in favour of his infant son Benedict, the fourth Lord Baltimore, who was brought up as a Protestant. In his time (1729) the town of Baltimore was founded. The fifth Lord Baltimore also governed his province in person for a short period in the 1730's. The line ended with Frederick, the sixth baron, a dilettante and a rake, who lived on the Continent, having got into disrepute. Dying, without a lawful heir, at Venice in 1772 he bequeathed his rights in America to his natural son, a minor, by a will which gave great offence to the people of Maryland. These dues and perquisites, estimated to be worth more than 35,000 dollars a year were, however, soon extinguished by the onset of the American Revolution.

At the census of 1790 there were reported to be 25,000 Roman Catholics in the United States of whom 16,000 were in Maryland. Like the Protestant Episcopalians they had no bishop until John Carroll, one of a celebrated Maryland family, was consecrated Bishop of Baltimore in 1789.

A proprietary government that failed was that which some Puritan lords founded on the island of Providence (1627). The patrons of the Massachusetts Bay Company, Lord Brooke, Lord Saye and Sele, and others, with John Pym as their business agent, desired to found a colony from which to harry the Spaniards and, in the same year as they despatched the peaceful Plymouth colony, they attempted a settlement near the Honduras Coast. Its history is obscure and disreputable. From the island unaptly named Providence, the Englishmen settled in Tortuga, which was merely a pirates' lair. The Spaniards drove them out of Tortuga in 1635 and Providence in 1641. These proceedings established an English interest in a region to which Cromwell laid claim some years later. As a young man he had been one of the promoters and, in 1641, even thought of emigration. English traders frequented the Honduras Coast from early times, certainly from the time of the Providence Company, perhaps long before. About the year 1638 the settlement of Belize (traditionally a corruption of the name of Wallis, an English pirate) was founded by traders who landed to cut log-wood from which a fast black dye was extracted. Treaties with the Moskito Indians, often renewed in later times, date from these first contacts. The log-wood cutters of the Moskito Coast who hunted the wild cattle for ships' victuals were known as the buccaneers, that is eaters of dried beef.

6. THE FREEDOM OF THE SEAS

'The use of the sea and air', said Queen Elizabeth, 'is free and common to all', an enlightened doctrine far more liberal than the common thought of her age, or of ours. Philosophers long wrangled about *jus naturale*, God's Law of Nature revealed by reason to every rational being, and *jus gentium*, the Law of Nations, that least common denominator of the laws of all civilised nations which they applied in their dealings with one another. But the common practice and common sense of world-wide humanity proved that these laws, where there was no effective sanction, were empty words. International authority there had been and international sanctions had been imposed, but not often and not far afield. Normally in the fifteenth century such international authority as was admitted was exercised by the Pope. All nations had tacitly accepted the award of 1360 by which a Castilian Prince was given the crown of the 'Fortunate Islands' and, with the progress of discoveries during the following century, a series of awards and arbitrations came without question from the papal court. When in 1493, after Columbus's first voyage, Pope Alexander VI decided that the new islands east of a certain meridian should pass to Portugal and west of that meridian to Spain, no new precedent was created nor had any of the parties the least conception of what they were dividing. Columbus had found what he believed to be a group of islands off the coast of Asia. The American continent was neither named nor thought of. Nor was it clear whether the Pope was acting as an international sovereign or as a mere arbitrator. The award was several times amended by direct negotiation between Spain and Portugal.

With the progress of exploration, as the vast extent of the New World was revealed, uncertainties arose as to the relative positions of some new lands, especially because, then and long after, there was no accurate method of fixing the longitude, and therefore no accurate map. There were negotiations and further arbitrations, first over the division of South America and, thirty years later, over the continuation of the meridian on the other side of the world where it passed through the Spice Islands themselves. At last the Treaty of Barcelona in 1529 made the decision, which stood for about 200 years, and determined some frontiers which still remain. In the Atlantic the dividing line allotted the sea coast of Brazil to Portugal and the whole American continent excluding Brazil to Spain; in the Pacific the Philippines were allotted to Spain and the rest of the East Indies—as then known—to Portugal. The Spanish hemisphere was gradually construed to include not only the Islands and the 'Spanish Main' of South America, but the surrounding seas and the whole of the Pacific, or Great South Sea, which the Spaniard Balboa had first observed from a Peak in Darien, and which Magellan had first navigated in a Spanish ship. From all this empire of land and water on which, as the kings of Spain boasted, the sun never set, they claimed to exclude all foreign trade and settlement. Nor was it an empty title for they backed their claim with the sanction of strong fleets and armies.

Queen Elizabeth's response to the Spanish imperial policy has already been mentioned. She would respect Spanish sovereignty only when there was effective occupation and she would not admit any principle of dominion over the sea. It was not until the following century that a clear legal doctrine of the freedom of the seas was evolved. Not only did the Spaniards and Portuguese assert their rights over certain oceans, but the English, in other reigns than Queen Elizabeth's, were no less assertive. As long ago as the reign of King John the demand had been made that every foreign ship should salute the ships of the English king in the Narrow Seas, a claim that was only at last waived in 1872. During the early seventeenth century this pretension to rule the Narrow Seas led to fishery disputes between England and the Netherlands. The Dutch lawyer Hugo Grotius put out the first systematic treatise on the freedom of the seas in his *Mare Liberum* which he afterwards incorporated into his general work *De Jure Belli et Pacis* (1625). A learned lawyer's controversy followed, the best known English exposition being the *Mare Clausum* of John Selden (1635). The English were now taking a higher line and demanding the right to levy tolls, even to exclude foreign ships from trading and fishing in the British Seas, whereas Grotius had declared that by natural law the fisheries of all seas should be free to all. From these discussions emerged the first principles of a newborn science of international law, which guided the Peace Conference at the end of the Thirty Years War, and every European Conference until the Germans overthrew all law and restraint in our own age. The greater Grotius founded the whole science; the lesser Selden enunciated the proposition, which has been generally accepted, of Dominion over Territorial Waters, 'so much as was capable of being controlled from the land'. It is curious that the Spanish jurists contributed powerfully to these academic discussions on the side of freedom of the seas, though their own King in diplomatic negotiation paid no attention to their arguments.

The Dutch claimed free fishing rights in vain from the English; the English, Dutch, and French together claimed free trading rights from the Spaniards, in vain. But in the course of the long changes of war and diplomacy the Spanish statesmen devised a new principle. Treaties made before the discovery of the New World applied to the Old World only. New treaties were to be drawn with reference to the Old World and should leave consideration of the New World out of court. Hence as early as 1559 Spain had made a treaty of peace with France with the exception that beyond the Pope's line of demarcation 'might should make right and violence done by either party to the other should not be regarded as a breach of the treaty'. The principle that whether there were peace or war this side there should be 'No peace beyond the line' cropped up in negotiations all through the seventeenth century. This it was that justified at law Drake's exploits and those of the Buccaneers a hundred years later.

All this logic-chopping in the grave chancelleries and universities of Europe worked out very differently on the high seas, where every captain was supreme judge on his own quarter-deck. Was there any law of the sea above that of the stronger hand and the swifter blow? Had not seamen since crafty Ulysses been a lawless race? Were not the English voyagers true successors to the vikings who brought home whatever harvest the ocean furrows bore?

> Some we got by purchase,
> And some we had by trade,
> And some we found by courtesy
> Of pike and carronade...
> At midnight midsea meetings,
> For charity to keep,
> And light the rolling homeward-bound
> That rode a foot too deep!

Were not all Bristol men slave-traders, all Cornishmen wreckers, all Sussex men smugglers, all Manxmen pirates since time out of mind? If rumour lied in saying so, there was no denying that every ship went armed and every shipman, like Chaucer's, was prepared to defend his craft and lading, neither giving nor asking quarter:

> If that he fought and had the higher hand
> By water he sent them home to every land.

Even in the British seas, in time of peace, the Barbary rovers might seize an English ship to carry her crew into captivity in Algiers. An injured sea-captain might take out Letters-of-Reprisal from the king to avenge his private wrongs by making war on his private enemies though the kingdom was at peace; and when the king went to war he would issue Letters-of-

Marque to sea-captains authorising them to wage war on his enemies at their own charges and for their own profit. So obscure was the line between plunder and reprisal, between piracy and privateering under letter-of-marque, so weak was the control of kings over their more distant subjects that, in effect, there was no law beyond the limits of strong government; and, by the King of Spain's admission, no law but that of violence 'beyond the line'.

7. THE COLONIES IN THE INTERREGNUM

THE English Civil War had but a slight effect and that a retarding effect on the progress of the colonies. Emigration fell off since shipping was restricted. As for political changes the colonial assemblies on the whole treated the Long Parliament and Cromwell with the same degree of passive obstruction that they had shown to James I and Charles I. King and Parliament in turn failed to bring them under a proprietary government. So far from taking sides with the English Puritans the Massachusetts Assembly rejected the legislative authority of Parliament: 'Our allegiance binds us not to the laws of England any longer than while we live in England.' Parliamentary sovereignty could not be accepted 'lest in after times...hostile forces might be in control, and meantime a precedent would have been established'. The New England States combined, in 1643, into a confederation which foreshadowed their republican future.

When King Charles was beheaded there was a royalist reaction in the southern colonies as in Scotland and Ireland. Virginia under Governor Berkeley, and Barbados under Governor Willoughby, with Antigua and Bermuda, declared for Charles II. After a year or two the Parliamentary navy, reorganised and led by Blake, was able to detach a squadron to reduce them by blockade. There was no fighting worth recording. One by one, in 1652, the colonies submitted and were reinstated in their former liberties, some royalist governors having been superseded.

The Commonwealth governments had an exalted view of the rights of the Sovereign People of England. They attempted to monopolise the profit of the seas they claimed as their own and at the same time to resist similar claims advanced by other empires, thus forcing certain issues at international and commercial law. A new code of commercial law for the Empire was inaugurated in the Navigation Acts passed by the Rump Parliament. 'Whereas there are in divers places in America colonies which were planted and settled by the people, and by authority of this nation, which are and ought to be subordinate and dependent upon England;...be it enacted...' and so on; thus runs the preamble of the Act of 1650. The second Act of 1651 begins: 'For the increase of the shipping and encouragement of the navigation of this nation which, under the good providence and protection of God, is so great a means of the welfare and safety of this Commonwealth, be it enacted....'

The effect of the two Acts was absolutely to prohibit the ships of foreign nations from trading with the colonies; to ensure that no goods should be brought from any part of Asia, Africa or America into England or the colonies except in English ships manned by crews of which the greater part were English; and to ensure that with certain named exceptions no European goods were to be brought into England save in English ships or ships of the country whence the goods were brought.

The aim of these acts was naval and political. They were intended to subordinate the colonies, to maintain the merchant navy, and to deprive the Dutch of the carrying trade between Asia and England. They were hardly concerned with the increase of trade and not at all with the free growth of the colonies.

The Acts of Navigation remained in force, though many times amended, for 200 years. They achieved their main object by forcing an issue with the Dutch shippers and depriving them of their carrying trade to England. They did in fact preserve and develop England's world-wide sea power. As for the subordination of the colonies, the Navigation Acts had but a slight effect. Over long periods and vast areas they were ignored; they were never in any colony effectively enforced; and when a serious attempt was made in the eighteenth century to enforce them on thirteen of the American colonies the attempt led to the disruption of the Empire.

The Dutch who at last, by the Treaty of 1648, had won their independence and a foothold in Spanish America, were at the height of their commercial greatness in 1652. During the Thirty Years War they had captured from the Portuguese the greatest prize of the Age of Discovery, the Spice Islands. Theirs was the wealth of the East Indies. In every sea they were the successful rivals of the English, in the Caribbean, in the Baltic, in the Iceland fisheries, in the coastal trade of New England, in the Gulf of Guinea, and in the East, where they had completely ejected the English East India Company from its 'factory' at Amboyna. The Navigation Acts were bound to bring to a crisis the fever heat which antagonised Englishmen and Dutchmen in all parts of the world. But the *casus belli* was sentimental not economic; it was Tromp's refusal to salute the English flag in the Narrow Seas, which the English claimed as their own dominion, as proudly as ever the King of Spain claimed the Pacific Ocean. The first Dutch War (1652–4), though of great interest strategically, had no profound effect on the colonies. The Dutch were more concerned with trade than with plantations; their settlements in America and Africa and Asia were trading posts not colonies; and it was their trade that suffered by Blake's victories and the seizure of 1500 Dutch ships.

The end of the first war was hastened by the rise to supreme power of Oliver Cromwell who had a totally different imperial policy. He was of the old school, and favoured alliance with all the Protestant powers against the Pope and the King of Spain, whom he would attack at their most sensitive point, in the West Indies. Before peace with the Dutch was concluded Cromwell was proposing a joint attack by both powers on the Spanish Empire. As Spain and Portugal had shared the world in 1493, now Holland might take Asia, England might take America, and the power of Spain be overthrown. Though this grandiose and truculent plan came to nothing, Cromwell persevered alone with a 'Western Design'. He presented Spain with a quite unacceptable series of demands and, on her refusal, reopened the buccaneering type of war, which had been so successful in the first half of Queen Elizabeth's reign but so unsuccessful in her later years, after the Spaniards had made preparations to defend themselves. Blake showed the English flag in the Mediterranean and captured the treasure fleet at Santa Cruz, while another expedition sailed against Hispaniola as in the days of Drake.

Cromwell's experiment in empire-building showed little appreciation of realities. It was based upon an anti-Spanish foreign policy that was fifty years behind the times, and was

carried out with utter neglect of fifty years' experience of colonisation. He supposed that a Spanish army could be defeated by a
mob, and that a successful colony could be planted with London
unemployables. The expedition that he sent against San Domingo
was disgracefully defeated and as a consolation seized the island
of Jamaica where there was but a weak Spanish garrison (1655).

For about sixty years the Portuguese dominions had been incorporated with those of Spain so that the greater part of the
New World, east and west, had been in the hands of those whom
English Protestants held to be their natural enemies. At the time
of the English Civil War the Portuguese had regained their
freedom. Charles II completed one of Cromwell's designs by
renewing the ancient treaty with Portugal. The alliance was
cemented by the King's marriage with a Portuguese princess,
who brought to England as her dowry the sovereignty of Bombay
and Tangier. Bombay will be considered in a later chapter;
Tangier provided a European complication. King Charles found
himself master of two fortresses, Dunkirk, which Cromwell had
captured from the Spaniards, and now Tangier, commanding one
gate of the Mediterranean. He rid himself of Dunkirk which was
expensive and useless, but retained Tangier for twenty years.
It served as a cantonment for a small standing army which he
wished to maintain though his people disapproved. The time
had not yet come when England had the necessity or the strength
to stretch her sea-power so far south. It was no strategic loss and
a saving of revenue when, in 1683, Tangier was evacuated.

8. THE AMERICAN COLONIES UNDER
CHARLES II

CHARLES II, his brother James, Clarendon, Shaftesbury and
other leading statesmen actively concerned themselves with the
colonies and brought into their counsels such eminent advisers
as John Locke and William Penn. Broadly, it may be said that
their chief concern was with trade and shipping, the mainstays of
the nation. Colonial trade, it was assumed, was subordinate to
the interest of the English market; the colonists were conceived
as Englishmen living overseas for the purpose of increasing

English trade, but entitled to the protection of the same laws and the enjoyment of the same liberties as if they were living at home.

Cromwell's Navigation Acts were therefore re-enacted and were amended, as conditions required, into a code of commercial law known as the Acts of Trade. Much argument took place over the schedule of 'enumerated commodities' which were to be reserved for the home market. These were tropical products such as 'sugar, tobacco, cotton-wool, indigo, ginger, fustic, logwood and braziletto', which were always scarce and of which it was thought desirable that there should be an English monopoly. Alterations in the schedule led to much legislation at home and much litigation in the colonies, where all attempts to enforce the law through revenue officers or to prosecute offenders in the Courts of Admiralty provoked fierce legal struggles in the colonial courts. From the beginning the colonists resented the intrusion of royal officers into the colonies as a breach of their chartered rights. For the present little harm was done, because the Acts could not be enforced. Smuggling was common through the Dutch settlement at Manhattan and through the buccaneering ports in the West Indies.

While the colonists were beginning to nourish a grievance against the mother-country over trading restrictions they could have no complaint over political rights. They enjoyed a far higher degree of self-government than Englishmen at home. The three New England provinces were confirmed in their liberties even to the extent of being authorised to elect their own governors.

(1) JAMAICA

Cromwell's last years had been spent in the ill-conducted war with Spain by which Jamaica had come into British hands. When the war ended in Europe it dragged on 'beyond the line' since Charles II was unwilling to restore the island. Thus for years Jamaica was at war while the rest of the world was at peace. It was most notably the island of the buccaneers, a great haunt of smugglers and a receiving house for stolen goods. Where the line was to be drawn between smuggler, pirate, privateer, buccaneer and man-of-war's man in Jamaica was indeed hard to say. The age has its hero in the Welshman Henry Morgan (1635–88), who led a raid across the Isthmus to the city of Panama

(1670), where Drake himself had failed. He looted and burned the town, seizing a vast treasure from the baroque church which still stands in ruins near the entrance to the Panama Canal. Though cruel and rapacious Morgan was a privateer not a pirate. Recalled to England to give an account of himself, he was exonerated, knighted and appointed Lieutenant-governor of Jamaica by Charles II.

The Spanish power was now fast declining; the cities of the Isthmus fell into decay after 150 years of greatness and were of little account until their resurgence in the twentieth century.

Although a large island, nearly as extensive as Wales, with a good harbour, Jamaica had been neglected by the Spaniards. When it was captured, the population did not exceed 1500 Europeans and about as many negro slaves. Some of the latter escaped into the wooded interior which rises in altitude to 7000 feet, reverting there to savagery. A desultory war was waged for many years against these wild negroes (known as Cimaroons, or Maroons—that is, 'men of the mountains') until, in 1738, they were pacified and 'settled' on the land. The Europeans at first were not remarkable for civilised virtues. Mutinous soldiers, Irish prisoners-of-war, vagrants and convicts made bad colonists, who lived in idleness and despondency until most of them died of yellow fever. The best were the overflow from the other colonies, 1500 from Nevis and even more from Barbados. By 1658 the population was said to be 4500 whites, 1500 slaves, and the Maroons.

During Cromwell's time the island was kept under military rule which proved as expensive as inefficient. Little real progress was made until King Charles II set up a colonial government of normal type with a royal governor, and an elected assembly, bound by English common law (1663). A long constitutional wrangle with the home government over the revenue ended, in 1728, with the voting of a permanent civil list. The Captain-general of Jamaica was a great personage, sometimes an English duke.

Cocoa was the first crop to be grown and marketed by small-holders, but, as in Barbados, sugar plantations organised on a larger scale soon prevailed. Jamaica sugar and rum fetched a higher price than the produce of the other islands. Though sugar was profitable, war and buccaneering made the real wealth of Jamaica. During the eighteenth century piracy was gradually suppressed and slave-grown sugar became ever more important. The population grew, and changed in character, from 8500 whites and 9500 slaves in 1673 to about 30,000 whites and 300,000 slaves in 1800. As slavery increased, so the slaves grew more restive, sometimes and notably in 1760, rising in revolt. Nature, too, was restive; a new town built at Kingston, after the destruction of Port Royal in an earthquake (1692), eventually became the capital.

(2) LEEWARD AND WINDWARD ISLANDS

The tangled claims of rival proprietors to the lordship of West Indian islands were again canvassed after the Restoration of Charles II. Lord Willoughby got the reversion of the Carlisle grant, subject to compensation for the other claimants, after appeals and counter-appeals to the Privy Council. In 1663, the financial obligations of the colonies were consolidated by an act of Parliament which levied an export duty of 4½ per cent on all the exports from the islands in the Carlisle Grant (Barbados and the Leeward Islands), to raise a fund from which the claims of the Crown and the Proprietors were to be satisfied. This duty is the sole example in the history of the British Empire of a tribute levied by the mother-country upon its dependencies, the sole example, that is to say, of that profit-making imperialism which all other empires in the history of mankind had regarded as the purpose for which dependencies were brought into existence; and this modest little revenue tariff was imposed only in order to liquidate legal liabilities. It survived for 170 years until, after strong remonstrances from the colonial assemblies, it was repealed by an act of 1838.

With a revenue guaranteed from his share of the export duty Willoughby returned to his proprietary lordship. His two periods as Governor (1650–2 and 1663–6) were full of activity. He had founded a thriving little colony of 100 settlers at Surinam in British Guiana (1650), had sent Sir Thomas Warner's half-breed son to come to terms with the Caribs of St Lucia, and was encouraging the expansion of all the island settlements, when the war against French and Dutch (1664–7) brought him to a halt. He beat off de Ruyter from Barbados, but lost Surinam to the Dutch, and temporarily lost St Kitts. On an expedition to its relief in 1666 he was drowned.

After the death of the fifth Lord Willoughby, his brother the sixth baron carried on his work with spirit and energy. In 1671 the great area of 'the Caribees' was split into two governments of the two geographical regions windward and leeward of the French colony of Guadeloupe. An early attempt to federate the Leeward Islands was made in 1698, but the General Assembly at St Kitts lapsed during the wars. Their greatest figure was Christopher Codrington (1668–1710), born in the West Indies, son of the Captain-general of the Leeward Islands. The Codrington family owned Barbuda and made the prosperity of Antigua, where lesser planters were jealous of their pre-eminence. Young Codrington, a gallant soldier and an Oxford man, succeeded his father as Captain-general in 1698 and governed the islands well. At his death, in addition to his legacy of £10,000 for founding the Codrington Library at Oxford, he left two plantations in Barbados to the Society for the Propagation of the Gospel, for the foundation of Codrington College which has a remarkable history. For a hundred and twenty years the Society managed these slave-plantations while educating the slaves and treating them benevolently. They founded a grammar-school for white boys and, in 1830, a college which trained white and coloured students for the ministry.

The Windward Islands, excluding Barbados, were not much settled in the seventeenth century. They were the home of the most numerous and ferocious of the Caribs. The French from Martinique and the English from St Kitts had made some attempts at settlement but without success. A strange story is that of 'Indian' Warner, Sir Thomas Warner's half-breed son, who was sent by Lord Willoughby to colonise Dominica, the most beautiful and fertile of the islands. More Carib than Englishman he became a chief in the island and, having quarrelled with his father's people, was treacherously killed by Philip Warner, his English half-brother. After this failure French and English mutually agreed to leave the Caribs alone. Except Martinique (French) and Barbados (British), all the Windward Islands, south of Guadeloupe, were treated as independent and declared so in several treaties, even as late as the Treaty of Aix-la-Chapelle, 1748. Nevertheless some infiltration of white settlers took place. Dominica and St Lucia, on either side of Martinique, acquired a French-speaking population.

(3) NEW YORK, PENNSYLVANIA, CAROLINA

In 1664, when the English and the Dutch were again at war, a plan of campaign against the Dutch settlements on the American coast was devised by James, Duke of York, and carried out by a small force of English and colonial troops without bloodshed. At the Peace Treaty of 1667 the Dutch retained the English colony of Surinam which they had captured, and ceded 'New Amsterdam' as they called their colony in North America.

Thus fell into English hands, in 1664, the island of Manhattan, the estuary of the Hudson river and the coast-line between New England and Virginia. The captured region was reorganised as two proprietary colonies under the names of New York and New Jersey. The Duke, as Proprietor of New York, established a civil government with liberty of worship and trial by jury, but without an elected assembly. Some Dutch traders had been settled on the coast since 1609, the year when Henry Hudson explored the river that bears his name. In 1626, in spite of English protests, they had bought from the Indians for a parcel of trade goods the rocky tip of the island of Manhattan in the mouth of the river, the best anchorage on the coast and the best line of advance into the interior. Here on the island they had built a trading post which grew into a little town. The anchorage was commanded by a fort at what is still called Battery Point. Wall Street to-day marks the site of the stockaded wall cutting off and protecting the tip of the island against the English who regarded the Dutch settlers as interlopers in their province of New England. Outside the wall the Governor like a true Dutchman planted a pleasure-garden which he called the Bowery. The estuary of the Hudson they called, as it is still called, the North River, the South River being the Delaware 200 miles away.

At the British conquest there were about 7000 Dutchmen in the colony, most of whom remained as British subjects. From the beginning the Manhattan colony was cosmopolitan; it included some Swedes from an earlier Swedish settlement which the Dutch had captured and incorporated, besides the Dutch and English. French Huguenots fled there for refuge and before the end of the century there was also a colony of Jews. It was never and is not now a typical American town, but a doorway from

4-2

Europe, a port of call. Of the many races that have come ashore in the Hudson none has left a stronger impress of personality than the sturdy Dutch originals. Stuyvesants and Rensselaers, Cortlandts and Van Burens, Schuylers, Vanderbilts and Roosevelts, the old 'knickerbocker' families, have been New York's leading citizens.

More remarkable was the Quaker colony of Pennsylvania, which arose from the odd friendship between the papist Duke of York and William Penn the Quaker leader. At several stages in his career the Duke attempted to build up a political party by reconciling all the dissident minorities in England against the central stronghold of the Anglican Church. Of the minorities the two most bitterly hated in Old and New England were the Papists and the Quakers. The quietism and pacifism which mark the Quakers to-day did not distinguish them in their first generation. Their contempt for rank and ceremony in an orderly society, their refusal to adopt conventional manners and customs led to their being regarded as dangerous revolutionaries. They were bitterly persecuted everywhere, but nowhere so harshly as in Massachusetts. The world was glad to see the last of them and to get them safely disposed in the Duke's new colony. Penn was a rich aristocrat to whom the Crown owed money. The debt was discharged in 1681 by a grant of land in the southern part of New Jersey where Philadelphia, the City of Brotherly Love, was founded. King Charles himself invented the name Pennsylvania for the Utopia which Penn was to found in the woods. It was described in one of its advertisements in London as 'a very unusual society for it is an absolutely free one and in a free country. Every one may be concerned that will, and yet have the same liberty of private traffique as though there were no society at all.' His colonists were drawn from many sources, not only Welsh and Irish Quakers but members of pietist sects from Germany and Switzerland. In 1683 arrived the first shipload of German Mennonites, better known to European readers as the Anabaptists of Munster. About 20,000 German Protestant refugees came to America, mostly to Pennsylvania, during the next forty years. In the 1730's another sect, the Bohemian Hussites generally known as Moravians, came to America under their leader Zinzendorff. They, too, found a home in Pennsylvania which became the most German part of the New World, preserving the frugal piety of old rural Germany, which was destined to be destroyed and perverted in the Fatherland.

Though many of Penn's schemes proved to be impracticable, he has two striking achievements to his credit. He laid out the city of Philadelphia on a rational plan based upon Wren's rejected plan for rebuilding London; and he established honest and friendly relations with the Indians. Penn was a slave-owner; it was only in later times that the Quaker state took the lead in the fight against slavery. In 1702 a new state named Delaware was carved out of Pennsylvania, the frontier between them being known as the Mason-Dixon line, from the names of its surveyors. This line was to be the northern boundary of 'Dixie', the land of negro slavery.

Early in Charles II's reign a fantastic project was begun for a large proprietary colony to be planted to the southward of Virginia, under the name of Carolina. Among the numerous courtiers who formed the proprietary body, the leader was Lord Shaftesbury the Whig. He employed John Locke to draft a constitution (1668) for the colony, an extraordinary document which bears no mark of the liberal principles associated with its author's name. Locke supposed that the colonists could be subjected to a rigid feudal system, as vassals of their absentee landlords, without self-government and without common-law rights. No effort was made to put this absurd scheme into practice, and not much effort to enforce the authority of the Proprietors. Carolina (or Carolana), the unexplored wilderness between Virginia and Spanish Florida, was already inhabited by a few interlopers from Virginia and the West Indies. Ignoring the vapourings of the Proprietors they formed an assembly in 1668 and elected their own governor. Charleston, afterwards capital of North Carolina and the largest city in the old South, was founded in 1670. During the next few years the Proprietors attempted, with slight success, to assert their authority. They could not prevent the growth of free institutions like those of all the other colonies. On the whole their influence was negative and Carolina a backward area until the development of the cotton plantations, a century later. The Carolina grant, which also covered the Bahama Islands, was the cause of endless frontier disputes with Spain.

The Atlantic seaboard between French Canada and Spanish Florida, though there were disputes at both extremities, was effectively occupied by the English in the seventeenth century. The settlements still, in 1700, lay along a coastal fringe communicating with one another by water. Inland lay unexplored forests from which the Indians occasionally emerged, in strange attire, to barter furs for gunpowder or rum, and to indulge in sudden inexplicable fits of violence.

9. THE RED INDIANS

WHAT every schoolboy knows about America is the myth of the noble red man, the American Indian. Like other legends it has grown with time. Those whom the Virginia colonists first met were forest Indians settled in villages and clearings along the shores and creeks of Chesapeake Bay. They were never numerous and soon outnumbered by the immigrants. On the whole, they were friendly disposed towards the pale-faced newcomers until, finding their plantations encroached upon, their forests cleared, their game driven off, they retaliated by a raid on the settlers, in 1622. Thereafter they were treated as enemies. In the North they traded with the Dutch and the French for furs, but found little friendly dealing among the Puritans of New England to whom they were like the Amalekites, idolatrous heathen, to be smitten hip and thigh; worshippers of Baal whose blood was to be shed without remorse, so that the Lord's chosen people might inherit the land; or in the homely idiom of the frontier 'the only good Indian was a dead Indian'. Against these harsh words and harsher measures good Roger Williams of Rhode Island and William Penn of the City of Brotherly Love protested in vain.

The Indians, according to the frontiersmen, were treacherous, implacable, bloodthirsty and crafty. But those men of peace who laboured among them found them also generous, honourable and nobly eloquent. They could be both in turn or both at once, like other human beings. Their pride and simplicity, their stoic courage, their mastery of woodcraft, their swift changes from silent dignity to unbridled passion, their aquiline beauty and picturesque adornments soon became the property of every romantic writer. A legend which began in the forests fringing the Atlantic shore gained new life in later days, when the frontiersmen encountered the horse-riding Prairie Indians of the far west.

The Indians who captured, threatened, and at last befriended Captain John Smith were not acquainted with the wheel, forged no metals, wove no textiles, plaited no cords. Their dress was a hunting shirt, leggings and sandals made of soft deerskin fringed and patterned with lines of sea-shells. Their axes and knives and arrows were tipped with jade, their bows were strung with deer-sinews, their ropes were strips of bark. They warmed themselves in robes of beaver and bearskin; they crowned their chiefs and warriors with a headdress of wild-turkey feathers. They lived in gypsy tents of skins or, in their older settlements, made sheds of slanting poles. The women worked in their small gardens tilling sweet potatoes and maize (which the Americans came to know as Indian corn); the men idled and gamed when not engaged in hunting or in war.

Like contemporary Scottish clans each Indian tribe occupied a small plantation and claimed a common right over vast ill-defined hunting-grounds. Some neighbouring tribes were hereditary enemies, others hereditary friends, but war was the exception and peace the normal state; even though some young brave might think fit to advance his private prowess by prosecuting the blood feud against a neighbour and taking his scalp when there was no public war. The young men lived together in clubs bound by a secret freemasonry to which they could be admitted only by passing terrific tests of courage and endurance in initiatory rites. When tribal quarrels boiled over, after the harvest and the cele-bration of the Corn-dance, or when the young braves forced the hand of their more cautious elders, the tribe with solemn dedication went on the war-path. All fleshly pleasures were renounced. The warriors shaved their heads, leaving a single tuft of long, black hair, the scalp-lock, which an enemy—if he were man enough to do it—might cut, bleeding scalp and all, and claim as the trophy of personal victory. Naked to the waist and daubed with war-paint, that is with patterns of soot and red ochre, the braves maddened themselves in the frenzied war-dance and followed the trail to battle.

War was fought under strict rules, and resolved itself into Homeric single combats between champions whose renown was measured by the number of scalps taken. Honour and glory once sated, the warriors were ready to meet in conference, to make long speeches enlivened with miming and dancing and to declare truce by the solemn smoking of the pipe of peace and the burying of the hatchet, until the urge for war should stir again. All this pomp with a very moderate amount of actual fighting was altogether different from the ruthless endless war of extermination, without quarter on either side, which arose when the white man drove the red man from his tribal hunting-grounds.

Like their cousins the Aztecs, who immolated human victims to their gods by hundreds, the Indians of the north had some notions of human sacrifice. They took delight in torturing and killing their prisoners of war, partly out of a perverted lust for cruelty, but chiefly for an obscurer reason, a half-understood theory of expiation. They cleaned the land from the guilt of blood by the ceremonial shedding of the blood of a victim, a scapegoat. This calculated cruelty provoked horror and hatred among the pale-faces who did not stay to reflect that their own persecution of heretics and witches derived from the same psychological impulse.

The Indians were also capable of nobler conceptions. The great world-spirit, the distant, uncomprehended *Manitou* had revealed himself to the red men through a culture-hero, a gay, smiling youth, who came among the people from the unknown and returned to the unknown again. He had taught them the arts of peace, to fish with lines, and to construct frail craft from sheets of birch-bark, to plant the maize whose sheath-like leaves of delicate green and golden tasselled head were the robes of the corn-spirit sacrificed, buried and brought to life again by the secret rite of the Corn-dance, which represented and stimulated the yearly miracle of the life and death of the corn. In the end of things he would return to lead the red men to happy hunting-grounds beyond the shining, unknown levels of the Great Lakes in the land of the Setting Sun. Longfellow's *Hiawatha* is an idealised version of one such (Ojibway) myth.

This was the life of the Indians before the coming of the white men, that dread invasion against which Hiawatha himself had forewarned them, or so that life has been dramatised by the pale-faced storytellers. But the red man has been so much written up by poets and novelists, and so much written down by practical men who were concerned with stealing his property that the plain truth is overlaid and lost. Some such generalisation as is here attempted will serve to show what the Indians have been thought to be. This picture of a doomed way of life has had a profound effect on the progress of America and on the attitude of the white men to the coloured races in all parts of the world.

The very language in which it has been described, the war-path and the pipe of peace, the braves with their gruesome trophy of bleeding scalps, the trail and the happy hunting-grounds are now the current coin of the English language, the common-places of Anglo-Saxon thought, which perpetually mould ideas. Even the primitive speech of the savages has been called in to enrich the Anglo-Saxon vocabulary with *canoes* and *tomahawks* and *moccasins* and *wigwams*; with the *squaw* and the *papoose*; with the tribal *totem*; with the *pow-wow* where the *sachems* meet in solemn debate concluded by the passing of the *calumet*[1] from lip to lip, in token of peace concluded with the *Yankees*[1] who had penetrated their forests.

In Virginia and in Maryland the invading white men came as farmers whose concern with the Indians in the first instance was the acquisition of land. Before the seventeenth century was over the Indians were driven back from the coastal plain into the wooded foothills of the Appalachians. They had not retired without many bloody struggles nor without getting some material gains from the pale-faces. They now used guns from Birmingham and knives of Sheffield steel and embroidered their leather work with English glass beads instead of the lines of shells called *wampum* which had been their currency. Coin was still scarce in America where much retail trade was done by barter. Among the white men, Virginia tobacco and Jamaica rum were commonly used as currency so that before long the fire-water of the pale-faces was traded with the Indians for beaver-skins. From the days of Caliban to the last days of the frontier in the 1880's the curse of the red men was the trader who supplied them with fire-water and fire-arms; their ferocious tendencies were mad-dened to frenzy by the one and their power to take vengeance on the white man multiplied by the other. At first the Indian traders were mostly Dutchmen from Manhattan and Frenchmen from Quebec whose settlements commanded the routes into the interior, through country controlled by a powerful confederacy of tribes.

The Five Nations (Mohawks, Cayugas, Senecas, Oneidas, Onandagas), known to the French as the Iroquois, who roamed

[1] *Calumet* probably French-Indian, *yankee* probably Dutch-Indian patois.

through all the lands about the River Hudson and west as far as
the Great Lakes, were combined into a confederacy ruled by a
council of fifty sachems. Even when a sixth nation (Tuscaroras)
joined the league their numbers probably did not exceed 30,000.
A muster of 940 braves who accompanied the British to Fort
Niagara was described as 'all the Mohawks and almost all the
Six Nations'. By 1644 they were in alliance with the Dutch to
whom they supplied beaver-skins in exchange for muskets, with
which the Iroquois drove the French Indians (Hurons and
Algonquins) north across the Great Lakes. When the English
came to New York they took over the alliance and the trade.

The penetration of the Indian country by French traders and
missionaries began when Frontenac was Governor of Quebec
(1673–82 and again 1689–98), and made Fort Frontenac, now
Kingston, his advanced post on Lake Ontario. His invasion of
the province of New York during the war which began in 1689
definitely confirmed the Iroquois in their alliance with Great
Britain. By the Treaty of 1701, made with commissioners from
New York, they placed themselves under protection of King
William III, acknowledging themselves tenants of the Crown for
the whole of their vast territories, an area of 800 miles by 400
miles, extending from Albany to the site where Chicago now
stands and including 'the great falls of Oakinagaro'. To this
treaty which still protects some of their descendants the Iroquois
on the whole remained loyal, especially the Mohawks whose
chief, 'King Hendrick', was the most powerful in the league.
They were reputed as British subjects 'appendant to the colony
of New York'.

The Society for the Propagation of the Gospel (S.P.G.) first
sent missionaries among the Iroquois in 1704 and for long with
small results. Their first success was the conversion of some
Mohawk chiefs and among them King Hendrick, who was then
escorted in great state to London, a triumph for the missionaries
and a guarantee that the alliance would be maintained in the
French War which had again flared up on the frontier. Hendrick
was presented to Queen Anne and protested his gratitude and
friendship in the name of the three Mohawk totems, Bear, Wolf
and Turtle.

10. WAR AND COMMERCE, 1688-1721

(1) THE REVOLUTION OF 1688

THE reign of Charles II is marked in British imperial history as a period of expansion in every part of the world in accordance with a comprehensive and, on the whole, an enlightened policy. Those years saw the acquisition of Bombay and New York, the foundation of Philadelphia and Charleston, the building of Cape Coast Castle and of Fort James on the Gambia, the development of the African slave trade (against which as yet no protest was made in any quarter) and the Hudson Bay fur trade, the attempted grouping of small colonies into dominions, the preparation of a commercial code for the whole Empire in the Acts of Trade, and the direction of policy through a single department, the Board of Trade and Plantations, which was permanently established in 1696. In all these undertakings the Duke of York had played a part, which he continued to play when, as James II, he succeeded his brother on the throne. His hand was felt in the administration of the American colonies and when his policy collapsed in the English Revolution of 1688, the imperial system in the colonies was sorely shaken. But with moderation the same imperial policy was renewed under his supplanter.

James was for firm efficient administration in each colony by a strong executive which might draw support from some elective assembly but would never submit to being controlled by it; foreign foes and domestic faction alike would be curbed by a standing army and navy; but within the frame of this autocratic rule common-law rights and religious toleration were to be ensured. Sir Edmund Andros, a conscientious and experienced administrator and a Protestant, was selected as the instrument of this policy. He was appointed successively governor of several colonies and, in 1686, Governor-General of New England, in partnership with a Surveyor-general of customs who was to enforce the Acts of Trade. The scattered factious Puritan commonwealths were to be united into a loyal dominion where even Quakers and Papists, even Indians, might enjoy their own. But the New Englanders were as determined as the men of Old England that they would not have legal equality on those terms. They plainly saw where jesuitry had led the Huguenots who trusted the paternal rule of Louis XIV. When Andros attempted to call in and revise their precious charters he met resistance in every colony. The news of the overthrow of James II reached Boston in 1689. Without hesitation and without violence the citizens rose and deposed his servant Andros, restoring the former governor. For the next few years there was confusion in several colonies; in Maryland where Catholics and Protestants again came to blows; in New York where rival factions alternately seized power; and in Boston. Meanwhile, a war had broken out in Europe. The French seized St Kitts in the West Indies and, with Indian help, encroached on every frontier: Newfoundland, Canada, Hudson Bay.

King William's War (1690–7) and Queen Anne's War (1702–13) were fought by Grand Alliances pledged to restrain the overwhelming power of Louis XIV of France. In each war the English government was the mainspring of the alliance and from the two wars the commercial and naval power of England derived great advantages. The trading interests regarded these as their war aims, but the governments were more concerned with political plans: in the first war with resisting King Louis' intention to restore King James II to the throne of Great Britain and Ireland, and in the second with preventing King Louis from seizing possession of the moribund Spanish Empire. These wars, of the English and Spanish Succession, are among the few examples in our history of a predominant part taken by British generals and armies in the land campaigns on the main continental front. But the political and strategic genius of Marlborough went far beyond the direction of his own battles in Bavaria and Flanders. He, first of Englishmen, conceived and inspired the plan of naval control of the Mediterranean in order to threaten what his descendant, Winston Churchill, called 'the soft underbelly of Europe'. After 1704 a decisive factor in all British strategy was the maintenance of a fleet in the Mediterranean, to prevent a combination between the enemy squadrons based on the ports of southern Europe and those based on the Atlantic ports. To make this strategy aggressive, to carry the war to the enemy's coast has required advanced bases far deeper into the Mediterranean than Gibraltar Bay. Hence the Balearic Isles, Corsica, Sicily, Malta, Corfu, Crete and Cyprus have at one time and another been occupied by British fleets and armies.

Gibraltar was seized from the French party in Spain by a neat little combined operation, in 1704, and was then retained in spite of counter-attacks by French fleets and Spanish armies, the first of many such attempts at siege. The Rock has now been in British hands for 240 years, a period of time rather longer than the former period during which it was subject to the united Spanish monarchy. Its population, of mixed Mediterranean descent, has hitherto shown no desire to return to Spanish rule.

Four years after the capture of Gibraltar a further step forward was taken by the seizure of the land-locked harbour of Port Mahon in Minorca, the most suitable base in the Balearic Islands for operations against the southern coast of France. Throughout the eighteenth century, British Mediterranean strategy was based upon Gibraltar for defence and Minorca for attack.

From the merchants' point of view these operations had the intention and the effect of defending our trade with the Levant. Protection for the Smyrna convoys meant as much to the merchants of London as protection for the treasure fleets to the merchants of Seville. The presence of a British squadron in the Mediterranean also had a restraining effect on the 'Barbary Pirates', the Moslem states of North Africa which lived by plunder and slave-raiding. The petition in the Litany for God's pity on 'all prisoners and captives' serves to recall our ancestors' perpetual fear of being kidnapped into slavery in Algiers or Tunis.

Outside Europe the campaigns were unimportant and for the most part unheroic. Even the greater naval operations were treasure-hunts, the only true-blue hero being the stout, old 'tarry-breeks' Admiral Benbow who died of wounds after an ill-fated action off Santa Marta. What seafaring men remembered of these wars was the plundering and destruction of a Spanish fleet worth fifteen millions sterling off Cartagena, and the burning of the treasure fleet in Vigo Bay (1702) when millions of pieces-of-eight went to the bottom, and lie there still. In the West Indies there were raids and plundering expeditions, mostly around the island of St Kitts which was lost to the French and retaken. 'Trade in general seems at a stand and nothing on foot but privateering', wrote a Jamaican in 1708. 'The war will leave to the world a brood of pirates to infest it.'

The northern colonies made a poor showing against the French, since their affairs were in great confusion after the overthrow of Andros, while French Canada was strong and united under Governor Frontenac. A champion arose at Boston in the person of Sir William Phipps, a rough, honest fellow, who got the confidence of the townsmen. He led a colonial expedition against Port Royal in Acadie, but achieved nothing beyond sacking the papist church. 'Not a blow was struck,' he said, 'for want of courage and conduct in the officers.'

In that year (1691) a new charter was issued making Massachusetts a royal colony with Phipps as Governor. He repeatedly tried to organise combined attacks on Quebec, that failed, mainly because of the unwillingness of the New Englanders to co-operate or to contribute funds. Three years later their pride had been so humbled by Indian raids and bankruptcy that they threw themselves on King William's mercy: 'we implore your royal aid...for the rescuing of a languished province...we prostrate ourselves at your feet'. But they remained republicans at heart.

Meanwhile the French with their Indian allies came down from Lake Champlain to raid New York Province. The most brilliant figure in the war was d'Ilberville, a French-Canadian, who ranged the whole interior of America from Hudson Bay to the mouth of the Mississippi, harassing the English. He drove away the agents of the newly established Hudson's Bay Company, and captured the English settlements in Newfoundland. But his exploits were barren since the victory of the allies in Europe obliged the French to give up all their conquests at the end of the war.

(2) THE TREATY OF UTRECHT

In the public history of Europe the Treaty of Utrecht, 1713, showed some disreputable features, but it was epoch-making for the British Empire. It gave the British navy control of the Mediterranean Sea, it made the first breach in the closed economy of Spain, and it narrowed and defined the French holdings in North America. In the first place Gibraltar and Minorca were ceded by Spain to Great Britain. Valuable as these fortresses were for naval operations, they made sore spots in the sensitive Spanish pride. Since the Treaty also placed a Bourbon Prince upon the Spanish throne it was almost inevitable that in any future war the King of Spain would join with France in the hope of recovering his lost fortresses; hence the concern felt in England over the repeated Family Compacts, in the eighteenth century, between the kings of France and Spain.

It will be necessary to pursue at some length the effect of the other clauses of the Treaty:

(1) France ceded her territory in Newfoundland and Nova Scotia to Great Britain with certain reservations, which will be discussed in a later chapter.

(2) Spain gave formal permission for a limited English trade with the Isthmus of Panama. She also admitted the right of British to cut logwood on the Moskito Coast.

The Treaty of Utrecht thus put an end to the old days of uncontrolled warfare against Spain 'beyond the line'. For a hundred years the kings of Spain had fought for their monopoly with pertinacity and courage. On the whole they had provided naval protection by concentrating the commerce of their Empire in armed convoys which converged each year at Porto Bello. There the manufactured goods of the Old World were exchanged for the luxuries of the New World and especially for bullion which was conveyed to Europe in the annual treasure fleet. Neither Drake nor Grenville had succeeded in grasping this prize, which only once fell into British hands, when Admiral Blake captured it at Santa Cruz (1657). Designs to seize the treasure fleet dominated our strategy in each successive war, but in vain; it was too well guarded.

While giving this naval protection to their ships the Spaniards had failed in giving economic protection to the commerce on which those ships lived. Not gold and silver, but sugar, rum, molasses, tobacco, indigo, and logwood were the true wealth of the Spanish Indies and the Spanish Main. The most valuable import that could be exchanged against these exports was a steady flow of negro slaves to work the plantations. It was not the naval raids against the treasure fleet that broke the power of Spain, but economic penetration. The Dutch, the French and the English had occupied and planted many of the most profitable islands in spite of Spanish resistance. They had built up in those islands a trade that flourished largely because it was unrestricted. Not that the Kings of England and France were less anxious than their brother of Spain to control and monopolise their own colonial trade; they tried but had not the power to do it.

The interlopers were often buccaneers and smugglers, occasionally pirates, but primarily traders. They came to import goods
that the Spaniards sorely needed, English manufactured stuffs
and negro slaves from Africa. They sought a market and if
necessary would fight for it, but not often, because nothing suited
the Spanish settlers better than to buy. The Spanish officials
and even governors often connived at the free trade. Jamaica,
where the best sugar was grown and the best rum distilled, was
the smugglers' market for the two commodities so potentially
demoralising, rum and slaves.

The eighteenth century was to see a more humdrum struggle
for the West Indian sugar trade, a prize of greater value than
chests of doubloons or pieces-of-eight. For this trade France
and England fought five great wars over the prostrate limbs of the
fallen Spanish Empire, but wars of a quite different character
from the Protestant crusade of Drake and Ralegh against the
'inquisition-dogs and the devildoms of Spain'. That had been
total war, 'ideological' war, with no respite and no quarter. The
struggle with France was commercial and political with occasional
resort to force when diplomacy failed. The wars were limited in
duration and in violence by the principles of international law
which, since Grotius, the nations had begun to apply. When
legitimate war had been distinguished from lawless violence,
piracy could be defined. It flourished among the unnumbered
reefs and bays and islands of the Caribbean, above all in the
Bahamas, which contained so many hiding-places for rogues.
But pirates after Utrecht were denounced, pursued and punished,
by all honest governments alike, as enemies of the human race.

(3) THE BAHAMAS: PIRATES

The Bahamas had been included in the grant to the influential
proprietors of Carolina (1670) but without much effect. The
Cloud-cuckoo land which John Locke devised for Lord Shaftesbury and his associates remained in the air, hardly even taking
root at Charleston, while the numerous sandy islands of the
Bahama group were exploited by adventurers on their own
account. The island of New Providence [1] was settled in 1666 by a

---

[1] New Providence in the Bahamas is to be distinguished from the older colony
of Providence off the coast of Honduras.

party of pioneers from Bermuda who elected J. Wentworth as their governor and maintained him in spite of the Carolina grant. Their port at Nassau was a rallying point in the irregular perpetual war with Spain and, as buccaneering declined into piracy, so Nassau became a free port where not too many questions were asked. A convenient centre for blockade-running in all the wars, it has been noted for contraband trade until recent times.

Not all governors were honest. John Avery, who captured the Great Mogul's daughter in the Indian Seas (1695), returned to disperse his crew and realise his gains in the Bahamas, where he was in league with the Governor. The wealth of Asia slipped through his fingers leaving him to die a beggar at Bideford in Devon. William Kidd, whom the government of Massachusetts hired to fight the pirates, concealed in the Bahamas some part of the loot of six French ships before returning to London to face the charge of having himself turned pirate. Some unsavoury tales of official collusion came to light, and more were smothered away, before he was hanged at Execution Dock (1701). Edward Teach, known as Blackbeard, was a pirate from Jamaica who made his base at New Providence. The terror of the Carolina coast, he held Charleston to ransom, exploiting a rivalry between two governors. Teach's treasure is probably mythical though his orgies and his bloodthirsty habits are recorded facts. A change for the better came when Captain Woodes Rogers, the circumnavigator, acquired the governorship of the Bahamas from the *fainéant* Lords Proprietor. In 1718 Teach was killed in a seafight and the pirates' lairs routed out. The celebrated Captain England went to Mauritius where his crew marooned him, others to Madagascar. Several who 'declared war on the human race' began to operate from Sierra Leone, so that their exploits blacken the history of Africa rather than America.

(4) THE ASIENTO AND THE TRADING COMPANIES

As part of the general settlement which accompanied the Treaty of Utrecht, France surrendered to England the 'Asiento', the profitable contract for supplying negro slaves to the Spanish colonies, a bargain which revolted the consciences of the Victorian English, but which rejoiced the harder hearts of their ancestors in the reign of Good Queen Anne. For the southern Spanish colonies a British slave-market was to be established at Buenos Ayres;[1] for the Indies the depot for the trade in human flesh was at Jamaica. The management of the trade was eagerly contested. It was already a privilege of the Royal African Company to buy negroes in West Africa and to ship them overseas. The distribution at the forward end was now allotted to the newly formed South Sea Company which before long was importing 5000 negroes a year through the main depots of Vera Cruz, Panama, Cartagena, Havana, Porto Bello and Caracas. But this happy state of affairs was destined not to last. The obstruction of free-traders and smugglers, British and Spanish, many of them officials of the colonial governments, was too strong. In 1750 the Spaniards withdrew the Asiento, buying out the South Sea Company for £100,000 and throwing the market open. British merchants and shippers flocked to this desirable trade and soon made the port of Liverpool, from which the slavers sailed, second only to London among British seaports.

In spite of the attitude of the City of London, where monopolies were disliked, four great chartered companies were formed or reformed in these years. The East India Company (see below, chapter III, 3) was refounded, after a fierce commercial struggle, in 1696. The Hudson's Bay Company, first chartered in 1670, suffered severely in Queen Anne's War and was saved by the Treaty of Utrecht; it will be more fully considered in the next chapter. The Royal African Company (1664) and the South Sea Company (1711) enjoyed a boom created by the Asiento Treaty. The decline of Spain produced a new wave of commercial adventure on the Spanish Main and in what were loosely described as the South Seas. The name properly belonged to the Pacific Ocean, the unknown waste of water seen to the southward from the Isthmus of Panama, containing, it was believed, the Antarctic continent and the fabled gold mines of King Solomon. Adventure at sea was the subject of the two greatest romances of the age, *Gulliver's Travels* and *Robinson Crusoe*, books which from that day to this have never lost the attention of 'the best audiences in the world, the children and the wise men'. Robinson Crusoe's island was not in the South Sea but off the Atlantic Coast of the Spanish Main; and the great 'bubble' company, though it placed the name of the South

[1] Probably the origin of the British commercial colony on the River Plate.

Sea in the prospectus, actually traded to the Caribbean and the River Plate.

The treaty permitted the British South Sea Company to send each year one ship, laden with British goods, to the annual fair at Porto Bello. This system, having once opened the door, gave every opportunity for further illicit trade in the commodities which the Spaniards so earnestly desired. The first such ship, the *Royal Prince*, laden with goods to the value of £256,000, made a successful voyage in 1717. But the limitation to a single voyage proved unworkable. Not more than ten of these annual voyages were made before the method was abandoned.

The Asiento agreement and the sailing of the first ship to Porto Bello sent South Sea shares soaring from £100 on issue in 1711 to over £1000 in 1718. Then a financial scandal involving the directors and two members of the cabinet broke the market. The shares came tumbling down, but were held at a figure above par by the skilful intervention of Robert Walpole, who at this crisis became what was beginning to be called 'prime minister'. The Company was saved, and survived in obscurity till 1853, providing in its later years a clerical post for Charles Lamb.

The South Sea Bubble was one of three great financial disasters caused by a phenomenon then new but now familiar, a hysterical rush to invest and play the market at a time when money was cheap, followed by an inevitable slump when the actual trade proved insufficient to justify the high price of shares. It had its counterparts in the Darien Scheme (1698), a Scottish venture in trading and colonisation, and the similar French Mississippi scheme (1720). In each of these instances the financial collapse involved the livelihood and even the lives of confiding settlers, a far more deplorable affair than the losses of the speculators.

The Darien scheme was the classic example of folly in colonisation. Although individual Scots had begun to make their mark in the colonies, no successful Scottish settlement had been planted and Scotland was excluded by the Acts of Trade from the benefits of commerce with the English colonies. The newly formed Board of Trade (1696), and Randolph its surveyor-general in America, resisted all attempts of the Scots to share these benefits, with the result that the Scottish merchants pressed for a colony of their own. In 1698 William Paterson, the founder of the Bank of England, floated a company for Scottish emigration to the

Isthmus of Darien, a quite unsuitable location, which was hampered by the nullifying stipulation in the charter that there should be no settlement in Spanish territory. The shares were taken up with avidity in Edinburgh while the project was denounced in London. William III, as Kings of Scots, had carelessly approved the scheme; as King of England he carelessly allowed his parliament to repudiate it. No protection against the Spaniards was to be afforded for this Scottish rival to the English trading ventures. About 2000 settlers and most of the scanty floating capital of Scotland were launched and sunk in the expedition to Darien. No adequate site was found and no market for the profusion of trade goods. The settlers, marooned on an unhealthy shore, met bitter opposition from the Spaniards to whom they eventually surrendered. Their funds were exhausted and the jealous English government made no move to help them. Some died, others drifted to the other colonies, and the colony came to an end, or rather failed to come into existence. This lamentable affair was a principal factor in persuading the Scots to forgo their independence in order to accept a commercial union with England. An indemnity from the English Treasury to the Scottish investors in the Darien Company was an article of the Act of Union.

(5) 'THE CITY'

Trade, shipping, the Navy—not colonisation—were the true imperial interests of Englishmen in the hundred years after the Restoration of Charles II. By 1688 the annual tonnage of ships cleared from English ports outward bound was 190,000; by 1701, 273,000; by 1738, 476,000; by 1763, 561,000. Money to invest was growing ever more plentiful and the great complex of financial interests which we call 'the City' had come into existence. Joint-stock companies were being formed for every sort of undertaking and especially for banking and insurance which gave a new stability to the market. Nothing contributed more to this stability than the funding of the national debt. In earlier times the greatest problem in every large national undertaking was that of providing a continuous flow of ready money other than on short-term loan. How could cash be found to repay the cash borrowed? The financier William Paterson arranged in 1694 to advance large credits to the government on a long term, the sum to be borrowed from subscribers who were to be repaid with terminable life annuities. In course of time the annuities were converted to payments of interest at a fixed rate which, long after, stood for generations at 3 per cent. This was the origin of the Bank of England which kept national credit firm through wars and slumps and made London the money-market of the world. Good credit in its turn secured the 'three-per-cents' as the stock for the cautious investor. Every landed man could now have a stake in the national finances as well as in his county and would find an interest in overseas trade, the foundation of national wealth. The whole solid system enabled 'the City' to invest its growing surplus in trading ventures.

Hardly less important was the system of marine insurance. Ned Lloyd's coffee-house was a favourite rendezvous in Charles II's reign for sea-captains and for shipping merchants. Here investors gambled on the chance of shipwreck by guaranteeing, for a price, to repay the value of vessels or cargoes lost. Before the end of the century the *habitués* of Lloyd's had formed a ring of underwriters who examined and classified ships and cargoes and insured them at agreed rates. The name of Lloyd's which has been absorbed into every European language, the regularity of insurance, the firmness of the London markets, the cautious management which, for 250 years, has justified the phrase 'Safe as the Bank of England', and especially the integrity of the London merchants, form the solid base on which trade and empire have been built. They would never have grown and endured had not 'the word of an Englishman', *palabra inglés* actually stood for honest dealing and prompt payment the world wide, a reputation enjoyed by the English individually but not by their government which has more commonly been described as *Albion perfide*.

'The City' was strongly protectionist. It presumed, perhaps rightly, that our commercial greatness had sprung from the Navigation Laws, and fought bitterly to retain these advantages for the home country, opposing the extension of free trade to the colonies and to Ireland. But within the frame of the laws protecting English trade, privilege was unpopular. 'The City' did not approve of royal monopolies or chartered companies, but desired freedom for all English merchants. There were, however, powerful 'interests' which sometimes overruled the preference for free competition. From the earliest times individual colonies retained their agents in London to look after their commercial and other interests.

Walpole was in office from 1721 to 1742, a long period of peace and prosperity. While trade flourished with the East and West Indies, while 'moderate men grew big' in the City of London, the American colonists were imperceptibly growing into a nation, were extending their pioneering labours into the wilderness, and were finding themselves confronted by a new military and naval power even more formidable than that of Spain. The French government was carrying out a set policy of limiting the English frontiers by ringing them round with naval and military posts.

(6) HUDSON'S BAY COMPANY

On 25 October 1666 a Huguenot adventurer named Chouart had audience of King Charles II. He had been to Canada where he acquired a seigneury from which he took the title of Sieur des Groseillers. In the City of London they called him 'Mr Gooseberry'. He had been fined by the Governor of Quebec for illicit trading in the far west and therefore brought his expectations to another market, offering to lead an English expedition from Canada to Hudson Bay, a proposal which was well received at court. When the Dutch War ended, in 1667, a holding company, in which the Duke of York, Prince Rupert, and half the King's ministers took shares, was formed to finance a preliminary expedition. In June 1668 two ships set sail; one went astray; the other, the *Nonesuch* with Mr Gooseberry on board, reached Prince Rupert's River in Hudson Bay, made a pact with the Cree Indians, built Fort Charles, and wintered in the Bay with 'nature looking like a carcase frozen to death'.

The voyage appeared to justify the King in issuing a charter to the Hudson's Bay Company on 2 May 1670: 'having undertaken an expedition...for a discovery of a new passage into the South Seas, and for the finding of some trade for furs, minerals, and other considerable commodities, and by such their undertakings have already made such discoveries...the Governor and Company of Adventurers of England trading into Hudson Bay [are granted]...the whole trade of all those seas, streights, and bays, rivers, lakes, creeks, and sounds...that lie within the entrance of the streights commonly called Hudson's Streights together with all the lands...upon the coasts and confines of the seas aforesaid...which are not now actually possessed by any of our subjects, or by the subjects of any other Christian prince or state....' The whole of this unknown tract of land was given away to the officers of the Company 'in free and common socage', with authority 'to judge all such persons as shall live under them according to the laws of this country' and to 'make war or peace with any prince or people that are not Christian'. While thus disposing of one-third of a continent, the King had no more notion of the extent of his grant than the Pope had in giving half the world to the King of Spain.

The Directors, with Prince Rupert in the chair, soon set to work. From 1671 they despatched three ships annually, in June, laden with some such cargo as '200 fowling pieces and powder and shot, 200 brass kettles; twelve gross of knives, and 900 hatchets' which were to be exchanged for beaver-skins against the return of the ships in October. The trade boomed at the rate of one beaver for a pound of tobacco, six for a laced coat, and twelve for a fowling piece. Five forts, at which landing parties could meet the Indians and, if necessary, pass the winter were established at Albany River, Hayes Island, Rupert's River, Port Nelson and New Severn. The Duke of York succeeded Prince Rupert as second Governor, the third was John Churchill (afterwards Duke of Marlborough), whose name was given to Fort Churchill in 1686. By that time the Company was paying a huge annual dividend, sometimes 50 per cent. In 1690 they watered the stock to three times its former value and still paid 25 per cent. But the French now began to react sharply against this attempt to penetrate western America from the northern seas. The French-Canadian, d'Ilberville, was sent overland from Quebec to resist their progress, with no small success. During King William's and Queen Anne's wars the Hudson's Bay Company lost much of its trade, and all its forts except one, to the French. The Treaty of Utrecht restored the trade and territory of the Hudson's Bay Company though without compensation for war damage.

The following fifty years (1713–63) saw the struggle between France and England for the hinterland of North America. While the English had begun to move inland in great numbers from the eastern seaboard and had now established trading posts on the

northern seaboard, the French, until their defeats in the Seven
Years War, held the inland waterways. In 1684 they had reached
Niagara. In 1682 La Salle sailed down the Mississippi. In 1717
De La Noue reached the head of Lake Superior. In 1731 Veren-
drye pushed westward as far as Lake Winnipeg. In 1743 one of
his parties had a distant view of the Rocky Mountains. In 1751
they built a fort on the Saskatchewan not far from the site of
Calgary. Meanwhile the Hudson's Bay Company was sharply
criticised in London for failure to carry out the terms of the
charter; they had been content to collect beaver-skins without
searching for the North-west Passage. A Royal Commission
justified their actions. The share-capital had been increased from
£10,000 to £100,000 upon which they annually· exported trade
goods worth £4000 and imported furs worth £12,000. What
more could be asked of a trading company in the unromantic age
of Walpole and the Pelhams?

11. NEWFOUNDLAND[1]

THE history of Newfoundland is unlike that of any other colony.
For 300 years fish and the fisheries constituted its only topic.
The Newfoundlanders turned their backs upon the interior of
their island, dismissing it contemptuously as the 'barrens',
and looked outwards to the offshore fisheries. A 'plantation' in
Newfoundlander's jargon was the name given to a fishing establishment; a 'fishing-room' meant the claim over a strip of beach
on which fish could be dried; and fish meant cod. All the English
settlements were fishing villages along the shores of the south-
eastern corner of the island, and the Avalon Peninsula, with no
connexion by land better than steep footpaths through rocks and
woods. There was no carriage-road in the island before the
nineteenth century.

The seasonal fishing-fleet from the west of England arrived in
May as soon as the ice was thawed and left in October or November before the winter storms set in. As early as 1549, an Act of
Parliament was passed, making admiralty regulations for the
'better encouragement of the fisheries of Iceland and Newfoundland'. Even before Gilbert's ill-fated voyage (1583), which is

[1] For map, see p. 579.

taken as the substantial claim to sovereignty over the island, a naval officer had been sent to adjudicate the quarrels of the fishermen. Before the end of the century a customary practice had grown up that the skipper of the first ship to arrive at Ferryland, on the eastern shore, should be recognised as the 'Fishing Admiral' for the season. In 1633 the custom of the fishing-fleet was authorised by Star Chamber in the form of a Fishing Charter issued to the Mayors of Southampton, Weymouth, Melcombe, Lyme, Plymouth, Dartmouth, East Looe, Fowey and Barnstaple, the nine west-country ports from which the ships sailed. Under supervision of the nine mayors the fishing-fleet was a floating republic with the Fishing Admiral as President and judge. The charter was based upon the customary law of the sea as prescribed in the ancient codes of Oléron and Wisby.

During the next few years three separate attempts were made to colonise Newfoundland by projectors working in the tradition of Sir Humphrey Gilbert. A fortified settlement would enable the British to monopolise the fisheries, excluding ships of other nations from the use of anchorages and 'fishing-rooms'. Such a plan for conducting the fisheries from a base in the island provoked hostility from the holders of the Fishing Charter who worked from bases in England. In spite of their activity a charter for a colony was obtained through the influence of Francis Bacon. John Guy, William Colston and others were incorporated, in 1610, as the Company of Adventurers and Planters of London and Bristol[1] for the Colony or Plantations in Newfoundland. The first party of settlers, led by John Guy of Bristol, wintered at Cuper's Cove in Concepcion Bay in 1610–11, founding there the oldest British colony which still survives; they numbered about a hundred. There was little progress until the plantation was reinforced by the support of Sir George Calvert (see above, page 36) who settled with his family at Ferryland in 1629. On his departure for Maryland, the colony languished. Some colonists, however, remained when the reversion of the Company's charter was given to Sir David Kirke in 1637. For some years Kirke lived in the stone house built by Calvert at Ferryland, with a few

---

[1] J. D. Rogers, the historian of Newfoundland, points out the recurrent dualism of the charters in this age. The rivalry between London and the west-country ports appears frequently in the titles of the companies. The west country resented London interference.

Scottish emigrants whom the French had driven out of Nova
Scotia. He first fortified the narrow entrance to the harbour of
St John's. The triumph of Cromwell in England led to Kirke's
recall and a return to the principles of the Fishing Charter.
Cromwell would have removed the Newfoundlanders to his
new colony of Jamaica and, after the Restoration, the Council of
Trade and Plantations continued in that mind.

The colony was saved by the influence of the Navy. When at
last a decision was taken, in 1675, to remove the settlers, a report
was rendered on the island by the naval officers who convoyed the
annual fishing-fleet. In their opinion it was necessary for strategic
reasons to maintain a base in Newfoundland. The report showed
that there were then twenty-eight distinct settlements on the
coast between Cape Race and the south-east corner of the island.
The settled population engaged in the fisheries was 523, of whom
361 were women and children. To these were added a casual
population of 1342 visitors who stayed in the island over a winter
or two, fur-trading, boat-building or growing vegetables for the
fishing-fleet. In consequence of this report the Council of Trade
reversed their decision in 1680, allowing the settlers to remain.
The new status of the island was regulated by an Act of 1699
establishing a double government. The fisheries were still to be
governed by the Fishing Admiral in accordance with the charter
of 1633, but the Convoy Captain, that is the senior naval officer,
was to be governor of the settlements. In the winter, when both
the Fishing Admiral and the Convoy Captain had departed, the
Newfoundlanders were left ungoverned.

Fear of the French had caused the Navy to take an interest in
the problem. In 1662 Louis XIV had founded the settlement of
Placentia on the ice-free southern coast where he stimulated the
French fishers with bounties and a more liberal Fishing Charter
than the English enjoyed. Newfoundland suffered much in the
ensuing wars. In 1696 the celebrated French frontiersman,
d'Ilberville, raided and sacked St John's at midwinter with a
band of men who crossed the island from Placentia on snow-shoes.
Too late, the War Office spent £3000 on fortifying St John's in
the following year. Twice again, in Queen Anne's War, the
French overran the English settlements, taking advantage of the
fogs which interfered with naval support. In 1711, the Convoy
Captain summoned a General Assembly of the islanders to

organise a militia, the first beginnings of a formal administration in the island. Since that date Newfoundland has been securely held as a British possession, with a peculiar status recognised in the eleventh clause of the Utrecht Treaty (1713). The French King admitted British sovereignty over the whole island, promising to withdraw the French settlers from Placentia. While abandoning the southern shore the French fishermen were still allowed a concession to 'take and dry fish' on the unoccupied northern and western shores, a concession productive of many disputes since these coasts were unsurveyed and were defined in the Treaty by reference to places not marked on any map. The Treaty also had the effect of concentrating the French settlements and shipping around the Straits of Belle Isle and the St Lawrence Gulf. The settlers from Placentia were removed to Cape Breton Island which became a French fortress.

12. PHILANTHROPY IN AMERICA

THE early New Englanders were a dour race, addicted to a frugal industrious way of life and indifferent if not hostile to the more genial virtues. Like their 'unco guid' fellow-calvinists in Scotland against whom Robert Burns railed, their religion, their laws, their habits were exclusive and intolerant. They were strict sabbatarians with little liking for cakes and ale, and were much inclined to impose civil penalties for breaches of the moral law. Theirs was not a missionary creed. The children of light withdrew themselves from the darkness of the outer world. The heathen were to be rooted out of the land; heretics and schismatics were driven into the wilderness. They were bitter in their hostility to all other Christian sects, especially to the Church of England. Papists were persecuted in New England and Quakers were hanged. It is not surprising that they shared the prevalent horror of witchcraft, as the most blasphemous of all heresies. One of the last and worst examples of the legal persecution of supposed witches in any Protestant country occurred at Salem, Massachusetts, where nineteen victims were executed in 1692. When Sir William Phipps became the first Royal Governor he shared the prevalent hysteria but soon came to his senses (perhaps because the witchfinders laid accusations against his wife), and put a stop to the legal proceedings, for which he was warmly commended by King William.[1] Tolerance was a bitter pill for the Boston Puritans, and another was the enlarged franchise under the new royal charter.

With their defects the New Englanders had corresponding strength of character. Like the Scots they were far ahead of the English in public education, having provided a school for every township of fifty householders. Church and school formed the basis of village life, their management being the nucleus of the New England town meeting, the assembly of all the citizens for direct democratic government. They elected their officers annually and voted them a salary, a system quite unlike that of the English townships where the local officers served, gratis, in rotation. Hence the status and function of justices, sheriffs and the lesser village officers differ profoundly in Old and New England.

One in 200 of the early Massachusetts settlers, forty of their eighty ministers, were graduates of Oxford or Cambridge, but scholarship inevitably declined in the hard pioneering age. There was a printing-house at Boston in 1639, and a strict censorship of the press, in a society with no disposition towards polite literature. Its first important production was an Algonquin Bible produced in 1661–3, the first bible printed in America. This was the work of the Rev. John Eliot (1604–90) of Jesus College, Cambridge, the 'apostle of the Indians'. In 1646 he began his mission to the Algonquins and at first received moral and financial support both from the General Court of Massachusetts and from the Long Parliament in England. The great sum of £11,000 was raised on both sides of the Atlantic for his work which culminated in the foundation of a Christian-Indian township (1651). He claimed 4000 converts. Later came the inevitable struggle by the Indians to retain their hunting-grounds. In the Indian war of 1674, known as 'King Philip's War' his converts were killed or scattered and his work brought to an end.

The beginning of a more humane culture derives from the legacy bequeathed by John Harvard of Emmanuel College, Cambridge, in 1636, £1000 and a library of books for the foundation of a college in New England. It began in a very small way as a training college for the ministry and, during the eighteenth

[1] *Calendar of State Papers (American)*, 12 Jan. 1692–3.

century, grew slowly into a small provincial university with a strictly classical curriculum. It should be remembered that Harvard College was unimportant when compared with the contemporary Spanish University of Mexico which already included faculties for classical studies, anthropology and native Mexican culture; but it played a part in forming the American nation. By 1693, 107 out of 123 of the clergy in New England were Harvard men. In the course of 200 years Harvard created the characteristic Boston School of writers and philosophers, austere, lucid, restrained in thought and style, the first native literature to appear on the American continent. After 300 years the modest foundation of John Harvard has grown into one of the greatest, wealthiest and most learned of the world's universities, notable for research and still retaining at Cambridge, Massachusetts, some faint flavour of the older Puritan university where Milton and Cromwell spent their youth in the placid English Fenland.

The next American university was founded at Williamsburg, Virginia, in 1691, where the original buildings have been piously preserved. Yale followed in 1716 and from that time colleges for higher education have kept pace with the growth of the American nation. The later universities, especially Princeton (1746) followed the Scottish rather than the English model.

The general sense of the American colonists favoured the free churches and most commonly those with Calvinist principles. But free-churchmen, Anglicans, infidels, all alike shared a hatred of 'popery', a prejudice even more virulent among the Americans than among the English. While there were as yet few Roman Catholics in the colonies, and no Catholic Irish vote, the colonists were becoming increasingly restive over French penetration into the hinterland of North America and its corollary, the spread of French Jesuit missions among the Indian tribes.

By a typically English legal fiction all colonists, for purposes of English law, were deemed to be freemen of the county of Middlesex who happened to be residing abroad. Like other Englishmen they were presumed to be members of the established Church unless they rejected its services by some legal form of dissent or recusancy. Though most colonists were, if they observed any religious forms, Dissenters, they came under the ecclesiastical jurisdiction of the Bishop of London who had commissaries in several of the colonies to exercise a spiritual control over the Church established by law in New York, Maryland, Virginia, and the Carolinas, and the principal West Indian islands, according to the usages of the Church of England. It must be admitted that the Anglican clergy in these colonies were lax and indolent on the whole. The Church flourished only among the aristocrats of Virginia who affected an English way of life, and in the cosmopolitan town of New York. The facts that the Church was losing ground, that it failed to reconcile the Puritans of New England, that it showed no missionary fervour to convert Indians or negroes were recorded by all observers. The first attempts at reform were made under the auspices of Queen Anne, 'the Church of England's Glory', by the foundation of the Society for the Propagation of the Gospel (1701) and the Society for the Promotion of Christian Knowledge (1698), the former concerned with missionary efforts and the latter with Christian education. The S.P.G. made notable progress especially in the Carolinas, in reviving churchmanship and in missions to the Indians, which aroused much suspicious hostility among the New England Puritans. Schools for the sons of chiefs were an early necessity; for this purpose Dartmouth College (New Hampshire) was founded in 1749. The S.P.C.K. concerned itself with issuing versions of the Bible in the Indian languages. But equally useful was the protection which the missionaries tried hard to get for the Indians against the unrestricted trade in rum, the cause of their worst misfortunes. Rum, it was universally agreed, perverted the most civilised Indian into a bloodthirsty savage. So vital was this restriction and so dangerous was the trade in rum that even the moderate use of strong liquors has been denounced as vice, in America, for two centuries.

Church activity was as yet on a small scale. The Anglican Church in America consisted of a few isolated parishes 3000 miles away from their diocesan bishop. It was recruited by occasional immigrant clergymen, in many cases poor representatives of their order. It could not flourish until rooted in American soil. Since the earliest days Churchmen had recognised this and had desired the establishment of a bishopric, a proposal that produced the most violent political reactions. In Georgian England a bishop was conceived as a political at least as much as a pastoral functionary. The days were not forgotten when proud prelates had ruled the land from high places in government. They still enjoyed

wealth and patronage, advised the Crown, presided in ecclesiastical courts. Puritans, who had fled to New England to escape
from this accursed thing, and Whiggish aristocrats in the southern
colonies, who were not at all desirous to buttress the power of
the Crown, alike objected. The conception of a bishop who had
merely spiritual authority and that only over his own flock was
unfamiliar. The Board of Trade was unlikely to move in this
troublesome controversial matter. The Anglican Church in
America had no bishop until after the Revolution; its activities
were regarded with hostility by most colonists, who suspected
that its sympathies lay with the King's royal prerogative rather
than with colonial rights, even with justice for the red man rather
than with unlimited progress for the white.

A persistent and noble effort was made by the idealist philosopher Berkeley to raise the standard of religion and learning
in the colonies. As a rising young Irish clergyman he was
launched into Society by Dean Swift (1724) with the odd testi-
monial that Berkeley's heart would break if his Irish benefice
were not taken away from him. Swift added to his letter the
recommendation that it would be more useful to 'keep one of the
first men in the Kingdom at home'. He was determined to found
a college in Bermuda both for white settlers and for the sons of
Indian chiefs who were to be trained as clergy and teachers for
the New World. Berkeley persevered so far as to get from the
House of Commons an almost unanimous resolution that it
would be proper to endow the proposed college with £20,000
from Crown property in the West Indies which had been allotted
to the colonial Church by Queen Anne. So promising a beginning encouraged Berkeley to migrate to America with his own
small fortune and a sum of £3000 raised by private subscription.
After waiting for some years in Rhode Island, he was at last convinced that the Whig government had no intention of releasing
good money for any such quixotic purpose. Walpole, the Prime
Minister, characteristically, after subscribing £200 to Berkeley's
private fund, let him know that the Treasury had no intention of
issuing the grant of £20,000; Berkeley 'had better give up his
expectations'. A bishop was heard to say at Westminster that
the resolution had been a mere compliment: 'all was done out of
regard for the man, not the design'. Another 'very good lord'
went further: 'learning', he said, 'tended to make the colonies

independent of their mother-country...the ignorance of the Indians and the variety of sects in our plantations was England's security'.

After a ten years' struggle Berkeley lost hope of getting the money. He had spent his private funds for the benefit of the Anglican Church in Rhode Island and for the new college at Yale, and had assisted in the foundation of a college at New York which was destined to become the University of Columbia, before returning to a philosophic career and an Irish bishopric. His contribution to the future of America was faith in a New World where no longer 'infidels would pass for fine gentlemen, and venal traitors for men of sense'. Among his papers there exists a copy of verses containing the celebrated lines:

> Westward the course of empire takes its way,
> The four first acts already past,
> A fifth shall close the drama with the day,
> The world's great effort is the last.[1]

Though Berkeley, perhaps from modesty, described these lines as 'wrote by a friend of mine', they declare his hope, his vision.

Another philanthropist in London tried to get the reversion of the money promised to Berkeley. This was General James Oglethorpe, a Tory soldier and suspected Jacobite. He devoted many years to relieving the condition of insolvent debtors who were confined, in great numbers, in English prisons. In 1732 he and others, including good Captain Coram of the Foundling Hospital, were appointed by the Crown as 'Trustees for the Colony of Georgia' which was to be planted between the Savannah and the Altamaha rivers. Philanthropy, the motive of the founders, was backed in this instance by prudence on the part of Walpole's government which judged that a British outpost so far south would serve to check the northward progress of the Spaniards from their fort at St Augustine in Florida, and that at small cost to the Crown. In this instance, therefore, £10,000 was voted and actually paid out.

In 1733 Oglethorpe led his first colony of 114 settlers to Georgia intending to direct their settlement with paternal benevolence. 'The Society will use their utmost endeavours to

---

[1] Correspondence of Berkeley with John Perceval, who acted as London agent to him and to General Oglethorpe.

prevent luxury and oppression in the officers, idleness and vice in the people. They intend to send no governor, to prevent the pride that name might instil. The power of the government they intend to invest in an overseer and council of honest and discreet men.... They [the settlers] are to be regularly armed and exercised yet the lands where they establish are to be regularly purchased from the Indians and all measures used to keep peace and friendship with them.... The Indians shall upon all occasions be treated with the strictest justice and utmost humanity. No rum...will be allowed to be sold to the Indians....All men are from the beginning to be established as freemen and not as servants....Mankind will be obliged for the enlarging civility, cultivating wild countries, and founding of colonies, the posterity of whom may, in all probability, be powerful and learned nations.'

In spite of these excellent intentions the ne'er-do-wells of London were ne'er-do-wells still in Georgia. Few men were found 'honest and discreet' enough to put down luxury and idleness alike except Oglethorpe himself, a born dictator. His colonists, small-holders each occupying a fifty-acre allotment, found work in a sub-tropical climate, without negro labour and without rum, so uncongenial that their unhappy fate was selected by Goldsmith in his *Deserted Village* to illustrate the horrors of emigration. Oglethorpe alone kept the colony going. He was on excellent terms with the Indians and successfully fended off Spanish encroachment, fighting a brilliant little campaign with his colonials against a column of Spanish regulars from St Augustine in the War of 1739. He attracted industrious Scottish emigrants from the Carolinas, and German Protestant refugees expelled from Salzburg by a persecuting archbishop, so that, when he retired in 1743, his colony was taking root. By 1752, when the charter was revoked and normal colonial government instituted, Georgia had assimilated to its northern neighbours. Besides 5000 white settlers there were now 2000 blacks and no embargo on slavery or rum.

But Georgia made one distinct contribution to American life by providing the cradle of the Methodist Revival. Oglethorpe, like many of the reformers of the age, was a Tory High Churchman and took with him to Georgia two young Oxford clergymen of good abilities and unimpeachable High Church principles,

John and Charles Wesley. Though they did not remain long in
Oglethorpe's Utopia their life-work was directed and formed by
their American experiences. Berkeley, Oglethorpe and the
Wesleys had much in common, the intention to regenerate an old
corrupt society in the pure air of the New World whether by
education, by enlightened government, or by evangelism.

Wesley's successor as Oglethorpe's secretary was George
Whitefield (1714–70) another Oxford parson. While the Wesleys
returned to reinvigorate the moral life of the English, Whitefield
remained as the apostle of Methodism in America. He soon left
Georgia and preached 'at large', during six visits to the colonies,
quite breaking with the Anglican system. His was salvationist
doctrine of a simpler type than that of the Wesleys whose
religion was flavoured with German mysticism and the pietism of
William Law. John Wesley was a scholar and a precisian, George
Whitefield an evangelist who spoke like a prophet from the Old
Testament. His message spread far beyond the narrow con-
venticles of Boston, beyond the musty loyalties of tide-water
Virginia. He, not the Puritans of Massachusetts, created American
Protestantism with its moral fervour, individualism, and self-
reliance, a proper religion for frontiersmen. He made a deep
impression even on Benjamin Franklin. Before Whitefield's
death his Methodists far outnumbered the New England Inde-
pendents, who have dwindled to a small minority even in the
City of Boston. It may be mentioned that he gratified his
colonial audiences by justifying negro slavery from the Old
Testament.

II

BRITISH NORTH AMERICA IN THE EIGHTEENTH CENTURY

Argument: The compact group of English colonies on the Atlantic sea-board was hemmed in by French settlements at strategic points on the waterways to the interior. Friction in Acadie, western Virginia, and also in Newfoundland, was a contributory cause of the great wars which ended in the triumph of the British at the Treaty of Paris, 1763.

When the French had been expelled, the English colonists in America became conscious of their opportunity and their destiny. They resisted attempts by the British government to reorganise the whole Empire on a rigid though enlightened plan with a common fiscal policy, local self-government, and safeguards for subject races. Invoking a coalition of the European powers against the mother-country, they won independence. A substantial minority of loyalists laid the foundations of a new British Commonwealth in Nova Scotia and Canada.

1. ENGLISH AND FRENCH IN NORTH AMERICA

AFTER twenty years of peace England drifted into war with Spain in 1739. Walpole, after skilfully avoiding earlier adventures, was at last hounded into a martial policy, by the Opposition leaders who hoped to make it a means of replacing him in office, and by the ignorant who hankered after the old days of Protestant warfare and treasure-hunting on the Spanish Main. There was no lack of matters for contention: occasionally the Inquisition still claimed an unwary English heretic as its victim; the King of Spain objected to the English settlement of Georgia; there were smugglers everywhere, and endless legal disputes over the Asiento. What followed was known derisively as the War of Jenkins' Ear from the tendentious story, put out as propaganda by the Opposition leaders, of an English skipper whose ear had been cut off by a Spanish coastguard.

This disreputable struggle at sea was the first phase of a general European war precipitated by the rapacity and treachery of Frederick the Great of Prussia. In Macaulay's glowing words: 'The whole world sprang to arms. On the head of Frederick is all the blood which was shed in a war which raged during many years, and in every quarter of the globe, the blood of the Column of Fontenoy, the blood of the mountaineers who were slaughtered at Culloden. The evils produced by his wickedness were felt in lands where the name of Prussia was unknown; and, in order that he might rob a neighbour whom he had promised to defend, black men fought on the Coast of Coromandel, and red men scalped each other by the Great Lakes of North America.' Wicked as Frederick was, this accusation is not fair to him. All the causes of war between French and English had long previously been recorded and each party in North America had often already played off against the other the ferocity of the red men; while in Southern India civil wars already raged among the black men before French and English were drawn into the strife (see page 161).

The war had one positive effect upon the growth of the empire, through the pacification of the Scottish Highlands. The break-up of the clan system led to the first emigrations of landless highlanders to America, a great loss to Scotland and a great gain to America. It also led to the formation of the highland regiments which have taken so heroic a part in the colonial campaigns of the British Army from Ticonderoga in 1758 to Tunis in 1943.

An uneasy feeling that the French were encircling the colonies by establishing a chain of posts to the westward had been in the minds of the English colonists for many years. Their own settlements had been formed in the Atlantic estuaries, and for long clung to tide-water. Inland lay trackless forests full of wild Indians. The westward movement had at first been made by systematic colonisation. In New England groups of approved settlers had been assembled to occupy, clear, and cultivate selected sites, they had gone in parties and had provided for themselves churches, schools, and town-meetings. In the southern colonies the advance inland had been by the surveying of large estates which were granted or sold under authority of the Lord Proprietor. On the fringe beyond the farthest clearances social life was unrestrained by the conventions of the tide-water settlements. Far inland, hunters, trappers and traders followed the Indian trails up to the passes of the Alleghanies and beyond to the headwaters of the unknown rivers that flowed westward. There neither King George's writ ran nor the writ of the Colonial Assembly. The frontiersmen, despising the square-toed citizens of Boston and Philadelphia, wore a deerskin dress not unlike that of the Indians, lived in the woods, and rivalled the Indians in woodcraft. Of these pioneers the most celebrated was that model hero of a hundred boys' adventure stories, Daniel Boone (1734–1820) who explored Kentucky. There were wilder characters than Boone, runaway sailors and servants breaking their indentures, who took to the woods to live entirely with the Indians. Such 'renegades' were often held in wretched slavery, but sometimes by practising a useful handicraft made themselves indispensable to their Indian masters as intermediaries and interpreters between the white and the red men. The trader, the missionary, and the government agent often got their first foothold in Indian tribal society by the help of some demoralised renegade. Occasionally these unfortunates cultivated an insane fury against the civilisation from which they were outcasts, went on the war-path with the Indians and got vengeance with the scalping-knife for the injuries they supposed themselves to have suffered.

By the year 1750 the frontiersmen at a hundred points found themselves in opposition to similar pioneers from the French colonies. It was vain to talk of legal rights. French-Canadian and half-breed, Yankee hunter and renegade, alike accepted no law but the law of might, and all encroached upon the hunting-grounds of the Indian when strong enough to defy him. There was, however, growing up a body of legal principles which were much discussed by lawyers in Boston and in London. It was beginning to be agreed that, in opening up new country, effective occupation of a coastline gave the occupier a prescriptive right to the hinterland. Some colonial charters, vaguely foreseeing the problem, had granted the Proprietors a strip of land running inland from the known Atlantic Coast right across unknown America to the Pacific. But whereas this westward limit of the colonies was legally uncertain, nature had given them a definite geographical limit in the watershed of the Alleghany Mountains, a barrier to settlement for more than a hundred years.

The story of the French settlements in North America had been very different. It began, as did the story of the English, with the fisheries off the Newfoundland coast and the search for the North-west Passage. In 1534 Cartier had sailed up the broad estuary of the St Lawrence to the point where the gulf narrows into a river channel and on to the limit of navigation. The first of these points is Quebec; the second, where Cartier was taken by friendly Indians to survey the prospect from the Hill of Hochelaga, he renamed with enthusiasm Mont-royal (now Montreal). Beyond claiming sovereignty little more was done by the French until the reign of Henri IV when the first attempts were made at colonisation. Port-royal in Acadie was settled in 1605 and Quebec in Canada by Champlain in 1608.

La nation canadienne, that very tough and homogenous entity, was made by two great men, Frontenac who served two terms as governor (1673–82 and 1689–95), and Laval, bishop from 1662 to 1681. At first the policy of Louis XIV's government was to concentrate the colonists; but, later, Colbert instructed Frontenac to find a passage westward into the 'South Seas'. Hence, La Salle's voyage down the Mississippi, in 1682, was a disappointment; the stream did not flow west. And hence the frontier farm, a few miles west of Montreal, was derisively called *La Chine* (China). The first wealth of Canada proved to be in the fur trade which drew both French and English traders to traffic with the Indians far in the interior. Frontenac's campaigns against the English, in his second term of office, might more properly be described as French-Indian campaigns against the English-Indians of the Hudson Bay posts and of New York province. At this time the French and French-Indians established themselves on the Great Lakes, at Fort Frontenac (Kingston, Ontario).

From 1664 onwards French colonial policy was directed to the object of building up an empire upon the basis of certain selected strategic points which were to be seized and held by naval and military power. Where necessary, colonists from France would be imported by direct action of the home government and when planted they would be kept under strict political control. This was to be a political empire quite unlike the sprawling individualist expansion of the nation of shopkeepers. Only in naval policy in the Mediterranean can we find anything in English history at all resembling the French occupation of Pondicherry, Mauritius and Goree, of Martinique and Guadeloupe, of Quebec, Montreal and Acadie. The weakness of the plan lay in the difficulty of attracting home-loving Frenchmen overseas. No more than a dribble of emigrants arrived in Canada, mostly Norman peasants, docile, pious and industrious, who cultivated small-holdings on the banks of the St Lawrence. French-Canadian society showed marked characteristics, all of them evident at the present day.

The settled peasantry, the *habitants* lived in village communities at the water's edge from which a narrow strip of land running back into the forest was cleared and cultivated. Each of these strips was a *seigneurie* granted to some French gentleman and organised on the model of a Norman manor. Life in a French-Canadian village was the repetition of life in France under the *ancien régime*, and retains today more survivals of that way of life than does village life in France. The seigneurial system survived in full strength into the nineteenth century. The *habitants* were as prolific as they were frugal. From an estimated 60,000 in 1750 they have increased to 2,000,000 in six generations, almost without reinforcement by immigration, and by slow progress have formed innumerable free village settlements inland from the original *seigneuries*.

But Canada too had its frontier and its frontiersmen. There were settled *habitants* and there were nomadic *coureurs-de-bois*. These latter like the hunters of New England, went long journeys into the woods. They had less colour-prejudice than the English, intermarried freely with the Indians and after a few generations were mostly half-breeds. Their commerce was in furs of beaver, racoon and bear; their skill was in rivers rather than in the trail and the packhorse. Their way to the interior was by canoe up to the headwaters of the rivers, then by carrying their canoes across the watershed or *portage* to another river down which they could descend to the next trading post. It must be admitted that the French were far more successful than the English in their relations with the Indians. Long afterwards, in 1826, a Chippewa chief said of the French: 'They never mocked at our ceremonies and they never molested the places of our dead. Seven generations of men have passed away and we have never forgotten it.'

The French government, then in close alliance with the Jesuit Order, was quick to see the advantage of planting French missionaries among the Indians. With the most enterprising traders, and even ahead of them, were to be found the French Jesuit priests whose zeal and heroism even to martyrdom do honour to human history. They were the first Europeans to see

Niagara Falls and the Great Lakes, or at least to record that they had seen them. But to the English colonists, with their hatred and horror of Roman Catholics, they were merely French spies of a peculiarly sinister sort. Against this background of *habitants*, *coureurs-de-bois* and Jesuit missions the ministers of King Louis XIV composed their designs for the mastery of North America.

French trading posts and mission stations appeared at numerous strategic points along the waterways of the interior. The year 1720 saw the foundation of Louisburg on Cape Breton Island at one end of the chain, of Fort Niagara in the centre of it, and of New Orleans at the mouth of the Mississippi forming the other end, 3000 miles away. Between 1720 and 1730 French and English settlers came into direct contact at the head of the Hudson River. Here there were two ways inland, west by the Mohawk Gap to Lake Ontario, and north by Lake Champlain to Canada. The English occupied the Mohawk gap with trading stations at Saratoga and Oswego; the French came down Lake Champlain and built military posts at Crown Point and Ticonderoga. Even when French and English were at peace, French Indians were at war with English Indians in this region. In the 1740's the French rapidly pushed on, occupying with brilliant strategic insight what have proved to be the sites of the cities of the Middle West, Fort William at the head of Lake Superior, Sault Ste Marie between Lakes Superior and Huron, Detroit between Lakes Huron and Erie, Chicago on the *portage* from Lake Michigan to the Illinois River, St Louis at the junction of the Missouri with the Mississippi, and finally at the head waters of the Ohio, the Fort which the French named Duquesne after the Governor of Canada, but which the Virginians renamed Pittsburg, after the great English commoner.

All this fertile, well-wooded land between the Hudson River, Lake Ontario, and the head of the Ohio was the hunting-ground of the Iroquois, who showed the greatest political abilities and the greatest faculty for civilised progress of all the Indians; acted as a single unit; and were even disposed towards peace and the arts of peace. This does not of course imply that, when they went on the war-path, they were any less intent than their fellow-savages upon plundering, scalping and torturing their victims; this was the code of war as they conceived it. The Mohawks, whose lands lay along the Mohawk River, at the vortex of the struggle were *par excellence* the 'English Indians'. They have been the loyal friends of the British for over 250 years. In the wars the Mohawks always, and by their influence the whole Six Nations as a rule, have fought on the British side. During negotiations at Albany, when each of the other tribes buried a hatchet, the Mohawks refused, saying: 'We bury none, for we have never broken the ancient links.'

The problem of rights over the hinterland should be considered as triangular. Land-hunger, the motive that brought French and English into strife between Fort Ticonderoga and Fort Duquesne, was a hunger to occupy the little plantations and the vast hunting-grounds of the Six Nations. Penetration inland was a matter of supreme interest to the colonial assemblies of Massachusetts, New York, Pennsylvania and Virginia, but Indian wars were quite another matter. Each colony might reluctantly raise its militia and vote a sum of money for repelling an Indian raid on its own frontier, but one and all consistently refused to combine in any joint scheme for defending the whole region, for administering the whole area of undeveloped land, for settling the Indians, or for resisting the French. On several occasions the governors met in conference, but their good intentions were nullified by lack of soldiers, by lack of funds, and by the narrow view of the assemblies which refused to provide them. The fiercest strife was on the northern frontier of New England.

In the French War of 1690–7 ferocious fighting between bands of French and British partisans in Nova Scotia ended in the recognition for the third time of the French rights in Acadie. Since the country was neither mapped nor explored this recognition did not mean much. During the previous thirty years fisheries had been established by New Englanders in the harbours of the Atlantic coast, while the French had drained and cultivated their holdings at the head of the Bay of Fundy. Some of the younger Frenchmen, according to the custom of Canada, took to the woods as *coureurs-de-bois*, mingling with the Indians and joining in their raids against the Puritan Yankees. For the most part the *habitants* of Port-Royal, Grand-Pre, and the other settlements were a pious and tranquil peasantry who had no politics other than obedience to their priests.

In Queen Anne's War Port-Royal was captured (1710) by an expedition from New England and was renamed Annapolis. To the delight of the New Englanders, Acadie, 'including Port-Royal', was at last ceded to Great Britain at the Treaty of Utrecht, though the boundaries of the province remained a subject of dispute. The British asserted that the act of cession covered the whole of Nova Scotia, with much of what is now New Brunswick; the French protested that the special mention of Port-Royal implied that Acadie was something else and smaller, merely the Atlantic coast of the peninsula. The status of the Acadian *habitants* in the Bay of Fundy thus became the crux of an international quarrel. The new British governor at Annapolis offered them protection, the use of their own laws and religion, and a representative assembly on condition of their taking an oath of allegiance to King George. Some hundreds, living near Annapolis, took the oath; the great majority ignored the appeal and stood neutral.

Beyond the confines of Annapolis and the fishery harbours King George's writ did not run. The woods were infested by French Indians and 'neutral' Acadians with whom there was no peace. It was the real or supposed influence of the French priests over the Indians that roused the anger of the New Englanders. Religious bigotry added to the barbarity of Indian warfare. Both sides offered rewards for scalps; each party accused the other of atrocious murders.

Mutual animosities increased when, about 1720, the French design to control the waterways of North America took shape. The outer bastion of the French strategic line from the St Lawrence to the Mississippi was Cape Breton Island, separated from Nova Scotia by a narrow strait. There the French founded the fortress of Louisburg, building up its strength, over a period of five and twenty years, at a cost of three million *livres*. When war broke out again in 1740, renewed Indian fighting and a French raid on Annapolis provoked the great expedition of the New Englanders against Cape Breton Island. They raised a force of 4000 colonials under a militia officer, Colonel Pepperall; formed their own fleet of transports; and landed on the island in April 1745, as soon as its shores were free of the winter's ice. A British naval squadron, under Commodore Warren, following somewhat tardily, came too late to cover the landing, but supported the assault on Louisburg. When some outer forts had been taken, batteries were mounted to bombard the main works and the siege was vigorously pressed, against strong resistance, for forty-nine days. At last the capture by Commodore Warren of a seventy-four-gun ship carrying essential stores obliged the French to capitulate. The garrison of 650 veteran troops and 1300 militiamen surrendered on condition of being carried back to France, with the 4000 civilian inhabitants. The plan 'for the reduction of this regularly constructed fortress was drawn up by a lawyer and executed by a body of husbandmen and merchants'. The motive force that impelled this army of civilians was to a large extent religious; they marched beneath a banner for which George Whitefield had provided the motto: *Nil Desperandum, Christo Duce*; their chaplain bore an axe with which to destroy the images in the popish Churches. They justified themselves as Protestant crusaders.

But the English government as yet had little interest in Canada. Macaulay has preserved an anecdote, perhaps apocryphal, of the appreciation of the campaign by the Duke of Newcastle, then Secretary of State. 'Oh—yes—yes—to be sure—Annapolis must be defended—Troops must be sent to Annapolis—Pray, where is Annapolis?' And again: 'Cape Breton an island! Wonderful!—My dear sir, you always bring us good news. I must go and tell the king that Cape Breton is an island.'

At the Treaty of Aix-la-Chapelle, 1748, the conquests made by the colonials in America were restored to France in exchange for Madras (see page 162), a bargain which both affronted and alarmed the New Englanders. Louisburg was a nest of privateers, an American Dunkirk; a fortress commanding the Inland Sea, an American Gibraltar, as great a threat to the New Englanders as was Fort Duquesne to the Virginians.

2. FORT DUQUESNE, ACADIE, AND QUEBEC

THE war of 1739–48 and the interval of uneasy peace that followed it brought to the fore three of the greatest figures in early American history, Benjamin Franklin (1706–90), Sir William Johnson (1715–74) and George Washington (1732–99). Franklin first appeared in politics as forcing the hands of the Quaker Assembly of Pennsylvania which would not vote funds for its own defence even when the Indians were raiding the colony. Franklin raised a corps of volunteers and paid for it by a lottery. In 1754 he laid before a Conference of Governors at Albany a plan for a Union of the American Colonies with a central authority to control Defence, Indian Trade and Indian Lands; but this plan which might have destroyed the causes of the American Revolution at their root came to nothing. The colonies were far too jealous of one another to make any such agreement. Responsibility for defence of the frontier was firmly handed back to the British government, which called upon the British tax-payer to provide £200,000 and an army for the defence of New York province.

Johnson was a wild Irish lad who had been shipped to New York to seek his fortune. In 1738 he opened a store for Indian trade on the Mohawk River and threw himself with avidity into the life of the frontier. He hunted with the Indians, excelled them at their own warlike sports, and in the end married an Indian princess. He was initiated into the Mohawk tribe as a warrior, was given an Indian name, and appeared wearing Indian dress with war-paint to represent the Indian cause at the Conference at Albany. The State of New York appointed him a salaried Native Commissioner. In the war of 1739–48 he commanded bands of Iroquois against the French Indians with the rank of colonel. During the interval of peace he built himself a great house, Johnson Hall, on an estate granted to him beside the Mohawk River. There he lived like a squire, planting orchards and wheatfields, building his flour-mill and his saw-mill, and settling his lands with hardworking Germans and Dutchmen and Highland Scots. He kept open house for his Indian friends who camped about his estate by hundreds. It was his labour to keep them at peace, to protect them from exploitation, and to encourage the work of the missionaries among them. However, he quarrelled with the parsimonious Assembly at New York and resigned, until his Indian friends persuaded him to become their agent again, and their leader when the colonial war with France broke out again, in 1754, as the result of a skirmish on the Virginian frontier.

By 1750 pioneers from Virginia had crossed the passes of the Alleghanies and were beginning to establish themselves in the Ohio valley in rivalry with the French. The Virginian government employed a young man of good cavalier family, George

Washington, to survey these lands for development. In 1753 he was sent with a party of frontiersmen to establish himself on the headwaters of the Ohio, thus claiming dominion over this region by 'effective occupation'. He was expelled in the following year by a superior French force under Governor Duquesne, who then built the stockaded fort which was to bear his name. France and England were still at peace. This frontier scuffle had little effect on the leisurely proceedings of the European powers where the 'Diplomatic Revolution' or 'Reversal of Alliances' was leading to a new war between England and Prussia on the one part and France and Austria on the other. It was not thought that a final breach in Europe would be forced, even by the sending of General Braddock with four regiments of regular troops to restore British control over the Virginian frontier. Braddock marched over the hills and through the forest defiles with a column in close order and a train of baggage until he was ambushed by French-Indians and his column was thrown into confusion. Braddock was carried to the rear, wounded and dying, muttering 'better luck next time'. Young Major Washington brought off the retreating column with credit, learning some useful lessons both about the weakness of regular troops in guerrilla fighting and their steadiness in disaster. 860 men were lost out of a strength of 1460, including 61 out of 87 officers.

The affair at Fort Duquesne which made the name of George Washington is better known than contemporary events in Nova Scotia. For some years past schemes proposed by Captain Coram and others for the colonisation of Nova Scotia had been discussed. In 1749 a plan for a military settlement on this troublesome frontier was approved by Lord Halifax,[1] the President of the Board of Trade. The Bay of Chebucto, which differed from Louisburg in being ice-free except in the severest winters, was selected for the settlement. Just at the time when the French were reoccupying Louisburg (June 1749), Governor Edward Cornwallis arrived with a colony of 3760 settlers to found the city of Halifax in Chebucto Bay. Most of the settlers were discharged soldiers to whom grants of land were promised according to their rank: 50 acres for soldiers or seamen, 300 for lieutenants, 600 for senior officers. Parliament had voted £40,000 for preliminary expenses and undertook to supply a free issue of

[1] George Dunk, Marquess of Halifax (1716–71).

rations, arms and implements until the plantation should take root. Further grants-in-aid were voted during the next seven years, the whole cost to the British tax-payer of founding Halifax being £415,000.

The site was covered with virgin forest to the water's edge. At first no thought of cultivation could be entertained. The Governor set the men to work for wages, clearing the town-site, laying out streets, contructing a wharf and a saw-mill, and building 300 log houses inside a strong stockade, against the approach of winter. In 1750 the garrison was withdrawn from Annapolis to Halifax which became the capital of Nova Scotia. A second settlement at Lunenburg (1753) was planted by a colony of 1430 Germans collected by public advertisement and shipped from Rotterdam. During the interval between the wars (1749–55) Halifax was strictly a military post maintained by its soldier-settlers in opposition to the great fortress of Louisburg which the French made stronger even than before. The British were so annoyed and restricted by the raids of French-Indians that they made little progress inland from their settlements.

When the news came from Virginia of Braddock's disaster at Fort Duquesne the provincial governments at Boston and Halifax were convinced that they must remove the perpetual threat from the Acadians and their Indian allies. The decision was promptly taken to clear the country of the 'neutrals' who had refused to take the Oath of Allegiance. All those who could be caught, to the number of 7000 or 8000, were forcibly deported (1755) in transport-ships to New York, Pennsylvania and Georgia. Some had been taken in arms against the British but most were the peaceful *habitants* of Grand-Pré and other villages in the Bay of Fundy. The searches and deportations, mostly carried out by colonial troops from Boston, continued for some years. Meanwhile the inevitable Seven Years War had broken out in Europe (1756). The second capture of Louisburg, by Wolfe in 1758, and the subsequent conquest of Canada removed the necessity for further persecution. When the whole of New France was ceded to the British in 1763, the surviving Acadians were allowed to remain in the few villages from which they had not been evicted. About 1300 of them settled in the district of Clare in the extreme south-west of Nova Scotia; some have drifted back from their place of exile to their old homes, other to the Magdalen Islands.

No excuse will suffice to justify the barbarous method of deporting these simple peasants whose land and stock were simply confiscated. Their case has, however, been sentimentally overstated in *Evangeline*, which so deeply moved the pity of our grandparents. The Acadians, who may or may not have been the innocents described by Longfellow, had brought about their own ruin by passive resistance against a lawful (and liberal) administration. While they refused British protection, the French blandly repudiated all responsibility for them. Neither subjects, combatants, nor rebels, they suffered the fate of the stateless, in the no-man's-land between the warring powers.

The year 1758 brought the war in Nova Scotia to an end. Since that date the province has been at peace except for privateering raids in the two American wars. The Naval dockyard at Halifax dates from that year (1758) as does representative government in Nova Scotia. Peace with the French at once led to peace with the Indians who made a treaty with the government of Nova Scotia in 1761 by solemnly burying the hatchet in the presence of the Provincial House of Assembly.

The Seven Years War (1756–63) raised the glory of British arms higher than ever before or since. The four central years of the war, 1757–61, when Pitt was in high office, form the only period in British history when national policy has been systematically directed to imperial ends, and when combined operations have been based on a true strategic initiative. Neither Cromwell nor Marlborough nor William Pitt the younger nor Lloyd George nor Winston Churchill has had the will and the power and the strategic insight and the understanding of imperial necessities to fight a war as the governments of France in the eighteenth century and of Germany in the twentieth century have planned and fought. The elder Pitt is the only British statesman who has made war an instrument of policy, almost the only 'imperialist' premier in British history, using that word in its derogatory sense.

The war had caught us, as usual, unprepared. After the pinprick at Fort Duquesne there had been a series of greater defeats, the loss of our 'factories' in Bengal, the loss of Minorca, the loss of Hanover. Montcalm, the French Governor of Canada, was winning successes about Lake Champlain. French-Indians were raiding into New York State, where they plundered the Mohawk

Valley. Only the influence of William Johnson steadied the Six Nations and prevented a general Indian rising. The first good news was to come from Bengal where Clive, in 1757, won the Battle of Plassy, but victory did not take shape until the combined naval and military operations under officers of Pitt's choice were begun in 1758. The outworks of French Canada were simultaneously assaulted by three widely separated columns. In the west, as Braddock's dying words had foretold, Fort Duquesne fell to 'better luck', or better management; in the centre, not so luckily, the British were bloodily repulsed from Fort Ticonderoga. In eastern Canada young General Wolfe's army landed under fire on an open beach and took the fortress of Louisburg, the decisive stroke of the campaign. The year of Victories, 1759, saw naval successes in the Bay of Biscay, the Mediterranean, and the Caribbean, military successes in Germany, and especially the threefold advance on Canada. In July, Johnson took Fort Niagara, and what is more remarkable prevented his Indians from committing outrages after the victory. Amherst, the Commander-in-Chief, at last stormed Ticonderoga and passed Lake Champlain, but the judgment of history has rightly adjudged to Wolfe the decisive part, and the greater honour. The two resounding volleys and the charge of the Highlanders, at sunrise on 13 September 1759, decided the battle on the Heights of Abraham, the campaign for control of the St Lawrence Valley, the future of the English-speaking nations. North America was to be English not French, and economic mastery of the world for at least 200 years went with the decision. This was the cause in which the two young champions Wolfe and Montcalm both had died. Wolfe's dying eyes saw that his was the victory.

Though the decisive battle had been won, there was much hard fighting before the conquest of Canada was complete. In 1760 all the columns converged on Montreal where the French capitulated. In Europe, too, the greater campaigns on the continental front were, for quite separate reasons, drawing to a close. There were desultory negotiations in which Pitt was ready to consider a peace of compromise, exchanging Canada for the West Indian Island of Guadeloupe, and even Gibraltar for the lost fortress of Minorca. But the war was renewed when Spain injudiciously revealed its alliance with the toppling power of France. At once Pitt's pugnacious instincts revived, and he urged an immediate declaration of war in order to seize the yearly treasure fleet.

It was on this issue that he quarrelled with the young King George III who consistently worked for peace on generous terms. 'Let any war be ever so successful,' wrote the King, 'it will be found upon examination that it has impoverished the nation, enriched individuals, and raised the name only of the conquerors.' However, into war with Spain we drifted without the guiding hand of Pitt at the helm. During the last two years of the war while peace negotiations dawdled on, at the ponderous gait of eighteenth-century diplomacy, British fleets were acquiring French and Spanish possessions in all quarters of the globe; from Spain Havana in the West Indies, and Manila in the East; from France the Sugar Islands of St Lucia, Guadeloupe and Martinique, and the African slave stations of Senegal and Goree. While the King and his minister Bute steadily worked for peace and reconciliation, without crippling annexations, the City, through the mouths of Alderman Beckford and the demagogue John Wilkes, demanded a crushing final triumph over French commerce. This was the 'interest' that supported Pitt and from which he won his title of the Great Commoner. It was, said Beckford, 'the West Indies where all our wars must begin and end'. We must be satisfied with nothing less than a complete exclusion of the French from the Newfoundland fisheries and from the West Indian sugar trade. We must retain Havana, Guadeloupe and Goree. Pitt, who two years earlier had been moderate, was now flushed by victory and vindictive against France and Spain.

It thus appears strange to posterity that the Treaty of Paris (1763), which left the British masters of all North America and with their rule firmly planted in Bengal, should have appeared to the City and the Whigs a shameful diplomatic defeat, a betrayal of Pitt's achievements by Bute and the young king. 'The Peace of Paris is like the Peace of God,' wrote Wilkes profanely, 'it passeth all understanding.' To retain Canada but to give up Guadeloupe seemed as absurd to commercial men of that age as a contrary decision would seem to-day to us. The future wealth of Canada was hidden from all but a few visionaries, while sugar was good for cash and credit on change in Lombard Street. Voltaire wrote that the nations were at war 'pour quelques arpents de neige vers le Canada, et qu'elles dépensent pour cette belle guerre beaucoup plus que tout le Canada ne vaut'.

France ceded to Great Britain by the Treaty of Paris Canada with Acadie and Louisiana, and admitted the English claims over Bengal. Great Britain restored to France her Newfoundland fishing rights, most of her West Indian Islands, Goree in Africa; she restored to Spain all the recent conquests. Minorca again passed to Great Britain.

3. THE AMERICAN COLONIES IN 1763

To those who study the tides and currents of human history no phenomenon can be of more lasting interest than the gradual separation of two great nations, two streams derived from a single source, flowing at first together in one channel, then parting, dividing their course, varying their character, as they pass through different environments, absorbing tributary streams that increase the distinction between them, until the original resemblance is faint and distant. No simple explanation can be given, nor can any final conclusion be reached to account for the causes, the occasion, the beginning, or the completion of the cleavage. To generalise is to give a false impression. This hiving-off, or casting-off, or breaking away of the United States from the British Empire can be and has been reduced to a formula and inflated into a myth, but the causes lie deeper. The successive political crises, when set against their psychological, economic and geographical backgrounds, provide a plan of historical causation leading to an almost inevitable schism.

Not so has the story of the American Revolution been presented to the world. A potent and lasting force in American history has been the revolutionary myth. To create the revolutionary fervour in 1776 it was necessary to invent and to propagate a legend of resistance against tyranny and oppression, and this legend has become part of the American heritage. Long ago American historians with painstaking sincerity set themselves to disentangle the truth from this fantastic tale; but history is of little interest to the public except where it creates enthusiasm, and the myth will never be destroyed until some more compelling political event is inflated by a new political artist into a myth of greater power. Whatever the profound historians may demonstrate in their works of learning, the people of America will continue to be nourished upon the anti-British tirades of the Declaration of Independence, the nursery tales of Paul Revere and Patrick Henry and the Boston Tea-Party, the allusions in a thousand songs and speeches to the glorious escape from the jaws of the tyrant King. This is not a sentimental trifle, it is the deeply-rooted almost instinctive foundation of the American national character, which must be appreciated if America is to be understood. That their own historians should have proved the legend of the downtrodden colonists and the wicked King George III to be a fable is a matter of very slight importance. The tale of Troy was a fable and that too built the character of a nation. What matters is that the Americans believe themselves to have come into existence fighting for liberty, no unworthy faith, and in that faith they stand for liberty to-day.

It is, however, less lucky for us that we should be cast as the villains of this drama. Though the British cause in 1776 has been largely rehabilitated by the efforts of American historians, the mud that was originally thrown sticks. Naturally the British are less powerfully affected by the myth than are the Americans, because what was the birth of America was a mere episode in British history; but so far as there is a traditional tale of the Revolution about which Britons have felt deeply, that tale is told exclusively from the American point of view. The Whig historians of the nineteenth century excelled their transatlantic colleagues in propagating the American myth, and to-day every allusion to the American War on a public platform or in a news-paper in this country is expected to be apologetic and slightly shamefaced. The attitude is symbolised in the erection of a monument to our great adversary, Washington, in Trafalgar Square. The time is likely to be far distant when the Americans, in a mood of magnanimity, will erect a monument to George III, as evidence that old scars are healed and old scores forgotten. Here, in short, is living history, old enthusiasms that still cause the heart to glow, old quarrels that still divide, old passions that are not resolved by logical demonstrations, old faiths that are still fruitful in works.

A neglected aspect of the story is the consideration that thirteen only out of the twenty-seven British dependencies in the West

7-2

broke out into rebellion. Though there were mutterings of complaint in several others they remained loyal when put to the test. The island colonies were influenced by their sense of dependence on the Royal Navy. Canada had particular reasons for adhering to Great Britain. The significant cases are the two youngest of the mainland colonies. Georgia in the extreme south threw in her lot with the Revolution late and reluctantly, while Nova Scotia in the north remained triumphantly loyal.

Immediately after the pacification of 1763 steps were taken to allure settlers from New England to Nova Scotia with promises of land. The cultivated fields of Grand Pré, protected by dykes against the roaring tides of Fundy were occupied by settlers from Connecticut who founded the township of Horton in 1760. The fishing port of Yarmouth was developed, in 1761, by seamen from the Massachusetts coast. A projector named Alexander McNutt settled the Acadian lands at the head of the Bay with colonists from New England, largely Irishmen (1761–7). This district, Onslow, alone of the Nova Scotian settlements, favoured the Revolutionary party in the American Revolution. The abandoned site of Annapolis, marked by ruinous stone walls and orchard trees, was reoccupied in 1764. As early as 1765 Highlanders from Scotland were settling in the district of Pictou. The whole population of Nova Scotia, in 1764, was estimated at 13,000. The island of Saint John (known as Prince Edward Island after 1799) was granted away by the Crown in 1767 to a group of absentee proprietors. In spite of this handicap 150 families had settled there by 1770 when it became a separate colony.

In 1763 there were no accurate statistics of the population either of the British Isles or of the colonies on the American mainland. It was estimated that there were between eight and nine millions in Great Britain and Ireland. Though the fact was not fully appreciated, the population was beginning to increase very rapidly, and where the fact was conjectured it was not ascribed to the correct cause, a fall in the annual death-rate. Improved hygiene and sanitation and greater variety of diet were imperceptibly conquering diseases produced by dirt and malnutrition, especially among children. The rapid rate of increase was even more noteworthy in the colonies where conditions of life were healthier. Although natural increase in America was assisted by immigration, the former was by far the greater factor.

The population of the mainland colonies in 1760 was estimated at about 70,000 French-Canadians, about 1,200,000 colonists of British origin, and about 400,000 negro slaves, three-quarters of them south of the Mason-Dixon Line. There was no reliable estimate of the Red Indian population, but they were not numerous.

The four New England colonies were a compact group in which Massachusetts, containing Boston the only large town, took the lead over its smaller associates, New Hampshire, Connecticut, and Rhode Island. Their peoples were of entirely English Protestant stock. This region was self-supporting in foodstuffs but not much more. The Acts of Trade prevented New England from developing manufactures, but craftsmanship flourished in the smaller village trades, and the New Englanders were already renowned as skilful shipbuilders. The Navigation Acts which restricted them in other directions protected them in this, so that they monopolised the American coastal trade and were active in the fisheries.

The middle colonies, New York, New Jersey and Pennsylvania, contained two large towns, New York city and Philadelphia, and the best routes to the interior. New York was, as it still is, the most cosmopolitan city in America, and was the centre of English mercantile interests. Wheat, Indian corn and pork were produced in the middle colonies in quantity to allow a surplus for export. Among the inhabitants of the middle colonies were many Protestant Dutchmen and Germans, but the Irish Roman Catholics had not yet begun to make their appearance. The Roman Catholic Church was everywhere persecuted except in Pennsylvania—even in Maryland, once a Catholic sanctuary.

Delaware and Maryland in a small way, and Virginia in a large way were the tobacco colonies. The London merchants sent their ships up the navigable creeks of Chesapeake Bay to buy tobacco in bulk direct from the estates of the growers, so that the tobacco-planters needed no commercial centre and used little currency. Though they lived a liberal life in their manor houses surrounded by ill-conditioned easy-going families of slaves, their wealth was less solid than it appeared, and suffered all the disadvantages of dependence on a single crop. If the market failed, Virginia had to live on scanty credit.

The Carolinas and Georgia were beginning to develop a vicious slave economy far different from the household slavery of Virginia. The planters were capitalists who had found a profitable crop in rice, and were soon to find one still more profitable in cotton. Slaves were bought and sold like cattle, were worked in gangs, and deprived of all protection by the laws, the slave-code being far more atrocious than those of the French and Spanish colonies. Rewards in money were offered for the recapture of runaways, the figure being sometimes as high as £50, if alive, and, if dead, £10 each for scalps.

The only large town in the south was Charleston, the market and the pleasure-resort of the planters. Of the four principal towns in the colonies, Boston, New York, Philadelphia, Charleston, none had a population exceeding 30,000.

The external trade of the colonies which had been both fostered and restricted by the Navigation Acts had developed largely on the 'triangular' route. New England ships carried the foodstuffs of the northern and middle colonies to the sub-tropical southern and West Indian colonies. They in their turn sent their tobacco, sugar, rice, indigo and other 'enumerated commodities' to the English market, and the returning trade brought English manufactured goods to Boston and New York from where they were distributed through America.

The administrative control of colonial commerce by the Acts of Trade was less real than its secondary consequence, financial control by the 'City'. Since the whole volume of colonial exports passed to England and since new supplies of capital for colonial development came from England also, many of the greater properties were owned by English capitalists or mortgaged to English banks. There was a perpetual shortage of currency in the colonies, and no money-market. Spanish dollars —pieces-of-eight—passed current everywhere, but local trade was largely by barter, rum or tobacco being the usual mediums of exchange. Little local banks issued notes, on doubtful security, until Parliament intervened with an Act for restraining note-issues. Though intended to prevent inflation and fraud it was an item in the account booked up against the Imperial Government. Another was control of the frontier.

4. TAXATION AND REPRESENTATION

CANADA was no sooner conquered than the colonies began to grow restive, even before peace was concluded with France. During many years every observant visitor to America, every designing foreign statesman, and several political philosophers had prophesied a breach between Old and New England as soon as the French menace should be removed. It has been recorded in John Wesley's *Journal*, and in the dying words of Montcalm that the sole link between England and her colonies was fear of the French on the frontier. The saying of the French economist Turgot was accepted as a commonplace that colonies are destined to drop off from the parent tree like fruit when ripe. The time of maturity had come and was first recognised by ambitious lawyers who had always found it easy to get notoriety in the colonial courts by twisting the lion's tail. The year 1761 is marked by several court cases in which irresponsible advocates, such as James Otis of Massachusetts and Patrick Henry of Virginia, challenged the authority of the British government to intervene in colonial affairs. Otis, in particular, fought a test case on the legality of search-warrants, a curious parallel to the case which the irresponsible demagogue, John Wilkes, fought in England a year or two later.

These cases stood upon historical precedent. 'What we did', wrote Jefferson, the Virginian democrat, 'was with the help of *Rushworth* [editor of legal documents of the Cromwellian period] whom we rummaged over for the Revolutionary precedents of those days.' The appeal was to the old principles of the constitution, to the seventeenth-century Whig writers, especially John Locke, and to the conveniently elastic 'Laws of Nature', an appeal which was strictly in line with that of the contemporary English radicals. From beginning to end every phase of the American Revolution had its counterpart in England. The constitutional struggle was fought throughout the Empire and almost came to civil war in England and in Ireland as well as in America; but far deeper than these pedantic lawyers' quarrels were the true issues, the emergence of a new nation that could no longer be held in subordination, and the failure on either side of the Atlantic to devise an adequate imperial constitution.

At the end of the Seven Years War the British government found itself in possession of vast conquered territories which perforce were held under martial law. Canada, with its French-speaking Roman Catholic population, was kept in that status for some years. The little-known wilderness called Louisiana, lightly populated by primitive nomadic Indians, was a more difficult problem, as the Indian lands had been encroached upon by French-colonial pioneers from the north and English-colonial pioneers from the east for several years past. It was, after 1761, controlled by British regular troops and their Indian allies. The intention of the British government was to form an extensive Indian reservation in the Ohio basin and to protect the Indians from exploitation by rum-runners and land-sharks. The immediate practical solution was to proclaim (1763) the whole hinterland between the watershed of the Alleghanies and the Mississippi a reserve for the Indian nations, to be administered by the military Governor of Canada, a well-intentioned policy which unfortunately pleased nobody but the French politicians. The English colonists were infuriated at finding their westward march again blocked by a military power far greater than that of Governor Duquesne; the Canadian *coureurs-de-bois* disliked the proclamation which limited their activities also; the Indian tribes resented transference from the French to the British allegiance without consent or consultation; and the French found it easy to plant agents among the Indians to foment the irritation. No display of force, no cunning of statecraft could have availed to prevent the frontiersmen from percolating into these fertile and almost empty lands, or to restrain the Indians from savage reprisals on the intruders. In 1763 and 1764 the whole frontier was ablaze from Lake Ontario to Georgia. The Indian tribes, capable at times of a high degree of political organisation, had found a leader in the Ottawa chief, Pontiac, who even succeeded in detaching the Senecas, one of the six tribes of the Iroquois, from their alliance with the British. Uncounted families of pioneers were driven from their settlements, robbed and scalped, until the Indian confederacy was broken up by two columns of British regulars who had been trained and equipped for Indian warfare. They were clothed, for protective coloration, in dark green, armed with rifled guns, and trained to fight in open order. The regiment is now called the King's Royal Rifles. In these cam-

paigns the colonial assemblies far away in safety by the tide-water
showed their worst form. With secure complacency they thrust
the financial burden of the campaign upon the British exchequer
and, in general, refused to allow their local militia to join in any
united operation. Each colony would defend its own frontier and
grudgingly vote funds for that alone. It was the last service
of Sir William Johnson to pacify the tribes after Pontiac's war.
He travelled far and wide through the Indian reserve, penetrating
to the Mississippi and to Detroit and finally presided at an
assembly of the Indians at Fort Stanwyx in 1768. Johnson died
in 1774, and his work for the Indians hardly survived him.

The British government was now at peace with the world and
disposed towards economy. The national debt had reached the
figure of £130,000,000, a sum on which the annual interest
amounted to one-half the national revenue, and this sum had
been spent on the conquest of French North America. Canada
and Louisiana had been conquered by British arms and British
money; they were still defended by these agencies alone. The
yearly cost of the army of occupation was estimated at £400,000,
spent in the colonies. The case put forward by George Grenville,
as Chancellor of the Exchequer in 1764, was that a part of this
additional liability should be collected from the colonies, and in
equity his case was unanswerable. But to demand the repayment
of a debt of honour and to endeavour to collect the debt by force
are rarely the acts of a wise statesman. After courteously consulting the colonial agents in London and rejecting their advice,
Grenville introduced into Parliament a bill for collecting a small
revenue in the colonies in the form of a stamp duty on legal documents. As is the way with colonial measures the bill attracted
little attention and was passed by a 'languid' House. At the same
time Grenville took measures to enforce the customs regulations
which were authorised by the 'Acts of Trade'.

The outbreak of protest and obstruction with which these
moderate measures were greeted in America came as a complete
surprise. They had the effect which neither the French nor the
Indian wars, neither the ingenuity of Franklin nor the policy of
the British military commanders could produce; they crystallised
American opinion and at last formed the disjointed colonies into
a single nation. All the politically-minded among the settlers
believed themselves to have a legitimate grievance and were more

united in opinion than ever before. A 'continental' congress to concert joint measures against the Stamp Act was at once convened, and the history of the United States was begun.

At the root of their new-found hostility to Great Britain was a conviction that the western lands should be their own, both by the moral law which entitled a pioneer to the lands he has discovered, planted, and converted to the use of man, and by constitutional law declared in the charters which the Stuart kings had granted. They saw the establishment in their midst of a standing army—in itself, they believed, unconstitutional—for the express purpose of limiting their westward expansion. They observed the new decision to enforce and to stiffen the code of commercial restrictions which had been so laxly administered, so easily evaded for a hundred years. These tendencies seemed to have been drawn by the Stamp Act into a general aim, to subject the colonies to the British Parliament, at the moment when their national destiny of freedom and expansion lay at last open before them.

There was as yet no outcry for independence; the colonies demanded their chartered rights, which were derived immediately from the King and not from Parliament. They resisted the attempt by Parliament to override their own assemblies and appealed against Parliament to the King, claiming very much what has come to be known in the twentieth century as Dominion Status. The form of the struggle thus became direct disagreement on a point of principle, whether Parliament could legally impose a direct tax on the colonies. The Americans summarised their case in the slogan, 'No Taxation without Representation', which was hotly discussed in both Houses of Parliament. The case for the Government was stated by Lord Chief Justice Mansfield in terms of 'virtual representation'. Democracy was no part of the British Constitution. Eight of the nine million inhabitants of Great Britain were without votes, but none the less had their interests upheld in Parliament. The House of Commons represented shires and boroughs and corporations not flocks of voters; it virtually represented all substantial interests, and through them every British subject could make his voice heard. This was plain fact. The fisheries interest, the shipping interest, the tobacco interest, the sugar interest, the slave interest were powerful in both Houses and, as for the general interest of the

American people, that was virtually represented by a range of talent such as Parliament has rarely known. By what system of suffrages could they have elected such men as Pitt, Shelburne, Burke, Fox and Wilkes, who ranging from the right to the left wing of politics defended the American cause from the Opposition benches. But the interplay of English politics at that moment, unhappily for America, had placed all the talent with the Opposition and all the votes of the dumb back-benchers with the Government. Let the disreputable Wilkes talk democracy; it was out of the question then and for another hundred years in aristocratic Britain. Let the sentimentalist Burke preach generosity rather than legality: 'It is not a question whether it is your right to make these people miserable but whether it is not your interest to make them happy'; it had no effect on the votes of the Government supporters. It was Pitt who swayed the opinion of the House. He proclaimed and gloried in the absolute sovereignty of Parliament, which could legislate for all parts of the Empire and in all cases, with this one Whiggish exception, that it could not 'take a man's money out of his pocket without his own consent'.

This was but one issue in a political struggle and not the crucial issue which led to the fall of Grenville's government, a few months after the passing of the Stamp Act. The next government, under Rockingham, a feeble, inept politician, repealed the Stamp Act but tacked to the repeal a general Declaratory Act, asserting the legislative authority of Parliament over all colonial assemblies, though it took no steps to implement it. The colonists had won the first round, having defied Parliament and resisted the tax. But the Declaratory Act served to confirm them in the suspicion that the British government had further tyrannical designs. The Act is one of the few examples in English history of an attempt to define constitutional principles by statute, to convert our unwritten constitution to a formal written model. It remained as a cause of friction with various colonial legislatures until, in 1931, the substance of it was repealed by Ramsay MacDonald's 'Statute of Westminster'.

The problem of paying for the defence of the American frontier remained, and a new administration which shortly replaced that of Rockingham set about solving it in a way suggested by the Declaratory Act. The next Chancellor of the Exchequer, Townshend, admitted that he thought the distinction between direct and indirect taxation 'nonsensical', but since the colonists accepted the legality of the latter and rejected that of the former he would proceed to raise a little revenue, all of it to be spent in and for the colonies, by way of customs duties on tea, glass, paint and other articles of secondary importance—the colonists had always agreed in theory to the Acts of Trade and why not to this? Having introduced his imprudent Budget he died shortly after.

Three or four years of revolutionary education had meanwhile made colonial opinion much firmer, so that the opposition to these duties was more systematic than that to the Stamp Act. The anti-British agitation had never died down in New England; it now broke out in Virginia under the leadership of Patrick Henry. Again a Continental Congress was summoned and again a series of resolutions was voted, protesting loyalty to the King, but determination to resist the encroachments of Parliament. An Association was formed on the model of the Scottish Covenanters' League to resist the payment of duties and to denounce those American 'Tories' who were obedient to the British Government. There rapidly spread through the colonies a system of local committees who organised a boycott of dutiable goods and, what is less justifiable, a boycott of all those persons who took the loyal side. As in all revolutions those who shouted loudest for liberty were the first to deny it to those who differed from them.

At this juncture there was a violent change in the balance of British politics. The young King George III had spent the first years of his reign in breaking up the domination of the Whig noblemen who for two generations had monopolised the spoils of office. A series of political manoeuvres had served to divide them into smaller factions, to split up their voting power, and to build a national party in opposition to them. He had succeeded, at least so far as to place in office (1770) the amiable, loyal, and pliant Lord North with a sufficient majority in both Houses of Parliament. The vacillations of the 1760's now gave place in the 1770's to a clear, consistent, and firm policy which might perhaps have produced some effect if it had been begun ten years sooner.

King George and his minister North were determined upon the principles of the Declaratory Act. The imperial sovereignty of Parliament must first be enforced and acknowledged. Secondly, order must be restored in the colonies; the unquestionable duty of a sovereign government was to maintain public tranquillity and due process of law. Thirdly, if the colonies would submit and place themselves under his protection, the King would assure them their chartered rights and would make any reasonable accommodation in the matter of the cost of their defence. This attitude was a great disappointment to the colonies; they were now not complaining about a tax of ninepence in the pound on tea, but about something which had become a point of honour with them, a matter of prestige. They had appealed to the King for protection against the demands of Parliament, but the King had taken his stand with his Parliament against them.

5. INDEPENDENCE

THE years 1770 to 1774 were largely taken up with unsuccessful attempts to restore order in Boston, where the town mob was systematically urged to riot and sedition. It was not difficult to inflame a sea-faring population, renowned for smuggling, against the officers of the revenue. The task was skilfully done by Samuel Adams, a radical lawyer with a fiercely anti-English bias. He was apt at provoking riots and inventing tales of atrocities against the officers whose duty it was to suppress them. At first the British government behaved with restraint and conciliation. After a riot in which a handful of soldiers were obliged to fire on a mob in self-defence, the so-called 'Boston Massacre', the government withdrew the soldiers from the town to avoid other incidents. Order reigned again in New England until the agitators provoked a mob to loot and burn the King's ship *Gaspée*, the most disgraceful of their actions, and finally to stage the riot known as the 'Boston Tea-Party', in December 1773. This arose from the last attempt to implement the Declaratory Act by imposing a token customs-duty on the colonies. The obnoxious duties levied by Townshend had been withdrawn, excepting that on tea which was retained as a test case. In order to oblige the East India Company which had large stocks of tea on hand, shipments were to be sent direct to America, thus avoiding the duties payable in English ports. The colonies were to pay a nominal duty of ninepence in the pound as a matter of principle and would get their tea nevertheless far cheaper than before. But to admit the principle was just what they would not do. The tea was refused everywhere in America and remains a little-used commodity there to this day. The Boston consignment was destroyed in a riot which exhausted the patience of King George's government. It was decided to restore order in New England by coercive measures. Without much difficulty North got through Parliament a series of bills for closing the Port of Boston, for suspending the charter of Massachusetts, and for placing New England under the military rule of General Gage, the Commander-in-Chief.

This desultory quarrel had now been going on for more than ten years, a long period in the history of party politics. On the British side, the rights and wrongs of the American colonists had taken their turn for the public notice with other imperial problems. Riots incited by radicals in Boston had not loomed so large as riots incited by radicals in London over the Middlesex Election. The constitutional relation between Parliament and the colonial assemblies was no more urgent a problem than the relation between Parliament and the East India Company. This last was much before Parliament in the early 1770's when Burke and Pitt (now Earl of Chatham) had more to say about Bengal than Boston.

At the time when their Empire in the West was dissolving into revolution, though they did not yet appreciate the danger, the Lords and Commons of England had their eyes fixed upon the East. A liberal policy for India, the new doctrine of 'trusteeship' for subject races, were the topics of debate. Even the Treasury was moved to co-operate when an enlightened Chancellor, ranging from one end of the imperial landscape to the other, thought to help Indian trade by importing to America, under a special tariff, the tea which the Americans chose to throw into Boston Harbour.

Canada, too, was taking up Parliamentary time. By the Quebec Act of 1773 the boundaries of Canada were confirmed as including the Ohio Basin, and the French-Canadians were permitted to retain their own civil law and religion. The last clause gave great offence in Protestant New England.

The coercion of New England by statute did not at first seem to be either a difficult undertaking or a desperate measure; but the colonists felt it as the latter and were resolved to make it the former. Suppression of chartered rights, martial law, the iron hand withdrawn from the velvet glove, these were the signs of tyranny which they had long dreaded and now saw revealed.

During the autumn of 1774, civil war rapidly drew on. Gage and his small army found themselves blockaded in Boston where they were dependent for supplies upon a hostile rural neighbour- hood. The dispossessed Massachusetts Assembly, nearby at Salem, was in regular correspondence with the Congress at Philadelphia and both were openly concerting measures of resistance. No overt act of war took place however until April 1775, when Gage sent a column of troops to destroy a rebel magazine at the unhappily named village of Concord. On the way back the troops were attacked by armed bands at Lexington. They fought their way through to Boston with a loss of sixty- five men killed. A few weeks later the colonists boldly took the initiative by occupying and entrenching Bunker Hill which overlooks the harbour. On 17 June, Gage ordered out a brigade of British regulars to clear the hilltop. He so much under- estimated the fighting qualities of the Americans as to neglect both the superior power of manoeuvre possessed by his trained troops and the help which the warships of the fleet might have given him. He counted on dislodging the Americans by a display of force in a frontal attack. The Americans were dislodged, but only at the third assault and after inflicting 1200 casualties on the British, a loss they could not afford. This, if anything, should be remembered as the Boston Massacre.

A few days earlier, Congress had voted authority for raising a Continental Army to be commanded by George Washington; but even as late in the struggle as this its full implications were not understood. It was on either side an attempt to establish a prin- ciple by direct action and not yet an absolute war. The news of Bunker Hill was an effective solvent of sentimental ties. The British realised they must fight relentlessly if they were to retain the colonies, and the Americans, having killed so many redcoats, felt that they were capable of victory.

During these months, belated attempts at conciliation were made by both sides. A final petition known as the Olive Branch, in the form of an appeal from his American subjects for protection against his British subjects, was sent to the King, who refused to receive it since it came from Congress which was in armed rebellion against him. Simultaneously he offered peace and protection to any colony which should propose its own plan for the cost of its own defence; but this proposal was rejected out of hand by Congress as an insidious attempt to sow dissensions between the colonies. The news of Bunker Hill had put an end to hopes of conciliation.

It was the aim of the British government and of their generals in America to crush the rebellion in New England before it should spread to the other colonies. This policy might have been attained in one of two ways: the rebels might have been crushed by superior military force, punished by martial law, and reduced to such misery as would have obliged them to submit, for the time at least; or they might have been confronted by some magnanimous stroke of policy, a generous offer of concessions which would have reconciled the moderate men and left the convinced revolutionaries in a small minority. Neither of these paths was taken. The King's proposal of 1775 offered too little and arrived too late; on the other hand, General Gage had neither the power nor the inclination to terrorise the country. The Army was helpless in Boston; when concentrated there it achieved nothing, when dispersed in detachments it was destroyed piecemeal by the guerrilla bands. New England proved to have an ideal social system for carrying on partisan warfare. Every able-bodied man was a hunter accustomed to the use of arms; every township was self-supporting and self-governing. The occupation of the capital, Boston, by a hostile army made almost no difference to the farmers who grew their own food and managed their own affairs in the town-meeting. The British commanders might have attempted to clear the country, hanging all men found in possession of arms, but no such drastic measure was ever proposed. On the contrary, several of the generals, especially Howe, who succeeded Gage as Commander-in-Chief in 1776, were much inclined to political sympathy with the rebels. They would have welcomed an accommodation and hated, as soldiers always do, this active service in aid of the civil power, a war against their fellow-subjects. It was with relief that they decided to withdraw from Boston and conduct a campaign from a more suitable base, the loyal city of New York.

The British government conceived the plan of isolating the incorrigible New Englanders and of rallying the friendly ele-

ments in all the other colonies. In Nova Scotia these were a safe
majority; in Canada it was to be hoped that the toleration recently
granted by the Quebec Act would at least tend to keep the
habitants tranquil; New York, whose life and commerce depended
on the British connexion, was pretty well secured; in Virginia,
the Old Dominion, though there was much disloyal talk, surely
there were many loyal sons of the cavaliers; in the Carolinas and
in Georgia there seemed to be little sign of rebellion. Meanwhile
a contrary policy was adopted by the Congress leaders whose
interest it was to spread the revolution into every colony. By
means of their network of corresponding committees they gained
control of the organs of government in the twelve adjacent
colonies from New Hampshire to South Carolina and at last in
Georgia, the thirteenth. Where they had constitutional power
they used it to disfranchise the loyalists and to confiscate their
property; where there was no legal authority they incited mobs
to plunder and ill-use the loyalists; and where this method was
beyond their strength they levied guerrilla war. In 1776, Canada
was invaded by an army from New England. The Governor, Sir
Guy Carleton, defended the ramparts of Quebec, eventually
driving off the invaders with the help of Scottish and French-
Canadian loyalist volunteers. Since Congress had fiercely protested against the grant of religious toleration to the Canadian
Roman Catholics it is not surprising that an appeal to the
Canadians to rise in revolt against the government that guaranteed
this toleration was a failure.

The loyalists in the Thirteen Colonies were numerous but unorganised. They included in their ranks the majority of royal
officials, of Anglican clergy and their families. Among those
who may be classed as officials were many whose duties took them
among the Indians. Missionaries, Native Agents and officers of
the irregular corps which guarded the frontiers were disposed to
see the Indian point of view in the struggle for the hinterland and
to favour the imperial policy of creating Indian reserves. Sir
William Johnson's death in 1774 was a loss to moderate and
British interests; his son Sir John was a loyalist leader. Robert
Rogers, the most celebrated frontiersman of his day, whose
Rangers have been an inspiration to all later practicians of
irregular warfare, was a loyalist.

In the cities all that connexion which nowadays is called 'Big Business' tended to the British side. Those who had interests on both sides of the Atlantic felt the advantage of the Acts of Trade and could afford to scoff at the pettiness of colonial politics. At the end of the war they withdrew with their wealth to the comforts of Old England, and maintained their personal contacts and their commercial dealings with the new America. In this class there was an ebb and flow with the fortunes of war. Alexander Hamilton was not the only loyalist who ended as a revolutionary nor Benedict Arnold the only revolutionary who reverted to the loyalist side. Families were divided; Franklin's son was a loyalist.

These were distinguished individuals. The great bulk of the loyalists was composed of recent emigrants to America and was to be found in the newer colonies. The Highlanders in Nova Scotia and the Scottish elements in the other colonies in general withheld their support from the Revolution. The inland settlements of the Carolinas and Georgia had been planted by Jacobite emigrants after the failure of the '45. Their traditional politics were Tory and, by a strange reversal, they had transferred their loyalty to the Tory King George, though his grandfather had been their enemy and his uncle, Cumberland, the destroyer of the Highland clans. Among the Scottish loyalists who fled from the fury of the American Whigs, as she had fled thirty years before from the fury of the English Whigs, was Flora MacDonald, the saviour of Prince Charlie.

On the other hand the Scotch-Irish, as Ulstermen were called in America, were solidly on the revolutionary side. They had begun to move across the Atlantic in Charles II's time when the Navigation Laws bore as hardly on Irish as on colonial manufactures. By 1750 it was estimated that they numbered about 50,000, from whose number Washington drew the best regiments of his Continental Army. The Scotch-Irish provided a high proportion of the political leaders in the early years of the Republic.

Ten years earlier there had been no suggestion of independence in any colonial assembly or in the correspondence of any responsible American leader. Every petition and remonstrance has been expressed in the language of legality and of loyalty. But the long struggle over the Stamp Act, the Declaratory Act, the Acts of

Trade, and the Tea Duties had forced thousands of simple colonists to re-examine the fundamentals of their politics. Gradually and reluctantly they discovered that their loyalty to the King of Great Britain had died. The stalk had withered, the fruit was ripe and ready to fall from the tree. The Americans roused themselves and awoke a nation of republicans and demo-crats, actively hostile to the Court of St James's and to the whole galaxy of social, legal and ecclesiastical lights that circulated around it. This change of heart was not made casually, nor absolutely, nor without moments of weakness and regret. In 1775 and 1776 there were many hesitants. Even after his appoint-ment as general, Washington declared that he 'abhorred the idea of Independence'. But when the change came, when the inhibi-tion was released, the conversion produced a flow of energy and power and a bitter hatred of the divorced partner in the broken alliance. The inhibition, the mental struggle, the release and the compensating violence are all clearly expressed in the preamble to the Declaration of Independence, which was chiefly the work of Thomas Jefferson:

When in the Course of human events, it becomes necessary for one people to dissolve the political bands which have connected them with another, and to assume among the powers of the earth, the separate and equal station to which the Laws of Nature and of Nature's God entitle them, a decent respect to the opinions of mankind requires that they should declare the causes which impel them to the separation.

The Declaration next proclaims the 'self-evident truths' that all men are 'created equal', are endowed with 'inalienable rights' to 'Life, Liberty and the Pursuit of Happiness', and have instituted governments to secure these rights. But 'whenever any Form of Government becomes destructive of these ends, it is the Right of the People to alter or to abolish it and to institute new governments'.

Prudence, indeed, will dictate that Governments long established should not be changed for light and transient causes; and accordingly all experience hath shown, that mankind are more disposed to suffer, while evils are sufferable, than to right themselves by abolishing the forms to which they are accustomed. But when a long train of abuses and usurpations, pursuing invariably the same object evinces a design to reduce them under absolute Despotism, it is their right, it is their duty, to throw off such Government....

No doubt the Americans persuaded themselves that there was in fact a direct design in Great Britain to establish 'an absolute Tyranny over these States', though it is hard to reconcile the evidence they adduced with the melancholy tale of fumblings and vacillations in British colonial policy then and thereafter; in George Grenville's parsimonious book-keeping, or in the illogical compromise with which it had been overruled, or in the experimental tariff of custom duties levied and varied and countermanded by Townshend, Grafton and North, or even in the stubborn determination of King George to suppress sabotage and riot.

'Let facts', say the authors of the Declaration, 'be submitted to a candid world.' The King of Great Britain has 'obstructed the administration of justice'; 'has erected a multitude of new offices and sent hither swarms of officers to harass our people'; 'has kept among us, in time of peace, standing armies'; 'has affected to render the military independent of the civil power'; 'has combined with others [i.e. Parliament] to subject us to a jurisdiction foreign to our constitution'. He has given his 'assent to their Acts:...for cutting off our trade...for imposing taxes on us without our consent...for abolishing the free system of English laws in a neighbouring Province [Quebec],...and enlarging its boundaries so as to render it...a fit instrument for introducing the same absolute rule into these colonies,...for taking away our Charters,...for suspending our Legislatures. He had abdicated Government here by...waging war against us ...has plundered our seas, ravaged our coasts, burnt our towns. ...He is at this time transporting...mercenaries to complete the works of death, desolation, and tyranny...and has endeavoured to bring on the inhabitants of our frontiers the merciless Indian savages.' The violent rhetoric of this document shows how far the revolutionary sentiment had moved in America between 17 June 1775 and 4 July 1776.

6. WASHINGTON AND FRANKLIN

AFTER the failure to extend the Revolution to Canada the American cause languished and the quarrels between the various colonies revived. The mere show of force by the British Army in New York and by the Navy at many points in American waters appeared to be breaking the spirit of the rebels so that a restoration of the old order was confidently expected. The members of Congress seemed as unwilling to make sacrifices for the American as for the Imperial cause, and occupied themselves largely with obstructing the needs and questioning the authority of General Washington who now bore the whole burden of responsibility for the Campaign. It was his intention and his achievement to make his ragged 'Continentals' into an army and to keep that army in being as a nucleus for the national revolt. He must pin the British down, harass their outposts, and threaten their flanks, but avoid a pitched battle in which he was likely to be defeated. While the Continental Army remained in the field, the British regulars could not be dispersed to pacify the country, and the country would remain in the possession of the colonial guerrilla bands.

Washington was a strange leader for a people's war. High birth and breeding, a coat-of-arms which is to be seen quartered with the coats of the noblest houses on several English heraldic monuments,[1] great wealth which made him by repute the richest man in America, and a cold haughty manner seemed to have designed him for command over the loyalists; but from the moment when he accepted the generalship of the Continental Army he never wavered. His character and his purpose were fixed, his resolution was unchangeable. When he made up his mind for independence thousands of moderate men followed his decision. When he offered his sword for the protection of the Boston rioters, accepting their part as better justified than that of their opponents, thousands of respectable men who had shrunk from the onset of violence took side with him. By temper a

[1] Argent, three mullets gules, three bars azure. A well-known story tells how this design was worked into the first American flag by Washington's household. The mullets (stars) replaced the Union Jack in a flag based on that of the East India Company, a red ensign with six horizontal white stripes.

conservative aristocrat he set himself to impose discipline on his ill-found soldiery and to acquire for them the status of regular combatants. Lack of money, lack of equipment, and an inclination shown by his men to desert every summer at harvest-time hampered him more than the unenterprising movements of the English generals. Though there were 700,000 adult males in America his army never reached a strength of 25,000; he never put as many as 18,000 in the field; he ended the war with a mere 6000 regulars; and this from a population of nearly two millions. He overcame all difficulties, partly by employing Prussian soldiers of fortune as drill-masters, mostly by the force of his own rock-like personality. He cared nothing that his dignity and reserve destroyed his popularity. The ribald soldier's song, 'Yankee Doodle', in one of its early versions ridiculed him for being so 'tarnal proud', for being a 'macaroni with a feather in his hat', but he ignored the criticism. His army never won a battle but it won the war.

After the defiant challenge of the Declaration of Independence (4 July 1776) the Americans for more than a year achieved very little. There was an indecisive campaign about New York from which Washington retired, having had the worst of every engagement, to winter quarters south of the Delaware, a wretched winter and the lowest ebb of American hopes.

While he and his men shivered, keeping up their spirits by occasional raids on the British outposts, King George's government was preparing plans and providing troops to bring the war to a crisis. But though there were loyalists in America there were also rebel sympathisers in England, and in general the cause and the campaigns were unpopular. Lack of recruits, never too plentiful in Old England, forced upon the government the hateful expedient of building up the strength of the Army with German mercenaries, sold into slavery by their unnatural monarch, the Duke of Hesse. The hiring out of conscripts was normal among the kings of Europe but aroused horror among the republicans of the New World who did not always pause to recollect that they too were slave-traders.

The conduct of the war was largely in the hands of Lord George Germain, the holder of a new office, the Secretaryship of State for Trade and the Colonies. A shallow clever man, he had never quite lived down the imputation of cowardice made against

him many years before when he was serving as a young officer
at the Battle of Minden. He was now prolific of grandiose plans
and optimistic forecasts, and much inclined to interfere with the
puzzled, unwilling generals, though his information was by
necessity two or three months out of date. It was alleged, perhaps
unjustly, that the campaign of 1777 failed because he forgot to
post a despatch to General Howe before going away for a holiday,
an occurrence amusingly described in Mr Bernard Shaw's *Devil's
Disciple*.

Two alternative plans were proposed for the year's operations.
One was the assemblage of a force in Canada to march down by
Lake Champlain, the path so often fought over in the French wars,
to occupy the line of the Hudson. New England would thus be
cut off from the interior and from the other nine colonies, and
might be reduced at leisure. The other plan was for a march south
from New York to complete the recovery of the middle colonies
by dispersing the Congress and its supporters from Philadelphia,
and to rally the southern loyalists. Owing to a confusion of
plans, the fault partly of Germain but partly of the rival generals,
both plans were simultaneously attempted. Howe marched
south, captured Philadelphia, and sent the Congressmen flying
helter-skelter into Virginia, while Burgoyne came down from
Canada as far as Saratoga on the Hudson, where he found himself threatened on all sides and with no prospect of help from
Howe. His little force of about 1900 British regulars and 1600
Hessians had cut themselves off from their base and could not now
reach their goal. After gallant and costly attempts to fight his
way through the American militiamen, who outnumbered him
three to one, Burgoyne surrendered on terms. His men were to
be marched to the coast with the honours of war, the officers
remaining with their men, and were to be repatriated to England.
Every clause of the convention was broken by the American
Congress. The rank and file were separated from their officers
and held as prisoners while inducements were offered them to
desert to the Revolutionary side, a policy which had some
success with the German mercenaries.

The news of Saratoga (October 1777) changed the face of the
war. It revived American hopes; it shattered British complacency; it served to persuade the Bourbon Kings of France and
Spain to give recognition, military aid, and eventually open

alliance to the Americans. Carleton wrote from Canada on hearing the news, 'this unfortunate event, it is hoped, will in future prevent Ministers from pretending to conduct operations of war in a country at three thousand miles distance', but his hopes were

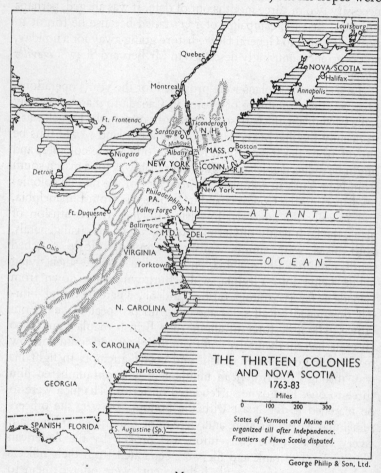

THE THIRTEEN COLONIES
AND NOVA SCOTIA
1763-83

Miles
0   100   200   300

States of Vermont and Maine not organized till after Independence. Frontiers of Nova Scotia disputed.

George Philip & Son, Ltd.

Map 2

not realised. Lord North did, however, make a final attempt at conciliation in order to reunite the empire against the French. He sent commissioners to America with almost unlimited powers to offer any concessions short of Independence, but Congress refused to make any reply.

Benjamin Franklin had been for many years the London agent
of several of the colonies, holding also a salaried post as deputy
Postmaster-General for the Colonies. In this capacity he had suggested some useful modifications in the Stamp Act. Like other
Americans he had shared in the exultation over Pitt's victories
and like King George had 'gloried in the name of Britain'. As
far back as 1754 he had proposed the plan at Albany for uniting
the colonies within the Empire, and twenty years later he was
still engaged in discussions and negotiations to this end. As
Washington was the most eminent among the colonists in
America, so Franklin was the most eminent American in the eyes
of the polite world of Europe. But though he favoured a rugged,
colonial simplicity and appeared to be bland, expansive, even
jocular, his was a subtle scheming nature. He had got the better
of the mealy-mouthed Quakers in the petty politics of Pennsylvania, and was quite capable of outwitting the counsellors of
King George and of King Louis. His reputation stood, in 1770,
on his researches into electrical phenomena which had led to the
invention of the lightning-conductor, and on his endeavours to
promote popular education. He had founded an academy, a
public library, and a newspaper in Philadelphia; and the series of
moral aphorisms which he issued under the pseudonym of 'Poor
Richard' were forming the character of the American business
man. He was the industrious apprentice turned philosopher.

At what point he ceased to work for imperial reform and
began to work for American independence it is hard to say. In
1763 he had fully approved of 'some revenue arising out of the
American trade to be applied towards supporting troops', that
is, the plan of the Tea Duties which, ten years later, he resisted.
During the Stamp Act debates he spoke ominously at the Bar
of the House of Commons of resisting 'by force of arms' the
payment of direct taxes. He was at all times exasperated by the
supercilious tone of condescension which so many Englishmen
adopted (and still adopt) in speaking of the Empire. 'Every man
in England', he said bitterly, 'seems to consider himself as a piece
of a sovereign over America; seems to jostle himself into the
throne with the King, and talks of *our subjects in the colonies.*'
His antipathy increased as the dispute dragged on, until an event
in January 1774 made him an open republican. The Assembly of
Massachusetts, shortly before its suppression, petitioned for the

removal of the Governor, employing Franklin to argue their case before the Privy Council. The evidence against the Governor was based upon some stolen letters which had come into Franklin's possession, and had been published in spite of Franklin's promise that they would remain private. The Solicitor-General roundly called Franklin a thief, not without some justification. From that moment Franklin became a dangerous and powerful enemy to Great Britain.

After the Declaration of Independence, Franklin was sent with two other agents to represent the American Congress in Paris. The court of France had been watching the troubles in America with malicious delight. The French defeats in the Seven Years War still rankled and the humiliation of England seemed desirable. Accordingly the French government adopted what is known in the diplomatic jargon of to-day as a 'non-belligerent' policy. They gave the Americans open goodwill and easy terms for obtaining munitions. French volunteers, among whom the most celebrated was Lafayette, were encouraged to join the Continental Army. Paris became the centre of a network of underground activities, conducted in a highly melodramatic style by Beaumarchais, the author of *Figaro*. Gun-running, the equipment of privateers in French ports, *espionage* and *sabotage* were organised on the largest scale. False reports of British atrocities were invented and put out as propaganda. An elaborate and unsuccessful plot was contrived to introduce into England spies who were to burn the Naval dockyards, but the ringleader was caught and hanged. Franklin threw himself into these activities and reinforced them with diplomatic measures. The news of Saratoga enabled him to persuade the French court that the time had come for revenge on England. In February 1778 he negotiated a treaty of military alliance with France which thereby recognised the independence of the United States. In the following year Spain, which also had scores to pay off against England, joined the alliance. France and Spain were to fight for American freedom, but Franklin had not the slightest intention of allowing them to compensate themselves at America's expense.

7. GREAT BRITAIN FIGHTS THE WORLD

WITH the appearance of the Bourbon powers upon the scene the interest of the war shifted from the land to the sea. As is usual in the interval between major wars, the Navy had been stinted of supplies and was quite unequal to a struggle with France and Spain, while the First Lord of the Admiralty, Sandwich, was perhaps the weakest member of Lord North's mediocre administration. On the other hand, the French Navy had been enlarged and re-equipped with more powerful ships and was commanded by the most able admirals in French history. The loser in the last war is often the best equipped at the beginning of the next. While the main theatre of naval operations was, as before, the West Indies, fleets, armies and supplies were also diverted from America to protect the coast of England from threatened invasion, to defend Gibraltar which was besieged by the Spaniards, and to fight the French in India. England itself was in such peril that the unpopular campaign in North America fell into a secondary place, as was recognised by Pitt whose last speech in the House (1778) was a rousing appeal to the nation to forget past differences and unite against the French.

Nevertheless, the British forces were firmly based, by land and sea, on Halifax and New York and were not dismayed by the defeat at Saratoga and its consequences. General Clinton began the methodical recovery of the southern colonies, where very numerous loyalists rose in arms to join the British wherever they appeared. Georgia was subdued in 1778, the Carolinas in 1779 and Charleston the capital of the south in 1780. Even as late in the war as this, there was a drift of disheartened colonials to the loyalist side, the most noted example being Benedict Arnold, one of Washington's trusted generals, who, like the French Admiral Darlan in 1940, suddenly decided on co-operation with the enemy. Even Washington wrote, in April 1781, 'we are at the end of our tether, now or never our deliverance must come'. It was coming. In South Carolina civil war was raging between loyalist and revolutionary bands, the former steadied by a force of British which Clinton had detached under Cornwallis, the latter by an army of French regulars under Rochambeau who had landed in Virginia. This reappearance of the French in America meant that command of the sea was lost. When Cornwallis fell back to Yorktown on the shore of Chesapeake Bay intending to ship his army to Charleston, he found the French Admiral De Grasse blockading the entrance to the Bay, instead of the expected British squadron.

After a short siege by a force twice as large as his own and half composed of French regulars, Cornwallis was obliged to capitulate with 7000 British soldiers on 17 October 1781, the fourth anniversary of Burgoyne's surrender at Saratoga. The British officers, studiously ignoring the 'rebel' officers of the Continental Army, handed their swords to Rochambeau's French staff; but the gesture was vain. Though the decisive manoeuvres had been made by a French admiral and a French general it was the stability of Washington that had maintained the American cause through so many waverings, and the subtlety of Franklin that united Europe against the British. These two were the makers of American Independence.

The news of Yorktown reached London in November 1781. It led to an immediate agitation for the overthrow of Lord North's government, and for an end to 'this unnatural and unfortunate war' with America. The King, who believed his royal honour involved in maintaining the unity of the Empire, was the last to yield. North himself had long been anxious to resign, but was not allowed to do so until March 1782. The new government under Rockingham opened preliminary negotiations with Franklin in Paris, while the war with France and Spain was prosecuted with vigour. The campaign in America had lapsed, leaving the British in possession of Canada, Nova Scotia and New York.

Until 1779 the naval war in the West Indies had been indecisive; fleets had manoeuvred, fought and parted; islands had changed hands. These actions, which then seemed vital are, for posterity, but distractions from the campaign on the American coast. They had the effect of quieting the unrest among the self-governing West Indian colonies who had agreed with the Thirteen Colonies in resisting the Stamp Act and the Tea Duties. Under the menace of the French fleet they remembered their debt to the British Navy, and their revolutionary fervour died away.

The war had taken a turn for the worse in 1779, when Spain joined the alliance against Great Britain with the avowed intention of regaining Gibraltar and Minorca. The great siege of Gibraltar, which was gallantly, defiantly, defended for three years by Sir George Eliott, focused the patriotic sentiments of the British.[1] In December 1779, Rodney fought his way in with a fleet to revictual the garrison, then sailed for the West Indies. All through 1780 the fortress was blockaded while the general prospects of the war worsened. In 1781 another convoy fought its way in with supplies for the besieged garrison of Gibraltar, but Minorca, too far away for relief, surrendered to the Spaniards. The northern nations banded together in an armed neutrality to resist the British claim to search neutral ships for contraband, that corollary of sea power which in every European war has embroiled the British with the neutral powers. In particular the Dutch had carried on so brisk a trade in what the British held to be contraband, and had given such unconcealed support to the American privateer Paul Jones, that Britain declared war against Holland (1780) and now faced the open or secret enmity of all Europe. Rodney's operations in the West Indies were then turned against the Dutch West Indies, the centre of the contraband trade with America. It was at this crisis, when the eyes of the British government were on the Rock of Gibraltar and the West Indies, that De Grasse sailed for Chesapeake Bay, bringing Washington the deliverance he desired.

Then came Yorktown, the fall of Lord North's government, and the first overtures for peace. But while preliminary proposals were exchanging between agents who were not fully accredited, before even the slow processes of diplomacy had been set in motion, the tide of victory turned. On 12 April 1782, Rodney's smashing victory over De Grasse near the island of Dominica quite altered the complexion of the negotiations, though it caused some confusion among the English Whigs who had been denouncing Rodney as an incompetent creature of the Tories. English politics were intolerably obscure and factious. The different groups who had combined to oust Lord North had no clear political aim except to scramble for the spoils of office. The death of the mild sentimentalist Rockingham led to another scuffle from which Shelburne rose to the top for a few months until he was displaced by an indecent coalition of two life-long opponents, Fox and North, who agreed only in dislike for

[1] It may very fairly be compared with the great siege of Malta, 1940–3.

Shelburne. Shelburne was responsible for the peace terms with America, France, Spain and Holland, but the definitive treaties were not signed until September 1783, by which time Fox and North were in office.

The terms of peace with Spain, also, were modified by the last actions of the war. When the diplomatic struggle was already far advanced the Spaniards endeavoured to achieve their war aims by a direct assault on Gibraltar. The attack was launched in September 1782 by a huge fleet of warships, by a powerful army on the landward side, and by specially constructed floating batteries carrying heavy artillery. Eliott destroyed the batteries with red-hot shot and repelled every assault. Next month Rodney appeared, drove away the Spanish fleet and raised the siege. Thus the war ended with a flicker if not a blaze of glory. The hearts of oak had fought again, and again conquered the fleets of Spain and France, even if the soldiers had failed in a war fought reluctantly against their own kinsmen.

The Thirteen Colonies were lost, but much had been saved largely by the efforts of four men, Rodney in the West Indies, Eliott at Gibraltar, Carleton in Canada and Warren Hastings in India.

The discussions in Paris were prolonged and complicated, not least by the successive political changes in England. All parties agreed that the thesis of the Declaratory Act was now untenable; American independence must be admitted, but the boundaries of the United States were a troublesome problem. The British were anxious to detach the Americans from the French alliance and to prevent the French from re-establishing their power in North America. Franklin was not at all disposed to exchange English for French patronage, but was bound by treaty with France not to make a separate peace. Having scored his point on American independence he welcomed the British victories over France and Spain which enabled him to play off his enemies against his allies. He presented four principal conditions: independence, definition of boundaries, restriction of the limits of Quebec to what it was before the Quebec Act, and freedom of fishing on the Newfoundland Banks; and these became the basis of the treaty. He also added a number of 'desirable' conditions, some merely facetious such as the cession of Canada, an indemnity and an admission of error on the part of Great Britain; but these were not taken seriously. The British negotiators stoutly held out for the rights of the loyalists, demanding personal security for them and legal possession of their property, to which Franklin blandly replied that Congress had no authority to overrule the decisions of the separate colonies on this point. The British had to be content with a recommendation to the colonies to end the persecution.

France got very little from the war except her revenge. The rights of fishing off Newfoundland with the use of St Pierre and Miquelon, which had been in dispute since the Treaty of Utrecht, were defined in a form favourable to France. She recovered two islands in the West Indies and several trading posts which the British had captured in India and Africa. The Dutch actually lost by their intervention in the war; they were obliged to admit the right of the British to trade without interference in the Eastern Seas.

The Spaniards failed to get what they wanted, Gibraltar, but otherwise got considerable advantages. They retained possession of Minorca but returned to Great Britain some captured West Indian islands. After long three-cornered discussions and much finessing, the Spaniards were confirmed in their possession of Florida, including what was then called West Florida at the mouth of the Mississippi and, in addition, the whole unexplored region beyond that river. No one, least of all the Spaniards, realised what wealth lay hidden in that vast domain. The United States, though possessed of the Ohio basin, were again obstructed in their westward march.

The definitive treaties of Versailles which ended the story of the first British Empire were signed on 3 September 1783. At the complimentary banquet, or so the wits alleged, the French plenipotentiary proposed the health of King Louis comparing him, with traditional flattery, to the Sun in splendour. The Englishman who followed turned the compliment by proposing King George who 'like the Moon rules the waves'. 'And I give you', said Benjamin Franklin, 'the health of General Washington who, like Joshua of old, bade the Sun and the Moon to stand still and they obeyed him.' He was right, the kings of Europe were all losers. King George had lost something but King Louis more. France had bankrupted herself in fighting other people's battles, had gained nothing solid, and had infected herself with a contagious disease fatal to the system of *le roi soleil*. Liberty,

Equality and Fraternity acquired in the forests of the New World were soon to raise the blood of France to fever heat. Spain, too, was to learn that it was not only English colonies in America that fall off like ripe fruit from the parent tree.

8. THE UNITED STATES AND CANADA

MANY tangled problems remained to be solved in America when the treaties were ratified: financial settlements between merchants with interests on both sides of the Atlantic, the survey of the new frontiers, the evacuation of the loyalists and the withdrawal of the British garrisons. Sir Guy Carleton, then commanding at New York, was unwilling to leave that loyal city until, in November 1783, he had arranged for the removal to Nova Scotia of all loyalists who sought his protection.

The American Congress which had urged the thirteen colonial governments, in 1777, to disfranchise and expropriate the loyalists now did nothing to restore their property and civil rights, nor made any gesture of conciliation. The heats engendered by civil war are not quickly cooled. The revolution, like all revolutions, had been the work of an active politically-minded minority. A large part of the population, as in all civil wars, stood neutral until the war forced itself into notice. John Adams, the revolutionary leader, estimated the active revolutionaries as one-third and the active loyalists as one-third also. A large number, more or less willingly, volunteered to serve King George in those areas where the King's soldiers were in control and, like the guerrilla fighters on the other side, melted away, when the fortunes of war changed. A surprisingly large number in the North, where they could put themselves under Carleton's protection, decided to go into exile with him and remain under the British flag. Throughout the war the British generals had been hampered by increasing crowds of loyalist refugees who, as the British cause deteriorated, were gradually concentrated in New York. About 30,000 were transported by sea to Nova Scotia.

The settlement of Shelburne was founded, not without many setbacks, by an organised party of 471 families who sailed in eighteen ships from New York. Douglas was founded by the 84th (New York) Loyalist Regiment. Montagu's and Tarlton's

Regiments from Carolina settled at Guysborough. Many legal and administrative officials from New York settled along the St John and Miramichi rivers, where a few immigrants from Scotland had already broken the ground. In 1784 this region was formed into the separate colony of New Brunswick which, though a small province, has taken a notable part in Canadian history, its founders having had a high level of political and intellectual ability.

Cape Breton Island was also made a separate colony (but reunited with Nova Scotia in 1820). While the site of Louisburg remained a deserted ruin, a new settlement was founded at Sydney (1783) and was soon attracting immigrants from Scotland at the rate of a thousand a year. New Edinburgh, another Scottish colony, was planted by Andrew Stewart in the same year. A steady emigration of discharged highland soldiers, to the Pictou district of Nova Scotia, followed the Peace of 1783.

Halifax remained the social and commercial centre of the Maritime Provinces. A leader among the newcomers there was the Rev. Charles Inglis, ejected from his rectory of Trinity Church, New York. In 1787 he was consecrated Bishop of Nova Scotia, the first creation by the Crown of an Anglican bishopric in the colonies. Politics in Nova Scotia in the next generation turned on denominational rivalries between the Anglican loyalists, the Acadian Roman Catholics and the Scottish immigrants. This, and a laudable interest in education, provided the little colony eventually with four rival University Colleges.

The loyalists were refugees from persecution, emigrants of another type from any hitherto described. Many whose political principles had driven them into the wilderness were unwilling pioneers, some were elderly professional men, some were infirm and old, most had been robbed of all their property. To the hardships and obstacles always encountered by the settlers in a new colony was added much personal misery for the loyalists in the Maritime Provinces. The Nova Scotians took a pride in overcoming these misfortunes, accepted the jocular nickname of 'blue-noses', and took as their motto the defiant words: 'We bloom amid the snow.'

When Pitt became Prime Minister in December 1783, he appointed a Royal Commission which sat from 1783 to 1790 and spent over £3,000,000 in making 'a liberal and a handsome compensation' for the loyalists, the poorest among them receiving the largest grants. Carleton, who was active in the organisation of the new settlements, obtained from the Crown, as a mark of royal favour, the distinction that the loyalists and their descendants should write after their names the letters, 'U.E.', to record their devotion to the cause of a United Empire.

Another group of immigrants were loyalist negroes from the southern colonies. From Nova Scotia they sent delegates to consult the Anti-Slavery Society about their future. Clarkson urged them to migrate again to Sierra Leone (see page 225), the new home for liberated slaves. Eleven hundred of them took his advice in 1792. Seven years later, some hundreds of Maroons from Jamaica (see page 225) also arrived in Nova Scotia. They too preferred to go on to Sierra Leone in 1800.

It fell to Carleton's successor, Haldimand, to provide for another loyalist emigration by land into the province of Quebec. At least another 20,000 loyalists from the back of New York State found their way by Lake Champlain to the St Lawrence or through the Mohawk Gap to the shores of Lake Ontario. These were mostly settlers of another type, farmers from Sir William Johnson's great estate, led by his son Sir John; Gaelic-speaking Highlanders, twice-exiled, who had no more love for Whigs in New England than for Whigs in Edinburgh; time-expired soldiers; Rangers from the frontier who had fought under Robert Rogers. Sir John Johnson brought with him two whole regiments, the Royal Greens, which he had raised and commanded; and with him came large numbers of British Indians, including most of the faithful tribe of the Mohawks, who were granted lands at Brantford and Quinté and own them to this day.

Much attention was paid to surveying townships and to allotting equitable grants of land. Soldiers might be allotted up to 200 acres free, and civilians 100 acres, but, in order to concentrate the settlers, the normal grant was sixty acres of virgin land and a town lot. The townships were surveyed in strips running back from the water's edge, along the Upper St Lawrence and on the banks of the Great Lakes. Thus began the British settlement of Upper Canada, later known as Ontario. It contained some strongly-marked Scottish areas where the kilt, the bagpipes and the Gaelic speech have never fallen into disuse.

Fair these broad meads, these hoary woods are grand,
But we are exiles from our native land.

From the lone sheiling in the misty island,
Distance divides us, and the waste of seas;
But still the blood is strong, the heart is Highland,
And we in dreams behold the Hebrides.

Scotsmen continued to migrate in parties to Canada and the Maritime Provinces, throughout the whole period of the Highland clearances. A notable emigration was that of the Glengarry Fencibles, a Highland Regiment brought out by their commanding officer at the Peace of 1802. They were Gaelic-speaking Catholics and their leader, Alexander Macdonell, became the first Roman Catholic Bishop of Upper Canada (1826).

The appearance of a large British population in part of the province of Quebec led to a demand on their part for revision of the Quebec Act. The French-Canadians, however, desired no such change; the Act was their charter of liberties ensuring them their own religion and civil laws. The immigrant loyalists wanted political rights like those enjoyed by the Maritime Provinces, where there was normal colonial self-government. They petitioned Parliament for these advantages, which Pitt conceded, deliberately. Though a reformer he had no sympathy with the advanced democracy of the United States and was anxious to establish a 'mixed' form of government in Canada, avoiding the errors which had led to the American Revolution. Carleton, now Lord Dorchester, who returned to North America in 1786 as Governor-General over all the surviving British provinces, was of a like opinion. He was of a cautious soldierly temper, suspicious of agitating politicians, and concerned above all to maintain a strong central government. In his long Canadian service he had grown to sympathise with the French point of view. 'This country', he wrote, 'must to the end of Time be peopled by the [French] Canadian race who have already taken such firm root.' After consulting Carleton, Pitt brought forward a proposal which was thus described in the House of Lords: 'Parliament are about to communicate the blessings of the English Constitution to the subjects of Canada because they are fully conscious that it is the best in the world.'

By the Canada Act, 1791, the Province of Quebec was split in two, Lower (or French) Canada, and Upper (or British)

Canada. Each was to have its own assembly, laws, language, and established Church, but the Governor-General, with more than royal powers, was supreme over both. Members of the lower house were elected as in the English shires by all freeholders with lands worth forty shillings a year. The nominated upper house was to have been composed of hereditary peers; but this intention, as Carleton warned Pitt, would never work and was quietly left unfulfilled. The French Canadians were not much pleased with the elective assembly which was alien to their traditions, but they were strengthened in their local patriotism by the establishment and endowment of the Roman Catholic Church. The Anglican Church was similarly established and endowed with one-seventh of the undeveloped waste land of the province. English common law was introduced into Upper Canada. 'To avoid the occasion of a misunderstanding similar to that which had formerly taken place,' said Pitt, 'no taxes were meant to be imposed by the Parliament respecting Canada, but such as might be necessary for the purpose of commercial regulation.'

The two provinces of Canada and the four Maritime Provinces may now be left in a stage of quiet development for twenty years. The 'Maritimes' grew their own food and exported masts and timber; Canada as yet exported little besides furs. All six provinces were weak and poverty-stricken, compared with the United States now in their boisterous youth. The destiny of Canada, its wealth in the north-west, lay hidden in the future. Many English and all American observers believed that sooner or later these sickly infant provinces would come to maturity under the Stars and Stripes.

Meanwhile relations between Great Britain and America continued to be very unfriendly. Owing to dissatisfaction at the treatment of the loyalists, the British refused to evacuate some frontier posts in the Ohio region. During the twenty years of revolution the population of the Thirteen Colonies had increased almost to three million and had overflowed westward into the disputed territories of the Ohio basin. Raids and reprisals by Indian bands, by loyalist rangers and by guerrilla fighters who were neither one nor the other, had deluged the advancing frontier with bloodshed and 'atrocity' stories. Never was a struggle nor its outcome more inevitable. By the end of the war the projected

Indian reserve contained a million scattered American settlers who hardly laid aside the rifle to take up axe and plough-rein. Gone for ever were the hunting-grounds and the domain of the redskins, but from this domain the British refused to withdraw their outposts at Oswego, Niagara, Detroit.

When war against the French Revolution broke out in 1792, and American hotheads urged Washington to renew the military alliance with France against England, he preferred to send Chief Justice Jay to negotiate a settlement of outstanding disputes. The Treaty of 1794, known as Jay's treaty, ends the struggle for North America. The frontier as far west as the source of the Mississippi, beyond which the Spanish territories lay unexplored, was agreed and surveyed as it remains to-day. The British withdrew their garrisons into Canada. Jay also hoped to gain concessions on the disputed question of the right to search neutral ships in time of war; but here he made no progress and the dispute has been a fruitful source of ill-will in every succeeding war. There were Americans so naïve as to suppose that Great Britain could be persuaded to admit the United States to all the economic advantages of the Acts of Trade even though they had contracted out of the Empire. Such a triumph would have been beyond the powers of any negotiator and was far beyond the powers of John Jay. He was thought to have failed in his mission when he got no more than a limited right for American ships to trade directly with the surviving British colonies. The final severance between the two branches of the English-speaking race was thus accomplished in a niggling spirit with a complete absence of magnanimity on either part. Dignity was shown almost alone by George III in his reception of John Adams, the first American minister at the Court of St James's. He said that as 'he had been the last to consent to the separation so he would be the first to meet the friendship of the United States as an independent power'.

9.   A RETROSPECT

WHAT justifiable complaints could have been made by the colonies in the eighteenth century against the mother-country? Not tyranny but neglect and condescension. For long years they were left to themselves until their problems happened to force the attention of the home government. A simple well-meant regulation was then imposed upon the colonies by officials who never doubted that they were superiors providing for their inferiors. When the propriety of the regulation was challenged by the colonists, the superior officials were so obliging as to recall it and substitute another, but never so critical as to question their own superiority. Not only were the colonial governments inferior jurisdictions, the colonists themselves were socially inferior people, a subordinate class. London society was unwilling to believe that Washington could be a gentleman or that Franklin would not be patronised. Too frequently the stay-at-home English have regarded the colonies as a refuse heap for misfits and failures, from the governor, often the feckless member of some political grandee's family, to the 'remittance man', that well-known figure in every colony, the black sheep paid to go abroad and stay abroad. As James Mill said, the colonial service was regarded as 'a system of outdoor relief for the upper classes'. Far worse was the disposition to export the vicious dregs of the old country, on Dogberry's principle that the best police report was to 'thank God you are rid of a knave'. The English penal laws were then the severest in the world, crimes classed as felony and punishable by death being numerous. Jeremy Bentham's model prisons had not yet imposed upon society a universal belief in solitary confinement as the proper treatment for convicted criminals. If not hanged, it seemed reasonable and cheap to dispose of felons by selling them into slavery for a term of years or for the term of their natural life. From 1707 till 1770 convicted felons were transported, by contract with ship-owners who placed them as indentured labourers in the American colonies. There was a brisk demand for the labourers but a very well-justified series of complaints against the practice from colonial statesmen.

Hardly less irksome than this low conception of colonial life was the 'Treasury Point of View'. Moneyed men in the City, and their political associates in Downing Street assessed the colonies as items in a balance-sheet. The plantations themselves, financed indeed by capital raised and owned in the City, were estates which ought to show a net annual profit. The colonists, very commonly mortgaged deeply, were the financial dependants of merchants at home and should be proud to act as their agents. The Treasury, keeping a watchful eye on the balance of trade, would favour any colony showing a healthy figure of raw materials sent home and a healthier figure of English manu- factured goods brought out; but a colony that called for a grant- in-aid was worthless and should be written off.

It was, however, recognised, in the eighteenth century, that every colony had one concealed asset which might be turned to the advantage of the Treasury, its undeveloped 'waste lands'. These by custom were the domain of the Crown, when effective occupation of any part of the region had been established by subjects of the Crown. The limitations of that hinterland were uncertainly defined, a problem which had already arisen in the case of the Ohio basin and which would arise again in each new colony on the coast of an unexplored continent. Fruitful in trouble was the inevitable clash between the frontiersmen, urged by restless ambition to go up and occupy the land, and the projectors of Whitehall making grants and restrictions on small- scale maps. Land-hunger was more powerful than distant, ill- informed, civil servants with no more than a languid interest in the ways of the wilderness.

When intervening to allot the 'waste lands', on whatever principle, it has always been the part of the Crown to protect the aborigines against frontier lawlessness. No solution was found in the history of the Thirteen Colonies, nor has it yet been found, to the problem of imposing a higher civilisation upon a primitive race without exposing the latter to exploitation and demoralisation. To assert that the 400,000 or 500,000 Indians were the rightful possessors of America and that by some law of nature it should have been reserved for them rather than for the 200,000,000 who now live there is ridiculous. Perhaps, as men lived and thought in the seventeenth and eighteenth centuries, no other fate than racial war was possible for the American Indians. Their expulsion from the fertile eastern lands was but one episode in the 5000 years' struggle between the predatory, nomadic tribes of the Stone Age and the agricultural peoples who have learned to be civilised by the use of metal implements. Let Englishmen be proud that their government attempted to protect and to civilise the savages; and let them not be surprised that they got no thanks from the settlers who lived under the threat of the Indian scalping-knives.

Philanthropic endeavour among the Indians was conducted by missionaries and largely by those of the official Anglican Church. Just as the Jesuits in Canada were regarded as the political agents of the French King, so in the Thirteen Colonies the Anglican clergy, and especially the missionaries of the S.P.G., were King George's men. There was more than a suspicion in America, as in later colonies, that missionary work among the savages was itself politically reprehensible; it stirred them to rebellious sentiments and acts. At the period of the American Revolution the authority of the clergy was slight; in the next age it was too much enlarged. As a class the clergy were loyalists, and the Tory party in England was soon to come under the influence of a religious revival. During the succeeding fifty years, when the Tories were almost continually in office, colonial policy was to be swayed by the missionary 'interest' more strongly than by any of those commercial 'interests', in the fisheries, in sugar, in cotton or in oil, which at other times have formed the motives of the Colonial Office.

Downing Street has fought many colonial campaigns, some arising out of, and some leading towards, greater wars in Europe. In all these campaigns the settlers in the colonies concerned have played a gallant part when it was their interest to do so. The colonists willingly shed their blood and somewhat less willingly spent their money to conquer Louisburg and Fort Duquesne. It was not until late in the nineteenth century that any colony saw fit to take part in an imperial campaign beyond its own frontier. Overseas trade, sea-power, and, by the same token, the expenses of the Navy were imperial concerns. The King's ships would naturally defend the trade which the King directed to his own advantage. As in England so in the colonies, the jolly tars were regarded with affection, but the soldiers were on another footing. All the old English dislike of militarism, the fear of martial law, flourished in the colonies which were as proud of their own 'constitutional' militia as they were suspicious of King George's red-coats. They had no control over these soldiers and were unwilling to pay their expenses. On the other hand, Downing Street had no liking for campaigns fought in the interests of colonists who would not meet the bill. Thus in each colonial war there was rivalry and friction, as young Washington found in his first campaigns under Braddock, between the formal regular officers with their ponderous stereotyped art of war and the undisciplined militia, so apt at a guerrilla skirmish on their own ground, so ineffective in a pitched battle.

All these causes of friction were essentially English; the traditions, the prejudices they had inherited from their English forefathers produced the mental atmosphere of the American Revolution; an equally English complacency and narrow-mindedness in the House of Commons produced the resistance to it. These ingredients, on one side and the other, have recurred in every later imperial crisis, though not always with such deplorable results. The foundation of the Irish Free State and of the Union of South Africa give evidence of the effect of 'magnanimity', a quality for which Burke called in vain in the 1770's, to dissolve prejudices and restore peace.

When the Americans had got their independence they made no clean break with the past. Their new constitution was not founded upon any Utopian design nor upon any historical precedent other than the existing colonial forms of government. The Thirteen Colonies, when they became sovereign states, retained the chartered rights they had received from English kings. Supreme control over some aspects of government they surrendered to a President and a Congress who were to play the part which the King and Parliament of England, as they supposed, should have ideally played under the old regime. Written constitutions, so unfamiliar to the home-staying English, came naturally to Americans accustomed as they were to chartered rights; and the veto over unconstitutional legislation assumed by the Supreme Court of the United States was but a repetition of the former right of the Crown to disallow Acts of colonial legislatures. The English common law remained, with all its imperfections, the basis of American law, though very differently administered in the United States. New England influence spread throughout the Union the concept of direct democracy, the people's justice. So much was power decentralised that in the backwoods, where the writ of the state could hardly run, the town-meeting usurped all the functions of government. Judges were directly chosen by the citizens, and if no other judge, then 'Judge Lynch'. Politics were strictly local; in a new country with bad communications, though there may be wide open spaces, there is often a narrow mental outlook. The township means more than the state, the state more than the Union. In these little, remote, self-governing communities, direct democracy sometimes degenerated into mob-rule or dwindled into anarchy. This primitive struggle to preserve the people's justice is the tradition of the 'Wild West'.

American political ideas and prejudices were derived from English sources; and in many other ways the United States was long dependent upon the British Empire. A flag, a president, a constitution could not alter the fact that the external trade of America was still in the hands of the British. Almost the whole tonnage of shipping entering American ports sailed under the British flag, the whole of it under protection of the British Navy. More than one-half of American exports went to Great Britain. The Americans were a nation of primary producers still backward in industrial development; for all manufactured goods, other than those produced in village workshops, they were obliged to rely upon the British, the one industrialised nation. This dependence tended to increase rather than to decrease as the Age of the Machines drew on. The southern states, enlarging the scope of their agriculture, sold increasing quantities of raw cotton to the English market; the northern states, eager to mechanise their crafts, bought their heavy machinery in Great Britain. While the Americans never lacked inventiveness, coming early into the field with labour-saving devices such as the harvester and the sewing-machine, they came late into the field of pure scientific research (excepting the work of the many-sided Franklin).

When the fringe of cultivation was not far inland, when no part of the United States was far removed from the life of the frontier, the struggle with nature occupied men's minds and produced appropriate practical qualities. Not in the first generations after independence could an indigenous school of Art or Letters be expected to arise. The culture of New England, which came nearest to it, was still provincial, not quite sure of itself, though it had the merit of being rooted in the soil. Elsewhere there was long a tendency, which has been repeated in more recent British colonies, for men of talent like the painters Copley and West, the writers Washington Irving and Fenimore Cooper, like Franklin himself, like Whistler, Sargent and Henry James a hundred years later, to settle in the more congenial society of Europe.

The American miracle was not their War of Independence, nor their constitution nor—what now seems remarkable—their technical ability; it was the conquest of a continent. No other event in the nineteenth century is so important as the westward march and expansion of the Americans. No other record exists in human history of colonisation on so gigantic a scale. The million and a half of white colonists, advancing in a hundred years from the Ohio to the Pacific Ocean, had multiplied seventeenfold to constitute the 26,000,000 white Americans of 1860. In these hundred years the bulk of the increase was caused by the natural fertility of the original English colonists and by the steady flow of immigrants from Great Britain. The newcomers were drawn in the first eighty of these hundred years mostly from England and Scotland, in the last twenty from Ireland. The American population, excluding negroes, drew level in 1860 with the population of the British Isles, though that too had been increasing at a surprising rate. The daughter had achieved an equality of stature with the mother-country. But even then the colonial period was not concluded. The flow of emigration continued; America was still a 'plantation' requiring new settlers to break the virgin ground, and attracting an increasing proportion of them from continental Europe. Again, the population doubled itself in a generation and continued to rise, though less steeply, until in 1930 there were 109,000,000 white men in the United States against 45,000,000 in Great Britain; but of the emigrants in the first years of the twentieth century only about one-quarter had come from the British Empire.

The western wilderness had now been subdued; the United States was highly industrialised; world markets other than the

English market invited American raw materials and manufactured goods; American social customs, jargon, hobbies,
beliefs, no longer derived from Europe, were in their turn
changing the character of European society. The American
universities, once the pale copies of unreformed Cambridge and
Glasgow, now devoting their boundless wealth and zeal to
research, experiment and record, were as well able to teach as to
learn from Europe. The colonial age ended when, in 1921, the
door was shut to European emigrants. The last link of dependence on Great Britain was financial subordination to the City of
London. America had been developed in its earlier heroic age by
British emigrants and through all its history by British capital.
At the beginning of the First German War the United States was
still a debtor nation with much of its resources mortgaged to the
City, to those same 'interests' which 150 years earlier had backed
the policy of the Elder Pitt. The two German Wars liquidated
these British capital investments, leaving the United States at last
mature and free. England had called the New World into existence to redress the balance against oppression in the Old, at the
cost of her own supremacy.

III

THE EAST INDIA COMPANY, 1600–1833

Argument: The Mogul court was more powerful and luxurious, in some ways more civilised, than that of any contemporary European king. At the end of the seventeenth century the attempt of the Mogul emperors to unite India had failed, largely because of a Hindu reaction led by the Maratha chiefs.

Early European visitors, deeply impressed by the wealth of Asiatic rulers, could at first effect little except in buying oriental luxuries for cash. The rivalry between Portuguese, Dutch and English was a struggle for sea-power and concessions at sea-ports. About the year 1740 French and British adventurers were drawn into the anarchic struggles of a dissolving empire. Sepoys led and trained by Europeans dominated every battle-field, but in the general course of world-affairs sea-power gave the British party victory over the French.

At a late stage Parliament intervened to curb the irresponsible 'nabobs' who had enriched themselves in the general anarchy. British India was thereafter governed by contract. The Company, withdrawing from trade, provided an administrative service under the control of a royal governor-general who ensured that public morality should conform to Western standards.

1. THE INDIAN BACKGROUND

'EVERY schoolboy knows', wrote Macaulay a hundred years ago, 'who imprisoned Montezuma and who strangled Atahualpa, but we doubt whether one in ten, even among English gentlemen of highly cultivated minds can tell who won the Battle of Buxar, who perpetrated the massacre of Patna, whether Sujah Dowlah ruled in Oude or in Travancore, or whether Holkar was a Hindu or a Mussulman. It might have been expected that every Englishman who takes an interest in any part of history would be curious to know how a handful of his countrymen, separated from their home by an immense ocean, subjugated, in the course of a few years, one of the greatest empires in the world. Yet unless we greatly err, this subject is, to most readers, not only insipid but positively distasteful.'

By the eloquence of his essays on Clive and Warren Hastings Macaulay himself has done much to remedy the fault. Though few now read Prescott's *Conquest of Mexico, and Peru* every schoolboy has heard at least of the Siege of Arcot, the Black Hole of Calcutta, and the Trial of Warren Hastings, some of the most familiar episodes in our imperial history. But English knowledge seldom goes deep enough to understand the British Raj as an episode in the age-long history of India, one in a series of foreign dominations. Perhaps the most extraordinary chain of events in all political history is that by which, almost imperceptibly, a company of English merchants crept into the throne of Aurangzeb as residuary legatees to the Mogul Empire. The pomp of Indian princes, among whom the English took their place, dazzled their eyes, giving them a false view of Indian prosperity. It was long before they realised that India, in fact, was miserably poor, a country where millions lived on the edge of starvation, where the Malthusian checks of war, famine and disease intermittently operated to prevent the natural increase of population and to force down the standard of living. The Indian social system which it fell to the English to maintain was already stratified with deposits from the remote past.

Modern archaeological research has revealed the ruins of civilisations in the valley of the Indus as old as Ur of the Chaldees and not dissimilar in culture. What dark-skinned nations dwelt in them it is hard to say, but they were long-established and far removed from barbarism when, in the second millennium before Christ, the Aryan invaders came through the passes of the Himalayas. All that is known of the Aryans is derived from some poetic fragments, the oldest surviving literature in the world. Sanskrit, the language of these ancient writings, had for many centuries been known only to indigenous scholars when Sir William Jones (1749–96), the Chief Justice of Bengal, brought it to the notice of the academies of the West. Warren Hastings encouraged the study of the Ancient Laws of India and founded the Bengal Asiatic Society (1784). In his presidential address (1786) Sir William Jones declared that Greek, Latin and Sanskrit had a common origin. Jones's translations from the Sanskrit led to the comparative study of grammar and mythology by a line of industrious German scholars, from Schlegel and

Jacob Grimm to Max Müller, who classified the Indo-European group of languages.

The Aryans, as described in the *Vedic Hymns*, were a nomadic, pastoral, fair-haired conquering race which had occupied the plains of north-western Hindustan; later they spread south into the tableland of the Deccan, and east to the Ganges delta. They devoted themselves to hunting, war and poetry. Their heroes were of divine origin and kept their blood pure from admixture with the dark-skinned aboriginals. At an early period their rigid marriage customs led to a division into three exclusive castes of the 'twice-born' conquering race—the Brahmins, the Warriors, the Merchants, and a lower caste of the conquered labourers, all of whom were restricted to marriage within their caste. In the course of centuries the lower castes have been infinitely subdivided, a process which caused progressive racial degeneration by in-breeding weakly types. The caste system was maintained by a system of stultifying taboos prescribing limits to the actions and habits and customs of every caste, and quite preventing rational improvements in the arts of life. Since many common functions and articles were tabooed as 'unclean' the structure of Hindu society required a class of universal slaves, *pariahs*, to perform the necessary menial tasks. These depressed classes, together with the heathen aboriginals of the jungle, and the foreigners who ignored the taboos, were deprived of social rights in this world and hopes of salvation in the next, but were none the less necessary if the world's work was to be carried on.

Hindu reformers of the present day very properly point out that the caste-system is no original or essential feature of their religion, but an accretion of some later age; yet this monstrosity exists, though with infinite local variations as the rigid frame of Indian society, and has its defenders. A sense of fraternity and a rule of self-government bind the members of each caste into a social unit, all together constituting the frame of a corporative state. The industrial castes are highly organised as craft guilds, maintaining wage-rates and standards of work, and allowing none of their members to starve. The village communities are ruled by councils of elders representing all castes, high and low. Caste has given such complete stability to society that the history of India has been a mere military pageant. Armies marched, kingdoms rose and fell, but the laws of caste and the lives of the caste-ridden remained unchanged. The incidence of good or bad kings was like the incidence of good or bad harvests, an event from which no other than the immediate consequences were to be expected or desired; there was no political or constitutional progress and, until the nineteenth century, hardly any economic change. Before the coming of the English, the rulers of India were without exception despots, having no check upon their whims and lusts except the check imposed by irrational taboos. There have been great and benevolent monarchs in Indian history such as Asoka in the third century B.C. and Kanishka in the second century A.D., but their influence was merely personal.

Our knowledge of Indian history is, however, incomplete. The Sanskrit classics, though they constitute one of the world's great literatures are limited in scope. Unlike other early literatures they are singularly poor in chronology; they are rich in poetry but not in history. The tendency of Hindu philosophy has been increasingly towards the contemplative and away from the active virtues, a tendency much strengthened by the system of Buddhism which originated in Hindustan during the sixth century before Christ. Though there are now few adherents of the Buddhist religion in India proper, the cosmology ascribed to Prince Gautama has been largely absorbed into the Hindu religion. Nothing has done more to mould the character of modern India than the doctrine of *Karma* with all its implications; its submissiveness, its quietism, its renunciation of power and will, its picture of human life as an unbroken chain of reincarnations leading forward to *Nirvana*, negation, the nihilist heaven.

But the religion of the Brahmins was capable of far more surprising accretions. Every godling could be adopted into the Hindu pantheon. Where every act of life was hedged round with caste taboos there was fertile soil for coarser superstitions. All sorts of fetishism and idolatry flourished, from the cult of the cow, the totem animal of the cattle-breeding Aryans, to the bloody rites of Kali and the masochistic festival of Juggernaut. *Suttee* and *Thuggee*, temple prostitution, female infanticide and human sacrifice were practised in the name of the Hindu cult. These rites were but the earthy symbols of a transcendental religion comprehended only by the refined whose purity of life and integrity of motive were above reproach. Not many *mahat-*

mas were to be expected in a single generation. They breathed a rarefied air where religion was defended by every sophisticated argument, for Hindu metaphysicians, like Hindu lawyers, were remarkable for intellectual subtlety.

So catholic is the multiplicity of shrines, ceremonies and idols admitted into the Hindu cult that the Portuguese who came to Calicut in 1498 entered a Hindu temple to pray, supposing from the images, the lights, the bells, the incense and the shaven priests that they were in one of their own churches. Such were the standards of Christianity when Rodrigo Borgia was Pope.

The worst deterioration in Hindu society was their treatment of women, who originally had equal rights with men. Child-marriages and premature child-bearing were enjoined by Brahmin law. Child-widows, if not forced to perform *suttee*, were the most wretched of slaves. This was and is the charge that must be laid in the balance against the virtue and charm of Indian domestic life where the wife and mother is supreme in her own household. *Purdah*, the seclusion of women, is a modern custom in India and due to Moslem influence. The evils of child-marriage, added to the effects of malnutrition, an enervating climate, the dysgenic effects of caste, and the insanitary customs imposed by superstition have all combined to keep physical standards in India among the lowest in the world.

Between the eleventh and the eighteenth centuries many armies of Afghans, Turks, Persians and Mongols invaded India through the Khyber Pass. All were Moslems and, flooding into the plains of Hindustan, brought successive waves of Moslem influence to submerge or at least to wash over the Hindu culture. In the foothills of the Himalayas, in the Indus Valley, and in the plains of Bengal, Moslems settled or Hindus were forcibly converted to Islam. Throughout India, Moslems won lordships and estates with the sword and often retained them in the midst of a Hindu population. Elsewhere there were Hindu revivals and recoveries, so that all India is full of religious anomalies. Hyderabad, a Hindu state, had a Moslem ruler; while Kashmir, a Moslem state was ruled by a Hindu. The Moslems, believers in one God, one faith, one law, iconoclasts and puritans, active to propagate their faith, intolerant of alien customs, rationalists, democrats in religion, despised the Hindus as mere idolaters; on the other hand, the Hindus condemned the Moslems as *mlechchas*, unclean cow-eaters without caste. Much could be absorbed into the Hindu cult but not the religion of Islam. The moral systems of the two cults are so radically opposed, the cleavage so absolute between the two societies that strife has been inevitable and recurrent. Several attempts from one side and the other to reconcile them in some comprehensive system have failed, but what is more remarkable is, by contrast, the amity in which Moslems and Hindus have often lived together for long periods in some Indian provinces. In particular Moslem rulers have been obliged to depend upon the skill and intelligence of Hindu administrators.

The Mogul Empire which at last provided India with an effective administrative system, was founded by Babur, the King of Cabul. By a victory won in 1526 at Panipat, the scene of several of the decisive contests of Indian history, Babur became master of the Jumna valley with its cities of Agra and Delhi. Among the spoils was the jewel called the Koh-i-noor, the symbol of imperial power. Babur left written memoirs which reveal him as a man of culture and observation; he composed verses, enjoyed good living, and was much more than a conquering tyrant. He thought little of the dreary plains of Hindustan compared with his own cool mountain kingdom. The people were ugly and unsociable, without genius or courtesy, they had 'no good horses, no good flesh-meat, no grapes or melons, no ice or cold water, no good bread, no baths or colleges'. But at Agra his descendants lived and reigned, built magnificently and astonished the world.

His grandson Akbar (1556–1605) extended his sway over the whole of Hindustan, imposed peace and organised his conquests. The Empire was divided into fifteen provinces each ruled by a feudal governor know as the *Nawab*, a word vulgarised by the English as 'nabob'. Since time immemorial the Hindu village communities had paid a fee or tax to the King of at least one-sixth and sometimes one-half of the annual value of the land. The original payment in kind had often been commuted for cash. Akbar attempted, but with only partial success, to convert this vague customary arrangement into a feudal-system by assigning the farm of villages or districts to his feudatories who undertook in return to support him in the field with an assigned number of armed horsemen. Within his province the Nawab was supreme and, like a feudal vassal in Christendom, might on occasion assert himself by force against his sovereign. The provinces were composed of smaller fiefs held by princes known as *rajahs*, or by some other title. Many of the rajahs were Hindus, the successors of ancient monarchs now tributary to the Moguls; but others were new fiefs created at the Emperor's will. The rajahs in turn claimed military service from their tenants, the 'landed gentry' of India whose feudal obligation and status varied locally as in medieval Europe. The *zemindars* of Bengal may be taken as typical. They lived upon a revenue drawn from the village communities, whose patrons and protectors they were, and passed on a proportion of that revenue, perhaps through some intermediate rajah, to the nawab who in his turn passed on a proportion to the court of the Great Mogul. Whether the zemindars should be regarded as the actual proprietors whose revenue was rent or whether they were government officials collecting a tax is a question for political economists. The provincial system and the method of collecting revenue in the form of a rent or tax on land outlived the Mogul Empire and were taken over by the East India Company.

Though the revenue system, like all systems of tax-farming, was oppressive it had the merit of regularity; and throughout Akbar's reign Hindustan was, by Asiatic standards, well and peaceably governed. Akbar was a sagacious politician and a cultured man of the world. As he grew older he lapsed from Moslem orthodoxy and developed a sceptical curiosity about other cults. He attempted a synthesis of Hindu, Christian and Zoroastrian theologies, held round-table conferences of religious leaders, invited the Jesuits from Goa to expound their doctrines at his court and married three wives—a Moslem, a Hindu and a Christian. India seemed to be drawing towards national unity, even to be developing a national language in *Urdu*, the language of the 'horde', its structure being Hindustani, its vocabulary largely Persian. But Akbar's successor, Jahangir (1605–27), drifted back to Moslem orthodoxy. The Empire reached its greatest extent and magnificence under the succeeding Emperor Shah Jahan (1627–58), the builder of the Taj Mahal, who ruled all India excepting the southernmost tip, now the state of Travancore. The long reign of Aurangzeb (1658–1707), a bigot and a persecutor, was largely spent in wars against rebellious Hindu vassals. The culture of the Mogul court was Persian; all the

Mogul princes loved gardens and landscape, they spent the hot weather in Kashmir; all were patrons of painting and architecture in a Persian style.

Moslem domination, intensified by the intolerance of Akbar's successors, had produced a noteworthy Hindu reaction. A puritanical Hindu sect known as the Sikhs had arisen among the warlike peoples of the Punjab. The high-born Hindu princes of Rajputana were restive, and a new military power, the Maratha confederacy, had appeared in the western Deccan. The most useful mounted troops in the polyglot armies of the Moguls had been drawn from the Maratha tribesmen, light cavalry who lived by war and plunder. During Aurangzeb's reign a Maratha general, Sivaji, conceived the plan of building up the Maratha tribes into a nation that might control or defy the Emperor. By making raids on all their neighbours and by exploiting the progressive weakness of Aurangzeb's successors the Maratha chiefs extended their power across central India from the Arabian Sea to the Bay of Bengal, keeping all India in terror for a hundred years. Though they set up a political administration over the provinces they subdued and looted, and though the Maratha principalities had long histories, it is almost impossible to describe their system in a few words. Sivaji founded the kingdom of Sattara near Bombay. It maintained a dynasty of rajahs but, in a single generation, their authority lapsed into the hands of their chief ministers, whose office also became hereditary in another dynasty known as the Peshwas of Poona. So far as anyone was head of the Maratha confederacy it was the Peshwa. His unruly vassals, or colleagues, were Scindia of Gwalior, Holkar of Indore, Bhonsla of Berar, Gaekwar of Baroda and others, in each case the bearer of a name which became a hereditary title. It was fear of the Marathas that drove the East India Company to remove their mainland factory from Surat to the safer island of Bombay; a few years later Calcutta, a thousand miles away, was fortified against their raids by what is known as the Maratha Ditch. They destroyed the peaceful administration of the Empire, allowing, if not obliging, the Nawabs to act as independent rulers in their provinces. While destroying the central government they failed to defend Hindustan against the disastrous Persian and Afghan invasions from the north-west.

2. THE PORTUGUESE AND DUTCH IN ASIA

ASIA, in the sixteenth century and long after, was pictured in Europe as a series of fantastic monarchies, the farther the more fabulous.

The myth had some foundation; at Constantinople, the world's most populous city, the Caliph of Islam known in Europe as the Grand Signior, or more simply as the Grand Turk, ruled over dominions far wider and perhaps as well-governed as those of the Holy Roman Emperor. Beyond the Turkish dominions the Soldan of Egypt reigned until, in 1517, the Turks added his kingdom to their own; beyond Egypt were the lands of the 'Sophy', the Shah of Persia. Hindustan was ruled by a king whose court at Agra surpassed in magnificence the most ambitious dreams of Rome or Paris. Sir Thomas Roe's description of Jahangir provided the model for Milton's description of Satan enthroned in Hell: 'High on a gallery, with a canopy over him and a carpet before him, sat in great and barbarous state the GREAT MOGUL.' Eastward of Mogul territories lay the 'Celestial' Empire of the Great Khan of Cathay about which Marco Polo had woven tales which sober men treated as gross exaggeration; his statistics of cities and their populations, of armies, and fortifications, and offices of state, though modern enquiry has verified them, outran belief. Even stranger tales were told of outlying kingdoms, such as the forbidden island realm of Cipangu, or Japan, which only in the twentieth century revealed its true character to the western world. Laputa and Brobdingnag seemed almost as likely to exist.

Early travellers from Europe approached these strange lands in a mood of childlike wonder, without the least sense of racial superiority, and rightly. In law and medicine and mathematics the Asiatics, and especially the Brahmins, were the masters of European scholars until the Revival of Learning in Europe. But to the unlearned travellers from the west, cruelty, wealth and power seemed to distinguish those regions where

> the gorgeous East with richest hand
> Showers on her kings barbaric pearl and gold.

To be sure the peoples of Asia were for the most part heathen and many of them worshippers of the false Mahound, but in

social refinement and political organisation they were not conceived as being inferior to the peoples of Christendom. The
colour-line had not yet been drawn on the map. Whites and
blacks wondered at one another and on occasion developed a
physical repugnance, but the lightly pigmented Saracens of the
Levant, who were the most familiar of Asiatic peoples, were not
'black-a-moors' and were not classed with them. Religion not
race set up the barrier.

The Saracen kings barred the way to the more distant, more
exotic lands, filled with hypothetical treasures, where certain
luxuries much desired in Christendom could actually be pro-
cured: the silks of China, the fine cottons and muslins of Bengal,
the shawls of Cashmere, the rubies of Golconda, the pearls of
Ormuz, ivory from East Africa—cinnamon from Ceylon, pepper
from Malabar, cloves and nutmeg from the Moluccas. What
reached Christendom of these delights was paid for in cash, a
steady drain of silver from west to east which lasted throughout
the Middle Ages and helped to build up the treasure hoards of the
Asiatic princes. The desire for a short-cut to the supposed riches
of the East, outflanking the Turks northward or southward, was
the motive of all the Renaissance explorations, especially of
those two voyages which Adam Smith described as the two
'greatest and most important events recorded in the history of
mankind', the discovery of America by Columbus in 1492 and the
rounding of the Cape of Good Hope by Vasco da Gama in 1497.

The Spaniards in discovering America had missed their aim.
Deluded at first by some resemblances between the Spice Islands
and the new-found lands which they called the West Indies, they
were consoled, when the error was revealed, by the actual
treasures of Mexico and Peru. After these had been looted, the
sons of the conquistadores slowly learned what was the true and
lasting wealth of the New World. Meanwhile the Portuguese
had begun to exploit the fabled riches of Asia, with motives
which, though mixed, were not so much commercial as quixotic.
They were a nation of sailors and sea-crusaders, seeking power
and glory, though not disdaining gold as a means to those ends.
Throughout their two centuries of greatness their policy was
concerned with opposition to the Turks and their Moslem allies.
South about Africa there must be a way to the sea-ports of
southern Asia which Marco Polo had described; and there a

Christian empire might be founded upon sea-power, to grasp the wealth of the Indies and to rally the Christian communities of the East against the Moslems. Were there not Christian Copts in Egypt, and Nestorians in India planted by St Thomas the Apostle? Was there not a Christian kingdom in Ethiopia, and might there not be a greater in the land of Prester John, could men but find the way there?

When Vasco da Gama landed at Calicut in 1498 he had the luck to find himself on the shore of a Hindu kingdom, in his eyes a friendly state because hostile to the Moslems. Successive Portuguese expeditions engaged themselves in the politics of western India with the object of establishing a base from which to operate against Moslem trade in the Arabian Sea. To this end, the greatest of Portuguese empire-builders, Albuquerque, made his capital city at Goa, in 1510, and spent his force in getting a foothold in the Persian Gulf. The trade of Asia largely went in Arab ships from the Malabar Coast to the Red Sea and the Persian Gulf, whence it passed overland through the dominions of the Soldan of Egypt. The Portuguese gradually extended their power from Goa to Ormuz, Mozambique, Colombo and Malacca, four points from which they could control all the sea-routes of the Indian Ocean. Building fortresses and maintaining fleets against the Soldan they made little effort to spread inland or to develop their own commerce. The trade remained in the hands of Asiatics who already made use of a complete system of commercial banking, bills of exchange and marine insurance, more highly developed than anything of the kind in Europe. Albuquerque encouraged his men to marry Asiatic wives and breed soldiers; he was more desirous of conquering and converting the heathen than of buying and selling with them. Before many years Goa contained more priests than merchants, and naval expeditions to the Red Sea were equalled in heroism by the expeditions of the Jesuit missionaries. At Goa St Francis Xavier died and was buried in 1542. But the power and pride of the Viceroyalty and Archbishopric of Goa declined with Portuguese sea-power, when, from 1580 to 1640, Portugal was subjected to Spain and was accordingly involved in the disastrous naval wars against the English and the Dutch.

The sixteenth century which saw the rise of the Portuguese maritime empire in the East saw too the rise of the equally foreign Mogul dynasty. Babur, the first of the Mogul emperors, from his kingdom of Kabul, was forming designs for the conquest of northern Hindustan while his contemporary, Albuquerque, was getting control of its western seaboard. Akbar, the contemporary of Queen Elizabeth, was the greatest monarch and the most enlightened statesman of his age. While he dominated the Indian mainland, and the Portuguese the Indian seas, Dutch and English interlopers appeared upon the scene.

In the east the Dutch outstripped their English rivals by an initial investment of capital five times as great. During the first ten years of its existence the English East India Company sent seventeen ships to Asia, the Dutch sent 134. The Dutch East India Company, a powerful trading corporation unhindered by state control, determined at an early date upon a policy far more ambitious than that of the English and different in design from that of the Portuguese. The Dutch traders sought to control and exploit the populous regions in which the desired tropical products were produced. By the year 1607 they had established themselves in Java and the Moluccas; in 1609 they made their headquarters at Batavia, the capital of their eastern empire for more than 300 years. In 1641 they seized Malacca from the Portuguese and after years of sporadic fighting expelled them from Ceylon in 1658. In 1652 they formed the first settlement at the Cape of Good Hope. These establishments did not involve them in the politics of the great Asiatic empires but were firm bases for commercial power. Their political strategy was intended to exclude their rivals, the English and the Portuguese, rather than to triumph over infidel monarchies. In despite of Portuguese armadas and Dutch commercial skill, the English began, in a small way, to seek a share in the trade of Asia.

3. THE EAST INDIA COMPANY, 1600–1709

THE voyages of Fitch and Lancaster stimulated sufficient interest in London for the foundation of a trading company. Accordingly a body of merchants, under the presidency of the Lord Mayor, petitioned the Queen to charter a project 'for the honour of their native country, and the advancement of trade and merchandise within the realm of England, and to set forth a voyage this year to the East Indies and other islands and countries thereabouts'. The charter was issued on 31 December 1600, granting to the 'Governor and Company of Merchants of London, trading to the East Indies', an exclusive right 'to traffic with any countries, islands, or ports beyond the Cape of Good Hope to the Straits of Magellan, not yet occupied by any friendly power'. The Governor and Directors, who were to be elected annually, were given authority 'to hold court and make ordinances and impose penalties...not contrary to the laws of this our realm', presumably within the limits of such 'factories' as they should establish.

The first Governor, Sir Thomas Smythe, whose interest in Virginia has already been mentioned, set his face against colonisation. 'The Portuguese,' he wrote, 'notwithstanding their many rich residences, are beggared by keeping of soldiers. They never made advantage of the Indies since they defended them. It has also been the error of the Dutch who seek plantations here by the sword. Let this be received as a rule, that if you will profit seek, seek it at sea and in quiet trade.' For the beginning of this quiet trade a joint stock of £30,133. 6s. was raised by 101 subscribers.

The first three voyages of the Company were made to Java, Sumatra, and the Moluccas, but after the peace with Spain and Portugal in 1604 it was decided to seek a concession from the Great Mogul for trade with the Indian mainland. The Portuguese, without doubt, would raise objections but perhaps might not, now that peace was restored, resist the English merchants forcibly.

The Company had rejected Mildenhall's advances (see above, page 14), with the intention of sending their own accredited agent, William Hawkins, to the Mogul court, in sufficient state to impress the Indians. His ship, the *Hector*, the first vessel to show the English flag on the Indian coast, anchored at the mouth of the Tapti River on 24 August 1608. After many months of negotiation with the local governor and in spite of counter-efforts by the Portuguese, Hawkins at last went up-country to Agra in April 1609. Jahangir (1605–27), who had succeeded to the throne but not to the greatness of his father Akbar, was a jolly toper, brutal, virile and obstinate. Though he had abandoned Akbar's heresies in favour of at least an external loyalty to Islam, he still extended toleration to the Portuguese Jesuits and appreciated the effects of Portuguese sea-power. While Hawkins could not break down the Portuguese influence at court, he achieved something by becoming the tyrant's boon companion, conversing with him fluently in Turkish. He lived three years at court in Asiatic style, married an Armenian Christian wife at Jahangir's behest, and was invested with a feudal fee 'of four hundred horse'.

Though Hawkins could get no *firman* from the Emperor, trade began in a small way. In 1613 the English were allowed to found an agency ('factory') for trade at Surat, to the chagrin of the Portuguese and their friends among the Surat merchants. Within a few months, though there was peace in Europe, English and Portuguese came to blows. An English fleet in 'Swally Hole' at the mouth of the river blockaded the Portuguese in Surat and drove off a punitive squadron sent by the Viceroy of Goa. The English ship *Hope* brought home the first Indian cargo, of indigo and cotton, in 1614. Jahangir took offence at Portuguese pretensions, favouring the English on the whole, especially when Sir Thomas Roe, a scholar, courtier and wit, arrived in 1616, as ambassador from King James I. To the further annoyance of the Portuguese the English also extended their trading activities into the Red Sea.

All accounts emphasise that nothing was done at the Mogul's court without an inducement, the difficulty being to provide any sort of present which would take the fancy of the richest ruler in the world. To compete with rajahs who brought their lord trains of elephants harnessed with gold was difficult for the factors of a London company. Jewels were out of the question; the Mogul appeared in a new outfit of them every day in the year. Broadcloth, though unrivalled in its own market, was not much in demand in the hot weather. The Englishmen racked their brains to think of ingenious 'toys'. Whereas a set of virginals was a total failure, a cornet proved such a success with Jahangir, who blew through it for an hour on end, that the cornet-player was persuaded to stay at court and turn Mohammedan. English mastiffs, fierce enough for baiting tigers found favour, but Sir Thomas Roe concluded that nothing went down so well with the Emperor as a few cases of Burgundy wine. It was not these things but the robust character of the strangers that made their fortune. Jahangir used to say, or so the English reported, that 'one Portugal will beate three of them [Hindus], and one Englishman three Portugals'.

Since Hawkins's time there had been several English residents at Agra, not only a 'factory' of the Company's agents, but also other visitors. Several voluminous accounts survive, in *Purchas's Pilgrimes* and elsewhere of Hindu ceremonies, of the feudal government of the Mogul's Moslem lords, and of the bidding against the Portuguese for commercial favours. The most amusing of the tourists was the eccentric Tom Coryat who walked to India overland for a wager laid in the Mermaid Tavern and, thanks to the tolerance extended in the East to those whom Allah has afflicted, went where he liked, talking whimsical paradoxes in any one of a dozen languages at an average expense of twopence a day. His ambition was to ride an elephant but he performed greater feats. He had the courage to climb a minaret at Agra and mimic the muezzin's cry with his own invocation: 'La Alla, illa Alla, Hazaret-Eesa, Ebn-Alla.' 'There is no God but the one God, and the Lord Jesus Son of God.' Coryat's adventures, until his death at Surat in 1617, were chronicled in letters to his friends at the Mermaid with special messages for Ben Jonson, Donne and Inigo Jones. Shakespeare cast a side-glance at him in *Measure for Measure*.

The trade of the Company was at first very profitable. One cargo of cloves bought in Amboyna for £2948 was sold in London for £36,827. Profits averaged 150 per cent on each successful voyage, that is, if the ships returned at all. But the trade was carried out in the teeth of opposition from all sides; the Company was one of those hated royal monopolies against which Parliament continually protested. Interlopers crept in, among them Sir William Courten—whom we have already noted as an interloper in the West Indies—with a special licence from King Charles I to trade with Asia, the Company's charter notwithstanding. There was strife with the Portuguese in the Indian Ocean and with the Dutch in the Spice Islands. There the Dutch prevailed, after the incident known as the 'Massacre of Amboyna'. The English dogged the heels of the Dutch traders and intrigued for a share of the trade which the Dutch claimed as their monopoly. In 1623 the Dutch merchants on the island brought a charge of conspiracy against the agents of the English Company, examined them under torture, in accordance with Roman-Dutch law, and executed the ten Englishmen of the party, with their leader, Towerson.[1] This was a shocking episode, even in a trade war where no hands were clean, and led to much bad blood. The tale of Towerson's torture and death lost nothing in the telling and was brought up again and again as propaganda against the Dutch Republic. It was a principal cause of the First Dutch War, thirty years later, and was only allowed to be forgotten when an indemnity of £88,000 was paid by the Dutch at the Peace Treaty of 1654.

Nevertheless the English were effectively excluded from the Spice Islands. They maintained a precarious foothold at Bantam in Java until 1682, but mainly depended for their oriental goods upon middlemen in Indian seaports. Hence the East India Company concentrated its efforts upon its 'factories' on the Indian mainland where it negotiated with Indian rulers for concessions.

The volume of trade, though it was sufficient to pay a good dividend on the capital of the Company, was never large. The Company imported indigo from Agra, saltpetre and sugar from Bengal, Malabar pepper, cotton yarn and piece-goods from Madras, calico from Calicut, and raw silk from Persia. The difficulty was to find a market for European goods with which to balance the trade. English broadcloth, which the Company was obliged by charter to carry abroad for sale, was welcomed by those few who could afford to buy it. Some was sold in Agra, but it was in small demand among the naked impoverished millions of Hindustan. Most of the imports were paid for in silver bullion sent out in bars or coined as Spanish pieces-of-eight, the universal currency of that age. This system of exchange encouraged the English merchants to speculate in secondary trading ventures from Indian ports to Persia and to China which, among other consequences, had the effect of introducing coffee and tea to the English market. 'That excellent and by all Physitians approved China Drink called by the Chineans Tcha, by other nations Tay alias Tee' was advertised for sale in London in 1658.

Groups of agents representing the Company were settled in the 1630's and 1640's in 'factories' at numerous points in India;

[1] Gabriel Towerson, probably the son of William Towerson, the West African trader (see page 10). Gabriel married William Hawkins' widow, the Armenian lady given him by Jahangir.

at Agra, at Masulipatam, at Balasore, and elsewhere, the principal establishment, or Presidency, being at Surat. On the eastern coast, though there was trade to be done in cotton cloth, there was no good harbour. As useful an anchorage as any was the roadstead off the village of Madras. In September 1641 the factory at Masulipatam was removed to this site where a walled settlement was built by Francis Day, on land leased from a Hindu princeling, and named the Presidency of Fort St George. That part of India was then disputed between rival rulers; in 1647 it fell into the hands of the Sultan of Golconda who confirmed the English in their possession of Fort St George, granting them the right to administer the port and district of Madras, on condition of paying him a fixed tribute from the revenues. Thus the East India Company became the feudal vassal of an Indian ruler.

Meanwhile the rivalry between England and Portugal had ended. A truce was agreed in 1634 between the Viceroy of Goa and the English merchants at Surat. A few years later Portugal regained its independence from Spain and at once began to draw towards its old alliance and friendship with the English government. Cromwell restored and Charles II confirmed the ancient treaties in such terms as to admit English trade to those seas and seaports in the East which the Portuguese had formerly claimed as their own. It was as part of a plan for combined resistance against the Dutch that the Portuguese ceded the island and castle of Bombay to England, in the marriage treaty between Charles II and Catherine of Braganza. The English fleet needed a base on the Malabar Coast from which to co-operate with the fleet from Goa. The status of the East India Company was so much raised in that decade that King Charles showed practical good sense in handing over the administration of Bombay, in 1669, to the East India Company for a nominal rent. The Presidency was removed from Surat to Bombay in 1687.

In Bengal the merchants welcomed the English buyers, though Dacca muslins and Agra saltpetre were subject to restrictions and charges imposed by the Mogul's governors. Several attempts were made to occupy some vantage point in the Ganges delta from which the trade of the Bay of Bengal could be controlled by blockade, but unsuccessfully until Job Charnock occupied the site where now is the city of Calcutta (August 1690). In 1691 he negotiated an agreement to pay the Nawab of Bengal an annual fee in return for an exemption from customs duties. In 1696 the Company acquired the right to fortify the factory, and in 1698 bought the *zemindari* or feudal authority over three neighbouring villages, which involved the collection of the land-tax and the payment of a share of it to the Nawab. On this ground was built Fort William, which became a Presidency in 1700 and grew rapidly into a city under English rule.

The three Presidencies of the Company were placed in fortified factories or depots, at Fort St George, Fort William, and Bombay Castle, the nuclei around which grew the new cities of Madras, Calcutta and Bombay. In each the primary function of the Company, to sell English wares in exchange for the wares of India, was replaced by the more exacting and more profitable task of administering the government and the revenues of a rapidly expanding sea-port town. The Indian peninsula, at the end of the seventeenth century, had been reduced to anarchy by internal wars, and offered no security for peaceful trade outside the European factories. Traders and ships gathered at Calcutta and Bombay, leaving Surat and Masulipatam and even Goa to wither away, until the customs collected by the English merchants outstripped in value the profit of their trading ventures. The three English factories were cities of refuge.

This change in the character of the Presidencies in India, though its full effect was not appreciated, was reflected by changes in the organisation of the East India Company. Like other royal foundations it had seen bad times during the Civil War, had made some recovery in Cromwell's later days, and had been re-established in its privileges at the Restoration of Charles II. A new charter, issued in 1661, was several times revised during the next few years, always with a grant of extended powers to the Company. The Directors were authorised to coin money, to appoint governors of fortresses, to enlist soldiers, to arm ships, to hold Courts of Admiralty, to enforce martial law within proper limitations, even to levy war and to negotiate treaties 'with any people that are not Christians'. In short the three Presidents in India might exercise powers wider than those of a royal governor in North America.

On the other hand the effective control of the shareholders over the Directors was limited by restricting the right of voting to those proprietors who held shares exceeding £500 in nominal

value. Actually the shares, which maintained a steady annual
profit of 20 per cent or 25 per cent, were at a high premium.
John Evelyn recorded that he bought a share for £250 in 1657
and sold it to the Royal Society in 1682 for £750. Ten years
later he would have got a higher price.

Sir Josiah Child, the goldsmith and banker, was Governor of
the Company during the years of expansion, and dictated the new
policy. 'The increase of our revenue', he wrote in 1688, 'is the
subject of our care as much as our trade. 'Tis that must make us
a nation in India.' It was his object to establish 'such a polity
of civil and military power and to create such a large revenue...
as may be the foundation of a well-grounded English dominion
in India for all time to come'. Though the reader should not be
misled into supposing that the words 'nation' and 'dominion'
meant to Child what they meant to us, there is no mistaking here
a new sense of imperial destiny.

But the Company by no means enjoyed tranquil progress. It
was a Tory stronghold and was hotly attacked by the Whigs
after the Revolution of 1688. The House of Commons carried a
motion in 1694 resolving that the Crown could not deprive
Englishmen of the right to trade with the Indies; only an Act
of Parliament could do that. Accordingly a new statutory East
India Company was chartered by Parliament, 1698, in opposition
to the old royal Company. For several years the two companies
were in competition, all the advantage going to the old Company
which had capital and credit and bases in India. It also scored a
tactical victory by buying up a block of shares in the new
Company, thus acquiring a controlling interest. The Government, hard put to it for money with which to finance Marlborough's Wars, favoured whichever of the two would make the
larger investment in war loan. Eventually, after long negotiation, the companies amalgamated, in 1709, in a form which lasted
for about sixty years.

The impact of India upon English public opinion took the
form of a growing rumour about the great fortunes which were
to be made in the East. Among the first of the wealthy upstarts
known as 'nabobs', was Governor Thomas Pitt, the grandfather
of the Great Commoner, and the owner of the largest diamond in
the world. Many strange tales were told of its origin in the
Golconda mines. As far as Governor Pitt was concerned, the

facts are plain. With a set purpose of investing his fortune in jewels he bought the diamond in the open market for 48,000 *pagodas* (say £16,000), smuggled it home in 1701, and sold it some years later to the Regent of France for 2,000,000 francs (say £125,000). With the proceeds of this shrewd deal he acquired possession of the pocket-borough of Old Sarum, a wise provision for his family.

4. DUPLEIX AND CLIVE

WHEN Aurangzeb died at a great age, in 1707, the Mogul Empire began to disintegrate. The most powerful of the Nawabs, Nizam-al-mulk, Viceroy of the Deccan, converted much of his fief into the independent state of Hyderabad, with difficulty maintaining his position against the Marathas who terrorised all central India. In the North the Sikhs made, lost and made again a kingdom about Lahore. Meanwhile at Delhi a series of puppets preserved the state and title of Mogul Emperors. Even so they existed only on sufferance after the Persian invasion of 1739. A great army led by Nadir Shah came through the Khyber Pass, scattered the worthless soldiers of the Mogul, annexed all provinces west of the Indus, plundered Delhi of £100,000,000 and withdrew contemptuously with the state jewels, the Peacock Throne and the Koh-i-noor. After Nadir Shah's death his eastern conquests were seized by a Durani chief who formed them into the kingdom of Afghanistan, whence four times in the next twenty years his men raided India as far eastward as Delhi. The sole power that might have restored some stable rule by resisting them was that of the Marathas; but in 1761 the Afghans inflicted on the Marathas a crushing defeat which they followed with the massacre of 200,000 men at Panipat, so often the field of India's decisive battles. All hopes that the Marathas might form a predominantly Hindu empire ended at Panipat. India was partitioned between Moslems and Hindus, although for almost another hundred years the lineal descendant of Timur, Babur, Akbar and Aurangzeb maintained a shadowy precedence over the other princes of the Empire. During these years the new seaport towns garrisoned by the merchants of the various trading companies from Europe enjoyed peace and attracted commerce.

Inevitably the restless rivalry of French and English induced them to take a hand in the political struggle.

As in Canada, so in India the first enterprises of the French had been made under Henri IV, but with little success until, fifty years later, Colbert produced his comprehensive schemes for building up naval and commercial power. The French factory at Pondicherry not far from Madras was founded in 1673, and that at Chandernagore not far from Calcutta in 1690. During the wars of King William's and Queen Anne's reigns, hostilities did not break out between English and French in India, though there was fighting between the French and Dutch; but the succeeding age, when all India was lapsing into anarchy and the Mogul Emperor was unable to offer any pretence of protection, was the age of French colonial expansion. The same years which saw the penetration of Louisiana from New Orleans to Fort Duquesne saw the appearance of French political designs throughout India. A brilliant series of governors, intermittently supported by French naval power, plunged into the chaos of Indian politics with the clear intention of sharing in the partition of the Mogul Empire. Much earlier the prescience of Sir J. Child had proposed a like policy to the English Company, but there was neither naval nor diplomatic support for it. The Directors in Leadenhall Street were anxious for their dividends and the government in Whitehall was in no mood for adventure.

The French appreciated that all their efforts depended on sea-power and to that end occupied the two islands of Mauritius, (1690) and Réunion (1720) then known as Isle de France and Isle de Bourbon. During the short period that Admiral La Bour-donnais was Governor of Mauritius it seemed likely that the French might become the rulers of India.

On land, French political influence dates from about 1735 when the Governor of Pondicherry began to intervene in party strife in the Deccan. In 1740 when the Marathas invaded the Carnatic, a province including both British Madras and French Pondicherry, the ruling prince fled for protection to the French Governor, who won fame throughout India by defying the Marathas. The titular Emperor at Delhi rewarded the Frenchman by raising him to the rank of Nawab which placed him far above the English merchants of Madras in Indian estimation. That was the year when Frederick the Great provoked world-wide war by invading

Silesia. In 1742 Dupleix succeeded as Governor of Pondi-cherry (ranking also as Nawab). It was his studied policy to make French influence supreme by using the forms of government to which Indians were accustomed. He lived magnificently, exploit-ing his imperial rank with more than oriental splendour. He was the titular equal of the Nawab of the Carnatic and even of the greater Nizam, the Viceroy of the Deccan; and behaved as his subjects expected him to do. His army of 7000 native infantry and artillery, trained by European methods, was more than a match for the irregular cavalry which composed the Indian forces. In four years he made himself master of southern India and might have been its legitimate ruler, but for the fortunes of war in Europe.

Meanwhile La Bourdonnais from his base at Mauritius operated off the Coromandel Coast, forcing the surrender of Madras in 1746. The English merchants appealed to their protector, the Nawab of the Carnatic, but in vain, since Dupleix utterly defeated him by land. This was the campaign which established, for 160 years, the superiority of European over Asiatic armies. The French victories, however, were barren since news arrived from Europe, early in 1749, that the Peace of Aix-la-Chapelle had been signed. The French government had renounced its conquests in Asia, restoring Madras to the English in exchange for Louisburg which the English had conquered in Canada.

At that time rival heirs were disputing the succession to both the Deccan and the Carnatic. Dupleix supported a candidate for each, with diplomacy and with force; and seemed likely to restore his control of southern India by establishing his men in these two governments. Again the shadowy authority of the Mogul was invoked to legitimise the power of the Frenchman.

A new English governor, Saunders, who had taken over the Madras Presidency resolved to resist French influence in the Carnatic by suporting the rival prince. In the desultory campaign which broke out, the English sepoys appeared as auxiliaries on the one part and the French on the other. Among the European volunteers was young Robert Clive whose fiery spirit had revolted both against the humiliating position of the English and against his own fate. He had been sent out as a 'writer' to Fort St George, and found himself possessed of other talents which might be made more profitable in India. His seizure and defence of Arcot (September–October 1751) turned the fortune of this

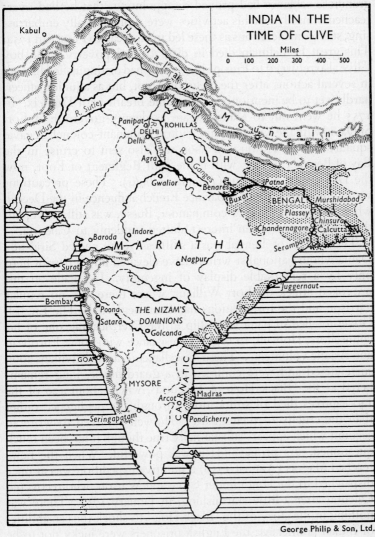

INDIA IN THE
TIME OF CLIVE

Miles
0   100   200   300   400   500

Kabul

Himalaya

R. Sutlej

R. Indus

Panipat
DELHI
Delhi
Jumna
ROHILLAS
Agra
O U D H
Ganges
Gwalior
Benares
Patna
Buxar
BENGAL
Murshidabad
Plassey
Chandernagore
Chinsura
Serampore
Calcutta

Baroda
Indore
M A R A T H A S
Surat
Nagpur
Juggernaut

Bombay
Poona
Satara
THE NIZAM'S
DOMINIONS
Golconda
C I R C A R S

GOA
MYSORE
Arcot
Madras
Seringapatam
C A R N A T I C
Pondicherry

George Philip & Son, Ltd.

Map 3

petty war. The boy was one of those born leaders who could bend stubborn Englishmen to his will, and whom soldiers of a more primitive race worshipped as a warlike *avatar*. The spell of Dupleix's successes was broken. A general sense that Dupleix's grandiose schemes had proved disappointing, that he had over-reached himself, that his activities were diplomatically embarrassing, such considerations as these led to his recall to France in 1754. This great Frenchman died in disgrace and poverty. The boy Clive also returned to Europe in 1753; he had distinguished himself in several actions after the Siege of Arcot, but as a junior officer, hardly yet to be mentioned in the same breath with Dupleix. In 1755 he went out to Madras again as deputy-governor of Fort St David with the King's commission as lieutenant-colonel. A naval squadron under Admiral Watson was also sent to cruise in the Bay of Bengal carrying with it the 39th Regiment of Foot, now the Dorsetshire regiment (*Primus in Indis*). These precautions were intended to counter-balance French influence in the Deccan where Dupleix's military commander, Bussy, was still active, but the centre of European interest shifted suddenly to Calcutta.

The Nawab of Bengal was a shiftless youth named Siraj-ud-Daula whom nationalist writers have elevated into a patriot hero only by a remarkable display of ingenuity. He made an un-provoked attack on Fort William, where there was no regular garrison and the fortifications had been neglected. The English Governor fled in panic to a ship in the river, leaving one of his counsellors, Holwell, to organise resistance with some European and Asiatic volunteers. These miscellaneous armed civilians soon surrendered and were confined in a guard-house, long remembered as the 'Black Hole of Calcutta', where about 120 of the 140 captives died of suffocation, through the negligence rather than the cruelty of their guards. Holwell survived to write an account which appears substantially true though it has been much questioned. As propaganda it was powerful. When the news reached Madras (August 1756) a punitive expedition was at once dispatched to the Hugli under Clive and Watson, who recovered Calcutta after a little skirmishing, in January 1757. There was nothing in the story of the 'Black Hole' to shock the sensibilities of Indian politicians; the English prisoners were lucky not to be robbed, tortured, and impaled on stakes, the usual fate of de-feated armies in the wars of the Moguls. An insistence upon adherence to treaties and to the conventions of civilised warfare was new in India and marked the rising power and prestige of the European nations. Clive and Watson at first demanded no more than a firm undertaking from Siraj-ud-Daula that he would restore the plunder of Calcutta and guarantee the immunity of Fort William, but the policies of the place and age were not conducted so straightforwardly.

There followed six months of intrigue and chicanery during which Siraj-ud-Daula twisted and turned in endeavours to avoid making restitution to the English Company. His hopes lay in stimulating the French at Chandernagore to assist him by neutralising the English at Calcutta; his fears that, while he embroiled himself with these dangerous foes in the Ganges delta, the Afghan armies would march down from the headwaters of the Ganges to take him in the rear. The wretched Nawab, who had proved as untrustworthy to his own subjects as to his English neighbours, was surrounded by traitors. There was not a courtier in his palace at Murshidabad, nor a magnate in Bengal, who was not willing to conspire against him, for a price. Hindu bankers and bureaucrats who had no love for their Moslem oppressor were the leaders in the plot. History rarely records such another web of corruption and treachery, and it must be admitted that the English lowered themselves almost to the moral level of the other conspirators. The Council at Calcutta formed the design of replacing the Nawab by his general Mir Jafar, employing as go-between a certain Omichund, who then attempted to blackmail them. Clive and his friends outwitted Omichund by showing him a falsified copy of the agreement, to which they had forged the signature of Admiral Watson. Through these intrigues Clive moved with ruthless insight and decision. The French problem was solved by the seizure of Chandernagore after an attack by sea and land. The overthrow of Siraj-ud-Daula was begun on the day after the signing of the false agreement. On 23 June 1757, Clive won the Battle of Plassey with 800 Europeans and 2000 sepoys against Siraj-ud-Daula's 50,000 men. Mir Jafar stood neutral with his contingent, uncertain whether his treachery was to bring him the prize; and came in to Clive's camp after the victory in terror of being contemptuously abandoned. He was, however, installed as Nawab of Bengal, after Siraj-ud-Daula had been put to death according to the custom of the country. Clive, who might have taken the loot of Murshidabad and, like Dupleix, might have made himself Nawab into the bargain, was contented with a gratuity of £200,000, and 'stood astonished at his own moderation'.

Mir Jafar found no peace after slaying his master. During his short uneasy reign he began at once to work up an alliance with the Dutch Company at Chinsura as a counterpoise against the English. The Dutch, failing to read the signs of the times, seized some English ships in the Hugli and prepared an attack on one of the lesser English factories (1759). Clive fell upon them and routed their Malayan sepoys, compelling Chinsura to capitulate. Thereafter the Dutch were not permitted to fortify or garrison their factory and remained in Bengal only on English sufferance. Clive returned to England a second time in 1760, in the middle of the Seven Years War.

After the recall of Dupleix there had been uneasy peace between the European settlements in the south. No major act of war took place until, in 1758, Lally, a soldier of Irish extraction, arrived at Pondicherry as French Governor, Commander-in-chief, and Director of the French East India Company. Again it seemed that an audacious compound of diplomacy and military force would make the French supreme. Lally, though endowed with brilliant gifts, was hasty and overbearing and contemptuous of native customs; he failed to reproduce Dupleix's masterly knowledge and use of Indian political methods. But far more significant was the flimsy foundation of his power. The French depended upon diplomatic skill and military prowess while the British now controlled the commerce and shipping of the richest Indian provinces. The basin of the Ganges and the estuary of the Hugli provided men, money, supplies and a base for sea-power, the essentials in which Lally was always deficient. Southern India was too poor and Mauritius too far away to supply his campaigns by land and sea. The naval operations of the war are of slight interest. Though the British fleet won no decisive victory it maintained a sufficient degree of command over the Bay of Bengal. A grandiose attempt by Lally to mount a combined attack by land and sea against Madras broke down when his fleet was obliged to fall back upon Mauritius, after an action with the British squadron from Calcutta. In 1760 Sir Eyre Coote, with some regular regiments, decisively defeated Lally's dwindling forces at Wandiwash, and proceeded to reduce the French factories in the Carnatic, one by one. The land campaigns were not so arduous as in later days. Officers were carried in palanquins at the head of their regiments, which were followed by long trains of camp-followers. At the Treaty of Paris in 1763, the

British restored the French factories, but on condition that they should be unfortified trading posts, as they remained thereafter. The French King undertook not to maintain troops in India, thus ending the great design formed by Dupleix. The suspicion and, if it is rightly so called, the ingratitude which pursued Clive and Warren Hastings to their graves was paralleled in the story of their French rivals. Dupleix, La Bourdonnais, and Lally all died in disgrace, but their influence did not perish in India. For many years French diplomacy was directed towards stirring up resistance against the English, by means of agents and soldiers of fortune at the courts of Indian princes.

While Coote was expelling the French sepoys from the Carnatic, the Council of the Presidency of Bengal were enjoying the privileges of an Indian ruling-class. They were men who had gone to India to make their fortunes and for no other purpose; they found themselves the colleagues of Indian financiers such as Omichund and Nuncomar to whom it had never occurred that government existed for any purpose, but to enrich the governors. It had long been the custom of servants of the Company to augment their meagre salaries by private trade on their own account. Since they enjoyed exemption from all tariffs and restrictions, wealth from private trade was easily got. Latterly they had taken to politics which was still more lucrative since nothing was done in India except for a consideration. Gratuities measured by *lakhs* of rupees, that is amounts of about £10,000, were commonly given to conclude a deal. Twenty *lakhs* had been Clive's reward for making Mir Jafar Nawab. It was afterwards enlarged from Mir Jafar's bounty by a grant to Clive of the quit-rent paid by the Company for the site of Calcutta. Clive thus became ground landlord of Fort William with an estate of about £30,000 a year.

The profitable trade of king-making offered more opportunities when Clive had gone home. Mir Jafar refused to be a puppet of the Company. He was almost as bad a ruler as Siraj-ud-Daula, had played the Company false with the Dutch, and like other traitors had no true friends. He in turn was dethroned in 1760 in favour of Mir Kasim, in spite of the protest of a junior member of Council, Warren Hastings: 'That he is a usurper is certain, and one of our making.' . . . 'We are bound if not in justice, in honour and policy to support him through these troubles. . . .'

The following year, 1761, saw the battle of Panipat where the Maratha power was crushed by the Afghans. India slipped further down towards chaos; there was now no prospect of a Hindu political revival. There was, however, still a Mogul Emperor, Shah Alam II, who was disposed to place himself under protection of the English since the Marathas had failed him. The Company at Calcutta toyed with the idea of placing their own man upon the throne of Delhi but the situation got out of their control. The new Nawab of Bengal, Mir Kasim, resisted their encroachments, limited their trading privileges and allied himself against them with his neighbour, Shuja Daula, the Nawab of Oudh (who as titular Vizier of the Mogul Empire was often called the Nawab Vizier). In 1763 the quarrel came to open war which Mir Kasim conducted on the usual principles. His multitudinous armies fled from every battle and he consoled himself by employing an Alsatian mercenary to kill about 200 English civilians who fell into his hands, at Patna. In October 1764 Major Munro defeated the forces of the two Nawabs at Buxar. Mir Kasim was overthrown and the more serviceable Mir Jafar was restored to his place in Bengal. Relations, with Oudh and with the Emperor were still under negotiation when, in May 1765, Clive returned to India for the third time. While in England, in spite of violent criticism, he had used his wealth to buy sufficient East India shares to control the Court of Directors and had thus been chosen as Governor of Bengal. His third visit to India was for a new object: he was now no longer a fortune-hunter but a reformer.

His first task was to negotiate a settlement between the Mogul and his two vassals, the Nawabs of Oudh and Bengal. Resolving that the Company, which hitherto had made and unmade governments in Bengal without show of legality, should become openly responsible he obtained from the Mogul the cession of the *diwani* of Bengal, that is the management and collection of the revenue. The servants of the Company at Fort William thus ceased to be merchants and became revenue officials with the title of Collectors. Under the feudal system current in the Mogul Empire, rights of jurisdiction naturally grew out of landholding, so that the Collector of a district was also a magistrate. The English Governor now acted constitutionally in Bengal as a business agent for the Nawab to whom he paid a regular civil list from the revenue. The remainder of the *diwani*, amounting to about £4,000,000 a year had to provide tribute to the Mogul, the normal expenses of government, and a dividend for the shareholders in London. A similar cession of the *diwani* to the Company was made at the same time for some districts in the Carnatic known as the Northern Circars.

Having secured his position in Bengal Clive was not disposed to advance further up the country. He undertook to establish the Nawab of Oudh in his dominions and to support him with the Company's troops, if the Nawab would foot the bill. The Mogul, too, was gratified by the restoration of a part of the province to his direct rule. Oudh was to be a strong protected barrier between Bengal and the unsettled regions of Upper India.

Bengal now entered upon 170 years of peace and constitutional government; but corruption, when it is the custom of the country and when men with very small stipends are habitually offered very large bribes, is not easily put down. Clive had made his own fortune and why should not his juniors follow his example? He was inexorable; private trade and the receipt of gratuities by the Company's servants were to end. Recalcitrants were replaced by men from Madras whom Clive could trust, while newcomers from Europe were obliged to sign a covenant renouncing these corrupt practices. More difficult was the management of the Bengal Army, whose officers mutinied when Clive reduced their allowances. He cashiered and replaced the mutineers. As an inducement to serve under these altered conditions he assigned that part of the revenue derived from the monopoly in salt, appropriately, for increasing the salaries of the Company's officers. Remuneration was at a high rate, though a mere fraction of the ill-gotten gains of Hindu or English officials in earlier times. The Governor received about £25,000 a year, and half-a-dozen other officials sums between £5000 and £10,000.

When the Nawab Mir Jafar died, in 1765, he left the Governor a legacy of £60,000. Clive devoted the whole of it to a benevolent foundation, known as Lord Clive's Fund, for assisting retired servants of the Company. He also paid generous allowances from his private fortune to deserving friends, especially to his first patron at Madras, Colonel Stringer Lawrence. Clive finally retired to England in 1767, to live in gloomy magnificence as the richest and most deeply suspect of all 'nabobs'.

A great famine which afflicted Bengal in 1770, the first of many such calamities to throw responsibility for relief upon a British-Indian government, drew the attention of Government at home to the incongruous position of the Company and led to Lord North's Regulating Act for the better government of Bengal. When Clive was attacked, he defended himself in his place in Parliament with reckless eloquence, hurling reproaches at his critics and at the Court of Directors. After bitter debates the House of Commons agreed to two resolutions: first, that provinces acquired in war by the forces of the Crown should belong to the Crown alone, and, secondly, that Clive had misused his powers as Commander-in-chief to obtain large sums of money from Mir Jafar. There they paused and, instead of proceeding to deprive the East India Company of its lands and Clive of his money, they resolved with illogical magnanimity 'that Lord Clive had rendered great and meritorious services to his country'. There was a chance that he might render still greater services. The year of the Regulating Act was also the year of the 'Boston Tea-Party' and it was Lord North's intention to send Clive to America to pacify the rebellious colonies, but this was not to be. Clive had suffered throughout his life from fits of depression; he died in 1774, by his own hand—as it is believed—at the early age of forty-nine.

Clive himself had formerly proposed to Chatham that the Crown should take over the government of Bengal; it was indeed absurd that a trading company should rule a province three times more populous than Great Britain, after conquering it with the help of the King's soldiers and the King's ships. But in eighteenth-century eyes nothing was more sacred than the rights of property and no act of state more culpable than confiscation. To rob the East India Company of its possessions was as unjust in the eyes of the Whigs as to tax the Americans without their own consent, a policy which Parliament had just renounced. It was first proposed that the Company should pay a tribute to the Crown, but the debates on Clive's administration led to a demand for more drastic measures. Although there had been a boom in East India stock the truth emerged, to the discomfiture of Burke and Fox who had been speculating in the shares, that the Company was insolvent and required financial backing from the Crown. Two acts were passed: one authorising a Treasury loan

of £1,400,000 to the Company; the other, the Regulating Act,
reorganising the constitution of the Court of Directors and providing for the appointment of a royal Governor-General for
Bengal with a right of supervision over the Presidencies of
Madras and Bombay. There was to be a Council of State of four
members and a Supreme Court of Justice. For the post of
Governor-General Lord North selected Warren Hastings, who
was already Governor of Fort William, as 'a person to whom
nobody would object'.

5. WARREN HASTINGS

CLIVE and Warren Hastings were both sons of impoverished
Tory gentry from the Welsh Marches and both were packed off
to India as writers to make their fortunes. There the resemblance
ends. Clive, as a boy, was a rude and reckless Tony Lumpkin;
as a man, he was harsh, imperious, uncultivated. He never
mastered any Asiatic language. So unstable and unhappy was his
nature that his faculties were fully extended only when he had
battles to fight and obstacles to overcome.[1] Warren Hastings
was an elegant classical scholar from Westminster School. In
the midst of his wars and political struggles he found time to
study the ancient Sanskrit poems, and to read and write in courtly
Persian. He corresponded with Dr Johnson, who recommended Sir William Jones to him, patronised Hindu learning,
and founded a Moslem College in Calcutta. He was a handsome
man though slight in stature, with engaging manners in society.
His long, happy, married life had begun with a celebrated love
match. But the most striking feature of his character was unshakable resolution, *mens aequa in arduis*. He was icy cool; and
it is hard to acquit him of Macaulay's judgment: 'His principles
were somewhat lax. His heart was somewhat hard.'

At the time of the passing of the Regulating Act in London,
Hastings in India was deeply engaged in the affair of the Rohilla
War. Clive had bequeathed to his successors an engagement by
which the Nawab of Oudh could claim military assistance from

[1] Like T. E. Lawrence, of whom Mr Churchill wrote: 'He was one of those
beings whose pace of life was faster and more intense than the ordinary. Just as
an aeroplane only flies by its speed and pressure against the air, so he flew best
and easiest in the hurricane. He was not in complete harmony with the normal.'

the Bengal Army. The Company's troops had been raised as mercenaries and, like other mercenaries, could be let out on hire as the Madras Army had been employed during the wars of the Carnatic. In 1773, therefore, Hastings agreed, for a price, to allow his army to be used by the Nawab of Oudh to drive out a predatory tribe, the Rohillas from a fertile valley which they had seized in the north of the province. The *casus belli* was adequate and the Company's participation was in fulfilment of a treaty, but the hiring-out of British mercenaries to an Asiatic ruler— and that was what the transaction looked like—seemed hardly reputable. It has never been repeated.

Three new members of Council, appointed under the Regulating Act, arrived in India in 1774, when Hastings was just concluding the Rohilla War; they made it clear within a few days of their arrival that they had come to thwart and, if possible, to supplant him. The ablest among them, Sir Philip Francis, was almost certainly the author of the bitter political diatribes known as the *Letters of Junius*. So base was the malignity and the envy shown by Francis towards Hastings that he defeated his own end. He excited the pity of posterity for his victim who, whatever else he may have been, was a most ill-used man. Cruel indeed was the fate of Hastings against whom reckless charges of oppression were framed by the poisoned pen of 'Junius', proclaimed in Westminster Hall with all the eloquence at the command of Edmund Burke, and recorded for the succeeding age by the ponderous philippic of Macaulay. Hastings never flinched From 1774 until 1776, he was in a minority in his own Council with no overriding power. His achievements in administration and diplomacy were made in the teeth of open avowed opposition from the men with whom he had to do his daily work. The death of one of them, in 1776, eased him by giving him a majority in Council of a single vote. In 1780, he freed himself from criticism by challenging Francis to a duel and severely wounding him. Thereafter he was master and had only to expect the vengeance that his defeated rivals were plotting for the day of his return to England.

The humiliation of the Governor by his own Council had produced a crop of false witnesses eager to ingratiate themselves with the rising power, by slandering that which seemed near its setting. The vilest of them was a certain Nandu Kumar, known to the English as Nuncomar, who supplied Francis with a series of scandalous charges against the Governor. It proved unnecessary for Hastings to refute these charges, since an action for forgery, brought by a Bengali merchant, was already pending against Nuncomar. A bench of English judges, newly appointed under the Regulating Act, took it upon themselves to assert the purity of English justice by making an example of Nuncomar, found him guilty and sentenced him to be hanged. Hastings, not the man to spare an enemy in such a situation, let the law take its course. Francis, on his part, recognising that Nuncomar dead was a far more potent weapon against the Governor than Nuncomar alive, ignored the appeals of his condemned associate for help, and made no move for a respite. It would be more convenient to assert that the Governor and the Chief Justice had conspired to suppress a witness against themselves by a judicial murder. The Chief Justice, Sir Elijah Impey, was impeached on this charge when he returned to England and was acquitted after completely justifying his action, but slander is not easily obliterated and was again used by Macaulay long after Impey's death to besmirch his memory.

The incident has more than political significance. It is an example of the danger of imposing a Western code of laws upon an Eastern people. The judges intended to vindicate honest principles by punishing a liar. The Bengali officials, who regarded forgery and perjury as the merest peccadilloes, drew from the occurrence the lesson that it was highly dangerous to thwart the Governor-General, placing upon the prosecution of Nuncomar a construction that Francis was quick to exploit. The true fault, as Macaulay pointed out, lay with the House of Commons which passed the Regulating Act in a form so carelessly drafted that the judges in Bengal could not know what classes of persons came into their jurisdiction nor what code they were to administer. Nuncomar's case was the first of many legal muddles. All the delays, the picturesque survivals, the quaint anomalies of the English common law, together with its ferocious code of pains and penalties were now entailed upon the Bengali baboos, whose subtle minds were not slow to discover in the system a thousand ways of eluding judgment.

The enduring work of Warren Hastings was to repair the ravages of the famine and to establish a just and economical government in Bengal. Not content with the collection of the revenue, he took over complete control of the *diwani*, removing the administrative capital from Murshidabad to Calcutta, and appointing Englishmen as collectors throughout the province. In repeated journeys he satisfied himself as to the rights of the actual tillers of the soil, preventing unauthorised exactions. He continued to fight against corruption in the government service and against clandestine attempts by the Company's agents to trade on their own account. He simplified customs duties and removed internal *octrois*. He established a civil police. He strove to convert Bengal into a peaceful prosperous province with honest finances and equal laws, and to root out the arbitrary oppression of the peasants, which had long been the bane of India. But he would have done this better if he had not himself been incurably careless about money matters. Some of his own household were allowed to be laxer than himself.

Though he made and kept Bengal an oasis in a waste of confusion, Hastings could not keep the peace without diplomatic adventures and even preventive wars. As administrator of Bengal, the Company's government was tributary to the Great Mogul. Hastings escaped from this ignominious state and saved a large sum annually, by repudiating the tribute when the Mogul again fell into the power of the Marathas. The principle of his foreign policy was 'to extend the influence of the British nation to every part of India not too remote from their possessions without enlarging the circle of their defence or involving them in hazardous or indefinite engagements; and to accept of the allegiance of such of our neighbours as shall sue to be enlisted among the friends and allies of the King of Great Britain'.

Though Hastings surmounted all obstacles in the relations between Bengal and its neighbouring provinces he found it difficult to impose his will upon the junior Presidencies of Bombay and Madras. They involved themselves in wars of which he disapproved and called on him to save them from the consequences of their own folly. However harassed by his disloyal Council, however short of troops and funds, he found means of relieving them.

Bombay, unlike the other Presidencies, was a royal colony, on an island. Nevertheless, the Council had begun to dabble in mainland politics, hoping, by playing off one Maratha prince against another, to get possession of some Portuguese settlements which the Marathas had overrun. The Bombay Army soon found itself engaged in a war which was sadly mismanaged. Though Hastings thought this war 'impolitic, dangerous, unauthorised and unjust', he recognised that he must prevent a triumph of the Marathas over the Company. He sent two columns from Bengal, in 1780, to march across India, one to take charge of the campaign near Bombay, the other to strike at Gwalior, the capital of Scindia who led the Maratha armies. The escalade of the Rock of Gwalior (August 1780), hitherto thought impregnable, relieved the pressure on Bombay, enabling Hastings to look southward where much greater dangers threatened. There was every prospect that the English would find themselves at war with the Nizam and the Sultan of Mysore as well as with the Marathas, and that the whole combination of enemies would be supported by a French fleet. It was a triumph to secure the north by bringing Scindia to terms in October 1781, and to sign a definitive treaty with him at Salbai in 1782.

The trouble in the south began with the tangled finances of the Nawab of the Carnatic (known to the English as the 'Nabob of Arcot'). He was publicly indebted to the Company and privately indebted to some of the Company's servants and to other European adventurers. Like other debtors he found himself in a position to sway the policy of his creditors. Supremacy just then in the Deccan was disputed between the Nizam and a Moslem soldier of fortune named Hyder Ali who had made himself Sultan of Mysore. Though the English at Madras made a very good thing out of advancing money to the Nawab, they made a very sorry show of protecting him against the rival threats of the Nizam and Hyder Ali. A break came over the claim of the Company to the *diwani* of the Northern Circars, which Hyder coveted.

In July 1780, while Colonel Popham on the other side of India was marching on Gwalior, Hyder Ali invaded the Carnatic, plundering and ravishing the whole province to the walls of Fort St George. Here also the Council, which had blundered into war in spite of the Governor-General, appealed to him for help. Here again Hastings promptly sent men and money, with his best officer Sir Eyre Coote, now old and testy. No decisive victory was won, but Coote at least checked Hyder Ali's progress and inspired him with respect for British troops, at the battles of Porto Novo and Pollilore, in 1781.

The resources of the Company were strained to the utmost by the wars of the Bombay and Madras armies, but worse was to come. Hyder Ali had drawn supplies from the French in Mauritius and was to receive far greater assistance. Early in 1782, a well-found French fleet, more powerful than the British squadron and commanded by de Suffren, a first-rate admiral, appeared in Indian waters. Four stubborn actions were fought that year between de Suffren and the British Admiral Hughes, an obstinate fighter with no great talent. De Suffren occupied the Dutch harbour of Trincomali in Ceylon, cruised off the coast, and put a French army ashore in the Carnatic. Hughes achieved no more than keeping his fleet in being. In 1783, by an action off Cuddalore, de Suffren compelled Hughes to put back to his base to refit abandoning the Madras Army (like Cornwallis at Yorktown a few months earlier) ashore between a hostile army and a hostile fleet. But the luck turned when news arrived in June that preliminary articles of peace had been signed at Versailles. The French again withdrew their armies from India thus forfeiting all chance of exploiting in Asia the prestige their forces had won in America. The Treaty of Salbai had placed the Bombay Presidency in a state of predominance over the Marathas, but in the Madras Presidency there was no such ascendency. There the French had merely withdrawn leaving the Sultan of Mysore supreme. During the war Hyder Ali died leaving his throne to his son, Tipu, an equally ferocious soldier, but a far less able ruler than his father. He made peace with the Company by the Treaty of Mangalore, 1784, after humiliating the envoys who came to discuss terms and, in general, behaving as a conqueror. There was, however, peace throughout India in the last year of Warren Hastings' rule.

The turning-point had been the hot season of 1781, when Scindia was brought to terms with the Bombay Presidency and when Coote checked the progress of Hyder Ali; that too was the crisis of the world war. Ten thousand miles away Cornwallis was turning to bay in the peninsula of Yorktown; Minorca was lost; Gibraltar was closely invested by land and sea. There had been little that Hastings could count on, beyond his own resources.

The Mysore and Maratha Wars cost money which Hastings had no means of supplying except from the treasury of Bengal. So far from helping him to conclude these wars which had been forced on him, the Directors in Leadenhall Street pressed him to send money for dividends and the House of Commons merely passed a vote of censure on his conduct. Hastings was obliged to get money where he could in the manner of other oriental rulers. Like a European king in the Middle Ages he demanded special war-contributions from his richer vassals and did not hesitate to crush his enemies by crippling demands. Two special instances were remembered against him, those of Chait Singh and the Begums of Oudh. In each case money was due and a special contribution not unreasonable. Chait Singh was a nobleman of Benares who had conspired against Hastings in the past and was not to be spared. When his contribution was not forthcoming it was doubled, and further delay led to the imposition of a huge fine. When Chait Singh protested Hastings went with a small escort to arrest him, but was forced to flee from a rising of the townsmen of Benares. He returned to confiscate Chait Singh's fief and property. The Begums were princesses of Oudh, who owed money to the Nawab, who owed it to the Company. Hastings brought relentless pressure on the Nawab to extract the money from these very retentive old ladies by any means. It was at last forthcoming. In each instance the victim had offered Hastings a large personal bribe; in each case he had accepted it, turned the money over to the treasury, and renewed his demand. Such extortion, by English standards, was disgraceful, though the common form of India during the decline of the Mogul Empire.

Meanwhile a tide of criticism had been rising against Hastings in England. After the Treaty of Versailles the state of India was the vortex of party strife in which the Coalition government of Fox and North was swept away. The Younger Pitt, on coming into office, proceeded with the India Bill of 1784, which will be further considered in the next chapter. It led to the retirement of Hastings who arrived in England in June 1785, expecting to be a centre of controversy and quite undaunted. He was an active man of fifty-three who might have hoped for office and honour but, after spending almost all of his adult life as an autocrat in India, he was unacquainted with the ways of English politics.

The Whig leaders slowly mustered their forces. Two years passed before the Commons resolved to impeach Hastings, and another nine months before Parliamentary time could be found for this obsolescent ritual. Such were the delays of procedure and the difficulties of collecting evidence from the other side of the world that the trial dragged on over 148 days in seven sessions of Parliament. Burke and Sheridan, the principal managers for the Commons, opened their case in 1788 with fervid eloquence based upon the model of Cicero's denunciation of Verres, but the proceedings dragged. Charge after charge, the cases of Nuncomar and the Rohilla War, were dropped, as the accusations proved to be mere verbiage. All the more vehemently they pressed the accusations of extortion from Chait Singh and the Begums, but no more could be proved than that, with war threatening on every hand, he had acted with injudicious harshness. At last, in 1795, the Lords who had heard the case with scrupulous attention to law and equity, acquitted Hastings on every charge.

By that time the wars of India had been overshadowed by the nearer catastrophe of the French Revolution. The public had lost interest in Hastings; the membership of the House of Commons had been quite reconstituted by a general election. The spectacle of a great Englishman, baited and abused in public over a period of seven years and ruined by the cost of his defence, had provoked a reaction in his favour, which had been anticipated in the cool judgment of Adam Smith: 'The servants of the East India Company acted as their situation naturally directed, and they who have clamoured the loudest against them would, probably, not have acted better themselves. In war and negotiation, the councils of Madras and Calcutta have upon several occasions conducted themselves with a resolution and decisive wisdom which would have done honour to the Senate of Rome.'

Certainly Hastings had never lacked Roman virtue and could forgo ambition with the piety of Cincinnatus. His lifelong ambition had been to restore the estate and name of his family. What was left of his modest fortune assisted by a pension from the Directors of the Company enabled him to buy and to maintain the lands held by his ancestors since a time before the Norman Conquest. For more than twenty years of retirement he lived a plain country life, content to be Warren Hastings of Daylesford, in the County of Worcestershire, Esquire.

6. CONSOLIDATION OF BRITISH INDIA,
1783–1813

Since the Regulating Act had been passed in 1773, a dominion constituted on just principles in America and ruled by just laws had been lost, owing to the dullness and vacillation of its rulers. During the same years a British dominion had been formed in India by methods of doubtful morality, but by men of great vigour and boldness. British India never lacked mighty men of valour. If Hastings had been supported by legitimate sovereign powers what might he not have achieved? But the Regulating Act was a failure: it did not succeed in subordinating the Directors of the Company to Parliament, nor the Governor-General to the Directors, nor the Councils of Madras and Bombay to the Governor-General, nor even in making the Governor-General master in his own Council-chamber. The enormities ascribed to Hastings were largely the fault of the framers of the Act who had burdened him with an impossible task.

Though all agreed that the Crown must take over the supreme government of Bengal, the method was the occasion of a party struggle. When the Coalition government was in office in 1783, Fox brought in a bill for replacing the Court of Directors of the East India Company by a Parliamentary committee, a measure which savoured of confiscation and alarmed the champions of property. King George, who hated him, found means to make a majority against Fox by rallying his own supporters in the House of Lords, and dismissed the Coalition. William Pitt, the King's chosen Prime Minister, produced his India Bill (1784) for setting up an unpaid Board of Control consisting of six cabinet ministers and privy councillors who would have no motive for directing Indian affairs on narrow party lines. A royal governor-general was to be appointed with authority, in case of necessity, to override his council, the commander-in-chief, or the Governors of Bombay and Madras. The Directors were left in possession of all remaining patronage. Under this dual control of the Crown and the Company, British India was administered for seventy years.

The essence of the system was the personal authority of the Governor-General who became not only the greatest subject of the Crown but, for his term of office, the most powerful of the world's rulers. In the days before it was possible for Whitehall to interfere by telegraph, the Governor-General had unrestrained executive power over a population which increased to more than one hundred millions. He was supreme lord of war and peace. It was Pitt's intention that the office should always be held by some great nobleman, exalted by rank and wealth over any temptation to corrupt practices, a man actuated only by honourable motives. Surely, if ever aristocracy is justified it is in this series of great rulers, the most beneficent, the most disinterested dynasty the world has known. No other absolute monarchs have maintained for so long a period such firmness with such moderation, nor has the reputation of the Viceroys of India for honourable dealing declined in the present age which has outlived respect for aristocracy.

First of the line was Charles, Marquess Cornwallis, the general who had been defeated at Yorktown. The reputation he had lost, through no fault of his own in America, he regained many times over by his judicious rule in India. It may be convenient to recall here the roll of his successors: Sir J. Shore (1793), Marquess Wellesley (1798), Sir G. Barlow (1805), 2nd Earl of Minto (1807), Viscount Hastings (1813), Viscount Amherst (1823), Lord W. Bentinck (1828), Lord Auckland (1836), Earl of Ellenborough (1842), 1st Viscount Hardinge (1846), Earl of Dalhousie (1848), Viscount Canning (1856), 8th Earl of Elgin (1862), Lord Lawrence (1864), Earl of Mayo (1869), Lord Northbrook (1872), Earl of Lytton (1876), Marquess of Ripon (1880), Marquess of Dufferin (1884), Marquess of Lansdowne (1888), 9th Earl of Elgin (1894), Lord Curzon (1899), 3rd Earl of Minto (1905), 3rd Viscount Hardinge (1910), Lord Chelmsford (1916), Lord Reading (1921), Lord Irwin (1926), Lord Willingdon (1931), Marquess of Linlithgow (1936), Lord Wavell (1943), Viscount Mountbatten (1947).

Cornwallis, eminently a safe man, was determined to carry out his instructions. His character was beyond reproach, and he was armed with a moral and legal authority unknown to Clive and Hastings. For advice upon the administrative and judicial reforms which he intended, he was able to rely upon Sir John Shore who had long experience of India, and upon Sir William Jones. He was a zealous enemy to patronage and jobbery. The higher posts under government were taken away from survivors of the age of corruption, whether Indians or Englishmen, and given to covenanted servants of the Company, Englishmen of character and of experience. In order to carry on the fight against private trade he found it necessary again to raise the scale of salaries. But the principal reform associated with his name is the Permanent Settlement of the revenue of Bengal (1790), which was carried out after long consideration both by Cornwallis in India and by Pitt in England. In intention it fixed the amount of land-tax payable annually by the *zemindars*, who had previously been subject to arbitrary and variable assessments; in effect it secured them in the freehold possession of the land. It has been a subject of unending controversy whether this conversion of feudal vassals into landlords on the English model was a benefit or a hardship to their tenantry, the tillers of the soil.

The Act of 1784 had stated that 'the pursuit of schemes of conquest was repugnant to the honour and policy of the British nation', yet Cornwallis found, like his predecessors, that the unsettled state of India obliged him to go to war. There was no appeasing Tipu Sahib who ruled in Mysore by the same right as the English in Bengal, that is by right of conquest and, like them, was determined to be paramount in India. Very soon after the Treaty of Mangalore Tipu was openly urging the French to join him in expelling the English. When, in 1790, he attacked Travancore, an independent Hindu state to which the English had promised friendship and protection, Cornwallis was bound to intervene. After fighting Tipu in two arduous, methodical campaigns he deprived him of some strategic points essential to the defence of the Carnatic and obliged him to surrender two of his sons as hostages for good behaviour. They were honourably treated and well educated in Calcutta.

Cornwallis retired in 1793, leaving Sir John Shore as deputy during an interregnum of five years, until the arrival in India of Richard, Lord Mornington (better known as the Marquess Wellesley), who brought with him his two brothers, Henry and Arthur Wellesley. The war against the French Revolution had, by 1798, reached an acute phase so that Wellesley, like Warren Hastings twenty years earlier, was confronted with the problem of maintaining British power in India, while at home the British government stood alone against a world of foes. Tipu was busily inciting the French and Turks, through his agents at Paris and

Constantinople, to carry the war against England into the East, while French adventurers in India formed Jacobin clubs and drank the health of 'citoyen Tipu'. A few weeks later came the news that Bonaparte had landed in Egypt with positive intentions of marching to India in the footsteps of Alexander the Great. Wellesley at once declared war on Tipu, sending several columns into Mysore, one under his brother Arthur (who characteristically thought the French threat to India mere moonshine). On 4 May 1798, Sir David Baird carried the fortress of Seringapatam by storm. Tipu died gallantly defending the breach. All the sea-coast of Mysore, the passes of the Ghats, and the fortress of Seringapatam were placed under the direct administration of the Governor of Madras, to prevent the French from penetrating southern India by sea. Tipu's family was pensioned off, while search was made for the heir of the original Hindu rulers. The legitimate line was then restored to the throne of the compact inland state of Mysore, which became the model native state of British India.

The two Moslem Sultans of Mysore, Hyder Ali and his son Tipu, were alien soldiers of fortune, as was Robert Clive. They staked their swords and their lives on the chance of creating a new independent kingdom with French help. They lost, and no sympathy need be wasted on them. Wellesley was high-handed in his settlement of southern India, but he was also high-minded. The *Pax Britannica* conferred benefits upon all the people of the south, of a kind quite beyond the reach of Tipu's imagination.

The Nizam, too, was firmly attached to the British alliance by the Treaty of Hyderabad, 1798. Unlike the Hindu kings of Travancore who had never been subject to the Great Mogul, and unlike Tipu the soldier of fortune, the Nizam was hereditary viceroy of a group of provinces in the Mogul Empire. The viceroyalty persisted, though allegiance passed from the Mogul Emperor to the Kaisar-i-Hind.

The Nawabs of the Carnatic had once been provincial governors under the Nizam and, like other Indian office-holders, had made the post hereditary. By the end of the century the Nawab had transferred much of the administration, including the *diwani* of several districts to the English at Madras. All his powers were mortgaged to his creditors. Wellesley was determined to provide an honest administration throughout the province, by straightening this tangle. On the death of the Nawab in 1801, he obliged the heir to accept a pension and brought the whole of the Carnatic under the Madras Presidency.

The land-revenue system in the south had been simple during the Mysore Wars. The landlord, with the help of his armed retainers, took all that he could find of the produce of the soil, while the tenant kept all that he could hide. Wellesley ordered a permanent settlement of the revenue, as in Bengal, but luckily his instructions were gradually modified. The man on the spot, Sir Thomas Munro, preferred the more flexible form of tenure known as *ryotwary*, his intention being to revive the authority of the village councils or *panchayets*. By consulting them about the assessment he hoped to increase the confidence of the peasants and so to encourage them to bring more land into cultivation. Security for the tenant was the aim in Madras rather than security for the landlord, which the permanent settlement had achieved in Bengal. The Madras *ryotwary* system prevails also in Bombay and Assam, the Bengal *zemindari* system in several other provinces.

The pacification of Mysore was completed by Arthur Wellesley who won his spurs hunting down the armed robber bands into which Tipu's army of mercenaries had disintegrated. All India south of the Godavari River was now at peace and has remained so for 140 years, a great part of it under the rule of legitimate native princes. Law and order have prevailed except for occasional outbreaks of fanaticism among the Moplahs, a turbulent Moslem tribe of the Malabar Coast. The peoples of southern India, in general, are not pugnacious and, for four generations, they have been unused to war. The Madras Presidency, so long in the full current of world politics has been a quiet backwater, the happy land that has no history.

In the north, Wellesley asserted the British claim to supremacy with even greater emphasis. The province of Oudh, largely on account of its partial dependence on the Company, which gave free play to all forms of corruption known to Europeans or Asiatics, was a scandal to lovers of justice. Again, as in the Carnatic, Wellesley made a clean sweep, by obliging the Nawab to cede certain vital frontier districts, to disband his dissolute unruly army, and to accept the Governor's brother, Henry Wellesley, as a general supervisor of the administration. This despotic action, though severely criticised, soon brought unexampled prosperity to the people of the rich Ganges and Jumna valleys.

There was now but one power in India strong enough to challenge the British—the Marathas, who were waging one of their frequent civil wars, Scindia and Holkar versus the Peshwa. Wellesley renewed old agreements with the Peshwa, by the Treaty of Bassein (1802), and accordingly incurred the hostility of the other princes. The Peshwa undertook to renounce all engagements with other European powers, to exclude all other Europeans from his service, and to restrict his diplomatic activity to intercourse with the British only. His enemies were then driven out of Poona by British arms. Wellesley won a decisive victory at Assaye (1803) over Scindia whose army was trained and commanded by Frenchmen. During the campaign against Holkar, who defended himself with skill, General Lake occupied Delhi (1805) and became the protector of the old blind emperor Shah Alam. Provided that the rites and symbols of monarchy were respected, the Great Mogul seemed indifferent whether Englishmen or Marathas were his guardians.

Holkar still held out in his principality of Indore when, in 1805, the English government recalled Wellesley. The Maratha Wars had proved an unlimited liability which they would not underwrite in times of greater danger nearer home. Cornwallis, now an old man, was sent back to India to patch up peace. He soon died, leaving the incomplete negotiation to a deputy governor of mean abilities, Sir G. Barlow. Wellesley had left the British supreme in eastern and in southern India and by so doing had conferred untold blessings on the peoples of India. The timidity of the home government, which prevented him from completing his task of pacifying the Marathas, condemned central India to thirteen years of misery and rapine. They postponed the inevitable decision between the Maratha hordes who lived by plunder, and the nation of shopkeepers whose representative was now patron and protector of the Great Mogul.

During the later stages of the Napoleonic Wars, when Lord Minto was Governor-General, British India was not much troubled. Though Napoleon's designs on Asia were several times renewed they were countered by naval measures which will be considered in another chapter. The occupation of Mauritius

(1810) from which all French attempts upon India had been launched, put an end to French ambitions in the East.

Lord Hastings (not a relative of Warren Hastings), who was Governor-General from 1813 to 1823, was obliged to renew the wars and to fight throughout his term of office. He had first to secure the northern border of British India against the tribes of Nepal who encroached upon it, village by village. After some severe fighting in which the British by no means had their own way, the Maharajah of Nepal was brought to terms by the Treaty of Sagauli (1816) which restricted his frontiers. Since that day this remote Hindu state has maintained its freedom and its convenanted friendship with British India, excluding all foreigners from admission and exporting men for the celebrated Gurkha regiments, some of the bravest soldiers in the world. The Nepal War gave the British access to the hill station of Simla. Lord Amherst retired there for the hot season of 1827 and, after 1848, Dalhousie went there regularly. It became the summer capital of India in 1864.

Having secured the north Lord Hastings was able to attend to the Maratha frontier. Some thousands of armed brigands known as the Pindaris had taken advantage of the total anarchy of the Maratha states to live by plunder and to raid British India. To subdue the Pindaris required the concurrence of the Maratha princes which meant prolonged negotiation, and probable war with one or other of them. When Scindia was persuaded, unwillingly, to co-operate against the Pindaris, the Peshwa took the opportunity to denounce his treaty with the British and marked the occasion by sacking the British residency at Poona. He was joined by Holkar and the Bhonsla. After two years of fighting (1816–18) the Third Maratha War ended in the reduction of the whole of central India. The confederacy of the Marathas was dissolved. Its titular head, the Rajah of Sattara, was confined within the limits of his small principality; its actual head, the Peshwa of Poona, was deprived of his dominions but gratified with an enormous pension. The other principal Maratha chiefs, Holkar, Scindia, Bhonsla and Gaekwar, were confirmed in the possession of their principalities with straitened frontiers and under British supervision.

The destruction of the Maratha power led to the release from oppression of several Hindu principalities of far more respectable antiquity. These, the Rajput States of Jaipur, Udaipur, Jodhpur, and others, regained their freedom under British protection.

When Lord Hastings became Governor-General he refused to make any show of homage to the Mogul Emperor. He proposed to 'extinguish the fiction'. Thus the imperceptible process was completed by which the King of Great Britain became the sovereign of a great part of India. The Mogul remained as 'King of Delhi'. In the same year, 1813, the monopoly of the East India Company was broken down by the admission of all comers to a share in the trade of British India.

7. 'JOHN COMPANY'

SINCE they had become a political power the Directors of the Honourable East India Company had quite changed the character of their operations. Their profits were derived from the land-tax raised in the provinces they ruled, rather than from the import and export trade with Asia. East India stock was more valuable than ever, but for a new reason; it controlled a share of the patronage of British India. The perquisites of a director-ship were said to be worth £10,000 a year. The twenty-four Directors were elected from the Court of Proprietors, that is of the shareholders, numbering about 1800, who possessed holdings of stock with a nominal value exceeding £1000. By the Regu-lating Act the annual dividend was limited to 10½ per cent which meant about 3½ per cent on the average cash price of the shares, but it is doubtful whether even this moderate rate of interest was justified by the balance-sheet. Though provinces, when thoroughly pacified, brought in a steady and increasing revenue, it was rarely sufficient to pay the cost of the wars of conquest. The Company steadily increased its indebtedness to the Crown on account of war loans. Its transactions showed a profit in London but an annual deficit in Calcutta which was regularly met by borrowing. Thus there was a great appearance of prosperity even when the Company, on a close scrutiny, would have been found insolvent.

Though not so important as formerly, the trading monopoly still persisted in India until 1813, and in China until 1833. The Company was obliged by its charters to export English woollen goods to Asia and still made a show of doing so. But small was the chance of finding a market among the millions of exploited peasants whose sad experience was that any display of unwonted finery led to an increase in the land-tax. It was this apathetic acquiescence in misery that so appalled Cornwallis and Wellesley, and inspired their efforts to give security of tenure by permanent settlements of the revenue. As in earlier times, the Company still sent bullion to the East, but in declining quantities. Towards the end of the eighteenth century the annual imports from England averaged at about half a million sterling in woollen goods and half a million in silver dollars. To this was added in Calcutta a proportion of the revenue of Bengal and Madras after the cost of administration had been met. The sum of these accounts constituted the Company's 'Investment' with which Indian goods were bought for export. About half of the Investment was spent on saltpetre, fine muslins and cotton piece-goods for direct shipment to England; the remainder was invested in opium for export to China. There it was sold in the Company's factory at Canton, to provide funds for the most important purchases made by the Company, the yearly crop of China tea, amounting sometimes to 27,000,000 lb. weight, and saleable in London for over £4,000,000 sterling. By comparison the shipments of cotton goods were decreasing in value. Lancashire was beginning to spin and weave American cotton, and soon, in the early nineteenth century, would be exporting cheap cotton cloths to India.

Tea was still a secure monopoly because China was still closed to foreigners. The Portuguese, alone of Europeans, occupied a treaty port at Macao. The merchants of the British Company were restricted to a single building at Canton which they approached by water. They might sell opium at the annual fair and buy tea, by contract with the Chinese merchants' guild, but not set foot outside their factory nor hold intercourse with the Chinese people. Though the 'foreign devils' were treated with contempt by Chinese officials, they lived in great luxury inside the factory which was reputed the best place in the Company's gift. The President might make as much as £20,000 a year.

There was luxurious living in all the Presidencies. Calcutta, described by one traveller as 'the most magnificent city in the world', stretched for a league of porticoed villas and lawns along the shores of the Hugli at Garden Reach. Its citadel, Fort William, reputed the strongest fortress outside Europe, had been built by Clive at a cost of £2,000,000. The city contained two Anglican churches, a Government House built by Wellesley on the model of Kedleston Hall in Derbyshire, a library founded by Sir William Jones and enriched with oriental MSS. taken in the sack of Seringapatam, and many merchants' houses designed like English mansions in the classic taste. The population of Calcutta in 1800 may have been 4000 or 5000 British and half a million Indians, the greater part of them huddled in the Black Town, a filthy slum which lay to the north.

Madras had a population of about 2000 British officials and 300,000 Indians. Though the government of the Presidency was conducted in the old buildings of Fort St George, most of the British inhabitants lived outside the walls, or inland at a hill-station. Formerly the capital of British India, Madras, still retained sufficient social prestige to expect that its governor should be a lord. Bombay stood much lower in social estimation. The population was not more than 150,000, many of them Portuguese half-castes. There were not more than 1700 British residents and none so rich and proud as the judges and counsellors at Calcutta with their salaries ranging up to £10,000 a year, or as the 'nabobs' of the Bengal commercial branch who still grew rich on perquisites.

Hardly less important than the commercial interest of the Company was the shipping interest. The East India Docks in London have a long history which began in the reign of Queen Elizabeth. Throughout the eighteenth century they contained several shipyards at which were built the bluff deep-hulled three-masters known as East-Indiamen, the biggest merchant ships afloat. The Company's ship *Hindostan* rated as a 1200 tonner (in 1799) was, by measurement in tons burthen, a larger ship than H.M.S. *Victory*, and five or six ships of not much smaller dimensions were built in London river every year. At war prices they cost £60,000 to build and equip for their first voyage, and after about six voyages were only fit to be sold out of the service. The East Indiamen were armed against pirates, sometimes with as many as thirty guns, mounted in broadside on the main deck and firing through ports painted, man-of-war fashion, in the Nelson chequer of black and white. In general appearance they much resembled frigates of the Navy and were even occasionally mistaken for seventy-fours. In war-time they were sometimes requisitioned for service as ships of the line. Ships of this special class, built and maintained for the East India trade, were retained under charter by the Company during the whole of their useful life, so that the owners inevitably acquired an interest in the Company's affairs. The shipping interest made larger profits than the Company's commercial branch and constituted a solid block of voters in the Court of Proprietors.

The captain of an East Indiaman was an important personage who held a position in society not much inferior to that of a naval officer. He bought his commission for about £8000 and hoped to clear at least £2000 a voyage. His officers were picked men wearing uniforms and swords. Nelson himself as a young man made a voyage as an officer in this service. The maintenance and discipline of ships and crews was as regular as in the Navy, with the advantage of profit from private trade, a surer expectation than the chance of naval prize-money. In addition to the regular lading of the Company's goods, or of troops conveyed at government charge, the captain, and his crew in due proportion, might fill a part of the cargo space with private merchandise. By this means quantities of English comforts and luxuries were carried to Bengal for sale to Englishmen abroad: the heavy wines of Madeira and Oporto that inflamed the legendary Anglo-Indian 'liver', and the special brew for tropical consumption still known as India Pale Ale. On the return voyage the bottom of the hold was filled with the captain's private venture in china-ware, a cargo not liable to damage by leakage of water, above which the Company's purchase of tea was stowed high and dry.

Still more lucrative a perquisite was the captain's right to charge fees for cabin accommodation in accordance with the passenger's rank, £250 for a general, £110 for a subaltern or 'writer'. Special accommodation for ladies might cost £500 or more for each berth. The ships left London crammed with cargo, passengers, and livestock—cows, goats and poultry for the voyage—leaving small space for amenities, even for those who had paid highly. Private berths were spaces in the 'tween-decks screened off with canvas and furnished at the passenger's expense. The only approach to comfort was the captain's after-cabin, opening on to the stern galleries through casement windows. Here honoured passengers were permitted to dine.

The voyage to India was slow, since safety and comfort were more desirable than speed when there was no competition. Four months to Calcutta and six or eight months to Canton was fast enough until, in the nineteenth century, the Yankee clippers broke in on the monopoly and forced the pace. They sailed no better than the old Indiamen but were kept at top speed in all weathers. During the Mutiny when speed was essential for all, the best voyages were made by the old bluff-bowed ships. Even before that an Indiaman had reached England from Ceylon in seventy-seven days.

But the 'Investment' at Calcutta was mostly put into the 'country trade' carried in ships built on the Malabar Coast. Dr C. N. Parkinson[1] has demonstrated that when the British first went to the East their ships were inferior in sailing qualities both to the dhows of the Arabian seas and to the Chinese junks. The shipbuilders of Surat, and in later times of Bombay, turned from their own traditional design to ships modelled on the British Indiamen, and bettered their instruction by building them of teak. They made the change not because they thought British ships more seaworthy but because of the terror of the British name. In seas infested with pirates British ships rode secure, for it was known that British sailors could and would fight. The best protection for less pugnacious mariners was to sail in what looked like a British ship. Hence there grew up a shipbuilding trade in each of the Presidencies, fostered by Indian capital but served by British managers and craftsmen. The Bombay dock-yard, owned by successive generations of the Parsee family of Wadia, built admirable ships for the 'Country trade', the Indian Marine and even for the Royal Navy.

The East India Company had a navy long before it had an army. In the first expeditions to Surat it was found necessary to establish a few ships in the Arabian Sea in opposition to the Portuguese. When Bombay became a presidency it regularly bore on its establishment an 'admiral' with a flotilla of country-built ships. In every war fought east of the Cape of Good Hope this unadvertised force, known at first as the Bombay Marine

[1] Author of *Trade in the Eastern Seas* to which I am much obliged for the information given in this chapter.

and later as the Royal Indian Marine, has played an adventurous part. Its ships supported Clive's campaigns, fought beside the Royal Navy against de Suffren, battled with Maratha pirates during the first Maratha War, assisted in the capture of Ceylon and, in later times, made voyages to war-fronts in Persia, China, even as far as New Zealand. Throughout the history of the East India Company the Marine Service never ceased to operate against the pirates of the Persian Gulf. After the abolition of the slave trade a new mission was to hunt down the Arab slavers. Gradually its organisation was merged into that of the Royal Navy. In 1827 its officers were given naval rank and a naval officer became superintendent. When Company rule ended, in 1858, it ceased to be an independent fighting service. The Indian Marine had frequently undertaken more peaceable but equally useful tasks. It established a steam-packet service to Egypt, in 1838, for the carriage of mails to Europe by the Overland Route. It surveyed the coasts and islands of the Indian Ocean. After 1858 it undertook the provision of river and coastal gunboats and the transport of troops between India and England, while the maintenance of sea-power in Eastern waters became a responsibility of the Admiralty.

The Indian Army is of more recent origin than the Marine Service; it can hardly be said to have existed before the days of Clive. There had been guards at the French and English factories from their beginnings but they were *peons*, armed servants, rather than soldiers. Perhaps an exception is the company of Englishmen sent by Charles II to Bombay, in 1662, though they were not, in fact, the nucleus from which the Indian Army grew. *Sepoys, Sipahis, Spahis,* that is, native troops drilled by Europeans, appeared first at Pondicherry about 1720. To meet this new French threat the Company brought out to India a King's officer, Major Stringer Lawrence, who was to organise a force of British sepoys. Since Fort St George was in enemy hands it was at Fort St David that he formed the first Sepoy regiment (1748), in which Robert Clive obtained a captain's commission. Having improvised the army which re-established the English power in the Carnatic, Stringer Lawrence set to work during the interval of peace to organise a permanent force. His plan (1759) was to raise seven battalions of sepoys each established on the model of the British infantry and to attach to each battalion two British subalterns and three serjeants, many of them volunteers from the 39th Foot. This little force, the prototype of many more, won for Stringer Lawrence the name of 'father of the Indian Army'. It also extracted from the Frenchman, Lally, a reluctant compliment: 'Their sepoys will venture to attack our white troops while ours will not even look at their black ones.'

In his later days in Bengal, Clive commanded an army of this type but three times as large. He built up the units into formations resembling what in a modern army are called Brigade Groups, each consisting of a troop of cavalry, a battery of artillery, a battalion of European infantry and seven battalions of sepoys. In 1805 the strength of the Company's armies was: in Bengal 64,000, in Madras 64,000, in Bombay 24,500. Of these about 22,000 were Europeans, more than two-thirds of the white population of British India.

The European troops were not King's regiments but bands of European adventurers, by no means all Englishmen. They were mercenaries fighting for their fortune. In earlier and worse times their recompense was plunder; in later, better-regulated times it was prize-money such as is still paid to sailors. £13,000,000 was divided among the officers and men who took Seringapatam. 'Loot' was one of the earliest words adopted from Hindustani into English.

The sepoys, also, were miscellaneous soldiers of fortune, flotsam of the tide of troubles that swept over eighteenth-century India, largely Moslem Moplahs in the south, and in Bengal, caste Hindus who were not remarkable for military virtues. Like all mercenaries they grumbled at their wages and mutinied on pretexts their employers thought frivolous: because a new type of shako disarranged their caste-marks, because they suspected they were to be sent overseas, away from the sacred soil of Mother India, because their cartridges were greased with pig's and cow's fat, or simply for a larger share of prize-money. Long before the great mutiny of '57, men told tales of Hector Munro's suppression of the mutiny in the Bengal Army in 1764, of Gillespie's ruthless action against the Madras mutineers who killed 200 Englishmen at Vellore in 1806, and of many other outbreaks.

The British officers were almost equally insubordinate. The very first English soldiers in India had mutinied under their Captain, Richard Keigwin, and had set up a military government

Plate 5 A

ROBERT, LORD CLIVE
(1725–74)

Painted towards the end of his life, by N. Dance. *See p. 162.*

Plate 5 B

REN HASTINGS
1732–1818)

in India, about 1775,
Kettle. *See p. 171.*

Plate 6A

RICHARD, MAR
WELLESLF
(1760–184
By J. Pain Davis. S

Plate 6B

CHARLES, MARQUESS
CORNWALLIS
(1738–1805)

After his return from America,
1783, painted by T. Gains-
borough. *See p. 180.*

at Bombay in 1683. Clive's difficulties with the officers of the
Bengal Army have already been mentioned. The 'white mutiny'
of the Madras Army, in 1809, revealed their discontent. Now that
the years of anarchy were over, they had no prospect of winning
wealth or honour or promotion, these favours being reserved for
officers of the King's regiments. Officers of the Company's
Army were sent out to India very young, without training or
supervision, to live in discomfort on meagre salaries, starting at
£120 per annum. No share of the fabled riches of the East came
their way in time of peace. Sir Thomas Munro wrote, when as a
boy he joined the Madras Army, 'my dress grows tattered in one
quarter whilst I am establishing funds to repair it in another, and
my coat is in danger of losing the sleeves, while I am pulling it
off.... I have dined to-day on porridge made of half-ground flour
and I shall most likely dine to-morrow on plantain fritters, this
simplicity of fare being the effect of necessity, not of choice.'
It was no wonder that good officers were scarce.

In the early days Europeans showed little colour-prejudice.
Since there were only 250 white women among the 4000 white
inhabitants of Bengal it is not surprising that young officers
formed connexions, often quite respectably, with the women of
the country. An apartment known as the *Bibi-khana*, or women's
quarters, is still to be found in the older cantonments, though long
since put to other uses. Thus a half-caste population sprang up,
contributing to the many Eurasians of modern India, to whom a
recent snobbish affectation has attached the inaccurate name of
Anglo-Indians. A touch of country blood did not disqualify a
man for a commission in the Company's Army, and rightly;
but caste prejudice, the custom of India, prevailed even among
the English and eventually condemned mixed marriages. The
practice of openly keeping Indian women as mistresses was
frowned upon as the professional status of the Company's
servants was raised. The higher moral tone of English society
in the nineteenth century worked against it, and improved
communications with Europe permitted Englishmen in India to
visit their families on furlough, or to bring out their wives to the
East. In the old days a commission to serve the Company in
India was a life-sentence, if not a death-sentence. There was no
furlough and only about one in four of the cadets who went out
as young lads lived to retire at Bath or Cheltenham.

The covenanted servants of the Company, the body which was to grow into the Indian Civil Service, numbered about 2000 in the year 1800. Since they had prospects of power and promotion, if no longer of unlimited wealth, appointments were sought after and candidates were young men of ability. The first effects of intervention by the Crown in the affairs of the Company had been to raise the standard. Cornwallis set his face against the jobbery by which the Directors put their clients into the most highly-paid posts, without regard to talent or experience. All higher officials, excepting the Governors, Counsellors and High Court Judges, who were appointed by the Crown, were to be covenanted servants with sufficient experience of Indian affairs. Incidentally this ruling closed the higher offices against natives of India.

Wellesley lifted the reforms on to a higher plane. His hatred of oppression and dishonesty was equalled by his belief in the need for enlightenment. He supported the Church establishment in the Presidency cities and encouraged the work of the chaplains. It was his desire to raise the moral and intellectual level of the Company's servants, an aim which he hoped to reach by education. No longer adventurers or traders, they were to be statesmen and soldiers worthy to represent a Christian king. In 1800 he founded a college at Calcutta where the young civilians were to be trained in literature, science and oriental languages. When it proved more convenient to carry out this training before the young men left England, the East India College was founded at Haileybury in 1806. For fifty years fifty young men were sent out annually from Old Haileybury to the civil service of 'John Company', as they affectionately nicknamed it; and few educational establishments can boast more eminent pupils. The College was conceived as something like a university, providing courses in Law, History, Political Economy and Oriental Languages, for students who commenced with a public school education. The staff were men of distinction, the most celebrated being the Rev. T. R. Malthus, the Professor of History. Among names remembered in India of men who bore the stamp of Old Haileybury are John Lawrence, the Colvins, father and son, Charles Trevelyan, Bartle Frere; but the College left its stamp on hundreds of others. They were strongly tinged with evangelical Protestantism and, if not all devout men, equally demonstrated the stoic habits of the Puritan. Scrupulously honest and even-handed, conscientious in the discharge of their duties, fearless, ruthless, and insensitive, they gave their lives to the service of India, ruling it with a disinterested fervour that has no parallel in history. This was the spirit, also of the Indian Army, when its officers, after 1812, were trained for their profession at Addis-combe. The spirit survives in many outlying provinces of the British Empire:

> Some beneath the further star
> Bear the greater burden
> Set to serve the lands they rule,
> Save he serve no man may rule,
> Serve and love the lands they rule,
> Seeking praise nor guerdon.

Slowly the pattern of English life in India changed. The old corrupt fortune-hunters, the 'nabobs', the men who went to the East, to 'shake the pagoda-tree' (*pagodas* being the gold coins of Golconda), were replaced by new men to whom Empire was a trust and work for it a pious duty. The age of Philanthropy was dawning.

IV

THE SOUTH SEAS: CONVICTS: SLAVES

Argument: The Pacific Ocean, hitherto almost unknown, was explored by rival French and British expeditions in the intervals between the wars of the eighteenth century. Captain Cook's three voyages revealed the general plan of the southern world. Picturesque accounts of the South Sea Islands opened a new field to traders, missionaries, and colonists. The whaling industry was vastly expanded.

Australia provided a sufficiently remote repository for convicts who could no longer be transported to America. By 1820 New South Wales, having attracted pastoral settlers and island-traders, had outgrown its original form as a convict-settlement under martial law.

The evangelical revival produced an agitation against the slave-trade which, since 1713, had been regarded as a staple of British commerce and sea-power. When it had been declared illegal, in 1807, after a long Parliamentary struggle, the British made strenuous efforts for an international agreement to suppress the trade.

The British colonies on the Gambia and the Gold Coast were by-products of the slave-trade. Sierra Leone was founded by the reformers as a refuge for freed slaves.

1. THE EXPLORATION OF THE PACIFIC

THE island-studded southern ocean, covering nearly one-half of the surface of the globe, was explored and mapped during the eighteenth century, but to tell its story it is necessary to hark back beyond the Renaissance voyages, beyond Marco Polo, to the Graeco-Roman geographers who knew very well that the earth was round. They were, however, disposed to guess that the southern hemisphere was likely to resemble the northern in containing more land than water. An unbroken expanse of water through 350° of longitude in the forties and fifties south of the equator seemed so unlikely as to be incredible. All that was known of this southern world for several hundred years was comprised in some vague misunderstood allusions which Marco Polo made, on hearsay, about rich kingdoms in the southern seas.

The first Europeans to penetrate those seas were the Portuguese who reached Malacca in 1511, the China Coast in 1516, and New Guinea in 1526. This progress step by step from places known to places conjectured seemed less significant than the Spanish approach by way of the New World, the vision seen by Balboa in 1513 'upon a peak in Darien'. Six years later Magellan set out to find a south-west passage into the southern ocean and emerged from the western outlet of his Strait on 28 November 1520. His track across the sea, to which he gave the well-omened name of Pacific, lay northerly through the Ladrones Islands to the Philippines where he met his death, leaving to his crew the task of concluding the first voyage round the world.

The great length of Magellan's voyage imposed such hardships on his crew that few attempts were made to repeat his exploit for many years. No ship succeeded in returning to America on an easterly course until 1565, when it was found that favourable winds prevailed in the north temperate latitudes. From that time an annual service of galleons sailed from Panama to Manila and back, rarely altering course from this easy route. Drake's addition to geographical knowledge, after capturing the Manila galleon, was his expedition up the coast to California, presumably undertaken in the vain hope of finding a short way home through the western entrance of some North-west Passage; his route across the Pacific revealed nothing new.

Further noteworthy discoveries made by the Spaniards were the Solomon Islands which were visited by Mendaña in 1565. Thirty years later he set out to plant them with a colony of settlers but, so faulty was the navigation of his day, neither he nor other voyagers could find them again. One of his successors, Torres, passed through the straits which bear his name, in 1606, but kept the discovery secret, as was the custom in that age of jealous, exclusive empire-building. All these discoveries remained hidden for nearly 200 years in the archives at Madrid, and the Solomon Islanders were still some of the most primitive peoples in the world when, in 1942, the clash of civilisations came rudely to their notice.

As the Spanish power faded from the Pacific the Dutch, who had ousted the Portuguese from the East Indies, began to enter the ocean from the western side. About 1611, Dutch skippers, often delayed like the Flying Dutchman himself, by the heavy

weather off the south-east coast of Africa, learned to take the
great circle southerly from the Cape, through the roaring 'forties
where the westerly gales are constant, to the longitude of their
East Indian possessions. Then striking north for Java they
picked up the dry harbourless coast of Western Australia, which
they called New Holland. Traditionally, the first Dutch skipper
to make the landfall was Dirk Hartog, at Shark Bay, in 1616;
though it seems likely that another ship from the Moluccas had
visited Northern Australia ten years earlier without making much
of it. The Shark Bay landfall became a regular sailing mark, no
more, and though the Dutchmen touched the coast at various
points they found nothing to tempt them to stay.

Van Diemen, the Governor of Java, sent out a number of
voyages of discovery, the principal being that of Tasman, whose
task was to find a way into the Pacific south about New Holland.
His first discovery was the island which he called Van Diemen's
Land, but which posterity has preferred to call Tasmania. Thence
he sailed away easterly until his path was barred by a high rocky
coast running north and south for several hundred miles. Some
of his men, putting ashore for water, were attacked, killed and
eaten by savages of efficient ferocity. Thus repulsed from what
he thought was the Southern Continent across his path, Tasman
cautiously turned away north for Java, rounding Australia,
though he did not sight its eastern coast, and passing to the
north of New Guinea. He had thus proved New Holland an island,
or a group of islands; but by his unlucky landfall on the west
coast of New Zealand (13 December 1642) he perpetuated for
another hundred years the legend of the Great Southern
Continent.

There was now a pause in the exploration of the Pacific.
The shape of western America was pretty well known as far north
as California; beyond that there might or might not be the outlet
from the North-west Passage. The China Seas and the East
Indies were known if not charted. North of the latitude of Japan
was a matter of guesswork so that there was nothing to prevent
Dean Swift from locating there the flying island of Laputa,
and Brobdingnag the land of the giants. South of the equator,
from Cape Horn to Tasman's bleak discoveries, the map was
blank; there might be ocean, but it was supposed that there
was land.

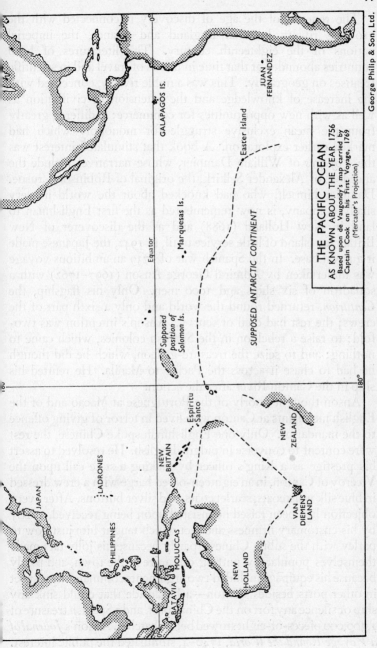

THE PACIFIC OCEAN
AS KNOWN ABOUT THE YEAR 1756
Based upon de Vaugondy's map carried by
Captain Cook on his First Voyage, 1769
(Mercator's Projection)

JUAN FERNANDEZ

GALAPAGOS IS.

Equator

Easter Island

Marquesas Is.

Supposed position of Solomon Is.

SUPPOSED ANTARCTIC CONTINENT

Espiritu Santo

NEW ZEALAND

LADRONES

JAPAN

NEW BRITAIN

PHILIPPINES

MOLUCCAS

BATAVIA

VAN DIEMENS LAND

NEW HOLLAND

George Philip & Son, Ltd.

Map 4

The renewal of the age of discovery is connected with the growing rivalry between England and France, the imperial nations of the eighteenth century. The literatures of both countries abounded at that time in books of travel and in scientific treatises on geography. This was a noble rivalry, concerned with the increase of knowledge and the extension of civilisation as well as with new opportunities for commerce; it differed greatly from the mean exclusive struggle for monopoly which had marked earlier exploration. A book that stimulated interest was the *Voyages* of William Dampier, whose narratives include the anecdote of Alexander Selkirk, the original of Robinson Crusoe. Dampier himself, who had knocked about the world in very shady company, is now remembered as the first Englishman to land in New Holland (1688) and as the discoverer of New Britain, an island of little service until, in 1942, the Japanese made it a naval base. In the Spanish war of 1739 an ambitious voyage was undertaken by Admiral George Anson (1697–1762) with a squadron of six ships and 1000 men. Only his flagship, the *Centurion*, returned round the world and only a sixth part of the crews; the rest had died of scurvy. Anson's intention was two-fold: to raise a rebellion in the Spanish colonies, which came to nothing; and to seize the treasure-galleon, which he did though he had to chase it across the Pacific to Manila. He refitted his ship in the Canton River after the action.

Anson thought poorly of the Portuguese at Macao and of the English merchants at Canton who lived in terror of giving offence to the mandarins. Only one Englishman spoke Chinese, the rest were content to converse in pidgin-English. He resolved to assert his prestige as a King's officer by making a state call upon the Viceroy of Canton, in an eighteen-oared barge with a crew dressed in blue silk waistcoats, scarlet coats, and silver buttons. After every objection had been raised he insisted upon being received, partly by his customary firmness and tact which taught him just how to parley with the subtle Chinese, partly because his jolly tars made themselves popular by putting out a fire in the town, and partly because his equipage included two arguments commanding respect in other ports besides Canton—a broadside that could sink any ship or silence any fort on the China coast, and a Spanish treasure of 1,300,000 pieces-of-eight stowed below hatches. Anson's *Journal of a Voyage Round the World*, 1740–4, stimulated the public interest.

At the end of the Seven Years War many eyes were turned towards the maps of the Pacific Ocean, both in France and England. George Grenville's schemes to organise the Empire included a plan for rediscovering Drake's 'New Albion', an obvious next step after the conquest of Canada. The writings of Alexander Dalrymple, who by some means had learned the Spanish secret of the discovery of Torres Strait, moved the Admiralty and the scientific world to action. Three naval expeditions under Byron, Wallis and Carteret crossed the Pacific between 1764 and 1767; two were unfortunate in hitting upon no major discovery, but Wallis in 1767 discovered Tahiti and wrote a stolid account of it. The following year a French expedition under Bougainville again visited the island, and his account profoundly affected the French philosophers by revealing the South Sea Islands as an earthly paradise. The crews of one expedition or the other repaid the easy hospitality of the Tahitians by infecting them with syphilis.

In 1769 a transit of Venus across the Sun was due to occur, a rare astronomical phenomenon which would enable geographers to make some useful corrections in the mathematics of navigation. As these were of practical value to the Navy and of scientific interest to the learned, it was agreed by the Admiralty and the Royal Society to send an expedition, jointly, to a place in the Pacific Ocean from where the transit could best be observed. The promoter was a wealthy young amateur, (Sir) Joseph Banks, (1743–1820) who advanced funds, and accompanied the expedition with a team of scientific assistants. The Admiralty provided a ship, a crew and a commander, Lieutenant James Cook (1728–79). Rarely does the historian have the privilege of describing so admirable a career as that of Cook. The son of a Yorkshire farm labourer, he went to sea in a Whitby collier, educated himself, studied his profession and became a master-mariner. At the outbreak of the Seven Years War he volunteered into the Navy before the mast and served with Admiral Saunders' squadron in the combined operations which led to the fall of Quebec. His skilful pilotage in the awkward waters of the St Lawrence under the French guns led to his selection, after the war, to survey the coasts of Newfoundland, a task which he accomplished so accurately and thoroughly that he was marked down by the Admiralty as 'fit for greater enterprises'. In 1768 he was missioned to command the barque *Endeavour* which was to take Sir Joseph Banks and his party to the newly discovered island of Tahiti.

Cook's instructions were, after completing the observations at Tahiti, to search the 'forties for the Southern Continent, to report upon its products and peoples, to cultivate their friendship and to annex convenient trading posts in the King's name. On leaving Tahiti he went away south and then west, intending to come down upon the east side of the inhospitable land discovered by Tasman, and made his landfall on 13 October 1769. For six months he cruised in New Zealand waters surveying the coasts and studying the native peoples. His charts, which remained in use for eighty years, proved that this was no part of a continent but a long and narrow group of islands extending from north to south through a thousand miles.

From New Zealand, Cook bore away north to search for the eastern coast of New Holland. He skirted along a line of cliff which, from some fancied resemblance to the Welsh coast, he named New South Wales. Further north he found himself in danger between the land and the shoals of the Barrier Reef which he followed for several hundred miles, a feat of navigation achieved by equal skill and luck. By way of Torres Strait he returned to England where he was loaded with honours. On the coasts both of New Zealand and of New South Wales he had made formal acts of annexation to the British Crown, but these were disregarded by the government at home.

In 1772 Cook was despatched again to search the southern seas for land. Making his base among the savages in a New Zealand harbour he crossed and recrossed the Pacific, as far south as latitude 70° where his way was barred by the Great Ice Barrier. He thus disposed of the ancient myth; there was no continental mass north of the antarctic ice. This second of Cook's voyages round the world was remarkable in that only one man of his crew died of disease, a record indeed when in earlier circumnavigations a crew was lucky if more than a minority came home alive.

In his third voyage Cook disproved the other great myth of Pacific geography, the existence of a navigable North-west Passage in the temperate zone, by cruising along the western coast of North America beyond Drake's 'New Albion', beyond

he limit of Spanish exploration and into the Behring Sea. A by-
product of the voyage was his discovery of the Hawaiian Group
which seems to have escaped the notice of the numerous earlier
navigators in the central Pacific. The rest of the tale is well
known. His men were at first received at Hawaii with Polynesian
liberality, he himself was treated with divine honours as a great
chief—all Polynesian chiefs were of divine origin. But the ships
outstayed their welcome. Quarrels arose between the rough
sailors and the islanders, who had the easiest notions of private
property and coveted the iron tools and weapons of the strangers.
On 14 February 1779, Cook was killed in a brawl on the beach
while trying to recover a stolen ship's cutter. His last word to
his boat's crew was to cease firing. When their quick tempers had
subsided the Hawaiians regretted his death and endeavoured to
make amends.

The publication of the account of Cook's voyages aroused an
extraordinary outburst of interest in England. His achievements
were greater than those of any earlier navigator; he had outlined
on the map the shape of lands and seas, hitherto unknown or
hardly known, amounting to one-quarter of the whole surface
of the globe; he had charted the coasts of New Zealand, New
South Wales, Hawaii and scores of smaller islands; he had
disproved the two ancient myths of the navigable North-west
Passage and the habitable Southern Continent; he had sailed
three times round the world, had taken his ship into the Arctic
and the Antarctic regions and, most remarkable of all, had done
this almost without loss of life. Cook has been credited with the
discovery of a preventive or of a cure for scurvy, but this is
beyond his due. It was the common knowledge of his age that
scurvy was a disease caused by malnutrition and curable by
proper diet. It was Cook's triumph that he prevented its outbreak by enforcing rules of health. He insisted on cleanliness,
ventilation, daily exercise, variety in diet and on the use of a
decoction of *sauerkraut* when no other fresh vegetables were
available. He took great pains to keep his crews cheerful and
encouraged dancing on the foc'sle. He was a naval not a medical
reformer.

With Cook's death ends the fantastic age of exploration by
sea. The general plan of all the oceans was known and only
details remained to be discovered. No longer need mariners be

lost in uncharted oceans, since Harrison's Chronometer, firs used by Cook, at last solved the old problem of finding the longitude. Though his adventures received the widest publicity though the best society of his day attempted to lionise him, Cook remains personally unknown. Among his voluminous officia papers there is hardly an anecdote or a characteristic saying to tell us what kind of man he was. His portrait at Greenwich reveals him as a tall, handsome man with a pleasant expression and a shrewd inquisitive eye; but he had no small talk and no aptitude for letter-writing. All accounts, including those of the Polynesian natives who were mightily impressed by him, agree that he was aloof, dignified and taciturn. His life, as Newbol pointed out, is summed in the names of the four ships he com-manded: *Endeavour*, *Resolution*, *Adventure* and *Discovery*.

The sailors of that age were in general careless of human life and brutally callous in their treatment of primitive peoples. The habit of kidnapping savages as slaves, the universal contempt for their religious and social customs, provoked sudden outbursts of vengeance, which the sailors regarded as treachery and punished with indiscriminate massacre. Among the light-hearted islanders of the Pacific, gaiety and good humour would turn in an instant to fighting frenzy when their honour was offended. Almost alone among the voyagers, Cook spared no effort to make a friendly honourable approach to the islanders. It is then all the more tragic that he should have lost his life in a brawl arising from a misunderstanding.[1]

2. THE SOUTH SEA ISLANDERS

THE aboriginals of New Guinea, and the belt of islands known as Melanesia to the eastward of Australia, are among the most primitive peoples in the world. In person they are tall, slender and negroid, with profuse heads of hair. When first discovered they lived by fishing and hunting, wove no cloth, made no use of metals, domesticated no animals, knew little of agriculture and lived in rude huts of branches. Descent was traced through the

[1] When this and the following section were first written I hoped that they would have been revised by my brother, A. H. Carrington, whose knowledge of the Pacific and of its exploration was, perhaps, unequalled. His death in 194 deprived me of that advantage. C.E.C.

female line since, as Malinowski asserted of the Trobrianders even in the twentieth century, they had no understanding of the process of paternity. The mysterious sense of unity with some animal totem united the family-group in so close a relationship as to compel marriage outside the group in order to avoid incest. The whole complex of beliefs, varying widely from region to region, but based upon some such folk-belief raised an impassable psychological barrier against European understanding and influence. Their political, their economic, their religious life were utterly unlike ours. The barrier has never been broken down. In general the Australian blacks and the Melanesian islanders have remained at their former level of culture and have not acquired European ways of thought in 200 years of contact. Of late a more enlightened school of colonial administrators has abandoned the attempt to 'civilise' these natives, adopting instead the 'zoological-gardens' policy of isolating them in their mental and physical wilderness. All the experience of colonisation goes to prove this segregation impracticable, although in some instances the islanders themselves have shown signs of welcoming it. But that ancient solvent of fossilised cultures, external war, has of late been at work in Melanesia.

Very different from the primitive negroid Melanesians were and are the gay sophisticated peoples of the zone of volcanic islands and coral reefs stretching through sixty degrees of the central Pacific from Fiji to Easter Island, from Hawaii to New Zealand, the mysterious Polynesians. They, too, used no metals but ground exquisite tools and weapons of a neolithic type from obsidian and jade. In the northern islands they wove cloth on the loom, but through most of the region beat out bark into fabric as fine as cotton cloth, excelled in basket work and patterned mattings of delicate fibre, embroidered their clothing with the gorgeous plumage of tropical birds. They cultivated the yam, the bread-fruit, and the sweet potato. They lived at the sea's edge as expert swimmers, navigators, fishermen; they named and studied the stars, knew the ocean currents, and could plot the map of the Pacific though they knew nothing of even the simplest form of writing.

Yet once, as they knew and told in their epic poems, they had been a greater people. Their culture showed all the signs of degeneration not of progress. For perhaps a thousand years

they had lived the life of lotus-eaters in the fortunate isles where
the sun was always warm and the earth almost unaided produced
her kindly fruits; but they had come from an earlier home in a
land which all the islanders alike remember and revere, the
fabulous land of 'Hawa-iki'. They had spread through the islands
in half-decked double canoes that could beat against the wind.
They retained, as priestly secrets, traces of a monotheistic
religion, and knew that they had once built holy places of dressed
stone. Relics of the lost theogony remain at Easter Island, the
farthest and strangest Polynesian outpost where gigantic stone
idols and terraces of masonry remain to confound the imagina-
tions both of visiting ethnologists and of the islanders themselves. Everywhere decadent traces of the lost culture remain in
the broken-down conventional patterns which all the Polynesians incise on the door-posts of their houses, the figure-heads
of their canoes, and the tattooing of their faces; designs containing representations of gods whose names and attributes
alone survive after their cult has been forgotten.

The Polynesian migrations ended with the occupation of New
Zealand by the Maoris about the year 1350. Then the art of
navigation was forgotten, as it seems to have been forgotten by
our own Anglo-Saxon ancestors after their invasion of Britain.
The Maoris never returned to the north, nor were voyages made
across the wider gaps between other island-groups; the ocean-
going double canoes fell into disuse and were remembered only
in legend. Yet when Bougainville and Cook introduced the
Polynesian race to the attention of the learned, comparative
studies proved that in the islands which had held no inter-
communication for 400 years the same traditional histories were
told and the pedigrees of chiefs were consistently traced to the
same ancestors, not only as far back as the age of dispersion
through Polynesia in the fourteenth century, but to a common
origin a thousand years earlier in 'Hawa-iki'.

Descent in Polynesia was traced through the male line and
pride of birth was no higher in Scotland. The chiefs were heaven-
born and endowed with supernatural powers, especially in having
an innate reservoir of force which they called *tapu*, anglicised
as taboo. The chief was bound by rules of caste, as strictly as any
Brahmin, in order to preserve and insulate this dangerous
potential which might strike an intruder dead as with an electric

shock. The chief's person and property, his house, food and weapons were *tapu*, polluted if touched by an inferior, and touched only with peril. The chief by a mere word might lay a *tapu* upon any thing or place, charging it, as it were, with a current so that all the magical restrictions attaching to his own person attached to the *tapu*-ed place or thing. No Polynesian dared break a *tapu*, on pain of punishment by the chief whose honour was thereby defiled, but much more for fear of supernatural penalties. The fact that *tapu* was something of which Europeans were quite unappreciative, whether through ignorance or through contempt, was the cause of almost every clash between the two races. The prestige of a chief increased with his triumphs in politics and war, making his *tapu* ever more effective. An intention in battle was to master and acquire and add to one's own the prestige of the opposing chief, an end best achieved by killing and eating him. Thus contests of skill and courage, in war and intrigue, were a natural occupation of chiefs and were concluded by a ritual cannibal feast.

Captain Cook earnestly and generously studied the Polynesians but never grasped their state of mind. They, too, studied him, obviously a great chief, aloof and dignified on his *tapu*-ed quarter-deck. The game ended without malice when they clustered round, each stabbing at his body to share in the prestige they gained by his death, each hoping for a mouthful of that strong meat.

The Polynesians are a tall, strong, stoutly built race varying in colour from light brown in the northern islands to a deeper colour in New Zealand and Fiji where there may be a strain of negroid Melanesian blood. Their language has hardly more than dialectic variations from island to island. Tribes held their land in common and made a festival of harvesting a crop or launching a new boat; no such event passing without feasting and dancing. The men were bold and active, the women graceful and licentious. This idyllic life reached its easy climax in Tahiti, the goal of every sailor sick for the land.

The Maoris who had voyaged to New Zealand found themselves in a temperate climate where the hard necessities of life made them a tougher, fiercer people. The yam would not grow at all and the sweet potato only in the north. There was no edible quadruped in New Zealand and a shortage of all meat after the invaders had killed off the *moa*, the gigantic flightless birds that once abounded there. The lack of other proteins led the Maoris to eat men for food. It made them the most ferocious enemies that the European adventurers have ever encountered.

In spite of their sexual morals which to Puritan sensibilities seemed so degraded, and the cannibalism which was so abhorrent, the Polynesians were shrewd and lively enough to adopt the culture of the invading Europeans. Of all 'coloured' races they have inspired least colour-prejudice and have interbred freely with the whites inside and outside wedlock. Their sea-going propensities led them to enlist gladly as sailors in the ships of the early navigators, and to renew their long-lost contacts with the world. Islanders appeared in London, kept their wits about them, and bought muskets with which to advance their honour in island feuds. When the missionaries came, the islanders welcomed them and made use of them. In the principal groups the people were rapidly converted to Christianity. In short, it took the Polynesians no more than two or three generations to advance a thousand years in culture, but not without misfortunes and mal-adjustments to which I shall refer later.

3. 'BOTANY BAY', 1788–1820

YOUNG Mr Pitt's cabinet in the period of reconstruction after the American War was filled with mediocrities, among them the Secretary of State, Lord Sydney, known to posterity for having given his name to the metropolis of the south Pacific. It was his task to cope with two urgent problems, the settlement of the American loyalists and the provision of a new land of exile for convicted felons since they could no longer be shipped to Virginia by contract. Several plans of colonisation were proposed both for the honoured and the dishonoured groups of emigrants, together or separately. Sir Joseph Banks suggested New South Wales for the felons and, after debate, the House of Commons resolved that 'the plan of establishing a colony of young convicts in some distant part of the globe...where the climate is healthy and the means of support attainable, is equally agreeable to the dictates of humanity and sound policy, and might prove in the result advantageous both to navigation and commerce'.

Plate 7

CAPTAIN JAMES COOK (1728–79)

ted in 1776 by N. Dance, at Greenwich. Another painting in the National Portrait
ry is strikingly different but this was reputed a good likeness by Cook's friends.
. 201.

Plate 8

CAPTAIN ARTHUR PHILLIP (1738–1814)

Founder of Sydney and New South Wales.
By F. Wheatley. *See p. 209.*

That indefatigable map-maker, Cook, had sprinkled the chart of the Pacific with names of capes, islands and mountains generally selected out of compliment to his patrons in the Navy, but occasionally with a touch of whimsicality. In his voyage along the coast of New South Wales he had noted but not entered an opening in the cliffs which he named Port Jackson, after an admiralty official. He had gone ashore in a marshy cove at a few miles' distance, near the site where is now the Great airport of Mascot. Cook's holograph journal, now at Canberra, shows that he first called this landing-place Stingray Harbour, then altered the name to Botanist and then again, by a happy transition, to Botany Bay on account of the variety of unknown plants collected by Sir Joseph Banks. The odd name caught the popular fancy and was to be long used as a general nickname for the convict settlements though, in fact, the site was not occupied by the convicts. 'Botany Bay', and all that it implied, were as well known as Jack Ketch and Tyburn Tree to two whole generations of the criminal classes and those who studied their ways.

Time passed in deliberations, and comparisons with sites in other continents, until the housing of convicts had become a scandal. As there were then no detention prisons they were held, in shocking discomfort, in hulks of ships moored in English harbours. Philanthropists like John Howard and projectors like Jeremy Bentham protested both against their present condition and against the plan to exile them among the savages, but sheer necessity prevailed and Botany Bay was selected. Parliament passed an enabling act and, in 1786, a naval officer, Captain Arthur Phillip, was appointed Governor of New South Wales. On 18 January 1788 he arrived at Botany Bay with a fleet of ten ships containing 529 male convicts, 188 females and a guard of 200 marines. Without hesitation he rejected the chosen site, where there was no anchorage and entered the gap which Cook had named Port Jackson. Phillip instantly recognised the harbour with its hundreds of miles of winding shore and deep sheltered waters as 'the finest in the world, in which a thousand sail of the line may rest in perfect security'. Posterity has justified his choice to which the pride of the free people of New South Wales in their incomparable harbour is an everlasting tribute. On 26 January the flag was broken; the marines fired a *feu-de-joie*, and healths were drunk to the royal family and the success of

the new colony; tents were pitched, to be replaced soon by huts
built of local stone near the head of the harbour, beside a bay of
deep water which Phillip named Sydney Cove.

Early days at Sydney were quite unlike the beginnings of any
other British colony. From the first day there was rule and
method and strong administration, by a governor who exercised
powers little short of dictatorship. He could draw on the Treasury
for money with which to import food, and could use the forced
labour of the convicts for making wharves and roads and public
buildings. The colony was a town rather than a plantation. It
cost the Treasury at first about £95,000 a year, which was
thought so excessive that proposals were made in Parliament to
put an end to the experiment. 'We have lost New England',
wrote one political economist, 'but New Wales has started up.
How many millions it may cost may be the subject of the calcula-
tions of succeeding financiers a century hence, unless by the
exertions of some able statesman that source of future waste
and extravagance is prevented.'[1] Phillip, however, saw clearly
from the beginning that he was laying the foundation of something greater than a convict prison. He insisted on the importance of making a start at agriculture and repeatedly urged the
Government to send out free settlers. He is described as a thin,
meagre little man; 'intelligent, active, persevering; with firmness to make his authority respected and mildness to render it
pleasing'. 'I have no doubt', he said, 'but that the country will
hereafter prove a most valuable acquisition to Great Britain.…
It will require patience and perseverance.' 'Settlers appear to be
absolutely necessary.' When ill-health obliged him to retire in
1792, a number of time-expired soldiers and sailors had begun to
cultivate small-holdings about Sydney, with the help of convict
servants 'assigned' to them by the Governor. At least one convict had already been set free, with a grant of thirty acres as a
reward for good behaviour.

The political history of New South Wales for the next thirty
years is a somewhat dismal tale of petty tyranny and its consequences. A succession of retired officers of the Army and Navy
held the appointment of Governor, for which they were selected
on account of their supposed capacity for disciplining a population of felons. The Governor had no power of pardon, but had

[1] Sir J. Sinclair, *History of the Public Revenue.*

absolute discretion in 'assigning' convict servants to the few free colonists, and absolute control over undeveloped lands; he could thus make any settler at will a rich man or a pauper. There was no representative element in the government, no trial by jury. The discipline imposed upon the convicts was ferocious. Floggings were frequent, hangings 300 times as numerous in proportion to the population as in England; but worst of all was the threat to transport convicts who misbehaved to the punishment camps formed in Van Diemen's Land (1804) and Norfolk Island (1825). The tales of happenings there recalls Buchenwald and Dachau, yet Governors King, Hunter, Bligh, Macquarie and Brisbane were conscientious reasonable men and their powers, except in respect of the punishment camps, were not misused.

The Governors were quite dependent upon the support of the military garrison, a sort of Pretorian Guard, called the New South Wales Corps. The officers of this regiment formed a 'racket', to buy up the entire cargoes of incoming ships and to maintain high prices for their own profit. The liquor trade, both in imported and locally distilled spirits, came entirely into their hands. Thus the government of New South Wales, for some years after the departure of Phillip, was marked by cruelty to the convicts, corruption organised by the warders and arbitrary interventions by well-meaning though despotic Governors. The picture would be black if civil government were the chief concern of colonial history, but the background of the story of New South Wales is of another colour.

All the Governors from Phillip onwards complained bitterly of the poor human material that formed a large part of the population. London pickpockets lacked the physique, the country training and the industrious habits needed for pioneering though some of them, when their time was out, lived well by their wits at urban occupations in Sydney town. There were also country lads in plenty, many of them victims of the iniquitous English game-laws, in exile at Botany Bay, where they often made good and lived to raise respectable families. It has been estimated that four-fifths of the convicts were transported for crimes which would now 'be dealt with by the summary jurisdiction of a police court or possibly pardoned under a First Offenders' Act'. These flattering assumptions must not be carried too far; it was

well said of the convicts (though not, as is often alleged, by
Barrington, the *doyen* of pickpockets) that:

> From distant climes, o'er widespread seas we come,
> (Though not with much *éclat* or beat of drum);
> True patriots all; for be it understood,
> We left our country for our country's good...
> And none will doubt but that our emigration
> Has proved most useful to the English nation.[1]

During the wars of the French Revolution political prisoners
in large numbers swelled the population of Sydney, quite altering
its character. Many ardent spirits, whose views were too advanced
for Pitt's anti-Jacobins, found themselves interned at 'Botany
Bay', among them men of education and virtue, such as the
Scottish political 'martyrs' who were sentenced to transportation
by Lord Justice Clerk Braxfield, and in later times the Dorset
farm labourers known to Trade Union history as the Tolpuddle
Martyrs. There were also several hundred Irish rebels who
attempted a mutiny in 1800.

Convicts were first worked in gangs on roads or public buildings, then, as their character and abilities became known, assigned
to free settlers as labourers, house-servants or even in positions
of trust as clerks or secretaries. Then released on ticket-of-leave
they were allowed to take up land, and finally became free settlers,
'emancipists'. It is not surprising that social barriers remained.
The officers of the New South Wales Corps, the best society of
Sydney, mixed only with those who had come to the colony as
free men, and frowned on the Governor if he showed favour to
an 'emancipist', of whatever degree of personal worth. Among
the first free emigrants were the sailors, since Sydney assumed at
once its destined place as the centre of south Pacific trade. The
ocean swarmed with sperm-whales which, before the end of the
eighteenth century, attracted British and American whaling-ships
in plenty. By an odd chance the colony lay within the area over
which the East India Company claimed trading rights and
therefore was outside the restrictions imposed by the British
Navigation Acts. The Company assumed no sort of control,
leaving Sydney open to the navigation of the world, a great boon
to the shipping interest of the United States. As wealth and

[1] The origin of this celebrated satire has been much disputed. It was probably
written and first published in London.

commerce grew, the influence of the New South Wales Corps waxed fat with it, all the more when the officers found a natural leader in Captain John Macarthur, the son of a Highland chief who had fought at Culloden. In this very corrupt society, Macarthur retained his personal integrity and, by honest if grasping means, became the richest man in the colony. He was 'keen as a razor and rapacious as a shark'.

In an age when economists were obsessed with the necessity of increasing the acreage of wheat and tended to neglect other forms of productive wealth, Macarthur demonstrated that the future of New South Wales was to be pastoral rather than agricultural. In 1794 he was breeding sheep, in 1797 he imported fine-wooled merinos from South Africa, and in 1806 a ram and five ewes from King George's own model farm at Kew. So rich and progressive a settler, an officer and a gentleman with friends in high places at home, could afford to defy the Governor and did so. Honest Governor Hunter, who did his best to break the monopoly in rum held by the officers of the corps, was himself recalled as a result of their intrigues in London.

The contest between the masterful Macarthur and the administration reached its climax in 1806–8 when the redoubtable Bligh of the *Bounty* was Governor. William Bligh had been with Cook at Hawaii in 1778 and had been given the command of another scientific expedition. He was to collect specimens of the bread-fruit plant in Tahiti and transfer them to the West Indies, where it was hoped that bread-fruit would make cheap food for slaves. The lotus-eating life of Tahiti was too seductive for Bligh's crew who mutinied, setting him adrift with a few companions in an open boat. Bligh's boat-voyage of 1500 miles to Timor is a classic tale of sea-adventure. The mutineers of the *Bounty* after various adventures arrived at Pitcairn Island, one of the remotest islands of eastern Polynesia, with some Tahitian women. Thus was founded in 1789, a few months after the landing at Botany Bay, the second British colony in the Pacific. The mutineers had fled far from the shipping lanes and remained forgotten until 1813, when a warship stumbled across their hiding-place. One of the mutineers was still alive, the ancestor of a numerous progeny which inhabits Pitcairn Island to-day.

Bligh returned to a distinguished career in the Navy, but had the misfortune to be involved in a second outbreak, the Mutiny at the Nore in 1797. This, too, he survived, to fight gallantly at Camperdown and Copenhagen where he was singled out by Nelson for special praise. In 1806 he arrived at Sydney, still a martinet with a truculent manner, and set himself to destroy the corrupt influence of the New South Wales Corps. 'The law, sir! My will is the law, and woe unto the man who dares to disobey it.' 'Damn the Secretary of State! He commands at home. I command here.'

Bligh correctly appreciated that using rum as currency was the vicious principle by which the power of the Corps was upheld. His attempts to suppress the trade in rum led to open hostility and at last to rebellion by the officers. For the third time in his life Bligh found himself a prisoner in the hands of mutineers. Macarthur's influence was so great that he lived down even the offence of deposing and imprisoning the Governor. Two years passed (1808–10), during which Bligh escaped and endeavoured to regain his authority, until Downing Street solved the problem, somewhat meekly, by sending out a new Governor, Macquarie with a new regiment of soldiers. To save Bligh's face he was reinstated as Governor for one day. The New South Wales Corps ended its disgraceful history by returning to England where it was reorganised as the 102nd regiment of the line. Governor Macquarie had many of the same troubles to contend with as his predecessors, but not thereafter a corrupt and mutinous garrison.

While the Governors were struggling with Macarthur's growing influence, there was much to be done away from Sydney town. The first settlement was a natural gaol, bounded by the sea and the rugged chain of the Blue Mountains which no colonist passed for twenty years. The shape of the country was quite unknown. Beyond the Blue Mountains there might be another Mississippi valley, or an arm of the sea dividing New South Wales as an island from the land far in the west known as New Holland. Two young naval officers, William Bass and Matthew Flinders, explored the southern coasts in a tiny private yacht. In 1798 they sailed through Bass's Strait proving that Van Diemen's Land (or Tasmania) was an island separated from New South Wales. Later Flinders, in a sloop provided by the Admiralty, made a survey of the whole south coast of the continent as far as Cape Leeuwin (1801–2), thus proving New

Holland and New South Wales to be parts of a single island continent, to which he gave the name of Australia. His expeditions were intended largely to forestall the French who were supposed to have designs in the South Seas.

At every stage in the exploration of the Pacific, the French and the English ran neck and neck. Wallis at Tahiti, Cook off the New Zealand coast, Phillip at Port Jackson, and Flinders on each of his voyages anticipated a rival French expedition by a few days or months. Back in the polite eighteenth century, the age of reason, national rivalries did not extend into the republic of science. When Cook set out on his last voyage, during the American War, the belligerent powers had issued instructions to their colonies to treat Cook as a neutral, and to afford him every help in a task which was for the interest of humanity; but times were changing. The ideological wars arising out of the French Revolution were precursors of the hideous total war of our time. 'The age of chivalry was gone.' Thus Flinders found the attitude of the French at each meeting less friendly. During the Peace of Amiens, Napoleon stretched out tentacles into every continent and every sea, preparing designs even against Botany Bay and, when the war was resumed, the republic of science took up arms. Flinders put in at the French island of Mauritius in 1804, and was arrested as a spy. Napoleon, to do him justice, intervened by ordering his release, but the French Governor found excuses for detaining Flinders until, in 1810, Mauritius was captured and annexed by a British fleet.

While Bass and Flinders explored the Australian coast, other and less successful pioneers tried to force their way inland. The first great discovery, in 1797, was a coalfield at a place on the Hunter River to which the name of Newcastle was given. It was not till 1812 that Gregory Blaxland found a way across the Blue Mountains. When no path could be found through the steep gullies he made his way over the tops by keeping to the rugged ridges, through sparse woods of eucalypt, into the grassy plains beyond. Governor Macquarie built a road across the ranges, but took care to restrict access to the new territories. The gaol wall had been broken down and he must see that his prisoners should not escape. This he might achieve, but not prevent the march of a nation. The free settlers were on the move as the Americans had moved over the Blue Ridge into the Ohio valley.

MacArthur's merinos were multiplying and eating up the land. Australia was no longer synonymous with Botany Bay, but was becoming a pastoral colony in which wool, not convict labour, would be the source of wealth.

At last Downing Street became aware of the change and sent J. T. Bigge as Royal Commissioner to enquire into the state of New South Wales. He reported that between 1788 and 1820, 22,000 men and 3600 women had been transported to Australia as convicts. The population, in 1820, was 30,000, of whom 2000 had come as free settlers and 1700 had been born in the colony. 12,000 were still serving their sentences while the remainder were 'emancipists' in various stages of release. About one-fifth of the population were at the subordinate settlement in Van Diemen's Land. There were in the districts round Sydney 4000 horses, 68,000 cattle, and 110,000 sheep, but the colony was not yet self-supporting in other foodstuffs. Bigge's Commission was a first step towards the Colonial Reform movement which will be discussed in a later chapter.

4. THE SLAVE TRADE AND THE AFRICA COMPANIES

THE early adventurers in Africa had been gold-seekers; until late in the seventeenth century slave-trading was a side-line. Each of the voyaging nations by that time had established its fortified posts in the Gulf of Guinea, some of them strong stone castles with bastions, turrets and crenellated walls in the best style of Renaissance military architecture. Christiansborg, Kormantin, Cape Coast Castle, Elmina, built respectively by the Danes, the British, the Dutch, the Portuguese stand in majestic decay along the strand of the Gold Coast, like the ruined castles that crown the headlands of North Wales. As in other parts of the world so in West Africa, the original primacy of the Portuguese was overthrown by the Dutch, whose power was again overshadowed by the French and British in the eighteenth-century wars. A changing pattern of factories along the coast has followed the fortunes of war in Europe, the rise and fall of chartered companies, and the influence of individual traders with the native kings. Never has there been a systematic allotment of

pheres of influence between the trading nations. The map is
till a chequer-board marked out in colonial areas by the chance of
history, without reference to geographical or ethnological factors.

The earliest of the British Africa companies was that chartered
by Queen Elizabeth in 1588 for 'trade to Senega and Gambra'.
t lapsed and, thirty years later, King James issued a charter to
certain 'Adventurers of London to Gynney and Bynney'. This
company was fortunate in producing a man of parts, Richard
Jobson, who went on their third voyage to the Gambia River in
1620 as supercargo. Refusing to trade in slaves he penetrated
far up the river in search of a fabulous mountain of gold. Though
he never found it he never lost faith, returning to publish a book
of travel, *The Golden Trade* (1623) giving an accurate account of
the country and promising rich rewards to merchants who would
trade to the Gambia. A persistent enthusiast, he continued to
spread stories of the golden mountain. Among those he inspired
was Prince Rupert who visited the coast in 1652 on his naval
campaign and took a Roundhead ship in the Gambia river.
After the Restoration Rupert helped to form a new company,
the Royal Adventurers (1660), 'for discovering the golden
mines'. The first expedition was led by Robert Holmes, the
swashbuckling admiral of Pepys's Diary, who seized a fort from
some Courlander merchants, on an island in the estuary, naming
t Fort James (1661). After three years of negotiation Fort James
was ceded by the Duke of Courland to King Charles II and thus
may be called the oldest British colony in Africa. It was sublet to
a group of traders known as the Gambia Adventurers, who lost
their money. Farther up the coast, de Ruyter with a Dutch fleet
was esconced at Goree, near Cape Verde, and came to blows with
the British in 1664. Thus English and Dutch rivalry in the
Gambia was the immediate cause of the Second Dutch War for
which some people blamed Robert Holmes. The French
succeeded the Dutch at Goree in 1678 and in the next generation
war was intermittent between the French at Goree and the
English at Fort James.

Meanwhile another company had been formed by Sir Nicholas
Crisp (his first endeavours as far back as 1631) to trade with the
Gulf of Guinea. His people had formed trading posts at Sierra
Leone and Kormantin, which, with Fort James at Gambia,
long remained the centres of British interest. Crisp also lost his

investment and sold out, in 1657, to the East India Company
These interests were taken up by the Royal Adventurers who
occupied and rebuilt an old abandoned fort near Kormantin in
1662. Its name was Cabo Corso which the English corrupted a
Cape Coast Castle. It resisted a siege by de Ruyter himself in
1665 and was recognised as British by the Treaty of Breda
(1667) at the end of the Second Dutch War. The British settled a
Accrà in 1676.

The Royal Adventurers, bankrupt like many such companies
surrendered their charter in 1672 to the Royal African Company
of England, which was allowed a monopoly, so far as the King
of England could grant it, of the slave trade. This was the
African Company which survived for seventy years, maintaining
forts and striving to maintain its monopoly in seas where every
advantage lay with the free-trader. Except for the Senegal and
Gambia estuaries, which faced the broad Atlantic and were
strategic bases in the naval wars, the West African coast had
neither ports nor cities. Trade was done in little ships which
put in at random wherever parcels of gold-dust, ivory, palm-
kernels, or slaves could be got by hard bargaining with triba
chiefs. There were no great markets, no openings for big business
and every monopolising company, French, Dutch or British
failed to show a profit.

Though the Royal African had turned its attention to slave-
trading, the coast still provided what store of gold bullion the
English government could get. Some sovereigns, valued at
twenty silver shillings, had occasionally been minted since
Henry VII's time. With the gold brought by the Royal African,
a new gold coinage was struck in 1663 bearing an elephant, the
badge of the Company. These coins soon won the familiar name
of 'guineas' and tended to increase in value since gold was scarce
in the seventeenth century and silver plentiful. When Isaac
Newton was Master of the Mint he observed that in popular
esteem gold was taking the place of silver as the standard of
value, at an enhanced price. Through his efforts a recoinage was
effected in 1717 and the guinea fixed at twenty-one shillings, an
arrangement which had the effect of making gold a legal tender.

The trade in a commodity so easily alienated as gold-dust,
together with the irregularities of interloping trade, made West
Africa a favourite haunt of the pirates when the West Indies

became too warm to hold them. Sierra Leone, then no-man's-land, was a pirates' anchorage. There harboured Edward Davis in his ship significantly named *Bachelor's Delight*, and there, too, his fellow-Welshman Howel Davis who captured Fort James by a stratagem. The greatest of all pirates was the martinet Bartholomew Roberts who kept naval discipline and, by good management, plundered 400 ships in four years (1719–22) along the Guinea Coast. When he was killed and his ship, the *Royal Fortune*, taken after a formal sea-battle with H.M.S. *Swallow* she was found to contain forty guns, 157 men and £4000 in gold-dust. Fifty-two of these pirates were tried and hanged at Cape Coast Castle.

The slave trade with America was organised as a commercial routine by the Royal African Company in 1672. Beginning with a modest export of 5000 slaves a year they reached a much higher figure, though the statistics are unreliable. From 1698 to 1713 the interlopers succeeded in overreaching the Company, by obtaining an Act of Parliament which took away the monopoly but saddled the Company with the cost of maintaining the forts, from the receipts of a 10 per cent duty on imports. This proved so insufficient that the Company found relief in the Asiento Treaty (see page 66) by which, from 1713 to 1750, the African Company produced the slaves and the South Sea Company shipped them to America. That system in its turn gave way again to free trade in slaves through the last and most prosperous age of the slave trade, from 1750 to 1807. By an Act of 1750 the trade was thrown open to the 'Company of Merchants', a free association which all might join, while a grant-in-aid of £10,000 a year was allotted to the African Company which survived solely to maintain the West African forts.

Buying and selling strong young negroes of both sexes was a matter of hard bargaining in a well-organised market. It depended first on the customary codes of the African kingdoms which defined the status of slavery. Normally the slaves were prisoners of war, though the European buyer rarely studied their origins. They were produced in droves by recognised middlemen at the factories and were sold by auction after a careful physical examination. Three pounds a head was a fair purchase price, in the eighteenth century, for slaves who might fetch thirteen or fourteen pounds in Charleston or Jamaica, if they

survived the 'Middle Passage'. Warlike African kings made a
good revenue by raiding more primitive tribes for captives who
could be sold profitably on the Coast. Never has there been a
time in Africa when the more advanced peoples of the coast
have not ravaged the interior for this sort of merchandise; the
negro slave trade is depicted on the frescoed walls of temples in
ancient Egypt; it is not yet extinct on the shores of the Red Sea.
Without doubt the brisk demand from America stimulated the
supply and brought into the business the fearless, rapacious
Moslem dealers from the north who searched all Africa for
heathen 'Kaffirs', fetching them to market in caravans that
travelled hundreds of miles, through the deserts of the interior
uplands, and the fever-stricken forests of the coastal belt. The
young and strong were brought to market with no little care, for
they were worth money; the infants, the old, and the infirm got no
mercy. When the lordly Saracen emirs of the Niger, and the
negro rulers of the ancient kingdoms of Dahomey and Benin and
Ashanti, as well as the middlemen on the Coast, had all to get a
fair commission on the deal, it was no easy task to buy slaves at
an economic price. The trade brought good business to English
merchants. In return for exporting men the West Africans
bought Brammagem goods, iron pots and kettles, copper and
tin, beads and linen and 'manillas'. There was even a brisk demand
for English broadcloth.

Liverpool and Bristol grew rich on the slave trade. The
Lord Mayor of Bristol said in 1739 that it was 'the great support
of our people'. Liverpool boasted of being 'the principal slaving
port not only in England, but in Europe'. But the good people
of these cities never set eyes on the results of their handiwork.
They built ships designed to carry the maximum load of slaves in
the minimum deck-space, fitted them out for the 'Coast' but
never saw them again until they returned empty from America to
refit. The largest ships each carried about 700 slaves, who were
occasionally let out in batches on the main deck for air and
exercise, since it would not be profitable to let them die, but
otherwise were shackled between decks with space to lie at full
length but not to stand upright. 'The French, Portuguese and
English slave ships', said a Dutch commercial rival, 'are always
foul and stinking.' It was the general saying at sea that you could
recognise a slaver by the smell if you got to leeward of her. In

all long voyages 200 years ago, sickness and mortality were to be expected. The death-rate on the 'Middle Passage' from Africa to America, explains the width of the margin between the buying and the selling price of slaves.

It is not for those who have lived in the 1930's and 1940's to upbraid other generations for callous indifference to human suffering. All men have a strongly developed faculty for ignoring the troubles of unknown remote nations when those troubles put money into their own pockets. The slave trade was regarded in Great Britain for 150 years as the foundation of imperial prosperity. 'The most approved judges...have ever been of opinion that our West India and Africa trades are the most nationally beneficial of any we carry on....The Trade of Africa is the branch which renders our American Colonies and Plantations so advantageous to Great Britain, that traffic affording our planters a constant supply of negro servants for the culture of their lands....The Negro-Trade therefore, and the natural consequences resulting from it, may be justly esteemed an inexhaustible Fund of Wealth and Naval Power to this Nation.' So wrote an anonymous essayist in 1749, echoing the general opinion of his contemporaries. In the next generation contrary voices began to be heard until, at the end of the century, the outcries of the philanthropists against the horrors of the slave trade drowned the arguments of the merchants in favour of its continuance.

Humanitarianism was becoming the fashionable cult. The poetic figment of the 'noble savage' had appeared in popular literature, a noteworthy example being Robinson Crusoe's Man Friday (1719). Religious leaders disapproved of slavery and denounced the slave trade. The Quakers petitioned Parliament against it; Wesley preached against it; even that stout Tory, Dr Johnson, startled an Oxford Common Room by drinking a toast to 'the next insurrection of negroes in the West Indies'. These academic objections, however, had little effect upon the moneyed men of the West Indian Interest. Political agitation could only be formed upon some evidence which would stir the political conscience of the nation. It came in the realisation that there were 14,000 negro slaves actually in England, brought there by West Indian 'nabobs', and that the common law was vague about their status. Could slavery exist in this free country?

Long ago when Domesday Book was compiled, there had been considerable numbers of slaves, not to mention that majority of the population held in the semi-servile status of *villeinage*. This feudal slavery had never been abolished by any general law of emancipation, but had imperceptibly dwindled and disappeared. A lingering remnant of villeins had been released from bondage by proclamation of Queen Elizabeth quoting as an authority the old tag of the Stoics 'that all men are by nature born free'; but even in the eighteenth century some vestiges of villeinage survived, especially in Scotland. There seemed to be no rule of law precluding the existence of negro slavery in Georgian England.

The first of the abolitionists was Granville Sharp (1735–1813), a civil servant who undertook the cause of the slaves in England. He made it his business to defend runaway slaves whose masters claimed ownership in the courts. Five such cases were decided on minor points of law before Sharp could oblige the courts to give a decision on the major issue: was slavery recognised by the laws of England? A negro named James Somersett had been brought to England by his master, cast adrift in the streets when ill and useless, and kidnapped back into slavery when his master found that he could be of use again. Sharp applied for Somersett's release on a writ of *habeas corpus*. The case came before Lord Chief Justice Mansfield who tried hard to get it settled out of court, as he was most averse to interfering with property rights, the first consideration of law and politics in that age. But equity prevailed with him to set free James Somersett and 14,000 other slaves, thus destroying property worth half a million pounds, with the decision (1772) that 'the state of slavery was so odious that nothing can be suffered to support it but positive law'. At once the difficulty appeared that the wrong done by slavery is not undone by the act of emancipation. Some thousands of derelict negroes were now thrown upon the world with no means of livelihood, so that Sharp found himself obliged to organise further relief for them. The agitation against slavery now began to gather force, but some years passed before it crystallised into political activity.

In 1785 a young man named Thomas Clarkson (1760–1846), when riding down from Cambridge to London, halted to rest his horse on a green hillside near Ware. As he sat, he reflected on the

University prize he had just won for a Latin essay on *Slavery*,[1] and resolved to devote his life to uprooting its evils. A monument now marks the spot where the resolution was made which he so nobly fulfilled. He made himself known to Granville Sharp and other abolitionists and, in 1787 called, with a copy of his essay, upon William Wilberforce (1759–1833), a Yorkshire Member of Parliament who was thought to be a likely recruit for the cause. This little group of enthusiasts, who were to do battle with the powerful West India Interest, formed part of a large circle which came to be known derisively as the 'Clapham Sect' or the 'Saints'. Society was at that time swept by a wave of religious revival which in the course of a generation permeated and altered the life of the whole nation. Its tendency was evangelical, towards a simple personal devotion and an absolute reliance on the Bible; its aim was to spread religious education at home and abroad. National education, so that every child could read the Bible, and foreign missions, were the main external activities of the Evangelicals; the abolition of slavery, for the spiritual rather than the physical benefit of the slaves, was a by-product. Clarkson, Sharp and Wilberforce met regularly, with other Evangelicals such as Zachary Macaulay, Hannah More, and the converted slave-trader John Newton, at Clapham where one of their number had a villa. Much that concerned the Empire during the next forty years emerged from their discussions.

Clarkson inspired Wilberforce to take up the cudgels in the House against the slave trade, and Wilberforce approached his friend Pitt. Although the first resolution (1788), that the House should take the slave trade into consideration, was moved by Pitt and supported by Burke and Fox, this was but the beginning of the task. The method of the Abolition Committee has become the classic means whereby great progressive movements in England achieve their ends. Clarkson toured the country collecting information from ships' captains at Bristol and Liverpool, interviewing visitors from the colonies, and thus building up a body of evidence on which to base his propaganda. He organised corresponding branches of the Abolition Committee, addressed meetings, published statistical reports, circulated popular appeals including copies of a poem by Cowper and a cameo by Wedg-

[1] *Anne liceat invitos in servitutem dare.*

wood with the motto, 'Am I not a Man and a Brother?' His correspondents collected signatures for petitions which Wilberforce presented to the House of Commons. Clarkson's outside agitation was used by Wilberforce to sway opinion inside the little world of the governing class. Tory members marked the growing influence of the Evangelicals among their constituents; Whig members marked the rising voice of democracy, a slightly discordant note in the abolitionist chorus.

Though Pitt never wavered in his personal hostility to the slave trade and invariably supported Wilberforce with his own voice and vote, he was unable to make abolition a Government measure. It was to him but one necessary reform which must take its turn among his efforts for the national revival and one which, pressed too hastily, would split his party and frustrate his larger policy. If one large section of his supporters were Evangelicals, another constituted the West India Interest. It was the general opinion in the City among shipping and commercial men that abolition would spell ruin to trade. They therefore supported the West Indians, as did the Navy. Rodney defended the trade in the House of Lords on grounds of strategy. But among these cautious men there were many who approved of a regulation of the conditions under which the trade was carried out, leading to a 'gradual' abolition at some future date. From 1791 onwards several bills were enacted for preventing the overcrowding of slave-ships and for encouraging with bounties the humane treatment of slaves at sea. Against these concessions there were reactionaries of the right wing who foresaw the direst consequences. The West Indian Assemblies, that of Jamaica most truculently, resisted every form of change, being convinced that concessions to the negroes would lead not only to commercial ruin but to mutiny and massacre in the colonies. 'How can we hesitate a moment', asked Pitt in the House, 'to abolish this commerce in human flesh which has so long disgraced our country and which our example will contribute to abolish in every corner of the globe?' Yet the members hesitated: 'The leaders, it is true, are for abolition', said a back-bencher. 'But the minor orators, the dwarfs, the pygmies will, I trust, this day carry the question against them. The property of the West Indians is at stake; and though men may be generous with their own property, they should not be so with the property of others.'

All that Pitt could get was a resolution of the House of Commons carried by 193 votes to 125 that 'the Slave Trade ought to be gradually abolished' (1793).

Meanwhile Clarkson had made a tactical error. On the outbreak of the French Revolution, in that enthusiastic dawn when it was 'bliss to be alive', he had visited Paris and established correspondence with committees of advanced democrats. Liberty, Equality and Fraternity made an explosive mixture which the Tories, alarmed by Burke's eloquence, determined to exclude from the British Empire. They were not surprised at the reports from San Domingo where the mulattos, intoxicated with their new-found liberty, had massacred 2000 Frenchmen, and at sympathetic riots in neighbouring British colonies. They succeeded in holding off further action by the abolitionists 'until the end of the war'. Nevertheless, year by year, Wilberforce kept the cause alive by rising in his place in the House to propose immediate abolition. During those years, since the British Navy blockaded French and, for part of the time, Spanish commerce, the British slave trade flourished as never before.

A practical measure undertaken by the abolitionists during these years of struggle was the settlement of emancipated slaves at Sierra Leone, which has the best natural harbour in West Africa. In 1787 Granville Sharp sent out a party of 340 negroes from London under Dr Smeathman, with some white vagabonds. The first colony aroused the hostility of a local chief who dispersed the settlers and burnt their camp. Nothing daunted, the abolitionists began again on a larger scale, this time obtaining a charter from the Crown to form a colonising company, on the old pattern, with Sharp as president (1791). The settlers were further reinforced by 1200 negro loyalists who had fled to Nova Scotia from the Thirteen Colonies. Thomas Peters, a Nova Scotian, was the first headman of Freetown. But the settlement was again destroyed (1794), this time as an act of war by a French Jacobin expedition. The Governor, Zachary Macaulay, one of the Clapham 'Saints', by firm administration set the colony on its feet after this setback until, four years later, Freetown was a little town with 300 houses, 1200 inhabitants and a growing trade with the interior. Yet it required a grant-in-aid that grew year by year. By 1804 the Sierra Leone Company appealed to the Crown for £25,000, having exhausted all its funds. Since, clearly the settlement was a financial failure, the charter was with-drawn and Sierra Leone was taken over by the Colonial Office in January 1808.

In addition to the fever and the plagues of insects which per-vaded all settlements along the Coast, the founders of Sierra Leone encountered difficulties similar to those which, in the same years, were hampering the founders of New South Wales. The negro colonists were quite unfitted for pioneering. Their lives had been spent as slaves in white men's countries, many of them in temperate climes, so that they were just as much strangers in Sierra Leone as were the white officials. They had no knowledge of African agriculture and, like all freed slaves, a great dislike for unnecessary exertion. Their contempt for the uncivilised 'bush-niggers' was only equalled by their inferiority at all the arts of living in tropical Africa. It is a great tribute to the efforts of Macaulay and his colleagues that anything was made of Sierra Leone. During the long years when the Navy was engaged in suppressing the contraband slave trade, cargo after cargo of negroes from all parts of Africa, at all stages of culture and speak-ing a hundred different languages, were liberated at Freetown.

A sudden turn in English party politics produced the opportunity for abolishing the slave trade. Pitt died in January 1806, after governing by means of a coalition of the right and centre. His right wing had prevented him from giving unqualified support to Wilberforce. The succeeding administration which lasted for a few months only, until the death of Fox its leader, was a govern-ment of the centre and left. Several Radical politicians, among them Henry Brougham, now spoke from the Government benches in support of abolition. Unlike Pitt who had subordi-nated all other questions to the necessities of the French War, Fox regarded the slave trade as a vital problem looming larger even than the war with Napoleon, in which he was a belated and reluctant participant. The two groups of abolitionists, the Radicals who desired political freedom for the negro and the Evangelicals who desired his moral progress, were united, while other circumstances at that moment divided the slave-owners. The conquest of several Dutch and French slave-colonies had upset the market for slave-grown crops. It seemed clear that the time had come for a reorganisation of the whole 'interest', since the moderates were ready for a compromise. When Fox moved a resolution for immediate abolition the defenders of slavery spoke with an uncertain voice and lost the vote in both Houses. The Act prohibiting the 'dealing and trading' in slaves, in British ships, under penalty of fine and confiscation, became law on 25 March 1807. Fox died while the Bill was before Parliament.

Much remained to be done before the trade across the Atlantic could be ended. French, American and Spanish slavers still abounded and seized the trade which the English had abandoned. It therefore became a cardinal principle of British diplomacy in every negotiation to press for international action. The Continental powers found some difficulty in appreciating this obsession of English diplomats.

The long struggle of Great Britain to abolish the international slave trade involved her in difficulties with all the slave-owning powers. At the Congress of Vienna the eight great powers agreed upon a declaration, dictated by the quixotic British to bring the slave trade to an end 'by all the means at their disposal'. The British alone took steps to carry out this undertaking. From 1807 onwards, even in the crisis of the French War about one-sixth of the effective strength of the Navy was diverted to the 'Preventive Squadron' on the African Coast. On that dangerous and unhealthy duty, ships' companies lost 5 per cent by deaths in every cruise, but had the consolation of receiving prize-money at the rate of £5 for every slave they released. The squadron cost the British taxpayer £750,000 annually. Though they rescued over 3000 slaves a year it was soon discovered that the Squadron alone would never solve the problem. The greater the difficulty of transporting slaves to the Spanish and Portuguese colonies, the worse was the treatment of these unfortunates on the Middle Passage. They were stowed tighter in the slave-ships and were ruthlessly thrown overboard if capture by a British cruiser seemed inevitable. Very large numbers still slipped through to the Argentine and Brazil and many were still smuggled into the United States, though Jefferson had forbidden the import of slaves in 1808.

No improvement was possible until the Squadron was given the Right of Search over suspected slave-ships, and this the jealous nations were slow to concede. A mutual arrangement was ineffective since none but the British were making any systematic attempt to hunt the slavers down. Agreements were reached with France in 1831, with Spain in 1835, and with Portugal in 1839. Only after a virtual blockade of the Brazilian ports was that branch of the trade brought under control. Slavers were then obliged to find refuge under the Stars and Stripes, for only that flag resisted the Right of Search. The Abolition of Slavery in the United States itself (1863) marked the end of the Atlantic Slave Trade.

V

WAR, TRADE, AND PHILANTHROPY,
1793–1833

Argument: Adam Smith's *Wealth of Nations* convinced thinking men that the attempt to make the Empire a fiscal union had been unwise. The independence of America, since trade with the former colonies increased, was not felt as a loss. The French Wars, 1793–1815, were not fought to acquire territory. British interest at the Peace Conference was to build up French and Dutch strength with the result that only a few strategic points were added to the British Empire, though all French and Dutch colonies had been occupied. Trade and sea-power were preferred to dominions.

Many frontier disputes in America, embittered by the wanton War of 1812, were settled by negotiation during the next forty years, not without some offence to Canadian loyalists. A renewed interest in whaling, sealing and the fisheries led to the exploration of Arctic Canada. In spite of the Monroe Doctrine British interests predominated in South America, especially in the Argentine. A sore point was the British claim to the Falkland Islands, another whaling base from which penetration into the Antarctic was begun.

Evangelical hostility to the protectionist slave-owners of the West Indies helped the cause of free trade as well as the cause of liberty. The abolition of slavery and compensation of the slave-owners was a triumph of Parliamentary skill and administrative efficiency.

1. WILLIAM PITT AND *THE WEALTH OF NATIONS*

WILLIAM PITT the Younger, Prime Minister from 1783 to 1801 and from 1804 to 1806, has already made several appearances in this history. The struggle over Fox's India Bill was the occasion of his being summoned to form a ministry, but the first fruit of his administration, the India Bill of 1784, though a measure of such importance, was prepared and managed by his colleague, Robert Dundas. The bills authorising the foundation of New South Wales and separating Upper from Lower Canada were under the charge of Lord Sydney. After some hesitation Pitt voted for the impeachment of Warren Hastings as a form of judicial enquiry into abuses, while dissociating himself from the prejudiced violence of Burke. On the question of the slave trade, though he gave his personal support to Wilberforce, he was unable to unite his political followers in favour of abolition, which, accordingly, was not taken as a Government measure. In each of these instances, whether it was a case of providing for plundered loyalists, or oppressed Hindus, or kidnapped negroes, or condemned felons, Pitt's actions were guided by a spirit of philanthropy, not by a policy of empire-building.

He cared more for trade than for plantations. As Chancellor of the Exchequer in Shelburne's administration (1782–3) he had conceived a programme of commercial and financial reforms leading in the direction of free trade, a tendency new and radical at that date though it was to be the commonplace of the nineteenth century. 'Monopoly is always unwise,' said Shelburne, 'but if there is any nation under heaven who ought to be the first to reject monopoly it is the English. Situated as we are between the Old World and the New, and between southern and northern Europe, all that we ought to covet upon earth is free trade and fair equality. With more industry, with more enterprise, with more capital than any trading nation upon earth; it ought to be our constant cry, let every market be open, let us meet our rivals fairly, and we ask no more.'

Such modes of thought were confirmed by the researches of a quiet scholar, Dr Adam Smith of Glasgow and Oxford. During the crisis of the American Revolution, in 1776, he had published a treatise entitled *An Enquiry into the Nature and Causes of the Wealth of Nations*. Like some others of the world's great books it was remarkable not so much for the enunciation of any strikingly original thesis as for the presentation in plain language of principles which had gradually been forcing themselves upon the notice of all enlightened men. He did not bring about a revolution in the science of political economy, he proclaimed the triumph of the new doctrine in terms so clearly defined and supported by such a mass of evidence that his book instantly became a classic. All progressive thought upon the subject for a hundred years was obliged to begin where Adam Smith left off. All who disagreed with him were thrown upon the defensive. 'Sir, we are all your pupils', said Pitt when Adam Smith was presented to

him at a dinner-party. His thesis, that monopoly is always dis-
advantageous, that the free exchange of commodities benefits
both parties, and that the British, although 'a nation of shopkeepers', had grossly mismanaged their business, was built upon
a close analysis of the East India Company's monopoly and of the
effects of the Acts of Trade upon Great Britain and her colonies.

'Nations have been taught,' he wrote, 'that their interest consisted in beggaring all their neighbours. Each nation has been
made to look with an invidious eye upon the prosperity of all the
nations with which it trades, and to consider their gain as its own
loss. Commerce, which ought to be a bond of union and friendship, has become the most fertile source of discord and animosity.
The capricious ambition of Kings and Ministers has not been
more fatal to the repose of Europe than the impertinent jealousy
of merchants and manufacturers.' Thus 'the sneaking arts of
underling tradesmen are erected into political maxims for the
conduct of a great empire'.

'It is the interest of the merchants and manufacturers of every
country to secure to themselves the monopoly of the home
market. Hence the extraordinary duties upon goods imported by
alien merchants, hence the prohibitions upon foreign manufactures, hence the restraints upon importation from those
countries with which the balance of trade is supposed to be dis-
advantageous.'

All forms of monopoly fell under Adam Smith's condemnation
since their effect, in his view, was to restrict the growth of trade
by diverting capital from more profitable markets to some market
selected for an 'impertinent' reason. The restrictions upon
colonial trade raised the price of colonial products and reduced
their volume, thus hampering colonial development; while the
encouragement given to the English merchants to trade by
preference with the colonies diverted them from better markets
nearer home.

'The wealth of a neighbouring nation, though dangerous in
war and politics, is certainly advantageous in trade. As a rich
man is likely to be a better customer to the industrious people in
his neighbourhood than a poor, so likewise is a rich nation.'

'France is the nearest neighbour to Great Britain. France
besides is supposed to contain 23,000,000 of inhabitants. Our

North American colonies were never supposed to contain more than 3,000,000, and France is a richer country than North America. France could afford a market at least eight times more extensive and, on account of the superior frequency of the returns, four and twenty times more advantageous than that which our North American colonies ever afforded. Such is the difference between that trade which the wisdom of both nations has thought proper to discourage, and that which it has favoured the most.'

Since on other grounds he condemned the management of affairs by joint-stock enterprises, the East India Company, a joint-stock company controlling a trading monopoly, was the object of his special disapproval. 'The single advantage which the monopoly procures (a high rate of profit which depresses other industry) to a single order of men is in many different ways hurtful to the general interest of the country.' He shrewdly pointed out that the supposed profits derived by the nation from the East India monopoly were in fact paid to the Directors of the Company out of the pockets of other Englishmen, who were not only deprived of the right to trade with Asia on their own account, but were obliged to buy Asiatic goods at an artificially enhanced price.

The trade with India and America in itself, was 'always and everywhere beneficial; the monopoly of that trade always and necessarily hurtful'. Adam Smith's strictures were concerned with finance and commerce, not politics. He wrote to rid the British people of their illusion that it was the mercantile system that held the Empire together. 'It has been not an empire, but the project of an empire, a project which has cost immense expense without being likely to bring any profit; for the effects of the monopoly of the colonial trade are, to the great body of the people, mere loss.'

'To propose that Great Britain should voluntarily give up all authority over her colonies was to propose such a measure as never was and never will be adopted by any nation in the world.[1] If it was adopted, however, Great Britain would not only be immediately freed from the whole annual expense of the peace establishment of the colonies but might settle with them such a treaty of commerce as would effectually secure to her a free trade,

[1] These words have an ironical ring after 1947. C.E.C.

more advantageous to the great body of the people, though less so to the merchants, than the monopoly which she at present enjoys.'

'By thus parting good friends, the natural affection of the colonies to the mother-country, which, perhaps, our late dissensions have well-nigh extinguished, would quickly revive. It might dispose them to favour us in war as well as in trade, and instead of turbulent and factious subjects, to become our most faithful, affectionate and generous allies.'

It should be remembered that these words were published in 1776, before the breach with America was irreparable. They were then far in advance of public opinion. Seven years later when the Thirteen Colonies were lost, such ideas, though bold and revolutionary, were beginning to make headway. So cautious a statesman as Pitt, though he acknowledged the influence of Adam Smith, was not the man to liquidate the British Empire in order to test the validity of an economic theory. In fact the hard necessities of politics obliged him to strengthen the bonds of Empire and to fight a bitter war in its defence. The main task of his administration, until war distracted his efforts, was to reform the whole fiscal system of Great Britain, gradually and prudently, according to Adam Smith's doctrine, by reducing and simplifying all duties which acted in restraint of trade, by a rational system of accounting, by adopting Adam Smith's rules of fair taxation, and by his commercial treaties with France. These were the first moves towards the free trade policy of the next generation; but the full implications of that policy: the suppression of the chartered companies, the repeal of the Acts of Trade, and the eventual dissolution of the Empire were still academic considerations. No practical politician of that age brought them into his programme.

Since 1776, the whole character of the Empire had changed. The three great wars with France, of 1740, 1756 and 1778, had been fought, so far as the British were concerned, largely over colonial rivalry in North America. The stake had been the present security and future prospects of a group of small self-governing communities, the most important and the most populous of which were inhabited by men of British blood and origin. Their value to Great Britain, apart from sentimental considerations of prestige, had been conceived as resting on the control of their trade. The prestige had gone for ever and the best informed students were of the opinion that the attempt to control their trade was an economic error. But all was not lost. The valour of Carleton and Elliot and Rodney and Warren Hastings, had preserved the framework of an empire of a quite different nature. There was Canada with its nucleus of docile French-Canadians, not very numerous and of no great account hitherto in the City of London. This colony must be retained, because of the debt of honour to the loyalists who had migrated into it, and because of the fur trade of Hudson Bay, the fisheries of Newfoundland, and the masts and spars from the Maritime Provinces. These practical shipping and commercial interests gave new strategic importance to the naval base at Halifax. There were the West Indies, the sugar islands, prize of so many battles, though not so prosperous as formerly. Some said that this has been their constant complaint, that their former happy state was mythical, but the West Indian Interest commanded sometimes as many as eighty votes in the House of Commons, and was strongly backed by the Navy. There was Bengal. In the years when we had been losing the sovereignty over two or three million white men in America we had been acquiring the sovereignty over twenty-six million Indians, three times as great a population as that of Great Britain, consisting of impoverished peasants to whom we could sell little or nothing. Could they be regarded as anything but an encumbrance which the impetuous servants of the East India Company had loaded on the shoulders of the Crown? If the Company would pay its way and keep quiet that would be the best of a bad business. As Pitt surveyed the population of the Empire in 1792, the unreconciled French-Canadians, the wretched peasants of Bengal, the slaves in Jamaica, the convicts in New South Wales, there was little cause for imperial pride.

But to turn from plantations to trade was to see a brighter prospect. His nine years of peaceful administration (1783–92) had raised the revenue of the nation to unprecedented heights while, at the same time, the French were lapsing into bankruptcy. 'Our good old island,' wrote one member of the Government, 'now possesses an accumulation and completion of prosperity beyond any example in the history of the world.' The nation of shopkeepers had become aware of their economic destiny and had learned that the loss of the Thirteen Colonies did not at all impair their aptitude for importing raw materials and exporting manufactured goods.

2. THE FRENCH WARS, 1793–1802

UNLIKE the three previous wars, which had been fought for colonial rivalry, the War of 1793 was a war of ideas, though the Prime Minister of Great Britain was slow to notice the difference. Pitt's foreign policy, after concluding the Commercial Treaty with France, had been chiefly concerned with such distant affairs as the dispute with Spain over the Pacific coast of North America and the encroachment of Russia in the Black Sea. His confident hopes of another fifteen years of peace were shattered in 1792, by the fall of the French monarchy, the first victory of the French revolutionary army over the Prussians, and the September Massacres in Paris. Even then, though anti-Jacobin horror was rising in England, he saw no reason for war until the French denounced the treaties which restricted the commerce of the Scheldt and prevented the fortification of Flanders. After some weeks of quarrelling, in which the British demonstrated their ancient sensitiveness about the Flemish coast, and the French appealed from old engagements to new abstract principles, the French declared war on 1 February 1793, a few days after the execution of Louis XVI. To the Jacobin leaders it was a war on 'behalf of all peoples against all kings'. To Pitt and the English middle-classes it was a war for the maintenance of commerce as guaranteed by treaty.

As is customary the British armies and navies were dispersed in ill-contrived expeditions without sufficient preparation or clear objectives. Pitt's 'inveterate prudence and instinctive horror of indiscretion' prevented him from concentrating his forces for some bold stroke, but not from frittering them away. The first year of the war was spent in despatching three combined forces, after much vacillation, to Gibraltar, to the West Indies and to Flanders. A large allied army of Prussians, Austrians and British was formed in Flanders for a victorious march on Paris, but was defeated in detail. The British under the Duke of York fell back from Dunkirk and were eventually withdrawn from Holland, the first of three evacuations which in that war concluded attempts to open a western front. Wellington, who had his baptism of fire under the Duke of York, used to say that the campaign taught him one lesson: how not to do it.

While professional opinion in the services looked to Flanders, the cabinet and the City hoped for solid successes in the West Indies, and on their side the French government was similarly biased. Between 1793 and 1798 each belligerent poured into the West Indies a stream of warships and transports carrying scores of thousands of soldiers, most of whom were destined to die of yellow fever. Almost any sacrifice of soldiers' lives, any diversion of the Navy from other tasks, was thought worth while to protect sugar islands and to seize those of the other powers. Added to the influence of the sugar-importers was now that of the manufacturers in Lancashire whose raw cotton came chiefly from the West Indies. The cotton importers, like the sugar importers, were firm monopolists unconverted to Adam Smith's principles of free trade.

When Pitt introduced the Income Tax in 1797, in calculating incomes from overseas investments he adjudged that four-fifths of all such incomes were derived from the West Indies. British investments there were worth £70,000,000. One-eighth of all British shipping cleared from West Indian ports. But these commercial assets were small compared with the wealth of the French island of San Domingo, or Dutch Guiana, or Spanish Trinidad and Cuba. The Spaniards were at first our allies, though later they went over to the French side. The Dutch were the allies on whose behalf we had entered the war; it was one of our primary objects to protect the Dutch colonies even though the enemy should overrun the Netherlands. We had friends too in the French islands, where the white planters invited British aid to restore the royalist regime, and to suppress the negroes who, in every island, were in a state of rebellion. None of the colonial campaigns was a simple issue. In each, loyalties and motives were divided. In almost every Dutch and French colony there was strife between those who dreaded British commercial competition and those who hated the Jacobin revolutionaries.

In 1794 British fleets and armies arrived in the West Indies to begin the bloodiest of their many wars for the sugar islands.

Since Cromwell's assault on the Spanish Indies every European war had brought about a dismal repetition of these ill-advised

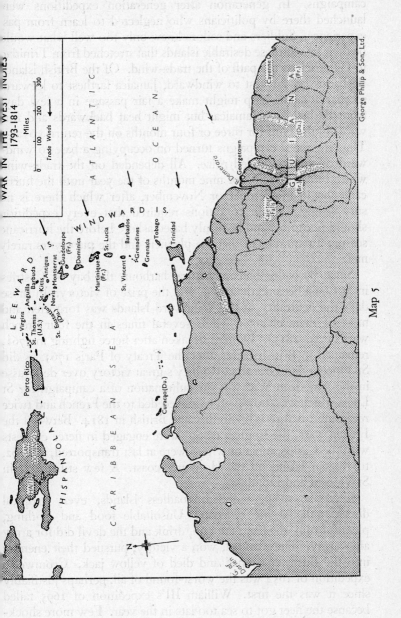

Map 5

campaigns. In generation after generation expeditions wer
launched there by politicians who neglected to learn from pas
experience. Soldiers and sailors knew only too well what woul
be their fate in these desirable islands that stretched from Trinida
to Cuba across the path of the trade-wind. Of the British island
Barbados lay farthest to windward, Jamaica farthest to leeward
so that a sailing-ship might make a fair passage in a few day
from Barbados to Jamaica, but might beat backwards and for
wards in the Gulf for three or four months on the return voyage
Thus the naval campaigns turned on occupying a base to windward of your intended prize. All depended on the trade-wind
which blows steadily for nine months of the year until the hurri
canes begin in October or November, after which there is n
sure sailing. These conditions required that every expeditio
should put to sea and be firmly based ashore before the hurrican
season, a requirement that the planners and the purveyors rarel
met.

Since Barbados had no natural harbour, the bay of Castrie
in St Lucia became the means and the prize of victory. In those
days the neutrality of the Windward Islands was forgotten anc
most of them changed hands several times in the four French
wars (1756–1815). Dominica, taken after fierce fighting in 1761
remained in British hands after the Treaty of Paris 1763, as did
St Vincent and Grenada. Rodney's great victory over de Grasse
in the American War was the culmination of a campaign for S
Lucia which was, however, twice receded to the French and twice
recaptured before it finally became British in 1814. Between the
French wars, the English troops were engaged in fierce contests
with the Caribs, most of whom were at last transported, in 1802,
to Ruatan Island off the Honduras coast. A few still linger in
St Vincent and Dominica.

In those steep, wooded, roadless islands, every tropical
disease afflicted the redcoats. Unsuitable food and clothing,
plentiful rum, the heat, the rain, drink and the devil did for army
after army. They landed, won a victory, pursued their enemies
into the Bush, encamped and died of yellow jack. Cromwell's
expedition of 1654 was the worst-found of all, perhaps justifiably
since it was the first. William III's expedition of 1695 failed
because the fleet got to sea too late in the year. Few more shocking stories can be read than that in which Smollett described

Roderick Random) the attack on Cartagena in 1740. Not only
the English regulars, but almost all of a contingent of American
volunteers died of fever. Of the 12,000 men who took part in
the grandiose campaign of 1762, 5000 died and were buried in
Havana. The war against the Caribs of St Vincent, in 1772,
was almost as deadly. A few years later St Lucia and Martinique
were swallowing up soldiers who might have weighed down the
scales on the side of victory if they had been with Cornwallis in
Virginia. A hundred years of colonial wars with France saw
whole armies dissolve and perish in the West Indies. More than
300,000 Englishmen died for the avarice of the sugar-planters
and the ignoble lust to plunder the Spaniards. But of all these
operations the most futile were the campaigns of the Younger
Pitt, which cost 100,000 casualties while contributing nothing to
the main course of the war against Revolutionary France.

In 1794 the British got an easy foothold in Martinique and
Guadeloupe and restored the royalist regime, to the great gratification of the French planters. It is not surprising that the
negroes and the mulattos, unwilling to lose their promised
liberty, combined with the Jacobin armies to fight against the
British. By July, rebellion, and yellow fever to which the negroes
were almost immune, had liquidated the British conquests, except
in Martinique. Revolt then broke out in the British island of
Jamaica, where the Maroons held the soldiers in check for about
two years. An expedition against San Domingo far to the west
also proved peculiarly costly and ineffective.

The pressure of the Lancashire cotton-spinners persuaded the
government to send out a still larger expedition in the winter of
1795–6, again at the wrong time of year. The operations proved
as unsuccessful as before in reducing San Domingo but progress
was made in the Windward Islands. This expedition is remarkable for two developments in the history of the British Army,
the provision of a medical staff which studied the prevention and
cure of tropical diseases, and a reformation in the treatment and
training of troops by Sir John Moore, who learned in these campaigns the lessons on which he built up the army that at last
defeated Napoleon. Moore's caustic comments did not endear
him to his superiors: 'In the West Indies, industry and cultivation do not contribute to the happiness of the inhabitants. All
tends to the profit of the master.'

'With a Roman instead of a modern exercise and discipline th
troops in the West Indies might, I am convinced, be kept healthy.

San Domingo, the principal objective, was not subdued
After troublesome campaigns the British withdrew, leaving i
under the rule of the negro patriot, Toussaint l'Ouverture.

Early in 1795 the troops of the French republic burst into
Holland proclaiming a new age of liberty. The Prince of Orange
fled to England, as his descendant was to do when similarly
attacked by the Germans in 1940, while the invaders set up at The
Hague a revolutionary government which they designated the
Batavian Republic. The Prince called upon the Dutch colonie
to place themselves under British protection and to maintair
the war against France. The very rich colony of Demerara ir
Guiana, which had largely been developed by British capital
fell in with the Prince's desire and invited British protection, bu
in other parts of the world, suspicion of British motives and age-
old commercial rivalry, even, perhaps, some sympathy with
French principles, provoked the Dutch to resistance. The British
were so eager to occupy the Cape of Good Hope that their army
arrived before the instruction from the Prince of Orange, so
that the Dutch Governor made some show at resistance before
surrendering. Nelson's keen eye had marked down the harbour
of Trincomali in Ceylon as the key to naval warfare in the Indian
Ocean; it fell into British hands in 1796, after a tortuous intrigue.
A Scottish professor named Hugh Cleghorn hit upon the device
of buying over the regiment of Swiss mercenaries whom the
Dutch employed to garrison the island. Having struck his
bargain in Switzerland with the proprietor of the mercenaries,
Cleghorn accompanied him to Ceylon to withdraw them from
the Dutch service. Faced with this situation, or perhaps on
account of his personal preferences, the Dutch Governor surrendered Colombo after a slight show of resistance.

While the commercial people had kept their eyes on the war
in the West Indies and the advantages of occupying the Dutch
colonies, the Admiralty had been increasingly concerned with the
war in the Mediterranean, where conquests were estimated for
their direct strategic value. In 1792 we had no naval base in
those waters east of Gibraltar. Our first endeavour to control
the French southern coast, by co-operating with the royalists in

Toulon, was a failure. The British fleet was expelled, in 1793, by the Jacobins, largely owing to the efforts of Bonaparte who commanded the artillery.

At this juncture the restless inhabitants of Corsica broke out in civil war. One party, among whom were the family of Bonaparte, adopted the cause of the French Revolution, while their rivals, led by the aged patriot Paoli, threw off the French yoke to elect George III as their king. Thus for two years (1794–6) the island of Corsica was a self-governing dominion of the British Crown. Nelson took part in the Corsican campaign—in which he lost an eye—and recorded his dissatisfaction with the unenterprising conduct of his superior. The French Toulon fleet was allowed to put to sea and to support the operations along the Riviera by which Bonaparte conquered Italy. The British then took a further step forward by occupying Elba, but with no effect.

At this stage of the war (1796) the Spaniards joined the French, supposing theirs to be the winning side, a step which seemed to make the maintenance of British sea-power in the Mediterranean impracticable. Since hostile forces held Minorca and the whole coastline of Spain, France, and Italy, it seemed wise to withdraw the British fleet to Gibraltar. Corsica was evacuated, an unheroic measure which, however, gave the turbulent islanders little cause for regret. Having found already that representative government and trial by jury were inconsistent with devotion to their *vendettas*, they readily lapsed into a simpler state of freedom when the British fleet was gone. Strategically the island was no great loss since it had no port on the north or east coast conveniently placed for naval operations against France or Italy.

But war with Spain meant renewed activity in the West Indies. The British soon got control of the Spanish and Dutch colonies, and of such French islands as were not in a state of negro anarchy. They had already occupied Ceylon and the Cape of Good Hope. Otherwise, after negotiations for peace had come to nothing, they were again, in 1797, fighting alone against the forces of France and Spain. All central Europe was in French hands and the French fleet was unquestioned master of the Mediterranean Sea. This costly and unprofitable war had outlived the anti-Jacobin enthusiasm of 1793 and was most unpopular. The Radicals clamoured for peace, the three-per-cents were down to forty-eight, Ireland was in a state of rebellion, even the Navy mutinied.

At this crisis Bonaparte was preparing to strike at Asia through the Mediterranean. Though still a junior general, without legitimate authority to dictate policy, ambitious fancy led him to follow the eastward path of Alexander the Great. The overthrow of the Venetian Republic, in 1797, had given him control of the Alpine Passes, of the Dalmatian Coast, and of Corfu which guards the entrance to the Adriatic. He secured his flank by seizing Malta, the key of the central Mediterranean narrows,

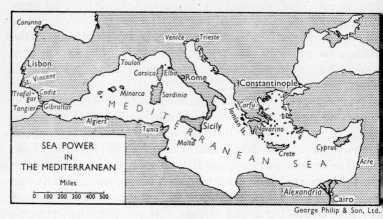

George Philip & Son, Ltd.

Map 6

and transported an army to Egypt under convoy of the Toulon fleet. The conquest of Egypt was but his first intended step. Far beyond, in the Indian Ocean, the Governor of Mauritius had been at work inciting Tipu Sahib ('Citoyen Tipu') to drive the British from India with the help of a French fleet. These plans for a single co-ordinated offensive based on Malta and Corfu, developed through Egypt and Mauritius as far afield as Mysore, with the intention of breaking the power of England in the East, were bolder, grander in conception, more far-reaching than any earlier combination against the British Empire. It required political imagination, audacity and responsibility in a high degree to meet the threat, in days when there was no electric telegraph for exchanging information and instructions between London and Calcutta; nor were these virtues lacking.

Nelson had already persuaded the Admiralty to send the fleet back into the Mediterranean. Having no suitable base for blockade he failed to intercept the Toulon fleet but, with uncanny insight, guessed the destination of their voyage. His total victory over the French fleet at the Battle of the Nile (1 August 1798) disrupted the whole design. Though it was the decisive blow, it was but one move in a strategic plan which almost equalled Bonaparte's in grandeur, excelling it in one respect, that of being simultaneously improvised by statesmen in three continents.

Another expedition sent from England captured Minorca and drove the French from Malta after a long siege. These naval victories made Nelson supreme throughout the Mediterranean. Naples, Sicily and Malta came under British protection. It was, however, unlucky that Bonaparte escaped to France, leaving his army marooned in Egypt. Meanwhile Lord Wellesley, far away in India, had acted with equal resolution. Tipu was defeated and killed at Seringapatam in 1798. Not content with that, Wellesley had sent an Indian army from Bombay to the Red Sea to co-operate against the French in Egypt; and even Popham, the Governor of the Cape, had been able to spare troops for a similar expedition. As these two armies converged from the far south and the far east upon the doomed Frenchmen, a third and more powerful expedition was launched against them from England and arrived first of the three. It was General Abercromby's force from England that destroyed the French army at the Battle of Alexandria (September 1801). A few days later preliminaries of peace were signed at Amiens.

3. THE BRITISH EMPIRE AND NAPOLEON

THE long wars against the French revolutionary armies had left the nations exhausted and inclined to pacifist sentiments. In Europe the dynasts had been toppled from their thrones, or sat in them uneasily by favour of the French. Elsewhere in the world, the richest islands and plantations had come into British hands through the prowess of the Navy. Though Britannia ruled the waves she longed for peace, for the day when she could disarm. When the day came, she disarmed with indecent haste, without regard to future perils. The pedestrian statesman Addington, who succeeded Pitt as Premier in 1801, was for peace at almost any price. He sent the ubiquitous, invaluable Cornwallis to negotiate terms at Amiens with the dictator of Europe, demanding no conquests, glories, triumphs or spoils. All the colonies of France, Spain and Holland, except Ceylon and Trinidad, were to be restored; even Tobago and Demerara which had been developed by British planters with British capital, even Malta where the inhabitants protested against the restoration. On the Continent, the dictator Bonaparte undertook to respect the frontiers and the liberties of surrounding states. But generosity was wasted on Bonaparte; he had undermined and weakened the authority of every state in Europe; his quislings were appointed, his fifth-columns were ready, in each of the subservient unarmed states adjacent to France. He flooded the world with inflammatory propaganda, protesting with unrighteous indignation at each diplomatic impropriety committed by any nation, at the time when he was violating frontiers, instigating political murders and annexing, one by one, the neighbouring states whose independence he had guaranteed. The inevitable breach with Great Britain came in the negotiations over Malta. Since the sixteenth century the island had been quietly decaying under the somnolent rule of the Knights of St John. These worthies, once an order of crusaders who had defied the Turks from their island fortress, had degenerated into a close corporation of hereditary noblemen, the last Grand Master having been a Frenchman. Their dwindling revenues were too small for administering the civil population, not to speak of garrisoning a military station sought by all the powers. For financial reasons the Knights placed themselves under the protection of the Czar, which further confused the issue. Like other Mediterranean cities, Valetta had some tradition of self-government, of having elected its own *Consiglio Popolare*, long ago before the coming of the Knights; and this tradition had been revived by the Jacobins during the short period of French occupation (1798–1800). By the Treaty of Amiens, the British agreed to withdraw from Elba, Egypt and Malta. Of these three, Malta provided a problem, since it could not be merely vacated. Some provision for its good government and military security must be made, a matter of delicate negotiation between Great Britain, Russia, France and the Maltese. Luckily the British remained in possession, proposing that they should garrison the island pending a settlement and refusing to accept the islet of Lampedusa as an alternative. This provided Bonaparte with the grievance he sought. With outcries about English perfidy he declared war in the spring of 1803. The Peace of Amiens had lasted only eighteen months, but long enough for him to have treacherously occupied Holland, Switzerland and Piedmont.

The restless ambition of Bonaparte (who at this time proclaimed himself the Emperor Napoleon) reached out to all parts of the world. During the interval of peace he had sent great armies to restore French control over San Domingo, but without success. Tropical disease defeated the French as it had defeated the English. Discouraged from further empire-building in the New World by this failure, he attempted to cut his losses by a plan which would ingratiate the Americans. He had acquired from Spain, by treaty, the undeveloped territory west of the Mississippi known as Louisiana. Instead of developing a French colony in this region (which now contains a population of fifty millions and several of the world's greatest cities), he offered to sell it to the Americans, to their great surprise, the agreed price being no more than fifteen million dollars (1803).

The first great crisis of the war, the threat to invade England, falls outside the scope of this book. From 1803 to 1805 the Grand Army lay encamped about Boulogne while the fleets of England maintained close blockade of the ports from which the French convoying squadrons were to sail. When, in August 1805, the Grand Army struck camp to march to the Danube, when in October Nelson destroyed the combined fleets of France and Spain off Cape Trafalgar, the course of events again diverted Napoleon's eyes to the East, persuading him to ignore the Atlantic and to destroy the islanders by boycotting their trade.

Routes to the East again became objectives of strategy. The British still held Malta. In 1806 Napoleon sent his brother to carve out a satellite French kingdom for himself at Naples. The British countered by occupying Sicily which for eight years (1806–14) was under British control. The Treaty of Tilsit (1807) between Napoleon and the Czar, contained provisions for partitioning the Turkish Empire, which led to further advances by the belligerents into the neutral eastern Mediterranean. A British squadron under Duckworth sailed through the Dardanelles but returned when the Turks refused to be drawn into alliance. The clash came in the Greek islands which were ruled by Pashas nominally subject to the Sultan. The French annexed the Dalmatian coast and islands, and threw a garrison into Corfu, the key of the Adriatic (1808). At the request of the inhabitants the British came in to 'protect' Cephalonia, Zante and the other Ionian islands. With sea-power and island bases the British had now stopped Napoleon's advance to the Levant.

All the foreign colonies which had been taken in the 1790's and given back at the Treaty of Amiens were again at Britain's mercy. Before Trafalgar there were no forces available for colonial campaigns, none even for Wellesley's Maratha War; after Trafalgar objectives might be selected at will. The West Indies were reduced during 1808, 1809 and 1810 without much fighting. The Cape was again occupied in 1806, in spite of stronger Dutch resistance on this occasion. The Admiral, Sir H. Popham, knew that the cabinet was dallying with plans for raising the Spanish colonies in revolt. With one eye on friends of his own among the Spanish revolutionaries, and the other on associates in the City, who were watching the South American market, he decided to liberate, or occupy, the Spanish colony at the River Plate. Borrowing some troops from his colleague General Baird, he crossed the South Atlantic and seized Buenos Ayres (June 1806). But since it soon appeared that the *gauchos* had no desire to exchange Spanish for British domination he found himself besieged and was forced to withdraw to Montevideo after a capitulation. The British government was so deeply committed that it was obliged to send a relief expedition, which arrived too late. In June 1807 General Whitelocke again attempted to assault Buenos Ayres, already at that date a city of regular stone buildings. Whitelocke's converging columns lost touch and were defeated by the Spaniards, who showed their historic skill at street-fighting. This shabby affair ended in another withdrawal on terms agreed at a parley. When he returned, Whitelocke was cashiered, and the speculators lost their money. Two years later, when Napoleon's injustice had goaded the Spaniards into war with France, Spain and her colonies were again allied with Britain. The River Plate was to become a profitable field for

British commerce and investment, even for British emigration, but not as a conquered province.

The Dutch colonies in Asia were quickly gathered in, Batavia itself in 1811. East and West, all the tropical colonies of the European powers and all the strategic points defending them were under British protection, and might all have been annexed if that had been the desire of the British government. Meanwhile Napoleon, then at the height of his power, ruled Europe directly from Danzig to Corfu, from Brittany to the Black Forest; his allies and dependants ruled Russia, Sweden, Denmark, Germany, Spain, though the Spaniards backed by British armies and navies were in revolt against him.

The death-blow to all Napoleon's Asiatic schemes was the taking of Mauritius by an expedition from India in 1810. From that base General Decaen had sent expeditions to survey a new colony in 'Terre Napoléon' on the Australian coast. From Mauritius he had supplied Tipu Sahib and sent agents to the Marathas. The Cape route was barred, the Mediterranean was a British sea, the friends of the French in India were defeated. The loss of Mauritius meant that there was no rallying-point left in Asia for French agents or French forces.

4. NEUTRAL RIGHTS AND THE WAR OF 1812

SINCE all wars fought by Great Britain are contests in the use of sea-power, the British, more than any other nation, have been concerned with the growth of international law in respect of blockade, contraband, right of search, and neutrality. Some general principles which emerged during the wars of the Dutch and English against the Spanish monarchy, had developed during the eighteenth century into positive rules of maritime law about which there was a tolerable measure of agreement among the civilised nations. Some of these rules were quoted as valid in treaties and were enforced by admiralty courts of all the great powers, to the general satisfaction. But the growing strength of the Navy, from age to age, enabled the British to conduct war by means of blockade ever more stringently, a process which has implied a steady encroachment upon neutral rights in the interest of belligerents. In the eyes of British lawyers, this has been a normal continuous process in constructive jurisprudence, while lawyers of other nations, whose interest has been intermittent, have often regarded it in a quite different light. Encroachments were championed or opposed according to the momentary status of the nation concerned, whether as an enemy or an ally of Great Britain, or as a neutral. Such has been the weakness of international law that Great Britain could never afford to disarm herself by conceding the right of search, while other powers have protested against it when fighting Great Britain but used it gladly when engaged as Great Britain's ally.

During the great wars with France, the neutral Baltic powers assumed an intermediate status known as Armed Neutrality to resist interference by the belligerents in their regular sea-trade. In effect these alliances operated against Great Britain since it was the British Navy that habitually made war by blockade. Further, the British Navy depended upon the Baltic trade for masts and spars and hemp, a consideration which obliged the government to treat the Northern powers with discretion. Not until the end of the Napoleonic Wars did the output of naval stores from New Brunswick and Nova Scotia arrive in sufficient quantity to provide a substitute.

War by blockade reached a new intensity in 1806 and 1807, when Napoleon attempted to turn the tables on the British by laying an embargo on their whole trade with France and the occupied territories. The British retaliated by declaring an absolute blockade on all the ports of Europe where Napoleon's writs hould run. From 1807 to 1812 the trade-war continued, the precursor of the trade-wars of 1914 and 1939, and, like the two later examples, to the great advantage of the maritime over the continental power. So secure was British naval strength that all western Europe was deprived of its external trade by our hold on the Ionian Islands, Sicily, Malta, Gibraltar and Lisbon, to which were soon added Heligoland, and Anholt in the Cattegat. The peoples of Europe could export nothing but, by large-scale smuggling, they imported a fair quantity of British goods through the ports which the British had occupied. At first the armed neutrals of the Baltic were ill-disposed towards Great Britain. The Czar allied himself with Napoleon in 1807, the two together agreeing to seize the Danish fleet. The British fore-stalled Napoleon's move by raiding Copenhagen, the second such occasion, as Nelson had similarly forced the Danes out of their neutrality, by an unprovoked attack in the previous war. Later, when the British blockade had begun to tell against continental Europe, the Baltic powers saw where their true interest lay. The War of Liberation in the north began with the alliance in 1812 between Great Britain, Sweden and Russia, the Czar having soon quarrelled with his brother-autocrat.

At the moment, when the crisis of the naval war was past, the Americans intervened on the side of the Tyrant of Europe. Surely no event in the history of Great Britain or of the United States is so entirely discreditable to either nation as the War of 1812. In America it is still remembered as a sort of epilogue to their War of Independence; in England it has been altogether forgotten, and better so. It grew out of national prejudices, it was fought with an utter lack of magnanimity by both combatants, it resulted in nothing but bad blood. It is sad that the candid historian should be obliged to exhume so unsavoury an episode.

Washington had bequeathed, as his political testament to the Americans, the doctrine of isolation, advising them not to enter into 'entangling alliances'. This policy had been continued until the trade-war of 1807 had obliged the Americans to define their attitude to the British blockade of Europe. Unfortunately for them, Jay's Treaty of 1794 had accepted the British interpretation of neutral rights in time of war. Now that the British Navy commanded every sea and exercised these rights in an extended form, the Americans, like the Baltic neutrals, began to raise objections. Negotiations, which should have reached an agreement, were compromised by repeated tactless interferences on the part of British naval officers. The American public was irritated when a British warship stopped the American frigate *Chesapeake* and deprived her of half her crew on the score that they were British subjects. On the one hand it might be alleged that right of search was justified by treaty, that the Navy was entitled to impress British seafaring men, and that American ships then, as throughout the nineteenth century, were manned largely by British deserters. American crimps openly seduced them with bounties in every port of the New World. On the other hand so insolent a treatment of a foreign navy was foolish and exasperating. Tempers rose as negotiations progressed, the more hot-headed among the Americans crying out to renew the old war against the British tyrants, and the British infuriating the Americans by treating them still as rebel colonists. Canning, in the House of Commons, alluded to the Americans as 'not a people we should be proud to acknowledge as our relations'. Liverpool, the Prime Minister, condescendingly suggested that the Americans 'ought to have looked to this country as the guardian power to which she was indebted for her comforts, for her rank in the scale of civilisation, for her very existence'.

As an American historian has said, this contest 'was waged by one free people against another free people in the interest of Napoleon, the real enemy of them both'; but it did not appear in that light to firebrands in Congress. Henry Clay of Kentucky demanded war with Great Britain 'because I believe her prior in aggression, and her injuries and insults to us more atrocious in character'. Clay came from the west where they had other causes of quarrel with the British. In the region of the Great Lakes where there was free movement of the tide of new settlers across the unmarked frontier, the British were still the protectors of the Indians, still spoke of creating a wide Indian reservation in the lands that the Kentuckians desired for themselves. 'The conquest of Canada is in your power,' Clay asserted. 'I verily believe that the militia of Kentucky are alone competent to place Montreal and Upper Canada at your feet....Is it nothing to us to extinguish the torch that lights up savage warfare? Is it nothing to acquire the entire fur trade?'

The British government, deeply engaged in the Peninsular War, in the Blockade of Europe, and in the Baltic negotiations, could spare but little attention to this side-issue in America. The general situation had, however, reached a stage where they were able to loosen the Blockade by withdrawing the Orders in Council which the Americans thought obnoxious. This was done on 16 June 1812, the moment in history when Napoleon began his fatal attack on Russia, too late for appeasement. President Madison, a weak inadequate man, more concerned with catching western votes than with any higher consideration, was pushed by the westerners into declaring war, on 18 June. Though he could not know it, the principal *casus belli* had vanished two days earlier.

The dismal story of the war may be told in three phases, the American raids on Canada, the frigate actions at sea, and the British raids on the American coast.

The western frontiersmen began the assault on Canada. Even Jefferson, who should have known better, said it would be 'a mere matter of marching'. An incompetent braggart named Hull led a small army into Canada from Detroit, proclaiming that he would deliver the Canadians from 'tyranny and oppression' and would restore them 'to the dignified station of freemen'. A mixed force of British regulars, British and French-Canadian volunteers and friendly Indians, about 1300 men in all under General Isaac Brock, fell upon a superior number of their would-be deliverers and drove them back in headlong ignominious flight. Hull surrendered Detroit with all the stores assembled for the invasion. Thus western Canada was saved, largely because the Indian tribes had rallied to the side of their British protectors. Troops from New York now attempted another invasion near Niagara which again was hurled back by the Canadians with heavy loss. Brock, the victor of Detroit, was killed in this action.

In the two successive campaigns of 1813 and 1814 the Americans showed more spirit. Realising the value of water communications they built small armed ships on Lake Erie, which were handled skilfully by Commodore Perry. With this advantage they regained the west and brought better-managed expeditions into the field. But though they made at least eleven separate attempts to invade Canada every one was repulsed, the severest battle being fought at Lundy's Lane (1813). Meanwhile the victorious conclusion of the war in Europe had allowed the despatch of many of Wellington's veterans from Spain for service in North America. By midsummer of 1814, 16,000 British regulars ensured the defence of Canada. The honours of war, however, went to the Canadians, a nation of less than 600,000, deeply split by racial differences, who had combined to resist the unprovoked aggression of a powerful nation six times as numerous, until help came. The war had been anything but chivalrous. While the Americans complained of the British employment of Red Indian auxiliaries, the Canadians complained that the American filibusters, who had come with promises of deliverance, had plundered and destroyed whatever they could reach. The village of Newark (now Niagara) and the town of York (now Toronto) had been wantonly burned by the invaders.

The war at sea was equally ineffective. The United States had no battle-fleet, but some useful small craft, and three large, heavily-armed frigates, each of them almost a match for a line-of-battle ship. They fought a number of well-conducted single-ship actions against British frigates and usually had the best of it owing to their heavier broadside. These actions, though very heartening to the Americans, had no effect upon the course of the naval war. No more had the action in which H.M.S. *Shannon* forced the *Chesapeake* to surrender in sight of Boston, to the disgust of

> The people of the port who came out to see the sport
> With their bands a playing Yanky-doodle-dandy-O.

Throughout the war British command of the sea was never challenged. The British could—and did—land troops at any point they chose on the American coast. 1814 was a great year for privateering. The Halifax privateers were busy off the New England coast and the New England privateers off the coast of Old England. The great difficulty of the Americans was disposing of their prizes since the British Navy was ubiquitous. Most of the ships they took were retaken and set free.

By 1814 the war had reached a stage of pitiable futility. But for this malicious pin-pricking the world was rapidly returning to peace. Large sections of the American people had been opposed to the war since its commencement and were anxious only to renew their trade with Britain. Commissioners from New England arrived at Washington in 1814, proposing to contract out of the Union in order to make a separate peace. However, the British had fleets and armies in America and must do something with them. An army landed in Chesapeake Bay and after inflicting a sharp defeat on an American force at Bladensburg (24 August 1814) occupied Washington, then a raw new settlement consisting of a few half-finished government buildings set in the wilderness, among temporary huts and pegged-out streets without houses. After frightening President Madison away and eating his breakfast, the troops burnt the government buildings as a reprisal for the American burnings in Canada, and withdrew. It was a legitimate act of war but, like all reprisals, most ill-advised. One Peninsular veteran, Harry Smith, wrote of the affair: 'At Bladensburg we licked the Yankies and took all their guns with a loss of 300 men, whereas Colborne [his old commander] would have done the same thing with a loss of forty or fifty, and we entered Washington for the barbarous purpose of destroying the city. Admiral Cockburn would have burnt the whole, but General Ross would only consent to the burning of the public buildings. . . . Fresh from the Duke's humane warfare in the south of France we were horrified.' The Americans began again to build their capital and refurbished the President's damaged house with a coat of white paint, from which it has since been known as the White House.

A still larger expedition was then sent against New Orleans, and ended the war with a complete fiasco. A combined operation, carried out by a squadron under command of one of Nelson's 'band of brothers', and an army of Peninsular veterans under command of one of Wellington's generals, utterly broke down through mismanagement. These troops, who had stormed Badajoz and forced the passes of the Pyrenees, failed to take a temporary fortification defended by Andrew Jackson and the local militia. The Americans were much gratified; while on their part the British Infantry had won such glory in Spain as not to be disgraced by one setback. The worst of it was that peace had been signed at Ghent (24 December 1814) before the battle was fought; New Orleans was but another sample of the malignant folly which characterised the War of 1812 from start to finish.

The Treaty of Ghent settled nothing, merely appointing commissions to adjust boundaries. It contains no reference to neutral rights or impressment of sailors. However, after a war which disgraced both nations, peace was restored. *Esto perpetua.*

5. THE EMPIRE AFTER WATERLOO

NEGOTIATIONS among the allies during the War of Liberation led to a series of treaties which were mostly concluded in 1814 after the occupation of Paris, and were but slightly affected by Napoleon's ephemeral reappearance for the Hundred Days' Reign in 1815. The continental powers gave almost the whole of their attention in these negotiations to the Balance of Power in Europe. It was hardly realised that the most striking effect of the war had been to endow Great Britain with overwhelming commercial and financial power. The British were now, without question, the most secure, the most opulent and the strongest among the nations. They might have retained the captured colonies of France, Spain and Holland if extension of territory had been their aim, but it was not. The objects of Lord Castlereagh and the other British diplomats were to rebuild the ancient kingdom of France under a stable legitimate government, to create a strong monarchy in the Low Countries under the House of Orange, to secure the world-wide British trade and shipping by the military occupation of certain strategic points, and to persuade the other power to join in suppressing the slave trade.

With a few exceptions, the additions to the British Empire at this time were military outposts and, accordingly, were administered by military or naval officers under the close supervision of the Secretary for War and the Colonies. This Crown Colony government was a new system quite unlike the easy-going representative government of the earlier colonies. Since the American Revolution there had been a wide diffusion of Adam Smith's opinion that colonies should either be released from their allegiance or firmly held in the imperial system so that some real advantage could be got from them.

One colony taken from the Dutch in the earlier war, Ceylon, had been retained throughout the Peace of Amiens and remained in British hands. It had at first been handed over to the East India Company to be incorporated into the Madras Presidency, but the Madras revenue system, which was quite unsuited to the customs of the Cingalese, had produced complete chaos. In 1802 the Government resumed control, converting the island into a Crown Colony. Its first governor, Frederick North, though he got into grave trouble by unwise interference in the politics of the unsubdued kingdom of Kandy, restored the old system of civil administration, with the Dutch code of laws, and relied upon the support of the 'burghers', that is the half-caste Dutch settlers.

Three Dutch colonies in South America had welcomed the British occupying forces sent there at the request of the Prince of Orange. They were Essequibo, Berbice and Demerara. Even before the British occupation many English planters had settled in this rich undeveloped land where Ralegh had once searched for El Dorado. The settlements prospered during the twenty years of occupation and, in 1812, the British renamed the capital of Demerara—Georgetown, treating it as their own. The three settlements were ceded in 1814 and in 1831 were combined into the Crown Colony of British Guiana. It was for long a wilderness of unknown extent perhaps 500 miles in depth behind 300 miles of coast. Its inland frontiers were not delimited until 1904, when the King of Italy acted as arbitrator.

Far more difficult was the case of the Cape of Good Hope, which was desired solely for its position on the route to India. British policy was directed to building up Dutch power in Europe and, while strengthening the frontiers of the Netherlands, seemed justified in taking responsibility for a fortress in the southern hemisphere which the Dutch were quite unable to defend. All the rich islands in the East Indies were restored to the House of Orange and, for the loss of Colombo, Capetown and Demarara, the Dutch willingly agreed to accept an indemnity of £6,000,000. The Dutch negotiator Falck summed it up: 'Our own interest ought to have brought us to abandon properties that are always onerous and compromised by the least chance of war. What good fortune to find people complaisant enough to pay us for abandoning them!'

Two Spanish colonies, Tobago and Trinidad, were retained, frankly in compensation for the great expenses which Great Britain had incurred. Tobago, like Demarara, was one of those colonies with a chequered history of conquests and reconquests, its first white settlers having been British.

The history of Trinidad, a rich island about the size of Lancashire, deserves a backward glance. It was discovered by Columbus and settled by the Spaniards in 1580. Ralegh overran the infant colony at Port of Spain in 1595 and caulked his ships from the Pitch Lake. Some of the grants to courtiers in early Stuart times included Trinidad among the English 'Caribbees' but the island was not settled by Englishmen, nor was it actively developed by Spain.

In 1780 a Spanish governor named Chacon, showing more than ordinary spirit, invited French colonists who raised the white population in a few years from 3,000 to 18000. In the war of the French Revolution an English squadron under Captain Vaughan became embroiled with these Frenchmen, a breach of Spanish neutrality which provoked Spain into joining the French in alliance against England (1796). The Spanish dons soon found that they had more sympathy with the English than with the

French Jacobins so that, when General Abercromby invaded Trinidad (1797), there was little opposition. At the Peace of Amiens the Spanish colonists petitioned against the return of the island to Spain. Trinidad became a British Crown Colony but retained its Spanish law, with the mild Spanish slave-code but the harsh Spanish legal procedure which permitted the examination of an accused person by torture. The first Governor, Thomas Picton, was severely censured by the humanitarians for maintaining it. But Trinidad prospered, and in 1834 its 22,000 slaves were valued at a higher price than those of any colony but British Guiana.

Most of the French colonies were restored to the rule of King Louis XVIII, except St Lucia in the West Indies, and Mauritius in the Indian Ocean which were retained as British naval stations. The unfortified French factories in India, and the fishing rights off Newfoundland were again restored to France.

In European waters, British naval power was guaranteed by the occupation of Heligoland, Malta and the Ionian Islands which, with Gibraltar, ensured for the Navy power to renew the blockade, a wise measure taken in no other general treaty, and strongly conducive to the peace of Europe. The good intentions of governors brought up in the tradition of English liberty produced a curious series of constitutional experiments in these European islands. Almost every island in the Mediterranean was held by a British landing-party at some time between 1792 and 1815. Corsica had for a time placed itself under British rule. The Maltese in 1800, after the expulsion of the French, had invited the sovereignty of the British. The islanders of Cephalonia and Zante had followed their example in 1809. Sicily was in British occupation for eight years, Corfu for the last year of the war. In Corsica the attempt to impose British Parliamentary institutions upon the islanders had lamentably failed. A similar attempt was made in Sicily, in 1812, but without success. There was a party in Malta, the Italianate aristocracy, who likewise demanded representative government under the British Crown. In 1812, a commission of inquiry went to Malta charged with the task of giving the Maltese 'as large a share of civil liberty as is consistent with the military circumstances of the island'. The place was a fortress and must be ruled as one. Warned by the failures in Corsica and Sicily the commission strongly recom-

mended against representative government. 'The majority of
people want nothing better than a more intimate and indissoluble Union with Great Britain.' During the war the island,
by doubling its volume of shipping, had acquired a degree of
prosperity never before known. With that and with an efficient,
honest administration the people would be perfectly satisfied.
There was no truth in the assertion that they nourished a tradition of former self-government. In consequence of this report
Malta too became a Crown Colony with a Council including the
Bishop and other Maltese officials, and with a martinet, Sir
Thomas Maitland, for Governor. He was a benevolent autocrat,
tirelessly efficient, scrupulously honest and somewhat contemptuous of the people he devotedly served. It was perhaps an
error to replace Latin by Italian as the language of administration, since the bulk of the people spoke neither, but only the
Arabic patois peculiar to the island.

Maitland's advice was taken over the Ionian islands, Corfu,
Cephalonia, Zante, Ithaca, Cerigo, Paxo and Santa Maura. They
had begun by petitioning Great Britain 'to restore their independence'. General Oswald who began the occupation in 1809
had undertaken to 'establish a free independent government', a
pledge which was guaranteed by the powers in a treaty (1815).
The islands were to be 'a free republic under protection of the
King of Great Britain'. Someone produced a federal constitution
on paper for the Septinsular Republic, but 'King Tom' Maitland
pointed out at the beginning that 'the only real and true method
of administring government here for the benefit of the people,
is in fact to maintain all the powers in the hands of His Majesty's
Lord High Commissioner'. 'The old nobles of the head families
look with disgust at anything like protecting the people from
their tyrannical and arbitrary control.' However the forms of the
constitution were preserved with some advantage to the political
education of the islanders.

British rule over the island of Odysseus and its larger neighbours lasted more than fifty years. Obligations in the Ionian
Sea forced British statesmen, somewhat unwillingly, into close
association with the Greeks during their national revival and the
War of Greek Independence. Missolonghi, where Byron died,
Navarino, where Codrington destroyed the Turkish fleet, were
but a short sail from the British Ionian Islands. When Greece

was set free the basis of the Treaty of 1815 was removed, and the British protectorate became an anomaly.

The necessity of interning Napoleon after Waterloo brought into prominence the island of St Helena where, since 1673, a resident officer of the East India Company had provided for the occasional needs of ships. This remote but healthy island[1] in a temperate climate was lent by the Company to the Crown for a few years (1816–21). For greater security against attempts to rescue the Emperor, the garrison of St Helena was supported by outposts on the two nearest islets, Ascension, and Tristan da Cunha hitherto uninhabited and 700 miles away. A time-expired soldier, Corporal William Glass, remained on Tristan da Cunha with his wife and two other families from St Helena. The Colonial Office lost interest in the settlement which was not regarded as a British colony until 1875 when authority was resumed upon a report made by the *Challenger* surveying expedition. Corporal Glass had died in 1853. The little colony, reinforced by a ship-wrecked crew and by other wanderers, reached the number of 225 persons in 1945.

Ascension also was reoccupied, after the *Challenger* expedition, but as a naval station. It has been an important junction on cable routes and may achieve a new importance as an air base. It was administered by the Admiralty, and was rated as a warship. In 1922 the island was resumed by the Colonial Office for the benefit of Cables and Wireless Ltd. and was thereafter administered as a dependency of St Helena.

6. THE INDUSTRIAL REVOLUTION AND THE EMPIRE

READERS of history are familiar with the notion of what is called the Industrial Revolution, though it is often represented as a sudden change accomplished about a hundred years ago. In the stable mid-Victorian age, when the British were consolidating their gains and no other nation was yet industrialised, such a

---

[1] St Helena is a rugged, hilly volcanic island about as large as Jersey. As well as Napoleon another famous man once lived there, Edmund Halley who used it as an observatory in 1676–7. With the disappearance of sailing ships its value as a port of call has declined. The population in 1946 was 4992, the only industry the cultivation of New Zealand flax.

view of the early nineteenth century appeared to be correct. The development of steam-power by British engineers had given a lead to British industry which the nation maintained and improved by means of its natural advantages: its unlimited coal-fields with adjacent beds of iron ore, its soft damp climate uniquely suited to the manufacture of textiles, its geographical position athwart the trade routes of the world. To these gifts of nature were applied the unrivalled technical ability of our metal-workers, the accumulated wealth of the City which had made the saying 'safe as the Bank of England' proverbial, the admitted probity of British merchants, the sea-faring tradition which maintained half the world's shipping under the British flag, and the prowess of the Navy which from Halifax, Gibraltar, St Lucia, Capetown and Colombo ensured a safeguard for the King's dominions and a 'security for such as pass on the seas upon their lawful occasions'. All these blessings, all these achievements had been, and were again to be, multiplied in the new machine age which the British had created. The nineteenth century belonged to Great Britain as surely as the seventeenth century to France, or the sixteenth century to Spain.

Although this wealth was based upon world-wide trading connexions, it was not dependent upon overseas dominions. British merchants had long abandoned, if indeed they had ever approved, the old mercantile system of trade within an enclosed empire. So far had the principles of Adam Smith triumphed, though full free trade was still far off, a Utopian dream. Meanwhile diplomatic action was directed towards opening markets; and fiscal reforms (after the Corn Law of 1815) towards loosening restrictions. Against this tendency, powerful groups of monopolists fought to retain their obsolescent privileges. First should be mentioned the landed interest at home, though their struggle to protect British agriculture against the advocates of cheap imported food and low wages lies outside the scope of this chapter. Next in importance was the West India Interest, by now highly organised to defend the sugar trade with a block of Tory votes in the House of Commons. Through their influence prohibitive duties on foreign sugar kept the price of colonial sugar up to 8d. a pound in the English shops.

The West India Interest was derived from the fusion of two groups, the absentee West Indian proprietors who lived in

England and the London merchants who traded to the West Indies. They had not always seen eye to eye, for example in 1733 when the planters persuaded Parliament to pass the Molasses Act in spite of the Shipping Interest.

As early as 1670 a number of planters met in London to recommend to the government of Barbados the appointment of a salaried agent who should represent their interests at home. The appointment was made in the following year and was soon imitated by Jamaica and other colonies. During Queen Anne's War the Commissioners of Trade and Plantations regularly consulted the colonial agents on such subjects as instructions for convoys. A Planters' Club was formed in London before 1740.

The trading interest first met at the Jamaica Coffee-house, a resort of sea-captains where, before 1700, letters were accepted for despatch to the West Indies. About the year 1750 there came into being a society of West India merchants, whose minute-books survive for the years 1769 to 1843; it was one of many regional trading associations. Monthly meetings were held; membership was by election; funds were raised by a voluntary levy of a penny on each cask of sugar shipped; and a paid secretary was appointed.

Trade dislocation during the American War caused such alarm that public meetings of planters and merchants were held in London and Bristol with the result that a standing committee was formed, in 1782, to represent their common interests. A secretary and treasurer were appointed, and Lord Penrhyn was the first chairman. This was the origin of the West India Committee which has an unbroken history to the present day, as one of the most influential of 'pressure-groups'.[1]

Three important chartered companies had survived into the new age. The East India Company still stood for the monopoly in China tea, and inevitably, since the Chinese Empire admitted no other merchants. Otherwise, after 1813, the Company had become a subsidiary organ of government. The Africa Company, since the abolition of the slave trade, had few functions beyond maintaining its mouldering fortresses on the shores of the Gulf of Guinea. In 1821 it was dissolved, after handing over its responsibilities to the Crown. The Hudson's Bay Company

[1] See L. M. Penson in *Eng. Hist. Review*, vol. 36.

alone survived as a body of traders with sovereign rights. Its territories were inaccessible and inhospitable; its system of trading posts was economical and effective, and it escaped the steady fire of criticism which other companies had to endure.

The newer generation of manufacturers, exporters, ship-owners and investors were turning away their eyes from the old monopoly trades, far afield to expanding markets which Adam Smith had not foreseen. Trading connexions with Europe, broken during the blockade, were not quickly renewed with the impoverished war-weary continental nations. While their commercial strength had been reduced during the wars, British trade had been growing in every other quarter of the globe. Naval superiority made it possible for British ships to carry British goods throughout the world in spite of Napoleon. After the war British capital established the trade and maintained the lead over other nations. The skill of British manufacturers and the wealth of British investors were now so great as to outweigh by far the advantages of a political monopoly. 'We had the ships, we had the men, we had the money too', and could afford to buy and sell in any market, whether the Union Jack flew over it or not. At this stage in British history, the old conception of the Balance of Trade was nullified by the appearance of 'invisible imports' which constituted an ever-growing proportion of the commercial turnover. Payments for shipping, banking and insurance; interest on foreign loans, and salaries to British technical experts residing abroad, all well-earned, were none the less a tribute paid by foreign nations to the British. In this sense several of the United States and large parts of South America were subject to the commercial empire of the City of London almost to the same degree that Jamaica and New Brunswick were subject to the Colonial Office.

In 1810, during the blockade of Europe but before the outbreak of the American War, North and South America took more than half of British exports, amounting in value to £26,000,000 out of £45,000,000, a high proportion in a boom year. After the reopening of the Continent, during the depressed years from 1815 to 1818, the United States alone took about a quarter of a smaller total. In the early 1820's, when the total exports averaged at about £36,000,000 annually, rather more than one-sixth went to the United States, almost one-sixth to Latin America and almost one-twelfth to the British West Indies. Canada absorbed a tiny fraction. Together the exports to the Americas amounted to about £14,000,000, a sum which equalled the exports to the Continent of Europe.

Cotton cloths were much the largest item in the British export trade. Before the war they had been negligible in value; by the 1820's they had risen to about £16,000,000 annually, whereas woollens, so long the staple of export, now came to no more than £6,000,000; Australian wool was not yet on the market. Iron and steel, the next on the list, made up less than £1,000,000. Liverpool, once the port of the slave trade, now prospered on slave-grown cotton, carrying 'Manchester goods' abroad and bringing back timber from eastern Canada in summer, and raw cotton in winter from the Gulf of Mexico. The Lancashire cotton trade had almost entirely grown up since the American Revolution. In 1775, while England still depended upon cotton piece-goods from Bengal, no more than 4,700,000 lbs of raw cotton had been imported, from the West Indies. The demand of the Lancashire mills for raw cotton during the next few years swelled the imports to 33,000,000 lbs in 1792, 57,000,000 lbs in 1802, 143,000,000 lbs in 1822 and vastly greater figures in later years. Three-quarters of this mass of raw material now came from the United States, especially from the 'sea-islands' off the Carolina coast where long-fibred cotton was grown in quality comparable with the finest from Bengal. Only fine muslins such as those which Henry Tilney priced for Catherine Morland were now brought from the East Indies.

While the Company retained its trading monopoly it was not likely to press for an increased export of Manchester goods to India. But, no sooner was the monopoly broken and traders admitted freely to British India (1813) than the people of India, and even of China, began to buy more of the cheap cottons from the Lancashire mills than they had ever bought of the fine cottons from the hand-looms of Bengal.

The Hudson Bay fur trade had given way in importance to the new import of timber from the Maritime Provinces of Canada. In 1802 the Baltic supplied almost the whole demand for masts and spars, in 1820 the Maritime Provinces supplied three-quarters of a demand that was steadily increasing. There were 1500 ships and 18,000 seamen employed in the Atlantic timber trade, a fruitful nursery of men for the Navy, and a great addition to the merchant service, since, in winter, when the St Lawrence was ice-bound, the ships were employed elsewhere. Nova Scotia ships and shipmasters played no small part in the making of a maritime empire. The Canadian trade was small in volume but important for its reactions on the whole naval and shipping interest. It therefore attracted some attention and earned preferential treat-ment. In the long struggle over the Corn Laws, Canadian wheat was brought into the system of imperial protection, though no-body then supposed that the surplus of Canadian harvests could ever be enough to swamp the English market.

Such preferences were concessions to imperial sentiment and were frowned upon by progressive economists and greedy exporters. Nevertheless the Tories were in office for eighteen years after Waterloo and were not to be rushed into radical experiments in free trade. The two statesmen principally con-cerned, Peel and Huskisson, continued the prudent, cautious methods of Pitt. War finance had been economical. Though the national debt had risen to over £800,000,000, that is seventy pounds per head of the population, imports, exports and revenue had also risen. The revenue (£103,000,000 in 1805, £120,000,000 in 1808, £131,000,000 in 1811), had reached £162,000,000 in 1814, which included £30,000,000 for the service of the national debt. Staggering as these amounts were by the standards of the previous age, the country seemed able to bear them, after the period of post-war disturbance had passed away. Normal trading conditions were reached when Peel, in 1819, stabilised the money market by restoring the gold standard.

Trade was secured by the campaign to suppress piracy in every sea, especially by the reduction—long overdue—of the strong-holds of the Barbary pirates in North Africa. The naval opera-tions by the Americans against Tripoli (1814) and by the British against Algiers (1816) may be considered as episodes in the abolition of the slave trade, since these African states lived by piracy and slave-trading.

Further steps towards a scientific tariff, rather than towards free trade were taken in 1823–5, when Huskisson was at the Board of Trade. The independence of the Latin-American republics was recognised and they were admitted to trade with the Empire on the same terms as the United States. Other nations were allowed to negotiate on terms of reciprocity for a share in the colonial trade. Much of the obstructive tangle of the Navigation Laws was swept away, but the main provision reserving trade within the Empire to ships registered under the British flag was retained, as perhaps it should have been retained to the present day. Preferences were granted to colonial goods, but the colonies were not yet permitted to fix their own tariffs. Though the dominions of the Crown were favoured and protected, their interest was not permitted to overrule the greater advantage to be derived by the mother-country from trade outside the Empire. India and the colonies provided some essential commodities such as tea, and sugar, and naval stores but on such a scale as to be able to buy back no more than one-third of the exports of Great Britain.

Sentiment could hardly count for much when the Empire was composed of such varied and substantially un-English component parts. Only in Canada was there a loyalist population of British origin. If the protected Indian states were taken into account the whole population of the Empire overseas exceeded one hundred millions, but of these less than one million were Europeans and less than half a million were British. The rest were French-Canadians, Cape Dutch, Bengali peasants, negro slaves and aboriginals of savage countries. In 1750 the population of the British Isles had been estimated at eight millions, while there were one-quarter of that number, about two million whites, in the American colonies. In 1821, the population of Great Britain was fourteen millions, with perhaps another six millions in Ireland, twenty millions in all, while the British overseas together made up less than a fortieth of that number, perhaps 250,000 in Canada, 100,000 in the West Indies, 50,000 in India, 30,000 in Australia, and smaller groups in other colonies. It was no wonder that the colonials carried little weight in Downing Street.

No one then living could foresee the future progress of the Industrial Revolution when steam-power should be surpassed by electric-power of which Great Britain had no privileged supply; when coal would be largely replaced by oil fuel of which she had no supplies at all; when Bombay, and even feudal Japan, would snatch away the textile trade from Lancashire, despite their less favourable climates; when America and Germany would be more intensively industrialised than England, and Russia bid fair to outstrip them both; when the population of Great Britain would be stabilised at forty-five millions while the despised colonies in a century would produce between them a British population of at least fifteen millions, a higher proportion of British overseas to British at home than before the separation of America.

7. THE HUDSON'S BAY COMPANY AND THE NOR'WESTERS

ONE effect of the Hudson's Bay monopoly had been to discourage exploration beyond the regular paths of the fur trade. With the exception of one lad named Henry Kelsey, who penetrated the country of the horse-riding Blackfeet Indians in 1690 and was the first European to see the prairie darkened with herds of buffalo, the Company's traders did little to explore the west during their first hundred years. The British conquest of Canada in 1763 opened the field to interlopers who threatened the monopoly. As early as 1768 a Scottish trader from Montreal went far into the west and soon, it was estimated, 500 *coureurs-de-bois* passed annually through Grand Portage at the west end of Lake Superior, taking westward with them the smallpox which killed off most of the Assiniboine Indians.

At last the Governors of the Hudson's Bay Company were stirred into competitive activity and began the systematic exploration of the far north-west which they called Rupertsland. Samuel Hearne was sent from Hudson Bay in 1768 to make a pact with the Athabasca Indians and to find a river flowing west. He wished to travel light, his Indian guides insisted on taking their squaws with them: 'Women,' they said, 'although they do everything, are maintained at very trifling expense, for as they always stand cook, the very licking of their fingers, in scarce times is sufficient for their sustenance.' He found his river and followed it, to the shores of the Arctic Ocean. The elusive North-west Passage had receded again. He also found that the Indians on the banks of his river, the Coppermine, made arrow-heads of pure copper, a new indication of the mineral wealth of Arctic Canada. A result of Hearne's voyage was the establishment of a Hudson Bay Post at Cumberland House on the Saskatchewan River.

The interlopers from Montreal became numerous and energetic, almost all of them Scotsmen. Simon McTavish first formed a group of them into a new fur-trading organisation, the North-western Company, in 1784. The Nor'westers were simply traders, with no royal charters or noble governors, and no legal rights of socage or jurisdiction. Their internal history was stormy with a long succession of amalgamations and schisms which led to fierce rivalries between groups. Agents went about the west competing for the allegiance of Indian tribes with gifts of rum. They fought one another for profitable areas and combined to fight the Hudson's Bay Company to northward and the American fur-traders to southward. In 1800 they reached a degree of equilibrium, moving their headquarters westward to Fort William (named after William McGillivray, one of their leaders) at the head of Lake Superior. 'The partners held a lordly sway over the wintry lakes and boundless forests of the Canadas', wrote Washington Irving with pardonable exaggeration. Their power, he said, was 'almost equal to that of the East Indian Company over the voluptuous climes of the Orient'. In 1800 they employed 50 clerks, 71 interpreters, 1120 canoemen and 35 guides; they exported annually 100,000 beaverskins and 80,000 other furs. One of the Nor'westers, James McGill, used his wealth to found a college at Montreal (1821) which has become a celebrated University.

Another Nor'wester of very independent views was (Sir) Alexander Mackenzie. In 1789, encroaching in undoubted Hudson Bay Territory, he reached and named the Mackenzie River, descending it to the Arctic Ocean. In 1793, portaging from the Peace River to the Fraser, he turned west and made the first crossing of the Rocky Mountains. On 22 July 1793 he reached the Pacific Ocean at Bella Coola, unperturbed among hostile Indians and timorous companions.

Twelve years passed before Mackenzie's discoveries were exploited, perhaps because of distractions in the Company's organisation. Between 1806 and 1811 two exploring parties from the North-western Company revealed the general topography of British Columbia just in time to save it from annexation by American rivals from the south. Simon Fraser, an Empire Loyalist, followed the course of what is now called the Fraser River; David Thompson followed the Columbia down to its mouth where he found the Americans already established in a trading post which they called Astoria (1811).

Until Mackenzie's expedition of 1793 there had been no crossing of the Rocky Mountains north of the Mexican border. Westward progress from the Thirteen Colonies had come to a halt where the tributaries of the Missouri rose in the dry prairie of the Middle West, then inaccurately described as the Great American Desert. Only in the far south had the continent been crossed by the Spaniards from Mexico, and that not long previously. In 1774 the Santa Fé route had been opened from New Mexico to the mission at Los Angeles in California. Otherwise all communication with western America had been by sea. Some account has been given in chapter IV, 1 of Byron's unsuccessful attempt and Cook's successful attempt to trace the Pacific coast in the latitudes which Drake had once visited; but this region in 1790 was a mere coastline on the map with no white settlement north of San Francisco. The effective survey was made by Captain George Vancouver (1792–4) who had learned his business as one of Cook's lieutenants. The coast was disputed by four claimants: the Russians, the British, and the Spanish by virtue of naval discovery, the Americans by virtue of cession from the British. Between 1790 and 1814 there was much diplomatic friction over these claims.

The affair of Nootka Sound, which led to the Spanish Armament crisis of 1790, is of great importance in the history of the west. In consequence of Cook's discoveries ships had come to the coast of what is now British Columbia to hunt for skins of the sea-otter (see page 462). In 1789 John Meares, the pioneer of the trade, was arrested, and his ship confiscated by a Spanish warship in Nootka Sound. Pitt took a strong line in Parliament, mobilising the Navy in preparation for war with Spain, a course in which he was strongly supported by the shipping interest in the House. The resulting negotiations, in which the Spaniards gave way on the main issue, led to far-reaching decisions. The attempted monopoly of the South Seas was at last abandoned. The King of Spain limited his claim to dominion 'so far as discoveries have been made and secured by treaties and immemorial possession', while navigation and fishing in the Pacific were thrown open to British subjects except within ten leagues of coasts occupied by Spain. In the Nootka Sound area the northern limit of the Spanish Empire was fixed at the Columbia River.

Ten years later Spain ceded the whole province of Louisiana to Napoleon, who sold it to the United States (1802). There remained great uncertainty as to the northern limits of Louisiana. The Americans claimed, and acted on the claim, that their purchase included a long stretch of the Pacific slope including what are now the states of Washington and Oregon. By this assumption they became Pacific neighbours to the British at the mouth of the Columbia River if, that is, they admitted the British right to Nootka Sound. Hence the efforts of the fur-traders on either side of the Columbia to stake out a claim for their respective countries, and hence the sudden determination to explore the routes across the Rockies.

About the same time that David Thompson was exploring the Columbia River, the American expedition of Lewis and Clark was wintering in Oregon, having spent two years in traversing America from St Louis on the Mississippi. John Jacob Astor, a Montreal fur-trader and the founder of the Astor family fortune, moved to New York with the intention of repeating the exploits of the North-western Company on the American side of the frontier. In 1810 he founded the Pacific Fur-trading Company with the ambitious plan of first sending his traders round the Horn to the Pacific coast and then supporting them by a chain of overland posts. After severe setbacks Astoria on the Columbia River was thus established. The War of 1812 brought rivalry with the British to blood-heat. The Nor'westers descended the Columbia, captured Astoria and renamed it Fort St George but, at the peace of 1814, were obliged to restore their prize. Thus a temporary frontier was fixed between Oregon and British Columbia under circumstances which left much room for future bickering.

Again the Governors of the Hudson's Bay Company attempted to assert their rights against the encroaching Nor'westers, the moving spirit being now a Scottish philanthropist, Thomas Douglas, 5th Earl of Selkirk (1771–1820). Like his friend Sir Walter Scott, he was a Lowlander deeply moved by the misfortunes of the Highland clansmen. The publication of Mackenzie's *Voyages through the Continent of North America* suggested to him that the displaced Highland crofters might be

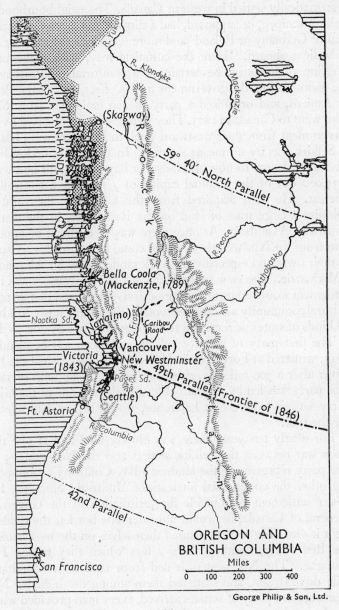

OREGON AND
BRITISH COLUMBIA

Miles

0 100 200 300 400

George Philip & Son, Ltd.

Map 7

systematically settled in western Canada. The neighbourhood of Lake Winnipeg, he supposed, had a climate 'not more severe than that of Germany or Poland' and more temperate than that of the Atlantic seaboard. 'Here the colonists may, with a moderate exertion of industry, be certain of a comfortable subsistence.' He memorialised the government to this effect, during the Peace of Amiens, and organised a party of 800 emigrants from Skye who went to Canada in 1803. They were, however, diverted by the government from their westward goal, to Prince Edward Island.

Selkirk was by no means satisfied. In 1810, after taking legal advice, he began to buy up Hudson's Bay stock until he owned £35,000 out of the nominal capital of £105,000, a controlling interest. He then acquired from the Company the right to colonise a large tract of land on the Red River, in the district known as Assiniboia. At once there was an outburst of opposition from the Nor'westers who had come to regard this territory as their own, and especially from Alexander (now Sir Alexander) a Mackenzie. The view of the Hudson's Bay Governors was that settlement would confirm their prescriptive right, and that an agricultural community would grow food for the trading posts, to which all kinds of stores were carried from great distances by dog-sledge.

The first party of seventy Selkirk emigrants left Scotland in 1811, wintered at Fort York in Hudson Bay and reached the Red River after a 700 miles overland journey in the autumn of 1812. The party was led by Captain Miles Macdonell, one of the Glengarry settlers from the St Lawrence, whom Selkirk had selected for the task.

For nearly ten years there was bloody feud and at one time open war between the Selkirk settlers and the Nor'westers, the one party representing the Hudson's Bay Company's monopoly, the other the commercial interests of Montreal. Since the Red River settlement lay outside the jurisdiction of the Governor-General of Canada, he would not intervene but left the rivals to fight it out. The settlers planted themselves on the west bank of the Red River, building there a fort which they named Fort Douglas. The Nor'westers issued from their Fort Gibraltar, a mile downstream, and scattered them among the Indians. Next year a second party of settlers arrived, every man provided with a musket and bayonet and an Indian pony. They too were driven away and Macdonell, captured by the Nor'westers, was packed off to Montreal. The third party in 1814 still clung to Fort Douglas but not much more. In 1815, a larger and better-organised party arrived from Sutherland led by Robert Semple, while simultaneously Selkirk from Montreal despatched experienced Scots and French-Canadians to their assistance. The Nor'westers, led by Cuthbert Grant, brought matters to a head by a direct assault upon Fort Douglas. Semple rashly sallied forth and was killed with more than twenty of his men in the Battle of Seven Oaks (June 1816).

Selkirk, exasperated at his failure to get support from government, now took the law into his own hands like a true Scottish nobleman of the old times. He enlisted a band of soldiers, largely Swiss mercenaries discharged in Canada at the Peace of 1814, and set off for the west with his fighting tail. He seized Fort William, arrested the partners of the North-western Company, and confiscated their private papers; then despatched Macdonell with men and guns to regain Fort Douglas far away on the Red River. Violence on the most distant frontier might pass unchecked by government but warfare on Lake Superior was another thing. The fur-traders of Montreal got a warrant for Selkirk's arrest; which he refused to accept. The Selkirk settlers were again in possession of their land and could defend it, but the struggle continued in the Canadian courts where charges and countercharges were laid and argued for several years. The dominant faction at Montreal, known as the Family Compact, were hot against Selkirk and resisted the conciliatory efforts of Lord Bathurst the Colonial Secretary. Selkirk was a 'canting rascal and hypocritical villain. He has got possession of our Fort William. Well, we will get him out of it and the Hudson's Bay knaves shall be cleared, bag and baggage, out of the North-west.' 'Fort William', said Selkirk, 'had served, the last of any in the British dominions, as an asylum for banditti and murderers, and the receptacle of their plunder.' Both companies were obliged by the courts to restore their conquests; the charges of murder against the Nor'westers broke down, since the Battle of Seven Oaks had been fought outside Canadian jurisdiction but, after long litigation, Selkirk was mulcted of heavy damages for his seizure of Fort William. He died in 1820 a disappointed man, too soon to see the reconciliation. His happiest years had been spent at Red River (1817–18) administering his little colony.

In 1821, the North-western Company was absorbed into its older rival, giving the Hudson's Bay Company undisputed power over territories stretching from Labrador to Vancouver Island, from the Yukon to Lake Superior. Selkirk's rights to the lands occupied by the Red River settlers were resumed by the Company in 1836 after a composition with his heirs.

The years between their union with the Nor'westers (1821) and the surrender of their vast estates (1870) were the great age of the Hudson's Bay Company; their policy being much enlivened by the ruthless energy of the free traders who had joined them. Sir George Simpson (1792–1860), who became governor of the northern department in 1823, was the driving force of the new trade; he was 'ever the fastest of travellers', and his progress in state on the Red River with a crew of scarlet-liveried Indians and with a Highland piper in attendance was long remembered. In 1841 he crossed the North Pacific in order to make an overland journey round the world through Siberia. He was a good friend to the Indians, not least for restricting the allowance of spirits given to them at the trading posts; though the saying in the west was that 'a beaver-skin was never lost to the H.B.C. for want of a bottle of rum'. The ferocious Blackfeet Indians met Simpson at Edmonton, imploring him with the rhetoric due to a wonder-working chief that 'their horses might always be swift, that the buffalo might abound, and that their women might live long and look young'. His policy was to fix the Indians in certain areas where they might trade with the Company's agents, but to extinguish their vague claims to undefined hunting-grounds. A 'Hudson's Bay Company Indian' was always a term of praise in the west.

Later he settled at Lachine, near Montreal, now the gateway of the west, but once the westerly limit of the first French settlement. Thence the French-Canadian *voyageurs* set out for their long journey westward by water, to St Anne's and the Ottawa River, past the Calumet rapids and over the portage into Lake Nipissing, then by the French River to Georgian Bay, through the rapids of Sault Ste Marie (by-passed by a canal in 1855) into the cool, deep waters of Lake Superior, until Thunder Cape brought the prospect of the rude luxury of Fort William.

From the western forts the trains of dog-sledges set out in winter to travel forty miles a day across the snow with pro-

visions for the distant trading posts, some so remote that they
were only visited once a year with their mail and a complete
year's file of the *Montreal Gazette*. Months later the sledges
returned freighted with beaver-skins. At one far post between
Labrador and Hudson Bay a young man named R. M. Ballantyne
was stationed in the 'forties. He returned home to write books for
boys (*The Young Fur-Traders*, 1856, *Ungava*, 1857, *The Dog*

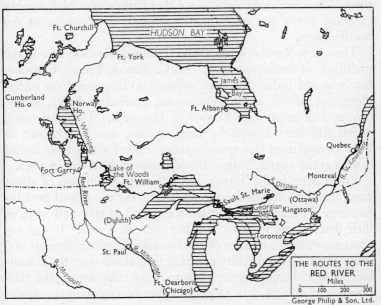

Map 8

Crusoe, 1860) which, though they have not retained the celebrity
of his *Coral Island*, are still known to the present generation of
boys and girls.

The Red River settlement became the central depot for the
Hudson Bay territories. Selkirk's colony never flourished.
Sections of land were laid out along the river bank and sold for a
mere registration fee. Their frontage having been surveyed, their
depth ran conventionally 'as far back from the river as a man could
see looking under a horse'. The few settlers, after enduring every
setback and surviving every plague, began about 1826 to get
bumper harvests, proving that Manitoba could rival the black
soil of Russia in fertility; but as yet they had no more than the

local market and only rudimentary communications with the world. North to York Factory on Hudson Bay, east to Fort William on Lake Superior, south to St Paul on the Mississippi the journey was more than 400 miles by any route, even to the outposts of civilisation. The best outlet was southward over the American border to St Paul by the celebrated York boats designed to cross the portages from Hudson Bay to the Red River, or by the no less celebrated two-wheeled Red River carts which went in caravans across the open prairie through the country of the hostile Sioux.

Those few Scottish settlers who remained were lost among the multitude of buffalo-hunters, H.B.C. traders, French-Canadian boatmen and Indians of many tribes who frequented the settlement, and formed, in two generations, a turbulent, brave, adventurous, half-breed race known as the *métis*. The settlement, which had been known by many names, was best known as Fort Garry, from the great, square, stone fortress with round towers at the angles, built at the junction of the rivers in 1836.

Fort Garry, in the 'forties, had a floating population of about 5000, mostly half-breeds who assembled for the annual buffalo-hunting. Tourists came out from England to take part in it, as their descendants went to hunt big game in Kenya. 'It was not uncommon to see officers of the Guards, Knights, baronets and some of the higher nobility coursing their steeds over the boundless plains and enjoying the pleasure of the chase among the half-breeds and savages.' In 1840, a leaguer of 1200 wagons moved out from Fort Garry for the annual round-up and slaughter of the buffalo herds, under an elected captain and an agreed code of camp rules. The *métis* counted on making more money by riding down and shooting buffalo on these annual expeditions than by the rest of the year's work. The buffalo were killed for their skins and for their tongues, said to be the most delicious meat in the world.

It was a great day for Fort Garry when, in 1844, Dr G. J. Mountain, the Anglican Bishop of Quebec, arrived by canoe to inspect the C.M.S. mission which had laboured there since 1820. He ordained three clergy and confirmed 800 persons. At his instance the diocese (later the arch-diocese) of Rupertsland was formed in 1849. The first Archbishop, Robert Machray who held the see from 1864 to 1904, found 12,000 inhabitants on the Red River, a few hundreds only being of his communion. He was a

powerful organiser of missions and schools, a pillar of the
Anglican Church and of the British connexion in the west, the
true founder of the University of Manitoba, and a wise counsellor
to the Colonial Office on confederation. In the far north the
Anglican missions have made progress among the eskimos who
are mostly attached to that communion, while the Canadian
Indians, through their old association with the French, adhere to
the French-Canadian Catholic missions, established in the north-
west since 1818. Selkirk had found the Red River in the days of
the Nor'westers a place without religion; 'no trace of temple or
idol or place of Christian worship'. He had promised his Highlanders a Scottish minister; but when at last one came in 1851 he
proved of small service as he had no Gaelic. Presbyterian influence in the west came later with emigration from Ontario;
the early Methodists came over the border from the United
States. While Machray was the religious and educational leader
of the British settlers, an equivalent part was played among the
far more numerous *métis* by the French-Canadian, Father A. A.
Taché (1823–94) who, after long missionary labours in the west,
became the first Roman Catholic Bishop of Manitoba in 1871.

8. FRONTIER PROBLEMS IN AMERICA: NORTHERN AND SOUTHERN SEAS

(1) THE CANADIAN FRONTIER

THE Treaty of Ghent, at the end of the War of 1812–14, left
many outstanding subjects for dispute, of which some were
settled at a further conference in 1818. By what was called the
Rush-Bagot Treaty of that year both nations agreed to disband
their naval forces on the Great Lakes, a triumph for the cause of
disarmament; and progress was made in delineating the Canadian
frontier in those regions where it had been left uncertain at the
Treaty of 1783. While it was not difficult to fix it at the forty-
ninth parallel of latitude across the featureless central plains the
eastern and western extremities were uncertain because the
country was unmapped. The respective rights of British and
American fishermen off Newfoundland were also defined.

As the United States increased in wealth and power, far more rapidly than its northern and southern neighbours, republican fervour produced an expansionist policy. At every corner of the Union, in Maine and Oregon, in Florida and Texas, the Americans seemed anxious to meet the fate foretold for those who remove their neighbours' land-mark. A thousand speeches and newspapers proclaimed the intention to assume, sooner or later, a protectorate over all North America, if not actually to annex it. This was, it was said, the 'manifest destiny' of the New World; it was extended to South America by President Monroe's message to Congress in December 1823.

During the Napoleonic Wars the Spanish Empire in America had withered away. While Spain itself had been liberated with British help, the trade of the Indies and the Spanish Main had passed into the hands of British merchants. By 1822 the southern provinces, the modern Argentine Republic, had virtually been independent for several years, while in Mexico, Central America and Colombia (then much larger than it now is) the Spanish power was moribund. Peru and Chile were in revolt. In that year the United States recognised the independence of the Spanish colonies and Chambers of Commerce in British cities petitioned Canning to do likewise. Though the United States stood forth as their champion it was Great Britain that supplied them with money, shipping and soldiers of fortune, Great Britain alone that could prevent a reconquest from Europe. But to recognise their independence would be an affront to Spain which Canning could not justify, it must be 'a matter of time and circumstance'. He accordingly appointed consular agents in 1823, and despatched commissioners to report on the affairs of South America.

The kingdom of Spain was too distracted and weak to undertake any great campaign for the recovery of *España Ultramar*. It was only when a French army intervened in Spanish affairs in 1823 to restore a despotic king that Canning took action. 'I determined', he said, 'that if France held Spain, it should not be Spain with the Indies. I called the New World into existence to redress the balance of the Old.' He positively warned the French off any attempt to restore the Spanish power in South America. A few weeks later President Monroe announced the policy which came to be known as the Monroe Doctrine, the isolation of the Americas from European imperialisms. Though Monroe appeared to echo Canning's decision he was swayed by other considerations. The message to Congress was not drafted with British collusion and was, in part, a threat to British interests. 'The American continents', said Monroe, 'are henceforth not to be considered as future subjects for colonisation by any European power.' From its context it is clear that he aimed this shaft at the Russians and the British who were staking out claims on the unoccupied North Pacific coast of America. 'With the existing colonies and dependencies', he went on to say, 'we have not interfered and shall not interfere, but with the governments who have declared their independence and maintained it, we could not view any interposition...by any European power, in any other light than as the manifestation of an unfriendly disposition towards the United States.'

This unilateral declaration, though it has come to be accepted as a fundamental rule of international affairs, at first had little effect. The South American governments were far more concerned with what Canning did than with what Monroe said. While Canning made it clear to the Americans that the British would oppose French designs on Mexico, and harboured no designs of their own on Cuba, he pressed on with commercial negotiations. Sir Woodbine Parish (1796–1882), his commissioner at the River Plate, convinced him in 1824 that the new state there (later known as the Argentine) deserved diplomatic recognition. A commercial treaty (1825)[1] of reciprocal free trade between Great Britain and the Argentine not only conferred untold blessings on the people of both nations for a hundred years but convinced Canning that he had deflated the Monroe Doctrine. South America was again drawn into the circle of the older nations. The recognition of the other Spanish-American republics followed in 1825.

The Canadian frontier was the scene of further friction in the 1830's. Not only did Canadians and Americans clash at several points during the Canadian Rebellion of 1837 (see below, page 340), each accusing the other of frontier violation, but the infiltration of American lumbermen over the New Brunswick frontier along the Restook (or Aroostook) River led to something that approached guerrilla warfare. Since the seventeenth century the New England states had maintained claims to this country, which

[1] See Appendix IV, 'The British in South America'.

the British resisted on the grounds that it had passed to them with the sovereignty of French Acadie. An arbitration by the King of Holland in 1829 was not accepted by either party. As usual the crux of the question was geographical, to decide which was the 'St Croix river' and where lay the 'north-west angle of Nova Scotia' mentioned in the Treaty of 1783. When Peel came into

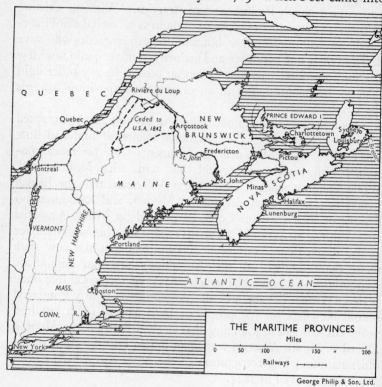

George Philip & Son. Ltd.

Map 9

office he despatched Lord Ashburton as a special envoy to settle this and other questions by direct diplomacy. The negotiations leading to the Ashburton-Webster Treaty, 1842, may perhaps be regarded as reasonable since David Webster was bitterly assailed in Congress for giving way to the British while Ashburton was equally abused by the Canadians.[1] The district

[1] It should be remembered that the infiltration across the unknown, unmarked, frontier went both ways. Over a million French-Canadians have made their way into New England and remain unassimilated.

between the Restook and St John Rivers, rather more than half the disputed area but less than the award made by the King of Holland, was ceded to the United States. One positive result was that the American State of Maine thereafter lay across the direct route from Quebec to Halifax, thus hindering the progress of communications. Peel and Ashburton did not regard this as of equal consequence with their success in gaining some American co-operation against the slave trade. Almost at once a new conflict arose over the frontier in the Far West.

The dispute with Russia was settled after negotiation in 1824. The Russians undertook not to extend their settlement southward beyond latitude 54° 40′ N. They retained not only Alaska but the coastal strip known as the Alaska Panhandle which barred access to the sea from the northern part of the Hudson's Bay Company's territories. (In 1867 Alaska and its Panhandle were sold by Russia to the United States.) The Spanish territories, limited by the Treaty of 1819 to the coast south of latitude 42°, became a province of the Mexican Republic three years later. Between 54° 40′ N. and 42° N. the coastal strip was known as Oregon and was visited by British and American sealing-ships. Inland the country was 'freely open to the citizens of both powers without prejudice to the claims of either'. The Hudson Bay traders frequented the Fraser valley and Vancouver Island, the Astoria traders frequented the Columbia valley.

In the eighteen-forties the first covered wagons reached the west by way of the Oregon Trail. The advent of settlers made it imperative to settle the sovereignty of the fur-trader's Alsatia. The democratic candidate for the presidency in 1844, James Polk, went to the polls on the slogan: 'fifty-four forty or fight', that is: exclude the British from the whole of Oregon up to the Russian frontier; but the British took the prospect calmly. When Polk was safely elected he stopped the agitation since it was not his real aim to multiply the free states of the north-west; it suited him better to support the filibusters of the southern frontier who were infiltrating Texas, New Mexico and California, regions where the southerners might increase their influence by forming new slave-states. The whole of this southern region was ceded to the United States in 1848 after the American invasion of Mexico. Meanwhile, Polk had been glad to negotiate with Great

Britain the Oregon Treaty of 1846 which partitioned the Oregon territory according to the spheres of interest of the fur-trading companies. Some years later the new American state of Washington was formed south of the line, and north of it the new colony of British Columbia, within its present frontiers.

(2) CENTRAL AMERICA

When the Gold Rush of 1849 sent hundreds of thousands of emigrants to California, some plodding over the desert and others tossing round Cape Horn, the old project, talked of since the days of Philip II of Spain, for a canal across the Central American isthmus was brought forward. American filibusters were active both in Nicaragua and Panama, seeking for concessions which might enable them to annex territory as they had annexed Texas and California. In 1846 the Americans got their first concession for a canal through the Isthmus of Panama. By the Clayton-Bulwer Treaty of 1850, Great Britain and the United States bound themselves not to annex territory or extend their dominion at the expense of the Central American republics. On their late record the Americans exposed themselves to deep suspicion, and they, too, were deeply suspicious of British designs on Nicaragua, another possible site for an isthmian canal. The presidential election of 1852 was again fought on the popular platform of restraining British imperialism, which was again challenged in respect of the frontiers of British Honduras.

The English 'baymen' in the seventeenth century ranged along the Caribbean coast of Central America for 600 miles from Campeachy Bay in what is now Mexico to the San Juan River which divides Nicaragua from Costa Rica. At two points, Belize and the Moskito (or Mosquito) Coast, these Englishmen were the first European settlers and could claim effective occupation since the seventeenth century. The British claim to Belize is unquestionable *de facto*; the town was founded more than three hundred years ago by Englishmen in a region which was never occupied by the Spaniards or by their successor states. The basis of the claim *de jure* is the Treaty of Madrid, 1670, by which the king of Spain ceded to King Charles II, in full sovereignty 'all lands, provinces, islands, colonies, and dominions in the West Indies or in any part of America which the said king of Great Britain and his subjects have and possess at present'. During the next hundred years the English interpreted this claim widely, while the Spaniards restricted it to the right of cutting logwood at Belize. In each of the eighteenth-century treaties, the English privilege was more strictly defined and notably at the Treaty of 1783 after the disastrous American War. 'His Britannic Majesty's subjects', declared the treaty, 'shall have the right of cutting logwood between the Rivers Wallis (or Belize) and Hondo. These stipulations are not to be taken as derogatory in any way from the rights of [Spanish] sovereignty.' This was the narrowest definition in the Series and, three years later, was modified by a Convention which again widened the British privilege.

In the same year (1786) a 'superintendent' was appointed by the British Government to administer the settlement according to their customary code, known as Burnaby's Laws. There were then about 200 whites, 200 coloured men and 900 slaves engaged in the wood-cutting trade. They asserted their loyalty by manning a flotilla which defeated a Spanish squadron off St George's Bay, near Belize, on 10 September 1798, a day of which the anniversary is still a holiday in British Honduras. At the end of the War, in 1814, a treaty with Spain renewed the *status quo ante*.

Much farther down the coast the British protectorate over the Moskito Indians rested on a different sanction. From Charles II's reign onwards a series of treaties of alliance had been made between British Governments and successive 'kings of the Moskitos', of whom one paid a state visit to London in 1796. The Moskitos had never been conquered by the Spaniards. But the Moskito Coast was very loosely administered by a Captain-general, usually despatched from Jamaica. Whereas on the mainland there were only woodcutters' camps among the Indians, there was in the Bay Islands a long-established colony of English settlers. At the Convention of 1786, the British had undertaken to withdraw from the Moskito Coast and the Bay Islands, but the settlers clung to their homes.

Though the Spanish colonies declared their independence in 1821 it was not until 1838 that the republics of Guatemala, Nicaragua, and Honduras were established in their present boundaries. They soon began to press for boundary settlements with the British Colony. Palmerston took a high line in these negotiations, especially over the Moskito Coast which, he said, 'has for upwards of 180 years been acknowledged as being under the protection of the British Crown'. He intervened several times with naval forces against Nicaraguan filibusters. But after the Clayton-Bulwer Treaty this 'protection' could hardly be maintained. Sir C. L. Wyke was despatched to Central America to negotiate treaties with the new republics. On 30 April 1859, a treaty was signed at Guatemala City, making provision for the demarcation of a boundary between Guatemala and British Honduras, and clearly stating (Article 1) that 'all the territory north and east of the boundary belongs to Her Britannic Majesty'. Article (7) of the Treaty led to prolonged negotiation. It declared that the two parties would 'mutually agree conjointly to make their best efforts for establishing communications between the fittest place on the Atlantic Coast near Belize and the capital of Guatemala'. After seven years the discussions lapsed since the cost of a road deterred both parties. Sixty years later, when a far better line of communication had long been opened to the Atlantic through Puerto Barrios, the Guatemalan Government threatened to denounce the Treaty on the grounds that Article 7 had not been implemented. Again long discussions took place until, in 1938 Lord Halifax proposed to refer the issue to arbitration, which the Guatemalans prudently declined.[1]

After coming to terms with Guatemala, Wyke negotiated next with Nicaragua, the point at issue being to ensure the rights of the Moskito Indians. A Treaty renouncing the British 'protection' but declaring that they should retain autonomy within the Nicaraguan State was signed on 28 January 1860 and, as recently as 1905, the Foreign Office used its influence on behalf of the Indians. The British then withdrew from the Nicaraguan Coast, leaving the isthmus free for the American imperialists of the next generation. Less reputable was the withdrawal of British authority from the Bay Islands. The Government withdrew; the British settlers did not. A visitor in 1937 described the islanders as being about 4000 in number, half of them of pure British stock. They were engaged in trading fruit and copra in their own schooners and were stubbornly resistant against the efforts of the Honduran government to latinise them.

[1] After 1814, British Honduras was regarded a colony by the Colonial Office, though not brought under normal 'Crown Colony' administration until 1870. The trade in logwood was superseded by a trade in mahogany, and later by that in *chicle*, one of the constituents of chewing-gum.

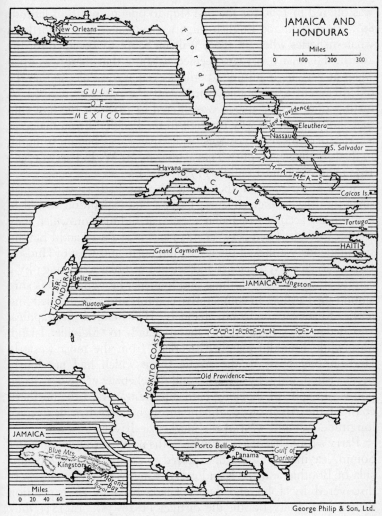

JAMAICA AND
HONDURAS

Miles

0   100   200   300

George Philip & Son, Ltd.

Map 10

(3) THE ARCTIC

A renewed interest in polar exploration may be traced to the
development of the whale-fisheries, both in northern and southern
waters, after Cook's demonstration that long voyages could be
made without loss of life. Exchequer bounties were given as an
inducement to Greenland whalers, and a special award of £5000

was offered in 1776 for the first ship to operate north of latitude 80°. More than 200 English ships were engaged in the northern whale-fisheries when, in 1806, William Scoresby qualified for the award. His many voyages seemed to show that there was open water at very high latitudes, perhaps even at the Pole, so that the old dream of a navigable North-west Passage was revived. A further reward of £20,000 was offered in 1818 for the first ship that should make its way through to the Pacific. From that year a series of authorised voyages of discovery was begun, bringing to the fore the names of two naval officers, Sir W. E. Parry (1790–1855) and Sir John Franklin (1786–1846).

Since knowledge of the Arctic regions had actually waned since the Elizabethan voyages, Parry's first expedition served to confirm the accuracy of Baffin's 200-year-old map on which they were recorded. Then between 1819 and 1821 Parry and Franklin simultaneously attacked the icy region north and west of Hudson Bay. Parry evolved the art and science of polar voyaging; by a careful study of diet, clothing and hygiene, he wintered his ship among the ice-floes in comparative comfort and sent out sledging parties to survey the frozen channels. He extended geographical knowledge westward from Baffin Land to Melville Island. Meanwhile Franklin marched overland from the most westerly Hudson Bay posts to the Arctic shore which had previously been visited only by Hearne and Mackenzie at two isolated points. In spite of shocking hardships he traversed the northern coast of the American continent through thirty-five degrees of longitude east and west of the Mackenzie River.

Parry's route had taken him far to the north through Lancaster Sound, leaving vast areas unexplored to southward. The peninsula of Boothia and the island called King William's Land were discovered by John and James Clark Ross in an expedition financed by Felix Booth, the distiller (1829–31). In 1831 they claimed to have identified the position of the Magnetic Pole. The outline of the coast westward from Hudson Bay to the limit reached by Franklin was filled in by Thomas Simpson, an official of the Hudson's Bay Company, in 1836–7. The general shape of the land-masses in the Arctic was by this time pretty well understood.

During the next few years Clerk Ross was leading an expedition to the Antarctic under the patronage of Franklin who had

been sent as Governor of Tasmania. In 1845 Franklin returned
to the north with Ross's two ships, to complete the series of
expeditions by an attempt to force the North-west Passage.
Three years later, since no news of him had been received, the
Admiralty sent a relief expedition. While no certain trace was
found, the rumour grew slowly into a certainty that Franklin's

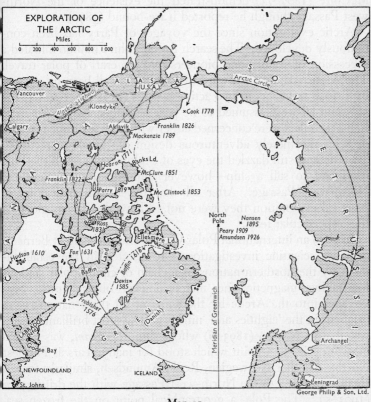

EXPLORATION OF THE ARCTIC

Miles
0   200   400   600   800   1 000

Vancouver

A L A S K A (U.S.A.)

Arctic Circle

Klondyke?

× Cook 1778

Calgary

Aklavik

× Franklin 1826

Mackenzie 1789

Hearne 1771

Banks Ld.

Franklin 1822 ×

McClure 1851

Parry 1819

Mc Clintock 1853

North Pole

Nansen × 1895

Peary 1909
Amundsen 1926

Ross × 1831

Ellesmere Ld.

Hudson 1610

Fox 1631

Baffin Land

Baffin 1616

Davis 1585

Frobisher 1576

G R E E N L A N D (Danish)

Meridian of Greenwich

Archangel

LABRADOR

Goose Bay

NEWFOUNDLAND

ICELAND

St. Johns

Leningrad

George Philip & Son, Ltd.

Map 11

voyage had ended in disaster. His wife raised funds for a search-
party, and then for others. Not less than seven fully-equipped
expeditions and many lesser ones were organised to discover the
fate of Sir John Franklin; by the Admiralty, by Lady Franklin,
by the Hudson's Bay Company, and by American sympathisers.
Though his ships were never found, evidence accumulated that
Franklin had discovered, but had failed to force his way through,

a westward channel south of Prince of Wales's Island. In 1846 he died. After two winters his men had abandoned their ice-bound ships intending to make their way overland to Canada, but all perished on the journey. The story was revealed at last by Sir F. L. McClintock (1819–1907), a masterly exponent of sledge-travelling, in 1859. Another of the searchers, Sir R. McClure (1807–73) demonstrated the existence of the North-west Passage though he reported it ice-bound (1850).

Arctic exploration since the voyages of Parry has been continuously developed. The search for Sir John Franklin initiated a succession of seamen and pioneers into the craft of polar travel. The Arctic islands northward of Canada had all been discovered by British travellers in two active periods (1578–1631 and 1818–59); and all were assumed to be part of British North America. Later travellers were concerned either with pure scientific research or with the merely adventurous design of 'breaking records'. Two dreams still dazzled the eyes of explorers: to reach the Pole itself and to sail a ship—however unprofitably—through the North-west Passage. After all that the British had done in practical exploration they were not to have the barren glory of these spectacular feats.

In 1879 an international Polar Conference was held at Berne to organise scientific investigations. It resulted in the establishment by the northern nations of a chain of circumpolar stations for taking magnetic and meteorological observations. Sea-voyages into the Arctic by the ships of all these nations were frequent in the 'eighties and 'nineties. The most brilliant exploit was that of Nansen (1893–6) whose ship, the *Fram*, was carried in drifting ice to a point which stood for many years as Farthest North. Another Norwegian, Roald Amundsen, similarly took a small ship through the North-west Passage with the drifting ice (1903–5).[1] The Pole, a geographical point on the frozen sea, was reached (1909) by the American, Robert Peary, who trained his team of Eskimo and European assistants as for an athletic contest.

[1] In 1937 the Hudson's Bay Company established a post at Fort Ross in Bellot Strait. Occasional trading voyages east and west from that post by the Company's ships have actually put the North-west Passage to commercial use.

(4) THE FALKLAND ISLANDS
AND THE ANTARCTIC

The exploration of the Southern Seas also was due to the activity of the whalers. In addition to the extension of geographical knowledge they were largely responsible for the early settlement of the southern colonies. Many voyages were despatched through the enterprise of Messrs Enderby, the shipowners, into the seas southward of the Falklands where Cook had noted the existence of South Georgia. The South Shetlands were discovered by the whalers in 1819, South Orkney in 1822. So many ships frequented the Falklands in these years that they became a subject of dispute among the powers; and it will be convenient to recapitulate their history at this point.

As early as 1592 the Elizabethan navigator, John Davis, discovered a lonely rainy group of islands 400 miles north-east of Cape Horn. They were rarely visited for a hundred years until another English sailor, Captain J. Strong, called there in 1689 and named them the Falkland Islands. On his voyage round the world (1740–4) Anson remarked upon their strategic value for controlling the South American trade routes, whereafter they received attention from the British, French and Spanish admiralties. The French navigator, Bougainville, landed a few settlers on one island of the group, which he called Les Malouines, in 1764. Without knowledge of this French move the British Government instructed Admiral Byron to annex the islands on his way to the Pacific in the following year. His formal act of annexation was confirmed by the building of a blockhouse on another of the islands, at which a small party of British soldiers were left, in remote isolation, to show the flag (1765). Two years later France ceded her claim upon the islands to Spain. So soon as he heard of the British outpost the Spanish Governor of Buenos Ayres took steps to crush it, by a show of force in the islands and by diplomatic pressure in Europe, with the result that the little garrison was withdrawn. The British government was sharply criticised in London for this compliance and all the more because they still claimed theoretical sovereignty over the Falkland Islands, even after removing the evidence of its reality (1774). For some years afterwards the islands were unoccupied and their sovereignty in dispute. The Spaniards claimed that the British relinquished their pretension to possess the islands by the Nootka Sound Convention (1790).

When Buenos Ayres revolted from Spain the nascent national feeling of the Argentine Republic was reasserted in the Falkland Islands which were proclaimed a dependency in 1820, under the name of Las Malvinas. Settlers sent from the Argentine found a fleet of fifty British and American whalers in the anchorage. But at that time there was friction between the Argentine and the United States. When the Argentine authorities arrested the crew of an American whaler for riotous conduct, an American warship bombarded and destroyed the Argentine settlement, leaving the Islands again desolate and in dispute. The British claim had never been allowed to lapse but was maintained by Sir W. Parish. In 1832 at the instance of the Royal Navy it was again asserted and has since been maintained. The Colonial Office took charge of the group in 1843 setting up an administration at a new settlement which was named after Stanley, the Secretary of State (1844). Again a tiny garrison was established, its strength (according to a return made in 1858) no more than thirty-five soldiers. At first a whaling-station and a strategic *point d'appui*, the Falkland Islands were then developed as a great sheep-run. S. F. Lafone, the merchant and rancher of Montevideo acquired a large estate (1845), which he stocked with sheep and managed with Scottish shepherds and South American *gauchos*. In 1851 his interest was bought out by the Falkland Islands Company which G. T. Whittington had founded some years earlier in London.

Crown Colony government on normal lines dates from 1892, the year which also saw the foundation of an Anglican bishopric. In 1938–9 the population was estimated at 2378, 'mostly British'. The islands contained 600,000 sheep, which produced about four million pounds of wool annually. But in recent years a new importance has come to the Islands from the whale-fisheries. Since northern waters have been over-fished the whalers have returned to the south and now get about five-sixths of the world's supply of whale-oil from the Antarctic. Dundee whaling-steamers began to make their base at the Falklands in 1892.

In 1923 the Colonial Office appointed a research committee to investigate the distribution and habits of whales, in order to preserve them, and the whaling industry, from extinction. It was generally know as the Discovery Committee, from the name of

Captain Scott's ship, *Discovery*, which was acquired for its use. The work of research and the consequent control of the whalers was administered by the Governor of the Falkland Islands whose authority was extended, in 1917, to cover all the islands and territories to the southward of the Falklands between the fiftieth and eightieth degrees of west longitude. On the island of South Georgia a resident magistrate was sent to preside over the most southerly settlement in the world.

In the two German Wars the Falkland Islands proved their worth as naval bases. Old Anson's prudence was justified five generations after his death by two naval victories, at the Falkland Islands, December 1914, and at the River Plate, November 1939.

The general exploration of the South Polar regions was not much advanced for sixty years after Cook crossed the Antarctic Circle, at several points, in 1772-3. A naval expedition under Sir James Clark Ross established the fact, in 1839-42,[1] that a mountainous mass of high land lay within the Great Ice Barrier. He penetrated the wide inlet known as the Ross Sea, and saw the two volcanoes which have been named Mount Erebus and Mount Terror, in honour of his two ships. Ross had demonstrated that, after all, there was an Antarctic Continent, part of which he annexed under the name of Victoria Land. Sixty years passed before any systematic attempt was made to investigate it. This long period was bridged by the life of the botanist, Sir Joseph Hooker (1817-1911), who accompanied Ross as a young man and survived to give his advice upon Scott's first and second voyages.

In 1898 an expedition under the Norwegian, Borchgrevink, wintered on the Antarctic Continent, and thereafter voyages of discovery were frequent. Three large expeditions were organised by British scientific bodies with help from the Royal Navy in 1901-4, 1908-9, and 1911-12, the first and third under Captain R. F. Scott, R.N. (1868-1912), the second under his lieutenant (Sir) E. H. Shackleton (1874-1922). Those who were best qualified to know gave the highest praise to Shackleton for his journey by sledge, in 1909, over the high plateau of Antarctica to a point within two degrees of the Pole. Since these expeditions were

---

[1] Wilkes's American expedition (see p. 786) visited the other side of the Antarctic Continent during the same years. He was probably the first to sight the land mass.

concerned with investigating the geography, climate and natural resources of the Antarctic, the race for the South Pole was incidental. Nevertheless the heroism of Scott's last journey, in which he and his four comrades lost their lives, is not likely to be forgotten. Amundsen, who had prepared Nansen's old ship,

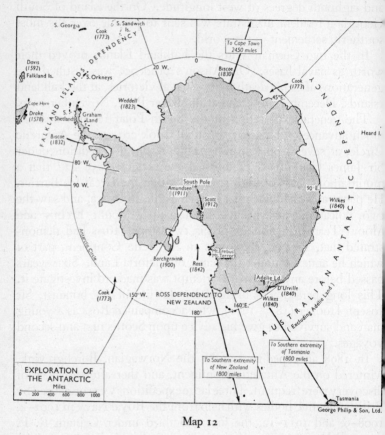

Map 12

the *Fram*, for a secret record-breaking exploit, unhampered by any intention of scientific research, had reached the Pole on 14 October 1911, a few weeks before Scott.

The systematic exploration of the Antarctic Continent was carried on by Shackleton in a series of voyages which placed him in the front rank of explorers. After his death, in South Georgia in 1922, his work was, in part, continued by the Discovery Committee which has been already mentioned. Hardly less valuable were the explorations carried out between 1911 and 1931 by Sir Douglas Mawson (b. 1882), an Australian scientist. In 1928 the Americans entered the field, despatching a series of expeditions under Admiral Byrd who first used aircraft for Antarctic exploration, working from a base which he called Little America.

The discovery of some signs of useful minerals, the growth of the whaling industry and the need for meteorological stations in the Antarctic led to disputes over sovereignty where seamen of several nations had declared annexations though none had effectively occupied the territories they claimed. In addition to the Falkland Islands Dependency another sector lying between longitudes 160° E. and 150° W., from New Zealand southward to the Pole, was formally annexed to New Zealand in 1923, under the name of the Ross Dependency. Similarly, in 1933, the Commonwealth of Australia declared that the sector between Australia and the Pole, that is between the 45th and 160th meridians of East Longitude, was the Australian Antarctic Dependency. These sectors of the southern continent were uninhabited. In January 1948, it was announced that Australia had annexed Heard Island south of Kerguelen and South Africa Prince Edward Island far to the south-east of the Cape.

9.   THE ABOLITION OF SLAVERY: THE EVANGELICALS

WHEN the British slave trade was abolished in 1807 the Evangelicals indulged in the hope that slavery would wither away. By cutting at the root of the supply they would oblige the slave-owners to study the welfare of slaves who could not easily be replaced. Marriage and the nurture of children would be encouraged. Domesticity, they believed, would raise the moral level of the slaves, inculcating habits of industry and a desire for self-improvement until eventually the planters themselves would realise that hired free labour was in every way superior to forced labour. The next step of the abolitionists was accordingly the foundation of the African Institution (1807), to form a general staff for the army of pioneers, merchants, and missionaries who were to repair the wrong done to the peoples of Africa in the past, by bringing them the blessings of civilisation. At the same time their political influence was turned to the field of diplomacy where all other nations were to be persuaded to follow the British example.

The gradual realisation that the prohibition of the slave trade in British ships was not enough led to the revival of agitation in 1823. Clarkson and Wilberforce were growing old though, in retirement, they lived to applaud the passing of the Act of Abolition in 1833. The lead was now taken by Sir T. F. Buxton, Joseph Sturge of Birmingham, and a rising light of the Clapham sect named James Stephen. These were the founders of the Anti-Slavery Society, an influential body with a royal duke as President. Their intention was 'amelioration' of the conditions of slavery leading to gradual emancipation or, as Stephen put it, 'an emancipation of which not the slaves but the masters themselves would be the willing authors'.

Demerara was the scene of their first attempts to ameliorate the conditions of slavery, with the immediate effect of an outbreak by the slaves, who thought that the reign of anarchy had begun (1823). The planters complained that the missionaries were preaching sedition. Even in sedate Barbados a 'party of respectable gentlemen' assembled to destroy the Wesleyan chapel. But the Evangelical tide was flowing in Whitehall. Lord Bathurst, the amiable undistinguished Colonial Secretary, was persuaded to issue draft instructions to colonial governments, which they were to issue as ordinances for preventing the ill-treatment of slaves. A register was to be kept and returns made to the Colonial Office. Protectors of slaves were to be appointed for each colony; and two new bishoprics were created, at Barbados and Jamaica. These proposals met with a poor response from the Colonial Assemblies, especially from Jamaica, the colony where slavery was most extensive. The 30,000 whites of Jamaica, standing on their chartered rights of self-government as proudly as the planters of Virginia in 1776, declined to be overruled by the Colonial Office. Far worse than the recent example of British Guiana was the anarchy prevailing in Haiti and San Domingo, their near neighbours, where concessions to the slaves had led to the massacre of their French masters and a generation of bloody misrule. The Jamaican Assembly would show no sign of weakness lest their 300,000 slaves should make another Haiti of their island. From 1824 to 1827 the Colonial Office urged concessions which the Jamaica Assembly found means of nullifying.

English politics were too feverish during the next two or three years for the Anti-Slavery Society to make headway. The issue turned on property rights; the same defence, which property owners made for the right to nominate members in a pocket-borough, served as a defence of slave-owning. The fifty-six votes which the West India Interest commanded in the House of Commons were votes alike for slavery in the colonies and for an unreformed Parliament. The Anti-Slavery Society by agitating against the West India Interest, threw the nonconformist middle-classes into the struggle for reform. Nomination boroughs and West Indian slavery were to be swept away together.

When the Whigs came into power in 1831 hopes of emancipation rose. The new government tried to bargain by offering adjustments in the tariff in favour of Jamaica, if the island would remodel its slave-code. The offer of this bribe was repudiated by the Assembly and the rumour of it produced a slave-rising in 1832, the year of the Reform Bill. In the first reformed Parliament Buxton moved and carried a motion for the Abolition of Slavery. Negotiations between the Colonial Office and the colonies on the form of the bill occupied the early months of 1833. The bill (3 & 4 Will. IV, cap. 73), drafted by James Stephen (who sacrificed his sabbatarian principles to complete it between a Saturday and Monday), became law in August 1833 and took effect on 1 August 1834.

Some of the more extreme abolitionists had desired to free the slaves without compensation, on the ground that there was no common-law right to slave labour which, they said, was no better than stolen property; but the view prevailed that England shared with the colonies the guilt of the slave trade and would suffer with the colonies if the sugar-plantations were ruined. It was expedient, in the words of the Act, 'that provision should be made for promoting the industry and securing the good conduct of the persons to be manumitted'. Slaves of working age were therefore to be retained as indentured apprentices by their former masters and still held, for a provisional period, to compulsory labour; but the hours of labour would be restricted to forty-five a week, a reduction by one-quarter from the sixty hours usually enforced on slave-plantations. In compensation for the loss of this quarter of their labour, and for the expectation of the labour of slave children (who were finally emancipated on 1 August 1834), the government first proposed a loan of £15,000,000, which was raised after some shrewd bargaining to a grant-in-aid of £20,000,000. On the other hand the period of apprenticeship was reduced from twelve years to six, and eventually to four years, at the instance of the Anti-Slavery Society. The last slaves in the colonies were emancipated in March 1839.

The payment[1] of this vast sum in cash to thousands of claimants in many countries presented an administrative problem which was solved with great skill and economy, but with inevitable delay. The first necessity was to provide the funds, a sum equal to two-fifths of the national revenue, in a time of financial depression. After several banking-houses had declined the task Rothschild undertook to raise a loan of £20,000,000, by instalments, on the principle that the money would be deposited with the Commissioners of the National Debt, until payment with accumulated interest, to the particular slave-owners was authorised. The subscribers to the loan received annuity bonds which were charged to the Consolidated Fund. The adjudication of claims and the distribution of compensation were placed in the hands of a body of five Commissioners from whose decision there was no appeal except to the King-in-Council.

The chairman was Mr C. C. Pepys, afterwards first Earl of Cottenham. James Stephen was one of the commissioners. They met, in rooms rented from John Murray the publisher, on 14 October 1833. Their first task was statistical: dividing the slave-colonies into nineteen 'units' they prepared from the current slave-registers the number of slaves in each 'unit' at the most recent return. Next they prepared a valuation of the average price of slaves of various classes during the eight years, 1822–30, arriving at the preliminary figure of 780,993 slaves with an aggregate capital value of £45,281,738. To arrive at these figures it was necessary to invite the co-operation of Assistant Commissioners appointed and paid by the governments in each 'unit'. The allotment of slaves to various classes: headmen,

---

[1] Historians, for the most part, are reticent on the method of emancipation. The only succinct account I have seen is in an unpublished thesis in the Library of the University of London, *The History of Slave Compensation* by R. E. P. Wastell (1932). I am obliged to him for permission to use his statistics.

field-workers, tradesmen, domestics, superannuated old people, young children, etc., proved a complex task since conditions varied in different colonies. 'Appraisers' were next appointed to visit every slave-owner in order to classify his slaves, an easy task in a small concentrated colony like Barbados, a difficult one among the scattered Bahama Islands or on the rugged frontier of Cape Colony, where one appraiser was killed in a Kaffir raid. Having gathered and analysed this information, which occupied them throughout 1834, the Commissioners in London could calculate what sums of money were due to each colony for slaves of each class at the average local price for that class. Claims for compensation were to be filed by slave-owners, before 1 March 1835, with the Assistant Commissioners who certified them and sent them to London. The great fault of the system was that claims were payable only in London, the intention being that slave-owners should collect their money through their London agents.

The first claim was paid, to a Jamaican claimant, on 10 September 1835. The total number of claims filed was 44,441, a number somewhat in excess of the actual number of slave-owners since some filed more than one claim. The Commissioners, when the procedure was running easily, dealt with 160 claims a week but, even at that rate, five years were required for settlement. By 31 October 1840, £15,125,347 had been paid on account of 39,790 uncontested claims. Correspondence about the contested claims dragged on for several years longer until, by 1845, the whole sum of twenty million pounds with the accrued interest had been disbursed, less the cost of administration which did not exceed the modest figure of £150,000. No more than six appeals were carried to the Privy Council and in only one case was the decision of the Commissioners reversed.

The process required the co-operation of the colonial legislatures at every stage and won it inasmuch as the slave-owners wanted their money. The unpopularity of the measure made it difficult everywhere to persuade men of character to act as appraisers. Some colonies had been remiss at keeping their slave-registers and now suffered for it. In Mauritius, and perhaps elsewhere, the returns had been falsified in order to avoid taxation; the planters were punished by qualifying for so much the less compensation. Meanwhile, before the claims were paid, it was everywhere admitted that apprenticeship was a failure.

Antigua and Bermuda cancelled it, giving their slaves full emancipation from the first day of freedom. On the other hand Jamaica, where two-fifths of all British slaves were concentrated, made the rules of apprenticeship so harsh that it was indistinguishable from slavery. By 1838 the abolitionists were in full cry against the Jamaica planters, persuading Parliament to sweep away apprenticeship without further delay. The Jamaica Assembly refused to co-operate further and talked of secession from the Empire. Lord Melbourne's threat, in 1839, to suspend the constitution of Jamaica was the issue on which his tottering administration was turned out of office. That point, and that alone, was scored by the West India Interest, with unwonted help from the Radicals who rallied to defend colonial self-government, as well as from the Tory Opposition.

The effect of adjusting the rate of compensation to the local price of slave-labour was to help the new colonies where land was cheap and labour scarce, but to handicap the old colonies where the soil was exhausted and the slaves numerous. The highest rate paid for any class was £230 for each 'headman' in British Guiana, a territory with boundless resources then rapidly being developed. The lowest rate was for 'inferior field labourers' in the worn-out over-populated Bahamas, the beggarly sum of £19. So sad was the plight of the Bahama planters that they petitioned the King for a special rate, but without success. The colonies with an expanding agriculture received more than those which had seen better days.

All the colonies were short of currency since in slave-economy men lived by barter. The distribution of a substantial part of twenty million pounds sterling, in small payments throughout the Empire, had a steadying effect upon their banking systems. Not the least of the obstacles which the Commissioners surmounted was the lack of any standard currency. In many colonies Spanish dollars (pieces-of-eight) passed as a token coinage with a most uncertain rate of exchange. The Commissioners arbitrarily valued the Spanish dollar at four shillings and fourpence with advantage to some colonies and disadvantage to others. In the long run the sterling payments and the fixed rate of exchange were a benefit to all.

The unknown factor is the proportion of the payments that actually reached the colonies. What was the value of a sterling draft on London to a boat-builder employing three or four slaves as carpenters in Bermuda, to a logwood cutter working on the Honduras coast for a merchant in Jamaica, to a Boer farmer about to trek inland with a train of Hottentot herdsmen? These men had no London agents, perhaps no banking accounts; the Boer farmers had no contacts with London of any kind. All they could do was to sell their claims to some speculator at a discount. On the other hand in the old colonies many of the plantations were owned by absentees who spent the money in London, while many more were mortgaged to London agents who collected the compensation money by power of attorney. Again it was the older colonies that had the worst of the bargain. Not only were they paid at the lowest rate, but their receipts were most reduced by the exactions of absentees and mortgagors. New plantations in Trinidad, Mauritius and British Guiana were more likely to get the benefit of the money.

Thus slavery in the colonies was abolished at great expense to the British tax-payer. Where the British flag flew there was freedom for men of every creed and colour. Let a foreign slave set one foot on British soil, touch with his extended hand the timbers of a British ship, and his freedom would be guaranteed by all the might of Britain's arm.

The Emancipation Act did not apply to the territories of the East India Company. The importation of slaves to British India had been ended in 1811, but the institution of domestic slavery survived much longer. It was deeply embedded in the social organisation of the people, and was regulated by Mohammedan Law. Further it did not display the hideous features of economic exploitation which were essential to plantation slavery in the colonies. The principle of Permissive Emancipation was introduced by the ordinance of 1843 which merely abolished the legal status of slavery, thus placing master and slave under the same rules of law as employer and employee. Slavery in India then diminished and disappeared. Not till the issue of the penal code of 1861 was slave-holding made a criminal offence. Permissive emancipation followed the same course in Malaya (1843), Ceylon and Hong Kong (1844) and in other Eastern dependencies. Domestic slaves held by bush tribes were emancipated in Burma as recently as 1925 and in Sierra Leone (by an irony of history) later still.

The men who had abolished slavery soon looked for new worlds to conquer. During the years of agitation, reports had come in from the missionaries in South Africa of the wrongs inflicted, as it was alleged, by the settlers upon the natives. Lord Glenelg, Colonial Secretary from 1835 to 1839, had picked a quarrel (see page 316) with Sir Benjamin D'Urban, the popular Governor of South Africa, over the Kaffir War of 1835, which led to a new philanthropic movement in London. Sir T. F. Buxton of the Anti-Slavery Society was appointed chairman of a Parliamentary committee on the state of the aborigines in the British settlements. The report of the committee, largely based on missionary evidence, was a mine of information upon the state of many savage races. It drew attention, for the first time, to the distinction between such primitive races as the Australian Blacks who hardly seemed capable of civilisation, and more adaptive races, such as the Polynesians of New Zealand and the South Seas, over whom the missionaries had soon gained a favourable influence. It recounted the history of the Hottentots and the Kaffir Wars in terms most reprehensive to the Boers and to the British governors, and proposed some definite recommendations. The protection of natives in the colonies should not be entrusted to the colonial legislatures but should be the prerogative of the imperial government. Indentured labour and 'pass-laws' forbidding the free movement of natives should be condemned as a form of slavery. The right to buy tribal lands from natives should be denied to the settlers and confined to the agents of the imperial government. Above all, the missionaries should be supported and maintained by the government as the natural protectors of the natives against exploitation.

Although these recommendations were never codified in any act of Parliament they were adopted by the Colonial Office as rules of guidance so long as the Evangelicals dominated its counsels, especially when Lord Glenelg held the seals. An easy lethargic man, he was confirmed in the faith and stirred to activity by the appointment of James Stephen as Permanent Under-Secretary in 1837. Outside the Office their efforts were supported by Buxton's new organ, the Aborigines Protection Society (1837), a body of philanthropists as powerful as the Anti-Slavery Society had been.

These years were the heyday of that surge of religious emotion which the ungodly characterised as 'Exeter Hall'. The Evangelicals, no longer an obscure group of pietists meeting at a villa in Clapham, had grown into a multitude of earnest and devout Bible-Protestants, of whom an increasing majority were radical and non-conformist, not Tory High-Churchmen like their founders. The May Meetings held annually at Exeter Hall in the Strand were religious conventions, of a type more frequently seen now in America than in England, where devotional fervour was concentrated on some field of Christian endeavour, most constantly upon foreign missions. Empire, to the crowds at Exeter Hall, was an opportunity for civilising and converting the savage and the slave, and under that flag the Colonial Office marched for many years.

The two ancient societies (S.P.C.K., 1698 and S.P.G., 1701) had languished during the free-thinking eighteenth century. They were now surpassed in enthusiasm by the new evangelical societies: the Baptist Missionary Society (1792), the undenominational London Missionary Society (1795), the Scottish Missionary Society (1796), the Church Missionary Society (1799), the Wesleyan Missionary Society (1813). All this activity was supported by the British and Foreign Bible Society (1804), and was equalled by a parallel activity in the United States. At the end of the nineteenth century British Protestant Missions were spending an income of £4,000,000 a year. In the Pacific islands, in Central Africa, and especially in China the social and political influence of the Protestant Missionaries was profound, not only because they converted the heathen, but because all missionaries were teachers and the most successful were often medical men.

In thus describing the Protestant missions it is not intended that the even greater efforts of the Roman Catholics, should be underrated. Since the foundation of the 'Propaganda' by Gregory XV in 1622 there has been no time when the Missionary Orders have not encircled the globe; but their work falls largely outside the scope of this book. The historian of the British Empire must however be aware of a noble rivalry, in the great age of Protestant missions, between them and the French missionary bodies, especially the Marists (1816) and the Society of Picpus (1817) in the Pacific, the Oblates of Mary (1845) in North-western America, and the White Fathers (1868) in Central Africa.

VI

THE BRITISH AT THE CAPE,
TO THE YEAR 1852

Argument: The Dutch evolved a characteristic society at the Cape in
the eighteenth century, with the help of imported slaves; they had little
to do with the Bantu peoples. Traditionally hostile to the monopoly of
the Dutch East India Company, they resisted British administrative
reforms after the cession of 1814, and especially those prompted by
the Evangelicals.

Extension eastward engaged the colony in Kaffir Wars, all the more
after the plantation of a British settlement near Grahamstown in 1820.

Boer dissatisfaction with British rule promoted the Great Trek, the
first penetration of the interior by European settlers in any considerable number. After complex disputes three new states were formed.
Natal as a British colony, the Orange Free State, which was at first
under a shadowy British suzerainty, the Transvaal as an independent
republic.

1. THE CAPE OF GOOD HOPE, 1488–1826

BARTHOLOMEW DIAZ passed the Cape of Good Hope on a
voyage of discovery, probably in May 1488. Nine years later
Vasco da Gama, with a larger expedition equipped for military
and diplomatic exploits, was driven off the Cape by storms and
made a landfall farther up the coast, at a place which he named
Natal, the day being Christmas, 1497. But his concern was
with India, the Arab Sultanates, and the realm of Prester John.
Then and thereafter the Portuguese passed on from the stormy
Cape to the good hope of empire in the East; though Almeida,
one of the makers of that empire perished, as it happened, in a
scuffle with Hottentots at the foot of Table Mountain. The first
Portuguese holding in East Africa was Mozambique (1508) from
where they dominated the coast as far south as the Zambezi by
the end of the sixteenth century. On the west coast their first
holding, a true colony, was founded at St Paul de Loanda in
1575. Strange to relate they made little use, in their great century,

of the anchorage at Table Bay, though ships of all the maritime nations called there occasionally for water and fresh meat which they bought from the Hottentots. Lancaster was there in 1591, and in 1620 two English captains took possession of the Cape for England, without effect since the government repudiated their action. Negotiations, which came to nothing, were even then in progress for a joint occupation by the Dutch and English East India Companies.

The prize lay there for any man's possession. The hippo-potamus wallowed in the marshes of the Cape flats; lions ranged the slopes of Table Mountain when, in 1647, the crew of a Dutch East Indiaman wintered in Table Bay, having lost their ship. After their rescue in the following year, they reported on the healthy climate, the fertile soil, the friendly disposition of the Hottentots, and the amenities of their life when camping at Green Point. The Dutch Company, which had found St Helena (1633) too near home, and Mauritius (1638) too far afield for half-way ports of call, then sent Jan van Riebeeck to occupy the Cape. On 6 April 1652 his three small ships cast anchor in Table Bay. His business was to provide victuals and refreshment for Dutch East India shipping, and no more. In his first report he pressed for the despatch of settlers to raise crops and cattle, but was severely snubbed. Their High Mightinesses wanted no more than could be grown by his garrison and servants, and would not hear of the admission of outsiders to their chartered territory. Not till 1657 was van Riebeeck permitted even to settle nine families of his people on farms of their own, and then only on condition that they traded exclusively with the Company. His attempts to develop his little colony were consistently overruled by inspecting officers sent out from Holland. Though he duti-fully endeavoured to enclose the settlement by a line of forts and ditches, its growth could not be restrained. By 1658 the handful of settlers united seditiously against the restrictions, and by 1660 he was at war with the Hottentots who felt the encroachment of the white men upon their narrow grazing-grounds.

In 1662, when van Riebeeck relinquished his command, the colony numbered 1394 persons, of whom thirty-six were 'free burghers' settled with their families. There were some white labourers and a few Malayan slaves brought from the Dutch East Indies. Cattle-breeding, which meant further encroachment on Hottentot land, was the most promising trade, if we except selling provisions illegally at high prices to British and French ships, when all should have been preserved for the Dutch ships at a fixed rate. The colony grew in strategic importance during the French and English wars of the 1670's. Capetown Castle was built by 1674. Between 1672 and 1677 conclusions were reached with the Hottentots; by a deed between the Company and various tribes, all the land as far north and east as the 'Hottentots Holland' Mountains and Saldanha Bay was ceded to the Company in return for trade goods which, the Hottentots alleged, were not paid to the rightful vendors. Hence another war which ended in a dispersal of these tribes beyond the confines of the colony.

The age of restriction ended with the coming of Simon van der Stel as Governor in 1679. Setting himself at once to the task of colonisation and expansion he planted thirty families with a minister and a teacher in the fertile inland valley which he named Stellenbosch (1683). The policy of the Company was now to attract Protestant emigrants who would form a local militia to garrison the fortress; and accordingly some approved families of Dutch, German and French Protestants were admitted, among them about 200 Huguenots after the Revocation of the Edict of Nantes. These French refugees, besides improving the culture of the vineyards and the quality of the wine, added a lively flavour to the phlegmatic Dutch temper of the settlers. The Afrikaner race would have been the poorer without that sparkling admixture of Gallic blood, and African history different without such names as Marais, de Villiers, Delarey, Joubert, Duplessis, Malan.

Van der Stel retired in 1699 to the dignified white manor house of Constantia which he built and which still stands among his oak-trees and vineyards on the sunny eastern slope of Table Mountain. His vintages carried by the India ships east and west soon attained worldwide fame. He loved the land and the cultivator, the *land bouwer*, somewhat distrusting the new generation of cattlemen; for in South Africa with its long dry seasons and periodic droughts every cattleman must be a rover like the Hottentots before him. But the wandering *trek-boer*, not the husbandman of the old Western Province around Capetown, became the national type.

Two hundred years ago the well-known comment was made that Boer farmers feel crowded when they see the smoke of a neighbour's chimney, a sentiment encouraged by their land laws. New farms were granted by the Governor well spaced-out. The farmer, in addition to his cultivated ground could buy a grazing licence for about 6000 acres round the farm at a nominal price, marking off its boundary, or so it was said in jest, by the rough test of 'riding-off' from the farmstead for half an hour at a walking pace.

During the eighteenth century the population grew rapidly, more by a high birth-rate and a healthy environment than by immigration. There may have been 500 Boer families in 1700; there was a white population of 21,746 in 1798 expanding outwards from four centres: 6000 about Capetown, 7000 about Stellenbosch and 4000 in each of two new settlements Swellendam (founded 1743) and Graaff-Reinet (founded 1785). There were also 25,000 slaves, many of them imported Asiatics, mostly in the neighbourhood of Capetown, the progenitors of the unfortunate 'Cape Coloured' race. The older farming districts were largely self-supporting and but little affected by the obstructive rule of the Company's Governors. In such settlements as Stellenbosch might best be seen the great farms built in the characteristic colonial style, which is now so much admired. These were the homes of a sober secretive frugal race, outwardly calm and inwardly passionate, notable for shrewdness and subtlety and a stubborn unbending courage; a nationality distinguished from the 'Hollanders' with whom they were already losing contact. The golden age of Boer legend, when this simple society enjoyed halcyon days, was the time of Governor Tulbagh (1751–71).

On the frontier the less disciplined members of this intractable race, the trek-boers, lived another life. Mounted on hardy ponies, they moved easily in search of pasture and of 'game' to settle always farther out, bringing on their family and goods in covered ox-wagons with Hottentot drivers and 'coloured' slaves walking alongside, until they chose a home where sweet water could be drawn from some 'fontein'. The first great trek was the eastward movement to the Fish River in the 1780's which led to the settlement of Graaff-Reinet.

The farther they were removed from the paternal hand of the Governor at Capetown the more republican became the settlements. Early in the century the outlying groups had developed the two characteristic organs of Boer self-government, the Commando and the Church-session (*Kerkraad*). Strict Calvinists of the Heidelberg Confession, it was natural for the elders of the *Kerk* to assume control over the local welfare of the community, though the minister was, in the early days, appointed by the Governor. The annual assembly of the Church for the *Nagmaal*, or Communion, became too a secular function where politics, marketing and matchmaking flourished. Defence was provided by the local militia in which every man served, bringing his own horse, gun and rations. Each local band, or commando, elected its officers. Commandos were first raised in the early Hottentot wars and were systematically organised during the eighteenth century for the war of extermination against the Bushmen. In 1778 the trek-boers first came into contact with Bantu Africans of the Xosa tribe, a foe that could give real opposition. After war and negotiation the Fish River was taken as the eastern boundary, which the Graaff-Reinet settlers defended against Xosa raiding parties, with little or no support from the Governor. There was not much expansion northward over the mountain ranges. The Orange River was discovered in 1760 but its banks were not settled until many years later.

At least twice during the eighteenth century the 'free burghers' were irritated into sedition by the petty despotism of the Company's Governors; they were exasperated when the Governor tried to check the Kaffirs on the Fish River with fair words instead of hard blows. Always conservative and unenterprising, the Company declined in wealth and power throughout the century, abating nothing of its oppressive demeanour. The dividend was reduced from 25 per cent to 12 per cent and then was left unpaid. The volume of Dutch shipping at the Cape dwindled so that Capetown rarely knew prosperity unless a French or British fleet revictualled at this 'tavern of the Indian Ocean'. When de Suffren left a garrison at the Cape in 1781 his French officers brought an air of frivolity to the little town with the gaiety and fashion of the old regime. That ended in collapse when the British naval victories, at the end of the American War, disposed of de Suffren and destroyed Dutch trade. From this blow the Dutch East India Company never recovered, but lapsed into bankruptcy. The French Revolution had its echoes in

the far south where the settlers at the Cape grew restive against
their moribund rulers. When the British forces under General
Craig arrived in 1795, the settlers on the eastern frontier were
already in revolt, having thrown off their dependence upon the
Governor at Capetown.

The relations of British and Dutch in the French Wars have
been discussed above (see page 240). The allegiance of the
Cape was most uncertain since Craig brought a letter from the
exiled Prince of Orange calling on them to admit an English
garrison, producing a situation somewhat like the Dakar Incident
of 1940, though with a different ending. The tradition of the
Dutch Company, always suspicious of British rivalry, led the
Governor to make at least a token resistance which deeply embarrassed General Craig. The Governor capitulated only when
British reinforcements arrived. Soon a Dutch naval force arrived
to restore the situation but achieved nothing because the sailors
proved loyal to the House of Orange and joined with the British.

For seven years British military governors found themselves
faced with just the same problems as their Dutch predecessors.
Their interest was in making the Cape into another Gibraltar,
which brought a boom of wartime prosperity to the Capetown
merchants; they were much averse to frontier wars against the
Kaffirs in the eastern districts. The attempt to wave an olive-
branch in the face of Kaffirs on the war-path soon raised some of
the burghers of Graaff-Reinet in revolution against the British
for the same reasons that had raised them against the Dutch
Company. But, at the peace of 1802, the Cape was receded to the
Dutch, that is to the Jacobin Batavian Republic which was
maintained in Holland by French money and French arms. The
new Governor announced a programme of administrative reforms, alarming the conservative Boers by a promise of secular
education and equality for all religions, but had neither time
(February 1803 to January 1806) nor funds to accomplish much
before the second British conquest by Sir Home Popham. Again,
after a show of resistance, the Governor capitulated on terms of a
guarantee to the inhabitants of their property, privileges and legal
system.

At first the only change made in the Dutch system of administration was the sending of justices on circuit to the outlying
districts. Although they were Dutchmen administering Roman-

Dutch law, their actions caused deep resentment among the frontier farmers. The missionary influence already felt in the last decade of Dutch rule was far more powerful after the British annexation. Reports were finding their way to London about the treatment of the Hottentots by their white masters, with the result that the justices made it their duty to investigate complaints. The circuit of 1811, long known as the Black Circuit, was felt by the burghers to be an insolent attempt to stir up a rebellion of native and 'coloured' servants. The British, like the Dutch before them, raised a Hottentot corps of military police. A crisis came in 1814 when a frontier farmer named Bezuidenhout refused to appear in court to answer charges of cruelty to a native. Having fired on the sheriff who attempted to serve a summons, he was killed in the resulting scuffle. His brother then formed a band of armed men and declared open rebellion, inviting the alliance of Kaffir chiefs. Most of his sixty followers surrendered to a burgher commando backed by troops, when the outbreak had manifestly failed; but Johannes Bezuidenhout made a running fight until he too was mortally wounded. Five of the rebels were sentenced to death and hanged at Slagter's Nek (1815). These unsuccessful rebels have been elevated by some extremists into a high place in Afrikaner martyrology. Bezuidenhout's myth, like John Brown's, goes marching on, though neither legendary hero gets much glory from the addict of factual history.

The affair of Slagter's Nek was determined by the stern decision of Lord Charles Somerset (1767–1831), a new Governor who left his mark on South Africa. His appointment was a Tory job, or so said the Whigs at Holland House: 'he was a horse-jockey who went to the Cape to make money'. To be sure his salary was the enormous sum of £10,000 a year and he anticipated it largely. He was an arrogant, overbearing aristocrat quite out of sympathy with Evangelicals or intellectuals of any colour, not an attractive figure. But much was done in his day, perhaps the better because this horse-jockey rode rough-shod over obstructors. He quarrelled with Sir John Cradock his predecessor in office, with Sir Rufane Donkin who acted as his deputy, with Dr Philip the agent of the London Missionary Society; but he knocked the colony into a shape that endured, held the frontier, settled the eastern province, and promoted agricultural improvement at a model farm.

When Somerset arrived, the frontier had been brought into better order than for years past by Colonel J. Graham, who founded the military post of Grahamstown (1812), covering it by a chain of forts along the Fish River. The new Governor proposed to hold this line with mobile columns of mounted infantry; and would have done so, had not Whitehall suddenly withdrawn his cavalry establishment, as an economy after Waterloo. It was ridiculous, in their eyes, that he should want 3000 troops at the Cape 'to guard against a few Caffres'. However, the garrison of Grahamstown, 500 miles to the east, was obliged to fight for life against a determined attack by 10,000 natives in 1819. After their defeat Somerset pushed back the frontier to the next river valley making a 'neutral zone' beyond the Fish River. He next began to demand settlers to form a militia— an English militia—in the Albany province on this side of the frontier.

Several projects had been formed, some speculative and some philanthropic, for settling parties of labourers at the Cape, as a remedy for post-war unemployment; and some hundreds of emigrants had actually sailed when a comprehensive proposal was launched in July 1819. The Chancellor, Vansittart, moved a vote of £50,000 which was to be spent by Bathurst, the Secretary for War and the Colonies, on assisted emigration to South Africa. *The Times*, not usually favourable to such schemes, gave its support with an enthusiastic account (18 June 1819) of 'our noble station at the Cape of Good Hope which has the finest soil and climate in the world'. The scheme for an organised emigration was that intending emigrants were to apply for permits to the Secretary of State, each head of a family making a deposit of £10 which would be returned to him by instalments in the colony. The first to apply from any town or village was appointed 'head of a party' and was authorised to select suitable emigrants from the other applicants in that locality. No party of less than ten persons was accepted. Within a few weeks fifty-six parties were formed comprising 3487 men, women and children with a combined capital of £14,000 deposited in cash. The smallest party was composed of fifteen persons from Carlisle, one of the largest was 220 from Cork. Twenty-four ships of about 400 tons burthen were chartered in various ports. The London fleet was delayed by ice in the river, this being the last occasion (December 1819) when the Thames was frozen at London Bridge.

The Irish party went to Saldanha Bay, the Welsh to Caledon, but the main landing was on the open beach of Algoa Bay in the early months of 1820. Two or three thousand emigrants spent the southern autumn in tents among the sand-hills waiting for wagons and ox-teams to draft them away to the settlements around Grahamstown. Thomas Pringle, the poet of the 'Eighteen-Twenty Settlers', thus described the camp on the seashore:

It consists of several hundred tents, pitched in parallel rows or streets, and occupied by the middle or lower classes of the emigrants....There were respectable tradesmen and jolly farmers, with every appearance of substance and snug English comfort about them. There were watermen, fishermen, and sailors from the Thames and the English seaports, with the reckless and weather-beaten look usual in persons of their professions. There were numerous groups of pale-visaged artisans and operative manufacturers from London and the large towns, of whom...a proportion were squalid in their aspect, slovenly in their attire, and discourteous in their demeanour.... Lastly there were parties of pauper agricultural labourers sent out by the aid of their parishes, healthier perhaps than the class just mentioned, but not apparently happier in mind.

Within a few months all were settled south and south-east of Grahamstown between the Kowie and the Fish Rivers. The most remote settlement was that of 400 Highlanders led by Captain Grant. They had particularly asked 'not to be mixed in with any others as speak a different language'.

Since Somerset was on leave of absence in England the colonists were received by his deputy, Donkin, who named the landing-place Port Elizabeth, after his wife. Donkin found himself obliged to issue rations against deductions from the settlers' deposits and, when these were exhausted, at government expense. Though the settlers were located before the coming of the spring the wheat crop failed for three successive years 1821, 1822 and 1823. Persistent blights, in spite of experiment with rustproof varieties, made it clear that this was not a district favourable for wheat growing; nor were many of the settlers expert cultivators. As always in a new colony some of the immigrants were ne'er-do-wells and many more, known as 'cockney gardeners', were incorrigibly urban in habit. When the deposit money and even the government rations were exhausted they drifted off into the older settlements to become tradesmen or objects of charity in

the towns. By May 1823 the original thousand families had
dwindled to 438. The leaders of parties stayed, the labourers
drifted away.

When Lord Charles Somerset came back, his masterful love of
interference led him to tyrannise over the settlers, often spitefully
undoing what Donkin had done for them. He kept his eye on
them as suspect 'radicals', a term of abuse in his vocabulary;
but on the other hand he secured their land-titles and eased their
burden of financial obligation. Donkin had allowed pasturage
leases which Somerset refused. Keeping cattle led to dispersal of
the settlers and tempted the Kaffirs to raid. Sheep-walks were not
permitted until 1825. The settlers were forbidden to hold slaves,
though their Dutch neighbours were slave-owners, as was the
Governor himself.

It has been customary to say that the 'Eighteen-Twenty Settlement' was a failure, because the settlers failed to make their
fortunes out of wheat in the first few years. Many of the best of
them stayed on the land. Some took up trading in ivory and
ostrich feathers with the Kaffirs; others, in 1827, introduced fine-
woolled sheep, thus finding what thereafter remained the true
pastoral wealth of the eastern province. The settlement was
decried by men with short views and mean minds. Time and
working capital are needed to found a colony. In their first three
years the 1820 settlers fared better than the first Virginians and
no worse than the first Dutch at Table Bay. To judge the worth
of the seeds planted on the open beach of Algoa Bay we must
look to-day at Port Elizabeth with its harbour-works and heavy
industries, at Grahamstown with its justly celebrated University
College and schools. By 1842 Grahamstown was a flourishing
town of 700 houses with 5000 inhabitants, a church, a school,
two newspapers and a bank.[1]

[1] See Isobel Edwards, *The Eighteen-Twenty Settlers.*

2. SOUTH AFRICA, 1820–38

WHEN Lord Charles Somerset returned to the Cape for his second term of office (1821–6) his manner was more overbearing than before. He watched what he supposed to be subversive movements, through agents among whom moved obscurely the mysterious figure known as 'Oliver the Spy'. Still the military governor of a fortress and of its victualling area, he saw no reason for allowing political privileges to the inhabitants. Under the changed conditions, as population and prosperity increased, his arbitrary behaviour provoked hostile criticism from two sides. The Eighteen-Twenty settlers demanded civil rights, advancing their claim through a newspaper which the Governor, and the Colonial Office, severely restricted. But the agitation was felt in England and fomented there; the first number of the *Manchester Guardian* (5 May 1821) featured an article on the oppression of the settlers in Cape Colony. Even more effective was the influence of the Rev. John Philip, the agent of the London Missionary Society at the Cape, who began, soon after his arrival in 1819, a long crusade on behalf of the Hottentots and, as if it were *a priori*, against the Boers.

In 1823 the Colonial Office sent a Commission led by J. T. Bigge (who had already made a similar investigation in New South Wales) to report and advise upon administrative reforms, whereupon the tongues of the critics were loosened. The effect of Bigge's Commission was the granting of the elements of civil rights and constitutional procedure in 1825. Some check was put upon the arbitrary action of the Governor by the provision of a nominated advisory council. Trial by jury was instituted, and an independent judiciary appointed. With the growth of liberties the criticism of Governor Somerset grew louder. Further attempts to restrain the liberty of the press led to his recall. His long survival as Governor had been due to the influence of the Somerset family which commanded twenty-two votes in the House of Commons. He and his patron Bathurst fell together in 1826, when attacked by Sir Rufane Donkin in the House and denounced by *The Times* newspaper.

The colony was divided some years later for administration into an eastern and a western province, the eastern province including the Kaffir frontier and the new English settlements, under Stockenstrom, an Afrikaner, as Lieutenant-Governor.

A less prudent reform was the replacement of Dutch by English as the language of administration and of the law courts (1827). It seemed justified since the Boers were now completely cut off from the culture of the Netherlands and had no system of Afrikaans education. Their dialect, which varied locally, had not yet crystallised into a literary language. Even the Dutch Reformed Church with its tiny establishment of seven congregations (1795) languished for lack of a succession of ministers. The scarcity was remedied by an appeal to the Scots who were of the same communion and whose racial character agreed well with the canny, dour, and yet essentially generous Boers. A powerful contribution to Afrikaner culture was made by the Scottish ministers who went to the Cape in response to this appeal. Among them Andrew Murray and his two sons should be specially mentioned; though strictly orthodox Presbyterians they brought into the Dutch Church a liberal and devout spirit and a respect for learning which the 'doppers' of the old age had lacked. The young Andrew Murray was the first minister at Bloemfontein; John Murray was a principal in founding the University of Stellenbosch (1859), for a long time the chief source of Afrikaner culture.

Though some slight attempts had been made by one of the ubiquitous Moravian missionaries (1737–44), and by Dutch Evangelicals (1786–95), to convert slaves in the colony, systematic missionary endeavour began to flourish with the intervention of the undenominational London Missionary Society in 1799. These English missionaries formed a Hottentot community near Algoa Bay, at Bethelsdorp (1808), which the Boers regarded with suspicion, and all the more when John Philip (1775–1851) began his polemical career as agent for the Society. He maintained a correspondence with Wilberforce and the other Evangelical leaders in England, influencing through them the policy of the Colonial Office, at least so long as Lord Glenelg was Secretary of State (1835–9). Philip frequently made tours of inspection of the mission stations which multiplied through Africa in the 'thirties and 'forties, conferring with tribal chiefs upon political as well as upon religious matters. Sometimes he seemed to show an almost malignant hostility to the Boer frontiersmen, yet it would be unjust to underrate his disinterested passion, his lifelong struggle, for justice on behalf of his native clients.

The gravamen of his charge against the Boers was their treatment of the Hottentots. In the full fervour of the Evangelical Revival he blamed the Boers for behaving as white men behaved to almost every aboriginal race until his own generation. The older Boers never doubted that the heathen savages were a lower order created to serve the Chosen People, and were deserving of kindness in proportion to their docility. They were good masters to their domestic slaves—liberal masters in Capetown where slaves owned property, practised crafts and traded on their own account. There was even a recorded case of a Dutch boy bound apprentice to a slave to learn his trade. But manners were rougher in the pastoral districts and on the frontier, where few farmers were so poor as not to own a tail of Hottentot herdsmen, not slaves by law but none the less forcibly held to labour, a system defended by precepts from the Old Testament.

The nickname 'hottentot' means 'stammerer' and alludes to the peculiar use in their language of palatal 'clicks' similar to those used for encouraging horses. By European standards they were an ugly race with yellowish skins, everted lips and strangely protruding buttocks, but they were tamable and were skilful with cattle. The first generation of Boer settlers had broken up their tribal system and reduced a large part of the race to servitude, but unknown numbers, perhaps 30,000, still wandered round the outskirts of the settlements, living largely by cattle-raiding. Among them, since the early Boer settlers were not so fastidious as their descendants, were many half-breeds who formed themselves into new tribes known as Griquas, or more bluntly as 'Bastards'. So scattered and interbred were they by the middle of the nineteenth century that it was said that no pure Hottentots remained. The Griquas were the peculiar care of the London Missionary Society.

In the dry scrub of the western province there lingered still more primitive tribes of 'Bushmen', so stunted in appearance, so secluded in habit that they seemed hardly human. Among the Bushmen the Old Stone Age survived—and still survives—as it once was in palaeolithic France and Spain. The drawings in a free bold style, which may be seen in Pyrenean caves, of animals long extinct, are paralleled by the hunting-scenes which the Bushmen draw on their rock-shelters in South Africa. They possessed nothing to tempt European cupidity, having neither landed property nor cattle but, being predatory hunters, they regarded the settlers' herds as fair game and so provoked reprisals. Before the British came they had been extirpated from the colony by systematic 'drives' and massacres. Hottentots and Bushmen were neither numerous nor formidable. The new tribes of Xosa[1] Kaffirs, whom the settlers confronted across the Great Fish River, were men of a different mettle.

Kaffir is an Arabic word meaning 'unbeliever', used by Moslems to describe all non-Moslems and especially heathen slaves. It came to be applied in a more limited sense by the Portuguese to the negro peoples of Central Africa who were the perpetual prey of the Arab slave trade, and finally by the Dutch to those tribes with whom they came in contact in south-east Africa.

The *Bantu* peoples were for long the dominant race of southeast Africa. Their prototype is the Ethiopian of Scripture, 'black but comely', who has not changed his skin these 3000 years and may be seen to-day just as he is represented in Egyptian frescoes of the wars of Pharaoh Rameses. The Bantu are a tall, strong, upright people with skins of chocolate brown to deep black. They use spears of hammered iron, wear girdles of oxtails, and delight in bracelets or anklets of copper wire. They are people of the savannahs, following the game-herds and the cattle-pasture in the dry uplands of thorn-scrub and sparse trees, where there are no lakes, few navigable rivers and but rare patches of forest. Men's work is herding cattle since wealth is counted only in numbers of cows. The women hoe the mealie-patch while the men squat on their heels beside the reed-thatched beehive huts. Legitimacy and the permanence of domestic life are secured by the custom of *lobola*, the ceremonial pledging of cattle from the bridegroom's to the bride's family. But cattle are a form of currency, not a consumable commodity, so that numbers, not quality, matter. Some tribes live largely on milk, and few of the Bantu, though cattle are all their care, make beef a staple diet.

[1] The name begins with a click introduced into a Bantu dialect from the language of the adjacent Hottentots.

For his food the Ethiopian, like the lion and the leopard, was parasitic on the countless herds of giraffe, zebra and quagga; the gazelles and antelopes of many species, which ranged over the Veld until times within living memory, but which now are rare except in parks and reservations. Deprived of their former food supply by the destruction of the game, the Bantu cow-herds have not learned to breed cattle for beef. Unwilling vegetarians, they subsist on an inadequate diet of mealie porridge which has lowered their resistance against disease.

Herding cattle, hunting game, and making war they held to be the proper occupations for a man. They were as fierce and predatory as the Europeans who appeared in South Africa simultaneously with them. Among the Bantu, in general, young men were of no account until they had won in war the cattle which meant the price of a bride. Wars were cattle-raids and were very bloody, so that the death of many warriors made polygamy the rule.

In private character men and women are simple, loyal, good-humoured, docile and brave. They are extremely superstitious and suffer much from mental persecution by witch-doctors. Among their *taboos* is commonly one against using the names of the dead, a prohibition which precludes records of the past, so that the Bantu have no recorded history. Perhaps the dynasty bearing the obscure title of Monomotapa, with whom the Portuguese trafficked from Mozambique in the sixteenth century, were a Bantu dynasty of superior abilities. They may have built the dry stone walls about the mysterious ruined citadel of Zimbabwe in Rhodesia, but no tradition was recorded; no other Bantu tribe with which we are acquainted was capable of the task.

During the eighteenth century Bantu tribes were drifting southwards through the Transvaal in numerous small warring bodies, among whom there arose a military genius, quite untaught by the lore of Europe or Asia, in Chaka, King of the Amazulu (died 1828). He formed a standing army of young warriors organised in regiments (*impis*) and armed with short stabbing spears (*assegais*). They were drilled to march in double time and to fight in a loose formation not unlike that of the Roman legions. No young man might settle down with a wife until he had served in an *impi* and blooded his spear, a rule which, for a hundred years, made the Zulus awkward neighbours.

Chaka established his dynasty in Zululand, ruled the greater part of what is now Natal, and raided all South Africa, setting in motion a wave of migration that was met by the contemporary Boer migration on the banks of the Great Fish River.

Tension between the Boers and the British missionaries grew over three distinct native problems: the treatment of the Hottentots, the abolition of slavery, and the defence of the Kaffir frontier. The Hottentot policy had been propounded in Governor Caledon's ordinance (1809) which declared that every native should have a fixed place of abode and not leave it without permission from the *landdrost* (district magistrate). This honest attempt to 'locate' the nomadic tribes was the first of the 'pass-laws', still so hotly discussed in South African politics. Missionary agitation against this restrictive ordinance had led to an inquiry into the treatment of natives and in consequence to the Black Circuit (see above, page 306) which so offended Afrikaner pride. 'Nearly one hundred of the most respectable families on the frontier' had been implicated by their coloured servants in charges which were sometimes false or frivolous. When a reaction set in, John Philip went behind the back of the Governor to Wilberforce and Wilmot Horton, the Evangelical leaders through whose influence Bigge's Commission was sent to Africa. In 1828 Philip had the signal success of instigating Buxton, the chairman of the Anti-Slavery Society, to denounce the pass-laws in the House of Commons with the result that the Governor was obliged to withdraw them. By the '50th Ordinance' (1828) he gave equality of status to all free men in the colony, irrespective of colour, an even greater affront to the patriarchal Boers.

Philip's hour struck when slavery was denounced throughout the Empire on 1 August 1834. The act of emancipation had been long foreseen and was but the climax of a gradual series of legal changes. No slaves had been introduced into the colony since the Batavian Republic took control in 1803. The visits of slave-ships to Table Bay had been forbidden since 1808. The slave-code had been ameliorated in the 1820's by legal restrictions upon the power of the slave-owner and by the appointment of an official Protector of slaves, as in the British West Indies. Further the appearance of a white labouring-class had somewhat relieved the perennial demand for hands. The effect of the Proclamation of 1834 was to convert the 39,021 slaves in the colony, mostly of Asiatic or mixed origin, into apprentices under indentures which held good until 1838, a change of legal status rather than of economic or social position. The masters were annoyed but not ruined, their chief concern being that compensation, in the form of drafts payable in London, amounted to no more than £1,247,701 or rather less than half their expectation. Five-sixths of the slaves thus emancipated were in the old-established western provinces.

Emancipation was administered by a new Governor, Sir Benjamin D'Urban (1777–1844), like most governors in that age a military man with a distinguished record in the French Wars. Philip at once began to urge upon him a new frontier policy. They were to set up a Griqua state and a series of Bantu states protected by the British missionaries against exploitation by the Boers. At this moment (December 1834) the eastern frontier flared up in one of its periodical conflagrations. Cattle-raids, which the Kaffir chiefs condoned as common form, led to reprisals, which the settlers similarly condoned, and so to a fierce frontier war in which the eastern province was saved from desolation by the brilliant and ruthless operations of Colonel Harry Smith. D'Urban's difficulties were increased by a sharp despatch from the Colonial Office rebuking him for carrying the war into the enemy's country. 'The Kaffirs', wrote Lord Glenelg, 'had right and justification on their side.' Glenelg obliged D'Urban to withdraw the frontier to the Fish River, abandoning the new province which D'Urban had just annexed. He also forbade settlers to take up land north of the Orange River. These weak concessions, this truckling to men and measures that the Boers detested, brought the frontiersmen to a decision to migrate beyond the reach of the British Governor.

3. THE GREAT TREK AND ITS
CONSEQUENCES

FOR some years past adventurous parties of *voortrekkers* had made exploring and hunting trips through what is now the Transvaal, as far north as the Limpopo. One of the boldest of them, Hendrik Potgieter, after a brush with the formidable Matabele tribe had fallen back to Thaba 'nchu at the foot of the mountains of Basutoland. Here was the rendezvous to which assembled in 1837 about 3000 Boers in a vast camp of covered wagons. They had trekked north from all parts of the frontier, but mostly from the Graaff-Reinet district, a journey of about 300 miles. Harry Smith, who knew and liked them well, wrote of the *trek-boers* as men 'of strong prejudices, most credulous in all respects, especially where the government is concerned, jealous to a degree of what they regard as their rights, constantly at variance with one another, and evincing a want of mutual confidence'. When Piet Retief, who planned an eastward march towards Natal, was elected 'Governor of the United Laagers', Potgieter and his followers broke away and trekked northward into the country he already knew. His mounted men engaged the Matabele *impis* in a running fight along the River Marico (November 1837) driving them into regions so remote that they were hardly heard of at the Cape for another fifty years. While Potgieter's party entered into possession of the treeless, sparsely-inhabited High Veld around Potchefstroom, Retief's wagons had moved on to Winburg, where they halted while he scouted ahead to find a pass down the high scarp of the Drakensberg into the coastal plain. Coming here by land, he met again the intrusive British, who some years earlier had reached Port Natal by sea. English guides led Piet Retief to the royal *kraal* of Dingaan, who had succeeded the great Chaka as King of the Zulus, in the land upon which the trekkers hoped to settle. The kraal stood in the hot coastal belt not far from the mouth of the Tugela river. Retief sought to win the favour of the King by leading a commando against a rival chief to recover stolen cattle; but Dingaan, having seen the skill of the Boer warriors, thought it all the more reason for getting rid of them. Having allayed Retief's suspicions by granting him a concession of land, the King enticed him and his men,

sixty-nine in number, into the kraal unarmed and murdered them.
The deed of gift was found on Retief's dead body. At the same
time Dingaan's *impis* fell upon the scattered trekkers struggling
through Natal, and murdered all they could master (6 February
1838). To make a clean sweep he also drove the English settlers
from Port Natal.

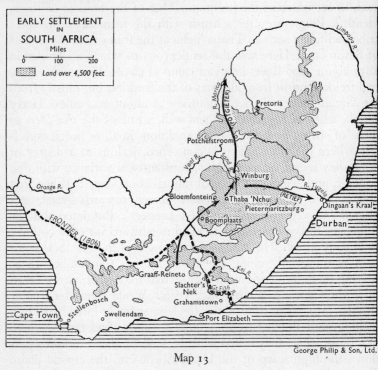

Map 13

George Philip & Son, Ltd.

The Great Trek and its consequences made painful reading in
Downing Street. Glenelg endeavoured to shift the blame by
recalling D'Urban on the grounds that he had failed to stop the
Trek. The next Governor, George Napier, was held in impo-
tence by a succession of impracticable instructions. He was to
stop the trekkers but was not to fight. Even the reoccupation of
Port Natal, reluctantly ordered in January 1839, was countermanded in December; for the Boers, with epic courage had
settled their own account with Dingaan. The trekkers who were
still assembled on the High Veld, under a new leader, Andries

Pretorius, invaded Zululand, provoking Dingaan to attack. They formed a *laager* in a bend of the Blood River, protected on two faces by the deep stream and on two by the interlocked and barricaded line of fifty wagons. On 16 December 1838, always remembered in South Africa as Dingaan's Day, the Boer elephant-guns were ranged behind the barricade against the assault of the Zulu spearmen. Three thousand Zulus were slain for a loss of three Boers; Dingaan fled a fugitive to the Bush leaving all Natal in the power of the trekkers. Pretorius at once formed the first of the Boer free states, the Natal Republic (1839–43) with its capital at Pietermaritzburg. He solved the Zulu problem by setting up, as a rival to the discredited Dingaan, his brother Umpanda who was duly enthroned upon a sacred stone at the Boer capital, and was properly subservient to the Boers. Dingaan was hunted by his tribal rivals and killed in 1840.

English adventurers by sea had long previously secured a foot-hold on the coast of Natal. In 1823 a retired naval officer, Lieut. F. G. Farewell, had taken a ship up the coast from Port Elizabeth with a party of traders among whom the most striking figure was H. F. Fynn, an innkeeper from Capetown. They formed a little settlement at Port Natal on the rich warm coastal plain which had been swept bare of inhabitants in Chaka's wars. Fynn visited the Zulu tyrant (1824) and won his favour by curing his wounded leg. In a hazy, ignorant fashion Chaka thereafter favoured the handful of English traders, giving them some sort of title to their settlement and even exchanging compliments with the Governor at the Cape; though he permitted no trade except with himself upon his own terms. They never numbered more than forty white men, mostly elephant-hunters who lived an easy half-savage life such as is described in Rider Haggard's early romances. In 1835 they devised the plantation of a colony, laying out the site of a city which they called Durban in honour of the Governor; but the plan was cancelled by Glenelg who saw no profit in it. On the other hand he went so far as to send a magistrate to Natal with authority under an Act of 1836 to exercise criminal jurisdiction over British subjects anywhere south of the twenty-fifth degree of latitude, another offence to the Boers, who saw it as an extension of British sovereignty. In 1835 three American missionaries arrived at Port Natal, and two years later an English clergyman, the Rev. F. Owen, sent by the Church Missionary Society, was actually allowed to live at the royal kraal of Dingaan. Owen drew up the deed granting a concession to Retief's Boers and was the horrified witness of their murder.

The whole short life of the Natal Republic was occupied in futile disputations with the British government and quarrels among the republican leaders. In the panic of 1838 the settlers at Port Natal had withdrawn by sea, leaving to the Boers possession of the whole country, after their triumph on Dingaan's day. Two years of negotiation followed (with two changes in the office of Secretary of State) while Downing Street, blowing now a little hotter or a little colder, maintained the divergent propositions that Natal was not British territory, that some of its native inhabitants were under British protection, that the Boers in Natal were British subjects, and that British subjects remained subject to British jurisdiction anywhere south of the twenty-fifth parallel.

Lord Stanley (Peel's Colonial Secretary), while stoutly refusing either to annex Natal or to admit Boer independence, went so far as to send troops to reoccupy Port Natal in April 1842 with the object of protecting tribes who complained of Boer oppression. A local commando of Boers took arms, besieging the little British garrison until a youth named Dick King brought aid from Grahamstown after riding inland 600 miles through the wild Kaffir country. This little war forced the issue. The Cape Governor sent as Commissioner an Afrikaner, Henry Cloete, to come to terms with the Natal Republic. The Boers, however, solved the problem for themselves by trekking again. While in Natal there was endless trouble with fierce and numerous tribes, and endless irritation by the feeble-forcible British government, up on the High Veld there was freedom for the trekkers. The Natal Republic dwindled and disintegrated, as the farmers straggled north again over the passes of the Drakensberg. In August 1843 Natal became a British colony after some heated conferences with the republican remnant at Pietermaritzburg.

The same forces which obliged the British to intervene in Natal equally drove them to intervention north of the Orange River. Though this was the political frontier, beyond it were allied native kingdoms, under the influence of British missionaries and now threatened by the encroachment of the trek-boers. There were the Griquas and, beyond them, the most virile native race in South Africa, the horse-breeding Basutos, securely based upon their healthy highlands. The British made their first treaty with Moshesh, the Basuto king, in 1843. All through the High Veld, from the Orange to the Vaal and far beyond, there were now 10,000 Boer settlers loosely organised in commandos which formed petty republics, then split and trekked again. Parties of settlers took up land at will, determined to subdue the heathen to honest labour and to be free of the vexatious British. These little states had neither revenue nor administration, hardly even a fixed abode, and were constantly engaged in native wars. Into this confusion there was thrown a new Governor of the Cape, Sir Harry Smith of the Rifle Brigade (1787–1860) who was also appointed the Queen's High Commissioner for all South Africa.

In February 1848 Smith, who knew and liked the Boers and had great self-confidence, took the bold step of declaring British sovereignty over the area between the Orange and the Vaal. Some form of unity for South Africa was already seen as an inevitable goal by the wisest observers. This method might have led to the establishment of free Boer states and protected native kingdoms under the British flag, had not Pretorius the hero of Dingaan's Day, determined to fight. He led a commando to Bloemfontein, where a British agent had resided since 1846, and was neatly and soundly defeated by that very old soldier, Harry Smith, at the smart little action of Boomplatz, 29 August 1848, 'one of the severest skirmishes' he ever saw. Pretorius then fled north across the Vaal River in an irreconcilable mood.

Smith was chosen by the historian of the British Army as the pre-eminent fighting soldier of his generation. After a baptism of fire at Buenos Ayres, he served through the seven campaigns of the Peninsular War. He was present at the burning of Washington and the repulse from New Orleans, and yet returned to Europe in time to have two horses shot beneath him at Waterloo. Throughout the 'thirties he was busily engaged in the Kaffir Wars. Next serving in India he won the brilliant action of Aliwal against the Sikhs, and then returned to the Cape as Governor. After the storm of Badajoz he had rescued two Spanish ladies from the licence of the soldiers. One of them, a young and spirited girl, became his wife and accompanied him on all his campaigns. Her gaiety and courage, his shrewd sense and cool bravery, and the risks they encountered together made the favourite romance of the Peninsular veterans. Their names are commemorated in the two South African towns of Harrismith and Ladysmith.

After the annexation of the north the whole colony enjoyed a brief period of calm under Smith's vigorous and popular administration. The Cape itself was now the centre of a prosperous colony with an expanding home market and a useful export trade in wool. Full self-government, for which the colonists had frequently petitioned Downing Street, had not yet been granted though Smith and the Secretary of State were corresponding over a draft constitution (at last promulgated in 1853). Meanwhile the administration had been progressively improved. The Governor's advisory council had been converted (1833) into a legislative council of the normal Crown Colony type. The larger towns were provided with elective municipal government in the 1830's, the country districts with elective road boards in 1843. A comprehensive educational system, including some schools for coloured children had been instituted in 1839. The South African College, which grew into the University of Capetown, dates from 1829; Victoria College, Stellenbosch, the first Afrikaans university from 1859. The Dutch Reformed Church was given self-government in 1843; the Anglican bishopric of Capetown dates from 1847. One heavy storm blew up over the threat to introduce convict labour, which Smith light-heartedly had invited. When a shipload of convicts arrived in 1849, such a flurry of petitions and threatened resignations blew up that he was forced to refuse them admittance and to divert them to Van Diemen's Land.

In 1850 war broke out again on both frontiers. A renewed struggle with the Kaffirs proved so prolonged and expensive that Smith (like most of his predecessors) was recalled (1852), though the Duke of Wellington protested in Parliament that no man could have done better. While he fought his last campaigns on the eastern frontier other British troops had been forced to intervene in a quarrel between the Boers and the Basuto. Small British columns were twice repulsed by Moshesh from the Basuto highlands to the disgust of the British taxpayer and *The Times* newspaper, which complained lustily of the expense incurred in these never-ending frontier wars. Successive governments had grown heartily sick of the South African problem and all, of whatever political complexion, were anxious to limit their liability. At the time of Smith's recall a conference was taking place at Sand River between the Boer leaders and two British commissioners to define precisely what was the sovereignty proclaimed in 1848. A tardy but reasonable agreement was reached in January 1852 disclaiming British authority over the more distant area beyond the Vaal River. There the British had neither rights nor obligations and there the *voortrekkers* might at last be free. Thus the four rudimentary unorganised Boer states in the far north gained their independence and eventually (1860) coalesced into the Transvaal Republic. But the expenses of the Kaffir war were not yet over and the Basuto were still untamed. The British taxpayers fretted while a great European war threatened in the Near East. The next government went further in limiting liability. In February 1854 at another conference at Bloemfontein the British abdicated their sovereignty over the Orange Free State.[1] The Sand River Convention gave a legal definition to an existing situation and relieved the Transvaal Boers of the threat of unjust persecution. The Bloemfontein Convention was a mere confession of weakness, an act of negation, which persuaded the Boers that a bold front could bluff the British out of any position. There were many British settlers in the Free State, especially in Bloemfontein which was already the seat of an Anglican bishopric, and there is no evidence that the Boers desired independence. Numerous mission stations were centres of British influence among the natives. Two powerful nations, Griqua and Basuto, were deeply embroiled in complex disputes with Boers and British. From these entanglements the British could by no means withdraw.

> Weep, Britain, for the Cape whose ill-starred name,
> Long since divorced from Hope, suggests but shame,
> Disaster, and thy captains held at bay
> By naked hordes. . . .

So wrote a minor poet, considering Kaffir and Basuto victories, governors disgraced after splendid careers, ministers of the

[1] Previously known as the Orange River Sovereignty.

Crown weakly abdicating lawful power; but finding consolation in the story of a shipwreck. Off that rocky, stormy, south-east coast of Africa haunted by the spectre-ship of Vanderdecken,[1] scene of countless piracies and wrecks and founderings in deep water; where so long ago as 1782 the *Grosvenor*, East-Indiaman, took to the bottom a million pounds in gold, while the English men and women who sailed in her were cast away and lost among the savages; where so lately as 1909 a modern liner, the *Waratah*, vanished in a calm sea, on a course that should not have taken her out of sight of land, leaving no trace of her 150 passengers; between Capetown and Port Elizabeth the troopship *Birkenhead* struck a reef in 1852. She carried drafts of young recruits from four British regiments on their way to join the columns fighting in the Kaffir war. In order to hold her on an even keel while the civilians took to the boats, the soldiers were paraded on the quarter-deck and stood in their ranks until the ship went down; 357 out of 506 officers and men perished. That is all, but the story has never been forgotten. The King of Prussia gave orders that it should be read out on parade before every regiment of his army.

[1] Several accounts of the Flying Dutchman are given in Martin's *History of the British Colonies*, vol. IV (1835). She was twice reported from H.M.S. *Leven* in 1823.

VII

THE COLONIAL REFORMERS, 1830–46

Argument: The Malthusian theory led to discussion of relieving unemployment by emigration and, eventually, to Wakefield's theory of systematic colonisation. Lord Durham's report on Canada, largely inspired by Wakefield, was the gospel of the Colonial Reformers. Planned emigration to Australia under control of a Board of Commissioners overcame much opposition and many unexpected difficulties. Wakefield carried out a series of experiments in colonisation on the model of the seventeenth-century colonies, the first in South Australia, the last at Canterbury in New Zealand.

1. EDWARD GIBBON WAKEFIELD

PARLIAMENT was plagued, in the 'thirties and 'forties of last century, by the activities of some persons called the Colonial Reformers. They can hardly be described as a group or party since they rarely acted in concert; at first drawn from the Radicals they later found support among the enlightened Tories. What they had in common was a determination to take the British Empire seriously even if its destiny were disintegration. What they opposed was the idle indifference of British politicians, expressed by one of their number in the truism that 'any government would rather lose a colony than lose a division in the House'. When they first appeared, the Empire, so far as it came into the calculation of politicians, was estimated at its strategic value. There were good naval and military reasons for retaining Gibraltar, Malta, Corfu, the Cape, Mauritius, Ceylon, Newfoundland, Halifax, Bermuda and the Windward Islands. Though free trade was the fashionable doctrine of the new age there were also grounds for protecting the fisheries, the North American timber trade, and West Indian sugar even in despite of the economists; or, at any rate, there were strong interests in favour of their protection, in the House of Commons. Nor could certain sentimental considerations be excluded. There was a debt of honour to the

Canadian loyalists, and even some sort of a duty towards those of our neighbours whom we had exiled to Botany Bay. But on the whole the population of these strategic outposts and other casual dependencies, consisting largely of disaffected Frenchmen, disaffected Dutchmen, white convicts and negro slaves, was felt as a burden rather than a blessing to the imperial government.

With the flowing tide of Evangelical Revival there came a change in this view of the colonies, taking its most definite form when Lord Glenelg, the son of Charles Grant who first sent missionaries to India, was Secretary of State (1835–9). He, and Sir James Stephen, his Permanent Under-Secretary from 1837, gave policy a new direction. It was their glory to free the slaves, and to protect savage races in several parts of the world from exploitation by land-hungry settlers.

But settlers also have rights, and their case was put by the Colonial Reformers. The new factor in the problem was the growing belief that emigration might be a cure for unemployment. The economic principles of the Reformers were utilitarian, deriving from the Malthusian doctrine (1798), that population, which tends to increase by a geometrical progression, must always outrun food supply, which can at best only be increased by an arithmetical progression.[1] This was the basis of Ricardo's theory of marginal rent (1817) and McCulloch's theory of the fixed wage-fund (1826) which together established the new Political Economy as the 'dismal science'. Low wages and chronic unemployment appeared to have been entailed upon the human race as the conditions of material progress. All the evidence then to hand, from the few and imperfect censuses, supported these theories. The population of Great Britain was rising at an astonishing rate: from 10,000,000 in 1801, to 12,000,000 in 1811, 14,000,000 in 1821, and 16,000,000 in 1831. And, although trade was expanding, unemployment seemed to be growing still more rapidly. The Poor Law of 1834, felt by humane men to be a desperate remedy, a cruel necessity, was not the end; the 'Hungry 'Forties' were to follow. Among the Classical Economists the link with the Colonial Reformers was John Stuart Mill (1806–73) who propounded the maxim that 'colonisation, in the present state of the world, is

---

[1] 'When goods increase, they are increased that eat them: and what good is there to the owners thereof, saving the beholding of them with their eyes?' Ecclesiastes v. 2.

the very best affair of business, in which the capital of an old and wealthy country can possibly engage'.

The plain answer to the problem of unemployment seemed to be emigration. To a generation that thought badly of the Americans and never read colonial history, the names of Governor Winthrop, Penn, Baltimore, and Oglethorpe, meant nothing at all. The reasons why some colonies had succeeded while others had failed were quite forgotten, if indeed they had ever been understood in Whitehall. Colonisation was conceived as meaning no more than shipping paupers overseas; and very enlightened colonisation no more than paying their passage overseas to some place where there was already a British governor. The exponent of this simple plan was Sir Wilmot Horton (1784–1841), a philanthropist, who was Under-Secretary for the Colonies in the 1820's. Though he achieved something in the way of providing cheap unskilled labour at the ports of entry in established colonies, his methods could not create new settlements for which capital and skill and organisation and patience were needed. In fact, less than one-seventh of the emigrants from the British Isles in those years were transported by his efforts, to which the Treasury contributed about £20,000 a year. Of that great and growing wave of emigrants (which will be further discussed in chapter IX), some went in conditions of great misery from the slums of British towns to similar marginal employment in Canada or the United States; some were shipped off as paupers at the expense of the parish in accordance with a provision of the new Poor Law; some luckier families were drawn overseas by the attraction of relatives who had already established themselves in a colony; some went in one of the organised parties which are described elsewhere in this book.

The beginnings of a systematic plan of land development in the colonies were to be seen in 1826 when the Canada Land Company was incorporated by Royal Charter under the provisions of an Act of Parliament of 1825. An area of 2,400,000 acres between Lakes Huron and Ontario was sold to the Company for 3s. an acre with the stipulation that one-third of the purchase price was to be spent on bridges, roads, schools and other improvements. The land thus thrown open was to be sold as a commercial transaction to immigrants brought in by the Colonial Office. The originator of this scheme, which made steady progress for many years, was John Galt (1779–1839), the Scottish novelist, who paid

two visits to Canada in 1824 and 1826. Though he made no fortune for himself, he began the settlement of western Ontario.
Seven years later the British American Land Company was similarly incorporated but, taking up land at Sherbrooke in the eastern
townships of Lower Canada, it provoked bitter opposition from
the French-Canadians to whom English land-titles and English
settlers were equally unwelcome.

These were schemes that partially succeeded among many that
failed utterly. Land speculation in the colonies was a byword
among investors who learned painfully that colonisation schemes
were usually Utopian and sometimes fraudulent. New light on
the subject was derived from researches made by a convict in
Newgate. In March 1827, a young man of fashion named Edward
Gibbon Wakefield stood his trial at Lancaster Assizes for abducting an heiress from a girls' school. Brougham prosecuted and
Scarlett defended in a case without parallel. Wakefield's own
statement, put in as evidence, revealed in him extraordinary elements of recklessness, ingenuity, and bad judgment. He was
thirty years old and this was not his first elopement. When very
young he had made a runaway match and had loved his first wife
dearly. After her death, his brother and his young stepmother
urged him to marry a fortune which would enable him to stand
for Parliament, in the liberal interest. Together they plotted the
abduction of Ellen Turner, a girl of sixteen who was quite unknown to them except by repute. She was inveigled from her
school on some pretence and persuaded to set off with Wakefield,
who now saw her for the first time, on a journey in a post-chaise
which actually brought them to Gretna Green. In those few hours
Wakefield's eloquent tongue revealed the imposture and persuaded her to marry him. The celebrated blacksmith of Gretna
gave evidence of her willing gaiety at the ceremony (and died of a
chill caught on his way home from the trial). Wakefield was sentenced to three years' imprisonment in Newgate. His Parliamentary ambition was restricted to an appearance at the Bar of the
House to protest unsuccessfully against Sir Robert Peel's Bill for
annulling the marriage. This was the end of Wakefield's public
career, his last performance, in a blaze of lurid light, before
fashionable society.

Three years later a changed man was released from Newgate, or
rather a man who showed the other side of his nature. The *flâneur*

who had known Lord Byron in Italy and seconded a duellist in Paris was also the friend of Francis Place the Radical, and was first cousin to Elizabeth Fry. As a convict he studied the reform of the penal code and wrote pamphlets in picturesque and rather violent language upon capital punishment and convict transportation, this last being the bridge that brought him to colonial reform. The reviewers spoke warmly of his work, especially Rintoul of the *Spectator*, with whom he was thereafter closely associated. But his method was to work, he said, like the mole in obscurity. He was, as Ellen Turner knew, remarkably persuasive and, for the next thirty years, was somewhere in the background of every colonising venture and every agitation for colonial rights, rarely showing himself, not often signing his innumerable essays and pamphlets, but preferring to speak through the mouth of some unexceptionable young politician who was free of the taint of Newgate.

The *Letter from Sydney* (1829), fathered upon a young colonist named Robert Gouger, was actually written by Wakefield in prison. It can hardly be believed that the author was a young man who had never seen a colony. It purports to describe the life of a settler who has land and capital in New South Wales but no labour. The English artisans whom he has taken out have left him to set up on their own account as mere subsistence farmers; the convict servants assigned to him are idle and dishonest. He is alone and helpless in the midst of his fine estate surrounded by timber which would be worth a fortune if he could fell it and cart it to Sydney seventy miles away. There may be minerals underground but to what advantage? He cannot 'hew down a tree with a banknote or cleave the soil with a sovereign'.[1] Returning to Sydney he finds society utterly corrupted by sycophancy to the despotic Governor and by the wretched vices of the convicts, a society where he 'must needs associate familiarly with depraved men and women; where to break the law is a merit, and to elude its grasp an honourable achievement; where, above all, human beings are continually hanged in rows, as cattle are slaughtered in the French *abattoirs*'. The shortage of women leads to a prevalence of immoral habits over which he does not mince words. And what is the remedy for all these evils? To supply free labour

[1] This graphic and oft-quoted phrase is used by Wakefield's first biographer, Dr R. Garnett. I cannot trace it to Wakefield's writings.

in a fixed ratio to the amount of land occupied. Sydney capitalists, feeling the shortage of labourers, demand that more convicts should be imported but 'however earnestly we may desire it, we cannot expect that the increase of crime will keep pace with the spread of colonisation'. How otherwise can labourers be attracted to the colony and prevented from dispersing into the bush as small proprietors, with no market for their produce and no civilised society for their families?

All can be accomplished if the simple rule is kept of disposing of the public land at a uniform fixed price, and applying the land-fund thus created to paying the passage-money to the colony of selected young emigrants of both sexes, preferably newly-wed couples. This was the doctrine of the 'Sufficient Price' which Wakefield maintained against all critics for the rest of his life. Karl Marx, in a diatribe marked by his usual sardonic perversity, described the Wakefield plan as a new method of capitalist exploitation, whereas it was the opposite in intention and in effect. It aimed at preventing any man, rich or poor, from monopolising more land than he could use; it produced close settlement by resident proprietors, assuring them of a home market. Wakefield's mistake was to suppose that it was a panacea for all colonial ills. '*Concentration*', he said, 'would produce what never did and never can exist without it—*Civilisation*.'

Within a few years the Wakefield doctrine became the common form of all colonial land-laws. His supporters and his critics alike used his terminology; colonial statesmen accepted or diverged from his norm. The doctrine was adopted, with some hesitation by the Colonial Office for New South Wales in 1831, was approved by a Committee of the House in 1836, and was ratified in an act of Parliament in 1842, though never with sufficient firmness to satisfy its author. Wakefield would never admit that the price had been fixed at a high enough rate in any one instance to demonstrate the full effect of his principle; but when pressed he would never name a standard figure. It must vary according to the local demand for labour. Experience taught him, in the course of years, to shift his ground, to take some few steps to meet critical attacks from this or that quarter, but his main position he doggedly defended.[1] It became an obsession, a '*cacoethes colonizandi*',

---

[1] The development of his ideas and their gradual effect upon policy are closely studied in *The Colonisation of Australia*, by R. C. Mills.

said Sir William Molesworth,[1] 'for which he would send to the devil any person or thing that stood in his way'.

If this were all, the Wakefield plan would be a dry corner of history, interesting to economists only, but the gaol-bird who formulated the doctrine of the Sufficient Price had a deeper insight into human affairs. He saw that colonies are made by women as much as by men, that the settler's wife is as valuable a figure as the settler in building a new nation. He first appreciated that a new plantation requires families not single men. He looked forward to a day when the proportion of children to grown-up people in the colonies 'would be greater than ever was known since Shem, Ham and Japhet were surrounded by their little ones. The colony would be an immense nursery, and would offer the finest opportunity that ever occurred, to see what may be done for society by universal education.' This was neither a question of relieving the English Poor Law unions nor even of founding raw new societies; 'they would be so many *extensions* of an old society' requiring not only pauper labourers, but surveyors, architects, engineers, miners, botanists, chemists, printers, schoolmasters, publishers, 'and even reviewers'; surgeons, lawyers, bankers, clergymen, singers, milliners, 'and at least one good Political Economist at each settlement, to prevent us from devising an Australasian tariff'.

Could such a society be conceived without self-government? Would such men as William Penn and Lord Baltimore have crossed the Atlantic if they had known that they would remain subject to the whims of an Under-Secretary at the Colonial Office? The settlements recently attempted in Western Australia and at the Cape were the first examples, in the long history of the Empire, of colonies begun without representative institutions. The errors of the struggle with the American colonies might be avoided in the new Empire for which he pleaded. The colonists 'might either take a share in framing the general laws of the empire, by means of their representatives in the British Parliament; or they might frame their own laws in a Colonial Assembly, under

---

[1] Sir W. Molesworth, Bart. (1810–55) was an independent and a *franc-tireur* in politics, who had been expelled from Cambridge for offering to fight a duel with his tutor. He was the reputed leader of the Colonial Reformers in Parliament after the deaths of Lord Durham and Charles Buller. He, too, died young, shortly after Palmerston had made him Colonial Secretary.

the eye of a viceroy, incapable of wrong and possessing a veto like the King of England, but whose secretaries, like the ministers of England, should be responsible to the people'.

The modern reader of Wakefield's *Letter from Sydney* may well be astonished at his foresight (though neither Wakefield nor any other political economist could foretell the vagaries of the birth-rate in the ensuing century). He is not least illuminating when he writes of political geography: of the errors of diet formed by con-servative Englishmen who have settled in a new province which is the antipodes of Naples; of the emergence of a new physical type in the 'Mediterranean' climate of New South Wales; of the central position of Australia facing the great arc of south-east Asia where lives the greatest mass of the world's peoples; and, as an afterthought, of the possibility of peopling Australia with Chinese coolies if it cannot be peopled with free white men.

2. FIRST EFFORTS OF THE COLONIAL REFORMERS

WAKEFIELD formed the first of his Colonisation Societies in 1831 and reconstituted it as the National Colonisation Society two years later. There were not more than about forty members, then young obscure men but, in several instances, marked for future distinction. They included John Stuart Mill, George Grote the historian, Rintoul of the *Spectator*, Hobhouse who had been Byron's friend, Sir Francis Burdett, Charles Buller, Sir William Molesworth, and other liberal M.P.'s. Robert Gouger, Wake-field's stalking-horse, was secretary. Several Radicals, whose in-terest in the Empire was disruptive rather than creative, though not members of the Society, must be numbered among the Colo-nial Reformers. J. A. Roebuck, a harsh critic of Wakefield's theories, which he did not understand, was London Agent for the restive French-Canadians. Joseph Hume, always to be found with every small minority, actually moved in the House during the debates on the Reform Bill that the colonies should send their representatives to Westminster, a proposal which the honourable members received with shouts of laughter. A few years later, he had swung round and was speaking openly for colonial indepen-dence, as did a much saner man, Sir William Molesworth. Indeed t would be difficult to find any statement of colonial policy by a front-bench politician in the eighteen-thirties, putting aside the utterances of extremists, which did not assume that independence was the goal of the colonies, whether temporary adjustments in the imperial connexion were thought desirable or not.

Wakefield had first to persuade his own circle that a constructive policy might make the colonies worthy of preservation, his own nucleus of disciples who stood by him faithfully being Mill, Rintoul, Buller and Molesworth. They had a signal triumph in converting Jeremy Bentham, then in the last year of his long life (1831), to the doctrine of the Sufficient Price. Less successful was the attempt to convert Wilmot Horton who attended one of the early meetings but broke out in furious opposition on finding that Wakefield's principles of emigration were destructive to his plans. An early convert was Lord Howick, son of Lord Grey of the Reform Bill and afterwards an energetic Secretary of State. As Under-Secretary in 1831, he was responsible for the decision that free grants of land in New South Wales should be forbidden and that all unappropriated land should be put up for sale at a uniform price of 5s. per acre. Though the mischief was done as regards the best land round Sydney which, long previously, had been given away to favourites of the government, and though Wakefield thought 5s. a miserably insufficient price, here at least was a beginning.

In 1829, a somewhat hare-brained scheme was launched for settling a colony at Swan River in what is now called Western Australia. Robert Gouger intended to join the party until Wakefield convinced him that the scheme must fail. It combined all the errors in the art of colonisation which he had already demonstrated. It failed; and Wakefield thereafter used it, not always quite scrupulously, as the standard example of how not to do it.[1] Several of the Colonial Reformers then proceeded to plan an experiment in systematic colonisation on Wakefield's model, selecting for the site of the experiment the fertile lands discovered (but not yet explored and mapped) by Captain Sturt near the mouth of the Murray River. There were six changes in the office of Secretary of State in the seven years (1830–6) required to launch the colony. Each of the six successive rulers of the Empire had to learn the doctrine anew, each must be convinced, and each

[1] For the history of the Swan River Settlement, see chapter VII, 6, page 363.

be stimulated into forcing Parliamentary action in the busy times of the Great Reform Bill. Whatever their party and however faint their interest, the six Secretaries of State were agreed on two points: the colonists should not be released from control by Downing Street, and the colony should not cost the British government a penny.

The first inquiry was politely repulsed by Wellington's government on the grounds that colonies were an expense and we could afford no more of them. In August 1831, three members of the Society, Colonel Torrens, Major Bacon and Gouger, approached the next government, Lord Grey's, with an elaborate plan for founding a joint-stock company with the double role of financing a 'Wakefield' colony and appointing a governor, to control it until it should include 5000 citizens after which it should receive self-government. Sir James Stephen, the permanent Under-Secretary, persuaded his chief to reject this plan as 'wild and unpracticable', unsound financially and above all 'republican'. His opposition, maintained throughout the transitory reigns of several phantoms in the Secretary-of-State's chair, won him the enmity of Wakefield, who never forgot an injury. They should have thought of introducing a House of Lords into Australia, he said, with 'a Viscount Kangaroo and a Bishop of Ornithorhyncus'.

In March 1833, when Lord Stanley was at the Colonial Office, they tried again. Wakefield had just written a new work, *England and America*, in which he compared the generous charters of Penn's and Baltimore's colonies with the petty restrictions imposed by nineteenth-century governments. The reformers now asked for a Chartered Company, not financially interested, but controlling both the finances and the government of the infant settlement through trustees. Stanley positively refused to relinquish political control. Luckily the next incumbent, Spring-Rice, was a school-friend of Wakefield and was persuaded to adopt the financial provisions; though the hope of getting self-government for the new settlement was abandoned. To get a bill through in the busy session of 1834 would have been an impossible task had not Wakefield by some means won the good offices of the Duke of Wellington who now gave his support to the scheme. No sooner had the South Australia Act become law, in August 1834, than the ministry went out, so that no action was taken for another year. The appointment of commissioners became a party matter, most of the original enthusiasts being put out to make room for friends of the ministry. By this time Wakefield's patience was exhausted; he had quarrelled with Gouger over the price of land which, at 12s. an acre, he thought far too low. The new men on the commission were, in his opinion, ignorant amateurs, though their secretary, Rowland Hill (afterwards the postal reformer), was one of the Wakefield school.

For a long time he was abroad at his beloved daughter's deathbed and, in 1835, when he returned, he affected to wash his hands of South Australia which could be regarded as a 'Wakefield' Colony only in an imperfect sense.[1] The settlement, at last planted in 1836, was not called after Wellington as the claims of gratitude should have required, but after Queen Adelaide in the hope of earning the favour of King William IV.

The next activity of the Colonial Reformers was to brief the Parliamentary Committee on Colonial Lands, 1836. Here Wakefield departed from his usual custom of pulling strings in the background. His public evidence before the Committee triumphantly displayed the causes of failure at Swan River and the dangers of failure at Adelaide inasmuch as the Sufficient Price had not been enforced. Though Sir George Grey (of Fallodon[2]), the government representative, voted against each proposal of the reformers, the general sense of the Committee favoured their views. They recommended 'that the whole of the arrangements connected with the sale of land should be placed under the charge of a central Land Board, resident in London', a salutary proposal which was carried out by Lord John Russell after no more than three years' delay.

In the next session the reformers raised the question of the evils of convict transportation. Public attention had been roused by a thoughtful book which Archbishop Whately had published in 1834. He argued that the strongest objection to transportation was that in many cases it meant not punishment but reward. All

---

[1] For the settlement of Adelaide see chapter VII, 6, page 365.

[2] The student of colonial history may be confused by the intermittent appearances of three statesmen named Grey in the mid-nineteenth century. Henry, 3rd Earl Grey (known in his father's lifetime as Lord Howick), was Colonial Secretary in 1846. His cousin Sir George Grey of Fallodon was Colonial Secretary in 1854. Sir George Grey, the Colonial Governor, was of another family. (See Appendix III.)

convicts were brutalised and degraded, but many eventually made their fortunes at Botany Bay and lived in vicious luxury ever after. Transportation failed either to reform or to punish. The work of the Parliamentary Committee of 1837 emerged as a landmark in the history of penal reform, then actively pursued by many who were not much concerned about the colonies. Peel, Russell, Howick and Sir George Grey of Fallodon sat on the Committee as well as Buller and Molesworth, the last-named being chairman. Upon the main issue there was little difference of opinion. It was agreed that the system of transporting convicts in the mass to the colonies should be discontinued as soon as possible, but that penitentiaries should be maintained abroad as well as at home for the reception of convicts sentenced to hard labour. The foreign convict stations, which should be located where there were no free settlers, were required solely because of the lack of accommodation in English prisons. The planting of colonies with exiled criminals ended on 1 August 1840, to the great disgust of the Legislative Council in New South Wales, where ruin for the colony was gloomily predicted.

From 1788 to 1836, 75,200 convicts had been sent to New South Wales; 27,759 had been sent to Van Diemen's Land since 1817. In 1836 there were 25,254 men and 2577 women held as convicts in the former, 14,914 men and 2054 women in the latter. At Norfolk Island there were, in the year 1837, about 1200 convicts, mostly transported again after committing further crimes in New South Wales. There were also 1500 convicts in Bermuda, mostly soldiers and sailors detained for offences against military law.

Van Diemen's Land, Norfolk Island and Bermuda were retained as penitentiaries; no fewer than 35,378 convicts were transported to Van Diemen's Land between 1841 and 1852 when at the urgent request of the free colonists the island was at last released from this burden of depravity. Norfolk Island was abandoned in 1855. The government was hard put to it to find a home for convicted criminals and the Colonial Office was often pressed by the Home Office to accept some batches. In 1846 when Gladstone was at the Colonial Office he varied the procedure by founding in Queensland a settlement for ex-convicts, emancipists from New South Wales. When Lord Grey succeeded him the scheme was abandoned, though the township of Gladstone survived. Here

Plate 9

A MEETING OF THE ANTI-SLAVERY SOCIETY

t Freemason's Hall in 1840. Thomas Clarkson, eighty years old, is speaking. The figure
ith dark hair at the top, on the left, is Daniel O'Connell. Beneath and in front of him
Sir T. F. Buxton. Joseph Sturge is on Clarkson's left. Painted by B. R. Haydon.
e p. 292.

Plate 10

LORD DURHAM (1792–1840)

'Radical Jack.' An engraving after a portrait by G. Richmond. *See p. 341.*

and there capitalists, finding themselves without labour in the days of emancipation, sighed for slaves or convicts, and even begged the Colonial Office to provide them. In general, as free emigration progressed, the decent feelings of the settlers everywhere revolted against accepting the off-scouring of the criminal class. In 1849 an attempt to ship ticket-of-leave men to the new colony of Melbourne was met by the stern refusal of the settlers to admit them and, what is more, they were refused admittance at Sydney also. New Zealand also kept its shores clean.

In the same year a shipload was turned away from Capetown. Lord Grey (formerly Howick), then Colonial Secretary, thought this attempt at transportation justified. 'What will be the consequence when two or three thousand convicts are turned loose upon society in the United Kingdom?' That they should be turned loose among honest men at Melbourne or the Cape seemed to him a matter of less consequence. The Parliamentary debates of 1849 reveal an enlightened approach to the problem, with much sensible discussion of the punitive, deterrent, and reformative effects of transportation. The Tory opposition on the whole denounced it, while the Whig ministry made a guarded defence of the policy of transporting small numbers of selected convicts under careful control. *The Times* took a large part in the controversy with much pregnant quotation from Gibbon Wakefield, but came down on the side of Lord Grey. 'If you do not transport to South Africa', asked the Thunderer in a leader that is often misquoted (27 March 1849), 'whither will you transport your convicts? If you do not send them to your colonies what will you do with them?' English society was saved by the weakness of one colonial governor, Fitzgerald of Western Australia, who expressed his willingness to receive his quota. Accordingly, 9720 male convicts were sent to Western Australia between 1849 and 1868, when the iniquitous system ended.

Naval requirements had brought about the despatch of convicts to Bermuda. The loyal conservative Bermudans had been shaken in their allegiance during the American War. The schooners they built and rigged so skilfully were used for the inter-colonial trade, and the islanders were sorely tempted to maintain the supply of Washington's army, until the rival influence of the King's Navy prevailed when Bermuda was required as a blockading station. The dockyard was not founded, however, until 1810. Not long afterwards the capital was removed from St George to the new township of Hamilton (1815). The population fell in times of peace. From 15,000 in 1780 it declined to 8500 in 1837. Since there were no plantations, slavery in Bermuda was merely domestic; the 4000 negroes worked for 1000 white proprietors and were not available for public works, even after the abolition of slavery. As early as 1824 gangs of white convicts were employed in making the dockyard. Until 1863, an establishment of 1500 convicts, military and naval offenders, was maintained there, each batch returning to England on completion of sentence, so that the islands were rid of them.

The Andaman and Nicobar Islands, the home of very primitive tribes, were occupied, for use as a penitentiary, by the Indian Government in 1857. The Andamans won notoriety for the murder, by a convict, of Lord Mayo, the Viceroy (1872).

3. THE CANADAS AND LORD DURHAM'S MISSION, 1822–39

POLITICAL life in Canada had not developed happily under the constitution of 1791. Though there was often a single Governor-General for the two provinces of Upper (or British) and Lower (or French) Canada, there was constant friction between the two provincial governments and the two races; friction in each province between the elected assemblies and the nominated councils; friction between the legislatures and the executive officers.

In Lower Canada the issue turned on control of the public purse. From 1818 onwards, every session took the form of a wrangle between the Governor and the Assembly over voting the civil list, which the Governors wished to be allocated as in England for a term of years, but which the Assembly attempted to grant or withhold, item by item, at will. The leader of the popular party was Louis Joseph Papineau (1786–1871), the Speaker of the Assembly. After numerous changes of Governor, references to Downing Street, debates in the House of Commons, and after the failure of a Royal Commission to adjust grievances, a complete deadlock was reached. From 1831 to 1835 the Assembly was repeatedly prorogued without transacting any legislative business, having refused to vote Supply. Their grievances were put forward in a series of demands (February 1834) for unconditional control of the revenue, for an elective upper chamber, for repeal of the imperial statutes which had modified French feudal tenures, for cancellation of the charter of the British American Land Company, and for various restrictions upon Crown patronage and the power of the executive. The Whig government in London made some concessions to these demands but authorised the Governor to pay the overdue expenses of government by appropriating the funds then in the Colonial Treasury. At the news of this decision the Assembly protested furiously and was prorogued for the last time (August 1837).

Meanwhile a parallel agitation had been felt in Upper Canada though there the issue was not embittered by a racial feud. An enthusiast named Robert Gourlay had struck at the root of the matter, at a political convention at Toronto in 1822, by making suggestions for public control of land settlement which found their way into the plans of later reformers. The deadlock in Upper Canada was formed by the permanent composition of the Governor's Executive Council, the 'Family Compact', which persisted, unchanged and irresponsible through the terms of office of governor after governor. Control of the revenue and the land-grants was theirs, it seemed, for life. The strongest man among them was an Anglican clergyman, John Strachan, a Loyalist and great Church organiser but a tactless politician, who was determined to maintain the rights of his own communion in a province which was increasingly Scottish and Presbyterian. In 1839 he became Bishop of Toronto.

The leader of revolt against the Family Compact was William Lyon MacKenzie (1795–1861), a somewhat violent journalist who became the first Mayor of Toronto when it was incorporated as a city, in 1834. He drifted away from the more moderate reformers to make common cause with Papineau in Lower Canada and with the Radical, Joseph Hume, in the British House of Commons. Hume gave great offence to the loyal Canadians, who wanted only an improved constitution, by foretelling a crisis in Canada 'which will terminate in independence and freedom from the baneful domination of the mother-country'. A new Governor, Sir Francis Head, failed as all his predecessors had failed to come to terms with the reformers, though he did work for a time with the most able of them, Robert Baldwin (1804–58), the reputed inventor of the device known as responsible government. Not to weary the reader with too many repetitions, it may be said that similar crises had repeatedly occurred in each of the three Maritime Provinces and in Newfoundland, the most eminent reformer in the east being Joseph Howe, the editor of the *Nova Scotian*.

In the autumn of 1837 Lower Canada was in a state of passive rebellion. The Assembly was prorogued, the revenues were not collected, the administrative machine had run down and stopped. Actual bloodshed was limited by the preventive measures of the military commander Sir John Colborne, who in his day had delivered the decisive counter-attack at Waterloo and was not to be caught unaware. He concentrated troops at Montreal and was ready for anything. On 23 October, when the movement of reinforcements from England was stopped by the freezing of the St Lawrence, a republic was proclaimed at St Charles, on the Richelieu River, the road to the United States, by an English Radical named Nelson. Colborne sent a party of troops who dispersed these rebels almost without fighting and took Nelson prisoner. Papineau, who had gone to join with Nelson, fled over the American frontier rather ignominiously. Stimulated by the rumour of these doings a few villages west of Montreal had armed and entrenched themselves. In December Colborne marched against these misguided peasants and defeated them, killing about seventy in a skirmish at St Eustache, which ended the rebellion in French Canada. Montreal was calmed by the efforts of Mgr Martigue the Bishop, who denounced rebellion as sin.

It seemed more alarming that a revolution should begin at Toronto in the land of the loyalists. There MacKenzie assembled a band of frontiersmen, some of them filibusters from the American side, with the intention of seizing the city which had been denuded of troops for the concentration at Montreal. But at the first show of force his followers melted away and he, too, fled over the American frontier. A 'provisional government' for Canada was then formed on American soil and, for some months, riots and raids were reported from several points on the unpoliced border.

The news from Canada provoked Lord Melbourne to characteristic action. Something must be done, and two nuisances might be cured together if a dangerous rival could be sent to do it. He therefore decided, in January 1838, to send the Earl of Durham to

North America with a multiple authority as Captain-General, High Commissioner and Governor-in-Chief of all the provinces, including Newfoundland. Lord Durham (1792–1840), the first of his line to accept a peerage, was head of an ancient family, the Lambtons of Lambton Castle, whose wealth had been vastly increased by the development of collieries. As a young man in Whig society he had been celebrated for his off-hand remark that a man should be able to 'jog along on £40,000 a year'. He had made his name in Parliament as one of the committee appointed to draft the Great Reform Bill, and had broken with Lord Grey, his father-in-law,[1] when the passing of the Bill was not followed by further radical reforms. Marked down as an extreme liberal he was nevertheless too proud, too pure-bred a Whig, to be classed as one of the doctrinaire Radicals. A brilliant, queer-tempered man and a bad colleague, he was admired and feared and excluded from office. Guizot, the French ambassador 'perceived in his haughty melancholy a strong imprint of egotism and vanity'. *The Times* described him as 'vainglorious, perverse and reckless'. Melbourne sent him as ambassador to Russia in 1836 and was glad to be able to send him next to Canada. The first statesman of cabinet rank ever to be made governor of a colony, Durham had no intention of submitting to departmental instructions from the Colonial Office. Conceiving his mission as a Viceroyalty, he used pomp as an instrument of power, laid careful preparations, travelled in state at great personal expense, and proposed to act with bold decision when he should be quite ready. He selected his staff with care and deliberation, choosing as confidential secretary Charles Buller (1806–43), a young liberal M.P., the friend and pupil of Carlyle. Buller's lively critical memoir is the best account of Durham's mission. He also wished to appoint two expert advisers, Wakefield for the public lands and Thomas Turton for the judicial system; but the high-minded Glenelg positively forbade the appointment of the disreputable Wakefield who, nevertheless, accompanied Durham privately, with 'no ostensible employment'. Turton's career, like Wakefield's, had been clouded by a domestic scandal which was disinterred and flaunted in Durham's face by his political enemies. The long delay from January to April before Durham sailed for Canada was an error which 'took the bloom off the mission'. The

[1] For Durham's family connexion see Appendix III.

crisis seemed to have subsided and the pomp which Durham affected seemed superfluous, all the more as it was tarnished by the Turton scandal.

On reaching Quebec Lord Durham was well received by the British-Canadians but with 'sullen and distant apathy' by the French. He set himself at once to the actual routine of government in Lower Canada where all was anarchy. At the end of six weeks his imperious activity had so far restored order that he took the step of celebrating the young Queen's Coronation day (28 June 1838) by proclaiming a general amnesty to the hundreds of rebels who were under arrest, excepting eight named leaders whom he banished to Bermuda, forbidding them to return on pain of death. Those other rebel leaders who were still plotting further rebellion from their retreat in the United States were also threatened with death if they should re-enter Canada. The amnesty gave general satisfaction throughout North America, even going some distance towards mollifying the French. According to Buller it was approved in a despatch from Glenelg to which was added an autograph letter from the Queen.

In July, Durham visited Upper Canada, making a short stay at Niagara where he impressed the filibusters by holding a review of troops. He minimised the importance of the petty tumults on this unruly frontier, setting himself to secure cordial relations both with Washington and with the neighbouring Americans. He had already sent his brother-in-law on a complimentary visit to President Van Buren and now took pains to pay courteous attentions to American visitors at Niagara, a welcome change from the haughty aloofness of earlier British officials. 'A million of money would have been a cheap price', wrote Buller, 'for the glass of wine which Lord Durham drank to the health of the American President.' Next he turned his attention to the affairs of the Maritime Provinces which sent deputations to represent their grievances to him at Quebec.

He was now at the height of his career, busy and triumphant when rumours reached the Dictator (as his staff affectionately nicknamed him) that renewed attacks had been launched against him in Parliament by his rival, Brougham, as well as by his opponents, the Tories. Lord Melbourne's government, basely giving way, passed an act restricting the scope of Durham's commission and disallowed his ordinance of 28 June, on the grounds that he had exceeded his authority by the banishments to Bermuda. Addresses poured in to the Dictator from all parts of British North America assuring him of much loyal support, but Durham's pride would not allow him to remain in office after such a snub. He instantly resigned and went further by attacking his political enemies in a proclamation (9 October 1838) announcing his departure. He assured the Canadians that he would defend their interests against 'some persons too apt to legislate in ignorance and indifference'.

On 1 November 1838, Durham sailed from Quebec in a ship with the ill-omened name of *Inconstant*. 'The sky was black with clouds', wrote Buller, 'bearing the first snow-storm of the winter, and hardly a breath of air was moving. The streets were crowded; the spectators filled every window and every housetop; and though every hat was raised as we passed, a deep silence marked the general grief for Lord Durham's departure. His own presentiments depressed him and those about him, for he had told me and others that he did not expect to reach England alive.' No sooner was he gone than rebellious outbreaks were renewed in both provinces and were again suppressed by Colborne without much difficulty (November 1838).

Durham's health, never strong, had broken down under the strain of his efforts and disappointments. Commissioned in January 1838, he had reached Canada in May; he resigned in October and was back in England in December. The Durham Report which refashioned the British Empire, was debated in Parliament on 11 February 1839. After completing his report he took little part in public life. He died eighteen months later at the early age of forty-eight.

4. THE DURHAM REPORT AND ITS CONSEQUENCES

It was not to be supposed that Lord Durham's report was all original or all new. Since he had taken pains to consult the most enlightened opinion in Canada and England no one need be surprised that many of his recommendations had been anticipated by students of Canadian affairs. He would have been foolish indeed if he had not taken their advice. He even appealed to the sympathy of the young Queen by pointing out that her father, the Duke of Kent, had foreshadowed one of the recommendations when serving in Canada in 1799. Nor is there any truth in the bitter jibe made by Brougham to Macaulay as they walked together in Lincoln's Inn Fields on 13 February 1839: 'The matter came from a swindler [Wakefield], the style from a coxcomb [Buller], while the Dictator furnished only six letters, D.U.R.H.A.M.' The Report is graced here and there with flashes of Buller's lively wit and is strengthened with the close contexture of Wakefield's forceful argument in those passages dealing with subjects in which he was expert; clearly Durham would not have employed these men if he had not intended to make use of their talents. He was no niggling bureaucrat, but a bold statesman with a contempt for small views and petty vanities and selfish interests. The breadth of vision, the nobility of sentiment in the Report are his own. His prescription for producing a free, prosperous, and loyal nation was threefold: he called for political union, administrative reform, and the device which is known, not very lucidly, as responsible government.

The Report is lengthy; it extends to more than 300 pages, excluding the appendices, in the standard edition prepared by Sir C. P. Lucas, nearly one-half of it being devoted to the future of the French in Lower Canada. Were they to be absorbed into a common citizenship with the British or were they to become (as in fact they have become) a *nation canadienne*? Of Lower Canada Lord Durham wrote: 'I expected to find a contest between a government and a people: I found two nations warring in the bosom of a single state: I found a struggle, not of principles, but of races; and I perceived that it would be idle to attempt any amelioration of laws or institutions until we could first succeed in terminating the deadly animosity that now separates the inhabitants of Lower Canada into the hostile divisions of French and English.' Lord Durham was far from displaying any national prejudice against the character of the French, who were not wanting in those virtues which 'common consent attributes to the nation from which they spring. They are mild and kindly, frugal, industrious and honest, very sociable, cheerful, and hospitable, and distinguished for a courtesy and real politeness, which pervades every class of society.' He paid a particular tribute to the Catholic clergy who 'to a very remarkable degree, conciliated the goodwill of persons of all creeds'. 'I know of no parochial clergy in the world whose practice of all the Christian virtues is more universally admitted.' But, having paid these tributes, he enlarged upon the conservative habit of mind of the French; deplored their obstructiveness against all forms of improvement and especially those forms of improvement which extended British influence into French-Canadian districts; and described the breakdown of all administration and the loss of public confidence which the recent rebellion had brought about. The French were irreconcilable. 'I feel confident that the accuracy and moderation of my description will be acknowledged by all who have seen the state of society in Lower Canada during the last year. Never again will the *present generation*[1] of French-Canadians yield a loyal submission to a British Government; never again will the English population tolerate the authority of a House of Assembly, in which the French shall possess a majority.'

The causes of dissension among the British in Upper Canada were altogether different, and not deep-rooted. Theirs were faulty institutions which could be remedied by a return to the true English principles of government. The rebellion in Upper Canada was not a national movement but the 'foolishly contrived and ill-conducted attempt' of a handful of persons in an exasperated country. 'Almost the entire body of the reformers of this province sought only by constitutional means to obtain the objects for which they had so long peaceably struggled before the unhappy troubles occasioned by a few unprincipled adventurers and heated enthusiasts.' At the threat of an invasion by ruffians from across the border the general population 'turned out with unanimity to defend their country'.

The disorders were occasioned by defects in the constitution which were common to Upper and to Lower Canada, even though there were underlying and graver causes in the case of Lower Canada only. 'It may fairly be said that in all these colonies [including Prince Edward Island, New Brunswick, Nova Scotia and even Newfoundland] the natural state of government is that of collision between the executive and the representative body. In all of them the administration of public affairs is habitually confided to those who do not co-operate harmoniously with the popular branch of the legislature.'

[1] My italics.   C.E.C.

In addition to these two principal weaknesses—the racial feud and the inadequate political institutions—there were many particular defects in all parts of the administration and all of them aggravated in Lower Canada by the hostile attitude of the French. The judiciary was insufficient; the juries were corrupt—in Lower Canada so partial that civil justice was no longer administered; there was no police force, except in Quebec and Montreal where Durham himself had instituted it. Stipendiary magistrates and a Supreme Court of British North America were much to be desired. There was no general system of public education except, and this is the one exception in their favour,[1] among the French whose Church made itself responsible for parish schools. It was no credit to the British, as good Bishop Macdonell pointed out in a letter couched in courteous and loyal terms, that the government, having suppressed the Order of the Jesuits (1774) in Canada, had applied their educational endowments to the Secret Service fund. A fundamental defect was the absence of municipal institutions. 'The people should have been trained for taking their part in the concern of the Province, by their experience in the management of that local business which was most interesting and most easily intelligible to them. But the inhabitants of Lower Canada were unhappily initiated into self-government at exactly the wrong end.'

Durham made an acute remark upon the parochial character of politics in a colony. 'I know of no greater difference in the machinery of government in the old and new world than the apparently undue importance which the business of constructing public works appears to occupy.... If an individual is asked how his own legislature has acted, he will generally say what roads or bridges it has made, or neglected to make, in his own district.' In this respect the British provinces were far more backward than the neighbouring American states where public works were developed by self-governing municipalities. The report frequently turns aside to draw unflattering parallels between the two sides of the frontier. (It is fair to say that the author of *Martin Chuzzlewit*,

[1] Durham appears to be confining these strictures to the British minority in Lower Canada. A common-school system on the American, or Scottish, model had been instituted in Upper Canada in 1816, in Nova Scotia even earlier. Canadian Education, perhaps, owes more to Egerton Ryerson (1803–82), the Methodist leader, than to any other man. He was Superintendent of the schools of Upper Canada from 1844 to 1876.

who visited Canada and the United States a year or two later, did not find conditions in the Great Republic so rose-coloured.) 'On the American side, all is activity and bustle. The forest has been widely cleared; every year numerous settlements are formed, and thousands of farms are created out of the waste; the country is intersected by common roads; canals and railroads are finished or in course of formation. Good houses, warehouses, mills, inns, villages, towns and even great cities, are almost seen to spring up out of the desert. . . . On the British side of the line, with the exception of a few favoured spots, where some approach to American prosperity is apparent, all seems waste and desolate.' There were only fifteen miles of railway in Canada; the roads were so bad that wheat could be shipped more cheaply from Toronto to Liverpool than from the farm where it was grown, ninety miles away, to Toronto. Local improvements were made the instruments of political jobbery. The development of roads and canals from the seaports of Lower Canada to the rich resources of Upper Canada was obstructed by the French who refused to contribute to the cost. The revenue of Lower Canada, deriving largely from customs-duties, showed a surplus which was never usefully employed; the finances of Upper Canada were burdened with debt, partly as a result of French unhelpfulness but partly the consequence of their own improvidence.

The backwardness of public works was closely connected with the misuse of public lands, and here Wakefield contributed his quota to the report. On the other side of the frontier the 'system of the United States appears to combine all the chief requisites of the greatest efficiency. It is uniform throughout the vast federation; it renders the acquisition of new land easy; and yet, by means of a price, restricts appropriation to the actual wants of the settler; it provides for accurate surveys; it gives an instant and secure title; and it admits of no favouritism. That system has promoted an amount of immigration and settlement, of which the history of the world affords no other example; and it has produced to the United States a revenue which has averaged about half a million sterling per annum.' On the other hand, excepting the experiments of the Canada Land Company, there had never been any regular system in the British North American colonies. Grants of land, far larger than the requirements of any settler, had been made profusely to the favourites of government without accurate survey, without secure titles, without access or communications. The practice of reserving one-seventh of the land for the clergy had merely sterilised one-seventh of the land, since the clergy could not take it up. Both large and small grants were commonly sold off to speculators for a nominal price when it was found that there were no facilities for cultivating them. Even the grants to loyalists and old soldiers had been made at the maximum expense to the government and the minimum advantage to the grantees. Not one-tenth of them had persevered to cultivate the land granted. The most shocking case was Prince Edward Island which had been entirely alienated, in sixty-seven grants to proprietors who were mostly absentees, with the effect that of nearly 1,400,000 acres in that fertile island only 100,000 were under cultivation. Emigration to Canada had dwindled from 50,000 in the year 1831 to 5000 in 1838 because of the political disturbances, the appalling reports of misery in the emigrant ships, and the failure to settle the newcomers effectively on the land. And of the emigrants who landed, an unknown number—perhaps half—had drifted over the border into the United States.

This accumulated record of lethargy and corruption did not oppress the buoyancy of Lord Durham. His recommendations were few and practical and he closed his report with an optimistic forecast. Having considered and rejected the confederation of the North American colonies he decided 'that tranquillity can only be restored by subjecting Lower Canada to the vigorous rule of an English majority; and that the only efficacious government would be that formed by a legislative union'. This would deprive the French of no political liberty or privilege but would tend to absorb them into the English majority, in the course of time, as the French of Louisiana had been absorbed into the English-speaking majority of the United States, an analogy which he developed at some length. He proposed to solve the problem of the relations between executive and legislature by 'precisely that limitation of their respective powers which has been so long and so easily maintained in Great Britain'. Each colonial governor should be instructed, 'by a single despatch' requiring no legislation, 'to secure the co-operation of the Assembly in his policy, by entrusting its administration to such men as could command a majority'. This was the device known as responsible government, the Governor under such a system being made responsible to the Assembly in the colony rather than to the Secretary of State in Downing Street. Responsible government was the crux of the matter and became the subject of fierce controversy at home and in every colony. It implied the discontinuance of that vexatious interference by the Colonial Office in the affairs of the colonies, excepting in certain matters of high policy which were reserved for the imperial government. Durham proposed to reserve three subjects only, the form of the colonial constitution, the regulation of foreign affairs and external trade, and the disposal of the public lands which should be held, he said, as the birthright of the crowded millions of Great Britain rather than the private property of the first-comers to a new settlement.

He intended that the Union should embrace all the British colonies in North America including Newfoundland, since all had common problems of communications and defence and almost all were separately concerned in diplomatic disputes with the United States. 'The preservation of the present general sympathy of the United States with the policy of our Government is a matter of the greatest importance'; but the disposition of the American frontiersmen towards filibustering could not be neglected. Whether all the colonies were to be united or not, the immediate union of Upper and Lower Canada was urged as a measure that would admit no delay, while the establishment of a common currency, a postal union, a customs union and a supreme court for all the colonies were hardly less desirable. Municipal administration should everywhere be introduced on a uniform plan. The public lands should be taken under imperial control and administered on the principles discussed above. The clergy reserves should be abolished. Several useful suggestions were also made for preventing corruption in the assemblies and the law-courts.

But the most unexpected feature of Lord Durham's recommendations is his forecast of what might be done by centralising the public works under a single government. 'The great discoveries of modern art [sic], which have entirely altered the character and the channels of communication between different countries, will bring all the colonies into constant and speedy intercourse with each other. The success of the great experiment of steam navigation across the Atlantic (1833) opens a prospect which will materially affect the future state of all these provinces. ...The formation of a railroad from Halifax to Quebec would entirely alter some of the distinguishing characteristics of the Canadas....it would supersede the lower part of the St Lawrence, as the outlet of a great part of the Canadian trade, and would make Halifax, in a great measure, an outport to Quebec.'...'The great natural channel of the St Lawrence gives all the people who dwell in any part of its basin an interest in the government of the whole.'

Here was a country, wrote Lord Durham, where 'an almost boundless range of the richest soil still remains unsettled. The wealth of inexhaustible forest and the most valuable minerals have as yet been scarcely touched. Around each island and in each river, are to be found the greatest and richest fisheries in the world. The country which has founded and maintained these Colonies at a vast expense of blood and treasure, may justly expect its compensation in turning their unappropriated resources to the account of its own redundant population; they are the rightful patrimony of the English people.'

'I cannot participate in the notion', he wrote in his peroration, 'that it is the part either of prudence or of honour to abandon our countrymen when our government of them has plunged them into disorder, or our territory, when we discover that we have not turned it to proper account. The experiment of keeping colonies and governing them well ought at least to have a trial.'

The Durham Report was received in French Canada with dismay, in British Canada with bitter criticism from those who feared that it would deprive them of the spoils of office. The Colonial Reformers everywhere accepted it as a new gospel. It was avidly read in South Africa, Australia and the West Indies, but at Westminster attention was diverted by a storm in a political teacup. Lord Melbourne's government went out in May 1839 and was reconstituted after the incident known to students of the constitution as the 'Bedchamber Question'. Nothing could be done for North America at such critical times. However, when the political shuffle and the new deal were completed, the colonies were found to have benefited by the appearance of Lord John Russell at the Colonial Office. Though Molesworth had moved a vote of censure on Glenelg in 1838 the latter clung to his job until February 1839, unmoved by the Great Trek and the Canadian Rebellion which, said Brougham wickedly, 'must have cost him many a sleepless day'. Yet he could not be displaced until a suffi-ciently fat sinecure was found as a consolation for him. Russell persuaded the cabinet to accept the greater part of Durham's recommendations but not 'what is absurdly called responsible government'. He either did not understand or would not accept Durham's revelation that self-government for the colonies im-plied an abdication of power by the Colonial Secretary. He still intended that colonial governors should be guided by his instruc-tions and not by the advice of a colonial ministry; and, when the Tories returned to office in 1841, his successor Lord Stanley was of the same opinion.

Between 1839 and 1845 Canada was ruled successively by three able and eminent governors-general: Poulett Thompson (afterwards Lord Sydenham), 1839–41, who was killed in a riding accident; Sir Charles Bagot, the negotiator of the Treaty of 1818 with the United States, whose ill-health obliged him to resign after a few months; and Sir Charles Metcalfe, 1843–5, who, after thirty-seven years in India, was slowly dying throughout his term of office. Between them they carried out many of Durham's administrative proposals and moved cautiously towards his constitutional policy.

Sydenham scored a great personal success by persuading the administrations of Upper and Lower Canada to accept the union. An act was accordingly passed through the imperial Parliament in 1840 and a joint Canadian legislature was summoned in 1841 at Kingston. Under the new constitution the Civil List was assured to the Governor. With the aid of a loan of £1,500,000, negotiated by Russell's aid, Sydenham established a Public Works Depart-ment and launched a programme of improvements. The system of allotting Clergy Reserves was abolished[1] by the Union Govern-ment which, in spite of Wakefield's theories and Durham's recommendations, was given unhindered control of public lands. County courts and rural district councils were instituted tenta-tively in Upper Canada. So far so good, but the clash between the executive and the legislative branches of government was post-

[1] In spite of Sydenham's best efforts to put an end to the system, the Clergy Reserves persisted until 1854, through the powerful influence of Bishop Strachan in London. Finally the Imperial Parliament passed an act enabling the Canadian Parliament to settle the question. The rights of the Established Church, and similarly the seigneurial tenures, were commuted upon reasonable terms in that year.

poned only by tact and compromise. Bagot's term of office was chiefly taken up with diplomatic affairs. This was the period of the American Presidential election fought on the issue of annexing much British territory in North America (see chapter v, 8, page 278). The Ashburton-Webster Treaty, 1842, delimiting the frontier between New Brunswick and Maine, owes something to the steadying influence of Bagot. He did his best to rally moderate men from the English and French parties in the legislature into a popular administration, and lost the confidence of the Colonial Office by doing so. Metcalfe was sent out as a strong man to retrieve the position by reasserting the authority of the Crown. His method was to act as Prime Minister, forming a Cabinet and appealing to the country to support his policy. At the bitterly contested election of 1844 he got a bare majority. It was a gallant fight which brought Sir James Stephen of the Colonial Office to the gloomy opinion that 'Canada appears to have shaken off, or laid aside, the colonial relation to this country, and to have become, in everything but name, a distinct state....There are this moment, in Canada, almost as many Europeans as there were in the United States when they declared their independence—a very pregnant fact.'

While Whig and Tory leaders in England agreed in confusing this simple issue, the plain way out was again demonstrated by a colonial statesman, in the little province of Nova Scotia. The principle of responsible government, which Robert Baldwin had propounded and which Durham had recommended, was flatly demanded by Joseph Howe in his published *Letters to Lord John Russell* (September 1839). His six years' struggle followed the same lines as that in Canada but achieved an earlier victory. In 1846 the Whigs again returned to office in England with Russell now as Prime Minister, and Henry, 3rd Earl Grey (1802–94) as Colonial Secretary. Now at last the office at Downing Street was in the hands of a statesman who neither regarded the colonials as an encumbrance to the garrison of his fortresses, nor assumed that missionaries were always right and settlers always wrong, nor subordinated colonial reform to party advantage. On 3 November 1846, Grey instructed the Governor of Nova Scotia, Sir John Harvey, to apply the principle of responsible government, his despatch being quoted as 'applicable to all colonies having a similar form of government'. The triumph was due to the steady,

Plate 11

SIR JAMES STEPHEN (1789–1859)

'Mr Mother-country', from a bust by A. Munro, said by his daughter
to be an excellent likeness. *See p. 390.*

Plate 12A

W. C. WENTWORTH
(1793–1872)

Leader of the popular party
New South Wales. *See p. 354*

Plate 12B

JOHN MACARTHUR
(1767–1834)

Founder of the pastoral wealth
of Australia, leader of the 'exclusives'. *See p. 213*.

loyal and constitutional propaganda of Howe and to the support given him by Charles Buller in the House of Commons.

Lord Elgin introduced responsible government in Canada in 1848, the first ministry being formed by Robert Baldwin and the moderate French leader, Louis Hippolyte Lafontaine. Such was Grey's confidence that he even suggested the admission to office of Papineau, the returned rebel—if the majority should ask for him; but Papineau's influence had faded. The frenzy of Canadian politics could not be expected to be calmed for ever by so simple, though salutary, a change. In 1849 Governor Elgin incurred great unpopularity with the Tory Canadians by insisting upon reparation to French sufferers in the late rebellion. In the ensuing riots he was stoned in the streets, and the public buildings at Montreal were burned. Another cry, for secession from the Empire, was raised when Canadian preferences were abolished by the successive movements of the imperial government towards Free Trade. The answer to this complaint was provided by Elgin's Treaty of Reciprocity with the United States, 1854 (see pages 545-6).

5. LIFE IN THE AUSTRALIAN COLONIES, 1820-50

At the census of 1828 Sydney town was found to contain 13,000 inhabitants, about one-third of the population of the colony. A thriving port with a considerable trade in ship-chandling, it was better supplied with public works, the result of convict labour, than other colonial capitals. Though Governor Phillip began with some notions of town-planning they were forgotten during the corrupt days of the New South Wales Corps, with the result that the city grew up planless in the gullies sloping down to Sydney Cove. Governor Macquarie (1809-21), a man of a liberal and improving turn of mind, encouraged educated men among the 'emancipists' to come forward and take their place in society when released from the status of convicts, a policy which Macarthur and the older generation of 'exclusives' bitterly resented. Among the emancipists whom Macquarie favoured was a Bristol architect, Francis Greenway (1777-1837), transported for fraudulent bankruptcy. He was encouraged to build several public offices and churches (notably St James's, Sydney) in a severe but elegant Regency style that can still be detected here and there in the older settlements of New South Wales. Had Greenway remained in favour Sydney would have been a more spacious city today, for he prepared street-plans and even indulged in a fancy, a hundred years before his time, of bridging the harbour. But his schemes were obstructed by the 'exclusives' and finally stopped, on grounds of economy, by Commissioner Bigge. Greenway died in obscurity and Sydney grew haphazard, depending for its singular beauty upon its natural surroundings, not its architecture.

The emancipists found a voice in William Charles Wentworth (1793–1872) when, as a result of Bigge's Commission, a limited measure of civil liberty was granted. The New South Wales Judicature Act (4 Geo IV, c. 96) checked the Governor's sole authority by providing a nominated Legislative Council, a Supreme Court, and trial by jury in civil causes.

Wentworth was not, himself, an emancipist; he was born at Norfolk Island, the son of a lawyer who had made his own way to Australia to avoid disgrace. As a young lad, Wentworth was selected by Macquarie for the post of Deputy Provost-marshal which must have inured him to the harsher features of life in a convict colony. In 1813 he accompanied Blaxland at the crossing of the Blue Mountains, a contrasting experience from which he returned a convinced enthusiast for the wealth and greatness of a free colonial empire.

Pausing, like Rhodes fifty years later, in his colonial career, he visited England, became a fellow-commoner at Peterhouse, Cambridge, and was called to the Bar. On his return he founded a newspaper, *The Australian* (1824), which conducted an agitation for reform. Though he appeared as the leader of the despised emancipists he was at heart an aristocrat, as ruthless as Strafford whom he claimed as his ancestor, as greedy for power as Ralegh whom he greatly admired. Two successive governors (Sir T. Brisbane, 1822–5, and Sir R. Darling, 1825–31) endeavoured to come to terms with Wentworth, as their contemporaries in Canada were endeavouring to do with Papineau, but without success. They were successively recalled after failing to reconcile their obedience to the Colonial Office with their duty to their turbulent subjects. The former had fallen foul of the exclusives, the latter of the emancipists. A more subtle effort for reform was made by the Chief Justice, Francis Forbes, who recommended in a confidential letter to the Colonial Office (October 1826) the same remedy that Robert Baldwin prescribed for the woes of Canada, perhaps the earliest suggestion of responsible government. Like Baldwin's, Forbes's appeal fell on deaf ears. New South Wales was not yet self-supporting in food nor could it show a balanced revenue-account. Convicts cost the imperial government £24 a head per annum, a subsidy to the colony which destroyed the claim to self-government.

Van Diemen's Land was separated from New South Wales in 1824 and made a distinct colony under Sir George Arthur, a puritan and a martinet. This beautiful and fertile island with its soft English climate was made hell by 'man's hate'. Nearly half the population (7449 out of 16,924 at the census of 1828) were convicts, many of them second offenders in punishment camps; the other half, the settlers, waged a perpetual war of extermination against the blacks, pathetic relics of the Old Stone Age with whom no civilised contact seemed possible. Nothing could make them understand the white man's notions of property in land or the difference between untended sheep and wild game. No considerable effort was made to come to terms with them until Governor Arthur decided to bring them to parley and to locate them for their own protection. To do this he was obliged to drive the country, at a cost of £30,000. Elusive to the last, they slipped through his cordons, vanishing into the Bush; or merely died to avoid the menace of civilisation. The survivors, penned at last in one peninsula, were removed to Flinders Island where forty-four still lived in 1847. The last full-blood died in 1876.

Between the settlers and the convicts in each of the penal colonies was a marginal population of runaways who had taken to the Bush, and lived by stealing sheep or raiding the remoter homesteads. These were the bushrangers—the name is first recorded at Sydney in 1806—who reached their prime in Van Diemen's Land. Michael Howe, the worst of them, was hunted down and killed in 1818. An atmosphere of false romance idealised these southern Robin Hoods; among them Martin Cash, who twice escaped from the punishment camp at Port Arthur, came nearest to deserving it. Governor Arthur was obliged to wage a regular campaign against the bushrangers of his day. For two years Matthew Brady, 'governor of the ranges', defied the Governor of Hobart Town until he was taken (1826) by a bold pioneer,

John Batman, afterwards renowned as the founder of Melbourne.
The colony, so cursed in its birth, now knew tranquillity and the
free settlers blessed the name of Governor Arthur. He reappeared
in imperial history as the 'timid and inert' governor of Upper
Canada who brought that province to disaster in 1838, having
found that ruling free men was a harder task than ruling prisoners
and savages. As Wellington said of Governor Brisbane, 'there
are many brave men not fitted to be governors of colonies'. The
most popular of the island's Governors (1837–43) was Sir John
Franklin the explorer, a founder of schools and public works.

Hobart, beneath its snowy mountain and beside its blue harbour, grew up an Italianate town with buildings of dressed stone.
Like Sydney it took shape before the Gothic Revival reached
Australia. Settlement in Van Diemen's Land spread northwards
from Hobart and southwards from Launceston, which was founded
in 1806. The older districts contain several stone mansions, built a
hundred years ago, where run-holders lived magnificently, like
Virginia planters, upon the labour of assigned convict servants.
While there was some settlement on the warm east coast, the
rugged, harsher west coast remained (and remains) undeveloped.

Under the squatter aristocracy who began to enjoy an easy
generous life in Tasmania and New South Wales, with more
luxury than comfort or refinement, framing their social round
upon the wool-sales, the horse-shows and the race-meetings, the
work of the station-hands was monotonous and lonely. A sheep-
run (which in England would have been called a sheep-walk) was
merely a string of 'stations' at each of which a shepherd lived
alone in a bark hut guarding his flock against drought, bush-fires,
dingoes, and marauding blacks, his only variety being made by the
periodic visit of the overseer with his week's or month's rations.
When he could endure the isolation no longer, the shepherd threw
up his job, drew his cheque—at a rate of no more than £25 a year
in the 'thirties—and cashed it at the nearest public-house. There
he stayed in drunken oblivion until his cheque was 'out', when he
took the road as a 'sundowner' or 'swag-man' to tramp in search
of another job. The wandering swag-man bearing a bundle, like
Christian in the old woodcuts of the *Pilgrim's Progress*, boiling
his 'billy' of tea and cooking his 'damper' of kneaded flour in
the ashes of a wood-fire, claiming as a right a night's lodging in

his own blankets under any roof, is perhaps the typical figure of pastoral Australia, immortalised in the jargon of *Waltzing Matilda*,[1] the national song. Though many an immigrant tried his hand at shepherding, or tramped as a swag-man in search of employment, the greater number of those who worked for wages in the stations, out back, were old hands spoiled by the convict system for any more civilised way of life. Shepherding was no occupation for a married man. For roughing it in the bush the squatters preferred men 'without encumbrances', drawing single rations. Later in the century came the migratory gangs of shearers, the aristocracy of Australian labour, who moved from station to station at shearing-time.

With the extermination of the wild black-fellows and the dingoes from the south-east, it was no longer necessary to fold sheep at night. The older type of shepherd was replaced by the mounted boundary rider, whose talk was of horses and dogs and the state of fencing, which became general in the 'fifties. Wages rose steeply on the stations when labour was drawn off to the gold-diggings, and native-born Australians now made the majority up-country. Known as 'wild colonials', 'currency lads' (by contemptuous contrast with the 'sterling English') or as 'cornstalks', they had been marked down early in the century as a new physical type. The author of the *Letter from Sydney* had grown lyrical over the grace and sparkle of the 'currency lasses'. The men were taller than the English but sparely built; loose-limbed and small-featured, plain-spoken, irreverent, equalitarian, impatient of discipline. Rovers rather than settlers, they were natural horsemen, addicted to racing and gambling; they lived by overlanding stock, bullock-driving, horse-breaking. The literature of colonial Australia, rich in picturesque tales of the squatters, preserves an admirable account of the type in *Robbery Under Arms* (by 'Rolf Boldrewood', 1888).

Fresh-faced immigrants from feudal English villages had thriftier habits and a more cautious temperament. Station life with black-fellows lurking in the scrub was too lonely; debauchery at the bush public-house, where the landlord might be in league with

---

[1] The words are by A. B. Paterson (1864–1941) whose ballads are more truly redolent of Australian life than those of the better-known Adam Lindsay Gordon (1833–70). Though Gordon adventured and died in Australia, he was essentially an English writer.

the bushrangers, was too reckless. They tended to remain at first in Sydney or within the limits of settlement. These 'New Chums' or 'limeys' (not yet known by the expressive modern nickname of 'pommies') were at first treated by the old hands with pitying contempt, but not for long. 'Every first emigrant to a colony', the Colonial Reformers used to say, 'regards the second as his enemy.' Within a few years the New Chum had become a colonial and was ready in his turn to resist the influx of newer chums whose arrival might be expected to lower the rate of wages.

MRS CAROLINE CHISHOLM

The census of 1841 revealed still twice as many men as women in Australia, with the result that young women who arrived at Sydney often went astray. The care of female immigrants was undertaken as a voluntary task by Mrs Caroline Chisholm, an officer's wife (1810–77), who found herself unoccupied in Australia when her husband went off to the China War. She prevailed on Governor Gipps to provide her with a building which she managed as an immigrants' hostel; then, in spite of ridicule, she undertook to chaperon parties of young women up-country to respectable situations where they were likely to find good husbands. She arranged to seek out and bring to Australia the wives of men who had emigrated or had been transported alone. With untiring energy she united broken families, sent for relatives of colonists who had made good, found places for the lethargic and timid and, in the course of six years (1841–7) is said to have 'settled' 11,000 immigrants. All was done by direct personal influence and contact, without regulations or administrative expense. She travelled all over New South Wales in a bullock-dray to see for herself that her girls found good homes.

In 1847 she returned to England to force her schemes upon Lord Grey. Her connexion was not with the Colonial Reformers but with pure philanthropists such as Shaftesbury and Sydney Herbert. Through their help she founded the Family Colonisation Loan Society for advancing small sums of money to families of emigrants, who were pledged to return their borrowings by instalments remitted from the colony. By 1854 she had despatched 3000 emigrants and, a fact which is more remarkable, the Society was solvent with £15,000 in hand. She interviewed intending emigrants, giving advice on their needs, inspected emigrant ships, and finally took over the whole responsibility, chartering ships in the name of her Society, and conducting a party personally to Australia in the first ship. Next she appointed her obliging husband as her agent for the reception of immigrants in Sydney while she despatched more ships from London. The total number of those she assisted is unknown. In 1854 she returned to a less active life in Australia. The changed circumstances there, brought about by the gold-rush and the grant of self-government, were bringing to an end the period of philanthropic colonisation.

The attitude of the British public towards emigration had also been completely changed by the practical endeavours of such workers as Mrs Chisholm no less than by the preaching of the Colonial Reformers. The change may be observed, for example, in the works of Charles Dickens between the publication of *Martin Chuzzlewit* (1843), in which emigration to America is painted in the blackest colours, and of *David Copperfield* (1850) in which Australia has become the land of promise. The kindly fun made of Micawber's preparations is reminiscent of Mrs Chisholm's advice to emigrants. Dickens was one of her strongest supporters, giving much space to her propaganda in *Household Words* (1850–2). It may also be noted with regret that the character of Mrs Jellyby (*Bleak House*, 1852) has been thought by some critics to present some features of an unkind parody of Caroline Chisholm.

EXPLORATION

The 1820's saw a great impulse outwards from the narrow bounds of coastal New South Wales, at first around the coasts and later across the ranges. Melville Island in the far north, which had been surveyed by a naval expedition, was occupied in 1824 with the hope that a trade-route to the East Indies might be opened. The settlement was discontinued when the trade came to nothing. Other annexations were made when Governor Darling took alarm at the appearance of a French scientific expedition, under Dumont d'Urville, in Australian waters (1826). He hastily sent parties of soldiers and convicts to occupy Westernport (in what is now Victoria), King George's Sound (Western Australia) and Moreton Bay (Queensland). A regular convict settlement was formed at Moreton Bay a few years later (1833); the other settlements were abandoned when no longer serviceable. The west coast was proclaimed British territory by Captain Fremantle in 1829, as a preliminary to the Swan River settlement. Australia was never formally annexed to the dominions of the Crown as a single territory. Lord John Russell used to relate that when he was at the Colonial Office (1839–41), 'a gentleman attached to the French Government' called on him to ask how much of the continent was British. 'I answered him "the whole", and with that answer he went away.'

In the same generation the overland routes were explored from Sydney. When Blaxland had found a way through the mountains a settlement was formed beyond the pass, at Bathurst. Though there was a growing desire to penetrate into the grassy plains which rumour reported beyond the ranges, not much, except unauthorised squatting, was done in Governor Macquarie's time. The interior of Australia was quite unknown and its character misjudged by early explorers. In 1817 and 1818 the government surveyor, John Oxley, traced the course of some of the rivers running north and west from the rugged bush-clad slopes of the Blue Mountains, until he lost them among swamps; from which he deduced that all central Australia might prove to be a salt-marsh. Later the pressure of the flock-masters on more accommodating governors led to the despatch of several exploring parties. They set out in ox-wagons (known in Australia as 'drays'), sometimes carrying whale-boats dismantled in sections, and accompanied by gangs of convicts who were spurred on with promises of early release and grants of land. Not far behind the exploring parties, and sometimes ahead of them, went the 'overlanders', the roving pioneers, driving their mobs of sheep in search of well-watered grassland.

In 1824 Hamilton Hume's party crossed the Murrumbidgee on a raft and worked south-west through the snow-clad ranges until they emerged at the western end of Port Phillip near the site of Geelong, to find sealing-gangs, landed from ships, already encamped there with huts and planted gardens. Three years later Allan Cunningham, a botanist from Kew, struck north from Bathurst into the fertile tableland, which was to be known as the Darling Downs, and reached them again by another route over Pandora's Pass from Moreton Bay. But the river-system, the topographical key to south-east Australia, remained hidden until it was revealed by the chivalrous Captain Charles Sturt (1795–1869), the knight-errant of Australian history. He correctly divined that the Murrumbidgee, and the Darling which he discovered, were tributaries of a greater river which must flow into Spencer's Gulf; then found the river and named it the Murray (1829). For twenty-six days he floated down the torrent in a whale-boat, which he had brought overland from New South Wales, until he

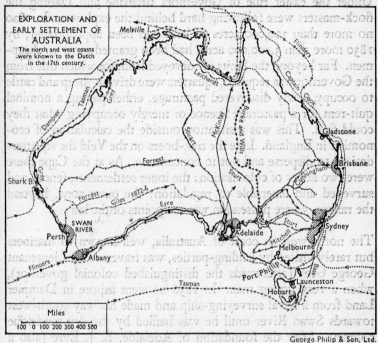

EXPLORATION AND
EARLY SETTLEMENT OF
AUSTRALIA
The north and west coasts
were known to the Dutch
in the 17th century.

George Philip & Son, Ltd.

Map 14

saw the breakers of Encounter Bay. Then he and his men rowed back against the flooded stream for fifty-six days, on rations reduced to half a pound of flour a day for each man.

Sturt's deductions were questioned by another Peninsular veteran, Major Thomas Mitchell, who was not convinced until he had made several journeys through the Murray basin. From the junction of the Darling with the Murray he struck south to the ocean at Portland Bay, finding there a settlement of unauthorised squatters from Van Diemen's Land. On his return journey Mitchell surveyed the route afterwards used by the overlanders who brought stock from New South Wales. From the top of a mountain he saw, through the heat-haze of an Australian mid-summer (December 1836), 'white objects which might have been tents'. It was the camp of John Batman who had just come from Van Diemen's Land as agent of the Port Phillip Association.

The topography of New South Wales was now revealed. Under the easier rule of Governors Brisbane and Darling the flock-masters were following hard behind the explorers. In 1820 no more than 300,000 acres of land had been appropriated; by 1830 more than 3,000,000 acres had been granted away to sheep-men. Far beyond the limits of surveyed land, for which title from the Governor was required, squatters were driving sheep and cattle to occupy newly discovered pasturage, either paying a nominal quit-rent for a pasturage licence or merely occupying what they could find. This was a situation outside the calculation of eco-nomists in England. Like the trek-boers on the Veld the squatters desired to disperse and not to concentrate. As at the Cape there were two zones of colonisation: the inner settlements, fenced and surveyed and amenable to regulation; the outer zone, beyond the ranges, where possession was ten points of the law.

The north-western coast of Australia, well-known to mariners but rarely visited by landing-parties, was traversed by Lieutenant George Grey (afterwards the distinguished colonial governor), when a very young man. In 1836 he went ashore in Dampier Land from a naval surveying-ship and made his way south-west towards Swan River until he was baffled by the dry sandstone country. After the foundation of Adelaide, E. J. Eyre (also a colonial governor in later life) brought cattle overland from Port Phillip. He led two expeditions from the new settlement, reaching Lake Torrens to the northward and King George's Sound (1841) far to the westward along the shores of the Australian Bight. In 1844 Captain Sturt went north-east from Adelaide over the un-suspected mineral wealth of Broken Hill. He returned from the wilderness with ruined health to confirm Eyre's reports that cen-tral Australia was a desert. Eyre and Sturt had shown exemplary leadership and resolution but had found no new pastoral paradise.

The mountainous south-east corner of Australia was first penetrated by a Pole, Count Strzelecki, who gave the name of Mount Kosciusko to the highest peak (1840). Another European adventurer, Ludwig Leichhardt, made three journeys (1842–8) from Queensland to the tropical north. He crossed the continent from Sydney to Port Essington, east of the site of Darwin. From his third expedition he never returned. As in the case of Sir John Franklin, the relief expeditions sent in search of Leichhardt were productive of much practical knowledge. One of the searchers, A. C. Gregory, crossed the continent on the other diagonal, from Brisbane to Adelaide (1858). Sturt's lieutenant and admirer, J. M. Stuart, took up his master's quest from Adelaide and at a third attempt (1862) reached the northern coast. It was largely generous rivalry on the part of the citizens of Melbourne that led them to launch another expedition with the object of crossing the continent on a parallel course farther to the east, from Melbourne to the Gulf of Carpentaria. Burke and Wills, to whom the leadership was entrusted, mismanaged the journey. 'Then the wood failed, then the food failed, then the last water dried.' Both lost their lives (1861), a tragic story better remembered in Australia than some more fruitful but less dramatic tales of travel. Professor E. Scott drily remarks of John McKinlay's later expedition, which reached the Gulf of Carpentaria, finding the relics of Burke and Wills by the way: 'The most picturesque exploits were not always the most valuable. A good bushman like McKinlay did not produce so readable an account of his travels as did George Grey; but the object of exploration was not to add to the literature of adventure.'

6. AUSTRALIAN LAND AND EMIGRATION IN THE 'FORTIES

THE colony at Swan River, which Wakefield selected as the target of his scorn, was first planned in 1828. As early as 1697 the river had been visited by the Dutch navigator, Vlaming, who discovered there the real existence of the black swan, a bird formerly known to fable only. Swan River estuary, opening into the Indian Ocean, 2000 miles from Sydney, was otherwise forgotten until it attracted the attention of a naval officer, James (afterwards Admiral Sir James) Stirling (1791–1865). It was his ambition to emulate Raffles by making at Swan River another Singapore. Getting no sort of encouragement from the Colonial Office, he managed to enlist the aid of John Barrow, Secretary to the

Admiralty and, after much lobbying, was appointed military governor—with one company of soldiers—of the country annexed by Captain Fremantle, in 1829 (see above, page 360).

Just then Thomas Peel (cousin of Sir Robert) and others came forward in London with a scheme for taking up land and importing settlers, a plan which Stirling hurried into execution without proper preparation. The coastline was annexed on 2 May 1829; in June Stirling proclaimed the colony; and in the next nine months thirteen ships arrived with 1500 immigrants, to find that there was no anchorage, no survey, no currency and no treaty with the aboriginals. The soil was light and the fertile patches lay inland. The natural tendency to disperse was intensified by huge land-grants, to the Governor among others. The food-supply was precarious because the settlers arrived at the wrong time of year for sowing. For some years the colony was half-starved between ships' visits. Peel brought out 300 settlers, 60 of them indentured labourers, to work on his estate of 250,000 acres; all had drifted away in six months, to squat on other fertile land, or to try their luck in the other colonies. The Sydney press was bitterly hostile to the Swan River scheme and did all in its power to draw away the precious labourers to New South Wales.

Meanwhile Stirling made the best of things, with robust good-humour and a sailor's inventiveness. He laid out the town-sites, of Perth a few miles inland beside a broad lagoon, and Fremantle on the dusty shore. The settlers grumbled that these towns were good for nothing but 'sand, sorrow, and sore eyes', a description which will surprise those travellers who have seen the flowery banks of Swan River, a century later. The colony cost the British Government £41,000 for a commencement, and a grant-in-aid of £6000 a year, which was put on a regular basis when a constitution, of the type then usual in Crown Colonies, was granted in 1834. Three years later, when Stirling retired, the population had crept up to 2032 whites, of whom 688 were women. The black-fellows had been driven off by the 'Battle of Pinjarra' (1834), a punitive raid led by the Governor against a marauding tribe. Of 1,500,000 acres allotted to holders of land-grants, only 1400 were under crop. The settlers were already talking of the advantages of convict labour. In 1848 the population had crept up to 4600, who lived without much prosperity. Their plea for a reinforcement of convicts was gladly granted when the Colonial

Office in 1849 could find no other place in the Queen's dominions where convicts were welcome.

The story of the obstacle race run by the South Australia Association has been told in an earlier chapter. Long before the settlers sailed, the projectors, especially Wakefield, had despaired of founding the model colony they had first proposed. Twice had the first body of settlers been assembled and twice dispersed before the progress of negotiations with Downing Street permitted their despatch. Land sales flagged amid these deferred hopes until an enterprising banker, G. F. Angas, floated a commercial company with a capital of £200,000 to give the colony a start. The 'sufficient price' had at last been fixed at £1 an acre.

In May 1836 the Surveyor, Colonel William Light (the son of Francis Light of Penang), sailed to Spencer Gulf and chose the site of Adelaide in the open country recently discovered, but not explored, by Captain Sturt. Those who thought the project fantastic might observe with irony that an earlier explorer, Captain Lemuel Gulliver, had located the kingdom of Lilliput just here on the map. The first batch of 600 colonists arrived too soon (December 1836), before the survey was completed. Within a few months there was complete deadlock between the Resident Commissioner for land sales and the Governor, Sir John Hindmarsh. The site and the survey were sharply criticised, and the settlers could not or would not take up their land. Meanwhile hypothetical sales of land in England continued and new batches of colonists continued to appear, one of the most useful groups being 600 German peasants sent out by Angas. By 1838, Wakefield's doctrine of concentration seemed only too successful; almost all the 3600 inhabitants of South Australia were still at the capital, living on rations provided at the expense of the Company. Hindmarsh and the Resident Commissioner were then recalled and replaced by Colonel George Gawler, who was invested with the powers of both. Light had resigned in disgust after planning the garden city of Adelaide, and the survey of the interior was taken over by the explorer, Charles Sturt. Gawler struggled with the unbalanced finances of the settlement for two years, drawing bills on the Commissioners for current expenses, while all the revenue was diverted to bringing out from England a stream of emigrants who could not be absorbed into the infant economy of the settlement. This was the Wakefield plan reduced to an absurdity.

In 1839 Lord John Russell, who had reason to doubt the integrity of the Commissioners, dissolved the Commission, replacing it by a Land and Emigration Board which for the next thirty years administered the sale of Crown lands and the despatch of 'assisted' emigrants throughout the Empire, a useful administrative reform. Colonel R. Torrens (1780–1864), one of the founders of South Australia,[1] became chairman of the Board.

By 1841 Adelaide was taking root as a colony but was bankrupt as a financial concern. Gawler demanded and got a loan of £155,000 to meet current expenses. But he, like so many colonial governors of that age, was held responsible for the chaos he had inherited and was recalled. To meet the crisis Russell took the audacious step of appointing as Governor a young soldier not yet thirty years old, Captain George Grey,[2] who had distinguished himself as the explorer of north-western Australia. Grey had the advantage of coming in as the luck was turning. More than half the inhabitants had already moved out of Adelaide on to the land. More than 7000 acres were under cultivation and more than 200,000 sheep were grazing in South Australia before Gawler departed. The new Governor worked no miracles other than those always achieved by economy, promptness, and resolution. Since there was now food in the land he stopped the issue of free rations, a decision which soon drove the labourers into the fields. But he was no more able than Gawler to pay his way without drawing bills on London. Already 16,000 emigrants had been despatched when, in 1842, the next Colonial Secretary, Lord Stanley, obtained an act of Parliament for constituting South Australia a colony of the normal type, and for writing off the loan of £155,000 as a grant-in-aid, a modest price for such a settlement. In that year copper was discovered at Kapunda. In 1845 when Grey was transferred to New Zealand the population of South Australia was 38,000, the revenue £82,000 and the aggregate land sales had reached half a million sterling. What meant more, as Grey noted, was 'the calibre of the new settlers. There was a worth, a sincerity, a true ring about them, which could not fail of great things.'

[1] His son Sir R. R. Torrens (1814–86), South Australian statesman, was author of the Torrens Act for registering land-titles, 1857. Later, returning to England, he was M.P. for Cambridge.

[2] See footnote above, page 335, for the Grey family.

South Australia has generally been taken as the test-case of systematic colonisation, and has been quoted by Australian writers in condemnation of the Wakefield plan. In spite of the obstructions and delay of the Colonial Office which foisted upon it an unworkable constitution, in spite of the misuse of funds by the Commissioners, whom Wakefield had condemned as 'ignorant and careless', it was a striking advance upon all earlier experiments in that generation. Its birth-pangs were slight indeed compared with those of Swan River. But colonies are made by men, not by agrarian laws. The quality of the settlers was the difference, and that was as essential to Wakefield's system as the Sufficient Price.

The Colonial Reform movement began to attract attention in New South Wales in these times of outward expansion. Systematic colonisation by means of the land-fund appeared to Australian sheep-farmers as a restrictive attempt by doctrinaires in Downing Street to interfere with natural growth. They were vociferous against the Colonial Office throughout the 1830's, on account of its supposed subservience to the Wakefield school at the same time when South African farmers were complaining of its subservience to the missionaries. The Colonial Office pleased nobody, and would please nobody, until it accepted the logic of responsible government for the colonies. Successive Governors at Sydney, with increasing reluctance and diminishing effect, tried to confine the squatters to the 'limits of settlement', the original nineteen counties of New South Wales. As well might they try to confine the Arabs of the desert or the trek-boers of the African Veld. New land, discovered every year, was taken into possession by the overlanders. Wentworth, himself a squatter on a great scale, promoted the squatting interest in the press and at public meetings, since there was not until 1842 any representative assembly in which he could form a constitutional opposition. Macarthur and the other 'exclusives' in the nominated Legislative Council found themselves in sympathy with him on this issue, so that, with the growing preponderance of the new generation of freeborn Australians, the distinction between 'emancipists' and 'exclusives' slowly died away.

Sir Richard Bourke, Governor from 1831 to 1837, was obliged to administer the regulation of 1831 though he disapproved of it. It obliged him to ear-mark the revenue from land sales

South Australia has generally been taken as the test-case of systematic colonisation, and has been quoted by Australian writers

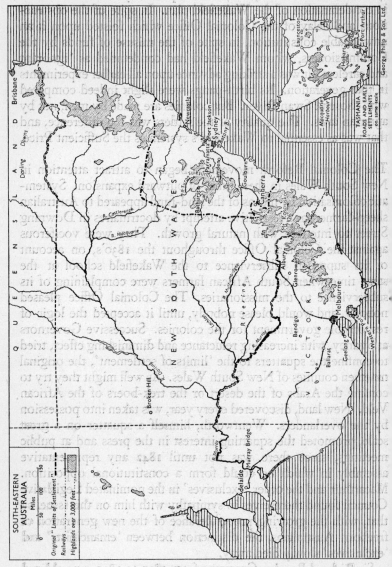

SOUTH-EASTERN
AUSTRALIA

Miles
0   50   100   150

Original "Limits of Settlement"
Railways
Highlands over 3,000 feet

TASMANIA
ROADS AND EARLY
SETTLEMENTS
on same scale

George Philip & Son. Ltd.

for subsidising emigration; and, after 1834, he had to pay the cost of gaols and police from colonial funds. Macarthur in the Council (until his death in 1834) and Wentworth in the press combined to denounce these instructions, demanding control of their own revenues through an elective assembly. Wentworth, with Dr J. D. Lang and others, founded the Australian Patriotic Association, whose London agent was Charles Buller, the reformer. In 1836 Bourke persuaded the Colonial Office to allow him to throw open Port Phillip to settlement on the same terms as the nineteen counties and to grant licences to squatters outside the 'limits of settlement'. With this incentive the squatters dispersed more rapidly than before. A thousand of them took possession of 44,000,000 acres of land. Bourke was long remembered in Sydney as the most popular of governors and, like most popular governors, was recalled for displeasing the Colonial Office. The Australians gave him the credit for founding religious equality, trial by jury, and the freedom of the press.

Sir George Gipps, a man of great force of character, was Governor at the crisis of the fever for land (1838–46). It was one of his tasks to prepare the negotiations with the Maori chiefs, in 1840, which made them subjects of the Crown. Wentworth took a hand in that, securing for himself by a private bargain with one of them a grant of half the South Island of New Zealand. In disgust, Gipps denounced and nullified this deal, making it his reason for excluding Wentworth from public office. Not at all abashed, Wentworth gloried in the attempt, saying that Drake or Ralegh would have done the same.

In a climate subject to periodic droughts, wool prices tended to fluctuate violently and all the more when arbitrary changes in the land-regulations led to speculative buying. During the great slump of 1843, when all parties in the colony were clamouring for Gipps's recall, he made regulations for preserving the rights of the Crown (that is of posterity) against mere land-grabbing, while securing genuine sheep-farmers in possession of their runs. Every squatter was obliged to buy a section of 320 acres within five years of occupying a run, in order to secure his right to pasture his sheep on the rest of it. Otherwise his claim lapsed. In spite of fierce opposition Gipps held to this principle until a compromise, not essentially different, was embodied in an imperial Act of Parliament (1846), giving to squatters in 'unsettled lands' a leasehold of fourteen years with rights of pre-emption. This was on the whole a triumph for the pastoral over the agricultural interest and for the practical experience of the colonists over the theories of the Colonial Reformers. Control of the waste lands of the Empire from Whitehall had proved impossible. Wherever responsible government was granted, control of undeveloped land quickly passed to the colonial parliament and became the focus of colonial party politics.

A proportion of elected members were at last added to the Legislative Council of New South Wales in 1842, with no distinction in the franchise between emancipists and free emigrants. In forming an administration Governor Gipps brought forward a young English lawyer, an Oxford man named Robert Lowe (1811–92), whom he thought the ablest man in the colony, as a counterpoise to the influence of Wentworth. Lowe proved to be an independent of advanced views. During the 'forties, politics at Sydney took the form of a duel between Wentworth, the leader of the squatters, who became increasingly aristocratic in his outlook, and Lowe, who led the new democratic interest of the free immigrants, opposing the claim of the squatters to unlimited land, and protesting against the continued importation of convicts. Lowe's most useful achievement was to organise the schools of the colony. In 1850 he returned to the wider world of London, becoming eventually (as Lord Sherbrooke) Chancellor of the Exchequer in Gladstone's administration. His colonial experiences made him bitterly cynical on the subject of democracy without literacy; he first said of the English electorate: 'We must educate our masters.'

When Lord Grey was at the Colonial Office (1846–52) self-governing institutions were granted to all self-supporting colonies. He made some motions towards federating Australia, a cause which received little support, except from Wentworth who was a man of large ideas. Out there the general tendency was centrifugal and the social cleavage between New South Wales, South Australia and Swan River too wide for adjustment, as wide as the geographical distance between them. In 1850, Grey obtained an Act of Parliament for giving each of the Australian colonies an elective legislature with a limited power of constitutional amendment, but reserving control of the waste land and the land-revenues to the Crown. Wentworth and the squatters received this offer without enthusiasm. During the next five years, in which no less than seven gentlemen held the office of Secretary of State, Downing Street yielded concessions step by step to the colonies. Control of the waste lands was transferred to the new legislatures by an act of 1855. Responsible government was hammered out in practice, not formally granted.

Wentworth's policy in New South Wales was to restrict the franchise and to restrain the assembly by a nominated upper house, even by a hereditary House of Lords. But the electorate, consisting largely of new immigrants with Chartist notions, insisted on a wide franchise, an elective upper house, and the ballot. Finding himself out of sympathy with the new democratic Australia, Wentworth retired to England. He is remembered as the founder of the University of Sydney (1849–52), the first true university in the British dependencies.

Port Phillip was separated from New South Wales as the self-governing colony of Victoria (1850). This was the one example in Australia, one of few in the whole Empire, of successful colonisation without a plan. In 1834 Edward Henty had left the fiasco of Swan River to set up a shore-whaling station in Portland Bay. In 1835 John Batman, an unauthorised squatter from Van Diemen's Land, had obtained a concession of 600,000 acres at Port Phillip from an aboriginal chief, who was certainly unaware of the nature of the bargain. Batman was the pioneer of the Port Phillip Association, a group of adventurers who brought in stock from the confined valleys of Van Diemen's Land to the wide plains of Port Phillip. They were soon joined by overlanders following Mitchell's track, known as 'the Major's path', from New South Wales. Governor Bourke persuaded the Colonial Office to permit land sales and pasturage licences at Port Phillip on the same terms as at Sydney. In 1836 he sent a magistrate to Port Phillip where a township of squatters had sprung up.

Early in 1837 Governor Bourke arrived at Port Phillip and instructed the government surveyor, Robert Hoddle, to lay out the site for a town on gently sloping ground, overlooking the Bay, beside the River Yarra. Hoddle's original sketch (now in the Savage Club at Melbourne) is the noblest conception of all town-plans in the Dominions, a rectangle described about four parallel avenues, each one hundred feet wide, interspersed by narrow service streets. Bourke named the new colony Victoria after the

24-2

young Queen (1839) and the town (incorporated in 1842) Melbourne after her first Prime Minister. At the last census before the discovery of gold, which set the town booming, the population of the district was over 32,000 and of Melbourne itself over 10,000 (1846).

All this progress came by infiltration of voluntary settlers neither planted by the Crown nor by any colonising company. It cannot, however, be justly compared with the settlement of Adelaide, a new plantation on a virgin site. Land, capital, stock and willing pioneers were available for development at Port Phillip. The first stage of colonisation was over in New South Wales and Van Diemen's Land, the next region for settlement was explored, and the frontier was ripe for a forward move when John Batman took the initiative. This was not, as the foundation of Sydney and Adelaide had been or as the foundation of Massachusetts and Maryland had been, a first venture into a new land; it was a second step like the advance of the Americans into the Ohio basin. It was carried forward by the boom in sheep-farming and enormously advanced in the next generation by the discovery of gold. Behind the advancing squatters moved up the rank and file of the invading colonists. Between 1831 and 1842 land sales had produced £1,090,000 of which £950,000 had been spent on providing passages for 50,000 free immigrants. Without this steady stream Port Phillip might have grown as slowly as Swan River.

Van Diemen's Land shed its unhappy past and was reborn as the free self-governing colony of Tasmania in 1855. Moreton Bay was separated from New South Wales in 1859 as the self-governing colony of Queensland. Western Australia (or Swan River), lapsing into the status of a convict colony from which the others had just emerged, was not yet qualified for self-government.

7. NEW ZEALAND AND THE MISSIONARIES, 1792–1848

COOK'S annexation of New Zealand, ignored by successive governments, was nullified by an Act of Parliament of 1817 which alluded to the islands as a place 'not within His Majesty's Dominions'. Occasional visitors to New Zealand noted chiefly the ferocity of the natives who, on several occasions, cut off boats' crews and devoured them. The massacre of the whole ship's company of the *Boyd* in 1809 had an alarming effect; yet white men did visit the islands and even settled there. The first recorded residents, a sealing-crew, spent the summer of 1792 ashore, in the far south where no native tribes were settled.

As early as 1791 efforts were made from Sydney to develop a trade in timber for spars and in the tenacious fibre of the New Zealand flax. These shipping stores attracted the British and American sperm-whalers to the Bay of Islands, a region broken by deep-water inlets among the forests of gigantic *Kauri* pines. Here dwelt numerous natives, children of the sun, who throve better in the sub-tropical north than in the cool windy south. Deserters from the ships and runaway convicts from Botany Bay sometimes made their way ashore at the Bay of Islands where, if they were not quickly knocked on the head and eaten, they might hope to make themselves useful to some chief as boat-builders, blacksmiths or interpreters. The first of these 'white [pakehà] maoris' was George Bruce, who married a chief's daughter in 1807. In the 'twenties and 'thirties every chief aspired to keep a tame white man, a *pakehà*, perhaps a mere pimp and bootlegger who got rum and muskets for his master in return for sending native women aboard the ships, perhaps an honest trader, or even something more. The great chiefs regarded the missionaries as their *pakehàs*, their agents with the outside world, much as a Frankish or a Saxon king regarded his bishop in the seventh century. Thus English civilisation at its worst and best began to penetrate New Zealand.

But the Maoris were far too virile and intelligent to wait for civilisation to come to them; many shipped before the mast to discover the world for themselves, and so came to the notice of the Apostle of New Zealand, the chaplain to the convict establishment at Sydney. The Rev. Samuel Marsden (1764–1838) of St John's College, Cambridge, was a straightforward practical Christian of the old school, not an enthusiast from Clapham. Since he could not obtain the services of ordained clergy he agreed with the Church Missionary Society to establish two respectable laymen, William Hall a carpenter and John King a rope-maker, at the Bay of Islands to prepare the way for Christianity. 'Till the attention of the heathen is gained, and moral and industrious habits are induced, little or no progress can be made in teaching them the Gospel.' In December 1814 Marsden conveyed his party to New Zealand under protection of two friendly chiefs, inaugurating his mission on Christmas Day with a sermon preached, through an interpreter, upon the text: 'Behold I bring you tidings of great joy.'

Since Hall and King were not sufficiently well-educated to master the Maori language, Marsden's next step was to despatch one of the two chiefs—his name was Hongi—to England. He stayed at Cambridge in the house of Samuel Lee, the Professor of Arabic (1820) who prepared a Maori grammar and dictionary in which the language was transliterated with elegance.[1] Until his death in 1838 Marsden supervised his missions in New Zealand, visiting the country seven times and, when sixty years old, making adventurous journeys on foot into the unknown interior. There was little evidence of progress until the arrival (1822) of Henry Williams, a naval officer turned clergyman, who impressed the savages with that quality of moral greatness (*mana*) which they instantly appreciated. 'This island was a very hard stone', said a Maori chief, 'and Archdeacon Williams broke it.' He and his brother, William Williams, were the patriarchs of a clan which has served New Zealand faithfully in Church and State for a hundred years. The Williams family has given bishops to the Anglican Church of New Zealand in three successive generations.

In his anxiety to find clergy, Marsden had invited the Methodists to send a mission. When it came (1823) he aimed at co-operation, with the result that spheres of influence were agreed upon, the Anglicans taking the north-east and the Methodists the north-west

---

[1] Readers may note the different effect of the elegant transliteration of aboriginal place-names in New Zealand and the commonplace transliteration of aboriginal place-names in Australia. The apparent ugliness of some Australian names is a fault of the Europeans who reproduced them in writing, not a defect in the native language.

coasts. In London there was no such happy issue since the two societies failed to come to terms. Those who doubt the efficacy of missionary endeavour would do well to study the change in the habits and morals of the Maori people achieved by the influence of a handful of missionaries in a single generation (c. 1820–50). Tribal warfare, cannibalism and slavery gradually disappeared without the exertion of political or economic pressure. The Maoris were neither conquered nor expropriated, but converted.

Before the consummation of this change, which Marsden did not live to see, the Maoris indulged in a last orgy of bloodshed. The chief, Hongi, whose 'mild manners' had made so good an impression, did not restrict his English acquaintance to Cambridge professors. He had been escorted to England by Thomas Kendall, one of Marsden's lay missionaries, who very improperly helped him to sell land-concessions to speculators for cash with which he bought guns. On his return to New Zealand he revolutionised the art of war. His raids and conquests, until his death in 1831, devastated the North Island, exterminating whole tribes, and greatly complicating for posterity the titles to tribal lands. The pressure of his campaigns affected, among others, an audacious and cunning chief named Te Rauparàha ('The Convolvulus Leaf') who took the war-path southwards. Making his headquarters on an island in Cook Strait, he dominated all the central region of New Zealand, almost annihilating the few and scattered tribes of the South Island. Gun-running for these wars led to a greater and even more disreputable trade between Sydney and the little Alsatia at the Bay of Islands, where the missionaries competed for the attention of the natives against the worst ruffians of the South Seas.

Rumours of land sales to missionaries and *pakehà maoris* had drawn the attention of speculators in colonisation to the possibilities of New Zealand. Mr Lambton (not yet Earl of Durham) had sent out a ship-load of emigrants who were frightened away by the mere aspect of a Maori war-dance (1826). There was also a cosmopolitan adventurer called the Baron de Thierry [1] who, as an undergraduate at Cambridge, had obtained some sort of land-concession from Hongi, and had notions of carving himself out a

---

[1] C. P. de Thierry (1793–1864) of Magdalen Hall, Oxford, and Queens' College, Cambridge, son of the Baron de Thierry, a French refugee. Born at Brussels, he had served in the British Army.

kingdom in New Zealand, with Dutch or French if not with English help.

Land-speculation, gun-running, escapes of convicts, increasing trade, and complaints by the missionaries about the outrageous proceedings in New Zealand at last obliged the Governor of New South Wales to intervene. The final abomination was the case of the brig *Elizabeth* (Captain Stewart) which was hired by Te Rauparàha to convey his war-party on a marauding expedition (1830). The English sailors, having decoyed a hostile chief and his family on board to be kidnapped and murdered, allowed the murderers to cook human flesh in the brig's galley and to enjoy a cannibal feast on the deck. It proved impossible to fix any charge against Captain Stewart except that of taking service under a foreign potentate in contravention of the Foreign Enlistment Act, and on that count the evidence proved insufficient. In 1831 Governor Darling decided to send James Busby as British Resident at the Bay of Islands. Since he had no more than moral authority either over whites or Maoris he could do little beyond rallying the support of the respectable inhabitants to the cause of law and order. He encouraged the formation of a confederacy of native chiefs, the United Tribes of New Zealand, for their own defence against exploitation (1835), and especially against the pretensions of the Baron de Thierry.

In his evidence before the Parliamentary committee of 1836 (see chapter VII, 2, page 335) Wakefield began his campaign for the colonisation of New Zealand. 'Very near to Australia there is a country which all testimony concurs in describing as the fittest country in the world for colonising, as the most beautiful country with the finest climate, and the most productive soil.' In 1837 he formed the first New Zealand Association with a strong committee including most of the Colonial Reformers. Their first draft of an enabling bill for colonising New Zealand received the usual short-shrift from James Stephen. He thought the project 'vague and obscure' and that it would 'infallibly issue in the conquest and extermination of the natives'. Here he expressed the view of the Church Missionary Society which, at last, was beginning to receive good reports from its agents in New Zealand. A sharp duel of pamphlets and addresses to the Colonial Office ensued between Wakefield and Mr Dandeson Coates, the secretary of the Church Missionary Society. Coates refused an interview with a deputation from the Colonial Reformers, sending them word that he proposed to thwart them by every means in his power. Nevertheless the missionaries and their parent society did not intend that New Zealand should remain a scene of chaos and anarchy. They, too, desired annexation by the Crown in order to create a missionary paradise of meek, unworldly converts under their own spiritual direction. Both parties alike demanded that the Crown should intervene to impose law and order. It was the failure of the Colonial Office to act that incited Molesworth to propose his vote of censure (March 1838) against Lord Glenelg, already deeply discredited by the collapse of his policy in Canada and in South Africa.

As in the case of South Australia, the only terms on which the Colonial Office would approve an experiment in colonisation were that they should retain absolute control while incurring none of the financial risk. And, on these terms, some encouragement was given to the New Zealand Association just before Glenelg was at last ejected from Downing Street. The Association, a philanthropic body, was accordingly replaced by a joint-stock company to the great mortification of Wakefield who was again forced to appear, against his will, in the character, which his enemies falsely attributed to him, of a land-speculator. The project, he said, had been begun by men with large minds and small purses and would be continued by men with small minds and large purses.[1]

During the greater part of 1838 he was with Durham in Canada. The Durham Report was no sooner issued than the Reformers turned to the formation of the New Zealand Company with a nominal capital of £200,000 and Lord Durham as Governor. But alas! the new Colonial Secretary, Lord Normanby, flatly refusing to be bound by his predecessor's decision, would give no direct or indirect sanction for the formation of a colony. The Directors accordingly decided to force the issue. They had bought a ship of 400 tons, the *Tory*, and had appointed, as leader of the colony, Wakefield's younger brother William, who had outlived the disgrace of his share in Ellen Turner's abduction as

[1] Presumably a hit at Joseph Somes, the great shipowner, who became chairman of the Company after the death of Lord Durham. I acknowledge here my debt to the memory of Somes whose estate provided endowments in New Zealand, to which I owe my education. C.E.C.

a colonel in the Spanish service, and had fought with distinction in the civil wars in Spain. Since preparations were well advanced, the elder Wakefield posted to Plymouth, on 4 May 1839, to despatch his brother with the *Tory* before the government could find means to prevent it. The sailing of the *Tory* on 5 May had the desired effect. Lord Normanby was now obliged to issue an instruction 'with extreme reluctance' for the annexation of New Zealand if only to protect the natives from the British colonists. On 13 June he informed Lord Durham that he had decided to send Captain William Hobson, R.N., to negotiate with the United Tribes of New Zealand for a cession of sovereignty. The one benefit he conferred upon the infant colony was an instruction that no convicts should be sent there.

Colonel Wakefield in the *Tory* sighted the South Island of New Zealand on 16 August 1839; in September he negotiated an agreement for the purchase of a wide tract of land from Te Rauparàha and other chiefs; Captain Hobson arrived at the Bay of Islands on 29 January 1840; and by this time there was also a French champion in the field. The story of the French designs on New Zealand has been somewhat confused by romantic exaggeration, in the local legend of the 'Race for Akaroa' between French and English warships. There was a race, but it took place in Europe between Edward Wakefield and a similar projector in France, a Captain Langlois, who was also trying to stimulate his government to action. He too formed a colonising company and despatched a shipload of emigrants without authority. Wakefield was the winner, both in getting his expedition under way and in forcing the hand of his government. Supposed French designs upon New Zealand were used by the Colonial Reformers as a means of bringing pressure on the English government. About the real activities of French free-lances there could be no doubt. Baron de Thierry in New Zealand was negotiating with the French government through his brother in Paris. Far more weighty was the work of French missionaries at the Bay of Islands. As in Canada a hundred years earlier, the missionaries, however innocent their motives, were regarded both by the savages and by most Europeans as the agents either of the Catholic or the Protestant power.

Jean Baptiste Pompallier (1802–70) was a learned and pious French priest who founded a missionary order (now generally known as the Marist Brothers) for the evangelisation of the Pacific islands, under the authority of a brief from Pope Gregory XVI. Having been consecrated a bishop *in partibus*, he arrived in New Zealand as Vicar-general in January 1838, with a letter of introduction to de Thierry. He made an error in not striking out a new claim but settled at the Bay of Islands in open rivalry with the Anglicans, who received him as an enemy.

As soon as Captain Hobson arrived at the Bay he commenced negotiations with the Maori chiefs for a treaty which was drawn up at Busby's house near the estuary of the Waitangi River. Williams the Anglican missionary, as interpreter, urged the chiefs to give their assent. Bishop Pompallier, who appeared at the conference in his canonical robes, was plainly hostile to the treaty but, on being assured that the British would guarantee freedom and protection to all Christian sects alike, he abstained from active opposition.

On 6 February 1840, the first signatures were obtained to the Treaty of Waitangi, the method being that each chief drew on the paper a copy of the design tattooed upon his face. Duplicates of the treaty were then carried by the missionaries to several parts of the islands for the collection of further signatures. Forty-six chiefs made their mark at Waitangi, and 456 others during the next few months, constituting a large majority, but by no means all, of the magnates of the Maori nation. The Treaty, to which the Maoris attached and still attach great respect, is a short document in three articles:

(1) The signatory chiefs 'cede to Her Majesty the Queen [*Te Kuini Wikitoria* in the Maori version] all the rights and powers of sovereignty which the said chiefs...exercise or possess...'.

(2) H.M. the Queen 'confirms and guarantees to the chiefs and tribes...undisputed possession of their lands...but the chiefs yield to Her Majesty the exclusive right of preemption'.

(3) Her Majesty extends her protection to the natives of New Zealand and 'imparts to them all the rights and privileges of British subjects'.

The Treaty was, in a sense, a counterblast to the action of Colonel Wakefield who had already begun to occupy the lands he professed to have bought, several hundred miles to the southward of the Bay of Islands. The site of a town had been selected and named Wellington, as a belated tribute to the old Duke who had helped the Colonial Reformers to steer the South Australian Bill through Parliament. The first shipload of emigrants had arrived, a fortnight before the signing of the Treaty. Hobson expressed his intention of visiting Wellington but was prevented by a paralytic stroke which left him an invalid, a dying man. But when the settlers, following the old model of the Pilgrim Fathers, held a meeting and formed a provisional government, the news alarmed him into action. He felt this to be a sort of declaration of independence and denounced it as high treason. He resolved to implement the Treaty of Waitangi by proclaiming British sovereignty over the North Island (21 May 1840). As if this trouble were not enough a French corvette appeared in June to protect the French emigrant ship which was then on its way to the South Island. Hobson thereupon despatched H.M.S. *Britomart* to the South Island to proclaim British sovereignty there also (17 June 1840). Further signatures were obtained to the Treaty of Waitangi including that of the redoubtable Rauparàha.

The site selected by the French colonists was the lovely secluded bay of Akaroa. The French corvette arrived there on 11 August to find that the *Britomart* had cast anchor in the harbour on the previous day, and that a magistrate had held a court, as formal evidence that the proclamation of 17 June was effective. A shipload of sixty French immigrants, arriving shortly after, decided to remain under the British flag, at Akaroa where some of their descendants still dwell. The French naval officers accepted the *fait accompli*, as did the French government, some years later, after an acrimonious debate in the Chamber of Deputies at Paris. So ended the French designs on New Zealand. Pompallier confined his labours to the mission field and became a British subject. The Baron de Thierry lived in obscurity at Auckland until his death in 1864.

8. EARLY SETTLEMENTS IN NEW ZEALAND

MEANWHILE several shiploads of emigrants had arrived at Wellington. Their way had been smoothed by the whaling-parties which, since about 1830, had settled in Cook Strait and the South Island. In 1840 there were 600 of these shore-whalers, making sixty boats' crews dispersed at about thirty settlements. Unlike the deep-sea whalers who hunted the toothed sperm-whale, they slaughtered the whale-bone whales who came to calve in the shallow water, usually killing the calf because the cow-whale would never leave its body. Such wanton destruction could but result in a short life for the trade. Though the fishery soon declined, a single shore-whaling station still operated a hundred years later, in 1932, at Te Awaiti. This station had once been the home of 'Dicky' Barrett, the doyen of the shore-whalers, who directed Colonel Wakefield to the site of Wellington and negotiated between him and the Maoris.

Colonel Wakefield claimed to have acquired a property in about twenty million acres of unexplored land on either side of Cook Strait. It was described in the deed of purchase merely in geographical terms as lying between certain degrees of latitude and longitude; it was paid for in two ways, by complimentary gifts to the chiefs of trade goods to the value of £9000, and by the guarantee that one-eleventh of the land, when surveyed and developed, would be formed into native reserves. The New Zealand Company always maintained that the reserves, immensely increased in value by the coming of civilisation, were the important consideration.

From the beginning of the story there was open conflict between the missionaries, who supported the Treaty of Waitangi, and the settlers, who supported the Wakefield land-purchase. On the one hand it was asserted that the settlers were mere 'land-sharks' expropriating the natives by a fraudulent contract which no law-court would uphold; on the other hand the settlers claimed that all reasonable native rights were scrupulously guaranteed by the New Zealand Company, whereas the Treaty of Waitangi was merely a legal fiction, a 'device to amuse and pacify savages for the moment'. When Lord John Russell became

Colonial Secretary (September 1839) he sent instructions to Governor Hobson to treat the Wellington settlers with 'kindness and consideration'. Their action, right or wrong, had preceded the signing of the Treaty and could not therefore be treated as a breach of it. In February 1841, after long negotiation, he gave a charter to the Company, thus justifying Wakefield's action in despatching the *Tory*. Notwithstanding the Treaty it was agreed that the Company might occupy four acres in New Zealand for every pound it had spent in colonisation. This would have been an equitable solution had events not moved in a contrary direction in the colony. There was a delay of three to six months between the issue of a despatch in London and its reception by the Governor at the Bay of Islands, and perhaps as long again before the Governor's action took effect at Wellington. The Letters-patent setting up New Zealand as a distinct colony, no longer subordinate to New South Wales, were issued in November 1840, but not promulgated in New Zealand until May 1841.

Not finding a suitable site for a capital city in the Bay of Islands, Governor Hobson cast about until he hit upon a commanding position, the isthmus between the two harbours of Waitemata and Onèhunga (October 1840). Here he decided to build a city, calling it Auckland after the Viceroy of India, his former patron at the Admiralty. It was a stroke of genius, or would have been, if either funds or labour had been available to develop it; but to foist an official capital, a Washington or a Canberra, upon a tiny struggling community was financially absurd. The population for some years consisted of officials and their families, with a few speculators from Sydney who manufactured a highly profitable boom in town lots, although there were no genuine settlers and no prospect of any. Nine-tenths of the paltry revenue of the country was spent on Governor Hobson's 'Folly'. His efforts in his last year were spent in trying to persuade the Wellington settlers to remove to Auckland, theirs in trying to persuade him to remove the capital to Wellington. So far from moving north the settlers were spreading into new areas in the south, rejecting Hobson's choice.

In 1841 the Company despatched two new ready-made colonies to different parts of the vast domain they claimed to have bought. A subsidiary company, formed in the west country under the patronage of the Earl of Devon and the Mayor of Plymouth, sent a small but select body of emigrants to found New Plymouth at the foot of the giant volcanic cone of Tàr=nàki (or Mount Egmont). Another colony occupied a site on the southern side of Cook Strait, and called it Nelson.

In July 1841 there arrived at Wellington a government commissioner armed with authority to arbitrate upon land-claims. Within a few days the settlers were convinced that his interest and intention was to urge the natives to repudiate their bargain with Colonel Wakefield. Two years of desultory negotiation were required for the allocation of the land to which Lord John Russell had declared the Company entitled. Long before that time had passed, the exasperated settlers were squatting where they could, while the natives had realised that strong factions among the white men would support them in repudiating any land sale. Hobson died in September 1842, a well-meaning honourable man, but unequal to the office he held, even if he had been in good health. During the full year required to arrange for a successor the Governorship was held by a deputy, Lieutenant Shortland, R.N., an incompetent underling whose reign was chiefly marked by jobbery, extravagance and delay. When at last the new Governor arrived, disaster had overtaken the colony.

The leader of the Nelson settlers was Captain Arthur Wakefield, R.N., another sprig from that remarkable family-tree, but unlike Edward and William, a man of blameless, indeed distinguished, reputation. After a long dispute with the ferocious Rauparàha about the ownership of a block of land at Wairau, the Nelson settlers determined to arrest him on a charge of arson since he had driven away a surveying party and burnt their hut. The warrant was served by Arthur Wakefield, a police magistrate and a posse of special constables, upon this renowned barbarian in the midst of his armed followers. High words led to fighting in which the civilian constables cut a poor figure. In an endeavour to stop the bloodshed Arthur Wakefield surrendered, and was massacred with several other Englishmen as a reprisal for the death of a Maori woman who had been accidentally shot during the brawl.

The Wairau Massacre has many counterparts in the long history of the relations between savages and civilised men, but the sequel is unparalleled. The action of the Boers after the murder of Retief in 1838 was in striking contrast. Far from leading to war and reprisal the news of the massacre led to an instant revulsion of feeling against the settlers. The Company's three little colonies began to put themselves in a state of defence until they were sternly forbidden by the Acting-Governor to form Home Guards. To their request for protection he let it be known that he was far more concerned with protecting Rauparàha against their reprisals. The captain of a warship which was sent to the Chief's village, though an old shipmate of Arthur Wakefield, addressed his murderer as 'Friend Rauparàha', taking him by the hand. No claim was made for recovery of the property stolen from the dead men. The missionaries, one and all, took the side of the natives. When the news reached England, Lord Stanley, the Colonial Secretary, declared in the House that the victims had 'violated the rules of the law of England, the maxims of prudence and the principles of justice'. How he came to this conclusion is not evident as no investigation had been held and the material witnesses on the other side were dead. Since Stanley himself had disallowed the Governor's ordinance granting municipal government to the settlements there was no means of empanelling a coroner's jury at Nelson.

Great hopes were entertained from the arrival of the new Governor, Captain R. Fitzroy, a celebrated scientist and navigator. As soon as he arrived (December 1843) he visited Wellington and, after upbraiding the leading settlers at his levee, passed on to a more congenial interview with Rauparàha, whose account of the massacre he instantly accepted as conclusive.

On the one hand stood an old bloodthirsty cannibal, renowned among his fellows for treacherous cunning, who for twenty years had been bargaining with white men, treating them with a nauseous alternation of bluster and fawning, who had signed the Treaty of Waitangi, and the Wakefield land-concession, and had repudiated both; whose sole claim to the Wairau lands lay in the fact that he had killed and eaten the former owners; whose tribe, not having occupied the lands, would suffer no material loss by their sale. On the other hand lay the dead bodies of a naval officer, a magistrate and twenty special constables killed in the execution of what they believed, however 'imprudently', to be their duty. The Church, the State, and the historians have agreed to blame the dead men. Such was the strength of early Victorian philanthropy.

During the two years when Governor Fitzroy held sway (1843–5) New Zealand lapsed into chaos. The Maoris every-

Plate 13

SIR GEORGE GREY, K.C.M.G. (1812–98)

'Good Governor Grey'. An engraving after a painting by G. Richmond,
about 1841. *See pp. 386 and 607.*

Plate 14

GEORGE AUGUSTUS SELWYN (1809–78)

Bishop of New Zealand. An engraving after a painting by G. Richmond, about 1842. *See p. 387.*

where repudiated land sales, obstructed surveys, and treated the English with the contempt due to cowards. In the north they truculently declared that Rauparàha should not be allowed to monopolise the glory of killing *pakehàs*. Progress at the Company's settlements, though emigrants continually arrived, was exceedingly slow. At Auckland the land-boom had collapsed, leaving the government sorely embarrassed. Governor Fitzroy, like the early Governors at Adelaide, was forced to draw bills on New South Wales without authority or backing. Being a convinced free-trader he abolished the customs duties, the sole reliable source of revenue, intending to replace them by direct taxes, which he could not collect. Being an honest man he quarrelled with his subordinates, from Deputy-Governor Shortland downwards, since there was not one of them who was not speculating on his own account. Yet the whole machinery of government at Auckland was so corrupt that he could not keep his hands clean and was actually blackmailed by one of his own officers. Suddenly, in desperation, he tried to solve all his problems by overruling the statutory price of land and reverting to the bad old principle of making grants for a nominal fee. This was too much for Lord Stanley who dismissed him with ignominy in 1845. The man selected to revive the bankrupt disorderly colony was Captain George Grey, who had just completed a similar task in South Australia. He was no more than thirty-three years old.

Grey's first problem was a native campaign at the Bay of Islands. In sheer high spirits, one of the tribes, spoiling for a fight, had repeatedly cut down the flagstaff bearing the Union Jack at Koro-ràreka (now called Russell), the old whaling-port. In March 1845 the defence of the flagstaff developed into a battle in which the Maoris sacked the town, allowing the inhabitants to escape by sea to Auckland. Troops from Sydney, and a naval brigade conducted a little bush campaign, not very successfully, against the Maori warriors, who then revealed their prowess. They based their tactics upon building at each suitable point a fortress (*pa*), sited, entrenched, and stockaded with a skill that won the admiration of regular officers, and defended with a courage that defied their efforts. After several failures under other officers, George Grey took personal command. He established his prestige (*mana*) as a great warrior by taking the *pa* of Rua-peka-peka ('the bat's nest') which brought the campaign to a close in January 1846.

From that day the northern tribes have maintained friendly relations with the British.

All observers reported a change in the habits of the Maori. In the northern war there was no cannibalism and no massacre of non-combatants. The tribesmen were Christians, observing the rules of civilised warfare. They complained ruefully that Rua-peka-peka fell only because the Governor launched the assault on Sunday morning when the Maori warriors were at church parade.

Grey had that quality which unsuccessful commanders describe as 'luck' in the successful commanders who supersede them. He had a sense of timing and the resolution to act only when the time was ripe. He was able to do what Hobson and Fitzroy could not, because he insisted upon being given the necessary resources. Whereas Hobson had been expected to make New Zealand self-supporting with its own revenues, and secure with an escort of five policemen, Grey demanded and got 2000 soldiers and a grant-in-aid to cover an estimated deficit of £25,000, his whole budget being £49,000. He set to work briskly at settling land-titles, reverting to the high-price system, and soon came to an agreement with the Company about their claims. Utterly ruthless when confronted with corruption or inefficiency, he discharged most of the officials who had served under the previous Governor.

His greatest success was with the Maoris whose language and traditions he studied, finding time to write a standard work on *Polynesian Mythology*. It was his custom to honour the leading chiefs with public and private attentions, usually inviting one or two to attend him on his journeys. After his success in the northern war he went south to Wellington and taught the tribes who adhered to Rauparàha a salutary lesson. Having defeated them in two or three skirmishes he set them to road-making for good wages. When one chief proved recalcitrant, Grey quickly brought him to another mind about the uses of a road by presenting him with a horse and trap. As for Te Rauparàha, the Governor had taken his measure. A party of sailors was sent ashore by night to kidnap the old warrior. They carried him, kicking and biting, aboard a warship where he was held in honourable captivity for several months. Though the Colonial Office was deeply shocked by such a deed, it was instantly effective. All the Maoris understood that the Governor had greater *mana* than the old chief, who died at a great age, in 1848, soon after his release.

The estimated population of New Zealand about the time of Grey's arrival was 120,000 of whom nine-tenths were natives.[1] Most of the white minority lived in the south, most of the native majority in the north. Grey was obliged, like his predecessors, to give most of his attention to the north and, accordingly, to Auckland rather than to Wellington.

The same point of view was taken by another Englishman, of hardly less moral and mental stature than Grey. This was George Augustus Selwyn (1809–78) who became Bishop of New Zealand in 1842. He was ideally qualified to reconcile Maoris with English, and missionaries with settlers. Not only was he a scholar and a High Churchman, but the Maoris were quick to recognise him too as a great chief. He had all the powers of body and mind required to dominate a community of pioneers. He would make stupendous journeys on foot, alone, from one settlement to the next, swimming the rivers, and sleeping rough. He loved the whalers and visited their camps to marry them to their native wives and to baptise their half-caste children. In return they paid him the compliment of saying that the Bishop could handle a sailing-boat better than any man in the South Seas. It was the Bishop who intervened in the fight at Koro-ràreka in an attempt to prevent the destruction of the town.

Among the problems he had to solve was the complaint that the missionaries themselves were not clear of the taint of land speculation. Even the saintly Henry Williams had provided an estate for his own family, and stoutly asserted that he had acted with honour in doing so. Marsden's policy of civilisation before conversion had made every mission station a farm colony by which the missionary was expected to earn his livelihood. He could not therefore escape the benefit of the general rise in land prices.

---

[1] Approximate figures 1844–5:

Natives (of whom 40% were Anglican; 15% Methodist; 5% Roman Catholic; and the rest heathen)		109,000
Whites: Bay of Islands	500	
Auckland	2000	
Wellington	4000	
Nelson	3000	
New Plymouth	1000	
etc.	500	
		11,000
		120,000

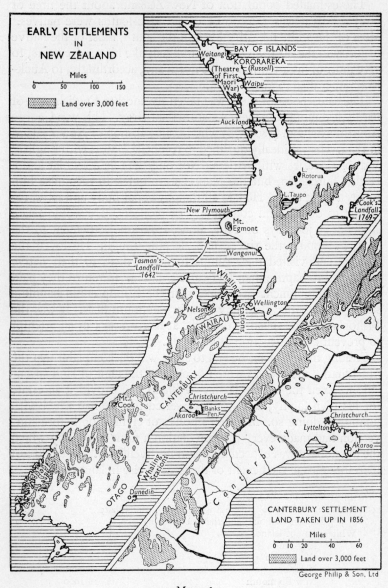

**EARLY SETTLEMENTS
IN
NEW ZEALAND**

Miles

0   50   100   150

Land over 3,000 feet

BAY OF ISLANDS

Waitangi

KORORAREKA
(Russell)

(Theatre
of First
Maori
War)

Waipu

Auckland

L. Rotorua

L. Taupo

Cook's
Landfall
1769

New Plymouth

Mt.
Egmont

Wanganui

Tasman's
Landfall
1642

Whaling Stations

Wellington

Nelson

WAIRAU

Mt.
Cook

CANTERBURY

Christchurch

Akaroa

Banks
Pen.

Whaling
Stations

OTAGO

Dunedin

Canterbury Plains

Christchurch

Lyttelton

Akaroa

**CANTERBURY SETTLEMENT
LAND TAKEN UP IN 1856**

Miles

0   10   20   40   60

Land over 3,000 feet

George Philip & Son, Ltd

Map 16

Selwyn's contribution to Church History was the organisation of the New Zealand Church on an elective basis. He and Governor Grey, mindful of similar experiments in Upper Canada, drew up a constitution for an autonomous colonial Church in communion with Canterbury, placing the temporalities in the hands of lay trustees, a device which, through Selwyn's influence, has spread throughout the whole Anglican Church. Selwyn and Grey, fast friends and allies, were a pair whose like could not easily be found even in that age of great Englishmen.

9. THE COLONIAL REFORMERS AND NEW ZEALAND

WHILE his two brothers, William at Wellington and Arthur at Nelson, were practising the art of colonisation in New Zealand, Edward Gibbon Wakefield had paid two visits to Canada, on private business in connexion with the North American Colonisation Company of Ireland, a land and irrigation company which had bought the Seigneurie of Beauharnois on the St Lawrence as a commercial speculation.[1] None of his biographers has much to say of this period of his life (1841–3). But Wakefield could never abstain from political activity. He was elected to the second Canadian Parliament for the district of Beauharnois, a predominantly French constituency which had been the scene of bloodshed and sedition throughout 1838, the revolutionary year. As was his custom he exercised his powers most vigorously behind the scenes as confidential adviser to Governor Metcalfe urging him to 'finish what Durham began'. The news of his brother's death in the Wairau Massacre recalled Wakefield to England (1843) as champion of the New Zealand settlers.

Since the death of Lord Durham (1840), and especially while Wakefield was abroad, the leading position among the Colonial Reformers had been taken by Charles Buller who, until his early death in 1848, was regarded by his own generation as a politician of great promise. His career, like that of his contemporary, the young Disraeli, was retarded only by an excess of wit which sometimes degenerated into flippancy. He made it his business to

[1] *Bulletin of Dept. of Hist. and Pol. Science.* Queen's University, Kingston, Ontario, December 1925.

deride the Colonial Office and its Permanent Under-Secretary, James Stephen, whom he caricatured under the figure of 'Mr Mother-country'. Despatches from Downing Street and speeches at Westminster made a practice of exhorting the inhabitants of the British colonies to submit dutifully to a mysterious fiction called the Mother-country. Buller set himself to discover who or what was this Mother-country to whom colonials did in fact pay a pathetic and unrewarded tribute of loyalty. It was not the young Queen whose actual power was no greater in imperial than in domestic politics; it was not the British public whose ignorance of the colonies was equalled by their unconcern with them; it was not the House of Commons which could hardly be persuaded to make a quorum for discussing a colonial bill; it was not the Secretary of State, a transient party-hack who never held office long enough to master the multifarious business of his office. In the last resort some irresponsible and obstructive clerk in Downing Street was all the Mother-country that a colonial could identify. 'We will not flatter the pride of our colonial readers', wrote Buller, 'by depicting the real arbiter of their destinies as a person of lofty rank or of the first class among what we call states-men.... He has a modest home in the outskirts of London with an equally modest establishment; and the colonist who is on his road to "the Office" little imagines that it is the real ruler of the colonies that he sees walking over one of the bridges, or driving his one-horse shay, or riding cheek by jowl with him on the top of the short coach, as he comes into town of a morning.... Mr Mother-country's whole heart is in the business of his office. He alone knows on what principle the predecessors of the noble or Right Honourable Secretary acted before: he alone, therefore, can point out the step which it is incumbent to take.'

Colonists who wait in the dismal ante-room of 'the Office', in the belief that they are appealing to the sovereign, find that this right of appeal is 'a mere device for prolonging the tortures of the unhappy victim who, bandied about from colony to England, from Secretary to Secretary, from Under-Secretary to Under-Secretary, from clerk to clerk, wastes away hope and existence, as a subject of Mr Mother-country's systematic procrastination'.

This and much more like it was no doubt personally unjust to James Stephen, a shrewd, prompt civil servant with a legal training and an evangelical conscience, but as a denunciation of the principle of Colonial Office rule it was fully justified. Neither Stephen nor anyone else was competent to direct the government of forty scattered provinces, some of them distant by the length of a six-months' voyage, and all known to him by hearsay only.

Repeated attacks by Buller, and the representations of the New Zealand Company Directors, led to the appointment of a Parliamentary committee on which the Reformers were strongly represented. In April 1844 the committee made a report which gravely embarrassed the government. After examining, and publishing, a mass of evidence largely supplied by Wakefield, they declared that the action of the Company in despatching the *Tory* to New Zealand had been 'highly irregular and improper', but that the Treaty of Waitangi, on the other hand, had been 'injudicious'. The implication that all the land of New Zealand, whether occupied or not, was the property of the sparse Maori tribes had been 'an error productive of injurious consequences'. Lord Stanley, the Colonial Secretary who had stoutly championed the Treaty of Waitangi, was obliged to accept this rebuff, but beyond informing the Governor of New Zealand, he took no further action.

The growing strength of the Reformers during the next few months must be considered as a phase of the revolution in English politics. Free Trade, an issue which was to affect the colonies as profoundly as the mother-country, was bringing about the break-up of the old Whig and Tory parties; and the agitation over New Zealand was used as another wedge to split Sir Robert Peel's majority. Buller took an active part in the Corn Law debates, surprising the House by blurting out: 'You advocates of Free Trade wish to bring food to the people. I suggest to you at the same time to take your people to the food.'

In June 1845 he achieved a triumph by moving a resolution that was, in effect, a vote of censure on Lord Stanley. The importance of the debate is not so much in what was said as in the fact that a colonial question was discussed for three whole days in a full House, an event that is rare in imperial history. When the House divided, Buller mustered 173 votes against a Government majority of 233. The Whig leaders Russell and Palmerston, the 'anti-corn-law' leaders Cobden and Bright, supported Buller, as did Disraeli, who was then working up his vendetta against Peel. Gladstone supported the Government. Peel himself spoke powerfully in defence of his subordinate, justifying the Treaty of Waitangi and assuring the House that all would be well now that Governor George Grey had taken charge. But the debate was so damaging to the administration that Lord Stanley soon resigned, ostensibly because of a difference with Peel over the Corn Laws.

When at the crisis of the Irish famine the Tories split and the Whigs returned to office (July 1846), Lord John Russell gave the seals of the Colonies to the third Earl Grey, who, as Viscount Howick, had adopted the Wakefield theories in 1831 and had voted for Buller's motion in 1845. Unfortunately he was one of those many people who disliked Wakefield and whom Wakefield hated. Lord Melbourne said of Grey, explaining his character to Queen Victoria, 'he is a very clever man but a very obstinate man, and excessively eager about what he takes up, and very angry when everybody don't immediately adopt his views'. He was now determined to solve the New Zealand problem in his own way, in consultation with his namesake, Governor Grey, and without reference to the intriguing Colonial Reformers. An interview between Lord Grey and Wakefield in August 1846 ended in a personal quarrel which the two participants described in flatly different terms. A few days later Wakefield was removed from the scene by a paralytic stroke—which confined him to private life for about a year. Physically he never recovered from this attack—he was fifty years of age—mentally he grew more violent, quarrelsome and secretive. In his absence the New Zealand Company had lost its grip on political affairs and had been degraded into a commercial company for administering the Crown's right of pre-emption over the central and southern parts of New Zealand. The government of the country was to have been regulated by a new and highly democratic constitution which Lord Grey had prepared and offered to the Governor. To the surprise of all concerned, the Governor instantly rejected it on the grounds that such a constitution would enable the whites, who formed one-tenth of the population, to tyrannise over the natives, who formed nine-tenths. Even more surprising was the fact that Lord Grey acquiesced. The settlers in New Zealand now began to regard Governor Grey as their enemy and no better than his predecessors; while the Colonial Reformers in London began to think that Lord Grey was a renegade from their principles.

A plan had long been germinating in Wakefield's fertile brain for interesting the Churches in colonisation, outflanking thereby the opposition of the missionaries. At Adelaide, Wellington, Nelson and New Plymouth there had been something wanting to complete the parallel with Maryland and Pennsylvania. The missing factor was religion as a motive force. He had begun to consider Anglican, Presbyterian, Irish Catholic and Jewish settlements, which involved him in a network of new intrigues. The foundation of New Plymouth, by a philanthropic association acting as an extension of the moribund New Zealand Company, foreshadowed the method by which Church Associations might found colonies. The Otago[1] (1848) and Canterbury (1850) settlements concluded Wakefield's career with a degree of success attained by few political projectors.

Mr George Rennie of Edinburgh had for some years been urging the New Zealand Company to found a Scottish colony, when the Disruption of the Scottish Church (1843) provided the necessary impetus. A Lay Association of the seceding Free Churchmen was formed in 1845 to organise a Free Church colony, the promoters being the Rev. Thomas Burns (the poet's nephew) and Captain William Cargill, a Peninsular veteran. Little progress was made until 1847 (the time of Wakefield's return to active life) when an agreement was reached between the Lay Association and the New Zealand Company. The former body was to select and despatch Free Church emigrants, the latter was to acquire and survey the site, and settle the emigrants upon the land. 2000 sixty-acre sections were to be sold to settlers at £2 an acre, while 400 additional sections were to be reserved as an endowment for churches and schools.

In November 1847 the first ship sailed from Gravesend with 100 Scottish emigrants, the second from Greenock with 240. In April 1848 they landed at Otago harbour in the south of New Zealand and founded the township which they called Dunedin. The harbour was renamed Port Chalmers after the hero of the Free Church. As in all the Wakefield colonies progress was much slower than had been anticipated. By December 1852 only about one-eighth part of the allotted land had been sold. The population consisted of hardy Lowland labourers (2000 in 1852, 3800 in 1856) who accepted the patriarchal rule of honest old Captain Cargill;

[1] Pronounced to rhyme with 'virago'.

and found the climate and the landscape not unlike their native Scotland. But for some years the colony languished, though its future was to exceed the hopes of its founders.

In November 1847, while convalescing at Malvern, Wakefield had become acquainted with a young Irish squire, John Robert Godley (1814–61), who proved to be the ideal promoter for a Church of England colony. Godley was a Tory and a High Churchman, a classical scholar of Christ Church, Oxford, and a friend of Gladstone (who, it should be remembered, was at that date still a Tory). He had travelled widely and had recently published a thoughtful book on his experiences in America. It was reported that he had almost persuaded Peel, in 1845, to anticipate the Irish Famine by advancing £10,000,000 to trustees who would transfer a million Irishmen to Canada. Godley brought into the circle of the Colonial Reformers a new group of young men whose ideals were very different from those of the matter-of-fact young Radicals of Wakefield's youth. Godley's friends were earnest, pious and enthusiastic, the products of the reformed public schools, the Oxford Movement, and the Romantic Revival. Wakefield had little difficulty in inspiring Godley with his enthusiasm for a Church colony, which Godley was to organise on the Wakefield plan. Twenty years of propaganda and experiment at last bore fruit. One Church dignitary alone, Dr Hinds, the Bishop of Norwich, had from the beginning stood with the Colonial Reformers; now many of the most dignified clergy gave their support to Mr Godley's scheme. Archbishop Sumner joined them as chairman of what was known as the Canterbury Association (March 1848). The membership was far more eminent than that of Wakefield's previous colonising bodies. In addition to two Archbishops, Sumner and Whately, seven other bishops lent their names. The lay members, many of them Godley's college friends, included Lord Shaftesbury, Lord John Manners, Sidney Herbert, the Earls of Lincoln and Devon, several other peers and fifteen members of Parliament. Among these notables, two now threw in their lot with the Colonial Reformers and devoted much of their public life to colonial questions; these were the fourth Lord Lyttelton (1817–76) and Mr C. B. Adderley,[1] afterwards Lord

---

[1] Perhaps best remembered by the main street of Capetown which bears his name, in gratitude for his Parliamentary efforts to save the Cape from being made a convict colony, 27 March 1849.

Norton (1814–1905). Godley was managing director of the Association until, in 1849, he was ordered abroad for his health. He then undertook to go to New Zealand as leader of the Canterbury Settlement, leaving the management of the Association at home largely to Lyttelton and Adderley.

Though Wakefield's name did not appear among the notables of the Canterbury Association he was never more active than in 1848 and 1849. His letters reveal a network of negotiations of extraordinary complexity. No one observing a stout florid John-Bullish figure, riding slowly over the Surrey Downs, followed by a pack of the rare Talbot hounds and beagles which it was his hobby to breed, would have supposed that this was the Machiavellian Mr Wakefield, whom *The Times* denounced as a dangerous and discredited swindler, whose past history was unmentionable, whose present activities were a spider's web of doubtful intrigues. Yet Wakefield was indispensable. He boasted that thirty-six members of Parliament called one week-end at his little house at Reigate to consult him on colonial questions. He had to manage the press, to write the propaganda, to appoint the officers of the Association, even to select a bishop for Canterbury, though he was a better judge of a prize bulldog than of a colonial bishop. He drafted the constitution of New Zealand one afternoon sitting with Adderley in the garden of the latter's house. Provided that he remained in the background all went well. In 1849 he instituted a new Colonial Reform Society to which he attracted his new Tory friends[1] from the Canterbury Association, as well as his old Radical associates. Colonial Reform was now respectable as was proved by the belated adherence of *The Times*. For twenty years every project connected with the hated names of Durham or Wakefield had been belaboured by the Thunderer. In 1849 the tune was changed, the Canterbury Settlement with its episcopal backing could not be denounced in the old clap-trap style.

The proposal was to transfer, to some part of New Zealand where there were no native inhabitants, what *The Times* described as a 'complete slice of England cut from top to bottom'. The settlers were to comprise not only labourers as at Otago, but gentle and simple, professional men in due proportion, teachers and clergy and at the top of the social scale a nobleman and a bishop

---

[1] Hume and Roebuck, Cobden and Lowe joined the Society, Peel and Disraeli refused Adderley's invitation to join.

as the natural leaders of an English, and Anglican, society. Two and a half millions of acres of land were to be purchased from the New Zealand Company and sold to settlers at the price of £3 an acre, which even Wakefield thought sufficiently high. The land-fund derived from sales would be disposed of at the rate of 10s. for the purchase price of the land, 10s. for survey and development, £1 for the emigration fund and £1 for the endowment of churches and schools. Every buyer of a fifty-acre section would be entitled to a quarter-acre town-lot in the capital city, and to a pasturage lease over the undeveloped land beyond the limits of settlement. At first, only members of the Church of England were admitted as land-purchasers.

Lord Grey somewhat grudgingly approved the scheme, though he took exception to some details, for which a royal charter was issued in November 1849. The New Zealand Company was dissolved in 1850 after disposing of its assets to the Canterbury Association, the whole transaction being legalised by the Canterbury Settlement Land Act (13 & 14 Vict. cap. 70) which became law on 14 August 1850.

While Godley was preparing to receive the settlers in New Zealand, Wakefield urged on the land sales in London. During the summer of 1850 the first band of settlers was chosen. Meeting frequently at their office in the Adelphi they formed a constitutional association, discussed their plans, heard lectures on New Zealand, and assembled the necessities of civilised emigration. Several settlers took with them frame houses in sections; a committee was appointed (under another of Wakefield's brothers) to acclimatise English plants and animals; and among other accessories the first ships carried an organ, a church bell, school equipment, and a printing press. The first actual achievement of the settlers was to collect a reference library of 2000 volumes from a grant made by the University of Oxford. Their keenest enthusiasm was for the foundation of a cathedral and a college, at the first commencement of the colony, to be 'a centre from which arts and morals should be spread through the southern world'. This combination of cathedral and college was derived from the constitution of Christ Church, Oxford, and Christchurch was accordingly to be the name of the principal town in Canterbury Settlement.

In spite of support from all quarters, and publicity hitherto unparalleled, the land sales again fell short of expectations. In the first year land to the value of £39,450 was sold whereas the terms of the charter required £50,000. The Association was saved from insolvency in May 1850 by a personal guarantee given by Lord Lyttelton and some others. They were now so deeply committed that they decided to launch the colony on a smaller scale than had been first intended and without the exalted leadership of a nobleman. Four shiploads of settlers were assembled in London and were dubbed by Martin Tupper, the popular poetaster of that day, the 'Canterbury Pilgrims', the name by which they are still remembered in New Zealand. A public dinner to the whole party was given by the Association at a cost of £742; and a farewell sermon was preached to them by the Archbishop in St Paul's. The First Four Ships sailed from London River on 7 and 8 September and arrived at the New Zealand harbour which they were to call Port Lyttelton between 16 and 27 December 1850. They carried 127 cabin passengers (at £42 a berth), 85 intermediate passengers (at £25 a berth), and 534 steerage passengers (at £15 a berth). No party of emigrants so well-chosen, well-prepared and well-led had landed in any colony since the golden days of Charles II. Never had any emigrants arrived to find such complete arrangements for their reception. Godley stood there to receive them on a wooden jetty. Four large 'barracks' had been erected on the hillside for temporary shelter. A hundred Maori labourers were at work making a road inland. The million acres had been roughly surveyed and three town-sites, Christchurch, Lyttelton and Sumner had been laid out. Governor Grey and Bishop Selwyn, both inclined to dislike Wakefield colonies, had been won over by Godley's transparent honesty, and both arrived to welcome the settlers. At first the Utopian dreams of the projectors seemed to have come true; but as a matter of fact the Canterbury Association was penniless and deep in debt.

10. CANTERBURY SETTLEMENT, 1850

EVERY new colony produces some new problem which the planners have not foreseen; in Canterbury it was the road from the port to the capital. The Canterbury block was a shelving alluvial plain formed by the outfall of torrential rivers from the Southern Alps, with a landscape and a climate like northern Italy. There was no harbour or anchorage off the surf-beaten sandy beach. Midway along the shore and projecting into the sea there rose a humped volcanic mass of hills, named Banks' Peninsula, penetrated from seaward by four deep-water inlets. One of these harbours was Akaroa where the French settlers had made their home in 1840; another was Port Lyttelton where Godley received the First Four Ships. But the exit from Port Lyttelton (or from Akaroa) to the fertile plains was over the crest of the range, a journey which Godley compared to a crossing of the Ogwen Pass from Bettws-y-Coed. Lack of funds compelled him to curtail construction of a mountain road so that for some years the settlers carried their goods by packhorse over a rocky trail, or transhipped them into whale-boats which must cross a dangerous sand-bar before rowing up the swampy stream to Christchurch, five miles inland. This was the first taste of 'roughing it', which dispelled the rosy dreams of the gentlemen in tall hats and ladies in crinolines among the Canterbury Pilgrims.

A school was opened, and a newspaper—vehemently demanding self-government in its early issues—was published at Lyttelton within a few days of landing. In February 1851 the centre of activity shifted over the hills to Christchurch where land was selected by the purchasers in order. While the settlers took up their sections, built huts of the scanty timber, and began to till the ground, Godley, as resident magistrate and as agent of the Canterbury Association, was responsible for law and order; for the survey and road-making; for the issue of land-titles and pasturage leases; for negotiating the limit of their reserves with the handful of Maoris who occupied three or four villages in Canterbury; for coming to terms with the French at Akaroa; and for regulating the position of some settlers from Wellington who had squatted in Canterbury before the coming of the 'Pilgrims'. Godley welcomed them, in spite of the displeasure of the land-purchasers, since they could sell provisions which would tide the 'Pilgrims' over to their first harvest.

Such tasks as these, which in every other new colony had led to bickerings and disputes, Godley carried out with firmness and patience. The foundation of churches and schools, which had bulked so large in the prospectus, took much of his time. The bishopric proved very troublesome since the bishop-designate fled at the first glimpse of colonial hardships, to the great disgust of Bishop Selwyn. The college (later known as Christ's College) made a start with a grammar school, a hospital, a library, and primary schools in each township but all on a tiny scale and under rough conditions. Godley's plan for the control of the Church endowments by a body of lay trustees proved to be the solution of the vexed problem of providing for the clergy from the waste lands of a new colony.

As political leader of the Canterbury settlers, Godley placed himself at the head of the opposition to Governor Grey, demanding the constitutional rights which the Governor withheld. On the other hand, although he was the agent of the Canterbury Association he declined to be bound by instructions from London if he found them unsuited to the conditions of the colony. He would not submit to regulation either by the Governor, 500 miles away at Auckland, or by the Association, 13,000 miles away in London. 'The form of the constitution', he said, 'might be a question for discussion, but it must be *localised*. I would rather be governed by a Nero on the spot than by a board of Angels in London, because we could, if the worst came to the worst, cut off Nero's head, but we could not get at the board in London at all.' Having realised very soon that pastoral farming, not agriculture, would make the wealth of Canterbury he began to grant pastoral leases to sheep-farmers from other colonies, who brought their stock and their experience to the new settlement. As this was in flat defiance of the original plan which allowed grazing-rights only to land-purchasers, he found himself at loggerheads with the Association in London. In Godley's view it was time for them to abdicate in favour of the settlers.

The Canterbury Settlement, founded with such high hopes, had already been written off as a failure by the faint-hearts, and as a failure it has been described in several histories. The mistake made by the promoters had been to suppose that it could be estab-

lished in a year or two. In December 1852 Godley returned to
England, where Gladstone gave him a high appointment in the
Civil Service (see chapter x, 2, page 536). His farewell speech to
the Canterbury settlers, a decent thriving community of 3400
persons, propounded his own faith. 'Now that I have been a
practical colonist,' he said, 'I often smile when I think of the Ideal
Canterbury of which our imagination dreamed. Yet I am not sure
that the reality is not in many respects sounder and better than the
dream.' He defended the Wakefield plan, claiming that at Canterbury there was a more concentrated population, a larger proportion of resident landowners and, consequently, a more civilised
society than in earlier colonies, none the less because 'a barrister
was not ashamed to dig nor an army officer to drive cattle'.

Six years later he was able to announce to a meeting of sympathisers in London, as agent for the Canterbury settlers, that the
population had reached 7000, with 2000 immigrants coming in
each year, that the debt to Lord Lyttelton had been repaid, that
the colony had been self-supporting from its third year and was
exporting food to the Australian gold-fields, that revenue at the
rate of £14 per head was raised without hardship and that exports
were valued at £30 per head. Between 1861 and 1867 the little
colony was able to finance from its own resources a railway,
piercing the hills between Port Lyttelton and Christchurch with
what was then the longest tunnel in the world. Within thirty
years the Cathedral and College were built much as they had
been planned, and the Canterbury block now sustains about
250,000 New Zealanders with a remarkably high standard of
comfort.

The New Zealand Constitution Act (15 & 16 Vict. cap. 72) had
been initiated by Governor Grey who thought the time ripe, at
last, for giving the colony a democratic and federal constitution.
Though Lord Grey concluded his policy of granting self-
government to the 'white' colonies by preparing the New
Zealand Bill the Whig government fell before it was enacted. The
next Colonial Secretary, Sir John Pakington, a Tory and a friend
of the Colonial Reformers, saw it through Parliament. The
colony became a federation of six strong provinces, five of them
Wakefield settlements, and the sixth the 'official' settlement of
Auckland.

Plate 15

EDWARD GIBBON WAKEFIELD (1796–1862)

The founder of six settlements in Australia and New Zealand. From a portrait by
C. A. Collins painted for the New Zealand Company in 1849 and now in the Canterbury
Museum, New Zealand. The dogs are said to be by Landseer. *See p. 325.*

Plate 16

HENRY, 3RD EARL GREY (1802–94)

Authorised responsible government in several colonies. 'A very clever man but a very obstinate man.' *See p. 392.*

With this happy ending to the struggle for systematic colonisation and self-government, Wakefield's life-work seemed to have
been completed. His political testament, *A View of the Art of
Colonization*, had been published in 1849, a book full of wise
reflexions, marred by bitter personal attacks on Lord Grey. The
governing classes had at last been converted, as was demonstrated
by the last of Wakefield's foundations, the Colonial Reform
Society. Wakefield now fulfilled an old promise of ending his
days in the colony he had founded. He arrived in New Zealand
soon after Godley's departure. 'I would have fancied myself in
England,' he said of Canterbury in 1853, 'but for the hard working industry of the upper classes and the luxurious independence
of the common people.' It was however in Wellington, which his
brother William had founded, that he spent his last years, fated,
to the end, to provoke suspicion and dislike. When one of the
Wellington constituencies elected him to the first New Zealand
Parliament (1853) he was accorded the honour of moving a resolution calling upon the Acting-Governor to institute responsible
government. For Governor Grey had gone on furlough, discreetly avoiding an encounter with Wakefield. Not many weeks
passed before Wakefield's inveterate love of intrigue had alienated
all his friends. The champion of responsible government was
bitterly denounced for exercising a malign secret influence over
the Acting-Governor.

He was now growing old and soon retired from public life. For
some years he lived quietly at Wellington and died, in 1862, at the
age of sixty-six, almost a forgotten man. The graves of the two
brothers, William and Edward Gibbon Wakefield, are in the old
cemetery overlooking Wellington harbour. They have no monument other than the Dominion of New Zealand itself.

VIII

EMPIRE IN THE EAST, 1814–79

Argument: The demands of trade and sea-power established British authority first in the seaports and then in the adjacent territories of Ceylon, Burma, Malaya, Borneo and the China coast. Singapore was the creation of one man who forced the hand of the British government, Sarawak of one man who played a lone hand.

The dynamic of the West broke through the fragile crust of conservatism that protected the old kingdoms of Asia. China and Japan were violated and forced to move with the times. Liberals and Evangelicals set out to reform India on Western lines. Less justifiable were the diplomatic intrigues that led to wars and conquests on the North-West Frontier. British India was integrated by Lord Dalhousie, against whose system the ill-organised spontaneous 'Indian Mutiny' reacted in vain, with the effect only of stiffening the ruling British caste.

1. CEYLON, BURMA, SINGAPORE, SARAWAK

CEYLON

AFTER seizing Ceylon from the Portuguese in 1658 the Dutch had occupied three or four seaports on the coast, but had never penetrated the interior. There were, as there still are, considerable settlements of Europeans and half-castes recruited from both nations at Galle, Colombo and Trincomali. Of these the Dutch element, known as 'burghers', made the deepest mark upon the life of the island. The settlements, under good Dutch laws and a Dutch system of administration, exported cinnamon and pearls.

The cupidity of rival nations was directed towards Ceylon, during the eighteenth-century wars, chiefly on account of the harbour of Trincomali which all strategists remarked upon. Nelson and Wellington had each made note of it. It had been held in turn by Hughes and de Suffren in the seventeen-eighties, and passed to Great Britain at the final cession of the island in 1814. Meanwhile the interior was held by the kings of Kandy who, generation by generation, excelled other oriental tyrants in pride, cruelty, and treachery. This was the island where every prospect pleased but only man was vile. The Dutch left the kings of Kandy alone. The East India Company, on many occasions, tried to come to diplomatic terms with them but were always repulsed with contempt. When they accredited an envoy to Kandy in 1762 he found his representations somewhat hampered by being obliged to approach the King's throne on all fours through a long hall and under a barrier. Prostrate on the ground, he then conveyed his message through four intermediaries to the royal ear. As was usual at such courts intrigue and bribery were the only ways to favour.

The story of the British occupation of Ceylon (1796) has been told in another chapter. Since the island had been occupied by troops of the East India Company it was for three unhappy years subjected to the Madras Presidency. But when the Madras revenue-system proved so unsuited to the customs of Ceylon as to provoke rebellion, it was decided (1798) to convert the island into a Crown Colony on the new model. Accordingly Frederick North, a man of talent and energy, was sent as Governor under the Colonial Office. His domestic policy was liberal and practical. Abandoning the Madras system he won the confidence of the cultivators and enlisted the support of the 'burghers', by restoring Dutch principles of administration and by introducing a specially prepared code of Roman-Dutch law. Externally he engaged his government in disgrace and disaster by intervening in the affairs of the kingdom of Kandy. He supported a candidate for the throne during a palace revolution and, naturally enough as politics went in that country, was cheated by the upstart whom he thought to make his tool. A peculiarly revolting series of treacheries and tortures was concluded by the massacre of a party of British soldiers, isolated at Kandy, who tamely surrendered on promise of their lives (1803). Since war against Napoleon was just then being renewed, no troops were available to avenge the massacre until 1815. The King of Kandy had filled the interval with sadistic acts of cruelty which provide material for bazaar story-tellers to this day. He overreached himself by seizing and mutilating a party of Cingalese merchants who were British subjects and, when a punitive expedition was sent against him, could think of no better means of resistance than by executing the messengers who successively brought news of their approach. His kingdom was overthrown and annexed to the colony of Ceylon. The

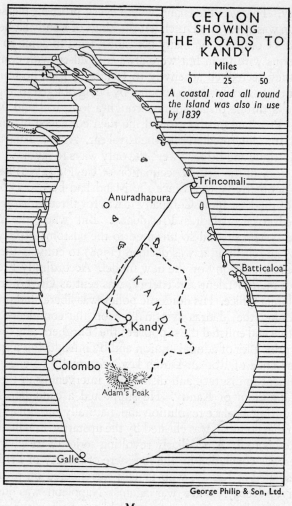

Map 17

forests and hills of the interior were not pacified until 1824, perhaps not securely until the completion of the military road from Colombo to Kandy in 1831 (reinforced by a railway in 1867), since when the political history of the island has been for the most part uneventful.

Among the administrative troubles of the government were some arising out of duties and privileges inherited from the former dynasty. For more than 2000 years the kings of Kandy had enjoyed great temple revenues as guardians of the sacred relic reputed to be Buddha's tooth. These temporalities were now attached to the British government, which for some years received the rents and administered the estates until, in 1844, the Colonial Office repented. 'A Christian administration must not be associated with the practices of an idolatrous religion.' The decision caused much offence in Kandy and led to a local insurrection.

At that time there was also economic unrest in Ceylon. Formerly cinnamon gardens and pearl-fisheries, both coastal industries, had formed all the commercial wealth of the island. Coffee had been introduced in 1836. In the few years before Peel's Free Trade government reduced the protective duties (1845) there was a boom in coffee-planting, in the virgin lands of the kingdom of Kandy. A few British planters moved in, followed by Tamil labourers from the Malabar Coast, to the number of 70,000 in a year. Unrest at this economic revolution, all the more when a slump came in 1846 and 1847, contributed to the outbreak of disorders. Nevertheless plantation coffee (exports to Great Britain were worth £363,000 in 1845, £2,750,000 in 1870) soon became the main source of Ceylon's wealth, while exports of cinnamon declined in quantity and more in quality. Though an increasing acreage of the best coffee-plantations was developed by the skill of British planters a substantial proportion (a third in 1850, a seventh in 1870) was owned by natives of the island. Rice was also cultivated intensively on the coast. The rising standard of living of the cultivators was marked by the increasing imports of foodstuffs and cotton cloth. Tea-planting was begun by the government of Ceylon to save the island from disaster, when, in 1876, a disease of the coffee plant killed off all the plantations. During the eighteen-eighties tea-planting extended and prospered until by the end of the century 390,000 acres of plantations produced, in a year, 146,000,000 lb. of tea. This was a more highly organised industry than coffee-planting. Tea-plantations required British supervision and the investment of £10,000,000.

BURMA

The kings of Ava, the inland part of what is now called Burma, resembled the kings of Kandy. Like most Asiatic rulers their origin was reputed to be divine and their sovereign powers accordingly unquestioned. In general, diplomatic relations were impossible since the Burmese monarch would converse with no one but the ambassador of a heaven-born king and then only if the ambassador first abased himself before the throne. Notwithstanding this arrogance, the Burmese kings were, in diplomatic theory, subject to the Chinese Empire.

In 1823 the King of Ava ordered his armies to march into Bengal and conquer the English, though, it appears, he did not very well know what or where Calcutta might be. Very ill-found expeditions took the field against him, suffering heavy losses from malaria, but there was little fighting. A sea-borne expedition to Rangoon made little progress up the rivers; a column from Manipur failed to penetrate the jungles of Assam; while a third combined operation under command of Captain Marryat, the novelist, led to the capture of the Akyab peninsula. The provinces of Arakan, Manipur and Tenasserim, which were inhabited by jungle tribes, not of Burmese race, were occupied, ceded to the British in 1826, and incorporated into the Presidency of Calcutta.

Prosperity soon came to the Arakan district from the cultivation of rice for the Indian market, which made Akyab the greatest rice-exporting seaport in the world. Administration was, however, bad. Direct government from Calcutta led to alternate neglect and delay, and to niggling interferences with the Resident. (Fanny Burney's brother, Admiral Burney, was the first to hold the office.) No funds and no forces were available to suppress *dacoity*, the form of brigandage which has always flourished when times are bad in Burma. There were no overland communications with India then, or a hundred years later when they were so sorely needed. The roads from the coast to the interior were jungle trails across parallel ranges of wooded mountains. Inland the kings of Ava were as intransigent and truculent as ever.

The second Burmese War broke out in 1852 over disputes between British merchants and the Burmese Governor of Rangoon, a cosmopolitan seaport. Repeated acts of petty tyranny against British citizens led to intervention by the Viceroy, Lord Dalhousie, who was then actively engaged in his policy of annexing misgoverned provinces as though the propriety of British expansion were a Law of Nature. The operations against the southern coast of Burma were carried out, again without meeting serious resistance, by Admiral Austen (Jane Austen's brother); and were followed by the annexation of Rangoon, Martaban, and Pegu. Again the expedition stopped short of invading Burma proper, the inland districts where the Burmese race dwelt. The trade with Rangoon was in hardwoods, and the annexation led to the growth of a prosperous shipbuilding industry at Moulmein. Teak was also exported for building ships on the Clyde.

THE STRAITS SETTLEMENTS

The great island of Sumatra imposed a barrier, a thousand miles long, across the sea-ways to China from the West. Though the Sunda Strait at its southern extremity was commanded by the Dutch port of Batavia, the Malacca Strait at the northern extremity had never been brought completely under Dutch control. The old fort of Malacca, once Portuguese, then Dutch, was declining; its trade with Sumatra dwindled, as the sultans of that island successfully maintained their resistance against commercial or any other progress. As early as 1771 Francis Light, the master of a 'country ship', had approached Warren Hastings with a proposal for a British post at Penang but nothing was done until peace was restored. Intervention in the American War brought no advantage to the Dutch. On the contrary by the treaty of 1784 the Dutch renounced their exclusive claim to the trade of the East Indies. Thereafter for about ninety years there were repeated disputes between the British and Dutch governments, and repeated claims and counter-claims by British and Dutch empire-builders on the spot, before the division of spheres of influence was completed. Sumatra, at first treated as neutral ground on which both nations had some paltry trading-posts, was a contentious region.

In 1785 Francis Light renewed his efforts, making a private treaty with the Sultan of Kedah who ceded him the island of Penang, 'as long the sun and moon should give light' for a pension of 6000 dollars a year.[1] This was a commercial transaction and lovers of the romantic must abandon the old fictitious tale that

---

[1] By a further Treaty in 1800 a strip of coast on the mainland of Kedah, Wellesley Province, was added to Penang and the payment raised to $10,000. Later still, in the general treaty of 1826, another foothold on the coast, known as the Dindings, was ceded to the Company, and was receded to Perak in 1934.

Light received the island as a dowry upon his marriage with the Sultan's daughter. Light then persuaded the acting Governor-General of India, Sir John Macpherson, to take over Penang as a province under the name of Prince of Wales' Island (1786). From the beginning Macpherson proposed that it should be a free port for the trade of all nations. For many years Penang showed a large annual deficit, and was valued chiefly as a naval station. Macpherson refused to be drawn into a defensive alliance with Kedah against the king of Siam, though Francis Light had promised an alliance to the Sultan.

When the Dutch Republic was forced into alliance with the French Jacobins, the rivalry between Dutch and British grew hotter in the Indies. The seizure of the Dutch colonies was more strongly resisted there than in Ceylon or at the Cape where the Orange party favoured a British alliance. Malacca was taken by a British force in 1795, receded at the Peace of Amiens, taken again in 1807 and receded once again after Waterloo. It was the base in 1809 for Lord Minto's hard-fought campaign for the conquest of Java in which Stamford Raffles (1781–1826) made his name as intelligence officer.

The extension of British trade and British sea-power into Malaya was brought about by the personal efforts of far-seeing pioneers and not by acts of policy such as those which led to the occupation of Ceylon and Lower Burma. These acts, though they substituted the rule of law for frantic tyranny, peace for perpetual strife, and wealth for poverty, were somewhat high-handed: but Singapore and Sarawak were occupied by the British without intrusion upon any man's rights. The work of Stamford Raffles and of 'Rajah' Brooke was entirely advantageous to the peoples of the archipelago and to the commerce of the world. Though both men were exposed to the ignorant abuse of partisans in England, both earned the lasting gratitude of the Asiatic nations whom they served.

When Lord Minto found Raffles invaluable, he was appointed administrator of Java, and set himself to mitigate the harshness of Dutch rule. He was a linguist, a student of oriental life, devoted to the Malayan peoples. 'The Malay races', he said, 'when treated with sympathy, are of all eastern peoples, the easiest to rule.' He prohibited the slave trade, regulated the conditions of slavery, abolished forced labour and the legal use of torture and mutilation, and attempted a settlement of the revenue on the Madras system. Like his contemporaries in India he favoured direct administration in European style, failing to appreciate the method of the Dutch which, though severe, was a kind of Indirect Rule. These sudden reforms assumed that Java would remain in British hands and were brought sharply to a close when the Dutch colonies were, in 1814, restored to the kingdom of the Netherlands. Raffles was marked down as a hasty and domineering young man who moved too fast and incurred unjustified expenses. However he was appointed Lieutenant-Governor of Bencoolen, a decayed trading-post in Sumatra, where he continued his researches and studies, in strategy as well as in the natural sciences. He made botanical discoveries and sent home ethnological specimens for the British Museum.

He was convinced, and repeatedly urged his conviction upon the governments in London and Calcutta, that the Dutch 'animosity against British trade was never greater than at this moment', that they were still determined to monopolise the East Indies. The remedy was for the British to occupy some strategic point: 'a port which should have a commanding position at the southern entrance of the Straits of Malacca, in the track of our China and Country trade...which might give us the means of supporting and defending our commercial intercourse with the Malay States, and which...might enable us to watch the march of Dutch policy'. 'There are ports of which we may take possession...and princes at liberty to make treaty with us in favour of our commerce. To the Dutch intimidation of the natives we can oppose protection. To their imposition of heavy duties...we can oppose the facility of obtaining our goods free of duty.'

In 1818 when on a visit to Calcutta, he was encouraged by the Viceroy, Lord Hastings, to pursue his schemes. 'Sir Stamford, you may depend upon me.' This seemed enough. On 30 January 1819 he signed a treaty with the Sultan of Johore for ceding the island of Singapore to the East India Company. 'You have only to glance at the map...', he wrote, 'our station completely outflanks the Straits of Malacca, and secures a passage for our China ships at all times and in all circumstances. It has also been my good fortune to discover one of the most safe and extensive harbours in these seas....' 'What Malta is in the West, that may Singapore become in the East.'

But Raffles's enthusiasm and a hint from Lord Hastings were not enough. The Dutch took deep offence, which even the British Governor of Penang thought well-justified. Each nation accused the other of breaches of the treaties of 1784 and 1814 and with good cause, since the agents of the Dutch Company were at

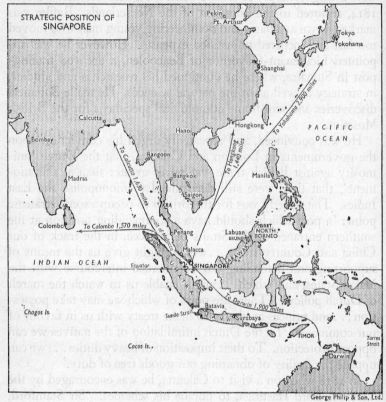

Map 18

least as active as Raffles. The matter was referred to diplomatic negotiation in London which took its leisurely course during the next four years. At this time Canning was much engaged in discussions with the Dutch minister Falck over a wide range of subjects, and noted that

the fault of the Dutch
Was offering too little and asking too much.

However, in 1824 an amicable treaty was signed. The British ceded to the Dutch their factories in Sumatra, the Dutch to the British their factories in India. The Dutch recognised the British claim to Singapore, and both governments agreed to allow no new settlements in the East Indies without authority from Europe. Canning wrote with typical British complacency to Raffles: 'Your extreme activity in stirring up difficult questions...did oblige me to speak my mind to you in instructions of no very mild reprehension. But I was not the less anxious to retain the fruits of your policy....' Raffles had contracted with the Sultan of Johore for the site of a factory and an area within range of a cannon-shot about it. Compounds were to be surveyed for European, Chinese, and Malay inhabitants. The English were to advance money for building 'a respectable mosque' near the Sultan's palace. The town was to be administered jointly by the English Resident and the Sultan's representative. British common law was to be enforced 'with due consideration to the usages and habits of the people'. In return for a final cession of the island the Sultan was paid 60,000 dollars and a pension of 2000 dollars a month. Though the island contained the ruins of an ancient city, the site had been deserted for many hundred years and was, when Raffles came there, uninhabited but for a few families of fishermen and pirates. Raffles had indeed committed the government without their knowledge to the founding of a city which would rival Batavia. Though the chancelleries of Europe were satisfied for the moment, the competition between Dutch and English empire-builders never slackened in the East.

The founder of Singapore returned to England in 1824 still a young man of forty-three and full of restless energy. On the way he lost, by shipwreck, his savings and his ethnological collections. His reward for service was to be presented by the East India Directors with a bill for £20,000 which he had overspent in their interest. The last two years of his short life, for he died in 1826, were devoted to the encouragement of foreign missions and, as first President of the Zoological Society, to the foundation of the London Zoo.

When Raffles left Singapore the population was said to be about 10,000, including many Chinese merchants. From its foundation it was a free port open to the trade of all nations, a new feature in the political economy of Asia. The slave trade, slavery,

and even debt-slavery, the oppressive Malayan system that enabled a creditor to seize the person of his debtor, had been abolished. It had been Raffles' intention to administer his city on
English rather than on Indian principles and to associate the mercantile community with the government. Merchants had already
been commissioned as Justices of the Peace. But, in 1826, when
the government of the three 'Straits Settlements', Singapore,
Malacca and Penang, was organised by the East India Company
and the last holdings in Sumatra were surrendered to the Dutch,
a change took place for the worse.

After they had lost their monopoly of the China tea-trade, in
1833, the East India Company lost interest in the Far East. These
outposts, with their Malayan peasantry and Chinese townsfolk, had
little in common with Bengal and brought it no advantage. Malacca,
once a rich city and for centuries the outlet for the trade of Sumatra,
was now cut off from that trade and dwindled in importance. By
contrast no mere neglect could stop the port of Singapore from
growing, so long as there was free trade. In 1832 the population
was returned as 22,000 including 91 European men, 28 European
women and 8500 Chinese. About 5000 Chinese arrived annually
to disperse themselves throughout Malaya and, in 1832, 420 full-
rigged ships aggregating to 120,000 tons cleared the port, carrying
a trade worth over £3,000,000. Thirty years later the population
was 90,000. But no thanks were due to the East India Company.

Penang, after a brief appearance as a separate Presidency
(1804–5) when it had been the base of naval operations, also sank
into obscurity. No progress was possible outside the British and
Dutch seaports in the East Indies until there was common
security for life and property. Throughout the archipelago all the
sea-ways were infested by Malay and Dyak pirates, whose swift
prahus could outsail most merchantmen and many warships. The
war against the pirates, a concern for the Admiralty, not the East
India House, was the chief British activity in the Straits Settlements. It was this that brought James Brooke as a volunteer to
Sarawak. Only steamships could solve the problem and steam
required coaling-stations. In 1844, reports of coal in the island of
Labuan led the Admiralty to take it over as a naval station for refitting and refuelling ships, by treaty with the Sultan of Brunei.
The measures against piracy had become effective by about 1852
when the sea-ways through Malaya were reported clear.

SARAWAK

Sir James Brooke (1803–68) of Sarawak, though a mere gentle-man-adventurer, did more good than most of his contemporaries. Having fought gallantly as a young soldier in the first Burmese War, and spent some roving years, he returned home to inherit a fortune which enabled him to indulge his fancy for voyaging. He loaded his own schooner, the *Royalist*, with trade goods and set sail for Singapore (1838), where he heard tales of the archipelago which fired his curiosity. Most of the larger islands were ruled by Moslem sultans, and inhabited by simple aboriginals. The *Dyaks* of Borneo, for example, were dark-skinned savages, living com-munally in huge thatched huts raised on piles above the tidewater, each hut housing a whole clan. They were so easily at home in the water as to be almost amphibious. Their chief occupation, their sport, their religion was head-hunting. Their rulers, the Malay in-habitants of the larger settlements, lived by slave-raiding. Beside the more or less legitimate sultanates were many villages of mere pirates recruited from Dyak head-hunters and Malay slavers in-discriminately.

The Sultan of Kuching eagerly fastened upon Brooke, asking his advice about Dutch and English strength. The English from Singapore sought trade, the Dutch forbade him to engage in it. 'Which was the cat and which the rat?' Brooke was at first un-willing to take part in Malay politics but, when begged to assist a vassal of the Sultan against a usurper, he reluctantly agreed to make a demonstration. The mere sight of a body of English sea-men was enough to put the usurper's men to rout. Brooke made himself so useful that the Sultan invited him to become Rajah of the subordinate state of Sarawak. 'The principal people were assembled and the agreement being read to them, the Raja in-formed them that henceforth I was to hold the government. I expounded my principles, and really I believe they were well pleased. We had great firings and rejoicings' (29 September 1841). But neither Malay landlords nor pirate chiefs rejoiced so heartily when they discovered that Brooke really meant to enforce even-handed justice and preserve the peace. He protected the cultivators against oppression and began to wage war against the pirates. 'What', said one pirate chief when tried and found guilty, 'am I to be put to death only for killing a few Chinamen?'

To change the character of two nations was no light task. 'I work like a galley-slave,' he wrote, 'I fight like a common soldier, the poorest man in England might grumble at my diet, luxuries I have none, necessities are often deficient. I am separated from civilised life and educated men.... Could money tempt a man to this?'

His campaign against the pirates drew the sympathy of the naval officers at Singapore, who on two or three occasions sent warships to help him, so that some degree of regularity was gradually given to his position. In 1847 he returned to England for a visit, was knighted, and was appointed Consul-General for North Borneo. Protests from the Dutch, that his activities were a breach of the treaty of 1824, were rebutted by the government.

When Brooke returned to Sarawak in 1848, he had to fight harder than before against new pirate bands which had arisen during his absence. He was not helped by an agitation worked up against him by a dishonest assistant, who denounced him to the Aborigines Protection Society. 'He had gone out as a private adventurer, had seized a territory as large as Yorkshire, and then drove out the natives. Under pretence that they were pirates, he subsequently sent for our fleet to massacre them.' His career was so odd that a Parliamentary enquiry was reasonable, but commissioners, who sat for three months at Singapore, abandoned further enquiry when they failed to find any evidence that was not entirely in Brooke's favour. He had pacified all the coast of North Borneo under legitimate authority and without incurring expense to the British government. The true test of his beneficence was that the population of Sarawak had more than doubled in ten years.

In 1857 he retired to England, hoping to persuade the government to give recognition to his rule over Sarawak. This proved so difficult a task that in despair he even offered the territory to France, but at last, in 1864, he achieved his end. His nephew succeeded as Rajah under British protection and founded the dynasty which ruled unchallenged until 1941.

2. WARS WITH CHINA, 1833–60

EAST of Suez most kingdoms were exclusive; they went further than the empires of the West, which endeavoured to monopolise trade, by endeavouring to close their frontiers absolutely against all contacts with the outer world. In Japan, from 1638 to 1853, the exclusion was complete, and in other kingdoms would have been so if the kings had been masters of their own frontiers. To these balanced societies with their self-sufficient economy, the very idea of progress, if it ever occurred to men's minds, was abhorrent. All changes, all *novae res*, were alike undesirable. Undoubtedly the universal belief in the Divinity of Kings contributed to this conservatism. The physical and moral order of society depended upon the rites of kingship so that aliens who would not submit to the system were indeed 'foreign devils'.

Hast thou not signed a decree that every man that shall ask a petition of any God or man...save of thee, O king, shall be cast into the den of lions? The king answered and said, The thing is true, according to the law of the Medes and the Persians, which altereth not.

Until the nineteenth century the kings of the East were able as a rule, to maintain their inviolability. Then there burst in upon them an influx of foreign devils: the British being the most powerful owing to their ubiquitous navy; the Americans, the Dutch, the French not far behind; the Russians and the Germans following. All alike were innovators, despisers of authority, anxious to turn the world upside-down. All demanded, as if they had a moral right to it, access for traders, access for missionaries, access for diplomats who scorned to perform the *kow-tow* and blasphemously insisted upon coming as equals before the thrones of the Divine Kings.

Rightly or wrongly, the energy of the Western nations prevailed. When once the frontiers were pierced, when Western traders, or missionaries, infiltrated into the forbidden lands, no power on earth could stop the disintegration of the old rigid societies. Whether the penetration was economical or ideological or military, the destructive effect was the same. The old way of life could not be maintained, the new culture must replace the old.

After a hundred years the process is almost complete, though two small and inaccessible countries, Tibet and Nepal, have still

(1949) resisted infiltration. Among those which have dissolved and recrystallised, no sentimental regrets need be wasted upon such bloodstained anachronisms as the kingdom of Kandy, nor upon Japan, which was adjusted to the new age with such shocking efficiency. The great drama is the dissolution of the Chinese Empire which, since the T'ang dynasty in the seventh century A.D., had sheltered one-quarter of the human race, in a rigid constitutional frame, under the rule of the 'Son of Heaven'. The peoples of the river valleys of China were cut off from the rest of the world, on the north and west by mountains and deserts, on the south and east by seas and by the tributary kingdoms of Korea, Annam, Siam, Burma and Tibet. When the Empire lost its protective crust of tributary states it was soon infested with the seeds of decay. The emperors knew little of the outer world and saw little good in knowing more, since the 'foreign devils' were, throughout the period, inferior to the Chinese in most of the arts of life. After resisting, with a fair measure of success, the encroachments of traders and diplomats, the crystalline structure of Chinese life was dissolved by an even more powerful solvent, the influence of Protestant Christianity.

The East India Company never succeeded in establishing diplomatic relations with the emperors of China. Like the traders of other nations the Company's servants were held off at arm's length, and were admitted (see chapter III, 7, page 187), on sufferance only, to a temporary foothold at Canton. Though officially treated with contempt by Chinese governors, they were actually received on friendly terms by the Canton guild of exporting merchants, known as the 'Hong'. The Chinese government reluctantly allowed its merchants a restricted commerce with the 'foreign devils', only on condition that they remained in isolation, outside the Chinese system of law and administration. It will be seen that this is a variant from the Moslem custom of permitting to foreign traders a right of local self-government by 'capitulation'.

In spite of these humiliations, the Company's servants were comfortable and prosperous at Canton. They found the Hong merchants, who were no less anxious to sell tea than the British were to buy it, so businesslike as to give the Chinese people a lasting reputation with the nation of shopkeepers as good customers when their national characteristics were understood. The

Plate 17

SIR STAMFORD RAFFLES (1781–1826)

The founder of Singapore. From a painting by G. F. Joseph, dated 1817.
See p. 408.

Plate 18

'RAJAH' BROOKE (1803–68)

From a painting by Sir F. Grant dated 1847. *See p. 413.*

Chinese government imposed a tax of 6% on all dealings with the foreigner, allotting the proceeds to a fund from which bad debts incurred by their own merchants were paid. The difficulty was to find a way of balancing the trade, since the Chinese desired little in the way of British goods. As an alternative to paying for the tea in coined silver, the Company (in 1773) hit upon the unlucky device

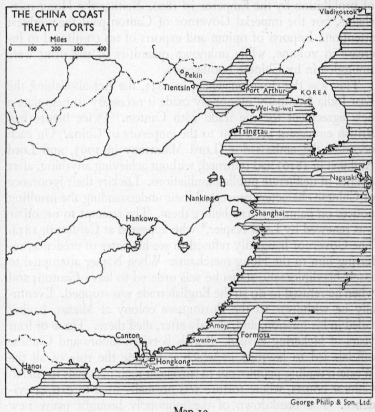

THE CHINA COAST
TREATY PORTS

Miles
0   100   200   300   400

Vladivostok

Pekin
Tientsin
Port Arthur
Wei-hai-wei
KOREA
Tsingtau
Nagasaki
Nanking
Shanghai
Hankow
Canton
Amoy
Formosa
Swatow
Hanoi
Hongkong

George Philip & Son, Ltd.

Map 19

of importing opium from Bengal to China, thus fixing the trade in drugs upon both countries. The use and abuse of drugs, though almost unknown in the West, was widely spread in the East; eighteenth-century traders were not likely to have been squeamish about dealing in it, even if a moral objection had been raised, but at first there was none. Country traders, Portuguese from Macao, Americans and Dutch, joined freely in importing opium from

Turkey and Persia as well as from Bengal; but the British, owing to their firm trading connexions at Canton, had the best of the market. A new method, introduced from the Dutch Indies, of smoking opium as a habitual indulgence, instead of occasionally eating it as a remedy against fatigue or hunger, began to fasten itself as a national vice upon the Chinese, and provoked an edict of prohibition by the Emperor in 1800. Neither the Hong merchants, nor the imperial Governor of Canton paid the slightest attention. Imports of opium and exports of tea continued to increase in volume, while unknown quantities of the drug were smuggled in by Chinese bootleggers.

This was the situation when, in 1833, the Act abolishing the East India Company monopoly made it necessary to negotiate a new agreement for the trade with Canton. Twice before had British embassies been sent to the emperors of China. On each occasion the ambassador (Lord Macartney in 1793, and Lord Amherst in 1816) had returned, without achieving anything, after a series of deliberate public humiliations. Luckily their ignorance of Chinese characters prevented their understanding the insulting notices on banners borne before them. The attempt to negotiate was renewed by Lord Napier,[1] who appeared at Canton in 1834. The Governor haughtily refused to see his letter of credence, referring him to the Hong merchants. When Napier attempted to assert his diplomatic status he was ordered to leave Canton; and when he refused to do so the English trade was stopped. Eventually he withdrew to the Portuguese colony at Macao, having failed in his mission, and, shortly after, died there. Three or four years of bickering ensued. Brawls between sailors and Chinese officials led to lawsuits in which it became the rule of all the Western trading peoples not to surrender their nationals to trial in Chinese courts, where torture was normally used to extract evidence. The breakdown of the monopoly brought many new dealers into the trade, largely Americans, whose fast clipper-built ships were, at this time, getting supremacy at sea. Napier's successor, Sir C. Elliott, though acting for the British only, assisted all the 'foreign devils' by the presence of a British naval squadron which lay in the sheltered anchorage behind the uninhabited island of Hong Kong, at the mouth of the Canton River. Quar-

[1] William, 8th Lord Napier (1786–1834), not one of the celebrated Napier brothers.

rels about jurisdiction and prestige did not prevent an increase in the exchange of opium for tea. Elliott's reports stimulated Palmerston to insist upon a new settlement, but the ministry was so bitterly opposed in parliament that they could secure a majority of only nine votes for their Chinese policy.

In 1838 the Emperor sent a new Governor to Canton to root out the opium trade. Without warning he shut up the British merchants in their factory, seized the stock—20,000 cases of opium, worth more than £2,000,000—and destroyed it without compensation. After repeated attempts at compromise and repeated snubs from the Chinese Governor, Elliott broke off negotiations and returned to Macao. A final breach was made when a fleet of Chinese junks demanded the surrender of some British sailors for trial in a Chinese court. Attempting to seize the men by force, they were fired upon by two British warships at Hong Kong. In February 1840 the British were formally excluded from the trade of Canton, and retaliated by blockading the port. Thus began what has been called the 'Opium War', a shabby business indeed, but not half so disreputable as the enemies of Britain have represented. The cause was not British determination to import the drug, but a blank refusal on the part of the Chinese government to meet other governments on terms of equality, to discuss informally, to negotiate officially, to make binding agreements on commercial matters, or to admit that 'foreign devils' had any rights whatsoever.

A brigade of British troops from India, under Hugh Gough, operated with naval support along the coast (August 1841–June 1842), forcing the surrender of successive towns. Wellington, the oracle, described the skill with which these combined operations were conducted as 'unparalleled'. When the force sailed up the Yang-tse to Nanking, the southern capital, Chinese intransigence gave way. Three imperial commissioners were sent to sue for peace on the deck of a British warship. For centuries the Chinese had made no agreements with the outside world save in the form of 'unequal treaties', the other contracting party being obliged to accept what the Chinese contemptuously offered through subordinates. The Treaty of Nanking, 1842, between the Chinese Emperor and the Queen of Great Britain, was the first of a series of 'unequal treaties' biased in the other direction. It was described as a treaty of 'peace and friendship' and might have merited the description if it had been interpreted with goodwill on either side, since the principle of friendly negotiation was admitted. In fact it inaugurated a long contest between the European powers for commercial and strategic advantages, each tending to weaken the authority of the Chinese Emperor. The Chinese agreed to pay an indemnity of about £5,000,000 for damages at Canton, and ceded the island of Hong Kong to Great Britain. They admitted European traders to five 'Treaty' ports (Canton, Amoy, Foochow, Ningpo, Shanghai), and granted foreigners in those ports the right of trial in their own consular courts, the rule of 'extra-territoriality'. A supplementary treaty also contained a clause granting, in advance, to Great Britain any advantages which might thereafter be granted by treaty to any more-favoured nation. France and the United States (whose government had heartily supported the British action) were not slow to negotiate similar treaties, each demanding the 'most-favoured-nation' clause, a perpetual stimulus to competitive encroachment; and other nations followed. As an American historian has written: 'The nationals of countries which did not resort to war with China enjoyed all the privileges of the countries which assumed the burden of war and Chinese resentment.' The resumed opium trade trebled in volume during the next twenty years, though still, from the point of view of Pekin, a trade in contraband goods.

Since this illegitimate trade was conducted by connivance with corrupt officials beyond the reach of the Emperor's feeble grasp, since the Treaty Ports were invaded by unruly foreigners who were hated the more for their extra-territorial privileges, since each of the foreign nations was always on the watch for claims to be advanced under the most-favoured-nation clause, relations between provincial governors and 'foreign devils' steadily deteriorated. The success of the British in the 'Opium War' led to what was called the 'gunboat policy'. A show of force, even the bombardment of a Chinese town by light naval craft which could penetrate the navigable rivers, proved the simplest way to intimidate a truculent governor. Such warlike acts might be undertaken without reference to Europe and without fear of Pekin.

Among the Western nations, the Americans have the best diplomatic record in the Far East. They claimed extra-territorial rights, enjoyed most-favoured-nation treatment, and smuggled opium, but always urged moderation. They deplored the 'gunboat policy', and until the end of the century annexed no territory in the East. On the other hand they sent Protestant missions to China at an early date (1830), introducing the ferment of liberal democracy through the channel of the mission schools.

The French, whose policy was more aggressive even than that of the British in the 'forties and 'fifties, came into the field as champions of the Roman Catholic missions, which had been established in China since the sixteenth century. In 1845 they persuaded the Emperor to issue an edict granting, though in vague terms, a general toleration to Christians. Thereafter missionary influence flourished, and their extra-territorial rights in remote inland provinces became a fruitful source of conflict.

Chinese good sense and Western adaptability combined, at the Treaty Ports, to set local government and commerce upon a business footing, especially at Shanghai. It was British enterprise that established the Foreign Settlement in 1845, as a quarter of the town where the consular courts of the Treaty Powers held exclusive jurisdiction. Four years later the French obtained a concession for a similar quarter, for their own nationals only. When, in 1854, a minor rebellion put the Chinese administration to flight, an improvised Board was set up by Chinese and foreign merchants to control the customs. Since in efficiency and honesty it was so far superior to the official establishment as to render a much larger revenue to Pekin, the Board was extended to cover all the ports, after the suppression of the rebellion. In 1863, Robert Hart, a servant of the Board, became Inspector-general of the Chinese Customs Service, the one branch of the imperial administration which remained efficient through all the revolutions of Chinese affairs until the Japanese invasion in 1937. The Foreign Settlement at Shanghai prospered and attracted population by its honest government. Similarly the rocky island of Hong Kong soon became a thriving city, with suburbs on the adjacent mainland.

Hong Kong, Singapore, Bombay, three of the world's great cities, are alike tributes to the blessings of British rule. Each of the three was an almost uninhabited island until developed by British industry; each was also an island in a sea of anarchy. The oppressed peoples of the neighbouring mainlands flocked to enjoy, under the British flag, the security, the justice and the equal laws which their own governments were unable or unwilling to provide. Each of the three islands was acquired by treaty without injury to any earlier inhabitants, and there is no reason to suppose that any of the three cities would be more than a village to-day if the British had not made it so.

While the Treaty Ports prospered, inland China was collapsing. All the southern provinces were scourged by the Taiping rebellion, which brought slaughter and famine behind it. A fanatic and mystic, who had been baptised by an American missionary, proclaimed himself a Messiah, born to establish the Kingdom of Heaven in China. At first the missionaries regarded him with some favour as a reformer until he raised mercenary armies, over-threw the government of provinces, and massacred the inhabitants of cities. He captured Nanking in 1853, with much bloodshed. Chinese civil servants, rotten with venality and sloth, and drugged with opium, could not cope with the Taiping fanatics; Chinese soldiers, miserably equipped members of a despised profession, could make no stand. The harassed Emperor lost province after province to the rebels while, in the same years, the British were encroaching upon his tributary kingdom of Burma (1852), and the French upon his tributary kingdom of Annam (1858).

To add to these troubles the Western powers renewed their pressure for further trading and diplomatic privileges. The French produced a list of grievances culminating in the murder of a French missionary priest, while Palmerston called upon the House of Commons for action against China on twenty-two distinct counts, the most serious being the seizure of the British ship *Arrow*. An official named Yeh, the imperial Commissioner at Canton, had thrown the British captain and Chinese crew into prison where several of them died. The state of the Chinese prisons was the only genuine grievance, for the case against the *Arrow* was justified. Palmerston's aggressive patriotism was then potent in British party politics, as he well understood. Public indignation against Commissioner Yeh, who actually behaved with dignified propriety but whom *Punch* made into a slightly comic ogre, helped to put 'Pam' in office with a larger majority after the election of 1857, and precipitated the second China War. Lord Elgin and a French colleague were sent to present demands to the court of Pekin. 'Fifty-seven was the Mutiny year. Though Canton was blockaded by the Navy, the troops designed for China had to be diverted to India, so that it was not until 'fifty-eight that military pressure could be applied. Like the first war, this was a struggle for prestige, correctly summed up in Sir F. H. Doyle's celebrated verses upon the *Private of the Buffs*, who was taken prisoner when drunk and executed out of hand near Canton, for refusing to perform the kow-tow. He too, like the Great Earl of Elgin, was Britain's ambassador. 'Let dusky Indians whine and kneel, an English lad must die.' Though ignorant, rude and drunken, 'he only knows that not through him shall England come to shame'.

Canton was again occupied by British troops and Commissioner Yeh carried off to exile in India. But the state of China was so chaotic that, while these operations were taking place in the south, the foreigners at Shanghai in central China were organising the imperial campaign against the Taipings, and in the north Elgin and his French colleague were attempting to negotiate with Pekin. They demanded the establishment of permanent legations at the Emperor's court; extra-territorial rights for Europeans, wherever they might be; a guaranteed toleration for all Christians whether Chinese or foreign; and more Treaty Ports.

The British contention upon the opium question was that it was useless and unjust to attempt to prevent the drug habit by legislative action against a single foreign source of supply, when much opium was home-grown, and more smuggled through other channels not protected by commercial treaties. The Chinese must begin by internal reforms, by stopping the demand and disciplining the corrupt officials who openly encouraged the trade. It was the American envoy who proposed a new solution to the opium problem, that the trade should be regulated, not ineffectually prohibited. This proposal was accepted, with the consequence that the opium trade became legal. Since administrative reforms did not follow, no action was taken for many years to decrease the consumption of the drug, or the demand for it.

It may be convenient to recapitulate here the later history of the opium trade between India and China. An agitation against opium-smoking was begun in 1906 by missionaries in China, backed by the new Liberal majority in the British House of Commons. The Chinese government then undertook to restrict the sale of opium to the addicts and to prevent the further extension of the habit. Cultivation of the opium poppy in China was to be reduced by one-tenth every year, so that the country would be ready for prohibition in ten years' time. The Indian government immediately concurred in reducing the export of opium to China by one-tenth annually. Such great progress was made in suppressing the habit that the Indian government was able to put an end to the trade in 1913, four years earlier than was expected, a serious loss to the Indian revenue. When the Japanese invaded Manchuria in 1931 one of their first actions was to restore and encourage the growth of the opium poppy, with the deliberate intention of debauching the Chinese population.

Though a treaty had been negotiated at Tientsin in December 1858 the representatives of the powers were determined that, as a matter of prestige, it should be ratified at the Emperor's court. This led to further diplomatic bickering throughout 1859, and to renewal of the war. The Chinese barred the approach to Pekin by strengthening the Taku Forts at the mouth of the Peiho River. Naval squadrons then forced an entrance after bombarding the forts; and despatched a small mixed expedition to occupy Pekin (August 1860). This was the occasion when the American Commodore Vatnall, though commanding a neutral squadron, cheerfully joined in the action with the words, 'blood is thicker than water'.

The Emperor fled from his capital, taking with him as hostages the British consul, Sir H. S. Parkes and other British and American diplomats. All were ill-used and some died, which added to the indignation of the Treaty Powers. Accordingly, as a reprisal, Elgin ordered the destruction of the Emperor's Summer Palace, a piece of architecture built to the plans of French Jesuit architects during the eighteenth century, in the Chinese Rococo style which was not fashionable in 1850.

The Emperor was forced to submit to the treaty, although the price of submission had risen still higher. Tientsin itself, the harbour of Pekin, became a Treaty Port, to ensure access for the Powers to the fortified legation quarter which they established at Pekin. The British colony at Hong Kong was enlarged by the cession of the mainland suburb of Kowloon. The Powers also exacted a large indemnity. It is worth noting that the Americans afterwards restored a large part of their share.

China was now 'open', and was ready for reconstruction. An

American officer was employed to organise measures against the Taipings, with success until he was killed in action. His place was taken, in 1863, by Colonel Charles Gordon, R.E., who suppressed the rebellion. In the same year, Robert Hart became Inspector-general of the Chinese Customs Service. China now entered upon a new phase of history. The powers vied with one another, all in turn using the most-favoured-nation clause to extend their spheres of influence and to get railway contracts for their nationals. Missionaries penetrated deeper, protected by extra-territoriality, spreading belief in Western education and distrust of the age-old Chinese learning, the path to promotion in the Imperial Service. The more the Treaty Ports prospered, the greater the unrest in the unexploited provinces. But the new culture was anarchic, giving no impetus to constructive reform at the Emperor's court.

Very different was the history of Japan. During the years of exclusion, the Dutch (like the British at Canton) had been allowed to visit Nagasaki for a restricted trade under humiliating conditions. As in China so in Japan, several attempts by Western nations to accredit ambassadors had been rudely repulsed. In 1853 the barrier was broken by an American naval mission under Commodore Perry, who scrupulously avoided the use or even the threat of force. A coaling-station on the way to China, and a promise of commonly humane treatment for shipwrecked American sailors were his first objectives. By tact and firmness he extracted from the Shogun, the hereditary vizier who then ruled Japan, a Treaty Port and a most-favoured-nation treaty. The Dutch followed with similar demands. Since the Crimean War was then being fought, the Russian and British naval squadrons in the East were deeply concerned, and each negotiated a similar treaty with Japan in the hope of scoring off the other. When commercial relations were established, the Treaty Powers were surprised to find that the Shogun was not the sovereign of Japan. There was in the background a concealed Divine Emperor, the Mikado, whose courtiers were bitterly hostile to the 'foreign devils'. Many incidents occurred in which the hired bullies of the conservative nobility murdered unarmed traders who relied on treaty-rights. Against the wishes of the American government the 'gunboat policy' was used against Japan. In 1864 a combined squadron, in-

cluding an American ship, bombarded the naval port of Shimonoseki. The sufferer in the contest was the Shogun who lost face
with the imperial court, by submitting to the Western Powers
when they demanded an indemnity for the murders. A new
Mikado, Mutsuhito, who had just ascended the throne (1868),
took advantage of the situation, to resume the royal power which
the Shogun had misused and to treat with the Western powers for
his own advantage. These were no 'unequal' treaties. There
would be no opium trade, no special privileges for missionaries,
no loopholes through which 'foreign devils' could creep to disrupt the Japanese economy; but unlimited trade, so that the
Mikado's men could buy such weapons as had trounced the
Shogun at Shimonoseki.

3. BRITISH SOCIAL REFORMS IN INDIA, 1813–56

WHEN the charter of the East India Company had come before
the House of Commons for renewal in 1793 an effort had been
made by Wilberforce to authorise the foundation of Protestant
missions to India, but in vain. The interest of the Company was
opposed to any such disturbing factor; their policy was to protect
the laws and customs of their Indian subjects. Behind Wilberforce
stood Charles Grant, an Evangelical, lately returned from the
Company's service and now devoted to the uplifting of the
peoples of the East. Pushing his interest in Leadenhall Street he
became a Director and returned to the charge when the charter
was again to be renewed for a second period of twenty years. By
1813 the two causes of evangelicalism and free trade had prospered, with the result that the power of the Company over the
moral and material welfare of India was whittled away. No longer
had the Directors a monopoly over the trade between England
and India, but all British citizens, and accordingly the missionaries,
were at last admitted freely to any of the Company's ports.
Furthermore the Governor-General was authorised to apply some
part of his funds to the promotion of learning in British India.
Christian missions and Western education in India, trace their
origin to the charter of 1813, though they had some earlier
foundations to build upon.

Round the coasts of India there had long been Christian settlements of various kinds: Portuguese Catholic missions which the English still regarded with suspicion and even hostility in the early nineteenth century; remnants of the ancient Churches of the East, known as Syrian Christians, on the Malabar Coast; and even a few evangelical Protestant missions which had infiltrated where the Company could not prevent them. Lutheran Protestants had been working for a century at the small Danish[1] factory of Serampur, sixteen miles from Calcutta, chiefly among the Eurasians. In 1793 an English Baptist named William Carey had gone alone as a missionary to Bengal. After rebuffs from the Company he settled at Serampur where he exhibited a talent for Church organisation, founding schools for Eurasian and native children, translating the Scriptures into vernacular versions which he printed and distributed, and conducting his mission so economically that it paid its way. He received help and encouragement, unofficially, from Lord Wellesley.

All that the Company had done for Christianity was to provide English chaplains at its own factories and when, in the new age of religious revival, an English bishopric at Calcutta was founded, the bishop's status was that of a chaplain-general subordinated on the one hand to the Governor-General and on the other to the Archbishop of Canterbury. Though all the missionary societies had combined in urging his appointment, the government did not send him abroad with a general mission to convert the Hindus. The first bishop, Thomas Middleton, was not able to do more than found some Mission schools around Calcutta. The second bishop, Reginald Heber (1783–1826), the author of the missionary hymns and of an account of travels in India which was widely read, made a great impression as an ecclesiastical statesman and as a pastor. He was much concerned with uniting the efforts of all the Protestant bodies and with bringing the Syrian Christian Churches into communion with them. The evangelising of India, or at least of the low-caste Hindus and the outcaste peoples, began to be spoken of as a possibility. As in other parts of the Empire the mission schools had an effect which extended far beyond the ranks of their converts.

A parallel movement in secular education began with the foundation of the Presidency College in Calcutta by David Hare, a

[1] Serampur was sold to Great Britain by Denmark in 1845.

free-thinking English tradesman, and Ram Mohan Roy, a learned Brahmin (1823). The Presidency College was the source of the flood of Western liberal ideas which has so profoundly changed the intellectual life of India. Ram Mohan Roy (1772–1833) was the first Brahmin scholar to be deeply versed in European languages and culture. A man of saintly life and sincere wisdom, he desired, as the dilettante Mogul emperors had desired, to make a synthesis of Eastern and Western thought, to reject the superstitious beliefs and vicious practices which had accrued to Brahminism, and so to regenerate the life of India. In 1833 he died while on a visit to England, where he had been received with honour and had given evidence before a committee of the House of Commons.

The arrival of Bentinck as Governor-General in 1828 implied that government would now begin to liberalise the laws and institutions of the Indian peoples. Lord William Bentinck (1772–1839) was a specimen of that characteristically English type, the aristocratic Radical; he combined liberal principles with a despotic temper. When he came to Calcutta, he had long experience of war, diplomacy and administration. He had been a soldier, and a martinet. Twenty years earlier, in Madras, his enforcement of the *minutiae* of military parade had been a principal cause of the Sepoy mutiny at Vellore. He commanded a division in Spain under Wellington who had a low opinion of his judgment and capacity, yet he was advanced to higher command. He conducted an invasion of Sicily and was responsible for providing the island with the stillborn parliamentary constitution of 1812. In Sicily, as afterwards in Bengal, Bentinck was remembered as the patron of liberty. He returned to the East pledged to 'found British greatness upon Indian happiness'.

The first part of his term of office was occupied with a firm consistent campaign against cruelty and oppression. He found himself obliged, much against his will, to take over the administration of two provinces in the south which were misgoverned by their protected native rulers. Of these two, Coorg remained part of the Madras Presidency, while Mysore, after fifty years of British rule, was restored in 1881 to its historic dynasty. Bentinck also forbade the internal trade in slaves in India, though the status of slavery was not abolished until 1862. The censorship of the press was discontinued in 1836.

Since time out of mind the peoples of India had suffered—and suffered almost willingly—from the misdeeds of the *thugs*, a sect whose cult of the hideous goddess Kali defies Western credulity. They were a secret society who worked in gangs to provide themselves with victims for human sacrifice. Having ingratiated themselves with solitary travellers, they lured them into lonely situations, and murdered them, with no other motive than religion, of the kind that is so potent to persuade men to do evil. Fear and superstition and perjury combined to render conviction for *thuggee* almost unobtainable in the courts. The *thugs* were sought out and hunted down by the long and patient efforts of Colonel William Sleeman, though they cannot be said to have been completely extirpated.

Almost more horrible because so widely spread and widely approved was the Hindu custom of *suttee* or widow-burning, which was no part of the pure religion of the original Aryans, but an older superstition prevalent among many primitive races. Perversely, the exalted view of the marriage vow taken by caste Hindus led to the incorporation of this vile custom into the Hindu religion. It was a pious duty, and a duty often joyfully embraced, for a widow to reunite herself with her lost husband, through the fire. The propriety of such behaviour was hotly defended by the consensus of Brahmin opinion, and would have been capable of defence on grounds not quite irrational if the custom had been confined to voluntary suicides. But the effect of another anti-social custom, child-marriage, deprived the defenders of *suttee* of what rags of decency they affected to shelter behind. A large proportion of the sacrificed widows were girl-children thrust into the flames before crowds of sightseers who assembled to gloat over the spectacle. Europeans since first they came to India, had protested against *suttee* and occasionally interfered to protect the victims. Job Charnock, the founder of Calcutta, is said to have married a Hindu widow whom he had rescued from the fire. But the politic necessity of respecting Indian religious rites had prevented British governors from putting an end to this practice.

The early Protestant missionaries, especially William Carey, had set themselves to force the issue. They remonstrated with organisers of *suttee*, usually in vain, begged mercy for involuntary victims and tried to dissuade volunteers. The British generation that abolished slavery was horrified at the revelation that little girls were burned alive by hundreds annually in British India; but the Governor-General was placed in a dilemma which has reappeared a dozen times in the history of Christianity. He was pledged as an enlightened ruler to respect the laws and customs of the Indian people, but equally pledged as a civilised man and a Christian to protect the helpless from cruel oppressors. What if cruelty to children were a religious rite held in great honour? Even Ram Mohan Roy, who denounced *suttee* in his teaching, thought its legal prohibition unwise. Lord William Bentinck made the decision, in 1829, to prohibit the practice of *suttee* by law, declaring all 'abettors in the act guilty of culpable homicide'. The abolition caused a wave of resentment among the more devout and conservative Hindus. Sir Charles Napier met the objections of the Brahmins of Sind with characteristic plainness. 'You say *suttee* is the custom. Well, we too have a custom which is to hang men who burn women alive. You build your funeral pyre and I will build a gallows beside it, and let each of us act according to custom.'

It is doubtful whether Bentinck won much gratitude, even from the Hindu women whose lives he saved, since they had been taught to regard *suttee* as a heroic duty which might fall to their lot, such a chance as human beings often face with equanimity. As with the slaves who were set free, so with the young widows whose lives were saved, the act of philanthropy produced a new problem, of providing for the released unfortunates. Since the abolition of *suttee*, the fate of the despised widows, deprived of martyrdom and left without social status, has been the shame of India.

In 1833 the charter of the East India Company came up to be renewed for a fourth period. The renewal followed upon the passing of the Great Reform Bill and was inspired by the principles of the new age. Respect for its 200 years of history preserved the Company, as yet, from dissolution but not from drastic reconstruction. It now entirely ceased to be a trading company. The last relic of the old commercial days, the monopoly at Canton was swept away with its perquisites, leaving the Directors as an auxiliary organ of the British government, in modern phrase a Public Utility, which undertook to rule British India by contract, under supervision of the Board of Control in Whitehall. The principles of Free Trade, invoked to condemn the monopoly, were based upon the secure right of private property, and therefore afforded no threat to the Proprietors, the holders of the gilt-edged East India stock. A guaranteed 10% dividend on every share of the nominal value of one hundred guineas was made a first charge upon the revenue. On the other hand public control was strengthened by an increase in the authority of the Governor, who was henceforward designated Governor-General of India. Bentinck during the two last years of his term, was the first to whom the title properly belonged.

The new charter contained the memorable words: 'No native of the said territories or any natural-born subject of His Majesty resident therein, shall by reason only of his religion, place of birth, descent, colour or any of them, be disabled from holding any place, office or employment under the said Company.' The tendency since the time of Cornwallis had been to restrict the higher appointments under government to civil or military officers brought out from England and, since the time of Wellesley, to train them for their duties at one of the Company's colleges. In order to reverse the tendency, education of Indians for the public services became an urgent need if the words of the charter were to lead to action.

The problem of Indian education came to the notice of Thomas Macaulay (1800–59) who went out to Calcutta in 1834 with a new appointment as Legal Member of the Council. He was a cocksure young parliamentarian and lawyer, the son of Zachary Macaulay who had been Governor of Sierra Leone. But unlike his father—that pillar of the Clapham Sect—young Tom Macaulay was a decided Whig and not in the least degree a pietist. So recent were the days when men had prospered by 'shaking the pagoda-tree' that Macaulay saw nothing indiscreet in announcing that he had sought the appointment in India with the primary intention of making money. He would save enough of his salary of £10,000 a year to provide himself in three years, with an independent income for life. Whatever his motives during his three years' service, he did more than many a Governor-General to mould the character of the Indian nation, by his labours in devising a penal code and by his recommendation that English should be the medium of instruction in India.

In some remote past age the dominant race of Hindustan had formed its character upon the Sanskrit literature, and had made the Laws of *Manu* the customary basis of land and village life. Then had come centuries of Moslem domination, reaching their climax in the age of Akbar when Persian was the language of the court and Urdu the dialect of camp and market. Persian was still the language of diplomacy and of legislation under the East India Company. The most cultured of the early governors, such men as Warren Hastings, successors of Moslem rulers in Bengal, had admired and had encouraged Moslem culture. As successors to Mogul governors and rivals of the Mogul's nawabs their view of India was tinged with a Moslem colouring. Meanwhile the break-up of the Mogul Empire had been accompanied by, and partly caused by, a Hindu revival. Conquests in central India had altered the balance, bringing the British into contact with Hindu dynasties and sects, while the Moslem minority, no longer the rulers of the land, ceased to impose their culture upon it.

The rationalist theology and law of the Moslems might well have been adapted to the needs of the nineteenth century, but for the vitality of the Hindu undercurrent. Warren Hastings had founded a Moslem Madrasa (or college) at Calcutta for the training of a governing class among the Bengalis. A few years later, in 1792, a Sanskrit college was founded at Benares with the support of Lord Cornwallis; but the antiquated mythology which passed for learning among the Brahmins was of little value in the modern world. Bishop Heber, after attending a lecture in 1824, 'wondered that such rubbish should be taught in a government college'. This was the object of Macaulay's scorn in his 'Minute on Education' (1835): 'Medical doctrines which would disgrace an English farrier, astronomy which would move laughter in the girls of an English boarding-school, and history abounding with Kings thirty feet high.' Was such literature and such philosophy capable of being modernised? Were the languages of India adequate to express the notions of the modern world? Macaulay treated the suggestion with derision. Others were of a different opinion. B. H. Hodgson (1800–94), an orientalist of repute, argued vainly for Bengali, the language of 37,000,000 people, 'competent to express any imaginable mode of thought'. The great advantage of Bengali was the existence of a system of vernacular instruction; there were said to be 100,000 village schools in Bengal. But to what advantage, said Macaulay, when one considered the nonsense taught in them.

On 7 March 1835 the decision was taken by the Governor-General in Council that 'the great object of the British government ought to be the promotion of European literature and science

Plate 19

LORD DALHOUSIE (1812–60)

Governor-General of India. From a painting by Sir J. W. Gordon dated 1847.
See p. 443.

Plate 20A

JOHN, LORD LAWRE[NCE]
(1811–79)

Governor-General of In[dia]
1864. From a drawing by [...]
Lewis. *See pp. 448 and 92[...]*

Plate 20B

LORD CURZON
(1859–1925)

Governor-General of India in
1899. From a painting after J. S.
Sargent. *See p. 934.*

among the natives of India and that all the funds appropriated would best be employed on English education alone'. The appropriation was at first no more than £20,000 per annum rising to £70,000 in the 1850's, and was spent chiefly on the provision of text-books. Small as this sum now appears, it was as much as was appropriated for education in England in the 1830's. Bishop Heber had already noticed that the desire to learn English was widespread in the mission schools, and that the less enlightened followers of Ram Mohan Roy merely showed an apish tendency 'to imitate the English in everything'. Candidates for government office soon found that a knowledge of English was an advantage worth striving for; they were officially notified in 1844 that English-speaking applicants would be preferred. The cleavage between the old and the new learning widened. It was remarked that both Hindu and Moslem aristocrats, the old governing class, were holding aloof from government service under the new conditions, while a middle-class of half-educated *babus* with a pedantic smattering of government-English was arising. But the English language was never forced upon the *babus* of Bengal; they strove for it at their own expense as a means to employment. Neither in India nor in England was universal education by the state yet thought practicable or desirable. At last, in 1854, the Board of Control in London instructed the Governor-General to frame a 'properly articulated scheme of education from the primary school to the university'—articulated though, of course, neither universal nor compulsory. One of the last acts of the government before the Mutiny was to found examining universities at Calcutta, Bombay and Madras, on the model of the University of London.

The tendency of the Victorian English to despise the native culture of India was partly due to their own abounding self-confidence. Britain so patently led the world in all that the age regarded as progress. Partly too it was justified by the corrupt state of the Province of Bengal when the British first acquired it. The conquerors could not doubt that physically, mentally and morally they were the better men, possessing advantages that might be conferred upon the Indians. The missionaries assured themselves that by their efforts idolatry would die out in a generation. The teachers believed that Macaulay's system would create an educated upper-class with English notions of politics and ethics. The lawyers believed that the penal code would inculcate English notions of legality. They were hardly aware that their contempt for native Indian culture depressed the status of the Indian upper-classes. Either the Indians must ape the British or lapse into dependence. As early as 1817 Sir Thomas Munro, in recommending eventual self-government, reproached the Company for debasing the natives of India. The Victorian philanthropists hastened the process. Since India was to be Westernised, her indigenous products fell into contempt. Indian handicrafts were ruined, undersold by Free Trade in cheap manufactured goods. Architecture and the Fine Arts, which the Mogul Emperors had patronised, were neglected by the British philistines.

4. WARS IN THE NORTH-WEST, 1839–49

THE peaceful and progressive administration of Lord William Bentinck was followed by the unhappy times of Lord Auckland (1836–42), when a foreign policy which was always aggressive and often unscrupulous led the Indian government into unjustified and unsuccessful war. He bequeathed to his successor Ellenborough a strategic tangle which could be straightened only by further and still more ruthless campaigns. Lord Auckland was prim, earnest and weak. His mission in India was to second the foreign policy of Palmerston by checking the growing influence of the Russians in Central Asia. Since the Treaty of Tilsit (1807), Russia rather than France had become the rival to British power in Asia and throughout the century the Russian frontier was steadily advanced (see chapter XVIII, 1, page 921). Wellesley had sent Sir John Malcolm in 1799 on the first of a series of diplomatic missions to Persia but without attracting it into the British sphere of influence. On the other hand the Russians compelled the Persians to cede territory in 1813 and when, in 1838, further Russian advances were made towards Bokhara the pressure began to be felt in regions where the British too had interests. Herat in western Afghanistan was next menaced by Persia, a threat which was thought in India to be a concealed Russian move. Auckland began to prepare strong diplomatic action largely on the advice of Alexander Burnes, an adventurous young political agent with a reputation for Central Asian travel.

The kingdom of Kabul, through which run so many celebrated lines of communication, has not always been the debatable ground that it was in the nineteenth century. Once it was the secure patrimony of the dynasty of Timur and only lapsed into anarchy on the decline of the Mogul Empire. Tom Coryat and other early travellers plodded their way through Kabul and the Khyber Pass without any sense of particular peril in that part of their journey. But since Nadir Shah of Persia had stripped the Moguls of these hereditary provinces (1739), all that lay between the Sutlej and the Oxus had been the prize of rival military chiefs.

The Sutlej is the most easterly of the five tributaries of the Indus which give their name to the Punjab, a wide corn-growing plain. Here the Khalsa, the military brotherhood of the Sikhs, lorded it over a largely Moslem peasantry. These robust puritans, the most stout-hearted race encountered by the British in India, valiant as foes and faithful as friends, had been united under the rule of Runjeet Singh, in friendship with the British government since the treaty of 1808.

In the peaceful years river traffic down the Indus grew in importance and promised much for the future. Its limitation was the tribute levied upon the trade by a group of Moslem robber-barons who had possessed themselves of certain fortresses commanding the stream, especially the walled city of Sukkur. Their title was based only on recent conquest, their sole interest in the river-valley was predatory, their sway was admitted by all to be tyrannous in the extreme; they ruled three confederate provinces, Khairpur, Hyderabad and Mirpur, through tributary chiefs, the whole body being known as the Amirs of Sind. In 1838, when arbitrating between Runjeet Singh and the Amirs, Lord Auckland obliged the latter to accept a British agent by the first of a series of treaties which the Amirs always accepted with reluctance and always violated. There was in short no ground for an agreement; Auckland wished to extend British influence and to safeguard the commerce of the Indus; the Amirs wished to live by preying upon it without his well-meaning interference.

The third party to the struggle was the Amir of Afghanistan who held the wild Pathan tribes with a most uncertain grip. Afghans and Sikhs were hereditary foes by race, religion and history. The fluctuating frontier between them became, when the Punjab was annexed, the turbulent North-west Frontier of India.

Runjeet Singh had long maintained at his court at Lahore an exiled Amir of Afghanistan named Shah Suja from whom he had extracted the Koh-i-noor, the fetish of the empire of Hindustan. While Runjeet had no intention of burning his own fingers he was

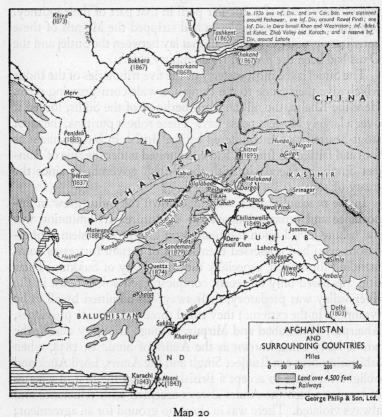

In 1936 one Inf. Div. and one Cav. Bde. were stationed around Peshawar; one Inf. Div. around Rawal Pindi; one Inf. Div. in Dera Ismail Khan and Waziristan; Inf. Bdes. at Kohat, Zhob Valley and Karachi; and a reserve Inf. Div. around Lahore

AFGHANISTAN AND SURROUNDING COUNTRIES

Miles
0 50 100   200   300

Land over 4,500 feet
Railways

George Philip & Son, Ltd.

Map 20

quite willing that the British should go to the trouble of replacing Shah Suja on the Afghan throne. Auckland first sent Alexander Burnes to negotiate with Dost Mohammed, the reigning Amir, but later overruled him, on the advice of Macnaghten, a rival political agent, and decided to restore Shah Suja to power. It was agreed with Runjeet Singh that a British army should march with Shah

Suja to Kabul, but not pass through Sikh territory; the Army of the Indus must go through the Bolan Pass—that is through territory of the Amirs of Sind. Pressure was again brought on the Amirs to give them right of way which was reluctantly permitted. Karachi, an ancient, silted-up, ruin of a seaport was occupied as a base in 1839. At first all went well; the march to Kandahar and Kabul was accomplished. The military administration was good and the only opposition, at Ghuznee, was overcome in a smart little action. Shah Suja was placed on the throne in place of his rival, who fled. The military operation was completed by a return march, north about, through the Khyber Pass. British garrisons were entrenched at Karachi, Quetta, Kandahar, Kabul and Jelalabad with the intention of retiring as soon as Shah Suja should be firmly seated. Two years later the garrisons were still in position. Shah Suja's authority extended not a yard beyond the reach of the British bayonets. While the soldiers, always unhappy when engaged on police work, would have been glad to withdraw, the political officers, especially Macnaghten, pressed for a forward policy, attempting to pacify the mountain tribes, alternately with bribes and punitive expeditions.

The morale of the army, or at least of its higher command, was low, since relations were strained between the civil and military powers. The Commander-in-Chief, who held that the British frontier should remain at the Sutlej, and refused responsibility for adventures in the 'Far West', was overruled by Auckland's political officers, the most offensive among them being Macnaghten, whom Wellington in England described as 'the person employed to command the army'.

In November 1841 the city of Kabul rose in rebellion. Shah Suja's authority vanished and Dost Mohammed reappeared. Burnes was murdered in the first onslaught, Macnaghten a few weeks later while attempting to divide the Afghan chiefs by a dubious intrigue. The garrison commander, an elderly invalid named Elphinstone whom Macnaghten had consistently snubbed, would have built a fort, had not Auckland disallowed the expenditure. Finding that he had no means to stand a siege, Elphinstone capitulated, agreeing to quit the country with his army under safe conduct. Since the state of the passes would not permit a withdrawal southward to his base he set out northwards for Jelalabad in the depth of winter (January 1842) with a column consisting of 700 English soldiers, 4000 sepoys, 12,000 camp-followers and a few English ladies. Whether Dost Mohammed intended that the army should escape is of slight importance, he could not have prevented the Pathans from harassing the retreat. All through the snowy passes the tribesmen attacked the column with increasing audacity. At one of many attempts to parley, Elphinstone and the Englishwomen surrendered to Dost Mohammed on the undertaking that they would be protected and that the attacks on the column would cease. The first condition was observed, the second was at once violated. In the rearguard the one British regiment, the 44th (Essex), making repeated counter-attacks, fought and died to the last man. The column straggled, dissipated and was destroyed. A solitary survivor, Dr Brydon, an army surgeon, reached Jelalabad.

Meanwhile the two authors of the war had disappeared from the scene. Runjeet Singh had died in 1839 leaving no legitimate heir to control his regular army of 50,000 men, trained by European soldiers of fortune and supported by 300 guns of a type more modern than those used by the British. 'Jealous of our power and contemptuous of our mismanagement', they observed the disaster at Kabul with pugnacious interest. Auckland too had gone, in February 1842, on the expiration of his term of office, a sadly discouraged statesman.

The next Governor-General, Lord Ellenborough, had exalted ideas about prestige. As soon as the passes should be open in the spring, Afghanistan was to be again invaded so that 'face' might be saved by a token victory. The southern garrisons which had been firmly held, produced a column under General Nott while, in the north, a column from Peshawar under General Pollock forced the Khyber Pass and relieved Sir Robert Sale in Jelalabad. The two columns converged on Kabul. The prisoners, excepting Elphinstone who had died, were released unharmed through the exertions of Sir R. Shakespeare, the reputed original of Thackeray's Colonel Newcome. Prestige having been restored, as Ellenborough supposed, by this promenade, the troops were withdrawn, leaving Dost Mohammed in possession of Afghanistan. As a symbol of victory Ellenborough ordered that the gates of Ghuznee should be brought back to India, supposing that they were trophies carried off by the Moslem conqueror Mahmud in the thirteenth century. The gesture was somewhat ineffective since

the antiquaries decided they were not authentic; and in any case
the Hindus had long forgotten their existence. To crown his victory Ellenborough issued a medal to all ranks who had taken part
in the campaign, the first such issue. The custom spread until,
after agitation in the press, a belated medal was issued even to the
survivors of the Peninsular War, against the wish of Wellington.
Time had been when he had represented the most powerful of the
world's kingdoms at the Congress of Vienna, wearing dark well-
cut plain clothes which marked him out among the beribboned
and bejewelled courtiers of the European monarchs. He would
have hated to see the British soldier's breast gaudy with stars and
crosses as if he were a Portuguese or a Prussian.

Fate struck a blow at the Amirs of Sind by sending Sir Charles
Napier in 1842 to command the Bombay Army. Although the
forward policy had just been abandoned, after the disastrous retreat from Kabul, Napier had no intention of allowing that to influence his behaviour in Sind where he had troops deployed at
Karachi and the crossings of the Indus. The most brilliant member of a handsome, gallant, pugnacious family, Charles Napier
(1782–1853) was an elderly soldier who had done a hundred
things but had never fulfilled his ambition of commanding an
army in battle. In politics he was an advanced Radical, in character a pure dictator. During the Chartist troubles he had kept the
peace in the north of England by assuring the Chartist leaders that
he supported the whole of their policy but would shoot them without a qualm if they provoked riot and disorder. To deal with the
Amirs was a simpler problem; if they would not act fairly by him
he would 'knock them over like ninepins', and would welcome
the chance. Our erroneous policy had led us into difficulties from
which there was no way of escape without the use of force. 'Auckland began by an act of injustice', said Napier. 'A course of injustice cannot be closed without hardship on someone. It is likely
to fall on the Amirs and on a crew more deserving to bear it
hardly could it alight.... I do not think the Amirs fools, I think
them cunning rascals. They saw our defeat which encouraged
them to break treaties. They hoped to have a second Kabul affair.
Now what is to be done? That which is best for...the good
government of the population, and we must not sacrifice it to an
endeavour, utterly hopeless I may say, to give to these tyrannical,
drunken, debauched, cheating, intriguing, contemptible Amirs a

due portion of the plunder they have amassed from the ruined people.'

Napier kept his political officer, James Outram,[1] under control; he first nicknamed him the 'Bayard of India', and afterwards over-ruled and abused him. Outram was for peace and was still nego-tiating hopefully when Napier and the Amirs were openly arming. It is hard to say who struck the first blow. On 17 February 1843 with a small force of raw unseasoned troops, Napier defeated ten times as great a force of Baluchis at Miani, a battle picturesquely described by his brother, William. 'Thick as standing corn, and gorgeous as a field of flowers, stood the Beloochs in their many-coloured garments and turbans; they filled the broad deep bed of the Fullailee, they clustered on both banks, and covered the plain beyond. Guarding their heads with their large dark shields, they shook their sharp swords, beaming in the sun, their shouts rolled like a peal of thunder, as with frantic gestures they rushed for-wards, and full against the front of the 22nd [Cheshires] dashed with demoniac strength and ferocity.' Charles Napier now reached his ambition by winning a battle in the field, which gave him the mastery of Hyderabad. He followed it up by a desert march in the hot weather to Mirpur where he subdued another of the Amirates. These two were annexed as the province of Sind. The third, Khairpur, whose Amir had observed the treaty and remained friendly, became a protected native state.

This brilliant little campaign was a masterpiece of Indian war-fare, as the old Duke of Wellington declared. Napier was the idol of his men, restoring their confidence in their leaders and the con-fidence of the government in its generals. He was a forceful ad-ministrator with a strong sense of justice and complete indiffer-ence to criticism, the creator of the model province of Sind. To his foresight India owed the port of Karachi, the commerce of the Indus, and the future prospect of the irrigation of the Indus basin. And yet the Sind campaign is the most blatant example of mere aggressive warfare in British history. Napier had no misgivings about his work. He did not say of it '*peccavi*', 'I have sinned';

---

[1] Sir J. Outram (1803–63). 'His life was given to India. In early manhood he reclaimed wild tribes by winning their hearts; Ghazni, Khelat, the Indian Caucasus witnessed the daring deeds of his prime; Persia brought to sue for peace; Lucknow relieved, defended, and recovered, were fields of his later glories. Many wise rulers, many valiant captains, hath his country sent hither, but never any loved as this man was by those whom he governed or led on to battle.' (Epitaph.)

though a contemporary witticism suggested that he might have said it. His comment was that it was 'a very advantageous, useful, humane piece of rascality'.

All his work and all his words were characteristic and original, as was his appearance. 'Beneath a huge helmet of his own contrivance' he revealed 'a fringe of long hair at the back and in front a large pair of round spectacles, an immense hooked nose, and a mane of moustache and whisker reaching to the waist'. His men affectionately called him Old Fagin from a character in a recent best-seller. Some indications of that eagle's beak, that lion's mane, are conventionally represented on his monument in Trafalgar Square 'to which the most numerous contributors were private soldiers'.

The Sind campaign was by no means the last of the troubles in the north-west. Lord Ellenborough was obliged to intervene in Scindia's state of Gwalior because he dared not leave so powerful a prince in doubtful friendship on his flank when troubles with the Sikhs was blowing up. Dissatisfaction over these campaigns led to Ellenborough's recall and replacement by Lord Hardinge (1844), but not to any settlement with the Sikhs. British victories in Sind and Gwalior brought the British armies in greater force upon their frontiers and provoked the trial of strength which they desired. In 1845 the Sikhs crossed the Sutlej with the intention of marching on Delhi.

Hardinge was an old soldier and, more in the manner of a knight-errant than a viceroy, he accompanied the army as a subordinate to his friend Hugh Gough, the Commander-in-Chief. Gough had made a reputation by his combined operations on the China coast in 1841, so that much was expected of him. But war against the Sikhs with their well-served artillery, their European staffs, and their stout Punjabi infantry proved a very different matter from hunting Chinese coolies led by mandarins. This was war between well-matched opponents, the only advantage to Gough being the leavening of British infantry in his army. After two costly combats with a doubtful outcome at Moodkee and Ferozeshah, Gough forced an issue at Sobraon (10 February 1846), a furious and bloody triumph for the British infantry. The campaign was fought by a force which would now be reckoned at three infantry divisions, whose nine British battalions lost 3400 men in killed and wounded. Sobraon enabled Hardinge to impose the Treaty of Lahore on the Sikhs, restricting their frontiers and obliging them to accept a British Resident, Henry Lawrence, at Lahore. His team of assistants were men of such force of character, such manly honour as the world has rarely seen.

Hardinge deprived the Sikhs of the mountainous tracts, outside the Punjab proper, which Runjeet Singh had taken from the Afghans, and imposed a war indemnity of £1,500,000. Part of the hill-country, the principality of Jammu, was ruled by a Rajput client of Runjeet Singh, named Gulab Singh, who assisted the British cause and negotiated the terms of the treaty. Gulab undertook the payment of the indemnity in return for the principality of Kashmir of which he became first Maharaja. By this rather shabby bargain the backward Moslem state of Kashmir, renowned for its natural beauty, passed under the control of a Hindu court and aristocracy.

The Treaty of Lahore was never more than an armistice. When the next Governor-General, Lord Dalhousie, arrived in 1848, his hope was for another period of peace and progress like Bentinck's term, but his first great effort was required against a Sikh national revolt. The first Sikh War had not produced so decisive a British victory as to reconcile the warlike Punjabis to a union with British India.

The cause of the second Sikh War was the murder of the British agent at Mooltan, the signal for a general uprising against the other British political officers. Dalhousie again unleashed Hugh Gough, a fighting Irishman who never had enough. 'Unwarned by precedents, uninfluenced by examples, the Sikh nation has called for war', declared Dalhousie, 'and they shall have it with a vengeance.' Again the Sikhs displayed their valour; they very nearly got the better of Gough at Chillianwalla (1848) where the British troops lost two colours, four guns and 2000 men. In response to public agitation Napier was ordered out to supersede him, but Gough 'never was bate and he never would be bate'; he finished the whole epic struggle by a crushing victory at Gujerat (1849), and by a pursuit to the banks of the Indus before Napier arrived.

The Punjab was now annexed and reorganised as a province of British India. Politically the most striking effect was to advance British rule to the line of the Upper Indus and thus to present the problem of the North-west Frontier which remained unsolved for a hundred years. John Lawrence, Henry's brother and successor, wished to stop at the river-line, since no practical advantage came of pressing on into the barren hills beyond. The military view tended to the orthodox strategic doctrine that all river-lines are weak unless covered by strong bridgeheads. Peshawar, which had been so often disputed between Sikhs and Afghans, at least should be held. It was occupied in 1850 and secured by the extension of the Grand Trunk Road, westward to Lahore and eventually to Peshawar, where George Lawrence, a third brother, was Deputy-Commissioner. The Punjab was quickly pacified by the personal influence of Lawrence's men over the Sikh soldiery. A Corps of military police was formed and then a new army, the Punjab Irregular Frontier Force whose reputation as the 'Piffers' is not yet forgotten in India. Their leaders, Herbert Edwardes, John Nicholson, Hodson of Hodson's Horse, were to see their work justified in 'fifty-seven.

5. LORD DALHOUSIE AND THE INDIAN MUTINY

THE organisation of Sind and the Punjab should be considered part of the achievement of James Ramsay, Marquess of Dalhousie (1812–60), who was Governor-General from 1848 to 1856 and one of the three or four greatest in that long and famous line. The unwieldy Bengal Presidency was also reorganised under his direction as two provinces each under a Lieutenant-Governor. He fostered commerce and the communications on which it depends. In addition to his two great roads, the Grand Trunk from Lahore to Peshawar and a hardly less vital artery from Agra to Bombay he linked the whole country with 4000 miles of public telegraphs, a more complete service than there was at that date in England; and introduced a halfpenny rate for letter-postage. He lighted the coasts and improved the harbours. He built the first railways in Asia, two short lines running inland from Bombay and Calcutta. Exports and imports were doubled and the revenue, though much enlarged, showed a surplus in his last year. At the end of his time his government was planning a comprehensive scheme of Indian education. He had arrived in India an active young man of thirty-six; he departed an old man of forty-four, worn out by incessant travel and responsibility but confident that India was set in the path of progress.

Politically he was no less enterprising but on far more dangerous ground. After the second Sikh War he found himself faced with a second Burmese War (see chapter VIII, 1, page 406) and, forcing the issue with spirited efficiency, annexed Lower Burma without compunction. He took a firm line with that superannuated phantom, the King of Delhi who still preserved some of the trappings of the Great Mogul. Thirty years before Dalhousie's day Bishop Heber had described the fantastic squalor of the court of Delhi, where hordes of beggars bivouacked in the purlieus of a palace greater than the Kremlin, where nothing was ever mended and nothing cleaned, where the King's throne was so coated with filth that its ornaments could not be distinguished. Princely gifts were exchanged between the Bishop and the old King according to the rule of oriental courtesy, but all was pretence since the government at Calcutta prescribed and provided what each English visitor should offer to the King, and confiscated the King's present in order to balance the account. The monarch had nothing to say except to complain fretfully that Lord Amherst had insisted on taking a seat in his presence. 'At Delhi,' wrote Heber, 'all was dirty lonely and wretched; the baths and fountains dry; the inlaid pavements hid with lumber and gardener's sweepings, and the walls stained with the dung of birds and bats.' The Mogul Empire had been a fiction since that day when Shah Alam had thrown himself upon the mercy of Clive, 'a fugitive without money, without troops, dependent on the English for his daily bread'. But fifty years passed before Viscount Hastings took the step of discontinuing the pretence that as ruler of Bengal he acted in the name of the Mogul. Amherst declined to do homage in 1827, meeting him on equal terms as the viceroy of an equally dignified monarch. Still the royal title, the pension of twenty-six *lakhs* of rupees (£200,000 a year) and the mysterious prestige of monarchy survived when Dalhousie took the decision that the Mogul monarchy should end with the life of the present incumbent. The last King of Delhi, Bahadur Shah, was eighty years old when Dalhousie left India.

This deferred sentence was not felt to be so significant as the annexations made in accordance with Dalhousie's doctrine of 'lapse'. The immemorial rule of Indian law gave to an adopted heir all the rights of a natural heir including that of succession to a throne. Dalhousie decided not to admit the principle in newly-created native states where the rulers held solely by an act of grace from the British *raj*. In such instances, when the legitimate family died out, the principality would lapse to the British government and not pass to an adopted heir. Cases occurred in Satara (1848), Nagpur (1853) and Jhansi (1854), each being a principality granted by the British to a conquered enemy after the Maratha Wars. The fourth case was the great and rich kingdom of Oudh which, since the days of Clive, had been intricately associated with the Bengal Presidency. The kingly title, first of its kind in India, had been assumed by the Nawab of Oudh upon British authority. The Company's troops had garrisoned the province and guarded the King's person for near a hundred years. And though Oudh was rich, its government remained in the scandalous state of all Indian governments in the eighteenth century. One Governor-General after another had urged reforms upon the kings of Oudh but without visible result. Corruption and misrule grew worse until it was commonly said that our own troops protected the King from the vengeance of his subjects. In 1856 Dalhousie was so heartened by the progress in Sind, the Punjab and the three lapsed Maratha states that he decided to intervene in Oudh under the terms of the treaty of 1837. Upon the advice of Outram and Sir Henry Lawrence, both of whom were opposed to annexations in general, he forced the King to abdicate, and placed Lawrence as British Commissioner at Lucknow, the capital of Oudh.

Dalhousie's momentous term of office was now drawing to a close. His successor, Lord Canning, had already arrived in India when the annexation was completed. In the same year (1856) the Persians had taken advantage of the diversion caused by the Crimean War to resume their encroachments towards the east. After long, unfriendly negotiation the British declared war to prevent their occupation of Herat. Outram was sent with the Bombay Army to Bushire on the Persian coast. After defeating the Persians in several small engagements, he obliged them to withdraw from Herat and to give an undertaking that the slave trade would be suppressed in the Persian Gulf. Having completed his task, Outram and his army returned to India (March 1857) in time to take part in the campaigns of the Mutiny year.

What was the Indian Mutiny, that fierce conflict which so profoundly moved our great-grandparents? It was not a proletarian revolution like those which began to agitate Europe in 1848; no general strike precipitated the urban workers into direct action; no agrarian riots threatened the property of the landlords; no national guard sprang into life. Nor was it a feudal tumult like those in which Clive and Dupleix had so audaciously intervened during the decline of the Mogul Empire; the greater princes held aloof, excepting two or three who nourished personal grievances, or used their influence discreetly in support of the government. Nor was it a communal struggle, though it began among the high-caste Hindus; nor a revolt of the newly conquered provinces, for Sind and the Punjab remained calm. It was not a general protest against British administration, for the unrest scarcely spread into the Bombay and Madras Presidencies. And yet it was something more than a mutiny of the Bengal Army.

Acute observers had been foretelling for years past that the pace of reform had been dangerously forced. 'The crusading improving spirit of the last twenty-five years', said Outram shortly before the Mutiny, 'would cause a resounding clash.' English law, English teaching, English religion, English interference with age-old customs pointed the way to a new India which would be Anglicised and centrally administered by means of road, rail and telegraph in despite of caste and race. The vernacular press, uncensored since Bentinck's day, harped upon grievances and denunciations; it was free to agitate and obstruct, but impotent to inform the illiterate masses. Bentinck had alarmed the orthodox by his liberal intentions; Dalhousie had threatened vested interests by strengthening the hand of government. The Evangelicals were at work in the civil departments and the officers' messes, speaking hopefully of a day when heathen practices should be extinct in India, and the English no longer be required to act as 'churchwardens to Juggernaut'.

But unrest does not make revolution, without resolute leading and a plan of action. Only in the Bengal Army does it appear that there was any conspiracy to revolt, and the mercenary armies of the East India Company had been chronically mutinous. It should be remembered that there was not one Indian Army but three, under separate administration and command, in the three Presidencies, with the nucleus of a new fourth Army in the Punjab. At one time the Mutiny looked rather like a civil war between the Punjab irregulars and the Bengal sepoys.

The Bengal Army, recruited largely from high-caste Hindus, had all the faults common to idle mercenaries. Since the Sikh Wars, when some regiments had behaved badly, they had been unemployed. Discipline was relaxed, the officers were elderly and easy-going, the sepoys chafed at military infringements of their caste rules. Service overseas in Persia or Burma was disliked and resisted. Grievances accumulated, to reach a climax in the rumour that their new cartridges were wrapped in paper greased with cow's fat as a deliberate British affront to caste. Early in 1857 the greased cartridges led to several minor mutinies in Lower Bengal which were suppressed without difficulty. The High Command was slow to take alarm, supposing that the withdrawal of the greased cartridges would restore tranquillity. Then and later, British officers, with pardonable pride, refused to believe that their own men would break faith, whatever the rascals in other regiments might have done. Some shrewd observers, noticing the faulty distribution of troops in the Bengal Presidency had foreseen the greater danger. Napier had pointed it out, and Henry Lawrence, fourteen years earlier, had published an accurate forecast of the events at Delhi. But the sudden bloodthirsty outbreak of the garrison at Meerut on that hot Sunday evening (10 May 1857), came as a surprise to the British residents and the Commander-in-Chief at Simla.

The mutinous sepoys had two obvious alternatives before them: to restore the military kingdom of the Marathas or to restore the Mogul Empire. They chose the latter. Marching off to Delhi in the night, they occupied the Palace and placed themselves under the allegiance of the bewildered, purblind Bahadur Shah, thus associating the Moslems with their cause. Letters had been passing between the court of Delhi and the Shah, from which arose a whole new crop of rumours that a Persian army would soon be marching to Delhi as it had done 120 years earlier. Moslems and Hindus were soon at loggerheads. The rebellion produced no statesman, so that the sepoys who fought bravely enough for the capital were championing a hopeless cause. The so-called siege of Delhi resembled the siege of Troy. Within the walled city were thousands of warriors and an old doomed feckless King. The engagements took the form of turbulent sorties by the garrison against the camp of the besiegers who were few, headstrong and heroic. It seemed that by nothing but a miracle could they take the city. Meanwhile in May and June the Mutiny spread like an epidemic through the Ganges valley. Sepoy regiments murdered their officers and marched off to join the mutineers at Delhi. Civilians, if they could not hold their districts, gathered the European residents in a body in some stronghold. The administration vanished. Petty princes armed their retainers to take vengeance on personal enemies, or on their creditors. Landlords, dispossessed in the revenue settlements, resumed their old estates. The police took to *dacoity*. But the villagers, the overwhelming majority of the Indian people, showed no resentment to the British, often helping them to places of safety.

From the first the conflict was ruthless and bloody. The repeated treacherous murders of officers by their men led to uncontrolled reprisal. All the main centres of communication between Calcutta and Allahabad were held or recaptured by small bodies of British troops, often by the personal authority of solitary British officers, who gave no quarter to sepoys or their associates. Beyond Allahabad all the countryside was dominated by the rebels and all the larger towns except Cawnpore, and Lucknow, as far west as Agra. Cawnpore surrendered on 27 June to Nana Sahib, the adoptive heir of the long-deposed Peshwa and therefore a claimant to the leadership of the Maratha confederacy.

At this crisis, when Lord Canning at Calcutta was separated by two anarchic provinces from his Commander-in-Chief, who lay outside Delhi with a handful of British troops, while the infection of mutiny was still spreading, India was saved from a relapse into chaos by the firmness of two brothers, John Lawrence (1811-79) at Lahore and Henry Lawrence (1806-57) at Lucknow. The sons of an Irish Protestant soldier, both had spent many years in India fighting in Lord Auckland's wars and afterwards reorganising the conquered provinces. They had much in common, both being rugged, simple, headstrong, unyielding men with firm notions of duty; and Lahore had not been large enough to hold them both. After a disagreement Henry had been posted away to other appointments and had arrived at Lucknow, the capital of Oudh, only a few weeks before the Mutiny. He found that province in turmoil after the annexation of 1856, seething with complaints that the monetary compensation promised by the government had not been paid. The aristocracy, a body of 300 hereditary landowners known as the *Talukhdars*, Rajputs of great wealth and feudal influence, had been deprived of all their rights pending a revenue settlement which had not yet been adjusted. Such a state of affairs was not disconcerting to Henry Lawrence who knew the land and the countryfolk of India better than any Englishman alive, and had, in fact, quarrelled with his brother by asserting the rights of a similar class in the Punjab. In the first days of the Mutiny he made the Residency at Lucknow a firm bastion, and even maintained some personal influence over the Talukhdars. But by the end of June the Residency was a besieged fortress and the only outpost held by the Government in Oudh. Lawrence was mortally wounded on 2 July and died urging his officers never to surrender.

The relief of Lucknow was the first step to be undertaken by the government in Calcutta before a way could be opened to Delhi and the west. A psalm-singing old ironside general named Havelock first undertook this campaign, smiting the Amalekites without mercy as he fought his way up-country. On 17 July 1857 he discovered the bodies of 200 British women and children treacherously murdered at Cawnpore, and took exemplary vengeance. But when he reached Lucknow he could do no more than reinforce the garrison with part of his small column under James Outram.

Meanwhile 500 miles away John Lawrence had acted at Lahore with resolution founded on the clearest vision. When the news from Meerut reached the north-west by telegraph his officers on the frontier had instantly formed a 'movable column' of reliable British and Sikh troops to march to any threatened point. Herbert Edwardes ensured the friendship of the Amir of Afghanistan, John Nicholson quieted the frontier tribes and so schooled one sepoy regiment which mutinied that his name is still a legend in the hills. Some Hazara tribesmen insisted on worshipping him as a god in his lifetime, though he did his best to flog them out of their creed. Before the end of May the movable column was swinging down the Grand Trunk Road to Delhi, the Guides marching a steady twenty-seven miles a day through the hot weather in their new dust-coloured (*khaki*) uniforms. Lawrence urged the Commander-in-Chief to audacious action. 'Reflect on the whole history of India. Where have we failed when we acted vigorously? Where have we succeeded when guided by timid counsels? Clive with 1200 men[1] fought at Plassy, in opposition to the advice of his leading officers, beat 40,000 men and conquered Bengal.' Lawrence would have abandoned Peshawar to save Delhi had that been inevitable, but so firm was the frontier that it proved unnecessary. 'Hold on to Peshawar to the last', telegraphed the Viceroy on 7 August. The new roads and telegraphs vastly increased Lawrence's resources. Bartle Frere in Sind, and Elphinstone at

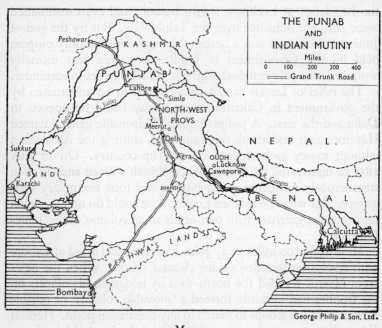

THE PUNJAB
AND
INDIAN MUTINY
Miles
0   100   200   300   400
===== Grand Trunk Road

George Philip & Son. Ltd.

Map 21

Bombay, kept open his communications with the west and sent him troops after quieting their own provinces. The princes of Rajputana and Kashmir, even the great Maharaja Scindia, held firm to their treaties with the British and to their faith in Lawrence. With tact and firmness he anticipated mutiny by disarming and disbanding many regiments of unreliable sepoys, so releasing 10,000 British troops for the campaign at Delhi. These he reinforced with more than 30,000 Sikhs, who never swerved from their military allegiance.

[1] Actually 3000.

The little British force on the Ridge overlooking Delhi fought every day throughout the summer against vastly superior numbers. It was reinforced in June by the movable column from the Punjab and later by other troops who brought with them a bewildering succession of commanders. In the heated discussions of policy the strong men from the Punjab dominated the councils, urging an assault on the city which was delivered against terrifying odds in September. John Nicholson was mortally wounded while leading one of the storming columns. On the day after the fall of Delhi, a dashing leader of irregular cavalry, Major Hodson, was sent to seize the person and family of the old King, Bahadur Shah, who was arrested, tried and transported to Rangoon for the remainder of his inglorious life. Hodson also arrested his two sons and, when a crowd of palace retainers threatened, or seemed to threaten, an attempt at rescue he shot the two princes with his own hand. Thus with the death of the last heirs of Tamburlaine the Great ended the ill-considered attempt to restore the Mogul Empire. Hodson's plea that the princes were 'shot to prevent their escape', a plea so sadly familiar in the revolutions of our own day, has never quite rung true.

After the recapture of Delhi the mutineers were thrown on the defensive. The Punjab movable column pushed on, and in October 1857 made contact with the loyal troops near Lucknow. The next problem was to reduce the province of Oudh where alone the Mutiny had assumed the form of a national rising against the British. Lord Canning, while always attempting to spare the lives of rebels who submitted, had made an error in declaring forfeit the lands of those Talukhdars of Oudh who had not stood by the Government. His mercy earned him the scorn of the soldiers who called him 'Clemency' Canning, a name he accepted as an honour; his confiscations drove the Talukhdars to join the mutineers. A year's hard fighting (October 1857 to October 1858) was required before Sir Colin Campbell, the new Commander-in-Chief, restored order in Oudh by the employment of numerous troops from England. The withdrawal of Canning's proclamation and the promise of a new land-settlement perhaps had more effect than Sir Colin's battles.

Until the last phase the Mutineers remained anonymous. The old King of Delhi had been no leader; for a time Nana Sahib cast himself for the part but proved as irresolute as cruel and treacherous.

A mere idle voluptuary, his sole interest had been a quite un-justified claim that the British should have added to his vast wealth by paying him the Peshwa's pension. His troops were scattered in the hills where he escaped the gallows by vanishing. His lieu-tenant, Tantia Topee, a Maratha soldier, broke away south into the hills of Central India. Here he was joined by the sole heroic figure among the rebels, the Ranee of Jhansi, girl-widow of a Maratha prince whose territory had lapsed by Dalhousie's rule. While Colin Campbell pacified Oudh, the Bombay Army under Sir Hugh Rose fought the last Maratha War against Tantia and the Ranee who were joined by mutinous soldiers from the armies of Scindia and Holkar. The Ranee was killed at Gwalior in May 1858, fighting in soldier's uniform at the head of her troops. Tantia held out till April 1859 when he was hunted down and very properly hanged for his share in the massacre at Cawnpore. Long before these smouldering embers were trodden out the East India Company had been dissolved and the Queen's government pro-claimed throughout India.

6. BRITISH INDIA, 1858–76

WHEN the charter of the East India Company came before Par-liament in 1853 for its fourth periodic renewal, it was generally felt that the system of 'double government' could not last much longer. Forty years had passed since the trading monopoly had been withdrawn from the Company, twenty years since the com-mercial branch had been closed, so that the position of the Pro-prietors had become anomalous. They merely held shares in what might be described as part of the funded debt of the British Dominions. Now their authority was further whittled away; the Crown strengthened its control by assuming the right to nominate one-third of the Directors, and weakened the Company by taking away the patronage. In accordance with current reforms in the home civil service, new appointments to India, after 1853, were made on the results of competitive examination. Old Haileybury College was closed down in the Mutiny year after celebrating the fall of Delhi in its last term.

Public opinion tended to fix the blame for the Mutiny upon the Company. The Directors defended themselves in a dignified petition to Parliament composed by John Stuart Mill, pointing out that political sovereignty had already passed away from the Company so that the servants of the Crown must be held responsible. In its day the Company's government had been 'not only one of the purest in intention, but one of the most benevolent in act, ever known among mankind'. During the last generation it had been 'one of the most improving governments in the world'. It had governed and defended India 'without the smallest cost to the British exchequer, which cannot be said of any other of the dependencies of the Crown'. The Company had constantly held that 'its first duty was to the people of India' and had 'seen with the greatest pain the demonstrations of indiscriminate animosity towards the natives of India' which the events of the Mutiny had provoked.

There was much truth in these assertions but not enough to justify the control of an Empire by a casual group of investors, as Palmerston jauntily pointed out in proposing a new India Bill on 12 February 1858. Before the Bill got through, his administration was overturned on quite another count, so that the short-lived Derby administration was responsible for the Government of India Act 1858 (21 & 22 Vict. cap. 106), which differed from Palmerston's Bill in some particulars. The government of India with all territorial rights and revenues and all tributes previously enjoyed by the Company was transferred to the Crown. The powers formerly exercised jointly by the Board of Control and by the Directors were to be exercised by an additional Secretary of State, acting upon the advice of a council of fifteen members. Seven councillors, in the first instance, were to be nominated by the Directors; the remainder by the Crown. Strict financial provisions prevented either the Secretary of State or the Governor-General from waging aggressive wars. The Secretary of State was instructed to render an annual financial statement to Parliament. The Company's armies and navy were absorbed into the armed forces of the Crown.

The Company submitted gracefully with a farewell message to its servants in India, September 1858. 'Let Her Majesty appreciate the gift—let her take the vast country and the teeming millions of India under her direct control, but let her not forget the great corporation from which she has received them nor the lessons to be learned from its success.'. . . 'The Coy has the privilege of transferring to the service of H.M. such a body of civil and military officers as the world has never seen before.'

The winding-up of the East India Company was a lengthy process since the dividend to stock-holders had been guaranteed by the Act of 1833 for a period of forty years. This sum, £630,000 a year, remained as a first change on the revenues of the Indian government until 1873, when the stock-holders were paid off in cash or in Indian government bonds. Until that final settling-day John Company retained a shadowy existence in the form of a chairman, five directors, a secretary, and a clerk, with no duties other than distributing the dividend. The palatial East India House in Leadenhall Street was taken over in 1858 by Lord Stanley, the first Secretary of State for India. Two years later he found it more convenient to remove to Whitehall whereupon the old house was sold and demolished.

On 1 November 1859, while war still raged in Central India, the Queen issued a proclamation to the 'Princes, Chiefs and the People of India':

> We have resolved to take upon ourselves the government of the territories in India, heretofore administered in trust for us by the Honourable East India Company....
>
> We announce to the native princes of India that all treaties and engagements made under the authority of the Company will be scrupulously maintained....
>
> We desire no extension of our present territories....
>
> We declare it to be our royal will and pleasure that none be in any wise favoured, none molested or disquieted, by reason of their religious faith or observances...that our subjects of whatever race or creed be freely and impartially admitted to office in our service...that in framing the law due regard be paid to the ancient rights, usages and customs of India....
>
> Our clemency will extend to all offenders save those convicted...of the murder of British subjects....
>
> When internal tranquillity shall be restored, it is our earnest desire to stimulate the peaceful industry of India, to promote works of public utility and improvement, and to administer the government for the benefit of all our subjects resident therein.

The last President of the Board of Control, Sir Charles Wood, later first Lord Halifax (1800–85), became Secretary of State for India in 1859. He in London and Canning as Viceroy reconstructed the administration in its new form after the turmoil of the Mutiny. Though much of the old system remained unchanged there was a new spirit in India. The old heroic age when adventurers like Nicholson ruled provinces by sheer force of character, without regard to precedents or regulations, had passed into a new age of efficient centralised administration. Much fun was made of the 'competition-wallahs', the discreet bureaucrats of the new dispensation by the salted, liverish, rough-and-ready 'quahais' of the old school. Everyone was tied by a telegraph-wire to Calcutta where lived the Viceroy, who was tied (after 1870) by a telegraph cable to Whitehall.

Although the Queen had proclaimed equality the sahibs more than ever constituted a new caste in India. As government grew more efficient and more impersonal the gap widened. The bad blood of the Mutiny lay between the sahibs who could not forget Cawnpore and the natives who could not forget the hangings and the shootings and the blowings from guns. The old easy relation between rulers and ruled was never resumed, at least not in the Ganges valley. It was quite out of the question for a sahib to set up a native domestic establishment. The British had reasserted their status as the master-race of India more firmly than ever. In mere physical courage, in endurance, resource and audacity, in unselfish co-operation, loyalty to their leaders, and in defiance of overwhelming odds they had proved themselves unquestionably superior to all the Indian peoples.

Before the Mutiny the task of the rulers had been to subdue the warlike races of the north and to restrain ambitious princes. Now the direction of the British effort was altered. The Princes who had been faithful to the treaties were the strongest buttress of the British *raj*. The virile martial races of the north, who had never swerved from their military allegiance, had earned the faith and friendship of the sahibs, while the mutinous 'pandies' of Bengal remained objects of suspicion and dislike. So small a share had they shown of military virtue that for two generations after the Mutiny few if any recruits for the Army were drawn from Bengal. But the history of British India in those years was not much concerned with war.

On their part the Indian intellectuals also withdrew from intercourse with the British. The Brahma Somaj of Bengal languished while a new reforming sect, the Arya Somaj founded by Dayanand Saraswati (1827–53) gained strength among the Hindus. This was not an attempt to reconcile East and West but a return to the pure undefiled religion of the early Vedas.

IX

MARKETS, MONEY AND MEN IN THE AGE OF FREE TRADE

Argument: In the old economy, staple trades in commodities not produced at home were protected by various devices. These monopolies and protective duties were swept away in an age when voters demanded cheap food and low production costs. Colonial interests were overlooked while trade with all the world expanded. Yet Royal Mail contracts, acting as a bounty to British steamships, gave them a new advantage. Steamships, coaling-stations and deep-sea cables were the nervous system of the new commercial empire. Its life-blood was the flow of capital for overseas investments. British commerce enjoyed continual prosperity from the 'fifties to the 'seventies. A series of gold-finds (all but the first in British territory) stimulated expansion, allowing several colonies to finance their own development. The United States was Britain's best customer, both as a buyer and a borrower, in mid-Victorian days; she also received the largest share of British emigration.

The first Empire had been made by Englishmen; Scottish and Irish emigration came later. A majority of the English race, a large majority of the Scots and an overwhelming majority of the Irish now live outside their lands of origin.

1. FREE TRADE

THE extent of this book does not permit a full enquiry into the effects of the policy of Free Trade, important though they are to the history of the Empire. Few will now deny that Free Trade was a prudent policy for English merchants to support during the period of commercial expansion between 1850 and 1875. Then, improved communications were opening new markets daily in every part of the world. Then, British mechanised industry was far in advance of all its rivals. If unrestricted imports led to an increasing return from unrestricted exports, then the British could hold the markets of the world against all rivals. Cheap coal and cheap labour could and did produce and distribute textiles and machinery for all markets at competitive prices. The surplus of a sure home market formed the broad margin for export; and the export market, in turn, was insured by the invisible export of shipping, services and capital loans (which will be discussed in the succeeding chapters). Even the surplus of population gave no trouble since the emigration of men had become as easy as the emigration of capital. America was a better market for British goods than was Australia. It therefore followed that emigration to America was a more advantageous means of disposing of the unemployed than emigration to Australia. Such, at least, seemed to be the belief of Mr Gladstone's government in 1870. The whole economy was unified by the gold standard. Successive finds of gold throughout the century brought each of the commercial nations into line and into closer relations with the dominant money market of London. The economics of Free Trade seemed unanswerable.

Though the academic economists preached *laissez-faire* as a panacea for all social ills, practical men tended to make a reservation in respect of their immediate concerns. While paying lip-service to Free Trade on principle, they were inclined to think that an exceptional preference should still be imposed to maintain the price of the particular line of goods they wished to sell or the particular rate of wages they had secured; just as their successors, a hundred years later, while admitting the theoretical necessity of a Planned Economy, still claim the right to bargain for better prices or wages in their own industry.

The first effect of mid-Victorian prosperity was to sweep away such slight enthusiasm for the Empire as had been engendered by the Colonial Reformers. Their work was done. The colonies were set free, and sentimentally associated with the mother-country only by common allegiance to the Crown. And the influence of the Crown ran low during the early years of Queen Victoria's widowhood. Free Trade and the utilitarian outlook were expected to weaken the irrational bonds of Empire while they strengthened the rational links of mutual commerce between all the nations of the world. Meanwhile the purchasing power of the colonies was but small. Since they bought less than one-third of what Britain exported and were not developing as rapidly as the United States, it was not to be supposed that the nation of shopkeepers would take much interest in them. British shipping required naval supremacy, that is to say coaling-stations. Otherwise the Empire was valued in terms of West Indian sugar, softwoods from Canada, Australian wool, and tea from the East Indies, until a cheaper supply should crop up somewhere else. The most interesting prospect lay in India, a vast potential market for textiles and not yet fit for self-government. When the Manchester men spoke indifferently of letting the colonies go they had no intention of losing their grip on India.

In general the colonies showed (as some still show) the instability and weakness of every economy based upon the export of a single crop. This Huskisson had recognised in his enlightened tariff reforms of the 1820's, giving preference to the colonial staples, and refusing to admit American goods at the same rate. But the colonies were not then self-governing, and Huskisson insisted that their tariffs should be determined by the British Parliament.

Other countries he met on terms of reciprocity, especially in making exceptions to the Navigation Laws.[1] He extended to the Latin-American republics the privileges given to the shipping of the United States, thus developing a brisk trade with the Spanish Main; but British and Nova Scotian shipping got the best of it. Guano from Peru was brought in great quantities to England as early as the 1820's. Huskisson's commercial treaty with the Argentine (1825) almost amounted to a fiscal union, admitting British merchants to Buenos Ayres on an equal footing with denizens. When steamships came into use in the 1840's the Pacific Steam Navigation Company established coaling-stations all along the coast of the continent. The value of British exports to Latin America in 1830 was £5,000,000, not far short of the goods worth £6,000,000 sent to the United States. British ranchers who began to raise sheep and cattle in the Argentine in mid-century were largely responsible for opening up the cool, empty grasslands of Patagonia.

West Indian sugar-planting had always been a chancy trade, exposed to violent fluctuations in the market and natural disasters by hurricane or earthquake. Perhaps it never had flourished except during the French Wars when scarcity produced high prices. Even before the abolition of slavery the older colonies were languishing.

The Whigs were determined to cheapen sugar which the working-classes consumed in ever greater volume. After a

[1] When they were finally repealed in 1849 little was left but a confused mass of exceptions and amendments.

long Parliamentary struggle Gladstone succeeded, in 1854, in removing the colonial preference, a step which reduced the planters
to despair. They were saved from collapse by the general rise in
prices in the 'sixties. Though impoverished by well-intentioned
philanthropists, neglected on principle by utilitarians, they continued to grow sugar and to live. The excellent Cape wines also
felt the weight of Gladstone's hand. Until he swept away the preferential duty (1861), 10% of all the wine drunk in England came
from the Cape; thereafter very little

The soft-wood trade of the St Lawrence had no defender when
the Admiralty turned to iron hulls and steam. Baltic pines would
content English buyers as well as those of New Brunswick or
Quebec and, in this case, no question arose of slave-labour in
either trade. The preference which Huskisson had allowed on
timber from British North America was swept away by Gladstone
in 1860. In spite of protests from the colonies he seemed justified
by the imports of the next few years. So great was the demand for
soft-woods that the annual import from the colonies steadily increased under Free Trade until 1867. But imports from the Baltic
increased more rapidly. Thereafter two-thirds of the British
supply came from the Baltic while the greater part of the Canadian
output went to the United States.

The great struggle over the Corn Laws touched the Empire at
one point only. The merchants of Montreal had prospered by
shipping their surplus of wheat from the St Lawrence to Great
Britain, and Peel had given them a preference of one shilling a
bushel in 1843. In spite of pressure from the Colonial Reformers
he refused to extend this preference to Australian wheat. The
whole advantage was abolished with the English Corn Law in
1846. Canadian wheat was a trifling consideration at that time,
hardly enough to sway the market price. No one foresaw the day
when England would depend for bread upon the harvest of the
prairie. No advantage accrued to England from the Canadian preference. A *douceur* to a struggling colony, it could not survive the
storm that swept away the Corn Laws.

It seems to posterity complacent in the extreme that the men
who withdrew colonial preferences and granted colonial self-
government should have still attempted to control colonial tariffs.
The Whigs took it very much amiss that Galt's government in
Canada, regarding the withdrawal of the preference on wheat as a

betrayal, should discriminate against British goods in the Canadian budget of 1859. They were still angrier when the Indian government attempted to discriminate against Manchester goods in the same year.

The East Indian trade is less easy to analyse. In the later days of the Company's commercial branch the only trading on a large scale had been the exchange of Bengal opium for China tea. India proper exported luxury goods and imported little, until English textiles, piece-goods woven in Lancashire of American cotton, began to find their way into Asia soon after Waterloo. An early visitor to Singapore reported the prevalence of English cotton cloths in Malaya even in 1830. Singapore and (after 1841) Hong Kong were free ports from which trade was distributed to all parts of the East. As soon as the new Indian government was formed it began (1859) a tariff struggle to protect the Indian industry against imported cotton goods. The prospect was changed by the American Civil War which put a stop for four years to the supply of raw cotton from the Southern States. Accordingly Lancashire bought up the Indian crop, the first large-scale importation of any form of Indian goods. When trade was resumed with the cotton-states of America the Indian merchants lost their short-lived trade and looked about for a substitute. Rice first came to England in quantity in the 'sixties and rice-pudding was then first seen in nurseries. Indian teak was also brought to England to build hard-wood ships which helped to drive the American clippers off the seas.

As the consumption of tea in England increased throughout the nineteenth century, the price fell steadily. When the China trade was thrown open in 1833 there was keen rivalry among ship-owners to seize this profitable trade from the slow East Indiamen. Samuel Cunard had been shipping direct to British North America since 1825 and now the Yankee Clippers came into the race. As in the southern wool trade the British ships had the best of it in the end. The great year of the tea-clippers was 1866 when nine Greenock ships left Foochow on a single tide. Three of them tied up together in London docks, having made an even passage round the Cape in ninety-nine days.

But by that date tea grown within the Empire was coming into the market. The wild tea-plant of Assam was noticed as early as 1820. After twenty years the first large plantation was made by the Assam Company which sent to London an inferior bitter tea consumable only when blended with Chinese. It was long before Indian tea improved in quality. By 1874 only 8% of British imported tea came from India, which now supplies much more than half. Tea-planting in Ceylon had not then begun.

Of Australian economy there is little to say here. Between 1820 and 1850 the export of wool, almost all of it to London, was multiplied tenfold. By the end of that period it was half the British supply and the best half in quality. The gold-rush of 1852 placed Australia on such a footing that the various states could finance their own development. Australia was less dependent than Canada or India upon the British investor, a fact which may have encouraged the self-reliant democracy of the Australians. The settlements scattered round the fringe of a continent trafficked by sea with one another and with England. Unlike the Canadians they were not burdened in their infancy with the cost of trunk railways.

The year 1860 saw the general triumph of free trade, the policy of the Open Door which for two generations was accepted by most progressives as a part of morality. It was clinched by Cobden's commercial treaty with France, the first of several treaties extending most-favoured-nation treatment to Continental countries. Great Britain thus deprived herself of the power to give preferences to colonial trade if ever thereafter she should wish to do so.

2. BRITISH SHIPPING AND CABLES

CAPTAIN COOK's achievements, which revealed the shape of the Pacific Ocean, also showed that long sea-voyages need not be prodigal of life. From the days of Magellan to those of Anson and Byron the hazards of a voyage to the Pacific had been so adverse as to deter commercial speculators. Cook was two years at sea without losing a man from preventible disease, and merchant ships soon imitated his measures against scurvy. It was not long before English ships came to be known as 'lime-juicers' and English seamen as 'limeys'.

The first commercial voyages into the Pacific, as it appears, were made by country-ships from the East Indian ports. On

Cook's third voyage his men had enriched themselves at Macao by selling skins of the sea-otter which they had brought from the Pacific coast of America. The news filtered through to Calcutta, into the receptive ear of John Henry Cox, an interloping trader. With connivance from friends in the East India Company he found his way to Canton, circumventing the Chinese authorities; and financed a series of voyages to seek for sea-otter skins. Cox was the backer of John Meares whose misadventures at Nootka Sound (see chapter v, 7, page 267) provoked the Spanish Armament in 1790. It is noteworthy that the Spanish Governor, after confiscating Meares's ship and goods, sold them obligingly to a Yankee skipper who was standing by to jump Meares's claim. Pitt's spirited reaction against the Spanish threats led to the opening of the Pacific to the trade of all nations. It was promptly invaded, in the 1790's, by numerous British and American whaling-ships, coming from East Indian ports or round the Horn.

The whalers were prepared to cruise for two or three years and to return only when their holds were filled with oil. In the words of the chantey, the whalemen 'never see the corn in the ear'. Though every whaler was a factory and depot-ship, it was common practice to leave a boat's crew for a season at a beach-whaling station on some prolific shore. As we have seen at Cook Strait, at Port Phillip, and in the Falkland Islands, shore-whaling stations sometimes grew into colonies. The whalers have no chronicle or statistics. Their activity and their profit grew with the demand for fine oil to lubricate the new machines, and declined as one species of whale after another was annihilated. Their contribution to the expansion of the British Empire must be indicated not computed. Though obscure in the records of the scientific historians it is clear enough in romance as the subject of a score of adventurous tales for boys.

The throwing open of the Pacific was followed by the abolition of the monopoly in the Indian trade (1813), and the China trade (1833–40); the repeal of the British Navigation Acts (1849); and the opening of Japan (1864).

Shipping plied on the old trade-routes, not much affected, for two generations, by the coming of steam-power. An engine had been put into a boat on the Clyde, by Symington, as early as 1789, but the first practical use of steamships derived from Robert Fulton's experiments and demonstrations in America, from 1807 onwards. Steamboats found their first opportunity on the American inland waterways. In the 1820's the celebrated stern-wheelers and side-wheelers, built like house-boats, were already plying up and down the Mississippi on wood-fuel. There was a steamer at Red River in 1839. In England inland water transport did not call for steam. The first British steamships were tugboats like that which for ever tows the *Fighting Téméraire* in Turner's picture (1839). The oldest sea-going steamship line in the world is the General Steam Navigation Company of London, founded in 1824 to carry passengers down to Margate, a run which was extended to the east-coast ports and Scotland.

Deep-sea voyages were beyond the capacity of the early steam-ships, simply because the ratio of fuel-consumption to engine-power was far too high. The ships could not carry enough coal to drive them across the Atlantic Ocean. Thus the claim to have made the first crossing by steam-power is put forward on behalf of several ships which carried auxiliary engines while depending in the last resort on sail. An American ship, the *Savannah*, crossed the Atlantic in 1819 with auxiliary steam, in seventeen days. It was a mere *tour de force*, leading to no further development. In 1833 the *Royal William*,[1] built and manned at Quebec through the endeavours of Samuel Cunard, made what is described as a crossing by steam which led to competitive attempts. The mer-chants of Calcutta and Bombay were also beginning to clamour for quicker communications than were provided by the slow East-Indiamen. It was indeed a great triumph for machinery when the *Enterprise* (470 tons and 120 h.p.) struggled round the Cape, mostly under steam, in 1825. She was piloted up the river to Cal-cutta by a young man named Thomas Waghorn (1800–50).

Logical progress towards steam communication pointed to carrying mails in fast steamships with a few passengers, while unhurried emigrants and bulky goods travelled under sail. The

[1] According to a writer in the *Mariner's Mirror* (January 1948) she was a paddle-steamer, schooner-rigged, with three tall masts; her length 176 feet, her engines developing 300 h.p.; her tonnage estimated at 363 tons 'burden' but actually much greater. Built for the St Lawrence trade she called at Boston in 1833, the first British steamer to visit an American port. Having been sold, she was despatched to England for disposal and left Pictou (Nova Scotia), 18 August 1833. When a gale disabled one engine she ran for ten days on her port engine only, and reached Gravesend on 12 September having averaged six knots, 'mostly under steam'. Sold as a warship to Spain she was the first steamship to fire a shot in action, 1834.

Admiralty had provided packet services of fast sailing-ships to carry mails since the seventeenth century. The regular services to Calais, the Hook of Holland, and Lisbon date from 1689, to Jamaica from 1702. Like most other public services in the eighteenth century they lapsed into an easy corrupt system of management by deputy. In the nineteenth century Post Office reform was begun by experiments with steam. The mails went from Liverpool to Dublin by steam-packet from 1819.

The first of the Royal Mail steamship companies is the 'P. & O.' which was founded by Arthur Anderson (1791–1868). He began his career as a blockade-runner in the Carlist Wars and specialised in taking light, fast ships from Falmouth to Lisbon. In August 1837 he advertised a service of five steamships to carry passengers and mails to Lisbon, Cadiz and Gibraltar, by contract for the General Post Office. His largest ship was of 900 tons with engines of 300 h.p. From Gibraltar the Admiralty already ran a steam-packet service in naval vessels to Malta but, for some years, the weak link was the run from Malta to Alexandria where the Overland Route began.

Thomas Waghorn, fascinated by steam and speed, had persuaded the Indian government to make some experiments in speeding the mail service, for which he agitated in Liverpool and London, making himself heartily disliked among the slow-coaches at the G.P.O. He plumped for the Overland Route. In Wellesley's day, despatches had been conveyed to India through Beirut and Basra, a road much beset by Bedouin robbers; Waghorn thought better of the route through Egypt and made a record trip from London by Trieste and Alexandria to Jedda in the Red Sea, in order to demonstrate its advantages. *The Times* now took up his case, threatening the East India House with awkward questions about its dilatory service of mails, until at last the Overland Mail was established in 1838. The Post Office extended its steam-packet service from Malta to Alexandria where Waghorn set up a travel agency for conveying passengers by stages through the desert to Suez. There they caught the mail-steamer, provided by the Indian government, to Bombay. The average time taken eastward to India was seventy-four days, and westward to England sixty-four days; the record run was fifty days.

Waghorn's service was conducted for five years (1838–43), the period from which dates the tourist traffic to Egypt, and the English 'colonies' at Alexandria and Cairo. Shepheard's Hotel was opened in 1844 as a rival to Waghorn's establishment. But the Post Office authorities disapproved of these interlopers. The Peninsular Steam Navigation Company was given a new contract in 1840 to take the mails through to India, which justified them in changing their name to the Peninsular and Oriental (P. & O.). In 1843 they floated a subsidiary company to manage the crossing of the desert, and put Waghorn out of business. He had transported 800 passengers in his last year.

Though he had lost all his money, Waghorn retained his energy and enthusiasm for rapid travel. He continued to harass the Post Office with schemes for sending the mails overland through Trieste. In 1845 and 1846 he was employed by the government to make further experiments. He twice achieved the timing of thirty days from Bombay, via Alexandria and Trieste, to London; but had great difficulty in recovering his expenses. He died in poverty in his fiftieth year (1850), having worn himself out with tropical voyaging. His furious energy and passion for speed were favourite subjects for the humorists of the age. He may well have supplied the model for Jules Verne's eccentric Englishman who went *Round the World in Eighty Days* (1872).

The organisation of the P. & O. Company in the days of the Overland Route was threefold. In Western waters they ran ships with English crews. East of Suez, after 1854, they used ships built for tropical seas and manned by Lascars (the hereditary caste of Moslem seamen from the coasts and islands of the Bay of Bengal). In Egypt they maintained resthouses, and caravans of 2500 camels and 400 horses, until they in their turn were supplanted by the Egyptian State Railways, which Robert Stephenson built for the Khedive (1858). The opening of the Suez Canal in 1869 was a sore blow to the P. & O. Company since their ships must now be refitted to make the whole voyage from England to India but, for many years more—until 1888—the mails and the passengers disembarked at Alexandria to go swiftly overland while the ship passed through the Canal dead slow, by daylight only.

The P. & O. Company designed steamships for comfort, even for luxury, on long voyages. In 1842 their crack ship was the *Hindostan*, a wooden paddle-steamer of 2000 tons with engines developing 520 h.p. at a pressure of 7 lb. Ten years later they could boast of the *Himalaya*, an iron-built screw-steamer of 3000 tons and 2500 h.p., able to carry 200 cabin passengers. A traveller to India described a voyage in the *Nyanza* (1800 tons) in 1869, with enthusiasm about the saloon and fitted cabins, for the P. & O. was the line of the empire-makers, the new governors going out to the scene of their triumphs. The fare, £95, included wines and spirits *gratis*, either at meals or when required. Dancing and games were enjoyed on deck but the other relaxations of modern cruising were not allowed. 'Strict etiquette was observed in clothing.' Since there were neither refrigerators nor electric fans, a cabin on the windward [1] side of the ship was a consideration.

The mail contracts were extended to China (1845), Australia (1856) and Japan (1864), until the P. & O. held something like a monopoly of Eastern travel. When competition came, the security of their government contracts enabled them to defy it and to lag behind in consideration for their passengers.

The year 1838 saw a contest for the Atlantic crossing by steam. Brunel of the Great Western Railway had built a ship named the *Great Western*, to extend his line of transport from Bristol to America. It made the round trip in fifteen days out and thirteen days home, but was preceded by a rival ship the *Sirius*. Among the observers of the contest was Joseph Howe of Nova Scotia who used his influence with the Home Government to give the mail contract to a steamship. Tenders were offered and the contract secured by Samuel Cunard, the Nova Scotian, for his Liverpool ship the *Britannia* which made the passage from Liverpool to Halifax in 15 days (1840), against Brunel's *Great Western*, a triumph for the Mersey as well as for Cunard. Regular sailings by four ships of the British and North American (Cunard) Line provided a fortnightly service to Halifax and Boston from September 1841. The P. & O. and the Cunard contracts were followed by the issue of mail contracts to steamship lines sailing to all parts of the Empire. The Royal Mail Steam Packet Company took over the Admiralty packet service to the West Indies; the Union Company (now Union Castle) to the Cape in 1857; the Allan Line, in opposition to the Cunard, obtained a contract for Canadian mails to Quebec in 1855. By 1860 the British government was paying a million pounds a year to steamship lines for carrying mails, a

---

[1] Port-side Outwards, Starboard-side Homewards. p.o.s.h. With regret I abandon this popular derivation, which is not substantiated, of the slang word 'posh'. C.E.C.

concealed subsidy which placed the British far ahead of their rivals
in marine engineering; for steamships could not yet be made to
pay without a subsidy. The Whigs had repealed the Navigation
Acts in 1849, as an act of devotion to the fetish of Free Trade,
and never noticed the protection they gave to the new shipping
industry in another way.

Yet all but the smallest steamships still depended upon auxiliary
sail in the last resort and, until the end of the century, were mostly
rigged with masts and spars. The first true ocean-going steamships, moved by steam-power and nothing else, were the ironclad
warships of the 'sixties. The Anglo-French rivalry of the years
1858–60 led to a race in naval armaments, similar to the Anglo-
German contest of fifty years later. Though French inventiveness
at first placed France in the lead, British superiority in marine
engineering and British industrial strength prevailed. Something
was learned from the improvised ironclads used in the American
Civil War, and more from the fast commerce-raiders fitted out in
European ports, but the problems of design were solved by naval
architects in the older countries. H.M.S. *Devastation*, launched in
1869, may be regarded as the model ironclad of the new age, an
'all-big-gun' ship with her armament in turrets placed amidships
and without masts or spars for carrying sail. Such ships produced
a revolution in naval strategy and tactics. Dispositions for war
were based on coaling-stations so that the value of the old naval
stations now depended upon supplies of coal. Cheap English
coal was towed about the world in hulks and stored at strategic
bases for the Navy. Similarly the Royal Mail Lines, especially the
P. & O., organised auxiliary fleets of coal-hulks.

While the British services turned to steam, the Americans, not
yet an industrial nation, concentrated on increasing the size, speed
and efficiency of their sailing-ships. The *Mayflower* had crossed
the Atlantic in sixty-six days. The news of the Declaration of
Independence, 150 years later, reached London by the easier
east-bound route in forty-four days. A substantial improvement
had been begun (1816) by the Blackball Clippers, actually the first
of all shipping 'lines'. Running to a schedule in fair weather or
foul, between New York and Liverpool, they averaged twenty-
three days eastbound and forty days westbound. Their ships were
built in progressively larger size, from 500 to 1200 tons; and at
last, in a few instances, reached 2000 tons. These were great four-

or five-masted sailing-ships, clipper-built, longer than British ships in proportion to their beam, and schooner-rigged to economise man-power. Though they held their own against the steamers in carrying emigrants and freight, their limitation was the difficulty of finding forecastle hands with sufficient stamina and strength. Yankee skippers were proud of their reputation for hard driving, which even British seamen admired and envied. It was no disgrace but good cause for pride to be

> mate of a bucko ship
> That always killed one man per trip.

On the longer runs they outsailed the mail steamers. The great days of the Blackball Line were the 'fifties when they grasped the Australian trade, going out with emigrants and coming home with wool. Driven recklessly before the westerly winds, with the landlubbers battened under hatches for days on end, they logged a steady sixteen knots through towering seas, a speed that no steamship could then achieve. British shipowners went into the trade, buying ships in New England and Nova Scotia or, later, building them on the Mersey or the Clyde. Some were celebrated, such as the *Cutty Sark* which is still afloat, or the even faster *Thermopylae* which carried mails to Melbourne under contract to pay a heavy forfeit for every day taken on the voyage in excess of sixty-eight. During the gold-rush of 1852 the two first steamships to reach Melbourne were sixty days out from London. The Blackball Liners, bought by Thomas Ismay of Liverpool, formed the nucleus of the White Star Line (1867), but teak-built British ships proved better than the soft-wood Americans.

As early as 1862 the Holt Line had built an economical steam cargo-ship, the first of many which at last drove the Stars and Stripes almost off the seas. The advantage of steam was certainty. Too often a sailing-ship, having made a record run from Cape Horn to the Lizard, lost its advantage beating against adverse winds in the Channel. Furthermore no less than 3% per annum of sailing-ships were lost at sea in the 'sixties. The proportion of steamships lost was less than half of 1%.

In 1830, American ships carried 90% of American trade; by 1890 they carried no more than 9%. The British had a million tons of steamships afloat in 1870 and held their lead well into the twentieth century. In 1910 Great Britain owned 40% of the world's shipping, her nearest rival being—not the United States—but Germany with 10%. Men were scarcer than ships. The unhonoured stokers and deckhands of the steamship lines inherited little of the glamour that had once surrounded the jolly tarpaulins who had been England's glory. The Merchant Service employed, in 1910, 280,000 seamen, of whom 80,000 were foreigners.

While speed in travel had obvious advantages, punctuality did not seem of equal importance in earlier days—could not until the addressee of a message or consignment had some means of knowing that it had been despatched. Perhaps the significance of the deep-sea cables has not been sufficiently noticed in history. Of all the mechanical devices introduced in the Great Century, surely these sensitive wires, sunk a thousand fathoms below any means of care or maintenance along an unsurveyed path of several thousand miles, are the most amazing. Merchants were sceptical of their use for many years, with good reason since they faded or failed intermittently.

Practical telegraphy was a by-product of railway-building and therefore, in the English railway age, was developed by private enterprise. The first telegraph line, built beside the Great Western Railway according to Wheatstone's patent of 1837, was thrown open to the public for sending outside messages in 1846. Telegraph lines multiplied with the new railways and surpassed them in 1851 by diving under the Channel from Dover to Calais. To stretch a cord across the Atlantic Ocean seemed too fantastically difficult a task, the crux of the problem being that no ship then afloat could carry a sufficient length of it. When a line was established from New York to New Brunswick, to Cape Breton Island and even to Newfoundland, an American engineer named Cyrus Field undertook to extend it across the Ocean (1856) with a financial guarantee from the British government. A ten years' struggle ensued, first on the principle of loading two ships with cables which were to be spliced together in mid-ocean and, when that failed, by packing the whole load into the hull of Brunel's *Great Eastern*, the ship built fifty years before her time. She was ten times as large as any other ship of her day, a 20,000-tonner of the same dimensions as the old *Mauretania*, but unmanageable since her engines could not develop sufficient power to hold her against bad weather, even though she was fitted with screws and paddles, and carried six masts rigged for auxiliary sail. A useless hulk, Brunel's Folly, she found her purpose as a cable ship.

When the line was at last laid from Land's End to Trinity Bay, Newfoundland, in 1866, transmission was so uncertain that it was still pronounced a failure. Not till the line was re-laid in 1872 was there regular communication. In the same years the deep-sea cables were rapidly extended, linking London with Bombay in 1870, with Melbourne in 1872, with Wellington in 1876. The world-wide linkage of London with the outer seas was completed in 1893–4, by the Eastern Telegraph Company, a British company controlling the main services to the Far East and the Islands. Some very lonely places gained a new importance as cable stations, among them Cocos Island, Norfolk Island, Fanning Island, and Ascension.

The reorganisation of the Post Office seemed to run counter to the *laissez-faire* principles of the age, so that it was odd to find Chambers of Commerce agitating in 1856 for cheap rates through the public ownership of telegraphs. This was achieved in 1868 in respect of inland telegraph lines. By an agreement between parties in Parliament the six telegraph companies were bought out for £6,000,000 and placed under management of the Post Office. The cable-services, excepting the Anglo-French cable which the Post Office took over in 1889, were still privately owned (as were telephone and radio services when, much later, they came into general use). In Canada, where the Far West looks across the sea to the Far East, cables round the world were more to the point than cables radiating from London. It is to Canada and especially to Sir Sandford Fleming, one of the builders of the Canadian Pacific Railway, that the Empire owed the conception of 'all-red routes', that is to say world-embracing links between all the countries coloured red on the map. This was the theme of the Ottawa Conference on imperial communications in 1894. A standard postal rate of one penny, or two cents, between all parts of the Empire as proposed by Sir W. Mulock, the Postmaster-General of Canada, and supported by Sir J. Ward, the Postmaster-General of New Zealand, was readily accepted. The 'all-red' cable route was more difficult. Though Canada and New Zealand were enthusiastic, Australia was lukewarm since her economy was nearer to the old world than the new. One of the triumphs of pioneering in Australia had been the overland telegraph line from Adelaide to

Darwin, linked to Java and the main Asiatic services, and completed in 1873. Having this service the Australians did not relish the expense of providing an alternative route across 6000 miles of ocean. However, the proposal for completing the circuit of the world by a trans-Pacific cable was strongly supported by Chamberlain when he came to the Colonial Office in 1895. Departmental committees in 1897 and 1899 urged its construction in spite of opposition from the Post Office and the Treasury. They were for leaving such matters to private enterprise, which won for them the influential backing of the cable companies. In 1900 Chamberlain got his way, overruling the other departments and securing the support of Australia. Tenders were issued for the laying of a cable to be managed jointly by the governments of the United Kingdom, Canada, Australia and New Zealand through a Pacific Cable Board. The cable was laid in 1902, at a cost of £2,000,000, from Vancouver to Fanning Island, Suva (Fiji), and Norfolk Island whence it divided into two branches running respectively to Queensland and northern New Zealand.

At the Imperial Conference of 1911 the Dominion premiers raised the question of applying the new technique of wireless telegraphy to 'all-red' communications. They were assured that the Postmaster-General, Mr Herbert (now Viscount) Samuel, was already negotiating contracts for an imperial wireless chain. Tenders were issued and agreements signed in 1912 with the Marconi Company. It was the suggestion that some members of the government had used their secret information to 'bull the market' in Marconi shares that caused one of the nastiest scandals of the age.

Modern commerce dates from the institution of the submarine cables which put the importing merchant in direct touch with his source of supply. He was now enabled to buy raw cotton or wool, sugar or tea, before shipment and to estimate the date of its arrival. Accordingly transactions on the exchanges at London, Liverpool and Manchester assumed the form which has become familiar.

Another consequence of regular sailings on the shipping-routes was the appearance of that typical English figure, the 'globe-trotter'. The English had long been known as a race of travellers but not of travellers round the world. Until the nineteenth century circumnavigations were still so rare as to be placed on record.

Seamen and emigrants went their ways but travellers for pleasure rarely strayed beyond the Grand Tour of France, Italy and the Rhineland. When the Travellers' Club was formed in 1819, the qualification for membership was to have travelled 'out of the British Islands to a distance of at least five hundred miles from London', this being the limit of mere commonplace touring. In the 'thirties and 'forties trips to America became fashionable. Literary men went there, like Dickens in 1842, to write a travel-book. Young men of fashion, like Lord Stanley when out of office in 1834, toured North America, took a glance at the Far West, perhaps even went to Red River for the buffalo-hunting. Twenty years later the steamship lines took them on to Melbourne and California. Lord Salisbury (then Lord Robert Cecil) was one of the first among young noblemen to extend the traditional Grand Tour to a trip round the world (1851–3). He thought poorly of colonial life. Sir Charles Dilke, after an extensive tour in 1866 and 1867, published his views in *Greater Britain*, a curious jumble of acute observation, perverse politics, and reckless prophecy.

J. A. Froude was another globe-trotting literary man whose descriptions of the colonies may still be read with profit; but the best among them was Anthony Trollope who combined business with pleasure by travelling to make reports for the Post Office. His robust, unsentimental books on *The West Indies* (1859), *North America* (1862), *Australia and New Zealand* (1873), *South Africa* (1878) are the best contemporary accounts of the colonies before imperialism came into fashion. The first royal tours were the visit to Canada in 1860 by the Prince of Wales, and a voyage to all the colonies in 1869–72 by his younger brother, the Duke of Edinburgh. After the 1880's globe-trotting had become so normal and easy as to deserve no further mention here.

3. THE EXPORT OF BRITISH CAPITAL[1]

BEFORE the French Revolution Amsterdam had been the financial capital of Europe. Dutch capitalists were believed to have held one-quarter of the shares in the British national debt, and Dutch bankers advanced money at a low rate of interest to London merchants who invested it at a high rate in the British West Indies. After Waterloo London became, for a hundred years, the unchallenged money-market of the world, with surplus capital always available for investment.

In the older wars the British had financed their allies by subsidies from the Treasury; the first foreign loan, as distinct from a subsidy, was that to Austria in 1794. When peace came, twenty years later, the agents of foreign governments flocked to London for money on commercial terms, and got it—perhaps too easily— from the great banking houses, among which Baring's was the most eminent. Many years passed before this new form of trading was accepted as worthy of political support. Neither Castlereagh nor Canning nor Aberdeen nor Palmerston regarded foreign investment as anything more than speculation by private persons or groups. Loans were rarely supported by a public guarantee, nor was any help given to the investors in collecting debts.

The first phase in the export of British capital was the financing of reconstruction in Europe after the wars, for which about £50,000,000 was pretty securely invested between 1815 and 1830. It was not by the wish of the Tory administration that a second phase followed of financing revolution in Greece and Latin America. The boom began with an advance to the republicans of Colombia in 1820 and continued until the bank failures of 1826, by which time about £20,000,000 had been subscribed for seven or eight revolutionary juntas. The shareholders for the most part lost their money. Two loans, nominally amounting to £2,800,000 had also been raised in 1824 by enthusiasts in London, for the Greek patriots. These also proved most unprofitable to the subscribers though very lucrative to the financial houses that issued

---

[1] In writing this slight essay upon an abstruse and contentious subject I have in general followed E. H. Jenk's *Migration of British Capital*, 1927. While paying a tribute to this scholarly and penetrating book I venture to dissent from the thesis which the author implies with delicate irony in almost every chapter, that few men and no Englishmen act on other than mercenary motives.

them. Joseph Hume the Radical made himself a rich man by commissions on the Greek loans.

The general history of these proceedings was that money was raised in London, and mostly spent there, on ships and arms and retaining fees to soldiers of fortune. When the financial houses had covered their own risk by deducting commission and interest in advance, the remainder was placed at the disposal of the revolutionary leaders. About one-tenth of the Greek loan was spent in Greece. So, in the case of the Mexican loans at the same date, about one-third of the £6,000,000 nominally subscribed was transferred to Mexico. But these were war loans which the revolutionaries accepted with open eyes. The difficulty was that affairs remained too unstable in Greece and Latin America for the burden of debt to be carried. In almost every instance the liability was repudiated at the next turn of the revolutionary wheel. When a new junta came, hat in hand, to the London bankers the terms for a new loan would be found to include some adjusted responsibility for the old one, with a mortgage upon the revenue to ensure payment of interest. This arrangement too would be repudiated at the next change of government, and would make the terms offered to future borrowers still more onerous. Thus the liability of Mexico to the bond-holders was doubled between 1821 and 1857 without any tangible advantage to the Mexicans; whereas the bond-holders received dividends only in the intervals between revolutions and only by foreclosing their mortgage on the Mexican customs.

In addition to these government loans much British money was invested in South American mining and engineering projects, beginning with a speculative boom (1825–6) when young Benjamin Disraeli was employed to write prospectuses for bubble companies, when Robert Stephenson went to Buenos Ayres to construct mine tramways, when Cornish miners were shipped to the Andes to improve mining techniques, and Scottish milkmaids to the Pampas to teach the *gauchos* to make butter. Though the bubble burst, these schemes were not entirely unproductive.[1] British capital, British technicians, and even some emigrants continued to find their way to South America and particularly to the

---

[1] Mr Dombey considered that to break one's heart on account of an adverse speculation in Peruvian mines was 'a very respectable way of doing it', as well he might when Dombey and Son grew rich by negotiating the loan.

River Plate. Commercial and banking houses established their agencies in South America to handle the exports from Great Britain. The financial connexion was supported by the shipping connexion, which was almost a British monopoly, and in due time the South American railways were built, largely with British capital and British skill. By the end of the century British investments in Latin America were worth not less than £300,000,000.

The 1830's saw an investment boom in the United States. About £30,000,000 was advanced by the London bankers to the agents of several states of the Union, with the effect of creating an inflationary movement in the South. Reckless finance produced the American banking crisis of 1837–9 which obliged nine states to repudiate their debts, three of them (Michigan, Arkansas, and Mississippi) finally and absolutely. American credit sank so low that the federal government itself was unable to raise a loan anywhere in Europe. 'Not a dollar', said Rothschild. It was against the background of this speculative misuse of surplus capital that Wakefield brought forward his plan for the simultaneous exportation of surplus men and money. Very little capital had been invested in the colonies during those years, the most noteworthy issues being for land development companies in Canada and Australia. The largest and most successful were the Canada Company (1826), the British North America Company (1834) and the South Australian Association (1834). It is hard to say how much capital they actually exported. In the case of the Emancipation Loan (1835) which was raised by Rothschild in London and charged to the British national debt, perhaps £10,000,000 was actually distributed in the colonies.

Overseas investment passed into a new phase with the boom in railway construction. Observers noted that it brought a new set of men into the money-market, raising the firm of Glyn Mills to the first rank among the banking houses. Even before the bad times of 1846–8 the railway contractors had begun to reach out into France and Belgium. Later, in the great age of expansion which we may attribute to the effect of steam, free trade, or gold discoveries, they carried their efforts into all parts of the world. The trunk lines were financed with British money, equipped with British rails and engines, surveyed by British engineers and, in many instances, constructed by British navvies. Greatest of the railway contractors, greater even than the Stephensons in the scope of his achievement, was Thomas Brassey (1805–70) who undertook 170 contracts for 8000 miles of railway in five continents between 1840 and 1865.[1] He employed 80,000 men in all, sending them abroad in organised parties of labourers with teachers, doctors and clergy. There were 4000 British navvies working for him on the Paris-Rouen railway alone. This was solid productive work quite unlike the speculative finance of the eighteen-twenties. It enabled him to survive the great crash of Overend Gurney in 1866 which brought down so many railway financiers. His foreign customers got value for money while Great Britain benefited by the direct earnings of the capital, by the sale of iron rails and locomotives, and by the wages paid to British engineers and labourers. But the monopoly was too rich to last. After the 'fifties and 'sixties industrial expansion was world-wide. Under the Second Empire Napoleon III tempted the savings of the frugal French out of the proverbial stocking into productive investment. The French began to finance their own railways and then to export their own surplus capital in competition with the British. No sooner was the Civil War over (1865) than the wealth of America began to be felt in the financial world. From year to year the Americans were less dependent upon importing British machinery, better able to finance their own expansion, more inclined to invest their occasional surplus of capital abroad, especially in Canada. Germany appeared as a third competitor after 1871. The Utopian dream of Free Trade had faded. Protective tariffs, strategic railways and guaranteed loans were the dominant factors in the politics of the late nineteenth century, even in the British Empire, though England itself clung to the doctrine of Free Trade.

One of the first of these imperialist projects was that for the Grand Trunk Railway of Canada (1852–64). Should the trade go by the American canals to the Hudson River and New York; or by the earliest Canadian railway—then the only international

---

[1] For example: 1841 Paris-Rouen Railway.
  1852 Grand Trunk of Canada Railway.
  1854 Turin-Mont Cenis Railway.
  1858 Eastern Bengal Railway.
  1862 Mauritius Railway.
  1863 Queensland Railway.
  1864 Central Argentine Railway.
  1864 Lemberg-Czernowitz Railway.

railway in the world—from Montreal to Portland, Maine (1853), or by a new route through British territory to the Maritime Provinces? The merchants of Montreal and Upper Canada were disposed to look southwards to the United States for their commercial routes, and to develop that trade on terms of reciprocity, though the easy route between Lower Canada and the open sea had been blocked by the Ashburton-Webster Treaty of 1842. The Colonial Office (under Lord Grey), and the influence of the Colonial Reformers, were for a railway through British territory at whatever cost. An Act of the Canadian legislature was passed to guarantee a British loan, financed by Barings and Glyn Mills, whereupon Brassey hurried to Canada to supervise the contract. The Grand Trunk Railway was routed for strategic rather than commercial reasons and never paid its way in sixty years. It cost the British investor about £12,000,000. Perhaps the best purpose it served was to induce the recalcitrant electorate of Nova Scotia to accept confederation with Canada.

During the early railway boom several proposals were made for railways in India. When Dalhousie became Governor-General (1848) they were revived but on a new principle. Watching with interest the methodical planning of state railways in France by Napoleon III he proposed for India a similar system which should avoid the haphazard speculative method of the English. His plans, which were approved in 1853, had made some progress when they were interrupted by the Mutiny. By that time about £14,000,000 had been invested by British shareholders who found that the price of stock stood firm. The settlement of India in 1858 was followed by a large increase in trade, particularly in cotton during the American Civil War. Accordingly India became the best field for the investment of capital. By 1870 about £150,000,000 of British money had been committed there, half of it in railways. It was noticed that Indian capitalists who invested freely in government bonds showed a strange unwillingness to take up guaranteed railway shares. Dalhousie's intention had been to limit Indian liability, to control costs, and to grant railway concessions only for a term of years. These safeguards were whittled away, through the influence of the moneyed men and the *laissez-faire* economists, in spite of the efforts of John Lawrence to preserve them. The Indian lines were well built and well designed, but at great expense. Too large a proportion of the Indian tax-revenue was always withdrawn to London in the form of 'Home Charges', which amounted in the 'sixties to £10,000,000 a year, mostly interest on guaranteed loans.

Personal control by a few great banking-houses over the market in foreign loans was never so great after the Overend Gurney failure of 1866. On the one hand the influence of governments was more directly applied; on the other hand the interest, and political power, of the small investor was beginning to be felt, owing to the principle of Limited Liability which was consolidated in English practice by the Act of 1862. With his liability limited and his interest secured by a government guarantee, the small investor found colonial bonds, paying 5% or 6%, increasingly attractive, though they were not classified as Trustee Stock until 1900. Except in rare instances, foreign holdings were still not secured by the British government but, after 1868, investors' rights were upheld by the influential Corporation of Foreign Bondholders, representing capital valued at £800,000,000.

All statistics of the export of capital are estimates and those of earlier date than 1854[1] are mere conjectures. Thereafter, accurate figures of new issues are available. The annual export of British capital in the 1830's may have averaged £30,000,000; in the 1860's it was £60,000,000. In 1872 it reached a record high figure of £83,000,000; and slumped in the succeeding years of depression. Between 1875 and 1880 more capital was withdrawn to London than was exported. Since by this date the United States and Germany were beginning to finance their own expansion, British investment went farther afield, largely to South America and to Australia which in the 1880's, for the first time, attracted capital in great quantities. It was in these years that the English became dependent for more than half their foodstuffs upon distant sources of supply, and paid for them in part by financial services. In 1890 the export of capital again reached the figure of £82,000,000. After a decline during the Boer War which swallowed up the available surplus, the export was again renewed in the twentieth century at a vastly increased rate, reaching the figure of £246,000,000 in 1912. During this phase Canada and the Argentine received the largest share.

In 1854 the total holdings of British investors overseas may have been as much as £500,000,000. In 1875, at the end of the first

---

[1] The figures in the following paragraphs are mostly derived from *The Migration of Capital* by C. K. Hobson.

great period of expansion, the sum has been estimated with a fair degree of probability at £1,300,000,000, of which £125,000,000 was in Indian and colonial railways, £118,000,000 in colonial government bonds, and £115,000,000 in other investments within the Empire. By 1909 the total sum exceeded £2,330,000,000, of which perhaps half was held within the Empire, one-fifth in the United States and one-fifth in Latin America.

Taking a longer view it may now be seen that investment within the Empire has been in every way more advantageous to Great Britain than investment in foreign lands. Not only was there no repudiation in the colonies, no writing-down of the value of shares for political reasons, no confiscation by revolutionary juntas, but colonial investments brought immediate and positive returns. Foreign loans were spent either on public works which brought no advantage to the lender beyond the interest on his money, or on armaments which were a menace to him. In the case of railway loans some part of the capital might be spent on British equipment, but of this there was no certainty. On the other hand much of the money lent to the Canadian Pacific Railway never left England; it was at once invested in British rails and locomotives. 'Of the loans for Indian railways, about one-third went to pay the Home Charges in London; something under one-third was spent on wages and administrative expenses, largely paid to English engineers; something over one-third on British rails and engines and in paying British ships to bring them to India.'

'Even those loans raised in New Zealand to pay for the Maori Wars and by the Indian Government to pay for suppressing the Mutiny went largely to people likely to increase the direct demand for British goods. Much went to produce, at lower prices, raw material for the industries of Britain and food for her people.' Still more valuable was the export of young men of the middle classes to the agencies of shipping, banking, and commercial firms. These men with the engineers, surveyors, doctors, and other technicians were the makers of the mid-Victorian Empire.

The years between 1850 and 1875 are a period unique in history for rapidity and magnitude of economic expansion. The export values (from Great Britain) increased by 40% between 1840 and 1850, by 90% in the next decade, and by 47% between 1860 and 1870. Wages, which had been almost steady between 1830 and 1850, rose by almost 56% between 1850 and 1874. Whatever method of computation is used, the national income and the amount of capital were growing prodigiously during these years. Between 1865 and 1875 the amount of capital increased by nearly 50%. The explanation of this efflorescence has been found in a great variety of circumstances: factory legislation, trade unions, the new railways and the new gold from California and Australia. But none of these by themselves explains satisfactorily the substantial rise in real wages. An important part of the explanation is to be found in the character and extent of English overseas investment between 1850 and 1875 and further in the fact that so large a proportion of it was to new and undeveloped countries within the Empire.[1]

At the conclusion of the third great phase of British expansion the total sum of British investments overseas was estimated (December 1913) at £3,763,000,000,[2] of which about 47% was invested in the British Empire, 20% in the United States, 8% in the Argentine, 6% in Continental Europe, 3% in China and Japan, 1% in Egypt. The proportion invested in the British Empire, 47%, was made up as follows: 14% in Canada and Newfoundland, 11% in Australia and New Zealand, 10% in India and Ceylon, nearly 10% in South Africa, 1% in West Africa and less than 1% in Malaya. Or, if the whole sum of £3,763,000,000 is classified by the nature of the investment, about 40% was invested in railways, 30% in government and municipal bonds, 5% in public utilities, and the rest in industry and finance. The annual income earned by these investments was, in 1913, about £200,000,000.

During the first German War British overseas investments were reduced by about £850,000,000, two-thirds of the reduction being securities sold in the United States. This was one of the steps which converted the United States from a debtor country, to the amount of £500,000,000 on balance in 1914, into a creditor country, to the amount of about £1,200,000,000 in 1922. These figures take no account of the war-time credits which France and Great Britain advanced to their weaker allies, or of the credits which the United States advanced to France and Great Britain, since almost all were, sooner or later, repudiated.

British investment overseas was resumed during the 1920's, too lavishly, in the view of some economists, in proportion to the progress of trade, though never on the scale of the pre-war years. By 1930, when the shadow of world-wide economic depression was deepening, the total figure of British overseas investments was

---

[1] H. J. Habbakuk in the *Cambridge History of the British Empire*, vol. ii.

[2] Estimated figures, based on *The Problem of International Investment*, Royal Institute of International Affairs, 1937.

back to something like the pre-war figure, but with a difference. Of the holdings 60% were now in Empire countries and only 5% in the United States. Canada, still a debtor country though highly industrialised, now owed more to the United States than to Great Britain. The older British investment (£540,000,000), mostly in government and railway securities, had been surpassed by the new American investment (£720,000,000) mostly in municipal bonds, public utilities and industry. Australia, on the other hand, had borrowed heavily, perhaps too heavily. Her indebtedness to London amounted to £494,000,000, 13% of the whole British overseas investment and a heavy burden on the Australian economy in the depressed 1930's.

4. THE GOLD-RUSHES, 1848–98[1]

DURING the eighteenth century the main source of the European supply of gold was Brazil which produced, at best, about 500,000 ounces annually. Production from the Gold Coast, averaging perhaps one-tenth of this amount, was not enough to sway the world market. The South American gold rushes, about the years 1730–50, saw the beginnings of that customary code of miners' law which spread through the whole world a century later. Though Brazilian gold was a Portuguese royal monopoly the restricted ownership of bullion proved illusory. It was used to finance the export to Brazil of goods, largely of English origin and handled by English commercial firms. There is little doubt that much of the advantage and some of the actual bullion drawn from the Brazilian mines helped to build up England's expanding trade.

The gold of the Ural Mountains, produced by servile labour in provinces remote from Western commerce, was used to finance the eastward march of Russia. The greater fields in Eastern Siberia were producing 900,000 ounces annually in the 1840's. Distances were long and roads were bad to the swamps and forests where the gold was found. Russia's backward industries could not provide machinery for mining until the opening of the Siberian Railway in 1891, yet the output steadily rose, to 1,400,000 ounces a year in the 'eighties, and to 1,900,000 ounces in 1914.

[1] For the information in this chapter I am obliged to Professor W. P. Morrell, who has allowed me to draw upon his standard work, *The Gold-Rushes*.

The mechanised mining which was made possible by railway development was largely financed by British capital. But this steady increase in gold production was part of the gradual growth of the world's industries which gives the nineteenth century its general character. The gold-rushes of the English-speaking peoples to California and Australia, to British Columbia and New Zealand, to South Africa and the Klondyke were phenomena of a distinct sort.

The Californian and Victorian gold-rushes of 1849–53 multiplied the world's total annual output six or seven times over. The stimulus of so great an increase in the gold backing to the currencies promoted an age of expanding trade and rising prices which lasted about twenty years. After 1866 the output of gold fell by a third but was still much higher than in the years before 1849. France and Germany adopted the gold standard; while the United States, which fought the Civil War on paper 'green-backs', was able to stabilise them at a rate convertible with gold. After twenty years of less rapid expansion the second group of gold-rushes, to the Rand and the Klondyke, produced another period of expansion. Between 1893 and 1913 the world's stock of gold was doubled.

The financial effects are surpassed in interest by the social and political effects. Whole new nations were called into existence by the emigration to the gold-fields in America and Australia, where a new type of society emerged. It is hardly too much to say that until 1849 the typical emigrant was a peasant in search of land, a natural conservative; after 1849 the typical emigrant was a digger, a man who would turn from working with pick and shovel on his own mining-claim to working with pick and shovel for a capitalist mine-owner or railway company. Such a man was a natural Radical strongly moved by the lessons of the hungry 'forties in Europe, sometimes a Chartist or revolutionary from the barricades of 'forty-eight. The prospector and the mining-engineer were now the leaders of the host, men very different in stamp from the *voortrekkers* of the older age. Thus the mining-camps of California pointed the way to the social changes which, with local variation, would appear successively in each of the British Dominions.

The gold-rush of 1849 was a by-product of the filibustering activity which added Texas, New Mexico, and California to the

United States. Settlers of the type that infiltrated these Latin-American provinces, overthrew their government, and seized control by force of arms were the most adventurous even of the frontiersmen. There were prospectors among them who had learned the technique of gold-hunting in the smaller fields of North Carolina. California was still under martial law, without settled government, when gold was found on the Sacramento River (24 January 1848). By the end of the year 10,000 men had flocked to the scene of the discoveries, but the main force, numbering over 80,000, the "forty-niners', of whom only one-tenth were women, did not reach this wilderness beyond the Rocky Mountains until the following year. They raised about 2,500,000 ounces of gold in the first season. Half the immigrants arrived by land from the Middle-Western states, over the newly-opened Oregon Trail. A quarter came by sea round the Horn in ships from New England, the remaining quarter by way of Panama. There was a railway across the Isthmus in the 'fifties, and talk already of an isthmian canal (see chapter v, 8, page 280). The Pacific Steam Navigation Company ran ships from Panama to San Francisco.

The miners, mostly Americans from the North, showed from the first their intention to make California a white man's country. There was no negro slavery, which put them out of favour with the dominant party at Washington: and, when Chinese immigrants appeared, they were met with plain hostility. Nor were other foreigners welcomed. The celebrated Vigilance Committee of San Francisco was formed largely to discipline certain unruly Australians, known as 'Sydney Coves' or 'Sydney Ducks', who had found their way across the Pacific. But the true character of the Californian miners was shown in their instant spontaneous organisation of democratic forms of government. The astounding fact is not that there was so much violent disorder, but that there was so little. At every new gold-field a diggers' committee enforced the two fundamental laws: 'jumping' another miner's claim or stealing his gold were instantly punished by the hand of popular justice. The extensive literature of the gold-fields—Bret Harte (1839–1902) was the first writer of repute—gives the impression that the miners themselves were industrious and law-abiding, though the chances of their profession disposed them to reckless gambling. Life at a new mining-camp was decent though rough. It was in the mushroom cities like San Francisco, which sprang into existence as depots for supplying stores and buying gold, that the harpies and the parasites, the swindlers, the card-sharpers, the confidence-men and the racketeers congregated. Since California had no law and no administration, these evils flourished unchecked, but not for long. As early as November 1849 the miners' committees elected a constituent assembly and formed themselves into a state. Their sternest trouble was to persuade the politicians at Washington to help or even recognise them, since the admission of another free state to the Union was a sore blow to the defenders of slavery.

By 1853 the number of miners had reached 100,000 and the output of gold 4,000,000 ounces. This was the climax of the boom from which California relaxed slowly into a less feverish condition. The independent diggers and prospectors had moved on by 1860, to carry into every continent the tradition of the 'forty-niners.

The diggers, who flocked to Australia when gold was reported there, wore characteristic costume: a red shirt open at the neck, moleskin trousers stuffed into the boots, a wide-brimmed slouch hat and an ostentatious pistol in the belt. Their jargon was already creeping into popular speech, with its talk of life at the diggings: of staking claims, and making lucky strikes, and getting down to bedrock, and watching how things panned out, and finding an expected Bonanza already a wash-out, and going stony-broke. The routine of a gold-field follows a typical course. First comes the solitary prospector, 'in a cavern, in a canyon, excavating for a mine', a pioneer of secretive habits, with an eye for country, washing samples of alluvial mud in every likely creek until the shining particles left in his pan satisfy him as 'payable gold'. He must keep his secret and register his find with the competent authority, often many hundred miles away, before pegging out a claim according to the lie of the land and the custom of the country. Now the secret is out and shrewd observers will be close on his track to peg out claims as near as possible to the original 'strike'. Claims in California were no more than ten feet square on some fields, and rarely more than thirty feet square, by diggers' law. If the first-comers strike it lucky, washing out an ounce or more a day for each hand in a gang of three or four, a rush soon sets in. Experienced diggers are followed by hordes of amateurs ('greenhorns', 'tenderfeet', 'new chums', 'cheechakos'—according to the jargon of the country), who may 'shout on seven-ounce nuggets' or may flinch at the hard labour of digging, starve through not knowing how to 'rough it', be bullied, or be cheated out of their claims. Soon the camp burgeons into a boom-town of tents and huts, vaingloriously named Eureka or Eldorado City, largely composed of saloons and gambling-booths where little sacks of gold-dust pass as currency. Now speculators in claims begin to make more money than diggers, and the price of a claim may be less than the price of the site for a provision store where a trader 'grub-stakes' the mining gangs. The cost of food and transport soars in a society that lives on an increasing flow of easy money. Inevitably, as the best sites are washed out, and the population grows, the profits of labour show a diminishing return, until the old hands begin to slink away in search of a new field. When the nuggets embedded in the superficial mud of the creeks have all been found, payable gold must be sought deeper where ancient watercourses have been buried, sometimes, as at Ballarat, beneath layers of hard clay, or, as in New Zealand, under beds of gravel, or, as in Alaska, deep in frozen mud. It becomes worth while to gather the smallest particles of gold by washing in a tank containing quicksilver with which the gold forms an amalgam; to sluice down and wash away the sides of ravines under hydraulic pressure; to break up frozen ground with jets of steam; and to pursue the veins of gold into the auriferous rock with drills and crushing machines. The speculators, the amateur miners and the human parasites who prey on them abandon the goldfield to the workers in a mechanised industry. Last of all, when that has ceased to pay, comes the 'fossicker', often an old solitary, who makes a meagre living picking over the 'tailings' of the mine for the crumbs of gold that have been overlooked, in a landscape stripped and scraped and scarred.

The finding of gold had several times been reported in Australia before 1851, but prospecting had been discouraged by governors who feared the anarchy of a gold-rush in a convict country. The Californian boom made such a restrictive policy untenable. Edgar Hammond Hargraves (1816–91), an Australian who went to California, returned convinced that he could find gold in his own land. According to an apocryphal story an American shouted after his departing figure, 'There's no gold in the country you're going to,

and, if there is, that darned Queen of yours won't let you dig it.'
Hargraves replied with mock dignity, 'There's as much gold in the
country I'm going to as there is in California, and Her Most
Gracious Majesty, Queen Victoria—God bless her—will appoint
me one of the Gold Commissioners.' He was right. In the spring
of 1851 he reported several finds, and in May a gold-rush began
to the Turon field in New South Wales. Sydney poured forth its
citizens even though it was race-week.

The Turon goldfield, though it will be familiar to readers of
that old-fashioned classic tale, *Robbery Under Arms*, was soon exhausted when 4000 diggers had washed 100,000 ounces of gold.
The most notable episode in the rush was the finding of a block of
quartz containing 1200 ounces by an aboriginal shepherd whose
master rewarded him with gifts of a flock of sheep and a team of
horses. Later in the year much more lucrative finds were made at
Ballarat (August) and Bendigo (September 1851). These were in
the new squatters' state of Victoria, lately separated from New
South Wales, and inhabited by 97,000 settlers and 6,000,000 sheep.
Only a few months earlier Lord Grey's Act had enabled the Vic-
torians to draft a constitution. Nothing had yet been done and
Governor Latrobe found himself obliged to control an unruly influx of diggers without adequate revenue or constitutional support. In September there were 7000 diggers at work; by December 20,000; by February 1852, 40,000 at Bendigo Creek alone. In
June 1852, 70,000 men at the various Victorian diggings were
washing out 30,000 ounces a month, at the time when the output
of California, too, was at its climax. One twenty-four-foot claim
at Ballarat produced gold worth £55,000, in five weeks during
which its ownership five times changed hands. By 1854 the population of Victoria had reached 400,000 and, by 1861, 540,000, of
whom half were immigrants from the British Isles. The Victorian
gold-miners were not experienced pioneers and prospectors as
were the 'forty-niners of California; they were for the most part
'new chums', including many Irish labourers, and some English
Chartists. They found no municipal government at Ballarat and
Bendigo, and a narrow freeholders' franchise for the legislative
council, while law was enforced by an armed corps of police who
were accustomed to disciplining convicts. No publicans' licences
were issued at the goldfields with the result that 'sly-grog-shops',
and the petty corruption that accompanies them, flourished. Yet

there was law and order. The miners' code was observed, and maintained by the police.

Governor C. J. Latrobe (1801–75), with no means of raising revenue except from miners' licence-fees (thirty shillings a month), in an empty capital city from which dockers, civil officials, Government House servants, and even policemen had decamped to make easy money at the diggings, yet did pretty well. He sent Gold Commissioners (of whom Hargraves was one) to allot claims; organised an escort for conveying gold to Melbourne; and established an Assay Office. In the time of his successor Sir C. Hotham (1806–55), the system broke down on the score of objection to paying licence-fees. A poll-tax that fell as heavily on the unlucky as on the lucky digger, in a community without responsible government, could not be collected without disorder. While dilatory plans were being made for constitutional reform, a riot provoked by a petty miscarriage of justice broke out at Ballarat. Impatience, ebullient democracy, and dislike of the police—who have never been popular in Australia—led to the growth of a republican movement, largely Irish in sentiment. A flag, with four silver stars on a blue ground, was adopted and a rude fortification built at Eureka near Ballarat, with no clearly defined purpose. Governor Hotham, acting promptly before the affair should get out of hand, sent a company of soldiers with some police, who stormed the Eureka Stockade on 3 December 1854. This violent irrational episode, in which four soldiers and thirty miners were killed, is the only land-battle ever fought on the Australian continent. Hotham insisted on prosecuting the defenders for treason but the juries refused to convict. The leader of the rebels Peter Lalor (1823–89), an Irishman bred at Trinity College, Dublin, having lost an arm in the Eureka fighting, lived to be the highly respected Speaker of the Victorian Legislature. The story of the diggers' stand for democratic rights is an honoured legend and the silver stars of the Eureka flag are still to be seen on the flag of Australia.[1]

[1] Since, at that date, there was no submarine cable east of Suez, the incident at Eureka on that southern summer morning was not quickly recorded in England, where all eyes were turned towards the Black Sea. The battle of Inkerman had been fought a few days earlier. Florence Nightingale had just arrived at the theatre of war, and a great storm which scattered the ships lying off the beaches announced the onset of winter. During the early months of 1855, the miseries of the Crimean campaign filled the newspapers.

The agitation died away when a democratic constitution that recognised the diggers' interests was proclaimed, in 1855. Mining constituencies were set up with a special miners' franchise. Elective assessors were added to the courts on the goldfields, which heard cases arising from disputed claims. The unpopular miners' licence was superseded by an export-duty on gold. Thus Australian democracy was born. Two previous eras, the age of the convicts and the age of the squatters, had come and passed. The future of Australia belonged to the new men whom the goldfields had formed into a type, the Australians who still familiarly hail one another as 'Diggers'.

The democratic forms claimed unsuccessfully by the English Chartists were freely adopted by the new state governments. Manhood suffrage was first introduced in 1855, in South Australia and, shortly after, in the other colonies. The secret ballot soon followed. The interests of the 'small men' were promoted by the agitators for easier access to the land which the great squatters monopolised. Hence the demand for Free Selection (see chapter x, 7, page 586) which became the law of New South Wales in 1861. But the miners tended to become urban rather than rural workers. Before the end of the 'fifties there were twenty factories making agricultural machinery in Australia and the agitation for an eight-hour day in industry had begun. Among the first acts of the new democratic government in Victoria was the laying of a poll-tax on Chinese immigrants. Though Palmerston had just concluded a treaty of friendly intercourse, at the end of the second China War, the miners would have none of it, but were already determined to preserve a White Australia.

In ten years (1851–61) gold worth £124,000,000 had been raised and the population of Australia had risen from 437,000 to 1,168,000. While the inevitable rise in wages and prices had threatened to ruin the farmer and the squatter, the actual effect had been to double the annual value of the wool-clip, which was worth £4,000,000 in 1861, and to increase the annual value of the external trade of Australia from £13 per head to £30. A great difficulty at first had been the difference between the cash price of gold, usually sold at a heavy discount, and the mint par value of the sterling currency. After some misgivings the Colonial Office, in 1855, permitted the establishment of a mint at Sydney where gold was freely bought at £3. 17s. 10¼d. per ounce, a fixed price which endured as long as the international gold standard. Prices then grew steadier, though intercolonial jealousy tended to disparage Sydney currency at Melbourne. As for the miners themselves, some had made fortunes, but few had made more than a bare living. It appears that in Victoria the earnings of the first 35,000, the men of 1852, were about £500 on an average. In 1853 the number of miners rose to 73,000 and the average earnings dropped to £170. Thereafter when there were more than 100,000 miners it is estimated that their annual earnings never reached the average figure of £100 a year.

The third gold-rush to a new country will be further discussed in chapter x, 3. In March 1858 Governor Douglas of Vancouver sent prospectors who confirmed reports of gold in the Fraser River. During the summer a rush of 25,000 miners, by sea from San Francisco, inflated the village of Victoria on Vancouver Island into a boom-town. Douglas asserted the right of the Crown by appointing a Gold Commissioner and charging licence fees to diggers at the rate of five dollars a month. In spite of opposition from unruly Americans, he got his way, founded his colony of British Columbia, and maintained the Queen's peace. In 1862 when the wagon-road had been driven far up-country, a second rush took place to the Cariboo district north of Lake Quesnel. It produced 200,000 ounces in 1863. But these proved not to be 'poor mens' diggings'. The extraction of gold from auriferous rock required machinery and capital, which were not then available, since more profitable gold and silver mines were booming in Nevada at the Comstock Lode.

In all the colonies prospectors were now at work and rewards were offered by speculators for finds of 'payable gold'. After British Columbia the next was in the antipodes where Gabriel Read reported a find beneath a bed of gravel in the South Island of New Zealand. In July 1861 the phenomena of a gold-rush startled the dour Scottish settlers of Dunedin, not then a prosperous colony. In the southern summer of 1861–2, 7000 miners went up to 'Gabriel's Gully' and found 400,000 ounces of gold; and larger crowds, deeper among the bush-clad mountains, found more in the following season. The Scottish colony had no sooner been inflated into a mining city and province, than the same fate came to the Anglicans of Canterbury Settlement. In the summer of 1864–5, even richer goldfields were found on the rainy west coast across the Southern Alps, a country so inaccessible, with no harbour and no road across the mountains, that a literary man among the Canterbury settlers had just imagined there the fantastic polity which he called *Erewhon*. In 1866 it was invaded by 30,000 miners, mostly from Australia, who risked the crossing of the bar at Hokitika, where many stout ships were wrecked, to win half a million ounces of gold in a season. Once ashore they found good order; it is reported that New Zealand miners did not carry guns.

The Victorian miners' code was legalised by the New Zealand Parliament, and the local government was administered (until 1873) by Canterbury Province, which undertook the construction of a mountain road over the high Southern Alps in 1865. Canterbury had already taken root and flourished before the west coast gold-rush brought an influx of new capital and labour. The prosperity of the province was then assured. But a state with strong foundations has a cohesion and stability of its own. The Canterbury settlers absorbed the new emigrants and used the new capital in directions that their founders would have approved. They now had the wealth to build the city with its cathedral and college which had been devised in the original plan. Close settlement continued on the plains; wheat was exported to neighbouring colonies; and sheep spread over the foothills of the Southern Alps. Similarly the Scottish element reasserted itself at Dunedin, to which Lowland and Highland emigrants continued to be attracted. Fifty years after the gold-rush to Gabriel's Gully, Christchurch was still aggressively English and Dunedin aggressively Scottish.

The gold-rushes of the 'sixties ended with the finds of 1866 and 1867 at Gympie in Queensland. Although the prospectors passed over the site of the rich Mount Morgan mines which, later in the century, were to be developed by machinery, at that date they only reproduced on a smaller scale the story of Bendigo and Ballarat. The finds were chiefly important for bringing 100,000 white immigrants into a colony which was beginning to depend on imported coolie labour.

Optimists could hardly doubt that the land of King Solomon's Mines would provide discoveries as rich as those of Victoria. In the 'sixties the prospectors were penetrating deeper into the Veld of South Africa until, looking for gold, they found diamonds. The first payable finds were in 1869, on either side of the River Vaal, the boundary between the two Boer republics. The British government had expressly repudiated all claim to sovereignty over the Transvaal, while still asserting a shadowy right to a protectorate over native races in the Orange Free State. A rush of British miners to a Boer farm named Vooruitzigt ('foresight') obliged the Governor of the Cape to organise a temporary administration like that of a goldfield, by virtue of his supposed obligation to the Griqua tribe (see chapter x, 10, page 622). In 1871 this district was annexed to Cape Colony and named Kimberley after Gladstone's Colonial Secretary. In that year 'a Mr Rhodes of Natal' found 110 carats of diamonds in twenty days. The character of the diamond-fields differed from that of the Australian goldfields in two respects. Though prospectors began by doing their own digging they generally brought in native labour for the heavier work when a claim was established. The European rush was succeeded, at every South African find, by an African rush of labourers in search of high wages. By 1872 there were 16,000 Europeans and 21,000 African natives at Kimberley. The other feature of the diamond-fields was the speculative nature of the product which could not, like gold, be converted into currency at a standard rate. The diamond industry was largely in the hands of Jewish traders among whom the most successful was Barnett Isaacs of Whitechapel ('Barney Barnato'). Very early in the history of Kimberley it became apparent that a glut of diamonds was spoiling the market. If profits were to be made after the first lucky strikes they would accrue to the men who cornered the claims and restricted the output. The richest mine was that of the De Beers Company who bought the freehold of 'Foresight' farm for £6000 (and later sold it to the government for £100,000). In deep pits, like the craters of volcanoes, 3600 separate claims were worked. From every one a rope and windlass was rigged to draw up samples of diamond-bearing clay to the pit's rim.

The Kimberley mine (on the De Beers estate) is said to be the deepest hole ever made by man. Claims were first pegged out on the 16th July 1871, 31 feet by 31 feet....In 1815 the greatest depth of the open working was 450 feet, the cavity excavated representing 9,000,000 cubic yards....The open area was stated to be 38 acres....Owing to the continual falling in of the sides the apparent depth is now somewhat reduced but the existing hole is still a remarkable sight....Mining was afterwards carried on by underground workings to a depth of 3601 feet, but has been discontinued since 1909.[1]

The De Beers Company steadily year by year bought out the claims until, by 1885, they were reduced in number to ninety-eight. Cecil Rhodes's masterstroke was to amalgamate all the De Beers holdings into a single mining-company, with financial backing from Alfred Beit and Rothschild. By 1888 he was in a strong enough position to force Barnato, his principal rival, to come into the combination. Thereafter Rhodes and his associates, controlling the diamond-fields, could keep the output steady at a value of about £4,000,000 a year.

Kimberley was a raw mining-camp in a desert, and retains the appearance of such a place to the present day. The railway reached it in 1885 but brought little in the way of the amenities of civilisation. Kimberley lived (and lives) by digging and trading diamonds and by little else. Beneath the surface of society an underworld lived on smuggling and illicit diamond-buying (I.D.B.), since diamonds, of all valuables, are the easiest to conceal. When in control of the whole capital and labour-force, Rhodes was able to put a check on I.D.B. by supervising the recruitment and the movement of native labourers who, for the period of their contract, live under strict discipline and are confined to closed locations behind barbed wire.

In the heyday of the diamond-fields, gold had been reported from several parts of South Africa, but generally in auriferous rocks which offered no easy return to individual prospectors. Several finds had been reported along the Witwatersrand before the attention of the Kimberley capitalists was attracted. In March 1886, J. B. Robinson (backed by Alfred Beit) bought land which contained a great part of the main reef, and began to develop deep-mining with native labour. In September 1886 the Rand was proclaimed a goldfield and prospectors flocked into the area. Within a year the new town of Johannesburg, named after the government surveyor, Johannes Rissik, had a population of 6000. But this was a rush of speculators rather than diggers. Prospectors staked out claims with the intention, not of working them, but of selling them to some great mining company with resources sufficient to organise excavation. The output even in 1888 was no

[1] *South and East African Year Book*, 1938.

more than 230,000 ounces and the main reef, 2400 feet below the surface, was reached only in 1893, after long technical experiment. By this time there were 35,000 native labourers in the mines; by 1899, the year when the Boer War put a stop to further progress, the number was over 100,000. The main reef proved to be 'an immense body of low-grade ore requiring elaborate large-scale work', quarrying not treasure-hunting. As at the diamond-fields the output could be regulated to suit the state of the market and the amount of available labour. In 1898 the 100,000 native miners produced 3,500,000 ounces of gold to justify a capital investment of £40,000,000.

Simultaneously with the prosperity of the Rand, industrial gold-mining reached great importance in Australia and New Zealand. In 1886 the Mount Morgan mines in Queensland began to employ profitable wage-labour, and in 1892 new gold-rushes took place in Western Australia. Coolgardie, 1892, and Kalgoorlie, 1893, attracted 70,000 emigrants, but these were not 'poor men's diggings'. The lack of water for washing gold in this dry country required irrigation works, organised by the state government on a great scale. The investment of £8,000,000 in three years implied that there was more speculation in shares than in claims; but the output reached 2,000,000 ounces in 1903. In Australia, unlike Africa, all the labour was done by white men and was proportionately expensive. Industrial gold-mines were also developed in the North Island of New Zealand. Advanced scientific techniques for extracting gold were notably introduced at Waihi near Auckland, from 1878 onwards. With an output of 500,000 ounces in 1902, this was the most profitable mining concern in the world.

The last of the great gold-rushes, to the Klondyke, presents the interesting feature of American and British methods side by side. Soon after the Alaska purchase (1867), Californian prospectors began to search for gold within the Arctic Circle, finding it at various points in the basin of the great navigable Yukon River. In winter they thawed out the frozen ground by lighting fires which enabled them to penetrate down to the 'pay-streak' at bed-rock; in summer they washed out the gold dust from the accumulated 'dirt'. In 1886 came a rush to Circle City. When (1894) the Canadian government found that disorderly American miners were flocking over the frontier, a mere unmarked meridian, they sent Inspector Constantine with forty troopers of the North-West Mounted Police to the Yukon. Two years later, in August 1896, an Indian found eighty ounces of gold in the narrow muddy Bonanza Creek which flowed into the Klondyke River, a tributary of the Yukon—in Canadian territory. Before winter set in, a 'city' had sprung up at Dawson. In the spring of 1897 a few hundred miners cleared $2,500,000; and in July the torrent of fortune-hunters began to appear. It is estimated that 100,000 persons set out for the Klondyke that year, but that only one-third of them reached the goldfield before winter. Some came by steamboat up the Yukon from the Arctic harbour of St Michael to Dawson City; some overland from Canada by way of the Peace River; the great majority came in ships from Seattle and San Francisco to Skagway, a 'mushroom' port in the Alaska Panhandle. Thence, equipped with stores and dog-teams, they had to climb the snow-bound Chilcoot Pass before crossing the divide into the valley of the Klondyke. Even among old prospectors, few were experienced in arctic travel; among the thousands of 'cheechakos' (amateurs) who passed through Skagway, the vast majority were unac-customed to any form of pioneering.

Alaska was anarchic until the arrival (1900) of federal officers. Skagway was a 'wide-open' racketeers' town without law or government, controlled by a gangster named 'Soapy Smith', who, until he was shot by a rival, took toll of all comers. All forms of corruption, dishonesty and violence flourished as far as the top of the Chilcoot Pass where the 'Mounties' maintained a frontier post. Since food was scarce and dear at Dawson City they turned back every immigrant who was not provided with 1000 lb. of supplies.

Inside Canada there was law and order, thanks to the 'Moun-ties'. The Dominion government sent a Commissioner of cabinet rank, Clifford Sifton, and a Supreme Court Judge, to administer the goldfields, and to collect a royalty of 10% on exported gold. Lawless as they were, the Americans yet showed great enterprise. They chafed at Canadian control, resisting the pay-ment of the royalty, but they invested capital in irrigation and in methods of thawing the ground by jets of steam. Between 1898 and 1900 they built a railway from Skagway over the White Pass to a navigable tributary of the Yukon, thus bringing freights down from $1 to 4½ cents a pound. By 1900 when individual mining was giving way to industrial processes the output of the goldfields reached 2,500,000 ounces. During the next few years payable gold was found in several parts of Alaska.

5. POPULATION CHANGES

EACH wave of migration has three phases. First come the pioneers, the 'legion that never was listed, that carries no colours or crest'. They are almost without exception men of strongly-marked individuality and force of character. Among them are always to be found a high proportion of traders, 'merchant-adventurers' in search of new untrammelled markets. In the seventeenth and eighteenth centuries the pioneers were largely seamen, lone hands like Henry Hudson or leaders of authorised expeditions like Captain Cook. In lawless places and unsettled times the pioneers included many hard-handed self-seekers and some mere ruffians, but it betrays a poor understanding of men and affairs to condemn out-of-hand even the buccaneers of the Spanish Main and the founders of the African slave trade; they took the world as they found it. The nineteenth century also had its characteristic types. As prominent then as the traders and the sea-captains were the prospectors and the missionaries. There were also the soldiers and sailors who hunted down and destroyed the slave-traders. Among the philanthropic pioneers of the nineteenth century, women appeared as well as men.

In our own day a new type, who may be regarded by posterity as the characteristic pioneer of the twentieth century, the scientific investigator, has entered the field. Anthropologists, ecologists and other research workers, men and women alike, now penetrate deepest into the wilderness to learn its secrets and master its afflictions.

Until the pioneers have blazed the trail there can be no colonisation but, such are their habits, no statistics are kept of their coming and going. I have found no way of making even a useful guess at the distribution throughout the world of the isolated traders, missionaries, prospectors, seamen, research workers and 'rolling stones' in general, whose place of origin is in the British Isles. Their irregular journeys are not recorded in the shipping returns, they haunt regions where censuses are often deficient, they pass easily from country to country. Quantitatively, their numbers are a lost item in the sum of the British population overseas; qualitatively they are more significant than any other group.

The second phase in the history of migrations is that of systematic colonisation. Those who have accompanied me so far as this chapter will probably agree that the common belief in an Empire which casually grew without direction is quite unjustified. Almost every British colony was deliberately founded by a formed body of settlers according to a preconceived plan and, generally speaking, the more complete the plan the more successful the colony. The settlers, for the most part, were groups of families and fairly representative of the society from which they had come. Their early success was the better assured if they were inspired by a common political or religious impulse. These systematic colonies may be classified in two groups: before the American Revolution (1607–1749), the best examples are Virginia, New England, Maryland, Pennsylvania, Georgia and Halifax; after the Revolution (1783–1850), Ontario, Red River, Albany (South Africa), the Australian settlements and the New Zealand settlements.

The third phase of colonisation, which persisted into the twentieth century, was the outward thrust of the frontier by the pressure of a growing population. After filling the temperate lands, or at least after exploiting their primary products, the colonists, whose numbers were everywhere swollen as much by the excess of births over deaths as by a torrent of new immigrants, flowed out into lands which previously had not been considered 'White Man's Country', into Texas, Arizona, Queensland, Rhodesia and even Arctic Canada. The lure was, in many instances, the prospect of finding gold, silver or diamonds. Boom-towns growing up where there has been a rush to the diggings seem to be the only exceptions to the rule of systematic colonisation. Of the great cities of the Commonwealth, Melbourne, Winnipeg and Johannesburg alone were not planned settlements, but even they did not spring up suddenly in the wilderness. They 'hived-off' from other thriving settlements within the jurisdiction of existing colonies. Apart from the gold-hunters, the emigrants in the third phase of colonisation are, for the most part, labourers in search of better conditions of work, perhaps driven out by adversity at home, perhaps led on by the rumour of prosperity abroad. But this casual migration of the third type can only follow upon the first and second phases. If the ground is not prepared before them, the casual migrants are a mere horde of refugees.

Until the end of the eighteenth century there are, generally speaking, no reliable statistics of the growth or movement of population. The first census of the United States was taken in 1790, of Great Britain in 1801, of Ireland in 1831. Before the establishment of the Colonial Lands and Emigration Commission in 1840 there are no reliable figures of the shipment of emigrants from the British Isles. Even after that date the reported figures are deceptive to the student unversed in the analysis of statistics. The gross figure of departures must be offset by the return of temporary visitors and dissatisfied emigrants, by the unknown number of passengers in transit from some other country through Great Britain, and of those in transit through one new country to another. To take an example, there has been, for more than a hundred years, an ebb and flow of migrants across the open frontier between Canada and the United States in the direction where greater prosperity was to be found for the time. This increase in the population of one country or the other is not indicated by the shipping returns from Europe.

Ten generations ago, in the age of Shakespeare and Ralegh, it is estimated that the inhabitants of England and Wales numbered about five millions, of Ireland something more than one million and of Scotland something less than one million. These seven millions (whom we shall call for brevity the British race, without implying thereby any ethnological doctrine) have increased and multiplied, in ten generations, about eighteen or twenty times over. Their descendants now number about 140,000,000 of whom rather more than half live in the United States and not much more than one-third in the British Isles. This is physically the most remarkable phenomenon in British history. While the British race has been so prolific, it is conjectured on scanty evidence that the population of Europe as a whole has multiplied no more than four or five times; and (on still scantier evidence) it is thought that the population of the world has increased at about the same rate as that of Europe.

Until the middle of the eighteenth century British emigration overseas was almost entirely English and agricultural. The two Scottish attempts at settlement, Nova Scotia and Darien, had failed miserably. The Southern Irish did not go far afield except by twos and threes to Newfoundland. On the other hand the Presbyterians of Ulster began to move to America when the pressure of the English Acts of Trade bore hardly on their industries. Some 20,000 are said to have crossed the sea before 1700. Bitterly anti-British, the Scotch-Irish, as they were called in the colonies, formed the backbone of Washington's Continental Army and provided several leaders to the Revolution. Still, at the first American census (1790), returns of the white population have been analysed as 80% English, 8% Irish (mostly Scotch-Irish) and 4% Scottish, while the other countries of Europe provided no more than 8% between them.

The mass-movement from the Highlands of Scotland to the colonies began in the middle of the eighteenth century. Maclean of Coll was endeavouring to ship away his clansmen as early as the foundation of Georgia (1733). The reduction of establishments after each European treaty of peace (1748, 1763, 1783, 1802, 1814) produced a flow of discharged Highland soldiers to the colonies. The pacification of the Highlands had put an end to the days when each proud chief was followed by a 'tail' of fighting men who lived on his bounty. When Dr Johnson made his tour of the Hebrides in 1773 he found the whole country inflamed with a fever for emigration, which he deplored. 'The lairds', he said, 'instead of improving their country diminished their people.' He spoke of rapacious chiefs 'making a wilderness of their estates' by their greed in demanding too high rents. It was the 'tacksmen', the better class of tenants, who were forced to emigrate. The depopulation of the Highlands, which Karl Marx selected as his classic example of the expropriation of the poor by the rich, makes an ironic commentary on the romantic legend of the north. The very chiefs who revived the tartans, the kilted dress, the bagpipes and the Highland games, who luxuriated in the sentiment of the *Waverley Novels*, were engaged at the same time in destroying the clans and driving away their kin. The crofts were first turned into sheepwalks and then by a further degradation into deer-forests which, in the fulfilment of time, must be leased to alien capitalists when the degenerate lords could no longer even boast their sheep. The descendant of that Maclean of Coll whom Boswell had criticised petitioned the Colonial Office in 1827 'for aid towards emigration. He himself sent out 300 souls from one of his islands, and he can now *spare* 1500.' The clearances of Coll,

Skye and Sutherland have been often selected as examples but I know no means of tabulating the general effect of the emigration, except by studying where the Scottish race now lives. To this I shall return later.

A single example will show the tenacity of Highland purpose and the fluid character of the statistics. A party of McLeods evicted from Sutherlandshire migrated to Pictou, Nova Scotia, and from there went on to St Anne in Cape Breton Island, but did not prosper. In 1851 their leader, the Rev. Norman McLeod, then an old man of seventy, ordained a further migration on the advice of his sailor son who wrote to him of the superior advantages of South Australia. Whereupon 130 Highlanders set off in a barque of 500 tons, which they themselves had built and manned, but, finding South Australia also not to their liking, they migrated again, to New Zealand (1854). Governor Grey settled them on land at Waipu north of Auckland, where several more shiploads followed from Nova Scotia, making a colony of 900 souls. The old patriarch, McLeod, long survived to preach to them in Gaelic. Their women used the spinning-wheel at least into the twentieth century, and their young men distinguished themselves in the German Wars.[1]

All attempts to estimate the numbers of Scottish, or of Irish, migrants are vitiated by the unchecked flow of internal migration between the three kingdoms. At all times in history there has been a reciprocal flow of population between Ulster and the Clyde. In the seventh century it set strongly towards Scotland, in the seventeenth century towards Ireland, and in the twentieth century towards Scotland again. Similarly there has long been a seasonal movement of unskilled labour across the Irish Sea towards England. Many return but many stay and are absorbed into the English population. Since the first Union with Scotland, in 1603, the drift of the Scots southward across the border has been remarked in every generation. There are a hundred columns of names beginning with 'Mac-' in the London telephone directory for 1947,

---

[1] I am obliged to my brother-in-law, the Rev. D. B. MacGregor, for drawing my attention to the part played in the emigration by the Scottish Episcopal Church, always closely associated with the American Episcopal Church. When the potato famine of 1847 assailed the Highlands, Episcopalians in the U.S.A. sent relief to their fellows in Scotland. Some of them chartered a ship, loaded it with food, and despatched it to the Bishop of Argyll, recommending that he should send it back to Portland [Maine?], laden with Scottish emigrants.

an observation which suggests, by a cursory comparison of the frequencies of certain surnames in proportion to the population, that there may be many more Scots in London than in Edinburgh.

There is however a difference between Scottish and Irish migration. Apart from the one Lowland colony (Otago, New Zealand) and certain mass-movements caused by the Highland clearances, the Scottish migrants, whether to England or abroad, are strongly individual. No traveller in the Empire can fail to observe how high a proportion of the leaders of colonial life are Scots. Doctors trained in the Scottish universities are (or seem to be, for there are no statistics) far more numerous than English or Irish doctors overseas. Many technologies, especially marine-engineering, seem almost Scottish monopolies. Very different is the status and repute of the Southern Irish. Though a peasant people they become town-dwellers when they go overseas. As in Liverpool and Glasgow, so in New York and Chicago and in the cities of the Dominions, the Catholic Irish form the urban proletariat, while the Scots everywhere are in positions of responsibility.

The rapid increase of the Irish population in the eighteenth century was not accompanied by the growth of industry, by agricultural improvement, or by any form of social insurance. When the population reached 8,000,000 in 1841, the island was grossly overpopulated. This is not the place to recount the wrongs of Ireland before the Union or the fallacious belief of English reformers that all would be set right by representation at Westminster, Roman Catholic emancipation and Free Trade. A wave of emigration, or rather of refugees escaping from misery, began about 1820 from Southern Ireland to North America. At first the rural slums of Connaught were merely decanted into the urban slums of New York and Quebec, in utter wretchedness. The pitiable conditions on the emigrant ships and at the docks were denounced in an appendix to Lord Durham's Report. But very soon observers noticed that the flow was strengthened and the intake rapidly absorbed. Of all emigrants the Irish have done most in the way of family self-help. One Irishman would no sooner find wage-labour at the high colonial rate than he would save money to bring out his friends and family. Thus the migration gained momentum and the newcomers found friends to receive them in the new lands. Wakefield said bitterly, 'the Irish do not colonise, they only emigrate miserably', a true statement but an insufficient one. They did in fact transport the majority of their race by their own efforts to another land. They were never pioneers and never founded a new settlement; they followed in the third phase of colonisation as proletarians. As in Old Ireland, so in the Dominions, the Protestants of Ulster have taken a different course. Ulstermen have taken as prominent a part in the commercial and professional world of British Canada as did the 'Scotch-Irish' in the Thirteen Colonies. Orange Lodges, preserving the Ulster tradition, have been prominent in politics, especially in Ontario.

Between 1815 and 1840 the gross total number of emigrants from the British Isles was about a million, of whom 499,000 went to British North America, 417,000 to the United States and 58,000 to Australia. The largest number in any one year was 103,000 in 1832. The export of Irish paupers had begun in 1823 but was not more than a small fraction of the whole emigration at this period.

Under the new Poor Law of 1834, English paupers were also shipped to the colonies at the expense of the rate-payers until, in 1840, the Wakefield system was partially adopted. In that year the South Australian Commission (see chapter VII, 6, page 366) was reconstituted as the Colonial Lands and Emigration Commission[1] with authority to collect the receipts of land sales and to apply the proceeds to despatching selected emigrants of good character. For twelve or fifteen years the Commissioners did useful work in issuing reports on colonial life, advising emigrants about their requirements, warning them against 'bubble' schemes of settlement—especially fraudulent attempts to divert emigrants to Latin America—and in publishing statistics. The conditions of life on emigrant ships were gradually improved, though the Irish rush of 1847–52 overwhelmed all attempts at organisation. The worst abuses disappeared after the shipping regulations had been consolidated in the Act of 1855. The gross number of passengers who left the British Isles during the thirty-three years that the Commission lasted was about 6,500,000, of whom nearly two-thirds went to the United States.

The North American emigration was uncontrolled. Most of the millions who crossed the Atlantic in those years paid their own passage-money (aggregating to £15,000,000) or were subsidised by their friends already in America. The Irish who went to the

[1] See W. A. Carruthers, *Colonial Lands and Emigration Commission*.

United States, nursing the memory of their oppression, fanned the flame of anti-British prejudice and remained bitterly hostile to all that reminded them of Britain. The United States until the 1840's had been violently Protestant in tendency. The Irish exiles created the first pressure-group and perhaps the strongest in American politics, the Catholic anti-British vote.

The year 1847 saw the beginning of the great Irish emigration. Flood-tide was reached in 1851 when 336,000 passengers, of whom 257,000 were Irish, left the British Isles. In 1852 the gross total figure was higher, 368,000, but the Irish element had dropped to 225,000. The attraction that year was the gold-rush to Melbourne. After 1854 the stream of migrants slackened off for a few years. No new goldfields were discovered, and the Crimean War provided employment for potential emigrants. But the strongest reason was the absolute decline in the population of Ireland. At a time when all other European populations were rapidly increasing, that of Ireland sharply fell, partly from actual famine but much more from the removal of so large a proportion of the men and women of marriageable age, as is proved by the great fertility of the Irish-Americans. Within a few years the Irish in America were far more numerous than the Irish in Ireland had ever been.

While hordes of miserable Irishmen were fleeing across the Atlantic to escape starvation, the Commissioners were conducting an orderly system of emigration to Australia. By good management they reduced the death-rate on the voyage from 5% to 0·5%. In 1847 they began to charter ships of their own for the long voyage and, by 1869, had carried 339,000 emigrants, in 1088 shiploads, at a cost of £4,864,000. More than £4,000,000 of this sum had been raised by land sales in Australia. But since the colonies had matured to self-government in the 'fifties, acquiring control of their own land sales, the spending of the fund by a Board in London had become an anomaly. After long agitation by Adderley, the Colonial Reformer, the Commission was terminated in 1872, its duties being divided between the Board of Trade and the agents of the colonial governments in London.

The statistics of inward as well as outward migration were first analysed and issued by the Board of Trade in 1873, from which date it is possible to quote a net figure of the annual loss to the British population by emigration. But it was not until 1912 that detailed particulars were recorded of the country of origin and intended residence of each ship's passenger. The annual net loss to the population of the British Isles by emigration, according to the Board of Trade returns, is as follows:

Net migration from the British Isles to places outside Europe, 1876–1930.

British nationality—excess of outward over inward passengers (numbers in thousands).

		Annual Averages			
Period	United States	British North America	Australia and New Zealand	All other places	Total
1876–80	47	8	28	4	87
1881–85	124	24	36	3	187
1886–90	110	20	22	7	159
1891–95	66	11	4	8	89
1896–1900	38	7	4	7	56
1901–05	58	36	5	18	117
1906–10	70	84	20	5	179
1911–13	49	132	67	9	257
1921–25	38	45	37	4	124
1926–30	31	39	24	5	99

That is an aggregate total of between six and seven millions. Again taking annual averages the net annual loss by migration is, generally speaking, about one-quarter of the net annual increase by the excess of births over deaths. Changes in the population of the British Isles during the last hundred years are shown in Fig. I overleaf, but the decline of the population of Scotland and Ireland should be accepted with reserve since it takes no account of Scottish and Irish migration to England.

The net annual average gain of the British Dominions and the United States in persons of British origin is given in Fig. II which shows the excess of outward over inward passengers between the British Isles and these countries during the period from 1876 to 1930.

It thus presents a general picture of the net emigration from the British Isles. The three pronounced dips in the curve (1884–5, 1894 and 1908) are each related to financial crises in the United States. The high peak of 1883 was a time of depression in England but of prosperity in the United States. The outward movement

Fig. I. *Population 1831–1931. England and Wales, Ireland, Scotland.*

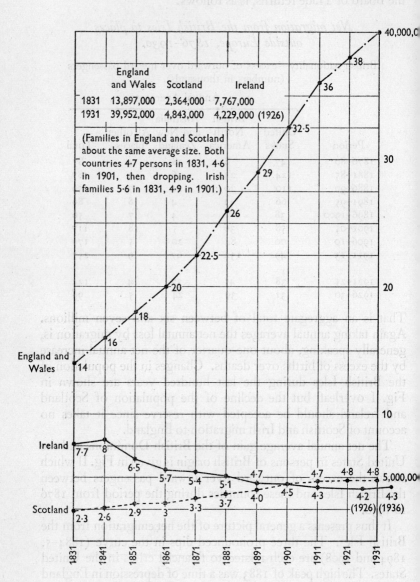

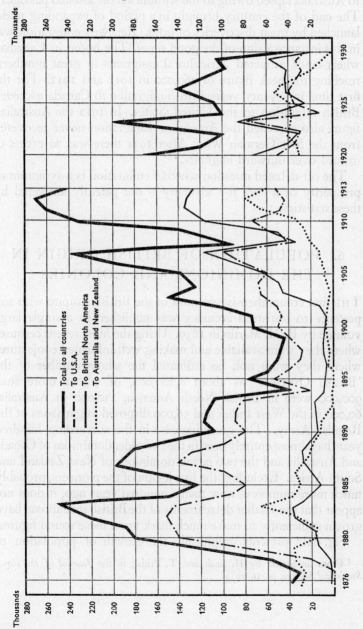

FIG. II. *Excess of outward over inward movement of British passengers between the British Isles and non-European countries, 1876–1930.*

of the middle 'eighties was a further Irish flight from agricultural depression. The early 'nineties were in general a period of contracting trade both in Europe and in the Dominions. Emigration to Australia lapsed owing to the withdrawal of 'assisted passages'. The end of the century brought in a period of expanding trade, launched by great discoveries of gold. Renewed emigration was in this instance a sign of the good times. The boom in Canadian wheat-lands attracted agricultural emigrants in great numbers, reaching the peak figure of 260,000 in 1911 and 1912. For the first time in seventy years British migration to Canada exceeded British migration to the United States. In 1912 the Australian figure also exceeded the American. Emigration never recovered from the first German War. After 1931 there was an excess of inward over outward migrants.

The oft-debated question whether emigration is a symptom of prosperity or a cure for adversity is not patently answered by these statistics.

6. POPULATION OF BRITISH ORIGIN IN THE DOMINIONS AND COLONIES

THE first comprehensive account of the British Empire with any pretence to statistical accuracy was published in a single large volume by R. M. Martin in 1839. Using the most recent censuses where they were available and making well-informed conjectures where they were not, he estimated the whole number of the 'British Overseas' as about 1,200,000, of whom more than 900,000 were in British North America, 130,000 in Australia, 60,000 in the West Indies and 56,000 disposed as garrisons of the Regular Army. The great increase in the succeeding hundred years has almost entirely been in the two older dominions of Canada and Australia and the two newer dominions of New Zealand and South Africa. Excluding the lost legion of the pioneers, probably much more numerous now than a hundred years ago, it does not appear that the smaller detachments of the British race abroad have grown sufficiently to make much mark upon these round figures.

Fig. III [1] presents graphically the growth of population of

[1] From an article by H. Leak and T. Priday in the *Journal of the Royal Statistical Society*, pt. II, 1933.

FIG. III. *Population of British origin in four Dominions compared with the population of Ireland and Scotland.*

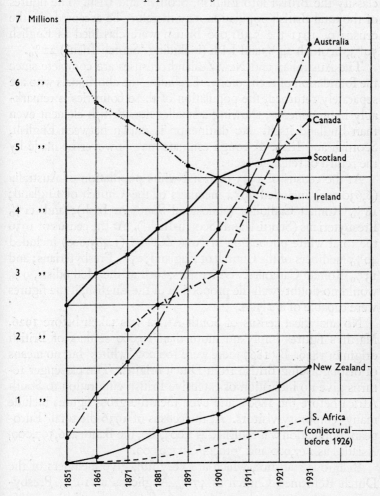

British origin in these dominions according to the census returns from 1850 to 1931. Since smaller numbers are in question the height of the scale is doubled in proportion to that of Fig. I and, for convenient reference, the populations of Scotland and Ireland are reproduced on the same enlarged scale.

The first complete census of Canada was taken in 1871. Since the Canadian constitution was designed to protect minority rights the censuses distinguish French- from British-Canadians and classify the British into English, Scottish and Irish. The figures of the total British population may therefore be accepted. In the census of 1931 the 5,381,000 British were classified as English 50%, Scottish 24% and Irish (including 'Scotch-Irish') 22%.

The Australian and New Zealand censuses are complete since the foundation of each colony. Excluding the aboriginals who are separately returned, the population of these countries is remarkably homogeneous, showing a smaller non-British element even than England itself. No distinction is drawn between English, Scottish and Irish. A rough estimate may however be made by the return of religious sects.

At the census of 1933 the total white population of Australia (6,630,000) included 39% members of the Church of England; 18% Roman Catholics (almost all Southern Irish); and 11% Presbyterians (Scottish and 'Scotch-Irish'). At the census of 1936 the total white population of New Zealand (1,485,000) included 40% members of the Church of England; 25% Presbyterians; and 13% Roman Catholics. Other sects, such as the Methodists, 9% would no doubt swell the proportion of the English, if the figures were capable of analysis.

No analytical census of South Africa was taken before 1926. Martin's figures imply no more than 10,000 settlers of British origin in 1839. By 1865 there were 100,000 'whites' but no means of distinguishing British from Dutch origins. The passenger returns give no indication of extensive British emigration to South Africa before the 1890's and even then the gross figures include many temporary visitors. At the census of 1936 the total 'European' population was returned as 2,003,000, the Bantu as 6,597,000, Asiatics as 217,000 and 'others' as 770,000.

Religious statistics, which are very full, give members of the Dutch Reformed Church as 57%, Anglicans as 19%, Presbyterians as 4·45%, other Protestants (largely English) as 9%, Roman Catholics as 4·8% and Jews as 4·7%. The small proportion of Presbyterians may be due to their absorption into the similar Dutch Church. Throughout South Africa there are many Afrikaner families of Scottish origin. The small proportion of Southern Irish may be due to their failure to compete against cheap native labour. Out of the two million who constituted the European population of the Union in 1936, perhaps 800,000 may be described as of British origin.

Three other 'white' settlements are worth noting precisely: Newfoundland with Labrador contained a population of 289,000 at the census of 1935; Southern Rhodesia contained 58,870 'Europeans' at the census of 1938; Kenya contained 20,894 'Europeans' at the census of 1930.

The aggregate figures for the populations of British origin in the four great dominions, and in Newfoundland, Southern Rhodesia and Kenya, will then amount to about 14,600,000, making no allowance for inter-censal increase, but taking in each instance the census nearest to the year 1935. To this must be added a figure, hardly more than a random guess, for the people of British stock in the British West Indies where races have been mingling too long for statistical analysis. R. R. Kuczynsky[1] gives an estimate of about 100,000. The Indian census of 1931 returned 300,000 'Europeans', 155,000 'British subjects' and 138,000 of the race euphemistically described as 'Anglo-Indians'. I know not how to regard these figures. Adding a random allowance for the unreturned numbers of the scattered pioneers throughout the world it seems that the British overseas in about the year 1936 numbered not less than 15,000,000.

Taking the figure of 1,200,000 for the decade ending in 1839 and the figure of 15,000,000 for the decade ending in 1939, and basing estimates at intermediate dates upon the census of the four dominions, we can now surmise the growth of the population of British origin in the Empire. Fig. IV presents as a graph the decennial census returns for the British Isles from 1831 to 1931 with a conjectural estimate of the whole 'British' population of the Empire, the total for 1931 being shown as 65,000,000. It also includes an estimate of the other half of the 'British' race no longer living under the protection of the British Crown. The decennial censuses of the United States (1790–1930) have distinguished, though not consistently, between 'white' and 'coloured' Americans. The graph of white Americans, also shown in Fig. IV, gives a starting-point for enquiry. In 1790 the white population was 92% British. It was not until the 1850's that the immigrants from the Continent of Europe began to outnumber those from the British Isles. The conscious endeavour of the

[1] *Population Movements*, 1936.

Fig. IV. *Estimate of the growth of populations resident or originating in the British Isles, 1830–1931.*

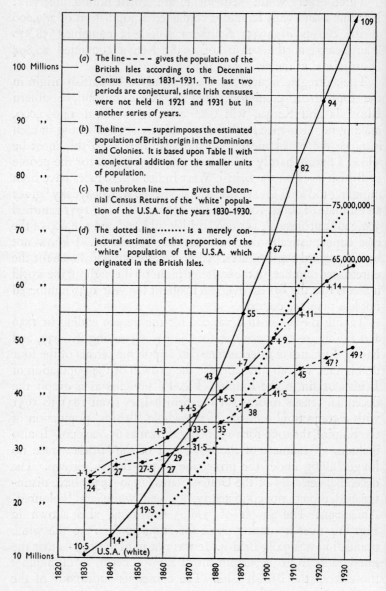

(a) The line – – – gives the population of the British Isles according to the Decennial Census Returns 1831–1931. The last two periods are conjectural, since Irish censuses were not held in 1921 and 1931 but in another series of years.

(b) The line — · — superimposes the estimated population of British origin in the Dominions and Colonies. It is based upon Table II with a conjectural addition for the smaller units of population.

(c) The unbroken line ——— gives the Decennial Census Returns of the 'white' population of the U.S.A. for the years 1830–1930.

(d) The dotted line ········ is a merely conjectural estimate of that proportion of the 'white' population of the U.S.A. which originated in the British Isles.

American people to mix the ingredients (or at least the white ingredients) in the melting-pot of the great republic makes it increasingly difficult to estimate the proportion of British stock.

The net emigration from the British Isles to the United States between 1830 and 1930 cannot be much less than 7,500,000. In the same period we know that about 2,300,000 emigrated to Australia and New Zealand and increased naturally to 8,000,000. Assuming that the 7,500,000 British emigrants to America increased at the same natural rate as those to Australasia and that the resident 'British' population of the United States increased at the same rate as the population of the British Isles, the total population of British origin in the United States in 1930 would be about 75,000,000.[1]

In conclusion I must refer to the scattered groups of persons of British origin living in other foreign lands, perhaps 200,000 in all. From the Argentine 1797 men and 532 women served as volunteers in the British forces in 1939–45 and another 1000 from other South American states. The British Argentine Society estimates that there are about 50,000 persons of British descent domiciled, and mostly naturalised there, among them the Welsh settlers at Chubut (see Appendix IV, pages 1048–9). The mercantile colonies in Egypt, China and elsewhere contain many British citizens who have not severed their connexion with home. In the Baltic and the Levant small and often ancient settlements of Englishmen and Scotsmen maintain their individuality. Finally there are the residential colonies in beauty spots and spas, mostly in France, Italy, Switzerland and the Atlantic Islands.

ASIATIC EMIGRATION

The great European emigration of the nineteenth century was paralleled by an Asiatic emigration produced by similar causes. The abundant population of south-east Asia also overflowed, the Chinese south-eastwards into Malaya and the Islands, the Indians south-westwards into the coasts and islands of the Indian Ocean. Statistical information of these folk-wanderings is scarcer even than of those previously discussed. The Asiatic emigrants appear

---

[1] These are indications not statistics. Another estimate by Julian Huxley and A. C. Haddon (*We Europeans*, 1935) gives the percentage of persons of British origin in the population of the U.S.A. as 53·6% in 1920.

generally as a discordant factor in the history of the British over-seas. Sometimes, as with the Chinese at the goldfields or the Hindus in Natal, they came as direct rivals to the European emi-grants; sometimes, as in the West Indies, Asiatics were introduced as indentured labourers upon terms which aroused the suspicion of philanthropists. To summarise emigrations which will be alluded to elsewhere in this book, mention should be made of the attempted infiltration of California and Australia by Chinese gold-diggers, the successful colonisation of Malaya by Chinese mer-chants and tin-miners, the settlement of Ceylon with Tamils from Southern India, and of Burma with coolies from Bengal and the colonisation of the East African coast from Durban to Zanzibar with Indian settlers of several castes and creeds.

But greater in scale was the importation of low-caste Indian coolies to the sugar-colonies, where labour was scarce after the abolition of slavery. The first experiment was made in Mauritius, which received 24,000 coolies between 1834 and 1839. A similar transportation to the West Indies was begun in 1837 but was stopped by the government of India, two years later, as an abuse. Herman Merivale of the Colonial Office said that 'in everything but the compulsion and the cruelty the immigration trade is but a repetition of the slave trade'. The whole history of indentured labour in the colonies repeats the same story. At its worst it de-generates into something not far different from slavery, but this worst has not often been seen under the British flag. At its best the labourer is still far from freedom. In many, perhaps in most, instances food and quarters and hygiene are well attended to be-cause it is the employers' interest to keep the workers healthy and contented. But all indentured labour implies a one-sided contract, which the coolies were often obliged to accept under pressure of poverty, and which conveyed them to a distant land where there could be no economic liberty for them. Payment often took the form of truck, and repatriation depended on the goodwill of the employer. In fact coolies did not often return to India, with the result that families were divided and, since men very largely out-numbered women, morals deteriorated.

In 1844 the West India Committee approached Lord Stanley, then Colonial Secretary, to ask for a controlled migration, which Stephen the Under-Secretary resisted until his retirement. Stanley, also, was 'determined to prevent the institution of any order approaching slavery' but obtained the consent of the Indian government for the transportation of 12,500 coolies a year under careful supervision by the Land and Emigration Commissioners. The movement went, naturally enough, to the prosperous new colonies rather than to the old exhausted plantations. By 1872, 80,000 Indians had been sent to British Guiana, 44,000 to Trinidad, 16,000 to Jamaica and 6000 to the other West Indian islands, while the far greater number of 350,000 had made the short journey to Mauritius, where efforts were also made but with little success to attract free African natives. In another direction, many thousand Indians emigrated to Fiji. Some 12,000 Chinese also found their way to British Guiana. In the 1860's negotiations for a steady flow of Chinese coolies broke down because the Chinese government demanded a clause in the contract guaranteeing a free return passage to China for each emigrant, and this the planters would not undertake.

7. THE WEST INDIES IN DECLINE,
1839–75

THE sugar colonies had not yet adjusted themselves to an economy without slaves when the second blow was struck by reformers in England. The preferences given to West Indian sugar were weakened and soon abolished. From the point of view of political economists at home, though not of planters in Jamaica, the new Crown Colony of Mauritius deserved the same treatment as its competitors, the British West Indian islands. As early as 1825 it had been admitted to a degree of preference; in 1835 the duties on sugar from the East Indian and West Indian colonies were equalised. Next an attempt was made during Peel's administration to discriminate by a tariff against sugar grown in countries where there was still slavery, although this led to diplomatic difficulties with Brazil. When Russell became Prime Minister in 1846 a general policy of free trade was adopted, to the dismay of the sugar planters. The West India Committee even found themselves allied with the Anti-Slavery Society on this issue in opposition to free trade in sugar. The two interests, strongly represented on a committee with Lord George Bentinck as chairman, held off the threatened blow. Russell had intended to reduce the preference by stages until a flat rate of 14s. a cwt., a mere revenue tariff, was reached. Through the efforts of Bentinck's committee the last stage was postponed until, in 1854, when Gladstone was Chancellor, an equal rate for free- and slave-grown sugar was fixed. Without much doubt the preference had been so high as to subsidise incompetence in the colonies and to restrict consumption at home. Yet to remove it altogether and to abandon the colonies to their own resources seemed to them a death-blow.

It was immediately followed by the banking crisis of 1847 which brought down the principal banks of Jamaica, British Guiana, Trinidad and Mauritius, in the train of their greater associates in London. The evils of plantation-colonies, their dependence upon a single cash-crop, their tendency to fall into the power of absentee-owners, their sensitivity to booms and slumps, were then peculiarly apparent. Wages in the West Indies fell by 50 % and, in several colonies, the attempts to reduce public expenditure led to struggles between governors and assemblies. Perhaps Trinidad, a Crown Colony governed just then by Lord Harris who had both ability and tact, came through the crisis with the least suffering, since he had instituted a systematic reform in local government, authorising the collection of rates for schools and police. Trinidad also preceded the other colonies in attempts to establish the free negroes as peasants on Crown land.

Jamaica was the worst afflicted of the islands. Hard times were followed by pestilence; in addition to the endemic yellow-fever, there were epidemics of cholera in 1850 and smallpox in 1852. The historic constitution of Jamaica, founded under King Charles II, was quite unequal to these strains. Since its foundation there had been intermittent struggles between the Governor and the Assembly over control of the revenue. In 1839 an attempt to reform this ancient model had led to the fall of Melbourne's government in England; in 1854 after some months of deadlock in Jamaica, the pride of the planters was abated and the island voted itself a new constitution. The Assembly was induced to give up its proud and reckless irresponsibility in return for a loan guaranteed by the British government. During the next five years Tobago, St Kitt's, St Vincent, Nevis and Antigua adopted similar constitutions which somewhat resembled the responsible government of the Australian and North American colonies.

The root of the economic problem in the sugar colonies was

shortage of labour since the abolition of the slave trade. When the introduction of indentured labour was authorised (1847), the Office reluctantly submitted to the demands of the planters that contracts for three or even five years should be permitted under the strictest supervision. There was some evidence, and the opinion of Lord Harris to back it, that long contracts were more humane since they enabled the labourers to settle down under supervision. The expense of shipment, and repatriation at the end of the indenture, fell heavily on the employers and most heavily where the voyage was longest. In these respects also Mauritius had the advantage being nearest to the source of supply in India. The planters of Mauritius financed their own immigration while the West Indians were obliged to raise loans in London with a guarantee from the Treasury. In Trinidad and British Guiana, where the largest numbers were introduced, they were encouraged by bonuses to remain as settlers when their indentures were out.

Of the other colonies, Barbados received very few; it differed from the other British islands in being overpopulated (1000 inhabitants to the square mile), with the result that there was no labour problem. Barbadians were said to be averse to travel; their pride in their island and its long loyal history was famous, and exclusive. Jamaica, on the other hand, was always short of labour. Wanting indentured labourers more than any colony, it received few because the missionaries and the coloured voters resisted their importation. The largest and richest of the older colonies,[1] Jamaica was always the most prominent in the view of the public at home, yet it was not a typical West Indian island. Though sugar-planting was the staple industry, the export of raw sugar made only 41 % of the island's external trade. There was an almost equally valuable trade in the celebrated Jamaica rum, and a

[1] Annual exports of sugar:

	Average of the years 1853–5 (cwt.)	Average of the years 1868–70 (cwt.)
British Guiana	931,000	1,567,000
Barbados	719,000	772,000
Jamaica	459,000	551,000
Trinidad	421,000	860,000

(No other British West Indian island had an output half as great as the lowest of these figures)

Mauritius	1,951,000	1,984,000

considerable trade in coffee grown by peasant-farmers. Jamaica planters were the aristocracy of the West Indies but Jamaica also had more small-holdings than the other islands. The administration, even under the constitution of 1854, was inefficient and corrupt. Wages were low and public services almost unknown. The government of the island, and the planters individually, were, as a rule, in debt.

During the last years of slavery and the first years of free labour the West Indies were described by many travellers.[1] The travellers concur in picturing a highly characteristic society. The exuberant beauty of the islands with their gaudy flowers and fruits forms a background to the indolent luxurious life of the planters, inclined to careless profusion and wasteful methods of using the land, but by no means deficient in the virtues of high caste, not unlike the aristocracy of old Virginia. Their life was clouded by the sense of slow decay. Living among abandoned plantations upon which the negro peasantry squatted they tended to assume that there had been better times in some half-mythical yesterday. Between the masters and the slaves (or ex-slaves) there was a patriarchal relation; West Indians never cringed as negroes did in the United States, but spoke up boldly to assert their loyalty and, especially in Barbados, their island pride. The negroes are described by all visitors as high-spirited, good-natured and idle, gaily dressed in coloured cottons, living as easily as they can, if the 'buckra' does not make them work, in a land where providence gives food for the lightest labour. Yet, 'between the idea and the reality...falls the Shadow'. The curse of slavery and caste lay on the islands. Social *malaise* expressed itself among native Christians, not far removed from African savagery, by relapses into the bloody rites of 'obeah'; in outbreaks of terrified cruelty by the white men against seditious negroes.

Charles Kingsley's account (*At Last*, 1870) is the most picturesque; Anthony Trollope's (*The West Indies and the Spanish Main*, 1859), written in his thumping downright style, is more to our purpose. Between the bombast of the patriots and the wishful thinking of the philanthropists his philistinish comments find a useful mean. Trollope arrived at St Thomas (then a Danish and

---

[1] A collection of their views may be found in an amusing essay entitled *West Indian Summer* by James Pope-Hennessy, 1943.

now an American possession) in the Virgin Islands in 1858. Since the coming of the steamships this first-rate harbour, though far to leeward, had superseded all the harbours of the Windward Islands to become the distributing centre of the West Indies. He thought it 'a niggery-hispano-dano-yankee-doodle place'. From there he made his way to Jamaica in burning heat, and disliked it, especially its towns. The naval dockyard was at Port Royal near the site of the old city, once the richest and wickedest city in the world, but drowned since the earthquake of 1692 beneath eight fathoms of water. The commercial port of Kingston four or five miles away was an insanitary slum without architectural pretension or decent streets, a wretched place compared with Havana or Martinique. Though the metropolis of Jamaica it was not the capital, which was placed at Spanish Town, a torrid empty city from which fled to the hills all whom the business of government did not detain.

At the great plantation houses among scenes of natural beauty the planters lived like squires and kept open house with crowds of domestics who managed to be both insolent and servile. All that was English was fashionable and all that was colonial, even their gorgeous fruits, despised. The colour-line was strictly drawn in every English house, 'except at the Governor's table'. It was the curse of politics, in Trollope's opinion, that had done most to reduce the wealth of the island. 'Her roads are almost impassable, her bridges are broken down, her coffee plantations have gone back to bush, her sugar-estates have been sold for the value of the sugar-boilers. Kingston as a town is the most deplorable that man ever visited, unless it be that Spanish Town is worse, and yet they have Lords and Commons. It has availed them nothing.' The Assembly largely consisted of coloured men and the white gentry tended to withdraw from it. 'Every man might vote who paid tax or rent', though few in fact took up the qualification. They would be much better off, he thought, under direct Colonial Office rule like British Guiana.

Barbados with its large population and fertile soil had no distress. There 'no coloured man votes at all. A coloured man or negro is doubtless qualified to vote if he owns a freehold; but then care is taken that such shall not own freeholds.' The future of the islands lay neither with whites nor blacks. A brown race, fitted for the climate with European energy and Asiatic physique, would emerge in the course of many generations and would inherit all.

Trinidad and British Guiana were lively commercial colonies filled with bustling vigorous Asiatic coolies, and not hampered by a corrupt 'lords-and-commons'. The Anti-Slavery Society before agitating against indentured labour should compare the progress of these Crown Colonies with the decadence of Jamaica. British Guiana, says Trollope, 'is the land of my choice when I settle out of England'.

Nevertheless the 'fifties, 'sixties and 'seventies were a period of modest progress in the West Indies as the increase in the export of sugar demonstrates. The calm was broken by one deplorable outburst, the rebellion associated with the name of Governor Eyre. Among the coloured voters of Jamaica was a man named George William Gordon, the son of a Scottish planter and a slave-woman. He made money in trade, attracted a following by his liberality and eloquence, was appointed a magistrate and was elected to the Assembly. Early in the 1860's he came to the fore as a dangerous critic of the government. He caused some alarm among the whites by comparing the state of Jamaica with that of Haiti, the negro republic, and was heard to make unguarded remarks about the future when the white men should no longer own the land. His enemies called him a seditious agitator, his friends a patriot. His clients spoke of his charities, which the opposite faction denominated bribes. After making rash charges against the officers of St Thomas parish at the south-east corner of the island and failing to sustain them, he was imprudently removed from his magistracy by Eyre, the Acting-Governor. Eyre and Gordon were thereafter political enemies.

A wave of unrest was passing over Jamaica. The American Civil War had raised the price and shortened the supply of foodstuffs which meant hardship to the thousands who lived improvidently on small-holdings and casual labour. More important perhaps was a religious revival which swept through the native population, an emotional explosion far removed from rationality. The new sect was known as the Native Baptists and their ceremonies, according to hostile critics, differed little from 'obeah'. But the powerful Baptist Missionary Society took the Native Baptists under its protection and, when Gordon joined the Native Baptists, Dr E. B. Underhill, the Secretary of the Society in London, took up the cudgels for Gordon. A petition was sent to the Queen asking her to relieve the sufferings of her Jamaican subjects, and was referred to the Colonial Office. Cardwell, who was then Secretary of State, rejected the advances of Dr Underhill and snubbed the petitioners in plain terms. He wrote that they 'must look for an improvement in their condition to their own industry and prudence'. This reply infuriated Gordon who spent the summer of 1865 moving about the island, making inflammatory speeches. It was not however proved that he ever crossed the bounds of treason or incited to violence. On 11 October 1865 a brawl broke out at Morant Bay in the parish of St Thomas which was regarded as the hub of Gordon's influence. It was the most backward of the twenty-one parishes into which Jamaica was divided, and had long been seething with unrest. The volunteer militia was called out, shots were fired, and the brawl grew into a bloody riot in which the court-house was burnt down and fifteen or twenty whites were murdered, among them a local magistrate who was Gordon's rival and enemy. The ringleader was Paul Boyce, a negro client of Gordon's.

The news reached Kingston forty miles away the next day. Governor Eyre had no more than 1000 regular troops, under General L. S. O'Connor, at hand. They were disposed with great skill and speed to close the road along the southern coast and the passes through the Blue Mountains to the north. Having thus prevented the rebellion from spreading beyond St Thomas's parish, the troops closed in upon Morant Bay, giving no quarter to negroes who could give no good account of themselves. Within a week order was restored. About eighty-five negroes were shot without trial; no less than 354 were executed by authority of courts-martial. On the day of the outbreak Gordon had been at his house in Kingston, quietly engaged in issuing propaganda leaflets. He made no attempt to join the rebels or to escape. By order of the Governor he was arrested, taken to Morant Bay and court-martialled on board a warship on 21 October. He was sentenced to death and hanged two days later. So skilful had been the dispositions of the Governor that it had not been necessary to extend the operation of martial law beyond a single parish, and the rising was over.

Eyre was quite unconscious of the storm he would arouse. Strong in his understanding of that which he had already quelled he met the Assembly on 7 November and, taking advantage of the state of panic which prevailed among them, he persuaded them to abdicate their powers to the Colonial Office. As there was no submarine cable as yet to the West Indies, Eyre's despatch describing the rebellion and its suppression did not reach London until 16 November. Cardwell at once congratulated Eyre on his promptness and vigour but warned him that the despatch contained 'many passages that will require to be explained'. As soon as the news was published a torrent of indignation was poured out, particularly in *The Times*, and by all the channels known to 'Exeter Hall'. On 16 December Cardwell recalled Eyre to London, pending the report of a Commission which was to go to Jamaica with the Governor of Malta, Sir Henry Storks, as chairman.

The fury of the philanthropists was unabated for six months and it was heated seven times hotter when the Commissioners reported in June 1866. They were by no means plain in their condemnation of Governor Eyre's actions. They decided somewhat equivocally that there had not been 'a general conspiracy' and that it had not been 'consciously provoked' by Gordon; but that there had been 'planned resistance to lawful authority'. Eyre was praised for his 'skill, promptitude and vigour' but blamed for maintaining martial law 'longer than was necessary'. Punishments had been excessive and in some cases 'positively barbarous'. The trial of Gordon was censured not so much as an act of tyranny as for technical irregularities. Not only had the defendant been arrested in an area where martial law was not proclaimed, but the court had also been irregularly constituted. Storks was then confirmed by Cardwell as Governor of Jamaica and Eyre retired on pension.

But this was not enough for the British public. The nation took sides for or against Governor Eyre, who was either the saviour of the white colonists or the cruel oppressor of the blacks. A strong committee, including John Stuart Mill, Herbert Spencer, T. H. Huxley, Thomas Hughes and Goldwin Smith, continued to assail him while he was powerfully defended by Carlyle, Ruskin, Tennyson and Kingsley. Several actions were begun against him in court, without success, for murder and other crimes, and the agitation did not subside for five years or more. Eyre maintained silence and lived in retirement for more than thirty years.

The riot at Morant Bay, the bloodshed, the panic, and the vindictive reprisals have many parallels in the annals of race-prejudice. Much crueller tales were told of the Jamaican slave-revolt of 1760. Much worse deeds than the execution of Gordon have since been done in nearer and more civilised lands. The reaction in London is the striking feature of this story. Eyre's persecutors and champions alike were imbued with a sense of responsibility towards the blacks that other ages and other conquering races have not known. It would not have been thought necessary in some great states to go to the trouble of preparing an apology for him.

Edward John Eyre (1815–1901) is now remembered, if at all, as an oppressive governor. His tragedy is that he was a life-long humanitarian. His youth had been spent as a pioneer in Australia where he accomplished the most exhausting desert journeys by his skill in placating the shy, suspicious black-fellows. Almost alone among Australian pioneers he had understood and loved them. Later, in New Zealand, as Lieutenant-Governor under Sir George Grey, he had emulated that great native administrator in managing the high-spirited Maori with sympathy and respect. He was an impulsive man, a hero in any physical crisis, and when left for years in Jamaica as a make-shift Deputy-Governor he gave rein to his impulses, acted, and bore the brunt of his action. In happier times, with a manageable constitution, he might have been a great colonial statesman, and Gordon his right-hand man.

Jamaica thus reverted to Crown Colony rule in 1866, with a nominated legislative council after 200 years of self-government. The other self-governing colonies in the West Indies followed suit until, in 1875, Barbados, Bermuda and the Bahamas alone retained their ancient liberties. The Leeward Islands were federated in 1870 under a single governor with a council elected by the nominated councils of the several islands.

Under the rule of the Colonial Office the islands were more efficiently and honestly administered and that is all. They continued to be neglected in all those respects where progress required the investment of capital with no immediate return in sight. All continued to suffer from too great dependence on a single cash crop in a highly competitive market. All lacked the steadying effect of a self-supporting peasantry, as every critic had pointed out since Rodney, who wanted to colonise St Lucia after its capture in 1783. Here and there some local enterprise made an exception, like the trade in lime-juice which brought prosperity to Montserrat. Every visitor commented on the uneconomic system whereby each planter was also the manufacturer of his own sugar. They ordered this better in the French colonies where the planters sold their cane to large centralised sugar-factories. Not until 1874 was the first sugar-factory opened in an English colony (St Lucia).

Among other changes may be mentioned the disestablishment of the Anglican Church in Jamaica where its adherents were a minority (1870); in Barbados Anglicanism still prevailed.

Outside the general run of the sugar islands, the Bahamas followed their own fortunes, prospering by the contraband trade and blockade-running during the American Civil War. The American tourist trade began soon after the peace. Bermuda, after a war-time boom, suffered an eclipse when the steamships captured the old coastal and island trade from her famous sailing-boats. In 1869 she began to supply early vegetables by steamship to the New York market. Otherwise she lived upon the dockyard.

X

THE NEW NATIONS OVERSEAS,
1846–1901

Argument: During the great mid-Victorian prosperity little notice was taken in London of the rise of the new nations in the colonies. Free Trade and self-government were supposed to have disintegrated the Empire. Canada's achievement in federating a plural society owed not much to British help or encouragement, except in respect of British capital loans. Confederation and the taming of the west were accomplished by a bold policy of railway-building.

Newfoundland was less happy in her political development. With one asset—fish—she had to complain frequently that her fishery-rights were bargained away by diplomats in London. At the end of the century she was in deep waters with over-capitalisation.

Between the gold-rush and confederation, Australia's history was uneventful, chiefly a matter of agrarian policy. The rise of a strongly nationalist labour party is its most significant feature. Confederation, though inevitable, was long delayed by differences of fiscal policy in widely-separated settlements. State socialism also made an early appearance in New Zealand.

An abortive attempt to federate South Africa in the 'seventies led to wars between the two white races, as well as to native wars. The Boers, who had some cause for believing themselves ill-treated, nourished a grievance against the British.

1. IMPERIAL POLICY, 1846–86

THE foundations of the new British Empire were laid in 1846 when the principles of the Colonial Reformers were adopted by Lord John Russell's administration. During the next twenty years the new nations crept into existence almost unnoticed by the politicians and the political historians. Even Froude and Seeley, when they attempted to popularise the history of the Empire, tended to dwell upon the old heroic days of the Spanish and French wars rather than upon the solid achievement of the years when they were young men. None of the events described in the previous four chapters of this book, with the exception of the

Indian Mutiny stirred the pulses of the British electorate or drew the serious attention of the chroniclers.

Two public events of the winter of 1845–6 have been made familiar to the modern reader. The first was the spiritual pilgrimage of an Oxford clergyman who could never quite reconcile the processes of an acute but credulous intellect with the demands of a sincere and tender conscience. In 1845 he left the Anglican Communion to seek an equally uneasy refuge in the bosom of Rome, a sore blow to the Church he left and an embarrassment to the Church he joined. The second event was political; the leaders of the two great parties, ungraciously bowing to the inevitable, entered into a rivalry as to which should saddle the other with the blame for enacting a measure contrary to the party interest of both. Newman's surrender to the pangs of conscience and Peel's to the logic of Free Trade are not without interest to the student of mankind, but they are mere sign-posts in the ecclesiastical and the economic histories of England.

Twelve thousand miles away from Oxford, another English clergyman, no less a saint than Newman and hardly less a scholar, a wiser man whose springs of action were not sealed up by introversion, intervened that winter between two battling armies to prevent a massacre, at the Bay of Islands in New Zealand. If we are to study the history of the English Church a hundred years ago, we must place Selwyn beside Newman as types of their age. Selwyn reconciled hostile tribes, preached down barbarous customs, saved the soul of a dying people, gave his province of the Church a new constitution, and returned to make his see of Lichfield a model for the whole Anglican Communion.

Nor was English statesmanship restricted to the grouping and regrouping of Whigs and Tories at St Stephen's during the debates over the Corn Laws. In 1846 John Lawrence began to form an administration that, for a hundred years, gave peace, prosperity and public works to the unruly province of the Punjab, much more than either Whigs or Tories could do for the smaller and less populous kingdom of Ireland. In 1846 Lord Grey solved the problem, which Russell, Wellington and Derby thought insoluble, of establishing responsible self-government in Canada without disrupting the Empire. Shepstone in Natal and Governor Grey in New Zealand were at that time devising ways of justly administering colonies where the aboriginals still made a large majority, while Rajah Brooke in Borneo was showing, by mere force of character, how English principles of justice could displace oppression and bloodshed. The people of New South Wales, with more prudence than their rulers, in that year proved their freedom by rejecting the convicts that Mr Gladstone attempted to foist on them. Beyond the old colonies where agriculture, commerce and immigration were beginning to flourish, the pioneers were never more active than in 1846. Sir George Simpson advancing trade in Rupertsland, David Livingstone preaching Christianity at Kuruman, Franklin exploring the Arctic, James Douglas staking out a claim to British Columbia, even Brassey building the *Chemin de Fer du Nord*, showed powers of leadership in matters more vital than leading the march into a Parliamentary lobby.

All these activities were remote from the general run of life in England during the hungry 'forties and the well-fed 'fifties. Emigrants vanished, were written off, and their remembrance was pigeon-holed, with no very clear notion what had become of them. Mr Micawber might, as like as not, be a magistrate at Port Middlebay. In his poem of the year 1845, Tennyson took a distant prospect of the South Sea Islands and rejected it, perturbed though he was by the 'great wind roaring seaward'. 'Not in vain the distance beacons', he cries as he bids 'a long farewell to Locksley Hall', but the reader is left doubting whether he goes far away. Globe-trotters were still rarities and often thought oddities in 1845. When Browning wrote a poem about his lost friend 'Waring' he imagined him as a sort of Rajah Brooke,

> a man upstarted
> Somewhere as a God,
> Hordes grown European-hearted,
> Millions of the wild made tame
> On a sudden at his fame.
> In Vishnu-land what Avatar?

This, though nearer the mark than Tennyson's fancy, was something too bold a prophecy of Waring's original, Alfred Domett C.M.G. (1811–87), who was a settler in Wakefield's colony at Nelson when Browning inquired for him, and later was Premier of New Zealand.

When James Mill described the Empire as a system of 'outdoor relief for the upper classes', it was a neat saying but not informative. In general the governing class did not emigrate,

though a few of their less presentable poor relations were jobbed
into colonial appointments. The supposed ignorance of British
statesmen about colonial conditions has been a joke in the
colonies for 200 years, and has given birth to a number of
traditional stories which, true or false, throw light on the myth
of imperialism. Smollett's Duke of Newcastle did not know that
Cape Breton was an island,[1] though he was responsible for the
combined operations against Louisburg. Castlereagh re-ceded
Java to the Dutch, because, it was whispered quite unjustly,
he couldn't find it on the map.[2] The omniscient Brougham
located South Australia as 'somewhere near Botany Bay'.[2]
'The Office' shipped water-casks to the expedition operating on
Lake Erie, not having been informed that the Great Lakes are
fresh.[2] True or false, the anecdotes of ignorance were capped by the
contemptuous references to colonial affairs. The oft-repeated tale
of the foundation of Williamsburg was put about, and perhaps invented as war propaganda, by Benjamin Franklin. The Virginians petitioned for a charter for their college, 'for the good of our
souls'. 'Damn your souls!' said the Attorney-General. 'Grow
Tobacco.' Much more recent is Melbourne's comment on the
dispute over British Columbia.[3] How could he be expected to take
any interest in a country where salmon would not rise to a fly.
Though Disraeli joined the imperialists he was never forgiven the
sneer that he uttered in 1852 about 'these wretched colonies,
millstones round our neck'.[4] When Sir George Grey was at the
Cape and Disraeli at the Exchequer, Sir George made up from his
own purse the allowances promised to friendly African chiefs,
which Disraeli had thought a suitable field for economy.[5] Froude
tells a story on good authority of a new ministry formed by
Palmerston. 'He was at a loss for a colonial secretary. At last he
said, "I suppose I must take the thing myself. Come upstairs with
me, H—, when the council is over. We will look at the maps and
you shall show me where these places are."'[6] The authenticity of
this story has been denied but there is no doubt about Palmerston's description of the Hudson's Bay Companies' territories as
'a wilderness in the northern part of America, where nothing lives
except fur-bearing animals and a few wild Indians but little re-

[1] *Roderick Random.*   [2] Wakefield, *Art of Colonisation.*
[3] Quoted by C. R. L. Fletcher, *History of England.*
[4] Letter to Malmesbury.   [5] Milne, *A Modern Proconsul.*   [6] *Oceana.*

moved from the lower creation, . . . confided to a company whose chief functions [are] to strip the running animals of their fur, and to keep the bipeds sober'.[1] However good a joke this was in the House of Commons it must have been infuriating at Red River. The series could be extended *ad lib.* to the present day. Was it much more considerate when the chairman of the Conservative Party contributed the following words to a debate, on 18 December 1935: 'Migration within the Empire should only be considered as a means of developing our best markets and permanently minimising the risk of unemployment.'[2]

A third Secretary of State, for War and the Colonies, was appointed in 1801. The double title serves to demonstrate the current theory of the Empire; colonies during the French Wars were valued largely for their usefulness to the War Office as strategic points of vantage. Nevertheless a permanent Colonial Department was formed with an Under-Secretary and a system of procedure. The tradition of the Colonial Office, which three generations of colonists decried, dates from this period when the Permanent Under-Secretary counted upon half, or less than half, the attention of the Secretary of State.

During the long peace after Waterloo neither the War Office nor the Colonial Office was thought to require the services of a statesman of the first rank, and, though Russell, Derby and Gladstone were among the many who flitted through the Office, their tenure of it came early in their careers. There is little evidence in the young Queen's correspondence that she cared much for imperial affairs other than the appointment of colonial bishops. Prince Albert's biographer credits him with an intelligent interest in Newfoundland dogs, but not in other denizens of the Empire. The affairs of the Grand Duchy of Pumpernickel fill page after page of these royal memoirs while the making of Canada and Australia passes unnoticed. The Duke of Wellington, whose prestige was almost royal, appears once in the civil history of the colonies, earning Wakefield's gratitude by some unspecified assistance in easing the passage of the South Australia Act, presumably a matter of arranging Parliamentary time. Otherwise the Duke's imperial interests were strategic. He was apt with oracular

[1] Hansard for 12 February 1858.   [2] Hansard.

comments on the Kaffir Wars and the combined operations in China, and is said to have planned the Rideau Canal and the fortifications of Quebec.

The longest tenure of the Colonial Office was that of Earl Bathurst (1812–27), a politician whose memory survives only in colonial place-names, although his partnership with Liverpool and Castlereagh directed the downfall of Napoleon. 'He was a High Churchman and a High Tory,' says Greville, 'but a cool politician; a bad speaker, a good writer; greatly averse to changes but unwillingly acquiescing in many. His conversation was generally a series of jokes.' A friend of Pitt, he was one of the old school, and reputed the last man in London to wear a pig-tail. Apart from this pen-picture we can form an idea of Bathurst from his gradual conversion to the necessity of an emigration policy, his belated but active support of the 1820 settlers, his ineffectual attempts to get justice for Lord Selkirk in the Canadian courts, and his reconciliation of the Hudson's Bay Company with the Nor'westers in 1821. He was at last discredited by complaints from the Cape against his client, Lord Charles Somerset. Lord Grey of the Reform Bill left no mark on the Empire except that his Colonial Secretary, Stanley, then in his whiggish youth, carried the abolition of slavery through Parliament. Later as Colonial Secretary in a Tory ministry (1841–4), and finally (when he had become fourteenth Earl of Derby) as a Conservative prime minister, Edward Stanley was known in the colonies as domineering and unsympathetic, though he had visited Canada and the West Indies. But much worse was the lethargic pietist Glenelg, under whom the colonies groaned from 1835 to 1838. He pleased no one but his Permanent Under-Secretary, (Sir) James Stephen (1789–1859), who took advantage of Glenelg's well-meaning compliance to make himself master in the Office. Melbourne, then Prime Minister, treated colonial problems with that heartless senile frivolity that so endeared him to London drawing-rooms. To him the Canadian crisis meant no more than a notable opportunity to score off his political rival, Lord Durham. Glenelg's ineptitude went well with Melbourne's policy of doing nothing constructive. When Lord John Russell unseated Glenelg in the last years of Melbourne's ministry, Canada, New Zealand and the Cape felt instantaneous relief. Russell seemed almost alone among English statesmen in his sympathetic understanding of colonial problems, whereas Peel's great ministry was remarkable in the history of the Empire chiefly as an obstruction against which the Colonial Reformers battered. It will not be necessary to repeat the list of achievements of Russell's administration (1846–52) when the third Earl Grey was Colonial Secretary. But the era of self-government which decentralised the Empire was also the era of Free Trade which threatened to disintegrate it. In Palmerston's heyday, though Indian affairs were prominent, the rest of the Empire again sank into neglect. Eleven Secretaries of State held office in thirteen years (1852–65), with little to show that it much mattered which was in, and which out. When at the onset of the Crimean War (June 1854) the Colonial Office was separated from the War Office, the status of the colonial department sank even lower in political estimation.

The death of Molesworth in 1855, after a few months as Colonial Secretary, ended the era of Colonial Reform. With Free Trade at home and responsible government overseas, the utilitarians of that age supposed that the imperial bonds were withering away; and the permanent officials at the Office seemed to regard themselves as engaged in winding up a dissolved partnership.

The desire to graduate to autonomy among the colonists was matched by a desire among English politicians and publicists to urge the nestlings to fly, the ripe fruit to drop off. They had already broken with the political traditions of the motherland; they were democratic and protectionist while she adhered to a qualified franchise and Free Trade. Little Englanders repeatedly challenged acquisitive statesmen to declare what colonies were good for. Cobden denounced them as part of the bad old system, 'the colonies, the army, the navy, the church and the corn-laws, merely accessories of our aristocratic government'. It would take fifty years, he thought, of the antiseptic effects of Free Trade 'to purge these impurities' from the constitution. Colonies were a limb of the discredited mercantile system and should disappear with it. Were the colonies useful for defence? Not in the opinion of many strategists. Canada in particular was a perpetual drain upon military resources and, worse than that, was a perpetual provocation to the United States. Why, asked Dilke, should we maintain at our expense an army to protect the French-Canadians who hated us against the Americans who should be our dearest friends? Was Canada anything but an offence to Anglo-American good feeling? John Bright spoke to this effect in the debates on Canadian confederation. Robert Lowe said to Dufferin: 'You ought to make it your business [as Governor-General] to get rid of the Dominion.'

The inexplicable feature in colonial life was loyalty, the protestation of the colonials that they wanted self-government within the Empire, not separation from it. This was regarded as sentimental folly which they should discard if they were to be taken seriously in a work-a-day world. Anthony Trollope rated the Australians soundly for their stupidity. If they did not want separation, they ought to want it; he told them so for their own good. Sometimes the criticism was sharper. The colonies clung to England because England paid the bill for their unjust native wars. Let them first be self-reliant if their loyalty was to be taken as disinterested.

The contemptuous attitude of Downing Street had produced a curious reaction against the use of the words 'colony' and 'colonial'. With a sigh of relief the Canadians cast off these servile names, adopting instead the name of Dominion, which to them signified freedom. In old English law and history a 'colony' had always meant a plantation or settlement of free men with rights under the common law, until the Colonial Office degraded the colonies in the nineteenth century. A 'dominion' meant an absolute lordship such as Henry VIII proclaimed over Ireland. The change from colony to dominion, if terms were precisely used, should have implied a lowering of status. But the brand of vassalage to the Colonial Office was felt to be the deeper disgrace, and dislike of the word 'colonial' persists to-day throughout the Commonwealth.

It is a paradox that statesmen were never more gloomy about the future of the Empire than at the moment of its maturity. After the conference that produced the British North America Act the Canadian delegates returned with their loyalism sadly shaken. Sir R. Cartwright of Upper Canada (1835–1912), asserted his belief that both Gladstone and Disraeli were disappointed because Canada had not asked for independence. Among the few British statesmen who were interested, most looked upon the foundation of the Dominion as the end of the story. Two successive Under-Secretaries were avowed separatists. Herman Merivale (1806–74), whose Oxford *Lectures on Colonisation* were revised and reissued in 1861, betrays in them a gross ignorance

of colonial life. In his opinion systematic colonisation had been a
failure, and Free Trade a cause which demonstrably prevailed
everywhere. He would wash his hands of the colonies and could
not see that any social ties need remain. The foundation of colonial bishoprics seemed to him superfluous. He found 'something
almost grotesque in the instituting of Orange Lodges in Upper
Canada and Pitt Club dinners in Australia'. Could English snob-
bery go further? Were not the Presbyterians of Ontario in precisely the same relation to William of Orange as the Presbyterians
of Ulster except that they had changed their domicile? Must the
Australians forget that Pitt had authorised the founding of New
South Wales? Merivale was Permanent Under-Secretary to the
Colonial Office from 1847 to 1861. The lowest ebb came under his
successor, 'a person called Rogers' who 'ruled the colonies for
fifteen years' according to a responsible statesman at Melbourne.
This was Sir F. Rogers, later Lord Blachford (1811–89), whose
official correspondence, especially with his assistant, Sir H. Taylor
(1800–86), is imbued with the desire 'to shake off all responsibly
governed colonies'. He could 'hardly realise the possibility of any
one sensibly thinking' of a contrary policy. Taylor went further;
he lamented to the Duke of Newcastle over the improved relations
with Canada as 'the worst consequence of the late dispute with
the United States'. Elsewhere he referred to Canada as 'a most
dangerous possession, a *damnosa hereditas*'.

The philosophy of separatism was expounded by Goldwin
Smith (1823–1910), who was Professor of Modern History at
Oxford from 1858 to 1866. Later he proceeded to an American
university, and lived for some years in Canada. On geo-political
principles he was convinced that the forty-ninth parallel was an
unreal frontier cutting clean across the economic subdivisions of
North America. Each Canadian region should and would be
drawn into union with its corresponding American region. Goldwin Smith took little trouble to conceal his contempt for the
colonials who had 'a strong propensity to the commercial vice of
protectionism, the natural resort of ignorant cupidity'; and were
also inclined 'to plunge into all the excesses of Universal Suffrage',
a truly horrid prospect. He was, says Bodelsen,[1] 'an austere

---

[1] The best summary of this topic, with ample references and bibliography, is
to be found in *Studies in Mid-Victorian Imperialism* by C. A. Bodelsen, first
published at Copenhagen in 1924.

aristocrat, intolerant of what he called muddled thinking'. Colonial loyalism in his opinion was infantile and unnatural. The desire of militarists to uphold the Empire for reasons of prestige was equally foolish since it could be shown that colonies were a source of military weakness. Could it be supposed that they would help Britain in her wars? This was a favourite theme of the Little Englanders, oddly falsified by later events. Even Dilke who was not a Little Englander plunged deep into error by asserting that 'Australia would scarcely feel herself deeply interested in the guarantee of Luxemburg, nor Canada in the affairs of Servia'.

To do them justice the separatists rarely envisaged a mere fragmentation of the Empire; it should be liquidated in an atmosphere of goodwill. It became customary to allude to the possible survival of a 'moral union' when the mother-country and the colonies should agree to part. The optimism of the Free Traders, which had some resemblances to that of the Marxians—their fellow-materialists—assumed that progress would soon eliminate national rivalries, that the nations would draw together when the shackles of the older dispensation were struck off. Pointing with admiration to the growing wealth and strength of the United States they sought to heal the schism of the English-speaking nations by an abdication of England's supposed domination over half the world. Let coal and cotton be the symbols of her sway, not ironclads and haughty proconsuls.

The conception of a commonwealth of nations bound together only by common allegiance to the Crown had occurred to the Colonial Reformers. There is a hint of it in the Durham Report and it had been expressly advocated by Adderley in 1846. Even the pessimistic Merivale thought it a possibility. The materialists ignored such a fanciful notion in the 1860's.

Of late years the tendency of historians has been to defend the Colonial Office against the abuse heaped on it by the reformers of the last century. The 'Office' was created by Sir James Stephen in the days of *laissez-faire* and public parsimony. No one then supposed it was the duty of Whitehall to direct the course of progress and mould society into new forms; that was the task of private enterprise and philanthropy. The duty of the Colonial Office was to preserve public order in the colonies, to ensure that government was carried out on honest, regular and, if possible, uniform principles, and to do so with the most rigid economy, in the interests of free and beneficent commerce. If no provision was made for education, health, and public works in the colonies, the justification was that these services were not provided by the Queen's government for the people of England a hundred years ago.

When some notorious misery cried out for relief, then, if the state of the finances permitted, public generosity might be invoked and a grant-in-aid provided; but this was conceived as an exceptional act of grace, not as a form of capital investment. Half the unpopularity of the colonies in Whitehall was caused by their repeated demands for grants-in-aid, which a reasonable system of guaranteed capital loans would have obviated. Money was voted for the colonies every year either from the British revenue or as an addition to the British national debt; £6,000,000 for purchasing the Cape of Good Hope; £20,000,000 for freeing the slaves; £370,000 a year for the convicts in New South Wales; £200,000 for the Swan River fiasco; £250,000 for establishing the colony of New Zealand; millions for the Kaffir Wars.

Management of money was very well understood in Downing Street. The Office consolidated the various agencies maintained by the colonies into the Crown Agency (1833), a controlled system for letting contracts, buying stores, investing balances and raising loans for the various colonies. Later a Colonial Audit Department was also formed to supervise their annual accounts (1889).

The grant of self-government in the eighteen-forties and 'fifties was, as Downing Street saw it, the shaking off of a financial burden. The 'Office' would no longer be obliged to go hat in hand to the Treasury for one grant-in-aid after another. Hence the bitterness over the Maori Wars when self-governing New Zealand was still drawing on the British Treasury. Sir F. Rogers was a good painstaking official (though his memoirs suggest that the colonies rarely entered his thoughts outside business hours); his contribution was the foundation of a real colonial service. Previously, governors, judges and other officials had been appointed by patronage, with the proportion of good and bad appointments that may be expected. In 1862 some cadets began to be selected for the colonial civil service by the Civil Service Commission after a qualifying examination. Gladstone's general reform of the civil services followed in 1870. The policy of the 'Office' was to standardise the service with interchangeable officials, especially the judges, although they might be obliged to understand old French law in Mauritius, Roman-Dutch law at the Cape and old Spanish law in Trinidad. An attempt was made to create a corps of governors trained in the service—Sir Hercules Robinson will serve as an example—though when Disraeli was in power he had a fancy for appointing noblemen with ancient names.

The first signs of a progressive, creative policy appeared in the early 'seventies and may perhaps be attributed to the appointment of Sir Robert Herbert (1831–1905) as Permanent Under-Secretary in 1871. He was unlike all his predecessors in knowing something about colonial life. Having gone out to Queensland as secretary to a governor he had stayed as a settler and politician, becoming the first premier of the state when it gained responsible government. In 1873 Lord Kimberley, as Secretary of State, initiated the forward moves in West Africa, Malaya and Fiji which his Tory successor completed. A more responsible view of Empire was taken; it was recognised that a civilised power could not merely ignore misrule on its frontier. Yet when the forward policy was fairly launched by Disraeli in 1874 Lord Carnarvon admitted that he dared not ask Parliament to guarantee a railway loan for Natal in the same session that had to face the cost of the Ashanti War. Both, in the eyes of the House of Commons, were equally unprofitable. Nothing but a public disaster would move the House to active benevolence.

The Colonial Office sent no 'experts' to the colonies; it had none to send. The one experiment, before Chamberlain's time, in scientific development was the association between the Colonial Office and Kew Gardens. So far back as 1788 Sir Joseph Banks had engaged the active co-operation of King George III in organising the exchange of useful plants between different parts of the Empire. The first experiment was the transfer of the breadfruit from Tahiti to the West Indies (achieved by the persevering Bligh on his second voyage). Other experiments followed until Banks and King George both died, in 1820. For some years little was done, though there was a public protest when the Whigs proposed to economise by selling the gardens. In 1841, after a Treasury inquiry, Kew was reorganised in close association with the colonial and Indian departments under Sir William Hooker (1785–1865) who was succeeded as Director by his son Sir Joseph Hooker. Very many investigations have been carried out at Kew and expeditions despatched to the colonies. Hundreds of botanists have also been trained at Kew for the colonial services. Among their greatest successes have been the establishment of the rubber-plant in Malaya, of the chicle in Honduras, cinchona in Jamaica, spices in the Windward Islands and of tea-cultivation in Assam.

Not much else of this kind was done until Joseph Chamberlain became Colonial Secretary in Lord Salisbury's third administration (1895). The essence of his reforms was the provision of capital on a large scale for development.

2. THE SELF-RELIANT POLICY AND
THE MAORI WARS

WHIG governments in the era of reform had been very properly concerned over the great cost of colonial defence. Between 1815 and 1860, from 40,000 to 50,000 British regular troops were dispersed about the Empire in twenty or thirty garrisons at a cost to the British tax-payer of about £3,000,000 a year, a large addition to the Budget in those thrifty days. Attempts to economise had been frustrated in the 'thirties by the Canadian Rebellion, and in the 'forties by the Kaffir Wars. Lord Grey, in 1846, had begun a careful programme of reductions on the very good principle that 'self-government begets self-defence', but the result had been a series of wrangles between particular colonies and the Colonial Office, with varying results.

This was one of the weaknesses revealed in imperial strategy at the beginning of the Crimean War. All the colonies had raised volunteer corps, presented loyal addresses and even voted token contributions (£20,000 from Canada) to imperial expenses, but the stern fact remained that many of our scarce line regiments were immobilised in distant colonies and never reached the seat of war. Offers of contingents of colonial volunteers were, strange to say, rejected by the War Office, where German mercenaries were preferred.

The Indian Mutiny and the China War repeated the lesson, with one shining example of co-operation. Sir George Grey, who was at the Cape during the crisis of the Mutiny, diverted to Calcutta several regiments that called on their way to the China War— including the 93rd Highlanders who relieved Lucknow—together with stores of food, his gold reserve and all the horses on which he could lay hands—including his own carriage-horses. There were those who said (and he was rather of that opinion himself) that he had saved British India.

The first reform had been to separate the War Office from the Colonial Office under a fourth Secretary of State (1854), whose Assistant Under-Secretary was J. R. Godley, the founder of Canterbury. A threat of war with France in 1859 made the question of imperial defence urgent. Palmerston, then Prime Minister, was for encouraging the volunteers, fortifying naval bases, and developing ironclad steamships in rivalry with the French Navy. In this crisis an inter-departmental committee representing the War Office, the Colonial Office and the Treasury produced a memorandum on colonial defence. Godley, with his enlightened views on colonial reform, wrote the majority report. He denounced the practice of locking up small garrisons in distant colonies as strategically unsound and demoralising to the colonials. The 'spirit of self-reliance', such as had been shown by the New Englanders who captured Louisburg, should be nourished by throwing the colonials upon their own resources. There were few precedents, before Waterloo, for employing British regular troops in colonial campaigns, except the disastrous precedent of General Braddock. In local campaigns against savages on their frontiers the self-governing colonies should fight for themselves. A clear distinction should be made between colonies and 'imperial posts' such as Gibraltar which should be held as part of a broad strategic plan for defending the whole Empire by sea-power.

The report was ventilated in Parliament by Godley's friends, Adderley and Gladstone, in spite of Palmerston's disapproval. A resolution was carried in favour of withdrawing the West Indian garrisons and throwing the self-governing colonies 'chiefly on their own resources'. But in that very year (1861) events in Canada (see chapter x, 3, page 552) required the despatch of 10,000 troops to the American frontier. The Canadians rose to their responsibility by forming a strong militia of 18,000 men, the best defensive measure taken in any colony. In 1863, the Colonial Office made a rule that colonies must contribute £40 a year to the Treasury for every British soldier they employed. During the next seven years superfluous troops were gradually withdrawn from the West Indies, from Canada—except for the two naval bases of Halifax and Esquimault—and even, partially, from the Cape. The test case came in New Zealand, where the Maori War had just been renewed. No one then supposed that the situation might ever be seen in reverse, that Canadian troops might come to defend the shores of Kent and Sussex, or New Zealanders fight and die for the Isles of Greece.

The release of the colonial garrisons had the healthy effect of turning public attention from land-power to sea-power. Naval theory had fallen behindhand since Trafalgar, to be revived in the writings of Sir John Colomb in the 'sixties, as a result of the debates of 1861. The conceptions of a 'fleet in being', the 'blue-water school', and the necessity of a 'two-power standard' date from this period, deriving their origin in part from Godley's report. Within a few years naval supremacy over France was assured by the excellence of British marine-engineering, so that the fear of a new Napoleonic war receded. The strategic balance in the Mediterranean had also shifted by the appearance of the new kingdom of Italy, attached to Great Britain by every tie of friendship and gratitude. The fortress of Corfu thus seemed less vital to the interests of the Royal Navy. Gladstone had been sent as High Commissioner to the Ionian Islands in 1858, and had come back with the report that, while the Islanders enjoyed all the blessings of civilisation under British protection, they desired nothing except union with the kingdom of Greece where these blessings were entirely absent. The opportunity of withdrawing gracefully came when the Greeks deposed their German King. After they had offered the throne successively to Queen Victoria's sons and to several British noblemen, the Greeks were persuaded to accept the Danish brother-in-law of the Prince of Wales. The fortifications of Corfu were then dismantled and the Septinsular Republic of the Ionian Islands released from British protection on the condition that it should be united to Greece under a free constitution (1864). Not many Englishmen now remember that the Ionian Islands were part of the British Empire for fifty years.[1] They show few signs of the British occupation except the survival of the game of cricket which, it is said, is still played in Corfu.

[1] A special Order of Knighthood had been founded in 1818 to reward services in Malta and the Ionian Islands. In 1868 the Duke of Buckingham, as Colonial Secretary, persuaded the Queen to constitute it as a colonial order, of St Michael and St George.

Malta, which was refortified in 1863, resumed its place as the
principal naval base in the Mediterranean.

Far away, in New Zealand, the new imperial strategy was tried
out in a frontier war.

THE MAORI WARS (1860–72)

The rapid colonisation of New Zealand in the 1850's led inevitably
to friction with the Maoris. The white population rose from
58,000 in 1858 to 256,000 in 1871, outnumbering the natives, and
eagerly demanding the right to acquire their unused tribal lands.
By this time the Maoris were mostly Christians but still retained
their social system. Since land was communally owned it did not
provide the property qualification required for the franchise under
the new constitution. They tended to withdraw from contact with
the settlers, keeping themselves to themselves, and maintaining
their lands in accordance with the Treaty of Waitangi. In 1858 a
number of tribes between Auckland and New Plymouth agreed to
elect a Maori king and to form an autonomous native state (as the
Basutos had done so successfully in South Africa). The 'King
Movement' was loyal and Christian, and might have been judiciously guided and encouraged, but Good Governor Grey, who
understood the Maoris and was a friend of the noble old savage
chosen as king, had left New Zealand. The new governor, Gore
Browne, snubbed the leaders of the King Movement.

A breach occurred in 1859 over the purchase of a block of land
at Waitara, near New Plymouth, from a minor chief whose right
to sell was overruled by a chief of higher rank. The rights and
wrongs of the Waitara purchase, involving obscure questions of
Maori tribal law, are hotly disputed to this day. In March 1860
Governor Browne decided to enforce the purchaser's title by sending troops to Waitara. At once the tribes rose and besieged the
New Plymouth Colony, a little coastal strip of cultivated land
lying beneath the majestic cone of Mount Egmont. There were
detachments of three British regiments, a sloop lent by the Victorian government and colonial volunteers, perhaps 3000 men in
all, to guard the settlement which was lightly invested throughout
the war. Some outlying settlers were killed before they could reach
safety and some laborious expeditions were made by the troops
against Maori villages, but without much effect.

In July 1860 the New Zealand Parliament met in a highly critical mood with no clear line of policy. The Waitara natives confided their cause to the Maori king, who had not taken part in the fighting, and there followed an uneasy truce. The Colonial Office, much dissatisfied with the affair, despatched Sir George Grey from the Cape to replace Gore Browne. Fifteen years earlier he had

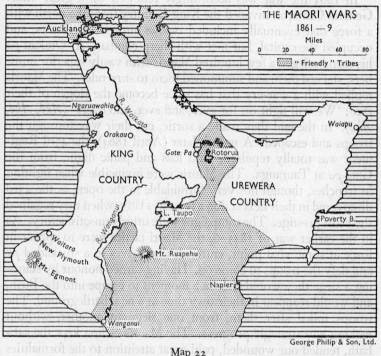

THE MAORI WARS
1861 — 9

Miles
0   20   40   60   80

"Friendly" Tribes

Auckland

Ngaruawahia   R. Waikato

Orakau   R. Otorohanga   Waiapu

KING   Gate Pa   Rotorua

COUNTRY   UREWERA
COUNTRY

R. Wanganui   L. Taupo   Poverty B.

Waitara   Mt. Ruapehu
New Plymouth
Mt. Egmont   Napier

Wanganui

George Philip & Son, Ltd.

Map 22

settled the first Maori War by his mere prestige. Then he had been the autocratic ruler of a Crown Colony. Could he repeat his exploit of pacifying the country now, when hampered by a constitutional ministry whose native policy he disagreed with?

The war-party had gained the majority in Parliament, led by Alfred Domett (see above, page 525). Grey was determined to pacify the tribes in his own way, and not by fighting. He sent an emissary, John Gorst,[1] into the 'King Country' and began to

---

[1] Better known as the Rt. Hon. Sir J. E. Gorst, Q.C. (1835–1916), in later life a Conservative politician in England.

make roads southward from Auckland. Reversing his predecessor's decision he restored the Waitara lands to the natives but, by an unlucky chance, another land-purchase near New Plymouth renewed the quarrel before the Waitara cession was completed. The tribes again closed in on New Plymouth, and Gorst was expelled from the King Country.

In 1863 the war was accordingly renewed on a great scale. General Cameron invaded the King Country from the north with a force that eventually included twelve imperial regiments, and occupied the capital, but met with sharp combat. At Orakau *pa* his men besieged a few hundred Maoris with vastly superior numbers, starved them and summoned them to surrender. The Maoris replied with a war-cry that has since become the slogan of their race: 'We will fight on for ever, and ever, and ever!' (*Aké, Aké, Aké*). In the end they made a sortie, cut their way through the troops and escaped. A month later (April 1864), the 43rd Regiment was totally repulsed, with loss and panic flight, from the Gate *pa* at Tauranga. The Maoris were invincible when fighting in trenches, though not very formidable in the open, as the 43rd discovered in their next action a few days later, when they regained their lost prestige. The campaigns were utterly unsatisfactory. As in the earlier war of 1845–6, the Maori tactics were to appear in force at some vital point, entrench themselves in a stockaded *pa* and defy the troops to come on. Having earned honour by standing a siege they would choose a moment to escape into the Bush, and would reappear in their own time at a new battleground. The troops toiled after them, from one siege to another, without making any strategic progress. The Maoris at first kept the sabbath, tended our wounded, paid great attention to the formalities of war, and practised a fantastic chivalry. ('If thine enemy hunger, feed him', for if he starves, there will be no fight which would be a pity.) They have been described as the Irishmen of the Pacific and have an inconsequent humour of their own. One tribe conceived a generous regard for the 65th (York and Lancaster) Regiment which distinguished itself in the fighting round New Plymouth. 'Keep your heads down, sikity-fif', they would cry out before firing a volley. But the Maori code drew no distinction between combatants and non-combatants, so that if a Maori woman was killed in the trenches the life of an Englishwoman was scrupulously taken in reprisal.

A darker shade came over the scene in 1864 with the relapse into paganism known as the *Hau-hau* cult. In a people only thirty years removed from brute savagery, disillusioned by what they thought the treachery of the whites, and rather unwisely nourished on the history of the kings of Israel, a reaction against Christian teaching is not surprising. The *Hau-hau* religion, a strange medley of pagan and early Jewish rites, appeared first near New Plymouth and spread across the North Island to the west coast. Human sacrifices were made, among them the ritual killing of an Anglican clergyman, Carl Volkner, at the Bay of Plenty (1865). But the *Hau-hau* movement declined and disappeared after three or four years without having spread to the far more numerous tribes in the north. The Maoris were as clannish and as much divided by clan jealousies as the Scottish Highlanders in the old days. Operations were generally aimed at single tribes and, as the war dragged on, the proportion of friendly tribes fighting beside the British tended to increase. Half the Maori race, including the tribes living north of Auckland which had fought in 1845–6, remained at peace, as did the tribes of Cook Strait and the South Island. The Maori king, though treated with respect on account of his high lineage, never enlarged his dominions or power. On the death of Te Whero-Whero, the first king, his son, a savage of ferocious aspect, was chosen to succeed him, though he showed no political sagacity. The King Country, a forest tract between the Waikato and Wanganui rivers, remained closed to white men, but the 'King' tribes lapsed into neutrality as the war dragged on.

By 1867 the cleared land around New Plymouth was firmly held, and the *Hau-hau* fever was dying down. Meanwhile the Governor, the Commander-in-Chief, and the Ministry were all at loggerheads. General Cameron had made no secret of the fact that he regarded the war as scandalous oppression of the natives, as did Bishop Selwyn. Cameron's successor, backed by the War Office, resisted every attempt of the Governor to interfere in his offensive campaign against the *Hau-haus*. Governor Grey, who had commanded the fighting troops in the first Maori War, never forgot that as Governor he was titular Commander-in-Chief. Disagreeing with the General's dispositions, he collected a force of settlers and friendly natives with whom he personally led a column to attack a Maori *pa*, while the General stood aside as a spectator.

As in the days of Washington and General Braddock there was serious and growing friction between the regulars and the irregular colonial troops. Whitehall, adopting the self-reliant policy, deplored the expense of providing infantry regiments, to very small advantage, for a war of doubtful morality in a rich self-governing colony. Sir F. Weld, a southern settler who became Prime Minister in 1864, was of like opinion, and maintained that if the colony paid for soldiers at the rate of £40 a head it should have control of them. Governor Grey, always a domineering autocrat, was at odds with all parties. At the conclusion of his term of office in 1867 he was (for the second time in his career), rather ignominiously dismissed by the Colonial Office. Bishop Selwyn went home in the following year, upon the urgent request of the Queen, to repeat his success as a Church organiser at Lichfield, where he died in 1878. With the removal of these two great men the patriarchal age ended in New Zealand. Selwyn was deeply grieved by the selfishness of the whites and the apostacy of the *Hau-hau* natives; he supposed himself to have failed in his mission. Grey was irrepressible; he announced that he had a second time restored peace and prosperity to New Zealand in spite of interference from Whitehall. But the war was not over. In 1868 an exiled chief named Te Kooti escaped with 200 followers from the Chatham Islands to Poverty Bay, where he massacred all the inhabitants of a village, including thirty-two whites, men, women and children. The British regiments were withdrawing one by one, the last in 1870, and a long campaign was fought by colonial irregulars and friendly natives against Te Kooti, who proved to be the one tactician among the Maori chiefs. In 1872 he escaped into the King Country where he was allowed to remain unmolested. A hero to his own people and, in spite of his ferocity, a man of principle, Te Kooti founded a new esoteric form of Christianity, the *ringatu* cult, which still survives.

The Maori Wars, which settled nothing, had cost the British government 1300 casualties among the regulars, and more than £3,000,000, over which there was an indecent wrangle between the colony and Gladstone's government. Most of it was added to the funded debt of New Zealand. In those days of bitter ill-feeling and recrimination New Zealand was far from being the favourite child of the mother-country, the model dominion that it afterwards became.

Hostility and contempt had also replaced the old good feeling between settlers and Maoris. The common talk of the colony was that, like the Australian Blacks, the Maoris were doomed to extinction. The labours of the missionaries were said to have been in vain. Such sentiments were reflected in the reports of visitors to New Zealand and may be read in an extreme form in J. A. Froude's *Oceana*, published as late as 1886. The Maoris had lost confidence in themselves and lapsed, if not into savagery, into apathy. Their numbers were declining, through the effect of white men's diseases, though not so sharply as the published figures seem to show. Early travellers had estimated the population at more, perhaps much more, than 100,000. The census of 1858 returned them as 56,000, that of 1896 as 35,000; but the next census showed an increase which has been rapid in the twentieth century. All these estimates and census returns are vitiated by the uncertain status of the numerous half-castes. Since there has never been a colour-bar in New Zealand and, it must be admitted, owing to the loose sexual morals of the Polynesian women in pagan times, miscegenation was at first frequent. The racial mixture produced a healthy and fertile strain in no way inferior to its parentage on either side. Some half-castes lived as Maoris with the tribes, others lived as white men in the settlements. The method of computing half-castes in the census returns was not consistent as between censuses, nor logical until 1926. The census of 1936 returned the Maori population as 67,000 and the half-castes as 15,000. No longer a dying race, the Maoris are now increasing at far higher rate[1] than the white New Zealanders, although their infantile death-rate is much higher.

The recovery of the Maoris, which is one of the glories of New Zealand history, can be traced back to events before the wars were concluded. In the first flush of victory the settlers insisted on punitive confiscations of Maori land, to the extent of nearly 3,000,000 acres, some of which was regranted to 'friendlies'. Not only did the confiscation plant a sense of injustice, it also produced an endless crop of disputes as to ownership which the courts have not yet disentangled. The Maoris are by nature litigious and have kept the Native Lands Court, established in 1865, fully employed. A better era dawned in the years 1869 to 1876 when Sir Donald

[1] The inter-censal increase of the whites was 1% per annum, of the Maoris 1·7% per annum, between 1926 and 1936.

Maclean, a clansman by birth and temperament, was Minister for Native Affairs. The two hostile areas, the King Country and the even wilder Urewera country north-west of Lake Taupo he left severely alone, trusting to time to bring about a reconciliation. Early in the present century the main trunk railway from Wellington to Auckland was driven through the King Country, opening it to white civilisation. In the more settled districts, impartial justice in the land courts, fair prices for purchased land, road-making, schools and the franchise restored the confidence of the Maoris in British justice. More and more they pinned their faith to the Treaty of Waitangi, their Magna Carta. On the whole they have retained their lands. With one-twentieth of the population of New Zealand they occupy about one-twelfth of the useful land. An almost quixotic reparation for century-old wrongs has been lately made by the Royal Commission set up in 1926 to give compensation, on a lavish scale, to tribes which, in the early days, sold their land for trifling sums.

A special Maori franchise with communal instead of geographical constituencies was set up in 1867. Like the white New Zealanders they enjoy universal suffrage, sending four native members to the Lower House. Two chiefs are usually nominated to the Upper House. For many years it has been customary to allot one seat in the cabinet to a Maori member and, so free are the New Zealanders from colour prejudice, it has passed without comment that on one or two occasions the native minister has acted as deputy in the absence of the prime minister.

Though the Maoris are still backward in literacy and public health, their progress has been remarkable in the twentieth century. Almost all of them work on the land, often as small farmers but, in the remoter tribal areas, they have adapted their communal tradition to modern co-operative methods. The Urewera, so recently the wildest of all the tribes, have excelled in co-operative dairying. Maori culture now shows little sign of decay. They have their own clergy, doctors and lawyers who are not inferior to their white colleagues. In the German Wars the Maori regiments have equalled their white compatriots in the soldierly virtues. In 1939, though conscription was not enforced in Maori areas, every able-bodied man was a volunteer.

3. CANADIAN CONFEDERATION, 1846–67

THE doctrine of *laissez-faire*, sponsored by the Radicals and adopted by the Whigs, prevailed as the fundamental belief of all reasonable men which only romantics and reactionaries opposed, through thirty years of expansion as the hungry 'forties gave way to the comfortable 'fifties, the well-fed 'sixties and the complacent 'seventies. In the colonies the effect was different.

Giving Canada self-government with one hand, the British took away with the other the preference on Canadian wheat, a small but growing trade already of great importance to the merchants of Toronto and Montreal, though not yet of vital importance to the poor of Great Britain. The merchants felt the loss rather than the wheat-growers as it meant a change in the direction of the trade but not in the demand. The harvest of Upper Canada now took the easy course southwards into the United States. Thus the Montreal riots of 1849, when the Parliament House was burnt down and when Governor Elgin was stoned by a furious mob, were provoked by discontented loyalists. The British government to which they had looked for protection injured them, as they supposed, by its fiscal policy and the Queen's representative flouted them by extending his favour to disloyal French-Canadians. A cry for secession to the United States was raised, with truculent unreality, by the party which in all its traditions was most strongly British. From this factious outbreak arose the movement towards a reciprocal free trade between Canada and the United States; it was the last of Elgin's great services to Canada that, unmindful of the insults of the English-Canadians, he negotiated for them the Reciprocity Treaty of 1854.

The first step was taken by the Canadian Parliament which passed an Act (1849) for admitting American foodstuffs to Canada free of duty, provided that the United States would make a similar concession to Canada. This led to negotiations which occupied several years. The Foreign Secretary, Palmerston, took a hand and raised the bid of the Canadians by offering the Americans free rights of navigation up the St Lawrence, access to the Newfoundland fisheries and the right to dry fish on certain parts of the Newfoundland coast, in return for free import of foodstuffs to Canada and coal to the Maritime Provinces. In 1853 a hitch in the negotiations led to a show of force. British and American naval squadrons were sent to the fishing-grounds, the one to protect British waters against illegal encroachment that was becoming customary, the other to assert American claims. This was but part of the diplomatic game which was concluded by the agreement of August 1853, ratified by the Canadian legislature in 1854, and by the American Congress in 1855. There followed a boom in Canadian wheat which flowed into the American market (124,000 bushels in 1849, 8,000,000 bushels in 1860), and thence overseas at the very high prices current during the Crimean War (1853–6). Prosperity led to railway development; the Grand Trunk Railway was opened for traffic between Montreal and Toronto in 1856, between Sarnia on Lake Huron and Rivière du Loup on the St Lawrence estuary in 1860, the longest trunk line on the American continent. It severely strained the financial resources of a young country.

The Reciprocity Treaty tended to link each region of British North America with its adjacent state in the Union, forming lines of communication north and south; and by reason of these natural geographic links many, perhaps most, observers foretold that each Canadian province would eventually be drawn into the American Union. The frontier, it was supposed, an imaginary line on the map drawn in defiance of strategic or economic factors, could not be maintained in a Free Trade world. The Americans, especially the New York manufacturers, expected to obtain in Canada a new expanding market for their wares. But the Canadian government, finding it hard to balance the budget when peace returned to Europe and wheat prices fell, introduced a revenue tariff on manufactured goods in 1858, and raised it in 1859, which caused annoyance both in the United States and in England. The consequence of self-government, as Galt[1] the Finance Minister brusquely pointed out, was that Canada now had fiscal independence and could retaliate when Great Britain withdrew Canadian preferences without consulting Canadian interests.

The crucial issue behind the struggle over tariffs was an issue still unsettled ninety years later, the question of the best outlet to the Atlantic Ocean for the products of the Middle West. Should they be carried by the British waterways through the Great Lakes and the St Lawrence, by-passing the Niagara rapids by the Wel-

[1] Mr (later Sir) A. T. Galt (1817–93), son of John Galt, q.v.

land Canal, and the St Lawrence rapids by the Rideau Canal; or should they be shipped into American territory at Buffalo and pass by the wider, deeper Erie Canal to the Hudson River and New York? The Rideau Canal, built by military labour at the cost of the War Office and upon the advice of the Duke of Wellington, was a strategic rather than a commercial route, intended for the quick concentration of troops, and could not take deep-sea shipping. Even when the Canadian waterways were used, the St Lawrence was frozen from November to April. If the east-west route was to be developed through British territory, the waterways must be reinforced by railroads; if not, the north-south routes into the United States would prevail. To extend the Grand Trunk Railway eastward to the ice-free port of Halifax, and westward as far as the limits of settlement, required a financial outlay far beyond the resources of the agricultural colony of Canada. A lien upon all the untapped wealth of the Far West would be required, and a working agreement with the government of Nova Scotia. Thus the federation of all the British colonies in North America gradually appeared as the alternative to their absorption one by one into the United States.

The colonies in North America fell into five groups all with widely varying interests. In the first place there was Newfoundland (including Labrador), the senior British colony. The Newfoundlanders looked eastward, to the sea. Their trade was with Europe and, although they imported some wheat from the St Lawrence, they regarded Canadians in general as competitors and potential poachers on their fishing-grounds. There seemed to be no commercial or other advantage to be derived from closer union with the mainland provinces. Though they sent delegates with a watching brief to the earlier conferences there was little likelihood of their joining the confederation. The mere suggestion of it provoked riots in St John's.

Secondly, the Maritime Provinces, Novia Scotia, New Brunswick and Prince Edward Island, formed a compact group with a strong local pride. They too looked seaward; the 'blue-nose' skippers of Halifax were the boldest seamen in the British merchant marine; their leader, Sir Samuel Cunard, was the pioneer of the steamship lines. If they were to ship the trade of Canada across the wintry Atlantic, they must be joined to Canada by rail. As long as this seemed impracticable their local pride, their higher standard of refinement and education, their conservative tendency, made them disinclined for union with the rougher inland provinces. Between the three there was that intense but friendly rivalry that often persists between neighbouring societies with independent histories. Prince Edward Island, the smallest and poorest, was also the most secluded. Its inhabitants nourished their grievance against their absentee proprietors (of whom Cunard was one) and went their own way. There was a physical obstruction to union with Canada in the shape of a mass of trackless wooded hills, which Lord Ashburton had ceded to the United States, between New Brunswick and Canada.

Thirdly there was the colony of Canada formed of the French and British provinces which had been united by the Act of 1841. By 1861 it was generally agreed that the Union had been a failure. In one respect Durham's forecast had proved quite wrong; so far from there being a fusion between French and English, the French-Canadians had drawn more closely together, preserving their nationality against English pollution. But he had been right in supposing that they would soon find themselves in a minority. The great emigration of the 'forties and 'fifties raised the British population of Upper Canada to 1,500,000, whereas the French, by natural increase, had not exceeded 1,000,000. Thus two nations, no longer warring, still lived uneasily side by side in the bosom of a single state. Canadian politics, between the grant of responsible government in 1846 and the confederation of 1867, were no more than an ingenious balancing of power between combinations of French and English politicians to prevent the dominance of either party.

Fourthly there were the vast territories of the Hudson's Bay Company, with their strange wild metropolis at Fort Garry on the Red River. The slow march of civilisation, the talk of transcontinental railways, the designs of capitalists from Upper Canada were beginning to cause dismay among the bold, ignorant *métis*, whose days of lawless freedom were numbered. But while Canada groped westward with its petty resources, the Americans were pouring across their prairies in thousands, financed by the wealth of the Atlantic states, backed by the influx of cheap Irish labourers three times as numerous as those who went to Canada. If the railway should not reach the Canadian west in time to link it with the St Lawrence basin, who could doubt that the tide of

American expansion would flow over into the Canadian prairie? No such doubt entered the mind of the Republican press in America where the 'manifest destiny' of the United States was freely assumed to include the whole North-west. St Paul in Minnesota was still the nearest town to Fort Garry. The Hudson's Bay Company itself, abandoning the route which gave the Company its name, communicated with Red River through St Paul.

Beyond the Rocky Mountains lay the fifth group of colonies, Vancouver Island and British Columbia, originally posts of the Hudson's Bay Company. Before the Oregon Treaty of 1846 the Company had occupied a dozen forts throughout the no-man's-land loosely called Oregon and, in 1843, had planted one on Vancouver Island at the site afterwards called Victoria. After the treaty, which ceded the southern part of the region to the United States, the Colonial Reformers pressed for the colonisation of the British area and the establishment of a naval base on the island. Lord Grey, in an expansive mood, proclaimed Vancouver Island a colony (1849) and provided it with a governor and a legislative council, though it had neither trade nor colonists other than the Hudson's Bay agents and their monopoly. Esquimault, afterwards the naval base, was established as a trading post in 1849. After two years without subjects or duties the first Governor, R. Blanshard, resigned in favour of the Hudson's Bay factor at Victoria, (Sir) James Douglas (1803–77), the true founder of British Columbia.

Some attempts had been made at systematic colonisation through a subsidiary formed, rather reluctantly, by the Hudson's Bay Company, and named the Puget Sound Land Company. They commenced a little trade in working coal for shipment from Esquimault to California. There were however no more than 2000 white inhabitants and no access to these little colonies except by sea round Cape Horn when, in 1855, gold was discovered on the Fraser River. At once British Columbia attracted 20,000 diggers from California. Douglas acted with exemplary energy. He was determined that there should be no repetition in British Columbia of the lynch-law which had prevailed in America's wild west, and preserved order with most meagre resources. He obtained an Act of Parliament (1858) for setting up a separate colonial government on the mainland with its capital at New

Westminster; and he organised this colony through the agency of a single company of the Royal Engineers, 150 officers and men, whom he borrowed for five years from the imperial government. Their task was to build a wagon-road, the 'Cariboo trail', for 480 miles north from the Fraser River through forests and mountains to the Cariboo Country, which yielded gold to the value of £5,000,000 in ten years. The sappers preserved order, maintained the government and, on discharge, many of them settled with their families in the country.

The Cariboo gold-rush was over before Canada became a dominion. The prospectors, the diggers, and the parasites who accompanied their march, moved off to other strikes of gold, in New Zealand or in Queensland, but left behind a formed and settled colony which had produced treasures and might again. During the American Civil War Esquimault was garrisoned by British troops and developed as a naval base which strengthened the interest of Whitehall in this remote dependency. The two colonies, Vancouver Island and British Columbia, were united in 1866 while their further union with Canada was under consideration. But an overland journey with wagons from Canada to the Cariboo Country was made for the first time only in 1862.

During the 'fifties the confederation of the Canadian colonies was occasionally discussed by statesmen in Canada and in the Maritime Provinces. It was not however a popular project. It was urged only by statesmen and financiers of more than ordinary enlightenment who were consistently snubbed, alike by Whig and Tory Secretaries-of-State, if they made proposals to Whitehall. A strange belief, for which it is hard to find a reason, long persisted in England that the confederation of a group of colonies would inevitably mean their separation from the Empire; and though most English politicians in the 'fifties believed that the destiny of the colonies was independence, not many wished to force the pace. Bulwer Lytton, Secretary of State in 1858, could boast the achievement of vetoing two schemes of confederation in a year, proposed by the Governors of Canada and the Cape.

At last a move was made in 1860 implying that the Crown had some sympathy with colonial loyalty, some affection for its subjects overseas. The young Prince of Wales was sent on a visit of ceremony to Canada accompanied by the fifth Duke of Newcastle (1811–64), Secretary of State for the Colonies in Palmerston's administration. It was the first time since the office was inaugurated that 'Mr Mother-country' had ever cast an eye on any of the provinces over which he claimed residual sovereignty. The Prince saw a great deal and gave much gratification to many honest folk whose loyalty had been sorely strained in the past; the Duke, who had long been one of the Colonial Reformers, saw more. Canadian confederation was a practical problem with two sides to it. The electors of the Canadian provinces must be roused from their parochial prejudice to see its necessity, and the scheme must be financed from London. He returned to England a friend and ally of the men who made the Dominion.

Among those with whom he conferred in Canada was Mr (later Sir) E. W. Watkin, the representative of Baring Brothers the bankers. From 1841 until 1873 the London accounts of Canada were held jointly by Baring Brothers and Glyn Mills. There is gold at the heart of every magic, black or white. Let those who suspect the malign influence of the international financier behind all public activities search out the part played by the Barings in the history of the British Commonwealth under Queen Victoria. Can a more beneficent family history be found than that of the descendants of Francis Baring whom Pitt made a baronet in 1793? A Baring negotiated the boundary of Canada and the United States in 1842; a Baring sat on the committee of the Canterbury Association; a Baring was Chancellor of the Exchequer in the administration that finally gave responsible government to the colonies; a Baring of the next generation was Viceroy of India; another reconstituted the government and prosperity of Egypt.[1]

In Canada, Baring Brothers gave their steady support to the policy of railway expansion which consummated the union of the provinces. Having overreached themselves in the railway boom of the 'fifties they sent Watkin to Canada to reorganise the confused finances of the Grand Trunk Railway. Newcastle's conversion to the policy of confederation was backed by Watkin's recommendation of a still bolder plan for railway development. A charter for an inter-colonial railway was issued in 1863.

What was only a distant prospect of Union was suddenly brought nearer by the outbreak of the American Civil War. One

[1] See Appendix III. Lord Sydenham, the Governor, who united the two Canadas, came of a banking family; his sister married William Baring, M.P.

group among the northern republicans had conceived the idea of uniting the American nation by provoking an external war against their old enemy, the British. The tariff struggle with Canada grew more bitter and much talk was heard of 'manifest destiny'. In 1861 relations worsened between Palmerston's administration in London and Lincoln's at Washington, until the year ended in provocation to Britain by the seizure of the British ship *Trent*. When war seemed imminent and the naval forces at Halifax and Esquimault were strengthened, it was humiliating to discover that troops sent in December to defend the Canadian frontier could reach it only by sledge over the snowy trails from Halifax. This was the best argument in favour of extending the inter-colonial railway.

In 1862 and 1863, when Lincoln's armies were making but poor progress, the Canadian frontier was at last safely guarded by 10,000 British soldiers and the Canadian militia. During these years a vigorous campaign for confederation was carried out in Upper Canada, the orator and pamphleteer of the party being D'arcy McGee (1825–68), once an Irish rebel but now a liberal imperialist in North America. In Nova Scotia, too, both Joseph Howe and Charles Tupper, the party leaders, were cautiously moving towards the same goal. In the summer of 1864, when Grant had assumed command of the armies of the Northern States and their eventual victory was assured, the demand for a closer union of some kind emerged as a political issue both in Canada and in the Maritime Provinces.

The weary exchanges of party faction in Canada had reached a total deadlock. All efforts to carry out efficient government by the moderate British and French leaders, Sir John A. Macdonald and Sir George Cartier (1814–73), had been nullified by the radical British-Canadian group, curiously nicknamed the 'Clear Grits', who were striving to establish a British ascendancy since the British now constituted a numerical majority. The deadlock was broken by George Brown (1818–80), the leader of the 'Clear Grits', who suddenly declared, in June 1864, his willingness to combine with Macdonald if an immediate move were made for confederation. The coalition of these lifelong adversaries was shortlived but it enabled Macdonald to open the negotiations.

Simultaneously the determination to confederate had been taken by the administrations of the three Maritime Provinces. A conference at Charlottetown, New Brunswick, in September 1864 resulted in a swift decision. Deputations were exchanged between the colonies and a general conference was summoned, in a mood of jubilation, to meet in the historic citadel of Quebec. On 10 October 1864 representatives of all the North American colonies, even Newfoundland, assembled, with the hearty approval of the Colonial Office, to draft a federal constitution. While Sherman was marching through Georgia, closing the net round the armies of the Southern States, the Quebec Assembly was at work. Their deliberations were secret, so that little is known of the obstacles encountered or the play of personalities, but the series of seventy-two resolutions which they adopted were substantially a draft of the constitution of 1867.

Serious difficulties first arose when the delegates returned to face their constituents. The year 1865 was marked by many set-backs. In each of the Maritime Provinces, general elections returned assemblies which repudiated the Quebec resolutions. The veteran Colonial Reformer, Joseph Howe, almost defeated the project by opposing it in Nova Scotia. He had favoured a confederation of the Maritimes but not their subordination to the distant economy of the Canadas. The proposed constitution did not sufficiently guarantee state rights. Meanwhile Macdonald and Cartier had their majority for confederation in Canada and were urging the Colonial Office to bring pressure on the Maritimes. This proved unnecessary since the pressure was applied by American bungling. In January 1865 the government at Washington gave notice that the Reciprocity Treaty would be denounced. Hoping by fiscal pressure to intimidate the British colonies they produced the contrary effect of closing their ranks against American threats. In April Lincoln was murdered, a few days after Lee's surrender, leaving the guidance of the republic in the hands of reckless and rapacious politicians with a large army at their disposal.

The pace was forced by that extraordinary gang of cruel idealists who called themselves the Fenian Brotherhood. More anxious to hurt England than to help Ireland, they planned outrages against English interests in every part of the world, delivering their boldest stroke on the Canadian frontier. In the winter of 1865-6 bands of demobilised Irish-American soldiers assembled at various points on the frontier, with some collusion from the local authorities, and without interference from Washington. There

was frontier fighting at Niagara from March to May 1866, and
a raid into Canada in which several men were killed. It was repulsed with ignominy by the Canadian militia, the fourth time
in a hundred years that the Canadians had defended themselves
from American aggression. The Fenian Raid tipped the scale in
favour of confederation. Though the Fenians of Maine were
properly restrained by the American authorities their presence on
the frontiers of New Brunswick taught the electors of that province the disadvantage of their isolation.

In the summer of 1866 delegates from New Brunswick headed
by Mr (later Sir) Leonard Tilley (1818–96) and from Nova Scotia
headed by Mr (later Sir) Charles Tupper (1821–1915) went to
London, having persuaded the reluctant Assemblies in their respective colonies to accept confederation. Later they were joined
by a strong delegation from Canada including Sir John A. Macdonald, Sir A. T. Galt, D'arcy McGee and Sir George Cartier the
French-Canadian leader. British legal and financial experts
attended the conference at the Westminster Palace Hotel in Victoria Street, where Lord Carnarvon, Colonial Secretary in Derby's
administration, took the chair. Differences of opinion between
the delegates and the Colonial Office turned on one small point
only, the limit of the Governor's power of pardon, a reminiscence
of Durham's misuse of the prerogative thirty years previously.
Among the delegates there was some dispute over the assumption
of the provincial debts by the federal government and the proportionate allotment of revenue to the provinces. An inducement that lightened the labours of the delegates was a loan of
£3,000,000, guaranteed by the British government and negotiated
by Baring Brothers, for the completion of the inter-colonial railway.

When agreement had been reached, on 24 December 1866, the
Parliamentary draftsmen were set to work. The British North
America Act (30 & 31 Vict. cap. III) was introduced in the House
of Lords by Carnarvon who had just become Colonial Secretary,
and in the Commons by the Under-Secretary, C. B. Adderley, who had been responsible for its drafting. It was opposed in
both Houses by speakers, on a brief supplied by Joseph Howe, but
carried without difficulty. In the Commons John Bright was put
up to explain that the interests of Nova Scotia could not be properly preserved in a protectionist dominion. He spoilt his brief
by an unworthy sneer at Canadian loyalty and a gratuitous hope

that Nova Scotia would secede to the United States, for which he was properly rebuked by a Conservative Privy Councillor. Robert Lowe, who had once been a democrat at Sydney, opposed the guaranteed loan. However the Bill was passed, with the languid indifference displayed to most colonial measures, and became law on 29 March 1867. The Dominion was proclaimed on 1 July, of which the anniversary is celebrated in Canada as Dominion Day.

Among the delegates the leading part had been taken by Sir John A. Macdonald, an adroit political manager. The reconciliation of so many diverse interests was his achievement, the form of the constitution was, in most respects, as he had designed. But whereas the term 'confederation' has been used in the previous pages, he would have preferred a legislative union, and by his efforts the federal constitution of Canada has many features which resemble the unitary constitution of Great Britain rather than the federal republic of the United States. It was Macdonald's wish to proclaim Canada a kingdom but this was vetoed by the Colonial Office lest it should give offence to the Americans. The selection of the title 'Dominion', in imitation of the seventeenth-century Dominions of Virginia and New England, is usually ascribed to Tilley of New Brunswick who, according to a reputable tradition, sought relief in Westminster Abbey from the wrangling of the delegates. The choir were singing the seventy-second Psalm:[1]

'Give the King thy judgments, O God: and thy righteousness unto the King's son.

Then shall he judge thy people according unto right: and defend the poor.

The mountains also shall bring peace: and the little hills righteousness unto the people.

He shall keep the simple folk by their right: defend the children of the poor, and punish the wrong-doer.

They shall fear thee, as long as the sun and moon endureth: from one generation to another.

His DOMINION shall be also from the one sea to the other: and from the flood unto the world's end.'

[1] Another version of the story gives the similar and even more apposite text from Zechariah ix. 10: 'his dominion shall be from sea even to sea, and from the river even to the ends of the earth.'

Unity rather than a federation of sovereign states is given as
the intention of the British North America Act in the preamble:
'Whereas the provinces of Canada, Nova Scotia, and New Brunswick have clearly expressed their desire to be federally united into
one Dominion under the Crown...with a constitution similar in
principle to that of the United Kingdom...and whereas it is
expedient that provision be made for the eventual admission into
the Union of other parts of British North America, Be it therefore
enacted...that it shall be lawful for the Queen to declare by proclamation that the three provinces shall form and be one Dominion
under the name of Canada.' A later clause declared that the
Dominion should be divided into four provinces named Nova
Scotia, New Brunswick, Ontario and Quebec, thus restoring the
autonomy of the old French colony.

The executive government of Canada, 'vested in the Queen',
was to be exercised by a governor-general with his capital city
at Ottawa,[1] but the military command of the troops was reserved
to a commander-in-chief who was directly responsible to the
Queen and remained so until 1904. Authority was given for the
creation of a Supreme Court of Appeal. Though it was instituted by a Liberal Government, in 1875, with the intention of
limiting the imperial power, appeals to the Privy Council were
still permitted even, by special leave, against decisions of the
Supreme Court itself. The tendency of Privy Council judgments
has been to strengthen state-rights against the federal authority
and they have been used by the provincial governments for that
purpose.

The Parliament of Canada, which was to be summoned within
six months[2] of the Proclamation of the Dominion, was to consist
of a nominated Senate and a House of Commons directly elected
by the constituencies. The Senators were to be appointed for life
by the Governor-General, in due proportion from the provinces
and in stated numbers. They were required to be over thirty

---

[1] The seat of government of the province of Canada had several times been
removed. The village formerly known as Bytown, headquarters of the construction works on the Rideau Canal, had been selected as the capital by Governor
Head in 1858, and renamed Ottawa. It differs from Washington and Canberra
in not being isolated in a Federal District; it is a municipality of the province of
Ontario.

[2] It first met on 7 November 1867 and ungraciously began its deliberations by
reducing the Governor-General's salary.

years old and to be in possession of a modest property qualification. The number of members to be elected to the House of Commons from each province was, in the first instance, prescribed in the Act. Out of a total of 181 members, Ontario had eighty-two, Quebec sixty-five, Nova Scotia nineteen and New Brunswick fifteen. General elections were to be held at intervals of no more than five years (the period in England being, at that time, seven years), and a redistribution of seats was to be made at every census.[1]

The provincial executives were subordinated to the executive of the Dominion by giving to the Governor-General the power to appoint and to dismiss Lieutenant-Governors of provinces. He also appointed the judges of the superior courts. Similarly the provincial legislatures were subordinated by enumerating the subjects on which alone they were authorised to legislate, the most important being municipalities, provincial taxation and public works. Education was more specifically allotted to the provincial administrations in a separate clause protecting the rights of the British minority in Quebec and the French minority in the other provinces. Provision was made for assimilating the laws of the English-speaking provinces, but the old French code was preserved in Quebec.

The Act declares that 'either the English or the French language may be used by any person in the debates of the Houses of Parliament of Canada, and of the Houses of the Legislature of Quebec', or by any person 'pleading in any court of Canada'. Acts of Parliament were to be printed and published in both languages.

The liability for the greater part of the provincial debts was assumed by the Dominion and a grant-in-aid proportionate to their populations was to be made annually by the Dominion to each province.[2] There was to be free trade between provinces.

[1] At the first census, in 1871, the population was returned as:

| Ontario | 1,626,851 | Nova Scotia | 387,800 |
| Quebec | 1,191,516 | New Brunswick | 285,594 |

The other provinces, not original members of the Dominion, were returned as follows:

| Prince Edward Island | 94,021 | North West Territories | 4,800 |
| Manitoba | 25,228 | British Columbia | 36,247 |

giving a grand total of 3,689,257, of whom 1,082,940 were French-Canadians.

[2] This was the clause to which Joseph Howe took exception in Nova Scotia. His friends at Westminster raised the matter in Parliament again in 1868. A compromise was arranged between him and Macdonald in 1869; but the grievance rankled until the schedules were revised by an imperial Act of Parliament in 1907.

The Act also declared 'the duty of the Government and Parliament of Canada to provide for the commencement, within six months after the Union, of a railway connecting the River St Lawrence with the City of Halifax'.

An omission from the Act catches the attention of the reader: no method was provided for altering the constitution. The Dominion remained (and remains) subordinate to the Parliament of Great Britain which alone can amend the British North America Act, notwithstanding the provisions of the Statute of Westminster. Though eighty years have passed since it was drafted, it has been but slightly amended. None of its fundamental principles has been changed in this long period which has seen repeated changes in the parent constitution of Great Britain. The British North America Act stands as one of the most efficient instruments ever devised by man. It was enacted at a moment in history when the federal principle was everywhere discredited, when the United States was emerging from bloody civil war into a decade of corruption and misgovernment, when the German Confederation had just been disembowelled by Bismarck, when even tranquil Switzerland was torn by religious dissension.

Canada has not escaped the endemic disease of all federal constitutions, the feverish struggle for state rights, but how mildly did the patient take it! In three generations which have seen the dissolution of so many empires, the fragmentation of so many composite kingdoms, the petty schisms of so many linguistic minorities, the two nations of Canada have dwelt together in unity at least, if not always in amity, a good and joyful thing to behold. They have had their tiffs, their agreements to differ, their jealous outbursts, but no more.

The leaders of the French minority (still hoping that their high birth-rate will some day make them a majority) have astutely seen in the British North America Act the safeguard of their autonomy, perhaps even of their survival as *la nation canadienne*. Their influence has tended to maintain rather than to disrupt the Dominion, though the balance of forces has often appeared unstable.

4. EASTERN AND WESTERN CANADA,
1867–86

Two island colonies in the east, Newfoundland and Prince Edward Island, stood aloof from the Dominion; two great regions in the west, British Columbia and the Hudson's Bay Territories, could not be effectively federated until better communications were provided with Canada. The Newfoundlanders emphatically preferred autonomy. Though most political theorists in Ottawa and in London long assumed that they would be obliged to join the federation, they did not, nor, until the present generation, did they show much inclination to look westwards. The people of Prince Edward Island were in a different position. Neither numerous nor rich, they feared that their local interests would suffer when absorbed into so great and diverse a nation. These local interests were bound up with the struggle against the land-monopoly. When the Dominion government undertook to buy out and extinguish the titles of these landlords, they quickly changed their tune, and in 1873 joined the Dominion upon their own petition. The Governor-General, Lord Dufferin, visited the island and found the people 'in a high state of jubilation, quite under the impression that it is the Dominion that has been annexed to Prince Edward Island'.

Preparations had long been made for extinguishing the Hudson's Bay monopoly. The old H.B.C. directors of Simpson's day had stood for fur-trading alone, and had resisted immigration. In 1863 a financial group, pledged to support federation and to construct a transcontinental railway, had acquired a controlling interest in the Company and had sent its agents into the west surveying and prospecting. The *métis* of Red River took alarm but their interests were not consulted. In the first session of the Canadian Parliament a petition was lodged, according to the provision of the British North America Act, for transferring the north-western territories from the Hudson's Bay Company to the Dominion. Lord Granville tactfully conducted the negotiations in London for the surrender of the Company's sovereign rights, in return for a cash payment of £300,000 and freehold property in some large blocks of western land (1869).

An age of empire-building ended with the loss of sovereignty by the East India Company in 1858 and the Hudson's Bay Company in 1869. These were the last survivors of the chartered companies which had played so great a part in the early history of British 'trade and plantations'. But, unlike the defunct East India Company, the Hudson's Bay Company survived (and flourishes) as a commercial body still active in the development of the northwest.

Bishop Taché, who passed through Ottawa in 1869, on his way from Red River to the Vatican Conference, warned the new government that the *métis* would resist annexation. Theirs was the reaction of the wild west against the approach of industrial civilisation. No steps were taken by the easterners to assure these proud ignorant buffalo-hunters that they would not suffer by the change. They feared the loss of their squatters' rights over the land and, in their fastness at Fort Garry, believed that they could defy the onset of Anglo-Saxon progress.

When an official from Ottawa arrived in the west he was refused admission to Red River territory. In December 1869 a young French-Canadian, Louis Riel (1844–85), called a 'national convention' of the *métis* at Fort Garry and was chosen president. A dangerous stirring of the racial feud was felt throughout Canada, all the more when Riel, a flighty, unstable demagogue, killed Thomas Scott, a British-Canadian who tried to make head against him. The 'Orange' party in Ontario demanded vengeance. Civil war was averted by the efforts of Donald Smith, afterwards Lord Strathcona (1820–1914), a Hudson's Bay official sent by the Canadian government as their commissioner to negotiate with Riel. He persuaded the *métis* to commit no more acts of bloodshed; reconciled the Hudson's Bay factors to the new dispensation; and simultaneously urged the government to send troops to Fort Garry.

An expedition composed of British regulars and Canadian militiamen was conducted to Red River in 1870 under Colonel Garnet Wolseley, who then made his name as a military administrator. Fort Garry was restored to the Dominion without fighting, and Riel fled over the frontier into the United States. The triumph belonged to Donald Smith who remained as Acting-Governor of the north-west. When Red River Territory became the province of Manitoba (1870), Smith was elected M.P. for Winnipeg, its new capital city near Fort Garry. French-Canadian opinion was pacified by Bishop Taché who returned from Rome in time to negotiate rights for his fellow-Churchmen in the west, like those they enjoyed in Quebec.

Riel was regarded as a patriot and hero by some sections of the French-Canadians. Though unbalanced he had heroic qualities. It is to his credit that he resisted attempts by Fenians and American filibusters to turn the Red River Rebellion to their advantage. In his years of exile he was repeatedly elected by French-Canadian constituencies to the Dominion Parliament but was not allowed to take his seat. The unfortunate *métis*, like the South African farmers, in a not dissimilar plight, trekked with their wagons and horses farther west to the Saskatchewan. Fifteen years later, in 1885, civilisation caught up with them again. The railway now spanned the prairie; the buffalo was almost extinct. In despair the *métis* persuaded Riel (still only in his early forties) to return as their leader. His rashness in attacking a police post provoked a bloodier outbreak which the British-Canadians were not again willing to condone.

Canadian troops, without British help, were concentrated from three directions by means of the new railways. The *méti* rising was crushed and Riel was hanged for his killing of Thomas Scott so many years before. In French-Canadian legend it is Riel that died a martyr. The worst danger of the rebellion of 1885 was its repercussion upon the prairie Indians. They too felt the constriction of the railways which limited their rovings. For the last time in Canadian history, many of them in that year were on the war-path against isolated settlers.

British Columbia, which had not previously enjoyed respon-sible government, joined the Dominion upon the petition of Governor Antony Musgrave and his Council in 1871, after they had been given a promise (which was not fulfilled) that a trans-continental railway would be constructed within ten years. As a preliminary measure Vancouver Island and the mainland had been united into a single colony in 1866. The islanders had no contacts and little sympathy with Canada; they doubted the necessity of building the railway, as well as the probability that it would be built, and were more concerned with their own plans for a colliery railway from Nanaimo to Esquimault. The mainland province had languished since the Cariboo gold-field was worked out. Federation brought no advantage so that the British Columbians received the Governor-General, Dufferin, with brusque demands for fulfilment of the railway promise, or separation. They were partly mollified by a further promise that the railway would come through, at least by 1890. The first estimate had been too rash; the second proved too cautious.

Canadian politics, in the later nineteenth century, like contemporary American politics, were largely concerned with railway finance, which meant too close a connexion between political parties and financial groups. Sir John A. Macdonald (1815–91), the maker of confederation and of the Canadian Pacific Railway, the dominant figure in Canadian life for thirty years, prided himself on being a hard-headed man of affairs. He was incorruptible but his friends and associates were not. The manner by which he combined and held together the moderate voters of British Ontario and French Quebec, his control of constituencies and elections, his agreements with opponents for particular ends were masterstrokes of political management. Though an indefatigable patriot he was not equipped with an acute sense of honour. 'Send me better men', he said, 'and I will be a better man myself.' His first attempt to let contracts for a transcontinental railway ended in a financial scandal which brought down his administration in 1873. The contractor had been a large contributor to Macdonald's party funds. The succeeding Prime Minister, Alexander Mackenzie, favoured a policy of railway construction by the state but, in his five years of office, made little progress in the west.[1] In 1878 Macdonald was returned to power with a large majority, on the popular platform of Protection and national development, which enabled him to renew his railway policy. He headed a mission to England in 1880 to raise capital for the Canadian Pacific Railway.

In 1881, the year by which the British Columbians had first been promised completion, the scheme was laid before the Canadian Parliament where it met severe criticism. In return for undertaking the building of the railway within ten years, the Company was to be given £25,000,000 and 25,000,000 acres of land on either side of the line. Though the investors were mostly British the controlling interest was held by Canadians, George Stephen (later Lord Mount Stephen); Sir George Rose, formerly Canadian Minister of Finance; J. J. Hill, a great railway-builder in the United States; and Donald Smith. Macdonald and Smith, who

---

[1] The inter-colonial railway to Halifax was opened in 1876.

had parted at the time of the scandals of 1873, were now reconciled. William Van Horne, an American, was the chief engineer.

Construction began in earnest in 1881, urged on by the driving force of Donald Smith. The central section across the prairie from Winnipeg to the Rocky Mountains was soon completed, in time for the passage of troops in the Saskatchewan Rebellion. The lake-strewn rocky wilderness north-west of Lake Superior, and the passage of the Kicking Horse Pass with its spiral tunnel proved far more expensive than the estimate. Twice, in 1883 and 1885, the Company had to appeal to Ottawa for further loans, of $22,000,000 and $5,000,000, which were willingly raised since Macdonald had obtained a large majority at the election of 1882 in support of his railway policy. With this aid the railway was completed more than five years sooner than the expected date. In November 1885 the 'last spike' was driven by Donald Smith at Craigellachie in British Columbia. The city of Vancouver, western terminus of the railway, was founded in 1886 and, with the coming of the railway, lumbering, farming and fishing brought new prosperity to the mainland of British Columbia.

The old north-west had been explored, pacified and exploited by the Hudson's Bay Company; the new west was made by the Canadian Pacific Railway. In these two groups of initials, H.B.C. and C.P.R., half the story of Canada is epitomised. The link between the two was Donald Smith, Lord Strathcona. Born in Scotland in 1820, he went as a boy to Canada to earn his living as a Hudson's Bay factor. He saw Lord Durham ride through the streets of Montreal in 1838—and was reproved for not raising his hat. For nearly thirty years he traded furs at Hudson's Bay posts in the wilds of Labrador, rising at last to be Resident Governor for the Company at Montreal. As an easterner he was sent to Red River to reconcile the men of the west with the policy of the Dominion. Later in life as M.P. for Manitoba, he spoke for the west in Ottawa. At sixty years old he solved the practical problems of the transcontinental railway, and lived another thirty years as the honoured elder statesman of Canada. He was raised to the peerage at the Diamond Jubilee of 1897. In the Boer War he raised a regiment of Canadian volunteers, Strathcona's Horse, which cost him a million dollars.

In 1880 a British Order in Council settled a question that had been left uncertain in the Act of 1867 by placing all territories on the mainland of British North America under the jurisdiction of the Dominion. Two new provinces, Alberta and Saskatchewan, were carved out of them in 1905. The remainder is administered as a dependent territory from Ottawa.

Western Canada differs profoundly from the western states of the American Union in one respect; it has never known an age of anarchy. The tradition of friendship and fair dealing with the Indians is derived equally from the old French regime and from the Hudson's Bay Company. 'The wild west' as it was in California and Texas never existed in Canada, except at Red River in the days of Lord Selkirk and the Nor'westers. There is no lynch-law north of the forty-ninth parallel. The two risings of the *métis*, in 1870 and 1885, were short-lived and not disorderly. The peaceful development of the Prairie Provinces and the North West Territories is due to that unrivalled corps, the Royal North-west Mounted Police. The 'Mounties', the admiration of all right-minded boys throughout the world—and of men who retain the generous instincts of boyhood—were established to relieve the garrison of British troops left by Wolseley in Manitoba: 300 men under Major McLeod rode westward in 1873 to posts on the plains, in scarlet tunics chosen because, an old Indian said, 'we know that the soldiers of our Great Mother wear red coats and are our friends'. In the Saskatchewan rebellion, at the Klondyke gold-rush, in locating the Indians on reservations, in checking the lawlessness which prevailed along the border, in enforcing the law at the loneliest posts beyond the Arctic Circle and in the high mountains, in suppressing the liquor trade to the Indians, hunting horse-thieves, fighting prairie fires, the Mounties have done their duty and retained the affection of the Canadian people. They now operate throughout Canada as a federal police force.

5. THE DOMINION OF CANADA, 1867–1917

THE domestic history of the Canadian people after they had achieved national unity falls outside the scope of this book. Certain threads in the pattern must yet be followed through if the whole story of British expansion overseas is to be recapitulated. These lines of argument are: (1) the growth of friendlier relations between the Dominion and its great southern neighbour after a century of invasions, raids and reproaches; (2) the development of a national economic policy based upon Canada's intermediate position as a buyer in the United States and a seller in the United Kingdom; (3) the great emigration in the early years of this century which, when applied to the natural resources of Canada, made the Dominion a world-power, perhaps now ranking sixth or seventh among the nations in wealth and influence; (4) the prudent statesmanship of the Canadian leaders who have so scrupulously respected the rights of the French minority while assuming Canada's true role as a nation of the New World and partner in the British Commonwealth.

Canada and the United States were never worse neighbours than at the conclusion of the American Civil War, in spite of the fact that many thousands of Canadians had fought as volunteers in the Northern Armies. Seward's hostility to the British, and Gladstone's sympathy with the Confederate cause, tended to increase as the long war grew fiercer. Blockade-runners used the port of Halifax for shelter and Confederate leaders after their defeat, even Jefferson Davis himself, took refuge in Canada. The Fenian Raids of 1866 and 1871 embittered relations already strained by the denunciation of the Reciprocity Treaty. In 1871 Canadian cruisers were engaged in seizing American ships which poached on the inshore fisheries while, at Washington, American Senators demanded the cession of Canada as compensation for damage done by the commerce-raider *Alabama* which had been equipped at Liverpool. The Canadians were somewhat gratified when Sir John Macdonald was invited to join the British delegation for negotiations at Washington. The discussions covered a variety of topics, the frontiers of British Columbia, fishery-rights off Canada and Newfoundland, and various claims arising out of the Civil War. To the British public, to Gladstone and to the historians, the *Alabama* dispute far outweighed all other considerations. Even those who admit that the American claims for compensation were exorbitant take the view that the British admission of error and acceptance of arbitration was an act of magnanimity that was worth the expense. To the Canadians, however, the Treaty of Washington (1871) was little more than a betrayal. Their claim against the Americans for damage by repeated raids across the frontier was tacitly dropped by the British. The Canadians did not regain the treaty for reciprocity in trade.

They objected to the admission of American ships to their inshore fisheries even though the concession was sweetened by an American payment of $4,500,000. (For the attitude of the Newfoundlanders see below, page 581.) Macdonald returned to Canada with little to show for his efforts and had to plead with his Parliament at Ottawa that they should accept the treaty for the sake of imperial unity.

Thirty years later the negotiations over the boundary of Alaska were equally unsatisfactory. Traffic to the Klondyke through Skagway had raised questions as to the status of the islands and channels off the Alaska Panhandle. Theodore Roosevelt truculently resisted arbitration. At last the issue was referred to a Commission consisting of three Americans, two Canadians and one Englishman who further incensed Canada by taking the American view, with the result that the decision (1903) went against Canada. In 1909 the Dominion set up its own department of External Affairs and in the same year an International Joint Commission, a standing committee for settling disputes with the United States, was appointed through the efforts of James Bryce, the British Ambassador, and Elihu Root, the American Secretary of State. Its work has been an outstanding success, very many minor difficulties having been settled by mutual agreement. In 1910 the vexed question of the fisheries was put to arbitration before the Hague Tribunal, at the instance of Newfoundland. The award gave general satisfaction. The strategic agreements which have drawn Canada and the United States so much closer together (1940–4) will be mentioned later.

The dream of renewing the Reciprocity Treaty haunted Canadian politics for half a century. It was the life-long hope of Sir Wilfrid Laurier who became leader of the Liberal Party in 1888. But Macdonald, who had been out of office since the financial exposures of 1873, had come back in 1878 pledged to a 'National Policy' of building up Canadian industries behind high protective tariffs, a great advance on Galt's Revenue Tariff which caused such alarm in 1859. Though he never quite forgot the possibility of reciprocity with the United States, Macdonald first desired imperial unity. This political imperialism was combined with economic nationalism for Canada. Formerly he had desired to erect Canada into a kingdom, a personal union with Great Britain under Queen Victoria's crown, and this rather than any scheme of federation remained his conception of Canada's future place within the Empire. Gladstone had withdrawn the last British regiments from Canada in 1871. Fiscal independence was reached in 1877 when Canada was excluded from the operation of British commercial treaties except in cases where she expressed a desire to be covered by them. In 1880 Macdonald demonstrated his theory of Canadian nationality by sending to London a High Commissioner through whom he communicated with the British government.

The immediate effect of Macdonald's protective tariff of 35 % is hard to estimate in a country developing as fast as was Canada in the 'eighties. Imports and exports, to and from the United Kingdom and the United States, continued to grow in various commodities and for various reasons. Local manufactures also sprang up, largely in textiles and in farm machinery; the latter became a staple industry both for local consumption and for export. As the prairie farms spread wider, new and larger devices were demanded and supplied, culminating in the combine harvester (1922). The celebrated firm of Massey-Harris was founded in Ontario in 1852, and by 1885 advertised its large and growing business with continental Europe. Between 1880 and 1890 the capital invested in Canadian manufacturing industries was doubled, while the number of manufactories, the number of employees, and the value of the gross output increased by about 50 %. Meanwhile, in a single year (1882), 60,000 settlers took up 3,000,000 acres of land in Manitoba. Three years later the Canadian Pacific Railway was completed. In 1882 the first steel ingots were produced in Nova Scotia; in 1883 the great beds of copper-nickel ore were found at Sudbury, Ontario. But the 1880's began and ended in commercial depression. After the long world-wide slump of the early 'nineties Laurier and the Liberals came into power, in 1896, on the crest of a wave of world-wide prosperity.

The gold-finds in the Rand and Western Australia were followed by the Klondyke rush (1897–8). About the same time lead and copper were first smelted at Kootenay in British Columbia, and the mineral wealth of Ontario was revealed. When the Northern Ontario Railway reached Cobalt in 1903 rich silver mines were at once developed. New wealth required new sources of power which was soon found in Canada's torrential rivers. The first hydro-electric station was built at Niagara in 1895 and the whole water-power of Ontario reorganised by (Sir) Adam Beck (1857–1925), a fighting financier and politician who grew rich, and made his country rich, by advocating and providing cheap hydro-electric power under municipal control. His Ontario Power Commission was formed in 1910.

Gold and silver, railways, industry in the east, cheap land in the west, new sources of power, boom conditions, at last produced in Canada the social background that the United States had known for fifty years. At the Chicago World's Fair of 1893 the Canadian West was given loud publicity. Canada was precipitated into prosperity, needing only population. The director of all this expansion was Sir Wilfrid Laurier (1842–1919), the French Canadian Liberal who was Premier from 1896 to 1911. A man of dapper figure and courtly manner, born of a family settled for 200 years in Quebec, fully bilingual, with a deep appreciation of English literature and a generous sensibility towards Old France, he was certainly as good a Canadian as John A. Macdonald. In external affairs, like Macdonald, he spoke for Canadian nationalism within the Empire. He too had been a convert to Protectionism but within moderate limits. To the Canadian dilemma between the rival economies of England and America he gave a different emphasis. He desired better relations with the United States, yet did not lose sight of imperial unity. It was Laurier the *canadien*, not Macdonald the imperialist, who first conceded a preferential tariff to British goods (1897). But Canada and Canadian interests always took first place. 'The nineteenth century', he said, 'has been the century of the United States; the twentieth century will be the century of Canada.'

Opposition among the farmers to Macdonald's high tariff brought Laurier into power. He commanded also the solid French-Canadian vote, the centre party that has balanced federal politics now for fifty years. Opposition came from two sides, from the loyalist commercial British-Canadians of the industrial east and from the isolationists, the *sinn fein*, of French-speaking Quebec. Between these two he steered a skilful course (as his successor, Mr Mackenzie King, has done after him), holding the nation together in spite of denunciations from one side that he was too French and from the other that he was too British.

The normal method of land development in Canada has been by the grant of Crown lands to railway companies who invited selected emigrants to take up sections of surveyed land *gratis*, hoping to reimburse themselves by the resulting traffic in farm produce. The wheat belt of Manitoba was opened up by the lines that began to radiate from Winnipeg, the geographical centre of Canada. Winnipeg is the boom-city *par excellence* of the British Empire. In 1874, when incorporated as a municipality, its population was 1800—buffalo-hunters and crofters sprung from Selkirk's Red River colony. In 1941 the city population was 222,000, the metropolis of a province with a population of 730,000, containing 5000 miles of railways and 7,000,000 acres of cultivated land. In 1875 an experimental load of 875 bushels of prairie wheat was sent east from Winnipeg; in 1942 the output of the Canadian prairie was 550,000,000 bushels of wheat, 650,000,000 of barley and 260,000,000 of oats.

The peopling of the prairie was organised by Sir Clifford Sifton of Manitoba (1861–1929), Laurier's Minister of the Interior, who also administered the Klondyke after the gold-rush. He advertised for immigrants to take up free homesteads of 160 acres each along the new railway lines. Between 1897 and 1914 about 3,000,000 immigrants came to Canada. A million of them crossed the border from the United States; another million came from the British Isles (see chapter IX, 5, page 507), the last wave of the great British migration that had peopled so many lands. Migration within the Empire from Britain to British Dominions at last exceeded the emigration to the alien United States. In 1911–13 the net gain to Canada in selected British immigrants was 150,000 a year. The third group of immigrants, also numbering about a million, came from the Baltic and from Eastern Europe. Several group settlements of persecuted minorities were transported to Canada by philanthropic action, but most came by spontaneous family migration in search of land and wealth. Some small groups, like the Doukhobors, have proved unassimilable but, as in the United States, the great majority of Scandinavians, Germans and Slavs have been completely assimilated. It should be noticed that they are absorbed into the English- not the French-Canadian element. Between 1901 and 1916, 73,000,000 acres of land in the west were taken up. The north-western prairies were constituted, in 1905, into the two new provinces of Alberta and Saskatchewan, with the reservation that the Dominion retained control of Crown lands and water-power until 1930.

Western Canada could not become the granary of the Empire until transport and storage were provided, and until a suitably hardy strain of wheat was evolved. As long ago as 1842 an Ontario settler named David Fyfe sent home to Scotland for samples of seed-corn. Among them one strain, of which he did not trouble to record the origin, established itself in Canada where it was known as 'Red Fyfe', a tough quick-ripening plant suited to the short northern summer. As cultivation spread north and west into lands where autumn frosts fell earlier, a strain of wheat that would ripen in a still shorter season was required. A scientific investigation was undertaken by Sir Charles Saunders, the Dominion Cerealist, who tried hundreds of strains between 1903 and 1909, hitting at last upon the strain called 'Marquis', a variant of 'Red Fyfe' that could be grown as far north as Peace River. From the foot of the Rockies to Winnipeg, and on to the shore of Lake Superior where the grain was shipped in steel freighters, the farms were strung out along the railway lines, and the grain stored in the tower-like 'elevators' that punctuate the Canadian landscape. The Grain Elevator Service, though commercially owned, provided what might (and eventually did) become a co-operative system. From 1904 it enabled the grading of wheat by quality according to Dominion standards.

The expansion of Canada north-westwards has been so largely a process of railway construction that railway finance has always dominated Canadian politics. Generally speaking the railwaymen were over-optimistic in building three transcontinental lines with numerous branches, a system whose extent was not for a long time justified by the actual or probable volume of traffic. By 1916 there were 40,000 miles of railroad in Canada, of which a quarter was built when Laurier was Premier. Some economy in administration was effected by the consolidation (1917) of lines into two main groups, the privately-owned Canadian Pacific and the state-owned Canadian National Railways, which between them own 90% of Canadian railways. It is typical of the easy relations now kept between the United States and Canada that the state-owned Canadian National Railway operates many miles of track running south through American territory. The complex problems of the waterways eastward from the Great Lakes to the Atlantic, and the control of hydro-electric power in rivers that cross the frontier, have been the subject of frequent negotiations since the original Rush-Bagot Treaty of 1818. Here the facts of geography must lead to co-operation in the future, unless they bring back the friction of the bad old days.

What could not be foreseen in the boom years before the German Wars was the coming of Air Transport which, among other novelties, has given the Canadians control over their new Empire in the Far North, the world's last open frontier, an opportunity for Canada in the New World as for Russia in the Old.

The future of Canada lay in the hands of scientific experts and technologists, a class which has produced Canada's most eminent citizens. To those names that have already been mentioned in earlier chapters there may be added some others. Sir William Dawson (1820–99), a Nova Scotian scientist, was for many years Director of the Canadian Geological Survey. As the author of a standard work on the *Geology of Canada* he was the father of the Canadian mining industry. As principal of McGill University, Montreal, he raised a little provincial college to the front rank among the world's universities. Perhaps its most eminent professor was Sir William Osler (1849–1919), a Canadian by birth and a great teacher of clinical medicine. Among physicians Canada, too, may boast the name of Sir F. Banting of Toronto (1891–1941), the discoverer of insulin. An engineer who took a great part in Canadian public life was Sir Sandford Fleming (1827–1915), who emigrated from Scotland as a boy. For a long period he was engineer-in-chief to the Canadian Pacific Railway but is perhaps better remembered for his persistent efforts on behalf of the Pacific Cable. Fleming originated the system of International Standard Time which was imposed throughout North America in 1883–4 and thence extended round the world. With him may be mentioned Sir W. Mulock (1844–1940) of Toronto, the organiser of imperial penny postage (1899). Alexander Graham Bell (1847–1922) emigrated as a young man from Scotland to Canada where his best work was done, but died an American citizen. His first effective telephone was made in 1876. The first public telephone-exchange was opened at Hamilton, Ontario, in 1878.

The last achievement of Laurier's government was the assumption of responsibility for the Royal Naval bases at Esquimault and Halifax (1910). This implied the foundation of the Canadian Navy which exposed Laurier to attack from both flanks, by the

French nationalists on the ground that he was doing too much for the Empire, by the British loyalists on the ground that he was doing too little. The double opposition brought about Laurier's fall in a renewed struggle over American reciprocity. Having learned that the Republican party favoured a new trading agreement, he despatched a minister to Washington, where a draft treaty of Reciprocity was prepared. He then appealed to the electorate on this issue and was overthrown (1911). It was the defection of the French-Canadian Nationalists, led by Henri Bourassa, that ruined Laurier's cause but the fruits of victory went to Sir Robert Borden and the Conservatives, who were pledged to Empire unity and a high Canadian tariff. No more was heard of reciprocity, though otherwise Borden's administration pursued the same line of action as Laurier's in external affairs. The outbreak of war enabled him to show his mettle.

In spite of the decisions taken at the Conference of 1911, the Dominions were not consulted in the crisis of August 1914. When Parliament met at Ottawa on 18 August, Borden proposed and Laurier supported a motion for associating Canada with the British war effort. Canadian autonomy was preserved in the sense that the Canadian Parliament decided what share, if any, Canada should take in actual hostilities. As the world knows it was a giant's share.

During Asquith's coalition government no steps were taken to consult the Dominions upon war policy. Early in 1916 Borden was demanding, and Asquith resisting the demand, that an imperial conference should be summoned. When it met at last in 1917, after Lloyd George had become Prime Minister, Borden moved the resolution that the Dominions should be recognised 'as autonomous nations of an Imperial Commonwealth', the first formal expression of Dominion Status. He took a large part in constituting the Imperial War Cabinet.

6. NEWFOUNDLAND, 1713–1914

DURING the later part of the nineteenth century Newfoundland took its place with the other self-governing colonies. Its peculiar position may be traced back to the great wars with France. The population of Newfoundland grew rapidly from about 3000 after the Treaty of Utrecht to 13,000 at the census of 1763, and to 20,000 at the end of the century. Among the residents were a large proportion of Southern Irish, the first large contingent of emigrants from Catholic Ireland in any colony. The Fishing Charter (1633) obliged English skippers to train up men to follow the sea by taking a proportion of 'green men' in each crew. They complied with the regulation by leaving port short-handed and making up the muster in Cork, with Irishmen who were allowed to slip ashore in Newfoundland at the end of the season, since there was no room for passengers when the ships were laden for the homeward voyage. The sea-fisheries employed more men, but the shore-fisheries made the better profit. St John's was now a town, the centre of a prosperous trade in boat-building and ship-chandling. In addition to the staple industry, the cod-fishing which lasted from June till October, there was salmon-fishing, whaling and sealing, trapping for furs in winter, and a growing industry in providing bait for the deep-sea cod-fishers who came from all the French and British dominions to the Great Banks.

The little ships of fifty or seventy tons from the west-country fishing-villages gradually gave way to larger ships, averaging 120 tons, from the principal commercial harbours. Dartmouth and Poole, alone of the nine chartered ports, continued to despatch ships throughout the eighteenth century. Jersey men and Guernsey men, first directed to Newfoundland when Ralegh was their governor, appeared as interlopers at an early date; they played a large part in the development of the maritime colonies around the St Lawrence Gulf, aided perhaps by their facility for smuggling French brandy. The old system of the fishing-fleet and the Fishing Admiral slowly decayed during the eighteenth century though it was not legally abolished until 1809, when it had long been a dead-letter. Annual voyages from England to the Newfoundland shore-fishery ended with the Napoleonic wars. The settlers, who owned 1100 boats, caught 348,000 quintals (approximately hundredweight) in 1763; 500,000 quintals in 1796; and averaged 900,000 quintals early in the nineteenth century, selling them at a price which varied from 10s. to 14s. a quintal in time of peace but went much higher in time of war. The fish was carried across the Atlantic in little ships from Jersey and elsewhere, known as 'sack-ships', to the Roman Catholic countries of southern Europe. The return trade was largely in wines which found their way to England by this devious route, or were traded in the West Indies for rum and molasses.

Commerce, naturally enough, led to a demand for regular civil government. In 1723, fifty citizens of St John's led by William Keene drew up a social contract for the management of their affairs. All power was still formally invested in the Convoy Captain whose interest lay in the shipping and the naval dispositions rather than in the administration of the settlements. Some progress was made in 1728 when the commission of the Convoy Captain was enlarged to give him the status of a civil governor. Keene and others were appointed justices of the peace with authority to act when the fleet should leave the station for the winter. Tolerable government in Newfoundland was preserved by the high character of the naval officers on this important station. Such men as Rodney, Graves, Palliser, Byron and Gambier were Convoy Captains in the age of the French Wars. But it is not surprising that settlers in so wild a country under such light control should prove unruly. Their patriarch, William Keene, fell a victim to disorder, in 1754, when he was robbed and murdered by a gang of Irishmen.

A sign of the uncertain status of Newfoundland arose at the time of the Stamp Act of 1765 which was resented there as in the Thirteen Colonies. It was not enforced since the best opinion held that Newfoundland was not a colony, but a 'free fishery'. Whatever sympathy the settlers had with the American rebels was quickly alienated by the action of Congress which laid an embargo on the trade of Newfoundland as on that of all British communities that would not join with them.

The best of the governors was Sir Hugh Palliser (1764–9). So rudimentary was the state of society that there was no legal property in land until, after Palliser's return to England, he obtained an Act of Parliament for converting the customary right to 'fishing-rooms' on the beaches into a lawful tenure. Until then the settlers, though established for 150 years, had been no more than squatters.

More important still was Palliser's decision that his province should not remain unexplored. He persuaded the Admiralty to send him Lieutenant James Cook with a surveying-ship to chart the west coast and the Strait of Belle Isle, thus making it possible at last to define the boundaries of the French 'Treaty Shore'. He also made a determined attempt to come to friendly terms with the Indians, a strange story that deserves a short digression.

When Sebastian Cabot returned from Newfoundland, he brought back to the Court of Henry VII three natives of the island as curiosities. The other early navigators made a habit of collecting such living specimens often by a simple process of kidnapping. These primitive Newfoundlanders were the original 'Red Indians' so called, not for their copper-coloured skins— they seem to have been fairer-skinned than the continental 'Indians'—but because they dyed their bodies with scarlet vegetable juices, as our own ancestors once did with woad. The Red Indians, who called themselves Beothucks, were few, shy and remote, skilful with the bow-and-arrow, and on occasion they were head-hunters. They were at constant feud with the Canadian Indians (Montagnais) who haunted the Strait of Belle Isle, and with the Eskimos who came from Labrador. Their suspicion of all outsiders grew, with ample provocation from the English fishermen and fur-traders, the roughest and boldest of mankind. Frobisher lost some men by a treacherous attack as early as 1576, but John Guy in 1610 at first found the Indians friendly. Before civil government began in Newfoundland perpetual merciless war had broken out between the Beothucks and the settlers.

Throughout the eighteenth century the isolated settlements were pestered by Indians who prowled by night to steal the invaluable tools and weapons of the white man and, on the other hand, any Beothuck man, woman or child encountered by the furriers in the woods was instantly killed like vermin. The opening-up of the northern bays at last compelled the authorities to take notice of this state of war. Sir Hugh Palliser, in 1768, was the first Governor to attempt a remedy. He and each of his successors for sixty years issued proclamations denouncing the murder of

Indians, but without effect in the remote bays where each settler had to fight for his own head. Further he sent out the first of a series of expeditions to explore the Indian country and by some humane means to make contact with the surviving Indians. There were thought to be no more than a few hundred of them, with their principal encampments on the Exploits River, near Grand Falls, where are now the Anglo-Newfoundland Paper Mills. Captain George Cartwright first explored this region (1768–9) without being able to make contact with the elusive Indians. Captain D. Buchan, R.N., actually met and attempted to exchange hostages with a party of Indians here in 1811, with unfortunate results. Owing to a misunderstanding the Indians took fright and killed two marines whom he had left in their hands. Later Governors hit upon the plan of offering rewards for bringing in alive an Indian who could be used as an intermediary with the tribe. In the course of many years, so shy were the survivors, only two captures were effected and neither without bloodshed. The attempt to make peace with the Indians was long prosecuted by Mr John Peyton who at last got possession of an Indian woman in 1819 but, since she unfortunately died before she could be trained as an interpreter, the effect upon the tribe was hardly favourable.

Meanwhile, the war of extirpation went on. In 1823 three Beothuck women surrendered in a state of starvation. Two died, but the third, an intelligent young woman called Shanawdithit, was brought to Peyton who placed her under care of a missionary. She died in 1829, the last survivor, so far as is known, of her race. The public conscience was at last aroused, and too late. In 1827 an institution was founded by a Mr W. E. Cormack under the patronage of Bishop Inglis of Nova Scotia and Judge Des Bayes of the Newfoundland Supreme Court to discover and protect the remnants of the unfortunate tribe. A series of voyages throughout the island seemed to prove that they had been destroyed. Cormack made the first crossing of the island from east to west along the watershed (1828), finding little except marshes, moss-hags and rocky knolls, where nothing but the caribou could live. Though the Beothucks had vanished, the Micmacs, a tribe of half-civilised Catholic Indians from French Canada, had taken possession. Their hunting parties habitually crossed the Strait of Belle Isle in canoes to penetrate the waterways of western Newfoundland where white settlers had never ventured. They were the first explorers of the island and, being armed with guns against the flint arrows of the Beothucks, they had destroyed the more primitive tribe in some long-forgotten war.

The Seven Years War which made the British supreme in North America brought no comfort to the Newfoundlanders. The campaigns brought renewed French raids upon the settlements, and the peace treaty whittled away their fishing-rights. While Pitt and his City friends were ready for 'another campaign or two' in order to exclude the French altogether, the government which took office in 1762 made concessions in this quarter. The Newfoundland seas were declared 'an open and free fishery for all the subjects of Great Britain' under supervision of the Governor of Newfoundland whose commission was extended to cover both shores of the Strait of Belle Isle. Thus began the claim of New-foundland to include Labrador. But the French, who were now excluded from the North American mainland, were consoled by the grant of two small islands, St Pierre and Miquelon (1763) off the south coast of Newfoundland, in addition to their rights over the north-western shore. This affront to the settlers of the senior British colony, at the end of a victorious war, was repeated, in humiliating terms, twenty years later, after the calamitous American War. The King of Great Britain was obliged by the Treaty of Versailles 'to take effective measures for preventing his subjects from interfering with the fishery of the French', that is to say he was to take part against his own people in a dispute of the utmost complexity. The limits of the French privilege on the 'Treaty Shore' were defined only after 200 years of diplomatic negotiation. The loyal Newfoundlanders, who had sent a regi-ment of volunteers to aid in the defence of Canada against the American rebels, learned to distrust the politicians of Whitehall who used their fishing-rights as the small change of diplomatic bargaining. Loyalty in Newfoundland tended to focus itself upon the Royal Navy to which they sent recruits and which brought visible blessings to the island. Their one advantage from the American War was the exclusion of New England fishing-boats from landing to dry fish, since they could no longer claim the privilege of British subjects.

The first full descriptive account of the colony was written in 1819 by the Rev. L. A. Anspach, the schoolmaster at St John's.

The previous twenty years had seen, first a great growth of population and prosperity during the Napoleonic Wars when a quintal of fish sold for 35s., and then a severe slump in 1814 when peace came and the quintal fell as low as 10s. That winter when times were at their worst, the timber-built town of St John's, a mass of wooden warehouses, shacks and drying-stages divided by narrow lanes, was burned to the ground. What stores of food remained were looted by gangs of hungry wretches. Three years later when just rebuilt, and while the fisheries were still depressed, the town was burned again. The winter of 1817–18 was long remembered as the worst in Newfoundland's history. For the first time the Governor wintered that year in the island, and died of it.

The settlements were gradually assuming the form of a regular colony. By 1822 the population reached 50,000 of whom about a third lived in St John's. Sir Thomas Cochrane, the first civil Governor, took the momentous step of building a road inland from the capital (1825). Before that time the island had known neither horses nor wagons. The only vehicles were little carts drawn by the celebrated Newfoundland dogs. According to Anspach the true breed were too fierce to be domesticated as pets, and what were known as Newfoundland dogs in England were but half-bred. Many years later, in 1884, the old breed had grown so troublesome for worrying sheep that they were all destroyed.

As in the other colonies a demand for self-government sprang up. A newspaper appeared in 1807 and in consequence a constitutional agitation, led by Dr J. Carson, an immigrant from Birmingham. The Colonial Office produced a constitution of the normal type, with a nominated council and an elective assembly, in 1832. Unfortunately the advocates of colonial self-government could find little to commend in the example of Newfoundland. While the fishing-settlements were indifferent, so long as the Colonial Office championed their fishing-rights, the town of St John's split into two hostile factions which frequently came to blows. Numbers were about equally divided between Roman Catholic Irish and Protestant English. Public officers were several times assaulted by mobs of the opposing faction. There was a crisis in 1835, and a deadlock in 1840, when the Speaker placed a judge of the High Court under arrest for refusing a *habeas corpus*. After petitions and counter-petitions a Parliamentary enquiry was held in London and the constitution was suspended. For fifteen years

NEWFOUNDLAND AND LABRADOR

Miles

0   50   100   150   200

Boundary as awarded by the Privy Council in 1927
⊙ Air Bases

A T L A N T I C

O C E A N

L A B R A D O R

Goose Bay ⊙

Belle Isle

Strait of Belle Isle

St. Lawrence

Anticosti

QUEBEC

Q U E B E C

Exploits B.

Gander

Grand Falls

Bonavista B.

NEWFOUNDLAND

Trinity B.

NEW BRUNS- WICK

PR. EDWARD I.

C. Breton I.

Harbour Grace

Placentia

Avalon

St. John's

Ferryland

Miquelon

St. Pierre

FRENCH SHORE

AMERICAN SHORE

George Philip & Son, Ltd.

Map 23

Newfoundland was reduced to the status of a Crown Colony until, in 1855, full responsible government was granted to this as to the other 'white' colonies. The population, by this date, was somewhat over 100,000. The Liberal (Roman Catholic) party at first assumed office and at once began to demand control over the fisheries. After a promising start in self-government the election of 1861 was exceedingly riotous and corrupt. The Conservative (Protestant) party which then came into power began a programme of development with roads, telegraphs and a geological survey. The pyrites deposits which old Frobisher had taken for gold, and the coal measures which had been noticed by Captain Cook, who had been a collier's lad, were at last surveyed. Attempts were made to develop Labrador.[1] The coming of the Atlantic cable to Harbour Grace in 1866 was a great event in the history of the island. There had been a service of steamships to Halifax since 1842.

The discussions over Canadian confederation led to a violent separatist agitation. The fishing interest was against any compromise with the competitive fishing interest of Nova Scotia. The commercial interest opposed incorporation in the Dominion for fear of increased taxation. In 1867 the population of Newfoundland was 142,000, of whom 22,000 lived in St John's. There were also 2500 'liviers' (coastal settlers) on the shores of Labrador. The annual revenue of Newfoundland was £137,000; the value of their imports £1,100,000, and their exports £1,000,000; and there was no funded debt. Though they bought foodstuffs in Quebec and coal in Nova Scotia, the great bulk of their trade was in fish sold direct to Europe. Their population lived on the eastern shore of the island looking towards the Old World. The Nova Scotians were their rivals, the French-Canadians their ancient enemies. They did not share the Canadian fear of aggression by the United States. Their pride and loyalty drew them towards

---

[1] Labrador had been transferred from Newfoundland to Canada by the Quebec Act of 1774 and was retransferred in 1809. Its status remained uncertain until the Privy Council decision of 1927 awarded the territory east of the watershed to Newfoundland and the remainder to Quebec. The decision was not a political award but a judicial finding on the actual status under existing acts and treaties. It went very decidedly in favour of Newfoundland which received territories on the mainland greater than the whole extent of the island. Since it was adjudged that the coastline followed the inlet up to Melville Lake, the site of the future airport, Goose Bay, fell to Newfoundland. It was leased to the Dominion of Canada in 1944.

England rather than Canada. In 1869 the Newfoundlanders decided to remain outside the Dominion. The election of that year fought on the issue of entering the Dominion was won by the furious campaigning of C. F. Bennett, the opponent of confederation. Governor Musgrave, who had worked hard for confederation, was transferred from Newfoundland to British Columbia, where his efforts were more successful.

Throughout the nineteenth century there was almost continuous negotiation with France and the United States over the fisheries. The naval officers on the Newfoundland station were frequently engaged in arbitrating local disputes and protecting British rights. By contrast with this tact and friendliness on the part of the Navy, the Foreign Office negotiated over the heads of the Newfoundlanders with but slight reference to their interest, in spite of vigorous protests by colonial ministries. Responsible government was inevitably limited by imperial treaty obligations. In addition to perennial disputes over the French Treaty Shore a new series of disputes had arisen over the American Treaty Shore. The Rush-Bagot Convention of 1818 had given the Americans the right to 'dry and cure fish in any unsettled Bay' of southern Newfoundland and on both sides of the Strait of Belle Isle. Elsewhere they might only take shelter or seek wood and water. In return the Americans abandoned their claim to the inshore fisheries of Canada and Nova Scotia. The treaty therefore pleased the mainland provinces but displeased the Newfoundlanders. But when the Reciprocity Treaty was signed in 1854, the Newfoundlanders were willing to admit American fishermen to their shores because they too had great hopes of selling and buying in American ports. These hopes were disappointed, since the Reciprocity Treaty was soon denounced, but at the Treaty of Washington (1871) which again admitted the Americans to their former rights on the 'American Shore' an inducement was given to the Newfoundlanders in an American payment of $1,000,000, a windfall which reconciled so poor a colony to the presence of interloping fishermen. The Newfoundlanders were as pleased with this turn of events as, for other reasons, the Canadians were displeased.

Meanwhile hardly a year passed without negotiation between the French and British governments over the 'French Shore'. Again and again the Newfoundlanders were infuriated by concessions to the French, which effectually deprived them of sovereignty over half of their island. A general settlement was negotiated in 1857 by Herman Merivale (the separatist Under-Secretary for the colonies, see chapter X, 1, page 531) making such outrageous play with Newfoundland sovereignty that there was a unanimous protest from the legislature. P. F. Little, the first Premier under responsible government, scored a triumph for the cause of colonial liberty by obtaining a complete recantation from the British government. Labouchere, the Secretary of State, assured him that 'the consent of the community of Newfoundland is regarded by Her Majesty's Government as the essential preliminary to any modification of their territorial or maritime rights'. No more was heard of Merivale's proposals and thereafter the government of Newfoundland took a hand in the perpetual negotiation.

Labouchere's despatch was regarded as the Magna Carta of Newfoundland, and was followed by some years of quiet progress until, about 1867, the spread of population began to reach the French Shore. Prospecting for minerals began and squatters settled in bays which the French claimed as under their jurisdiction. After long disputes and firm action by the Newfoundland government it was agreed in 1877 that they should appoint magistrates, even on the shore which the French claimed. Now a new difficulty arose. Between 1860 and 1880 the Newfoundlanders developed the industry of canning lobsters, and built twelve factories on the French Shore; to which the French very much objected. They retaliated by building two French canneries in 1883. The Chanceries of Europe and America were much concerned over the obscure point whether the right to 'take and dry fish' included a right to come ashore and can lobsters.

When the first colonial conference met in 1887 the Premier of Newfoundland, claiming his right to speak for the 'senior British colony', demanded in vain that colonies should control their own fisheries. The point at issue was now the definition of the term used in all the old treaties—'to take and dry fish'. But what was 'fish'? To a true Newfoundlander the word had always meant cod and nothing else. Bertrand Russell, as a very young man, was an honorary attaché at the Embassy in Paris in 1894. He records that he 'had to copy out long despatches attempting to persuade the French Government that a lobster is not a fish, to which the

French Government would reply that it was a fish in 1713, at the time of the Treaty of Utrecht'.[1] It was only in the series of agreements known as the Entente Cordiale (1904–5) that this musty old dispute was at last concluded. In return for concessions in Central Africa the French abandoned their claim to use the Treaty Shore, retaining no territorial rights in North America except possession of St Pierre and Miquelon.

Similarly the regulation of the 'American Shore' grew increasingly difficult as the population of Newfoundland spread round the coast. The problem of the southern shore was bait. The Newfoundlanders wanted to supply bait in their off-season to American deep-sea fishermen but wanted to exclude Americans from the shore-fisheries. A riot at Fortune Bay in 1878, against Americans who annoyed the Newfoundlanders by many breaches of customary fishing-laws (and not least by fishing on Sundays), led to a new crop of disputes and negotiations which went on for thirty years. In 1885 the Americans denounced the Treaty of Washington. Since some arrangement had to be made, Lord Salisbury sent Joseph Chamberlain, then out of office, to negotiate a *modus vivendi*. It was a landmark in the growth of good feeling between England and America but only a temporary settlement of the vexed problem. Throughout the 'nineties there were repeated negotiations which failed, largely because of the contrary influences of Newfoundland and Canada. This was one of the reasons why Newfoundland was not admitted to the Dominion in 1895. At last after a period of unusual exasperation Sir Robert Bond of Newfoundland obtained permission, at the colonial conference of 1907, to refer the whole dispute to the Hague Tribunal. Again there were long deliberations and bitter quarrels over the particulars. In 1909 a series of seven questions was placed before the Tribunal. The award given in 1910 and ratified by the Washington Agreement of 1912 at last satisfied all parties. In general terms it may be said that it was an interpretation of the Rush-Bagot Treaty of 1818 very similar to Joseph Chamberlain's *modus vivendi* of 1887.

Towards the end of the nineteenth century the Newfoundlanders employed about 3000 small craft, averaging forty tons, in the summer cod-fisheries off-shore. Attempts to lure them out to the deep-sea fisheries by bounties had little success; they were

[1] Bertrand Russell, *Autobiography* (Library of Living Philosophers).

reputed 'bad Bankers'. In their own way they caught 1,500,000 quintals of fish a year.

Until about 1890 the Newfoundlanders were men of one idea, interested in little besides the harvest of the ocean. Lead- and copper-mining had been attempted in a small way since 1857, followed some years later by iron-mining; a steam saw-mill to supply the local demand for timber had been started in 1871; and that was all. The growing world-demand for soft-woods began to affect Newfoundland about 1880 when a contract for a railway was let to an American syndicate. The promoters were to be granted 5000 acres of virgin forest for every mile constructed inland from St John's. The project failed and the rights were resumed by the government. In 1889 the government began a new negotiation with Robert G. Reid, a Scottish capitalist who operated in Montreal. During the next twelve years he acquired a financial control over Newfoundland like that which Cecil Rhodes was acquiring over South Africa, but without the wealth of the diamond-fields to give him local support. He built his railway westward; then obtained subsidiary contracts for branch lines and harbour works. He took over the contracts for ports and tele-graphs and tramways, until he held the whole state in fee. The national debt which had been negligibly small in 1871 was £1,000,000 by 1891, and £3,000,000 by 1901 while the increase in population was from 160,000 to 220,000. The great majority of the Newfoundlanders were poor and illiterate fishermen and lumbermen.

In 1893–4 the two commercial banks in St John's suspended payment, bringing down with them in their ruin the Government Savings Bank. The government, which had unwisely committed itself to a policy of development under the direction of an exter-nal capitalist, now looked around for a rescuer, throwing itself again, as in 1840, on the mercy of the Colonial Office. A some-what frantic appeal to Whitehall resulted in the despatch of a Treasury official, Sir H. Murray, who arrived with £10,000 in currency, a modest sum which proved sufficient to steady New-foundland's little finances.

But Lord Ripon, the Colonial Secretary would do no more un-less the Newfoundland Government would accept a Royal Com-mission of enquiry into their financial conduct. Almost desper-ately the Newfoundlanders turned to Canada. Thirty years earlier

Newfoundland had remained apart from Canada as unwilling to assume a share of her debts. Now Canada refused to underwrite the debt of Newfoundland. Her terms for admitting Newfoundland to the Dominion were $5,000,000 short of Newfoundland's necessity. Again Sir W. Whiteway, the Premier, appealed to the Colonial Office for a loan of £1,000,000, and again Ripon refused to fill the gap unless he should send a Royal Commission. The Newfoundlanders were again thrown on their own resources and saved themselves from bankruptcy by borrowing $3,500,000 on the London market at 4%, with the result that the country was mortgaged more deeply than before.

A few months later Joseph Chamberlain took charge of the Colonial Office. If he had been able to conduct the negotiations instead of the orthodox Ripon, it may well be supposed that some more generous forward-looking treatment would have been given to Newfoundland in her embarrassment; but it was now too late. Much as he disapproved the farming-out of the island's resources to a single capitalist, he was unwilling to overrule the constitutional act of a self-governing colony; the agreements with Reid were censured but upheld. Between 1898 and 1901 the monopolies were reorganised as the Reid-Newfoundland Company Ltd., a sort of public utility in which Reid still held the bulk of the shares.

Sir R. G. Reid (1842–1908) had gone out to the Australian goldfields as a poor Scottish lad. Training himself as a civil engineer, he moved on to Canada, worked for the Canadian Pacific Railway and made fame and riches. He built the Lachine Bridge and the International Bridge at Niagara. He was a great constructional engineer and, though he came to be known as 'Czar Reid' in Newfoundland, no one who knew him suggested that he was anything but an honest man. The error in Newfoundland was an optimism that led to capital development on a scale which the resources of the island could not justify. Newfoundland remained a poor and backward country of scattered fishing-villages that suffered inevitably from a low standard of literacy and public health, and a load of public debt.

7.　AUSTRALIA, 1851–1907

RESPONSIBLE government was established in the colonies of New South Wales, Victoria, Tasmania and South Australia by 1855. From the beginning all four showed democratic tendencies by adopting the Chartist policy which the British Parliament had rejected. Manhood suffrage, the ballot, equal electoral districts, Church disestablishment and secular education soon became the rule in each of these colonies. Queensland was admitted to the same degree of self-government in 1859 but Western Australia (or Swan River Colony), still a convict settlement, remained under the direct control of Downing Street. The fifty years of rule by separate governments are not easy to summarise. Each of the Australian colonies had its independent line of progress while none of them suffered from those wars, revolutions and shocking crises which magnetise the reader's attention. White Australia, both as a whole and in its constituent parts, has been the happy land that has no history of frenzy or slaughter.

The black spot in the record is the treatment of the aboriginals, whose lack of aggressiveness was their undoing. They were so utterly nomadic that they could not be expropriated. In general they vanished before the advance of the squatters, appearing now and then to steal sheep and spear lonely hut-keepers, but making no attempt at general resistance, since they had no real property to defend. When the blacks grew troublesome the settlers combined to drive them farther inland, giving no quarter to those they encountered. This intermittent undeclared war was less bloody than might have been expected. Perhaps the black-fellows never numbered more than 100,000, of whom but a small proportion roved through the temperate south-east. Most of them lived, and live, in the hot north where white men are scarce. When they disappeared it was assumed that they were dying out. A few degenerates lived in parasitic squalor around the white men's townships, their best employment being as 'black-trackers' for the police; the majority withdrew into the Bush where there was boundless space for the Stone Age culture to which they were so perfectly adapted. When Governor Denison wrote complacently to the Secretary of State in 1859 of their 'natural progress towards extinction', he was perhaps wrong, though most white Australians were willing to agree with him. For the most part the black-fellows were ignored, and perhaps better so, since they seemed incapable of civilisation. They have almost no place in the history of White Australia. At a census taken in 1941 their numbers were returned as 73,000 of whom one-third were still nomadic. Of late years the tendency of literary and scientific groups in Australia to detach their traditions from the northern hemisphere, so that a truly Australian naturalism may evolve, has led to some demonstrations of sympathy but to no effective contacts with the original Australians. Constructive social endeavours have been confined to a few philanthropists among whom should be remembered with honour the Spanish Benedictine, Bishop Salvado, who founded the monastery of New Norcia in the west as long ago as 1846. More recently a notable name has been that of Mrs Daisy Bates, C.B.E., a social worker among the blacks of Western and South Australia from 1901 to 1939.

The first great problem in each of the colonies was that of 'unlocking the land'. The Imperial Waste Lands Occupation Act, 1846, had given security of tenure to the squatters with rights of pre-emption. As in other parts of the world so in Australia the influx of land-hungry emigrants led to a political agitation for access to the unimproved land which the squatters monopolised. Nascent democracy was assumed to imply cheap freehold land for the small cultivator. The battle was joined in New South Wales where John (later Sir John) Robertson (1816–91) stood forward as the champion of 'Free Selection before Survey', and carried his case in the legislature after the introduction of manhood suffrage (1858). An Act was passed in 1861 restricting the leasehold of the squatters, and enabling any citizen to 'select' at will a farm of 320 acres on payment of 5s. an acre. All unoccupied land was thrown open for selection and, as grazing leases expired, the squatters' sheep-runs were also made available. Titles to selections were easily registered by the Torrens Transfer system.[1]

[1] Sir R. R. Torrens carried an Act for simplifying land-titles through the South Australian Parliament (1858), in despite of the bitter hostility of the legal profession. 'His shipping experience had suggested to him the query why land, the great object of acquirement in a new community, should not be made as easily and cheaply transferable as a ship, title by registration being substituted for title by deed.' The Torrens Act has been widely adopted, with amendments, in other colonies.

Thus the Wakefield plan for systematic colonisation and close settlement was altogether abandoned. But New South Wales was a grass country, not naturally suited to agriculture, and sheep, which are more efficiently managed in large flocks, remained its chief source of wealth. The squatters found it easy to secure the most desirable sections of their runs by putting in their dependants as 'dummy' selectors. By 'picking the eyes of the land', they deterred small farmers from encroaching. In the first ten years of free selection (1861–71) the flocks of sheep increased from 5,000,000 to 16,000,000 while the acreage of wheat increased only from 120,000 to 150,000. After another decade it was estimated that only 20,000 resident cultivators had made good out of 120,000 selectors, while 96 squatters still held 8,000,000 acres of land (1882). Free selection had failed in its purpose and had reacted very unfavourably on the character of the people. It provided infinite opportunity for land-speculation and petty corruption, and scattered the rural population far and wide, beyond the reach of churches and schools, beyond the limits of law and order. Bush-ranging revived, in the form of stealing stock which could always be hidden away at some remote 'selection'. Economically the squatters were still supreme though political control had nominally passed to the new working-class electorate. In the 'eighties more than half the population of New South Wales already lived in Sydney, the commercial centre of the South Pacific. Otherwise the flock-masters and the wool-dealers owned the country.

Similar agitations for free selection took place, with local variation, in the other colonies. The progress of cultivation was greatest in South Australia where large areas were naturally suited to wheat-growing. Land under crops increased in that colony from 6000 acres in 1841 to 2,000,000 in 1891, that is an average of seven acres of wheatland to every white inhabitant, whereas the average in New South Wales was less than two acres to each inhabitant. The South Australian economy depended upon the use of chemical fertilisers which were first introduced in the 'seventies amid the jeers of old-fashioned farmers. The application of phosphates in large quantities produced a rapid increase in the yield of corn.

In the next generation a more systematic policy of close settlement was resumed throughout Australasia. Blocks of land were selected by the Departments of Public Lands and thrown open to settlers on favourable terms, after survey, and in accordance with a policy of Public Works. A typical case, in New Zealand, is more fully described below, page 611.

At this time Tasmania languished, not yet having outlived the legacy of the convict days. Such prosperity as it attained in the 'seventies and 'eighties came from the development of resources which were not in direct competition with those of its rich progressive neighbours. Tin, lead and copper mining was begun in the 'seventies. Fruit and vegetables were also exported to the other colonies in a small way, but could not be sent farther afield before the modern age of refrigeration and canned foods.

The colony of Victoria, first launched into prosperity by the gold-rush of the 'fifties, continued to enjoy an age of expansion even through the world-wide trade depression of the late 'seventies. Its population rose from 541,000 in 1851 to 1,140,000 in 1891. In that generation the most eminent citizen of Victoria was Sir Charles Gavan Duffy (1816–1903), the Irish revolutionary of 1848, who resigned his seat at Westminster to emigrate to Melbourne where he was received as a hero in 1855. Constructive statesmen in the colonies (unlike Joseph Chamberlain and the imperialists of Whitehall) have mostly been ardent in their support of Irish Home Rule. Though Gavan Duffy prided himself upon being 'an Irish rebel to the backbone and spinal marrow', he was a firm constitutionalist in Victoria and a steady adherent of Australian federation within the Empire. He died a K.C.M.G. Gavan Duffy took up the cause of free selection in 1862 with much the same immediate results as in New South Wales. While he did not succeed in breaking up the big estates he did bring much land under cultivation (1,500,000 acres by 1880).

Victoria did not escape the revived pest of bush-ranging. From 1878 to 1880 the townships along the Murray River were terrorised by a group of squalid ruffians known as the Kelly Gang. The tale of Ned Kelly's last fight, at Glenrowan (27 June 1880), where his comrades were shot down and he was taken alive in a suit of home-made armour, is dear to the memory of the Australian adolescent. Though Kelly was a robber and murderer caught redhanded, 5000 Melbourne citizens led by a former cabinet minister petitioned (in vain) for his reprieve.

If the continent of Australia was considered on a small-scale map, the confederation of these similar colonies seemed obvious and inevitable. On the spot it was more plain that they were commercial rivals with different fiscal policies, and severed from one another by vast distances. Though men of large political views, like Gavan Duffy, advocated confederation they could not point to any immediate advantage that would generate enthusiasm for it. The problem turned on the need for a customs union, a topic upon which the Colonial Office held decided views. Since Free Trade was England's policy, and assumed by the English to be the policy of all sensible men, it showed a folly that was almost malignant in colonial politicians when they discussed tariff advantages. Gavan Duffy, though a Free Trader, had several sharp exchanges with Gladstone's Lord Kimberley on the competence of the colonies to make their own arrangements. But right or wrong, Free Trade was not the prevailing theory outside Great Britain; and the Australians, like many economists in foreign countries, were turning their minds towards a policy of protection and high wages.

Under Crown Colony rule the Australians had given to British manufactured goods a preference of 5 % which was swept away by the new democratic governments in the Free Trade epoch. Victoria lapsed from orthodoxy by introducing a light revenue tariff in 1857. The seeds of heresy thus planted were sedulously cultivated by David Syme (1827–1908), a Scottish journalist who made the Melbourne *Age* the most influential Australian newspaper. In 1862 he founded a Protectionist League with the avowed object of establishing a planned economy in Victoria. For forty years he was the true leader of the protectionist party and was responsible for introducing a tariff (1864) designed to protect local industry. In 1877 it was raised to give an average advantage of 25 %, and in some instances 45 %, to goods manufactured in Victoria. But this was only a part of Syme's intention, since he quite rejected the popular theory of *laissez-faire*. 'It is good', he wrote, 'for the whole community that the population should be fully employed and adequately remunerated. Then it may be necessary for the state to promote, by such means as it has in its power, the growth of manufactures.' This very moderate statement of protectionist economics was thought dangerously heretical seventy years ago. As an advocate of a planned society controlled by direct democracy, Syme was a powerful force in moulding the Australian national character. His autarchic system implied the setting of limits to the population lest an unrestricted influx of cheap labour should lower the rate of wages. He therefore campaigned against the encouragement of immigration from Great Britain. By his influence state-aided immigration of labourers to Victoria was ended in 1873, and by 1901 had ceased throughout Australia. The intake was confined to independent settlers bringing either capital or technical skill.[1]

If Australian history can be related in terms of the interplay of opposed forces, the late nineteenth century may be seen as rivalry between the Free Traders of Sydney and the protectionists of Melbourne. Both were prosperous when the world was impoverished. Though the price of wool kept pretty steady (until 1893) and though the acreage of wheat increased, critics at Sydney foretold that the Melbourne bubble would burst, since the protected industries had not made the state truly self-sufficient. The absurd situation continued of a customs barrier, and at times a tariff war, along the River Murray, which divided the rival economies of Victoria and New South Wales. When protectionists appealed to the Colonial Office for authority to frame a customs union, the Office frowned upon any other policy than Free Trade all round. No less than six inter-colonial conferences were held between 1863 and 1873 without an agreement upon a common fiscal policy. Not till 1873 was the Colonial Office persuaded (by Julius Vogel of New Zealand) even to sponsor the Australian Colonial Duties Act by which the colonies were enabled to enter into reciprocal agreements.

Meanwhile Australia was borrowing heavily in London. Sir Hercules Robinson who governed New South Wales from 1872 to 1879 was an advocate of bold borrowing. During the five worst years of depression (1876–80), when the export of capital to other countries had almost ceased, London advanced £22,000,000 to Australian governments and £11,000,000 to other Australian

[1] Syme was a prolific and original writer upon many themes. A biographer in 1892 gave the following account of his philosophy: 'Having rejected Free Trade, the mechanical competition of blind forces like greed and want, as an adequate motive for the development of human society; having condemned the competition of selfish interests in the machinery of government, he proceeds to combat the theory of natural selection as sufficient to explain the origin of species, and contends that all modifications of organisms originate in the cell, which is the psychological as well as the physiological unit. Mr Syme is an evolutionist without being a Darwinian.' *Dictionary of Australian Biography*, edited by P. Mennell.

borrowers. During the next five years (1881–5) these figures were surpassed and almost doubled. Between 1886 and 1890 the total investment of British capital exceeded £100,000,000. Unlike the investment in Canadian governments these were not specifically railway loans. Thanks to her long seaboard Australia did not need grand trunk railways for her early development. Each colony built its own short lines inland from the port to serve its own productive regions, without thought of any continental plan. Thus, casually, three different railway-gauges were introduced. The line from Melbourne to Sydney was opened in 1883 with a break of gauge where it crossed the frontier.

The discovery of a 'hill of gold' at Mount Morgan in Queensland (1882), and the opening of the Broken Hill silver mines in South Australia (1883), inflated prosperity still further, producing a boom in Melbourne which the protectionists believed to be a justification of their principles. It reached its apex in 1887 and began to fall off in 1889 when world prices were sagging ominously. The Baring crisis in London in 1890 brought down many banking-houses and plunged Melbourne, after long prosperity, into deep depression. Throughout the 'nineties misfortune after misfortune was heaped upon Australia. The price of wool, which for long had stood at above 1s. a pound, fell to 7d. in 1893. Then the silver market collapsed. The demonetisation of silver by India and the United States meant a fall in the market-price from 4s. 3½d. per ounce in 1883 to 2s. 1¼d. per ounce in 1893. The driest seasons ever known recurred again and again, until the drought of 1897–9 reduced the number of sheep in Australia from 100,000,000 to 50,000,000. Melbourne's business was stagnant and her policy discredited. Sydney seemed to survive the depression more comfortably, and gave the credit to Free Trade. But relief came from two new sources of Australian wealth. The first was refrigeration which enabled the squatters to export the carcasses of their sheep as well as the wool-clip; the second was the gold-rush to Coolgardie.

Until 1865 Western Australia had been dependent for more than half its revenue upon the subsidy provided for the penal establishment. In that year the British government announced its intention to discontinue the transportation of convicts, a decision which gave great satisfaction to the other colonies though it caused some dismay among employers of labour in Western

Australia. The free settlers countered by petitioning for self-government but were fobbed off with the right to elect some representatives to the legislative council, until such time as they should constitute a majority over the time-expired convicts, and until the colony should be self-supporting. Until the final grant in 1890 the Colonial Office endeavoured to impose free immigration as a condition of self-government. The new era in Western Australia dates from the closing of the convict establishment in 1868. A progressive policy was inaugurated by the Governor, Sir Frederick Weld who, as Prime Minister of New Zealand, had been an advocate of the self-reliant policy. He set to work to explore the resources of the country and to survey the routes to the other colonies, employing for this purpose a young man who was to be the creator of Western Australia as a modern state. John (afterwards Sir John[1]) Forrest was born in the colony in 1847 and educated at Bishop's College, Perth. Entering Weld's new survey department he made his name by a series of journeys which revealed much good pastoral country behind the forbidding coast-line. His chief work was the planning and construction of the overland telegraph line from Perth to Adelaide (1874–6) which bridged the gap between Western Australia and the other colonies. As an active member of the legislative council he encouraged land settlement and when, through his efforts, responsible government was at last granted (53 & 54 Vict. cap. 26), he became the first premier of Western Australia (1891).

The discovery of gold at Coolgardie in 1892 came aptly for the development of the new state. The survey of the gold-fields was a task which Forrest well understood. Irrigation, roads and railways were skilfully financed from the new-found wealth; and each area thrown open by the miners was surveyed for land-settlement. Between 1891 and 1911 the population of Western Australia increased from 49,000 to 282,000; the annual exports (including bullion) from £800,000 to £5,400,000; the land under crop from 89,000 to 850,000 acres.

Another exception to the rule of Australian society was to be seen in North Queensland, 2000 miles away from Swan River. The great province of Queensland is in part an extension of the

---

[1] Shortly before his death in 1918 he was raised to the peerage as Lord Forrest, the first Australian to be ennobled.

pastoral south-eastern region. The overlanders from New South
Wales had spread into the Darling Downs, creating there the
sheep and cattle runs, and the same problems of land and labour
that appeared in the older colonies. There too came the gold-
seekers, to Gympie in 1867 and to Mount Morgan in 1883. But
far to the north the climate grew so torrid as to raise doubts
whether North Queensland was white man's country. The coastal
lowlands under the lee of the Great Barrier Reef were suited,
like the coast of Natal, to tropical agriculture and there, as early
as the 1850's, some experiments had been made in growing sugar.

The importation of indentured labourers, known as *kanakas*,
from the Islands is generally traced to the efforts of Captain
Robert Towns (1794–1873), a Sydney skipper with an extensive
island trade. In 1863 he brought sixty islanders to work under
contract on a cotton plantation, which came to be known as
Townsville, in North Queensland. Within three years the number of kanakas on the plantations had grown to about 1200, and
white labourers were dismissed to give place to them. It was,
however, philanthropic objections raised by the missionary
societies that produced the first agitation against their employment. In 1867, the Colonial Office, incited by the missionaries,
brought pressure to bear on the new Queensland legislature which
passed an Act, in 1868, for supervising the contracts of labour and
the conditions on board the ships which brought the kanakas. So
far, so good. It was not in general alleged that the 46,000 kanakas
imported to Queensland under these regulations, during the next
five and thirty years, were actively ill-treated either on the voyage
or at the plantations; but there were grave moral objections to the
trade. Since the whole vast region of the south-west Pacific was
still no-man's-land, and since the European governments were in
no mood to enlarge their colonial empires, there was no means of
supervising the recruitment of labour. The islands exhibited all
the varieties of primitive culture from the palaeolithic savagery of
the New Hebrides to the highly-developed monarchies of Hawaii
and Tahiti. Some islands, like Tonga, had been formed by the
missionaries into theocracies, while others, such as Fiji, were
already contaminated by western commercialism at its lowest
level. The island traders lived by no standards but their own and
tended to degenerate, as men do in the midst of anarchy. The
more primitive Melanesians might be lured on board a trading-

schooner and merely kidnapped without fear of diplomatic reprisal. The candid, curious Polynesians, adventurous by nature,
might be induced to make their mark on a contract they could not
understand and so to sign away their liberty. This was the method
of the new Pacific slave trade which was known discreetly as
'black-birding'. Once shipped to the plantations, mission-boys,
braves, and degraded savages alike must work or starve; nor when
their indentures were worked out was there any means of ensuring
their return to their own islands among the thousands that sprinkle
the Pacific. The sad statistics show that in the 'eighties the death-
rate among the kanakas, all able-bodied men, averaged more than
sixty per thousand annually while the white death-rate in Queensland was less than fourteen. As savages do, they died from mere
lack of will to live.

Still stronger antagonism to the use of coloured labourers on
the Queensland plantations came from the white labourers. 'They
hated the kanaka brother whom they saw with as much zeal and
heartiness as the philanthropists in England loved the dusky
islander whom they had not seen.'

Queensland after the grant of self-government in 1859, when
the white population was 26,000, was more subject to the violent
fluctuations in prosperity which afflict young communities than
the other colonies. Its politicians were inclined to snatch political
and other advantages from these fluctuations rather than to lay the
foundations of a solid state. With all its faults the plantation-
system in the lowlands at first held out a prospect of successful
trade. The cotton-boom during the American Civil War brought
a short-lived prosperity. Then the planters turned their attention
to sugar, but on a falling market after 1880. An injudicious land
and emigration policy flooded the country with white emigrants,
for whom employment was lacking. The Overend Gurney Bank
failure (1866) deeply involved the Queensland government. From
this disaster they were saved by the lucky occurrence of the Gympie gold-rush (1867) which brought into the country more white
labourers and a stronger hostility to the kanaka immigration.

All Queenslanders alike were deeply interested in the problems
of the western Pacific, so that parties generally combined in their
efforts to induce the imperial government to annex the adjacent
islands. Queensland as a whole was perhaps the most imperialist
of the colonies. None the less its Labour Party led the fight for

a White Australia under a social-democratic government. A miners' member was elected to the legislature as early as 1873. The resistance of the planters took the form of a separatist movement. Repeatedly, between 1866 and 1900, they petitioned the Colonial Office to split the colony in two. Lord Kimberley stated the policy (1872), to which his successors in office adhered, that it would not be constitutional to subdivide a self-governing colony except on the advice of its responsible ministry.[1] When the Tories were in power at Westminster they supported this view still more strongly, since a grant of home rule to North Queensland would make an awkward precedent for Ireland. The last appeal of the planters was made in 1895 to Joseph Chamberlain, who firmly told them to wait until the impending federation of Australia should provide a solution to this with other problems.

The bank failures in Melbourne and the fall in wool prices of the early 'nineties again brought Queensland to insolvency, with the unusual consequence that the Bank of England, in disgust, 'severed relations' with the Queensland government. In the same year (1893) Brisbane was devastated by a flood which deposited a gunboat, permanently, in the Botanical Gardens. Sir Samuel Griffiths (1845–1920), the radical premier who had long fought the planters of the north, was so far intimidated as to permit a renewed importation of kanakas (illegal since 1890), lest the sugar trade also should be ruined. Later in the 'nineties Labour influence prevailed and Queensland politicians turned their attention to the closer settlement of land. In 1899 the voters of the state declared for confederation, by a majority of 7000 on a poll of 69,000, with the understanding that this was a vote for White Australia. The indentured kanaka labourers were deported (1904–6) under a Commonwealth statute. The census of 1941 showed no more than 3000 Polynesians as resident in the whole of Australia.

The Australian Labour movement won its first successes in Queensland and suffered there its first resounding defeat. A Radical journalist named William Lane (1861–1917) migrated from Bristol to Brisbane by way of America where he had acquired a socialist doctrine of an idealist character. Like most

---

[1] The Colonial Office did not hesitate, however, to interfere in respect of migration. In 1876 Carnarvon vetoed a Queensland Bill for excluding Asiatic immigrants. Lord Derby suggested a compromise, which was accepted in 1880, of restricting them by a test of literacy.

Radicals in the colonies he had fallen under the influence of Henry George (who made a triumphal tour of Australia in 1889) and regarded the squatters' monopoly of the land as the bar to progress. By combining the wage-earners against the land-monopolists he hoped to create some such Utopia as was pictured in the popular allegories of Edward Bellamy. Marxian materialism, then and for thirty or forty succeeding years, was almost unknown in Australia. The classical political economy of the utilitarians was altogether rejected by these Socialists who proposed to build society upon a basis of social security and not upon the iron laws of supply and demand. Accordingly the idealists who propounded these doctrines were dismissed by the orthodox as mere enthusiasts, while the practical men who endeavoured to implement them by direct industrial action were treated by the officers of the law as dangerous revolutionaries.

Through his newspaper the *Queensland Worker*, Lane agitated for 'socialism in our time', to be achieved by consolidating all manual workers into a single union. In 1885 he organised a trades and labour council for Queensland, in 1889 an Australian Federation of Labour. 1889 was the year of the London dock strike to which the Australian Unions sent lavish contributions in cash, even impoverishing themselves at a time when their own trial was coming. The times were unpropitious for a contest with the employers. A long period of depression set in, in 1890, with wool prices falling, banks calling in their reserves, money dear, and London investors in a shy mood.

The Queensland squatters made the first move by issuing a new code of wages and conditions, ignoring the rules of the Shearers' Union. Brisbane dockers then refused to handle 'non-union' wool. This was the first attempt by the 'wharfies' to dictate terms by declaring such-and-such a ship or cargo 'black', a method that has eventually given them the whip-hand in all countries that depend upon bulky exports for a livelihood. But Lane's organisation was inadequate to the test since enough non-union labour could be recruited. The leadership passed from Lane's hands into those of W. G. Spence, a trade-union organiser from Melbourne, who eschewed building castles in the air but concentrated on organising the Australian shearers on the best English trade-union principles. Though he composed the crisis at Brisbane, a seamen's strike, for 'recognition' of Lane's union of all maritime workers,

broke out at Adelaide and spread to the other ports, with the
unusual feature that the ships' officers joined with the crews in
striking. After serious rioting at Sydney and Melbourne (August–
September 1890) the strike was broken and the leaders indicted
for conspiracy, under obsolescent statutes. Consolidating their
position, the squatters forced the issue with the Shearers' Union,
which was broken in 1891, by what in English parlance would be
called a lock-out, if the nature of the migratory business of shear-
ing permits such a use. The violent methods which the shearers
commonly used against non-unionists, nicknamed 'scabs' from
the endemic disease of the sheep-runs, enabled the employers to
invoke the ancient penalties of old laws with their heavy bias
against strikers.

Australia was now in the doldrums. Hard times and disillusion
led politicians back to fundamentals. From the barren policy of
direct action they turned towards social reform by constitutional
means. The Australian electorate, the 'diggers', were the heirs of
the English chartists and, having achieved five of the six points of
the Charter, were disposed to legislate for a social-democratic
commonwealth such as the old Chartists would have approved.
A secondary influence, of growing strength, was that of the Irish
catholic immigrants, politically radicals but socially conservatives. In every Australian state (as also in New Zealand)
a code of labour laws was introduced with some system of
industrial arbitration at an early date. The first was carried
through the South Australian legislature by C. C. Kingston in
1894. For some years the employers maintained their hostility
to organised labour, and then reluctantly accepted the implications
of the new labour laws. By European standards, all parties
in Australian politics were Social-democrats, and none true
Socialists. The Labour parties seemed content to secure minimum
standards of social security and comfort without reconstituting the
structure of capitalist society; the right-wing parties—not pre-
suming to adopt such compromising names as Conservative or
Tory—were concerned with safeguarding the financial and commercial interests by which Australia lived, while acquiescing in
the socialisation of wage-labour. Both sides looked to prosperity
to ensure a high standard of life, without much regard as yet to the
social insurances against adversity, which all progressive parties
in England and Germany advocated.

The first 'Labour' government was formed by a group of William Lane's adherents in Queensland, in 1899, after Lane himself had withdrawn from the scene of his defeat. He departed for Paraguay in 1893, at the head of a shipload of disciples, with the intention of founding there a communist polity, which soon collapsed.[1]

Between its two phases, of industrial and political activity, organised labour took but a small part in the federating of the Australian Commonwealth. By 1904 the federal Labour Party was strong enough to form a makeshift ministry, and in 1908 a strong effective ministry, under Andrew Fisher. A cardinal point in their policy had been fixed by the Commonwealth Arbitration Court which, like the Supreme Court of the United States, had assumed almost a legislative function. A famous judgment, given in 1907, by the President, Judge H. B. Higgins (d. 1929), established the principle of the basic minimum wage as a fundamental in Australian industrial law. Reverting from utilitarian economics to the scholastic theory of the just price, he declared that wage-rates were not to be fixed by the 'higgling of the market' according to the laws of supply and demand but by 'the normal needs of an average employee, regarded as a human being in a civilised country'. This was 'the bedrock below which the Court cannot go'.

Australia of the convicts and Australia of the squatters had passed away, leaving in their place a new and homogeneous society which emerged from the troubles of the 'nineties mature and self-conscious. It had a strongly marked equalitarian tone best seen in the Sydney school of ballad-writers, journalists and caricaturists when the *Bulletin*, inspired by the talented Lindsay family, was in its ribald, radical youth. Despite the belief of the world outside, Australian society was essentially urban, taking colour from its sunny, thriving cities, not from the 'great wide spaces'. Yet its culture was of the open air. The Australians lived an easy, open-handed, carefree life out of doors, having shed many of the social inhibitions of puritan England, though they could still be

---

[1] With the support of his unions Lane raised £20,000 and, after an appeal for land to the government of New South Wales, which rejected it, he got a large grant from the government of Paraguay, on condition of settling 800 families. After a reconnaissance, a party of 220 Australians sailed to Montevideo, followed by a second party of 200. Lane made himself unpopular by enforcing a puritanical moral code and left the settlement in 1894. Changing his views, he went to New Zealand and became the editor of a Tory newspaper.

intolerant of social eccentricity. If, like the English middle classes, they were Philistines, their saving grace was a greater interest in music. Perhaps the most celebrated member of the Australian race has been the singer who took the name of Melba from her native city.

8. THE COMMONWEALTH OF AUSTRALIA

LORD GREY's intention to federate the Australian colonies, as a sequel to the enabling act of 1850, was not well received either by the Australians or by the Colonial Reformers in London. Molesworth objected on the grounds that the scheme was imposed from above, not based upon the popular will; and Wentworth, at Sydney, was inclined to the same view, though in general he was an advocate of federation. No further unifying measure was taken at that time than the issue to the Governor of New South Wales of an overriding commission as Governor-General. Even this appointment, which meant little, was allowed to lapse in 1861. The cause of Australian nationality was chiefly sustained by a fiery Scottish minister, the Rev. J. D. Lang (1799–1878), the founder of the Presbyterian Church in Australia and of Sydney Grammar School. A sturdy Protestant, he deplored the influx of Irish Roman Catholics and would have controlled immigration by the Wakefield plan. The union of all the scattered colonies into an Australian nation, if necessary outside the British Empire, was his lifelong enthusiasm.

In Victoria Gavan Duffy was the first to take up the cause of federation, but his efforts broke down on the fiscal issue. Commercial rivalry between Melbourne and Sydney was at its height and was not reduced by the unhelpful attitude of the Colonial Office. A counter-proposal from Sir Henry Parkes[1] at Sydney, with an alternative scheme to Duffy's, was disallowed in 1867. When at last the Colonial Office made a customs union possible (1873), the two colonies failed to come to an agreement.

The appearance of Germany in the Pacific directed the attention of the colonies to the problems of imperial defence, which were

[1] Sir Henry Parkes (1815–96), a Birmingham apprentice, emigrated to better himself in 1839. Entirely self-educated, he became a cultured man of letters and a lifelong worker for democracy, public education, Free Trade, and Federation. He died a very poor man, having been three times Premier of New South Wales.

discussed at an inter-colonial conference in 1883, the year when Queensland attempted to annex New Guinea. Six of the Australasian colonies agreed to form a Federal Council with limited powers to legislate on external affairs. It was authorised by an imperial Act of Parliament, in 1885, and met periodically until 1899. Since New South Wales and New Zealand stood aside from the Council, though the new administration of Fiji adhered to it, the status of the Federal Council was but meagre in Pacific affairs.

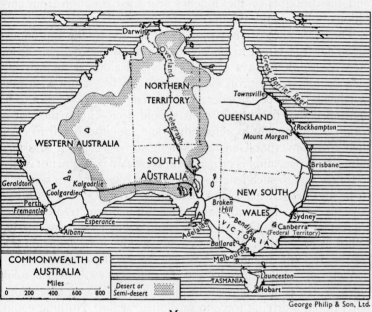

Map 24

George Philip & Son, Ltd.

A report on the defences of New South Wales prompted Sir Henry Parkes to make a further effort for federation in 1889. Proposals were discussed for a national convention, which was convened at Sydney in May 1891. After long and cautious discussions, with careful study of precedents in Canada, the United States and Switzerland, a draft constitution was prepared, largely by Sir Samuel Griffiths of Queensland. The delegates were strongly influenced by the argument of Bryce's *American Commonwealth* which had just been published, so that the draft which they adopted is rather an improved version of the Constitution of the United States than of the British North America Act. Its four main features, which were eventually incorporated into the Act of 1900 were states-rights, free trade between the states, a federal revenue based upon a federal tariff, and a federal system of defence.

The delegates parted in the full understanding that the framing of a tariff would divide the nation. The opposed views of Victoria and New South Wales were at this time irreconcilable. Furthermore the bank failures, the commercial crisis, the strikes and the droughts of the 'nineties distracted attention from ambitious political endeavours.

The conference of 1891 was almost startled by the appearance of Sir George Grey, in his eightieth year, as the delegate from New Zealand. Always original, he stood alone as an extreme radical imperialist, proposing Australasian federation as a first instalment of imperial federation on democratic principles. He demanded that the Australasians should decide upon their own form of government by referendum and should proceed to elect their own Governor-General. Among the delegates he was in a minority of one, and his principals in New Zealand were not ready to follow him to such lengths—1200 miles of stormy sea were felt to be an effectual bar against federating New Zealand with the Australian colonies which differed from it in origin, tradition, and current problems. On the other hand, a single delegate, Sir G. Dibbs of New South Wales, attempted to revive the demand for a republican United States of Australia; he too stood alone.

Victoria, South Australia and Tasmania now formed a solid block with a general agreement upon the principle of federation, but without a driving force to precipitate action. Nothing could be done until New South Wales should be induced to compromise. The federalists took the practical course of forming associations throughout the colonies to stimulate interest. The Australian Natives' Association (a 'native' in Australia means a white man born in the country) at last provided the motive force. At a public meeting at Bendigo in 1893, Dr John Quick proposed the method by which the electorate could be directly interested in bringing about a federation. An Act should be introduced into the legislature of each colony to authorise the summoning of a statutory convention; and the constitution approved by the convention should be submitted to a referendum of the whole people in each colony. The politicians at Sydney still hesitated until

Sir George Reid (1845–1918), the Free Trade leader, announced his conversion to the method of procedure, if not entirely to a federation with protectionist states. With heavy humour, he compared himself to a 'teetotaller keeping company with five drunkards'.

After enabling acts had been passed in each of the Australian colonies (1895), a convention was summoned to meet in 1897, first at Adelaide and later at other centres. A constitution, based on the draft of 1891, was agreed upon, after detailed negotiations on the composition of the federal senate, on railway rates, and on the federal tariff. Sir Edward Braddon (1829–1904) of Tasmania contributed a clause which aroused fierce opposition in New South Wales where it was thought likely to lead to increased taxation. The Free Traders at Sydney were making their last stand; and the Labour Party suspected that the Federation was a device of aristocrats and militarists. It was the part of Sir George Reid, a stout jolly man with a large personal following, to overcome these scruples and to allay these suspicions. Not without evasive movements he steered his party round.

In 1898 Victoria, South Australia and Tasmania submitted the constitution to referenda which gave overwhelming majorities in its favour. In New South Wales there was a bare majority but not the three-fifths required by the Act. Reid made this an excuse to hold out for better terms, extracting from Victoria the concession that a new capital city should be sited in an enclave of Federal Territory within the State of New South Wales. In 1899 the proposal was again submitted to the electors of New South Wales and was given a competent majority. Queensland adhered, in 1899, by a narrow margin of votes; Western Australia was admitted, belatedly, in 1900 after holding out for a gradual adjustment of its tariff over a period of five years.

There remained the reference of the scheme to the imperial authority. In the midst of the Boer War, to which all the colonies had severally despatched contingents of volunteers, a delegation presented itself to the Colonial Office with a *fait accompli*, asking for the incorporation of their constitution, as it stood, into an Act of Parliament. While Joseph Chamberlain, the Secretary of State, was an enthusiastic supporter of Australian Federation, he like Sir George Grey regarded it as a step to the federation of the whole Empire and was suspicious of any feature appearing to weaken the prerogative of the Crown. A firm but friendly dispute followed upon the right of appeal to the Privy Council, which the Australians proposed to abolish altogether, and which Chamberlain hoped to retain as the rudimentary organ of an imperial judiciary. The delegates professed their inability to amend what had been approved by the legislatures and the people of Australia. The utmost Chamberlain could do was to insert a saving clause which reserved to the Queen the right to grant leave for appeals from the High Court of Australia to the Privy Council in such cases as the High Court should approve.

The Commonwealth of Australia Constitution Act (63 & 64 Vict. cap. 12) received the Queen's assent on 9 July 1900. The Commonwealth was proclaimed on 1 January 1901.

The British North America Act had been the outcome of rivalry between the two races of Canada. Its effect was, in one way, centrifugal, breaking their unhappy union and creating subordinate governments, but securing their status under a strong central executive. The form of the Canadian constitution was monarchical; the function of the Governor-General was firmly prescribed; the Senate, a nominated body of elder statesmen, was intended as a buttress to the Crown; legal sovereignty was retained by the Crown and Parliament of the United Kingdom, which created, and which alone could amend, the constitution.

Very different was the Constitution of the Australian Commonwealth which, as the preamble of the Act declares, was founded upon a democratic social compact. 'Whereas the people of New South Wales, Victoria, South Australia, Queensland and Tasmania, humbly relying on the blessing of Almighty God, have agreed to unite in one indissoluble Federal Commonwealth, under the Crown of the United Kingdom of Great Britain and Ireland, and under the constitution hereby established... be it therefore enacted... that it shall be lawful for the Queen... to declare by proclamation', and so on. The Queen is enabled to give legal authority to a constitution already established by the people under the guidance of God.[1]

The constitution begins by describing the functions of the Federal Parliament, which consists of the Queen (represented by

---

[1] This appeal to a Higher Sanction was qualified in the body of the Act by a clause forbidding the establishment of any religious sect or the imposition of religious tests.

a Governor-General), an elected Senate and a House of Representatives. The Senators are to be chosen by the electorate voting directly as a single constituency in each state, by the method known as *scrutin-de-liste*. This was a concession to the democratic principles of the smaller states and had the effect of making the Senate a radical body quite unlike the general run of Upper Chambers. The franchise for both chambers was so framed as to permit female suffrage.

The powers of Parliament were enumerated in great detail, giving it control of all such matters as trade, commerce, taxation, currency, state railways, defence, immigration, nationality, the care of subject-races (other than aborigines) and relations with the Pacific islands. In case of disagreement between the two Houses they were to meet in joint session. The Governor-General's prerogative was not very precisely defined, though the power of the Crown to disallow Acts of Parliament was preserved. Nothing was said in the Act about responsible government. The jurisdiction of the High Court covered appeals from the Supreme Courts of the states which previously would have been heard by the Privy Council. In case of repugnancy between federal and state laws, the federal law was to prevail.

In all other matters residual sovereignty was retained by the states, and they have zealously striven for their rights. Each state maintains a viceregal establishment and each demands the right of direct access to the imperial government in matters within its competency.

Provision was made in the Act for creating new states and territories. States were empowered to surrender portions of their territory to the direct control of the federal government. Under this clause the Northern Territory, which by a strangely confusing nomenclature had been part of the state of South Australia, was transferred to the Commonwealth in 1910. The federal capital was also sited at Canberra in a small enclave of federal territory.[1]

[1] The site was chosen after long argument in 1909. The town-plan, the winning design in a public competition, was prepared by W. B. Griffin of Chicago. The works were inaugurated at a public ceremony in 1913 by Lord Denman, the Governor-General. H.M. King George VI (then Duke of York) opened the Parliament House in 1927, whereupon the removal of the government from its temporary quarters in Melbourne was begun. Canberra, now a city of 13,000 permanent residents, sparsely housed in an area designed for a much larger future population, lies in a beautiful well-watered plain ringed by wooded hills. Its chief disadvantage is its remoteness from the centres of population and industry.

The same clause enabled the Commonwealth to take over the government of Papua (British New Guinea) as a federal territory in 1905. No new states have been admitted since the adherence of Western Australia in 1900.

The final clause of the Act prescribes the method of altering the constitution, by national referendum, after the proposed alteration has been approved by both Houses of the federal Parliament. The sole check upon this sovereign power, other than some detailed provision for procedure, was the necessity of presenting the law thus approved 'to the Governor-General for the Queen's assent'.

9. SOCIAL-DEMOCRACY IN NEW ZEALAND, 1870–1914

At the end of the Maori Wars New Zealand was divided and dispirited. Under the federal constitution of 1855 the provinces controlled their own revenues, with the result that those which had been fought over in the North Island were insolvent while those in the South Island, especially the gold-mining provinces, were prosperous. A belated triumph for the settlers over the Maori interest was the transference of the seat of government from Auckland to Wellington, at the centre of the group of islands, in 1865.

The administration of Sir William Fox, formed in 1868, was pledged to stop the war and to initiate a policy of public works. His right-hand man was a young Jewish journalist named Julius Vogel (1835–99), who had come out to Dunedin by way of the Australian goldfields. In 1870 Vogel, as Colonial Treasurer, came forward with an audacious plan for developing roads, railways and immigration by means of a national loan of £10,000,000 to be secured upon the public lands. At that time the white population of New Zealand was less than 250,000. He succeeded in obtaining from the British government a guarantee for the first instalment of £1,000,000 for constructing trunk railways in both islands. Vogel was a clever financier and a sound administrator, and would have cut a better figure in history if the later years of his public career (1869–87) had not been marked by world-wide depression and restriction of trade. He continued to urge his policy of public borrowing, which left the country over-capitalised. As in Canada the railway programme proved more expensive than he expected, so that the main trunk lines were not completed until 1908.

Vogel had much in common with Sir John A. Macdonald who was carrying out a similar policy of national development in Canada, and both men modelled themselves upon Disraeli. But the difference between New Zealand and Canada was the tendency of all progressive administrations in New Zealand towards State Socialism. Vogel inaugurated a State Life Insurance Office in 1869 and a Public Trustee's Department in 1872; and simplified land transfer by introducing from Australia the Torrens system of registering land-titles. Among his unrealised ideals was that of forest conservation which the New Zealanders, to their cost, undertook far too late. A strong imperialist, he pressed in vain for the annexation of Samoa, when visiting England in 1873, and succeeded in obtaining an Act enabling the Australasian colonies to form a customs union. He was knighted in 1875. From this period of colonial co-operation and improved communications dates the submarine cable from New Zealand to Australia (1876), the subsidised service of mail-steamers to San Francisco, and the two steamship companies which have contributed so much to New Zealand's strength. The New Zealand Shipping Company (1873) carried colonial produce direct to the London docks and brought back emigrants. The Union Steamship Company, connecting all the Australasian ports with fast modern ships (1875), made Dunedin for many years the commercial capital of New Zealand. Dunedin was also the cultural capital, the first of the New Zealand cities to equip itself with a university college (1869).

In all these schemes of development Vogel took a hand, in spite of grave disabilities. In middle age he became deaf and so crippled that he was wheeled into the House in a bath-chair, but still remained indispensable. Though at first a 'provincialist' he changed his mind and, when serving as premier in 1873, launched the campaign which destroyed the provincial governments. Their control of the public lands obstructed his national policy.

The struggle over the provincial system recalled to public life a figure from the past heroic age of New Zealand. Sir George Grey (1812–98), since his dismissal by the Colonial Office in 1868, had been obliged to retire on pension. Returning to New Zealand he established himself in a handsome house on the little island of Kawau near Auckland. In this idyllic retreat he lived for twenty years as an elder statesman of the Empire, holding somewhat the same place in the public estimation as, fifty years later, was held by General Smuts. The range of his knowledge of books and men and countries was immense. No globe-trotter visited Auckland without paying his respects at Sir George's island. He had been the pupil of Whateley, the lifelong friend of Carlyle, the intimate of Selwyn in New Zealand and of Colenso in South Africa. He corresponded with Livingstone about evidences of Hellenistic exploration in Central Africa, and quite confounded the geologist Lyell by his superior knowledge of palaeoliths, having been wounded by one in a fight with an Australian black-fellow. As a collector of Polynesian lore he was one of the founders of the new science of anthropology. As a booklover he had founded the Cape-town Library and was forming another collection for the library of his beloved Auckland. He was above all a liberal imperialist with unrivalled knowledge of the colonies. He had explored north-west Australia, restored the finances of South Australia, governed New Zealand despotically as a Crown Colony, attempted to federate South Africa, provided New Zealand with a liberal constitution and, in all these capacities, had hectored and harassed the Colonial Office. Like Durham before him Grey, had tender spots. Both were quarrelsome and overbearing as colleagues though always courteous in manner. The sentiment of reverent loyalty which both men felt towards the person of Queen Victoria is an important characteristic of each. The Crown itself, not the Colonial Office, was the true link that made a United Empire.

When it was proposed to destroy the federal constitution which Grey himself had devised, he came forth from retirement to defend his handiwork. The province of Auckland elected him Superintendent (as the chief executive officer was called) and the city of Auckland elected him to Parliament (1875). He spoke of 'fighting to the death' for his province and appealed in vain to the Secretary of State. The financial interests of the richer provinces prevailed and in 1876 the loose federation of provinces was converted into a unitary state. Under New Zealand's flexible constitution this fundamental change could be made by a simple act of the legislature without reference to the British Parliament. Local government was devolved upon a multitude of county councils and other elective bodies which are perhaps too numerous for economy. Though the provinces were abolished, local rivalry

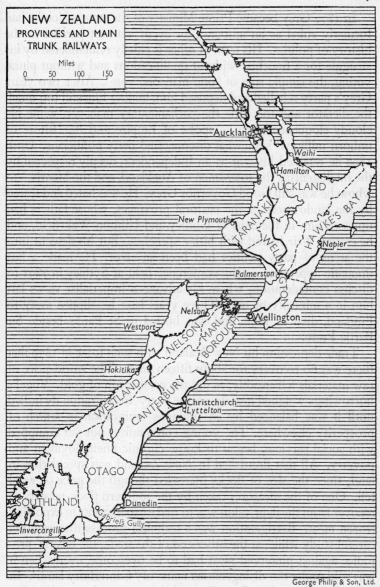

NEW ZEALAND
PROVINCES AND MAIN
TRUNK RAILWAYS

Miles
0   50   100   150

Auckland

Waihi

Hamilton

AUCKLAND

New Plymouth

TARANAKI

WELLINGTON

HAWKE'S BAY

Napier

Palmerston

Nelson

Wellington

Westport

NELSON

MARLBOROUGH

Hokitika

WESTLAND

CANTERBURY

Christchurch

Lyttelton

OTAGO

SOUTHLAND

Dunedin

Gabriel's Gully

Invercargill

George Philip & Son, Ltd.

Map 25

still remains strong, especially between the four larger provincial
centres, Auckland, Wellington, Christchurch (Canterbury Province), and Dunedin (Otago Province).

In 1877 Grey became Prime Minister of the state which he had formerly ruled as an autocrat, an event without parallel in the history of politics. His term of office is chiefly remembered by his struggle for a franchise without qualifications and without plural voting, the simple rule of 'one man one vote'. After two years Grey's party rebelled and deposed him, finding him still too much the dictator and too little the parliamentary manager, while his cloudy eloquence when he spoke of Empire and the 'future of unborn millions' somewhat disconcerted petty politicians. Until 1890 he retained his seat as an independent, deeply respected by the intelligentsia, the townsmen of Auckland, and the Maoris—to whom he was still Good Governor Grey. He was hated and feared by the landowners of the pastoral provinces, whose fathers had opposed him in the days of Godley and Gibbon Wakefield, and he earned their hatred with bitter speeches. But his descent into the arena of party politics had been an error. He made a last dramatic appearance at the conference held at Sydney in 1891 to discuss confederation, where his advanced imperialist views left him in a minority of one. Three years later he slipped away to England, died in 1898, and was buried in St Paul's beside Sir Bartle Frere.

Trade depression hit New Zealand with such force in 1879 that there was no recovery for about fifteen years. The world-price of raw materials fell steadily, as did the production of gold. Vogel's borrowings weighed heavily on the state. Immigration dwindled until it was balanced by an ominous emigration in search of prosperity elsewhere. The young community, not yet equipped with social services, began to know chronic unemployment and poverty. All that flourished in New Zealand was speculation in land, since the size of flocks increased though the price of wool fell. One of the measures taken by the southern flock-masters to recover from the depression was to make experiments in exporting frozen meat. Refrigeration was a technical process that required careful study while, at the other end of the trade, the buyers' prejudice against preserved meat had to be overcome, even when it was sold under the disingenuous name of 'Canterbury lamb'. In 1882 the sailing-ship *Dunedin* carried a cargo of mutton in her freezing-chambers from Port Chalmers (Dunedin) to London, where it was sold for 6½d. a pound, £1900 in all. By 1886, the export of frozen mutton fetched £400,000, by 1890 £1,000,000.

But Canterbury lamb was raised, fattened, frozen and marketed in a large way by prosperous runholders and merchants, without much direct benefit to the urban unemployed. It was the landowner's province, Canterbury, that produced the left-wing reaction in politics.

From 1886 until 1912 the Liberal Party held office in New Zealand with a progressive policy of state intervention. Its strongest man was Richard John Seddon (1845–1906) who became Prime Minister in 1893. Lancashire born, he had emigrated to the goldfields as a boy, first to Victoria then to the west coast of New Zealand where he took to provincial politics as a supporter of Sir George Grey. Rugged, forceful and unscrupulous, he mastered his little world, the small-town wage-earners of an isolated colony. To them he was 'King Dick' and a match for any monarch in the courts of Europe. He had little schooling and no social graces, and he made no secret of his intention to stand by his friends. 'It is unreasonable and unnatural', he said, 'to expect the government to look with the same kindly eye on districts returning members opposed to the government as on those which returned government supporters', and on that principle he spent the public money. Yet this favouritism (which has been practised by prouder monarchs) was the worst that can be told of him. While he exercised his political shrewdness and driving power in managing the House and the constituencies, his two lieutenants, Mackenzie and Pember Reeves, carried out a series of reforms that drew the attention of every student of politics. They were lucky in enjoying a period of trade recovery.

John M'Kenzie (1836–1901), Minister of Lands, was a dispossessed crofter from Ross-shire who nourished a Celtic passion for settling the people on the land. By his two Land Acts of 1892 he instituted a general principle of granting Crown lands to genuine occupiers on a lease-in-perpetuity at a fixed rental, and he took authority to buy up large estates for subdivision among small cultivators. At the same time a graduated land-tax was imposed, bearing heavily on unimproved land and on absentee landlords. The government also undertook to advance cash to settlers on mortgage at a low rate of interest. About 120 great estates were acquired and reallotted on lease to 3000 settlers. In 1893 there were 45,000 holders cultivating 10,000,000 acres. Ten years later there were 65,000 holders cultivating rather more than 13,000,000 acres. The Canterbury aristocracy showed great powers of resistance against M'Kenzie's policy of breaking up the great estates. Many of them paid their taxes, improved their land and maintained their social pre-eminence. But a further change began in the nature of New Zealand farming. Refrigeration was applied to the dairying industry which, unlike sheep-farming, suits the small man. Dairy-farming did much to develop the North Island, so long held in stagnation by war and poverty. In 1906 it drew level with the South Island and now far surpasses it in population and in wealth. Though many extensive sheep-stations remain, the typical New Zealand farmer (the 'cow-cockie') now milks fifty or a hundred cows daily on land leased from the government. Fat lambs and dairy cows require good pasture so that imported grasses have quite changed the character of New Zealand farming and the appearance of its landscape. Grass-seed grown for export has been a useful subsidiary in some states of the world market.

The relative changes in value (in thousands of pounds sterling) of the exports from New Zealand of wool, meat and dairy produce are as follows:

	1883	1893	1903	1913	1923	1943
Wool	3014	3775	4041	8058	10,905	10,000 (approx.)
Frozen meat	118	1085	3197	4450	9013	10,000 (approx.)
Butter and cheese	49	355	1513	3832	17,559	23,000 (approx.)

Exports of grain, which were worth more than £1,000,000 in 1883, shrank in these years almost to nothing. Exports of gold which exceeded £2,000,000 in 1903 also declined rapidly thereafter.

William Pember Reeves (1857–1932), Minister of Labour, was the son of an early settler and the fine flower of the Canterbury tradition, a scholar and a gentleman. He provided the intellectual stimulus to the social-democratic programme, of which he was the historian. If for nothing else he would be remembered as the author of *The Long White Cloud*, the best descriptive account of New Zealand or of any colony. After a short political career he went to London as High Commissioner, and later became Director of the London School of Economics and a prominent member of the Fabian Society.

New Zealand in 1890 was a backward country in respect of social legislation. Its one advanced public service was free secular and compulsory education at the primary stage, which dated from

1877. In a few years Reeves introduced a code of legislation which made New Zealand the model social-democracy. He began with factory laws, providing better conditions of labour than were enjoyed in any other country, but his fame rests on Compulsory Arbitration in Industrial Disputes (1894). Trade unions were obliged to register themselves and refer disputes to conciliation boards, with a right of appeal to the Court of Arbitration. Similarly employers were prevented from 'locking out' their workers by the same obligation. At first the Court was viewed with hostility by the employers and welcomed by the trade unions. After some years, as Ramsay MacDonald and other critics had foretold, the wage-earners found that compulsory arbitration restricted their freedom with the result that a left-wing labour movement, in opposition to the registered unions, appeared.

Seddon's administration also granted a non-contributory pension to the aged, and the right of voting to women. Female suffrage was closely involved with the so-called Temperance Movement which agitated New Zealand for many years, perhaps with good reason since drunkenness was reported by many early travellers to be the national vice. In order to secure the support of the Women's Temperance Society, Seddon instituted a referendum on the prohibition of strong liquors, to be held whenever there was a general election. This triennial contest made a strange distraction from normal party politics. Until 1919 the proportion of votes cast for prohibition steadily increased and thereafter declined without having (as yet) secured an effectual majority.

The beginnings of a national health service also date from Seddon's term of office. Their interest does not lie in administrative measures but in the record of New Zealand as the healthiest country in the world, due largely to the climate, the food and the absence of grinding poverty. The low death-rate and especially the low death-rate of infants (twenty-five per thousand in 1946) may be ascribed to the care of babies and nursing mothers according to the principles of Sir F. Truby King (1858–1938), a Dunedin doctor and one of the chief benefactors of our age. His methods have been adopted all over the world.

Seddon's visits to London for the colonial conferences of 1897 and 1902 were remarkable for his exuberant imperialism. His determination to urge the dubious policy of federating the Empire and to outstrip the other colonies in demonstrations of loyalty

were somewhat embarrassing to the other delegates. He was the
first colonial premier to despatch troops to the Boer War. In 1906
at the end of a visit to Australia, he sent a telegram to his cabinet
colleagues with the characteristic message: 'Leaving to-night for
God's own Country', and died suddenly on the voyage. He had
not lived to see the consummation of New Zealand's nationality
by its formal elevation to the status of a dominion (26 September
1907). Though the change of style made no difference in the realm
of constitutional law it would have gratified his pride.

After the death of Seddon a weaker Liberal administration remained in office under Sir Joseph Ward until 1912, when it was
replaced by the (right-wing) 'Reform' party which retained
power, either separately or as part of a coalition, until 1935. The
trend of New Zealand politics was not violently altered. The small
farmer's vote was the deciding factor in each election and the
national policy was tempered by growing indebtedness. Both
the payment for exported produce and the loans for development
depended on the London market. Manufacturing industries were
mildly encouraged by modest tariffs, but they protected secondary industries such as woollen mills, cheese factories and freezing
works which were developed directly from the primary products
of the land. Having small mineral resources, other than gold,
New Zealand has not developed the heavy industries.

Seddon's land-laws were modified to meet the desire of the
small farmers to acquire the freehold of their land on easy terms;
his Arbitration Laws were modified to meet the growing opposition of left-wing labour. About the year 1907 a new type of trade
unionism began to appear in the mining industries and among the
dockyard workers. They rejected arbitration and the registered
craft unions, and organised national industrial unions which attempted to combine into the New Zealand Federation of Labour
(1909), known as the 'Red Feds'. The doctrine behind this
revolutionary movement was American, borrowed from the
Industrial Workers of the World (I.W.W.), and Syndicalist in
type. The pure Marxian Communism of the Third International
made but slight progress in New Zealand. After several disputes
which displayed a rising ill-temper, a general strike of miners and
waterside-workers was attempted in 1913. It was promptly and
rather harshly suppressed by the government as an illegal activity
which defied the Arbitration Laws. It proved that the organised

proletariat in New Zealand was a tiny minority easily dominated by the farmers who supported the government.

In the following year domestic troubles were forgotten at the outbreak of the first German War. New Zealand had no foreign policy beyond faithful support of the British Crown. 'When the Empire was at war, New Zealand was at war.'

In the years of prosperity after 1896 and before the shadow of the Great Wars fell upon the world, New Zealand with its liberal constitution, law-abiding people, fertile soil and healthy climate was the happiest of lands. If ever men have drawn near to the Utopia of the philosophers it was in this farmers' democracy, a society without a millionaire and without a depressed class of paupers. Visitors from a vaster world, with deeper lights and shades, found New Zealand dull and provincial. Yet they took account there of a philosopher-statesman, an active philanthropist, a scientific genius, and a prose-writer of acute sensibility. A young nation of a million people in a virgin land has not done badly if in a single generation it can produce the varied talents of Pember Reeves, Truby King, Ernest Rutherford and Katherine Mansfield.

10. SOUTH AFRICA, 1852–76

THE twenty-five years between the Sand River Convention (1852) and the first annexation of the Transvaal (1877) are a comparatively tranquil period in South African history. Tolerably friendly relations existed between the two British colonies and the two Boer republics under the general guidance of Her Majesty's High Commissioner. But something new and troublesome was always cropping up and Africa was still the grave of reputations. Armed and warlike nations of the Bantu guarded their independence and tried to guard their land in many areas, looking to the High Commissioner with varying degrees of sincerity and hope, as their protector or ally against land-hungry Europeans. The Bantu frontier in the eastern province of Cape Colony, the fertile pastures at the foot of the mountains of Basutoland, the blood-stained country of the Zulus were always in dispute, always likely to breed war. In the republics the commandos fought many small campaigns; in the colonies British regular troops were always on active service, a great expense to the British Treasury. The

Colonial Office, goaded by complaints from the Treasury, was for limiting our liability. Had we any real interest in South Africa beyond Table Bay and Simonstown? It produced no staple crop to compare with Australian wool or West Indian sugar. But all who knew the country saw that liability could not be limited. We were deeply committed, through treaties with the natives, through the activity of the missionaries, through the settlements of British emigrants in the two colonies, and through the geographical fact that the hinterland is one vast country without natural boundaries. It was already infiltrated by Boers, Britons and protected natives, all alike regardless of the hypothetical frontiers. Men of vision foresaw in the 1850's that the whole land must some day be united either into an Afrikaner republic or into some sort of federal union under the British Crown, alternative and equally ennobling conceptions. The *voortrekkers* had dreamed of an Afrikaner Republic; the first proposal for a federation within the British Empire came from Sir George Grey, who had just equipped New Zealand with a federal constitution. In the Colony, an elective assembly had been instituted, with a liberal franchise. There was a property qualification but 'no distinction of class or colour'.

After a short vacation in England, Grey arrived at the Cape as Governor in December 1854, still a young man of forty-two years of age. The frontier province had been separated from the Colony under the name of British Kaffraria (1847), a savage country without revenue, administration or white inhabitants. Showing his usual skill Grey conjured out of the Colonial Office a grant-in-aid[1] of £40,000 a year with which to begin the work of civilisation. As in New Zealand his plan was to treat the native chiefs with respect but not to enhance their authority. He employed them as government officers on a salary which he could stop if they misbehaved. He blarneyed them, dominated them and bent them to his purpose. Roadmaking with hired native labour would bring trade, industry and civilisation into the country; industrial schools were founded, and hospitals where true science was to show the falsity of witch-doctoring. He was a patron of missionaries and especially of the Presbyterians at the Lovedale Institution (founded 1841), now so well known to all friends of the African peoples.

[1] When the grant was terminated in 1865, the government of Cape Colony was persuaded to take over British Kaffraria as a dependency.

But African tribesmen were not like his favourite Maoris. The Xosa tribes were frenzied by a strange superstition throughout the summer of 1856–7. A prophetess had foretold that on 18 February 1857 a world-shaking cataclysm was to bring in the golden age when the white men were to be driven into the sea. Meanwhile the people were to neglect their crops, kill their cattle and live on faith. The unfortunate natives took her advice with the result that perhaps two-thirds of the population of Kaffraria died of famine in 1857. There was little the Governor could do to help them. Grey was nothing if not resourceful and, observing that the frontier was no longer endangered, he sent away his troops to fight the Indian mutineers. When the wave of unrest among the tribes died down, in 1858, there were no more 'Kaffir Wars' for twenty years.

Capetown owes much to Grey's activity and benevolence. In his time railway construction in the colony and the harbour-works at Table Bay were first begun. The contract for a line of mail-steamers was taken up when he was Governor (1856). He persuaded the new Cape legislature to vote money for the importation of emigrants selected in the right proportions by sex and age, with the result that 8000 British settlers were brought in between 1858 and 1861. At the same time he supported a scheme whereby about 800 indigent children were brought from Holland and placed with Boer families. At the conclusion of the Crimean War he took over the King's German Legion of mercenaries, planting them as military settlers on the frontier, but when the Mutiny began, many of them were hastily withdrawn and sent to India. A private arrangement for bringing German peasant settlers from Hamburg was stopped by the Colonial Office, after Grey had committed himself to heavy expense. He paid the balance out of his own pocket and recovered the money from the settlers at their convenience. They contributed to the population of the new settlements at East London and King William's Town ("King").

Both officially and privately Grey was a benefactor to learning. In his roving adventurous life he had yet found time to collect medieval MSS., editions of the classics and numerous works on ethnology and folklore, published and unpublished. These he gave on his departure to the South African Public Library, which by his gifts came to hold a place among the world's important collections; and immediately set to work to form a new collection. He founded a high-school, the Grey Institute, at Port Elizabeth,

and actively supported the foundation of the college at Stellenbosch (1859), the main source of Afrikaner culture. 'I know no
people', he said, 'richer in public and in private virtues than the
Boers.'

Though the Orange Free State had been released from imperial
control, Grey succeeded in maintaining a friendly social connexion.
He provided the impoverished little republic with the funds for
its first educational institution which was named, after him, Grey
College, Bloemfontein (1856). After the Sand River Convention
the Church of England had withdrawn from the Free State. The
clergy now returned and Bloemfontein became the seat of an
Anglican bishopric (1863). Such were the terms of friendship between the Free State and the Colony that in 1858 he put forward
a proposal for a federal union of South Africa, with the direct
support and encouragement of the Free State government. In
1859 the reply came from the Secretary of State (Sir E. B. Lytton,
the novelist) in the form of an indignant snub. Her Majesty's
Government would in no circumstances renew her sovereignty
over the Orange Free State. Like several other good governors of
the Cape, Grey was recalled in disgrace, though it is fair to add
that, as was his habit, he had flouted the Colonial Office on many
occasions. No sooner had he arrived in England than a change of
government swept him again into favour. Palmerston's Colonial
Secretary, the Duke of Newcastle, sent him back to his post at the
Cape on the understanding that he would not meddle with so
dangerous a topic as federation. His second tour of office had
hardly begun when, in 1861, he was again transferred to New Zealand to cope with the Maori Wars.

At the Cape, progress was marked by public works, education and increased trade (exports in 1853, £733,000; in 1863,
£1,996,000—two-thirds of it being wool). The colony did not
take the expected step forward from representative to responsible
government until 1872, since the colonists were unwilling to
accept responsibility for their own defence and for administering
the populous native areas.

A quite different course of development was to be seen in
Natal. The Secretary of State said in 1846 that Natal had been
annexed solely in the interest of the native races, to be 'a centre
whence the blessings of civilisation and Christianity may be
diffused'. Two pioneers, Sir Theophilus Shepstone (1817–93) and

Bishop Colenso, in their respective ways devoted themselves to this task.

Shepstone spent thirty years (1846–76), as a native agent and later as Secretary for Native Affairs, among the tribes of Natal over whom he acquired strong personal authority, using the method which in the twentieth century is called indirect rule. He had little money to spend and few reliable assistants. Native law and customs were preserved and were, within reason, administered through the chiefs, by a few resident magistrates. Polygamy and *lobola*, on which the whole social system was based, were permitted and legalised. Even the frequent murders arising from the native fear of witchcraft were leniently treated. Tribal influence was so much encouraged that detribalised natives who had fled into British territory for refuge formed themselves into tribes. The native population of Natal steadily increased under the mild British rule. Shepstone's intention to form a large compact native protectorate was vetoed by Governor Grey, who proposed to encourage habits of industry by interspersing the tribal reserves in blocks among areas settled by Europeans. The opportunity of earning wages by regular labour was, he thought, the greatest of blessings which could be conferred upon the natives. On the whole they preferred idleness and poverty.

To the north of Natal, across the River Tugela, lay the land of the ferocious Zulus who abstained from hostility to the white man as long as they remembered Dingaans' Day. A new prince of the House of Chaka and Dingaan was rising to eminence in their internal wars. By 1856 he was master of Zululand and in 1872 Shepstone installed him as King of the Zulus; his name was Cetewayo.[1]

Until 1849 there were few white settlers in Natal. An emigration was then set on foot by a speculator named J. C. Byrnes who eventually went bankrupt. Having some partial understanding of the Wakefield plan he persuaded government to let him finance the selling of land in Natal in order to use the funds for sending out emigrants, but without provision for survey, public works, or for the concentration which the Colonial Reformers thought essential. Between 1849 and 1851, while 4000 emigrants went to Natal, few took up land. Many departed to Cape Colony while some went up-country as traders or transport-riders. The white

[1] Pronounced approximately as 'Ketch'wỳo'.

population of the colony when representative government was granted in 1856 was thought to be over 7000, most of them in the hot seaport of Durban, a bad harbour before it was developed, or in the pleasant little capital town of Pietermaritzburg up in the hills. They were a mere handful, among natives twenty times as numerous. The colony was still in its infancy; the exports in 1854 were worth no more than £40,000, the largest item being ivory. Sugar-canes from Mauritius, first planted in 1847, met with no commercial success until the legislature authorised the entry of Indian coolies, in 1856. By a law of 1875 they were allowed to settle in Natal when their indentures were out.

Pietermaritzburg, a social centre, a garrison and a cathedral town, produced an ecclesiastical scandal which resounded through the Empire. In 1854 Dr J. W. Colenso (1814–83), like Selwyn and Marsden a Johnian and a scholar, arrived as the first bishop. His name was already known to the world, and may still be remembered by the elderly, as the author of many mathematical school-books. A man of enlightened views, he formed an immediate friendship with Sir George Grey, a partnership like that of Grey and Selwyn in New Zealand. Natal was a missionary diocese and Colenso's work lay among the natives rather than among the few Europeans. His sympathies were engaged by the Bantu whose life and culture he appreciated. It was a shock to the straitlaced when he allowed native converts to live in respectable polygamy. Conversion was not to begin with divorce and repudiation. Among a hundred activities he found time to contribute to the 'higher' criticism of the Bible with a profound display of liberal learning which alarmed the orthodox. When he published a book denying the Mosaic authorship of the Pentateuch he was disowned and excommunicated by his metropolitan, the Bishop of Cape-town (1863).[1] Colenso ignored the ban, on the grounds that it was *ultra vires*. An appeal went to the Privy Council where, so far as there was any case, judgment went in favour of Colenso (20 March 1865) on the grounds that the Church of England is 'not a part of the constitution in any colonial settlement, nor can its authorities...claim to be recognised...otherwise than as

---

[1] Older readers will remember the somewhat similar schism in 1913, between the Bishops of Zanzibar and Mombasa after a Church Conference at Kikuyu. It convulsed the Church and agitated Society, but had no constitutional significance.

members of a voluntary association'. This judicial award had the effect of finally disestablishing the Anglican Churches in all the self-governing colonies, where episcopal authority had raised many constitutional problems in the previous hundred years. Four new colonial sees (Adelaide; Newcastle, N.S.W.; Melbourne; Capetown) had been created together in 1847, with an endowment from Miss Burdett-Coutts the millionairess, in the general belief that these bishops were public officials; they were so regarded by the Colonial Office.

The Colenso judgment did not, however, solve the local problem in Natal, where a schism persisted for years between Colenso's followers and those of the Bishop of Capetown. Saintly, learned and forceful, he remained an active figure in colonial life and a mighty champion of native rights.

The early history of the Orange Free State[1] is largely taken up with their wars against the Basutos who, in their knot of mountainous country, were welded into a nation by Moshesh, the wisest of the Bantu kings. Though not averse to fighting, he preferred conciliation and, by diplomacy, preserved for his people the independence and the territory they hold to-day. He was on good terms with a succession of High Commissioners whom he frequently asked to take the Basuto people under the protection of the Queen, rather as a counterpoise to Boer influence than from love of the British. The most powerful agents of civilisation in Basutoland were French Protestant missionaries whose efforts were purely altruistic. Although expelled by the Boers after one of the Basuto wars, on the accusation of conspiracy, there is little evidence of their taking any part in politics. They returned and are still active in Basutoland.

Sir George Grey twice intervened, in 1855 and 1858, between the Basutos and the Orange Free State. After a few years of peace, a far more serious war broke out in 1865. The Boers exhausted their resources in bringing Moshesh to terms, while appealing alternately for help to the Transvaal and to the Governor of the

---

[1] Properly speaking the Orange River Sovereignty from 1848 to 1854. Later, from 1900 to 1910 it was known as Orange River Colony. I have, for convenience, used one name throughout. Similarly the Transvaal should properly be called the South African Republic from 1857 to 1877 and again from 1884 to 1900.

Cape, in his capacity as High Commissioner. The decisive intervention was made by Sir Philip Wodehouse (1811–87) a stiff,
upright man who was transferred to South Africa after governing
British Honduras and British Guiana, and knew the ways of small
struggling republics as neighbours. But neither Free State
burghers nor Basuto tribesmen adhered to the settlement he imposed. Basuto cattle-raids, which Moshesh could not prevent, always provided pretexts for Boer encroachments. In January 1868
Wodehouse persuaded the Duke of Buckingham, Colonial Secretary in Derby's administration, to authorise, reluctantly, the
annexation of Basutoland. It was proclaimed on 12 March 1868,
the first of the long series of protectorates which were to form the
new colonial empire. With like reluctance the Cape government
made itself responsible for the administration (1871), upon the
method known later as indirect rule. The old chief, Moshesh,
died in 1870, at a great age.

Though the Basuto did not regain the disputed territory on the
plain, their hill-country was now secured, to the disgust of the
Free State burghers who felt that, but for the British, they would
have brought the Basuto to submission at last. A deputation from
the Free State to protest against the annexation was refused a
hearing by Buckingham in London.

In the eyes of Downing Street these struggles were irrelevant
and petty, battles of frogs and mice. Cape Colony was a small
unprofitable province; the republics were unimportant. Our sole
concern was to be rid of them. But when, in 1867, a child was
found at play with a toy which proved to be a diamond worth
£500, the picture changed. By 1869, a rush of 40,000 or 50,000
diggers (see chapter IX, 4, page 491), mostly British citizens, had
invaded the district known as Griqualand West, on the lower
reaches of the Vaal, near its confluence with the Orange River.
This large, loosely-defined, territory had been allotted, thirty
years earlier, to a tribe of Griquas, who thus conceived themselves
to be under British protection. But, by the Sand River Convention (1852), the British had renounced all authority over natives
located beyond the Vaal and, by the Bloemfontein Convention
(1854), they had abdicated territorial sovereignty in the region between the Vaal and the Orange Rivers. Their relation to the five
or six hundred nomadic Griquas was indeed obscure. Since no
boundaries, other than the Vaal River, had been defined in the two

Conventions, the western frontiers of the Transvaal and the Orange Free State were wide open.

During the 1850's this empty, arid, country had become celebrated by the labours of the missionaries, especially of Livingstone (see chapter XI, 2, page 647) whose exploits had fired the imagination of the English-speaking world. The tale of an attack by Boer filibusters on Livingstone's mission station, in 1853, was well-known. His country was the comparatively fertile strip of land that fringed the Kalahari Desert. Along it lay the 'Missionaries' Road' (or rather the two alternative roads) to the north, the gateway to Central Africa. One of the first to gauge the importance of the Missionaries' Road was David Arnot, a bold speculator from Capetown, who made himself agent for several native chiefs and especially for Nicholas Waterboer, Chief of the Griquas. Long before the discovery of diamonds, he was asserting Waterboer's claims and, when Waterboer's country revealed these new treasures, his time was ripe.

Each of the two republics sent commissioners to the diamond-fields, who set up administrations as at a goldfield, with some difficulty, as reports of new finds attracted diggers here and there. Along the Vaal River the Transvaal government attempted to give a monopoly to three favoured speculators, with the result that the protesting diggers proclaimed a new republic. Farther south some speculators from Port Elizabeth acquired from its owner, De Beers, the farm called 'Foresight' which proved to hold the richest claims. A magistrate from the Free State was sent to officiate at the De Beers site which at first was known merely as the 'New Rush' (July 1871).

Waterboer's case was very ably presented by David Arnot who was backed by Richard Southey, the Colonial Secretary at the Cape. So powerful was their reasoning that they persuaded the Acting High Commissioner, General G. C. Hay, to send magistrates to the disputed area. Hay's report to the Colonial Office was to the effect that the Orange Free State government was attempting to expropriate the Griquas, the darling tribe of the London Missionary Society. In May 1871 Gladstone's Colonial Secretary, Lord Kimberley, authorised the annexation of Griqualand West on two conditions, that Waterboer should desire it, and that the Cape Government should undertake the expense of administration. By this time a new High Commissioner had

THE DIAMOND-FIELDS

Miles

0   25   50   75   100

R. Limpopo

Kolobeng

TRANSVAAL

Mafeking

GOSHEN

Potchefstroom

The Keate Award

Vryburg

STELLALAND

R. Harts

Kurumano

Taungs

R. Vaal

ORANGE FREE STATE

Klipdrift

GRIQUALAND WEST

Kimberley

Winburg

Griquatown

R. Modder

Bloemfontein

R. Orange

BASUTOLAND

R. Orange

CAPE COLONY

George Philip & Son, Ltd.

Map 26. The Diamond-fields, the Keate Award, and the Missionaries' Roads to the north.

arrived, Sir Henry Barkly (1815–98), who had no sympathy with the Boers. A House of Commons man, he had been Governor of Victoria and knew something of diggers' democracy. He came to South Africa to institute responsible government at the Cape and was determined to settle the question of the diamond-fields.

Barkly persuaded the Transvaal government to refer the boundary question to arbitration before the popular Lieutenant-Governor of Natal, R. W. Keate, who had satisfied them well in a previous arbitration. Keate's Award (October 1871), scrupulously following the evidence presented, gave the whole of the disputed area north of the Vaal to independent native tribes, and excluded the Transvaalers entirely from the Missionaries' Road. Barkly accepted this as evidence of the general propriety of the case put forward by David Arnot and declared the annexation of Griqualand West (November 1871) without more ado.

His next endeavour was to introduce responsible government in Cape Colony, of which (Sir) J. C. Molteno (1814–86) became the first Prime Minister, in April 1872. Politics at the Cape resolved themselves into a struggle between the Afrikaners of the Western Province, who were liberal in tradition and opposed to imperial expansion, and the English of Port Elizabeth and Grahamstown, who favoured commercial development and a forward policy. Molteno, though English-born, was a westerner and stoutly resisted responsibility for the hinterland. For two years more the diamond-fields were ruled, California-fashion, by diggers' committees, until Barkly was obliged to set up Griqualand West as a separate Crown Colony (January 1873), with its capital at the New Rush, renamed Kimberley.

Griqualand was an undeveloped area of 17,000 square miles in which there were 150 Boer households lawfully settled as well as the gypsy Griquas. The diggers received the annexation without enthusiasm. Its first effect was to equalise natives and Europeans at law, so that liquor and guns were sold at random to the hordes of turbulent natives who had flocked to the diggings, natives who were as disorderly after their manner as the white diggers after theirs. Illicit diamond-buying (I.D.B.) flourished. As for Waterboer, in whose interest the Colonial Office acted, his rights were soon bought out for a pension of £1000 a year which he invested in liquor.

The Keate Award and Barkly's subsequent actions exasperated both republics. In the unstable Transvaal, President Pretorius was unseated in favour of a new President, who repudiated the award and the arbitration. Frustrated in the west he turned towards the east, searching for an outlet to the sea, somewhere clear of British territory. President Brand of the Free State accepted the new frontier under protest. When, at last, a land-court sat to disentangle the Kimberley properties the records nullified the claim of Waterboer to the land between the Orange and the Vaal, thus justifying the claim of the Free State to Kimberley.

The Boers were exasperated by British policy. Governor Wodehouse, an official who took the Downing Street point-of-view, had protected their enemies, the Basutos. Governor Barkly, a Liberal, had hastened to deprive them of a new source of wealth. What seemed hypocrisy in Gladstone's Liberal government had upheld these two hostile actions in the name of philanthropy. The British government seemed to ignore the Sand River Convention whenever a question of advancing the British frontier arose. Even the patient President J. C. Brand (1823–88), a friend of the British and once a supporter of union, was infuriated. The case of the Orange Free State was put forward by the Volksraad in a dignified manifesto, to which a very lame reply was given at the Cape. The Volksraad reminded the world that they had been excluded from British protection against their desire. 'In 1854 Her Britannic Majesty withdrew her sovereignty. Few in numbers, we were reluctant to take it over.' The republic had been formed, not by their own intention, but by necessity. Assuming that they were a sovereign people they had learned that the British did not so regard them. No course was left but to register a protest.

In the fourth European state in South Africa, the Transvaal, the organisation was so loose that it hardly deserved the pretentious name, assumed in 1857, of the South African Republic. The 'emigrant farmers' ranged over the Veld occupying land at will, maintaining their simple, hard, adventurous way of life as it had been in the days of the Great Trek, untainted by the modern corruptions which the British called Progress. Every burgher's son was entitled to a free grant of 6000 acres of land which he could appropriate at will in a country without maps or survey. It was not customary in the Transvaal to allot native reserves, but to allow the inhabitants to remain as tenants-at-will on their former holdings where they would provide labour for the newcomers.

The Republic was unruly rather than disorderly. A constitution was made and a capital city, Pretoria (1855), laid out, but no administrative system other than that of the commando and the kerk-session seemed necessary. Schisms arose in the Dutch Reformed Church as in the state. Parties of 'burghers' tended to trek farther out where they sometimes split off into new republics. There were bitter quarrels between rival groups, leading on one occasion (1862) to civil war.

Affairs in the Transvaal came to the notice of the world in 1875. In the uneasy shuffling which led to the partition of Africa, a dispute arose over Delagoa Bay where the British claimed to have annexed a landing-place in 1824, not far from an ancient mouldering Portuguese settlement. The case was put to arbitration before the French President who decided in favour of Portugal (July 1875). In the eyes of the Transvaal government, Delagoa Bay might become a new outlet for their trade to the sea-coast. Their credit, however, was so bad that they could not raise a loan sufficient to build a railway to Delagoa Bay, and their administration was so corrupt that such money as they raised was frittered away, leaving the republic insolvent (1876). Finally the republican commandos were worsted in a war on the eastern frontier against Sekukuni (Secoeceni), a chief who occupied the land through which the railway was to run.

11. SOUTH AFRICA, 1876–81

AFTER twenty years of representative government, Natal made a retrograde step in constitutional development. Shepstone had advised, and Bishop Colenso had protested against, the deposition and imprisonment of a chief named Langalibalele. The Colonial Office intervened by sending out a new Governor, the popular but autocratic General Wolseley, fresh from his triumph in the Ashanti War. 'Longbelly', as Wolseley jocosely called him, was released and the Natal settlers were persuaded, with the help of Wolseley's lavish hospitality, to vote away their own privileges. Like Jamaica, Natal was reduced to Crown Colony status (1875), for the benefit of the blacks rather than the whites.

This resumption of imperial authority was the work of Lord Carnarvon, again Colonial Secretary in Disraeli's administration, and was preliminary to a larger plan. Carnarvon believed that the time had come to federate South Africa, as Canada had been federated in his earlier term of office. While his motive was an enlightened theory of empire, the Tory Party as a whole was more concerned with avoiding the expense of native wars. There is little to show that Disraeli's love of prestige led him on to a policy of expansion in South Africa, nor did he set much store by Carnarvon as a colleague.

The problem was complex. Carnarvon must first persuade the two solvent and progressive states (Cape Colony and the Orange Free State) to come to an agreement, though they had just quarrelled over the diamond-fields. He must next persuade them to underwrite jointly Griqualand, Kaffraria, Basutoland and Natal. He must finally put pressure on the intransigent South African Republic (the Transvaal) to come in on some terms. His first approach, to the government of the Cape was flatly and rudely rejected by Governor Barkly and Premier Molteno. The Cape would undertake no new liabilities, not even the diamond-fields which had slumped owing to over-production and I.D.B. Carnarvon next sent his friend J. A. Froude, the historian, to make a confidential report. Though Froude was sadly disillusioned by what he found in South Africa he did not shake Carnarvon's determination to proceed. A second attempt was made in 1876 when delegates of the provinces were invited to London. Shepstone, who happened to be in London, was flattered by the award of a K.C.M.G. and brought into consultation; Froude, fresh from his South African journey, attended and advised; but the only plenipotentiary was President Brand from the Orange Free State, who was unwilling to discuss federation. He came to London solely to demand compensation for the territory of which he had been deprived, and accepted £90,000, a derisory sum when balanced against the wealth of the diamond-fields, but a comfortable windfall for the impoverished little republic. That, and the trade and currency brought in by the diggers, restored the finances of the Orange Free State which became a thriving farmers' democracy. Though the conference achieved nothing, Carnarvon obtained from Parliament a permissive Act (1877) enabling the South African colonies to federate.

Carnarvon's third attempt was by bold executive action. He sent Shepstone back to Africa with authority to intervene in the affairs of the bankrupt Transvaal where, it was believed, many of the people would welcome a union with the British colonies. Natal and the Transvaal, its hinterland, were to be the nucleus of the federation. At the same time Carnarvon selected as High Commissioner a man of such eminence and experience that he might be expected to do for South Africa what Lord Durham had done for Canada forty years earlier. Sir Bartle Frere (1815–84) had held the highest offices in the government of India with the greatest distinction. Scholar, traveller, diplomat, administrator, he was also an imperialist, a man of liberal views, and a friend of the missionaries. He was surely the man to bring to an end the miserable series of errors which composed the story of South Africa. Like Durham's, his mission failed; he returned to England after three years amid the execrations of English politicians, but with the love and respect of the colonials.

In January 1877 Shepstone went up to Pretoria where he was well received. The President made no stand against him. Having persuaded himself that there was no enthusiasm for the republic, Shepstone declared the annexation of the Transvaal to the British Empire on 12 April 1877. The Union Jack was hoisted at Pretoria by Rider Haggard, then a young man on Shepstone's staff, and later celebrated as the author of *King Solomon's Mines*. Sir Bartle Frere, who had just landed at Capetown, was confronted with the *fait accompli* of annexation. At first it seemed that all was well and this a successful step towards the Union of South Africa. The immediate problem was financial, since much money would be required to give the new colony a decent administration and there was no more than 12s. 5d. in the Transvaal Treasury. Unwilling as the Boers had been to pay taxes to their own republic they paid still less willingly to Shepstone, who proved a careless and incompetent financier. The inevitable grant-in-aid from the British Treasury was soon swallowed up.

Though almost all the officials of the republic took service with the new administration, it was with a bad grace. Among them the lead was taken by Paul Kruger (1825–1904), the hero of the Afrikaner people, whose whole history was typified in his life and exploits. An enormously tall, broad, coarse-featured man, with all the heroic qualities of the frontier and none of the graces of civilisation, he had come north as a boy of ten years old in the Great Trek. His exploits in hunting and in native wars were legendary. He had a deep, sincere conviction that he was called by God to lead his people out of the House of Bondage. Kruger went twice to London to demand the restoration of independence and was snubbed by two successive Secretaries of State.

Unfortunately for Frere, the years 1877 and 1878 were marked by every misfortune. The whole world was sinking deeper into one of the worst of depressions. While war in the Near East threatened to spread, while the London mob shouted and sang jingo songs against Russia, while Disraeli displayed his virtuosity at Berlin, there was neither care nor money for a spirited policy in Africa. These two years were afflicted by drought and famine which meant native unrest on every African frontier. All round the diamond-fields the tribes were up. Sir Bartle Frere was himself engaged in the last of the Kaffir Wars on the eastern frontier while, in the Transvaal, the British were as unsuccessful against Sekukuni as the Boers had been. In the southern summer of 1878–9 a general native rising throughout South Africa was expected. If it came it must be led by Cetewayo who had welded the martial Zulus again into a nation as in Chaka's day, with a standing army of 30,000 men. Since it was Cetewayo's rule that no man might leave the *impi* to marry until he had washed his spear in blood, the Zulus were, to say the least of it, awkward neighbours, as Shepstone well knew.

In the Transvaal the Boers had been encroaching upon Zulu territory and, when a boundary commission gave an award in favour of the Zulus, Frere decided to make it a means of bringing them to a better frame of mind. He sent Cetewayo an ultimatum agreeing to cede the disputed land on the conditions that the bloodthirsty celibate army should be disbanded, that Cetewayo should receive a British Resident, and that he should give his protection to missionaries in Zululand. When Cetewayo declined to answer, Zululand was invaded (January 1879).

The Zulu War might be selected by a satirist as the typical British colonial campaign. We had a respectable cause but presented it so badly that the invasion seemed an outrage. We began light-heartedly with careless tactics that produced a bloody defeat, which might have led to worse things but for the courage of two subalterns with a handful of men. Having brought the war to a successful conclusion by a laborious undistinguished campaign, we then left the country without making a settlement. Three years later we restored the *status quo ante*.

The main force in the invasion included the 24th Regiment (South Wales Borderers), which, as everyone knows, was caught unawares at Isandlhwana and massacred (22 January 1879). Natal then lay open to the Zulu *impis* but for the handful of men guarding the ford of the flooded Tugela river. The defence of Rorke's Drift by Lieutenants Chard and Bromhead with about eighty British soldiers stopped their advance. In these two engagements the Zulus lost 3000 men which took the edge off their keenness. When the various British columns had closed up, the Zulus were totally defeated at Ulundi (June 1879) and, shortly afterwards, Cetewayo was made prisoner. The ill-fortune that dogged these proceedings was completed by the death of the Prince Imperial of France who had accompanied the British as a volunteer. He was imprudently permitted to go on a dangerous reconnaissance and rather pusillanimously abandoned by his comrades in an ambush. Even in republican France this episode did British prestige no good. 'A very remarkable people, the Zulus!' said Disraeli. 'They defeat our generals; they convert our bishops; and they have settled the fate of a great European dynasty.'

Carnarvon had already resigned from Disraeli's tottering administration leaving the grim, cautious economist, Sir Michael Hicks-Beach, at the Colonial Office. Imperialism was again in retreat. Though Frere was held responsible for every error by the Government, and was vilified by the Opposition, he was not yet recalled. Half of his pro-consulate (Natal and the Transvaal) was taken from him in 1879 and given to the ubiquitous Wolseley, as High Commissioner for South-East Africa. Frere accepted the blame and the humiliation with dignity, remaining at his post until Gladstone replaced him, in 1880, by a respectable second-rate official, Sir Hercules Robinson (1824–97), afterwards Lord Rosmead.

Wolseley made the worst possible settlement in Zululand. Having deposed Cetewayo, he broke up the Zulu nation into its thirteen constituent tribes, one of them under an English renegade named John Dunn, and left them in their native barbarity. In 1882 it was thought advisable to restore Cetewayo who was at once plunged into war with a rival backed by Boer filibusters. He died in 1884.

In Basutoland, too, there had been mismanagement. The Cape government had attempted to contribute to the general settlement by disarming the Basutos, who resisted and refused to be disarmed. Next they called in no less a man than General Gordon to reduce these truculent savages; but Gordon was so eccentric as to make it plain that he had more sympathy with the Basutos than with the Cape politicians. In despair they handed back the administration to the imperial government (1884). As an imperial protectorate, Basutoland was well governed, above all when Sir Godfrey Lagden was Resident (1893–1901).

In the Transvaal, Wolseley's genial blustering manner was not effective with the Boers. While he enforced a rigid financial control through an official borrowed from the Treasury, he took no steps to carry out Frere's promise that the Boers should get self-government. He assured them that the 'Union Jack would wave over Pretoria so long as the sun shone and the Vaal flowed to the sea'. Meanwhile the Boers were well aware of the effect of a change of government in London. Gladstone's election speeches at Midlothian, denouncing the whole imperial and foreign policy of the Conservatives, had led them to expect relief when the Liberals should be returned to power. It came as a shock to them when the Queen's speech, in May 1880, declared that it was not the intention of Mr Gladstone's new government to restore the independence of the Transvaal.

On Dingaan's Day (16 December), 1880, the Boers rose by concerted action, proclaiming the revival of the republic. There were British troops in Natal, but only one battalion of the 94th, concentrated in the Transvaal. Marching towards Pretoria in column of route, with the band playing, it was ambushed at Bronkhorst Spruit. When the colonel refused a sudden demand to surrender, 350 of his men were shot down by concealed riflemen. Though deprived of this support two small detachments at Pretoria and Potchefstrom had no difficulty in holding out against Boer commandos. Wolseley had been succeeded as High Commissioner by General Sir George Colley (1835–81) who took the field in person, and thought it best to seize Laing's Nek, the pass through the Drakensberg, with the few hundred British troops at hand. After two unsuccessful skirmishes Colley led a column by night to occupy the commanding height of Majuba Hill. In the morning (27 February 1881) Boer skirmishers climbed the hill and drove the British down in headlong flight with a loss of 280 men. Colley, the High Commissioner, was shot dead on the hilltop. It was but a petty engagement, 550 British against perhaps a thousand Boers, but the news of it rang round the world.

Even before Majuba, Gladstone had changed his mind. He would find a formula for satisfying the Boer demands. Without setting in motion the main body of troops from Natal, Lord Kimberley, again Gladstone's Colonial Secretary, ordered a cessation of hostilities and called a conference at Pretoria (March 1881). The discussions were long and far from edifying. The military member of the Royal Commission wanted strategic safe-guards on the eastern frontier and a face-saving parade through the republic, but was overruled by his colleagues; the Treasury representative, true to the principles of Gladstonian finance, saddled the new state with a considerable share of the old debt, ensuring that its chronic insolvency would be perpetuated. Inde-pendence was indeed restored but 'subject to the suzerainty of Her Majesty', a dangerous phrase that contained the seeds of future trouble. A British Resident was to have a veto over native legislation but no such safeguards were ensured for the liberties of white British subjects. The apparent surrender to force and the vagueness of the conditions aroused bitter feelings of shame and antagonism in England. The irritating restrictions and the parsi-monious financial settlement aroused an equal resentment in the Transvaal. The Pretoria Convention was another link, and not the last, in the chain of errors and tragedies that followed the wrongful annexation of the diamond-fields. A blight lay upon every attempt to bring union to South Africa.

While on the Veld all went awry, the other British Dominions enjoyed two whole generations of busy progress, checked only by the periodic movements of the trade-cycle. The interplay of their party politics led to stronger combinations and larger groupings.

XI

PENETRATION OF AFRICA AND THE ARAB LANDS

Argument: The interior of Africa was quite unknown to Europeans in 1800. British penetration came from three directions, from the old slaving-posts on the West Coast, from the Cape, and from the Arabian Sea, which had long been a sphere of influence of the Indian government.

The exploration of the Niger basin, initiated by philanthropists, was for long unfruitful since West Africa was then the White Man's Grave. The Nile Quest and especially the career of Livingstone laid upon the world a moral obligation to pacify Central Africa and to suppress the Arab slave trade. British reluctance to annex territory, as exemplified in the Abyssinian War of 1867, persisted for some years later.

1. ISLANDS OF THE ARABIAN SEA

THE nineteenth century saw the establishment of British-Indian control over almost all the strategic points in the Arabian Sea. Since the earliest days of the East India Company the Bombay Presidency had been concerned with sea-power along the Persian and Arabian coasts, This expansion reached out, in the 1830's, to meet the expansion of British influence through the disintegrating Turkish dominions; a new factor in what was called the Eastern Question.

Many of the islands festooned from India to Madagascar had come under British authority during the French Wars. A side-issue of the Mysore campaigns had been the submission to the British (1792) of a mainland rajah whose rights extended over the Laccadive Islands. (They were annexed by the government of India after a period of misrule in 1877.) The conquest of Ceylon included the Maldives, whose Moslem sultans were tributary to the Dutch. The remote colony of Mauritius,[1] at that time in the full-

---

[1] A volcanic mountainous island fringed by coral reefs. In extent Mauritius is rather larger than Skye. The climate is mild. Culturally it is bilingual, English and French. Economically it looks to India and has a rupee currency. Imports mostly come from India, exports mostly go to England. Population (1936) 268,000 Indians, 132,000 Europeans and others.

stream of world-affairs, retains like Quebec some features of the French *ancien régime*. The sugar which the French aristocracy still exports to France is no longer cultivated by docile African slaves but by very numerous Hindu immigrants who may yet change the character of the islands. When Mauritius was taken in 1810, numerous groups of coral islands, some inhabited by French creoles, passed with it under British rule: notably the Seychelles, where the French Governor was retained in office after transferring his allegiance to the British; Rodriguez; and the Chagos Islands with the harbour of Diego Garcia, one of the most spacious anchorages in the world. Another of these islands, Réunion, was re-ceded to France after Waterloo.

On the opposite coast the Bombay Marine was often engaged against pirates and slave-traders. From these operations there arose diplomatic relations with several Arab sheikhs who had grasped independence from the enfeebled Turkish Empire. The sheikhs of the Trucial Coast agreed to receive a British political agent in 1820, as did the Sultan of Bahrein. In the Indian Political Department these rulers were oddly described as the 'pacificated chiefs'. (The Trucial Coast virtually became a British Protectorate in 1892; Bahrein in 1895.)

Palmerston's hand in the diplomatic struggle with France and Russia over the affairs of Turkey and Egypt in the 1830's was strengthened by the acquisitions of the Bombay Presidency. His policy was threefold and his three aims were achieved: by breaking down the influence which Russia had acquired over Turkey, by preventing a combination of France and Russia against British influence in the Near East, and by maintaining the Turkish Empire against further disintegration. The British acquisitions on the Arabian coast were not made at the expense of Turkey but with Turkish goodwill in order to prevent their falling into the hands of Mehemet Ali, the rebellious Pasha of Egypt. When a shipwrecked British crew was illtreated and redress refused by the Sheikh of Aden, an expedition was sent from Bombay (1839) to seize this commanding site, which had gained a new importance by the opening of the Overland Mail through Egypt in the previous year. Its value as a coaling-station and as a cable-station steadily increased throughout the century, as is shown by the population which increased from 1000 in 1839 to 44,000 in 1901. (Some inland districts ruled by the Sultan of Socotra were gradually brought into the British sphere and defined as the Aden Protectorate in 1934.)

Routes to the East gave ever-increasing importance to the Arab principalities. The Kuria Muria Islands were ceded to Great Britain for use as a cable-station in 1854. The French were fore-stalled at Perim in the mouth of the Red Sea by a sudden British annexation, in 1857, of this useful island which was regularly used as a coaling-station until 1936. The Sultan of Socotra accepted a British subsidy in 1876 and, ten years later, placed the island under British protection. The Sultan of Kuweit at the head of the Persian Gulf placed himself under British protection in 1899 in order to avoid submission to the Turks; his territory was interesting as a possible terminus for the projected Euphrates railway. The British diplomatic control over Southern Arabia was much enlarged by the War of 1914; the only formal annexation was the island of Kamaran, between Aden and Jidda, which was taken from the Turks and retained as a quarantine post for pilgrims on their way to Mecca in British ships. But all this authority was very lightly exercised and, outside the colony of Aden, the British political agents did little more than to maintain a discreet control over the external affairs of the sultans, some of whom have grown immensely wealthy, by development of oilfields under British protection. It would be difficult to define precisely what are the present limits of the British sphere of influence.

The gains in sea-power in the East somewhat offset the loss of prestige in the first Afghan War (1839–42). A by-product of that war was Napier's conquest of Sind which gave to the Bombay Presidency the Indus delta and the port of Karachi (1843). All these accessions made it easy to bring pressure upon Persia and accordingly upon Russia who was making her a catspaw in the war of 1856–7.

Sea-power in the Indian Ocean tended to involve the British Empire ever more deeply in the Arab world. Routes between Asia and Africa were traditionally the scene of Arab voyaging since the mythical days of Sindbad, the seafarer from Basra. From the land of frankincense and pearls, across the Gulf to the Horn of Africa, downwind to Zanzibar the island of slaves and spice, over the Mozambique Channel to Madagascar, where lingered the legend of gigantic birds, through seas where monsters basked like islands on the surface, to lands containing serpent-haunted valleys of diamonds and hoards of ivory in swamps where the elephants came to die, past islands where grew the *coco-de-mer* which some think to be the forbidden fruit of Eden, and so to the Malabar Coast: in all these shores and seas the Moslems were masters and, in the eighteenth century, had driven out the intruding Portuguese.

Among the Moslem rulers the greatest, in the nineteenth century, were the Imams of Muscat, hereditary leaders of an Islamic sect. As early as 1798 the Imam had been in treaty relations with the East India Company. Seyyid Said, who became Imam in 1804, ruled the Oman coast of Arabia and extended his sway southward along the East African coast beyond Mombasa. In 1832, he took the step of removing his capital to the flat, fertile island of Zanzibar (somewhat larger than the Isle of Man) which he planted with cloves. Indian and Arab traders soon resorted in great numbers to its natural harbour which became the commercial centre of the Arabian Sea, and a great slave-market. Zanzibar traders, known as 'banians', soon got financial control of all East Africa far inland. From Zanzibar there spread the *lingua franca* of East Africa, a Bantu-Arabic jargon known as Swahili. 'When you play the flute at Zanzibar men dance by the Great Lakes.'

As early as 1824 Captain W. F. Owen, R.N., while surveying the African coast, had been persuaded to declare a British Protectorate over Mombasa, which the Colonial Office instantly denounced. The interest of the British government in East Africa for another fifty years was confined to naval measures against the slave trade. Empire-building merchants, officials and missionaries were however drawn by the magnet of the commerce, influence, and unregenerate conservatism of the Sultanate of Zanzibar. The Bombay government established a political agent there in 1841. In the following year Dr Ludwig Krapf, a German in the service of the Church Missionary Society, who had previously failed to get a footing in Abyssinia, opened a mission on the Zanzibar coast. He was the first white man to see Mount Kilimanjaro (1849). The Sultan agreed in 1845 to put an end to the sea-borne trade in slaves between his African and Arabian provinces. Eleven years later he died, leaving a disputed succession which was settled in arbitration by Lord Canning, the Viceroy of India. Zanzibar became independent of Muscat under a son of Sultan Seyyid and was given a guarantee of independence by Great Britain and France (1861).

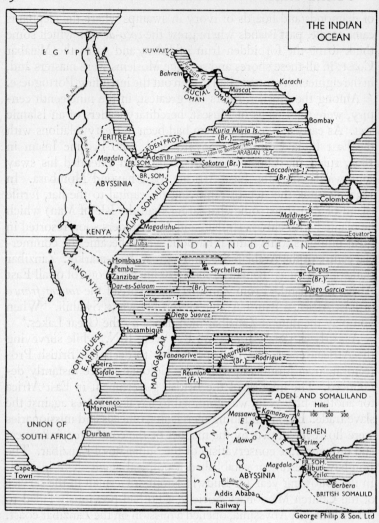

THE INDIAN OCEAN

EGYPT
KUWAIT
Bahrein
Persian G.
TRUCIAL OMAN
Muscat
Karachi
ERITREA
ADEN PROT.
Kuria Muria Is.
(Br.)
Aden to Bombay 1664 Miles
ARABIAN SEA
Bombay
Magdala
FR. SOM.
Aden (Br.)
Sokotra (Br.)
BR. SOM.
Laccadives
(Br.)
ABYSSINIA
ITALIAN SOMALILD.
Maldives
(Br.)
Colombo
KENYA
Mogadishu
R. Juba
INDIAN OCEAN
Equator
Mombasa
Pemba
Seychelles
Chagos
(Br.)
Zanzibar
Dar-es-Salaam
(Br.)
Diego Garcia
TANGANYIKA
Diego Suarez
Mozambique
Mauritius
(Br.)
Rodriguez
PORTUGUESE E. AFRICA
MADAGASCAR
Tananarive
Beira
Sofala
Réunion
(Fr.)
ADEN AND SOMALILAND
Lourenco Marques
Massawa
Kamaran
Miles
0 100 200 300
ERITREA
YEMEN
UNION OF SOUTH AFRICA
Durban
Adowa
Perim
FR. SOM.
Cape Town
Magdala
Aden
ABYSSINIA
R. Blue Nile
Jibuti
Zeila
SUDAN
Addis Ababa
Berbera
BRITISH SOMALILD.
Railway

George Philip & Son. Ltd

Map 27

Sir Bartle Frere as Governor of Bombay (1862–6) was a champion of the new imperialism. Among his protégés was William (afterwards Sir William) Mackinnon (1823–93), a Bombay shipowner who founded the British India Line in 1862. Frere did all in his power to advance trade in the Arabian Sea, sending agents to the various Sultans. He advised Mackinnon to run a service of steamers from Zanzibar to Aden. As patron and friend of Livingstone, Frere assisted in organising his last expedition and sent Livingstone's friend, Doctor (afterwards Sir John) Kirk (1832–1922), to the consulate at Zanzibar where he eventually became Consul-general. Frere defended Kirk against the attacks of H. M. Stanley, as will be seen in the next section. Kirk was singularly successful in winning the confidence of Seyyid Barghash who succeeded as Sultan in 1870.

Affairs at Zanzibar reached a new crisis since slavery and slave-trading were universal in spite of the treaty of 1845. When Frere was sent out on a special mission from England in 1872 he was unable, for all his suavity and experience, to persuade Barghash to come to terms. After Frere's departure Kirk was instructed to take a stronger line. He presented the Sultan and his assembled vassals with an ultimatum demanding immediate abolition of the slave trade and got his way without losing the Sultan's friendship. The great slave-market of Zanzibar was closed on 5 June 1873, and a few months later the Universities Mission began to build a cathedral on its site. The state visit of the Sultan of Zanzibar to England in 1874 was a notable occasion in both countries.

2. THE EXPLORATION OF AFRICA AND ARABIA

ALTHOUGH the whole coastline of Africa had been visited by Europeans through a period of 300 years the interior was quite unknown to the Western nations in the eighteenth century. Neither Portuguese, nor Dutch at the Cape, nor slave-traders of the Guinea Coast made many attempts to penetrate the savage and unhealthy hinterland. The system of lakes and rivers in Central Africa, which Pliny had vaguely indicated on hearsay evidence, was no better understood 1700 years later when Dean Swift wrote:

> So Geographers, in Afric maps,
> With savage pictures fill their gaps,
> And o'er unhabitable downs
> Place elephants for want of towns.

The Sahara and the equatorial forests alike proved fatal to European invaders who seemed to be less resistant to tropical diseases than Africans or Asiatics.

Yet it would be incorrect to describe Africa as undiscovered when it was merely undiscovered by Europeans. The region of the Upper Nile had been Christianised at least as early as the fourth century by Copts from Egypt, whose societies were overrun and largely destroyed by Moslem Arabs in the eleventh century. One relic of the earlier age survived in the kingdom of Abyssinia, embedded in Islam and lost to the view of Western Christendom, except that some legend of its existence continued in the fabulous tales of Prester John. The truth was revealed by Portuguese missionaries of the sixteenth century, whose experiences were made familiar to English readers by Samuel Johnson's translation (1735) of Father Lobo's voyages (1626). Elsewhere the Arabs had overrun the north coast of Africa in the early days of Islam. By the eleventh century they had spread westward from the Nile to the Niger and had reached the ocean by way of the Senegal River. The celebrated but mysterious city of Timbuktu was founded about A.D. 1100.

Moslem proselytism has been continuous among the negroes and has met with no small success. Even at the present day Islam is said to be spreading more rapidly than Christianity in Africa. The Moslem cities of the Upper Niger region attained a high degree of civilisation and, through Islamic law and the practice of pilgrimages, preserved their contact with the Arab world. Their weakness was their addiction to slave-raiding, with the consequence that human life was held in low esteem in Central Africa. It should be remembered that the Arabs were the purveyors of the merchandise which the European slave-traders handled as middlemen.

The pagan country to the southward could also exhibit patches of characteristic civilisation. Negro kingdoms, at Dahomey, Kumasi, Benin and elsewhere, were highly developed states with formulated constitutions and sophisticated arts and crafts. They were however damned in the eyes of Europeans since they practised witchcraft and ritual murder, immolating crowds of victims as sacrifices to their divine kings. In the last days of the African slave trade these 'customs' of the West African kingdoms provided the Arab raiders with a profitable side-line in the supply of victims for sacrifice. Perhaps both there and in East Africa the natives were sociologically decadent. It may be that the ruined cities of Rhodesia were once inhabited by negro nations at a higher stage of civilisation than the West African kingdoms but there is no agreement upon this point among the antiquaries.[1]

Some of the first European penetrations into the interior of Africa were made by officers of the consular services, an organisation of which the history is not well known. The British consular service came unnoticed into existence in the days of the old chartered companies. The earliest consuls in the Near and Far East were the servants of the Levant and East India Companies respectively, and passed into government employment when these companies lost their privileges, in 1825 and 1858. They had no sort of political status and can hardly be said to have belonged to an official hierarchy. But John Baldwin, an orientalist, held an appointment from the Foreign Office as Consul-general in Egypt as early as 1786. Commonly they received no salary but recompensed themselves, often handsomely, by charging fees for commercial services. A series of reforms instituted by the Foreign Office, in 1856, 1876 and 1903, gradually converted the consular service into a department of government, though it was still inferior in status to the diplomatic service, a typical paradox in the English system. The nation of shopkeepers treated the agency which helped them to live and grow rich as less important than an agency largely concerned with social relations between courts and aristocracies. Yet, in the old informal days, many distinguished travellers and cosmopolitans lived abroad in ease and affluence by holding consular appointments.

James Bruce (1730–94), who was brought up in the Lisbon wine-trade, became British consul at Algiers. Thence after travelling through Egypt he made his way to Massawa in the Red Sea and, in 1769, went up-country to Gondar, the capital of Abyssinia. After exploring the headwaters of the Blue Nile, which he took to be the main source of the Great River, he returned to Europe, by way of Egypt, in 1774. His experiences in Abyssinia were received with much scepticism by stay-at-homes so that, from that time, the Nile Quest shared with the search for the North-west Passage the reputation of being an almost insoluble problem. The main stream of the river was mapped by British, French and German explorers in the Egyptian service, by the year 1841, as far

[1] The *Cambridge History of the British Empire* takes the view that the Rhodesian remains at Zimbabwe and elsewhere survive from a Bantu culture that reached its climax 800 or 900 years ago.

south as Gondokoro. John Petherick, a Cornish ivory-trader, was British consul at Khartoum in 1853.

The antiquities of Egypt were fully revealed to Europe by the expedition of Bonaparte in 1798 and the learned men who followed after. Among them may be mentioned the German linguist J. L. Burckhardt (1784–1817), of Göttingen and Cambridge, who went up the Nile to Assuan, visited Abyssinia, penetrated to Mecca in disguise (1815), and described the ruins of Palmyra and Baalbek. From the earliest times the Arab lands have exercised a strange fascination over some of the strongest English characters. First in the role of these English eccentrics is the name of Lady Hester Stanhope (1776–1839), who lost her employment when her uncle Pitt, for whom she kept house, died in 1806, and her lover when Sir John Moore fell at Corunna in 1809. She set out in the following year for the Levant, where she came to exercise a commanding influence over the Bedouin, always respectful to those whom Allah has afflicted. Growing crazier as she grew older, she yet retained an air of the best society and, royally if oddly, entertained other English travellers at her mountain fortress in the Lebanon. One of her visitors was that very superior person, A. W. Kinglake (1809–91), when he made the tour through Sinai and Syria commemorated in *Eothen*. Syrian, Persian and Arabian archaeology drew a succession of French, German and English travellers to the Levant, among them Sir A. H. Layard (1817–94) who excavated Nineveh in 1845. He was employed as a political adviser by Palmerston and later rose to be ambassador at Constantinople during the Russo-Turkish War. Sir H. C. Rawlinson (1810–95), an Indian Civilian, was sent as consul to Bagdad. A profound Persian scholar, he distinguished himself by deciphering the inscriptions of King Darius at Behistun. Another sort of traveller was W. C. Palgrave (1826–88), who went through Arabia in disguise on behalf of a Jesuit mission. Later, abandoning his creed, he undertook a political mission to Abyssinia in 1865. The coastal region of southern Arabia and Persia was visited by many political agents from India, notably Sir Lewis Pelly (1825–92), who led a mission from Bombay in 1860.

At the time of the occupation of Egypt the British authorities employed as a linguist Professor E. H. Palmer (1840–82) of Cambridge, a self-educated young man with a remarkable knowledge of oriental dialects. A precursor of the more celebrated

T. E. Lawrence, he undertook to ingratiate the tribes of Sinai during the Egyptian War, but was killed by the Bedouin. Neither misanthropy nor political intrigue formed any part of the motive of Doctor Charles Doughty (1843–1926) who travelled alone through central Arabia in 1873–6 and wrote the strange rich odyssey, *Arabia Deserta*, to which all later travellers in that region are indebted. An unassuming Christian, he scorned disguise, moving freely and alone among fanatical Arabs, a poor man who went about doing good. He had a low opinion of Sir Richard Burton, who boasted of having made the pilgrimage to Mecca disguised as a Moslem.

Hardly less mysterious than the sources of the Nile was the course of the River Niger which was rumoured to flow past Timbuktu, but whether eastward or westward was not known. Perhaps it emerged on the Atlantic coast under the name of the Senegal or Gambia; perhaps in the Gulf of Guinea where there was a delta known as the Oil Rivers and an estuary known as the Congo. The investigation of this problem was undertaken by the African Association (1788) in which Sir Joseph Banks was a principal. This was the first of a series of efforts to open the way into the Niger basin in the joint interests of evangelism and commerce, which no one doubted to be ancillary to one another. The African Association (reorganised in 1830 as the Royal Geographical Society) despatched a number of expeditions to the Niger from north, south, and west, most of them failures with loss of life. Their general effect was to confirm Europe in the view that West Africa was the White Man's Grave.

The most celebrated of these voyages, since the author's memoir of it is a masterpiece, was made by Mungo Park (1771–1806), a young Scottish surgeon who entered the service of the African Association in 1795. Setting out from the Gambia he crossed the Senegal River, made his way to Bamako on the Niger and returned (1797) after struggling alone and unarmed through almost unbelievable hardships. For seven or eight years he lived the quiet life of a country doctor at Peebles, where he won the friendship of Sir Walter Scott; then he was again sent to the Niger at the head of a large expedition financed by the Colonial Office. In November 1805 he sent back word to the Gambia that he was descending the Niger in a boat built by his men. There the story ends. Years later, reports filtered through from native traders that he and his few surviving comrades were drowned in a scuffle with Hausa tribesmen. Several succeeding expeditions also came to grief.

The first European to enter Timbuktu was Major A. G. Laing (1793–1826) who made his way there across the Sahara from Tripoli and was killed by the Touaregs on the return journey. A Frenchman, Réné Caillié, made a successful visit in the following year (1827) from the west and planted the seeds of French influence. The problem of the Niger, meanwhile, had been attacked by another British expedition from Tripoli. Two officers, Lieutenant H. Clapperton, R.N. (1788–1827), and Lieutenant D. Denham, 23rd Regiment (1786–1828), crossed the desert to Lake Chad which they were the first Europeans to visit (1823). Two of their English companions died, and their progress westward towards the Niger was obstructed by the powerful Fula kings who ruled the walled cities of Kano and Sokoto. Clapperton made a second attempt, after returning to Tripoli, and on this occasion approached the Niger from the Oil Coast. He crossed the river to die at Sokoto. His work was completed by his personal servant, Richard Lander (1804–34), a valet, who had accompanied Clapperton on all his travels. Lander returned to England and persuaded government to finance a third expedition led by himself and his younger brother. They marched from the Oil Coast to the Niger, then paddled for two months downstream, emerging by the channel known as the Brass River (1830). The Oil Rivers were thus proved to be the outlet of the Niger. Richard Lander was killed in a fight with natives when on another visit to the delta.

The savannah country between the Niger and Lake Chad was made known in general outline by the travels (1852–6) of Dr Heinrich Barth of Hamburg, who was despatched from the north by the British government.

During the 'fifties the centre of interest shifted back from the Niger to the Nile, and at this point it will be proper to introduce the swashbuckling figure of Sir Richard Burton (1821–90), the translator of the *Arabian Nights*. He was bred at Oxford and, if he is to be given a professional label, we must call him a philologist. After serving in the Bombay Army he began a wandering life in Moslem India, winning fame in 1853 by his pilgrimage to Mecca which he described in a forceful literary style. Next he attempted to penetrate Somaliland with J. H. Speke (1827–64) a fellow-soldier from India; then served a campaign in the Crimea. In 1857 Burton was despatched by the Royal Geographical Society to corroborate the tale told by Dr Ludwig Krapf, the missionary, of snowy mountains and inland seas in the heart of Africa. He set out with Speke from Zanzibar. But Burton was a sharp-tongued fellow, ill to reckon with, and Speke parted from him on the shores of Lake Tanganyika, the first of the Great African Lakes to be discovered. Speke found the southern shore of Lake Victoria, and Burton disbelieved his story. Speke came home first and claimed the credit of the voyage with the result that he was sent by the Society on a further trip to find the source of the Nile. With a new companion, J. A. Grant (1827–92), he saw the main stream of the river issue from Lake Victoria (28 July 1862), but his travels added little to precise geographical knowledge since he was no surveyor. Speke and Grant followed the stream down until they met another English traveller coming up the river to meet them. This was Sir Samuel Baker,[1] a rich adventurer and sportsman who had come south from Egypt with his wife and a well-equipped party. Speke first among Europeans saw the source of the Nile; Baker explored and surveyed the region on information supplied by Speke. Later as Governor of the Equatorial Province (1869–73) Baker served the Khedive of Egypt in suppressing the slave trade. Speke was killed in a shooting accident soon after his return to England.

The discomfited Burton transferred his efforts elsewhere. He held consular appointments at Fernando Po, Damascus, Santos, and Trieste which enabled him to travel adventurously and to write vigorously about Arabia, West Africa and Brazil.

When the message was telegraphed from Khartoum in 1863 that the source of the Nile had at last been found ('The Nile is settled'), it produced a new enthusiasm for the opening of Central Africa. This wonderland of lakes and mountains, which Burton, Speke and Baker had revealed, must be explored, civilised and cleansed from the horrors of the slave trade. The stage was set for the entrance of the hero who appeared in the person of David Livingstone, then at the height of his fame.

[1] Sir Samuel Baker (1821–93) had spent several years in Ceylon where he introduced white settlers to plant coffee. His book, *With Rifle and Hound in Ceylon* is a classic of sport.

Through Livingstone's memoirs the public became acquainted with the features of African travel. They could picture the clear sunshine beating on the red dusty plateau that makes up nine-tenths of the continent; the files of negro porters, led by standard-

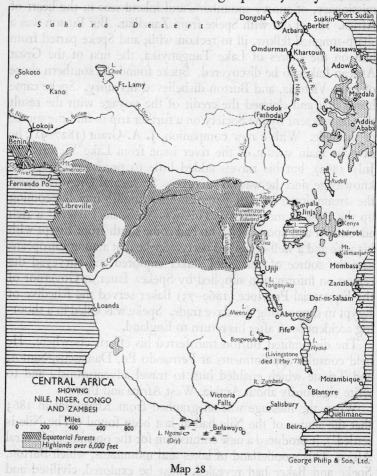

CENTRAL AFRICA
SHOWING
NILE, NIGER, CONGO
AND ZAMBESI

Miles
0   200   400   600   800

▨ Equatorial Forests
▨ Highlands over 6,000 feet

George Philip & Son, Ltd.

Map 28

bearers and drummers, bearing bundles on their heads through the tall grass in which grew like living things the domed or pinnacled ant-heaps; they could smell the hot spicy scents of the crowded markets where Livingstone's heart overflowed with kindness to-wards the smiling, hard-bargaining, cheerful Africans. In park-like glades the herds of game glanced up and vanished into the scrub as though scorning the slow-footed humans; the lions roared after their prey by night; the snow-white cranes and egrets and kingfishers flew over shining lakes and rivers towards glimpses of inaccessible mountains. And all was afflicted by the ten plagues of Pharaoh, with tsetse-fly, fever, hailstorms, swarms of locusts, and last of all with slaughter and death.

David Livingstone (1813–73) was working in a cotton-mill at Blantyre at the age of ten. He educated himself and was accepted for service abroad, in 1838, by the London Missionary Society. After awaiting an appointment for two years, which he spent in studying medicine at Glasgow, he was selected to serve with Robert Moffatt in South Africa. On the voyage to the Cape he persuaded the ship's captain to instruct him in navigation and thereafter 'took his daily observations as regularly as he said his prayers'. In 1841 he went up to Kuruman in Bechuanaland to join Moffatt, whose daughter he soon married.

Though eclipsed by his greater son-in-law, Robert Moffatt (1795–1883) makes no small figure in the sphere of missionary enterprise. He opened the 'Missionaries' Road' along the eastern fringe of the Kalahari Desert, settled among the Bechuana (1825), and even came eventually to exercise some influence over Moselikatze, the first King of the Matabele (about 1859). While Moffatt devoted his life to preaching and converting, Livingstone was rather a pioneer of missions, hailing with delight the decision taken by the Society, 'that we go forward to the dark interior'.

After several excursions westward across the Kalahari and northwards towards the Zambezi, in one of which he was mauled by a lion, he sent his wife and children to England and plunged into the unknown. In his absence his house and papers were ravaged by Boer filibusters who already knew him as a protector of natives against exploitation, and hated him.

The first of Livingstone's three great expeditions was his crossing and recrossing of Africa (1853–6) from the middle Zambezi to Loanda on the West Coast, and back to Quilimane on the East. In November 1855 he discovered the Victoria Falls. This series of marches, without white companions and on foot, among primitive tribes who were mightly impressed by his dauntless simplicity was perhaps his greatest and most typical exploit. Thereafter men from his favourite Makololo tribe, his 'faithfuls', followed him to the end of his life. On this expedition, too, he first came upon the beastly evidences of Arab slavers, and was obliged to admit that Portuguese traders backed their efforts. He then devoted his life to combating the slave trade by moral influence, his method being to let light into Darkest Africa so that Christian civilisation could prove its worth.

In 1856 Livingstone returned to England to find that the publication of his *Missionary Travels and Researches* made him famous. The precision of his observations won him recognition from the Royal Society, the Royal Geographical Society and the universities; and his appeal in the Senate House at Cambridge (4 December 1857) led to the foundation of the Universities' Mission to Central Africa. 'I beg to direct your attention to Africa', he said. 'I know that in a few years I shall be cut off in that country, which is now open; do not let it be shut again. I go back to Africa to try to make an open path for commerce and Christianity; do you carry out the work which I have begun. I leave it with you.' He resigned from the London Missionary Society (though not through any change of principle) in order to accept a post as consul at Quilimane which would enable him to explore the country north of the Zambezi, where he was to establish the Universities' Mission, with a government grant of £5000.

His second great expedition began when he left Quilimane (1858) in an ocean-going steam-launch at the head of a party including Dr John Kirk. This was not so happy an experience for Livingstone as his earlier travels. He was out of his element when in command of white men. Nor did the attempt to explore by river-steamer prove successful since the Zambezi, like most Africa rivers, is blocked by cataracts. Yet the explorers entered the Shiré country (where now the town of Blantyre is named after Livingstone's birthplace), and discovered Lake Nyasa. The country was ravaged by slave-raiders with whom it was difficult to avoid fighting when they obstructed progress. Two misfortunes fell in 1862, when Bishop C. F. Mackenzie, who had come out to start the Universities' Mission, died of fever, and when Livingstone's wife also died while visiting him. In 1863 the expedition was withdrawn for lack of funds.

Though Livingstone was deeply grieved, he abated nothing of his courage. Since he could find no market for his steam-launch he characteristically sailed it across the Indian Ocean to sell it in

Bombay before returning to London (1864), where he was lionised again. Lord Palmerston and the best Whig society made much of him. Though Livingstone was now past fifty and weakened by dysentery after his Zambezi voyage, he was persuaded by Sir R. Murchison, the President of the Royal Geographical Society, to return once more to Africa. The work of Speke and Baker must be completed. Had they indeed found the ultimate source of the Nile or was there another tributary stream beyond Lake Tanganyika? This was Burton's view, and Livingstone, who rather favoured it, sought confirmation in traditions preserved by Herodotus. Livingstone's third and longest expedition was geographical; he was to find and explore the central watershed of Africa between Lakes Tanganyika and Nyasa. For all his popularity the money provided was meagre, and he went to Bombay to collect the sale-price of his steamboat. There he won the enthusiastic support of the Governor, Sir Bartle Frere, who gave him a letter to the Sultan of Zanzibar and a detachment of Indian sepoys. Frere also arranged for Livingstone's old comrade, Dr John Kirk, to be appointed to the consulate at Zanzibar.

In 1866 Livingstone was mustering his resources at Zanzibar in an atmosphere that he heartily disliked. The taint of the slave-market corrupted slaves and slave-owners alike. His train of porters from this depraved society proved idle and mutinous from the start. Even Livingstone's example failed to charm them into honourable courses. The *banians* who provided his stores and the Arab chiefs who lorded it over the coastal region, though obliged to respect his authority as a British consul approved by the Sultan, yet knew that his life-work was to destroy the trade in 'black ivory' by which they lived. They thwarted him politely and frustrated all Kirk's endeavours to send replenishments to the advanced base which, on Speke's advice, he proposed to form at Ujiji, beside Lake Tanganyika. Once away from Zanzibar he was more solitary in Africa than ever before. His porters mutinied, deserted, pilfered; the sepoys proved useless for African travel; only his 'faithfuls' were any comfort to him. Soon an ominous recurrence of ill-health began to be noted in his journal. His mighty frame was wearing out, and the loss of his medicine-chest, stolen by a deserter, was a sore blow. He roved through Central Africa, seeking his river, for more than seven years (1866–1873) but was seen only once again by any white man.

No sooner had he vanished up-country than a tribal war broke out behind him cutting off all communication with the coast. Later the cholera came, decimating Zanzibar and depopulating the countryside. In 1866 one parcel of despatches came through, and then a rumour that he was dead. Next year a relief expedition went up Lake Nyasa, found evidence that he was alive, but failed to make contact. After a long pause another letter reached the coast in 1868; then nothing.

The world wondered, while the old man marched and countermarched about Lake Tanganyika in failing health. In 1868 he found Lake Bangweulu; in 1869 he came to Ujiji to find that the stores sent by Kirk had been looted. For a long time he was obliged to live on the charity of Arab chiefs whom he found 'very gentlemanly slavers'. They protected him, thwarted him, and made no secret of their real business. At last in March 1871 he discovered a broad clear river, the Lualaba, flowing north and made sure it must be the headwaters of the Nile, but by no means could he obtain a boat to launch on it. On 13 October 1871 he fell back to Ujiji shockingly ill, with neither food nor drugs nor trade goods and with a mere handful of followers; and there five days later the relief expedition of H. M. Stanley found him.

Livingstone was relieved by Stanley, not lost and found; for Stanley encountered him just where he was supposed to be. Refreshed by Stanley's company and re-equipped by his bounty, Livingstone resumed his quest without any thought of withdrawing before his task was accomplished. After the two parted, in March 1872, Livingstone explored the region between the Lakes for a whole year more, while disease and weakness slowly mastered him. He made no more great discoveries but would not falter, though his daily marches shortened. When he could no longer march he rode a donkey, and when he could no longer ride he was borne in a litter, but still pressed on. If he could he would have died marching and, since he could not, he died praying. On 1 May 1873 his 'faithfuls' found him dead, kneeling at his bedside. Not the least heroic episode in his saga is the decision of his 'boys', Susi and Chuma, to hold the expedition together. They marched back as they had come, through 800 miles of wilderness, from Lake Bangweulu to Zanzibar, carrying their master's body and the record of his work. On the way they met another relieving expedition which had come too late. Its leader, Lieutenant

V. L. Cameron, went on to finish Livingstone's task. The old man had been at fault; his Lualaba River was the Congo not the Nile.

Meanwhile Stanley had scooped the greatest newspaper sensation of the decade, and exploited it in lecture-tours and in a book: *How I found Livingstone*.

In the final opening of Africa, H. M. Stanley (1841–1904) played no small part. His own story was hardly less remarkable than the epic life of Livingstone, though by his own account it rather resembled a serial story in a magazine for boys. He ran away to sea from a Welsh workhouse after thrashing the Mr Squeers who had ill-treated him there. Later when befriended by an American named Stanley, the boy adopted his benefactor's name and nationality. In the Civil War he managed the surprising feat of fighting on both sides, first in the Confederate Army and then in the Federal Navy. After skirmishing with Red Indians in the West, and coming through a scrape with brigands in Asia Minor, he turned up at the Abyssinian War as special reporter for the New York *Herald*. By bribing the telegraph clerk he got his first 'scoop', an exclusive account of the fall of Magdala, which made him ripe for higher flights of journalism. In October 1869, his editor, Gordon Bennett, summoned Stanley to Paris to receive several assignments; he was to go to Persia and India for this and that, to attend the opening of the Suez Canal and, when he got around to it, he was to find Dr Livingstone, not because the Doctor needed help but because he made headline news. Fifteen months passed before Stanley came to Zanzibar and there he was so blatant in his gossip-columnist's method, so secretive about his real intention, so careless of the company he kept, that he antagonised John Kirk and all Livingstone's friends. Without their help he proved himself a master of the art of tropical travel, perhaps because he had unlimited funds; and marched up the country beneath the Stars and Stripes, in record time, not achieved without a liberal use of whip and gun. Forcing his way through opposition he arrived, as has been already told, at Ujiji.

As I come nearer [so runs his record [1]] I see the white face of an old man. ...He has a cap with a gold band round it; his dress is a short jacket of red blanket cloth, and his pants—well, I didn't observe; I am shaking hands with him. We raise our hats and I say, 'Dr Livingstone, I presume?' And he says 'Yes'.

[1] Letter to New York Herald, dated 3 November 1871.

The banality of that famous utterance, bringing world-wide movements and opposed generations into a single focus, like a snapshot of a historical crisis, was at once fixed as one of the undying myths of the Anglo-Saxon race. The old age and the new met and recognised one another. There was the simple old Scottish saint, as plain and resolute as one of his own covenanting ancestors, one of the most famous men alive but intent only on his self-allotted duty; and there was the Anglo-American publicity-hunter, nigger-driving through Africa with all the blare and bounce of the yellow press. Yet Livingstone drew new life from the adventurous youngster who brought him relief, friendship, conversation, news; and Stanley, in spite of his coarser fibre, knew that to serve Livingstone and win his affection was the supreme experience of his career. His flashy journalism is tinged with reverence when he speaks of the Doctor: 'In him there is no guile and what is apparent on the surface is the thing that is in him. His gentleness never forsakes him; his hopefulness never deserts him. Religion has tamed him and made him a Christian gentleman.' With this tale Stanley returned to England where he was genuinely shocked to learn that many people thought him vulgar and pretentious, while some doubted the truth of his story. He weakened his case by belittling Livingstone's other friends, especially John Kirk,[1] in order to heighten the effect of his own exploit. The Queen was one of the first to make allowances and to give him credit.

In 1873 Stanley was off again to Ashanti with Wolseley's expedition. In 1874 he was persuaded by Burnham of the *Telegraph* and Bennett of the New York *Herald* to undertake the exploration of the Congo. This was (1874–7) perhaps the most fruitful of all African expeditions. After tracing the whole course of the river he marched through the rain-forest to the Lakes, surveyed Lake Victoria, discovered Lake Edward and revealed to the world the kingdom of Uganda, the most advanced of African polities. The first to grasp the meaning of his discoveries was King Leopold of Belgium who sent to meet him as he returned, with consequences that will be considered in the next chapter. After four years of strenuous pioneering in the Congo State (1879–83) he made his

---

[1] The old controversy between Stanley and Kirk has been settled by Sir Reginald Coupland in *Livingstone's Last Journey* (1945), to which I acknowledge my indebtedness.

last expedition to Africa in search of Emin Pasha (see below, chapter xv, 2, page 812) and then withdrew from active travel though not from lecture-tours. As he grew older he became more favourable to British policy, resumed his British nationality, accepted a knighthood, stood for Parliament as a Liberal-unionist and married into one of the best families. He died in 1904 at the age of sixty-three.

By that time Africa was mapped,[1] partitioned and subjugated. A stream of missionaries and explorers, inspired by Livingstone's example, had followed the trail he blazed. The slave trade had been stopped or driven out of sight; and after it vanished tribal wars, cannibalism, human sacrifice. In the new Africa of the twentieth century the long laborious fight against ignorance, poverty and disease was beginning.

3. BRITISH TROPICAL AFRICA, 1808–75

THE abolition of the British slave-trade on 1 January 1808 quite changed the character of the British posts in West Africa. They were now reorganised to prevent the traffic by which they had formerly lived. In 1821 the moribund 'Company of Merchants' was relieved of its responsibility for the forts, which were taken over by the Crown. The royal governor of Sierra Leone was given general charge of all the West African stations from Gambia to Accra, along a coastline of 1500 miles. It will be convenient to recapitulate their history.

Fort James (or Gambia Castle) on James Island, a few miles up the Gambia River, had much declined in importance. Its value had been strategic rather than commercial, and its history belongs to that of the naval wars with France. The two rivers Senegal and Gambia, on either side of Cape Verde, were recognised as the best ways into the heart of Africa but seemed to lead only to dry savannah country where Jobson's 'golden trade' could not be found. Neither the French on the Senegal nor the British on the Gambia made any sustained attempt to probe the hinterland before the nineteenth century.

[1] Yet still there were dark recesses. In the twenty years after the publication of *King Solomon's Mines* (1885), which he located in the land afterwards called Rhodesia, Rider Haggard was able to find room in Africa for five other dream-kingdoms as subjects for later romances.

In the Seven Years War the British seized Goree, the French stronghold near Cape Verde, and annexed Senegal. From 1763 to 1783 the whole coastal strip between the river-mouths was administered as the crown colony of Senegambia, which never paid its way. At the end of the American War Senegal was re-ceded to France with little reluctance, and the region remained in the French sphere of influence. Fort James, several times demolished, abandoned, and reoccupied in the wars, was almost derelict at the end of the century, though still visited by traders. Mungo Park drew attention to its value by making it the base of his expeditions.

When the wars ended at Waterloo and the object of British policy was to close the Gambia estuary against slave-traders, a new site was selected on St Mary's Island near the river-mouth, to be used by the Preventive Squadron as a port of call. It was named Bathurst after the Secretary of State. Sir Charles Macarthy, the Governor of Sierra Leone (1814–24), a philanthropist and an empire-builder, attempted in Gambia as elsewhere to civilise by spreading British influence. In 1823 he bought from a native king an island, now called Macarthy's Island, 160 miles upstream. Then it seemed reasonable, since there were continual disputes with the French to the northward, to reassert the British right to the north bank of the river. Accordingly the French were excluded by a treaty with the King of Barra, who granted to the British (1826) what is called the 'ceded mile', a mile-wide strip of the foreshore along the right bank. The Gambia was a group of holdings in a river estuary and nothing more. Sixty years later (1888–94) when the French had penetrated all the hinterland a friendly settlement of spheres of influence was arranged. The islands and the 'ceded mile' were constituted as the distinct colony of Gambia, while the tribal areas along the river bank became the Gambia Protectorate, an enclave in the French zone. So inferior was British influence in this region that French money passed current in Gambia until 1922, when it was demonetised at great expense.

The port of Freetown beneath the Lion Rock of Sierra Leone became the base for the crusade against the slavers. Captured slave-ships were brought there for disposal by a court of vice-admiralty, set up in 1819, and later reinforced by an international tribunal. Hence a stream of liberated slaves came in to build up the colony. Mortality from disease had been shocking among the first-comers who gave to Sierra Leone the name of the 'White Man's Grave'. The liberated negroes suffered almost as much as the whites and, clinging to the town, showed no disposition to settle and cultivate land, or to fraternise with inland tribes. Nevertheless in Macarthy's time some progress was made; twelve villages were planted west of Freetown. The population, not much more than 1000 in 1808, had risen by 1833 to 200 whites and 33,000 British negroes. Sierra Leone had become a true example of a settlement colony. Much of its success it owed to British and American Methodist missionaries who entered this field as early as 1795. A further advance in enlightenment was the foundation of Fourah Bay College by the Church Missionary Society in 1827, the first institution for the higher education of Africans. However, the colony required an ever-increasing grant-in-aid, £95,000 in 1824, which infuriated economists in Parliament.

An uncertain note was struck when an American Society, whose motives Governor Macarthy mistrusted, began to despatch liberated American slaves to Sierra Leone. In 1821 they moved off into adjacent territory to found the settlement of Monrovia, named after the President. On the advice and under the protection of the British Colonial Office an independent state was formed and recognised, by Great Britain first among the powers (1847), as the Republic of Liberia. It owes its origin to American missionaries, British military protection, and to the energy of its first President, J. J. Roberts, an American coloured man, whom Palmerston and Queen Victoria received with honour when he visited England.

As at the Gambia, so at Sierra Leone, Governor Macarthy endeavoured to enter into treaty relations with the inland tribes, to the dismay of the Colonial Office which wanted no more territory. Farther to the east his policy led to disaster. Sierra Leone and Liberia were known to traders as the Grain Coast from the supplies of slender Guinea grain with which they revictualled their ships. The next stretch of coastline was the Ivory Coast, renowned for 'Olifants' teeth' but not much frequented by traders. Beyond that the Gold Coast, 'where Afric's sunny fountains roll down her golden sand'. Here all the trading nations kept posts clustered about the old castle of Elmina from which the Portuguese had been ousted by the Dutch. The Portuguese alone had claimed territorial rights and penetrated inland to dig for gold; they alone had imposed their culture on the Africans. Even the pidgin-English, which was gaining ground along the Coast, was studded with Portuguese words, such as *palaver*, *fetish*, *piccaninny*, *caboceer* (headman). But Christianity had made no progress against Mumbo-Jumbo, the celebrated bogy of the Mandingo peoples.

In 1751 the Rev. Thomas Thompson of the Society for the Propagation of the Gospel volunteered for service on the Coast since 'somebody must lay the first stone'. As chaplain at Cape Coast Castle he found it hard to get attention from the natives. No one knew their language and the *caboceer* 'took occasion to remark the immoral lives of many that profess Christianity'. Thompson did however send home three African lads to be trained as teachers, of whom one, Philip Quague the *caboceer*'s son, was ordained as the first African priest in the Anglican communion. He succeeded Thompson in the chaplaincy and when he died, after fifty years as missionary and teacher, the Company erected a monument at Cape Coast to his memory. This was but a small glimmer to enlighten Darkest Africa. A society living by the slave trade was not evangelically inclined and even when palm-kernels began to replace slaves as the staple of commerce it was not a squeamish trade. The 'coasters' were significantly known as 'palm-oil ruffians'.

The coastal natives, enervated by long contact with European traders, took alarm in the eighteenth century at the rise of a new military monarchy inland, the pagan kingdom of the Ashantis, whose divine monarch sat upon the Golden Stool at Kumasi, a fetish washed with the blood of lavish human sacrifice. In 1803 the Ashantis laid siege to Cape Coast Castle and were repulsed with difficulty. Friendly relations with the Fantis on the Coast made peace with their Ashanti tyrants impossible, as Governor Macarthy soon decided. In 1824 he led an expedition against them and lost his life in a skirmish. The skull of Governor Macarthy was for long kept and revered as a powerful fetish by the Ashanti Kings at Kumasi. After the Ashantis had been driven off the Coast by a punitive expedition (1826), preparations were made to withdraw altogether from the Gold Coast, since the forward policy had not been approved by the Colonial Office.

With some difficulty the traders dissuaded Downing Street from evacuation, suggesting instead a return to administration through a committee of merchants as in earlier days. From 1828 to 1847 the British posts were administered by Captain George Maclean, a young officer who had distinguished himself against the Ashantis. In the eyes of the Colonial Office he was merely a justice of the peace at Cape Coast Castle; his office was 'President' of the Committee of merchants; yet he was generally called the Governor and as a governor he acted, though his resources were something less than £4000 a year and a company of mercenary troops. Acting quite ruthlessly and entirely on his own authority he quickly made the British the paramount power on the Gold Coast, bringing the Fantis under his protection and driving back the Ashantis into their own country. All this was very shocking to the Colonial Office and very irritating to the Dutch at Elmina who found their power and trade taking an inferior place.

In 1838 Maclean's career took a curious turn. He married Miss Letitia Landon ('L.E.L.'), a literary lady who had some reputation at home for sentimental verses in the contemporary style. She died soon after reaching Cape Coast Castle (1839), of prussic acid poisoning, perhaps a dose taken in error. Maclean's headstrong manner had made him many foes, who hinted that he had murdered his wife, or at least driven her to suicide when she learned he had one wife already on the Coast. Maclean, the oppressor of the natives, now assumed the fiendish shape of Maclean the poisoner. The Aborigines Protection Society were furious against him and Sir James Stephen at the Colonial Office had to take serious notice. A globe-trotting philanthropist named Madden laid the wildest accusations, which were dispelled only when a Parliamentary Commission made a full report on the Gold Coast in 1842. Maclean's public actions were exonerated and approved, while the private scandals proved unfounded. Nevertheless the maker of the Gold Coast colony died a sadly embittered man, still in harness in 1847. Three years later his work was recognised when the Colonial Office again resumed responsibility.

At this time the annual exports from Great Britain to West Africa averaged at about £350,000, one-third of it in textiles, another third in guns and powder, and the rest in trade-gin. The imports, two-thirds in palm-kernels, were valued at about the same amount. The demand for vegetable oils, increasing throughout the century, directed trade farther to the eastward, into the head of the Gulf of Guinea. Beyond the Gold Coast lay the bloodthirsty kingdom of Dahomey with its main outlet to the sea at Lagos, a shallow fever-stricken lagoon on the Slave Coast, a name of evil omen. Beyond the Slave Coast lay the Oil Rivers which men were just beginning to accept as the undoubted delta of the Niger. Lagos and the Oil Rivers produced an increasing volume of palm-kernels, said to be worth £1,000,000 in 1861. In that year the town of Lagos, on an island in the lagoon, was acquired by purchase from the King who sold his rights for a pension. This was not done in the interest of trade but by the Foreign Office to disinfest a disreputable haunt of slavers. The Colonial Office advised against the annexation.

Naval control of the Gulf demanded that British influence should spread eastward. In 1828 Canning had negotiated with Spain the lease of a naval base on the deserted island of Fernando Po in the angle of the Gulf. This healthy mountainous island was administered for twelve years (1828–40) as a British colony and was the base of the various expeditions up the Oil Rivers. One of those who accompanied Richard Lander on his last expedition was MacGregor Laird (brother of John Laird, the Birkenhead shipbuilder). He founded the British African Steamship Company (1832), long since absorbed into the Elder Dempster Line, and for a whole generation urged the government to promote the trade of the Niger by subsidies to shipping. He steadily lost money but never lost faith.

Laird's commercial efforts were supported by Sir T. F. Buxton (1786–1845) the philanthropist, who wrote a book, *The African Slave-Trade and its Remedy* to propound a new plan for striking at the root of the trouble by civilising the slave-producing countries. Treaties of friendly relations with African chiefs would permit the infiltration of Africa by Christianity, social progress, and beneficent trade. A new Society 'for the Civilisation of Africa' was launched at Exeter Hall (1839) under the patronage of the Prince Consort; and Russell's administration was persuaded to raise the ban on a forward policy in Africa. Russell insisted however that there should be no annexations.

Buxton's philanthropic schemes and Laird's commercial schemes went well together and both could be directed from a base at Fernando Po. Their expedition to the Niger (ridiculed in *Bleak House*), with the intention of financing a mission station and model farm at the confluence of the Benue and Niger rivers by importing

Manchester goods, was a shocking failure which broke Buxton's heart. Laird's ship was lost and most of the pioneers died of fever (1841).

After Buxton's death (1845) Laird designed a river-steamer with a screw-propeller and sent it up the river under command of Dr W. B. Baikie (1825–64) in 1853. Later three trading-stations were established in the delta, under Baikie's supervision as British consul at Lokoja, but when Laird died, in 1861, there was a lull in these endeavours. Not, however, in missionary enterprise; one of Baikie's African assistants, Samuel Crowther, was consecrated in Canterbury Cathedral (1864) as Bishop on the Niger.

Meanwhile there had been political developments on the Gold Coast. The annexation of the Fanti country, in 1850, had led to troubles with the coastal tribes who were unwilling to pay taxes for their defence against the Ashantis, and led, furthermore, to disputes with the other trading nations. On this strip of coast there was the Danish fort of Christiansborg three miles from the British at Accra while Dutch and British posts alternated east of Cape Coast Castle. The collection of dues and taxes was intolerably complex. The Danes who had little care for colonisation solved the problem by selling Christiansborg (1850), for the trifling sum of £10,000. It is now the residence of the British Governor. The Dutch were less accommodating and relations between Elmina and Cape Coast Castle were unfriendly. In 1863 Ashanti raids forced the issue so that a desultory negotiation began for mutual exchanges of location. In London the missionaries wished to resume the forward policy, but a parliamentary committee led by Sir Charles Adderley, the colonial reformer, recommended strongly against any extension of British territory (1865). The dispute was ended in 1872 by the Foreign Office, which persuaded the Dutch to withdraw altogether from the Gold Coast in return for concessions in the East Indies.

Immediately a new Ashanti War broke out.[1] The King of Kumasi had his own point of view. The Dutch had paid him what they called a subsidy and he called a tribute. They were his com-

---

[1] In return for the Dutch cession of all rights and claims in West Africa the British ceded to the Dutch all rights and claims in Sumatra which, since 1824, had been regarded as a British sphere of influence. Like the British on the Gold Coast, the Dutch in Sumatra were at once involved in a long series of bloody wars, against the Achinese peoples who refused to admit the validity of the Anglo-Dutch agreement.

mercial clients as the British were the commercial clients of the coastal Fantis, and he did not propose to transfer his alliance to his British enemies. Gladstone's government made a bold move and sent Sir Garnet Wolseley, fresh from his Canadian triumphs, to the Gold Coast, with a brigade of British infantry. On 4 February 1874 Wolseley entered Kumasi after an almost bloodless campaign in which he showed his usual administrative skill. The King was bound to good behaviour by a very strict treaty and obliged to pay an indemnity in gold dust for his many raids upon the protected tribes. This was the first British move in the partition of tropical Africa.

4. THE ABYSSINIAN WAR, 1867–8

An almost forgotten episode in British history is the expedition against a usurper who had seized the throne of Abyssinia in 1855 and had assumed the name of King Theodore. Since 1848 there had been a British consular station at Massawa on the Red Sea, and Theodore, cultivating the society of the consul, Mr C. D. Cameron, urged him to persuade the Queen to accredit an ambassador to the Abyssinian Crown. When Cameron failed in this endeavour, since Theodore's throne was unstable and his behaviour barbarous, the tyrant vented his spleen by throwing Cameron into a dungeon and sending ten European missionaries to join him there (1863). When an emissary was sent from Egypt to expostulate, he too was thrown into prison. Successive British governments, with exemplary patience, spent four years in endeavours to obtain the release of the consul. But Theodore retained his prisoners as hostages, offering to release them only on condition of royal recognition of his status. He must be sent an ambassador with gifts and with a corps of technical advisers. When steps were magnanimously taken to meet the demand for technical help, Theodore made no conciliatory move but carried away his prisoners to a secure retreat in the mountain-fortress of Magdala. His rule was so bloodthirsty and the outlying tribes so hostile to him that there seemed every chance of his being deposed by his own people. When this expected rebellion hung fire, Disraeli at last decided upon a military expedition to rescue the prisoners. That only was his intention, and the Commander-in-

Chief, Sir Robert Napier (1810–90) was expressly warned that there would be no annexations and no indemnity. The invasion of Abyssinia was 'not to obtain territory, not to secure commercial advantages, but for high moral causes and for high moral causes alone...to vindicate the honour of our country and to rescue a few of our fellow-subjects from an unjust captivity'.

The expedition was prepared by the government of India; the troops were provided by the Bombay Army; and the bill (£8,600,000) was paid by the British Treasury. The campaign is of great interest in the history of warfare. Though badly equipped by the Indian government which showed itself rather remarkably ill-prepared for mobilisation, the whole expedition went like clockwork as soon as Napier took command in Abyssinia. He landed 12,000 soldiers with a greater number of camp-followers and a vast array of elephants, camels and mules on an open beach near Massawa and marched them 400 miles inland over the mountains, with great economy and trifling losses either from battle or disease. When the army was deployed before the fortress of Magdala, Theodore vacillated, offered to negotiate, released some of his prisoners, then determined to fight. The fortress was carried by assault on 13 April 1868 with the loss of a score of British soldiers. Several hundred Abyssinians, who fought with characteristic valour but without modern weapons, were killed, and Theodore shot himself when the battle was seen to be lost. All the captives were released.

Napier then withdrew as he had come, much harassed on his retreat by tribesmen who had given every help to his advancing army but regarded the withdrawal as evidence of weakness. The troops were re-embarked and the whole campaign concluded in a single dry season (October 1867 to June 1868), a very striking contrast in intention, execution and effect, to the bombastic Italian campaign of 1935 which cost ten times as much money, required ten times as many troops, shed more blood, was undertaken without a shadow of justification, and resulted only in oppression and misery for the Abyssinians.

For twenty years after the overthrow of Theodore, Abyssinia retained unquestioned independence and successfully resisted the encroachments of the Mahdi. During the 1880's French, Italian and British commercial interests grew on the Red Sea Coast. The French began to develop the port of Jibuti in 1881; the Italians the port of Massawa in 1885. Though a treaty between the Emperor Menelik and the Italians in 1889 gave Italy a position in Abyssinia which, in Italian eyes, amounted to a protectorate, all was lost in the war of 1896 when the Italians were defeated at Adowa. A rider to the Anglo-French agreement of 1904, the *Entente Cordiale*, was a joint agreement between England, France and Italy to respect the independence and integrity of Abyssinia. This was the principal treaty which the Italians broke in 1935.

XII

THE NEW IMPERIALISM:
SOUTH AFRICA TO 1912

Argument: Between 1865 and 1885 there emerged a new conception of
Empire as a duty. It can be derived from the doctrines of Froude and
Seeley and found final expression in the verses which Kipling published
in the nineties.

The new imperialism was to be seen at its best and worst in Cecil
Rhodes. Having attempted, and failed, to reconcile British and Boer
interests, he committed himself to a plan for uniting South Africa by
chicanery and force. His plan broke on the rock-like character of
Kruger. Though Joseph Chamberlain's emissary, Milner, failed to
restore good feeling or to come to terms with Kruger, he persisted,
through the long Boer War, in preparing for the Union which, in the
end, was approved by the shrewd sense of the Afrikaner leaders.
The War was a touchstone, sharply dividing the minority of 'Little
Englanders' from the 'imperialist' majority in England and the
colonies.

1. THE RISE OF IMPERIALISM

(1) GLADSTONE AND THE IMPERIALISTS

SEPARATISM at the time of Canadian confederation provoked a
reaction among the friends of Empire. A new 'Colonial Society'
was formed in London in 1868 and was incorporated a few
months later as the Royal Colonial Institute (now the Royal
Empire Society). Viscount Bury, who organised it, had in mind
a non-political society for the exchange of information, on the
model of the Royal Geographical Society. Australians and
Canadians residing in London took a prominent part in its proceedings. Among the early members were men of all opinions,
Lord Granville and Sir F. Rogers as well as Lords Carnarvon
and Salisbury; and the Prime Minister, Mr Gladstone himself,
attended the inaugural dinner on 15 May 1869. A discordant
note was struck by the American Ambassador who made a
jocular allusion, after dinner, to Canada's future in the United
States, for which he was politely rebuked by Lord Granville.

But soon there was formed within the Society a loyalist group that began to harry the government with leading questions about their intentions. Lord Granville, Gladstone's Colonial Secretary, was the particular object of their attacks, particularly for the tone of his despatch to the government of New Zealand on 7 October 1869. Though most English statesmen and many in the Colonies favoured the self-reliant policy and the withdrawal of the British troops, Granville [1] had announced his decision to remove the last regiments, so brusquely as to imply that he wished to goad the New Zealanders into secession; he was taxed with this in Parliament and in the press. Both Granville and his chief gave evasive answers. Gladstone's attitude to the Empire was always difficult to define. Morley's great volumes have little to say about it beyond Gladstone's protest in old age that he had never been a separatist. He took pride, wrote Morley, in having been one of the Colonial Reformers, a pupil of Molesworth and Wakefield; but this was in an earlier generation and, later on, his attention had become fixed upon other problems. Perhaps Chamberlain was right in saying that Gladstone 'never gave his mind' to imperial affairs.

Constructive efforts by the new colonial enthusiasts were snubbed by Gladstone's colleagues, and it is fair to add that they were repudiated as officious busy-bodies by one or two colonial statesmen, notably in Queensland. Viscount Bury led a deputation to ask the Colonial Office to summon a conference on the government of the Empire, and received a flat negative from Granville (December 1869). Early in 1870 a trade depression led to unemployment and to a demand for organised emigration. 100,000 working-men set their names to a petition presented by Sir George Grey (lately returned from New Zealand), J. A. Froude the historian, Sir R. R. Torrens of South Australia, and other notables. It was rejected by the Prime Minister. When Torrens pressed Gladstone in the House for an answer whether he

---

[1] A long and acrimonious correspondence between Granville and Governor Sir G. F. Bowen, on the subject of the withdrawal of the 18th Regiment, is to be found in *Accounts and Papers*, vol. L (1870). Several interventions by Sir G. Grey, then in retirement in England, are included. Granville's despatch of 7 October 1869 contains these words: 'The present distress of the colony arises mainly from two circumstances, the discontent of the natives, consequent on the confiscation of their land, and neglect of successive governments to place on foot a force sufficiently formidable to overawe that discontent. The abandonment of land, the recognition of Maori authority, and the maintenance of an expensive force are distasteful remedies which will not be resorted to while the colony continues to expect assistance from this country.'

wished to abandon the colonies, Gladstone was obliged to admit, with his usual circumlocution, that 'there ought to be nothing to preclude the hope, when the growth of a colonial possession is such as to make separation from the mother-country a natural and beneficial result, that that separation, so far from being effected by violence and bloodshed, might be the result of a peaceable and friendly transaction'.

The uneasiness of loyalists increased, and to say more, political managers began to notice that the electorate was not behind the separatists. Elder statesmen too, such as Russell and Earl Grey, expressed their concern in the Lords. The latter went so far as to recommend a strengthening of the bonds of Empire by resuming powers that had been decentralised. He would have federated the Empire under a committee of the Privy Council, to which the agents-general of the colonies were to be co-opted. In this he spoke as a convinced Free Trader who hoped to correct the 'absurd, unwise, mischievous' tendency of the colonies towards Protection.

Other critics were not so sure. By the year 1869 economic nationalism was apparent in France, Germany, and the United States as well as among the benighted Canadians and Australians. A new theory of Empire was emerging with its slogan: 'Trade follows the Flag.' Edward Wilson, an Australian journalist, used the phrase in a letter to *The Times* on 10 November 1869.[1] New lines of communication by cable and steamship were forging actual links between the mother-country and the colonies, which must direct the channels of trade. Colonial populations were growing so rapidly that these markets had an increasing importance.[2]

[1] It was about this time that the word 'imperialist' began to be heard in this connexion. Previously it had meant 'the adherent of an emperor' and nothing more. As late as 1878 Lord Carnarvon wrote in the *Fortnightly* that he was 'perplexed by a new word "imperialism" that has crept in'.

[2] Does Trade follow the Flag? Professor Hancock gives the following estimates in his *Survey of British Commonwealth Affairs*, vol. II (p. 81):

Proportion of the total external trade of Great Britain to and from Empire countries, by quinquennial averages (see also Appendix II).

Period	Per cent	Period	Per cent
1861–65	28·3	1901–05	25·6
1866–70	23	1906–10	26
1871–75	22·7	1911–15	39·4
1876–80	24·6	1916–20	31·7
1881–85	26·3	1921–25	33·5
1886–90	25·8	1926–30	34·8
1891–95	25·2	1931–35	37·9
1896–1900	24·5		

In fifty years, it was believed, Australia would be more populous than Britain; already Australians bought British goods at the rate of £10 a head whereas Americans bought only at the rate of 10s. But this was Mr Gladstone's blind spot. Nothing infuriated his opponents so much as his apparent indifference to the fate of emigrants, a subject on which Froude wrote with no little heat. The British government appeared to acknowledge no duty to the British unemployed. Let them go away, no matter where; perhaps best if they go to the United States where immigrants are welcome, since to placate the United States seemed to be the beginning and end of Gladstone's foreign policy.

The tide of separatism began to ebb visibly, so that even Gladstone realised that he had made a false move. Writers in the monthlies began to discuss schemes of federation, the prophets of the new era being Edward Jenkins, a Canadian, and J. A. Froude. In 1870 Ruskin's inaugural lecture, nominally on the subject of 'Art', startled Oxford and impressed the youthful Cecil Rhodes with a new political ideal. England should 'found colonies as fast and as far as she is able, formed of her most energetic and worthiest men; seizing every piece of fruitful waste ground she can set her foot on, and there teaching these her colonists that their chief virtue is to be fidelity to their country'. Even *The Times*, which scorned the efforts of the enthusiasts in 1869, had changed its tune by 1872.

The most sudden conversion was that of Disraeli who, in the first sixty years of his life, had shown no liking for the colonies. So lately as 1866 he had written to Lord Derby suggesting: 'Leave the colonies to defend themselves; recall the African Squadron; give up the settlements on the West Coast of Africa; we make a saving which shall enable us to build ships and have a good budget.' Attuning his ear to the new working-class voters whom he enfranchised in 1867 he was quick to notice that they did not share this contempt for their brothers who had emigrated. Political advantage might yet be gained from the Empire. Disraeli opened his campaign by a speech at the Crystal Palace (24 June 1872) which was intended to give a new plank to the platform of the Conservative Party. 'The colonies have decided', he said, 'that the Empire shall not be destroyed.' The Liberals who viewed everything 'in a financial aspect, totally passing by those moral and political considerations which made nations great', were to give way to statesmen of broader views. He lightly sketched the programme for an imperial tariff, a code of mutual defence and a system of 'security for the people of England for the enjoyment of the unappropriated lands'. The ripple (for it was not yet a powerful wave) of enthusiasm for Empire helped to float Disraeli into office in 1874, and there the matter ended.

The mythology of British history reports Disraeli as the champion and Gladstone as the opponent of Empire, but with slight justification. Neither appreciated the meaning of the two new phenomena: the rise of nationality in the dominions, and the conquest of the tropics by capitalist industry. Though Gladstone had an inkling of the nature of colonial democracy his career was concerned neither with advancing nor retarding it. On the other hand he was responsible as Premier for the annexation of the diamond-fields, and the armed occupation of Egypt. Though Disraeli yearned to hold the gorgeous East in fee, and acquired control of the Suez Canal in order to attain that end, his imperial policy largely consisted of grandiose gestures in the realm of foreign politics. He added Cyprus to the dominions of the Crown but made no use of it. Lord Carnarvon, his Colonial Secretary, enjoyed little of his confidence, taking his own line in South Africa while Disraeli ridiculed him behind his back.

(2) DILKE; FROUDE; SEELEY

The new imperialism was much stimulated by the efforts of several men of letters whose books appealed to a wider public than had been reached by the Colonial Reformers of the previous generation. Opinion was formed particularly by Dilke's *Greater Britain* (1869), Seeley's *Expansion of England* (1883), and Froude's *Oceana* (1886). Sir Charles Dilke (1843–1911) first came before the public as an author after making a voyage round the world. He was then a studious young Radical who alarmed the sedate by openly advocating the abolition of the monarchy, although he was a hereditary baronet. When he struck up a close friendship with Joseph Chamberlain, experts in politics began to speculate which of these two extremists would become Prime Minister in the Radical administration that must follow Gladstone's death or retirement. Dilke's early interest in the Empire was replaced by other political activities which marked him for advancement until, in 1885, his career was blasted by a scandal, a *cause célèbre* which ranked with the Parnell and Wilde cases in its effect on public opinion. When cited as co-respondent in a suit for divorce he was advised by his counsel not to give evidence on his own behalf. He thus carried the burden of a most dishonourable imputation, because, it is believed, he desired to shield another implicated party. Whatever the intention the effect put an end to his political ambitions. After an interval in retirement he resumed his imperial studies, producing several books of which the most important was *Problems of Greater Britain* (1890), a more restrained exposition purged of the taint of separatism and republicanism.

The value of Dilke's work lay rather in his analytical study of the Empire than in his inferences, for his observation was sounder than his judgment. Greater Britain to him meant, not Britain and her dependencies, but the English-speaking world. He foresaw a glorious future for the British race and hoped to see it morally reunited, by co-operation rather than by any legal formula. In such a union America and the 'white' colonies would take their place. He opposed the extension of British rule over foreign nations, civilised or uncivilised, but oddly made exceptions in the case of India and Ceylon. We must never relinquish India, he said, lest she should relapse into the anarchy from which we rescued her. He even recommended the colonisation of Kashmir by Englishmen.

Support from other quarters was provided by J. A. Froude (1818–94) and Sir J. R. Seeley (1834–95) who held the chairs of modern history at Oxford and Cambridge respectively. Froude was already distinguished as the historian of Tudor England when, in the 'sixties, he took up the cause of the colonies. He harped on naval and military exploits, and made a trip to the West Indies in the track of the buccaneers. He was active with Sir George Grey and R. R. Torrens in urging upon Gladstone the need for state-aided emigration. Froude became the most eminent of the new imperialists when his friend Lord Carnarvon was made Colonial Secretary by Disraeli. Carnarvon, who had carried the British North America Act through Parliament, sent Froude to the Cape as his confidential agent for the federation of South

Africa. Reversing the role of Balaam, Froude set out to bless the British South Africans and stayed to abuse them. A fastidious intellectual, he disliked the rawness of colonial society; a Tory with feudal instincts he found himself in sympathy with the patriarchal Boers. He was convinced (and rightly) that the annexation of the diamond-fields was sharp practice which had involved us in a series of errors. Realising that federation was unattainable he swung to the other extreme, suggesting that we should abandon all South Africa, except the Cape Peninsula which might be made into another Gibraltar.

Froude's disgust for Gladstonian liberalism made him a prophet of woe. He consoled himself by preaching the virtues of leadership as he believed them to have been displayed by the Elizabethans. He was not without a taint of that odious doctrine of hero-worship which his master Carlyle advocated so noisily, and to which a later generation gave an uglier name. Ten years after his visit to the Cape, Froude recovered his false step by his *Oceana*, the journal of a voyage round the world: 75,000 copies were sold of this, his most popular book, which is still worth reading, though his prejudices lead him into surprising comments. Unlike Dilke the radical, he has a hearty British contempt for foreigners and not least for Americans. What pleases him in the colonies is any evidence of English ways of life, the good old English qualities of self-help and personal responsibility. He warns his readers that the colonials will never accept any form of federation imposed upon them by Whitehall, nor will they ever willingly secede from the Empire. He asserts their loyalty, their simple devotion to the Queen, and asks in return that they should be treated with a little sympathy. The news of Gordon's death came when Froude was in Australia and stirred depths of feeling which he faithfully reported. He wrote at length and with good judgment upon the offer made by W. B. Dalley of New South Wales to send an Australian expedition to the Sudan.

One of Froude's observations on Australian life rings strangely in modern ears. From his experiences (of Government House society) he supposed that Australia would be the last refuge for English country gentlemen when democracy should drive them from their homes. Australia, at least, had nothing to fear from socialism and would never be threatened with a graduated income-tax. The heresies of Henry George would find no breeding-ground there.

Dilke and Froude were the publicists of radical and tory imperialism; Seeley was a profound scholar who neither visited colonies nor dabbled in politics. He was chiefly known as the author of *Ecce homo*, a theological 'sensation', until he published a series of Cambridge lectures under the title of *The Expansion of England*, proposing an entirely new line of approach to the history of the British people. So absolute was the success of his teaching that it is difficult now to recall what were the previous views of the average reader. Every historical compiler, for fifty or sixty years, has taken for granted what was new and startling when Seeley first propounded it. The older historians, he alleged, while concentrating on domestic affairs and European diplomacy, had overlooked the main factors which gave a meaning to the history of England in the eighteenth century, 'the simple obvious fact of the extension of the English name into other countries. In that century the history of England is not in England but in America and Asia.' 'There is something very characteristic in the indifference which we show towards this mighty phenomenon of the diffusion of our race and the expansion of our state. We seem, as it were, to have conquered and peopled half the world in a fit of absence of mind. While we were doing it, that is in the eighteenth century, we did not allow it to affect our imagination, or in any degree to change our ways of thinking.' 'We constantly betray by our modes of speech that we do not reckon our colonies as really belonging[1] to us; thus if we are asked what the English population is, it does not occur to us to reckon-in the population of Canada and Australia.' So far as the eighteenth century takes us, Seeley himself rectified the error. The ordinary educated Englishman has now a fair conception of the part played by Wolfe and Washington in the expansion of the British race. But Seeley's researches were not carried forward into the history of his own times. The Thirteen Colonies usually get adequate attention in the histories of England, while Canada and Australia are often not yet 'reckoned-in'.

---

[1] He means here that England and her colonies mutually belong to one another, not that the colonies are England's property.

(3) RUDYARD KIPLING

The two profoundest influences exercised by the English upon the history of the world may well be English commercial expansion and English lyric poetry. These lines of force do not often meet, and only in dealing with the 1890's need a historian of one concern himself with the other. There was then a poet whose verses were constructed with such curious art as to appeal to the artless and the illiterate, who for a moment made poetry popular with the middle classes, and who wrote on imperial themes. The doom reserved for all who are supposed to write down to the vulgar was pronounced upon him by the pontiffs of the cult of sophistication, until, after his death and after the Empire as Kipling described it had passed away, he was reinstated on a modest but respectable literary pedestal by Mr T. S. Eliot. It is not likely, however, that Kipling's work, except a few of his simpler ballads and children's stories, will be much read by future generations. He was a journalist of genius, but his writings are too topical and allusive to be understood when the allusions are forgotten and the topics stale. His career is a far more significant episode in the history of the British Commonwealth than in the history of English literature.

During the 1880's an ill-educated, middle-class lad was working as a hack reporter for an up-country newspaper in India. He hardly belonged to the governing class, was neither a soldier nor a civil servant; not even a 'box-wallah', the salaried agent of some great London firm; not quite a 'pukka sahib'. His experience of the world had been confined to a childhood spent in mean lodgings at Southsea, a boyhood curtailed at a second-rate school in Devon, a premature adolescence spent in that seamy side of life which is exposed to a provincial newspaperman. But his father was a scholar, an archaeologist, and his mother, whom Kipling thought the 'wittiest woman in India', had been one of the Pre-Raphaelite circle in London. The boy knew something of artistic craftsmanship as taught by William Morris, and something of the French impressionist writers on whom he modelled his style.

Kipling achieved a local fame, first among the British residents in the Punjab, then throughout India when he was taken up by

Lord and Lady Dufferin, until finally his reputation reached London. He wrote skits and parodies in the manner of Swinburne and Browning on Anglo-Indian life and politics; he filled odd columns in the *Civil and Military Gazette* with cynical short stories, owing much to Bret Harte and more to de Maupassant, which revealed, in this boy of nineteen or twenty, a terrific power of minute observation. 'This young man', said Oscar Wilde, 'has seen many remarkable things—through keyholes.' He was far from complacent about British rule. He distinguished then, as later, the unselfish unrewarded labour of the pioneer, up-country and alone, from the ponderous remote bureaucracy of Simla and Whitehall. His lip-service was to the Law, to the Flag; his real admiration was always for the irregular, the guerrilla-fighter. In a thousand solitary settlements young Englishmen of the middle classes toiled and improvised to pacify the savage, to turn the wilderness into a garden, to make wealth out of poverty, knowing that they would not be enriched by it. Here were the words for which they had waited, the sentiments they were too inarticulate to utter:

> By the bitter road the Younger Son must tread,
> Ere he win to hearth and saddle of his own,—
> 'Mid the riot of the shearers in the shed,
> In the silence of the herder's hut alone—
> In the twilight, on a bucket upside down,
> Hear me babble what the weakest won't confess—

Kipling's first literary creation was the cockney soldier, a guttersnipe without manners, morals or traditions, homesick for London: 'for the sounds of 'er an' the sights of 'er and the stinks of 'er, orange-peel an' hasphalte an' gas comin' in over Vaux'all Bridge'; rude, ignorant, and yet dimly aware of the honour and privilege of his task to serve 'the Widow of Windsor'; much exposed to the criticisms of pharisees and the romancing of stay-at-home novelists—

> It's Tommy this, and Tommy that, and 'Tommy, 'ow's your soul?'
> But it's 'thin red line of 'eroes' when the drums begin to roll—

attacks which Tommy repulsed on either flank with equal vigour. He was neither blackguard nor 'thin red hero'. This humblest of empire-builders, gay, humorous, impertinent, courageous, enduring; without a touch of ferocity; devoted to dogs and

Plate 21

RUDYARD KIPLING (1865–1936)

In his study at Burwash. From a painting by P. Burne-Jones, 1899. *See p. 671.*

Plate 22

LORD DUFFERIN (1826–1902)

Canada, Egypt, India, Burma. From a painting by G. F. Watts. *See p. 764.*

children and beer; imperturbable and unchanged whether his fate was to march with Howe to Bunker Hill, or Roberts to Kandahar, or Allenby to Jerusalem, or Montgomery to Alamein, Tommy Atkins had at last found a voice.

When first Kipling became known outside the narrow limits of the Punjab, he was recognised as the soldier's poet; he was next hailed as the poet of empire. In 1890 an Indian newspaper sent him eastward on a world tour to Burma, Japan, California and at last to London, where he lived solitary in lodgings and was unhappy though prosperous. He felt himself out of place, sharing the bitter feelings of so many young men from the dominions who have come to the land they were taught to call 'home', to find themselves strangers in a cold unfamiliar society. He married an American lady and took her back to New England which he liked even less. He shook the dust of America off his feet and rarely again wrote a line about the Americans without abusing them, unless they should have the grace to become anglicised. At last finding in South Africa the ideal empire for which he had been seeking, he divided his time for several years between Cape Colony and Sussex. In 1904 he settled finally in England, turning his back on the Empire and his mind towards other themes which lie outside the scope of this book. The period of his travels in North America and South Africa, and of the voyages to and fro, had filled his notebooks with dramatic incidents and pictures, with patches of local colour and snatches of technical jargon which he cunningly wove into the fabric of his later songs and stories.

To a whole generation homesickness was reversed by inoculation with Kipling's magic. Englishmen felt the days of England 'sick and cold, and the skies gray and old and the twice-breathed airs blowing damp'; heard the East a' calling; fawned on the younger nations, the men that could shoot and ride; were conscious of the weight of the White Man's Burden; learned to read and talk the jargon of the seven seas; while, in the outposts of Empire, men who read no other books recognised and approved flashes of their own lives in phrases from Kipling's verse: the flying-fishes and the dawn coming up like thunder across the Bay of Bengal; the smell of the wattles at Lichtenburg in the rain; the voyage outward-bound till the old lost stars wheel back and the Southern Cross rides high; the palm-tree in full bearing bowing down to the surf under a low African moon; the aching berg propping the speckless sky at hot Constantia; the wild tide-race that whips the harbour-mouth at Melbourne; the broom flowering behind the windy town of Wellington; the islands where the trumpet-orchids blow and the anchor chain goes ripping down through coral trash; the western railway where the trestle groans and shivers in the snow; the Golden Gate of San Francisco where the blindest bluffs hold good and the wildest tales are true. Such tales they heard by camp-fires, of mine and ranch, and moose and caribou, and parrots pecking lambs to death; of little wars with Sayyid Barghash of Zanzibar, and King Lobengula with the smoke-reddened eyes, and Fuzzy Wuzzy who broke a British square; and of Piet the Boer farmer, with his Mauser for amusement and his pony for retreat, who fought so much better than some crack English battalions.

South Africa, in the 'nineties, was in a high fever with the temperature rising. The open frontier to the north where there might be gold and certainly would be bloodshed, the labours of engineers at desert railways and deep mines, the scuffling and jostling of 'boom' towns, the visible march of trade and industry, and behind that the steady consolidation of pasture and ploughland, the creation under his eye of a new country by pioneers as bold and ruthless and far-reaching as Drake and Ralegh, were the ingredients of a composition he understood and admired, the triumph of individualists whose only high ideal was a schoolboyish sentimental loyalty. Rhodes and Jameson were the men after his own heart.

> If you can meet with Triumph and Disaster
> And treat those two impostors just the same
>
> Or watch the things you gave your life to broken,
> And stoop and build 'em up with worn-out tools.

This Rhodes did after the Jameson Raid. Rhodes is the man who

> Can talk with crowds and keep his virtue
> Or walk with Kings—nor lose the common touch.

But the poem was written of Jameson whose name, it has been said, is concealed in it as a cryptogram.

Kipling has often been described as if he were the poet of orthodox, conservative imperialism. He is the very opposite of that; he spoke for those whom he called the 'Younger Sons', the middle-class adventurers, the 'Sons of Martha' who accepted responsibility and were never too proud for any task; not the 'Sons of Mary', the governing class which accepted wealth and power as a right. He is the poet of the frontier-rebel, the filibuster, the buccaneer. He would have sided with Drake not Burleigh, with Ralegh not James I, with Washington not George Grenville, with Wakefield not Earl Grey. To the frontiersmen he gave a voice, but the stay-at-home English no more appreciated it than George III appreciated Benjamin Franklin. When Kipling addressed the English on their Empire it was always, as in *Recessional*, with a note of warning against 'frantic boast and foolish word'. But to that warning the English turned a deaf ear.

2. RHODES

By the Convention signed at Pretoria in August 1881, six months after the battle of Majuba, Her Majesty's Government guaranteed to the Transvaal 'complete self-government subject to the suzerainty of Her Majesty' and subject also to fifteen 'reservations and limitations'. A British Resident at Pretoria would watch over the interests of the 'suzerain', reporting upon them to the High Commissioner at the Cape. The control of the 'external relations of the State including the conclusion of treaties' was to be carried on through Her Majesty's diplomatic and consular officers. 'No future enactment affecting the interest of natives' was to have any effect without Her Majesty's consent. The Transvaal state was to be liable for debts incurred both before and during the British occupation. 'All persons other than natives conforming to the laws of the Transvaal State' were to be permitted to reside and work in the Transvaal without discrimination in respect of paying taxes. Nothing was said in the convention about granting them political rights, though Kruger gave a verbal assurance that all but 'newcomers' would be enfranchised. Resident aliens were to be exempt from commando service, and loyalists were not to be victimised. This last proviso was ignored by the Boer leaders as it had been by the Americans in 1783. On their part the British government undertook that the troops should be withdrawn.

No sooner was the republic established than Kruger, who was elected President in 1883, began to minimise and whittle away the suzerainty. He went to London to negotiate for better terms, which he extracted from the fifteenth Lord Derby, the next in the long line of Colonial Secretaries. Derby admitted that the word 'suzerainty' had no precise connotation but refused to abrogate it. The London Convention (27 February 1884) makes no mention of suzerainty, leaving the juridical situation more uncertain even than before. The new convention repeated most of the clauses[1] of the former one but made several concessions to Republican sentiment. The Transvaal state was permitted to resume the proud old name of South African Republic, and the British Resident was degraded to the status of a consul. What was not made clear was the relation of the second document to the first. Did the London Convention supersede the Pretoria Convention, in which case suzerainty was tacitly abandoned, or was it an amendment, in which case suzerainty remained? Apart from these sentimental concessions, the most important effect of the London Convention was a very precise delimitation of the Transvaal frontier. When Kruger returned to Africa it was to find trouble on his eastern and western borders.

According to their nomadic tradition some Boers had trekked east and west beyond the borders of the Transvaal. A group of trekkers, allying themselves with Dinizulu, the son of Cetewayo, set up the 'New Republic' in eastern Zululand. Locally the cause was typical Boer land-hunger, but behind it loomed Kruger's desire for an outlet to the sea, an ambition for which he might expect some support from Germany. The uncertain frontiers between British and Portuguese territory on either side of Africa left loopholes for German penetration.

Westward the clash came in Bechuanaland, a territory familiar to the British public from the exploits of Dr Livingstone. Every schoolboy knew of the Missionaries' Road along the comparatively fertile fringe of the Kalahari Desert, northward to the Zambezi and the half-revealed Great Lakes in the centre of the Dark Continent, which was said to hold the secret of King Solomon's Mines. This strip of pasturage, the mission-field of

[1] Especially on external affairs. 'The South African Republic will conclude no treaty or engagement with any state or nation, other than the Orange Free State, without the Queen's permission.'

Moffat and Livingstone, was seized, in spite of missionary protests, by Boer trekkers who set up two petty republics known
as Stellaland and Goshen (1882). The first British counter-action
was taken by the Rev. John McKenzie who hoisted the Union
Jack at his mission in Stellaland, with the approval of the Colonial
Office and the Aborigines Protection Society. The Boers tore it
down. Next, Robinson, High Commissioner at the Cape, sent a
man of his own choosing to replace McKenzie as Deputy Commissioner. This was Cecil Rhodes, then unknown outside his
own province. He was a wealthy young mine-owner and a
member of the Cape Parliament (since 1881). Rhodes occasioned
some alarm by announcing that he wanted 'to get rid of the
Imperial Factor in this question and to deal with it jointly with
the Transvaal'. It was his habit to blurt out his intentions.
'Tell the town-crier exactly what you are going to do,' he said,
'and then you have no trouble.'

In that frame of mind Rhodes went north to deal with De la
Rey, the leader of the Stellaland Boers. 'Blood must flow',
roared the infuriated De la Rey. 'Give me my breakfast,' said
Rhodes, making himself at home, 'then we can talk about
blood.' In a week's time the two were on the best of terms and
Rhodes was standing godfather to De la Rey's child; but the
missionaries disapproved of Rhodes's friendship with the Boers
and his hostility to the Imperial Factor. Whereas agreement
was reached over Stellaland, Rhodes was not able to come to
terms with the more northerly and still more primitive republic
of Goshen. Rather against his principles, for he mistrusted
soldiers, Rhodes was obliged to ask for military backing. The
Imperial Factor was produced, with unusual promptness, in the
shape of Sir Charles Warren (1840–1927) with a column of 4000
first-rate troops. The reason for this show of force was not the
presence of a few Boer filibusters, but fear of Germany.

In 1883, Karl Lüderitz, a German adventurer, had obtained a
concession from a native chief for a trading-station at Angra
Pequeña north of the Orange River estuary. For reasons of his
own, Bismarck had been finessing with the British Foreign
Office, not so much because he wanted territory in south-west
Africa as because it suited him to embarrass Great Britain with the
threat. The Foreign Office would not assert a prior British claim
unless assured that Cape Colony would undertake the cost of

administration. The pedestrian government at the Cape, not wishing to enlarge its native problem, would do no more, though it had taken over from Her Majesty's Government the little harbour of Walvis Bay, north of Angra Pequeña. In 1884 Bismarck, without enthusiasm, took the step of declaring a protectorate over the country thereafter known as German South-West Africa. The fear that he would claim the hinterland and exclude the British from the 'Missionaries' Road' to the north led to the despatch of Sir Charles Warren to the aid of Rhodes.

Thus the petty dispute between Rhodes and the Boer filibusters was swallowed up into the great diplomatic struggle for the partition of Africa, then approaching its crisis. These were subsidiary moves in the diplomatic game played at the Berlin Conference (November 1884–February 1885); the moves were made to an accompaniment of war-drums in the Sudan where Khartoum fell on 26 January. While Warren secured the Missionaries' Road, a cruiser was sent to St Lucia on the East Coast to secure the littoral of Zululand before the Boers of the 'New Republic' should break through to the sea.

In March 1885 Warren annexed Stellaland and Goshen, having overawed the republican Boers without fighting. The greater part was proclaimed a Crown Colony with the name of British Bechuanaland, while to the north the country of the great chief Khama (1828–1923), always a loyal friend of the British and of the missionaries, became the Bechuanaland Protectorate. Rhodes was profoundly dissatisfied, for Warren acted in the interest of the natives and the missionaries, absolutely excluding Boer settlers. Though this was triumph for the Imperial Factor, Kruger, who was penniless and friendless was obliged to accept it, but he mistrusted the approaches of the wealthy young financier. He met Rhodes in conference, in 1885, and recorded: 'This young man is going to cause me trouble.'

At this time Zululand had relapsed into tribal war. Though Cetewayo was released from internment he proved unable to reassert his sovereignty and died, a fugitive, in 1884. As on the west coast so on the east the imminence of German intervention stimulated the British government to action. Zululand was partitioned between Natal and the 'New Republic'. At the final settlement of 1888, the 'New Republic' was incorporated into the Transvaal. The coastal strip, including St Lucia Bay (which was thus denied to Germany), together with the remaining two-thirds of Cetewayo's patrimony, was annexed to the colony of Natal (1887) and governed in accordance with the Shepstone policy.

Few stories are better known than that of the East Anglian clergyman's son, Cecil John Rhodes (1853–1902), sent to the local grammar-school because there was not enough money for him to follow his elder brothers to Eton, then packed off to Africa to make his fortune and cure his weak chest. After an attempt at cotton-growing in Natal he found his way to the diamond-fields in 1871, among a host of other adventurers, but carrying a Greek lexicon in his baggage. The big, hulking lad, rapidly throwing off his delicacy in the keen upland air, shrewd in business, easy and open-handed though ruthless and resolute, was utterly different in grain from the devil-may-care adventurers, the get-rich-quick speculators, and the rough diggers with whom he associated. He was unconcerned with women, uninterested in sport; he had a secret source of strength in his Dream. 'When I find myself in uncongenial company,' he said, 'or when people are playing their games, or when I am alone in a railway carriage, I think of my great idea. It is the pleasantest companion I have.' He believed in power—*Weltmacht*—which must be based upon knowledge and wealth. Since knowledge was to be the first step he entered himself, when he was earning a mere hundred pounds a week, as an undergraduate at Oriel College, Oxford. Keeping his terms, at intervals, over a period of five years (1873–8), he returned to Kimberley between them to make more money. Though never a scholar, nor even what is called a reading man, he knew that Oxford scholarship was a source of power and, early in life, conceived the plan of extending to other Younger Sons of the Empire the boon which he had tardily and inadequately striven for. The Dream changed, as dreams do, enlarging its scope as the dreamer matured.

In 1880 he founded the De Beers Company at Kimberley, and entered the Cape Parliament as member for a constituency in the diamond-fields. His first *coup*, after gaining an influence over

Sir Hercules Robinson, was the mission to Stellaland (1884)
which has already been mentioned. During the next five years
he was more concerned with finance than with politics. 'One is
called a speculator', he said. 'I do not deny the charge. If one
has ideas, one cannot carry them out without having wealth at
one's back.' His achievement at Kimberley was to introduce
mechanised production on the largest scale, to buy out the
numerous claims of individual diggers, to prevent I.D.B. by
confining native labourers into compounds, thus acquiring control
of the whole field in order to restrict the output of diamonds
(see chapter IX, 4, page 491). The amalgamation with Barney
Barnato, which virtually created a monopoly, was completed in
1888, but Rhodes liked to recall that he bought out the last
independent claim, 'by searchlight', during the siege of Kimberley.

In 1887 he founded the Consolidated Goldfields Company at
Johannesburg, but Rhodes was never master of the gold-fields as
he was of the diamond-fields. Generous and careless in his
private affairs, he never knew how rich he was. By 1888 he was
one of the richest men in the world with a reputed income from
Kimberley of about £1,000,000 and from Johannesburg of about
£300,000 a year. He began to use this wealth for realising his
Dream; wealth would open for him the road to the north. South
Africa should be a federation of free states 'with the Union Jack
for protection'. Otherwise the Imperial Factor should be shut out.

'When Rhodes stood upon the Cape Peninsula,' said Mark
Twain, 'his shadow fell upon the Zambezi.' But why should
vision stop at the Victoria Falls, which he never saw with the
eyes of the flesh? In East Africa other empire-builders were
striving for wider British protectorates in competition with the
Germans. Even if they failed, the money of the richest man in
the world would talk. The German Kaiser would see the value
of a business deal. A British Dominion from the Cape to Cairo
was part of the Dream (though the phrase belongs to H. H. Johnston rather than to Rhodes). North of the Great Lakes the
Mahdi's empire was another obstacle. In the opinion of most
men it would be necessary to 'smash the Mahdi' before there
could be a southward advance from Cairo, but Rhodes thought
otherwise. He had once considered accompanying Gordon to
Khartoum in the belief that even the Mahdi might have been
brought to terms. One could 'deal with him' as one had dealt

with De la Rey in Stellaland or buy him out as one had bought out Barnato.

Even there the Dream was not terminated; it embraced the moral reunion, perhaps the federation, of the English-speaking peoples. 'We are the first race in the world,' he wrote to W. T. Stead, the Liberal journalist whom he converted to his views, 'and the more of the world we inhabit, the better it is for the human race. The absorption of the greater portion of the world under our rule simply means the end of all wars.' In later years he was not so crude though even his faults were always engagingly boyish. He found no inconsistency in combining this exalted racialism with a genuine liking for the Boer farmer.

In 1888 Rhodes was thirty-six years old, Kruger was sixty-three. The future of South Africa lay between these two: the young dreamer with his eye set on far horizons, eager to use his speculative wealth and fleeting energy, impetuous, hasty, constantly modifying his schemes; the old patriarch, narrow, rigid, and consistent, always harping with unshakable patience upon a single theme—'My people the Afrikaners...the independence of my people...my land.' 'The racehorse is swifter than the ox,' said the old President, 'but the ox draws the heavier load. We shall see who wins in the end.' Gold set the two contestants on an equal footing. Kruger learned to exploit the wealth of Johannesburg as Rhodes exploited the wealth of Kimberley. No longer the wretched ruler of an insolvent state, Kruger became, by no effort of his own or of his people, dictator of the richest community in the world. His revenue in 1885 had been £178,000; in 1887 it was £638,000; in 1889 £1,500,000; and in 1899 £4,087,000. The weakness of his position was that, while posing as the simple patriarch of a farmers' democracy, he was in fact a financial speculator just as Rhodes was. He too had taken service with Mammon. International capital, so long shy of the bankrupt pastoral republic, was willing to back the ruler of the Rand. In 1888 the Netherlands Railway Company was founded with Dutch and German capital to build a railway from Pretoria to the Portuguese frontier where, eventually, it linked up with a Portuguese line to Lourenço Marquez; it was opened to traffic in 1894.

Rhodes was not averse at this time to Kruger's eastward progress which diverted Boer attention from his own advance to the north. Beyond Bechuanaland lay the healthy uplands over which Lobengula, King of the Matabele, ruled barbarously. The Matabele, an offshoot of the Zulus, were perhaps the most ferocious of all the Bantu tribes. They had moved north from Zululand in the 1830's, 'eating up' tribe after tribe until the Boer *voortrekkers*, coming up behind them, had driven them far into the interior. Their land contained ivory and might contain gold, for it was seamed with ancient workings and the vestiges of forgotten cities. Missionaries, traders, and hunters had occasionally visited the Matabele country since the 1850's, but Lobengula was an unchallenged despot when Rhodes sent an emissary, C. D. Rudd, to him in 1888. 'Loben', a magnificent but rather simple savage, was plagued by British, Boer, and German concession-hunters who plied him with champagne while they worked upon his royal bounty. Rhodes's agent obtained a concession for all the minerals in Lobengula's country in return for guns and ammunition, a steamboat on the Zambezi, and a pension of £100 a month. Later 'Loben' grew uneasy and killed the counsellor who had advised him to grant the concession, but he kept his word to Rhodes.

Meanwhile the Aborigines Protection Society was in full cry against Rhodes who hurried home to London to obtain a charter. Appealing to the Radicals he won the support of W. T. Stead, the erratic editor of the *Pall Mall Gazette*, and placated the Irish in the House of Commons by subscribing to Parnell's funds. His triumph was to convert several eminent persons who had signed a petition against him, among them a Royal Duke, and Earl Grey[1] who was later Governor of Rhodesia. The Chartered British South Africa Company was incorporated on 29 October 1889 with a capital of a million pounds. Of this, £200,000 was subscribed by the De Beers Company, while the investing public rapidly took up the remainder and had long to wait for any return on their money.

Next the column of pioneers was organised to survey the resources of Lobengula's country. Though drilled as an army, the expedition, 180 prospectors and 300 of the Company's mounted police, was organised by a civilian contractor. Led by F. C. Selous (1851–1917), the greatest of big-game hunters, the column left Mafeking in August 1890 and, in the following

[1] The nephew and successor of Henry, 3rd Earl Grey. (See Appendix III.)

month, founded Fort Salisbury. The prospectors discovered no
'payable' gold. When the long road was opened, through 2000
miles of British Territory, from Capetown to Salisbury, settlers
began to trek north into 'Charterland' or 'Rhodesia'. The
pioneers had discreetly avoided Lobengula's *kraal* at Bulawayo,
keeping well to the east in the country of the Mashona, a people
subject to the Matabele. Here the settlers were allowed to take up
land, without much regard to native rights, but as tenants-at-will
of the Company. Rhodes encouraged Boers to settle as freely
as British, on the Company's terms, but when a body of Boer
trekkers from the Transvaal attempted to enter the country
independently they were sternly headed back.

With increasing difficulty Lobengula restrained his young
warriors from resisting the white invaders, while his own misgivings grew. At his side stood Rhodes's lifelong friend, the
little doctor, (Sir) Leander Starr Jameson (1853–1917), who cured
Lobengula's gout and held him to his promise.

> 'If gold is in my royal *kraal*, can they come and dig?'
> 'Yes, O King!'

During the march of the pioneers Jameson was alone among
the Matabele, and inflexible. In 1891 he became administrator of
the Chartered Territory. Soon the telegraph line arrived at
Salisbury (1892) and Rhodes's men were reaching out for further
conquests. North of the Zambezi he was buying out a trading
company on Lake Nyasa, while others of his people made a
bold move to reach the sea-coast in the Portuguese zone. A
sharp struggle for Manicaland, conducted both by filibusters on
the spot and by diplomatic exchanges in Europe was solved by
the Anglo-Portuguese agreement of June 1891. Sir H. H.
Johnston, consul at Mozambique, disagreeing with the brusque
methods of the Chartered Company, was largely responsible for a
friendly settlement which secured the Portuguese rights over
their territory, while giving the British a commercial outlet at the
new Portuguese seaport of Beira. Navigation of the Zambezi
was thrown open to all nations. A railway from the port of Beira
to Mashonaland was begun in 1892.

There came a time when Lobengula could restrain his young
men no longer. They began to raid Mashonaland, their tribal
custom being to hunt the Mashona as fair game, killing the

adults, carrying off the boys and girls, and driving the cattle. The war which Jameson thought inevitable had come (1893). He raised a force of volunteers and marched on Bulawayo, whereupon Lobengula burned his capital and fled. A few weeks later he died of fever in the bush, protesting with his last words: 'I did not ever wish to fight with Rhodes and Jameson. Go now all of you to Rhodes and seek his protection. He will be your chief and friend.'

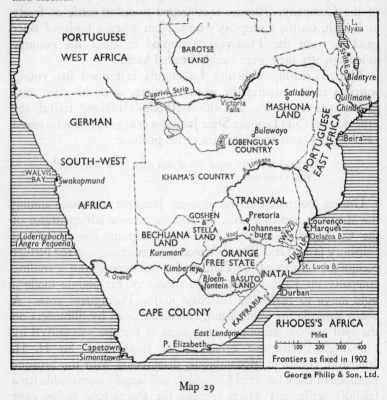

Map 29

Thus fell Lobengula, not without nobility. Yet he was a cruel tyrant, the oppressor of the Mashona and other subject tribes. To them the age offered no prospect of liberty. If not 'eaten up' by Lobengula their destiny lay between submission to the British or to the Boers. Perhaps they got the least of the three evils. And thus Kruger's Republic was hemmed in, as he bitterly complained, on all sides. His plea for *lebensraum* must however be qualified by the fact that his 50,000 burghers already occupied a territory as large as France.

The Matabele War is remembered for one heroic incident, the fight—to the last man and the last round—of Major Alan Wilson and his thirteen comrades at the Shangani River, where they were overwhelmed by Lobengula's rearguard (5 December 1893). The war record is dishonoured by Jameson's message to his troops: 'Each member of the force will be entitled to mark out a farm of 3000 *morgen* (6000 acres) in any part of Matabeleland.... The loot shall be divided, one half to the British South Africa Company and the remainder to officers and men in equal shares.'

3. KRUGER

IN the early 'nineties Rhodes was at the height of his career. He owned the diamond-fields and represented them in the Cape Parliament. His Chartered Company had occupied and virtually annexed the country they called, to his great delight, Rhodesia. In 1890 he became Prime Minister of Cape Colony, largely on the Boer vote.

For several years past a nationalist movement had been emerging among the settled Afrikaners of the colony. Initiated by hot-heads at the time of Majuba 'to defend our language, our nation, our people', the Afrikander Bond was a partly political and partly cultural society. Its founders had envisaged it as a revolutionary group for establishing 'the United States of South Africa under our own flag', but the cautious temper of the Cape Colonists had prevailed, through the influence of J. H. Hofmeyr the elder (1845–1909), a loyal friend of the British. The preservation of the Afrikaner national character under the British flag was his policy which in many respects agreed with that of Rhodes. The period 1890 to 1895, when Rhodes and Hofmeyr were cabinet colleagues, was an age of progress and good feeling, when Rhodes revived the Dutch colonial architecture, promoted agricultural research, built railways, and inspired the people of South Africa with his dream. The old cultivated society of the Cape expanded in the sun of prosperity. Even the English learned to sympathise with Afrikaner ways after reading the *Story of an African Farm* (1883) by Olive Schreiner, the sister of one of Rhodes's colleagues. This sober, humane book wears better than the other best-seller about Africa, *King Solomon's Mines* (1885), which pictures the boyish irresponsible spirit of the treasure-hunters who looted Lobengula's country.

Between 1884 and 1894 all the native territories between Cape Colony and Natal were successively annexed, to anticipate attempts at German penetration. This obliged Rhodes to adopt a consistent policy of native administration, a problem which had been shirked for 200 years. In Cape Colony, alone of the South African states, coloured persons might qualify for the franchise. The qualification was tightened, in 1892, to prevent the swamping of the European vote by natives from the new territories. Like most of his contemporaries Rhodes never doubted that the greatest benefits he could confer upon a native were to instil habits of industry and to provide opportunities of self-help. The new policy was embodied in the Glen Grey Act (1894), so called from the district where it was first applied. Tribal lands were converted into individual holdings with a rule of primogeniture to prevent subdivision. As in England younger sons must go out and work. The rare privilege of voting was then restricted by a property qualification in money. European settlers and liquor-traders were excluded from native areas. In the villages local government was entrusted to elected native councils. The development of this system throughout the Transkei 'is today perhaps the brightest feature in the complex of relations between white and black in South Africa'.[1]

Apart from the native problem which loomed ever in the background, the political issues were tariffs and railway rates. When the Transvaal was poor, Kruger had been willing to form a customs-union, which Cape Colony refused since it enjoyed the revenue from a tariff on the trade of the inland states. When the Transvaal became rich, Kruger could afford to set up a tariff wall against the other states, diverting his own trade from their railways to his Delagoa Bay Line. In spite of the customs-union formed with Cape Colony by President Brand in his last year, the Free State began to draw away from the Colony into the orbit of the hostile Transvaal.

Johannesburg was a typical gold-rush city, with a mixed

[1] J. H. Hofmeyr the younger. *Cambridge History of the British Empire*, vol. VIII.

population of engineers, prospectors, speculators, native traders, and the riff-raff such as always haunted a goldfield. Some came from the British Isles, more from the seaboard colonies, and many were Jewish traders from Central Europe, these last being known by the strange nickname of 'Peruvians'. The town contained few genuine Transvaal burghers. Though no census was taken between 1890 and 1904 it was generally agreed that by 1896 the newcomers, *Uitlanders*, outnumbered the whole Boer population of the republic two or three times over. It was known that they paid more than nine-tenths of the taxes. Over the town they had created and the revenue they provided, they exercised no control whatever. Kruger restricted the franchise by successive stages, making it almost impossible for anyone but the son of a burgher to be admitted to the roll. There was no municipal self-government, no status for English—the language of the majority—in courts or schools, almost no public works. When a petition for the franchise bearing more signatures than the whole Boer adult population was submitted, in 1894, it was rejected with scorn. Political power was to be reserved to 'the old people of the land'. Kruger hated the Rand, and its noisy profane inhabitants, yet never thought of relinquishing the wealth these Uitlanders produced. In seventeen years he made the forty-mile journey from Pretoria to Johannesburg only three times and then was treated with insolence by mobs of Uitlanders. He hardened his heart, like Pharaoh, against them, but he would not forgo his tribute. Even before the fatal year, 1896, he had begun to import arms from Germany and to build forts at Johannesburg with which to overawe the subject race. Kruger's contracts and monopolies, bearing heavily upon the Uitlanders, were corruptly administered by a horde of greedy officials. He began to irritate the best men among his own supporters by financial favours to advisers and capitalists from Holland and Germany. His morals, like Rhodes's, were somewhat stretched by financial megalomania.

The appearance of Joseph Chamberlain at the Colonial Office, in 1895, inspired that dull department with new activity. The federation of South Africa and of Australia was to be the first move towards an eventual federation of the whole Empire, which 'Oom Paul' Kruger must not be allowed to frustrate. Chamberlain scored a diplomatic victory by insisting upon the reopening of the Transvaal frontier when Kruger tried to close it. This convinced him that continued pressure would oblige Kruger to make concessions to the Uitlanders who were now talking openly of rebellion. Kruger watched them grimly. 'You wait', he said, 'until the tortoise puts out its head, and then you chop it off.' Never was there so open a conspiracy. The High Commissioner at Capetown (still Sir Hercules Robinson) conferred with Chamberlain and was instructed that, when the rising should take place, he was to intervene at Pretoria by summoning a national assembly. The possibility of using police from Bechuanaland to keep order was also discussed.

While the Uitlanders' Committee at Johannesburg conspired, with the utmost indiscretion and frequent disagreements, Rhodes at Capetown took a hand, attempting to control the situation through three agents, all medical men. One of the apocryphal sayings of Rhodes was that he liked employing doctors 'since they were not squeamish over a little blood-letting'. His agent in London, Dr Rutherfoord Harris, negotiated with Chamberlain for the transference of Bechuanaland from the Crown to the Chartered Company, ostensibly to ease the construction of a railway northwards from Mafeking to Bulawayo, his own ulterior motive being to threaten the Transvaal frontier. He tried in vain to draw Chamberlain into the conspiracy. Chamberlain took a strictly correct view of the railway project, merely authorising the cession of a narrow strip of land to the Company while safeguarding the territories of Khama and other chiefs. The grant was enough to justify Rhodes in concentrating a force of the Company's police at the railhead near Mafeking. This was the starting-point for Dr Jameson, the second medical man. The third, Dr Wolff, was Rhodes's agent with the conspirators at Johannesburg. The rising was planned for December 1895. At the last moment the conspirators lost heart since they could not agree upon their main objective. Some were for carrying out a palace revolution within the Transvaal to overthrow Kruger's party and purge the state; others were for annexing the Transvaal to the British Empire. They postponed the rising to a later date.

Dr Jameson then took the bit between his teeth. He precipitated revolution by invading the Transvaal with 450 mounted police (29 December 1895). The Uitlanders' Reform Committee tardily distributed arms and seized control of Johannesburg

Plate 23

DAVID LIVINGSTONE (1813–73)

Not painted from the life but based upon photographs. By F. Havill. *See p.* 647.

Plate 24A

CECIL RHODES
(1853–1902)

A studio portrait, about 1
See p. 679.

Plate 24B

JOSEPH CHAMBERLAIN
(1836–1914)

A studio portrait about 1902.
See p. 834.

with divided counsels and uncertain aims. While they were caught unawares by the Jameson Raid, Kruger was not. Strong commandos of burghers intercepted Jameson forty miles from Johannesburg at Doornkop, where he surrendered (1 January 1896) after a sharp fight against superior numbers.

History shows no mercy to a *coup d'état* that fails. If the Uitlanders had been a little bolder, or if Jameson's force had been better led, or if Kruger's reaction had been less prompt, this filibustering expedition might have been acclaimed with the similar campaigns by which Fremont gained California and Houston gained Texas for the United States; but the execution was as inept as the design was vicious. In trying to force the hands of the Uitlanders, of Rhodes, of Chamberlain, of Her Majesty's Government, Jameson brought dismay to all four. On hearing the surprising news Chamberlain instantly ordered him to return, disclaimed responsibility, and demanded his extradition when he was captured. Sir Hercules Robinson went to Pretoria —how much less proudly than he had expected—and found himself unable to protect the rebels from Kruger's just wrath. Rhodes saw that his cause was lost, betrayed by the rash folly of his best friend. There could be no doubt of his own guilt in loading and aiming the weapon that Jameson had let off at half-cock. The bubble of his reputation had burst. His cabinet fell away; his Afrikaner friends turned from him in disgust; his enemies in London triumphed at the exposure of his malignity. The Little Englanders did not doubt that Jameson, Rhodes, and Chamberlain were fellow-conspirators. A still clumsier intervention from another quarter diverted the displeasure of the English people. The German Kaiser was moved to send a telegram to Kruger congratulating him upon suppressing the revolt 'without calling on the aid of friendly powers'. Whatever the British public thought about the machinations of capitalists in Africa, they resented the Kaiser's hint that he might draw the mantle of his protection over the Transvaal. When 'Dr Jim' was sentenced to two years' imprisonment, at the Old Bailey, a large part of public opinion had so far rallied as to regard him as a hero in misfortune.

Very different was the fate of the Uitlanders. Though they had committed no act of violence and had meekly submitted at the request of the High Commissioner, Cecil Rhodes's brother and three other ringleaders were sentenced to death, fifty-nine others[1] to rigorous imprisonment with fines and confiscations added. It added little to the credit of Kruger's justice that these sentences were commuted, after months of haggling over the precise sums, for fines amounting to £250,000. They should perhaps be rather described as bribes since no account was rendered of the disposal of the money.

Troubles accumulated upon Rhodes's head in 1896. Most of the cattle in Rhodesia were destroyed that year by the *rinderpest* for which the natives blamed the white newcomers. Not only the Matabele but also the downtrodden Mashona rose in revolt, massacring 200 white settlers, men, women, and children. A general war of annihilation raged until Rhodes went north to his own country. With patient care he brought the chiefs to negotiation through an aged Matabele princess, Lobengula's stepmother, who has been described as the only woman Rhodes ever respected. Unarmed, he met the tribesmen, promising them justice and peace. He alleviated famine by giving them a million bags of mealies at his own expense. The Matabele transferred to Rhodes some of the numinous respect paid to their own kings and when, five years later, his body was buried in the Matoppo Hills, they acclaimed him with the royal salute never before given to any white man.

Meanwhile in England Chamberlain was facing the fury of the Radicals who had not forgiven his abandonment of the Liberal Party in 1886. He defended himself with brilliant energy against reckless accusations that he had directed the Raid, that he desired only to provoke war with Kruger, and—a venomous shaft from Lloyd George—that his interest in the munitions industry at Birmingham was at the back of his policy. Jameson he altogether disavowed, but to Rhodes he, rather quixotically, extended his protection, though he disliked the man and disapproved his methods. After bitter recriminations a Parliamentary enquiry was held in 1897. No evidence was brought to inculpate Chamberlain though some gaps in the testimony seemed to imply his guilt. His innocence of complicity in the Raid was not established until the publication of his *Life* by J. L. Garvin, in 1932. Chamberlain had known, as the whole world knew, of the imminent

---

[1] Thirty-four British, sixteen South Africans, one Canadian, one Australian, six Americans and five others, including one Turk.

rising at Johannesburg and had made plans for action when it should occur. But to provoke the rising by the use of Jameson's troops was the last thing he intended or desired. Such a coup could have no effect but to knock the good cards out of Chamberlain's hand. Rhodes appeared resiliently at the enquiry, fresh from his Matabele triumphs. As always he spoke with perfect frankness and self-possession, dominating the Committee. When a report was issued, in July 1897, no censure was pronounced upon Chamberlain, whereas Rhodes was pronounced guilty of 'misconduct and duplicity', though not of acting on 'stockjobbing motives'.

After crushing his enemies the Uitlanders, Kruger too was afflicted with *hubris*. He increased his expenditure on armaments, especially on heavy artillery which could not be used for any other purpose than to fight the British. The proved guilt of a few hundred rebels gave him the excuse for denying justice to many thousands of immigrant miners. Chamberlain continued to press for the grant of civil rights, a reasonable request and not made less reasonable by the Raid. In January 1897 he sent Sir Alfred Milner (1854–1925) to replace Robinson as High Commissioner. Milner's name was then unknown to the public. After carrying off many university prizes at Oxford and serving an apprenticeship under Cromer in Egypt, he found the opportunity for a great career in South Africa at the age of forty-three. Though a man of many friendships he was too precise and unbending to win the affection or respect of the Boers.

The Afrikander Bond, reacting from its association with Rhodes's 'Progressive' Party, now denounced British Imperialism and supported Kruger. Milner's determination to carry out Chamberlain's policy of federation engaged no sympathy in the troubled years after the Jameson Raid. His perpetual problem was the hostility of the Bondsmen in Cape politics where the only alternative government was that of Rhodes's discredited party. Milner disliked and distrusted Rhodes whose desire, he said, was 'to gain prematurely by violent and unscrupulous means what you could get honestly and without violence, if you would only wait and work for it'.

As negotiations dragged on, through 1897 and 1898, it became evident that the hour of accommodation had passed. Kruger would not grant an equable franchise to the Uitlanders since that meant rule in the Transvaal by a majority of British miners who were opposed to him and to the Boer way of life. Milner would not give way on 'suzerainty'. Unsatisfactory as he found Gladstone's ill-fated formula, he interpreted it in the sense that the British must remain the paramount power in South Africa. Milner asserted firmly, most plainly in a speech at Graaff-Reinet (March 1898), that he asked the Transvaal to do only what the Orange Free State had always done, that the British at the Rand claimed no higher privilege than the Afrikaners had always enjoyed in Natal and in Cape Colony. But Kruger now talked of nothing but independence, repudiating the suzerainty which he himself had accepted in 1881; and intensified his preparations for war. A conference at Bloemfontein in June 1899 ended in a complete deadlock. 'It is my country you want', said the President with the tears streaming down his old wrinkled face; then went away and hardened his heart. After the Bloemfontein Conference the Free Staters threw in their lot with the Transvaal as, indeed, they were bound by treaty to do. Though they had no cause of quarrel with the British, they too began to arm.

The franchise was far from being the whole cause of the dispute. Some observers alleged that the Rand capitalists cared little for the vote so long as they could work the mines profitably. What agitated the mass of the white mining population was petty corruption and oppression by Kruger's officials. The case of a miner named Edgar who was shot dead in December 1898 'while resisting arrest', by a party of armed police who broke into his house without a warrant, provoked a genuine agitation for justice. The murderer was held to bail for £200, acquitted, and congratulated by the court for doing his duty. The promoters of an orderly meeting of protest against the murder were arrested, held to bail for £1000 each, and charged with sedition. Edgar's case, more than any other event, rallied the democrats of the other Dominions to the side of the Uitlanders.

A little less rigidity shown either by Milner or by Kruger might, in the opinion of some critics, have averted war, though there were many Boer firebrands who welcomed the prospect. The time had come to drive the *rooineks*, the red-necked British Tommies, into the sea. One man who did not want war was Chamberlain. He urged Milner to show more patience and forbearance. Chamberlain had an uncertain hold over his colleagues in the government, especially over the War Office. Their contribution to the problem was to send as Commander of the troops at the Cape Sir William Butler, an Irish Home-Ruler who openly declared his sympathy with Kruger. Chamberlain was also involved, in 1898, in colonial disputes with the United States over the frontier of British Guiana, with Germany over Samoa, with France over Fashoda, and with Russia over encroachment in Manchuria. England's diplomatic position was something worse than isolation; she was at odds with all the world. Through Chamberlain's influence all these disputes were settled peaceably.

By the autumn of 1899 a breach with Kruger had become inevitable. While Salisbury and Chamberlain considered the form of their ultimatum, Kruger forestalled them by a provocative message (9 October 1899) demanding that Queen Victoria should send no more troops to her South African colonies. Salisbury rejected this insolent demand in a few plain words that meant war.

4. THE 'BOER WAR', 1899–1902

THE main battlefield, beyond which columns ranged widely, was a grassy plateau about as large as France, hot in summer and cold in winter, seamed by watercourses which in flood became torrential rivers, bounded on the east by a high mountain range and on the west by a desert. For the most part the open, roadless Veld consisted of undulating pastures from which cropped up here and there the characteristic flat-topped hills known as *kopjes*. In the centre lay the golden city of Johannesburg, its mining-stamps silent, its native labourers dispersed. Towards this city, the prize of victory, railways converged from each of the sea-ports, with very few lateral branch-lines.

In this theatre a small courageous nation fought and lost a war of independence, far more heroic than the American Revolution. Their utmost effort in the field was 60,000 men against the might of a world-empire. Their enemies mustered against them 400,000 soldiers in all, though never more than about 200,000 at a time. The British effort was based upon unchallenged sea-power, while the Boers, after expending their accumulated armaments, lived upon the country.[1]

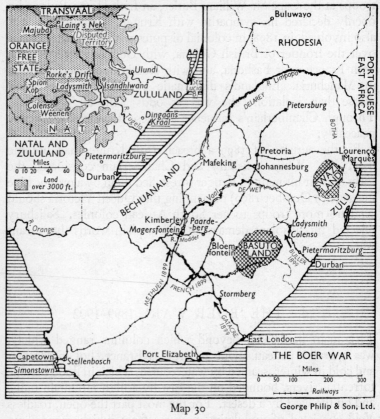

Map 30   George Philip & Son, Ltd.

The strangest feature of the war was the tacit assumption that it concerned white men only, though fought in the midst of

[1] Censuses were taken in South Africa in 1890–1 and in 1904, with the following result:

'European' population	1890–1	1904
Cape Colony	377,000	580,000 (mixed)
Natal	47,000	97,000 (mostly British)
Transvaal	119,000	297,000 (mixed)
Orange Free State	78,000	143,000 (mostly Afrikaner)

Natives and other non-Europeans outnumbered Europeans by at least four to one, the highest native proportion being in Natal and the lowest in the Orange Free State.

Milner estimated in 1901 that 52·3% of the Europeans were Afrikaners, 39% British, and 8·7% others.

a great majority of warlike Africans. The clashing columns swirled round the frontiers of mountainous Basutoland, respecting its neutrality. Whereas de Wet averred that the Basutos favoured the Boer cause, the Zulus on the eastern frontier certainly did not. If permitted, they would have fought beside the British and, on one occasion, they fell upon a commando of Boers, massacring them all by night. At the end the fiction of native neutrality was wearing thin.

Much of the apparatus which has become so painfully familiar to our generation, the khaki uniform, the block-houses and barbed-wire, the dugout shelters, the sand-bagged slit-trenches, the mobile heavy guns ,the visual signals in morse code, the bully-beef tins and the little piles of gleaming cartridge-cases that mark the site of an engagement, were first described in press reports from South Africa. But in other respects the Boer War was fought just too soon for modernity. It was almost the last phase in that age-long chivalrous partnership between the soldier and the war-horse. Indeed the necessity for finding 7000 horses a month came near to frustrating the British war effort. If the war had come five years later the internal combustion engine would have gone far towards solving Kitchener's transport problem. Ten years later, the aeroplane would have enabled him to locate the guerrilla bands. But in the age of the magazine rifle and the horse, Boer tactics were unsurpassed, and Christian de Wet perhaps the greatest of all partisan leaders. Battles were fought in extended lines at very long ranges, so that a man was thought to be a soldier if he could ride to his place in the battle-front and then shoot straight. Tactically, the lessons learned on the Veld had to be unlearned by the commanders in the ponderous close-range battles of the first German War; but in handling troops and in military administration the men of 1914 learned their trade in South Africa. Not only Kitchener and his two lieutenants, French and Ian Hamilton, took the lead against the Germans on their South African reputation, but among the young majors and colonels who made their mark commanding columns on the Veld appear the names of Haig, Plumer, Smith-Dorrien, Byng, Rawlinson, and Allenby.

Twice as many men died of disease in South Africa as were killed in battle. Preventive medicine and sanitary discipline were still rudimentary in 1899, and that great safeguard, inoculation against typhoid fever, was not yet in use. Pestilence was still regarded as the inseparable companion of war. Only in 1914, for the first time in military history, was the butcher's bill, to use the soldier's grim phrase, bigger than the doctor's bill.

The war produced a series of surprises, not least in its opening moves. What the world supposed to be a brutal conspiracy by a great empire to crush a small free nation began with a brisk offensive by the weaker party. The Boers invaded British territory on a wide front, instantly proclaiming the annexation to the South African Republic of every district they entered. At the front they outnumbered the British in men and deployed a heavier artillery. There were, in October 1899, about 22,000 British regular troops in South Africa, the greater part of them in Natal. Sir George White (1835–1912) had concentrated a force of about one infantry division in the mountainous salient angle between the frontiers of the two republics. On 12 October the Boers crossed the frontier and, on 20 October, were engaged with White's advanced detachment. After three sharp actions which betrayed the rawness of both armies, White was besieged in Ladysmith with a garrison of 12,000 men.

Far away in the west other Boer commandos invaded and annexed British Bechuanaland. They held a long stretch of the railway to Rhodesia, northwards to Mafeking and southwards to Kimberley, lightly investing each of these towns.

White's intention in holding Ladysmith was to protect Northern Natal until the arrival of General Buller with a whole Army Corps, which disembarked at Durban during November and concentrated south of the Tugela River with little interference from the Boers. After their first impulse was spent, the main Boer force of 30,000 men was content to close in on Ladysmith. Their military organisation was inadequate either to the task of launching an assault or of masking the fortress and pressing on. During this pause, while operations by either side hung fire, an armoured train reconnoitred up the line towards Ladysmith on 14 November. It was ambushed and wrecked and the crew taken prisoner, including the correspondent of the *Morning Post*, whose behaviour that day was far from being non-combatant. His name was Winston Churchill, his captor's Louis Botha.

Before Buller was ready to march to the relief of Ladysmith news of disaster came from the west. The three railway crossings

of the Orange River were the vital points in the defence of Cape
Colony and, at each of the three, troops were concentrated as
soon as they could reach the front. At the western crossing, on
the line to the diamond-fields and Rhodesia, Lord Methuen
(1845–1932) assembled a force of something less than one
division for the relief of Kimberley. His force, including the
Guards Brigade, was confronted by a strong commando under
General Piet Cronje, the most celebrated Boer fighter of the old
school. Cronje had forced the surrender of an English garrison,
in the war of 1880, by the slimmest of ruses; he had a sinister
reputation for harsh treatment of natives in several campaigns;
and, above all, Cronje had stopped, defeated, and arrested the
Jameson Raiders. Methuen made a frontal attack on his entrench-
ment at Modder River (28 November) and was held up with a
loss of 500 men. But when his flank was threatened Cronje
slipped away to a new position at Magersfontein. A fortnight
later, reinforced by Canadians, Australians, and the Highland
Brigade, Methuen attacked him again. The Battle of Magersfontein (9 December 1899) began with a night march by the
Highland Brigade, in close order, to an assaulting position within
200 yards of Cronje's rifle-pits. When the Boers opened fire the
Brigadier was killed by the first shots, leaving no one who understood the plan. The Brigade withdrew in disorder having lost
57 officers and 700 men in a few minutes.

Meanwhile Boer commandos had crossed the Orange River at
each of the other railway crossings. In the centre they were
skilfully contained by General French (1852–1925) and eventually
driven back, but, farther to the east, a brigade group under
General Gatacre was shamefully defeated. On the day after the
disaster at Magersfontein they marched into an ambush at
Stormberg where 600 regular soldiers surrendered in a body.

The news of Magersfontein and Stormberg came just as
Buller's ponderous preparations in Natal were complete. On
15 December 1899, he attempted a frontal attack on the Boer
positions near Colenso, with a force of four infantry brigades,
one cavalry brigade, and forty-eight guns (some of them converted naval guns). One brigade got well forward and one
battery of field artillery was rashly advanced to cover it, within
range of Boer rifle fire. When men and horses were shot down,
leaving the guns unmanned, Buller abandoned his intention,

went forward to the leading infantry, and vainly devoted his whole endeavour to saving the guns, at the cost of many lives. The battle tamely petered out and the troops were withdrawn across the Tugela River having lost 1120 men killed, wounded, or missing, for no result. After this curiously ineffective action Buller sent a message to White advising him to surrender Lady-smith on terms, a suggestion that White indignantly repudiated.

Magersfontein, Stormberg, Colenso made a black week (9–15 December 1899) for the British public. The whole con-tinental press set up a roar of malicious delight at the discomfiture of the hated British, who now appeared to be effete cowards. The American press was on the whole sympathetic to the British. It was not altogether fanciful to trace a resemblance between this campaign and their own Civil War. This too was, in a sense, a war to prevent secession and to protect coloured mens' rights. At this time also the Americans were deeply embroiled in a colonial campaign in the Philippines and appreciated some of our difficulties. As usual, disaster united parties in Great Britain. On 18 December the government announced its policy. So far from there being a capitulation as after Majuba, they now took measures for total war. The army reserve was called up, an appeal was made for volunteers, a large proportion of troops were put in training as mounted infantry, and Lord Roberts (whose son had died winning a Victoria Cross at Colenso) was ordered to South Africa as Commander-in-Chief, with Kitchener as his deputy and chief of staff. Meanwhile Buller in the eastern sector and Methuen 600 miles away in the west continued their campaigns while the striking force was built up in Cape Colony.

Calmly and methodically Buller prepared another attempt to force the line of the Tugela. On 21 January 1900, he concentrated on the left flank, passed a brigade across the river, and seized by night the crest of Spion Kop, the commanding hill, 2000 feet high, from which the *voortrekkers*, in 1835, had spied out the promised land. In the morning the 4000 men on the summit were exposed to heavy fire from Boer skirmishers, which made the situation only too reminiscent of Majuba. But they held their ground with a loss of 1500 killed and wounded, the heaviest roll of British casualties in any battle between the Crimean and the German Wars. As at Colenso, Buller flinched from further losses, withdrawing for a second time across the Tugela. Three weeks later he repeated the same sequence of moves at Vaalkranz, on the right flank, but escaped this time with lighter loss.

In February Lord Roberts began his general advance across the Orange River, with the result that the Free State commandos drew off from Ladysmith to defend their own country. Buller at last committed his whole force to an offensive on a wide front which carried him to Ladysmith after a week of desultory fighting. Among the first to ride into Ladysmith on 27 February 1900 was Winston Churchill, recently escaped from captivity and now a subaltern of irregular horse.

The operations for the relief of Ladysmith had cost Buller 5000 casualties, while more than a thousand men, one-tenth of the garrison, had died by battle or disease inside the besieged town. The garrison had resisted one general assault and had carried out several audacious sorties against Boer posts. They had been shelled continuously with six-inch guns. Starved as they were, on half-rations of horse-flesh, they nevertheless had the resolution to send out a column to pursue the Boers northwards.

Sir Redvers Buller (1839–1908) had seen service in all parts of the world and had won the Victoria Cross in the Zulu War. A skilled administrator, he took a leading part in Wolseley's reorganisation of the War Office, and when in command at Aldershot, won the hearts of the rank and file by his unremitting attention to the soldiers' welfare. In the field his manœuvres were masterly, his personal courage exemplary. Yet his battle tactics were feeble and vacillating. While the armchair critics denounced his incompetence, the men he commanded never weakened in their loyalty to him. There may be in Chelsea Hospital some veterans who would still name Buller as their favourite general. The waves of despondency and elation which swept through the English-speaking world at the news of Colenso, Spion Kop, and the Relief of Ladysmith are now forgotten by a generation which has known crueller wars. It may be a help to the imagination to suggest that the campaign was somewhat on the same scale as the first siege and relief of Tobruk in 1941.

By 15 February 1900 Roberts had concentrated three divisions for the invasion of the Free State. But first he sent cavalry under General French to ride round Cronje's flank to relieve Kimberley.

The siege of the diamond-fields had been no more than a blockade by Boer patrols, against whom a handful of regulars and a large force of local volunteers had acted vigorously. The defence was hampered by friction between the military command and Cecil Rhodes, who had quixotically thrown himself into the town to stand the siege among his own people. So large a bird fretted in so small a cage.[1]

The relief of Kimberley was the opening move in Roberts's general advance. Grim old Cronje was easily bolted from his defences. He slipped away to protect Bloemfontein but was caught on the wrong side of the Modder River, at Paardeberg, by five columns of British and Canadian troops, about 30,000 men. Kitchener, who was on the spot, ordered a converging assault on 18 February. As at Colenso and Magersfontein the troops were stopped by rifle-fire, with a loss of 1100 killed and wounded in the nine leading battalions. Kitchener then summoned Cronje to surrender, refusing to grant an armistice, and received a defiant answer. For a week Cronje stood up to continuous bombardment while the troops closed in on his flanks, bringing his trenches under enfilading fire. On 27 February 1900, the anniversary of Majuba, he surrendered with 3000 Transvaalers and 1000 Free-Staters, leaving the road to Bloemfontein open. Ladysmith and Paardeberg made a week as black for the Boers as had been the week of Colenso for the British. Roberts entered Bloemfontein on 13 March, while President Steyn and his government fled northwards. Kruger now attempted to intervene with an offer of peace, on terms of returning to the *status quo ante*, but Salisbury replied with a flat refusal and ordered the annexation of the Orange Free State (May 1900).

Typhoid and enteric fever broke out while Roberts halted at Bloemfontein. About 7000 cases passed through the hospitals, the deaths reaching fifty a day. Thereafter these diseases were endemic in all large standing camps, British or Boer. The cause was bad water, which was worse at Bloemfontein after a daring move put the Boers in possession of the water-supply. A British column was ambushed and cut to pieces near the waterworks at

---

[1] It was his last exploit. In failing health, though no more than forty-eight years old, he withdrew to Capetown and died there (1902) before the end of the war. He left the bulk of his huge fortune as a trust for sending young men from the dominions, the United States, and Germany to the University of Oxford.

Sanna's Post, 31 March 1900, by a new Boer leader, Christian de Wet. A burly, bearded man of forty, wearing dark glasses, he had been the implacable foe of the British since Majuba where he had fought as a boy.

By May, Roberts was ready to march north again. His total strength amounted to eleven divisions, eight under his own immediate command and three under Buller in Natal. With his main force he entered Johannesburg on 30 May and Pretoria on 5 June, brushing aside the slight forces with which the Boers opposed him. Kruger's celebrated forts at these towns were abandoned after firing a few rounds. The triumph seemed complete when Buller advanced up the line from Natal to meet the Commander-in-Chief, skilfully turning the formidable defences of Laing's Nek almost in sight of Majuba Hill. But the eyes of the world during these marches were focused on a secondary campaign. Far in the north-west Major R. S. S. Baden-Powell (1857–1941), with about 1100 colonial troops, was holding the perimeter of Mafeking against a fluctuating ill-led force of Boers. Baden-Powell's surprising ingenuity and jocular manner scandalised the enemy who thought that, by all the traditions of British warfare in South Africa, he should surrender or, at least, not make fun of them. His defence was maintained actively with many raids and sorties. When an assaulting-party of Boers broke into the town, the breach was sealed off and the attackers made prisoner. Five days later (17 May 1900) Mafeking was relieved by three converging columns from the north, the south, and the east. The sense that all fear of disaster had now lifted produced a hysterical outburst of rejoicing in London of such intensity that it added a new word to the language. Yet even 'mafficking' has its uses. It gave the hero of the siege such widespread celebrity that he was able to found (1908) the international Boy Scouts Association, the best thing that came out of the Boer War.

In June Lord Roberts turned eastwards from Pretoria against the main Transvaal army of perhaps 15,000 men under Botha. Though he struck them a shrewd blow at Diamond Hill he did not succeed in breaking up the army, which withdrew towards the Portuguese border into difficult country. With them went President Kruger and his government with the gold reserve, £2,000,000. The British reached the frontier in September to find that Kruger had escaped with his gold into Portuguese territory. When the Transvaal was, for the second time, annexed to the British Empire on 1 September 1900, the republican government remained in being. Kruger retired to Holland, well supplied with funds, to conduct a campaign of propaganda, though the legend persists that much of his treasure still lies hidden in the eastern Transvaal. He left Schalk Burgers behind as his civil representative with General Botha's army. One large commando under De la Rey broke away westward and lurked in the wild Magaliesberg Mountains of the western Transvaal.

Meanwhile Kitchener had turned south, in June, to conduct a similar campaign against the refugee government of the Free State. He broke up their main army of 8000 or 10,000 men, receiving many surrenders, but he did not catch President Steyn and, which was worse, he did not catch the dangerous de Wet, who escaped westwards with about 2000 men across the railway line into the country south of the Vaal River, thereafter his favourite hiding-place.

The two republics were annexed, their armies defeated and dispersed, their capitals occupied; the two British colonies were purged of invaders. It seemed that the war was over. In December 1900 Roberts went home, leaving the final pacification to Kitchener. The army in South Africa was drastically reduced and the service for buying remounts in foreign countries was discontinued. Most of the volunteers from Great Britain and the Dominions, who had enlisted for one year only, were sent home and released from service. Dr A. Conan Doyle, who had accompanied Lord Roberts's march as a war correspondent, completed and published his standard work on *The Great Boer War*. But the war went on, to the disgust of Kitchener, who regarded his task with aversion.

Three large, formed bodies of Boers kept the field, Botha in the northern Transvaal with President Burgers, De la Rey in the western Transvaal, and de Wet somewhere in the Free State with President Steyn. Their forces swelled or dwindled with their momentary successes or failures. Thousands of Boers had laid down their arms, unwillingly, to resume them again when some celebrated commando leader was in their district. Finding themselves almost everywhere among friends, the commandos could disappear into the population of scattered farmers, and reappear freshly mounted and supplied, in due time. By the strict laws of war the Boers were not regular combatants but *franc-tireurs*. They wore no uniform, unless a captured British uniform, but this was accepted as the custom of South Africa.

Their hope, in prolonging the war, rested upon three chances. The British might lose heart as they had seemed to do in 1881. But Gladstone was dead; a chain of authority through Salisbury, Chamberlain, Milner, Kitchener would hold more firmly. There was in England much dissatisfaction over the war and much sympathy with the Boers, but the radicals, with Lloyd George as their mouthpiece, were unlikely to carry the electorate. Should there be a Liberal reaction it would probably favour the Liberal imperialists from whom the Boers could expect no more than milder peace terms after victory. This chance was swept away by the 'Khaki' election of October 1900 which returned the Conservatives to power with a large majority pledged to imposing an unconditional surrender. The second hope was for foreign intervention like that which had won independence for the Americans. This too was doomed to failure. Though England was friendless and unpopular, no European power lifted a finger against her. Early in the war there had been about 2000 foreign adventurers (including 500 Irish and Irish-Americans) with the Boer armies but there was no Lafayette among them, and sea-power prevented foreign gun-running. Though the French press was most bitter in its hostility to the British, France was too weak to move. The German Kaiser, mercurial as ever, disappointed the Boers by adopting a friendly attitude to the British; that is to say, he tried to teach his grandmother, in the last months of her life, how to fight colonial campaigns. The third hope was to present Kitchener with an overpowering problem by raising the standard of revolt in Cape Colony, where there was much sympathy with the republics. In December 1900 a conference was held to discuss secession. Somewhat tamely the delegates contented themselves with petitioning Milner to stop the war. He replied brusquely that it was too late; the whole Empire was united for victory. The town where they conferred was protected by a garrison of Australian and Canadian volunteers. No more than 8000 'rebels' from the Cape joined the republican commandos. Much of Milner's activity was in controlling the Cape Parliament, which he persuaded to disfranchise the rebels. In general they were not harshly treated, though about thirty-five of their leaders, taken in arms, were executed after trial.

Kitchener met General Botha in February 1901, offering him self-government for the Boer States within the Empire. Botha, still hopeful for the future, stood out for complete independence and an amnesty for Cape rebels. Though the negotiation failed, many Boers urged the acceptance of Kitchener's offer. But when two of them visited de Wet's commando he executed them as traitors; he would fight to the bitter end.

The renewed guerrilla war placed Kitchener in great difficulties. His strength in men was down to 70,000 and in horses was miserably insufficient. His first problem in the early months of 1901, was to create a new army of colonial volunteers and yeomanry from England. Arriving untrained they were thrown into action piecemeal, on unseasoned horses. The quality of the troops deteriorated during the war, especially among the units raised in South Africa. While some crack corps, like Baden-Powell's mounted police, maintained the high standard of the volunteers of 1899, commanders depended most upon the steady line regiments now largely converted into mounted infantry. Unlike the 'five-bob colonials', they were still paid a bare shilling a day.

Even among the good troops there were in South Africa far too many 'white-flag incidents', when detachments surrendered tamely after a token resistance. Let some social psychologist explain why the same phenomenon occurred in 1940 and 1941, whereas it was almost unknown in 1914.

The Boer commandos, on the other hand, shedding their faint-hearts, improved in fighting quality as they declined in numbers. De Wet would take the field with about 2000 followers, each man mounted and leading a spare horse. Not delayed, as were the British columns, with ox-transport, his men carried their scanty supplies in light two-wheeled Cape carts which moved as fast as the commando. Food they requisitioned from the country; arms, ammunition, and clothing they captured from the British. When they took prisoners they stripped them and let them go. De Wet's technique was to appear and raid some line of blockhouses or railway posts, lure the British on until five or six columns were closing on him, then break back through the line at its weakest point and vanish to the other side of the country. De la Rey invented a terrifying type of mounted charge, with his men firing from the saddle as they approached, a tactical method which disconcerted half-trained troops.

Twice in the southern summer (1900–1) de Wet broke into Cape Colony, twice he was headed back by a sweeping movement of five or six columns, and twice he escaped. Other commandos infiltrated into the colony in small numbers, disturbing the countryside. Hertzog's commando even reached the sea at Lambert's Bay.

In the winter of 1901 Kitchener quartered the whole country with lines of barbed wire following the railways, and blockhouses which he manned with second-class troops. His best troops were organised in columns—at one time as many as sixty-four—with which he swept the country, area by area, burning farms where the inhabitants showed hostility. The weakness of his plan was over-centralisation. Columns were formed and grouped and moved by direct order of the chief, with no fixed chain of command and no operational staff as such things were understood in the German Wars.

More serious than the fighting was the problem of controlling Boer civilians in battle areas. As early as December 1900, Roberts had invited non-combatants from lonely farms to come in to 'concentration camps' (an ill-omened term borrowed from the Spanish in Cuba), where they would be fed and protected by the British. At once 50,000 presented themselves, a new puzzle for the harassed army staff. By May 1901 the camps contained 77,000 Boers and 21,000 natives; by October 118,000 Boers and 43,000 natives. Almost all were the households of men on commando and virulently anti-British. They were under no discipline and quite unaccustomed to life in large communities. Sanitation, shocking in the armies, was unspeakable in the camps. The diseases that decimated the armies rioted among the civilians, but it was an epidemic of measles among the children that killed the most. In March 1901 Miss Emily Hobhouse exposed the scandal in London with the result that the War Office immediately sent out a committee of ladies led by Dame Millicent Fawcett to investigate. By the end of the year the epidemics were mastered and Milner got the camps into tolerable order. A war in which the British were feeding the Boer women and children while fighting the men was in itself fantastic. Although the Boer leaders, especially Botha at the peace conference, expressed their gratitude to the British, the Afrikaner people cannot forget that 4000 women and 16,000 children died in British hands.

Kitchener made the error, in August 1901, of supposing that he had mastered the guerrillas. He issued a proclamation calling upon the survivors to lay down their arms by a certain date after which they would forfeit belligerent rights. It was ignored by the Boer leaders and led to a last vain effort in the summer of 1901–2. A new invasion of Cape Colony was carried out by J. C. Smuts, one of the younger Boer leaders, who penetrated so deeply that Capetown itself was put under martial law. Botha led the Transvaalers down the Zululand border to threaten a new invasion of Natal. De Wet appeared again in the north of the Free State and was more nearly captured than ever before—but not quite. As a final coup De la Rey caught his old antagonist, Methuen, at Tweebosch with a weak force of raw troops whom he drove in headlong flight. Methuen was wounded and captured (6 March 1902).

But all this activity was superficial. The Transvaalers presented themselves to Kitchener to ask for terms on 23 March. Kruger and his associates had departed leaving the field to younger men, Botha, Burgers, and Smuts, whose hands were clean and whose military honour was unstained. The chivalrous De la Rey admitted that 'the bitter end had come'. At least 4000 Boers had been killed in the field, 30,000 were prisoners of war, and not many more than 20,000 were left with the commandos. No longer could they hope for succour from English Liberals, continental monarchs, or Cape rebels. While the Transvaalers, who had instigated the war, ruefully admitted failure, the Free State leaders, who had come into the quarrel and lost all for mere loyalty, were still resolved to fight on. But when delegates from all the commandos met under safe-conduct at Vereeniging it was agreed, by fifty-four votes to six, to capitulate, though it was well understood that the terms would be no better than Kitchener had offered in March 1901. The last year's fighting had achieved nothing. De Wet opposed the settlement to the last, but gave way and signed in the end; President Steyn resigned his office and remained unreconciled.

The terms had been drafted in Kitchener's house at Pretoria and forwarded with a recommendation to the delegates at

Vereeniging, where they were accepted on 31 May 1902. In spite of strong censorship the news leaked out and was despatched to London by Edgar Wallace, as a scoop for the *Daily Mail*. The capitulation (often called the Treaty of Vereeniging) had been put into final shape by Smuts and Hertzog, the two Boer generals who had a legal training. Forty years later they were the dominant figures in South African politics. On the British side Kitchener was for negotiating generous terms, provided that British sovereignty was secured, Milner was for unconditional surrender and a dictated peace. The terms were in fact generous, especially the financial concessions which exceeded Boer hopes.

All South Africa had now been brought under the British flag at a cost of 22,000 British soldiers killed or dead of disease, 100,000 sent to hospital sick or wounded, and £191,000,000 spent on death and destruction, by the British tax-payer, on the War Office vote alone.

5. RECONSTRUCTION AND UNION IN SOUTH AFRICA, 1902–10

By Kitchener's generosity the settlement at Vereeniging had been drawn in the form of a treaty with the two republics, though in fact it was the capitulation of a disorganised and scattered army. The Boer leaders had undertaken to lay down their arms and to take the oath of allegiance to King Edward VII.[1] Prisoners of war were to be released on taking the oath. An amnesty was granted to the Cape rebels, but, in spite of all the efforts of the republican leaders, the rebels were not to receive the same consideration as the republican troops. They were to be disfranchised for five years with no assurance that legal proceedings would not be instituted against their leaders. Kitchener went so far as to promise that there should be no more death-sentences. For the future the treaty promised that the Dutch language would not be excluded from law-courts or schools, that civil government would replace military administration at the earliest possible date, and that 'as soon as circumstances permit, representative institutions leading up to self-government' would be introduced. The difficult question of a native franchise was to be

[1] Queen Victoria died before the end of the war, January 1901.

deferred until after the grant of self-government. To these terms was added the magnanimous promise of a 'free gift' of £3,000,000 from the British Treasury to the Boers for the reconstruction of their country. An indemnity paid by the victor to the vanquished is indeed a rare historical event. The terms were gratefully accepted and loyally carried out by the Boer generals. About 12,000 Transvaalers, 6000 Free-Staters, and 2000 Cape rebels came in to take the oath, thus clearing the field and ending the guerrilla war. The last remnants of opposition were seen among the prisoners held in camps in India who would not take the oath until persuaded to do so by General De la Rey in person.

The first month of peace was not over before Kitchener resigned the task he had so reluctantly carried out, and left the country. Milner, who had already made much progress with his plans for reconstruction, remained as dictator of South Africa for three years (June 1902–April 1905). Gathering round him the team of young men known as his 'Kindergarten',[1] he set to work to provide the two conquered provinces with an efficient administration, building up their institutions so as to make a secure foundation for self-government. ' "Never again" ', he said, 'must be the motto of all thinking, of all humane, men.' Never again must an ignorant oligarchy repeat the errors of Krugerism.

His instructions from Chamberlain were to take over the republican administration of the Orange Free State and adapt it to the new colonial regime, but to reconstruct the Transvaal fundamentally. Accordingly, he set up his headquarters as High

---

[1] John Buchan, in *Memory Hold-the-Door*, gives the following list: Military Secretary, the Hon. (afterwards Maj.-Gen. Sir) W. Lambton; A.D.C.'s, Lord Brooke, Lord H. Seymour (both Brigadier-generals in the 1914 War); Secretaries: Lord Basil Blackwood (killed in 1917), the Hon. H. Wyndham, C. G. Sellar; personal assistants selected for special tasks, Geoffrey Dawson (afterwards Editor of *The Times*), Lionel Curtis (Editor of *The Round Table*), the Hon. R. H. Brand, W. L. Hichens, the Hon. Philip Kerr (afterwards Lord Lothian and ambassador at Washington), and (Sir) P. Duncan (afterwards Governor-General of South Africa). Buchan (afterwards, as Lord Tweedsmuir, Governor-General of Canada and celebrated as a novelist and historian) was also one of the secretaries. Other accounts mention L. S. Amery (Secretary of State for the Dominions, etc.), (Sir) Fabian Ware, A. Browne, E. B. Sargant and others, as members of the group which, like all such groups, had a vague and fluctuating membership. Not all were Oxford men. The editor of the *Milner Papers* adds: Basil Williams, R. Feltham, F. Perry, and John Dove; but omits the military men and Mr Amery, who is described as an associate and equal of Milner rather than a client.

Commissioner and Governor of the Transvaal at Johannesburg during the war, deputing to a Lieutenant-Governor the easier task at Bloemfontein. In Milner's opinion the root of the problem was to restore the finances and, to that end, to set the mines at work. His treasurer, Patrick Duncan, was chiefly responsible for creating an honest system of finance and accountancy. Concessions issued by Kruger to his friends were cancelled and the foreign shareholders, including those of the Netherlands Railway Company, bought out. Before the end of the war half the pre-war white population had returned to the Rand, and one-third of the stamps were at work. The limitation on progress was the shortage of native labour. Prosperity on the Rand meant money for development, especially for completing a national railway system throughout South Africa. The opening of the country to British land-settlement would raise the standard of agriculture and produce a modern democracy absorbing Boer nationality into a greater synthesis, a new Union of South Africa which should be a model to the English-speaking world, the nucleus of a united Empire. The plan was a modern version of that which Lord Durham had once conceived for Canada. Strenuous attempts were made to settle British ex-soldiers on the land, with only partial success. The problem proved as intractable as after other wars. It was perhaps more useful that 4000 young English-women were brought in as immigrants.

During 1901 Milner began a reformation of the conditions of native labour, making a new agreement for the recruitment of natives in Portuguese East Africa, putting an end to the liquor traffic in the mines, simplifying the pass-laws in the native interest, preventing the enlistment of native labour by irresponsible agents, limiting the practice of corporal punishment, and introducing medical supervision, which lowered the death-rate in the compounds from fifty-four to thirty per thousand. Public health was shockingly neglected in the Transvaal, even among the whites, until Milner took that in hand, completely renovating the system. Local government, for which the Uitlanders had striven in vain, was organised by Mr Lionel Curtis, at first for Johannesburg and then for the other towns.

Simultaneously an agricultural department was formed with an experimental station and a notably effective bacteriological branch. Milner gave particular attention to experiments in afforestation. For all this administrative work the British Parliament gave a vote of credit, in 1901, of £6,500,000.

With the coming of peace these reforms were overridden by urgent necessity. Two-thirds of the white population of the Republics had been displaced. Nearly 32,000 were prisoners of war, 110,000 were in the concentration camps, 4500 had 'come in' and taken service with the British, 30,000 were at large on the Veld and likely to starve. Milner had taken charge of the camps in 1901, after the worst of the epidemics was over, and had reduced them to order. The Boers coming to reclaim their families were, in many instances, delighted to find them well-fed and happy, not at all as described in anti-British propaganda. A strange side-issue was the organisation of a schools system providing for a much larger number of children than ever attended school in the days of peace. The opportunity was taken of extending a modern educational system, for the first time, through the two provinces, with the help of 300 specially selected teachers from Great Britain and the Dominions. Some credit for the improved state of the camps in their later history may be given to Dame Millicent Fawcett and John Buchan. All the inmates had left the camps by February 1903, by which date the prisoners had also been repatriated.

The greatest problem was simply to restore the farmers to the land. Hardly a house was left standing on the Veld. The native farm-servants were dispersed, the stock was driven and commandeered. Even the towns were largely deserted. On the Rand 80% of the houses had been looted. Nature intensified this calamity with locusts, cattle-disease, rinderpest, and the worst harvest for forty years in 1902–3.

> Half her land was dead with drouth,
> Half was red with battle;
> She was fenced with fire and sword
> Plague on pestilence outpoured,
> Locusts on the greening sward
> And murrain on the cattle!

The grant of £3,000,000 was immediately applied to resettling the Boer soldiers and restocking their farms, which was not achieved without administrative errors on the one side and grumbling on the other. Since the fighting Boers, the 'bitter-enders' of 1902, claimed the whole sum under the terms of the treaty, the British government granted additional funds for those who had surrendered earlier. The promised gift of £3,000,000 was swollen to £7,000,000 in the end. The whole cost of reconstruction to the British tax-payer on all accounts exceeded £14,000,000 on the Colonial Office vote.[1] In November 1902 martial law was replaced by civil administration and, in 1903, the Field Force was reduced to a British garrison of 25,000 men. By 1910 it had been further reduced to 10,000.

Though the Boer generals scrupulously observed the terms of the treaty, they did not co-operate in the reconstruction. They shrewdly observed that their chance would come when a Liberal government should be returned to power in England, and maintained their connexion with the English 'pro-boers'. It was not difficult for them to accumulate grievances against Milner and to keep them prominently before the Liberal press. A deputation visited England in 1902. Though they were lionised by the fickle London mob, so recently addicted to mafficking, they got singularly little advantage from their visit. Chamberlain refused further concessions and, when they asked for larger grants-in-aid, blandly offered to help them recover Kruger's treasure by diplomatic pressure. But those funds, if they still existed, were not forthcoming. An appeal to their Continental friends produced a very small response, since foreign governments saw no further hope of damaging Britain through the Boers. A few months later Chamberlain visited South Africa. He too was well received by both parties, except in Bloemfontein where de Wet and Hertzog openly charged him with violations of the treaty. Chamberlain had little difficulty in convincing his audience, if not the two irreconcilables, that British actions far surpassed what had been promised.

Meanwhile shortage of labour seemed likely to frustrate all Milner's plans. Labour always had been scarce in South Africa. The Natal sugar-planters had been importing Indian coolies by indenture since 1860, and said that they never had enough. In Cape Colony Rhodes's administration had brought pressure on the natives to work for wages by the 'Glen Grey Act' of 1894, which imposed preferential rates of taxation to the disadvantage of natives who remained in their reserves. The demands of the

[1] Statistics given in *The Times History of the South African War*. The *Milner Papers* give a higher figure.

farmers everywhere for native labour during the reconstruction drew men away from the Rand. In 1903 there were no more than 50,000 natives in the mines and corresponding unemployment among the white technicians. Low output from the mines, coupled with a bad harvest, meant loss of revenue and retrenchment instead of progress.

Two solutions were propounded to the labour problem. A mining-engineer, Mr F. H. B. Creswell (b. 1866), proposed to break down the Afrikaner prejudice against manual labour by white men, and to work the mines with efficient white labour. This ingenious suggestion got much attention but required a moral revolution in South Africa. It could not be adopted suddenly in a crisis. Its effect was to consolidate the skilled white workers in the industry as a South African Labour Party led by Mr Creswell. After some hesitation Milner decided against it on the grounds of urgency. The alternative plan, to introduce coolie labour, was backed by the employers and could be adopted without delay. More coolie labour would at once require more skilled supervision and so benefit both Creswell's associates and Milner's plans.

In June 1904 the first batch of Chinese coolies was brought to the Rand, under indentures which the Chinese government scrutinised and approved. The terms were far more favourable to the coolies than those under which Indians were regularly brought to Natal, far more favourable than those which a Liberal government had authorised in 1894 for the importation of Chinese coolies to British Guiana. The indenture restricted the coolies to labour only in the one industry and contained provision for compulsory repatriation to China, thus answering the objection commonly raised by critics of the system. No serious objections against the conduct of the Chinese on the Rand, or against the terms of their indentures, or against their treatment by their employers were ever raised either in South Africa or in China. Between 1904 and 1906 prosperity returned to the Rand. The output of gold rose from £12,000,000 to £24,000,000 in value, and, as Milner had foretold, the white population increased by 30%. In June 1907, 17,000 Europeans, 54,000 Chinese, and 94,000 natives were employed in the mines.

But by this time the stage was cleared of many leading characters. Chamberlain left office in 1903, giving place to

Alfred Lyttelton who authorised Milner to bring in the Chinese. In 1904, his eightieth year, Paul Kruger died in Switzerland. Old animosities were forgotten in respect for his antique valour. His body was brought to Pretoria for burial with honours from the British administration. In April 1905 Milner returned to England having completed the first phase of reconstruction and laid the foundation of union. He was not the gloomy tyrant that he was supposed to be by the Little Englanders. He left South Africa in a flicker if not a blaze of popularity, with a parting tribute from General Smuts. 'I am afraid you have not liked us,' wrote the General, 'but I cherish the hope that as our memories grow mellower and the nobler features of our respective ideals become clearer we shall more and more appreciate the contribution of each to that happier South Africa which is surely coming, and think more kindly of each other. History writes the word RECONCILIATION over all her quarrels.'

Milner's last achievement had been to persuade Lyttelton to grant a limited measure of representative government to the Transvaal and the Orange Free State. It was clear that the Conservatives could not much longer cling to office. Milner's task was handed over to Lord Selborne who was thought to be *persona grata* to the Opposition leaders. Then the storm burst over Chinese labour. The Conservative Party, after twenty years of power, had exhausted its mandate. Balfour, Prime Minister since Salisbury's retirement in 1902, had not been prepared to follow Chamberlain's lead towards an imperial tariff and was left with an uncertain policy in a rising tide of unpopularity. On the other hand the Liberals, since Gladstone's death in 1898, were also ill led and aimless. Their left wing consisted of the Little Englanders whose creed was simply negative, a ferocious hatred of the Jingo Imperialists and a bitter antagonism to the policy they attributed to Chamberlain and Milner. Chinese labour on the Rand provided them with a rallying-cry against the imperialists. With total indifference to the fact that the terms of the contract of labour were far more favourable to the Chinese than to indentured labourers elsewhere they made of 'Chinese slavery under the Union Jack' a slogan that carried the electorate off its balance. With that odd illogicality that marks British political thinking, their platform orators denounced simultaneously the enslavement of the Chinese and the Chinese themselves. It was a poster of a hideous evil-looking Chinaman that most impressed some of the electors. Balfour resigned in December 1905. At the election in January 1906 there was a turnover of 250 votes[1] which put Campbell-Bannerman into Downing Street with a great majority. Though he was described by the Tories as a Little Englander his strength lay in the support of the Liberal Imperialists.

In March, a vote of censure on Milner, for the alleged ill-treatment of a Chinaman by one of his officials, was carried by 355 votes against 155, in spite of attempts to moderate its wording by the Under-Secretary for the Colonies, Mr Churchill, who had recently joined the Liberal Party.

The government soon found that Chinese slavery, which had won them the election, was very different in fact from what it had been represented to be. Mr Churchill was obliged to admit that one accusation, if not a lie, was at least a 'terminological inexactitude'. There were no abuses to redress in the system and no means of abolishing it without paralysing the work of reconstruction. To the disgust of their radical supporters the Liberals went no further than to discontinue the import of coolies after 1907. From that date their numbers declined until 1910 when the last batch returned to China, unnoticed by the British public, who had by then forgotten all about them. The native labour supply gradually increased, eventually to a total of over 300,000, who worked under conditions somewhat less favourable than the Chinese 'slaves'. Primitive Africans were far less able to prosper at the mines than the thrifty Asiatics.

Nevertheless the introduction of a new racial minority into a country so torn by racial feuds had been a political error. It alarmed many people whose judgment was cooler and whose ignorance was less abysmal than that of the Little Englanders. Especially it alarmed the democratic governments of Australia and New Zealand. Both Deakin and Seddon protested to the Colonial Office that they had sent troops to fight for the oppressed Uitlanders and not for the employers of Chinese coolies. Creswell's white-labour policy was what engaged their sympathy.

[1] 'Khaki' Election, 1900:

Election of 1900		Election of 1906	
Liberals	177 seats	Liberals	379 seats
Unionists	404 seats	Unionists	156 seats
Nationalist (Irish)	82 seats	Nationalist (Irish)	83 seats
Labour	9 seats	Labour	52 seats

A far more significant problem which was not solved was the regulation of immigrants from India. In 1904 there were about 100,000 Indians in Natal, many of them resident traders. When prosperity returned to the Rand, they began to infiltrate the Transvaal, to the dismay of the Europeans, who were able to control and confine African and Chinese labourers but could not treat Indians in the same way. They were British subjects and they had money.

At the instance of the Boer generals the Liberal government overcalled Lyttelton's grant of an elective council by the offer of full responsible self-government to the two Boer provinces in 1906. It was no surprise that the 'bitter-enders' now stepped forward, judging that their time had come. General Botha, supported by General Smuts, obtained a majority at the first election in the Transvaal, while de Wet and Hertzog both took office in the new government of the Free State. The imperialists took alarm, and all the more when the loyalist government of Dr Jameson at the Cape was swept away at the election of 1908. In three of the four provinces, the Boer leaders were exercising lawful power.

Even Natal, the British province, was no safeguard. The chief concern of the Natal government after the war had been to rectify its frontier by annexing from the Transvaal that part of Zululand which the Boers had filibustered in the 'eighties. Two Zulu tribes became restive in 1906 and committed outrages against settlers and police. Injudicious interference by the Colonial Office aggravated the trouble and emboldened the native warriors. They were suppressed with some severity in the last of the many campaigns fought by the British against the Bantu. But Zululand was still unsettled until, in 1908, the heir of the House of Chaka, Dinizulu, was arrested and exiled to St Helena. This native war distracted the attention of the people of Natal in the creative period of the Union.

All Milner's tireless energy and bold planning had been directed towards a legislative union of the four provinces. The 'Kindergarten' had put their minds to it from the earliest days, and when the first crisis of reconstruction was past Lionel Curtis had worked steadily to prepare public opinion. In 1907 Lord Selborne drew up a memorandum positively recommending Union to the government. The issue was forced by the breakdown of a conference on railway rates in May 1908. The delegates agreed that only a legislative union could solve their problems and recommended the provinces to call a national convention, which met at Durban in October 1908. Later they transferred their meetings to Capetown and came to a cordial agreement in March 1909. Neither the British government nor the High Commissioner intervened.

There were four main problems before the delegates. The first, the relation between British and Boers, was solved by the political sagacity, good sense, and magnanimity of the Boer leaders. The initiative was taken by the Transvaal delegates who arrived with a united front and a draft constitution drawn up by Patrick Duncan and R. H. Brand and supported by Botha, Smuts, and the British leader Sir Percy Fitzpatrick.[1] Similarly the delegates from the Cape forgot their political feuds. Observers remarked upon the tact and diplomatic skill of Dr Jameson, whom the Boers had once regarded as their most hated enemy. The feud between the two white races was, for once, forgotten.

The second problem was the relation between Europeans and Africans, a stumbling-block in the way of unity, since there was franchise for all 'civilised' men in Cape Colony but a rigid colour-bar in the other three provinces. Here the paramount power might be expected to intervene in the interest of the Africans.

The third problem was the tariff, about which the industrial Transvaal, the pastoral Free State, and the commercial Cape Colony had divergent opinions and, intimately bound up with the fiscal problem, was the fourth, the problem of railway rates. The traffic of the Rand was again slipping away from the Cape-town Railway to the Delagoa Bay railway. The Transvaal, the wealthy province, was looking east not south.

The delegates and the people of South Africa seem to have been surprised at the ease with which agreement was reached on all points. Only in loyalist Natal was there strong opposition[2] based upon a dislike of submitting to a Boer majority, and even

[1] Sir Percy FitzPatrick (1862–1931). Secretary of the Johannesburg Reform Association in 1896. Known to thousands of English-speaking readers as the author of *Jock of the Bushveld*.
[2] The attitude of Natal was complicated by its jealousy of the Cape. In its commercial policy Natal sided with the Transvaal, its hinterland.

there a referendum of the electorate gave a substantial majority (11,000 to 3700) for union. The other three provinces voted their approval by simple resolution of their legislatures. All four had given their assent by June 1909 and, in August, the South Africa Bill was brought forward at Westminster. The Union was proclaimed on 31 May 1910. Milner had given South Africa a modern administrative machine. The Liberals granted a democratic constitution. It fell to Louis Botha, the most moderate of the Boer leaders, to inherit Milner's responsibilities, as first Prime Minister of the Union.

By the South Africa Act (9 Edw. 7, cap. 9) the King was enabled to proclaim the legislative union of the four provinces 'on terms and conditions to which they have agreed by resolution of their respective parliaments'. Executive government was vested in the King who was to act through a Governor-General and his executive council. The Act made no mention of a cabinet or of the principle of responsible government, maintaining the old English legal fiction of a council summoned at the royal will. Nevertheless it specified that the ten heads of administrative departments should be *ex officio* members of the council and must be members of one or other House of Parliament. The 'seat of government' was to be Pretoria.

The two Houses of Parliament, known as the Senate and the Assembly, were to meet at least once a year and to be re-elected at least once in every five years. A peculiar feature of this constitution was the duplication of the capital. Though the executive was placed at Pretoria, the legislature was to meet at Capetown. The Senate was partly nominated by the Governor-General and partly elected by the Provincial Councils. The membership of the Assembly was closely prescribed in the Act with elaborate machinery for redistributing seats at intervals, since the different provincial franchises had been a point of dissension between the provinces. The colour-bar against native or coloured voters was preserved in the Transvaal, the Free State, and Natal, while the historic Cape franchise was also preserved.[1] The respective powers of the two Houses were to be much as in the constitution of the United Kingdom with the

[1] Civilised natives in Cape Colony were assured of their right to vote but deprived of their theoretical right to sit in Parliament. Actually no native had ever sat.

modification that a deadlock between the two Houses was to be resolved by their meeting together in joint session. The power of the Governor-General to reserve bills for the King's pleasure, and of the King to disallow them, was firmly stated in the Act. On the other hand a Supreme Court was to be created (to meet neither at Pretoria nor Capetown, but at Bloemfontein) for hearing all appeals. Only by special leave of the Crown could appeals be taken to the Privy Council. The Roman-Dutch law, somewhat modified by English principles and procedure, had been the civil code of all four provinces, and remained unchanged under the Union.

Although the South African Dominion was to be a union, and not a federation, the identity of the provinces could not be swept away. The distinction of franchise maintained their political survival, and the same franchise was to be used for the local government elections. An Administrator was to be appointed by the Governor-General for each province and a Provincial Council elected. The limits of provincial authority were clearly defined and, to avoid doubts, it was stated that provincial ordinances would be invalid if repugnant to any Act of the Union Parliament. The revenues, the assets and the debts of the provinces were taken over entire by the Union government as were the harbour-works and railways, by a clause of the Act which General Smuts called the Magna Carta of the inland provinces. The provincial authorities were given control over local taxation, municipal institutions, agriculture, and other matters of a 'merely local and private nature'.

But, as in Canada, a very powerful exception to this rule was the commitment of primary and secondary education to the provinces. Milner's system, while allowing the Dutch language to be legalised as a vernacular, had made English the language of instruction in all types of school. It had been his express intention to make English the dominant language on the grounds that every Boer gained many cultural advantages by learning English while the English colonist gained nothing by learning a dialect of Dutch. The despised 'taal', the dialect of the Boers, was not yet rated as a literary language. The law, the administration, and the Reformed Church used High Dutch, the language of Holland, which a back-veld Boer could hardly understand. The struggle for a national language began with the Dutch Reformed Church in the Orange Free State where children were withdrawn from the English-speaking schools and instructed in their own tongue in church schools. In spite of opposition from English-speaking Natal, the demand for the Dutch language was urged and urged successfully by Hertzog of the Orange Free State. The English-speaking delegates gave way gracefully on this point with the result that the whole of South Africa was made officially bi-lingual, not, like Canada, allowing local distinctions of language. 'Both the English and Dutch languages', says the Act, 'shall be official languages of the Union, and shall be treated on a footing of equality.' In the schools both languages are taught, the language of instruction being the one preferred by the parents.

To have condemned the English-speaking districts to accept an unwritten *patois* on equal terms with the language of Milton would have been a hardship but, as in other national revivals, the Afrikaners have created a literary language. Gradually breaking away from High Dutch they have standardised and purified the 'taal', under the name of Afrikaans, which was fixed by the publication of an authorised Afrikaans version of the Bible in 1931. The Afrikaner [1] nationalism of the Free State, led by Hertzog, 'the language fanatic', made bilingualism the criterion of South African parties. Resisting the endeavours of Botha and Smuts to unite Afrikaners and British, they developed the two-stream policy, the conception of a plural society.

In Canada the British North America Act is a fundamental law, which the Canadians can amend only by an appeal to the Parliament of Great Britain. In Australia an elaborate procedure for making amendments is incorporated into the constitution. In South Africa (as in New Zealand) the statute which created the constitution enabled the making of amendments by a simple act of the legislature, subject always to the Crown's right of disallowance. To this there were two exceptions in the South Africa Act. Part of the electoral machinery was declared un-alterable for a period of ten years, and the Cape franchise was to be modified only if there were a two-thirds majority in a joint

[1] At this point I reject finally the use of the name 'Boer' against which the government of the Orange Free State protested at least as early as 1871, describing it as an 'opprobrious nickname'. It seems to me, however, pedantic to suppress it in writing of earlier times when it had no opprobrious significance to English readers.

session of both Houses of Parliament in favour of altering it. Since more than one-third of the Assembly was drawn from the Cape Province, it could not be overruled on this issue by the other provinces.

The defence of the Cape franchise was one of the last endeavours made by the Crown to act as the guardian of native rights. Although the Act states that 'the control and administration of native affairs and of matters specially or differentially affecting Asiatics' should be vested in the Governor-General, it was soon found that in this as in other respects the Governor must act on the advice of his ministers. Accordingly the two great tribal areas, Zululand in Natal and Kaffraria in Cape Colony, have been effectually administered by the government of the Union. There still remained outside the Union, the three native territories of Basutoland, Swaziland, and Bechuanaland ruled directly by the Colonial Office through a High Commissioner. Of late years the appointment of High Commissioner has been separated from that of Governor-General. Provision was made in the Act for the transfer of these territories to the Union on the receipt of a petition from the Union Parliament.

Similarly provision was made for incorporating Southern Rhodesia into the Union but, in the generation after the passing of the Act, the political development of Rhodesia was in another direction.

XIII

THE BRITISH IN EGYPT, TO
THE YEAR 1914

Argument: Though British diplomats for generations past had been interested in routes to the East, Disraeli's purchase of the Suez Canal shares was a new political technique. When Gladstone authorised the occupation of Egypt he only half-approved action without the concurrence of the other powers and never mastered the consequent problems. With even greater reluctance he sent Gordon to Khartoum. When Cromer created Egyptian prosperity by administrative reforms it was perhaps the purest example of the New Imperialism. Neither for himself nor for England did he ask or get direct profit, privilege or even gratitude. The benefits of his work were enjoyed equally by the Egyptians, the British, and other nations trading to Egypt. Kitchener's conquest of the Sudan was almost the last act in the suppression of the African slave trade. When virtually under British rule the Sudanese for the first time enjoyed peace and welfare.

1. MEHEMET ALI AND HIS SUCCESSORS

FROM the day when Cleopatra applied the asp to her breast Egypt never again enjoyed national independence until the twentieth century. Whether well or badly ruled by successive dynasties of Romans, Saracens, and Turks the *fellaheen*, tilling the most fertile soil on the earth's surface, had long ceased—if they had ever begun—to feel national pride or the want of civic liberties. A good or a bad Nile (that is, Nile-flood) was all their care. During the decline of Turkish rule, in the seventeenth and eighteenth centuries, their condition had deteriorated. In spite of the Sultan's nominal sovereignty all the lucrative offices in Egypt had come into the hands of the Mamelukes, a military caste of Levantine, not native, origin, under whose oppressive rule the *fellaheen* were plundered, with the result that population was diminishing and land going out of cultivation. Egypt under the Mamelukes may be compared with central India under the Marathas. It was the Mameluke power that Bonaparte broke when he invaded Egypt in 1798.

Even though the French were defeated and, three years later, expelled, French social influence prevailed in Egypt. The French language began to supplant the Italian as the *lingua franca*. The governing class in the cities of Egypt adopted French manners and ways of life which largely persist to the present day. British influence in the Levant in the early nineteenth century was directed to two particular channels, the preservation of an overland route for mails to India through the Turkish dominions, and the support given by the Foreign Office to the Sultan of Turkey. Through the century British diplomats persevered in attempts to civilise the Turkish court. Purged of its ancient corruptions it was to be accounted one of the 'Powers' and admitted to the Concert of Europe. The effort failed, as all know, but should be recalled to memory when considering British policy in Greece, Arabia, or Egypt. The British went to Egypt in 1801 to expel the French, on behalf of their ally, the Sultan rather than to restore his unruly vassals, the Mamelukes. And with them went an illiterate Albanian named Mehemet (or Mohammed or Muhammad) Ali as an officer in the Turkish service. Little is known of his origin but that he was born in the vintage year, 1769; he was thus the contemporary of Bonaparte and Wellington and has been ranked by some writers as comparable with them in genius.

Five years later in another phase of the Napoleonic War a British army was again sent to Egypt, on this occasion without the Sultan's goodwill, to anticipate a French move. Mehemet Ali turned against the invaders, defeated a small British force at Rosetta (1807), and exposed the severed heads of 200 British soldiers as the prize of victory. With skilful statecraft he had mastered the various factions in Cairo and had been accepted as Pasha of Egypt by the Sultan. Though he negotiated a British evacuation of Egypt on moderate terms, promising that, if the British went, he would not admit the French, he was regarded as a hostile barbarian by successive British governments, all the more when he disposed of the Mamelukes by a general massacre, in 1811.

From 1807 to 1849 Mehemet Ali ruled Egypt as sovereign n all but name. Even when at war with the Sultan he never finally renounced his allegiance. But, like another Saladin, he sought with boundless ambition to unite all Arabs, perhaps all Moslems, under his single rule. With the help of his sons, notably the courageous Ibrahim, he conquered western Arabia including the Holy Cities (1812), the Sudan (1820), the Peloponnesus (1827), Syria (1832), and had some notion of overrunning all the Barbary States. Whereas he got much friendship and diplomatic support from France, he was thwarted again and again by Great Britain, especially when Palmerston was at the Foreign Office. Yet he never opposed British interests nor showed antipathy to the British, except when they invaded Egypt. In this long diplomatic struggle two crises are worth recalling here. Mehemet's attempt to attain sea-power in the Mediterranean was crushed when his very inefficient fleet was destroyed at Navarino (1827). Though the Foreign Office thought this an 'untoward event', since it forced the issue between the Sultan and the Greek rebels, the British people thought differently. Dreaming that Greece might yet be free they did not propose to see her subdued to Islam by the slave-trading Pasha of Egypt. Rebuffed at sea, Mehemet Ali advanced by land and conquered Syria. The Sultan saved the Turkish Empire from extinction by placing what remained under the protection of Russia at the Treaty of Unkiar Skelessi (1833). To Palmerston the prospect of the Russians at Constantinople was worse than the prospect of Mehemet Ali there. For years he worked to undermine the Treaty, and at last succeeded. When Mehemet seemed at the height of his greatness in 1839, Palmerston obtained an agreement for restoring the Sultan's authority by joint action of the Powers rather than by single-handed Russian action. Only France demurred, with the result that the British Navy settled the matter. Russia could take no part and the French stood aside discomfited. Alexandria was blockaded and Mehemet's garrison at Acre bombarded (1840). The old Pasha soon agreed to withdraw from Syria and Arabia, which were handed back to the misgovernment of Turkey. A blow at Russian prestige in Turkey, this was also the second blow struck by Britain at French prestige in Egypt; forty years later a somewhat similar crisis would result in a third blow.

Mehemet Ali was compensated for the loss of his external conquests by the establishment of his dynasty in Egypt. On consideration of paying an annual tribute to the Sultan, he and his heirs after him were to hold the *pashalik* in perpetuity. In 1867 the title of Khedive was substituted for that of Pasha.

Though driven back Mehemet Ali had much to show for his long laborious life. He had included the Sudan and the Red Sea littoral in Egypt, had restored law and order, had put an end to Mameluke oppression, and allowed no one but his own servants to extort money from the *fellaheen*. He built roads and attempted to inaugurate schools, hospitals, and factories though, for lack of honest officials and technical experts, they were slow to develop. At the end of his reign he began to construct the Barrage at the fork of the Nile near Cairo, the first of the great irrigation schemes of modern Egypt. He introduced the cultivation of cotton as a government monopoly. It was not to be expected of any oriental ruler of his day that he would discourage slavery, and in fact the conquest of the Sudan was regarded as the provision of a new field for organised slave-raiding. While he gave the people of Egypt firm and regular government, he oppressed them mightily like some Pharaoh of old with conscription and with the *corvée*, or forced labour at public works.

Ibrahim survived his father by a few months only. The next Pasha, Abbas (1849–54), was a cruel and avaricious tyrant under whom Egypt lapsed again into misgovernment. In his day the Czar Nicholas proposed to the British ambassador his preparations for the funeral of the Sick Man of Europe. Russia was to take the Balkans and England Egypt. The Sick Man was however set on his feet again by the Crimean War, and Egyptian affairs brightened when Said succeeded Abbas.

Proposals for a Suez Canal were now being actively canvassed. The growth of steamship lines had brought new urgency to the problem of routes to India (see chapter IX, 2, page 464) and, since steamships were hardly yet capable of so long a voyage, it was arguable that English predominance in railways was more to the point. A railway from Alexandria to Suez or even from Beirut to Basra was more practicable than a ship canal and, if a ship canal were preferred, would it not be simpler to link the waterways from the Orontes to the Euphrates, than to link two oceans through the Isthmus of Suez? Bold as the English engineers and investors were, they shrank from this project which, they thought, must be too expensive to pay its way. Palmerston was hot against the visionary scheme for a Suez Canal and tried to influence the pro-British Pasha Said against it. However, in 1854, the French consul Ferdinand de Lesseps (1805–94) got a concession. Before he had even formed a syndicate the English were in the field. Robert Stephenson built the first Egyptian railway, from Alexandria to Cairo in 1855 and carried through a light railway, now abandoned, to Suez in 1858. In association with the P. & O. Steamship Company it then provided a mechanised service for passengers and mails to India.

In the same year the Suez Canal Company was registered in Egypt, with a capital of £8,000,000 subscribed mostly in France. In 1859 Lesseps began operations by founding the town at the canal entrance which he called Port Said, after the Pasha. By 1862 contingent expenses for these ventures were mounting and Said's government was beginning to borrow money. Said died in 1863 and was succeeded by Ismail, the first Khedive of Egypt. The railways, the cotton-boom, and the general prosperity of the early sixties made a fine opportunity for an enlightened despot and Ismail was nothing if not that. He borrowed hugely, egged on by French, Austrian, Italian, Greek, and British financiers. In the sixteen years of his reign the national debt rose from £4,000,000 to £91,000,000 sterling, a heavy burden on a nation of no more than 6,000,000, most of whom were peasants with holdings of one or two acres. Taxation rose by 50%. The cost of the Canal was far greater than had been expected, £26,000,000 in all, of which a good part was borrowed by Ismail, at a rate of $12\frac{1}{2}\%$ interest, on behalf of the Company. Another obstacle overcome by de Lesseps was the continued opposition of Palmerston, who protested that the forced labour supplied by the Khedive was simply slavery. This was a taunt that provoked Ismail to the unprecedented extravagance of hiring labour for public works, and so increased his expenditure. Egypt was to move with the times and, accordingly, among the many Turkish and European experts brought into his service were several soldiers of fortune, German, Italian, or British, whom he employed to suppress the slave trade. After Sir Samuel Baker, the first Governor of the new Equatorial Province (1869–74), Ismail obtained the services of 'Chinese' Gordon as Governor-General of the Sudan (1874–9).

In Lower Egypt French influence still prevailed, and the manifest triumph of French enterprise as the Canal neared completion drew Ismail closer to Napoleon III, a ruler with whom he shared some common characteristics. Alexandria and even Cairo were largely rebuilt as cities in the French style, with a population swollen by Europeans, who increased in numbers from 6000 in 1852 to an estimated 100,000 in 1882. On 17 November 1869 the Suez Canal was opened in the presence of the Empress Eugénie, the Emperor Francis Joseph, the Crown Prince of Prussia, and many other notables. The proceedings were celebrated by the first performance, in the Opera House at Cairo, of *Aida* which Verdi wrote for the occasion. Egypt had arrived in the first rank of civilised powers. Though no Englishman of equal celebrity honoured the festivities, it was noted that the first ship to pay toll for a commercial passage through the canal was British, as were three-quarters of all that passed through during the next few years. By 1872 the receipts from tolls were exceeding the expenses of the Canal Company; but in 1875 the government of Egypt was insolvent.

Not only in Egypt but throughout the world a bleaker outlook confronted business men as the 'sixties gave way to the 'seventies. A long period of contracting trade was setting in, to reach its first acute phase in 1879. But Ismail, 'un galant à te faire dresser les cheveux' as Eugénie described him to her husband, continued to borrow and spend on luxuries and refinements as though the good times would last for ever. The fall of the Second Empire coming so soon after the Empress's visit might have warned him, but did not. In November 1875, Disraeli got wind of an attempt Ismail was making to raise money in Paris by mortgaging his interest in the Suez Canal. Acting on his own responsibility, since Parliament was not sitting, Disraeli authorised Rothschild to buy the Khedive's holding on behalf of the British government, for cash. Accordingly 176,602 ordinary shares out of the total of 400,000 were bought, at a little below par, for £4,080,000 sterling and became the property of the Crown.[1] The purchase was approved by Parliament, not without misgivings in the minds of the older members. It would have been natural if Disraeli, by some diplomatic stroke based upon sea-power, had obtained a fortress commanding the Canal, another

[1] In 1938 the British holding of shares was valued at £46,000,000. One-third of the Directors were by agreement British, three of them being appointed by the government. Dividends were paid to the Treasury and appeared in the Budget annually. The dividends averaged about £600,000 at first and rose to £1,699,269 in 1938–9. In 1938, 6171 ships (3028 of them British) carried 28,779,000 tons of merchandise through the Canal.

Gibraltar or Aden, but for the Queen's government to acquire shares in a foreign trading company was a new thing and felt by the fastidious to be degrading. It was part of the new vulgarity and on a par with Disraeli's other coup that winter, when he altered the age-old title of the Queen, calling her Empress of India, a new-fangled name which, in John Bull's eyes, was a step down in the world. The Queen responded by making her elderly admirer Earl of Beaconsfield.

During the financial crisis of 1876 representatives of the European bond-holders began to intervene in Egyptian affairs. Ismail was so well pleased with the £4,000,000 in sterling, received on account of his Suez Canal shares, that he agreed to submit the management of the Egyptian finances to an international office, the *Caisse de la Dette*, with two secretaries, an Englishman[1] and a Frenchman. Thus Egypt admitted bankruptcy and passed under what was called the Dual Control. At the same time the ancient 'capitulations' which, since the sixteenth century or earlier, had entitled Christian foreigners to remain under the jurisdiction of their respective consular courts, were modified by the creation of mixed consular tribunals, with jurisdiction over foreigners of every nation. For a year or two there seemed some slight improvement. Ismail accepted the financial advice of the two controllers and governed on regular principles through his Prime Minister, Nubar Pasha. But he was incapable of sustained economy and soon resumed his dance along the road to ruin. In 1879 when it was revealed that he had been intriguing against the Dual Control he was deposed by his suzerain, the Sultan of Turkey, at the request of the British, French and German governments. Ismail was so far resigned to his fate as to withdraw peaceably to Naples with a numerous court and 300 ladies of the harem. The Egyptians seemed not to care.

[1] The Englishman, Evelyn Baring (1841–1917), afterwards Lord Cromer, was bred a soldier but early showed the family talent for financial administration. His first civil appointment had been as private secretary to Sir H. Storks in Jamaica (see chapter IX, 7, page 520). Later he distinguished himself in India as private secretary to Lord Northbrook, the Viceroy, who was his cousin.

2.   A SPIRITED FOREIGN POLICY AND ITS CONSEQUENCES, 1874–85

In February 1874 Disraeli had at last become Prime Minister with a sufficient Parliamentary majority (350 Conservatives to 250 Liberals) for carrying out the programme that he had so long advocated. We are not here concerned with his admirable social reforms but with the 'spirited foreign policy' which was designed to give Great Britain her rightful place as the first of nations, renewing under Queen Victoria the glories of the Elizabethan Age. In Egypt and in India this policy had a profound effect upon the growth of the Empire, for Disraeli's eye was dazzled by the glamour of the East.

The bad harvest of 1874 was perhaps the operative cause of the revolutions which broke out in the Balkans in 1875. Turkish credit collapsed, and the Suez Canal shares came on the market when this financial uneasiness spread to Egypt. The next year saw a palace revolution at Constantinople where two successive Sultans were deposed, to make room for the redoubtable Abdul Hamid II (1876–1909). Then the Bulgarians revolted, whereupon the Sultan inaugurated his reign with massacres, which drew Gladstone from retirement to demand that the Turks should be expelled from Europe 'bag and baggage'.

The Prime Minister, more concerned by Russian intrigues than by Turkish atrocities, was of another opinion, which seemed justified when, in April 1877, Russia declared war on Turkey. Public opinion swung sharply to Disraeli's point of view and hardened against Russia when the Turks (as so often before and since) defended themselves with stubborn heroism. When the Russians at last broke through to the Aegean Sea (January 1878) Disraeli knew that the masses were behind him. The music-halls were echoing with the song: 'We don't want to fight but, by Jingo! if we do....' Accordingly he moved the Mediterranean Fleet to Besika Bay in Turkish waters and, a few days later, sent a squadron through the Dardanelles into the Sea of Marmora, to ensure, by fighting if necessary, that the 'Rooshians' should not have Constantinople.

Though this was a game of bluff, and successful, it was too bellicose for some of Disraeli's colleagues. (One who resigned was Carnarvon, leaving his schemes in South Africa unfinished and his High Commissioner, Sir Bartle Frere, without support from home.) In March the Russians imposed upon Turkey the harsh treaty of San Stefano, to which Disraeli reacted by mobilising the Army. To demonstrate the unity of the new British Empire he brought 7000 sepoys from India through the Suez Canal to reinforce the garrison of Malta. Tension was somewhat relieved by Bismarck who took a hand convening the Congress of Berlin (June 1878), from which Disraeli returned bringing 'Peace with Honour'. He might have obtained a protectorate over Egypt as the prize of diplomatic victory; he merely accepted, as a gratuity from the Sultan for services rendered, a protectorate over the island of Cyprus, to the general astonishment. The new protectorate was never put to any strategic use.

Meanwhile the funeral of the Sick Man of Europe was again deferred. Tenniel represented Disraeli in *Punch* (27 July 1878) as a tightrope walker, bowing and smiling to the audience, and carrying the Sultan, like an Old Man of the Sea, on his back. His foreign policy was indeed one of unstable equilibrium. Egypt just then was tranquil since Ismail was playing fair with his financial advisers, but in South Africa the Zulu War was threatening. The main contest with Russia had been triumphantly won but, on the very day that the Congress opened at Berlin, the Russians, according to their wont, retaliated on another front by sending a military mission to Kabul.

After the successes of 1878 a year of troubles followed. The powers were obliged to intervene again in Egypt and to depose the Khedive, while in South Africa Sir Bartle Frere entered upon the Zulu War, to the dismay of his friends almost as much as of his enemies. And now a new series of troubles began beyond the North-west Frontier of India. The effects of a spirited foreign policy there will be considered in chapter XVIII.

Afghanistan, South Africa, Egypt, and the wickedness of Disraeli's foreign policy in general formed the burden of Gladstone's rhetoric in his Midlothian Campaign. At the ensuing election Gladstone was returned to power with a majority of 349 Liberals against 243 Conservatives. He became Prime Minister on 23 April 1880. Under his administration, pledged to 'foster the strength of the Empire...and to reserve it for great and worthy occasions...to avoid needless and entangling engagements' in Europe, some shrewd blows were struck at British prestige. The public had to swallow the news of Maiwand (27 July 1880), Majuba (26 February 1881), and Khartoum (26 January 1885); but whether the blame is to be ascribed to Disraeli's faulty beginning or to Gladstone's faulty ending may be left to the judgment of the reader.

Tewfik, the new Khedive, began his reign with heavy handicaps: bankruptcy, foreign intervention and military mutiny. The bond-holders strengthened their grip in 1880, insisting upon economies, especially by disbanding superfluous troops. The Egyptian Army was very large, very inefficient, and officered by Turks and Levantines who were almost as alien to Egypt as the French or British. One of the few senior officers of native origin, Arābi Pasha, put himself at the head of a national movement in opposition to all foreign rule. The dynasty of Mehemet Ali, themselves aliens, had introduced a new alien aristocracy, had mortgaged their country to the Franks, had favoured the westernised cities at the expense of the *fellaheen*, had enriched themselves from an enormous royal domain of a million acres. The time was come to claim Egypt for the Egyptians. Arābi was something more than a mutineer; Cromer said that he led a genuine revolt against misgovernment; Dufferin described him as a champion of Islam.

Beginning with military tumults he thrust himself into the post of Minister of War and seemed likely to make himself dictator, as Mehemet Ali had done eighty years before him. By May 1882 disorder became so serious that Great Britain and France sent naval squadrons to Alexandria to protect, if necessary, the evacuation of the European residents. On 11 June fifty or sixty Europeans were killed in the streets and settled government was at an end. Arābi began to strengthen and to man the forts on the foreshore commanding the fleet anchorage. In London Gladstone, though opposed as always to war and annexation, reluctantly decided to restore the legitimate authority of the Khedive, now helpless in the hands of the mutineers. Once committed to the Dual Control we could not see Egypt sink into anarchy. But in Paris Gambetta, who would have co-operated with Gladstone, had just been put out of office and the Chamber voted against intervention in Egypt. Accordingly the French squadron withdrew before hostilities began. Sir Edward Seymour engaged

the batteries with eight ships of the line on 11 July 1882, when
his ultimatum demanding that Arābi should stand his gun-crews
down produced no reply.

It was a bright hot day with a calm sea. For nine hours ships
and forts hammered at one another at 1500 yards range until the
batteries were silenced one by one. More light would have been
thrown on the old problem of ships versus shore defences if
either side had been equipped with the right ammunition. Though
the Egyptian gunnery was far from negligible—the *Alexandra*

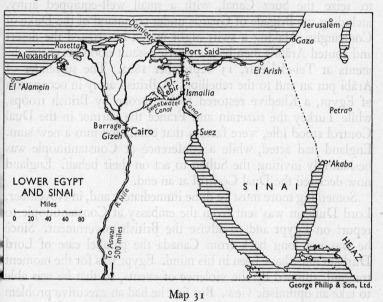

LOWER EGYPT
AND SINAI

Miles

0   20   40   60   80

George Philip & Son, Ltd.

Map 31

was hulled thirty-four times—the shells could not penetrate the
armour-belt which covered the vitals of the British ships. On
their part, the ships were provided chiefly with armour-piercing
projectiles which had little effect against earthworks. A decisive
blow was struck by the *Superb* which exploded the largest
Egyptian magazine with a well-directed shell; but, in the eyes of
the public, the honours went to Lord Charles Beresford's *Condor*,
a gunboat, which left its station to engage at closer range. At
dusk Arābi's soldiers fled from the forts and from the city, which
was promptly fired and plundered by the mob. On the next day
naval landing-parties restored order. The British casualties had

been six killed and twenty-seven wounded. This was the first occasion when the British Navy went into action with armoured ships and the last when it used muzzle-loading guns.

A year earlier France had acted alone in Tunis where England had equal interests, and the French occupation of Tunis lasts to this day. Now England by a similar stroke was to occupy Egypt, while France was all the more jealous because timid and vacillating. After the bombardment the Chamber again voted against intervention. In August Sir Garnet Wolseley landed at Ismailia to seize the Suez Canal, with a small well-equipped army, including the Brigade of Guards under command of the Duke of Connaught. Making a swift night march he crossed the desert and routed Arābi's men by a surprise assault upon his entrenchments at Tel-el-Kebir, 13 September 1882. The surrender of Arābi put an end to the rebellion. A British army in occupation of Egypt, a Khedive restored to his throne by British troops, while Turkey the suzerain and France the partner in the Dual Control stood idle, were factors that combined into a new sum. England had acted, while a conference at Constantinople was hesitatingly inviting the Sultan to act on their behalf. England now declared the Dual Control at an end.

Something more must be done immediately and, in November, Lord Dufferin was sent from the embassy at Constantinople to report on Egypt and to advise the British government. Since he was not long back from Canada the parallel case of Lord Durham must have been in his mind. Egypt was for the moment tranquil, stunned by the violence of events, so that he was able to take an optimistic view. But first he had an executive problem to solve. What was to be done with Arābi against whom legal proceedings had been taken with all the delays that the confused judicial system permitted? Dufferin cut all that short, as Durham had done on a like occasion, and deported Arābi to Ceylon. Whatever were its other effects, this decision demonstrated to the world that the Khedive was a puppet of the British.

Dufferin's report, issued in February 1883, spoke of implanting in Egypt 'those instincts of patriotism and freedom which it has been our boast to foster in every country where we have set our foot'. But, to do this, time was needed, 'time to consolidate' and to guarantee that the fabric built for the benefit of the Egyptians would endure. There must therefore be a British

occupation 'for an indefinite period of time'. This was uncomfortable reading for Gladstone and his Foreign Secretary,
Lord Granville, who harped continually on the theme that the
occupation was a cruel necessity which should be cut short as
soon as possible.

The Report proposed for Egypt a complex system of government based on indirect election. National institutions, on
Durham's admirable principle, were to grow out of municipal
institutions. The electorate, both for the General Assembly and
for the Provincial Councils, was to consist of representatives
elected by the village communities. But the powers of the
Assembly were at first to be strictly limited; the initiative was to
remain in the hands of 'the government', which would enjoy
'sympathetic advice and assistance' from British experts. In the
future, no doubt, the power of the purse would be assumed by the
Assembly; for the present Dufferin recommended the 'masterly
hand of a resident'; and that precisely was what Egypt got.
The constitution was established and, in September 1883, Sir
Evelyn Baring (later Lord Cromer) returned to Egypt as Agent
and Consul-general. For twenty-three years he was the ruler of
the land, as positively as Joseph in the days of Pharaoh the
Great.

This was not the whole substance of Dufferin's report: he
suggested a programme of public works, large-scale irrigation for
the benefit of the *fellaheen* to be undertaken by British engineers
from India; the formation of a new army with Egyptian officers
under the guidance of a British military mission; and a new
policy for the Sudan. The southern provinces of that territory
should be evacuated, as no part of Egypt proper, and the northern
provinces reorganised with a new outlet by railway from Berber
on the eastward bend of the Nile to Suakin on the Red Sea. The
weakness of the report was that it said little of finances, and
pressure by the foreign bond-holders was to make finance the
limiting factor.

Dufferin had no sooner departed than troubles began to
accumulate. In the summer of 1883, the cholera came to Egypt
and revealed the abject inefficiency of the Department of Public
Health. The hospitals built by Mehemet and his successors were,
not unjustifiably, regarded with dread by the people. The doctors
were as timid as they were ignorant and corrupt. In November

came news of a disaster in the Sudan where another rebellion had broken out, while in Cairo the government was more insolvent than before.

3. GORDON AND THE SUDAN

ARĀBI had not been the only leader of a national rising. As early as March 1881 reports came to Cairo of a prophet of martial tendency who had appeared on the Upper Nile. This was Mohammed Ahmed (1844–85), a boat-builder of Dongola, who was preaching holy war against all the corruptions of life in the Delta. Khedives and pashas and their parasites, Greek merchants and French financiers and English officials, westernised Egyptians and European dabblers in the East, all alike were damned as wine-bibbers, tobacco-smokers, breakers of the strict law of Islam, and were best despatched to hell if they would not instantly submit to Allah and the Prophet, and to Mohammed Ahmed the *mahdi* or 'guided one'. He denounced the whole world of Cairo as 'Turks' and they, with equal inaccuracy, spoke of him and his followers as 'Dervishes', the Levantine name for members of the ascetic orders of Islam. The Mahdi's men called themselves 'Ansar'. With his band of followers Mohammed Ahmed, who was beautiful in person and eloquent in speech, came near to conquering all Moslem Africa. The first and most faithful of his adherents was Abdullahi, a ruthless soldier of the Baggāra tribe. Though there have been many *mahdis* in the history of Islam and innumerable *caliphs* or *khalifās*—that is lieutenants—Mohammed Ahmed and Abdullahi are known exclusively to English readers as the Mahdi and the Khalifā.

An Egyptian official, sent to arrest the Mahdi, was repulsed with loss of life; a senior official with a larger force was captured and forced to submit to the Mahdi under threat of death. The movement spread through the provinces until every Sudanese governor was calling for military help while the mutinous Egyptian Army was defying Admiral Seymour's fleet at Alexandria. Unfortunately Gordon, who would certainly have understood and, at that early stage, might even have appeased the Mahdi, had gone, and was replaced as Governor-General of the Sudan by an ineffective Egyptian pasha. Though Dufferin mistrusted the policy, a half-hearted attempt was made to restore order in the Sudan. While as yet there was no new system in Egypt, a miserable army of 10,000 unwilling, untrained conscripts was assembled at Khartoum and placed under command of Colonel Hicks of the Indian Army. Trailing away south they were misled by treacherous guides, and ambushed by the Dervishes near El Obeid (November 1883). Hicks and his European staff died fighting; the rank and file were slaughtered since there was no way to run for safety. This was the first crisis to be faced by Sir Evelyn Baring who had just taken charge in Egypt: a second followed; the garrison from Suakin under Colonel V. Baker (brother of Sir Samuel Baker) was also routed by a chief named Osman Digna, who threw in his lot with the Mahdi. Suakin would have been lost had not naval landing-parties been sent to hold the port.

If the southern Sudan was to be evacuated as Dufferin proposed, it would be a difficult task to extricate the officials and garrisons, not to mention the traders and missionaries, from this wide and savage area. Baring now wished, as a measure of economy, to withdraw from the whole Sudan, even from the junction of the White and Blue Niles, where the town of Khartoum contained many Egyptian and a few European residents. For this task a strong man was needed and Fleet Street cried out for Gordon. Though Baring was less enthusiastic, Gordon's reputation seemed to meet the need. Gladstone adopted this way out of the difficulty and sent Gordon back to Egypt in January 1884.

If the task had been to break through all opponents and link up with Stanley in the Congo, if it had been to lead a crusade against Islam and the slave-raiders, if it had been to bear witness and die, a Christian martyr, in the Mahdi's camp, then Charles George Gordon would have been the man; but to temporise, to negotiate surrender, to cut his losses and abandon his allies was to him unthinkable.

Born in 1833 he had served in the Crimea and had gone to China to suppress the Taiping rebellion (see chapter VIII, 2, page 425). As 'Chinese' Gordon he was known to the world for quixotic bravery and no less quixotic unselfishness. He had refused the great rewards offered him at Pekin, accepting only a gold medal which he afterwards sold for charity. Wandering in many lands he had pored over the Bible, interpreting it quite literally, a single-minded mystic as was, in another style, the Mahdi. When Governor-General of the Sudan he repeated his Chinese exploits, after reducing his own salary from £10,000 to £2000 a year. It was remembered that he had ridden alone into a camp of 6000 slave-raiders and compelled them, by sheer force of personality, to obey him. He had visited South Africa to advise upon the problem of Basutoland and made a great impression on the young Cecil Rhodes. Gordon had his own ideas about managing the Sudan.

Much controversy has taken place over the terms of Gordon's appointment. Lord Granville's instructions were necessarily vague since Gordon was to act under the authority of the Khedive, while the Khedive must do as Baring told him. Thus the responsibility fell upon Baring and the operative document is the *firman*, issued after Gordon had reached Khartoum in February 1884, reappointing him Governor-General of the Sudan. His mission was 'to carry into execution the evacuation of those territories, and to withdraw our troops, civil officers, and such of the inhabitants, together with their belongings, as may wish to leave for Egypt... and after completing the evacuation [to] take steps for establishing an organised government for the different provinces in the Sudan'. Gordon had no doubt that the second part of the programme must come first.

He had already announced his own plan which included the creation of a number of Arab sultanates, and had even spoken of offering one of them to the Mahdi, but within a few days he felt the need of a counterpoise. To the astonishment of the world and the dismay of the Anti-Slavery Society he suddenly and vehemently demanded that Zebehr (or Zobeir) Pasha should be placed at his disposal. Now Zebehr, though very influential, was a notorious slaver and one of Gordon's old enemies. Furthermore Gordon was talking, at least as early as 27 February 1884, of 'smashing the Mahdi'.

The request for Zebehr, to cast out Satan with the help of Satan, was too much for Gladstone, though Baring did not think it altogether unreasonable. The refusal put Gordon out of all patience with his employers; he would play a lone hand, doing his duty by the people of Khartoum who trusted him. On 22 March a strange episode occurred; armed envoys appeared before Gordon appealing to him to embrace the Mahdi's cause.

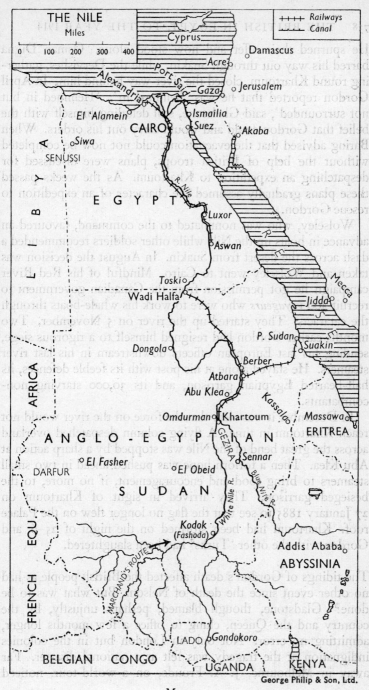

Map 32

He spurned their offer and now stood alone. Osman Digna barred his way out through Suakin, while the Dervishes, gathering round Khartoum, closed the river-way behind him. In April Gordon reported that he was 'hemmed in'. 'Hemmed in but not surrounded', said Gladstone, still deluding himself with the belief that Gordon could and would carry out his orders. When Baring advised that the evacuation could not now be completed without the help of British troops, plans were discussed for despatching an expedition to Khartoum. As the weeks passed these plans gradually assumed the character of an expedition to rescue Gordon.

Wolseley, who was nominated to the command, favoured an advance in boats up the Nile while other soldiers recommended a dash across the desert from Suakin. In August the decision was taken and Wolseley went to Cairo. Mindful of his Red River campaign he got permission from the Canadian government to recruit 400 *voyageurs* who were to work his whale-boats through the cataracts. They started up the river on 5 November. Two months earlier Gordon had resigned himself to a rigorous siege, sending his last European officers downstream in his last river steamers. He stayed alone at his post with its feeble defences, its half-hearted Egyptian garrison, and its 30,000 starving non-combatants.

In December it was clear that the force on the river would not reach Khartoum in time. A flying column despatched overland across the great bend of the Nile was stopped by a sharp action at Abu Klea. Then a forlorn hope was pushed ahead in two small steamers to bring food and encouragement, if no more, to the besieged garrison. They arrived in sight of Khartoum on 27 January 1885 to see that the flag no longer flew on the Palace roof. Khartoum had been stormed on the night of 25–6, and Gordon with the other 'Turks' had been slaughtered.

The tidings of Gordon's death affected the British people as had no other event since the death of Nelson. But what was to be done? Gladstone, though blamed, perhaps unjustly, by the country and the Queen, clung to office a few months longer, admitting no error. Not only in London but in the colonies indignation at the tragedy was felt as a national disaster. Far away in Melbourne, J. A. Froude, on a world-tour, noticed that the sense of shame, the anger with Gladstone, the demand for renewed action were universal. The campaign which the Canadian *voyageurs* had begun was to see Australians in action before all was over. While Wolseley maintained pressure on the Nile front he arranged for a brigade of troops to be sent from India to Suakin with the object of crushing Osman Digna and reopening the road to Berber. In this campaign Australian volunteers were in the field.

In 1885 the acting-premier of New South Wales was a Mr W. B. Dalley (1831–88), an Irish Roman Catholic who earned momentary fame by his initiative and is commemorated by a tablet in St Paul's Cathedral. He instantly raised and despatched to the Red Sea a corps of volunteers. On 23 March 500 infantry and 200 gunners from New South Wales left Sydney with guns and horses, and arrived at Suakin in time to take a small part in the action at Tamai. Offers of contingents from other colonies were rejected by the War Office.

At that moment operations were called off, since a counter-irritant to the Egyptian affliction had made itself felt farther east. In March 1885 the Russians occupied Penjdeh in Afghanistan. This new crisis raised a scare of war with Russia, which justified Gladstone in withdrawing finally from the Sudan and in sending home the colonial contingents. His handling of the Penjdeh Incident (see chapter XVIII, 1, page 924) restored to some extent the prestige lost at Khartoum. Wolseley also had lost prestige.

For half a generation Sir Garnet Wolseley (1833–1913) had been the indispensable commander, 'England's only soldier' according to the more cynical organs of the press. Gilbert had caricatured him, rather savagely, in the *Pirates of Penzance* (1880) as the Modern Major-General, a part which Grossmith played made-up to resemble Wolseley. Sir Garnet could do far more than 'thrash a cannibal'; he could solve any problem, cope with any situation; his name was a by-word for efficiency so that cockneys said, 'All Sir Garnet' to express what they now mean when they say 'O.K.' He fought through eleven campaigns in four continents and then reorganised the Army. Before he was twenty-seven he had served with distinction in Burma, Russia, India and China, and been three times wounded; he had visited the Confederate Armies in the field, where he struck up a friendship with Stonewall Jackson. Wolseley's reputation was made by the Red River Expedition and enlarged by the march through Ashanti. Next he spent two years as Governor of Natal, among native disturbances and threats of civil war, and returned there two years later to bring the Zulu war to a conclusion. In 1882 he fought the model campaign of Tel-el-Kebir which indicated him inevitably as the commander to relieve Khartoum. Essentially a scientific soldier, his tendency was towards minute planning and preparation. In his determination not to repeat the disastrous wild-goose chases into Africa made by his predecessors he over-insured his risks and took a week too long in mounting the expedition. When his men came in sight of Khartoum, too late, his reputation was somewhat blown upon. Scientific soldiers are rarely as popular as scatter-brained heroes. But it was by scientific methods that the Sudan was at last reconquered, and the rising star of Roberts in India, which was to outshine Wolseley's, was also that of a scientific soldier.

Wolseley did not again take the field, but became Commander-in-Chief when the old Duke of Cambridge was finally dislodged from the Horse Guards (1895). At last his schemes for reforming the Army could be initiated even though privilege and tradition were more stubborn foes than Ashanti tribesmen and Egyptian rebels. Even after his retirement in 1901 Wolseley kept pegging away from his place in the Lords (he had been raised to the peerage in 1882). In the long run he created a new professional tradition of attention to staff duties, technical proficiency, and education for all ranks, which made the British regular army of 1914 the best-trained and best-equipped in the world.

The Egyptian frontier was the training ground for the Army in the 'eighties and 'nineties. The keenest officers of Wolseley's school sought appointments in the new Egyptian Army, which saw much active service. They were stiffened by British troops based on Wadi Halfa and Indian troops based on Suakin, during the twelve years of the evacuation of the Sudan. Yet Egypt proved a bad training ground for war against a civilised enemy as the operations in South Africa were to prove.

Tactics in the desert campaigns were wonderfully old-fashioned. Though regiments no longer, after the Zulu War, carried their colours into action, the Guards and the Line still fought at Tel-el-Kebir in scarlet. It was the last appearance in battle of that traditional cloth derived from Cromwell's Ironsides, except that in the forlorn hope for the relief of Khartoum a party of twenty soldiers wore scarlet in the leading boat, for moral effect. Battles in the Sudan were fought by volley-firing in drill formations. Some machine-guns were used experimentally but with small effect owing to difficulties of ammunition supply. Troops habitually formed squares, with their transport in the middle, to receive charges of Sudanese spearmen, and even manœuvred across the desert in echelons of battalion squares. At the Atbara in 1898 the British brigade advanced against the *zariba* with three battalions in mass behind a single battalion in line. The brigadier, Gatacre, rode in the centre of the line beneath a huge Union Jack whose bearer was shot down in the mêlée.

Battles were very bloody, often ending with the annihilation of the losing side, in earlier years usually the Anglo-Egyptian force, and in later years usually the dervishes. Old soldiers long remembered the prowess of the 'Fuzzy-Wuzzies', the Haden-dowa tribe, who broke a British square at Abu Klea (17 December 1884), which was more than the Grand Army could do at Waterloo.

4. CROMER IN EGYPT, 1885–97

THE war in the Sudan prolonged the British occupation of Egypt beyond Gladstone's intention, and the disaster of 1885 implied that the defence of the Egyptian frontier against a dervish advance must fall upon the occupying power. All these troubles added further to the embarrassment of the government in Cairo, alarming the bond-holders without allaying their suspicions about British policy. De Freycinet, the French Minister who had failed to persuade his countrymen to share in the occupation, said bitterly of Great Britain: 'Elle ne pense plus à l'évacuation; elle oublie qu'il y a une Europe. Elle escompte l'avenir comme si l'avenir tout entier lui appartenait.' She was to have a pretty long innings but, whatever Great Britain was doing in Egypt, she was certainly not acting as the agent of cosmopolitan finance; she was spending on defence and development the Egyptian revenues which the bond-holders claimed as their due.

In June 1884, when Gordon was already 'hemmed in' at Khartoum, Lord Granville presided at a conference of the powers in London to discuss the Egyptian budget. On Baring's advice he proposed a guaranteed British loan to Egypt of £9,000,000 which, after paying off the deficit to the bond-holders and the reparation for the damage done by Arābi's plunderings, would still allow a modest million for irrigation. But to this proposal the other powers would not agree. Lord Northbrook (Baring's cousin) was then sent to make a further report, which provoked the French to fury since he actually suggested that interest should be withheld from the bond-holders for the urgent needs of administration. This shocking proposal was checked by the French members of the *Caisse*, now supported by German and Russian representatives, who cited the Egyptian Prime Minister before a mixed tribunal and compelled him to pay to the uttermost farthing. While the French thus vindicated financial probity, Wolseley was just launching his expedition to Khartoum. At the crisis of his campaign the French carried a still graver charge against the puppet govern-ment of Egypt and its British master. In defiance of the capitula-tions the police had attempted to suppress a French newspaper in Cairo merely for publishing a proclamation from the Mahdi calling upon all Egyptians to rise in rebellion. Again the action of the government was reversed by the courts. These two victories for the cause of usury and sedition gave great satis-faction to the enemies of Great Britain. There was, in short, only one asset over which Baring had a lien, the British holding in the Suez Canal shares, and the British accordingly abstained from drawing a dividend until Egypt was solvent.

Patient efforts by British diplomats at last (July 1885) produced a *modus vivendi* that worked until 1904. The political status of the British in Egypt was not defined but was tacitly accepted. The loan of £9,000,000 was raised and guaranteed jointly by the powers, but in such a form that the mischievous *Caisse* could and did exercise a veto over the spending of any surplus in the Egyptian Budget. But Egypt was released from bankruptcy and there was at last a balance of cash in hand for current expenses.

The next problem was to conciliate the Sultan of Turkey whose sovereignty over Egypt had been usurped by the British. When Lord Salisbury came into office he sent Sir Henry Drummond Wolff to negotiate (1887), with the general intention of drawing the Sultan into partnership. The conclusion of the British occupation within three years was foreshadowed and proposals were made that the Turks should be responsible for reconquering the Sudan. But to spend money on Egypt was not Abdul Hamid's intention; he maintained the classical Ottoman theory that an empire existed to pay tribute to its ruler, and that was all he cared about. Accordingly the British were again left to shoulder the responsibility. Drummond Wolff's mission was, it seemed, a failure as Northbrook's had been, and only a *modus vivendi* was arranged with Turkey. The British were to do all that must be done while the Sultan was to receive his accustomed tribute for doing nothing—£670,000 a year guaranteed by the British was a surer benefit than any earlier Sultan had got from Egypt.

Meanwhile Baring was quietly pegging away at reforms in the administration with the handicap that every item of new expenditure was questioned by the other members of the *Caisse*. They obstructed the abolition of the *corvée*; they refused, when the time came, to finance the reconquest of the Sudan; they hampered the building of the Aswan Dam. By sheer unremitting attention to economy Baring showed a real surplus of revenue over expense in 1888–9, but that was a 'bad Nile' year, so that it was not until 1889–90 that the benefits became apparent.

The reconstruction of the Nile Barrage was completed in 1889, bringing an increase of 10% in the land under cultivation at a capital cost of £460,000. Control of the numerous irrigation channels throughout the Delta was placed under a public works department organised on the Indian model and depending upon hired labour instead of upon the *corvée*. 1890 was the first of seven years of great plenty through all the land of Egypt, so that the previous seven years of famine were forgotten. Baring's policy was at first to lighten the burden on the *fellaheen* since there were as yet insufficient resources for large constructive plans. He removed the oppressive tax on salt, which ceased to be a government monopoly; abolished internal *octrois*; lowered the tolls on Nile shipping; reduced the postal and railway rates; and altered the incidence of the land-tax so that the poorer peasants were relieved of their obligation by about 30%. In spite of these remissions the national revenue was buoyant, exceeding £10,000,000 for the first time in 1890.

Ismail's old officials were, as a class, so corrupt and oppressive that it became necessary to bring Englishmen from the Indian services to reorganise one department after another—the police, the law courts, the department of internal affairs, and principally the army; and great as were the benefits conferred upon the inarticulate *fellaheen* it will not be supposed that the English newcomers were popular with the Egyptian officials whom they superseded. By the end of the century 960 out of 11,000 civil servants were Englishmen.

Rigid economy imposed by outsiders was bound to provoke unrest, which duly appeared when Abbas II, known as Abbas Hilmi, succeeded to the Khediviate in 1892. By then Baring (who became Lord Cromer that year) was firmly in the saddle; his cautious, conservative nature prejudiced him against premature changes and he made no political concession to the nationalist movement. In this he was supported by Lord Salisbury and by the Liberal Imperialist, Lord Rosebery, who became Prime Minister in 1893. 'The real feeling of the native population', said Rosebery, 'is not unfriendly. A policy of permanent importance, undertaken in the general interest of Europe and civilisation should not be modified in deference to ephemeral agitation among certain classes. Withdrawal [from Egypt] would be followed by a relapse into confusion.' It was clear, and Cromer emphasised it in his annual reports, that the British occupation must remain, and many years must pass before the Egyptians would be fit to govern. The census of 1897 showed that only eighty-eight per thousand of the men and three per thousand of the women could read and write.

The population of Egypt was returned as 9,734,000 of whom 608,000 were Christian Copts and 112,000 Europeans. The largest foreign colony was that of the Greeks who numbered 38,000. There were 24,000 Italians, 14,000 French, 6000 British Maltese, 4000 other British civilians, and 4000 British soldiers.

5. RECONQUEST OF THE SUDAN, 1896–9

THE twelve years since the fall of Khartoum had seen great changes in the Dervish Empire. The Mahdi had outlived his enemy, Gordon, by a few months only and lay buried in a domed shrine at Omdurman, a new suburb of Khartoum on the left bank of the Nile. All that was pure in the Mahdist movement died with him, leaving nothing but rapine and murder to mark the reign of Abdullahi the Khalifā (1885–99). Never was there a bloodier, more destructive tyranny. The population of the Sudan is said to have diminished by half under his rule. And with the death of the prophet, victory deserted the banners of the Dervishes, who fought still with careless heroism but no longer invincibly. They could make no progress against the equally fierce Abyssinians, though they did kill King John of Abyssinia by a lucky stroke; they could not take Suakin from the British; and they could not take Wadi Halfa.

Year by year the Khalifā threatened to invade Egypt and to drive the 'Turks' into the sea, but not till 1889, after two false starts, was the invasion attempted in strength. The Dervishes were decisively defeated at Toski near Wadi Halfa by Sir Francis Grenfell with a force of Egyptian troops. The threat vanished, but more remarkable was the resurgence of the Egyptian conscript army. Perhaps the greatest achievement of the British in Egypt was the work of the officers and sergeants (under Sir Evelyn Wood), who made the downtrodden *fellaheen* stand up and face their enemies.

There followed several years of comparative peace. Some news trickled through of events in the Sudan but no full account until the escape of Slatin in 1895. His book, *Fire and Sword in the Sudan*, informed the world, and his private information was of a kind that the Intelligence Corps knew how to use. Slatin, a free-thinking Austrian officer, had been one of Gordon's lieutenant-governors and, when alone among fanatics, had saved his life by affecting to turn Moslem. This apostasy earned him the contempt of some pious persons whose solider faith had not been tested by the threat of instant death. With two or three others in like case he survived ten years of degradation as the Khalifā's slave. Sitting in chains by the gate of Omdurman he had seen Gordon's head carried by in a bloody napkin. At last he escaped and, as Sir Rudolf Slatin Pasha, K.C.M.G., honoured by four nations, he lived until 1932 to do much good service for the Sudan.

The year 1896 was crucial in the history of Egypt; it saw the foundation of the Aswan Dam and the first steps to reconquer the Sudan. The change of policy on the frontier was partly due to the return to office of Lord Salisbury, partly to a desire to help the Italians who had been defeated by the Abyssinians at Adowa. At the request of Rome it was decided in London to advance into the Sudan, since pressure there would prevent the Dervishes from taking advantage of Italian weakness. Patience and economy had at last provided Egypt with sound finances and an adequate army.

In the preliminary campaign of 1896 the province of Dongola was cheaply and efficiently reoccupied, and the Egyptian Army thoroughly tested. The next year was chiefly taken up with making communications; for Sir H. Kitchener, Sirdar since 1892, had decided neither to go up the river in boats nor to cross the desert from Suakin with camels, but to build a railway across the bend of the Nile to Abu Hamed. Early in 1898 the main advance began. Osman Digna, entrusted with defending the right bank of the Nile, was defeated with slight loss to the Anglo-Egyptians at the Battle of the Atbara in April. By July the railway was brought forward to the Atbara River. Six weeks later the whole force, of one British division, one Egyptian division, a cavalry regiment, a camel corps, and a naval flotilla, was in position before Omdurman. The Dervish army now appeared in force to smite the infidels. Abating nothing of their old fury, they immolated themselves before the volley-firing—10,000 dervishes died and not one came to close quarters with the steady lines of infantry. The casualties on the winning side were less than 500, of whom a quarter were killed or wounded in the unlucky charge of the 21st Lancers.[1]

The Mahdi's tomb was demolished and stood a ruin until 1946 when his son restored it. In order to extinguish the cult the Mahdi's body was disinterred and mutilated. Like Cromwell's head which was similarly abused, the head of the Mahdi vanished and its whereabouts is not revealed. The Khalifā fled south

---

[1] *The River War* by Winston Churchill is the best account of the campaign. As a cavalry subaltern the author rode in the charge of the 21st Lancers.

with his faithful emirs. A year later he was brought to bay at Debreikat by General Wingate and died like a Saracen hero. Osman Digna, a hunted fugitive, was taken in 1900.

The cost of the campaign was about £2,500,000 of which more than a million was spent on strategic railways bringing direct benefit to reconstruction and trade. The Desert Railway was carried forward across the Atbara River to Khartoum in 1899. These advantages had not been foreseen by the *Caisse* which vigorously obstructed the spending of the Egyptian surplus on Kitchener's campaign. Part of the cost was paid from current revenue while the balance, £800,000, was provided by the British taxpayer in the form of a grant-in-aid.

6. CROMER IN EGYPT, 1898–1906

By this time the *Caisse* was very well endowed with the surpluses of a dozen prosperous budgets. From 1896 onwards, Cromer had managed to inaugurate a series of constructive reforms in Egypt as well as to finance the reconquest of the Sudan. A network of roads for wheeled traffic was developed to replace the old donkey-tracks through the Delta and, after 1898, was reinforced by 500 miles of light railway under private ownership. A concession was granted for the construction of these light railways to a Coptic company which raised the capital locally in Egypt, under strict supervision. In that generation no statesman yet saw any merit in nationalisation on principle, at the expense of economy and efficiency, and the Egyptian State Railways were neither economical nor efficient. They did not improve so rapidly under Cromer's regime as the other public services, largely because of the great growth of untrammelled traffic on the Nile. The Khedive's line of mail-steamers was also grossly inefficient and could not be modernised for lack of capital. Cromer made a good bargain for Egypt by selling the line to an English company which soon gave good service and paid its way. A National Bank was founded, with a subsidiary Agricultural Bank for advancing money to the *fellaheen* on easy terms. Cairo and Alexandria were lit by electricity, early among cities. Sanitation was less easy since surface drainage was a problem where the river was embanked high above the land. Hygienic and technical progress were slow in a country where the working-class was illiterate and the governing-class corrupt; and money was kept as short by the *Caisse* for education as for any other item. A small annual grant-in-aid to the Moslem vernacular schools was increased year by year as the revenue permitted.

The first full census of Egypt, taken in 1897, and the land-survey enabled the resources of the country to be precisely calculated. The reports of Sir William Garstin (1849–1925), an engineer borrowed from the Indian Public Works Department, made possible the systematic irrigation of the whole Nile Valley. All previous schemes had been designed to trap and use as much as possible of the floodwater while it was passing through Lower Egypt. The Barrage that French engineers had built across the apex of the Delta had been reconstructed by the British (1883–91) with the effect of doubling the cotton crop and adding about £5,000,000 to the annual income of Egypt. Though it held a head of seven feet of water above the normal level, the Barrage did nothing to protect the country against the disastrous effects of an unusually high or low or late flood. The lowest recorded year was 1877 at the nadir of the national fortunes. The weakness of the old Barrage was that it was founded upon desert sand; Garstin now proposed to control the entire stream in Upper Egypt by means of a new barrage founded upon rock. At the First Cataract, 500 miles south of Cairo, the Nile passes through a gorge of granite where the flood can be measured and parcelled out. Throughout human history the records of the flood show little variation from an average height of 25½ feet at the First Cataract in mid-September. In the worst years it is never more than three weeks late and never varies more than three feet above or five feet below the average. The first plan for damming the gorge at Aswan was made in 1893 by Sir William Willcocks (1852–1932), another engineer from India. Work was begun on the site in 1896 and by 1898 the dam was built, a granite structure one and a quarter miles in length holding a head of sixty-five feet of water. The estimated cost, £2,000,000, was advanced by a London financier, Sir Ernest Cassel, who devoted the profits of the deal to endowing Egyptian hospitals. The Egyptian Treasury repaid him by instalments, to avoid the problem of extracting funds from the *Caisse*. Four million acres were at once brought under permanent irrigation. In 1907 subsidiary works were added lower down the river and the crest of the Aswan Dam raised by twenty-six feet. The Nile was now tamed and with proper care Egypt need never again know deluge or drought.

In 1903 Cromer rendered an account of his twenty years of stewardship. The population of Egypt had almost doubled; the revenue had increased from £9,000,000 to £12,000,000; the external trade had trebled. Imports (one-third of them from Great Britain) had increased from £7,900,000 to £20,560,000; exports (nearly half to Great Britain) from £12,200,000 to £20,800,000. The national debt still stood at £101,000,000 mostly held abroad, but the £9,000,000 borrowed under Cromer's regime had brought more good to the Egyptian people than the £91,000,000 borrowed by Ismail in the bad old days. Furthermore the bonds which had paid 5 % on a market value of 87 now paid 3½% on a market value of 99. While all this was evidence of prosperity, the expense account was shocking. In eighteen complete financial years the aggregate expenses of the Egyptian state had been £193,000,000. Of this sum no less than £79,000,000 had been paid to the bond-holders as interest on loans which were largely unproductive, while £13,000,000 had been paid to the Sultan of Turkey as tribute. Subtracting military expenses, the Khedive's Civil List, and the deficit on the accounts of the Sudan, only £73,000,000, less than two-fifths of the national revenue, had been spent for the benefit of the people, including £11,000,000 on irrigation. With this meagre sum and in spite of the drain to the avaricious and obstructive bond-holders, Cromer had made Egypt orderly, prosperous and progressive.

The evident sign of progress was the rising tide of nationalism, the ever-increasing agitation against the foreigner. The slogan, 'Egypt for the Egyptians' was the rallying-cry of the students at the Moslem university of El Azhar, always the cradle of the movement. Egyptian nationalism has been a phase of the Moslem political revival, largely a pan-Arab movement, and has not owed much to the educated and intelligent minority of Christian Copts, though they may more properly be regarded as the heirs of Ancient Egypt. Cromer showed no sympathy with the nationalist movement which he thought premature and frivolous. It was directed from Paris, where anglophobia raged and where the nationalist leader, Mustapha Kamel, lived in exile; it attracted an increasing amount of support from the anti-imperialists in

England. In Cromer's last year of power (1906) opposition was much inflamed by the Denshawai Incident, which Bernard Shaw denounced in the preface to *John Bull's Other Island*. Four Egyptian peasants were hanged and others flogged, for killing a British officer in a riot which the indiscreet behaviour of the victim had done something to provoke. This seems to have been the worst offence of the exploiting tyrants.

The later years of Cromer's consulship were, however, marked by a triumph that transcended all criticism, the signing of the 'Entente Cordiale' Treaty, 8 April 1904, by M. Cambon and Lord Lansdowne. This comprehensive agreement, prepared by King Edward's state visit to Paris in 1903, and announced in the speech from the throne, on 2 February 1904, consisted of a convention on Newfoundland and West Africa, with four declarations, on Egypt and Morocco, on Siam, on Madagascar, and on the New Hebrides, solving many problems. His Britannic Majesty's Government declared that they had 'no intention of altering the political status of Egypt', while the Government of the French Republic undertook not to 'obstruct the action of Great Britain in that country.' The British also agreed to 'respect the rights which France enjoys in Egypt'. By a subsidiary agreement published in the form of a Khedivial Decree the *Caisse*, that crusted organ of obstruction, lost its power to overrule the spending of Egyptian money for Egyptian ends, and handed over its comfortable surplus of £6,000,000; but the capitulations and the mixed tribunals survived for thirty years longer. Lord Cromer resigned in April 1907, after delivering a last warning against nationalist agitators, and died in 1917.

As Egypt grew more prosperous the status of the British became more paradoxical. 'Here is a country', wrote Kipling, 'which is not a country but a longish strip of market-garden, nominally in charge of a government which is not a government but the disconnected satrapy of a half-dead empire, controlled pecksniffingly by a Power which is not a Power but an Agency, which Agency has been tied up by years, custom, and blackmail into all sorts of intimate relations with six or seven European Powers, all with rights and perquisites, none of whose subjects seem directly amenable to any Power which at first, second, or third hand is supposed to be responsible. That is the barest outline.'

'Among these conflicting interests and amusements sits and perspires the English official, whose job is irrigating or draining or reclaiming land on behalf of a trifle of ten million people, and he finds himself tripped up by skeins of intrigue and bafflement which may ramify through half a dozen harems and four consulates.'[1]

Thirty years had passed since Disraeli gave his solution to the Eastern Question and for thirty years the powers had been at peace in Europe: even the Balkan volcano was dormant. While administrative reform in Egypt progressed so rapidly under British rule, liberation seemed to be receding into the future. The Young Turk Revolution (1908) revived Egyptian agitation in the same year. Could the British cling to their superstition that democracy would not flourish in the soil of the 'Immemorial East' when a republican party had called a national assembly on the Bosphorus? In London the Liberal Imperialists made no move. The Egyptians were not yet thought fit to rule themselves and meanwhile Egypt had become the strategic centre of the British Empire. A single brigade of British infantry still affronted Egyptian pride by garrisoning Lower Egypt with its headquarters in Saladin's historic citadel at Cairo.

7. EGYPT, 1907–14

IN Cromer's time a consistent policy had been followed with a consistent aim in view, to set up an honest, efficient, and solvent administration which could take and keep control when the British withdrew. The process had taken longer than had been expected and, when he retired in 1907, Cromer thought it not yet complete. Liberating and pacifying the Sudan had been long and costly. While some optimists (though not Cromer) thought Egypt ripe for self-government, no student of affairs then supposed that the ruling class in Cairo was fitted to assume trusteeship for the Sudanese. Then there were the capitulations, a cause of perpetual friction, even though the Entente Cordiale had meant a slight change for the better. As the twentieth century progressed the likelihood increased that if England withdrew from Egypt, France or Italy would step in, fears which grew stronger when,

[1] *Egypt of the Magicians* (1913). Letters of Travel.

in 1911, France seized Morocco and Italy went to war for Tripoli. Cromer was a Whig of the old school whose belief in political liberty did not imply an unqualified adherence to absolute democracy achieved by universal suffrage in all circumstances. He could find no evidence in the class of wealthy Levantines, or in the rabble of Cairo, or in the ignorant *fellaheen*, of such civic virtues as would justify a grant of responsible government, and he set his face against political concessions. Yet since he regarded British rule as a transient phase, even though it might last long, he made no effort to popularise British institutions or to stimulate a sentiment of loyalty. For himself he never sought popularity and departed without receiving any spontaneous tribute of gratitude.

One of Cromer's last achievements in Egypt was the foundation of a Ministry of Education, begun, for lack of funds, in a very small way. As the first Minister he selected (1907) Saad Zaghlul, an official for whom he foretold a useful career. Like Arābi before him, Zaghlul was a man of the people, a *fellah*, and he established himself in the political world of Cairo by marrying the Prime Minister's daughter. Cromer's hope had been to form an indigenous system by inspiring a reform of the Koranic University of El Azhar, but he had failed to overcome Moslem conservatism. A European system of high-schools was then organised by Zaghlul's director of education, a Scotsman named Dunlop. In spite of Cromer's warning Macaulay's error was repeated in Egypt; national education was made to mean the creation of a needy class of black-coats whose sole ambition was to be clerks in government service. In the Sudan these errors were avoided by a practical system of education based upon the vernacular schools.

Cromer's successor, Sir J. E. Gorst (1861–1911), the son of that J. E. Gorst who had figured in the Maori Wars (see chapter X, 2, page 539), came as the nominee of the new Liberal government in London, with instructions to introduce political reforms.[1] Gorst's work in Egypt, like the contemporary Morley-Minto reforms (see chapter XVIII, 2, page 937) in India, was to increase local representation in the provincial councils. The effect of his guiding Egypt with a lighter rein was merely to strengthen the

[1] According to Lord Lloyd, *Egypt Since Cromer*. There is nothing about it, and almost nothing about Egypt, in Viscount Grey's memoirs.

Plate 25

SIR GARNET WOLSELEY (1833–1913)

'The modern major-general.' From a painting by A. Besnard, dated 1880.

See p. 739.

Plate 26

SIR EVELYN BARING, LORD CROMER (1841–1917)

The maker of modern Egypt. A studio portrait in 1906. *See p. 727.*

will of Abbas Hilmi, the Khedive, who took liberties with Gorst that he dared not take with Cromer. A new premier, Boutros Pasha, who could be held responsible for errors, was installed in the place of Zaghlul's father-in-law, the reliable old Fehmy Pasha. The Khedive was not displeased when the rising wave of nationalism broke against the British.

No one could suppose that the British were popular in Egypt. The maladies they had come to cure, a generation earlier, were now forgotten and, as Herbert Edwardes said of a similar situation in the Punjab: 'The patient is well now and he finds the doctor a bore.' In 1908 the Suez Canal concession came up for renewal. When it was renewed for forty years after a payment of £4,000,000 by the Company, the Nationalists summoned mobs and staged riots. Political crimes increased, culminating, in 1910, in the murder of Boutros Pasha, who was unpopular with the mob because he was a Christian Copt and because he had been one of the signatories to the agreement for the Sudan Condominium in 1899.

When Gorst suddenly died in 1911 no less a man than Lord Kitchener at the height of his reputation was sent to restore a situation that was a little out of hand. Not only was Kitchener powerful in person and character and prestige and experience, he was also a match for the Khedive and the pashas in the arts of oriental diplomacy. His term of office in Egypt was largely occupied with external affairs, since the Turco-Italian War (1911–12) was fought in the Western Desert just beyond the frontier. The Balkan Wars (1912–13) also stirred opinion in Egypt, a Moslem country where the Sultan of Turkey was still the nominal suzerain. During negotiations Kitchener laid bare a singularly corrupt and treacherous bargain between the Khedive and an Italian syndicate for control of the railway westward from Alexandria. With that black mark against him Abbas Hilmi was made to sing pretty small.

Though he did not much approve of imposing Western institutions on orientals, Kitchener continued the work of Gorst by reforming the legislature in 1912. The franchise was arranged so as to strengthen the agricultural interest, the real concern of the masses, and the legislative powers of the Assembly were increased. Egypt thus proceeded to a Parliamentary system of government. The chief gainer by this reform was Zaghlul, who resigned his ministerial appointment (1912) in order to devote himself to party politics, finding more scope for his talents in opposition than in office.

The political reform was intended by Kitchener as a step in agrarian reform, his principal interest in Egypt. In addition to legislation designed to free the peasants from oppression by moneylenders, he initiated the series of irrigation works in the Sudan in the tract called the Gezira between the Blue and White Niles. In 1912 the Sudan became self-supporting after drawing a subsidy from Egypt for thirteen years. A loan of £3,000,000, free of interest, was then advanced by the British government for irrigation works, which caused some alarm among Egyptian Nationalists. Were the British going to develop the Sudan by depriving Egypt of Nile water? Would they divert Sudanese trade from the Delta to Port Sudan? Matters were not helped by the lowest Nile flood yet recorded, in 1913. Kitchener, who was an engineer by training, personally supervised the works on the Blue Nile until they were brought to a stand by the outbreak of the first World War. In 1919, the amount of the loan was raised to £6,000,000 and the work was resumed; in 1924 the cotton scheme was in full operation, with a railway link to Kassala.

In August 1914 Kitchener was in London and the Khedive was visiting his friends in Constantinople. Neither returned to Egypt. When it became clear that Turkey would join with Germany there was a long correspondence between Sir Edward Grey and Sir Miles Cheetham, Kitchener's deputy, on the future of Egypt. A plan for British annexation was rejected since this would entail direct rule by British officials. The decision was taken to abolish the nominal Turkish suzerainty and to maintain the existing administration under British protection.[1]   On 2 November 1914 martial law was proclaimed. On 18 December Abbas Hilmi was declared to be deposed, and his elderly and respectable relative Hussein was proclaimed Sultan of Egypt. While assuming the rights forfeited by the Sultan of Turkey the British government undertook 'the sole burden of the war' in Egypt. These arrangements were accepted tranquilly by the Egyptians.

---

[1] Similar action was taken in Cyprus at the same time.

8. THE SUDAN, 1898–1925

WHEN Kitchener arrived at Khartoum in September 1898 he learned that another military force had established itself a few weeks earlier, 10 July 1898, on the upper reaches of the White Nile. This was Major Marchand's French expedition which was known to have set off from the Congo two years earlier. Without delay (10 September) Kitchener went up the river in a gunboat, leaving Sir R. Wingate to finish the campaign, and on 19 September found the French flag flying over a *zariba* at Fashoda (now known as Kodok). The two soldiers exchanged courtesies with martial punctilio, each endeavouring to treat the other as a guest in territory over which he himself had lawful authority. Undeterred by the knowledge that Kitchener had a victorious army on call, Marchand was at one stage inclined to show fight, though he commanded but nine Frenchmen and 150 *sénégalais*. One shot fired would have led to a European war, for England was diplomatically isolated and universally unpopular, while the French press screamed defiance. But Marchand and Kitchener kept their heads, as did the statesmen in London and Paris. Both Chamberlain, the mainspring of Salisbury's cabinet, and Delcassé the French Premier, were set on maintaining the agreement on Central Africa signed a few months previously, and both saw a chance of coming to terms. In November Delcassé, ordered Marchand to withdraw (see chapter xv, 5, page 830) and in March 1899 an agreement was signed, allotting the Nile basin as the British sphere of influence and the Congo basin as the French.

This enabled the geographers to recolour large regions on the African map, though years passed before the frontiers were delimited on the ground. Much of the watershed was unexplored and all was in a state of savagery. The Wadai province was not effectively occupied by the French until 1909, nor the Darfur province by the British until 1916. The frontier between the Sudan and the Belgian Congo was surveyed in 1906–9;[1] that between the Sudan and the Uganda Protectorate in 1913. Control

---

[1] A name that crops up in diplomatic writing of this period is the Sudanese district known as the Lado enclave. It was occupied by the Belgians and leased to the Congo administration until 1909.

of the headwaters of the Blue Nile was placed under the joint control of Great Britain, the Sudan and Abyssinia by a treaty in 1902.

The condominium, or dual sovereignty over the Sudan was proclaimed in March 1899. Supreme legislative power was vested in the Governor-General who, though nominally appointed by the Khedive, was selected by the British government and could not be removed without its permission. The higher posts in the administration were filled chiefly with British army officers, the lower posts chiefly with Egyptians, since there was no educated class in the Sudan. A customs union was arranged between the Sudan and Egypt.

All British progress in north-eastern Africa had been regulated, so far as it was regulated at all, by the Foreign Office. Cromer, like Kirk and Livingstone, was a consular officer and had no link with the Colonial Office. In some respects the Sudan has been the model tropical dependency, perhaps because the Foreign Office was able to appoint picked men from the universities and the services to its administration.[1] The Foreign Office has also been free of that tenderness towards missionary opinion which has been so marked in the Colonial Office. The Sudan was organised as a Moslem state in which the activity of Christian missions was severely restricted. Islamic law was enforced by the new government and the rudiments of an educational system were begun with vernacular schools. One of the first acts of the administration was the founding of Gordon College at Khartoum, at first (1902) as an elementary school and later (1913) as a teachers training-college. Here the English language was used for instruction.

Under the first Governor-General, Sir R. Wingate (b. 1861), who held office for seventeen years, peace brought an unforeseen prosperity marked, as always in a primitive country, by a rapid increase in the population. It was soon evident that Cromer had been right and Gordon wrong in their estimates of the value of the Sudan; with irrigation and communications it might be made fertile and rich. Of necessity this would take time, in a million square miles of wilderness inhabited partly by slave-raiding Bedouin and partly by dispersed tribes of naked pagans. Not till 1913 did the Sudan administration pay its way without a grant-in-aid from Egypt.

[1] The Civil Service was thrown open to qualified Sudanese natives in 1944.

When order was imposed the next problem was to improve communications. The outlet to the Red Sea, indicated by Dufferin twenty years earlier, was opened in 1905 by a railway from Atbara to Port Sudan, a new harbour north of Suakin. Access to the headwaters of the White Nile was eased by Garstin's great achievement in cutting a permanent channel through the 'Sudd', the masses of waterweed that choked the river for hundreds of miles. By 1904 a navigable channel was cleared to the Uganda frontier. The climax[1] of the British effort was the control of the Blue Nile by the Sennar Dam (completed 1925), which irrigated the rich Gezira cotton-lands at a capital cost of £11,000,000. Sudan cotton was to be produced co-operatively on the principle that the native cultivators should own the land, the Sudan Plantations Syndicate should manage and market the crop, and the government should supply the water. The receipts were to be divided in the proportion: 40% to the cultivators, 25% to the syndicate, and 35% to the government.

Wingate was succeeded in 1917 by Sir Lee Stack who introduced the principle of indirect rule into the Sudan, especially in the remoter districts where extant tribal authority could be upheld and given new responsibility. In the more civilised districts he progressively brought Sudanese natives into the higher grades of the administration. The murder of Sir Lee Stack by Egyptian Nationalists in 1924 was a severe setback to every good cause in Egypt and the Sudan.

[1] Schemes for the development of power and irrigation on a far greater scale were inaugurated in 1948 at Jinja, near the source of the Nile, with the approval of the Egyptian government. Several territories are concerned, and the plan is known as the Uganda Hydro-electric Scheme.

XIV

SOUTH-EAST ASIA AND THE ISLANDS

Argument: The forward policy in Burma had some justification, but not the subjection of Burma to direct rule by British-Indian officials.

In Malaya the forward policy was undertaken with the goodwill of the legitimate rulers, whose status was guaranteed. Chinese immigrants to Malaya submitted to the British administration complacently. British rule brought wealth and content to both the federated and the unfederated states, until the Japanese invasion. The first staple product, tin, was worked by the Chinese; the second, rubber, introduced by the British, provided the Malayan peasants also with a cash-crop for export.

Singapore grew and prospered on British and Chinese commerce, not as an outlet for Malayan produce.

Missionary kingdoms in the South Sea Islands were commercialised and dominated by British, French, American, and German traders. The appearance of a new slave trade moved the British government to a forward policy, strongly urged by the governments of Australia and New Zealand. The Pacific was accordingly divided among the powers into spheres of influence, in which coaling-stations, cable-routes, and, more lately, air-bases were of strategic importance.

1. THE BRITISH IN ASIA

WESTERN imperialism made short work of the independent kingdoms of Asia during the late nineteenth century. Administrative efficiency and mechanised industry backed by a growing supply of capital were assumed to be the evidences of moral and political superiority. Against these integrated forces static systems, however ancient and respectable, could not prevail and were not, by Western standards, justified in the attempt to do so. 'Better fifty years of Europe than a cycle of Cathay.'

It will be convenient to recapitulate the stages of European infiltration. The capture of Mauritius in 1810, which put an end to French imperialism in Asia for about forty years, left the British and Dutch to dispute the field. From about 1778 the Royal Navy had designs upon Ceylon which was occupied in 1792 and annexed by Great Britain in 1814, while Light's acquisition of Penang in 1785 had renewed the interest of the East India Company in the Malayan region where the Dutch had been supreme for 150 years. Though the enlightened policy of Castlereagh led to the recession of Java, commercial rivalry between British and Dutch on the spot was intense. It inspired Raffles to base British sea-power and trade in the East upon Singapore which the Dutch recognised in 1824 as a British possession. 'On the East Indiaman's route to China, all to the left hand was then in the British, all to the right hand in the Dutch sphere.' Two years later the king of Ava was punished for his intransigence by the annexation of Tenasserim and Arakan, that is to say the future teak-trade of Moulmein, the future rice-trade of Akyab. A further consequence was the commercial treaty of 1826 between Great Britain and Siam, strengthened, thirty years later by a further treaty giving extra-territorial rights to British subjects.

The forward policy of the years 1839 to 1842, like that of 1858 to 1860, may be derived from Palmerstonian diplomacy. Though the Afghan War ended in failure, its sequel was the advance of the British-Indian frontier from the Sutlej to the Indus (1843–6), and an extended control over the Arabian Sea, secured by the occupation of Aden in 1839. The same years were marked by aggressive diplomacy in China and what is called the Opium War. By the Treaty of Nanking, 1842, Palmerston gained his objectives of commercial agreements, treaty-ports, and a British colony at Hong Kong. Unlike the acquisitions of other European powers in China, Hong Kong was thrown open to the world's trade and even surpassed Singapore in thriving prosperity. These two free ports were the buttresses of British sea-power in Asia where the nation of shopkeepers could meet all competition on equal terms. British commercial supremacy was greatly aided by the coming of the steamship. Hence the demand for a coaling-station at Labuan (1846) between Hong Kong and Singapore, which led to the penetration of Borneo, in the Dutch sphere, already breached by Rajah Brooke's solitary exploit.

The opening of trade with China attracted the Americans who had occasionally traded to Canton since the eighteenth century. No sooner was California added to the Union than trade-routes were opened across the Pacific through Midway Island and Hawaii. Commodore Perry broke down the isolation of Japan in 1853 in order to establish a coaling-station on the route from California to China. The French, too, resumed imperial activity in the 'fifties, joining the British in demands for diplomatic relations with the court of Pekin, and competing against them for control of vital points. In 1859 they began the conquest of Cochin China by seizing Saigon, and in 1862 they established the French Concession at Shanghai.

Meanwhile a second forward move of British influence had been begun by Dalhousie's Burma War which added Lower Burma, with the port of Rangoon, to British India in 1852. The Persian War of 1856-7 meant a further advance into western Asia and was followed by the seizure of Perim in the Strait of Bab-el-Mandeb. The Mutiny itself, which seemed for a moment to mark the downfall of British power in the East, ended in triumph for the West. No sooner was the crisis past than troops were despatched to back Lord Elgin's aggressive diplomacy in China. Again it was the Palmerstonian policy that compelled the Chinese to give extra-territorial rights to all Europeans.

The next steps forward marked a change in the history of imperialism. Hong Kong, Singapore and their smaller satellites had been set up as trading posts or as ports of call for shipping. Except for conquests designed to round off the frontiers of the Indian Empire, annexations of territory were not approved in the age of Palmerston. But the merchants in the new seaports were beginning to press for annexations since anarchy in neighbouring territory was bad for trade. Jealousies broke out between the Western powers over spheres of commercial influence which, sooner or later, were converted into protectorates and finally into colonies. The Dutch began to extend their authority from the seacoast until they subdued all Java and Sumatra, not without heavy fighting (1871-1906). The French successively acquired Cochin China, Cambodia, Annam (1863-87). The British took one of the tin-producing Malay states under their protection in 1874 and, by 1914, had absorbed all the others. Thus the buffer states which had so long insulated the Chinese Empire from the world were overthrown, one by one, until only Tibet and Siam survived. A casualty in this clash of civilisations was the ancient and picturesque kingdom of Ava, which was somewhat wantonly destroyed in 1885.

The rate of industrial progress in Asia was greatly accelerated by the opening of the Suez Canal in 1869. New fields for

European manufactures, capital investment, and professional skill were thrown open along the trade-routes; new sources of raw materials—rice, tin, rubber, tea—were tapped; and the prosperity of lands newly devoted to production for export started waves of migration as multitudinous as those which peopled America. The coasts of Burma were invaded by Tamils and Bengalis, the Malay Peninsula by Chinese tin-miners, Hong Kong and Singapore by tradesmen and merchants from the troubled mainland of China. Indian coolies went as far overseas as Fiji, Chinamen as far as California.

(1) UPPER BURMA

Pegu, or Lower Burma, was organised as a province of British India in 1862. Lightly populated, with not more than 2,000,000 inhabitants of mixed race and culture, it was altogether Indian-ised, with a sepoy garrison, Sikh police, Bengali clerks and coolie labourers from Madras. Otherwise there was little social change until the Suez Canal brought a great expansion of trade. Intern-ally all communications went by river-boat and, after 1868, by the British-owned Irrawaddy Flotilla Company which plied upstream to the kingdom of Ava. The submarine cable reached Rangoon in 1870; the B.I. steamship service ran regularly from 1871; the first railway, from Rangoon to Prome, was opened in 1877. A prospect of trade through Burma with the untapped inland market of south-western China began to attract attention. One British traveller, (Sir) E. B. Sladen (1827–90), penetrated from Bhamo to Yunnan in 1868 and, though another agent of com-mercial expansion failed to develop the route,[1] it was generally felt that the hinterland should be opened by British rather than French initiative. Trade with China would 'follow the flag'. In 1867 a treaty of free trade had been negotiated between the King of Ava and the Indian government with an understanding that preferences should be granted to no other power. Yet, as early as 1874, a French agent obtained a treaty in a contrary sense giving preferences to French trade, which led to a deepening cleavage between the British and the court of Ava.

---

[1] The railway from Rangoon reached Mandalay in 1889, Lashio in 1902. The celebrated Burma Road from Lashio to Chung-King was not constructed until 1939.

Relations had been excellent on the whole since King Mindon ascended the throne in 1853. He received a British Resident and observed his treaty obligations, though he never formally acknowledged British sovereignty over the lost southern provinces. While he built and fortified a new capital at Mandalay he did not omit to honour older Buddhist shrines, and embellished the Shwe Dagon pagoda in British territory. Ava was tranquil and prosperous in King Mindon's day, drawing advantage from the new commerce of Rangoon. At the end of his reign, as French influence grew, there was a change for the worse, ending in a tiresome quarrel over ceremonial. The British Resident, refusing to abase himself before the throne according to the custom of the country, withdrew from court.

When Mindon died, in 1879, without naming his successor, the customary struggle for power broke out among the princes. A designing Queen seized the throne for her son-in-law, Theebaw, who secured his position by massacring about eighty rival princes and princesses. When Europeans expressed their disapproval, Burmese statesmen vindicated the procedure as traditional, and the only alternative to civil war. Since there was no British Resident, Western protests against the murder of the princes and the reign of terror that followed it were put forward by Anglican missionaries (no longer in favour since King Mindon's death). The merchants also appealed for British intervention, with complaints that law and order were breaking down, that the endemic form of political brigandage known in Burma as *dacoity* was spreading. At first the Indian government (having just burned its fingers by intervention at Kabul) was unwilling to intervene at Mandalay. A more active policy was dictated by events in Europe.

Anglo-French rivalry became acute in the years 1883 to 1885 when Jules Ferry was directing French colonial policy. While building up a French Empire in Indo-China he positively challenged British predominance in Burma which was to be brought into the French sphere and to become, with Theebaw's goodwill, a French Protectorate. After negotiations in Paris which served merely to reveal the French intention, Lord Salisbury (Prime Minister from June 1885 to February 1886) authorised strong action and Dufferin the Viceroy soon found a *casus belli*. By a strange coincidence the French government fell at the same moment with the consequence that Jules Ferry's policy was abandoned.

Theebaw, when short of money, had borrowed £100,000 from the Bombay-Burma Trading Corporation, a British firm with wide timber concessions in Ava. He demanded more and, when they refused it, threatened to cancel their concession in

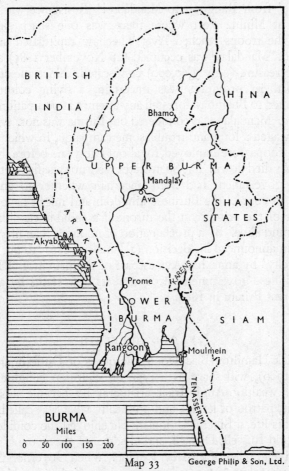

BRITISH

INDIA

CHINA

Bhamo

UPPER BURMA

Mandalay

Ava

SHAN

STATES

A R A K A N

Akyab

KARENS

Prome

LOWER

BURMA

SIAM

Rangoon

Moulmein

TENASSERIM

BURMA

Miles

0   50   100   150   200

Map 33   George Philip & Son, Ltd.

favour of a French firm. In order to crush the British firm, a case was trumped up in the courts at Mandalay with the effect of fining the Bombay-Burma Corporation the amount they had refused to lend. Dufferin now interposed with demands that the case should be put to arbitration, and that Theebaw should receive a British Resident at his court, whereupon Theebaw declared war, 9 November 1885. Lord Dufferin promptly sent a punitive expedition which concluded its first task by a fortnight's campaign. 9000 troops from India with 3000 followers were sent up the Irrawaddy in river steamers; 'can't you 'ear their paddles chunkin' from Rangoon to Mandalay!' Resistance was trifling except at Minhla Fort where there was one sharp skirmish. When the troops reached Ava, Theebaw capitulated and was deposed. Mandalay was occupied (28 November 1885) and the King's treasure (only £60,000) confiscated. Since the status of the northern provinces was uncertain, a flying column was despatched to Bhamo to forestall any attempt at occupation by the Chinese. Mandalay was conquered but Burma was not. Irregular forces waged a long and troublesome campaign, in which 30,000 British troops were employed, for about two years before the wave of *dacoity* died down. The Shan States were not pacified until 1890.

The government had been uncertain whether to annex or merely to control the Burmese kingdom and might have placed another of the princes on the throne if a suitable candidate had been found alive. By a proclamation of no more than fifty words Dufferin announced his decision (1 January 1886) 'to put an end to anarchy' by annexing Ava as part of the province of Burma. The Chinese government recognised its new status by a treaty with Great Britain in 1886.

(2) LORD DUFFERIN

Frederick Hamilton-Blackwood, Marquess of Dufferin and Ava (1826–1900), will serve as a type of Victorian enlightenment. Born a wealthy Anglo-Irish aristocrat he became a scholar, traveller, patron of letters, and politically what was called, at the end of his life, a Liberal-Unionist. He enjoyed the confidence of Lord John Russell, Disraeli, and Gladstone. As a young man he was active in relief of the Irish Famine. When Governor-General of Canada (1872–8) he had opportunities of showing his charm of manner and discreet judgment in the transference of the Hudson Bay Territories to the Dominion, a problem of great delicacy. Later he held several embassies in succession and was at Constantinople when Gladstone authorised the occupation of

Egypt. As High Commissioner (1882–3) Dufferin recommended the rejuvenation of Egypt under British tutelage, the plan which in fact was carried out. From 1884 to 1888 he was Viceroy of India. As in Egypt, so in India he worked on the principle that progress should take the form of a gradual development of British ideals and institutions and, accordingly, gave his patronage to the Indian National Congress. His wife, celebrated in verse by Browning, Tennyson, and Kipling, was a pioneer of the Women's Movement in India especially in respect of hygiene and education.

The two triumphs of Dufferin's viceroyalty were the discretion with which he handled his guest Abdurrahman during the Penjdeh crisis and the firmness which he showed towards King Theebaw six months later.

> I took a country twice the size of France,
> And shuttered up one doorway in the North.
> I'll stand by those. You'll find that both will pay.[1]

It is an ironical comment on the late Victorian scene that this *grand seigneur* fell into money troubles at the end of his life. He had unwisely lent his name to an investment company which was involved in the collapse of a swindling speculator named Whittaker Wright. Though Dufferin was cleared of any taint of dishonest complicity he showed that all his experience and skill could not guide him through the dark labyrinth of high finance.

(3) BRITISH BURMA

If the kingdom of Ava had been conquered twenty years earlier the British would have been content with a commercial treaty and extra-territorial rights, if twenty years later a more resolute attempt would have been made to govern by indirect rule. What Burma got was a rigid administration on Indian lines, impartial justice, and the economics of *laissez-faire*. The new Civil Service was British in its higher ranks, and in its lower ranks Indian because there was, by Indian standards, no educated class in Burma; that is to say there were no *babus* with a smattering of Western book-learning. But Burma was a Buddhist country with an indigenous written literature and a monarchy limited by the prestige of the Buddhist clergy. No other Eastern nation was

---

[1] R. Kipling, *One Viceroy to Another.*

better suited for an experiment in the protection and development of a native culture. The opportunity was lost, to the chagrin of some of the British-Indian officials sent to govern the country.

Through fifty years of British-Indian rule the political history of Burma was uneventful and the country, by the simpler tests of prosperity, flourished. Relations between British and Burmese were, in the middle years at least, friendlier than in caste-ridden Hindustan. The population more than doubled (15,000,000 in 1931); the revenue was buoyant; the external trade leaped up from an estimated value of 30,000,000 rupees in 1868 to more than 500,000,000 rupees in 1937. Rangoon grew into a modern city of 300,000 people, but a British-Indian not a Burmese city. A new source of wealth had appeared, in mineral oil which constituted one-third of the exports in value. An even larger proportion, two-fifths of the export value, was derived from rice grown by peasant-cultivators and mostly absorbed by the Indian market. Though this was the main occupation of the true Burmese people it does not appear that they were enriched by it. A well-informed critic [1] has estimated that the growing demand for rice encouraged the peasants to take too much land into cultivation with the effect of forcing them into debt, to village moneylenders who usually were Indian immigrants. The moneylenders in turn were financed by British bankers, millers, and, in the last resort, shippers, all of whom were living on the profits from Burmese rice. Even Curzon's system of co-operative credits was thought to increase agricultural indebtedness on the whole, by opening another channel for improvident borrowing. By 1936 it was estimated that more than half the rice-lands were effectively owned by brokers, bankers, and mortgagees. Municipal reforms and social services had done little for the countryside and it was a poor consolation to the Burmese peasantry that cheap Manchester goods had crushed their native textile crafts. Education, though more widely spread than in other parts of south-east Asia, meant the training of clerks and lawyers in an imported idiom, while Buddhist literature was forgotten and the influence of the Buddhist clergy ignored or alienated by the British administrators. We had failed 'to take the people along with us', as Elphinstone said of Bombay. Between 1900 and 1930, a

[1] J. S. Furnivall, *Colonial Policy and Practice*.

sinister symptom of social malaise was the increase of violent crime. The number of murders was doubled and of *dacoities* was trebled, in proportion to the population.

2. MALAYA

HALF-FORGOTTEN Hindu empires had left their mark upon the East Indies where some features of the caste-system prevailed, though these empires had long been broken up by Moslem conquerors. The Islamic cult was lax; among Malayan Moslems there was no equality but a Brahminical respect for royal birth. From Penang to Sarawak each point of vantage was the stronghold of a Moslem sultan, where every remote descendant of a ruling prince was a *rajah*, as punctilious about his honour as a Highland gentleman. The complaisant, improvident Malays acquiesced in the tyranny of their lords who lived, like Highland chiefs in the eighteenth century, by levying blackmail. Civilisation had run right down. Cities were abandoned, and what trade and industry existed was left to Chinese immigrants.

The Sultan of Kedah, who ceded Penang to Francis Light, was one of these easy-going tyrants. Being in some sort a vassal of the King of Siam he was aggrieved that the East India Company refused to help him to his independence. The Siamese overran Kedah and, after long confused negotiations, in which the Company was determined to shirk responsibility, Captain Burney made a treaty with Siam in 1826. Unfortunately it was drafted in a jargon not far removed from pidgin-English and capable of misinterpretation. The general effect was to recognise Kedah as a Siamese fief while Pérak and the other states to southward of it were admitted to be substantially independent.

Pérak and Sélangor had already (1818) made trade treaties with the Company, though they could provide no security for commerce. The Company was now obliged reluctantly to appear as their protector.

Two hundred miles farther south was the sultanate of Johore which included Singapore Island. Raffles's original treaty had been signed by one claimant to the sovereign authority at a time of disputed succession. This did not matter much when Singapore was a deserted province in an impoverished unpopulated kingdom, but when Singapore grew rich both claimants felt themselves entitled to demand a share of its wealth, and to question the validity of the signature on the deed of cession. The dispute dragged on until 1854.

These sultanates, and several others like them, were distracted and chaotic, poor in the midst of potential wealth, quarrelsome and proud, uncertain of their status, dissatisfied, unable to regulate themselves, riddled with the pernicious system of debt-slavery, and intolerably bad neighbours. The merchants of Singapore demanded that they should be brought into conformity with the civilised world.

When the Indian Mutiny signalled the approaching end of the Company's rule, the Singapore merchants petitioned for release from subjection to the new Indian government. Though the Viceroy, Canning, agreed that no Indian administration could do justice to Malaya, some years passed before a change was made, and it was not until 1867 that control of the Straits Settlements (Penang, Malacca, and Singapore) was transferred from the India Office to the Colonial Office. Meanwhile, since no public works were undertaken, a private company at Singapore had begun to construct modern harbour-works at what is now called Keppel Harbour.

The first reports to the Colonial Office pointed out the necessity of coming to terms with the Malay States, and again rivalry with the Dutch was a consideration. Their adoption of a forward policy in Sumatra, in 1871 (see chapter XI, 3, page 659), was a stimulant to British expansion. Civil wars were raging in several of the sultanates; a British ship was seized by pirates off Sélangor and a warship standing in to give assistance was bombarded from the coast. Faction fights between rival gangs of Chinese tin-miners in Pérak had flooded Penang with refugees and casualties. It was plain that something must be done. The Colonial Office, even under Lord Kimberley was disposed to an active policy, so that Sir Andrew Clarke (1824–1902), an official of wide experience who was sent out as Governor in 1873, was given a new commission empowering him to report 'whether it would be advisable to appoint a British officer to reside in any of the states'.

This was enough for Clarke who went up to Pérak and arranged, with the Sultan's goodwill, to place a Resident at his

Plate 27 A

LORD KITCHENER
(1850–1916)

Painted in 1899 as the 'Sudan machine' by C. M. Horsfall. *See p. 863.*

Plate 27 B

LORD LUGARD
(1858–1945)

A miniature painted by C. E. Lugard in 1893, when the Little Englanders described him as a 'hare-brained militaire'. *See p. 828.*

Plate 28

SIR GEORGE TAUBMAN GOLDIE (1850–1916)

Founder of Nigeria and of the United Africa Company. Painted by
Sir H. von Herkomer in 1899. *See p. 825.*

court. The treaty, signed at Pangkor in 1874, became the model on which the other states of the Malay Peninsula have successively been brought under British protection. Pérak came first because it was the richest and the most disturbed. The district of Larut had been invaded for about twenty years by Chinese tin-miners who shipped their ores through Penang, and Larut was in an uproar until the British Resident took charge. The Sultan of Sélangor was brought into a similar agreement in the same year, as was the principal chief of Negri Sembîlan ('the nine states').[1]

Clarke's 'residents' were advisers and no more. They had no troops and no financial control and were expressly forbidden to interfere with Malayan law and custom. Nevertheless they made some progress in restoring order, and by interfering with the rights of assault and robbery claimed by every gentleman, they made enemies. The next Governor, Sir William Jervois, decided to take a further step. Without obtaining previous permission from Downing Street, he changed the title of his officers from 'resident' to 'commissioner' and instructed them to take over the administration. This was hotly resented in Pérak where there was an inclination to repudiate the Treaty of Pangkor. The Resident, Mr J. W. Birch, was attacked and killed by Malayan swashbucklers (1875) when making a tour to proclaim the new system. Not more than a handful of white men had been seen in the inland districts and it was supposed by the Malays that to kill them would put an end to the nuisance.

Though Lord Carnarvon at the Colonial Office censured Jervois severely and removed him from his post, he also sent a punitive column with three British regiments to show the flag in Malaya. While the country seethed with excitement there was little fighting. The murderers took to the jungle, were hunted down and hanged, and Clarke's system was restored. No violent change took place, no startling new policy was initiated. Owing to the patient influence of the British officers law and order slowly spread, and owing to the industry of the Chinese tin-miners the country slowly grew rich. The Malays gradually learned to accept these blessings to which they did not contribute much. By influence rather than authority modern

[1] The remaining states of this loose alliance, a federation within a federation, accepted British Residents between 1874 and 1895. The fourth of the Federated Malay States, Pahang, applied for British protection in 1888.

methods of administration crept in. A great advance was the collection of revenue by an export duty on tin which enabled the sultans to free their subjects from a great variety of vexatious tributes and charges. Debt-slavery was abolished in 1884. The states were self-supporting by 1879 and the trade returns trebled in the 1880's. Revenue meant funds for public works and roads brought more prosperity. The first Malayan railway, from Larut to the coast, was opened in 1884. About the same time the Governor of the Straits Settlements, Sir Hugh Low, began to encourage plantations of *parà* rubber from Brazil.

A modern system of administration required trained public servants, who were not to be found among the Malayans. More British 'advisers' were required in the higher ranks; the police were recruited in India; Eurasians and Chinese filled the lower ranks of government service. This Civil Service, while politically employed by four Moslem sultans, was engaged in a single economic task, enriching the states by enabling tin to be shipped away through the British seaport of Penang. As elsewhere, the railways brought about the federation. The metre-gauge state railways of Pérak, Sélangor and Negri Sembílan formed a single system designed to extend northwards to the Siamese frontier and southwards to Singapore. A plan for federation was put forward in 1893 by Sir Frank Swettenham (1850–1946), one of the original 'residents' who had barely escaped when Birch was murdered in 1875. He proposed to unify the administrative system and to share the revenues between the richer and poorer states while leaving each sultan in nominal control of his own country. Islam was to be the established religion, and the Governor-General of the Straits Settlements would be High Commissioner for the Federated Malay States. The constitution was loosely drafted, needing no minute precision since it merely gave formal recognition to a system of government that had grown up in practice. All the administrative departments had been created by British officials who already worked by a common rule. The Federation was proclaimed on 1 January 1896 with Swettenham as the first Resident-General. An administrative centre was built at Kuala Lumpur in Sélangor State and was provided with a new harbour called Port Swettenham.

Wealth in the Federation began to influence the more backward neighbouring states and first, Johore, the desolate country lying between the Federation and Singapore. Abu Bekr, the heir of Raffles's ally, proved a ruler of ability (1862–95). Having been brought up in Singapore, in Western style, he made a great effect when visiting London, where he won the favour of the Queen and the confidence of the Colonial Office. For many years he was used as an intermediary with the other sultans though they despised him as an upstart. He built a new capital, Johore Bahru, on the road from prosperous Pérak to prosperous Singapore. In 1895 he gave Johore a written constitution, shrewdly reserving his rights as a Moslem monarch, and refusing to allow Johore to lose its identity in the Federation. His successor accepted a British protectorate on his own terms in 1914. A railway was built in 1903 across the Island from Singapore to a point on the strait opposite Johore Bahru and plans soon followed for a Johore State Line to link up with the railways of the Federation (1909). When the causeway was built across the strait in 1924 it became possible to make a continuous journey from Singapore to Bangkok along a line built and financed by the Federation.

Johore itself began to share in the general prosperity, as did the more backward states on the east coast of the peninsula. Tin had financed the development of Malaya and rubber maintained the rate of progress. Until the twentieth century the sap of several species of the fig family was casually collected by jungle tribesmen in various parts of the tropics and sold in the crude form to European merchants. The trade in 'wild rubber' was much abused by ruffians who found it easy to cheat and oppress the gatherers. The exposure of the Congo atrocities in the 'nineties was repeated in 1910 when Sir Roger Casement revealed similar stories of oppression from Putumayo in Brazil. To control the trade it seemed best to grow rubber-trees in plantations. The search for a suitable species, begun at Kew Gardens about the year 1860, was prosecuted at the Botanical Gardens in Ceylon and Singapore. For many years 'wild rubber' remained more profitable than 'plantation rubber', chiefly because the trees were of slow growth. About the year 1910 rubber plantations began to pay, though the price of the crop fluctuated fearfully. At the beginning of the century 40,000 tons of wild rubber at 3s. or 4s. a pound satisfied the world's annual need. At the time of the first Rubber Boom (1910–11), the annual supply was 80,000

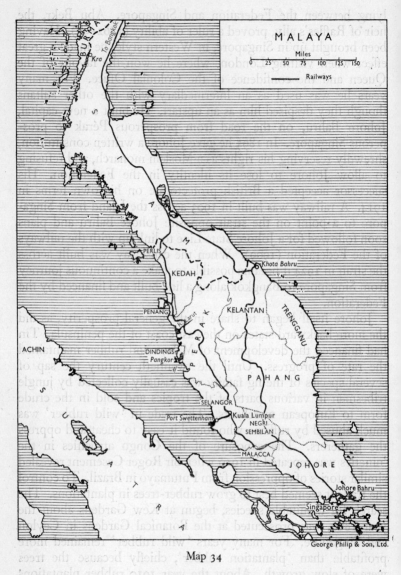

MALAYA

Miles

0   25   50   75   100   125   150

Railways

BURMA

To Bangkok

Kra

PERLIS

KEDAH

PENANG

Krian

DINDINGS
Pangkor

PERAK

ACHIN

SELANGOR

Port Swettenham

SUMATRA

Kuala Lumpur

NEGRI
SEMBILAN

MALACCA

Khota Bahru

KELANTAN

TRENGGANU

PAHANG

JOHORE

Johore Bahru

Singapore

George Philip & Son, Ltd.

Map 34

tons of wild and 10,000 of plantation rubber, sold at a price
which soared to 12s. a pound. In 1920 the supply was 350,000
tons, half of it from Malaya; the price reached a low figure of
1s. a pound in 1921.

The rubber plantations spread through Malaya, not only in the Federated States but through Singapore Island, Johore, the more backward states of the east coast, and the northern states which were still nominally vassals to Siam. And with prosperity went roads, railways, modern administration and English technical advisers.

The diplomatic rivalry between England and France for spheres of influence in South-east Asia had preserved Siam as an independent buffer-state between French Annam and British Burma. An attempt by the French to dominate Siam in 1893 provoked stiff diplomatic resistance from London until, after long negotiation, Lord Salisbury agreed to the convention of 1896, allotting western Siam as a British and eastern Siam as a French sphere of commercial influence. Such methods of treating oriental monarchies were common form in the 1890's. Although the French supposed themselves to have got the best of the bargain they were disappointed, since the trend of Siamese commerce developed south-westerly into the British sphere, linking up with the commerce of British Malaya. In 1905 80% of Siamese external trade passed through British hands. Yet the kingdom of Siam, more fortunate than Burma or Annam, while making use of British money and technical skill, retained its independence, which was guaranteed at the Entente Cordiale of 1904.

During the 'nineties there was much talk among concession-hunters in several countries of cutting a ship canal through the Kra Isthmus that joins Siam to Malaya. It had the effect of concentrating British diplomatic attention on this region, which lay in the British sphere of influence under the Anglo-French Agreement of 1896, though by Captain Burney's treaty of 1826 Siamese rights had been assured not only over the Isthmus but over the state of Kedah at the southern end of it.

In 1904 the Sultan of Kedah (successor of the ruler who had granted the leasehold of Penang to Francis Light) became insolvent through mismanagement. Appealing to his suzerain the King of Siam he was provided with a loan of $2,500,000[1] and a (British) financial adviser. British diplomatic influence was already at work to exclude any rival power from the Kra Isthmus,

[1] The Malayan dollar, like the rupee, fluctuated with the price of silver. Between 1890 and 1903 it sank in value from 3s. 4d. to 1s. 9d. In 1906 it was fixed at 2s. 4d.

and to connect the railway systems of Siam with those of the Federated Malay States. Since on both sides the technical advisers were British, the Anglo-Siamese treaty of 1909 presented no great diplomatic difficulty. The suzerainty over Kedah (and over its little neighbour Perlis) was transferred from Siam to Great Britain together with such shadowy rights as Siam asserted over Kelantan and Trengganu, the two remaining states on the eastward face of the Malay Peninsula. In return Great Britain made two substantial concessions; the debt contracted by Kedah was shouldered by the wealthy Federation, which also undertook to complete the trunk railway through that state, and the right of extra-territoriality in Siam was yielded up. These proceedings, though Gilbertian in character, gave satisfaction to all parties. The railway was opened for traffic between Bangkok and Kuala Lumpur in 1915.

Kelantan and Trengganu had not been exploited by Chinese tin-miners, nor were they growing rich in rubber, nor did they lie on the route of the trunk railway. Both states accepted British Residents in 1910 but steadily refused to be drawn into the Federation. The history of Kelantan is bound up with the concession granted by the Sultan in 1900 to a Mr R. W. Duff for the development of 3000 square miles of forest-land. Duff claimed that through his influence Kelantan was added to the British Empire but, when British suzerainty was established, the nature of his concession was so uncertain as to lead to years of litigation which several times reached the Privy Council and was not concluded until 1927. Finally the Federation financed a settlement by advancing funds to the state of Kelantan for buying out Duff's territorial claims.

During the Japanese invasion of 1942 the loss of Khota Bahru airport, in Kelantan, was fatal to the defence of Singapore.

Between 1909 and 1913 the Malayan region enjoyed immense prosperity and was spared the bane of controversial politics. It might not be fanciful to see in this loose system of states and islands a microcosm of the British Empire, a commercial organism clustered around its nucleus, the commercial city of Singapore. Its constitution was difficult to define, difficult even to discover, for it had no fundamental statute, indeed no unity except the homogeneous British governing-class, who behaved in much the same way in protected Sarawak, or federal Kuala Lumpur, or colonial Penang. The whole region lived and grew rich by overseas trade, by the export of staples to the world-market, by unrestricted migration, and by the provision of capital from the richer provinces for development in the poorer, an expanding economy where all had the benefits of social order and personal liberty, and the rulers thought it no part of their duty to redistribute wealth.

But Singapore itself was an entrepôt for the commerce of Asia, not an outlet for the produce of Malaya. A British and Chinese city, it stood fourth or fifth in importance among the world's seaports, as the terminal of eleven deep-sea cables, the port of call for fifty steamship lines. A cosmopolitan centre, it had been built upon Free Trade and throve by it. Though constituting with Malacca and Penang the Crown Colony of the Straits Settlements, it had little in common with them, for Malacca had lost its commercial value and Penang was the outlet for the tin of the Federated States. The revenues of Singapore were largely derived from the Opium Monopoly which, as in Bengal, was controlled and progressively diminished.

The four states of the Federation (Pérak, Sélangor, Negri Sembílan, and Pahang) were rich, tranquil, and well-governed, and were described, by a legal fiction which Englishmen found it easy to comprehend, as monarchies, though foreign critics[1] were surprised to find that the reigning sultans did not administer the executive power. The revenue of the Federation was derived from a tariff which disposed the states towards a protectionist policy, inevitably since their prosperity depended upon protected foreign markets—40% of the rubber and tin was bought by the United States, 40% of the food of the country was imported. Tin was almost entirely a product of Chinese labour and capital until, between the two World Wars, the introduction of heavy machinery for tin-dredging led to a demand for larger concentrations of capital and so to British investment. Rubber was chiefly grown on plantations managed by Englishmen though about a quarter of the crop came from Malayan small-holdings

[1] The most compendious account of British Malaya is to be found in Mr R. Emerson's *Malaysia*. This useful work of an American scholar is marred by the ritual anathemas that he feels obliged to utter whenever he mentions the accursed words, 'exploitation' and 'imperialism'. Though his concluding chapter is largely a series of admissions that the evidence belies his prejudices, he fails to muster enough courage to renounce them.

(165,000 in 1931). Throughout this area, so recently a roadless, lawless jungle, the tourist could motor on good roads for hundreds of miles between the smooth monotonous rubber-trees.

Outside the Federation a widespread group of dependencies was loosely attached to British Malaya by political or commercial bonds. Of the five 'unfederated states', three (Johore, Kedah, and Perlis) had been drawn into the artificial economy of the Federation while two (Kelantan and Trengganu) preserved more of their Malayan social life and economy. In the surrounding seas a number of British islands and coasts were linked with Singapore by trade-routes or submarine cables. In addition to Sarawak, mentioned in an earlier chapter, there were:

COCOS ISLAND

Cocos or Keeling Island, was far out in the Indian Ocean, selected by Darwin as the typical example of an atoll. Discovered by Captain Keeling of the Dutch service in 1609, it was never occupied until the nineteenth century. When a solitary named Alexander Hare settled there with some Malayan slaves in 1823, the Dutch disclaimed responsibility. Two years later James Clunies Ross, a Scotsman, arrived with his family, took charge of Hare's dependants and formed a patriarchal community of several hundred who live there still. This is the Coral Island, and Ross's life the exemplar of a hundred boys' adventure-stories. In 1857 the British government annexed Cocos Island. After placing it first under the administration of Ceylon, the Colonial Office attached it to the Straits Settlements in 1886. Ross and his family and servants lived by exporting copra in happy seclusion until in 1902 a cable-station was fixed upon the island, giving it a new importance. It was the scene of a naval battle in 1914 when the German cruiser *Emden* was sunk by H.M.A.S. *Sydney*. The great-grandson of the original Ross was killed in a Japanese air-raid upon the island in 1941.

CHRISTMAS ISLAND

Christmas Island in the Indian Ocean was annexed to the Straits Settlements in 1888. Its population of 1100 is employed in digging phosphates.

NORTH BORNEO

North Borneo had occasionally been visited by English traders since the sixteenth century. The Labuan Trading Company, formed by W. C. Cowie, was active there during the eighteen-seventies. A strip of coast was ceded by the Sultan to (Sir) Alfred Dent and other traders in 1878, whereupon they formed the British North Borneo Company which was chartered in 1881. Seven years later their position was strengthened by the declaration of a protectorate over British North Borneo. While external affairs were to be controlled by the Colonial Office, the domestic administration was entrusted to a Governor appointed by the Company subject to the approval of the Secretary of State. Administration of the Company's territories, which are rich in rubber and timber, was according to the usage of British India, and the Indian penal code was enforced.

LABUAN

Labuan, as a coaling-station and a harbour for refitting ships, was at first administered directly by the Admiralty. The coal-mines never paid (they were abandoned in 1911) so that the island always required a grant-in-aid. From 1848 to 1889 it was a Crown Colony, then was handed over to the British North Borneo Company, and finally in 1907 was annexed to the Straits Settlements. It had little value except as a port and market for local produce until, in 1894, a station on the Hong Kong to Singapore cable was placed there, with a branch to the mainland of Borneo.

BRUNEI

The Sultan of Brunei, who had parted with a large part of his dominions by these concessions, accepted a British Resident in 1888 for the remainder, which thus became a British Protectorate.

3. ASIA AT THE NADIR

TREATY-PORTS, the Europeanised Customs and Postal Services, and the alienation of the satellite kingdoms, had quite destroyed Chinese control over the imperial coasts, while the efficiency of these foreign administrations contrasted sharply with the weakness and corruption of the inland provinces where the Emperor's writ still ran. The common talk of the Western world was that the empire was on the point of collapse. A British admiral even wrote an authoritative work on 'The Break-up of China'. Should this collapse occur, it seemed probable that the British, by virtue of their predominant merchant shipping, their control of Hong Kong and of the major part of the trade of Shanghai, and of their growing interests in the Yangtze valley, might repeat in China their Indian achievement in grasping the sceptre of a declining empire, another triumph for commerce based on sea-power. This was the nadir of Asia. The Western powers believed themselves to be everywhere in the ascendant, having not yet noticed a portent in the farthest East, the rising sun of Japan. The Mikado's reforms were nothing but a joke when W. S. Gilbert made them the subject of a satirical comedy in 1885, and still failed to impress the young Rudyard Kipling when he visited Japan in 1889.

During the 'seventies Japan had advanced so far in Western methods as to begin aggressions upon Chinese dependencies by the 'gunboat policy'. The political infiltration of the satellite kingdom of Korea was brought to such a point that, by 1894, the Japanese were ready to stage a war against China on behalf of 'Korean independence'. China could no more resist the assaults of Japan than of the other powers, but Russia, France, and Germany greedily stepped in to prevent Japan from annexing more than its share of the Chinese fringe.

The Western penetration was led by a vanguard of Christian missionaries whose influence was more pervasive even than that of the missionaries of commerce. All were protected by extra-territorial rights. The Germans set the bad example of using outrages against missionaries as an excuse for demanding strategic concessions. Between 1895 and 1897 they compelled the Chinese court, as compensation for the murder of missionaries, to cede a site for a naval base, at Kiao-Chow, and an exclusive right to develop the province of Shantung, the heart of old China where Confucius was born. Development implied contracts for building railways which Chinese commerce sorely needed. The Russians at once drew level by establishing a naval base at Port Arthur. Since the advance of the Siberian Railway, in 1891, to the Chinese frontier, the Russians had been providing for themselves a sphere of influence in Manchuria, with the intention of bringing a branch of the railway through to the Korean coast. Their arrival at Port Arthur made a clash with Japan inevitable.

Since Germany and Russia had acquired naval bases in China, France and Great Britain must do likewise. Accordingly the British obtained the little port of Wei-hai-wei,[1] which, from 1898 until it was re-ceded to China, against the wishes of the inhabitants, in 1931, was an oasis of tranquillity surrounded by every kind of desolation. Occupied solely for reasons of prestige and not made a base for further aggression, it was of minor importance in the troubled history of twentieth-century China. Less justifiable was the acquisition of a larger area of the mainland adjacent to Hong Kong (1898) on a leasehold tenure for ninety-nine years.

While Germany, Russia and Japan scrambled for spheres of influence which they intended to annex sooner or later, the United States were in favour of maintaining the territories and supporting the power of the Chinese government, in order to encourage trade with the interior. This was the 'Open Door' policy which the Americans proposed to the other powers in 1899. The British, in spite of occasional lapses, had, on the whole, been of the same opinion; their sphere of influence, the Yangtze valley, was open to the commerce of all nations. These discussions were interrupted by a conservative revival in the north of China, instigated by the Dowager Empress. It was accompanied by outbreaks of fanaticism against the 'foreign devils' stimulated by a secret society which the foreigners nicknamed the 'Boxers'. Missionaries and native converts were murdered, and the foreign diplomats were besieged in the Legation Quarter at Pekin (1900). Again a combined expedition of the powers bombarded the Taku Forts, marched on Pekin, destroyed the Emperor's palace, and extorted

---

[1] From 1885 to 1887 the Royal Navy had temporarily occupied another base, Port Hamilton in Korea.

enormous indemnities. It is gratifying to record that the sums received on account of the 'Boxer Indemnities' were, at the instance of the United States, applied eventually to the education of the Chinese people.

But the Americans,[1] so long distinguished from the other powers by their peaceable procedure in Asia, had fallen from grace. Their successful war with Spain (1898) had dropped into their lap the Spanish colony in the Philippines. Alone of Eastern peoples, the Filipinos had long been converted to Christianity (by Spanish Jesuits) and were already imbued with Western ideas. They declared an independent republic, no doubt prematurely, obliging the Americans to restore order by a bloody little colonial campaign just like so many which the 'Imperialist' governments have been forced to fight. American opinion was sharply divided on the propriety of becoming a colonial power, though somewhat pontifically urged by Rudyard Kipling to 'Take up the White Man's Burden'.[2] The burden was assumed and, owing to their advanced social condition, the Filipinos were rapidly passed through the stages which, in British history have been called Crown Colony Government, Responsible Government, though without the fiscal independence of a British Dominion.

After a period of diplomatic isolation which was not so 'splendid' as had been hoped, the British were looking round for friends. Their perpetual anxiety about Russian intentions in the East, increased by the appearance of Germany as a naval power, even in the China Sea, directed Great Britain towards the alliance with Japan (1902). But Japanese intentions were not honourable. As preliminary steps towards the absorption of China the Japanese war lords expelled Russia from Port Arthur by the war of 1904, and Germany from Shantung by the war of 1914. Action against French, British, and American holdings in Asia would follow some years later.

A further incalculable factor was the second phase of the Chinese revival. After the conservative national movement which boiled over in the Boxer Rising, came the liberal movement derived from the influence of American missionary schools. The makers of the Chinese Republic were, or at least had been,

---

[1] American Protestant missionaries had been working at Canton since 1830.

[2] Published simultaneously in *The Times* and the *New York Tribune*, February 1899. Probably the first use of this celebrated phrase.

educated by Protestant Christians. Sun-Yat-Sen admitted the lesson he had learned from Western efficiency:

I compared Heung Shan with Hong Kong, and although they are only fifty miles apart, the difference of the Government oppressed me very much. Afterwards I saw the outside world, and I began to wonder how it was that foreigners, that Englishmen, could do such things as they had done, for example, with the barren rock of Hong Kong within seventy or eighty years, while in four thousand years China had no place like Hong Kong. After I had studied all this I went home to persuade the village elders to do the same thing on a small scale, at least to clear the streets and make a road to the next village; but they said, 'We have not got any money.' I replied, 'Labour can be had! We young men can start the work,' and so while I was at home I swept the street and cleaned the road. Many young men followed my example; but immediately we began to work outside the village there was trouble, and I had to give up getting Hong Kong on a small scale.[1]

4. THE SOUTH SEA ISLANDS

CAPTAIN COOK's third voyage led to the opening of the North Pacific fur trade, to the Nootka Sound Incident (see chapter v, 7, page 267) and so to the renunciation by Spain of her claim to monopolise the Pacific Ocean. When she lost her American Empire a generation later the old Spanish sea-routes across the mid-Pacific to the Philippines fell into disuse and Spain appeared no more as a Pacific power. The Portuguese had never made much showing there, nor had the Dutch, whose Indonesian Empire was not advanced eastward of Torres Strait. The partition of the Pacific into spheres of influence in the nineteenth century was made by Great Britain, France, the United States, and Germany, on the general principle that the British and American governments acted with great reluctance when already committed by pioneers of trade or Christianity, while the French and German governments took bold and ruthless decisions from considerations of European policy. In the British and American spheres the common form, in New Zealand, Hawaii, Fiji and elsewhere, was as follows: first came visits by whalers in search of supplies; then the establishment on the islands of castaways, deserters or 'beachcombers', who acted as interpreters and eventually set up trading posts; then the intervention of the

[1] Quoted in the *Spectator*, 24 March 1944.

missionary societies whose plan, as exemplified by Marsden in New Zealand, was to civilise the natives under their own chiefs; then the emergence of new political and industrial problems, with disorder and exploitation, until the chiefs themselves appealed to Great Britain or another power to step in and protect them.

The islands which, as Wallis, Bougainville and Cook described them, had been an earthly paradise, unhampered by economic pressure or by puritan morality, were depopulated by white men's diseases, ravaged by tribal wars which white men's deadly weapons made more bloody, and finally afflicted with a new form of the slave trade known as 'black-birding'. Yet the islands of the vast Pacific Ocean are so numerous that new primitive beauties were continually revealed to the explorer—new fields for Christian missions, new commodities for trade, new retreats for solitaries in search of the simple life. Nineteenth-century literature abounds in stories of South Sea Island adventure, the unnumbered progeny of *Robinson Crusoe*, though often differing from their great original in making light of the hardships and the solitude that he lamented. Generations of children have been reared on Marryatt's *Masterman Ready* (1841) and Ballantyne's *Coral Island* (1858), while even more popular, though far inferior, was J. D. Wyss's *Swiss Family Robinson* (translated 1814), in which island abundance was crudely exaggerated.

Yet there is some truth in the legend of these fortunate islands, as scores of real Robinson Crusoes have discovered, among them at least one man of genius, Hermann Melville, who lived in the Marquesas in 1841. Later when the islands were more civilised, Gauguin in Tahiti (1890–1902) and R. L. Stevenson in Samoa (1890–94) preserved the legend for posterity. The story is everywhere much the same, but for a single racial distinction. The brown-skinned Polynesians, a race of bold, confiding seafarers, promptly accepted Christianity, took part in trade, and moved with the times. Their frankness and generosity made them easy victims for the exploiter, though they showed no taste or aptitude for regular manual labour. The dark Melanesians of the western islands resisted Christianity and progress alike. The survival of head-hunting and cannibalism even into the twentieth century gave them a reputation for treachery and ferocity as they defended themselves from exploitation. But once caught by the 'black-birders', at some risk, and sold on the plantations they could be held to continuous work.

The first European settlements in the western Pacific were also directly inspired by Cook's voyages. The convict settlement at Sydney (1788) made a port of call for the whalers who, about 1796, began to leave the coast of Chile and work from the coast of New South Wales. An exception to the East India Company's monopoly, which restricted British trade in those seas until 1813, was made in favour of the whalers by Act of Parliament. Though there were many British whalers the New Englanders surpassed them, reaching their greatest activitity in the 1840's. Having once equipped crews and ships for a deep-sea voyage, they avoided civilised ports, preferring to call for refreshment at some island retreat. In 1838, sixty whalers put in at Papeete in Tahiti, seventy at Honolulu in Hawaii, a hundred at the Bay of Islands in New Zealand. Eight years later whalers made 500 calls at Honolulu.

The voyage of Cook's Lieutenant Bligh to collect specimens of the breadfruit plant from Tahiti was the occasion of the mutiny of the *Bounty* and the flight of the mutineers to remote Pitcairn,[1] the first of the beachcombing settlements. Others soon followed when brigs and schooners from Sydney began to visit the nearer islands for pearls, tortoiseshell, or whatever else was saleable. An early article of trade was *bêche-de-mer*, a holothurian also known as sea-cucumber, which was caught on the coral reefs, cooked, dried and exported to the China coast as a food delicacy. A gang of Americans were curing *bêche-de-mer* with the help of native labour at Levuka in Fiji, about the year 1835. Ships went to the Bay of Islands in New Zealand to refit with masts and spars of *Kauri* pine and with cordage made from the tough fibres of the plant known as New Zealand flax. Another valued product was

[1] Having been occupied by the mutineers of the *Bounty* with some Tahitian women in 1790, the island remained in obscurity until 1808. There had been quarrels and feuds from which one only of the original white men survived as a pattern of patriarchal piety. Ships occasionally visited Pitcairn until in 1856 the islanders who had increased in numbers to 192 were removed at their own request to Norfolk Island. Forty of them soon drifted back to their remoter Pitcairn. In 1936 the population was 202 persons. In 1898 the Island was placed under the Western Pacific Administration which governs through an elective council and an elective chief magistrate. Henderson, Ducie, and Oeno Islands are included in the 'district' of Pitcairn.

the rare sandalwood which could be sold for £100 a ton in China where a perfumed oil was extracted from the heart of the wood. If a few trees were found on any island they would soon be sought out and felled. There was a boom at Sydney in sandalwood from Fiji, which began about 1804 and lasted ten years until there were no more trees. Relations between the natives and the sandal-wood traders were bad, and worse when the traders began to work the more savage New Hebrides.

When American traders found sandalwood in Hawaii, about 1811, a native chief of great ability monopolised it, drawing from the trade a revenue with which he made himself King, taking the title of Kamèha-mèha I, and so began to administer and civilise the whole group. Similar attempts to found Polynesian kingdoms were made with more or less European advice in Tahiti, Tonga, Fiji, Samoa, and New Zealand. Many chiefs built and manned schooners to trade on their own account between the islands. The British Government, which had disclaimed Cook's annexa-tions in the Pacific, by an Act of Parliament in 1817, appointed consuls in some of the islands—in New Zealand (1832), and in Tahiti (1837).

All this commercial activity, though aggregating to a con-siderable value, was at first a small man's trade, conducted by barter, in ships rarely exceeding 120 tons, following no regular routes but visiting any likely island. Among the first to form regular lines of commerce was Peter Dillon, an Irish trader who ran cargoes of island produce to Valparaiso (about 1808 to 1838), founding a transpacific trade which drew the attention of the new governments of Chile and Peru to eastern Polynesia. No political action was taken by the British government beyond the appoint-ment of more consuls, and the establishment of an Admiralty Court (1823) at Sydney with jurisdiction over British seamen in the Pacific.

At the same time as the island trade was growing, the mis-sionaries were advancing into the Pacific, reaching some islands before the traders. The London Missionary Society, afterwards so powerful in Africa, was founded in 1795 to evangelise the Pacific. Its first mission set sail (August 1796) for Tahiti in the ship *Duff* with the Society's flag at the peak, 'three doves argent on a purple field, bearing olive branches'. Four ministers and twenty-six laymen formed the party. They worked for ten years in Tahiti without visible effect, so that some were disheartened and one or two even abandoned the mission to go beachcombing. Then came a sudden change when Pomaré, the principal chief, began to see the advantage of Western progress and of Christianity. His baptism in 1812 was followed, as were the baptisms of Anglo-Saxon kings, by mass-conversion of his people. Tahiti became a Protestant and anglicised state with written laws and a constitution compiled by the Methodist missionaries. In 1817 John Williams (1796–1839), the apostle of Polynesia, arrived to join the mission in Tahiti and instantly formed plans to advance to the other islands. 'I cannot content myself', he said, in words that sounded like Livingstone's, 'within the narrow limits of a single reef.' He built a schooner and in twenty years founded missions in the Cook Islands, the Marquesas, Tonga, and Samoa. This was not enough; in 1839 he set sail for the savage New Hebrides and was murdered at Erromanga by Melanesians whose only previous experience of white men had been a visit from some brutal traders in sandalwood.

While the Methodists had been at work in central Polynesia, the Anglicans of the C.M.S. had been working in New Zealand (see chapter VII, 7, page 374) since 1814. When Bishop Selwyn arrived in New Zealand in 1842 it was his dearest wish to extend his mission to the islands. By an accident of drafting, his letters-patent had given him episcopal authority over an area much larger than New Zealand, and of this he took advantage. He founded a college for native teachers at Auckland, naming it St John's after his own Cambridge college, and in eight voyages to the islands he collected native students. He founded the Melanesian Mission, and when Auckland proved too far distant, he transferred its headquarters to Norfolk Island (1851), which Her Majesty's prison-officers and many of the Pitcairners had abandoned. Selwyn also persuaded the Anglican bishops in Australia to organise New Guinea, Melanesia and the western Pacific in general into a missionary area under the Australian Board of Missions (1861).

(1) TAHITI

The first spheres of civilised influence in the Pacific were those of the missionary societies. The Protestant sects divided the field by friendly agreement, on the whole. No dangerous rivalry occurred between British and American missionaries (the latter had been working in Hawaii since 1820); but the appearance of French Catholic missions at once brought friction. Between 1833 and 1836 the Marists and the Picpus Fathers[1] came on the scene, forming mission stations where Protestants were already at work, entering into open competition for converts. Under Louis Philippe a short-lived phase of French imperialism occurred, when French and British empire-builders disputed several points of vantage. As a counter-stroke to their discomfiture over the British annexation of New Zealand, the French made short work of Tahiti (September 1842); French missionaries backed by French gunboats brought pressure on the Queen who appealed for protection to Queen Victoria, in vain. Tahiti was annexed in spite of the protests of the Rev. George Pritchard (1796–1883), a Methodist missionary who had been appointed British consul. The house of Pomaré was eventually overthrown and the island brought into the French colonial system, though it had been discovered by the Englishman Wallis, celebrated by the exploits of the Englishman Cook, and evangelised by English missionaries. France and the Roman Catholic Church prevailed.

Though Peel in Whitehall uttered a dignified remonstrance, no further action was taken, except negotiations between Great Britain, France and the United States at which it was agreed not to dispute over Hawaii too, but to recognise it as an independent kingdom. The French and British spheres of influence in the central Pacific were negotiated in 1888.

(2) HAWAII

The westward march of the American nation did not stop with the occupation of Oregon and California (1846–9); sea-power in the Pacific was the next step. Much interest had been aroused by the naval expedition of Commander J. Wilkes who visited many islands between 1839 and 1842. His were also the first ships to sight the Antarctic continent. It was American naval force

[1] The heroic Father J. Damian who worked on the leper island of Molokai (1873–89) was a Picpus Father.

that opened Japan to commerce in 1853, and American enterprise in the 'fifties that made the first practical proposal for a Panama Canal. Sea-power, based on San Francisco and looking to the trade of Eastern Asia, meant a growing interest in Hawaii and the intervening islands. Midway Island was annexed as a naval base in 1867. By the 'seventies there were 5000 Americans at Honolulu busily planting sugar-cane and bringing in Chinese coolies. The royal house struggled long for independence, appealing once or twice for British protection, but the case was hopeless. The dwindling remnant of Hawaians were outnumbered, in a generation or two, by Asiatic and even by American immigrants. In 1875 Hawaii was drawn into the American fiscal system by a Reciprocity Treaty and thereafter annexation was imminent, though President after President was reluctant to take the step. Political disorder, following the extinction of the house of Kamèha-mèha, made it inevitable. Hawaii was annexed to the United States in 1898 during the Spanish-American War. All the inhabitants, American, Asiatic and Polynesian, thereafter enjoyed the same rights of citizenship, including the American common-school system. Hawaii became by far the richest and most socially advanced of the Polynesian island-groups.

When Tahiti fell to France, and Hawaii came under American influence, there was no predominantly English group, though everywhere there were British missionaries and traders. This was a matter of deep concern to expansionists in Australia and New Zealand. Sir George Grey repeatedly urged the Colonial Office to adopt a forward policy in the Pacific, while Dr J. D. Lang, the Sydney Nationalist, incited the government of New South Wales to make annexations on its own account. The Australians were seriously alarmed by French activity in the adjacent island of New Caledonia, where the French made a convict station in 1850 just when the Australians had at last purged their own shores from the taint of Botany Bay.

(3) FIJI

In the Fiji Islands an attempt was made to set up a native kingdom under white supervision. The British consul, Mr W. T. Pritchard, the son and biographer of George Pritchard of Tahiti, persuaded the leading chief of the island of Levuka, Thakombau (or Cakobau) by name, to give him jurisdiction over the disorderly British residents, who then numbered about 200. Pritchard came to London in 1859 to urge annexation. Thakombau was willing, even anxious, to come under British protection, on one condition, that the British government would pay his debts. For several years the American residents had been pressing him for damages on account of a fire, started in a Fourth-of-July celebration, which had burned down their consul's house. The Americans demanded £9500, which was more money than Thakombau possessed. If the British would relieve him of this embarrassment and give him their countenance, he would make himself King of the Fiji Islands indeed. Pritchard's case for annexation was strongly supported by the Manchester Cotton Supply Association, since he assured them that under an orderly government cotton could profitably be grown in Fiji. But the Colonial Office, after sending out a special commissioner who reported adversely, decided against annexation in 1861, and repeated their decision as late as 1869.

Meanwhile the boom in cotton during the American Civil War had justified Pritchard's claim. Some hundreds of settlers from New Zealand and New South Wales arrived, and did pretty well until the revival of the American Southern States spoiled the market. Cotton-planting required field-labour and it was at this time, in the 1860's, that 'black-birding' broke out all over the Pacific.

The first recorded case on a large scale was the kidnapping of natives by a Peruvian ship for work in the phosphate deposits of the eastern Pacific Islands, in 1862. This was reported and stopped by French diplomatic action. In the same year began the importation of kanakas to Queensland (see chapter X, 7, page 594). During the 'sixties a dozen vessels of about one hundred tons were fitted out in Sydney in the style of the old slave-ships, for carrying from fifty to one hundred men battened below hatches. The most celebrated of the black-birders was Captain W. H. ('Bully') Hayes, a picturesque ruffian of great audacity who could be very genial with his friends of any colour. He became legendary, the Robin Hood of the Pacific.[1]

The Melanesians were hard to catch and fought for their liberty with poisoned arrows. A scuffle with 'black-birders' at Nukapu on the island of Santa Cruz was followed by a tragedy that could not be overlooked. In September 1871 Dr J. C. Patteson, the Bishop of Melanesia, went ashore in a canoe, unarmed as was his custom, at Nukapu. He too was recruiting, for another service, looking for native students to carry off to his college at Norfolk Island. The simple savages clubbed him to death in revenge for five of their comrades killed by the 'black-birders'. The death of Bishop Patteson was the salvation of the Melanesians. Exeter Hall was so incensed that the subject became a matter of high politics. In the Queen's speech, at the opening of Parliament in 1872, a tribute was paid to the martyr and a promise given that British subjects in the Pacific would be brought under control.

The regulation of the kanaka trade was intimately bound up with Fijian politics. Proposals were again put forward for annexing the islands to New South Wales, which Lord Kimberley at the Colonial Office half approved, if only New South Wales would foot the bill. For the fall in cotton prices was the death-blow to Thakombau's regime. Some planters would not pay

---

[1] According to T. Dunbabin (*Slavers of the South Seas*), William Henry Hayes of Cleveland, Ohio, had been a Mississippi pilot when, in 1859, he decamped to the islands in a ship obtained by false pretences at San Francisco. In 1864 he turned up at the New Zealand gold-diggings, already a celebrated sea-ruffian with a reputation as a ladies' man. Again getting unlawful possession of a schooner, the *Wave*, from Lyttelton Harbour, he went 'black-birding', his line being to supply the sugar-planters of Fiji with Polynesians from the lonelier islands. Niue Island was cleared in 1868. Hayes was arrested by J. L. Williams, the British consul at Samoa in 1870 and handed over to the American naval authorities as a pirate. The case lapsed, probably because all the witnesses were in collusion with the defendant. After a turn on the China coast, hi-jacking Chinese pirates, Hayes settled as a trader in the Marshall Islands in 1872. Tales are told of his flouting French and Spanish authority in other groups. He made his last cruise in 1876, having again stolen a ship from San Francisco. Not long out at sea, he ill-treated the ship's cook who retaliated by knifing him. There are several other versions of his life-story. Charges were laid against him in several ports on many counts, usually for barratry or for abducting women.

taxes, some were for calling in the Americans, and some would have set up a rival chief in opposition to Thakombau. A further complication was the incorporation in Melbourne of the Polynesian Company, which offered to pay Thakombau's debts in return for a grant of 200,000 acres in Fiji. This Melbourne Company, running in opposition to the Sydney traders, had some high notions of empire-building and talked of rivalling the East India Company.

Thakombau's chief secretary was J. B. Thurston who was at first regarded in London as a mere beachcomber. When he again asked for a British protectorate the result was another commission of enquiry which made a voluminous report favouring his proposal on the whole. There followed several serious and well-informed debates, in both Houses of Parliament. They turned on the necessity for a naval base in the Pacific, on the motives of Australian land-companies, on the need for policing the islands, and on the question who was to finance Thurston's government, which was now £87,000 in debt. Gladstone, who went out of office during these discussions (1874), spoke strongly against supporting a planters' administration. Finally the new Colonial Secretary, Lord Carnarvon, sent the Governor of New South Wales, Sir Hercules Robinson, with authority to arrange terms of annexation. All the principal chiefs submitted, as well as Thakombau, who sent his war-club to Queen Victoria in token of abdication. His constitution was already in suspense. The Fiji Islands became a Crown Colony in October 1874.

Parliament had passed an Act (1872) declaring that all labour-traders should be obliged to take out a licence from the British authorities, a first step towards regulating the kanaka trade. This had little effect until the Governor of Fiji was given further authority, in 1877, as High Commissioner for the Western Pacific with a wide extra-territorial jurisdiction over British subjects. Piracy and kidnapping were gradually suppressed under this system which was enforced by naval vessels using rough-and-ready methods against 'black-birders', and no less against head-hunters. A case could be made, and was made, for recruiting islanders as indentured labourers under proper regulation, and for schooling savages who attacked legitimate traders. Some naval officers preferred this point of view, discounting the complaints of the missionaries as too sentimental. The 'gunboat policy' of punishing hostile acts by bombarding villages was not

uncommon in the Pacific. When H.M.S. *Rosario* went to Santa
Cruz to enquire into Patteson's murder, a boat's crew was
attacked. The warship then shelled the guilty village of Nukapu,
to the dismay of the missionaries and of several members of
Parliament. Until the twentieth century many Melanesian tribes
retained an attitude of sullen hostility to officials, traders, and
missionaries alike.

The later history of Fiji may be quickly dismissed. The first
Governor, Sir Arthur Gordon, arrived to find the islands in
political chaos and one-quarter of the inhabitants dying of
measles. To set the country to rights he turned to Thurston
who again became Chief Secretary and the creator of the colony.
An Englishman by birth, (Sir) J. B. Thurston (1836–97) had
begun as an island trader and had been cast away for two years
on one of the Samoan Islands, where he had learned to understand
the Polynesians. He now proved to be a talented colonial
administrator, was knighted and eventually became governor.

A turn was taken in Fijian affairs when, with Carnarvon's
permission, Indian coolies were introduced to grow sugar.
Although the first shipload, in 1879, brought smallpox with them
this trouble was surmounted and many thousands settled in Fiji
with their families. The total population of the islands in 1936
was recorded as 195,000 of whom 98,000 were Polynesians,
85,000 Indians (the majority of them born in Fiji), and 4000
Europeans. The main item in the islands' wealth (1936) was
cane-sugar, almost all of it handled by the Colonial Sugar
Refining Company, an Australian corporation with a capital of
£3,000,000. The importation of coolies was stopped in 1916,
after which the policy of the Company was to lease small-holdings
to Indian residents and to buy the crop. Nearly half the cultivated
land of the islands remained, however, in Fijian ownership.

Fiji was (1936) the only Pacific Crown Colony with an elective
element in the Legislative Council. Of the unofficial members
three Europeans and three Indians are elected by those communities. In the early days several attempts were made by
the planters to federate Fiji with one or other of the white
colonies. It was a member of the abortive Australian Federal
Council in the 1880's. In 1900 proposals were made both by the
Fijian planters and by Mr Seddon that Fiji should be annexed to
New Zealand. On the strong representations of the Governor,

who mistrusted the New Zealanders, Chamberlain rejected the proposal. Throughout the partition of the Pacific, empire-building by the dominions was discouraged at the Colonial Office, though colonial governors, such as Robinson of New South Wales and Gordon of New Zealand, were sometimes charged with special missions to the islands on behalf of Downing Street.

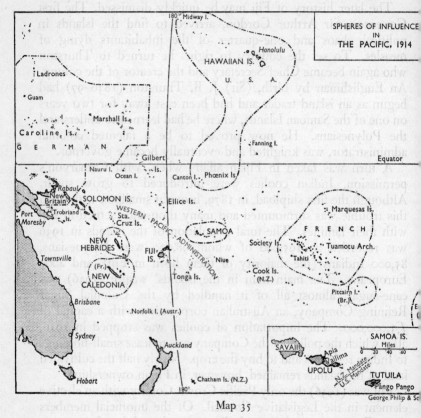

Map 35

Including Rotuma, and the many smaller islands of the group, Fiji is the most extensive as well as the most populous of the British Pacific island-groups. The two largest islands, Viti Levu and Vanua Levu are, respectively, about as large as Hampshire and Sussex. They are volcanic in origin, mountainous, and densely wooded on their windward, south-eastern slopes.

(4) NEW GUINEA

The Queensland government, from its first foundation, regarded New Guinea as a natural appanage which should be annexed to the colony. It first attracted the attention of the High Commissioner for the western Pacific when finds of gold were reported in 1878. During the next twenty years there were several 'rushes' of diggers from Queensland to goldfields in New Guinea and its adjacent islands, though the finds were small. The High Commissioner and the Colonial Office showed little sympathy with appeals from this quarter since Queensland planters were not thought suitable rulers for so primitive a race as the Papuans. Missions of several sects had tried in vain to convert them and had on several occasions been forced to withdraw.

In February 1883 Sir S. McIlwraith, the premier of Queensland, warned the Colonial Office that the Germans had designs on New Guinea. The Secretary of State (the fifteenth Lord Derby) took no notice. McIlwraith forced the issue in April by sending a magistrate who proclaimed the annexation of all of New Guinea that the Dutch had not occupied. In July Lord Derby repudiated the annexation, stating in terms that were plain to the point of rudeness that any annexation by a colonial government was *ultra vires*. He went on to suggest that if the Australian colonies would combine together and provide the cost, a protectorate over the coast tribes might be permitted 'after mature consideration'. In December an intercolonial conference at Sydney approved his plan and months of mature consideration followed. In October 1884 Derby authorised the protectorate, too late to secure the prize. Bismarck had sent the celebrated traveller, Dr Finsch, to stake out a claim and had secretly organised a New Guinea Company. He now blandly informed Great Britain that north-eastern New Guinea was a German colony. The British protectorate was restricted to the south-eastern sector, which vexed the Australians sorely.

In August 1885 Sir Peter Scratchley arrived with four policemen and no other resources to set up an administration at Port Moresby. He died after a few months, having had time to do no more than announce a policy of protecting natives from interference, of disciplining the diggers and beachcombers, of dividing the areas worked by rival missionaries. He also recommended that the protectorate should be made into a colony. His plans were carried out by Dr William MacGregor who was appointed Governor of the Crown Colony of British New Guinea in 1888, with a steamboat provided by the British government and a grant-in-aid of £15,000 from the Australian colonies. Mac-Gregor made a number of journeys into the interior, hitherto unknown, and formed a native police force, with which the colony was brought into good order. The staple product was gold, to the value in his time of £70,000 or £80,000 a year. In 1906 the colony was annexed to the Commonwealth of Australia under the name of Papua. Through almost the whole of its history Papua has been shaped by the firm hand of Sir Hubert Murray, administrator from 1907 until his death in 1940, when he was succeeded by his nephew. Apart from the goldfields, and some recent prospecting for oil, the colony was not much developed and, at the time of the Japanese invasion of 1942, was still largely unexplored. Some coastal plantations allotted to settlers on government leases were worked by indentured labour under government control. A grant-in-aid of £40,000 or £50,000 annually from the Australian government kept the colony solvent without allowing much for public works. Native welfare was entirely in the hands of the missionaries. Apart from pacification and protection, Murray's personal task, it cannot be said that Australia has done much for its dependency.

German New Guinea, with its adjacent islands and its naval base at Rabaul (established 1910), was allotted to Australia under mandate in 1920. It had been developed, even before Bismarck's annexation by a celebrated beachcomber, 'Queen Emma' Forsyth, a Samoan-American half-caste, who established plantations around Rabaul in the 'seventies. She married a German and died, rich, at Monte Carlo in 1914. The Mandated Territory proved to have much greater, or much more accessible, resources than Papua. A notable event in its history was the earthquake of 1937 when the town of Rabaul was destroyed. Thereafter the administrative capital was removed to Salamaua.

(5) SAMOA

British and German spheres of influence in the Pacific were agreed by negotiation (1885–6), in which the colonies were not asked to participate. Difficulties next arose in Samoa where attempts had been made to set up a native chief, Malietoa, as king under white guidance. Samoa was the Pacific headquarters of the Hamburg firm of J. C. Godefroy & Sons, the greatest traders in the Pacific. They were notable for their open and consistent opposition to missionaries of every sect; and were notable also as the originators of the trade in copra. About the year 1859 they began to buy the dried flesh of the coconut from native cultivators and to ship it to Europe in that form, instead of exporting coconut oil extracted by crude native processes. In 1875, Godefroy's shipped copra worth £175,000 from Apia in Samoa alone. But they had no political standing there and, in the 'seventies, British, German and American consuls all got concessions from chief Malietoa to use Apia as a naval base. A municipality was also set up in the town under control of traders of the three nations. After Godefroy's, the merchants of next importance were the New Zealand firm of Macarthur's. The New Zealand government was strongly disposed to annex Samoa when Queensland annexed New Guinea, but was warned off by Lord Derby. In Samoa too, German intrigues were suspected. Godefroy's were reconstituted as the German South Sea Company with something like a guarantee from Bismarck, and their agent continually interfered in Samoan politics with strong support from a German naval squadron.

In 1887 the Germans started a frivolous quarrel with Malietoa and declared war on him. A petty campaign dragged on through 1888 in which some landing-parties of German marines were unable to subdue the Samoans. Lord Salisbury stated that we had 'no interest in Samoa', though the New Zealanders were hotly incensed, and the Americans more so at the high-handed conduct of the Germans. When Americans were insulted in these dis-orders (they can hardly be called battles), a naval squadron was sent to uphold the honour of the American flag. The Senate voted an appropriation, and war threatened between Germany and America.

In March 1889, three German warships lay in the bay at Apia, an open roadstead under the lee of a coral reef. Three American warships were anchored near, their officers in such a mood that the courtesies commonly exchanged between friendly navies were omitted. One British warship was in the bay, the cruiser *Calliope* fitted with new compound engines and bunkered with fast-burning New Zealand coal. So high were tempers that no commander would move his ship from its station off the lee shore when the weather broke. A hurricane struck Samoa, driving all three German ships and all three American ships ashore with great loss of life. Only the *Calliope* kept her head to the storm and steamed out through a narrow opening in the reef.

The Apia hurricane blew away the war-clouds; animosities were forgotten in the common wreck from which the Samoans heroically rescued German and American sailors alike. A conference was called in Europe just then to deal with Zanzibar (see chapter XV, 2, page 813) and, as a side-issue, the *status quo* was restored in Samoa. In New Zealand and Australia the escape of the *Calliope* was felt to be symbolic. Her picture, riding the storm, hangs beside that of the King and Queen in many a barroom at Auckland and Sydney. Her flag, it was believed, would again float some day over the roadstead at Apia.[1]

Ten years later Germany took advantage of the entanglement of the other two powers, America with the Filipinos and Britain in South Africa, to renew her intrigues. As in Hawaii and Fiji so in Samoa the Polynesian kingship was unequal to the strains of commercial politics, and collapsed. Germany and America agreed to divide the Samoan group, taking respectively the harbours of Apia and Pango Pango, and to compensate Britain elsewhere. Chamberlain was glad to appease both powers at this juncture by agreeing to the partition and had only to consider the resentment of New Zealand whose Premier, Seddon, protested. The New Zealanders were mollified when Chamberlain placed the Cook Islands under their administration (1901), a benefit to the islanders, whom the New Zealanders have treated as generously as their own Maoris.

The German triumph over Samoa still rankled in New Zealand and was quickly reversed when war came. Western Samoa was

---

[1] The best account of events in Samoa in these times is to be found in *A Footnote to History* by R. L. Stevenson.

occupied by a New Zealand force in 1914, and allotted to New Zealand under mandate in 1920, with less satisfactory results. A nationalist movement sprang up among the high-spirited Samoans, who disliked direct rule by New Zealand administrators not much less than they had disliked rule by Germans. Having no trained service of colonial servants, the New Zealand government sent to Samoa military men who were unimaginative and unsympathetic. Throughout the 1920's there was continual friction with the nationalist association, known as the Mau, which was supported by some half-caste and white planters, notably by a Mr O. F. Nelson. The administrator unwisely banished Nelson and some others from the island, a step which led to riots and bloodshed in 1929. Better times came when the Labour government in New Zealand instituted Crown Colony government of a more enlightened type with a strong elective element in the Legislative Council.

(6) TONGA

The last survivor of the missionary kingdoms was Tonga, where the leading chief had set up a constitutional monarchy under Methodist supervision, taking the name of King George. A serpent crept into this Eden in the form of political corruption. After some years of arcadian ease strange rumours began to come from Tonga about the conduct of King George's 'premier', the Rev. S. Baker. At last the High Commissioner intervened (1890) and deported Baker as an undesirable British subject. He had set up an autonomous church in Tonga, breaking with the Methodist society, and had converted all the revenues of Church and State to his own use. The High Commissioner sent one of his own staff, Basil Thomson (afterwards better known in London as head of Scotland Yard) to purify the administration (1890–1). Tonga was proclaimed a British protectorate in 1900 and has since prospered as a native kingdom under indirect rule.

(7) THE WESTERN PACIFIC

The adjustment of spheres of influence with France and Germany led to the assumption of British protectorates over a part of the Solomon Islands (1893), the Gilbert Islands (1896), the Ellice Islands (1897), and some smaller groups. In the central Pacific the working of phosphate deposits by traders of several nations led to uncertainty about the status of several islands. Then cable-stations gave a further importance to other islands, and finally in the 'thirties airports and emergency landing-grounds renewed the interest. Ocean Island, a mass of calcium phosphate, was annexed to the Gilbert and Ellice Islands Protectorate in 1900.

Ocean Island and its neighbour Nauru have a curious history. One day in 1899 Mr (later Sir) A. F. Ellis took notice of an odd piece of rock, the souvenir of an island voyage, used as a doorstop in the Sydney office of the Pacific Islands Company, which Sir Arthur Gordon (formerly High Commissioner) had formed to develop some derelict coconut plantations in the central Pacific. Finding that the doorstop was a mass of hard compact phosphate from the German island of Nauru, he set further inquiries afoot which led to the reconstitution of the Company (1902) as the Pacific Phosphates Company. They made their working base at Ocean Island and commenced digging there until, in 1906, they were able to get a concession to work the German island where the deposits were more accessible.

When war broke out in 1914 Nauru was at once captured by an Australian cruiser. In 1920 it was allotted to the British Empire under mandate. After arbitration by Lord Milner between the governments of the United Kingdom, Australia and New Zealand it was agreed to set up a joint administration, and to market the phosphates for the public profit through a Phosphates Commission, which was to pay a small royalty to the natives of the island. They bought out the interest of the Company for £3,500,000 of which the United Kingdom paid 42%, Australia 42%, and New Zealand 16%. A million tons of phosphates were shipped from Nauru in 1938–9. In some years Ocean Island has produced as much; it became the headquarters of the commission and the seat of government for the Gilbert and Ellice Islands (until 1946).

Farther to the east some scattered islands on either side of the equator had been sporadically worked by trading companies for phosphates and copra, since the 1850's. At the end of the century the Pacific Trading Company (and its successors) and the Burns Philp Shipping Company of Sydney had interests there. Fanning Island was placed under British protection in 1888 and made a relaying station for the Pacific Cable in 1902. Several other islands were colonised and planted by Polynesians with some success under the direction of the Burns Philp Company. They were placed under the Gilbert and Ellice Administration in 1937–8. But America also claimed jurisdiction over some of the islands[1] and in 1939 an agreement was signed: Canton and Enderbury Islands in the (British) Phoenix Group were placed under a joint administration so that they might be developed as an airport for Pan-American Airways.

In general these annexations implied no more than the despatch of a 'resident' by the High Commissioner for the western Pacific. Even more shadowy was the jurisdiction set up jointly with France in the New Hebrides. In the first instance a Joint Naval Commission was instituted in 1887 to try offences committed by French and British subjects. After the Entente Cordiale this apology for an administration was inflated into a condominium, the worst of all forms of government (1906). Resident Commissioners of France and Great Britain were appointed, with jurisdiction over their own nationals and authority to co-operate in matters of police and public works. The result has been to leave the islands untouched by the economic development and the social services which either a French or a British colonial administration would have provided. Both the Australian and New Zealand governments lodged objections against the condominium.

By the year 1906 the partition of the Pacific was complete. Later changes followed the fortune of world wars, which divided the German sphere between Japan, America, and the British Dominions in 1920, and liquidated the Japanese sphere in 1945. Between the wars Hawaii, with its population of 400,000, of whom a quarter were American and a third Japanese, had a volume of trade ten times as great as any other island-group. It ranked in importance almost with one of the smaller British dominions. In comparison with Hawaii's total trade, £43,000,000 in 1938, that of the Japanese islands was only £4,500,000, although they poured settlers into their sphere. The mandated

[1] In 1939, Kingman, Palmyra, Jarvis, Howland and Baker Islands were American possessions. The Colonial Office list, 1946, describes Canton and Enderbury Islands as forming a condominium.

territory of New Guinea showed a trade figure about equal
to that of the Japanese group, owing to the development of gold
production in the 1930's. The international oil companies also
were interested in this territory. The Fiji Islands, exporting sugar
and fruit, had an external trade worth £3,800,000. Next in order
was French New Caledonia, rich in nickel and other metals,
with trade worth £1,795,000. Papua lagged far behind mandated
New Guinea with a trade worth £850,000. Tahiti followed,
with a trade figure of £650,000, mostly in copra shipped to
France. Nauru phosphates were worth about as much. Samoa's
trade amounted to no more than £358,000, and the figures for the
other groups were smaller still, mostly consisting of copra shipped
by one of the Australian companies.

XV

THE PARTITION OF AFRICA, 1884–1914

Argument: The partition of Central Africa was precipitated by Stanley's pioneering work on the Congo. The Berlin West African Conference, though convened by Bismarck for disingenuous purposes, created the Congo State and recognised British influence on the Niger. The Anglo-German partition of East Africa and the Anglo-French partition of West Africa were natural consequences. While British and German diplomats were in general agreement, there was hostility and friction between British and French on the Niger and on the White Nile, until the Entente Cordiale.

French policy was concerned with creating a solid block of territory from Algeria to the Congo under a single administrative system with a French commercial monopoly, which disgusted British Free Traders. It was the Liberal policy in the 'eighties to govern British tropical colonies by chartered companies which were gradually replaced by Lugard's new system of indirect rule.

The disgraceful history of the Congo State discredited all commercial imperialism.

1. THE COLONIAL OFFICE, KING LEOPOLD, AND BISMARCK

IN 1864 Sir Charles Adderley, the colonial reformer, moved for a Parliamentary committee on affairs in West Africa, asserting that the four West African 'establishments' cost the tax-payer a million pounds a year, and to no purpose. The attempt to create a civilised negro community at Sierra Leone had been, he said, a failure, the Gold Coast involved us in frequent unjustified wars, the Gambia and Lagos were less productive of trade than other areas not under British rule. The report of the committee, which was laid before the House of Commons in June 1865, contained these recommendations: 'All further extension of territory or assumption of government, or new treaties offering protection to native tribes, would be inexpedient...the object of our policy should be to encourage in the natives the exercise of those qualities which may render it possible for us more and more to transfer to them the administration of all the governments, with a view to our ultimate withdrawal from all, except, probably, Sierra Leone.' This was at the end of a session and, before Parliament met again, the death of Palmerston led to a change in the administration. Cardwell, the new Secretary of State, announced in 1866 that as a result of the Report the West African establishments had been drastically cut down.

Such a sequence of events would not have occurred a few years later. The imperialists of the 'sixties still devoted their attention to the self-governing colonies, and had not yet ranged themselves beside Livingstone in the crusade for the regeneration of Africa. The reluctant decision to establish a protectorate over Basutoland in 1868, and Wolseley's Ashanti campaign of 1873, marked the first sign of a forward policy. There was a stirring in the Chanceries, a new concern with the Dark Continent. Stanley's exploration of the Congo (1874–7) as reported by the *Daily Telegraph*, kept public interest alive. His account of a visit to the generous King M'tesa of Uganda led to the despatch of missionaries to that unspoiled kingdom, the first step towards the partition of East Africa. In the same year, 1876, Leopold of Belgium founded the International African Association, with national sub-committees in ten countries.

Leopold II, King of the Belgians (1865–1909) will serve as a horrid warning against the faults of imperialism, presenting all the features of that bogey of the Radicals, the colonial exploiter. An uncommonly clever and plausible man with all the moral backing of the respectable House of Saxe-Coburg, he was able to approach the problem of Africa with every appearance of progressive enlightenment. Having quickly noted the potential wealth of the newly discovered territories he assumed the post of patron to the pioneers; he was the man to open Central Africa for civilisation. Livingstone died too soon for him; Gordon was otherwise employed; de Brazza the French explorer negotiated with him and cannily withdrew on an expedition of his own; but H. M. Stanley was quite taken in by Leopold's royal courtesy. Together they formed a new society, the *Comité d'Études du Haut Congo* (1877), conceiving the plan that Stanley should bring all the tribes of the Congo by treaty into a federation, under protection of an international body which should be inspired by the purest philanthropy. Stanley returned to the Congo to spend four strenuous years (1879–83) carrying out the plan. On the north side of the river de Brazza was carrying out a rival undertaking on behalf of France and it was here that the international struggle for Africa began. Both pioneers returned in 1883, each of them bearing numerous treaties with native chiefs who had been attached to the French interest by de Brazza, or to King Leopold's interest by Stanley.

There were other Englishmen as well as Stanley in Leopold's employment and the Foreign Office showed considerable interest in their actions. Even under Gladstone's administration the British seemed to be pushing out every frontier, infiltrating the Congo and the Niger basins, as they had infiltrated Egypt and Bechuanaland, to the disgust of the French who regarded the whole affair as British greed masked by British hypocrisy. French and British empire-building went step by step in the 1880's. France stole a march on England by occupying Tunis in 1881; England stole a march on France next year in Egypt. France annexed Annam in 1883; England forestalled further French progress by conquering Upper Burma in 1885. The British traders got the better of the French on the Lower Niger in 1884; the French excluded English influence from Madagascar in 1886. There was deadlock between French and British claims in Newfoundland, deadlock in the New Hebrides.

In these troubled waters Bismarck perceived that there were fish for him to catch. He seems to have had no great desire for colonies before the year 1884. In that year he changed his tactics rather than his policy and began to annex territory not, it appears, for its own sake so much as to embarrass the British. It suited him to reinsure against another European war by appeasing the French; he would reconcile them to the loss of Alsace-Lorraine by encouraging them to look overseas and, with typical German crudity, he assumed that he could demonstrate his goodwill to the French by demonstrating his ill-will to the British.

German and Austrian scientists and travellers had played no small part in the pioneering tasks of the nineteenth century. The history of the British Empire would be poorer without the exploits of Heinrich Barth in Nigeria, Krapf and Rebman in East Africa, Slatin and Emin in the Sudan, Leichhardt in Northern

Australia, von Haast[1] in New Zealand, but these men came as citizens of the world from an older Germany without political unity. German states even had held colonies such as the Brandenburger forts on the Guinea Coast; and the Hanseatic merchants owned trading posts throughout the world; but a German colonial policy was a new thing. German traders and pioneers all over the world began suddenly to make inquiries about treaty rights with native chiefs.

In April 1883 Karl Lüderitz of Bremen bought the trading post of Angra Pequeña, where there had been a Lutheran mission for twenty years, from an African chief and, on 2 May, ventured to hoist the imperial flag over the first German colony.

The British statesman upon whom it fell to take notice of these proceedings was Gladstone's Foreign Secretary, the second Earl Granville (1815–91) who, fifteen years earlier, had incurred the wrath of the New Imperialists. Having previously declared himself uninterested in South-West Africa, he now rather feebly referred the matter to the Cape government which procrastinated, dreading the expense of extending the frontier. When, at last, the Cape decided to file a claim it was too late. Bismarck had confirmed the action of Lüderitz by taking South-West Africa under German protection in June 1884. It was missionary influence, exercised through Granville's radical colleague Joseph Chamberlain, that obliged him to set limits to German expansion by sending Sir Charles Warren to annex Christian Bechuanaland before the year was out. Provoked into reaction by German pinpricks, Lord Granville now became an imperialist in spite of himself. He had no antipathy to Germany, no objection to German colonisation, if only Bismarck would cease to be provocative. Where he saw antagonism was in West Africa, the scene of French aggression 'since the French imposed a hostile tariff wherever they went'.

Granville had already determined, in 1883, to exclude the French from the Niger Delta. On 16 May 1884 (just before Bismarck's action in South-West Africa) he gave instructions to Mr E. H. Hewett, the British consul for Benin and Biafra, to establish a British protectorate over the Niger Delta and as far

---

[1] Sir J. von Haast of Bonn (1824–87), F.R.S., etc., geologist, explored much of the South Island on behalf of the New Zealand Company. Later he was one of the founders of the University of New Zealand.

east as the Baptist mission station at Victoria [1] beyond the Rio del
Rey. The plan was to administer the country through a chartered
company, 'like that of British North Borneo'. Hewett hurried
back to Africa and, on 19 July, met a German expedition under
Dr Nachtigal on a similar errand, at the mouth of the Cameroons
River. Nachtigal had already (5 July) proclaimed a German protectorate over Togoland, thus separating the British colonies of
the Gold Coast and Lagos. He was now claiming territory farther
east. Reports of what occurred are somewhat scanty,[2] but
Nachtigal claimed the coastline southward from the Cameroons
Mountain and Hewett the coastline westward as far as Lagos.
In July and August Hewett worked along the coast, in October
and November up the main stream of the Niger and into the
Benue River, taking African chiefs under British protection by
treaty. Thus came into existence the Oil Rivers Protectorate of
which, said one prominent Little Englander, the very name made
him feel sick.

During those months, north-eastern New Guinea on the other
side of the world was taken under German protection, to the
dismay of the Queenslanders, and to the disgust of Granville's
radical colleague, Joseph Chamberlain. An even more ambitious
scheme of the German imperialists was launched by Karl Peters
who arrived in disguise at Zanzibar in the same month (November
1884), with a design of bringing all the mainland territories of the
Sultan under German rule. Land-grabbing in Africa was now
proceeding at so rapid a rate that diplomatic intervention was
urgently needed.

An abortive negotiation between Great Britain and Portugal
about their respective interests in the Congo estuaries gave
Bismarck the opportunity he sought of irritating Lord Granville
by a subtler stroke of diplomacy. Claiming that wider interests
were involved, he issued invitations, after careful preliminaries,
to a general conference on Central Africa. It met at Berlin on
15 November 1884 and closed on 26 February 1885 after ten
plenary sessions had been held. As is usual at such affairs much
of the most useful work was done by subcommittees behind the

---

[1] The Rev. W. Collings of the Baptist mission at Ambas River had been
urging annexation upon Gladstone since 1882. The most celebrated British
mission station on the Oil Coast was that of the Presbyterians at Calabar, the
scene of the labours for forty years (1876–1916) of Mary Slessor.

[2] According to S. E. Crowe, *Berlin West Africa Conference*.

scenes. At the opening session Bismarck himself presided. The British delegation, including a team of experts on Africa and a geographer from Stanford's in Long Acre, was led by Sir E. Malet, the ambassador at Berlin. A prominent part was taken by the delegate from the United States whose interest was philanthropic. The American people, having accepted H. M. Stanley as a national hero, regarded the schemes of the International African Association as a charter of liberty for Africa. Though the Association had no diplomatic standing, its influence everywhere prevailed through the efforts of Stanley, who was co-opted to the American delegation.

Great Britain, France, Germany, and Portugal were the powers immediately concerned in the partition of Central Africa. Before the Conference met, Bismarck had staked out his claim to the Cameroons. The French, regarding the plans of the Association as mere Anglo-Saxon humbug, were well content to work for a right of pre-emption over the territories that Stanley had marked out for it. So soon as the International African Association should fade away they would thus incorporate its territories with the colony which de Brazza had annexed for France on the north bank of the Congo. The English, to Bismarck's chagrin, were not at all discomposed by his conference. Granville recorded that the Liberals were delighted; they welcomed the opportunity of referring the whole African problem to a congress with such wide terms. It would enable them to exclude the protectionist French from a large part of Africa. Though it was far from Bismarck's intention, the diplomatic effects of the Berlin West Africa Conference were to drive Portugal into the arms of France and to demonstrate that Britain and Germany had nothing to quarrel over.

The 'Berlin Act', the General Act of the Conference, signed on 26 February 1885, professed to draw up a code of international regulations for the partition of Africa. Extending their view from the Congo Delta, the delegates took pains to define the whole region over which they asserted authority, the 'Conventional Congo Basin', which was declared open to the free trade and navigation of all nations. Within this region there were to be no paper protectorates. Sovereignty was to depend upon actual occupation and all the signatories were to be informed when any district was occupied. While the Congress was sitting each delegation made a separate treaty with the International African Association, recognising the sovereignty of the new Congo Independent State.[1]

While the French, with their right of pre-emption, supposed themselves to have secured the residual, that is the real, control of the Congo, they were neatly excluded from the estuary of the Niger. Only on 14 November, the day before the Conference began, did Consul Hewett obtain the last of the treaties that rounded off the Oil Rivers Protectorate. Accordingly, when the Conference turned its attention from the Conventional Congo Basin to the Niger the British delegation could demonstrate that this was already a British sphere within the conditions that the Conference had just approved. The hand of the delegates was strengthened by the appearance of George Taubman Goldie, an obscure but influential figure. As chairman of the National Africa Company he had been able to inform Lord Granville that on 1 November he had bought out the only French company trading on the Lower Niger. The external trade of the river was now wholly in the hands of British merchants.

There was then no reasonable course for the Conference to take except to declare the Niger like the Congo open in principle to the free trade and navigation of all nations, and to invite Great Britain to enforce the Berlin Act on the river and its branches 'so far as they are or will be under her sovereignty and protection'. Higher upstream the French were to do the same.

Before the Conference ended, the spotlight of publicity had been withdrawn from Stanley's triumph to Gordon's tragedy. On 5 February 1885 the news came to Berlin of the fall of Khartoum. Another African empire, as extensive as the Congo State, had lapsed into barbarism.

The Berlin West African Conference thus confirmed the British in the possession of another huge dependency and, in doing so, intensified Anglo-French rivalry. While endeavouring to internationalise Central Africa it created a state which became a byword for misgovernment. Declaring for Free Trade it set up systems under which the commerce of the Congo—and of the Niger—was monopolised. The suppression of the traffic in

[1] Often called the Congo Free State, though such a title is inaccurate, nominally and really.

arms, liquor, and slaves was approved as a desirable course of action, and shelved. It was left for the Brussels Conference, convened by Lord Salisbury, four years later, to take any active steps for an international campaign against these abuses.

Bismarck had widened the breach between France and England without ingratiating the French and had therefore failed in his main object. Under cover of this tortuous diplomacy he had taken possession of a colonial empire of 2,000,000 square miles without moving a soldier or a warship, while France in her sphere was employing thousands of soldiers and spending millions of money. The British method of colonial expansion in the 'eighties was a revival of the Elizabethan plan of colonisation by chartered companies.[1] The first of the new series was the British North Borneo Company 1881; the National Africa Company was chartered in July 1886 as the Royal Niger Company; the British Imperial East Africa Company in 1888; and Rhodes's British South Africa Company in 1889. It cannot be said that this attempt to combine commerce with administration succeeded, for only one of these companies showed a prosperous balance-sheet while carrying out its political obligations. After a few years the system was denounced by Cromer, who was much influenced by what he saw on a tour of inspection up the Nile and into the Congo State.

Cromer was one of the first to observe that King Leopold's Utopia had quite changed its character. Stanley severed his connexion with the Congo State in 1887, and after his departure most of the British officers were replaced by Belgians. In 1891 the Congo basin treaties were amended to allow the imposition of a tariff which soon grew into a state monopoly of external trade. Ivory and rubber were strictly monopolised and in 1896 a private estate, *la domaine de la couronne*, of 100,000 square miles was allotted to King Leopold in person. In addition to vast legitimate profits he drew from the *domaine* at least £4,000,000 for his privy purse. Though access to the Congo was increasingly difficult, ugly rumours began to creep back to Europe of the methods by which the Congo natives were persuaded to bring in a quota of raw rubber. But Leopold was very skilful at disguising his designs and delaying investigations, and stopping the mouths

---

[1] The chartered companies of the 1830's were land-settlement companies without political authority.

of men who knew too much with gold. But there was one mouth
he could not stop, that of E. D. Morel (1873–1924), a Liverpool
shipping-clerk whose duties with the Elder Dempster Line
frequently took him to Antwerp and Brussels, where he had
access to the facts about the Congo. For twelve years he fought
a duel with the King of the Belgians, maintaining an agitation in
London through the Congo Reform Association.

The Aborigines Protection Society led by Sir Charles Dilke
became restive about 1896 and in the following year Morel began
his investigations. The philanthropists next received support
from the Liverpool Chamber of Commerce which protested, in
1901, against the expulsion of all but the monopolist trade.
Parliament debated the Congo scandals nine times in five sessions.
Lord Lansdowne raised the question diplomatically in 1903 but
could not enlist support of any kind from the other signatories to
the Berlin Act. He sent a British consular agent, Roger Casement,[1] to the Congo where he fully verified Morel's charges.
Meanwhile King Leopold blandly evaded the pressure put on
him, and Belgian public opinion, naturally enough, rallied
round the genial and generous king, who ingratiated his European
subjects by enriching their cities with parks, galleries and theatres
bought with the blood of his African subjects. Had the perfidious
British no beam in their own eye? In his last year (1909) King
Leopold was so far moved by adverse critics as to bequeath his
estate to the Belgian nation, and so died in the odour of sanctity.
The Congo Reform Association was dissolved in 1910, having
completed its task, for, under constitutional rule the Belgian
Congo has become, in the eyes of some critics, the best administered of all European dependencies in Africa, showing some
of the most enlightened features of French and some of British
practice.

The course of events in the Congo State besmirched the
whole business of empire-building. Here was a new slave trade
worse than the old, to mark an end of Livingstone's dream.

---

[1] This was that Roger Casement, knighted in 1911, who afterwards exposed
the Putumayo atrocities in Brazil, and crowned his career of strange crusading by
fighting for Germany against British imperialism in Ireland. He was taken and
hanged for treason in 1916.

2. BRITISH, GERMANS, AND PORTUGUESE IN EAST AFRICA

It was estimated that forty-five distinct exploring expeditions were at work in Africa in the season after the Congress of Berlin. All the colonising powers investigated and annexed the hinterland behind the coastlines they had occupied and these converging forces met in that central region between the Great Lakes and the Congo.

In this very heart of Africa, Speke had found and Stanley had described the pagan kingdom of Uganda,[1] a rich and beautiful land inhabited by a sturdy negro race, living by settled agriculture, and organised as a community at a high level of political progress. Stanley had been much impressed by the worth of their king, M'tesa, whom he instructed in the rudiments of Christianity. Stanley's appeal in the *Daily Telegraph* (14 April 1875) led to the despatch in 1877 of a strong missionary body to Uganda, by the C.M.S. Two years later there arrived a French Catholic mission of the order known as the White Fathers. Both missions made some progress and each was patronised by a political faction. The two rival parties in Uganda during the next few years described themselves as *Fransa* and *Ingleza*. While bitterly opposed to one another theologically, the missionaries who inspired the two sects protested that they were not the agents of the French and British governments and were not responsible for the party dispute. Each mission in turn got the ear of the young King Mwanga who succeeded to M'tesa's throne in 1884.

Just then a third factor appeared. Karl Peters was annexing tribal territories right and left, to the south of Lake Victoria, with support from a German squadron at Zanzibar. Mwanga took fright and reacted against all three varieties of white interloper.

The C.M.S. missionaries innocently enough made great play with the news that an Anglican bishop had been consecrated for Central Africa, another great white chief. This was James

[1] The name Uganda is a corrupt Swahili form. Properly speaking the people are the Ba-ganda, the country is Bu-ganda, and their language is Lu-ganda. The Uganda Protectorate includes the more primitive kingdoms of Busoga and Bunyoro (1896) as well as the kingdom of Buganda.

Hannington (1847–85), an experienced missionary and traveller who had arrived at Zanzibar. Karl Peters' road to the south side of the lake was extremely unhealthy so that the Bishop decided, on the advice of Sir John Kirk, to approach his new diocese round the north shore, by way of the healthy Kenya highlands which had just been discovered by a traveller named Joseph Thomson (1883). This, to the King of Uganda, was the last straw; here was another invader from the north-east presumably coming to do what Karl Peters was doing from the south-east. He had refused to let Thomson pass that way and, when Hannington came, he sent soldiers who arrested the Bishop and killed him near the source of the Nile, October 1885. A reign of terror then prevailed. Many *Ingleza* converts were martyred in spite of efforts by the *Fransa* missionaries to save them. The blood of the martyrs was without doubt the seed of the Church in Uganda. The C.M.S. redoubled its efforts not only by sending another bishop but by influencing public opinion to undertake the civilisation of East Africa.

In June 1886 Lord Salisbury became Prime Minister, and for the next six years imperial expansion went apace. As his own Foreign Secretary, Salisbury conducted the negotiations with the other colonial powers. At the end of the year he drew up a convention with Germany, to which France[1] and the Sultan of Zanzibar adhered, dividing the mainland territories of the Sultan into a British and a German sphere of interest, the regions now known as Kenya and Tanganyika respectively. The German sphere was actively administered by the German East Africa Company, that is to say, by Karl Peters who lost no time in enforcing and extending his authority; the British sphere was undeveloped and the best part of it, the highlands, was almost uninhabited. (Sir) H. H. Johnston had approached a number of the chiefs in 1885 and urged Sir W. Mackinnon to form a British East Africa Company. Mackinnon now turned for further support to H. M. Stanley.

A message came through to Zanzibar in February 1886, from the Khedive's Governor of the Equatorial Province, to say that

---

[1] The price paid to France was a partial recognition of French rights in Madagascar. British traders and missionaries who had been active in the island for many years were thereafter excluded by the French. The dispute rankled until 1904. See also p. 795 for concessions to Germany in the Pacific.

he had escaped southward with a band of Sudanese troops from the Mahdi's tyranny, and needed help. He was one of Gordon's men, a German soldier named Edward Schnitzer, but usually known as Emin Pasha. Mackinnon persuaded Stanley to leave the Belgian service and to go in search of Emin, at the same time bringing the territories north of Lake Victoria into the British East African sphere. Stanley's last African journey (1887–9) from the Congo through unbroken stretches of rain-forest, inhabited by Pygmy peoples whom he first examined and described, led to the discovery of Lake Edward and Mount Ruwenzori and to the loss of two-thirds of his men. When he found Emin he could not bring him much relief, for his own resources were at an end, while Emin's men were in good heart and unwilling to be rescued. Emin refused to enter either the British or the Belgian service, naturally enough, since his own country was now in the field. He went back into the interior to work with Karl Peters in the interests of Germany, and was killed, some years later, by Arab slavers.

These large undertakings provided publicity. The sum of £240,000 was subscribed for the British East Africa Company which received a charter in September 1888, granting it rights over the British sphere. The Company was interested in three regions; the coastal strip through which all trade must pass, the empty but promising highlands, the rich but inaccessible kingdom of Uganda. Not much could be done with the highlands until the two other regions were well-ordered.

Sultan Barghash died in 1888 and with him ended the empire of Zanzibar. In the German sphere rebellion broke out against Karl Peters' oppression, whereupon Britain and Germany joined in blockading the coast against gun-runners. In 1889 the German government took over the administration. Next a civil war broke out in Uganda between Christians and Moslems. The B.E.A. Company raised a small force of troops under Captain F. Lugard and sent them up to Uganda to restore peace and prevent German encroachment. Lugard entrenched himself at Kampala, now the commercial capital of Uganda, and imposed order on the country, first stopping hostilities between Christians and Moslems, then between Catholics and Protestants.

The German problem was solved over the head of Lugard and Peters by the direct negotiation between London and Berlin of the celebrated 'Heligoland' Treaty, which was signed just after Bismarck's fall (July 1890) by Count von Caprivi. The frontier between the British and German spheres was finally adjusted and Zanzibar itself included in the British sphere. By a separate agreement the new Sultan accepted a British protectorate. In return for this concession England ceded to Germany the island of Heligoland.[1] Although there was rivalry between pioneers in Africa there was none, on this issue, between the British and German governments. The partition of East Africa was carried out in a spirit of friendship and co-operation—that is, among the diplomats. And Germany was the first power to recognise British rights in the Sudan.

Though Salisbury supported Lugard, his colleagues deplored the expense of garrisoning Uganda. Plans were being made to withdraw, until Lugard came home to arouse the missionary interest. When Gladstone returned to power for the last time, in 1892, Rosebery, his Foreign Secretary, was the only member of the cabinet who favoured African expansion. Harcourt, the Little Englander, spoke slightingly of 'militant bishops and hare-brained *militaires*' but Lugard the *militaire* persuaded the C.M.S. to pay the Company's expenses in Uganda for another year. It was said to be the plausible Rhodes who talked Gladstone round. Rosebery was authorised to send out Sir Gerald Portal who

---

[1] (*a*) The island of Heligoland formed part of the ancient Duchy of Holstein which has so often been the cause of dispute between Danish and German governments. In 1714 it was captured by the Danes and held by them until occupied by a British naval force in 1807. Having been valuable to the British Navy in the Napoleonic War as a centre of resistance against Napoleon's 'Continental System', the island was ceded to Great Britain in 1814 with a proviso that the inhabitants should retain their Danish laws. The population consisted of about 2000 Lutheran fisherfolk, speaking a Frisian dialect, and described as industrious and law-abiding. From 1814 to 1890 they were ruled, on the regular colonial principle, by a civil Lieutenant-Governor and an elective council of six members. There was neither a garrison nor any fortifications.

The cession of the island to Germany, though approved by Salisbury and Chamberlain, caused dissatisfaction among the exponents of sea-power. On the other hand the Germans, not yet interested in naval strategy, thought little of it at first. The island was valued as a holiday resort. In the two wars of 1914 and 1939, when it was strongly fortified, its uses were negative rather than positive, denying an area of sea to British approach. The works were destroyed by bombing in 1945 and the island was then left deserted.

(*b*) Another side-issue was the German insistence upon access to the Zambezi from S.W. Africa. They were granted the 'Caprivi Strip', a corridor twenty miles wide, which proved worthless.

solved the problem by declaring Uganda a British protectorate in 1893. Through all this turmoil the B.E.A. Company was spending money and making none. Its last chance of prosperity vanished when the British government imposed Free Trade on the coast, thus depriving the Company of its source of revenue. In 1894 the shareholders offered to surrender their charter and got harsh treatment from the Liberal government. Their rights were bought out for £250,000, leaving a deficit of £190,000 which they had spent on administration without thought of profit. In 1895 British East Africa (Kenya) was also placed under British protection. Zanzibar remained an autonomous sultanate advised by a British Resident. With the best harbour on the East African coast, the island grew richer by selling spices (120,000 tons of cloves in a year) than ever it was by selling slaves.

The B.E.A. Company had been unfortunate in having to deal with the Little Englanders. All was changed when Salisbury came back in 1895, and gave Chamberlain the Colonial Office. The neglected estate in East Africa was now to be developed. Work was at once begun on the Uganda Railway,[1] a metre-gauge line from Mombasa to Kisumu on Lake Victoria, a distance of 587 miles over a mountain escarpment 7000 feet high. The cost was £5,250,000, of which the capital and sinking fund were contributed by the British tax-payer without recompense. The line, completed in 1902, began to pay its running costs in 1906.

As Resident in Uganda, Sir H. H. Johnston reorganised the kingdom on the principle of indirect rule, making it the model African native state, though his land-settlement (1900) on the Indian pattern was adversely criticised. After the birth-pangs of Christianity, the martyrdoms and the religious wars, a mass-conversion of the whole nation took place under the influence of the C.M.S. missionaries, and Uganda is now a Christian country. The old quarrel between *Fransa* and *Ingleza* was healed through the good offices of the Pope who tactfully replaced the French missionaries by the English Mill Hill Order.

The development of Kenya was very different. In 1902 a land-company, the East Africa Syndicate, backed by the

---

[1] Perhaps the strangest episode in the history of railways is the war that was waged against the railway gangs by a pride of man-eating lions. (See *The Man-eaters of Tsavo*, by W. Paterson.)

Chartered Company of Rhodesia, was formed to settle the highlands with white emigrants whose history will be given in a later chapter.

Sir H. H. Johnston (1858–1927) whose name has already been mentioned as a pioneer of Kenya, was a man of enlarged views. A literary man and a scientist, he had already travelled widely in East and West Africa and had struck up a friendship with Cecil Rhodes, when he was appointed British consul at Mozambique in 1889, the year of the foundation of Rhodes's Chartered Company. Johnston was the propagator of the plan for a British axis through Africa from the Cape to Cairo, and was deeply involved in Rhodes's schemes for linking British South Africa, British East Africa and the British posts in Egypt by lines of telegraph and railway. The intrusion of Germany across the axis was a set-back, but was not irreparable since Germany was a friendly state. Rhodes was confident that he could 'square' the Kaiser and did so, getting permission to carry his telegraph-line through German East Africa.

The troublesome factor was Portugal, once an imperial state, and stirring again after centuries of slumber. Portugal had been 'annexing territory by the simple expedient of re-colouring the official maps' and now claimed a belt right across Africa from Angola to Mozambique, the whole Zambezi basin and all the country that Livingstone had explored.

Johnston took steps, as soon as he was appointed, to reassert British rights over the Shiré highlands, where Livingstone had planted the Universities' mission a generation earlier. Since 1876 there had been permanent British occupation by a Scottish mission at Blantyre, which made Nyasaland one of the predominantly Scottish regions of the Empire. In 1878 two brothers named Moir, working in close sympathy with the missionaries, founded the African Lakes Corporation, a trading company. Seven years later one of their directors, James Stevenson, made a road northward from Lake Nyasa and brought a steamer overland to Lake Tanganyika. Lugard's first African campaign (1889) was fought against Nyasa slavers on behalf of this enterprising and beneficent Corporation. Johnston declared a protectorate over Blantyre in 1889, whereupon a furious dispute arose with Portugal. The London press, notably *Punch*, treated

Portuguese claims with derision, since Portugal was on the brink of a republican revolution which, it was thought, would mean the disruption of her empire. At Lisbon corps of students volunteered to fight for their colonial territories against the grasping British. The Pioneers who entered Rhodesia in 1890 were half inclined to force the issue by seizing the coast, and some filibustering[1] actually put them in possession of what is now the Umtali district of Rhodesia. Johnston took exception to this swashbuckling procedure; severing his connexion with Rhodes, he worked for a diplomatic settlement with Portugal. During the negotiations, representatives of the Chartered Company took possession of the country northward as far as the frontier of the Belgian Congo. The treaty between Rhodes and Lewanika, the very intelligent king of the Barotse peoples, gave the Company control of the country to the north of the Upper Zambezi; and Livingstone's discoveries were thus denied to the Portuguese. The Anglo-Portuguese treaty of 1891 divided the whole area with the frontiers that still remain. After the clamour had died down the Portuguese found themselves in possession of as much territory as they could develop and have remained on excellent terms with the British in Africa. This settlement, with the Anglo-German Agreement of 1890, concluded the partition of the south and east of Africa.

A general belief that the Portuguese Empire would collapse led Chamberlain to inspire a secret and hypothetical treaty with Germany in 1898 for partitioning the Portuguese colonies in the event of Portugal disposing of them. There was no intention of forcing the issue, as was made clear to Germany by the ostentatious renewal of the ancient Anglo-Portuguese Treaty of Windsor in the same year.

Several sharp campaigns were fought around Lake Nyasa before slave-raiding was finally suppressed in 1895. The first administrator of the Protectorate (then known as British Central Africa and, after 1907, as Nyasaland) was Johnston himself. The African Lakes Corporation was bought out by the British South Africa Company (1893). Modern Nyasaland has an uneventful history. Until the cultivation of tobacco and tea were introduced early in this century, there was no staple for export. Commercial

---

[1] An early story of Kipling's, *Judson and the Empire* (*Many Inventions*), describes one of these episodes in the manner of the period.

progress was slow until the railway bridge over the Lower Zambezi made a new outlet for trade through Portuguese territory in 1937.

In 1895 the Chartered Company took over the administration of Rhodesia north of the Zambezi, founding two towns, Abercorn and Fife (1897), on the Stevenson Road between the Lakes. By 1899 the telegraph-line was through from the south to Lake Tanganyika. Sir Alfred Sharpe's journeys through this country had drawn attention somewhat away from the fanciful Cape-to-Cairo scheme towards the real mineral wealth of the Katanga district, east of Nyasaland. Before the emissaries of the Chartered Company arrived, a British officer in the Belgian service annexed the best part of it to the Congo State (1890). When copper, lead, and zinc were found at Broken Hill on the Rhodesian side of the frontier it was decided to push the railway northwards from Rhodesia to the Belgian border. In 1904 it reached the Victoria Falls, which were bridged in 1905; and in 1909 it was linked with the Belgian railway system.

3. BRITISH SOMALILAND: THE ITALIANS

THE origin of British Somaliland may be traced to the interest shown by the East India Company in the Arabian Sea. After the annexation of Aden the Company entered into treaties with two sultans across the Gulf in the Horn of Africa, paying them subsidies and controlling their external relations (1840). Little was known of the interior of this region until Richard Burton made his adventurous journey to Harrar in 1854. Twelve years later the British campaign in Abyssinia was planned to begin with a landing on this desolate shore where the influence of British India was not unknown.

At the climax of his career Khedive Ismail exercised some shadowy authority over all the southern coast of the Red Sea, but Egyptian authority vanished when Osman Digna declared for the Mahdi in 1883. French and Italian empire-builders had also coveted this land of rock and sand and scrub and now saw their opportunity. Centuries before the union of Italy the Popes had maintained some slender links with the Abyssinian Church so that Italian agents were never quite unknown in the

Red Sea ports. England forestalled Italy by occupying Socotra in 1875, as she had forestalled France by occupying Perim in 1857; in the Red Sea, Italian designs on the ports that led to Abyssinia were forestalled by France.

In 1883 the French began to develop the port of Jibuti, thus controlling the route by which eventually (1915) a railway was built into Abyssinia. Again the Italians had to be content with second best. They occupied Assab and Massawa, which, at great expense, they painfully made into the colony of Eritrea. Great Britain approved the Italian action and was willing to come to terms with France. A further series of treaties was negotiated with six Somali chiefs by the government of India, and an agreement was made with France in 1887 defining the limits of British and French Somaliland. In 1889, again with British approval, the Italians occupied the outer coast of Somaliland facing the Arabian Sea, empty country which tempted no other imperial power. Their intention was to establish a protectorate over Abyssinia which then would have access both to Italian Eritrea and Italian Somaliland, an intention which was dismally nullified when the Abyssinians routed an Italian army at Adowa (1896). Italian empire-building was resumed more patiently in 1900 when the Sultan of Zanzibar sold to Italy, with British consent, a strip of coast including the ancient port of Mogadishu. It was a very different matter when, twenty-four years later, Ramsay MacDonald ceded Jubaland, a further strip of the coast, to Mussolini as a delayed bribe for Italian participation in the war of 1914, without consulting the government of Kenya or the Sultan of Zanzibar.

Of the three sectors of Somaliland, the British was the least valuable, having neither the strategic value of the Italian nor the commercial value of the French sector. Its people are largely nomadic and there is no staple of commerce. There are no railways and the total value of exports in 1938 was no more than £207,000. In 1898 the administration of the protectorate was transferred from the India Office to the Foreign Office, and in 1907 to the Colonial Office.

The colony retains unchanged the Islamic culture of the eighth century and the events of its political history are survivals from that era. A Holy War was waged with considerable success against the British unbelievers by Mohammed bin Abdulla Hassan (1865–

1921), whom they oddly called the 'Mad Mullah'. There was method in every phase of his madness.

The Mullah declared his *jehad* in 1901 and won his first victory in 1903 over a small force of British and Afrikaner mounted infantry sent against him as soon as they were released from the South African War. It was necessary to send a strong punitive expedition which succeeded in driving him into Italian territory. A peace was arranged in 1905 by Italian mediation. Three years later he took the field again, robbing, mutilating and murdering tribesmen who favoured the British. The Liberals, then in power, shrank from the expense of defending this profitless wilderness and ordered a withdrawal to the coast. The inland tribes were equipped and encouraged to defend themselves. But the Mullah pressed home his advantage and defeated the irregular camel corps in 1913, killing their British commander. Again it became necessary to drive him back with a strong military expedition. During the first World War, when no troops were available, the Mullah overran and oppressed the country. Only in 1920 could sufficient troops be found to inflict a crushing defeat on him; the force comprised a brigade of Indian and African troops (King's African Rifles) and a camel corps, with naval and air support. The Mullah fled to Abyssinia and died there in 1921.[1]

4. THE FRENCH IN AFRICA

THE lion's share in the north-western half of Africa fell to the French during the 'eighties and 'nineties. Since the French imperialists made a systematic advance, against which the British in West Africa spasmodically reacted, it will be convenient to discuss the partition of West Africa from the French point of view.

Their oldest colony is Senegal, which has been in French hands since 1637, if we except some short periods when it was occupied by English or Dutch fleets in the old wars. Goree, near Cape Verde, was added to the colony of Senegal in 1677. So pre-

[1] During the second World War, in June 1940, a powerful Italian force from Abyssinia defeated the small British garrison and occupied the Protectorate, the only military victory won by the Italian Armies in their war against the British in Africa. British Somaliland was liberated without much difficulty, in March 1941, as soon as a British force could be mustered.

eminent is this among French possessions that the natives of the original settlement enjoy civic rights which no other French colonials enjoy without special qualification. The name *séné-galais* is commonly used in France for all kinds of African troops. As elsewhere in Africa the European settlements were confined to the coast and estuaries until the nineteenth century. It was only in 1827 that the French explorer Caillié reached Timbuktu, a year after the first British visit.

In 1854 General Faidherbe was sent to govern Senegal as a mark of political disfavour. He employed his exile in conquering the hinterland eastward and southward from the Senegal river as far as the British posts on the Gambia. From his time dates the conception of a French continental empire in Africa. He founded Dakar, a great modern seaport, contrasting strangely with the squalid British settlements. In 1882 the French advance reached the western frontier of Sierra Leone and, in the following year, General Gallieni, who thirty years later defended Paris from the Germans, was established at Bamako on the Upper Niger. All this region became the colony of French Guinea with a seaport, second in importance only to Dakar, at Konakry. Having encircled and compressed the British posts on the Gambia, the French penetrated the hinterland of Sierra Leone and Liberia. When British and French patrols accidentally exchanged shots, each supposing the other to be a party of slave-raiders, it was time to delimit the frontier of Sierra Leone also (1895). During the 'nineties the expeditions of Colonel Louis Binger into the 'Niger Bend' and towards the Ivory Coast extended the French zone to the sea on either side of the British Gold Coast. Conquering the barbarous kingdom of Dahomey in 1893, the French drove a wedge between the Gold Coast and Lagos.

The conquest of Algeria had been begun in 1830 when Charles X attempted to prop his falling kingdom by a foreign adventure. Having easily overthrown the Dey of Algiers, the French were confronted, after an interval of tranquillity, with a national rising under Abd-el-Kader, who maintained the war of independence until 1847. Under the Second Republic, when pacification at last seemed complete, Algeria was organised into three departments and incorporated into the French metropolitan state, a policy which, though reversed under the Empire, was resumed under the Third Republic and still prevails. The franchise has, however, been restricted to those Algerians, never very numerous, who qualify as French citizens. Strenuous attempts were made to encourage emigration from France and from the other Latin countries, until the European element amounted in 1936 to 987,000 out of a total population of 7,000,000. The garrison was strengthened by the celebrated Foreign Legion.

Another point of entry into Africa was the Congo delta where French philanthropists founded Libreville as a settlement for liberated slaves (1849). After journeys through the rain-forests of the Congo, Paul du Chaillu published in 1861 a true account of the gorillas and the Pygmy tribes, about which the world had previously been incredulous. From this direction de Brazza's journeys in the early 'eighties led the French into Central Africa.

The extension of French Algeria southwards until it was contiguous with Senegal, and beyond to the Ivory Coast, the Congo and Lake Chad, led to the emergence of a truly grand conception, *La France d'Outremer*, in which half the continent of Africa was to be absorbed, under a single centralised administration. All the inhabitants were to be advanced by progressive stages, without distinction of race or colour, to the full enjoyment of the same civic rights as other Frenchmen. French was to be the language of the whole organism, a French Union rather than a French Empire; and all citizens, black or white, would serve as conscripts in the French Army. The long process of imposing French civilisation was regarded as one of education, upon the principle, attributed to General Gallieni, *instruire la masse et dégager l'élite*. This was the very opposite of the British principle of indirect rule, and it has had some remarkable successes, notably in the towns. In French Africa the public works are, in general, conceived on a grander scale than in British Africa and the towns are more imposing. Uniformity of administration brings financial advantages which are evident to any visitor. Furthermore, colour prejudice has been overcome to such a degree that a West Indian negro (Félix Eboué, *premier résistant de la France*) has served as a notably successful Governor of the Equatorial Province. It remains to be seen, however, whether the attempt to convert the African *élite* into Frenchmen can succeed in this stormy century.

La France d'Outremer was organised on strictly protectionist principles. As Lord Salisbury bitterly wrote: 'Wherever Great Britain has undertaken the task of developing and civilising the interior, French trade profits equally with that of Great Britain; but the tendency of French arrangements is to obtain exclusive privileges for French commerce.'

The climax of French imperialism came in the years 1879–85 when Jules Ferry, a secularist and radical, played a part in French politics not unlike that played by Joseph Chamberlain in England. He established French power in Tunis, Annam, Madagascar and on the Niger.

It may be mentioned that Georges Clemenceau was the leader of a group comparable with the Little Englanders. He summed up the process of Imperialism as 'first the missionary, then the soldier, then the financier'. The pioneers of *La France d'Outremer* have not in general shared the anti-clerical views of the politicians in Paris. No sketch of French Africa would be complete without mention of the *Société des Missionnaires de Notre Dame d'Afrique*, commonly known as the White Fathers. The first house of their order was founded by Cardinal C. M. A. Lavigerie at Algiers in 1871. In 1879 their missions had reached Uganda, in 1891 Rhodesia. As in Canada 200 years earlier their rivalry with the English Protestant missionaries could not wholly be deprived of a political flavour.

Lavigerie preached through Europe a crusade against the slave trade, which was accepted as the common policy of all the powers at the conference convened by Lord Salisbury at Brussels in 1889. The sixteen signatories of the Berlin Act, at the instance of the British representative Sir John Kirk, agreed upon concerted measures (1890) to suppress the trade in slaves, arms and liquor throughout tropical Africa. The French and British wars of the 'nineties against the Arab slave-empires in the Sudan, about Lake Chad, and on the Niger, resulting in the final partition of Central Africa, were justified by the Brussels Agreement.

The French protectorates over Tunis and Morocco have a history of another sort. As in Egypt, so in Tunis, the form of the conquest was a military occupation after a financial and social breakdown. The French occupied Tunis in 1881, before the British occupation of Egypt, to put an end to disorders, and, like the British Army in Egypt, the French Army remained in Tunis for over sixty years. In 1898 Tunis was converted into a French protectorate which has been remarkably prosperous. By the Entente Cordiale agreement Great Britain recognised that the French sphere of influence was to include Morocco, excepting Tangier and the Spanish zone. German diplomacy, which had come badly out of the scramble for Africa, was for some years directed to fomenting trouble with France in Morocco. But the country itself was a pawn in the diplomatic game and was abandoned by Germany, when it had served its purposes in the crises of 1906 and 1911. Meanwhile a civil war in 1908 had led to French intervention and to the establishment of a French protectorate, which was organised by the greatest of French pro-consuls, the gallant and cultivated Marshal Lyautey.

Throughout this long process of expansion there was inevitable friction at many points between French and British pioneers in Africa, as between French and British diplomats in Europe. After the Berlin Conference the principal stages in Anglo-French negotiation were: the provisional agreement of 1890 on Central African zones of influence; the agreement of 1898 precisely delimiting these zones; the acceptance of British status in the Sudan in 1899, after the Fashoda incident; and the world-wide settlement of outstanding differences at the Entente Cordiale of 1904. These successive instruments by which Central Africa was finally partitioned will be further considered in a later chapter.

5. BRITISH IMPERIALISM IN WEST AFRICA

THE French penetration of West Africa from the Senegal River had brought about a series of frontier negotiations. The British Gambia Protectorate was delimited in 1889, the Sierra Leone Protectorate in 1895. In the latter instance the two powers had agreed to make their frontier the watershed between the Niger basin and the coastal region, with the result that the British had been obliged to advance from Sierra Leone taking over the administration (1895) of inland tribes who had little in common with the Westernised negro settlers of the old colony. Farther to the east, the status of the Ashanti peoples, as the French frontier closed in around them, forced a new crisis. Since Wolseley's war there had been anarchy at Kumasi. After long dissension a new

King, Prempeh, had been enthroned upon the Golden Stool with appropriate bloodshed, but not to the satisfaction of the British. He had not paid the indemnity imposed by Wolseley, and he had not suppressed the barbarous 'customs'. When human sacrifices were offered on a horrific scale in 1894, pressure was again brought upon him to fulfil his treaty obligations, and again the Little Englanders protested against this interference with sovereign rights.

This was one of the points at which Chamberlain imposed his authority when he came to the Colonial Office. 'Prempeh is a barbarous chief', he said, 'who has permitted human sacrifices,

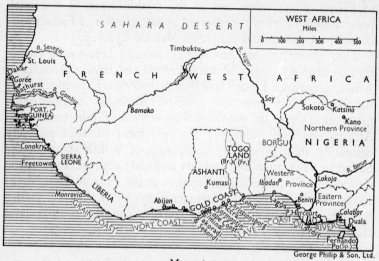

Map 36

attacked friendly chiefs and broken a treaty. The only proof he has ever given of civilisation is that he has engaged a London solicitor to advocate his interests.' It was necessary to establish a protectorate here also, and to do it before the French from the north or the Germans from Togoland should forestall us. Prempeh was deposed and a protectorate established after a bloodless expedition to Kumari in 1896.

In 1900 Governor Hodgson of the Gold Coast made an imprudent attempt to seize that famous fetish, the Golden Stool of Kumasi, in evidence of sovereignty, as Edward I had seized the Stone of Scone. The Ashanti rose in rebellion, besieging him and his bodyguard at Kumasi. Though he fought his way out, a little war was required to restore order. Ashanti was then annexed to the Colony (1901). Meanwhile the Stool had vanished. It was found in 1921 and was restored to the Ashantis as the palladium of their nation. The tribal guardians who had been charged with hiding it away had stripped it of its golden ornaments for their own profit. According to the principle of indirect rule they were tried and punished by tribal law.

Another war to suppress barbarous customs occurred in the Oil Rivers Protectorate in 1897. Benin city had long been execrated as the scene of frequent human sacrifices which the officials of the protectorate proposed to terminate. J. B. Phillips, the consul at Benin, attempted to interfere and was himself murdered in 1897. A naval landing-party made its way to the city without meeting serious opposition and found the place of sacrifice reeking with blood (February 1897). Benin was brought under indirect British administration through a council of chiefs. The offending king was exiled to Calabar but, in 1914, his heir was permitted to succeed to the throne of Benin. The celebrated Benin sculptures in brass and wood were at first regarded with disgust as the symbols of a disgusting cult and only later attracted the admiration of art critics.

British trade and influence on the lower reaches of the Niger were much advanced by George Taubman Goldie, a young soldier who went out to the Coast in 1877 to look into some family investments. He remained to organise a moribund trading company which, after several amalgamations, he reformed (1879) as the National Africa Company. It was Goldie's chief success to buy out the two principal French rivals and thus to justify the claims put forward in 1884–5 at the Berlin Conference.

On 10 July 1886 Goldie obtained a charter for his company which, until 1899, was known as the Royal Niger Company. The Directors were empowered to exercise jurisdiction over lands previously acquired by treaty from native chiefs and to levy customs duties, on condition of doing all in their power to suppress the slave trade. The Company was forbidden to create a monopoly. Commerce chiefly took the form of exporting palm-oil and kernels from the lower reaches of the river, but Goldie, whose headquarters were far up-river at Lokoja, had already entered into treaties with emirs in the dry uplands which produced hides and cotton. Over this country, too, he was given authority by a somewhat vague extension of the protectorate (1887) to 'all territories in the basin of the Niger and its affluents which are or may be subject to the government. . . of the Royal Niger Company'. Negotiations with the French were now inevitable. An agreement was signed in 1890 defining the French sphere of influence as all the Sahara region 'southward to a line from Say on the Niger to Baruwa on Lake Chad'. So far Goldie had the best of it. The great emirates of Sokoto and Kano fell within the British sphere while the French territory was sardonically described by Salisbury as having 'a very light soil'.

The great prize, Timbuktu, fell into French hands in 1893 after a *coup de main* by a young officer with nineteen men who were relieved and supported by Colonel Joffre (another name of power in 1914). The French then moved rapidly down the south bank of the Niger into the kingdom of Borgu, inland from their new province of Dahomey. Lugard, who had been brought over from East Africa by Goldie, forestalled the French by a rapid march, 'the race to Nikki', 1894, and won most of Borgu for the Company. Having gone so far the imperialists could not stop; they were obliged to fight the Emir of Nupé who made a habit of raiding across the river into Borgu. Goldie defeated him in 1897 and so began the subjugation of the Fula and Hausa kingdoms in the north. When he brought Nupé into submission to the Company, Goldie instantly abolished slavery throughout the Company's territories.

But the prospect of serious fighting against these warlike sultans persuaded Chamberlain that the Crown should take over Nigeria from the Company. He raised an imperial corps, the West African Frontier Force (1897), and placed it under Lugard's command, not only to subdue the sultans but to discourage the French from encroachment over the 1890 line. The Company had done well and had even paid its way. Nevertheless there were complaints that it had engrossed the Niger trade so thoroughly as to make a virtual monopoly which was forbidden by the charter and by the Berlin Act. The Liverpool merchants, interested in the Coast for generations, were loud in its condemnation. Accordingly the Crown took over the Nigeria Protectorate on 1 January 1900, buying out the political rights of the Company for £865,000 in cash and a concession for mineral rights.

While the Company was again being reorganised, the Foreign Office came to terms with France. By a general agreement (1898) the whole Anglo-French frontier in Africa from Lake Chad to Senegal was delimited, on the map, with some variations from the provisional line drawn in the agreement of 1890. Even then much of the country was inaccessible and the new frontier was not traced on the ground until 1904.

Goldie, the maker of Nigeria, withdrew unnoticed from the scene. Perhaps piqued at being thrust aside, he took no great part in public life, though he lived for another five and twenty years. Few lives have been more adventurous and strange than that of George Taubman Goldie (1846-1925). Extremely tall and thin, with a hawk-nose, a piercing eye, and a wizened complexion, he was known to his friends in later years as Rameses or the 'Mummy'. He was impatient, voluble and pugnacious, a man of unpredictable dislikes, endowed with genius rather than talent. Such was his horror of publicity that he destroyed his papers and forbade his heirs to authorise a biography, with the result that the history of the Niger Company is obscure. From the day when he walked out of the Army 'without troubling to send in his papers' he had taken his own line. He left England, he said, 'to escape from the sound of church bells'. He travelled widely and, by his own account, spent three years with the Bedouin for love of an Arab maid. Goldie was no sycophant: when summoned before the cabinet to be told that he could not have a charter for one of his earlier companies he stalked out and slammed the door. Then, he recounted with gusto, when they changed their minds, what should Gladstone do but take the charter away in his greatcoat pocket and leave the greatcoat in a railway carriage.

Such a man might hardly seem worth taking quite *au sérieux*, but never was there a sterner idealist. Having private means, he declined to take a penny of profit from the companies he directed. The suppression of the slave trade was his vocation and, after that, the suppression of the African liquor trade. Only by fighting the emirs could freedom be restored to their eighteen millions of subjects, and he was willing—and delighted—to fight for this freedom in Hausaland, or to work for it in his office on Ludgate Hill for sixteen hours a day. Goldie, the capitalist, abolished slavery throughout an area three times the size of Great Britain.

If the first half of the story of Nigeria can be told around the life of Sir George Goldie, the free-lance, the second half can be told around the life of his lieutenant, Lugard, a great public servant.

Sir Frederick, later Lord Lugard (1858–1945) was a man of unbounded energy, quick to take responsibility, and imbued with a high sense of duty to humanity. In him the conception of the White Man's Burden reached its purest form. He was bred a soldier and served with distinction in Afghanistan, Egypt and Burma. When the Empire was at peace in 1888 he set out for Africa to do something 'if possible in the suppression of the slave-trade'. After offering his services in vain to the Italians, he found his way to Lake Nyasa where he fought an arduous campaign against Arab slavers. His work caught the attention of Mac-kinnon who employed him to take over Uganda after the Anglo-German agreement of 1890 (see chapter xv, 2, page 813). Next Goldie summoned him to the Niger to implement the Anglo-French agreement. In West as in East Africa the speed of his movements was decisive. After a journey through the Kalahari Desert on behalf of Cecil Rhodes he was recalled to Nigeria to command the West African Frontier Force. When the Crown took charge in 1900 Lugard was the first Commissioner of the northern territories, which were associated with the British only by treaties of a general nature. It was his task to pacify the Hausa and Fulani emirates with their lordly Saracen aristocracies, their great walled cities, and their devotion to Mohammedanism in its most reactionary form. After three years of tactful effort he resolved, without consulting Whitehall, to compel the re-calcitrant emirs of Kano and Sokoto to fulfil their obligations. In a few weeks' campaign, early in 1903, he took those cities by assault in spite of their crenellated walls, and their martial defenders who far outnumbered his own men.

The French had completed the subjugation of their sphere two years earlier by a converging campaign against the slaver Rabeh. Its hero was Colonel Lamy who was killed (1902) in a victory won south of Lake Chad, at the city now called Fort Lamy. This, with Lugard's victory, completed the long wars against the Arab slave trade in Central Africa.

Lugard administered the northern emirates by indirect rule of which he became the classic exponent. The emirs and their courts continued to reign and rule according to Islamic law, but under the supervision of British Residents who were quickly linked with one another by telegraph. The slave trade and the liquor trade were suppressed. In later life Lugard published a book on *The Dual Mandate in Tropical Africa* (1922), the harvest of his forty years of experience. The doctrine he taught was that 'Europe is in Africa for the mutual benefit for her own industrial classes and of the native races in their progress to a higher plane, that the benefit can be made reciprocal, and that it is the aim and desire of civilised administration to fulfil this dual mandate'. After a spell as Governor of Hong Kong (1907–12), where he founded the University, he returned to Nigeria as Governor of both the Northern and the Southern Provinces.[1]

With his immense experience and industry, Lugard was able to bring about the union of all the territories about the lower and middle Niger, constituting them into the great artificial unit of Nigeria (1 January 1914).[2] The new state had a single centralised administration, though subdivided for some purposes into the 'colony'—that is the coastal region—the Southern, and the Northern Provinces of the Protectorate. The whole area is three times the size of Great Britain, 330,000 square miles, with a population of 20,000,000 showing every diversity of culture from primitive savagery to civilisation on the western model. There are not more than 5000 or 6000 whites in Nigeria. Indirect rule was retained in the Northern Provinces and partially introduced into the Southern Provinces, while the colony received a normal constitution with an elective element in its Legislative Council. Both the union and the principle of indirect rule have been adversely criticised, of late years, by the educated natives of the Colony (see chapter XIX, 1, page 977). Thirty years ago they were the means of producing a rapid increase in prosperity by

---

[1] The life of Lugard is not adequately told without mention of Miss Flora Shaw (1852–1929), whom he married in 1902. One of the great emancipators of her sex from the trammels of enforced domesticity, she became chief adviser to *The Times* on colonial affairs. In later life she was a worthy partner in her husband's public work. Earlier she had interviewed Zebehr Pasha in Egypt, assisted Sir John Kirk at the Brussels Conference, and been an expert witness of the Klondyke gold-rush and the Queensland kanaka trade. Her evidence was decisive at the Parliamentary enquiry into the Jameson Raid.

[2] The capital was established at Lagos. Though not geographically the outlet of the Niger region, it had been placed under the same administration as the Oil Rivers Protectorate in 1886. Its natural hinterland, Dahomey, had fallen into French hands.

linking the produce of the interior with the commerce of the coast. The total external trade of Nigeria was £5,000,000 in 1909, £12,000,000 in 1914, and £38,000,000 in 1937.

The Anglo-French Agreement of 1898 was no sooner signed than the world was astonished at the news of a French military mission at Fashoda (July 1898). Simultaneously with the advance from Senegal to Dahomey and the middle Niger, other French pioneers had struck northward from the Congo, reaching the southern shore of Lake Chad by way of the Shari River about 1891. A secret expedition under Major J. B. Marchand was despatched in 1894 by steamboat up the Congo. Following one of its northern tributaries, the Djur, they crossed the portage to a western tributary of the Nile, emerging four years later at Fashoda (see chapter XIII, 8, page 755). This journey was inspired by the anglophobe statesman Gabriel Hanotaux, whose colossal scheme was to drive an axis through Africa from west to east, from Senegal to Somaliland, thus breaking the British axis from the Cape to Cairo. Abyssinia was Marchand's objective and, when obliged to withdraw from Fashoda, he continued his journey eastward to Jibuti on the Red Sea. It did not fall to Hanotaux but to Delcassé to cope with the resulting crisis. He was unwilling to lose the benefit of the recent agreement which had given France so much. Ignoring the clamour of the yellow press, Delcassé and Salisbury made a new adjustment after Marchand's withdrawal. In March 1899 it was agreed that the watershed between the Nile and the Congo should separate the French and British zones of influence. The partition of Africa was then complete but for the survival of indigenous kingdoms in Morocco and Abyssinia, and for the republic of Liberia.

6. THE PARTITION OF AFRICA:
CONCLUSION

THE opening of Africa had taken about sixty years from the discovery of the Niger Basin (1826–32) to Stanley's last journey (1887), and not often has any prolonged exertion been inspired by purer motives. The desire for knowledge, evangelical fervour, a sincere belief in the virtues of Western civilisation, all pointed the same way. Explorers, missionaries and traders co-operated in what altruists described as a single beneficent task, the regeneration of Africa. The obvious fact that there were black sheep in the flock of pioneers did not detract from the value of the general advance. To modern readers of the literature of African travel, a striking feature is the universal horror of the Arab slave trade. All honest men agreed that it was the shame of the age, to be suppressed by the general effort and by every means. Slowly it became clear that political intervention, that is to say the partition of Africa among the civilised powers, was the sole way of accomplishing what all desired. Thus the European governments, which in the 'sixties and 'seventies were all unwilling to extend their commitments in Africa, vied with one another in the 'eighties and 'nineties in staking out claims. If Africa was to be partitioned, it was natural that each power would seek a profitable share.

The partition was accomplished in about twenty years (1879–99). It has been customary among recent historians to denounce this series of events as a disgraceful episode in history. If ever any historical sequence was inevitable—economically determined—it was this. In the age of steam-power, cheap manufactures, rising population, surplus capital and liberal philanthropy, nothing could have prevented these various forces from impinging upon Africa; the question was whether the impact should be orderly or disorderly. According to the Marxian myth the financiers, seeking an outlet for surplus capital, were the 'governors of the engine' which advanced through Africa. But it is difficult to trace their direct influence upon the expenditure in blood and treasure which the French lavished in the Sahara Desert, or upon Bismarck's tortuous diplomacy, or upon the creation of the South

African protectorates. It would of course be absurd to deny that speculative finance played a dominant part in the making of

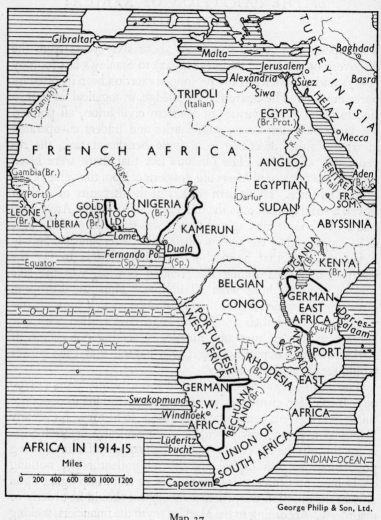

Gibraltar

Malta

Baghdad

Jerusalem

Basra

Alexandria

Suez

Siwa

TRIPOLI
(Italian)

EGYPT
(Br. Prot.)

Mecca

FRENCH AFRICA

ANGLO-
EGYPTIAN
SUDAN

Gambia (Br.)

Darfur

ERITREA (Ital.)

Aden
(Br.)

FR.
SOM.

(Port.)

S.
LEONE
(Br.)

GOLD
COAST
(Br.)

LIBERIA

TOGO
LD

NIGERIA
(Br.)

Lome

KAMERUN

ABYSSINIA

Fernando Po
(Sp.)

Duala

(Sp.)

Equator

KENYA
(Br.)

UGANDA (Br.)

S-O-U-T-H   A-T-L-A-N-T-I-C

O-C-E-A-N

BELGIAN
CONGO

PORTUGUESE WEST AFRICA

GERMAN
EAST
AFRICA

Dar-es-
Salaam

Rufiji

NYASALAND (Br.)

PORT.
EAST

RHODESIA
(Br.)

AFRICA

GERMAN

Swakopmund

S.W.

Windhoek

AFRICA

BECHUANA LAND (Br.)

Lüderitz-
bucht

UNION OF
SOUTH AFRICA

INDIAN-OCEAN

AFRICA IN 1914-15
Miles

0   200 400 600 800 1000 1200

Capetown

George Philip & Son, Ltd.

Map 37

Rhodesia and the Congo State, but it is a jaundiced view that cannot see what Rhodesia also owes to the ideals of Livingstone, what the Congo owes to those later Belgian administrators who have righted the wrong done by King Leopold.

On the whole, granted that it had to take place, the partition of Africa is rather above than below the average of international conduct. Far more blood was shed and far greater barbarities committed in the partition of America, which exterminated the aboriginals through vast regions, and caused generations of world war. After the Berlin Act there was much finessing among diplomats and much encroaching among pioneers, as they scuffled for advantages here and there, but there was neither war between the powers nor general massacre of the natives.

During fifty years Black Africa has enjoyed a higher degree of tranquillity, a more sustained advance in health and wealth, than ever before in her history. Though still ignorant and poor and sometimes downtrodden, the Africans have seen a new light and have begun to grope their way towards it, for better or worse. The two World Wars have done infinitely less harm in Africa than in Europe or in Asia. No longer the Dark Continent, Africa is now coming into the daylight. She has not been able to avoid the economic diseases of our age but in the heart of the continent, between the Limpopo River and the Sahara Desert, the Africans, whether under British, French or Belgian rule, have been lucky, as luck is estimated in the twentieth century.

XVI

DOMINION STATUS: THE FIRST WORLD WAR

Argument: A new constructive policy for the Colonial Dependencies was inaugurated by Joseph Chamberlain. His intention of federating the Empire by tariff reform was frustrated by British devotion to Free Trade and by emergent nationality in the Dominions. The Commonwealth evolved as a moral union not a *Zollverein*, while a new school of philosophers denounced the Colonial Empire as an instrument of exploitation. When urged to participate in defence the Dominions preferred to do so by founding armed forces under their own control. Yet on the outbreak of war all placed their resources at the disposal of the Crown.

Canadian forces fought exclusively on the Western Front. Australian and New Zealand forces, after taking part in the naval war in the Pacific, operated against Turkey and later on the Western Front. South African forces undertook as their main task two arduous campaigns in Africa. The Indian Army fought chiefly in the Middle East, a historic sphere of Indian influence. All the Dominions strengthened their economies by developing war industries, partly financed from their own resources.

Emerging from the War as mature nations the Dominions were separately represented at the Peace Conference. Their indirect influence was considerable in the regional pact made with Turkey at Lausanne; they took a direct part in the regional pact made for the Pacific at Washington.

1. CHAMBERLAIN'S IMPERIAL POLICY

JOE CHAMBERLAIN, the Birmingham Radical, is something of an enigma in English political history. His views were so extreme and his expressions so truculent that those who met him were surprised at his urbanity. He was a well-read, well-groomed man of the world, a dandy with an orchid and a monocle which did not seem to match his politics. A secularist and a democrat, he opposed the privilege of the Lords and (in his younger days) was more than half a republican. Though he succumbed, like all his contemporaries, to the prestige of the Great White Queen, he boldly resisted court influence and scrutinised royal expenditure with jealous economy. Having made his pile by twenty years' hard work he entered public life at forty as a rich man, the idol of his fellow-townsmen for whom he had carried out a series of municipal reforms. What he had done for Birmingham he now proposed to do for England, and later for the Empire. He was modern and smart, as hard and penetrating as one of his own steel screws. Pacifists called him a jingo; Tories called him a Socialist or worse; the mean-minded insinuated that he cared for nothing but 'the nail and sarspan business as 'e got 'is money by'. All these opinions were wide of the mark. He was a Social-Democrat, differing only in stature—for he was the greatest of them—from many of his contemporaries in colonial politics. Chamberlain's 'unauthorised programme', the culmination of his radical endeavours, which split the Liberal Party in 1885, would have seemed reasonable enough at the Cape or in Canada and a commonplace programme in Australasia. Had he been Lord Mayor of Melbourne instead of Birmingham his progress from municipal to national politics would have been triumphant. Disestablishment, secular education, licensing reform, municipal ownership of utilities, graduated income-tax, 'unlocking the land', manhood suffrage, with a glance forward towards old-age pensions and tariff reform: all these were practical politics in Victoria, Queensland, South Australia, and New Zealand. Nor would colonial statesmen have flinched from the hard knocks which Chamberlain was ready to give or take in the Party struggle.

Merriman of South Africa revealed to those who cared to take notice, in 1884, that Chamberlain, was a potential champion for the colonies. He alone among British politicians of the day was man enough to sweep the cobwebs from the Colonial Office. Until that time he had shown but slight interest in the Empire, and his official biographer has revealed little of the process of conversion. He was remembered as a bitter opponent of the annexation of the Transvaal in 1877, as a keen defender of its retrocession to the Boers both before and after Majuba. 'What is the use of being a great and powerful nation', he had said, 'if you cannot admit your error when you are conscious of it!' He had opposed Disraeli's 'spirited foreign policy', and had deplored the annexation of Cyprus. He justified the occupation of Egypt solely in order that we might establish Egyptian self-government and denounced the very suggestion that we ought to protect the interest of the foreign bond-holders. He showed much sympathy with the Mahdi and a great measure of distrust for Gordon.

But these were not his responsibilities as President of the Board of Trade in Gladstone's second administration (1880–5). His first direct action on an imperial issue was his proposal to the cabinet in 1884 that we should occupy Bechuanaland, not from any desire to enlarge British possessions but at the instance of his nonconformist constituents who wished to protect the Christian Bechuanas against the inroads of Boer filibusters. Chamberlain's widening interests led him at that time rather into the sphere of Foreign than of Colonial affairs. The despatch of Sir Charles Warren to Bechuanaland had another aspect, which Chamberlain approved; it was a show of force to counter Bismarck's attempts to dominate South African affairs, a demonstration that we meant to hold the Transvaal Boers to the terms agreed in the Convention of Pretoria. Chamberlain was incensed over the sharp practice by which Germany seized north-eastern New Guinea in the same year, and was accordingly thrown into partnership with the Australian leaders. 'Ware Australia!' he said in January 1885 in a speech aimed at Continental ears. 'It does not need a prophet to predict that in the course of the next half-century the Australian colonies will have attained such a position that no power will be strong enough to ignore them.' What he wrote to Dilke his confidant was, however, 'I don't care in the least about New Guinea and I am not afraid of German colonisation, but I don't like to be cheeked by Bismarck, or any-one else.' The Iron Chancellor, wrote Chamberlain's biographer,[1] did much to create the New Imperialism in Great Britain.

Chamberlain's education as an imperialist may be ascribed in part to his reading Seeley's *Expansion of England* in 1883. Shortly afterwards we find him consulting John Morley about the line they ought to take. Was there, or ought there to be, a radical-imperial policy? The answer to this question, as to many others in the history of the Empire, is bound up with the Irish problem, upon which Morley and Chamberlain were to part company. Irish affairs dominated English politics from 1885 to 1895. In the colonies opinion was substantially in favour of Irish Home

[1] J. L. Garvin, *Joseph Chamberlain*.

Rule; even Cecil Rhodes contributed to Parnell's party fund. At Westminster Chamberlain came forward with a policy to which he attempted to rally the new centre party known as the Liberal Unionists, but which proved unacceptable both for the British Isles and for the British Dominions overseas. A devotee of efficiency, a radical planner, Chamberlain would not agree to Gladstone's cleavage of the Union, since it weakened the central authority. He was for devolution, 'Home Rule All Round', provided that formal and effective sovereignty was retained by some representative body at Westminster, and frequently quoted the history of British North America as a precedent. He was consistent in striving to preserve sovereignty, whether in the Irish controversy, or in enforcing the observance of the Convention of Pretoria, or in attempting to retain the jurisdiction of the Privy Council in the Australian Constitution. Saving that residual power, Chamberlain advocated self-government for all the Queen's Dominions. But a residue of sovereignty at Westminster was rejected by the Southern Irish and by the Australians.

It astonished political circles when Chamberlain took the Colonial Office, a post of the second rank, in the coalition government which Salisbury formed in June 1895. At least since Kimberley resigned, twelve years earlier, the Office had lapsed into its earlier lethargy under a series of Secretaries of State whose names are hardly worth recording. However eminent in other respects, they were nonentities in the story of the British Empire. Yet these twelve years, 1883 to 1895, had seen the revival of enthusiasm for the Empire and a vast increase in its extent, though the Colonial Office was responsible for neither. This was the age of Chartered Companies and Protectorates sponsored by the Foreign Office. In his first administration, Salisbury had been his own Foreign Secretary; in Gladstone's fourth administration the Foreign Secretary was Rosebery who, though a Liberal, was more of an imperialist than the Tory Salisbury. These two had inaugurated the new policy. Rosebery, both when serving Gladstone and in his own short-lived administration (1894–5), had ploughed a lonely furrow—to use his own phrase of a later date—in a cabinet of Little Englanders. He had then gathered around him some younger members of his party who in the next decade, as the Liberal Imperialist group, created the modern Commonwealth and Empire.

A positive and constructive policy was required for these newly-acquired provinces and this Chamberlain was ready to apply. As the strong man of Salisbury's government he proposed to dictate foreign as well as colonial policy, and to do battle with the Treasury for the expenditure his policy would entail.

In his election speech (July 1895) he set the tone. 'Our colonies are in the condition of undeveloped estates.' Under such circumstances, he asked, what would a great landlord do? He would spend money in improving the property, especially in making communications. He would construct 'public works such as the Romans left behind'. By the judicious investment of British money, he said, 'those estates may be developed for the benefit of their population and the greater population which is outside'. This was something to cause a convulsion in Downing Street where cheeseparing had been the rule in the long years of Gladstonian finance. Chamberlain began by refurnishing the old offices which stood as Gilbert Scott had built them to Palmerston's order,[1] installing the new electric light and equipping his own room with an enormous globe. Then he set to work, much harder than any Secretary of State had worked there before. His subordinates, who called him 'the Master', soon learned that they might rely on his loyal support as he on theirs; the colonies that they might expect moral and financial backing, not spinsterish reproof.

Authority and funds were produced without delay for building state railways from Sierra Leone to the new protectorate (1896); from Sekondi on the Gold Coast to the Ashanti goldfields (1898); from Lagos, which was linked to the mainland by a road and railway bridge (1900), to Ibadan the metropolis of the Yoruba country, and eventually (1912) to Kano in the north. Chamberlain also gave Rhodes permission to run his railway through Khama's country, while carefully protecting the rights of the Bechuana against the Chartered Company—to Rhodes's indignation. He permitted the Reid contracts in Newfoundland to go forward though he denounced their political background. He ardently supported the Canadian plan (1898) for an 'all-red' Pacific cable. He even got a grant-in-aid for Cyprus. By his

[1] The first Colonial Office stood at the end of Downing Street, No. 12, where is now the Whips' Office. The department had moved into Palmerston's new block of buildings in 1875.

influence the Foreign Office decided to reoccupy the Sudan and to commence work on the Uganda Railway. One of Chamberlain's neatest strokes was the Colonial Stocks Act (1900), enabling the colonies to borrow at favourable terms on the London market, by classifying their bonds as trustee securities. All this was done in the teeth of the Treasury though its grim watch-dog, Hicks-Beach the Chancellor, had his successes too. He thwarted Chamberlain's eminently practical scheme for building up a Colonial Development Fund from the dividends on the Suez Canal Shares (then worth £670,000 a year).

For the West Indies, which Chamberlain specially desired to help, he was not able to do much beyond forming a Department of Agriculture. Their chronic depression was just then acute, and for the usual reason. The islands still depended on a single crop, sugar, which was over-produced and subject to competition with subsidised foreign beet-sugar. A strong commission in 1900 submitted a version of the report that has so often been made on the West Indies, that they could be made prosperous only by a better-balanced economy, and not by protection. In any case, protection for British sugar was out of the question, as Chamberlain found all protectionism to be in English politics. With great patience he brought about a convention at Brussels of the other sugar-producing countries (1903) whose representatives undertook to remove their subsidies. The scientific study and planning of tropical agriculture, which was the proper solution of the West Indian problem, had to wait until funds were available.

The greatest triumph of the new imperialism was the systematic offensive launched against the enervating diseases of the tropical colonies. Sir Patrick Manson (1844–1922), a Scottish surgeon, who had retired early after studying and combating parasitic diseases at Hong Kong, was appointed medical adviser to the Colonial Office in 1897. For several years he had been studying the process of insect-borne infection and had engaged the attention of a younger man, (Sir) Ronald Ross (1857–1932) of the Indian Medical Service, in the probability that mosquitoes carry malaria. This was but one link in a chain of scientific investigations by many students in various countries, notably in Italy. But popular history, which always simplifies, has done right in focusing attention upon that evening in Secunderabad, 20 August

1897, when Ross completed his study of the life-cycle of the malarial parasite. When Manson announced to the British Medical Association in 1898 that the problem of malaria was solved he met with much scepticism. A controlled experiment lasting two years was carried out in the Campagna by some of Manson's staff, with Italian help, before the whole process of infection through mosquito-bites was understood and demonstrated. Meanwhile Chamberlain and Manson had brought about the foundation of the London and Liverpool Schools of Tropical Medicine at which Manson and Ross respectively lectured.

Ross was a pugnacious, talented fellow, a poet and a propagandist. He was the sort of man who makes enemies and was sometimes accused, rather unjustly, of monopolising the credit for the great discovery. There was another side to that; he came into the colonial service and carried out investigations and lecture tours all over the world. He devised the administrative routine[1] of mosquito control which in fact was the method of fighting malaria. It was first imposed at Rome, where 'Roman fever' had for centuries been the scourge of pilgrims, and where old wives' tales had always associated fever with mosquitoes. Next the military cantonments at Ismailia were cleared (1902–5) on the initiative of the Suez Canal Company; then successively Port Swettenham in Malaya, Hong Kong, Mauritius and many other colonial regions. The Americans took up the method and, between 1904 and 1907, made possible the cutting of the Panama Canal, by first bringing disease-bearing insects under control throughout the Canal Zone. In the words of the Duke of Windsor, Ross had made one-quarter of the world habitable, an achievement which was recognised in his lifetime by the foundation of the Ross Institute (1926) with funds raised all over the world in his honour.

This spectacular triumph was but one campaign in the war against insect pests. Hardly less important was the struggle against sleeping-sickness which Stanley's porters had brought with them from West to East Africa. In 1899 Sir H. H. Johnston tackled the problem, which was understood if not mastered, when Sir David Bruce of the R.A.M.C. identified the tsetse fly as the carrier of the disease. Fly control in the interests of human and animal health became another task for colonial administrators.

[1] *Instructions for the Prevention of Malarial Fever*, by Sir R. Ross (1900).

Chamberlain's railways also helped to repair the ravages of the tsetse, for in the locomotive engine he had at last provided tropical Africa with a beast of burden that was flyproof.

For the fight against tropical diseases a general staff was provided in the Bureau of Hygiene and Tropical Disease, a department responsible to the Secretary of State but directed by an honorary committee of expert advisers. Similar organisations with honorary committees were formed for each of the new services that the Colonial Office was now expected to provide. Much was done in Chamberlain's time, and since then the extension of activity has been continuous. Merely to mention some of the departments which the Colonial Office has sponsored is as much as space will permit: the Colonial (now Overseas) Nursing Association was founded in 1896: in 1900 a Directorate was appointed to advise and help colonial students at British universities; in 1905 a (geological) Survey Committee was formed; in 1909 a Medical and Sanitary Committee; in 1913 the Imperial Bureau of Entomology; in 1920 the Bureau of Mycology; the Imperial College of Agriculture, so long desired, was opened at Trinidad in 1921; the (economic) Research Committee was formed in 1923; the Committee for Research in the Falkland Islands (usually known as the Discovery Committee) opened its marine biological station in South Georgia in 1925; the Imperial Economic Committee first met in 1925, and the Empire Marketing Board (discontinued as an economy in 1933) in 1926; the Colonial Medical Research Committee dates from 1927, the Advisory Committee on Native Education from 1928. Regional groupings of colonies for economic studies, and the formation of regional Currency Boards were especially encouraged when Milner was Colonial Secretary (1919–21).

Reform of the colonial administration was a gigantic task, begun by Chamberlain but not completed for thirty years. He attacked the problem by calling for a report upon the Colonial Civil Service from his Under-Secretary, Lord Selborne (1895). The Empire was not in any sense a single administrative unit. Some territories, having got self-government, were drawing away from the control of Downing Street; some were administered by the Foreign Office or the India Office; while, in all, the Treasury rule held good that each dependency should be self-supporting or, if not, should ask for a separate grant-in-aid. There were popular and unpopular, rich and poor, healthy and unhealthy colonies, all with their own systems. The first step was to transfer the protectorates to the Colonial Office, a process beginning with Nigeria in 1900 and completed, except for the Sudan Condominium, by 1913. The next step (after Joseph Chamberlain's time) was to separate the administration of the backward dependencies from the discreet, almost diplomatic, relation with the self-governing colonies. A Dominions Division was formed inside the Office in 1907 and made into a separate secretariat in 1925.[1]

To unify the service was no easy task. Since 1862 some appointments to cadetships in the Far East had been made on the result of competitive examination, and in 1882 this method had been widely extended. Chamberlain consolidated the entrance examination, in 1896, with that for admission to the Civil Service in general. Once inside the Service, officials were moved about, here and there, by patronage, actually upon the decision of the private secretary to the Secretary of State. West Africa, still the White Man's Grave, was an unpopular region and remained so until political experiment made it interesting, and hygienic reform took away its reproach. A beginning was made with the West African Medical Service which reduced the European death-rate from twenty per thousand in 1903 to five per thousand in 1935. The new slogan was to be that 'Health followed the Flag'.

It was not until Mr L. S. Amery was Colonial Secretary that unification of the services came in sight. He summoned the first colonial conference in 1927 from which arose the Warren Fisher Committee of 1929. The resulting plan for a unified service with the declared intention of helping the more backward, unhealthy, and penurious colonies was put into effect by Lord Passfield (Sidney Webb), the next Colonial Secretary, in June 1930. The Colonial Legal Service was formed in 1933; the Medical Service in 1934; Forestry, Agricultural, and Veterinary Services in 1935; Survey, Mining, Geological, Postal, and Customs Services in 1938. It should not be overlooked that the creation of this great bureaucracy seemed to hamper local autonomy and was suspected by native colonials in the lower ranks as likely to exclude them from the higher appointments.

[1] After 1930 an additional Secretary of State for the Dominions was usually appointed. In 1947 his title was changed to Secretary of State for Commonwealth Relations.

All these developments, foreshadowed by Joseph Chamberlain, had to wait for their fruition until adequate financial provision was at last made, in the Colonial Welfare and Development Fund of 1940, when Chamberlain's son was Prime Minister.

Proper attention to the colonial territories, in the event, occupied only a fraction of Chamberlain's attention. In every continent and ocean colonial policy was limited by diplomatic factors, with peculiar urgency in those days of 'splendid isolation' when Britain had not a friend in the world. Shortly after coming into office he had to face a crisis with the United States. Flaunting the Monroe Doctrine, President Cleveland made some political capital by inciting Venezuela to urge outrageous claims on the territory of British Guiana. But Chamberlain with his American wife and strong American sympathies was not to be upset by these ritual twistings of the lion's tail. He handled the problem with extreme patience and delicacy. The case was put to arbitration and decided in favour of the British colony (1897). In the very next year Chamberlain was able to assert his goodwill to America. All the European powers favoured Spain in the Cuban dispute, but Chamberlain persuaded his colleagues not to give her diplomatic support against the United States. He made no secret of his American partiality in the ensuing war. Forbearance in the Venezuelan dispute and goodwill in the Spanish War earned their reward when generous Americans allowed that there might be something to be said for the British case in South Africa.

Far more difficult were the world-wide disputes with France and Germany. Though unfavourably disposed on principle towards the French, Chamberlain came to terms with them in the African agreement of 1898 (see chapter xv, 5, page 827). His approach to Germany was very different. The hostility and chicanery shown by the Kaiser's government in all its relations with England exasperated him since his darling wish was for an Anglo-German alliance. The most he could achieve was to detach the Kaiser from the diplomatic support, almost the pretension of a protectorate, which he had offered Kruger. The price paid for this achievement was a series of concessions to Germany, in West Africa and in the Pacific, which caused dismay among imperialists of narrower views.

As if this were not enough Chamberlain had to deal with a dispute with Portugal in 1898 over the Beira railway, and an anxious situation in China where Russia and Germany were both seizing territory and new concessions. When France and Germany and Portugal had been brought round by skilful diplomacy, and when the Boer War took a better turn in 1900, there came trouble in Ashanti, where the Governor was besieged at Kumasi, and trouble in China where the legations were besieged at Pekin.

The settlement of all these problems, where colonial and foreign policies were intermingled, must largely be credited to Joseph Chamberlain. His larger plan for the Empire, a sovereign union based upon an imperial tariff, never came near success. The federation of Australia and the unionist plan for Ireland were to Chamberlain two stages towards this greater objective, the federation of the Empire. He resigned office in 1903 to conduct a campaign for Protection. His last word to the nation was his appeal to them to 'think imperially'. They did so, but in the sense of Liberal Imperialism which then was devoted to Free Trade.

Chamberlain's health gave way in 1906; he survived as an invalid until July 1914. It was during his retirement that the new Empire took shape as an inner ring of self-governing Dominions and an outer ring of tropical Dependencies, the former released from control, the latter scientifically administered from Downing Street. The cause of Imperial Federation was, however, lost.

2. THE IMPERIALISTS AND DOMINION STATUS, 1884–1914

IN the 1880's it had been generally supposed that, if the colonies were not to fall away, some positive measures must be taken to attach them to the mother-country. The Imperial Federation League was founded in 1884 through the efforts of C. Labilliere, who introduced W. E. Forster, its first President. Forster's name was a guarantee, since he was a Liberal and a Quaker, that the League was not composed of jingoes and expansionists. Federation of the Empire was a vague term used to cover many rival policies, which may be grouped under four heads:

(1) *Schemes for Legislative Union.*

Adam Smith had first advocated the admission of colonial representatives to the House of Commons in order to convert it into an imperial legislature. The plan had an engaging simplicity which appealed to those who held with Seeley that the colonies were merely extensions of the United Kingdom. It was occasionally revived in the nineteenth century, for example by Joseph Hume in 1832, and seemed more possible after steam and electricity had narrowed the estranging sea. It was, however, politically impracticable. No House of Commons would consent to admit new national minorities, perhaps as troublesome as the Irish Party, to upset the balance at Westminster; no colonial assembly, having achieved responsible government, would renounce its authority to delegates in England.

(2) *Schemes for an Imperial Advisory Council.*

As early as 1843, T. C. Haliburton of Nova Scotia had suggested such a plan. The firmest proposal came in 1879 from Earl Grey who desired to revive the old Council of Trade and Plantations as it had been in Charles II's day. To this committee of the Privy Council, the agents-general of the colonies should be admitted, to assist the Colonial Office in framing policy and to put forward the colonial point of view. But so deep was the distrust felt for the Colonial Office that the colonies had no desire to strengthen its hand; nor could agents-general be trusted to frame policy at a distance.

(3) *Schemes for a new Federal Constitution.*

Though very many such schemes have been brought forward during the last sixty years none has gained the approval of the electorate either in the United Kingdom or in any colony. All have an Utopian character. Several have been combined with plans for the reform of the House of Lords, an association of ideas that appealed to Lord Rosebery in the 'eighties. The conferment of peerages upon colonial governors and colonial grandees has in fact made colonial debates more enlightened in the Lords than in the Commons; but it showed a great lack of understanding of the Empire to suppose that a banker or squatter, who retired to live in London with a title, could remain a mouthpiece of Canadian or Australian democracy.

An elaborate scheme of federation was propounded by Sir George Grey in the *Contemporary Review* in 1894. It had the transcendent merit of allowing for local variety and could be applied to all self-governing dependencies, large or small. Each part of the Empire, he suggested, should be enabled to form its own constitution, to elect its own Governor, and to provide its own representation in a Federal Chamber which should legislate for the whole Empire. The British Isles, too, should be federated into the same organisation with 'Home Rule All Round'. Sir George Grey was always inclined to let his imagination run free. He had no doubts of the compatibility of democracy and loyalty; the reaction of the colonies to the London dock strike on the one hand and to the birth of the Prince of Wales on the other, as he thought, proved his point. Universal suffrage, and especially the women's vote, would ensure the blessings of unity and liberty.

Nor need the flight of fancy stop at the British frontier. The Arbitration Treaty with the United States must lead, he wrote, to a permanent Anglo-American council. The two great Federal Empires both based upon English principles, upon the English language, and upon Christian democracy must draw together to form the nucleus of the 'Parliament of Man, the Federation of the World'. Extracting from this dream of an old visionary the thoughts that were taking shape beneath the consciousness of statesmen, we find here a draft of the plan of federation towards which Joseph Chamberlain strove in vain, and a foreshadowing of the Covenant of the League of Nations.

(4) Schemes for Increased Co-operation.

All attempts at formal federation foundered on the hard facts of politics. The unsurmountable obstacle was the growth of national feeling in the Dominions. Not even Australia and New Zealand any longer admitted that they were extensions of England overseas. And this had never been true of the multiple societies in Canada and South Africa; they were new and might be called plural nations. Excluding the enthusiasts who, however eminent they were, never convinced the electorates, the general run of imperialists contented themselves with plans for increased co-operation in order to strengthen the links that bound the Empire in a moral and cultural Union.

From the days of Wakefield to the days of Chamberlain this theory of an Empire united only by the invisible bonds of friendship and loyalty was advocated by Adderley, the last survivor of the Colonial Reformers. Both he and his contemporary Gladstone ascribed the origin of the concept to some discussions between Joseph Howe of Nova Scotia and J. R. Godley of

Canterbury in the years 1853 and 1854. Still earlier, in the Durham Report, even in Wakefield's *Letter from Sydney*, we can trace the idea of an Empire consisting of self-governing nations linked solely by allegiance to the Crown. This idea, dormant during the reign of the cotton-spinners and the eclipse of the widowed Queen, emerged with the outburst of loyalty which greeted the Jubilee of 1887.[1] The strength of monarchical sentiment proved itself (and has continued to prove itself) far greater than any political economist thought possible, far greater in the age of democracy than in the age of aristocracy, perhaps greatest of all in the democracies overseas. These links lighter than air were in plain fact the strong confirmation of the Empire's unity, which the rationalists have been quite unable to explain away.

Lord Rosebery became President of the Imperial Federation League on the death of Forster in 1886. In that year Sir A. T. Galt of Canada and G. W. Rusden of Victoria led a deputation to Lord Salisbury, the Prime Minister, asking him to summon a Colonial Conference on the occasion of the Queen's Jubilee. Salisbury agreed and the first conference met in April 1887. It was a festival, a social occasion. The conference had no fixed composition, no agreed agenda; its function was to be 'purely consultative'. Canada alone had attained Dominion Status (though the term was not yet in use) and claimed to be received as a partner in Empire. The other representatives were guests not delegates, sent by Crown Colonies as well as by colonies which enjoyed responsible government. The representatives from New South Wales were specifically forbidden by their constituents to discuss the unpopular subject of Imperial Federation. Lord Salisbury's opening address, avoiding difficult questions of status and legality, appealed for co-operation, alluding to the possibility of an imperial customs-union, a *Zollverein* on the German model, and a defensive union or *Kriegsverein*. In spite of the jubilation and the cordiality, it was plain that the colonies made a disappointing response. The Canadians, if they needed naval protection at all, were inclined to provide their own. Admiralty influence was brought to bear in favour of a single imperial navy under one strategic control, but only the rudimentary Australian Union which excluded New South

---

[1] It may be proper to antedate the 'outburst' to 1886, the year of the Indian and Colonial Exhibition for which Tennyson wrote a ceremonial ode.

Wales, could be persuaded to make an annual contribution, and that only for a squadron to be based in the Pacific. The delegates parted in an atmosphere of enthusiasm which veiled the discontent of the professed imperialists.

In 1894 the Canadian government convened a conference at Ottawa to discuss some practical problems, chiefly of postal and telegraphic communications between the colonies. Preparations were made for intercolonial penny postage (achieved in 1898) and for direct links by mail steamers and submarine cables to join British territories across the Indian and Pacific Oceans. These were to form 'all-red routes' round the world, touching only at ports and islands which were coloured red on the map. The New Zealanders, urged on by Seddon, that swash-buckling democrat, demanded the annexation of all the anarchic islands of the Pacific; but in this as in other respects the colonial delegates were thwarted by Lord Ripon the Colonial Secretary. When Hawaii was annexed to the United States in 1898, in spite of Seddon's attempt to intimidate President Cleveland, it was necessary to divert the plans for the Pacific Cable, which was completed in 1902 from Vancouver to Fanning Island, thence branching through Fiji to Sydney and through Norfolk Island to Auckland.

A motion was proposed at Ottawa in favour of an imperial system of tariff preferences. When this too was vetoed by Lord Ripon, the delegates proceeded to discuss inter-colonial preferences, which were to be arranged even if Great Britain maintained Free Trade.

The Conference of 1897 was again summoned on a festal occasion to celebrate the Queen's Diamond Jubilee, though with Joseph Chamberlain at the Colonial Office, the opportunity of talking business was not wasted. The invitations were addressed only to the premiers of self-governing colonies, to meet for confidential discussion, which Chamberlain cautiously led towards the subject of Imperial Federation. The proposal was favoured only by Seddon of New Zealand and Braddon of Tasmania. With these two dissenting, the premiers agreed that 'the present relations between the United Kingdom and the self-governing colonies are generally satisfactory under the existing condition of things'.

In the view of the public, who were not aware of what passed at the private discussions, the hero of the Diamond Jubilee

Plate 29 A

SIR JOHN A. MACDONALD
(1815–91)

Premier of Canada. From a sketch
made about 1870. *See p. 562.*

Plate 29 B

R WILFRID LAURIER
(1841–1919)

er of Canada. A studio
it taken in London, probably
7. *See p. 568.*

Plate 30A

R. J. SEDDON
(1845–1906)

Premier of New Zeala
studio portrait taken in
probably in 1902. *See p.*

Plate 30B

SIR HENRY PARKES
(1815–96)

Premier of New South Wales.
A studio portrait in old age. No
picture of Parkes in the prime of
life is available. *See p. 600.*

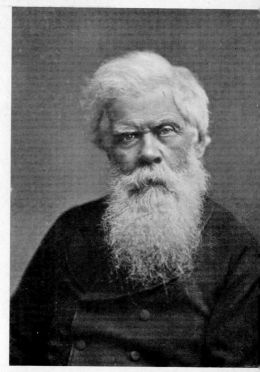

Conference was the courtly, scholarly Sir Wilfrid Laurier. After the death of Sir John A. Macdonald he stood head and shoulders above all other Canadian public men. His ideal of the national independence of Canada within the loose partnership of the Empire was a far more mature concept than that of the advocates of Imperial Federation. Kipling's eulogy of Canada ('Our Lady of the Snows', 1897) proved to be an understatement. Laurier's Canada was not content to be 'Daughter...in my mother's house and mistress in my own'; but proposed to be treated as a sister rather than a daughter nation. At successive conferences Laurier pricked the bubble schemes put forward for confining the living growth of the British Commonwealth within a rigid frame. As it has emerged from the test of the two German Wars the Commonwealth is not the creation of the professed loyalists, nor of the radical-imperialists; it is substantially the work of two magnanimous leaders of racial minorities, Laurier and Smuts.

While the public applauded Laurier for speaking the language of friendship and unity, the imperialists regarded him with suspicion as an opponent who outwitted them with evasive charm. 'That damned dancing-master', said Dr Jameson to Kipling, 'had bitched the whole show.'[1] Even Laurier's grant of a 25 % reduction in the duty on British imports was a move in the political game. It was so framed as to lower prices in Canada, to reassure the loyalists, to gratify Chamberlain, and yet not to hinder the prospect of a new Reciprocity Treaty with the United States, the rosy dream of so many Canadian statesmen. It was not an Imperial Preference but a concession granted to all countries 'which admitted Canadian products on terms as favourable as Canada offered'. Actually it favoured Free-Trade Britain; potentially it might lead to favours from Protectionist America. Laurier therefore responded coolly to Chamberlain's suggestion of an Imperial *Zollverein*.

The response of the colonies to the South African crisis of 1899 came as a welcome surprise. They at least did not regard the South African War as a struggle between British tyranny and Afrikaner rights. First to act were the Australian colonies which vied with one another in making offers of assistance. 'Labour', sympathising with the (white) miners of the Rand was as

---

[1] This remark, quoted in *Something of Myself* by R. Kipling (1937), presumably refers to the Conference of 1907.

enthusiastic as 'Capital'. Before the outbreak of war each of the states had offered to send troops, Queensland first—in July 1899. By the end of the war, by which time also the Australian states had been confederated, the total number of volunteers sent to South Africa exceeded 16,000. Like most Australians of that day, they excelled as rough-riders.

In the New Zealand Assembly on 28 September 1899, the Radical Premier Seddon moved a resolution, which was carried by fifty-four votes against five, to support Great Britain with troops. The first contingent sailed in October. In all, 6000 volunteers, selected from a much larger number of applicants, were equipped and despatched to the war at the expense of funds raised by voluntary subscription.

Sir Wilfrid Laurier was less certain of his ground, since the French-Canadians might be supposed to show some sympathy for Afrikaner aspirations. Nevertheless he carried a motion in the House, on 31 July 1899, supporting the action of the British government in the Transvaal. It was not then his intention to take part in the impending war. Under pressure from public opinion he permitted the enlistment of volunteers in October, and despatched about 8000 men to South Africa at a cost of $2,000,000, which was borne by the Canadian government. The election of 1900 was the occasion of much criticism of Laurier's policy both by the Conservatives and by Henri Bourassa (a grandson of Papineau), who raised an agitation in Quebec, not so much in favour of the Afrikaners as reasserting the claims of *la nation canadienne*. Between Bourassa and the Conservatives Laurier rode out the storm, but Canada took little part in the last phase of the South African War. Laurier's guarded support and independent action, his insistence on a policy that should unite all Canadians within the frame of Empire, were more statesmanlike than they seemed to some jingo imperialists.

The Conference of 1902 was again held in an atmosphere of loyal emotion. The Coronation of Edward VII consummated and exhausted the patriotic fervour which had renewed Chamberlain's mandate at the 'khaki' election of 1900. He moved more cautiously on this occasion, proposing to the colonial premiers a code of Imperial Defence which would involve an Imperial Revenue Tariff. He spoke of Great Britain as a 'weary Titan' obliged to offload some part of the financial burden of Empire

upon the lusty younger nations. The bill for war and reconstruction in South Africa stood as evidence of the need.

No agreement was reached upon Imperial Defence. Laurier,
standing firm behind the protection of the Monroe Doctrine,
saw no need for Canada to contribute to the Navy; nor would
he admit that Canada need be obliged to participate in England's
wars. Australia made an increased contribution to the Navy,
but insisted that it should be spent upon an Australian Squadron.
The best result of these discussions was the formation of a training
establishment in Newfoundland to bring back the seafarers of
the senior colony into the Royal Navy. On the other hand the
colonies were now agreed upon the principle of an Imperial
Tariff, which Laurier graciously encouraged by raising to $33\frac{1}{3}$ %
the Canadian Preference on British goods. But Chamberlain
had failed to convert his own colleagues.

Balfour was right in declining to commit the Unionist Party
to the policy of Tariff Reform in 1902. It took thirty years of
sad experience to convince the British electorate that Free Trade
would no longer serve its turn. The election of 1906 was so
resounding a defeat for those who had flirted with Tariff Reform
as to banish Imperial Preference from practical politics. The
Colonial Conference, due in that year, was postponed until the
new Liberal government was firmly seated, and met in 1907 in a
changed atmosphere. On this occasion the Conference was not
an appendage to a national festival. When Deakin of Australia
came forward with the customary proposal for Imperial Preference it fell to Mr Winston Churchill (then the Liberal Under-
Secretary for the Colonies) to decline on behalf of the United
Kingdom. He did so with the characteristic phrase that the
assembled premiers would be better employed in 'making roads
across the Empire, not building walls'. The Conference accordingly turned to more practical problems such as the organisation
of the all-red routes. From the discussions of 1907 there
emerged a rudimentary constitution for what was thereafter
known as the Imperial Conference. It was agreed that there
should be regular four-yearly meetings between the premiers of
'H.M. Government and the Governments of the Self-governing
Dominions' and that the Prime Minister of the United Kingdom
should preside. Each government should be entitled to one
vote. The provision of a permanent secretariat was approved in

principle but not found practicable. So many questions relating to Defence also arose that a subsidiary conference was summoned to deal with them in 1909, when the Armaments Race with Germany was gathering speed. It will be considered in a later chapter.

Dominion Status[1] may be said to have been admitted at the Conference of 1911. Though Asquith boggled at the principle of allowing the Dominions a share in the control of foreign policy, he admitted them to the *arcana imperii,* by bringing Sir Edward Grey to give the premiers a survey of international affairs, which was said to be fuller than any he had given to his own cabinet colleagues.[2] Andrew Fisher, the Australian Premier, put forward a complaint that the Dominions should have been consulted over the new code of international law, drawn up after the Hague Conference of 1907 and codified in the Declaration of London (1909). This Asquith would not accept (and it did not much matter as the Declaration was afterwards abandoned); but a resolution was agreed upon 'that the Dominions shall be given an opportunity of consultation...when time and the subject-matter permit...when preparing instructions for negotiation of international agreements affecting the Dominions'. This was not sufficiently explicit for the Australians; but was more than enough for the Canadians, who since 1884 controlled their foreign policy in their own hemisphere. Shortly before the Conference Laurier had been negotiating a commercial treaty with the United States. He did not wish to press Asquith for a share in Britain's foreign policy, and was content that Britain did not press him for a share in that of Canada.

Two legal problems were argued at length and inconclusively at the Conference of 1911, the reform of the Judicial Committee

[1] Though the concept of Dominion Status emerged at the Conferences of 1907 and 1911, the term was not generally used before 1918. It was made familiar by Mr H. Duncan Hall in his *British Commonwealth of Nations* (1920), a short historical study to which I acknowledge a debt.

The term defines the status of a government in relation to other governments under the same Crown; it implies nothing about the relation between a government and a people. During the controversies over the Indian Constitution it was misused by politicians who supposed that Dominion Status implied the enjoyment of a constitution like that of Canada, or Australia. The grant of Dominion Status to India would have meant a change in the relation between the Viceroy and the Secretary of State, not in the relation between the Indian government and the Indian people.

[2] What Grey said is to be found in Gooch and Temperley's *Documents on the Origin of the War,* vol. VI.

of the Privy Council and the admission of Indians to citizenship in the Dominions. Australia somewhat languidly proposed the foundation of an Imperial Court of Appeal; New Zealand would have added a judge from each Dominion to the Judicial Committee; Canada was for leaving well alone; and South Africa disliked all appeals to London. The discussion dragged on from Conference to Conference, delayed by the conservatism of the London lawyers who resisted the dilution of the courts at Westminster with men whom they regarded as obscure provincials.

A common citizenship was urged by the British government on behalf of British India against the opposition of the four Dominions, all equally hostile to Asiatic immigration. An appeal for democratic equality was countered by Laurier who said plainly: 'if Indians have no votes in British Columbia, neither do women in England', a shrewd blow at Asquith, then deeply embroiled with the suffragettes.

The climax of the Conference was the decisive defeat of a plan for Imperial Federation formally proposed by Sir Joseph Ward, who had succeeded Seddon as Premier of New Zealand. In his own country he had advocated an Imperial Advisory Council, and now overcalled his own bid by producing at the Conference a draft for an Imperial Legislature of 297 elected members. The plan was rejected by the other premiers and bitterly denounced by Laurier who was in the chair at that session of the Conference. On this occasion only was Imperial Federation, so often discussed in general terms, proposed in form by a responsible statesman. It is doubtful whether Ward would have gained the support of a majority even in the New Zealand Legislature, if the case had been put before them squarely. Three disqualifications deprived Ward of Seddon's former prestige and popularity, though he was an able administrator. He could not live down an ugly scandal in his professional career; he was a Roman Catholic; and he unwisely accepted a baronetcy. A few months after the Conference, his government was overthrown at a General Election (1912). Laurier's long term of office (since 1896) also ended at the Canadian Election of 1911.

As in 1899 so in 1914, the onset of war confounded the judgment of the critics. The Germans with their habitual crude insensibility supposed that the Empire would disintegrate, not realising that the petty quarrels over points of constitutional law were evidence of unity in greater matters. The probability was that the Dominions would insist upon their right to be consulted, would demand a voice in the direction of policy, would take as large or small a share in the war as suited them. As the world knows, all this adolescent captiousness was laid aside and forgotten in August 1914. The governments of the four Dominions placed their resources without stint at the disposal of the Crown. The constitutional leaders of opposition in Canada, in Australia, and in New Zealand approved. Only in South Africa did the irreconcilables attempt a schism. Much stronger opposition to the cause of Empire came from the Little Englanders at home where a new doctrine of anti-imperialism was in fashion with the intellectuals.

3. IMPERIALISM AND ANTI-IMPERIALISM

THE frantic boasts and foolish words, against which Kipling had warned his readers in vain, left a nasty taste in the mouth when the reaction came against the fashionable jingoism of the 'nineties. Neither the causes nor the conduct of the South African War could be regarded complacently by moralists. Those who doubted the honesty of the Rand millionaires, those who disliked the vulgarity of the halfpenny press, those who merely railed at Joseph Chamberlain,[1] combined in opposition against the imperialists, abusing them in more violent terms than had been applied to Lord North and George III. The chorus rose louder when the imperialist wing of the Liberal Party prevailed at the election of 1906. Asquith and Grey, with Rosebery in the background, were condoning the sin of Joseph Chamberlain who first had gone a-whoring after strange gods. The word 'imperialism', changing its meaning a second time, began to be used to signify the capitalist exploitation of backward regions, and this in a disreputable sense. What almost no one considered to be anything but virtuous in 1880 was considered by most advanced thinkers fundamentally vicious in 1920. The major prophet of the new cult was J. A. Hobson (1858–1940), whose book, *Imperialism* (1902), was a challenge and a rebuke to the Liberal Imperialists.

[1] 'And Joseph dreamed a dream, and he told it his brethren: and they hated him yet the more.'

He took up the story of the Empire, where Seeley had concluded it, to analyse the new financial policy of empire-building by means of protectorates and chartered companies. This, he recognised, was a quite different process from the agricultural colonisation of earlier days, and must, he asserted, antagonise the self-governing colonies by provoking wars which would involve them in expense and bloodshed. Such an empire could never be federated. If we were to grasp at still more colonial territories we should assuredly exasperate the Dominions until they declared their independence. The fault in British policy was using our surplus capital to establish financial domination over remote parts of the world instead of using it to raise the standard of life of the British working-classes. Since Free Trade had failed to spread through the world, the British had reverted to the old policy of aggressive nationalism. The South African War, said Hobson, was but another example of the wicked old methods of the East India Company. We had forced our trade and our capital loans upon India in such a way that even Free Trade had done her harm. We had failed either to civilise or to enrich the Indians, or to gain their affections; and there was every prospect of our repeating the process in China, unless the Japanese should forestall us.

Hobson's chief contribution to the economics of empire was the distinction he drew between colonies as fields for investment and colonies as fields for trade. Most of the wide colonial territories annexed since 1870 were poor and backward areas where there was but a small demand for British manufactured goods. The statistics proved that trade in consumer goods did not follow the flag to Bechuanaland or Borneo. Influences of quite another nature were at work there.

Whereas various real and powerful motives of pride, prestige, and pugnacity, together with the more altruistic professions of a civilising mission, figured as causes of imperial expansion, the dominant directing motive was the demand for markets and for profitable investment by the exporting and financial classes within each imperialist regime. The most potent drive towards enlarged export trade was the excess of capitalist production over the demands of the home market. In other words there has been over-saving and under-spending. This is due to a distribution of the general income which puts too small a share into the hands of the working-classes, too large a share into the hands of the employing and owning classes. Our concern here is with the urgent drive this situation impels towards the acquisition of foreign markets and areas of lucrative overseas investment.

The motor-power of Imperialism is not chiefly financial: finance is rather the governor of the imperial engine, directing its energy and determining its work: it does not constitute the fuel of the engine, nor does it directly generate the power. Finance manipulates the patriotic forces which politicians, soldiers, philanthropists and traders generate; the enthusiasm for expansion which issues from these sources, though strong and genuine, is irregular and blind; the financial interest has those qualities of concentration and clear-sighted calculation which are needed to set imperialism at work.[1]

Hobson's disdainful condemnation of imperialism can hardly be reconciled with the work of earlier critics. The reader may well wonder whether he and Froude were writing of the same train of events; and in a sense they were not. The Empire which Dilke and Froude described, which Seeley taught thinking-men to honour, was that which now is called the Commonwealth; the Empire upon which Hobson heaped abuse was the new colonial Empire which can hardly be traced back further than the annexation of Basutoland in 1868. A hundred years ago, the utilitarians had studied the effect upon the home market of a surplus of capital and, as Hobson admits, it was Gibbon Wakefield who proposed a remedy which then seemed adequate, the simultaneous exportation of surplus capital and surplus labour to a self-governing colony. In general the provision of capital was then the greater difficulty. When the great trade expansion came, in the 'fifties and 'sixties—the age of *laissez-faire* economics—when the flow of emigration was rapid and free, when capital for investment was coming to hand at an increasing rate, no one proposed to control or direct the flow. Nor did it occur to anyone to doubt that trunk railways, the glory and delight of the age, were justifiable. Over-capitalisation did not yet seem likely to be a burden to growing countries. Not even Karl Marx suggested that the Union Pacific Railway and the Suez Canal were hurtful in themselves. They were the characteristic expression of the age. To expand, to forward the march of industry, with unquestioned self-confidence, was assumed to be desirable, by all except a few Pre-Raphaelites and poets. The process was half-through before economists began to question its propriety.

The earlier writers, obsessed with population problems, conceived the Empire mainly as a field for the exportation of men; the later writers mainly as a field for the exportation of money.

[1] These are not Hobson's original words but a convenient summary which he provided for the revised edition of *Imperialism*, issued in 1938.

Froude omitted to notice, and would not have appreciated, the African phenomenon of the rise of Cecil Rhodes; Hobson too showed a lack of understanding when he implied that finance 'manipulated' the lives of Livingstone and Lugard. The impartial reader will hardly fail to notice a tendency in the anti-imperialists to impute base motives to all *entrepreneurs*, as if Willcocks designed the Aswan Dam in order to plunge the Egyptians into debt, as if Gordon and Livingstone were the puppets of finance.

The case may well turn upon the provision of public works in Egypt and India. Modern economists ascribe the bankruptcy of Egypt and the consequent British occupation to over-capitalisation. Loans, they say, were forced upon Ismail Pasha by French and British financiers who thereby made the Egyptian tax-payers their vassals. Whether intervention in Egypt was beneficial in intention or in effect are problems too complex to be solved in a chapter that treats of general principles. Gratitude is so rare in politics that its absence proves nothing. The fact, patent to every visitor to Egypt, is that the Egyptians got what they wanted from the Western usurers. England wanted to sell and Egypt wanted to buy the whole apparatus of industrial society; including its schools and its political economy; and the deal was put through. So far from exploiting the Egyptians, the British government, by stepping in, compelled them to husband their resources, prevented them from wasting their new assets. Cromer was sent to protect them from the rapacity of the bond-holders while providing them with a Western administration. Chamberlain urged that their burden of debt should be eased by a partial repudiation. The proof is to be seen in the end of the story. After long hesitation, since power is always loth to abdicate, Egypt was given self-government in 1922, and was promised independence by the treaty of 1936. It is now practicable because Egypt is financially strong enough to stand alone. What was intended has been done, though the Mahdi, the Young Turks, and the Fascists drew out the interval of time from five to fifty years.

Indian finance was a sore subject for the imperialists. Was Indian administration on too lavish a scale for so poor a population? Was too large a sum withdrawn from India annually to pay the salaries of officials in the Indian Office, and the pensions of the retired civil servants? Was India overburdened by the guaranteed rates of interest on loans, especially for unremunerative strategic railways? Was the cost of the wars[1] on the North-west Frontier entailed upon the Indian poor merely to gratify Disraeli's lust for a spirited foreign policy? The case was strongly argued by H. M. Hyndman in the *Nineteenth Century* (1879). The drain of money to England, 'the tribute' (see chapter XVIII, 2, page 933) rankled a little in the consciousness of loyalists who liked to assert that Queen Victoria was the only Empress in history who had never exacted a single penny from her dominions. What, men began to ask, was the Indian Empire, what was its purpose and future goal?

Seeley's *Expansion of England* has some illuminating comments on the lessons of Indian history, though he is inclined to take refuge behind paradoxes. He displays an almost whimsical pleasure in exposing the falsity of the 'bombastic' school of historians. The English, he says, never conquered India. Some English adventurers commanding armies of Indians defeated other armies of Indians, while the civil population stood neutral. It was not trade that engaged us in these conquests, since the East India Company thwarted and censured the warlike governors. Besides, trade with India was not worth much until the Company's monopoly was broken. The English did not even suppress the Mutiny with superlative heroism; they were on the winning side in a civil war between the Punjab and the Bengal Armies. Their physical power rested solely upon an army of mercenaries who might some day prefer to serve the Russians against them.

When military nations have mastered ancient static civilisations in the past, the result has usually been the subversion of the conquerors by their victims. So Roman *mores* gave way to Asiatic servility under the Empire. There was a moment, as Pitt pointed out in 1782, when the Rajah of Tanjore and the Nabob of Arcot kept their minions in the British House of Commons. English liberty might have been overthrown by Indian corruption, said Seeley, had not Cornwallis and Wellesley purified the Indian administration. Since then India had little effect upon England, but what effect had England upon India?

[1] Gladstone had departed from precedent in 1880 by advancing £5,000,000 from the British Treasury towards the cost of the second Afghan War. This problem has been intensified by India's contribution to the two World Wars. It is arguable either that they were fought for the defence of India, or that India would not have been involved in them but for her connexion with Great Britain.

The English rulers discovered there 'the arrested and half-crushed civilisation of a gifted race which has from the beginning been isolated from the ruling and progressive civilisation of the world'. 'It may be compared to Europe as Europe would have been if it had been unable to protect itself against the Tartar invasions of the tenth and thirteenth centuries.' 'The dominion of England in India is the empire of the modern world over the medieval. It is not a glorious light shining in darkness, but a somewhat cold daylight introduced into the midst of a warm gorgeous twilight.' The decision made as a result of Macaulay's minute on education 'to stand out boldly as teachers and civilisers remains the greatest landmark in the history of our empire'.

The confident spirit which created the nationalist movement in India by encouraging education in English liberal principles is the same as that which created the free port of Hong Kong, built the Uganda Railway, and conquered the Sudan. While the British exported men and money in the nineteenth century they never doubted their right and duty to export culture also. The White Man's Burden was an obligation to confer on less fortunate persons the evident benefits of cheap manufactured goods, sanitation, the common law, elementary schools, and Christian ethics, for all of which alike capital expenditure was first required. The corollary was that an obligation lay also on somnolent Asia and on primitive Africa. They owed it to the rest of mankind to reveal their hidden resources and to move with the times. Few observers in Edwardian days supposed that Europe and Asia alike were to be plunged into an era of wars and revolutions when faiths and empires would 'gleam like wrecks of a dissolving dream'.

4. PREPARATIONS FOR WAR, 1904–14

ENGLAND joined late in the international rivalry that led to the War of 1914. Throughout the period of the partition of Africa neither Liberals nor Conservatives showed any hostility to German schemes of empire-building. Since France was every-where our rival, especially in Egypt, it seemed best to play for German goodwill. Though Chamberlain disliked Bismarck's sharp practice in South-West Africa and in New Guinea, he still worked for an understanding with Germany by making large concessions in the Pacific, to the disgust of Australia and New Zealand. Rhodes too regarded the Germans as partners rather than as rivals in Africa, even though he did not want them in his sphere of influence.

On the other hand Kaiser Wilhelm II, from his accession in 1889, offered sporadic challenges to England which were reflected in the new offensive tone of the German press. The first serious alarm in England was raised by his intention, announced in 1900, to build a High Seas Fleet, which could exist for no other purpose than to challenge the British Navy. After Salisbury's retirement, in 1902, the policy of 'splendid isolation' was outmoded. Balfour's government, looking round the world for friends, formed the Anglo-Japanese alliance (1902) and the Entente with France (1904). Though the latter was not a military alliance it brought the British into the orbit of the European military rivalries and led very soon to conversations between French and British army-staffs. They were initiated by the Little Englander, Campbell-Bannerman, when England first gave diplomatic support to France against Germany during the Morocco crisis of 1906. Long-standing differences with Russia over Tibet, Afghanistan, and Persia were smoothed over by the Anglo-Russian agreement of 1907.

Looking backward it can now be seen, though it was not so evident at the time, that the teams were picked and the field chosen for the contest. The pace was increased by repeated additions to the German naval programme. When anxious inquiries and visits by august persons led to no friendly response from Germany, Mr Asquith was obliged to reply in kind. In March 1909, the First Lord announced a building programme of six new capital ships and was urged by the Conservative Opposition to make it eight. Now the shadow of war began to loom large, so that politicians of all nations and parties were obliged to take notice, in spite of the economists who demonstrated that war would not happen because it would not pay. It was averted at the second Morocco crisis in 1911, when the Entente once more held firm against the Kaiser's calculated affront to France in her North African sphere of influence. British unity was made plain in this crisis by the adherence of the Radical wing of Asquith's government. Lloyd George, who had once been a pacifist and a pro-Boer, warned off the German aggressor by a public speech in

London. About the same time Mr Churchill became First Lord of the Admiralty.

The Royal Navy had won the first round in the armaments race by building the *Dreadnought* (1906), an all-big-gun ship with turbine-engines; and the second round by increasing the standard armament of capital ships from 12-inch to 13·5-inch guns. Mr Churchill now won the third round by approving the design (1911) of ships to carry 15-inch guns, which would leave no room for coal-bunkers . Oil-fuel instead of coal meant perhaps as radical a change in British policy as the older change from sail to steam. Not coaling-stations but oil-wells were to be the nodal points of British strategy.

In 1901 wide concessions to prospect and drill for oil in southern Persia had been granted to a British company. Though mineral oils were a valuable article of commerce, they were no more than that, and still had no military importance when the Anglo-Russian treaty of 1907 placed the Persian oil-fields in the British sphere of influence. Wright's biplane had not yet come to Europe, the motor-car was hardly more than a luxurious toy, and the oil-burning battleship was not yet thought of. In April 1909, at the height of the British 'Dreadnought crisis', the Anglo-Persian Oil Company was formed to work the concession. The laying down of Mr Churchill's five new super-dreadnoughts in 1912 and 1913 (*Queen Elizabeth*, *Valiant*, *Barham*, *Warspite*, *Malaya*) made Persian oil a matter of high and secret policy. The British government accordingly acquired shares to the value of £2,000,000 in the Company which was to guarantee a supply of oil-fuel to the Navy. Thus the Persian Gulf became as vital an area to Great Britain as Suez or Gibraltar.

The naval developments did not pass unnoticed by the Dominions. Co-operation in imperial defence had come up regularly for discussion at the Colonial Conferences, since 1887 when first it was decided that colonies should protect their coaling-stations with fixed artillery, and that they should make voluntary contributions to the cost of the Navy. The rudimentary Australian federal council (which then included Fiji but not New South Wales) had undertaken to raise £126,000 a year towards the cost of a British naval squadron in the Pacific. Cape Colony, too, had offered to contribute the cost of a battleship in 1897, commuting it later for an annual sum of £50,000 from Cape

Colony and Natal together, a subvention that was unconditional, and so more welcome. At the Conference in 1902 Lord Selborne had appealed in vain for a united Imperial Navy. Both Canada and Australia were set upon navies of their own, for the good reason that their defence problems were not identical with those of Great Britain. Canada undertook the cost of maintaining bases at Halifax and Esquimault (from which the last British garrisons were withdrawn in 1906) but did little more. Australia bargained for retaining her Pacific squadron in return for making a larger contribution. In spite of the Anglo-Japanese alliance it was invasion from the north that the Australians feared.

The Russo-Japanese War, which reversed the tactical lessons of the South African War, led to discussions on armies at the Conference of 1907. A plea from Haldane for uniformity in training, organisation, and equipment drew a quicker response. A Committee of Imperial Defence had come into existence after the South African War (1904). Its work was now implemented by the appointment of a Chief of the Imperial General Staff under whom there were to be staff officers representing the Dominions. War plans for the whole Empire then came up for discussion at the special naval and military conference convened in 1909, at the height of the Dreadnought crisis.

Within a few days of the presentation of the British Naval Estimates, the premier of New Zealand, Sir J. Ward, had cabled an unconditional offer to present a capital ship to the Navy. Deakin the Australian Prime Minister capped him with the offer to raise and equip a squadron including one capital ship, provided that it was stationed in the Pacific. Both offers were accepted and before the end of the year H.M.S. *New Zealand* and H.M.A.S. *Australia* were on the stocks. The Australian Navy, consisting of the *Australia* and two cruisers, *Sydney* and *Melbourne*, was organised as one squadron of the British Pacific Fleet and commissioned in 1913. In addition to the gift from New Zealand, another capital ship, H.M.S. *Malaya*, was presented to the Royal Navy, in 1912, by the Federated Malay States, which were then enjoying great prosperity from the boom in plantation rubber. In Canada strategic decisions moved more slowly. Laurier was not prepared to admit in principle that Canada must engage in England's wars and would not commit the control of Canada's fighting services to staffs in Whitehall. There had been a sharp disagreement between Canada and Great Britain over the Alaska boundary in 1903, quickly followed by a quarrel between the Minister of Defence and a British general, Lord Dundonald, whom the War Office had lent to command the Canadian forces. Laurier's Militia Bill of 1904 had firmly removed the historic Canadian militia from command by any British generals and, by the same act, from all prospect of being reorganised as were the other forces in the Empire. Differences of equipment and administration were to place the Canadian armies at some disadvantage in 1914. Nor would Laurier co-operate in naval defence, either as New Zealand had done or as Australia had done.

It was not until Sir Robert Borden came into power in 1911 that an adequate Canadian naval programme was launched, too late for a Canadian squadron to take part in the first World War. However, by 1914 the Royal Navy had an adequate margin of ships to ensure safety and the magnitude of the Canadian war-effort far surpassed anything that could have been foreseen in 1911. At the conference of that year the statement by Sir Edward Grey persuaded the statesmen of the Dominions that world war was imminent and that the nature of the opening campaign could be accurately foretold.

Between 1909 and 1914 the territorial armies of all four Dominions were reorganised on the democratic principle of compulsory training for home defence, a principle against which English democrats fostered a strangely illogical prejudice. Preparations for a striking force of trained volunteers were also hurried on in Canada, Australia, and New Zealand.

It was at this stage that the figure of Lord Kitchener began to dominate the field of imperial defence. On his return from India the politicians could find no adequate post for a soldier-diplomat who had been powerful enough to unseat even Lord Curzon. He was despatched (1909–10) on a tour of the Dominions to advise them upon their mobilisation plans, and to his stimulus the creation of the formidable 'ANZAC' armies is largely due. His reputation, great as it was in England in 1914, was perhaps greater in the Dominions.

Horatio Herbert Kitchener (1850–1916) first appears as a serious-minded cadet who volunteered for service in the Franco-German War, an escapade from Woolwich that was to endear him to the French, forty years later. His first noteworthy employment was map-making for the Palestine Exploration Fund which led naturally to intelligence work on the Egyptian Frontier. Several sharp comments on Major Kitchener appear in the diaries where Gordon recorded his hopes of defying the inexorable facts of Anglo-Egyptian politics. Kitchener kept his counsel and, in due course, became Sirdar of the Egyptian Army with an unrivalled knowledge of men and affairs in the Near East. By his liberation of the Sudan he concluded a sequence of events that has been only too frequent in English military history, the methodical, orderly, and economical completion of a task at the second attempt, which at the first attempt had been bungled by unthinking optimists. As the avenger of Gordon, Kitchener became a national hero for whom G. W. Steevens, the war correspondent, devised the appropriate myth. This tall, slim, silent soldier with the cold eye and the heavy moustache was a monster of almost inhuman efficiency, the 'Sudan Machine'. On the whole the myth was justified by Kitchener's conduct of the South African war, the grave of so many reputations. But in the eyes of the British regulars Kitchener was rather a colonial administrator than a soldier, and one or two critics hinted that his two victories, Omdurman and Paardeberg, had been won by deplorably unsound tactics. Be this as it may, he had carried out his task, and largely by sheer force of personality. With a contempt for bureaucratic methods, he kept all authority in his own hand, all secrets under his own hat and, in his 'drives' across the veld, thought nothing of controlling a score of columns without grouping them under intermediate commanders. In India Kitchener was a more orthodox reformer; he reorganised the Indian Army on a mobile basis so that complete divisions of infantry and cavalry could be instantly despatched to a war-front; and this was the topic upon which he was qualified to advise the Dominions. From 1911 to 1914 he was Consul-General (a petty title for a great part) in Egypt and, in 1914, stepped as of right into the position of Secretary of State for War.

A soldier in a Liberal cabinet was nevertheless a fish out of water. Nor was the appointment altogether welcome to his fellow-officers. A new school of scientific soldiers had sprung up, with their eyes on Germany rather than on the Empire.

Plate 31

THE RT HON. J. C. SMUTS

On the occasion of his visit to an exhibition of works produced at the Cambridge
University Press, September 1931. Chancellor of the University of Cambridge
since 1948. *See p. 897.*

Plate 32

STATESMEN OF THE GREAT WAR, 1914–19

An imaginary portrait-group by Sir James Guthrie. The statesmen portrayed never actually met in one room. Names from left to right: (*Standing*) The Maharaja of Bikanir, b. 1880; General L. Botha, 1863–1919 (S. Africa); G. N. Barnes, 1859–1940; Sir R. Borden, 1854–1937 (Canada); Lord Balfour, 1848–1930; Sir E. Geddes, 1875–1937; A. Bonar Law, 1858–1922; Lord Morris, 1858–1935 (Newfoundland); Lord Kitchener, 1850–1916. (*Seated*) Sir J. Cook, 1860–1948 (Australia); W. M. Hughes, b. 1864 (Australia); D. Lloyd George, 1863–1945; Lord Milner, 1854–1925; W. F. Massey, 1856–1925 (New Zealand); Winston Churchill, b. 1874; Lord Grey of Fallodon, 1862–1933; Lord Oxford and Asquith, 1852–1927.

The rising generation that in every war rejects the traditions of the last, foretold a short campaign to be fought in Flanders by professional soldiers. The lessons of the South African war would be less useful than the lessons of the Picardy manœuvres in 1910, when the French had developed a new technique for using artillery in battle. This was the teaching of the Staff College and especially of Henry Wilson, the quickest-witted of the new generation of officers. Similarly the best naval opinion was opposed to autonomous naval forces in the Dominions. What mattered was a concentration of dreadnoughts under a single command in the North Sea. Behind the screen of the Navy the territorials would serve for home defence when the regulars had gone overseas. Colonial troops, if trained and equipped by British officers, might usefully provide 'contingents' to be incorporated into the British army, if the war should last long enough to require them.

5. THE NAVY AND THE EMPIRE, 1914–15

WHEN war came there were demonstrations of loyal adherence to the British cause from all parts of the Empire. It surprised no one but the continental powers that the Australian and New Zealand governments should place their resources unreservedly at the disposal of the King. New Zealand offered to despatch troops on 2 August, and Australia on 3 August, before the declaration of war. It was more significant that, when the Canadian Parliament met on 18 August, Laurier in opposition gave unconditional support to the war-effort of Borden who was in office. The Irish nationalists adhered to Asquith's government. Even in India, that is to say in articulate and instructed India, there were surprising demonstrations of loyalty. The Dominions overlooked the fact that they had been committed to war without prior consultation, the Indian legislative councils that there was no obligation on their armies to undertake anything but the defence of India. From all parts of the Empire, even from South Africa where the trumpet sounded an uncertain note, the garrisons of British regular troops were withdrawn[1] and concentrated for service in Europe.

[1] The last detachment of *rooineks* handed over the coastal batteries at the Cape in March 1916.

After transporting the B.E.F. to France, the next task of the Navy was to hunt down those German naval units that were at large, in order to free the seas for commerce and further movement of troops. In October 1914, a convoy of thirty-one ships carrying more than a division of Canadian volunteers was brought from Quebec to Plymouth, picking up on their way two ships with volunteers from Newfoundland and one with a British regiment from Bermuda. The whole strength of the Grand Fleet was disposed to cover these moves. At the same time two divisions of British regulars and three of Indian troops were transported from India to the Suez Canal, while three British territorial divisions were despatched to India to replace them. British detachments amounting to the strength of two more divisions were recalled and assembled from various colonial garrisons, and two divisions of Australians and New Zealanders were brought from their homes to the Mediterranean. By the middle of December all these voyages had been accomplished without the loss of a single ship or man, and the seas were swept clear of German raiders. The submarine campaign against merchant shipping had not yet begun.

During these anxious months when the B.E.F. was fighting from Mons to Ypres and the great convoys were at sea, the decisive moves of the naval war in the Pacific were made. In June the German Pacific Squadron, under Admiral Von Spee, had left its base at Kiao-chau in the Shantung province of China and had vanished, until in August it called at Rabaul in German New Guinea. Its movements were limited by supplies of coal and by information from its four main wireless stations at Rabaul, Apia (Samoa), Nauru, and Yap. The British and Australian navies faced a fourfold problem: to neutralise Kiao-chau, to seize the four wireless stations, to destroy Von Spee's squadron, and at the same time convoy the Australian and New Zealand troops to Europe. On their part the enemy might do much harm to our communications as well as to our commerce. The only cable stations they succeeded in disrupting were Cocos Island and Fanning Island, and these only for a few days.

Though not obliged by their treaty with the British to take part in the war, the Japanese undertook the first of these strategic tasks. Having been prevented by German diplomacy, ten years before, from annexing Port Arthur, they set to work, with relish, to deprive the Germans of Kiao-chau. It was besieged by a Japanese army with which a small English contingent co-operated, and was taken after a stubborn defence. The Japanese next made haste to expand into the German Pacific islands and in October 1914 seized Yap, to the no small concern of the Austra lians, who mistrusted these allies. In December the British government persuaded the Australian government to accept the principle that German islands north of the equator should fall to Japan and south of the equator to Australia. On these lines the mandates were finally allotted in 1920.

Meanwhile the Dominions had been no less quick off the mark. On 30 August a New Zealand expedition seized German Samoa; on 9 September the Australians seized Rabaul, on 10 September Nauru; thus the old ambition of the colonial imperialists was achieved, without fighting. All these moves were covered by the Australasian Squadron, which justified the existence of H.M.A.S. *Australia*, the only ship in the Pacific that could have both caught and fought the *Scharnhorst* or the *Gneisenau* if she had the chance. While the *Australia* was at Rabaul, Von Spee suddenly appeared off Apia to find it occupied by a New Zealand garrison too strong for any naval landing-party he could send against them. He vanished again into the Pacific, where no bases were now left for him, to meet his fate three months later at the battle of the Falkland Islands, 8 December 1914.

Though the Australian ships were not present at the battle, they had already completed their tasks by frustrating Von Spee's plans. Of two German warships still at large, one, the *Emden*, after a successful career of commerce-raiding, was sunk on 9 November 1914 by H.M.A.S. *Sydney* at the Cocos Islands, where she had put in to destroy the British cable station; the other, the *Königsberg*, was blockaded in the mouth of the Rufiji, an East African river, in October 1914.

The Australian and New Zealand Army Corps (ANZAC), mobilised for service in Europe, was detained in Egypt from November 1914 to April 1915. After the first Flanders campaign, which had opened much as the general staff anticipated, a deadlock set in while the centre of strategic interest moved to the Near East. Under its new nationalist ruler, Enver, Turkey had for some years been drifting away from the century-old friendship with Great Britain into complicity with the German militarists. Enver's pan-Turkish policy was designed to foster a strong national state in Asia Minor and the Caucasus, at the expense of Russia, rather than to maintain the ruins of the old Ottoman Empire. Slowly and reluctantly British policy moved round towards giving some support to the Balkan, Syrian, and Arab nationalists who saw new hopes of freedom. A last effort to retain Turkish friendship by guaranteeing yet once more the integrity of the Turkish Empire, now that the Young Turks had declared for reform and progress, was rejected by Enver, who preferred to accept a direct bribe from Germany, the use of the warship, *Goeben*, against the Russians in the Black Sea. Accordingly Great Britain declared war on Turkey (November 1914), Egypt was declared a British protectorate, promises of liberation were made to the Arab princes, and in due course came the campaigns in Gallipoli, Mesopotamia and Palestine.

6. TURKISH AND AFRICAN CAMPAIGNS, 1914–17

FIRST blows in the war against the Turks were struck by an Indian brigade sent to reinforce the garrison at Aden. They drove off a concentration of Turkish troops in November 1914. Other small detachments had also sailed for Bahrein and for Mombasa, both of them in the old Indian sphere of influence. From Bahrein it proved necessary to move forward to Abadan in order to protect the installations of the Anglo-Persian Oil Company. One commitment led to another until two Indian divisions were deployed, after some fighting, on the Shatt-el-Arab and the Tigris. Basra was occupied and a Turkish attack repelled (April 1915). Another Indian division took the shock of the first Turkish attack on the Suez Canal in February.

These were minor and defensive engagements. The first major operation of the Turkish war was the direct assault upon the Dardanelles, conducted in two phases both of which failed. The naval assault in February 1915 was followed, on 25 April, by beach-landings on the Gallipoli Peninsula in the face of determined opposition. The first wave, consisting of one British and parts of two ANZAC divisions, secured two beach-heads at a heavy cost in casualties. After bitter fighting for more

than seven months the troops were obliged to admit their failure
to break out of these beach-heads, though, for one moment in
August, a third landing at Suvla had seemed likely to bring
success. The Dominion troops were evacuated from the ANZAC
sector to Egypt in December 1915, the British troops from the
Helles sector in January 1916. The expedition had cost 30,000
lives, of which 7500 were Australians and 2400 New Zealanders.

The winter of 1915–16 was a gloomy period for the Allies.
While the deadlock in France was still unbroken the Germans
had overrun Russian Poland and Serbia. As the troops from
Gallipoli reorganised in Egypt they were again thrown on the
defensive by belated Turkish attempts to raise a *jehad* throughout
Islam. Luckily there was little response, though campaigns
were necessary against the Sheikh of the Senussi in the Western
Desert (February 1916), and the Sultan of Darfur in the remote
Sudan (April 1916). A more serious affair was the attempted
invasion of Egypt from Palestine by a Turkish force under an
able German officer. He was stopped and forced to retire by a
series of actions in which Australian and New Zealand mounted
troops played a notable part (March–April 1916). When the
ANZAC infantry was transferred to France that season, the mounted
troops remained in Palestine. As a result of these operations it
was resolved to take up an offensive-defensive role by moving
the armies forward from the Canal into southern Palestine as
rapidly as the construction of roads, bridges, railways, and pipe-
lines would permit. General Murray's ponderous advance came
to a halt after the two battles of Gaza early in 1917.

Progress in Palestine, however, fired the imagination of Lloyd
George, with the result that he detached troops from other
theatres and sent a new commander, Allenby, to 'give Jerusalem
as a Christmas present to the Allies'. This was not altogether
a matter of sentiment since it was supported by the military
counsel of General Smuts. Nor did Allenby fail; the Turks were
manœuvred out of Jerusalem by a masterly campaign, in
December 1917, and nine months later their armies were
annihilated at Megiddo.

Meanwhile the independent campaign conducted by the Indian
government in Mesopotamia had also ended in victory after an
early disaster. First conceived as a defensive move to cover the
Anglo-Persian oil concessions, it had been allowed to grow

into an offensive against Turkey with ill-defined objectives. The Viceroy was persuaded to authorise an advance on Baghdad by a striking force of one British-Indian division with improvised communications. After some audacious successes General Townshend (see chapter XVIII, 1, page 926) found the task too great for his resources and was invested at Kut-el-Amara (November 1915). Much greater strength, including the two Indian infantry divisions from France, was concentrated for his relief. The first-class campaign that ensued was a failure since it overstrained the administrative system of the Indian Army. After a humiliating attempt to make terms, General Townshend was instructed to surrender, on 29 April 1916, with 2000 British and 6000 Indian troops, the only example in the first World War of those capitulations by British troops which were so painfully frequent in the second. There seemed no alternative to doubling the stakes and speculating again, if prestige were to be repaired in Asia. Accordingly a new offensive under a new general, Sir Stanley Maude, was deliberately mounted for the following winter, and this time by the War Office. After three months of prudent and deliberate operations (December 1916–March 1917) Baghdad was captured and the whole basin of the Tigris and Euphrates shortly fell into British hands.

These changes of fortune were reflected throughout the politics of the Middle East; they reacted also upon the wider world. India's first enthusiasm for an altruistic war was sadly shaken by events in Mesopotamia. Nationalism revived in 1916, making the very reasonable plea that, if India was to fight beside the Dominions for the rights of oppressed nations, India too should have home rule. The same plea was heard from Southern Ireland, where the outbreak of war had been followed by delay in carrying out the contentious provisions of the Home Rule Bill. Recruiting appeals were aimed rather at consolidating loyal Ulster within the Empire than at conciliating the unwilling South. The Easter week rising (April 1916) in Dublin came just at the time of the surrender at Kut. Irish troubles reacted in the Dominions where there was little sympathy with English 'Unionism', especially in Australia with its large minority of Irish immigrants.

By the summer of 1916, when these political difficulties arose, a lull had set in on the Eastern fronts. The whole Canadian Army, the Australian and New Zealand infantry, an Indian cavalry division, and a contingent of South African troops were deployed beside the British in France and Flanders, where the decisive battles were to be fought. Before proceeding with their story it will be convenient to look back to affairs in Africa during the first half of the war. As in the Pacific, the strategic problem was to deprive the Germans of the signal stations and coaling stations which might succour their commerce-raiding warships. As early as 6 August 1914, a junior officer from the Gold Coast entered Lomè, the capital of Togoland, demanding its surrender, which was granted. A few days later a handful of African troops under Lt.-Col. F. C. Bryant seized the great wireless station at Kamina, the communicating link between Germany and all its African colonies, after a sharp skirmish. With that Togoland passed into allied occupation, 26 August 1914. The great territory of the Cameroons, twice as large as the British Isles, was a more difficult proposition. The decisive step was the seizure of Duala, the capital, on 26 September 1914, by a force of French- and British-African troops under General Sir C. Dobell. The Germans with their *askaris* withdrew, fighting, into the interior. After a period of preparation, converging forces, of British-African troops from the Benue River, and French-African troops from the French Congo, broke into the territory. There was some stiff bush-campaigning which did not end until, in February 1916, the main German force escaped into Spanish territory. The Cameroons were placed under allied administration on 1 April 1916 and divided, as was Togoland, into British and French spheres of influence. This smart campaign was a pleasing example of good co-operation between the services and between the allies.

The task of seizing the German stations at Lüderitzbucht (Angra Pequeña) and Swakopmund (near Walvis Bay) in German South-West Africa was offered to the Union government by the British, who thereby placed the premier, Botha, in a dilemma. He had already offered to release the garrison of 7000 British regulars, whom he had used only a few months earlier against white rioters in Johannesburg. If he made himself responsible for the defence of South Africa that would imply some action against the German bases. The peace of Vereeniging was but twelve years signed, the Union but four years established and, though he and Smuts accepted their obligations as members of the Commonwealth, he knew that many Afrikaners did not. On the very issue of the imperial liability his administration had been weakened, in 1912, by the defection of General Hertzog's group. Against Smuts's conception of South African unity within the greater unity of the Commonwealth stood Hertzog's conception of a 'two-stream' state in which British and Afrikaners were to live side by side, without mingling. The Afrikaner Nationalists had already claimed the right of neutrality in Britain's wars. The extreme wing, the irreconcilables of 1902, had a pro-German tendency since some of them had lived as exiles in German South-West Africa.

If Botha was to rally the nation, if indeed it was to act as a nation, he knew that he must draw to him the other heroes of their war of independence. Hertzog, dry, cautious, and legal-minded, gave no lead; while not denouncing the war he denounced the proposal for invading German territory. Botha appealed to Steyn, the former President of the Orange Free State, but Steyn refused to help. There remained De la Rey, now growing old, de Wet, and beyond that such intransigents as Colonel Maritz, who had lived in German South-West and had held a commission in the German colonial force. At this point Beyers, the general commanding the newly reorganised South African Defence Force, resigned in protest against Botha's war policy.

The Germans wisely took no action. Maritz, who commanded a post on the frontier, could be trusted to make enough trouble. He would draw Beyers into rebellion; Beyers would implicate De la Rey and de Wet, thus embarrassing Great Britain with a new Boer War. On 13 September, Beyers set off from Pretoria with De la Rey to visit a training camp nearby; whether to declare for peace or war no man can say. By a coincidence that passes belief, their car was fired on by a policeman engaged in a fight with gangsters, a fight that had no political significance. De la Rey was shot, and Beyers and Botha met in friendship, for the last time, at his funeral. The dead leader, old, chivalrous, and respected, had no guile in him. His removal seemed to knock away a central pillar about which the Afrikaners might have rallied.

When combined operations by land and sea were opened against German South-West (18 September 1914) the factions rapidly drew apart. Maritz proclaimed a rebellion on 9 October and, within a few days, was hustled into German territory by loyalist troops. Beyers then took the field in De la Rey's country, the Western Transvaal, where some rebels were already in the field. His commando too was dispersed and harried. On 8 October Beyers was drowned while trying to escape across the Vaal River. A more serious matter was the raising of de Wet's standard in the north-east of the Free State. Moderate men were not impressed by the complaint he made against the new government: they had fined him 5s. for striking a native. Though in a few days he was at the head of a band of 5000 armed men, the day of the Boer pony in warfare was ended, as he had been warned. When he was attacked by a column with some motor vehicles his following began to melt away. Yet the muse of history allowed him one more exploit to rival those of his youth. Escaping from the government forces with fifty men he rode across the Veld into Bechuanaland. The motor-cars did not catch him until 2 December. In February 1915 Maritz's men surrendered and all was over. Botha had wisely used none but loyal Afrikaner forces against the rebels, instructing them that the rebels were to be scattered and captured. 'Let the rebels fire first.' A few only of the leaders, de Wet among them, were tried and sentenced to short terms of imprisonment. They were soon released. One only was executed after trial, an officer who had rebelled without resigning his commission. Maritz withdrew into Portuguese territory and into obscurity.

As the only South African in whom all parties had personal confidence, Botha himself had commanded in the field against the rebels. Though still Prime Minister he next assumed the military command against the Germans. Both ports of entry to German South-West were occupied by small parties of South Africans under naval convoy, Lüderitzbucht in September, Swakopmund in December. The advance up the country from the two seaports to Windhoek, the capital, proved to be an administrative rather than a tactical problem, which Botha solved with great skill, hard marching, and not much fighting. On 9 July 1915 the German forces, including about 7000 armed Europeans, surrendered without having made any remarkable resistance. Another link in the German signals system was snapped.

The British government next appealed to Botha to send a

South African expedition against the Germans in East Africa. Being unwilling to leave his distracted country, where he had just fought a virulent general election campaign, he despatched Smuts with two infantry brigades and one mounted brigade. The East African war differed in character from the rebellion and the campaign in German South-West. Those had been white men's wars according to the tradition of South Africa; this was tropical campaigning in which both sides used great numbers of native *askaris* under white officers. Here also a battalion of Cape coloured troops fought valiantly.

East Africa was the only German colony where a successful strategic diversion was made, the one heroic exploit in German colonial history, largely because of the talent of von Lettow-Vörbeck, the commanding general. As early as September 1914 he made demonstrations against the Uganda Railway, thus engaging the attention of a brigade of troops from India. His strength was reinforced by the cruiser *Königsberg*, which was not discovered lurking in the Rufiji river until October 1914 and not destroyed until British monitors could reach the spot in July 1915. Even then its crew with their ship's light armament joined the German army in the bush.

Throughout 1915 Von Lettow defied the surrounding British colonies and made several harassing raids. When Smuts arrived at Mombasa, in February 1916, the Germans were established at Taveta in British territory, east of Mount Kilimanjaro. Having cleared British territory by a tough preliminary campaign Smuts rapidly prepared an advance southwards, with two divisions, through the Paré mountains, while his subordinate, van Deventer, made a wide flanking march, with one division, farther west. By June they had cleared the whole of the railway from Kilimanjaro to the port of Tanga. By September Smuts was at Morogoro, the German administrative capital, and in control of the port of Dar-es-Salaam. When the coast was secured the reduction of the German forces inland was no more than a 'mopping-up' operation, but a prolonged one. Smuts had driven his forces very hard at the cost of heavy losses from disease and from the climate. When he was recalled, in January 1917, to attend the Imperial War Conference he recommended that his successor, van Deventer, should complete the campaign chiefly with Indian and native African troops. Though hunted by van Deventer's men, by Rhodesians, Belgians, and Portuguese, von Lettow-Vörbeck still kept his army in being and was operating in Portuguese territory when the war ended.

7. THE WESTERN FRONT: MAN-POWER

DURING the early months of 1916 the strategic reserve of the Empire, about a dozen divisions, was removed from Egypt to France, since the advocates of a policy of winning the war in the west had prevailed with the war cabinet. The concentration of troops became far more intense than was ever attempted in the second World War. Just before the battle of the Somme 117 divisions, two-thirds of the German Army, based upon interior lines and well dug-in behind thickets of barbed wire, confronted ninety-five French and sixty-three British divisions. No way of winning the war appeared to the Allies except to batter their way through with grim persistence, which they displayed throughout the summer of 1916 and the whole of 1917. Of the sixty-three British divisions, fifty were infantry and three cavalry from the United Kingdom, two were Indian cavalry, three were Canadian infantry, four Australian infantry, and one New Zealand infantry. A Canadian cavalry brigade, a South African infantry brigade, an infantry battalion from Newfoundland and several other units from the Dominions and colonies were incorporated into British formations.[1] The number of soldiers engaged in particular actions again surpassed anything in the second War. For example, on 1 July 1916, zero day of the battle of the Somme, eighteen British and five French divisions were in the first line of assault against twelve German divisions. The British suffered 57,000 casualties in a few hours and the German losses were proportionate. On that day only one battalion from the Dominions was engaged, the Newfoundland battalion which lost all its officers and 700 men.

It will not be necessary nor would it be possible to distinguish the part played by the men from overseas in these unparalleled

[1] Canadian Forestry Corps, South African and Egyptian labour corps, several units of the Royal West Indies Regt., a Bermudan battery of artillery, a Rhodesian detachment with the King's Royal Rifles, even a British South American detachment serving with King Edward's Horse, etc. Units of British volunteers from Ceylon, Hong Kong, and Singapore served in Gallipoli and Palestine.

scenes of slaughter. The Canadians were the first troops from the Dominions to fight on the Western front; in April 1915 (a few days before the Australian landing at Gallipoli) the First Canadian Division had repulsed the treacherous attack made at Ypres under cover of a cloud of chlorine gas. After this heroic beginning the Canadians made their name in the desultory but fierce fighting that never quite died down in the Ypres salient, as the Australians made theirs at Gallipoli. From one division the Canadian strength was gradually built up to four divisions in August 1916. The British commanders and staff officers were replaced by Canadians as they acquired war experience, until finally Sir Arthur Currie (1875–1933), a career officer of the small Canadian permanent force, was given command of the Canadian Corps in 1917. The Arras and Vimy offensive in the spring of that year revealed the status of the Canadian force as an autonomous army, equal in military efficiency to any.

The reputation which the ANZACs brought from Gallipoli was confirmed in the battle of the Somme. The Australians also replaced their British commanders by gradual promotion of their own officers. Having expanded to five divisions they were divided into two Corps of which one, containing only Australian troops, was placed under command of Sir John Monash (1865–1931), a Melbourne engineer; the other, consisting of Australian and New Zealand troops, remained under command of a British general. The battle of the Somme also provided the most celebrated episode in the history of the South African Brigade, the defence of Delville Wood. Among the numerous and bloody assaults with limited objectives on German strongholds, perhaps the most thoroughly prepared and executed was the attack on the Messines Ridge by the New Zealanders in June 1917.

The crisis of the naval war came in the spring of 1917 and was prolonged for about a year. Though the submarine campaign against all merchant shipping led to President Wilson's declaration of war (April 1917), little military aid could be expected from a nation without soldiers and without arms. No American troops could be expected to operate in France until late in 1918 and no forces of decisive strength before 1919. Meanwhile all the other allies were collapsing. The French armies which had borne the brunt of the first two years were exhausted and disaffected; the Italians were routed at Caporetto (October 1917); the Russians dissolved into anarchy. When Trotsky attained power over the central provinces he repudiated the alliance and made peace with Germany (March 1918). The whole burden of the war was then carried by the British Empire. The slogging-match at Ypres in the autumn of 1917, in which all the forces under Haig's command were engaged in turn, reduced the strength of the British and Dominion infantry so low that the prospect for 1918 was bleak. It was eminently a British task to hold on until the Americans should be ready, to stand fast as Wellington had stood at Waterloo, waiting for night or Blücher.

All turned on man-power. It made a moral revolution in English life when Lloyd George imposed conscription in May 1916. Six months later New Zealand followed suit; but in Australia and Canada political complications arose. The Premier of Australia, Mr W. M. Hughes, was a radical imperialist with a great following among the working classes of New South Wales. Though Australia had long been committed to the principle of compulsory training for home defence with the reluctant consent of the Labour Party, conscription for service overseas was another matter. As in South Africa it raised the question: how far was Australia committed to fight England's war? The objectors approved the allied cause; they were proud, as well they might be, of their voluntary army; and yet they boggled at the proposal to send conscripts 10,000 miles away to fight under a supreme command which they could not control. After Turkey and France they might next be sent to fight in Russia, or in Ireland. A powerful voice against conscription was that of the Roman Catholic Archbishop Mannix of Melbourne, an Irishman with a traditional grievance against England and a large following among the Irish-Australians. The issue was put to a referendum, in September 1916, with the result that conscription was rejected by a majority in the proportion of eleven to ten. Of the Australian soldiers in France 72,000 voted for and 59,000 against conscription. A reconstruction of the government followed, still under Mr Hughes, who got a firm majority for the other items of his policy at a general election in 1917. Later he attempted another referendum which produced a similar result. Recruiting for the Australian forces overseas remained voluntary and of course produced a diminishing return.

Similarly in Canada Sir Robert Borden introduced a bill for a very modest measure of conscription in 1917. It was vehemently opposed by Laurier[1] on the grounds that his Militia Act of 1904 had laid down a fundamental principle of compulsory service for home defence. The bill was fought on racial lines. It was estimated that, of 400,000 Canadian soldiers who served overseas, more than half were British-born immigrants and less than 30,000 were French-Canadians. Again this did not imply sedition or antipathy to the war aims but a conviction that the war affected Canada only indirectly, and did not justify conscription. The act was passed but very loosely administered. Exemptions were so numerous in the Province of Quebec that few conscripts were enrolled. Passive resistance was common, and active rioting against the enforcement of the act occurred in some instances.

The full weight of the German offensive fell upon the British group of armies in March 1918. It was Ludendorff's last throw, his one chance of snatching at victory before the American reinforcements should come into line. The attack was delivered against armies sorely depleted in numbers. With the one exception of the New Zealanders, who maintained both the quality and the strength of their division until the end of the war, British and Dominion divisions had great difficulty in filling their ranks even upon reduced establishments. Lowest in strength were the Australians, the only surviving army of volunteers in the West. It was the more honour to them that they declined to reduce their establishments and allowed no stronger formations to excel them. Much was due to their commander, Monash, who, in the opinion of some critics, was the ablest general in France.

Ludendorff inflicted sore losses, the heaviest ever suffered by British armies, and scored some tactical successes, but failed to reach even one of his objectives. His deepest thrust was parried by the Australians at Villers-Bretonneux (March 1918). When the allies swung over to the counter-offensive the first blow, on 8 August 1918, Ludendorff's 'black day', was struck by a British, a Canadian, and an Australian Corps. New Zealanders and Australians took part in the decisive battle for the Hindenburg

[1] Laurier died in 1919, disheartened by his defeats in 1911 and 1917.

Line in September. Haig's victory despatch announced that on the last day of the war the Canadians had captured Mons.

The war record of the four Dominions had placed them at least on a level with the smaller European states, in the eyes of Germans, Frenchmen, and Americans. With that status they sent their own delegates to the peace conference. While three had won their European reputation on the fields of France, the fourth, South Africa, had conducted two independent campaigns nearer home. The place of South Africa in the world was assured by the extraordinary eminence of General Smuts, the most distinguished of the statesmen at Paris after the 'Big Three' (Wilson, Clemenceau, and Lloyd George). Having been summoned to the Imperial War Conference in 1917, General Smuts had been retained in London as a supernumerary member of the Cabinet. In that capacity he spoke for the Dominions on many occasions, familiarising the British public with the concept that came to be known as Dominion Status. His duties were those of a general adviser and factotum, equally useful at settling a strike of Welsh miners, reorganising the air defence of London, preparing plans for an independent Royal Air Force, advising on strategy in Palestine, or drafting a covenant for the League of Nations. At the end of the peace conference he expressed deep dissatisfaction with the financial clauses of the treaty.[1]

The war-effort of the British Commonwealth in man-power can be approximately expressed in tabular form, though accuracy is excluded by the roving habits of young British males. No enumeration can be made of Englishmen serving in overseas units or of men from overseas serving in English units. Let these round figures serve as an indication:

	Estimated population in 1914	Troops sent abroad	Killed, died and missing
British Isles	46,000,000	5,000,000	705,000
Canada	8,000,000	458,000	57,000
Australia	5,000,000	332,000	59,000
New Zealand	1,100,000	112,000	17,000
South Africa (whites only)	1,400,000	136,000 (mobilised)	7000

---

[1] General Smuts returned to South Africa in 1919, upon the death of Botha, whom he succeeded as premier.

War finance is not easy to summarise from statistics kept on different principles by different states. A simple factor is the list of free contributions to the British war funds made by large and small states according to their means, from the imperial gift of £100,000,000 made by the Indian Government, a normal year's revenue, to the £26,000 given by the Gambia. The great Dominions financed their own war-efforts and hastened their own economic development thereby. As always in wartime, primary producers flourished and, while direct taxation was doubled in several communities, it did not keep pace with farmers' profits. Prices of raw materials were stabilised by national supply and munition boards which in each Dominion, from 1915 onwards, began to experiment in bulk purchase of whole harvests and the annual output of mines, the beginning of a new technique which would end the era of Free Trade.

While borrowings were gigantic by pre-war standards, they did not impair the strength of the young communities, as was proved by the high proportion of the money that was raised locally, and by the buoyancy of revenues. Nor did any Dominion default when bad times came. No small part of the capital expense was laid out on public works and industrial enterprises that would be valuable after the war. The national debt of Canada rose from about £67 millions in 1914 to about £317 millions in 1919. The figures are complicated by exchange transactions between Great Britain and Canada, from which it appears that Canada borrowed, on balance, £48 millions in London and the remainder at home or in the U.S.A. During the same period the Australian Commonwealth debt was increased from £19 millions to £325 millions, of which increase about £114 millions were borrowed in London, the rest in Australia. The total cost of the war to Australia was estimated at £311 millions paid for, as to 15% from revenue, as to 85% from loans. There were also large increases in the public debts of individual Australian states. New Zealand, already heavily indebted in 1914, raised war loans to the amount of £80 millions and only sought for one-third of that sum in London.

As was proper, the accumulated wealth of the mother-country was poured out more copiously for expenditure that was almost all unproductive. The national debt rose from £650 millions to £8000 millions. Yet the City carried the load and remained the world's financial centre. Sterling was sterling still until the crash of 1931–3 when the British government defaulted on its financial settlement with the United States, after ten years of paying its debts and forgiving its debtors.

8. PEACE-MAKING, 1918–20

THE breaking of the Hindenburg Line by British and Dominion troops, on 26 September 1918, was the decisive blow that brought the war to an end. The news sent Germany's smaller allies to surrender post-haste and persuaded Ludendorff that he too must ask for terms. While that victory was being hammered out in France, General Allenby in Palestine was concluding his secondary campaign by the destruction of two Turkish armies. The pursuit with massed cavalry to Damascus (1 October 1918) and beyond, as audacious and mobile as any in the second World War, completed the destruction of the Turkish Empire and left the British supreme in Islam from Stamboul to Sarawak. The Dardanelles and the coast of Asia Minor were commanded by the Royal Navy; British armies of occupation were in Aleppo, Damascus, Mosul, Baghdad; South Persia was garrisoned by British Indian troops; an expedition had seized the key points in the Caucasus; Afghanistan and India were secure; Malaya was untouched by war. Arabia, Egypt, and the Sahara Desert were far behind the front. In those regions of Central Asia where British and Russian interests had been thought to clash, the British were masters since there was no settled government in the Russian Empire, though the new, unknown and untrusted, party of Bolsheviks (who had surrendered ignominiously to Germany at Brest-Litovsk) ruled precariously about Moscow and Leningrad. Three-quarters of the Russian Empire, its north and south coasts and its Siberian outposts were, if ruled at all, ruled by provisional governments that were still faithful to the Allies. At Archangel, at Odessa, at Vladivostok, and at many other points American, French and British detachments stood valiantly beside those Russians who had been faithful in the war against German militarism.

In January 1919 the delegations of the victorious Allies met in Paris. Lloyd George was there, renewed in authority by the 'coupon' election of December 1918 and supported by the representatives of Canada, Australia, South Africa, New Zealand, and the Indian Empire. And President Wilson was there, an *avatar* from the West, whose declaration of the Fourteen Points (January 1918) had inspired all the political minorities in the world with a new hope. Most of them were represented in Paris and most went away disappointed. The President spent two short periods in Europe, from January to February and from March to May 1919, and in that time the political situation rapidly deteriorated throughout the world. He had come believing that a pure and simple application of general principles could solve problems that were neither pure nor simple. He solved nothing and left the minority delegations to get the best terms they could. Those who were not satisfied returned to organise national revolts for their supposed rights.

By the middle of April, the British were deeply engaged in at least five distinct political disturbances:

(1) In Ireland the Sinn Fein party had boycotted the British Parliament. Their elected members had assembled in Ireland and issued a Declaration of Independence (21 January 1919). Though the Irish Civil War did not break out until later in the year Sinn Fein was a growing embarrassment to Mr Lloyd George. Sinn Fein got no hearing at the Conference.

(2) In India Gandhi's first campaign of non-co-operation (described in chapter XVIII, 3, page 945) was launched in March. The Amritsar incident and the declaration of war by the Amir of Afghanistan followed on 13 April 1919.

(3) A sudden outburst of anti-British agitation in Egypt had produced riots and murders, also reaching a crisis in March. The nationalist leader Zaghlul, having appealed in vain to the conference for a hearing, turned to terrorism and was arrested. In April Mr Lloyd George was obliged to send his favourite general, Allenby, to restore order in Egypt. These events will be discussed further in chapter XVIII, 5, page 959. For the present it will be sufficient to say that on 19 April 1919, the British protectorate over Egypt was recognised by President Wilson, a sore blow to the nationalists.

(4) The intransigence of the Turkish generals gave the supreme council some anxiety from the beginning. It was necessary to bring military pressure to bear upon them in Asia

Minor and this produced one of the first cleavages between the Allies. Wilson resisted the demands of the Italians, who dreamed of creating an Aegean Empire. Repudiating with moral indignation the claims they based upon secret treaties with the other allies, he caused them to withdraw from the conference in petulant chagrin. With the approval of Lloyd George, who was fired with romantic enthusiasm for the rejuvenation of Greece, Wilson encouraged Venizelos to occupy Smyrna with a Greek army (May 1919), in order to overawe the Turks, and to forestall an Italian *coup-de-main*. Though not immediately relevant to the history of the British.Empire the events in Smyrna were to be linked with it three years later.

(5) The military commitments in Russia were a severe drain upon British resources at the time when the armies were being demobilised. Far from urging intervention, the War Office spent the year in trying to disengage, a policy that Sir Henry Wilson, the C.I.G.S., preached in and out of season. It seemed, in the spring of 1919, that the Bolshevik regime was about to collapse under pressure from the White Armies of Kolchak and Denikin. Kolchak's farthest advance was in May, Denikin's later in the summer. If a *bourgeois* counter-revolution were on the point of succeeding it was clearly the policy of the Allies to nourish its social-democratic elements. The existing military missions therefore hung on a little longer. The small expeditionary force in North Russia was not withdrawn until September 1919, when its departure caused dismay from Archangel to Riga. Some technical and financial support was given to Denikin for a few months longer.

All these were side-issues and as such were overlooked until the greater issue of the European peace-treaties had been settled. The Treaty of Versailles was drafted in May and signed on 28 June 1919. Though this was followed by world-wide rejoicing (in an atmosphere of relief and optimism that was noticeably absent in 1945), it was soon appreciated that the side-issues were urgent and threatening. So far as the British were concerned the limiting factor was the disintegration of our armed forces. At the beginning of the year Britain and the Dominions possessed a greater effective strength by land, sea and air than France or America. Having taken the lion's share of the fighting in the last campaign the British might have had the lion's share of the spoil. They preferred to go quietly home. All the armies of the Commonwealth clamoured to be demobilised, with an enthusiasm that led here and there to good-humoured mutinies. Above all they were unwilling to take any part in the Russian civil war. Mr Churchill was sent to the War Office to satisfy this demand, which he met with such speed that a surplus of 3,000,000 soldiers in January was reduced to 2,000,000 in March and to none in June. By the end of 1919 he could find but one British and one Indian division for the requirement of all the little wars that threatened. Thus the withdrawal from Russia was inevitable, as was a more prudent policy in the Near East. In January 1920 the Supreme Allied Council somewhat ruefully agreed that it would be necessary to leave Constantinople to the Turks. This decision was taken in the month that saw the founding of the League of Nations.

It was not the League but the Supreme Allied Council, at conference after conference, that laid down the lines of the post-war settlement. The meeting at San Remo, in April 1920, was known as the 'prize-giving' since an assignment of mandates for conquered or liberated territory was agreed among the victorious powers. The preparation of the formal instruments for ratifying the mandates was to occupy the Mandates Committee of the League for three or four years. Meanwhile it was imperative to provide for the government of the dismembered Turkish Empire. The mandate for Irak was awarded to Great Britain with something like general agreement; that for Palestine was accepted by Great Britain after it had been tentatively laid at the feet of the United States. There was an optimistic belief in some quarters that the Americans might accept responsibility too for the unfortunate Armenians; but the tide of isolationism was running hard, and the election of the Republican Harding as President in November 1920, crushed any further hope of American co-operation in the Near East.

The French, having received a provisional mandate for Syria, proceeded to overthrow the Arab nationalists in Damascus and to expel King Feisal, whom T. E. Lawrence had installed there. They also met resistance in the ancient province of Cilicia. All these arrangements, together with a provisional Greek mandate for Smyrna were confirmed by the Treaty of Sèvres which was imposed upon the Turks in August 1920. Thus passed from history the Ottoman Empire which, in the sixteenth century, had been the most powerful state in the world and, in the nineteenth century, was still the terror of English Liberals.

In spite of the treaty, the year 1920 showed a marked turn for the worse. In October a complete reversal was caused by the death of King Alexander of Greece, from the bite of a pet monkey. The Greeks, always ready to turn to some new thing, recalled the exiled King Constantine, who had been regarded as pro-German during the war, and dismissed the Premier Venizelos, the friend of Wilson and Lloyd George. While Constantine embarked upon an aggressive campaign against the Turks (February 1921), hoping to carve out a Greek Empire, the Allies quarrelled. The French, rejecting any suggestion of friendliness towards King Constantine, made a treaty of alliance with Kemal, the new dictator of Turkey, since Turkey was the traditional ally of France.

Hope of overthrowing Trotsky's terrorist rule in Russia had also vanished in 1920. Kolchak had been disposed of in January, Denikin in July. There had even been a danger of the Bolsheviks overrunning Poland until the farthest ripple of their unorganised army was stayed by Marshal Weygand in front of Warsaw (August 1920). All through the year terrorism in Ireland too was blazing up into civil war until, in January 1921, Lloyd George was goaded into authorising a policy of reprisal which was as unwise as it was unworthy. India provided its share of the general unrest in a Moslem agitation known as the *khilafat* (or caliphate) movement, an expression of sympathy with the Sultan of Turkey who, as Caliph of Islam, was disparaged by the *feringhi* at the Treaty of Sèvres. Gandhi supported the *khilafat* agitation though not the bloodthirsty rising of the Moplahs which followed it. Only when Kemal deposed the Sultan and abolished the caliphate did the agitation among the Indian Moslems subside. The revolt of Islam affected the British most powerfully, at that time, in Mesopotamia where a sporadic guerrilla outbreak of the Arab tribes pinned down large numbers of British and Indian troops, at a cost to the British taxpayer of over £20,000,000.

9. THREE REGIONAL PACTS, 1921–5

(1) THE MIDDLE EAST SETTLEMENT, 1921–4

IT will now be necessary to look back five years to the diplomatic moves which first led the British into Arabia, Palestine, Syria, Mesopotamia, and Persia. The Turks had never effectively ruled Arabia, though Abdul Hamid had built the Hejaz Railway (1909) with the intention of doing so. Since his deposition Turkey had been in the hands of the Young Turks who disdained the spiritual power of the caliphate and were bent upon a nationalist 'pan-Turanian' policy. It was time for the Arab peoples to be free in name as well as in effect; and even before the outbreak of war in 1914 the Sherif of Mecca had secretly appealed to Kitchener for help in the cause of Arab independence. Kitchener, however, would not be drawn into any such intrigue.

When Great Britain declared war on Turkey (5 November 1914), these obscure designs could come out into the light, though with discretion so long as Turkish garrisons held the key-points in the Arab lands.

While there was still hope of success in both campaigns Sir Henry MacMahon, who had taken Kitchener's place in Egypt, made the first of the secret agreements with the Arabs. He gave an undertaking (October 1915), with the approval of the British government, that Great Britain would 'recognise and support the independence' of Arabia, Syria, and Mesopotamia, excepting Basra and Baghdad, where 'the established position and interests of Great Britain necessitate special measures', and the coast of Syria, where the population was not wholly Arab. A further reservation was that this was to apply only in those territories 'in which Great Britain is free to act without detriment to the interests of her ally, France'. Later, these pledges were renewed by an assurance that districts which liberated themselves should enjoy self-government.

It was not surprising that the Arabs were slow to move, since the MacMahon Pledge was followed by the investment of Kut and the evacuation of Gallipoli. All that winter (1915–16) Cairo was full of defeated generals reorganising their commands according to plans that changed every day. In February 1916 an intelligence department known as the Arab Bureau was formed in Cairo. It became the rallying-point of one of the most remarkable pressure groups in British history. The Arab Bureau drew upon the varied talents of Dr D. G. Hogarth of the Ashmolean Museum; his young protégé, T. E. Lawrence, who was expert in Syrian affairs; Sir Leonard Woolley, the excavator of Ur; Miss Gertrude Bell the Oriental traveller; George Lloyd afterwards Lord Lloyd; Aubrey Herbert the M.P. who was sent to buy off the Turkish general besieging Kut, and others.

One of their number, Sir Mark Sykes, was selected by the cabinet to negotiate (reluctantly) a new partition of the Turkish Empire with the other allies. Unfortunately the Foreign Office acted without reference to MacMahon's negotiations, with the result that the instrument called the Sykes-Picot agreement, of May 1916, could hardly be held consistent with the MacMahon Pledge. It was now agreed that northern Syria should become a French protectorate, southern Mesopotamia a British protectorate. Between the two 'an independent Arab state or a federation of states' was to be created, under tutelage; it was to be divided into French and British zones of influence. This was a bad treaty, and the worst of it was that it was kept secret for eighteen months until the Russian Revolution, when the Bolsheviks published it to embarrass the allies.

Without knowledge of the Sykes-Picot Treaty, the Sherif and his sons let loose their revolt against Turkey in June 1916, a courageous act, since the fall of Kut in April had reduced British prestige to its lowest. Lawrence joined the Emir Feisal in the Hejaz in January 1917; launched his harassing campaign against the Turkish railway garrisons in February; and by June was in possession of Akaba, the port from which the guerrilla war could be maintained. Meanwhile, and again without an adequate consultation of the parallel policy in Egypt, the British-Indian campaign in Mesopotamia had gone forward. The first resounding triumph of the Eastern war was the capture of Baghdad (March 1917), a feather in the cap of the Indian government. Direct rule on the Indian plan was set up in the occupied provinces of Mesopotamia, with a staff of 400 British officials, very few of whom, as Lawrence said tartly, could speak Arabic. With that the Mesopotamian campaign receded from public attention, though there were interesting political developments. Contacts were made with Czarist cavalry in North Persia and, when Russian influence vanished at the Revolution, a screen of military posts was drawn across South Persia, to cover the overland routes to India. In 1918 some advanced British detachments even garrisoned key-points in the Caucasus. Curzon succeeded in negotiating a treaty with Persia (1919), establishing what amounted to a British protectorate over the southern part of the country. At the last moment the Shah's government refused to ratify it and the British outposts were withdrawn in 1920.

The part played by Lawrence in the Arab Revolt has been variously estimated by the critics, and sometimes depreciated by those who have not understood his intentions. He was but one of several staff officers who advised the Arab partisans in the Hejaz; his two specific contributions to the campaign were a new guerrilla strategy which was to be an inspiration to many irregular fighters in the second World War, and a plan for carrying the revolt out of the desert into Palestine and Syria, under the banner of a Sherifian prince. While the Bedouin could easily be raised to arms the problem was to interest the peoples of the settled districts in the enterprise. In this Lawrence succeeded, extending the revolt through Syria to Damascus. He was never so naive as to suppose that his efforts were more than a fringe to the fabric of Allenby's campaign, that is in a military sense. His purpose and achievement were political, to show the Arab flag so that the MacMahon Pledge might be redeemed. Having set up an Arab administration in Damascus he withdrew. For his own part he believed himself engaged in honour to make the Sherif's son Feisal the Arab King; but the British Headquarters was not so deeply committed as was Lawrence to Feisal in person; and the Foreign Office, dubiously entangled in the Sykes-Picot agreement, was half-hearted. When Feisal, with Lawrence at his elbow, made his own plea for Arab independence at Versailles he could not prevail against the French, who stood firm upon the agreement. Accordingly Lawrence withdrew from public affairs in a mood of frustration, and Feisal was driven from Damascus by the French.

This was the deadlock which produced tumultuous fighting throughout the Middle East in 1920. The Treaty of Sèvres crystallised a situation that no one approved. In January 1921 Lloyd George made one of his bold improvisations. He transferred the mandates in the Middle East from the Foreign Office to the Colonial Office, that is from Lord Curzon to Mr Churchill, who then became Secretary of State for the Colonies.

Mr Churchill lost no time in summoning a conference at Cairo (March 1921). One of his first successes was to persuade Lawrence to join his staff and so to take part in repairing the wrong done to the Arabs. In April they created the Arab state of Trans-Jordania under the Emir Abdulla, the Sherif's eldest son. In June they sent the Emir Feisal to Baghdad to offer himself as candidate for the throne of Mesopotamia. Having been accepted by a plebiscite in which he gained 96% of the votes, Feisal was proclaimed King of the new Arab state of Irak in August. An Arab administration lightly supervised by a British High Commissioner, Sir Percy Cox, replaced the administration by British-Indian officials. A provisional mandate was issued by the Council of the League of Nations in October and was confirmed by a treaty of alliance negotiated in 1922 between the British and Iraki governments. The rebellion died away when a native administration was established. Not until 1924 was the final instrument that ratified these arrangements issued by the League.

Lawrence resigned from the Colonial Office in June 1922 to withdraw into the cloistered obscurity of life in the ranks of the R.A.F. In a letter to the Press he declared his satisfaction with the Middle East Settlement which, he said, might well stand firm for fifteen years. It was a triumph for the mandatory system, for British good faith, for Mr Churchill's political skill, and for the principle of indirect rule. One of the decisions of the Cairo Conference had been to withdraw the British troops from Irak and to maintain security with Air Forces supported by armoured cars. The military establishments, of thirty-two battalions in 1921, at a cost of £20,000,000 to the British tax-payer, was reduced to one Indian battalion in 1928 which with the other armed services cost £1,500,000.

Irak was deemed ready for a Parliamentary constitution with manhood suffrage in 1926, and in 1932 the British mandate was freely surrendered. In the last year of peace, 1938, the population was estimated at 3,500,000, the revenue at £7,500,000, of which a quarter was derived from state royalties on the production of oil. Trans-Jordania also was released from the mandate in 1946.

In February 1922 Lord Allenby declared the British protectorate over Egypt to be abolished. Though this was a step forward, a factor in the general settlement, it did not, as will be seen in a later chapter, lead to the same happy results as the reforms in Irak.

A NOTE ON THE IRISH TREATY

Following close upon the Middle East Settlement came the Irish Treaty. The year 1921 had opened with a bitter struggle between the Irish terrorists and the counter-terror of the 'black-and-tans'. Refusing to be deterred by these scenes of degradation, Parliament had passed another Home Rule Bill giving Ulster the right to contract out, and this at least made an opening for a forward move. In June 1921 King George V inaugurated the Parliament of Northern Ireland at Belfast. The influence of the Dominion premiers, then assembled at an imperial conference, was not without its effect upon the truce of July and the long negotiations in London. The treaty, which was accepted by most Irishmen in December 1921, gave to the new Irish Free State 'the same constitutional status in the Community of Nations known as the British Empire as the Dominion of Canada'. The revolt of the irreconcilables, the bitterest of all Ireland's woes, which followed the establishment of the Free State in 1922, need not be recounted here.

(2) THE WASHINGTON NAVAL TREATIES AND BRITISH SEA-POWER

Delegates from the Dominions to the imperial conference revealed some doubt about the wisdom of renewing the Anglo-Japanese alliance in its pre-war form. Hence they responded eagerly when President Harding issued invitations to a naval conference, to be held at Washington in November 1921. On the other hand they were piqued at the form of his invitation which was addressed to the British Empire as a single unit. The representatives of the Dominions thus appeared as members of the British delegation, which was led by Lord Balfour. Though all attempts to agree upon a general plan of naval disarmament failed, the leading powers consented to make humane restrictions upon submarine warfare, and to restrict the size of battleships. Instead of the former two-power standard, that is, a navy as powerful as those of any two potential rivals, the British were to maintain no more than parity with the United States. The Japanese were to restrict their naval strength to three-fifths of the British and American strength, the French and Italians with their narrower commitments were rated proportionately. The naval agreement made one of a series of seven treaties negotiated at Washington between November 1921 and February 1922. A Pacific pact of arbitration was signed. The German deep-sea cables were partitioned between the victorious powers. The integrity and independence of China were guaranteed by the nine-power pact.

It was indeed a landmark in history when the British Navy abandoned its mission to rule the seven seas. For about a hundred years the Palmerstonian tradition had prevailed, that it was Britain's duty to send a warship, and if necessary a combined force, to any unruly shore. Thus British naval squadrons had intervened in Crete, at Alexandria, off the Nicaraguan coast, in Yokohama Bay, as well as in defence of British territories. No longer, after Washington, could Britain police the world. Almost the last of these affairs was the Shanghai Incident of 1927–8. The abrogation of some treaty rights to the new nationalist regime of the Kuo-min-tang in China had led to an agitation against the concession at Shanghai also, and to anti-foreign riots. Order was instantly restored upon the arrival of a division of British regular troops, the only military operation of any consequence undertaken by the British Army between 1922 and 1938, and, of course, a demonstration of sea-power.

It came to light at the Washington Conference that strategy in the naval war had turned on cable communications. Though the American Western Union Company had got control of most of the Atlantic cables before the war, British pre-eminence in all the other seas had given the Royal Navy the run of the world's communications. After the seizure of the German signal-stations the German commerce-raiders were speechless. On the other hand the British naval effort was controlled by the British-owned services with their tentacles in every sea. The cables were administered, in war-time, by the Admiralty, which laid many new strategic lines, with the result that a return to unfettered commercial ownership after the War was hardly practicable.

The British government (in partnership with the Dominions) already owned the Pacific Cable and several strategic lines. In 1920 it bought back one of the Atlantic cables from Western Union. By 1921 the 'all-red' route was accomplished by nationally owned services through Penzance, Fayal in the Azores, Halifax, Vancouver, Fanning Island, and Fiji. This caused some hard thinking at Washington, when the American war-staffs realised where the strength of the British imperial links resided. 'The United States had missed the boat when Cyrus Field went to Europe.' Between the wars the competition of the American companies was terrific, where it could be applied, but there were many parts of the world where Britain's island colonies provided terminals for signal links whereas America had none. Competition drove the British companies to combination. At the Imperial Wireless and Cable Conference of 1929, a general merger was agreed upon with a return to private ownership. A new trust was created (reconstituted in 1934 under the name of Cables and Wireless Limited), with two nominees of the British government on the Board, to manage all the British overseas communications on commercial principles. They took over 165,000 miles of privately-owned cable, including the Eastern Extension, the Australia and China system, and the West-Indian system; 25,000 miles of publicly-owned cable including the Atlantic and Pacific 'all-red' routes; the new Beam Wireless system; and the manufacturing interests of the Marconi Company. Their uniform world-wide press-rate of a penny a word to every part of the globe, for signals that never failed, made Cables and Wireless the most powerful instrument of propaganda in the hands of any government. In the second World War it was a weapon as well as an organ of administration. Whether direct public ownership and management would have been preferable to commercial ownership under government supervision is an open question.

The real problem for communications is not public versus private ownership, nor British versus American predominance, it is Cables versus Wireless. The British network links seaports and was designed for sea-traffic. The new American imperialism is concerned with terminals for wireless links between air-ports, not following the old traffic-lanes, but great circles over land and sea.

The prudent British withdrawal, by the Washington naval treaties, from a position that had become untenable prescribed a new imperial strategy. The Pacific Dominions were drawn into the strategic sphere of the United States by their concern at the ambitions of Japan, in spite of the well-meant efforts of the Australian Labour leaders to avoid this realignment. They had opposed the Washington policy in the hope of bringing Japan to an accommodation. Nevertheless Australian defence became dependent upon American naval power in mid-Pacific, and required a complementary British force at Singapore.

While service opinion urged the construction of a fortified naval base at Singapore the plan was opposed, as provocative, by the pacifists who predominated on the left wing in all the English-speaking countries, and it received scant support from left-wing governments. A corollary of the Singapore strategy was that Hong Kong, which the British had made into the greatest free port in the world was outside the perimeter and militarily indefensible.

(3) CHANAK AND LAUSANNE

The triumphant diplomacy of Lloyd George's government which had retrieved so many desperate situations in 1921 and 1922 collapsed over the revival of Turkey. Kemal, the Turkish dictator, had stopped the Greek advances, in June 1921, at the Sakkaria river. For a year the armies faced one another, the Turks growing stronger and the Greeks weaker in equipment, morale and diplomatic support. The strong men of Lloyd George's cabinet, looking back from their successes at Cairo, Dublin and Washington, were deeply divided over Turkey. Almost alone Lloyd George retained his faith in the Greek renaissance, while Mr E. S. Montagu, who had to deal with the *khilafat* agitation in India, was as passionately pro-Turk. Curzon was for a friendly deal with Kemal, giving him all he wanted except Constantinople, while Mr Churchill warned Lloyd George that Kemal would fight, and that we had no army sufficient to stop him.

In March 1922, the allied powers feebly tried to intervene and were snubbed by both Kemal and Constantine. In August Kemal struck, drove the Greeks into the sea, and blooded his young soldiers by allowing them to sack Smyrna, in true Turkish fashion. On 11 September, Kemal was warned not to enter the neutral zone patrolled by allied detachments along the shores of the Bosphorus and Dardanelles. A week later the French withdrew leaving the British alone in the field. While Curzon at Paris tried to shame the French into some sort of co-operation, and while General Harington defied the Turkish advance at Chanak with one British infantry brigade, Lloyd George appealed to the Dominions for support. New Zealand immediately responded with an offer to send troops. Mr Hughes, too, would have fought again for the bloodstained slopes of Gallipoli, but his impulsive offer was sharply criticised by the Australian opposition. Canada had no sentimental interest in the campaign, and the Canadian government was justly angered by a premature release to the press of Lloyd George's appeal, which they regarded as an attempt to incite Canadian opinion behind the back of their government. Mr McKenzie King coolly replied that the question must be referred to the Canadian parliament; and the South African Government gave a similar reply. In the eyes of the world this looked like a rift in the unity of the Commonwealth; it was an irreparable breach in the Anglo-French alliance.

The Chanak incident, which for a moment looked catastrophic, blew away and vanished. By 28 September Mr Churchill could report that sufficient troops had arrived to hold the position under cover of the naval guns, while for their part the Turks had shown no disposition to attack. All the contestants were brought together at the Lausanne Conference (November 1922 to January 1923) where Curzon's firmness brought the Turks to reason. After six months more of stubborn argument they signed the Treaty of Lausanne which completed the pacification of the Middle East.

Peace was then for a few years restored to the whole world. Even the Bolsheviks had been received into the comity of nations at the Genoa Conference (April 1922). Churchill's Arab Settlement, Balfour's Treaty of Washington, Curzon's Treaty of Lausanne, were three great regional pacts all made within the framework of the League Covenant. All three reacted also upon the structure of the British Commonwealth. The Middle East Settlement seemed to have sown the seed of a new group of Islamic peoples freely associated in a new Commonwealth with the British; this had been Lawrence's dream. The Treaty of

Washington foreshadowed a new direction for the policy of the Pacific Dominions. Lausanne forced the issue of imperial control over foreign affairs.

Though the Dominions had been ready to fight beside the British at Chanak they were deeply perturbed at being committed to action by Lloyd George's chauvinism. It was the primary cause of a demand for declared equality of status. Chanak was the death-blow to Lloyd George's coalition government. Three years later when the Tories negotiated the Treaty of Locarno (October 1925), the last and most significant of the regional pacts, Sir Austen Chamberlain scrupulously excluded the Dominions from any obligation in a region where they were not vitally concerned.

XVII

THE BRITISH COMMONWEALTH,
1917–39

Argument: Dominion Status was generally recognised as a fact in 1919. Indications of a recession from that status in the 'twenties encouraged nationalists in the Dominions to press for a legal definition, which was given in the Balfour Declaration. Legal niceties required further clarification in the Statute of Westminster, 1931.

The world-wide economic depression of 1929–31 revealed fundamental weaknesses in the British economy. The century-old policy of multilateral trade through the Open Door was replaced by a series of restrictive bilateral agreements, negotiated at Ottawa.

While the Commonwealth made a good recovery and while the Dominions built up their secondary industries, Great Britain was no longer the greatest manufacturing nation. The surplus of men and of money for export was exhausted.

1. MATURITY OF THE BRITISH COMMON-
WEALTH, 1917–32

UNTIL the fall of Asquith's second administration, the claim of the Dominions to a share in the direction of war policy had been allowed to go by default. When Lloyd George formed his coalition, in December 1916, one of his first acts was to call the Dominion premiers[1] into consultation, thus reverting to the principle agreed in 1911. The Conference which held two sessions, in the spring of 1917 and the summer of 1918, was grandiosely but inaccurately known as the Imperial War Cabinet; its functions were not executive but informative. During the adjournments General Smuts was invited by Lloyd George to remain in London as a member of the British War Cabinet. Though a minister without portfolio, he was regarded as an honorary representative of the Dominions in which capacity he wore the mantle of Laurier, rather than of Seddon or Deakin.

[1] First Sir Robert Borden of Canada, when on a visit to London.

Jan Christiaan Smuts (b. 1870), farmer, lawyer, and philosopher; graduate of Stellenbosch and of Cambridge; admirer of
Cecil Rhodes before the Jameson Raid and adherent of Kruger
after it; Boer *guerillero* and British general; international statesman and shrewd, even harsh, party-leader; known all his life
long as 'Slim Jannie' by his own people who are held to be good
judges of slimness; he was no soft sentimentalist, no narrow
provincial to be charmed into acquiescence by diplomats and
courtiers. His belief in the utility of Dominion Status meant
more than any loyal tribute.

The Imperial War Cabinet proceeded to Versailles in a body
to constitute the British Empire delegation at the peace negotiations of 1919. All the Dominion premiers signed the treaty,
placing their signatures together below that of the British
Prime Minister. The Dominions and India were admitted as
full members of the League of Nations. In 1919 Smuts could say
in the House at Capetown: 'We have received a position of
absolute equality and freedom, not only among the other states
of the Empire, but among the other nations of the world.' In
Canada Sir R. Borden spoke to the same effect. But the law and
the convention of the constitution may differ, and the practice
may not entirely conform with one or the other. What was true
of Canada, which retained a High Commissioner in London
since 1879, which had claimed fiscal independence since 1854,
and negotiated directly with Washington since 1884, which
accredited its own ambassador to the United States in 1927, was
not so true of India whose autocratic ruler was the nominee of
a Secretary of State in Whitehall.

In spite of the good feeling between the Dominions and the
mother-country after a war in which imperial unity had been
valorously displayed, the 1920's were uncomfortable years for
imperialists. The compact group of four Dominions, as it had
appeared in 1911, was variegated by the addition of India to the
Conference of 1921. Newfoundland, at the other end of the scale,
was also treated as a Dominion. More significant was the admission
of the Irish Free State which, according to its Constitution Act,
was given the same status as Canada.

Recent events had obliged the Dominions to concern themselves far more actively with foreign affairs. It could not be
thought satisfactory that they should have been consulted about

the end of the war though not about its beginning. After the fall of Lloyd George in 1922 they lost ground, and repeatedly protested that they were neither consulted nor informed. It appeared that the Foreign Office[1] was not much influenced by the resolutions of Colonial Conferences. No British administration treated the Dominions so discourteously as that of Ramsay MacDonald, whose *volte-face* of recognising the Soviet government in 1924 was presented to the Dominions as a *fait accompli*. In Baldwin's time there was some improvement, as over the Treaty of Locarno.

The one point on which the Dominions all agreed was national autonomy; for them the issue of imperial federation was dead. Since it was clear that the resolutions of 1911 had not been carried out, some students began to press for a new declaration of status, a formula of Empire. In 1915 some of those men who, ten years earlier, had been known as Milner's kindergarten came forward as the 'Round Table Group' to work for closer organisation. All who care for the status of the Dominions owe a debt to Mr Lionel Curtis, the editor of the *Round Table Quarterly*, for his researches and for the stimulus he gave to public interest; but his main thesis, the necessity of closer union, was already a lost cause. Too many colonials agreed with the Australian Workers' Union in 1918 that it meant 'government of the Dominions of the Empire by the plutocrats of England'.

Since the vocabulary of 'imperialism' had been besmirched by the abuse of hostile propagandists, the Round Table Group brought into popular use the title of the British Commonwealth[2] of Nations.

The Conference of 1921 was negative in its effects. Resisting all tendency towards closer union the delegates parted, agreeing that it was better not to convert the aery links of loyal partnership into legal formulas that would be as brittle as they were rigid.

This, and the succeeding conference in 1923, led to the last

[1] The standard *Cambridge History of British Foreign Policy* (1923) makes no allusion to the claim of the Dominions to participate in the foreign policy of the Empire.

[2] First used by Lord Rosebery in a speech at Adelaide in 1884 and adopted by the Fabians.

'The words Empire, Imperial, Imperialist, and so forth, are pure claptraps. What the colonies are driving at is a Commonwealth; and that is what the English citizen means, too, by the Empire, when he means anything at all.' Bernard Shaw, *Fabianism and the Empire* (1900).

British efforts, hitherto, for systematic colonisation. An Empire Settlement Act was passed in 1922 to authorise state-aided emigration, especially for discharged soldiers. A sum of £3,000,000 a year was voted by Parliament for this purpose. Several attempts were made to finance the settlement of groups of families on agricultural land in the Dominions, with very limited success. Perhaps the best was the 'Three Thousand Families Scheme' for sending ex-soldiers to Canada; about 70% of them prospered sufficiently to repay their advanced passage-money. Most of the schemes broke down, as anyone who had read the reports of similar schemes in the 1830's might have known they would break down, since little effort was made to create new communities. The most ambitious was the '£34,000,000 Agreement' of 1925 with the Australian government, providing for advances of capital up to that sum by the British government on account of public works for land development. The Australians agreed to accept one British immigrant for each sum of £75 advanced. The scheme languished and died after only one-twentieth part of the £34,000,000 had been actually spent.

Mass-emigration, that is to say the export of surplus man-power, an important feature of British social life in the previous hundred years, came to an end in the slump of 1931. Its epitaph was pronounced by the inter-departmental committee over which Mr Malcolm MacDonald presided in 1934.[1] The Commissioners, blandly ignoring the whole history of the British Dominions, went further in assuming that group-migration also

[1] *Report of the Inter-Departmental Committee on Migration*, 1934. The last year of mass-emigration on a great scale, 1913, was also the first year for which complete analysed statistics were prepared. It was then for the first time possible to calculate the net outward migration from the U.K. to the Dominions, by excluding travellers for business and pleasure from the totals, and by setting off the inward against the outward migration.

Net outward migration

U.K. to—	1913	1929
Canada	165,000	53,000
Australia and New Zealand	56,000	11,000
Other parts of the Empire	3000	(−1000)
Foreign countries	80,000	24,000
Total	304,000	87,000

After 1929 the inward migration from the Dominions exceeded the outward figure to them.

was impracticable. Though, at the time when they were sitting, some of the largest experiments ever attempted in systematic colonisation were being carried out in Soviet Russia, the Commissioners seemed unaware of them; they did not even seem to have heard of the brilliant success of the Zionist settlements in Palestine under British mandate. Emigration, they asserted, in the British Commonwealth in the twentieth century, could only follow the method of infiltration.

When they turned to the field of statistics they were much better informed though no less dismal. The fall in the birth-rate had already extinguished the surplus of young persons in the British Isles who were of an age to emigrate successfully. The industrial revolution had destroyed the English peasantry. Land-hungry farmers' boys were now rare in Old England, not super-fluous. As for other workers, it was plain that English trade unionists did not want to go and Australian trade unionists did not want them to come. State-aided schemes of insurance against unemployment tended to fix wage-earners in their own country and to make them suspicious of interlopers. It would however be quite wrong to suppose that all migration had ceased because the tide was ebbing instead of flowing. The adventurous continued to move about the Empire where opportunity offered.

The distribution of talent continued in spite of the stoppage in the distribution of labourers. Throughout the period between the German Wars, common citizenship made travel easy for the white-skinned subjects of the King who could pay their way. The makers of the Empire have rarely been those members of the governing class, globe-trotting with first-class return tickets, against whom the Socialists declaimed; nor have they been dumb proletarians. The building-up of the Commonwealth continued as it had begun, as an opportunity for the adventurous middle classes. For them, for the engineers, the architects, the surveyors; for the medical men, the scientific investigators, the teachers; for the lawyers, the merchants, the accountants, the secretaries, the scholars, the clergy, Capetown, Melbourne, or Auckland were in no foreign lands; nor did their fellows from the Dominions find it hard to establish themselves in London. These are the men who formed the character and maintained the unity of the British Commonwealth of Nations.

Canada was troubled in 1926 by a constitutional dispute between Mr McKenzie King the premier, and Viscount Byng the Governor-General, over the prerogative right to dissolve Parliament. The last step in rounding off Dominion Status was the destruction of the political power of Governors. By a resolution of the Conference of 1926 they were declared to be the personal representatives of the King, not the agents of the government in Downing Street. The demand that the Crown should appoint some respected citizen of each Dominion as its Governor naturally followed, the first such appointment being that of the Chief Justice of Australia, Sir Isaac Isaacs (1855–1947), as Governor-General in 1931. It then became further necessary for the British government to appoint a political representative at the capital of each Dominion. By this means the hated rule of the Colonial Office was whittled away. Already during the war Lloyd George had granted what Asquith refused in 1911—direct access to the British Prime Minister for Dominion premiers who visited London. In 1919 a separate Dominions Department had been created within the Colonial Office; after 1925 an additional Secretary of State for the Dominions was appointed.

So much constitutional progress was made that the long-expected formula for Dominion Status had become a practical necessity. It was supplied in a long and somewhat metaphysical statement issued on behalf of the Conference of 1926, and known as the Balfour Declaration. Though Balfour drafted most of it, the significant words 'autonomous communities freely associated' were inserted upon the suggestion of J. B. M. Hertzog (1865–1942), the South African nationalist who replaced General Smuts as premier in 1924.

The Committee are of opinion [begins the Balfour Declaration] that nothing would be gained by attempting to lay down a constitution for the British Empire...it defies classification and bears no real resemblance to any other political organisation which has ever yet been tried....There is, however, one most important element in it which, from a strictly constitutional point of view...has now reached its full development—we refer to the group of self-governing communities composed of Great Britain and the Dominions....They are autonomous communities within the British Empire, equal in status, in no way subordinate to one another in any aspect of their domestic or external affairs, though united by a common allegiance to the Crown, and freely associated as members of the British Commonwealth of Nations.

With this the loyalists were more than content and were willing to let well alone; but not so thought Hertzog, austerely trained in the Roman-Dutch law, who returned to South Africa to announce: 'The old British Empire is no more.' What to General Smuts, the philosopher of 'holism' was the creation of a greater synthesis, seemed to the narrower mind of Hertzog to be disintegration. Some legal interpretations of the Balfour Declaration were referred to a committee of eminent jurists and, through their influence, the British government was persuaded to enact the measure known as the Statute of Westminster. Some good judges thought that the Act played into the hands of separatists without conferring any real advantage on loyalists. It was drafted in response to requests from learned lawyers in South Africa and Ireland, with some support from Canada where an appeal to the Privy Council had recently exposed a point of law that called for amendment. The Bill was proposed by the Colonial Secretary, Mr J. H. Thomas, in the House of Commons in November 1931, and carried after debates of more intensity than is usually shown over colonial questions. When the House divided on a substantive amendment, 350 members supported and fifty opposed the passage of the Bill. Sir Stafford Cripps gave the approval of the Socialist Opposition to the Bill in principle, as did Mr Amery for the Conservatives. Its leading opponent was Mr Churchill, who pointed out the grave danger that the Irish might use it as an excuse for repudiating the treaty of 1922. Such an event would form a bad precedent when negotiating the constitutional progress of India.

In spite of its bombastic nickname, the Act is no charter of liberties and enshrines no glowing sentiments. It will never be memorised for recitation by schoolboys in Australia, as is the Declaration of July 4th in America, or as was the Law of XII Tables in Ancient Rome. It is a neat constructive job of legal amendment largely concerned with repealing an Act of 1865 which none but Constitutional lawyers had ever heard of. It will therefore be necessary to hark back for a moment to Mr Cardwell's Colonial Laws Validity Act which had not been thought important enough to be mentioned in any standard work on Victorian political history until its repeal gave it prominence.

In the year 1865 Chief Justice Boothby of South Australia had reduced the officers of that state to fury by a series of judgments invalidating their Acts. Unfortunately he had the law on his side and, though no one complained of being a penny the worse, almost everything done by the South Australian government for months past had been *ultra vires*, on a strict interpretation of the constitution. After several fruitless appeals to the Colonial Office and the Law Officers of the Crown that Boothby might be silenced or removed, Cardwell, the Secretary of State, obliged the South Australians by slipping through Parliament, where it attracted no attention, a neat little Bill 'to remove doubts respecting the validity of divers laws enacted by the legislatures of certain of Her Majesty's colonies'. It set careful limits to the doctrine of 'repugnancy' whereby colonial laws were held to be nullified if they were found to be repugnant to a British Act of Parliament. However, by defining, it maintained the superiority of the British Parliament in some trifling particulars which were not irksome in 1865, though they had become so by 1931. Colonial laws might still be voided for repugnancy or in certain technical cases might be reserved for possible disallowance by the Crown. For years past these powers had not been used to control political activity, but only to solve technical problems when the courts found a conflict of jurisdictions. It was generally held that the colonies had no authority to legislate 'extra-territorially', that is to say for their own subjects and ships when at sea or in foreign ports. It is with the unromantic topics of repugnancy, extra-territoriality, and disallowance that the Statute of Westminster deals, not with the destiny of nations or the rights of man.

The Statute of Westminster (22 Geo. V. cap. 4) is properly entitled 'An Act to give effect to certain resolutions passed by Imperial Conferences held in the years 1926 and 1930'. Its preamble recalls that the governments of the Dominions concurred in making declarations at these conferences and that some of them required ratification at law. At the request of the Dominions (Canada, Australia, New Zealand, South Africa, the Irish Free State, Newfoundland) it was therefore enacted that the Colonial Laws Validity Act should not apply to any law made thereafter by the Parliament of a Dominion; that no law made thereafter in a Dominion should be void 'on the ground that it is repugnant to the law of England'; that the Dominions should have 'full power to make laws having extra-territorial operation'; that Acts of the Parliament of the United Kingdom should thereafter 'be deemed to extend to a Dominion only at the expressed wish' of that Dominion; and that certain sections of the Merchant Shipping Act, 1894, and the Colonial Courts of Admiralty Act, 1894, should thereafter not apply to the Dominions.

The rest of the Act, clauses 7 to 11, consists of cautious reservations in favour of four Dominions which had not shown much enthusiasm for its enactment. The Canadians, adhering to their fundamental law, were given a clause exempting the British North America Act, 1867, from the effect of the Statute of Westminster. The Australians had a clause to protect Australian state rights. The New Zealanders and Newfoundlanders insisted upon the formal declaration in the body of the Act that it should not apply to them unless their own Parliaments should adopt it. The royal assent was given on 11 December 1931. More than ten years passed before Australia took any steps to make the Act effective. Under the stress of naval war in the Pacific it was then found that extra-territorial legislation was necessary, and powers were accordingly taken under the Act. Canada adopted the Act in order to regulate the system of appeals to the Privy Council. The canny South Africans, though a separatist government under General Hertzog was in office, were content with abolishing the right of the Crown to disallow Acts of the Union Parliament. The New Zealanders did not adopt the Act and, at as late a date as 1947, obtained a separate Act from the imperial Parliament, giving them relief from the legal hindrances mentioned in the Statute of Westminster without accepting its constitutional implications.

The fears expressed by Mr Churchill began to be justified three months after the enactment of the Statute when Mr De Valera became President of the Irish Free State in the place of Cosgrave, a narrow pedant thus replacing a statesman as generous as Laurier or Smuts. Mr De Valera began by abolishing the oath of allegiance; then, claiming his right to select a Governor-General, he reduced the office to a mockery by appointing a nonentity and depriving him of all his functions. Throughout 1932 and 1933 Mr De Valera worked up a quarrel with the Dominions Secretary over the payment of guaranteed annuities, apparently on the grounds that it was an insult to an Irishman to expect him to pay his debts to an Englishman. His removal of the formula of the royal assent from Irish Acts of Parliament provoked Mr Thomas to reproach him for using the machinery of the Statute of Westminster to evade the terms of the treaty of 1922. Mr De Valera promptly challenged Mr Thomas to say whether the Irish Free State had the right to secede from the Empire or not, a question to which Mr Thomas gave an evasive reply. During his long term of office (1932–48) Mr De Valera was content to minimise the association with the Commonwealth, without forcing the issue of the right to secede.

As if to demonstrate the flexibility of the Commonwealth, the House of Commons, in the same week as the debates over Irish secession (December 1933), received the abdication of Newfoundland from Dominion Status, and restored a sort of Crown Colony government, at great expense to the British tax-payer.

2. THE OTTAWA AGREEMENTS

THREE generations had passed away since the first step towards Dominion Status had been taken by Lord Grey. The Whig government that gave new hope to colonial loyalists in 1846 by the grant of responsible government had seemed to blight that hope in the same year by adopting the full programme of Free Trade. Within twelve months of the enactment of the Statute of Westminster, by which MacDonald's coalition government abdicated legal sovereignty over the Dominions, the same government set to work to draw the Dominions into a new commercial union by preferential tariff agreements. In July 1932 an Imperial Economic Conference met at Ottawa with Mr R. B. Bennett,[1] the Canadian Premier, as chairman. Delegates arrived from the United Kingdom, Australia, New Zealand, South Africa, India, Newfoundland, and Southern Rhodesia. Though Mr De Valera had just imposed a tariff discriminating against British goods he impudently sent a delegate, who returned from Ottawa empty-handed but for commercial treaties with Canada and South Africa. His simple plan for engrossing all the benefits while evading all the responsibilities of the Commonwealth here overreached itself.

Some newspapers in England agitated for a comprehensive tariff under the name of Empire Free Trade; but Mr Baldwin, who led the British delegation, did not approach the problem in

[1] Later Lord Bennett (1870–1947).

that way. Eleven distinct bilateral agreements were negotiated either between Great Britain and particular Dominions or between one Dominion and another. 'The gist of the agreements was that Britain agreed to continue the existing preferences to Dominion products and to extend them to other commodities such as wheat, meat, and certain minerals. On the other hand the Dominions and India agreed to lower their tariff barriers against British goods in some cases and in others to widen the margin of preference.'

In effect the protectionist Dominions relaxed their restrictive codes, while Great Britain slipped farther into the abyss, away from the orthodox purity of Free Trade. In order to provide a margin for a preference to Canada, a duty of 2s. a quarter was imposed on the importation of foreign wheat. Preparations were also made to regulate the supplies obtained from Australia, New Zealand and South Africa, a move towards the systems of bulk-purchase which were common in the 1940's. Such heresy produced a political crisis at Westminster. The Old Guard of Free Trade, led by Philip Snowden, split the coalition and fought hard in the House against the triumph of the Birmingham protectionists, who had prevailed after forty years. Labour members opposed the Ottawa agreements on the grounds that Canada discriminated unfairly against Soviet Russia. But Free Trade was a lost cause in 1932, as *démodé* a doctrine as Protection had been in 1846.

The Ottawa Agreements, an expression loosely used to cover various subsidiary and amending agreements as well as the eleven treaties made in 1932, were drawn on the assumption that the British Commonwealth was still a political unit, an assumption that was not accepted by other trading nations. The quota system was regarded in some quarters as a breach of most-favoured-nation clauses in earlier treaties. The complexities of trade between Great Britain, Canada and the United States soon necessitated further negotiation. Most of the Ottawa Treaties were given a period of five years, and most were amended at the end of it, if not sooner. The Anglo-American Commercial Treaty of 1938 was in some degree an admission that the Ottawa policy was not enough.

Britain's unfavourable trade balance shifted after Ottawa, to the amount of £120 millions, now due to the Dominions instead of to foreign countries. The advantage to Britain was one of goodwill, no small matter in the 1940's.

It appears that the Dominions made a better bargain at Ottawa than the mother-country. Securing a market for their raw materials and foodstuffs, they were able to use their renewed financial strength in building up secondary industries which enabled them to dispense with imported British goods. The flow of British capital to the Dominions dried up, after 1931, while older loans were 're-patriated'. This latter process was much hastened during the second World War even to the extent of confounding the anti-imperialist doctrinaires, when India became a creditor country. The British income from overseas investment estimated at £230 millions in 1929 shrank, and recovered only to £184[1] millions in 1938. In those years the proportion of British imports drawn from the Dominions increased from 29 to 38% while the proportion of Dominion imports drawn from Great Britain decreased from 34 to 31%. The picture may be varied by examining it from a different angle, as the terms of trade are notoriously difficult to disentangle. It may be useful to tabulate some gross figures of the value of the external trade of the United Kingdom (in millions sterling):

	1929	1931	1937
U.K. imports from Empire countries	359	247	405
U.K. exports to Empire countries	348	187	264
U.K. imports from foreign countries	862	614	623
U.K. exports to foreign countries	492	268	332

Perhaps India and Australia derived the most direct advantage from the Ottawa agreements, and Australia all the more by devaluing its currency (see next section). Other regions responded less smoothly to bilateral agreements. A hundred years of Free Trade had set up triangular traffics on the greatest scale. Malaya, for example, sold the greater part of her tin and much of her rubber to the United States, but spent the proceeds on manufactured British goods. Canada, on precisely the other tack, sold her wheat to the United Kingdom and spent the proceeds on American manufactures. Multilateral trade was their life-blood and must so continue. It was the problem of dollar settlements, in these and other instances, that made the proposal for a closed imperial system merely quixotic, that gave the United States a

[1] Lord Kindersley's estimates, *Economic Journal*. Sir S. Cripps, in a speech on 10 February 1948, gave an estimate of £175 millions net in 1938 and £51 millions net in 1947.

whip-hand over British commercial policy after the second World War.

Canada, still holding the lead among the Dominions, had by 1945 achieved a mature economy to match her mature political constitution. Between the wars she had come forward as a large exporter of capital on her own account. Though British investments in Canada had reached the high figure of £440 millions in 1930, American investments were much greater, perhaps £800 millions. Canada also had a *per contra* account of £340 millions invested abroad, mostly in Great Britain and the United States. In the second World War she was able to repatriate much of her debt as a preliminary to making huge benevolent grants to the mother-country.

3. CANADA, AUSTRALIA, NEW ZEALAND, IN THE 1930's

THE Dominions emerged from the depression of 1931 much wiser, and in some respects stronger. South Africa, thanks to her unlimited supply of gold, survived the crisis at least so far as it was a currency crisis, with less dislocation than the others. Her problems, of land and labour, are so intimately connected with the general problems of African development that they are best considered in that context. Canada and Australia, though to the home-staying English they may seem to be two of a kind, reacted and recovered themselves in ways that show their social differences. The unity in diversity of the British Empire is nowhere more evident than in the contrast between tory Canada and radical Australia, two great nation-states with little in common except the invisible factor, the common heritage of British culture.

Canadian politics, as Lord Bryce wrote, 'live by heredity and, like the Guelfs and Ghibellines of Medieval Italy, by memories of past combats'. Liberals, the followers of Laurier and of his faithful successor Mr McKenzie King (Prime Minister 1935 to 1948), somewhat resemble Democrats in the United States. Their voting power depends in part upon the left-centre, the group that would be called Liberal in English politics, in part upon the French-Canadian bloc which may be compared with the Democrats of the 'solid south'. Conservatives, deriving their origin from John A. MacDonald, somewhat resemble Republicans in the United States; theirs is the party of the business-man. There has been little sign in Canada of that militant Chartism which has made Labour the characteristic creed of the Australian.[1]

As in the United States many attempts have been made to split the vote by the formation of a third, 'farmer-labour' party. As early as 1894, a farmers' organisation known as the Grange, parent of many such throughout North America, won a short-lived triumph in Ontario. Co-operative grain-growers' organisations were formed in 1906 and, during the next few years, the revolt spread through the farming community against the stranglehold of railway-rates and manufacturers' policies. A farmers' government held office in Ontario in 1919 and, thereafter in each of the Prairie Provinces 'progressive' parties carried the electorates on the strength of the farmers' vote. Between the wars, Manitoba, Alberta, Saskatchewan, made various 'progressive' experiments, though their programmes were restricted by the overruling power of the Dominion government at Ottawa. When the Conservatives held office, especially under Mr Bennett (1930–5), test cases sent to the Privy Council were used to strengthen the financial control of the federal government over the provinces, a recent tendency in all federations.

For their part the progressives showed a tendency to schism; the moderate elements looked to the prospect of effective power by combinations with the Liberals, who returned to office in 1935; the extremists resorted to economic heresy. In Alberta the electorate adopted the doctrine of social credit (1935) as expounded by William Aberhart, who proved unable to implement his programme owing to the resistance of the Canadian banking-system. A more effective because a more inspiring party was the Commonwealth Co-operative Federation (C.C.F.), founded by J. S. Woodsworth, a Labour leader from Winnipeg, in 1932. His doctrine was a fusion of agrarian, Fabian, and Christian-Socialist principles, his programme was one of direct democracy somewhat on the Australian model. By strong party organisation the C.C.F. won substantial minorities in several provinces.

[1] At the election of June 1949 the Liberals again obtained a large majority, their leader being Mr L. S. St Laurent, a *canadien* who succeeded Mr McKenzie King as premier, upon the latter's retirement. The progressive parties lost ground.

No longer a simple society of farmers dominated by railway finance, Canada has now become a complex industrial state, by far the richest of the Dominions. Even the French-Canadians have turned towards industrial capitalism and now constitute a large part of the urban proletariat, which cannot remain in social isolation from the modern world.

Excepting the progressives of the West, most Canadians like most Americans, looked to a renewal of the upward swing of the production-curve; that only would bring recovery to their expanding economy after the depression of the early 'thirties. In this respect they differed from the Australians who turned to measures of social insurance against a return of the depression. 'Down North' lay the metallic ores that were to be the foundation of Canada's future wealth. Already Canada produces vast amounts of gold, magnesium, zinc, asbestos, copper, lead, most of the world's platinum and nickel, a share of the uranium on which a still greater value is set. This is the justification of old Frobisher's dream when he brought home his ships freighted with pyrites which he mistook for gold. And these mineral resources are no longer exported for the profit of British and American capitalists. Already, to take one example of the contrary tendency, aluminium to the value of $184,000,000 in a year has been processed by cheap Canadian hydro-electric power from bauxite imported from the United States. With unlimited power and with further development of her iron ores Canada expects to escape from her dependence on the heavy industries of the United States, as she has already escaped from dependence upon British capital. The new alignment of world-strategy, focused upon Arctic Canada, gives a new meaning to her intermediate position between the economies of Britain and the United States, associated with both but subordinate to neither.[1]

The depression in world trade was felt in Australia when wool-prices began to fall, in August 1929. Gold was withdrawn from the country and sterling went to a premium in terms of Australian currency. On the advice of Sir Otto Niemeyer, a financial expert

---

[1] Space does not permit a study here of the importance of air routes in mastering the 'great open spaces' of the Dominions. It is significant that the missionaries, in Arctic Canada and inland Australia (where they initiated the 'Flying Doctor' service), sometimes led the way.

summoned from London, the premiers of all the states assembled in conference to agree upon a policy of restriction and economy. The internal debts, both of the federal and of the state governments, to the amount of £556,000,000, were to be converted to a lower rate of interest, and every state was to reduce its expenditure by 20%. Thus the external obligations of Australia, that is her payments of interest to British bond-holders, could be met, and her export trade might be maintained. The Premiers' Plan was on the whole successful, the bulk of the debt was converted and, in every state but New South Wales, expenses were reduced.

A constitutional struggle of great significance ensued between the Labour government, which in 1930 assumed office in New South Wales, and the federal government, which was supported by the governments of all the other states. Australian labour, since the crises of the 1890's and especially in the populous state of New South Wales, was devoted to a policy of high wages and self-sufficiency. The wage-earners of Sydney refused to admit that the claims of the bond-holders were paramount, even though the high Australian standard of life was based upon world-prices in the export market, even though Australia 'lived on the sheep's back'. The new Premier of New South Wales was Mr J. T. Lang, an able but truculent leader, who commanded a docile majority of fifty-five out of ninety votes in the Lower House. He had won the election on a platform of maintaining wage-rates and social services while balancing the budget by punitive taxation of the rich. He denounced the Premiers' Plan with the suggestion that 'Australia should pay no more interest overseas until the British financiers should fund the Australian debt on the same terms as Australia funded her internal debt'—not an unreasonable suggestion if it had been made the basis of friendly negotiation.

In January 1931 the Commonwealth Arbitration Court, the pillar of the Australian economic system, lowered the basic minimum rate of wages by 10%, and Mr Lang defied the Commonwealth. Between January and June the Lang Plan was tried in New South Wales, while the Premiers' Plan was imposed throughout the rest of Australia. Whether right or wrong in his appreciation, Mr Lang failed in his intention. Trade and revenues were shrinking in Australia and throughout the world, and nowhere more evidently than in New South Wales which, in April, defaulted on payments due for interest overseas. To save a general collapse the federal Government made itself responsible for the deficit, while Mr Lang redoubled his efforts, putting crippling taxes on all incomes over £500 a year. New South Wales was now demonstrably insolvent so that he was obliged to close the State Savings Bank. When he met with opposition in the Upper House he attempted to overcome it by the nomination of a large number of senators from his party, and was prevented from doing so by the State Governor, Sir Philip Game.

In January 1932 the Australian premiers again met in conference to face a situation that had grown far worse. The exchange rate had sunk to 25% below sterling and was pegged there. Not only recalcitrant New South Wales, but willing Tasmania and Western Australia also required help to meet their obligations overseas. The other states refused to carry an additional burden for a state that would not share the unpopular but agreed policy of retrenchment. The federal government thereupon passed a bill giving itself exceptional powers to collect the revenue of the state of New South Wales and to apply it to meeting the service of the state's external debt. Mr Lang fought the measure in the High Court, and by passive resistance in his administrative departments. A dangerous situation ensued in Sydney where an association of ex-soldiers, the New Guard, organised opposition to Mr Lang by methods that seemed to point to Fascism. They staged a demonstration at the opening of the great Sydney Harbour Bridge, in March 1932. A complete deadlock came when Mr Lang legislated for a capital levy in New South Wales, and the Parliament at Canberra devised a method of nullifying it by a federal act.

Governor Game had been urged to use his residual powers, earlier in the crisis, but, getting no encouragement from the Dominions Office in London, he had held his hand. When Mr Lang instructed his officials to ignore the new federal legislation the Governor would temporise no longer. He requested Mr Lang to resign, which Mr Lang brusquely refused to do. Governor Game then summarily dismissed him from office (13 May 1932) on the grounds that he was breaking the law of the land.

So high-handed an action by a governor, though legally correct, was an isolated instance in the history of the modern self-governing Dominions. It was justified at the ensuing state election when Mr Lang's party was heavily defeated (800,000 votes to 500,000). The new government in New South Wales conformed to the Premiers' Plan, while an ironical contrast was provided by Britain's attempts to repudiate her financial obligation to America. In June 1933 President Hoover admitted the impracticability of the agreed settlements, by accepting a token payment from Great Britain.

In the year 1933 a rise in wool-prices began to lift Australia out of the depression, from which she recovered with remarkable buoyancy. The Lang crisis was a landmark in the history of the Australian Commonwealth. To students of constitutional law the complex struggles between federal and state parliaments, between state governor and state premier, present many features of interest. Though Governor Game acted with propriety, and though his action was justified by the event, it was felt to be a dangerous precedent which strengthened the mounting wave of objection against imported English governors. Though federal policy prevailed over state policy, as in Canada, the crisis had again demonstrated the strength of state loyalty in Australia. Though all social and economic tendencies seemed to point forward to a time when the loose confederation should become a unitary state, a strong political reaction set in with separatist movements in more than one state (notably in Western Australia). Attempts to increase the financial powers of the federal government by amendments to the constitution were strongly resisted, until the second World War made a heavy schedule of federal taxation inevitable. Even then, proposals to maintain the federal revenue for reconstruction after the war were rejected by the whole Australian electorate and accepted, at a second referendum (1946), only in a modified and less effective form.

The third consequence of the Lang crisis was a still stronger tendency towards economic nationalism in Australia. Upon reflexion many Australians found merits in Mr Lang's plan, even though they rejected his political strategy. Had not Australia paid too high a price for the benefits of financial orthodoxy? Was there not some justification for Mr Lang's assertion that probity begins at home, that the obligation to the Australian producer should take precedence of the obligation to the consumer (and especially to the financier) overseas. All pointed to an increased effort towards a national economy that should not be

precariously balanced 'upon the sheep's back'. The growth of
secondary industry, already well advanced, was pushed on apace
during the second World War. As early as 1933 Australian
industries employed 30% of the wage-earners as against 19%
employed on the land. By 1935 the single firm of Broken Hill
Proprietary, with its subsidiaries, employed more steel-workers
than the total number of gold-miners. Steel, in the view of some
writers has 'replaced wool as the core of the Australian economic
structure'.[1]

New Zealand, too, suffered severely from the fall in the world-
price of primary products, in 1929–30. She, too, followed the
British example of attempting to balance her budget and to meet
her external obligations by stringent economies. Her currency
was depreciated with that of Australia. An unimaginative schedule
of reductions in wages and reliefs soon revealed the extreme
weakness of the social services. Once the most advanced of
democracies, New Zealand had been content to rest on her old
achievements without adopting the more recent devices of social
insurance which saved Great Britain from disaster in the bad
times. Accordingly the losses of the New Zealand farmers and
the sufferings of the unemployed, in so comfortable a country,
were taken hardly and have not been forgotten. While the drastic
remedies of deflation and restriction saved the national economy
from complete collapse they convinced the electorate that such
misfortunes must never be allowed to recur.

The Labour Party was returned to power in 1935 upon a
deliberate programme of insuring against the fluctuations of the
trade cycle, by legislative measures. In 1938 a complete system
of social security was introduced and audaciously founded upon
a guaranteed high standard of life for the wage-earner. Social
security was to be a first charge on production. Even in New
Zealand, which has few mineral resources, secondary industries
were eagerly developed, behind a wall of protective tariffs and
restrictions, in order to build up a strong home market as a shock-
absorber in case the price of exported foodstuffs should collapse
again. At least all the eggs would not again be in one basket.
The policy of bulk agreements for marketing produce at guaranteed prices secured the farmers' vote for the Government

[1] B. Fitzpatrick, *The Australian People.*

with the result that the Labour Party remained in office after the elections of 1938 and 1945, until 1949.

In 1939 New Zealand again, as forty years earlier, was the scene of an experiment in progressive Social-Democracy. At first it seemed unlikely that so brittle a fabric could stand the strain of competition in the world's produce-markets. The War, which removed the fear that Britain might not absorb all that the Dominion farmers produced, gave the New Zealand government its chance, a term of years when prices were high and the demand for foodstuffs was constant.

The change of government led to no change in New Zealand's traditional foreign policy. In 1939 as in 1914, the loyal Dominion was the first to align itself against England's enemies.

In New Zealand, as in Australia, the hopes for the future lay in the quality of the people and their work, most of all, perhaps, in the policy of certain powerful trade unions which, in the past, have not always been remarkable for their public spirit.

4. ECONOMIC DECLINE

WHETHER the Ottawa Agreements were beneficial to the parties or not, they were a clear indication of a change in the world's economy, the end of the dream of a liberal millennium to be achieved by the policy of the Open Door, the acceptance of a restrictive policy of quotas and controls. The change was an admission of failure on the part of the British; optimism and freedom were not enough to achieve world-wealth, as the Tariff Reformers had been pointing out for many years.

Every statistical analysis[1] of British trade, over the whole period of the two German Wars and the interval between them, reveals a continuous regression from Britain's former financial and commercial supremacy, not through any specific decline in British faculties, not even as a direct consequence of the long wars, but from deeper-seated causes and from tendencies previously noticed. 'Britain opened her home-markets freely and sacrificed her agriculture in order to attain and maintain her

[1] Notably that by A. E. Kahn (*Great Britain in the World Economy*, New York, 1946). In the following paragraphs I have made much use of his analysis and have quoted some short passages.

position as the world's leading exporter of manufactured goods. In the process undeveloped areas became customers and customers became competitors.... British technical advances enabled her to specialise increasingly in higher grades and qualities of manufacture...and so to adapt herself in part to the industrialisation of former agricultural customers.... But international trade has failed to keep pace with international production.' While the total production of the world was estimated to have increased, between 1913 and 1937, by 52%, the overseas trade of the world on the same reckoning increased only by 23%, and the British share of the world's export trade actually decreased from 13 to 10% of the total, all these percentages being quantity indexes.

More precise figures from the British censuses of production show that while the gross industrial production of the United Kingdom increased by 70% in sterling value between 1907 and 1930, the proportion of that production exported overseas declined in value from 30 to 22% of the whole. In the great age, bulky goods (cottons, woollens, iron, steel, machinery, rails, and coal) made up the bulk of the export trade, 65% in 1913; and it was goods of these types that other nations learned to produce with equal efficiency. Lancashire had once enjoyed so dominant a position as to defy her rivals in every market. In 1881 she owned half the world's spindles and looked forward to an ever-expanding trade. It reached its climax in 1913 when cotton goods worth £98 millions, a fifth of Britain's total export trade, were sent overseas. By 1937 Lancashire owned not much more than a quarter of the world's spindles and her export figure had shrunk to £45 millions. Significantly, the decline was greater in piece-goods than in cotton yarn. Mainly it was due to the rise of industry in Asia. In 1913 British India took 43% of Lancashire's exports; in 1937 half of this trade had been snatched away by Japan in spite of the restrictions upon Japanese trade imposed at Ottawa. Even more remarkable was the growth of the Bombay textile industry which, in 1936, supplied three-quarters of India's expanding home-market. Hand-weavers in the East were displaced by dark Satanic mills as, a hundred years earlier, the hand-weavers had been displaced in the West. And the former complaint of Indian economists, that Free Trade enabled Lancashire to undersell native craftsmen, was countered by the complaint of English Free Traders, that Indian economic nationalism (after

1921) ruined Lancashire without bringing any real benefit to the Indian people.

In the heavy industries, based upon iron and steel though the gross production figures may have seemed satisfactory, British primacy had long passed to the United States and to Germany. British exports of iron and steel declined absolutely, from 4971 thousands of tons in 1913 to 2574 thousands of tons in 1937. Behind this decrease lay the dark shadow of the depression in the coal trade, a direct threat to the foundation of Britain's secular wealth. Coal smelted the iron and steel, coal drove the mills that spun and wove the Manchester goods, coal bunkered the ships that carried the goods overseas, and coal itself almost vied with cotton as an article of export to less favoured lands. The production figures tell their own tale:

Year	British output in millions of tons	Bunker coal and exports in millions of tons
1860	80	7
1913	287	84
1932	208	53
1937	240	52
1947	200	[6 for export?]

Early in 1947 British commerce sank to a low level, which our grandfathers would not have thought credible, when an American ship delivered coal in Cardiff at £5 a ton.

But coal was no longer king in the age of oil and hydro-electric power, nor the Black Country pre-eminently rich in the world of non-ferrous metals and synthetic materials. Though Britain was not backward in developing the new light industries, they expanded to meet a domestic demand, and the goods exported had to face the competition of other industrial nations no less well-equipped than Britain. While the old staples of export diminished, the demand for imported foodstuffs did not diminish but grew to meet the needs of a population still growing and increasingly urban in character, with the result that the balance of trade became steadily more unfavourable to Great Britain.

Perhaps the worst symptom was the proportionate decrease in British shipping, which could not be expected to dominate the age of oil, though strategic considerations had induced the British, first among the nations, to convert their navy to the use of oil-fuel. In 1914 Great Britain built 60% and owned nearly 40% of the world's ocean-going ships; in 1937 she built less than 30% and owned 26%. The size of the whole world's merchant fleet had increased far more rapidly than the volume of overseas trade; and the British could no longer hold the advantage formerly given them by good, cheap, and plentiful coal over their decreasing share of that trade. Once British ships had set out bunkered with British coal, and often laden with it, to bring back bulky raw materials. Now too often the outward voyage was made half-loaded with light articles of smaller bulk. While British exports decreased in volume between 1913 and 1937 by 28%, British imports increased in volume by 32%.

In 1913, Britain's adverse trading balance of £158 millions, that is the difference between the sums received for exports and the sums paid for imports, had been handsomely offset by the 'invisible income', £210 millions from the interest on overseas investment, £94 millions from shipping services, and—perhaps—£35 millions from other sources, leaving a credit balance of £181 millions on the nation's external commerce. From this high figure of net profit there was continuous decline, though the processes were not always obvious. The Empire rode out the storm of the 1914 war, emerging still the most powerful state (or group of states) in the world, still the world's chief market for almost every commodity, including gold. Its strength between the wars was social and political; its economic weakness was revealed by the world-crisis of 1931 when the old mechanism of the London money-market[1] could no longer adjust the balance of payments among the trading nations. Debtors could not meet their obligations and producers could not get payment for their wares. Having nursed too long the hope that the free sterling market would survive, and that multilateral trade would recover, the British were obliged to capitulate in the general rout of the orthodox economy. Free Trade and the Gold Standard vanished together. Even the British repudiated financial obligations, even the Americans knew long years of contracting trade and mass-unemployment.

---

[1] The probity and competence of the London overseas banking-houses (Anglo-Austrian, Anglo-Egyptian, Anglo-Italian, London and Brazilian, London B.A. and River Plate, Hong Kong and Shanghai, etc.) did much to stabilise the world's economy. See H. Feis, *Europe, the World's Banker*.

While the gap between British import- and export-values had widened to £400 millions, the invisible income that formerly had filled it was now shrunken by a third. To save the British economy it was necessary to close the gap by securing the export market, the intention of the Ottawa Conference. And when Britain turned to bilateral agreements with her dominions and colonies, for bulk-purchase at prearranged prices, with discrimination against foreign competitors and especially against Japan, all the nations were obliged to make similar arrangements for themselves. High tariffs and economic nationalism had triumphed, and the measure of their triumph was the compulsion that lay upon the British to save themselves by taking that course.

Again the prudence of British finance was seen in the moderate degree of protection that was imposed at Ottawa. Britain and the Dominions suffered less and recovered more quickly than the United States where high tariffs were a corner-stone of policy. Between 1931 and 1937 a period of modest prosperity recurred, and without doubt the volume of trade among the nations of the British Commonwealth was increased. Again Britain and the Dominions had set an example in stability to the world, and entered upon the new trial of the 1939 war with faith and hope in their political and economic system.

But in the great depression that reached its depth in 1931, two factors that had contributed to Britain's greatness, the export of men and the export of money, disappeared, bringing to an end the age of British imperial expansion.

XVIII

BRITISH POWER IN ASIA: CLIMAX AND RECESSION

Argument : The unsettled North-West Frontier was India's weak spot. Forward policy in the 'eighties, as in the 'forties, provoked a series of frontier troubles concluded only by the Anglo-Russian agreement on spheres of influence.

Dalhousie's policy of integrating India by public works was pushed on by three generations of British officials. The good effects of famine- and disease-control and of irrigation were partly frustrated by the uncontrolled growth of population.

Political reforms were for long restricted to Indianising the public services. Only in its second generation did the Congress, a body formed under official patronage, press for a democratic constitution. British attempts to move by cautious stages towards Dominion Status were frustrated by the 'non-co-operation' of Congress, which also rejected British proposals for safeguarding the rights of minorities. Having failed to impose a federal constitution the British reluctantly turned towards persuading the Indian leaders to accept partition into two Dominions, as a temporary measure. Burma and Malaya, overrun by the Japanese in 1943, were re-constituted after liberation.

On a smaller scale the same constitutional problems occurred in Ceylon. A temporary constitution of an unusual type carried the colony over the transitional period to Dominion Status.

The British withdrawal from Egypt, long overdue, was repeatedly delayed by vexatious interferences. From 1922 to 1936 every attempt at a settlement was thwarted by Egyptian political faction. After 1936 the nationalists tolerated the presence of the British as a safeguard against Italian Fascism. The Palestine mandate, undertaken in good faith, proved unworkable. Abdication in the Middle East weakened British influence in the oil-producing areas.

1. THE NORTH-WEST FRONTIER, 1856–1939

DURING the whole period of the British-Indian Empire, the North-West Frontier presented unsolved problems of policy, strategy, administration, and finance. Lord Roberts summed up the impact of the Eastern Question on India as follows: when the British first got a footing on the south coast of India the Russians had not yet penetrated east of the Urals, their most advanced post being Orenburg, 4000 miles from Fort St George. No one then supposed that British and Russians could ever threaten one another. During the eighteenth century the Russians overran the Kirghiz Steppe while the British conquered Bengal. The distance between them had now shrunk to 2000 miles. By 1850 the conquest of the Punjab had brought the British to the line of the Indus while the Russians had passed Lake Aral and had reached the Jaxartes, no more than 1000 miles away. Between 1864 and 1873 the Russians overran Turkestan as far as Samarkand, enclosing Afghanistan from the north as the British did from the south-east, pushing and squeezing that amorphous state into something·like its present shape. The frontiers of the two empires were now no more than 400 miles apart.

On both sides the same problems presented themselves: the decision whether to advance, or to stand and consolidate, might be taken as a result of diplomatic negotiation in Europe; or be forced by the impetuous action of a high-spirited proconsul; or a government might be inveigled into action against its better judgment by the intrigues of an accredited, or unaccredited, or discredited, agent on the frontier. For, once committed to a forward step, no government could withdraw without loss of prestige. Advances were made usually by infiltration rather than invasion, by sending a military mission to establish a protectorate over a local ruler rather than by annexing territory. And each advance produced a reaction in the other camp. The Russians tended to cover their aggressions by bluster, the British by apologies and excuses, but both made similar advances, as a glance at the map will show.

Under Lord Auckland's rule the British in India had pursued the forward policy which led to the first Afghan War. From 1849 to 1869 policy was guided by the 'masterly inactivity', to use his own words, of John Lawrence who, as Commissioner of the Punjab and later (1864–9) as Viceroy, was always opposed to any advance beyond the valley of the Indus. He made a treaty of alliance with the Amir in 1855, backing it with a subsidy in 1857. But in those years Russia adopted the forward policy. Gortchakoff excused himself, in 1864, by a circular note to the powers pointing out the dilemma in which 'civilised states are placed when in contact with wandering tribes. They find it impossible to live in unity with such neighbours and must establish a system of control or see their frontiers a prey to chronic disorder. But when the frontier tribes are subdued they in their turn are exposed to the aggression of more distant tribes; and hence the frontier line must be extended until it comes in contact with a regularly organised state which can maintain order within its own borders.' Having made this declaration he commenced a regular campaign for the conquest of Turkestan. The Russian armies reached Tashkent in 1865, Samarkand in 1868, and established a protectorate over the Amir of Bokhara. In 1873 they occupied Khiva with the whole right bank of the Oxus and, in 1876, Khokand, far exceeding what they had revealed to the British as their intentions.

In 1876 Lord Lytton was sent out as Viceroy expressly to take up the challenge, resuming the forward policy in spite of protests from Lawrence, then in retirement in London. The British occupied Quetta (1877) after imposing a treaty upon the Khan of Khalat, a state which guards the road to Kandahar, as Peshawar guards the road to Kabul. The crisis became acute in 1877 when the Russo-Turkish war broke out in Europe, bringing the 'jingo' agitation in England. It seemed likely that we must fight so that the 'Rooshians' should neither have Constantinople nor Kabul. On the opening day of the Congress of Berlin which averted war from Europe, the Amir received a Russian military mission. When Lytton demanded that he should receive a similar British mission it was firmly turned back from the entrance to the Khyber Pass.

There followed the second Afghan War (1878–80) which in its sequence of events is strangely reminiscent of the first. Again a successful invasion was followed by a revolt, the murder of the British agent, a military setback, a swift recovery, and a withdrawal which left the Afghans free under a ruler of their own choosing. Late in 1878 a threefold invasion was launched from India, the right and left columns taking the traditional routes, the centre column, under Sir Frederick Roberts (1835–1914), taking a new shorter route to Kabul through the difficult Kurram valley. The Amir, who had favoured the Russians, fled and all the tribes rose in anarchy. Our columns halted when Yakub Khan, a rival prince, seized the throne and entered into a treaty with the British. In July 1879 Sir Louis Cavagnari was received at Kabul as the

British agent, and two months later was murdered in a rising of the townsfolk. Yakub disclaimed responsibility, placed himself under Roberts's protection and eventually abdicated. Roberts marched on Kabul to punish the murderers and demonstrated his power by dismantling the Bala Hissar, the ancestral fortress of the kings of Kabul, till then believed impregnable. During the winter Roberts's small force was in difficulties among the hostile but leaderless tribes. It was then that he showed a firm courage that distinguished him from his predecessor at Kabul forty years earlier.

After the abdication of Yakub Khan, Lord Lytton's next intention was to disintegrate the unruly amirate (which had neither historic nor geographic unity) into several small principalities, but there emerged a new pretender named Abdurrahman who showed promise of uniting the Afghan tribes. He was accordingly recognised as Amir early in 1880, about the time of the general election in England which overthrew Disraeli's government. Lytton resigned in April, but Ripon, the new Viceroy, though there was anxiety in India lest Gladstone should reverse the forward policy, stood firmly to the agreement with Abdurrahman. English Liberal opinion, mistrustful of the forward policy and its effects, had been expressed in bitter criticism of the reprisals inflicted by Roberts at Kabul.

At this uncertain moment the tribes rose about Kandahar and defeated a British column in the sharp little action of Maiwand, 27 July 1880, a battle which inspired several of Kipling's early works. Roberts set out with hearty support from the new Viceroy, to march with all his forces from Kabul to Kandahar where he restored the situation by a single battle, 1 September 1880. The troops then withdrew to India by the southern route through Quetta, leaving Abdurrahman on his uneasy throne. Somewhat to the surprise of most observers he controlled the tribes by firm oriental methods, maintained his frontiers against Russian encroachment, and kept faith with the British.

The war had provided the British public with a new hero in Roberts, who had been the protagonist, though not the commander-in-chief. His march from Kabul to Kandahar, though he thought it a lesser feat than forcing the Kurram valley, showed a prompt courage and a power of organisation that took the fancy of the public. He had led his column of 18,000 men, 11,000 animals, and 18 guns over 313 miles of mountain road in twenty-two days when the temperature varied from freezing-point at dawn to 110° at midday. No more than four men and twenty animals were cut off by the tribesmen who beset the flanks of the column to watch for stragglers, a striking contrast to the fate of that earlier column from which, in 1842, a single survivor had reached the goal. The severity of the whole campaign may be judged by the record of the 66th (R. Berks) Regiment, which in three years lost eleven officers and 367 men killed, mostly at the Battle of Maiwand.

As commissioner at Peshawar and later as commander-in-chief, Roberts set himself to securing the frontier by improved communication. The numerous marches and forays in which our troops were involved during the next few years were, fundamentally, road-making expeditions like those of General Wade in Jacobite Scotland. They were backed up by an expensive programme of strategic railways linking the crossings of the Indus. The railway reached Peshawar in 1883 (and in 1922 was extended to Jamrud in the Khyber Pass). On their side the Russians did likewise, building the Trans-Caspian Railway from Krasnovodsk to Merv, Bokhara, Samarkand, and Tashkent during the 1880's. The coming of the railway to Merv led to a renewed alarm and, when the news came of a Russian attack on an Afghan frontier-post at Penjdeh (1885), to another diplomatic crisis. Abdurrahman, who happened to be paying a state visit to the Viceroy, refused to be perturbed; he fixed the disputed frontier by negotiation with the Russians. It was delimited by a boundary commission in 1886–7.

Roberts (Lord Roberts from 1892) was not only a reformer, an expert in supply and transport, and the creator of a new Indian field army which absorbed the three old Presidency Armies and the Punjab Frontier Force, he also endeared himself to the soldiers by his lifelong endeavours to raise their status, to add to their comforts and to provide them with rational occupation and amusement. The young Kipling pictured him to the British public:

> What 'e does not know o' war,
> You can arst the shop next door—
>   Can't they, Bobs?
> Oh, 'e's little but 'e's wise,
> 'E's a terror for 'is size,
> An—'e—does—not—advertise—
>   Do yer, Bobs?

By the end of the century he was, perhaps with the exception of Dr W. G. Grace, the most popular figure in the British Empire. Sixteen editions of his *Forty-one Years in India* (1896), a large work issued at a high price, were sold within a year of publication.

The north-west frontier of India was delimited on diplomatic not strategic grounds. Though the advantages of a 'scientific frontier' for the defence of India against Russia were often discussed, they were abandoned in favour of preserving Afghanistan as a buffer state bound to India by subsidies and treaties of alliance. What then was to be the frontier between India and Afghanistan, and what was to be done with the broad belt of mountainous 'tribal territory'? Though the tribes of the Khyber region were Sunni Moslems, of the same stock as the Amir's people, they had never been brought to order either by the Amirs of Kabul or by the Sikh rulers of the Punjab. Always at feud with one another and with their neighbours they entered British territory in the cool weather for trade or wage-earning, and returned to the hills in the hot weather to live by rapine. The two experiments in a forward policy (1839 and 1879) had led to unprofitable wars. The problem remained unsolved and, on a low estimate, frontier campaigns between 1850 and 1920 averaged one a year, British casualties one a week.

The Punjab policy of inactivity was reversed by Sir Robert Sandeman (1835–92) who, as a young officer at Dera Ismail Khan, began to exercise a personal influence over the tribes. In 1876 he had persuaded the Khan of Khalat to accept a subsidy in return for allowing a military line of communication through his country. In 1877 Sandeman formed the British agency at Quetta. The whole of the modern province of Baluchistan was gradually brought to order by his method of paying personal visits unescorted to tribal *jirgas* and allotting subsidies judiciously to tribes that kept the law. His greatest success was the foundation of Fort Sandeman in the Zhob Valley in 1889.

Similar methods in the Pathan country farther north proved less effective. Abdurrahman showed signs of disapproval when British political agencies were established, with the goodwill of the tribes, in the Wana, Tochi, Kurram, and Malakand valleys (1892–5). A general settlement of British and Afghan spheres of influence was negotiated by Sir Mortimer Durand at Kabul in

1893. The 'Durand Line', often shown on maps as if it were the Indian frontier, was a diplomatic not an administrative boundary; it includes the territory of many tribes whose members were not admitted as British subjects.

Far to the north in the Pamirs the settlement of the frontier led to difficulties with the Russian government which were not smoothed away until 1895. The agency at Gilgit was permanently established in 1889 as a counterpoise to Russian influence. But the penetration of Hunza-Nagar in 1891 was not achieved without fighting, and a British military mission sent from Gilgit to Chitral (1892) got into serious trouble. A palace revolution in the fort of the Mehtar of Chitral had led to the request for a British agency; a second palace revolution repudiated the request and attacked the agent. (Sir) G. S. Robertson (1852–1916) was besieged in Chitral from January to April 1895, with a company of soldiers under Captain C. V. Townshend (1861–1924), later celebrated as the defender of Kut-el-Amara. Chitral was relieved by two converging columns, one of which marched westward over the passes from Gilgit in Kashmir, the other northward by a new route from Malakand. This very picturesque campaign has inspired countless romances for stage, screen, and circulating library.

There followed the usual hesitations, a matter of party politics in London, whether to withdraw or to remain in Chitral. The decision to open and maintain a road from the south was the spark which fired a train of risings along the frontier. An undercurrent of unrest ran through Islam from the Bosphorus to Egypt (where Kitchener had not yet restored British military prestige) even to the Khyber Hills. The tribes rose in turn, first the Mahsuds of Waziristan who had resisted the agency since 1894, then the Mohmands, north of the Khyber, then the Afridis south of the Khyber, in the Tirah district which gave its name to the 1897 war. Nearly 40,000 troops and 20,000 followers were engaged. Lieutenant Churchill of the 4th Hussars fought his first campaign against the Mohmands with the Malakand Field Force. One episode in the Tirah, the advance of the Gordon Highlanders at Dargai, 20 October 1897, became legendary on the London music-halls.

When Curzon came to India as Viceroy in 1899, 10,000 troops were still cantoned beyond the administrative frontier. Again reversing the forward policy he made radical changes. British territory beyond the Indus was separated from the Punjab and formed into a new North-West Frontier Province, directly under the Viceroy. The troops were withdrawn behind the administrative frontier into large garrisons which were then linked by strategic roads and railways. Law and order were preserved beyond the frontier by tribal levies commanded by British officers. And when next the untamable Mahsuds committed outrages they were subdued by blockade (1900–1), not invasion.

For twenty years the North-West Frontier was comparatively tranquil. The estimated trade of the new province was worth £2,500,000 by 1911. Only one considerable military campaign was required, against the Mohmands who had been raiding across the frontier in 1908. When the grim old Amir Abdurrahman died in 1901, his son Habibulla remained uniformly loyal to his treaty obligations. Habibulla's murder, in February 1919, was followed by a troubled period. The next Amir, Amanulla, supposing that all was already over with the British *raj*, sent a political mission to the new Soviet rulers of Russia, and declared a holy war against the infidel British. In April 1919 he incited the tribes, and the tribal levies, to join in an invasion through the Khyber Pass. In May Afghan troops and tribesmen were driven back and, in reprisal, the British seized two Afghan forts, Dakka on the road to Kabul and Baldak on the road to Kandahar. The Amir then asked for peace, which was granted by a treaty signed at Rawalpindi, 8 August 1919. It required a gruelling campaign along the whole frontier all through the hot season of that year to pacify the tribes.

The Amir's subsidy was withdrawn as a penalty, and the effect was rather to lessen the dependence of Afghanistan upon British India. No remarkable change was made in the tribal area between 1919 and 1947. The frontier was on the whole quiet but for operations in Waziristan in 1935 and 1936. By this time military control had been much eased by the use of air reconnaissance.

2. ECONOMIC DEVELOPMENT OF INDIA,
1858–1947

INDIAN unity was created by the British *raj*. A comprehensive plan of modern communications for India, designed by Dalhousie's new Public Works Department between 1849 and 1854, had been begun before the Mutiny. The Indian road system is almost entirely a British achievement. Though an early Mogul emperor had laid out a horse-track from Delhi to Bengal it had vanished before the English came on the scene. When Bentinck took office in 1828, there were no hard roads in India beyond the suburbs of Calcutta; elsewhere heavy traffic followed the waterways. He restored the Grand Trunk road from Calcutta to Delhi which Dalhousie extended towards Lahore and Peshawar in the 'fifties. It was completed in 1864. 'The road runs straight, bearing without crowding India's traffic, for fifteen hundred miles—such a river of life as nowhere else exists in the world. For the most part it is shaded with four lines of trees; the middle road—all hard—takes the quick traffic. Left and right is the rougher road for the country carts. A man goes in safety here—for at every few *Kos* is a police station.'[1] Another remarkable piece of construction was the mountain road to Darjeeling, finished in 1861.

The transition from roads to railways was slow. The first lines built before the Mutiny extended no farther than a few miles inland from Bombay and Calcutta, but Dalhousie had planned trunk lines joining the three Presidency towns. Capital and skilled labour were to be provided from England by private enterprise. The Indian government placed the contracts, guaranteed 5% interest on the shares, and retained an option to buy outright. The north-western trunk line was begun in 1859. A direct line from the Bengal system through Delhi to Lahore was opened in 1870 and extended to Peshawar in 1883. The Bombay railways, including the Great Indian Peninsular line which connects them with the Bengal system, date from the 1860's when Sir Bartle Frere financed development during the cotton boom. The east coast railway connecting Calcutta with Madras

---

[1] *Kim*, by R. Kipling (1901).

was not complete until 1891, the Assam railway to Chittagong not until 1895.

In 1869 the policy had been changed. The guaranteed interest on the £76,000,000 which had been invested—and so far unprofitably—fell heavily upon the government, which determined to take over responsibility for construction. Attempts were made to set a limit to the external debt by borrowing in India but her resources proved insufficient. After some years, construction by private enterprise was resumed except for certain strategic railways built between 1880 and 1900. Later the government preferred to exercise its right of buying out the private owners as opportunity occurred. By 1905, 28,000 miles of railway had been built, at a cost of £240,000,000, a far greater mileage in proportion to its area and resources than in any part of the world except western Europe or eastern America. About half had been built by the state, and all the principal trunk lines had come into the possession of the state. Though some of the branch lines had been constructed on a narrow gauge as an economy, half the mileage and all the trunk lines were built to the broad gauge of 5 ft. 6 in.

Irrigation works on a large scale also date from the time of Dalhousie, who in this instance followed the tradition of Indian rulers. Madras had ancient systems of canals; and the Punjab had been elaborately irrigated by Shah Jehan with canals long since silted up. Throughout India the construction of 'tanks'—the familiar word is of Indian or Portuguese-Indian origin—had been a frequent work of charity in the past. Dalhousie constructed the Ganges Canal (1842–54), causing some perturbation among the devout, who shuddered at any restraint upon the holy water of Mother Gunga. Lawrence began the modern irrigation of the Punjab by the Bari-Doab Canal, in 1859, in order to settle Sikh ex-soldiers on a million acres of improved land. This was the first of a series culminating in the Lower Chenab Canal, in 1892, which turned 3,000,000 acres of wilderness into rich agricultural land. The area irrigated was surveyed in lots and leased to bands of peasant immigrants who were grouped in new villages of 1500 inhabitants around the new town of Lyallpur (1905). In ten years the population rose from 8000 to 800,000, not without some inevitable miscalculations and hardships. The Triple Canal scheme on the Sutlej was greater still. Even earlier the Swat valley on the frontier had been pacified by irrigation, which turned the inhabitants from robber-tribesmen into peaceful cultivators. But all these are small when compared with the irrigation of the Indus valley initiated by Lord Lloyd, with works on a larger scale than even those in Egypt. The Sukkur barrage (1923) may well prove the most lasting monument of British rule in India. By 1938, 27,000,000 acres in all had been irrigated by 67,000 miles of canals at a capital cost to the Government of £109,000,000. In addition to the benefit to the cultivators, the net profit to the revenue was over £2,000,000 a year.

Good communications made it possible, for the first time in history, for the central government to cope with the periodic famines which afflict one province or another whenever the monsoon fails. Until the 1860's the possibility of famine relief was confined to measures taken locally, since there was no means of conveying or distributing food from more fortunate areas. In the old days Indian economy was strictly Malthusian; the population bred up to the limits of the food supply and was kept within those limits by the natural checks of war, famine, and pestilence. Perhaps the total population had never reached 100,000,000 before the days of British rule. The gradual cessation of internal wars may have permitted this number to be doubled in the hundred years after Clive's conquest of Bengal. No statistics are available before the very inadequate census of 1871 which recorded the population as 206,000,000, more or less. The figure rose to 294,000,000 in 1901[1] and 388,000,000 in 1931, and now exceeds 400,000,000, with a steadily greater pressure upon the food supply. From 1858 to 1947 there were no internal wars in India, while the government organised a gigantic famine-relief service, and made much progress in the prevention of tropical diseases.

In 1866 the crops failed in Orissa and the province was then isolated by the onset of the rainy season. The Government, conscious that they had not done so well as in the north-western famine of 1860, which had been relieved by means of the new railway, called for a report on which more active measures were based. But new problems arose in other areas. The Rajputana famine of 1868 led to an uncontrolled refugee movement out of the area. The Bihar famine of 1873 was handled too lavishly, so that 800,000 tons of undistributed food was left in the hands of

[1] There were then 600,000 Indian coolies indentured outside India.

the government. The Madras famine of 1876 cost the treasury £10,000,000 with less to show in relief than the £4,000,000 spent on the Bombay famine of 1877. In 1883 a comprehensive famine code was prepared in order to profit by this experience. Regulations were issued for action whenever a famine should be 'declared'. Instructions were issued for providing employment at fixed rates of wages on government contracts as the principal means of relief, for controlling the gratuitous issue of food in emergency, for granting agricultural loans in distressed areas, and for economy in financial administration. A sum of 15,000,000 rupees (say £1,000,000) was annually allotted in the budget for a famine relief and insurance fund. From this time famines were kept in check. The drought of 1898–1900 was the severest test to which the famine administration has been put and, on the whole, it stood the strain. In addition more than £1,000,000 was raised for the sufferers by private charity, 60% of it from the British Isles. The wartime famine of 1943 in Bengal was on quite another footing. Bengal was by then a self-governing province with a responsible Indian administration which did not do very well. It was not, however, a question of coping with a local scarcity but with a world-wide breakdown in the distribution of the rice crop caused by the Japanese invasion of Burma.

In 1828 there had been no more than 1600 'non-official' Englishmen in India, most of them engaged in the Bengal indigo trade buying the crop from native cultivators. During the 1830's and 1840's British planters began to grow jute, coffee, and tea.[1] None of these crops was raised on a great scale until the Crimean War created a demand for jute by cutting off the supply of Russian hemp. In 1855, a Mr Acland set up a jute-spinning mill at Serampur, and power-looms for weaving appeared within a few years. The jute industry was concentrated in Bengal, around Calcutta, and was closely linked with Dundee which provided Scottish capital and Scottish technicians. It steadily increased in value until the export of raw and manufactured jute became the largest item in Indian external trade, and almost a Scottish-Indian monopoly. Labour in the jute-mills has been largely casual, provided by migratory workmen

---

[1] Tea was planted at Darjeeling in 1840. By the end of the century 54% of the tea consumed in Great Britain came from India whereas 36% came from Ceylon and 6% from China (see above p. 156).

who supplement their peasant earnings with a period of work for wages. Though the conditions of life in the industrial towns were appalling by western standards the earnings were high by the standards of Indian poverty.

The growth of the cotton industry is also due to the chance of war. Spinning and weaving as domestic crafts are of great antiquity in India and, contrary to popular belief, they stood up well against the competition of the factories. At the census of 1901, when the agitation against industrial competition was blowing up, twenty-four per thousand of the Indian people were still returned as hand-weavers,[1] and home-spinning has since been inculcated as a social duty by the nationalists. But the spinning-jenny and the power-loom prevailed in India as in England, and as in Japan. The first Indian cotton-mill was set up in Bombay by a Parsee in 1851. The American Civil War, by stopping trade with Liverpool, enabled India to break into the market, by exporting raw cotton to England and by competing against Manchester goods in the Indian market. At the height of the boom, about 1865–6, when cotton to the value of £36,000,000 was exported from India, the price of land in Bombay city was trebled, great schemes of land reclamation were planned, and the trunk railways were urged forward. The population of the city rose from 200,000 to 800,000 in fifty years. One of the weaknesses of the Bombay economy was lack of power. Coal was at first imported from England and later from Natal. Not until 1915 was this problem solved by hydro-electric installations.

Unlike the jute industry of Bengal the cotton industry of Bombay was financed and managed by Indians. The labour in Bombay has been largely casual, and badly housed. Legislation to protect women and children in the mills was commenced in 1882. A revelation of bad working conditions was made to a Royal Commission in 1908 with the consequence that a code of factory legislation was issued in 1911. Workmen's compensation was introduced in 1922 in order to comply with the requirements of the International Labour Organisation, when India was admitted to the League of Nations.

The rivalry between Bombay and Lancashire led to a sharp struggle over the Indian tariff. As in most other countries a

---

[1] The census of 1931 returned 4,000,000 'textile workers' of whom only 489,000 were described as employed in mills.

demand arose for tariff protection to be given to the growing industry. Until 1890 imported cotton goods from Lancashire exceeded the Indian product. The Manchester men, with whom Free Trade was almost a religious dogma, protested bitterly against the import duty on cotton goods brought into India. Lord Northbrook, the Viceroy, replied that the duty was a revenue tariff which he could not afford to forgo at a time when India was passing through a currency crisis. Whitehall overruled him, insisting that he should nullify it by a countervailing excise upon cotton goods produced in India (1894). Otherwise India was a Free Trade country after 1882. India's subjugation for Lancashire's profit was a favourite grievance with the nationalists, though the Indian cotton trade continued to grow. Many years later, in 1917, when Indian legislative autonomy was becoming more assured, a protective tariff which discriminated against Manchester goods was introduced.

Trade and finance in the 'eighties and 'nineties were bedevilled by the currency question which affected India much as it affected the United States. Both countries had a convertible silver currency which declined in value relatively to the British gold currency because of a vast increase in the supply of silver bullion, through the Comstock Lode and Broken Hill discoveries. The sterling value of the rupee sagged from a steady 2s. in 1871 to an unsteady 1s. 0½d. in 1893. Since the home charges (that is, the payments to London for pensions and the interest on debts) were paid in sterling or the equivalent, the 'drain' was doubled. The Indian people were the poorer, and so were British officials whose purchasing power in terms of imported goods was halved. Those were the days of the obscure controversy on 'bimetallism' which may be left to the experts. The solution adopted was to peg the rupee at 1s. 4d. and, five years later when prices had settled, to place India on the gold standard (1899). Again, as hostile critics averred, India was to be dragged at England's chariot-wheel.

The service of the national debt[1] was a sore point for every Viceroy and a great cause of offence to nationalists. By 1908

---

[1] In 1860, after the Mutiny, the gross revenue of India had been £43,000,000, showing a deficit of £7,000,000. The Mutiny had added £42,000,000 to the funded debt, making £98,000,000 in all. The Budget was balanced by 1864. The land-tax then still provided 40% of the revenue.

the total sum was £246,000,000, of which £77,000,000 had been incurred for railways mostly run at a loss, and £30,000,000 for irrigation works which soon paid their way. Most had been borrowed at the favourable rate of 3%, whereas Japan, another oriental state engaged in moving with the times, was obliged to borrow at 5%. Such were the advantages of development within the British Empire in the happy Victorian age. After 1900, when the Colonial Stocks Act enabled prosperous white colonies to compete against backward India in the market, cheap money was not so easy to come by.

The turn of the century may be taken as the zenith of the British Indian Empire[1] and Curzon's Viceroyalty as its symbol. George Nathaniel, Marquess Curzon (1859–1925), arrived in India in January 1899 just before his fortieth birthday. An oriental traveller and scholar, he had already served as Under-Secretary of State and, in that capacity, had carried through Parliament the bill for broadening the base of the Indian provincial councils (1892). He was untiring and imperturbable. Taking every part of government into his own cognisance, he set his mind upon prestige and efficiency as the necessities of rule. While he regarded the vapourings of nationalist politicians with 'frigid indifference', he thought continually of bettering the conditions of the peasant masses. In his term of office there were no great measures of political reform since he could find no utility in them. He governed like a Mogul emperor, irradiating a tranquil people with the splendour of the throne.

His first task was to apply the famine code to Bombay and the Central Provinces during one of the worst droughts in Indian history, when 6,000,000 persons were relieved at a cost of £8,500,000. He next concluded a long series of petty wars by a new policy for the North-West Frontier which has already been described in the previous chapter. The fortune that favours

---

[1] Growth of Indian external trade, 1834–1904 (annual averages of 5-year periods in lakhs of rupees):

	Imports	Exports
1834–9	7	11
1854–9	27	26
1874–9	48	63
1894–9	88	113
1904 (single year)	144	174

bold players brought him to India when the world was moving into a period of prosperity. That old bugbear, the railway deficit, disappeared in 1900 when the state railways at last began to pay their way. Thereafter Curzon had an annual surplus which enabled him to remit taxation and help the peasants. A reform long overdue was the formation of an Indian Agricultural Department in 1903, with generous help from an American benefactor. By the Co-operative Credit Act of 1904 he initiated the rural co-operative societies which, forty years later, had spread to 124,000 villages, the most practical of all agrarian reforms.

Curzon next turned his attention to education, which he found very backward. Denouncing the 'cold breath of Macaulay's rhetoric', a top-heavy plan for training briefless barristers, he reorganised the whole system with fifteen teaching universities at the top and thousands of new village schools at the bottom. The problem of providing teachers for 400,000 scattered villages has, however, remained beyond the reach of Indian finance. Literacy has grown slowly from 8% in 1881 to 14·6% in 1941. It is noteworthy that the native state of Travancore, where there is a high proportion of Indian Christians, has a far higher literacy rate (38%) than any of the provinces. Female education is still deplorably backward throughout India.

Curzon did all in his power to raise the status of the ruling princes, especially at the Coronation Durbar held at Delhi in 1903. He founded colleges for the education of rulers' sons. It was typical of him that he discouraged princes and other Indian notables from wearing European dress. The historic glories of India were always in his mind and he was a generous patron to the archaeological department.

It might be supposed that he would adopt a spirited foreign policy which, in India, meant forestalling the spirited foreign policy of Russia. The whole Persian Gulf region was brought into the British sphere of influence by a sort of Monroe Doctrine, and was buoyed, lighted, and policed by the Indian Marine. In 1903 he paid state visits to all the sultans from Kuweit to Aden confirming them in their treaties of alliance. On the northern frontier he insisted upon sending a diplomatic mission to the 'forbidden kingdom' of Tibet, because the Dalai Lama had sent a mission to Russia. It was unfortunate that Sir Francis Young-husband's march to Lhasa (1904) should have met with resistance, at one point, since the intention was peaceable. The coping-stone of Curzon's policy was the Anglo-Russian agreement of 1907, completed after his resignation. It distinguished the Russian and British spheres of influence in Persia, and guaranteed the neutrality of Tibet.

There was in India another Englishman, Lord Kitchener, whose force of character equalled Curzon's. When Curzon the Viceroy and Kitchener the Commander-in-Chief differed on a point of army organisation, Curzon rather pettishly offered to resign. To his chagrin the home government supported Kitchener and accepted Curzon's resignation (August 1905), as if with relief in some quarters, at being rid of so dominant a personality.

About the time of Curzon's departure a change of tone could be observed in India. The Japanese victory over Russia in the war of 1904–5 was profoundly disturbing; it revealed that Czarist militarism was too incompetent to threaten the North-West Frontier, and it reversed the decision of 150 years of Asiatic warfare. An Eastern nation, using all the appliances of the industrial age, had defeated a Western nation, and with that the resurgence of Asia against Europe began. Indian politicians watched Japan with interest and could not suppress a sense of satisfaction when, forty years later, Japan won victories over the United States and Britain. Such considerations throw a light upon the opposition to British rule which was growing among the Indian intelligentsia. In spite of the Queen's proclamation in 1858 of impartiality 'to every race and creed', a liberal education did not break down the colour-bar. 'In this land of caste', wrote Mr Nehru, 'the British, and more especially the Indian Civil Service, have built up a caste which is rigid and exclusive. Even the Indian members of the service do not really belong to that caste, though they wear its insignia and conform to its rules. That caste has developed something in the nature of a religious faith in its own paramount importance, and round that faith has grown an appropriate mythology which helps to maintain it. A combination of faith and vested interests is a powerful one, and any challenge to it arouses the deepest passions.'[1] The hierarchy that governed India so long, with all its merits of regularity and impartiality, and a quite astonishing freedom from petty corruption, was, like all hierarchies, a little stiff and slow.

[1] *The Discovery of India*, by Jawaharlal Nehru (1946).

How could it not acquire a Byzantine formalism? It is to be feared that neither the Curzonian grandeur which actually impressed the masses, nor the aloofness of bureaucrats whose sense of duty was never relaxed, was the true cause of the new hostility. Much of the harm was done by the occasional discourtesies shown by young white officials to respectable Indians.

It was Curzon who pointed out that 'Indianisation' of the higher posts under government was proceeding so slowly as to be almost negligible. He wondered (as Hitler wondered after him) that so complex and gigantic an administration could be carried on by so small a number of responsible officers. The whole apparatus of government consisted of 6500 British and 218,000 Indians. Though all appointments to the Civil Service had been filled by competitive examination since 1853, and though Lord Lytton had eased the path for Indian candidates, only 92 out of 1355 senior appointments in 1904 were held by Indians. Enlightened British opinion favoured the Indianisation of the services rather than the introduction of democratic forms of government. Indianisation made up a large part of the 'Morley-Minto' reforms of 1909. The devolution of a large measure of financial control to the provinces in 1920 was also designed to place more power in the hands of councils with an Indian majority. But the central fortress of the Civil Service based upon the 250 district officers (known in some provinces as Collectors or Deputy Commissioners), the executants of government, was but slowly infiltrated. In 1939 the number of British officials had shrunk to 3000 out of the vastly increased total of 1,500,000. Though eleven out of the fifteen members of the Viceroy's Council and 90% of the judges were by that time Indians, an Indian majority in the executive branch of the Civil Service was attained only in 1944.

The officering of the Indian Army was on another footing. One of the many paradoxes in British Indian history is the status of this justly celebrated force which defended India for 200 years and won laurels outside India in three continents. As reconstituted after the Mutiny, a stiffening was added at the rate of one British battalion to every two Indian battalions. The artillery was retained in British hands, and all the commissioned officers were British. Recruiting ceased in those districts which had produced the mutineers, with the result that in recent years almost the whole strength was drawn from the peasantry of upper India, martial but not highly literate races which produced few men of sufficient education to become officers. In 1929, of a total of 158,000 Indian troops, 86,000 came from the Punjab, and 16,000 from the United Provinces. No other Indian province produced as many as 10,000 and Bengal produced none. A large contingent of 19,000 Gurkhas from Nepal, which was not part of the Indian Empire, made up the total. It was only in 1918 that the King's commission was for the first time granted to an Indian soldier, and only in 1943 that an Indian officer was appointed to the command of a brigade on active service.

Since the army was recruited from a rural inarticulate class having few contacts with advanced politics, it was customary for Congress leaders to decry and belittle them as mere mercenaries. But India is a land of hereditary trades and the tradition of military service among the Punjabis is as true and characteristic as any other Indian tradition. More than 1,100,000 Indians volunteered for service in the 1914 war, more than 2,000,000 in the 1939 war. And in the 1939 war, recruiting, into the technical branches as well as into the infantry, was successful in all provinces. A notable feature of army life was the development of primary education. During the 1939 war the whole force was instructed in the rudiments of the English language.

While the Indian Army in time of peace was not large, it threw a heavy load upon the expenditure of a poor country, about 30% of the whole annual revenue. This was quite four times as much as the proportionate cost of defence to any other British Dominion. Its justification lay in the fear of invasion in a country which has been so often invaded in the past, in the threat to internal security in a country where blood is shed every year in communal riots, in the turbulence of the North-West Frontier. To meet these threats the employment of one soldier for every 2000 civilians at a cost of half-a-crown a head does not seem excessive. There may be however a tiny seed of truth in the malicious suggestion that the War Office was gratified to be able to maintain a concealed strategic reserve in India, with the frontier as an area for battle-training.

India was able to take a more decisive part in the second World War because of the growth of heavy industry. Until the twentieth century the jute and cotton industries were the whole of India's manufactures. A little coal was mined at Raniganj in Bengal from 1851 onwards and a little pig-iron smelted from 1875. Mass-production on a great scale began with the foundation of the Tata iron-works in 1912. All the metallurgical processes of the modern iron and steel industry were developed with an economic use of by-products. The Tata firm endeavoured to settle a true industrial class by building a model industrial town at Jamshed-pur, and constructed a new port at Vizagapatam for the export of their wares. Heavy machinery and military vehicles for the Army were thus produced in India with Indian labour, capital and management.

The growth of industry quite reversed the plan of Indian capitalism. Fiscal autonomy was formally granted to the Indian government in 1921. A national Reserve Bank was entrusted with control of the currency in 1935. The last sign of subjugation to British finance was the so-called 'drain' of interest payments, against which nationalists had so often inveighed. In 1939 the ex-ternal debt of the Indian government amounted to £357,000,000, almost all of it productive. The whole sum was 'repatriated' during the war, to be offset against expenses incurred by the British government for war purposes in India. Thus the long tale of 'exploitation', that is the equipment of India with produc-tive capital, ended with the conversion of India from a debtor to a creditor country.

In 1938–9, the last year of normal trade, the total exports of merchandise were valued at £122 millions of which the United Kingdom received 34%, Japan 9%, the U.S.A. 8%, and Burma 6%. Jute, raw and manufactured, accounted for £19 millions (a low figure, below the annual average); cotton, raw and manu-factured, for £23 millions (a high figure, above the annual average); tea for £17 millions; oil-seeds for £11 millions. The total imports of merchandise were valued at £114 millions of which 31% came from the United Kingdom, 10% from Japan, 6% from the U.S.A., and 16% (rice) from Burma.

At the census of 1941 the total population of India was returned as 388,998,000, of whom 93,189,000 lived in the princely states and agencies. 206 millions were caste Hindus, 92 millions Moslems, nearly 49 millions members of the 'scheduled' (that is depressed) castes, 6 millions native Christians, and 5½ millions Sikhs. Only fifty-eight towns returned a population exceeding

100,000 and only 2·5% of the population lived in these towns. The immense majority were villagers.

Eighty years ago few Europeans doubted that roads and railways and irrigation, famine relief, internal peace and order, would make India prosperous and happy. Such optimism overlooked the stern insistence of the Malthusian law. The Indians were still a peasant people holding land on settled tenures and cultivating for subsistence. They multiplied at a greater rate than the produce of their fields, and have remained poor.

3. POLITICS IN INDIA, 1877–1947

PROFESSOR COUPLAND has published[1] a *catena* of pronouncements by British statesmen in the nineteenth century, all assuming that political freedom was the goal of British rule in India. Such statements were less frequent and less assured after the Mutiny. Disraeli's proclamation of the Queen as Empress (1 January 1877) gave no hint that the new regime was not to last as long as the Mogul Empire. Even the anti-imperialists who foresaw the rapid disintegration of the colonial system supposed that Indians would not be capable of self-government for generations yet. The possibility was fully discussed in *The Expansion of England* (1883) by Seeley, who wrote sardonically that 'a time may conceivably come when it may be practicable to leave India to herself, but for the present it is necessary to govern her as if we were to govern her for ever'. The time came, sixty years later.

Meanwhile the form of government in India was an absolute despotism. The authority of the Governor-General was unlimited, during his term of office, except by the displeasure of the British Parliament expressed through the Secretary of State, 4000 miles away. Until the submarine cable was laid, in 1870, the responsibility of the Governor-General was complete for the daily routine of government. Acting through his executive council he held the power of the purse. When he acted through the legislative council his ordinances had the force of law. These nominated councils had no power of amendment, criticism, or initiative; they were merely consultative bodies, not European

[1] *India: a Restatement* by Sir R. Coupland (1946).

parliaments but Asiatic *durbars* like those of the Mogul emperors. Executive and legislative councils, and similar councils in the provincial governments, were strengthened from time to time by the addition of nominated unofficial members, indirectly elected members, and members representing interests or communities; nevertheless they retained the character of *durbars* until the reforms of 1919–20.

Political reform in India, this plant whose early growth was stunted, put out three branches which grew and flourished at varying rates. Critics have sometimes confused the issue by failing to distinguish between the three lines of progress, any or all of which have been described as a movement towards Dominion Status. There was the liberation of the government of India from control by the Parliament of the United Kingdom; there was the replacement of British by Indian officials in the Indian government; and there was the limitation of the Governor-General's power by democratic institutions.

According to the best current opinion from Lord Durham's time onward, it was thought proper to plant the seeds of self-government in local affairs, and it was not done too soon. Modern municipalities were set up in Bombay in 1865, in Madras in 1867, but Calcutta was still the darkest and dirtiest of the world's great cities even after the municipal reform of 1892, and that of 1899, and perhaps much later. The District Boards, elected by the tax-payers of rural areas by Lord Ripon's ordinance of 1882, were used after 1892 as primaries for electing non-official members to provincial councils. The general report on these political experiments is that they aroused no more than a languid interest. On the other hand the townsfolk, especially of Bengal, showed great legal ability and activity so that Hindu lawyers soon reached an eminence in their profession which called for elevation to the Bench. The 'Ilbert Bill', 1883, which authorised the appointment of Indian judges, was withdrawn as a result of opposition by the British planters and merchants, who would have preferred an extra-territorial privilege as in Egypt and China. Theirs was the first of the attempts at communal schism.

Sir Bartle Frere once complained that the people of his province had no means of making a complaint to him except by starting a riot. It was the desire to tap Indian opinion that led to the convening of the first Indian National Congress at Bombay in

December 1885. Its conception is generally ascribed to the efforts of A. O. Hume (1829–1912, son of Joseph Hume the radical), who had ended his distinguished career in the Indian Civil Service by a disagreement with his superiors. He had taken an active part in the disputes over the Ilbert Bill. Hume obtained the benevolent patronage of the Viceroy, Dufferin, and of the Governor of Bombay, who offered to preside at the first meeting. The Congress, which opened with loyal tributes to the government, was more like a meeting of the British Association than of a political party. There were seventy-two participants (two of them Moslems) representing the Indian intelligentsia. All were imbued with English liberal notions and some with esoteric doctrines of synthesis between Eastern and Western thought. At this time the theosophist cult which had recently appeared was a powerful influence over the English and American friends of India and of the Congress.

No startling developments appeared at that or at the successive meetings, held yearly in different Indian cities, so that Lord Dufferin lost interest. But as the membership steadily increased, the members began to ventilate grievances and to discuss political reforms. They were largely responsible for denouncing the economic policy of the Indian government during the currency crisis of the eighteen-nineties, making common cause with Social-Democrats in England. Free Trade economy, which to the English appeared as the beneficent policy of the Open Door in Europe and in Asia, now began to be represented as colonial exploitation by monopoly-capital.

It has been said above that a crucial change of opinion in India came about the year 1905. A symptom was the unexpected explosion over the partition of Bengal in Curzon's last year (1905). The division of an unwieldy province into two manageable parts seemed to him a question of administrative routine dictated partly by requirements of police. It led to a violent outbreak of Hindu, or rather of Bengali, enthusiasm against the splitting of their nation, and to a campaign of political murder. The leader was G. B. Tilak, a high-caste Hindu who had started an intellectual revolt against European culture. His hero was Sivaji, the Maratha chief, who (like Robert Bruce) began his career with the cold-blooded murder of a political enemy. Tilak's defence of murder as a fine art was popular among the worshippers of Kali in Bengal, but less popular among the Moslems, since Sivaji's victim had been one. When the National Congress was an intellectual discussion-group it contained many Moslem members (156 out of 702 in 1890). In 1906 the survivors broke away to form the Moslem League. The next two sessions of the Congress were taken up with a struggle for mastery between Tilak's extremist group and the moderate, or constitutional group, which was led by Gokhale. Though the moderates won control by a narrow margin, Tilak's unamiable policy inspired his supporters in Bengal to commit one murder after another. In 1909 one of them achieved fame by the quite unprovoked assassination of Sir Curzon Wylie, a retired Indian official, at the opening of the Imperial Institute in London.

In the very unfriendly atmosphere created by these murders, Mr Asquith's Liberal-Imperialist government set to work to reform the Indian administration. Though very useful, the changes made by Lord Morley as Secretary of State, and Lord Minto as Viceroy, were not radical. Morley protested, when attacked by Curzon in the Lords, that he had not introduced, and did not intend to introduce, a Parliamentary system into India but to improve the existing system, by associating the Indian people more closely with their government. Indian members were thereafter nominated to the Secretary of State's Council in London and to the Viceroy's Executive Council in India, while the number of elected members in the provincial councils was very largely increased. In Bengal there was even an elected majority and, to conciliate nationalist opinion, the divided halves of the province were reunited.

As a strong Moslem deputation, led by the Aga Khan, pointed out to the Viceroy, the Moslems, a poor and largely illiterate community, would be under-represented even where they were a majority since the franchise was restricted to literates. Accordingly the principle was admitted, rather reluctantly, in the Morley-Minto Reforms, of separate electorates for Moslems.

It now seems surprising that Mr Asquith's government, so audaciously liberal in its dealings with South Africa, should have been so cautious in its dealings with India and Egypt. The explanation, perhaps, is the prevalence of terrorism. They were caught in the vicious circle of murder which obliges any government to withhold concessions and to impose coercion, thus provoking more murder. The Bengali terrorists were not placated. Though King George's Delhi Durbar (1911) aroused a mighty demonstration of loyalty in a country where royalty is revered, it was followed (1912) by an attack upon the Viceroy, Lord Hardinge, who was severely wounded.

The first German War was a period of rapid change in the conception of Empire. The theory of what came to be known as Dominion Status was never quite appreciated by Asquith, but rapidly won approval when Lloyd George became Prime Minister (December 1916). India, as a political unit, was admitted to membership of the Imperial Conference in 1917, and an Indian plenipotentiary signed the Treaty of Versailles with the other members of the British delegation. Such progress in external status was hollow until there was also internal constitutional progress. Congress was now taking a stronger political line. In 1916, having elected the English radical and theosophist, Mrs Annie Besant, as President, they demanded a 'substantial instalment' of self-government, which was not refused.

The next stage was the report (1917), by Mr E. S. Montagu as Secretary of State and Lord Chelmsford as Viceroy, upon which the Government of India Act, 1919, was based. The intention was expressed rather verbosely as 'the increasing association of Indians in every branch of the administration, and the gradual development of self-governing institutions with a view to the progressive realisation of responsible government in India as an integral part of the British Empire'. A measure of self-government was first to be introduced in the provinces and extended to the central government after a period of experiment. Never before in human history had so complex a political experiment been made on so great a scale. A wide range of subjects was devolved upon the provincial governments which now obtained control of their own finances. By the device known as 'dyarchy' these subjects were divided into two groups of which one, including agriculture, public works, health and education, was entirely transferred to the control of Indian ministers responsible to the legislatures. The other group, what Laud and Strafford would have called 'matters of state', was reserved for the provincial governor's prerogative. Representative though not fully responsible assemblies were directly elected, to advise both the Governor-General and the provincial governors, with the fullest powers of discussion and criticism. By what was called the Lucknow Pact, 1916, the Congress had submitted to the Moslem demand for separate electorates. At the capital of India (transferred from Calcutta to Delhi in 1912) the Viceroy's authority was still sovereign since the Act empowered him to override the veto of the assembly by 'certifying' the necessity of any Bill which he thought vital to the national interest. The 'certifying' power was very sparingly used. A corner-stone to the whole constitution was the creation in 1921 of a Chamber of Princes to advise the Governor-General upon the affairs of the Indian states.

The new constitution was pretty well received, as an instalment of favours to come, by the moderate Congress leaders and by the Moslem League. Before it was brought into being a new series of troubles threw all India into confusion and at this juncture the Mahatma Gandhi first appeared as a world-shaking figure. A Gujerati of the trading-class, M. K. Gandhi (1869–1948) was educated as a lawyer and called to the Bar at the Inner Temple. For seventeen years he practised among the Indian community in South Africa, where he evolved (see chapter XIX, 3, page 985) the political technique known as *satyagraha* or non-violent non-co-operation. In middle life he renounced his family and profession to become an ascetic, a traditional practice[1] highly honoured in India. Already eminent in public life, he placed himself at the head of a revolutionary movement early in 1919. One of the periodical outbreaks of terrorism in Bengal had led to a coercion bill (the Rowlatt Act) against which he staged a protest. Pledging his followers to non-violent resistance against the Rowlatt Act, he assured them that *satyagraha* would lead to Home Rule (*swaraj*) for India within a year. In the ferment of the post-war period his appeal had an effect which seems to have genuinely surprised him. Non-co-operation led to bloody outbreaks of violence all over India. In one instance when a great city was in the hands of a ravening mob a senior British officer inflicted reprisals with a ruthlessness equal to their own. This was General Dyer (1864–1927) who shot down 387 persons at Amritsar on 13 April 1919, and boldly asserted that by doing so he had saved the whole Punjab from anarchy. Whether this was brutal massacre, or excess of zeal, or merely error of judgment, it

[1] Some readers will welcome a reminder of Kipling's little masterpiece, 'The Miracle of Purun Bhagat', in *The Second Jungle Book*.

did infinite harm to the British cause, and perhaps ruined the prospects of the new constitution. An army sprang up of Congress National Volunteers who were by no means pledged to non-violence. At the same time a new political movement, the *khilafat* (or Caliphate) agitation, appeared among the Moslems who supported the lost cause of the Sultan of Turkey. And, on the day of Dyer's action at Amritsar, the Afghan Amir raised the tribes of the North-west Frontier (see above, page 927).

Nevertheless elections for the new legislatures were held in the autumn of 1920 and dyarchy was instituted. While many Congress moderates supported the new administration, Gandhi launched a campaign of 'civil disobedience' which implied a refusal to pay taxes. The issue was further confused by a rising of the Moplahs, a simple race of Moslems in southern India who merely supposed that the day had come for killing the Hindus and abducting their women (1921). Even Mr Gandhi repented when he saw that he had released a demon of violence. A reaction against his policy set in, especially after the wanton murder of twenty-two policemen who were burned alive by a mob at Chauri Chaura. In March 1922 Gandhi was arrested by order of the Governor of Bombay and sentenced to six years' imprisonment. At his trial he admitted and deplored the consequences of his campaign. The *khilafat* agitation also flickered out in 1923 when its rallying-point, the Caliphate, was abolished by the Turkish republicans.

India then entered upon a short period of political tranquillity. The Congress moderates, led by Mr C. R. Das, decided to co-operate to the extent of standing for election in order to agitate for further reforms inside the legislatures. Here too they failed; though it was the largest single party, the Congress rarely attained a clear majority, so that it was often outvoted by local combinations in the provincial assemblies. The next phase began when a Parliamentary Commission was appointed in London (November 1927) to report upon the working of the constitution. The result of their deliberations, generally known as the Simon Report[1] and published in 1930, is the best comprehensive account of Indian affairs between the Wars. Again the effect was spoiled by Indian intransigence. The Congress Party, piqued as well they might be by the membership of the com-

[1] Cmd. 3568.

mission, which was all-British, set up a committee of their own dominated by the two Nehrus, father and son, to draft a constitution that should satisfy nationalist opinion.

The Nehru Report (1928) declared for a unitary government without separate Moslem electorates, and with a plain threat to the Indian princes that they must reform their constitutions if they were to enjoy the benefits of Indian unity. It was not surprising that this had the effect of driving the Moslems and the princes into opposition. On 1 January 1929 an All-India Moslem Conference repudiated any unitary system, declaring that their rights must be safeguarded by the federal principle.

When the Simon Report was published, it was seen to follow the universal practice of the British Empire by recommending the protection of the minorities, that is, such a federal solution as the Moslems demanded. When thinking of Indian affairs it is perpetually necessary to recall the variety of the Indian scene, the distances, and the huge population which so far outnumber political groups in Europe or America. The Moslems, though a minority, were more numerous than the German nation; the depressed castes[1] were more numerous than the French nation; the Indian Christians outnumbered the inhabitants of California. The Sikhs outnumbered the inhabitants of Massachusetts; the fifteen largest princely states were comparable in population with the fifteen South American republics (excluding Brazil). No British government could allow such interests to be overruled without consideration. Otherwise the recommendations of the Simon Commission were a cautious step forward from the Montagu-Chelmsford report. Dyarchy was condemned, not on political but on administrative grounds, as unworkable. Full responsible government was recommended in the provinces, and the nature of the proposed federal government was referred to a 'Round Table Conference' of the various parties.

Again an amicable solution was prevented by civil strife. Gandhi was moved to launch another campaign in 1930 of nonviolent disobedience to the law. A Congress grievance was the very ancient revenue, far older than British rule, derived from the government monopoly in salt. Conscientious objectors were now marshalled in large parties which, after giving notice to the

[1] In Indian political parlance, the 'untouchable' depressed classes are known as 'scheduled castes'.

police, marched to the salt-pans in order that they might symbolic-
ally help themselves to this gift of nature that the government had
engrossed. The expected riots ensued and Gandhi was again
arrested.

Accordingly the first Round Table Conference was boycotted
by the Congress leaders. The exertions of the Governor-General
(Lord Irwin who afterwards became Lord Halifax) led to a
reconciliation, with the result that Gandhi was released from
prison to attend a second conference (August 1931) as sole
plenipotentiary of the Indian National Congress. His authority
now reached its highest point. Courteously, but with an air of
condescension, he dictated terms in London; he spoke, he said,
not for a party but for the Indian nation, for Moslems as well as
for Hindus, even for the princes. Like Lord Mansfield in the days
of the American Revolution he asserted the principle of virtual
representation. His was, he claimed, virtually the voice of India.
He demanded as of right an immediate solution of the constitutional problem at the discretion of Congress, with an admitted
right to secede from the Empire. Again the protests of the
minorities precluded any agreement. Gandhi returned to India
to organise further civil disobedience, and was again imprisoned.
While in the gaol at Poona in 1932 he won a signal victory. A
proposal had been made for setting up another franchise with a
separate electoral roll for the depressed classes. Gandhi told
the world that he would 'fast to death' if this were preferred to
his alternative plan for organising their franchise as a subdivision
of the Hindu electorate. When he grew weak by fasting, the leaders
of the depressed classes themselves abandoned their own interest
to save the life of the Mahatma. The 'Poona Pact', afterwards
incorporated into the Constitution of 1935, permitted separate
primary polling for candidates from the depressed classes, but
at the subsequent elections in Hindu constituencies high- and
low-caste candidates would stand together.

The relation of Gandhi the Prophet to the caucus of the
Congress Party defies explanation by a Western analogy. An
ascetic, and finally a martyr, he displayed the form of genius
known as saintliness with an utter disregard of side-issues and
prudential considerations. If a course of action were morally
right then the probable reaction might be neglected. Like Saint
Teresa, like John Wesley, he combined the most direct simplicity

(*sancta simplicitas*) with the shrewdest understanding of men and affairs. He could, as the saying goes, charm a bird from a bough, could captivate his persecutors and, between terms of imprisonment, was the friend of two or three Viceroys. His oracular statements which stirred new impulses in millions of impressionable minds were so phrased as to place his opponents uncomfortably in the role of sinners. Like the Pope he could err in his casual observations but not when speaking on faith or morals, *ex cathedra*. Gandhi withdrew from public life for long periods but, like Mr Gladstone, he was never so potentially dangerous to his opponents as in retirement. In due time the angel with the coal of fire would quicken his lips to prophecy.

He must be ranked with Lenin, Sun-Yat-Sen, and (unfortunately we must add) Hitler among the major prophets of the twentieth century. What had been the political activity of a group of intellectuals with an extremist left-wing was inflated by Gandhi the Mahatma into a crusade for setting India free from the trammels not only of the British *raj* but also of western capitalist economics, western social-democracy, western utilitarian standards. *Swaraj* attained by *satyagraha* was to be a victory of soul-force over materialism. The outcome was not peace but a sword.

In the face of Gandhi's absolutes the British government in Whitehall showed patience and perseverance. There could be no settlement in India if he condemned it. Any other government would have hanged him, instead of imposing those mild periods of internment during which he lived as he wished, interviewed his friends, and even conducted his propaganda until India should be tranquil enough to justify his release. Without despairing of his co-operation, British and Indian lawyers and statesmen hammered out a constitution which took shape in the Government of India Act, 1935, Mr Churchill vehemently dissenting. It granted full responsible self-government for the eleven major provinces of India and authorised a method of setting up a federal government to include the other dependencies and states. The opportunity had now come for Indian statesmen to grasp at liberty. Not only were they legally enabled to do what General Smuts had done in Africa, they could go further as De Valera had done in Ireland; for British liberties are constructive and *de facto* rights in British constitutional history have always run ahead of rights *de jure*.

While the minority parties gave a grudging acceptance, the Congress Party rejected the new constitution out of hand. After a year of tactical manœuvring between groups the Governor-General, Lord Linlithgow, persuaded the Congress leaders to participate in the provincial elections which, in February 1937, placed them in office in seven provinces. The 'working committee' of Congress announced these results as an 'overwhelming rejection' of the federal constitution. Though Congress was revealed as the largest single party, it was fair to say that barely half the electorate (29,000,000 men and 3,000,000 women) had voted and had given Congress 700 out of 1500 seats. Nevertheless so efficient was their party machine, so powerful their propaganda, that they felt confident of attracting Moslem votes away from the League and of overthrowing the princes by extending *satyagraha* to the Indian states. Until the outbreak of war in September 1939, the greater part of India was ruled by Congress ministries and legislatures, all of which were aligned in strict party discipline by the 'Working Committee'. The federation never came to birth. As the Working Committee gradually asserted itself, claiming to represent the people of India—to be already the real government of India—so did the princes and the Moslem League draw away into separatism. The clash between the Congress Party and the Governor-General over responsibility for Defence was the breaking-point.

When war came, since the new federal government had not been formed, there was no constitutional authority other than the Governor-General-in-Council. Only he could, as he did, announce India's participation. The Congress leaders, while expressing their general sympathy with the democratic powers, demanded that Britain should expound its war aims and place in the forefront of them an immediate surrender to Congress of the control of Indian defence. On this issue the Congress ministries in the provinces were ordered by the party to resign. Four large provinces (Bengal, the Punjab, Assam and Sind) were unaffected, but in the seven Congress provinces the Governors were obliged to rule with various combinations of the minority parties.

Between the wars, in the twenty years since Gandhi carried his resolution that the purpose of Congress was 'the attainment of *swaraj* by all legitimate and peaceful means', the party had become 'the best machine for propaganda in Asia', a totalitarian party

·claiming to be identical with the state. Its leader, afterwards the first prime minister of India, was Jawaharlal Nehru (born 1889), a Kashmiri brahmin, educated in England, widely read and widely travelled. Though a follower of Gandhi, he was a man of the world with a keen sense of what was practical in politics. The Nehru plan, which he and his father had drawn up in 1928, become the blue-print for liberated India, a unitary not a federal state. One of Nehru's achievements was the creation of a new political myth, by rewriting Indian history in terms that discredited the British achievement; but he was nothing if not reasonable. A part of his thesis which could hardly be controverted was that the British *raj* had outlived its function. The *sahibs* no longer retained confidence in their right to rule. 'The British,' he wrote, 'who had come here as representatives of a dynamic society, were now the chief up-holders of a static unchanging tradition. Among the Indians there were many who represented the new dynamic order and were eager for change, change not only political, but also social and economic.' The curse of India, if we except party politics, is peasant poverty; the hope, said Mr Nehru, lay in planned industrial development to occupy the ever-growing population. Though he has admitted that the wealth of Indian capitalists contributed to the Congress organisation for the election of 1937, it was not to Big Business that he looked for support, but to the mass of 'four-anna subscribers'. India, he implied, needed a social revolution and could not expect that the harassed band of surviving British officials would direct it. Traditional methods looked like reaction in Mr Nehru's India.

Though the whirligig of time seemed to display the successors of Warren Hastings, Dalhousie, and Curzon as superannuated mummers, they had still one tragic scene to enact before with-drawing from the stage. While Congress sulked and bargained, they raised and trained and equipped and put into the field an army of 2,000,000, a voluntary organisation, drawn from all parts of India, that actually outnumbered the Congress Party in membership.

The fall of Singapore, in February 1942, dictated the necessity of a new appeal for co-operation. Sir Stafford Cripps arrived in India, at the time of the retreat from Burma, to offer substantial concessions, a self-governing Indian union immediately after the War, with freedom for any dissident province or state to hold aloof. The offer was ignominiously rejected; Congress would listen to nothing but an unconditional surrender to their policy. At this moment Mr Gandhi's daemon prompted him to intervene with a firmer call for civil disobedience than any he had made before. Believing that the British cause was lost, he belittled the Cripps Offer as a 'post-dated cheque on a crashing bank'; and even if the British could still conquer he would not admit that they ought to fight. Anarchy was his panacea. The British, he said, should have submitted to the Germans in 1940, and the Indians should submit to the Japanese now, in 1943. *Satyagraha* would prevail; all that was necessary was that the British should 'Quit India', without delay, abandoning their campaign, their obligations, and their allies. The riots and sabotage that ensued were bloodier than any previous consequences of the Mahatma's acts of faith. Somehow the effete British officials surmounted these troubles, though the Japanese were on the frontier and Bengal was starving for lack of Burmese rice. While Mr Gandhi denounced it, co-operation between British and Indians held the frontier and defeated the main Japanese land armies, in the two severest campaigns of the World War. Not for an instant did Moslem and Hindu leaders check their feud. The intransigence of Congress led to the Moslem demand for the partition of India, a plan with which some Moslems had been dallying for years past. Mr Jinnah adopted the policy of independence for the Moslem state of Pakistan early in 1940.

In 1946 strenuous attempts were made to implement the Cripps Offer by means of a freely elected constituent assembly, but in vain, though Mr Attlee gave a firm assurance (16 May 1946) that the new Indian State might, if it so desired, secede from the Empire. When no agreement could be reached between the Indian parties he announced (20 February 1947) that the British would quit India, in any case, in 1948. The only practicable solution was partition, which a new Viceroy, Lord Mountbatten, persuaded Moslems and Hindus to accept, in June 1947. A Bill to constitute Hindu and Moslem India as two separate Dominions was passed by the British Parliament in July with the rueful consent of the tory opposition. Dominion Status as a temporary measure was proclaimed for India and Pakistan on 15 August 1947.

The British soldiers and civilians were then instructed to quit India in two months, thus taking Gandhi at his word, to the consternation of the Moslem leaders (in the North-West Frontier

Province, Sind, Baluchistan, the Punjab, and East Bengal), who were obliged to create a new administration, in this short time, for the new state of Pakistan. The demarcation of frontiers was not achieved without cruel massacres of minorities on both sides of the line, such bloodshed as India had not seen since the Mutiny year. Both states were, however established before the end of 1947, and both remained in association with the British Commonwealth. Whereas the schism between Hindus and Moslems was thus widened, the expected resistance of the other minorities did not arise. The policy of absorbing and integrating the princely states, from which so many viceroys—since Dalhousie—had shrunk, was boldly adopted by Mr Nehru who did not hesitate to use a show of force. With the exceptions of Kashmir, where war broke out between the adherents of India and Pakistan, and Hyderabad, where the Moslem ruling class made some opposition, all the states were peaceably incorporated within two years.

Gandhi, whose last public act was to mediate between Hindus and Moslems in Bengal, was murdered by a Hindu nationalist fanatic at Delhi, in January 1948. Jinnah, the creator of Pakistan, also died, a few months later.

4. CEYLON: BURMA: MALAYA

CEYLON provides a good example of the progress of a colony through all the stages of self-government. In the earliest days of colonial reform a cautious recommendation that liberal institutions should eventually be set up in the island was made by Sir W. M. G. Colebrooke, a commissioner who visited Ceylon in 1833. Nevertheless constitutional progress was but slight in the nineteenth century, though the colony was, on the whole, well-administered and prosperous.

At the time of the Morley-Minto reforms on the adjacent mainland of India, a similar step forward in Ceylon was authorised by the Colonial Office, upon the proposal of Colonel J. E. B. Seely then Under-Secretary of State. An elective element was introduced into the Legislative Council by means of a narrow and communal franchise. This seems to have provoked the latent antipathy between races with the consequence that there were communal riots in 1915. As in India the post-war enthusiasm for unrestrained democracy was met by further extensions of the elective principle, in 1920 and 1923, until twenty out of twenty-three unofficial members of Council were elected by the several communities. The balance of races had been estimated in 1918 as:

Sinhalese	3,300,000
Sinhalese Tamils (i.e. those long settled in Ceylon)	540,000
Indian Tamils (i.e. recent immigrants)	700,000
Moslems	300,000
European 'burghers'	20,000
Total	4,860,000

As in India, the majority party, the Sinhalese, agitated for sovereign control, while each of the racial minorities demanded autonomy. Lord Donoughmore's Commission reported[1] in 1928 on a constitution which had patently failed to acquire momentum. As so many commissioners since Lord Durham had pointed out in so many colonies, representation without responsible government was unworkable in Ceylon also; but, owing to the communal problem and the inexperience of the politicians, Donoughmore recommended a plan that fell 'somewhat short of full responsible government'.

In order to give the representatives of the people some administrative experience he proposed that the constitution should be reformed after the model of the London County Council rather than after that of the British Parliament.

The communal system was replaced by a single electoral roll with universal suffrage. The Council thus elected was to govern the country through its seven standing-committees, each dealing with a department of government and each electing a chairman who should be the minister for that department. The seven chairmen together with the heads of three 'reserved' departments constituted the cabinet which thus made the Governor a constitutional ruler. This ingenious device, a quite new experiment in British colonial practice, has influenced later constitutional progress in the West Indies and elsewhere. It establishes a relation between the executive and the legislature resembling what some political writers describe as presidential government. Under this system Ceylon tided over the period between the wars with a notable decline in communal antipathies, though the demand for full responsible government was frequently renewed.

[1] Cmd. 3131.

Between 1943 and 1945 another commission led by Lord Soulbury prepared further reforms, working on a draft supplied by the Ceylonese ministry. The constitution adopted in 1947 went even further than Soulbury's recommendation by granting Dominion Status to Ceylon without further delay (January 1948).

BURMA

Though the Burmese national revival followed the same course as the contemporary Indian movement, there were factors in Burma that did not apply in India. A Buddhist people could not fail to have sympathies with the Japanese and to be stirred by their victories over Russia in 1904. The nucleus of the Burmese revival was the Young Men's Buddhist Association, formed in 1906. But political reforms which were perhaps belated in India came too soon in Burma where political consciousness was confined to the clerks and students of the new towns. Provincial self-government, which followed after the Montagu-Chelmsford Report of 1917, gave the Burmese an elective constitution for which they were unprepared. At the election of 1925 no more than 17% of qualified voters troubled to go to the poll.

When in times of bad trade, in 1924 and again in 1930-1, agrarian riots took a political colour, the first fury of the rioters was spent on Indian moneylenders, the nearest agents of foreign finance. Later the agitation was more definitely anti-capitalist. Hence when the Simon Commission recommended (1930) the separation of Burma from India the offer of responsible government was received with suspicion by the nationalists as a plan to make Burma 'safe for capital'. However the plan went forward and Burma received a constitution in April 1937 of the most advanced colonial type, with safeguards for the racial minorities, both in the cosmopolitan towns and in the primitive tribal areas.

A weakness of the new constitution was the lack of trained officials; there were neither Civil Servants, police, nor soldiers of Burmese nationality. Only in 1939 were the first efforts made to recruit Burmese for the (British-Indian) Army. It is not altogether surprising that when the Japanese invaded Burma they had no difficulty in raising 30,000 volunteers. British Burma was attacked by sea and was overrun between March and May 1942. The British-Indian forces were too weak to do more than

fight a skilful series of rearguard actions covering the withdrawal of many thousands of refugees by the overland route to
India. The reconquest of Burma required three arduous campaigns (1943–5), partly conducted by amphibious forces along the
Arakan Coast but mainly by columns coming overland. These
last campaigns of the old British-Indian Army will remain as its
greatest glory. In the north the tribes gave valiant assistance;
in Burma proper the people were rather disposed to welcome the
departure of the Japanese than the return of the British.

A provisional British administration was restored in 1945
with a promise that, as soon as the state of the country permitted,
Burma should be offered the alternatives of independence or
Dominion Status. In January 1947, Mr Attlee and Aung San,
the Burmese Nationalist, met in London and agreed upon
procedure. A Constituent Assembly in Burma declared for independence which was authorised by a British Act of Parliament in
November 1947, in spite of strong opposition led by Mr Churchill.
Burma therefore left the British Empire, with the consent and
goodwill of the British government, on 4 January 1948. Aung
San had been assassinated some weeks before this consummation.

MALAYA

Fluctuations in the rubber-market during the slumps of 1921
and 1929 made the real history of Malaya in the thirty years before
the Japanese invasion. Political developments were less critical
than elsewhere in Asia. The wealth and administrative efficiency
of the Federation produced a bureaucratic growth at Kuala
Lumpur, which inevitably provoked opposition from the sultans.
Accepting their status as princes who reigned but did not
govern, they used their influence, which was considerable, to
resist the encroachments of the centralised administration.
Meanwhile the philanthropic intention of the Colonial Office to
protect the interest of the Malays, the least enterprising element
in the population, perhaps had the effect of enriching the princes
rather than the peasantry.

In 1909 a Federal Legislative Council was formed, at which
the princes took their seats beside some of the British officials.
As the proceedings were in English and dealt largely with
questions removed from their control the part played by the

princes was slight and even undignified. The most active among them was the Sultan of Pérak, a stalwart for decentralisation, who also demonstrated his breadth of view by proposing, in 1911, the gift of a battleship to the Royal Navy.

After several abortive plans for reforms in the federation Sir Cecil Clementi arrived as Governor in 1930 with instructions to prepare a Malayan Union, which implied both a loosening of the Federation and a tightening of the links with the other states. Whereas it was not difficult for him to get the support of the four federated princes, the 'unfederated' princes were unwilling to lose their autonomy, while Free-Trade Singapore deplored a customs union with the protectionist Federation. He met with so much opposition that Sir Samuel Wilson, the Permanent Under-Secretary of the Colonial Office was sent to make a special report. Some progress was made in decentralising the top-heavy administration at Kuala Lumpur, and in imposing upon Singapore the preferences agreed at the Ottawa Conference, 1932, but this did not bring about a Malayan Union. The tendency was towards administrative rather than political reform since a democratic constitution would have given a preponderant vote to the Chinese 'uitlanders' over the Malays in their own country.

With the approach of war other considerations gave way to the defence of Singapore. The preparation of a naval base had been made a matter of party politics in England and in Australia with the result that constructional work was intermittent. Australia had made no contribution, New Zealand had made a grant of a million pounds, the Federated States (on the motion of the Sultan of Sélangor) had made a grant of £2,000,000 and the Straits Settlements, while refusing a regular assignment from their annual budget, made occasional contributions amounting in all to $100,000,000. It should be noted that the intention was to make a protected naval base, not a fortress like Gibraltar which would have been an impossibility on that site.

When war came, all forecasts were vitiated by the facts: that French Indo-China, foreseen hitherto as friendly territory, was already in Japanese hands; and that no modern air cover, at that stage of the war, was available east of Suez. Singapore accordingly fell, in February 1942, the gravest military disaster in the history of the Empire overseas. On 5 September 1945 it was reoccupied by the British, without fighting, as a result of victories on other fronts.

Anarchy throughout South-east Asia seemed to call for another attempt to unite the Malay States. Sir H. MacMichael was accordingly sent to persuade all the Malayan rulers to accept a settlement which would convert the whole region, except Singapore, into a unitary colony with a common citizenship. These dictates were no sooner announced than an agitation arose against the hasty conduct of the proceeding. The Malay denizens, in particular, little as they interested themselves in politics, protested against a constitution which would unduly favour the shifting population of immigrant Chinese in the seaports and at the tinmines. On second thoughts the Sultans plucked up courage to assert their own and their peoples' rights. The Colonial Office reconsidered its decision, and accepted the advice of a committee representing the Malay Sultans, the British officials and a national association known as the United Malayan National Organisation (U.M.N.O.), which was led by the premier of Johore State. A draft constitution was approved in 1947 as a basis for the new Malayan Federation, proclaimed on 1 February 1948. It included both the former federated and the former unfederated states, together with Penang and Malacca. All received constitutions with nominated councils, and all were promised elective councils, 'as soon as circumstances permit'. The fear of Chinese communism rallied the Malayan peasantry to the federation.

Singapore became a Crown Colony with a legislative council to which six members were elected by universal suffrage.

At the time of the MacMichael negotiations (1945), the directors of the British North Borneo Company and the (white) Rajah of Sarawak were also persuaded to surrender their territories to the Colonial Office. The Brooke dynasty, having reigned in Sarawak for a hundred years, did not pass without a struggle. The heir-presumptive protested against the cession of sovereignty as the unconstitutional act of an absentee Rajah.

When the British restored peace and prosperity to Hong Kong and Singapore, the two *foci* of trade and civilisation in Southeast Asia, they could not restore the old balance of forces. Throughout the Pacific, American air- and sea-power were predominant while, on the mainland, communist armies threatened war. Strategically, all the British dominions and colonies, including Australia and New Zealand, were drawn into the American sphere.

5. EGYPT, 1914–47

THE war of 1914 deepened the antagonism of the Egyptians against British rule. The well-meaning declaration that the British would take upon themselves the whole burden of the war could in itself be taken as an affront to Egyptian pride. While the Turks still threatened the Suez Canal, and the Senussi tribesmen under Turkish influence harassed the western frontier, the tensions of war were felt by the Egyptians but, when General Murray carried the armies forward east of the Canal and into Palestine, Egypt relapsed into the humdrum indignity of a base area. When Egypt held the strategic reserve of the British Empire the troops had not fraternised with the inhabitants. One or two incidents are still remembered, in Palestine as well as in Egypt, when troops from the Dominions retaliated with riot and looting against Levantine slimness. And observers noted that polite relations in higher circles had worsened. In Cromer's day there had been social equality between the Pashas and the English officials. The newcomers, the hordes of military staff officers and temporary Civil Servants, did not conceal the fact that they thought themselves a ruling class. With more bureaucracy there was less efficiency, so that military regulations were sometimes enforced tyrannically as in the bad old times. Even the *corvée* crept back, in the form of a conscripted Labour Corps, to follow the armies. The one consolation was the high price of cotton, and even this was restricted since the British government took the whole crop at a fixed rate.

It came as a surprise only to the British government, absorbed in other matters, that Zaghlul the nationalist leader should apply, on 13 November 1918, two days after the armistice, to lead a delegation to the peace conference with all the other national minorities. His suggestion was brusquely refused. Then, too late, Lord Curzon suggested that Rushdi the Premier should send a delegation, but Rushdi cannily refused to go without Zaghlul. Early in 1919 Egypt broke out into anti-British rioting. Since Zaghlul openly incited it, he was arrested and deported to Malta. Lloyd George then sent Sir Edmund (afterwards Viscount) Allenby (1861–1936) as High Commissioner to Egypt, March 1919.

Allenby's first action was to insist upon the release of Zaghlul who then went unofficially to Paris but got no hearing. It was a severe rebuff when, on 19 April, President Wilson recognised the British protectorate in Egypt. Terrorist attacks continued against Englishmen. According to custom a strong commission was sent to Egypt under Lord Milner, in December, and was boycotted by the nationalists. After completing his report, which was not published until 1921, Milner was at last successful in coming to terms with Zaghlul in Paris. They agreed that the future relations of Great Britain and Egypt should be settled by a freely-negotiated treaty on the general lines of independence for Egypt, with declared reservations. Sixteen years were to pass before the precise terms of the treaty were agreed.

The year 1921, which saw the settlement in Irak, was a year of bedevilment in Egypt. Zaghlul revealed defects of character which invalidated all negotiation. With great shrewdness in diplomacy and great powers of political organisation, he had neither moral nor even physical courage. He was vain, timid, and irresponsible, always ready to run away from the consequences of his own action. While his diplomatic efforts won concession after concession, his appeals to the mob produced a series of bloody outrages. In December 1921, after inciting riotous assemblies in defiance of police regulations, he was again arrested and deported to the Seychelles. Quite undeterred by tumults, Allenby proceeded to abolish the protectorate by proclaiming the independence of Egypt, 20 February 1922, his second generous concession.

From that day the position of Britain in Egypt was reversed. The task of forty years was accomplished. No longer were the British concerned with purifying and modernising the administration for the benefit of the Egyptians, nor with internal security; they remained in Egypt to protect what the Egyptian government and the other powers had recognised as their legitimate interests. In the words of Allenby's proclamation these interests, upon which agreements were to be concluded 'by free discussion and friendly accommodation', were:

(a) The security of the communications of the British Empire in Egypt.

(b) The defence of Egypt against all foreign aggression or interference direct or indirect.

(*c*) The protection of foreign interests in Egypt and the protection of minorities.

(*d*) The Sudan.

The next problem was to come to terms with Fuad, who was enthroned in March 1922 as the first King of Egypt since the Ptolemies. Fuad was a nationalist of another sort, not swayed by Zaghlul's demagogy but determined to rule as kings rule in Islam. While he appreciated the value of British support in world politics he concerned himself with staking out a claim to rule the Sudan also. In this quarter he found Allenby firm. The British had no intention of releasing this favoured province, the pattern of colonial administration, to the House of Mehemet Ali who had conquered the Sudan only to use it as a hunting-ground for slaves, and whose successors had failed to protect it from the Mahdi's savage hordes.

For the third time, in 1923, Allenby belied his reputation, by releasing Egypt from martial law. This strong silent soldier, known as the 'Bull', showed himself more liberal than any politician. One effect was the return of Zaghlul, in time to direct his party campaign for the first democratic elections ever held in Egypt. When Parliament met, in January 1924, the nationalists (the *Wafd* Party) obtained so huge a majority that Fuad was obliged to make Zaghlul his first constitutional Prime Minister. About the same time Ramsay MacDonald became Prime Minister of England.

During his nine months as premier, Zaghlul revealed no talent for administration, no policy for the betterment of Egypt. He devoted himself to extracting diplomatic concessions from Ramsay MacDonald and to fostering an anti-British agitation in the Sudan. Since the Egyptian nationalists had been encouraged by British Labour leaders for many years, it came as a shock to Zaghlul to find that MacDonald would not relinquish British interests. Zaghlul revenged himself by cancelling some financial agreements with the British government, and by issuing boldly mendacious reports about British brutality in the Sudan. His activities were so far successful as to cause some petty mutinies in the Egyptian Army, and to stir up a pretentious 'nationalist' movement among the handful of Egyptian townsfolk at Khartoum who did not represent the opinion of one-hundredth part of the Sudanese peoples.

Ramsay MacDonald's government fell at the end of October and, on the 19 November, an event in Egypt brought down Zaghlul. The Sirdar of the Egyptian Army, Sir Lee Stack, was mortally wounded by assassins outside the Residency at Cairo. On this occasion Allenby acted with the firm hand that was expected of a soldier. Without waiting for authority from London he summoned the shrinking, terrified Zaghlul, confronted him with the affects of his propaganda, and gave him an instant ultimatum. He demanded an apology, an indemnity of £500,000,[1] and an immediate submission of the Egyptian government to British policy in the Sudan. The unreliable Egyptian regiments were to be withdrawn and, a more significant fact, the Egyptian government was to put a stop to its policy of obstructing irrigation works on the Upper Nile. They opposed an extension of the Gezira scheme out of jealous fears that Nile water would be unduly diverted from Lower Egypt.

Aghast at what he had done, Zaghlul hastened to resign after accepting the terms of the ultimatum. Though the withdrawal of the Egyptian regiments was not effected without further mutinies, the real welfare of the Sudan was assured by the completion of the Sennar Dam in 1925 and the consequent irrigation of another 300,000 acres of land. Allenby did not stay long to enjoy his triumph. His sudden *coups* were too much for the Foreign Office which foisted on him (Sir) Neville Henderson as an unwanted political adviser. Allenby thereupon resigned (1925); he was perhaps the last of those great military proconsuls in the tradition of Cornwallis who have shown themselves as just and liberal in administration as they were bold and ruthless in war. His successor, Sir George (later Lord) Lloyd, formerly Governor of Bombay (1879–1941) was reputed to have a still more forceful personality, though a civilian.

In Egypt it was the King's party that prospered by the crisis. Zaghlul was afraid to take office again, even though the *Wafd* won 140 out of 200 seats at the election of 1926. He had some cause for nervousness since two of his close associates were arraigned for complicity in the Sirdar's murder and, though plainly guilty, were acquitted only through a scandalous misprision of justice. Zaghlul died in 1927 at the age of seventy-four.

[1] When the money was received it was devoted to social services in the Sudan.

By manipulating interests King Fuad was able to rule for several years with combinations of minority parties and for one long period without summoning Parliament. Though he and his ministers were willing to come to terms with Great Britain they were well aware that any moderate settlement would be repudiated by the *Wafd*; they therefore temporised, and the treaty negotiated in 1927–8 was never ratified. Lloyd achieved one success by the agreement in 1929 for the control of the Nile waters jointly in the interests of Egypt and the Sudan. But, when MacDonald again became Prime Minister in 1929, he recalled Lloyd with ignominy upon the supposition that he supported royal dictatorship against Egyptian democracy. MacDonald obliged King Fuad to recall his Parliament by making the draft for a treaty conditional on parliamentary approval, with the result that the *Wafd*, once more in power, rejected the treaty.

It was not until August 1936, four months after the accession of the young King Farouk, that agreement was reached at last. The Italian invasion of Abyssinia in 1935 had obliged the Egyptians to face their problems with realism and, when the shadow of world war began to loom over the Suez Canal, negotiations were reopened by a 'United Front' of Egyptian politicians.

By the treaty of 1936 an alliance for twenty years was formed between Great Britain and Egypt. The British undertook to withdraw their troops from the Delta to cantonments in the Canal Zone, which they were to occupy and defend until the Egyptian Army had been modernised and re-equipped upon British technical advice. The condominium over the Sudan was to be maintained. In the following year the good offices of Great Britain were used to secure the admission of Egypt to the League of Nations, and the abolition of the capitulations by agreement between the interested powers. The pity of it was that only the factiousness of the Egyptian nationalists had prevented them from taking this step forward many years earlier.

About the time of the Anglo-Egyptian Treaty of 1936 the French made similar treaties with their mandatory states of Syria and Lebanon. With the exception of the unhappy Arabs of Palestine, all the Moslem peoples between the Mediterranean Sea and the Persian Gulf were then ruled by indigenous governments[1] and all, except Syria and Lebanon, were engaged more or less firmly in treaties of friendship and alliance with Great Britain. Even though the Sherifian House had been driven from Mecca (1925), by Ibn Saud, the head of the puritanical Wahabis, friendly relations held good within the terms of the MacMahon Pledge. In this block of Moslem monarchies it was natural that the kingdom of Egypt, richer, more populous, and more Westernised than any of them, should take a leading place. The Arab kings stood by their engagements to their British friends and former liberators, in the second World War as in the first. Again it was necessary for British and Indian detachments to occupy key points in Syria, Irak, and South Persia in order to crush or to forestall German attempts at infiltration with the help of local sympathisers. But in Egypt these problems appeared in a different light since there was already a political party which had long represented the British as being military oppressors. It was not difficult for German and Italian propagandists to work upon Egyptian nationalists as they could also work upon disruptive groups in Syria and Palestine. Wartime politics in Egypt took their tone from the atmosphere of defeat or victory and there was a time when the King's party was disposed towards appeasement of the Axis while the *Wafd* urged co-operation with the British. In general the situation was a repetition of what took place in the first war. Again the Egyptian government and army stood neutral while Egypt became the strategic reserve and, for a moment, the vital point of the British Empire. Again a specious prosperity failed to reconcile the Egyptians to the presence of great armies of occupation. Again, as soon as the emergency was passed, a clamour arose for the British to quit Egypt.

In 1946, though the Anglo-Egyptian Treaty had still ten years to run, Mr Attlee announced an immediate withdrawal of British troops from the Delta and an imminent withdrawal from the Canal Zone. The Citadel of Cairo was accordingly handed over to Egyptian troops on 31 March 1947, after a British military occupation of sixty-four years. As might have been expected, the Egyptians took this concession as a sign of weakness and immediately pressed for a withdrawal from the Sudan also. When

[1] Irak, Trans-Jordan, Saudi Arabia, Kuwait, Muscat and Oman, Yemen, Bahrein, Qatar, and the six chieftainates of the Trucial Coast.

the British government stood firm Nokrashy, the Egyptian premier, broke off negotiations and appealed to the United Nations Organisation against the treaty of 1936. The United Nations did not, however, encourage him to denounce it.

6. PALESTINE

ZIONISM, founded in Russia about 1860, had been formed into an international organisation by Dr Herzl of Vienna in 1897. Proposals for Zionist colonies in British territory had been many times advanced by philanthropists, notably by Chamberlain in 1903 (see chapter XIX, 3, page 998), but without success. Meanwhile the Rothschilds had actually planted seven farm colonies of Zionist refugees in Palestine from 1883 onwards. By 1914 there were about 80,000 Jews in Palestine, three times as many as a generation earlier. Most British Jews, regarding themselves as a religious body not a nation, were unsympathetic to the Zionist movement as were the Liberal leaders, Asquith and Grey. Yet it was a Liberal English Jew, Sir Herbert Samuel, who raised the issue in 1915 when the disintegration of the Turkish Empire was envisaged. The industrial chemist, Dr Chaim Weizmann, then began to work upon Balfour and the Conservatives. A story told by Lloyd George that Weizmann won the support of the British government in gratitude for his researches is entirely fanciful. In 1917 the Arab Bureau, and notably Sir Mark Sykes, took up the topic, initiating the proposal for a 'Jewish National Home', not a Jewish state, in Palestine. The document known as the Balfour Declaration was drafted by Lord Milner and adopted by Mr A. J. Balfour on 2 November 1917, that is to say before the conquest of Palestine. It was an aspiration not a grant. 'His Majesty's Government view with favour the establishment in Palestine of a national home for the Jewish people, and will use their best endeavours to facilitate the achievement of this object, it being clearly understood that nothing should be done which may prejudice the civil and religious rights and political status enjoyed by the Jews in any other country.' This clearly implies that no new Jewish nationality and therefore no Jewish national state was intended.

The juridical status of Palestine in 1918 was uncertain. In

succeeding Turkey, as the suzerain by right of conquest, Great
Britain inherited the obligation to maintain the civil and religious
liberties of several communities in Jerusalem and the other holy
cities. These would be maintained without question, whatever
was the status of the countryside which, after long centuries of
Turkish misrule and neglect, was poor and thinly populated. The
problem lay in interpreting some sentences in the MacMahon
Pledge (see above, page 886). Was Palestine excluded from the
Arab area by the reservation of 'the portions of Syria lying to the
west of the districts of Damascus, Homs, Hama, and Aleppo,' . . .
'since they cannot be said to be purely Arab'? These districts
had certainly not been liberated by a spontaneous rising of the
people, as Arabia and parts of Syria had been. Under the Sykes-
Picot Treaty, to which the other powers attached more weight
than to the MacMahon Pledge, they fell in the British zone of
influence. Thus the mandate would fall, on every count, to
Great Britain. It was understood that the Sherifian princes would
approve of a Zionist colony, a settlement scheme—that is to say—
not a state.

A civil administration for Palestine, with Sir Herbert Samuel
as High Commissioner, replaced the military government set
up by Allenby, in June 1920. The mandate was finally issued
with the approval of France, the United States, and the American
and European Zionists in 1923. It was Samuel's task to give
Palestine a modern administration and, in his memoirs, he claims
credit for improving the police, the law-courts, the departments
of education, health, and public works, for preserving antiquities
and amenities, and for making surveys on which the land-
settlement schemes were based. The greatest obstacles he
encountered were the sectarian jealousies of all the religious
bodies in Jerusalem. The form of government was that of a
Crown Colony with a nominated council, and a Civil Service in
which the higher officers were British.

For about five years progress was rapid, and public order no
worse than was to be expected in that turbulent country. Jewish
settlers came in pretty fast and were settled in about a hundred
agricultural villages at a cost to the Zionist organisations of
about £6,000,000. In addition to the 25,000 farmers, 30,000
Jews had swelled the village of Tel Aviv into a city with municipal
self-government. The immigrant community conferred with the

High Commissioner through its own semi-official committee, the Jewish Agency. Not the least remarkable achievement was the revival of classical Hebrew as a spoken tongue. Lord Balfour's visit in 1925 to inaugurate the Hebrew University at Jerusalem was the climax of this first happy phase. It was ominous that the Arab community called a general strike. In Syria a similar Arab agitation against the French mandate led to open revolt and, when Balfour visited Damascus, his life was threatened by the crowd.

Sir Herbert Samuel had done his best to appease Arab senti-ment. The statistics make it plain that the increase of wealth and population had materially benefited the Arabs as well as the Jews, but the steady increase of this alien minority from one-ninth of the population in 1922, to one-fifth in 1936, and nearly one-third in 1944 was a growing irritation. If immigration continued the Jews might soon become a majority, and a wealthy majority that would overrule the Arab interest. The newcomers were no longer simple pietists, content to live a 'minority life', if only it might be in the land of Israel; they were active young radicals with advanced views of political and industrial technique, remarkably free from traditions and taboos. It should be noted too that most came from lands where the state and the police were regarded as the enemies of the people.

Sir H. Samuel convened a General Moslem Council as a counterweight to the Jewish Agency, in the hope of promoting co-operation between the two. The Moslems proved to have no policy but flat negation. Electing as their president (1921) Haj Amin el-Husseini, the Mufti of Jerusalem, they rejected the inter-pretation put upon the MacMahon Pledge; they denied the validity of the mandate; they opposed the flooding of their country with alien Jews; they demanded that Arabs in Palestine should enjoy the same liberties as Arabs in Irak and Trans-Jordan.

If the later 1920's seemed to be a period of tranquillity and progress in Palestine it was only because events in Europe did not stimulate emigration. The misdeeds of Hitler let loose a flood in 1932 against which the Arabs violently protested. In 1933 the arrival of 30,000 Jews was recorded in Palestine while many more came irregularly; in 1934 there were 42,000 immigrants, in 1935 62,000. Three million pounds a year were invested in land-purchase. The Arabs protested in vain to the High Commissioner, to influential friends in London, to the League of Nations, demanding some limit to the Jewish National Home.

Since Arab opinion was unanimous and, on the whole, constitutional it seemed proper to take a step towards self-government. A plan for an elective Legislative Council (1936) was opposed by the friends of Zionism in Parliament since it would mean dominance for the Arab majority over the Jews. At this rebuff the Arabs broke out in revolt forming an organised army under Fawzi-ed-Din, a Syrian soldier of fortune. It was necessary to mobilise and despatch to Palestine a British infantry division. Though there had been many disorders during the previous fifteen years they were communal riots of Arabs against Jews; this was a regular campaign which cost the mandatory power 300 British casualties. Before it was over, a Royal Commission headed by Lord Peel was sent to make a report.[1]

Inevitably and reluctantly the Commission recommended that Palestine should be partitioned into a self-governing Jewish area, a self-governing Arab area, and a small enclave, under a renewed British mandate, covering the Holy Places. Neither the Jewish nor the Moslem community had been consulted and neither accepted the recommendations. It was particularly repugnant to the Arabs since it conceded to the Jews a change in status from a 'National Home' into a political unit. For two years a state of deadlock continued, with a desultory campaign by Arab partisans against the British. The influence of the Arab kings, counselling moderation in method, brought the war to a close in 1938; they were none the less adamant in their support for the Arab case. In 1939 Mr Malcolm MacDonald, the Colonial Secretary, made a concession to the Arabs that was a sore blow to the Jews and their world-wide Zionist backers. He proposed to limit Jewish immigration to a total of 75,000 during a period of five years while a new constitution was to be prepared, and thereafter Palestine was to be independent. From that time it was the Jews rather than the Arabs who opposed British rule. No

---

[1] The Palestine Royal Commission Report, 1937 (Cmd. 5479) contains a full impartial survey of the whole series of events. It is essential for any objective study of the problem. It recorded that the population had increased from 600,000 in 1922 to 950,000, of whom 400,000 were Jews; 97,000 settlers lived in 203 village colonies, 150,000 lived in Tel Aviv; £14,000,000 had been invested in British guaranteed loans, £63,000,000 by Zionists; 80% of the export was in citrus fruit; the revenue had risen from £1,000,000 to £4,500,000.

sooner were the Germans defeated in Europe than the Jewish extremists organised the smuggling-in of immigrants with help from the enemies of Britain in every country. A campaign of assassination was begun in 1944, when the British Resident Minister in the Middle East, Lord Moyne, was murdered by the Stern Gang in Cairo. Many murders of British policemen and officials ensued.

Between October 1946 and January 1947, repeated attempts were made by the British to bring Jews and Arabs to a compromise. When the final proposals were rejected by both parties, the British referred the issue to the United Nations Organisation. In September 1947, a committee of the United Nations recommended the recognition of an independent Jewish State but could not get agreement upon the terms of partition. In any case, the British were unwilling to undertake the task of imposing terms by force, against the will of both parties. Great Britain therefore relinquished the mandate on 15 May and completed the withdrawal of troops by 1 August 1948, whereupon Jews and Arabs resorted to war.

7. MIDDLE EASTERN OIL

The abdication of power in Egypt, Palestine, and Irak would, at an earlier date, have been estimated in terms of strategic routes to India. More recently it had been related to the supply of oil.

Petroleum products were first used extensively as fuel in the oil-lamps and oil-stoves of improved pattern which were introduced in the 1850's. It was a Scotsman, James Young, who first distilled finer essences from raw petroleum and an American, E. L. Drake, who succeeded in tapping subterranean deposits by drilling for oil near Philadelphia in 1859. The use of kerosene (paraffin) for American oil-lamps led to the first great expansion of the oil industry. In 1870 Rockefeller began to build up his organisation of refineries and pipe-lines which, in forty years, gave him control of nearly 90% of the American output. This was the origin of the Standard Oil Trust which was broken up, by the Sherman Anti-trust Law of 1911, into its twenty constituent companies. But this first great development was chiefly for home consumption; exports of oil from the United States were a small fraction of the output.

World-trade in oil was built up in those years by the London firm of M. and S. Samuel, East India merchants, who hit upon the plan of supplying the lamps of India and China with Russian and American paraffin. In 1890 they built their first oil-tanker, on the model of those used by the Russians in the Caspian Sea, and in 1897 formed the Shell Transport Company with a capital of £1,800,000 to deal with this branch of their business. The name 'Shell' was derived from their former profitable line of trading in curios made of oriental shells.

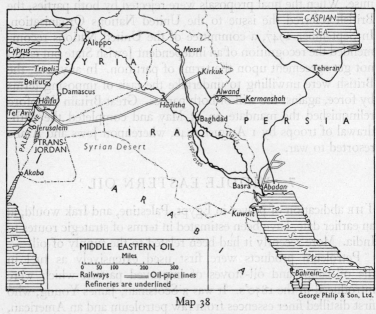

Map 38

George Philip & Son, Ltd.

Standard Oil now made a determined effort to capture the distribution of oil products throughout the world, with the result that the Samuels were forced into amalgamations to resist them. They acquired an interest in an oilfield in Dutch Borneo and entered into close relations with the Royal Dutch Corporation. By 1907 refining and distribution in the old world were in the hands of the Asiatic Petroleum Company (now reorganised as the Shell Petroleum Company), a combination of Shell, Royal Dutch, and French Rothschild interests. Meanwhile the introduction of petrol engines in the 'eighties and 'nineties was leading to a vastly greater demand for petroleum products. The output was estimated at 20 million tons in 1900, 50 millions in 1913, 250 millions in 1939. Though Shell was principally a distributing agency it acquired interests in all the world's oilfields except those of Soviet Russia, and those of Mexico which were nationalised in 1938. Shell owned a fleet of 191 ships in 1947, and Shell oil was the largest item in the traffic of the Suez Canal.

The need for an assured supply of petroleum was the dominant factor (as mentioned above) in the transference of the British Navy from a coal-burning to an oil-burning basis. The first steps taken by the British government were to acquire an interest in the Burmah Oil Company and through that in the oilfields of the Middle East. In 1901 Mr W. K. D'Arcy had obtained from the Persians an exclusive concession to prospect and drill for oil in an area of 100,000 square miles in South Persia. In 1907 prospectors struck oil at Masjid-i-Sulaiman. Two years later a powerful corporation, the Anglo-Persian (now Anglo-Iranian) Oil Company, was formed to work the D'Arcy concession. The Burmah Oil Company was one of its backers, but more than half the ordinary share-capital, to the nominal value of £7,500,000, was eventually taken up by the British government with a controlling interest on the Board. For a hundred years the Persian Gulf had been regarded as a British sphere of influence; the Anglo-Russian agreement of 1907 had recognised that fact; the oil concession (renewed in 1933) confirmed it. Strategically the head of the Persian Gulf was now a main base of supply for the Navy. The holdings of the British Treasury, in Suez Canal shares, in Anglo-Persian Oil, and later in Imperial Airways and in Cables and Wireless, made the Middle East the nerve-centre of the whole imperial organism.

The main outlet for Anglo-Persian oil was through the refinery at Abadan, for long the largest in the world, near the Mesopotamian frontier where there was water-carriage down the Shatt-el-Arab. The security of Abadan and its pipe-lines was the primary objective of the Mesopotamian campaign in the first World War.

As the demand for oil continued to grow, both British and American interests concentrated upon the Persian Gulf, bringing new wealth and diplomatic significance to the Arab sultanates. A concession for the oil of Kuwait was granted jointly to the Anglo-Iranian and to (Mr Mellon's) Gulf Oil Corporation, one of the successors to the Standard Oil Trust, as are the Texas Corporation and the Standard Oil Company of California which hold the concessions for Bahrein and Saudi Arabia. Among these interlocking interests the most complex was the Irak Petroleum Company formed in 1927 to develop the ancient oilfields of Mesopotamia, which are mentioned in the Book of Genesis. Its shares were held by a subsidiary of Anglo-Iranian, a subsidiary of Shell, a French group and two American groups (Standard Oil of New Jersey and Standard Oil of New York). Irak petroleum was mostly delivered at Haifa and Tripoli, by pipeline across the desert from Kirkuk, and shipped by Shell. Middle Eastern oil, unlike American and Russian oil, is produced primarily for the export market. Between the Wars, Western Europe lived upon it as it once had lived upon Tyne coal.

Other exporting oilfields are in Venezuela and Trinidad. Central America produces about 20% of the world's output, distributing much of it through the Shell organisation. In the twentieth century oil has meant power, as did coal in the nineteenth. It is yet to be seen whether new sources of power will supersede oil in its turn.

XIX

LAND, LABOUR, AND SETTLEMENT IN AFRICA

Argument: Indirect rule was the master-principle of British administration in tropical Africa between the Wars. It was extended to all the West Coast colonies, to Tanganyika, and elsewhere. The Colonial Office attempted to preserve peasant economies rather than to permit the plantation economy favoured by exporting corporations. Self-government, with safeguards for natives, was given to the white settlers of Southern Rhodesia. There, as in the Union, a policy of segregation, the organisation of a plural society, was the accepted solution of the racial problem. The Indians of Natal were a racial minority that resisted segregation. The clash between white and black Africa was most critical in Kenya where the Colonial Office declared native interests paramount.

1. INDIRECT RULE, THE NIGERIAN SYSTEM

DIRECT and indirect rule of the native races in colonies are varying tendencies, not opposed principles. Whenever rule is established by a stronger and more highly organised people over a weaker people with a simpler organisation the rulers must, in the first instance, employ some leaders of the subject race as their agents and must administer laws that those agents understand. No tyranny is so absolute as to be able at once to enforce the methods of the stronger civilisation upon the weaker, especially among primitive peoples whose laws are not distinguished from customs and whose language is not likely to contain words for other than customary, notions. The question that all colonial administrators must face is whether to assimilate the laws of the colony to those of the dominant race or to develop the laws and customs of the subject race so as to make them adequate to the needs of a progressive society. In every instance economic factors impose some form of compromise. No colony has ever been quite assimilated, and none has been left unaffected by the laws of the suzerain. There must be some assimilation together with some degree of local autonomy.

Generally speaking the Latin nations have favoured assimilation, or direct rule, in their dependencies which are thus brought under a uniform administration. There, indigenous societies are allowed to wither away, the traditional powers of princes lapse, and a new governing class, trained in the principles of the dominant race, emerges. This was the guiding principle of *La France d'Outremer*, at least in the last generation. But the most striking examples of direct rule in recent years may be seen in the Russian colonisation of Central Asia, where the indigenous peoples have been rapidly propelled into the paths of Soviet Communism. Confiscation and reallotment of the land was the decisive step.

There was a time when English Liberals spoke of westernising India by direct rule. Cornwallis had made a beginning, with the permanent settlement of Bengal and, when Bentinck was governor-general, the English common law and education in the English language were conceived as steps towards the English political and social system. The gradual progress of liberalism in India from 1828 to 1947, in spite of many setbacks, may be considered as an achievement for direct rule. When communal distinctions again divided the Empire which the British had united, the assimilation was shown to be incomplete. The age-old cleavage between Moslem and Hindu had not been closed by a century of liberal education for the new ruling class.

But British rule in India had not been constant to the direct principle. The feudatory princes whose territories were associated by treaty with British India continued to administer their own states with more or less supervision by British Residents. This was the origin of indirect rule, which has been extended to many parts of the British colonial empire since the early twentieth century. Though every colony has its variant it will be convenient to distinguish four main types:

(i) *Missionary Kingdoms*. The early Protestant missionaries supposed with supreme optimism that barbarians could be civilised within a few years by the influence of the Gospel. They strove to admit peaceful commerce to the mission-field while excluding the trade in arms, slaves, and liquor, hoping thus to convert savage tribes into liberal Christian kingdoms. It was necessary to implant habits of industry and to improve agriculture, which could rarely be done without a settled land-tenure. Willynilly the missionaries were sometimes obliged to acquire tribal land, as in New Zealand and Nyasaland, in order to carry out their policy; or to acquiesce in the creation of a landlord class, as in Uganda. Many attempts were made to establish evangelical Utopias in Africa and in the Pacific. In two colonies at least, Uganda and Tonga, something like success was achieved.

(ii) *Westernised Oriental States*. Almost the reverse of the missionary policy was adopted in the Malay States where Islam was the national cult. The impact of civilisation upon these comfortable retreats took the form of a boom in tin-mining. In order to use the new wealth for the benefit of the community it was necessary to introduce trained administrators and technicians who could organise revenue, police, and public works. Indirect rule in Malaya maintained the prestige of the sultans as the social and religious leaders of the indigenous race while creating under their authority an efficient Western administration. The prosperity of the Federated Malay States was almost entirely derived from the efforts of the immigrant communities. Their land was developed by mining concessions and rubber plantations. It has been the task of the protecting power to ensure that the profit of Chinese miners and British planters has been advantageous to the Malays also.

(iii) *Mere Protection*. From 1868 onwards a great number of tribes have been taken under British protection, often at their own request. Sometimes this implied no more than controlling their external affairs, suppressing barbarous customs, and arranging some sort of extraterritorial jurisdiction over European residents. Sometimes these protectorates asked and got from the Colonial Office a grant-in-aid, a dole to supplement their scanty revenue. They were among the neglected estates for which Joseph Chamberlain asked something more than bare justice. Indirect rule here was negative, the absence of positive direction. Basutoland, the first protectorate, over-populated, overstocked with cattle, and actually dwindling away by soil-erosion, will serve as an example.

(iv) *Lugard's System*. Indirect rule in the Niger territories arose naturally from the social and political situation. In 1903 Lugard found himself with a handful of white assistants in possession by conquest of northern Nigeria, a large well-populated pastoral and agricultural country. The northern peoples were ruled by a Fulani aristocracy, were accustomed to the Islamic law of land-tenure and taxation, were equipped with a common tongue in Hausa, the only native African language with a written literature. No other system was at first possible than to maintain the rule of the emirs under British authority. This again was very different from the Malayan plan. In northern Nigeria the British Crown was sovereign; the administration that carried out its orders was native in its composition and in its method. Since the British officers were few and scattered, the pressure of their hand was light. Slavery was abolished (1900), the liquor trade was rigidly restricted, and that at first was almost the whole change. No grants of land were made to Europeans since all was in the lawful possession of native landowners; nor were concessions for mining of much consequence at first.

The country prospered in peace and began to develop new lines of trade. About a quarter of the population lived in walled towns among which Sokoto was the seat of the principal emir. The largest town was Kano, which held 100,000 people within its crenellated walls of red, sun-dried brick. Kano had long been celebrated for its trade in tanned goat-skins which, sent by caravan across the desert, were known in Europe as Morocco leather. Now that the Niger routes were open Lugard proposed that the trade of Kano should find an easier outlet southward to the sea.

Under the system of indirect rule Kano remained, and still remains, an African city. Its scanty European population lives in a location outside the walls while the African municipality has entire control of light, power, police, sanitation, hospitals, and schools within. A principle of Nigerian administration is the financial autonomy of each emirate. There are more than sixty native 'treasuries' in the Northern Provinces, Kano being the richest with a revenue (1936–7) of £200,000 a year.

When Lugard united the various Niger states into the colony of Nigeria he extended the principle of indirect rule to the Southern Provinces, where there are more than one hundred 'treasuries'. South-western Nigeria, Yoruba-land, also a country of populous cities where the power of chiefs had always been limited by custom, took up the principle briskly. Ibadan, with nearly 400,000 inhabitants (and no Europeans in the city limits), is the largest self-governing African city. In the south-east indirect rule has been less successful among the Ibo peoples who were not previously organised in large social groups. In the coastal towns where European influences—good and bad—had long prevailed, municipalities of a Western type were instituted. It is here among the English-speaking westernised Africans that an agitation against indirect rule has arisen. Conceiving themselves as an emergent governing class, the future rulers of the country when self-government reaches a further stage, they protest that indirect rule nullifies the effect of education by buttressing the power of illiterate chiefs.

Meanwhile the story of Nigeria is one of growing prosperity achieved by improved communications. The railway from Lagos through Ibadan reached Kano in 1912; the eastern provinces were developed by the construction of a new harbour, named Port Harcourt after the Colonial Secretary (1913), near the old slaving-port of Bonny. The old lines of trade that followed the Oil Rivers were replaced by road and railway; the old trading posts, hulks moored in midstream, were replaced by storehouses ashore. A new cash-crop that brought in revenue was groundnuts from the north while palm-kernels from the south were exported in vastly greater volume.[1]

When the Crown took over the territories in 1900 the Niger Company reverted to its former role as an importing and exporting house with a far-reaching organisation, which expanded with the steadily growing demand for oils and fats. All the world's markets were then being searched for new sources of supply, especially by Lever Brothers who had a keen eye to West African affairs. In 1907 Lord Leverhulme (then Mr Lever) made the first of several approaches to the Colonial Office for a concession in Nigeria which was brusquely refused. It was intended that Nigeria should be developed by peasant cultivation, not by plantation methods and, in any case, the principle of indirect rule precluded the alienation of tribal lands. Leverhulme accordingly turned to the Belgian Congo where he obtained a

---

[1] The ground-nut, or pea-nut (*Arachis hypogaea*) is an American leguminous plant whose pods ripen underground. Palm-kernels are the seeds of the wild or cultivated African oil-palm (*Elaeis guineensis*). Oil is extracted from the endosperm by crushing the entire kernel.

concession for 1,500,000 acres. Though he failed to get control of West African production he got a firm grip upon its external trade, by acquiring the interests of the Niger Company for £8,500,000 in 1920. After a fierce commercial struggle he got control also of its principal rival, amalgamating the two in 1929 under the name of the United Africa Company, a reversion to the name given by Goldie to the first of its forerunners.

2. THE GOLD COAST

EVEN more rapid than the progress of Nigeria was that of the Gold Coast, though indirect rule did not run so smoothly there. The Gold Coast was a pagan country where tribal authority was strictly limited by custom, often by very barbarous custom. The power of chiefs, great and small, was traditionally associated with their 'stools' or thrones, a concept as difficult to rationalise as that similar traditional abstraction, the throne of a European monarchy. The restoration of the Golden Stool to the Ashanti people, and the punishment of its desecrators, were signs that indirect rule was at last being interpreted in terms that an African would appreciate. But the traditional revenues of each 'stool' were not easily adjusted to the needs of a modern administration, and the recognition of chiefs as administrative officers deprived the people of their cherished right to 'de-stool' unpopular chiefs. Indirect rule was gradually applied by recognising the 'stools' of the sixty-three paramount chiefs in the colony (1925), and by reviving the Ashanti Confederacy of seven clans in the Protectorate (1935).

The interest of Gold Coast history in recent years does not, however, lie in political but in agricultural organisation. Though mineral rights have largely been alienated to British mining companies, the land has been retained by the people, who mostly live in village communities and cultivate family holdings. Fifty or sixty years ago the cocoa-plant was introduced from Brazil, by way of Fernando Po, as a cash-crop to supplement subsistence farming. At that time the total world-output was no more than 70,000 tons. In 1939 it had increased to 725,000 tons of which more than half came from British West Africa. In the favourable climate of the Gold Coast, cocoa proved a suitable crop for cultivation by peasants using small patches of land sheltered by forest trees.

The cocoa-plant with its glossy foliage, pods of brilliant colours, and rich perfume made the fortune of the Gold Coast. Sir Gordon Guggisberg, an enterprising Governor (1919–28), had the courage to 'cash in' upon the boom in cocoa and to equip the colony with public works on a scale that less favoured territories could not afford. For nearly 400 years British ships had lain off-shore at Accra and Cape Coast, unloading and loading their freight in surf-boats manœuvred through the breakers by Kru-boys, the tribe of courageous longshoremen. Guggisberg built a harbour at Takoradi, at a cost of £1,250,000, and linked it with the interior by railway. Accumulated revenue also enabled him to found the Prince of Wales College at Achimota, for an initial cost of £600,000, an institution far more lavishly equipped than any other African college. It was conceived as a complete school of life for pupils of all ages and of both sexes drawing upon the traditions of African arts and crafts and of European academic studies. Though Christian and English-speaking, it threw open its doors to Africans of all races and religions. The conception was that of James Aggrey, an African scholar.

The fame of Achimota was widely celebrated among all those who studied Africa and all those who studied systems of education, not without provoking some jealous criticism. There seemed to be an element of the grandiose in building this luxurious academy when the schools in the bush were so inadequate, the peasantry so poor. In reply the defenders of Achimota asserted that nothing but the best was good enough. The peoples of the Gold Coast might take pride in this product of their own resources and exertions, a pattern for all Africa to follow.

The firm foundation of native society upon cocoa-farming enabled the peasants to make a stand against the exporters' monopoly. Not only the cultivation but also the marketing of the cocoa was in native hands through about 1500 native 'brokers', who employed twenty times as many 'sub-brokers' to collect the cocoa from the villages. As in other peasant societies these buyers performed the unpopular but useful role of village money-lenders whose interest was to hold prices steady and to tide the growers over bad seasons, with the frequent effect of forcing them into debt. The brokers had to make their bargain with the

exporting houses, about a dozen in number, among whom the
United Africa Company was predominant. During the boom-
years of the 1920's, cocoa averaged over £50 a ton in London;
in the 'thirties the average price was less than £30 a ton, largely on
account of the great increase in the world's output. The exporters
made a determined effort in 1937 to buy cocoa cheaper by
organising direct purchase from the growers, whereupon the
villages, standing by their traditional organisation, withheld
supplies. Being a true peasantry they could subsist on the produce of their lands even without sending their cash-crop of cocoa
to market, and could wait until the exporters gave way.

A Royal Commission, headed by Mr W. Nowell, made an
exhaustive report[1] which was debated by Parliament in 1938.
On the one hand it was shown that the United Africa Company
had been obliged to buy cocoa for several years at an uneconomic
price, which was offset by its many other interests in the import
and export trade of the Coast; on the other hand it was no less
evident that the system of the brokers was grossly uneconomic
with far too great a margin of middleman's profit between the cost
to the exporter and the receipts of the cultivator. The solution
proposed by the Commission was the formation of a cultivators'
organisation for co-operative marketing. When war broke out in
the following year new sources of temporary revenue and new
problems came to the Gold Coast, but the stand of the peasants
against monopoly-capital, however irrational, was a landmark in
the history of Africa.

Indirect rule on the Nigerian plan was introduced, with
appropriate modifications, into Sierra Leone and the Gambia.
On a smaller scale their recent history resembles that of the
two larger colonies. In all four, progress has been made towards
self-government by the admission to the legislative councils of
members representing the native 'treasuries' and the coastal
municipalities. The constitution conferred upon Nigeria in 1945,
though the most liberal of these experiments, is far from satisfying
the demands of the African intelligentsia, whose gaze is fixed upon
the political progress of British India. Many thousands of
African ex-soldiers who have served in Asia are aware of these new
developments.

The British have set their West African dependencies in

[1] Cmd. 5845.

movement at a rate which is too fast for the backward races and too slow for the progressives. It should be remembered that Nigeria and the Gold Coast are political fictions with no real cohesion beyond that supplied by the British system. They include peoples at all stages of culture and speaking many languages. Their frontiers are not natural but were devised to fit some international compromise or other, during the partition of Africa, with a total disregard of tribal boundaries. Indirect rule now appears as a temporary stage in the movement towards a more rational plan for tropical Africa, when Moslem emirates, Christian seaports and pagan villages—still more when French and British territories—shall readjust their relations. In the British sphere several moves have been made towards a union of the four colonies, but with little success, since inter-colonial communications are poor. Strategic necessity led to the despatch of a Resident Minister of cabinet rank, to co-ordinate West African affairs during the second German War. Later co-operation was confined to occasional conferences between the four Governors.

The rate of social progress is limited by African poverty. Fortunate as are the peasants of the four colonies in relation to other Africans, they are still miserably poor by English standards, and accordingly are miserably under-equipped with social services. To increase this wealth they will require capital investment on a scale far beyond the resources of the Colonial Development Fund. Private capital alone, as the world is now organised, can supply this deficiency, and such firms as the United Africa Company, unpopular as they are with radical philanthropists, have still a part to play.

In British Africa the Company concentrates on wholesale trading and leaves retail trading in the interior to native traders. In 1947, 1400 'buying-points' and 667 'stores', the vast majority of them under native management, were operated by the Company in the four colonies. They purchase about one-half of what the colonies export and distribute about one-third of what the colonies import. The Company is thus by far the largest buyer for the West African Produce Control Board which, since 1939, takes over the whole exportable surplus at fixed prices. The accusation that the Company is a strangling monopoly is met by the assertion that only 3% of the sums received in West Africa in 1947 were transferred to London to provide office expenses, taxation, and profits. Of the 97% retained in Africa, 73% was paid to the native producers or their agents, 13% was the cost of transport, 7% was spent in maintaining establishments in Africa, and 4% was taken for port-dues.

According to the published report of the Company, British West Africa is not that part of the 'Unilever Empire' from which a high rate of profit is derived, and in the view of the Company's officers a higher degree of industrial organisation would increase the prosperity of the cultivators. Only scientific control can check the ravages of the new pest, 'swollen shoot', which threatens to destroy the unsupervised peasant holdings of cocoa; only plantation methods, it is alleged, could increase the output and improve the quality of palm-oil, making the trade economically comparable with that of the Dutch Indies.

3. SOUTH AFRICA

NATIVE policy in South and East Africa has been fundamentally different from the West African policy since the earliest days of colonisation, the crucial distinction being the rule of land-tenure. At the Cape the Dutch pioneers were able to mark out claims almost at will in a land that was uncultivated and, except for nomadic Hottentots, uninhabited. Only when they moved far inland did they come into conflict with the Bantu tribes who, like themselves, were recent immigrants and pastoral farmers. Though the Bantu cultivated some small plots of land it was by 'shifting cultivation' which did not involve the legal conception of real property. The trek-boers were hardly less nomadic.

Under British colonial rule no change was made in the Boer system of providing every householder with a freehold from the unappropriated waste, but a determined attempt was made to enforce the equality of all races before the law. The Cape constitution of 1853 granted the franchise, with a property qualification, 'on equal terms to all male British subjects without distinction of class or colour'. In the Colony, where there were then few Bantu natives, the 'Cape franchise' was granted for the benefit of the more prosperous members of the 'Cape Coloured' race, many of them the progeny of the slaves who had been set free in 1834.

No such favours were conferred upon any pigmented peoples in the Afrikaner republics. The Transvaal constitution of 1858 expressly repudiated any form of 'equality either in Church or State', nor was there equality in land-tenure. While every burgher was entitled to a freehold farm, natives were permitted to occupy land in the European areas only as tenants-at-will, on condition of spending a proportion of their time working for a European landlord. The Afrikaners have always taken pride in their understanding of the natives, and the benevolent character of this feudal system at its best is demonstrated, in many instances, by its voluntary continuance through several generations. At worst it was no better than slavery. The Afrikaner republics continually encroached upon the tribal areas and, generally speaking, allotted no native reserves.

There was plenty of room in the Transvaal for whites and blacks; in Cape Colony the oncoming Bantu tribes were forced back behind the eastern frontier. Kaffraria was not deliberately made into a native reserve, it was left undisturbed because there was neither money nor inclination to develop it. The fear of German infiltration, more than any other cause, led to the nominal annexation of the Bantu territories between 1879 and 1894. Not here but in Natal was a constructive policy initiated, by Shepstone; it was the outcome of the confused struggle between British, Boers, and Zulus between 1839 and 1843. In his early experiment at what later was to be called indirect rule Shepstone fostered tribal administration and would have reserved tribal lands in large blocks, had not Governor Grey insisted upon interspersing settlers' and native holdings, in the well-meaning belief that native agriculture would be improved by European example. The failure of Shepstone's system, in the eyes of the settlers, was that it dried up the pool of native labour.

The feudal period of South African history ended with the discovery of the diamond-fields, which hugely increased the demand for unskilled labourers. It was at Kimberley, under British rule, that Rhodes originated the system of recruiting native labour in the reserves and confining the labourers in compounds for the period of their indentures. The natives were now to be civilised, as wage-earners under industrial discipline, a far harsher process than Boer feudalism. It was the British technicians and foremen at Kimberley who first drew the industrial colour-line between high-paid European and low-paid African labour. The Kimberley system was imitated on a larger scale by the gold-mining companies of the Rand.

There was an old precedent in South Africa for 'pass-laws', first imposed by a reforming Governor of the Cape (see chapter VI, 2, page 315) as a means of settling the nomadic Hottentots. These laws were revived with ever-increasing stringency to control the migratory labour from all parts of Africa to the mines. Natives were obliged, under threat of fine and imprisonment, to produce upon demand written evidence of their right to be outside their location. An attempt to extend the scope of the pass-laws to Indian immigrants in the Transvaal led to a political duel between two young men of promise, M. K. Gandhi and General Smuts.

In an earlier chapter an account has been given of the introduction of coolies to the sugar plantations of Natal. Many remained as residents and attracted a bourgeoisie of Indian traders and shop-keepers like that which was already established farther north in the dominions of the Sultan of Zanzibar. In 1894 Gandhi, then on a professional visit to Natal as a young lawyer, put himself at the head of an agitation against their civil disabilities, and especially against their virtual exclusion from civil rights in the neighbouring Transvaal Republic. A feature of his campaign was loyalty to the British Empire, upon which he grounded his claims. He demanded for his Indian friends the right, as British citizens, to move about the country freely and to practise any trade or profession. He recruited field ambulance units among the Indians of Natal to serve with General Buller's force in 1899, and again during the Zulu rising of 1906.

During the reconstruction after the South African War, when the Colonial Office was still in control, an attempt was made to restrict the movement of Indians into the Transvaal by a form of pass-law. There was nothing degrading in the laws themselves which are now the common form of all European countries; it was the discrimination in British territory against British Indians that was resented. In 1906 Gandhi launched the first of his campaigns of passive resistance, against the pass-law.

When self-government was restored to the Transvaal and still more when the Union was achieved, discrimination against the

Indians was stiffened. The dispute came up again and again at imperial conferences, where the Colonial Secretary appeared with a brief from the Secretary for India, while the new South African Dominion was supported by the other Dominions in asserting a right to control its own immigrants.

A crisis came in 1913 when a new South African marriage law had the incidental effect of invalidating many Hindu marriages in Natal. Gandhi forced the whole issue with a renewed campaign of non-resistance against unequal laws. He defied General Smuts by leading a march of Indians across the Natal frontier into the forbidden country of the Transvaal. 'Non-violent' transgression of the law produced violent repression, as it was intended to do, and overcame it by patience. This was the technique of *satyagraha* which Gandhi afterwards perfected in India. After a meeting between General Smuts and Gandhi a compromise was arranged and the validity of Hindu marriages was confirmed. But the racial policy of South Africa remained unchanged.

Meanwhile the woes of Indians in Africa provoked counter-measures in India. On Gandhi's motion in the Legislative Council the Indian government put an end to the despatch of indentured labour, to Natal in 1911, to the other colonies in 1917. 1 January 1920 was India's Abolition Day when the last indentures of Indian coolies overseas were cancelled. The resident Indians of Natal, a prosperous community with a high birth-rate, still presented a problem that grew more intense as racial discrimination increased. General Smuts took a firm stand in 1923, declaring that Indians must not expect equality in the Union. After a further struggle another compromise, the Cape Agreement of 1927, was negotiated between the South African and Indian governments who undertook 'continuous co-operation'. Hopes were entertained of solving the problem by encouraging a remigration to India, which was, in fact, set in motion. But of the 200,000 Indians in Natal—a racial group as numerous as the white population of that province—80% are African-born. They are prolific, and some of them are wealthy. Attempts by the Durban City Council to plan development by allotting zones for the different segregated races produced a further crisis in 1946, and new recriminations between the Indian and South African governments. South Africa's unanswerable case was that segregated Indians in Natal were far less restricted and oppressed than the 'scheduled castes' in India.

The annexation of the native territories to Cape Colony obliged the politicians at Capetown to reconsider their franchise law. It was reasonable enough to prevent the swamping of the electorate with illiterate voters by imposing an educational qualification in 1892, but the Glen Grey Act of 1894 (see chapter XII, 3, page 686) was a first step in another direction, towards segregation and towards indirect rule. After the South African War the problem was stated in plain terms at an inter-colonial conference (1903). Should the Transvaal system or the Cape system prevail in reconstructed South Africa? The conference proposed a scheme, which was not adopted, for political segregation with communal representation for natives, as in New Zealand. At the National Convention of 1908 Lord Selborne fought hard to extend the liberal Cape franchise to the other provinces and, on failing to do so, insisted upon securing it in the Cape Province by a special clause of the Act of Union. Even here some ground was lost, for, as the Act was framed, Cape natives and coloured persons lost their right (which had never been exercised) to stand for Parliament, though they retained their right to vote if qualified.

After the Union, the Transvaal native policy began to gain ground. The control of native mineworkers in 'compounds' was embodied in the law by the Mine Workers' Act 1911. A new land policy initiated in the Native Lands Act, 1913, to put an end to the unregulated 'squatting' tenure, took the form of scheduling certain areas as native reserves. Thus the principle of segregation was established. It was extended by new acts in almost every session of the Union Parliament. Distinct systems of local government for European and native areas were instituted in 1920. The Native Urban Areas Act, 1923, segregated natives in separate 'locations' in the towns.

While tribal organisation was rapidly decaying among the Bantu, modern industrial organisation was slow to develop among them owing to their illiteracy and poverty. The native reaction against the contraction in trade after the first World War took the form of a tumultuous agitation for more land. It was suppressed with great severity at Bulhoek in 1922. Far more serious than this echo from the past was the strike of the white mine-workers in the same year. The mining companies, in an effort to economise by lowering costs, proposed to use a higher propor-tion of native labour underground, that is to employ natives in what had been white men's jobs. The so-called 'Labour Party' staged a strike of white miners who were inflamed by violent racial and social bitterness. General Smuts again acted promptly and ruthlessly, breaking the strike by the use of military force.

Though General Smuts and the mine-owners appeared to have saved the country from revolution, their triumph was short-lived. It was General Hertzog, the leader of the Afrikaner Nationalist Party, that carried off the spoils. Since the South African War the character of the white community in South Africa had changed. As in America, so in South Africa, the frontier was closed. Since burghers could no longer find free land, a class of poor whites was drifting to the towns. In 1890 65% of the Europeans lived in the country, in 1936 65% lived in the towns. Furthermore the European residents in the towns had been mostly British, when Colonel Cresswell, the leader of the Labour Party, first opposed General Smuts in 1911. In 1922 the majority of his supporters were Afrikaners.

At the election of 1924 Hertzog was returned to power, and remained Prime Minister of the Union until the outbreak of war in 1939. His majority depended upon an alliance between the 'back-veld Boers', the *sinn fein* of South Africa, and the white trade unionists of the Rand. Their policy was segregation of the natives and white predominance. Though some of Hertzog's supporters flaunted their fascist sympathies, it would be unjust to condemn him on this score. Afrikaner politics are notoriously bitter and the weakness of his position was the continual fission of his party as extremist groups broke away. Hertzog, like Smuts, was a lawyer of scholarly tastes and humane principles, but of a somewhat rigid and narrow cast of mind. He genuinely believed in the equity of a plural society where native interests should be paramount in native areas and European interests in European areas. The native problem in South Africa is both complex and intractable and is not capable of solution by mere philanthropy. No other practical step than segregation in some form could be taken by any politician who hoped to retain the support of the white electorate. The weakness of Smuts's position was that, though he could command the vote of the liberals and progressives, he could not escape the logic of events. He too was pledged to segregation and white predominance, which he had enforced with bloodshed at Bulhoek. The limiting factor, as all white men knew, was that South African prosperity depended upon the gold-mines, that is upon white technical skill and black labour.

The segregation policy was urged forward. The Immorality Act, 1926, penalised miscegenation between Europeans and natives; the Native Administration Act, 1927, set up a distinct system of lawcourts; and, after a long struggle, the Cape native franchise was abolished in 1936. Hertzog had raised the issue by granting a universal male and female franchise to the whites in 1931 while leaving unaltered the qualifications for the native and coloured vote. When challenged on the old pledge of 'equal rights for all civilised men'[1] he boldly stated that in his opinion 'white' and 'civilised' were synonymous terms. At an earlier stage he had manœuvred to win the 'Cape coloured' vote by classing this community with the whites rather than the natives. Now the nationalists wished to segregate the coloured race also. Though not deprived of their votes, they were gradually excluded by trade union pressure from many branches of skilled employment, and thus forced downward in the social scale. Similarly the barrier between the whites and the Indians in Natal was raised by social pressure and municipal regulation.

The new status of the natives was determined by two Acts passed in 1936, the Representation of Natives Act and the Native Trust and Land Act. The statutory majority of two-thirds of the members in a joint session of both Houses was at last obtained for depriving of the franchise the 15,000 qualified natives. In the Union Parliament the native races were to be represented thereafter by four (white) senators indirectly elected, while local government in the Reserves was entrusted to native representative councils. Politically, this reversion from direct to indirect rule was realistic in form and beneficial in effect; the test of the new system was its solution of the agrarian problem. It was admitted that the Reserves scheduled under the Act of 1913 were

---

[1] This principle had been elaborated by Mr Churchill at the Imperial Conference of 1921: 'No barrier of race, colour, or creed should prevent any man of merit from reaching any position, if he is fitted for it.'

grossly inadequate. Authority was created to buy a further 15,000,000 acres at the public expense on trust for native use. Unfortunately these powers were not generously used and, ten years later, not half of the scheduled area had been acquired. Meanwhile the pressure of the native population upon the existing reserves had increased.

As a gold-producing country South Africa was able to surmount the currency problems of the world depression in the 1930's more happily than the other Dominions. As in England, an uneasy coalition government was formed, in which General Smuts served under Hertzog (1934-9). The anniversary of the Great Trek, celebrated in 1938, was the occasion of jubilation throughout South Africa and of a renewed outburst of separatist feeling among a section of the Afrikaners, some of whom openly declared their sympathy with Hitler's Germany. This violence played into General Smuts's hand in 1939, since Hertzog resigned to avoid participation in what he regarded as merely another pro-British war. As premier again, General Smuts played his cards with his customary decision and skill. Ignoring the opposition to his policy he ensured that South African troops should take a prominent and a gallant part in the expulsion of the Fascist forces from Africa. He despatched South African troops even to Italy and was justified by a large majority at the election of 1943.

The trade union policy of differentiating sharply between the wages of white technicians and black labourers prevailed between the two German Wars with consequences which were analysed by an economic commission as early as 1926. South Africa was not a rich country, not comparatively wealthy except in gold (*aurum inrepertum et sic melius situm, cum terra celat*). The national income was low, £96 per head per annum, whereas in Australia it was £178 and in Canada £260. High wages for the white worker were held up to something over £1 a day, only by forcing down the wages of the black worker to something under £1 a week. Twenty years later the ratio was the same, with some adjustment of the figures.

Native unskilled labour was provided by pressure of population in the Reserves and by the necessity to earn cash for paying direct taxation. A money economy was coming into existence, with a demand for manufactured goods. The census of 1936 gave the native population as 6,500,000 of whom nearly 3,000,000 lived in the Reserves; 2,000,000 more resided and worked as labourers on European farms; and nearly 1,500,000 were in the towns. Of these urbanised natives 387,000 were working in the mines and living in mine compounds, while a rather larger number (390,000) were domestic servants in white employment. In some respects the mineworkers were fortunate. They were recruited by agencies, such as the Native Recruiting Corporation, which provided for their journey and engaged them to work 313 shifts, that is about nine months, for a mining company. In the compounds they were fed and housed at least as well as they could feed and house themselves in the Reserves, were medically examined and treated, and were sent home with money in their purse. The discipline is not uncongenial to young Bantu. On the other hand the separation of families has a deplorable effect upon domestic morals as well as upon the efficiency of the family farm.

But it should be remembered that 48% of the mineworkers (1936) were recruited from outside the Union, 89,000 from Portuguese East Africa, 49,000 from Basutoland, and smaller numbers from elsewhere, even from colonies as far away as Nyasaland.

Not in the mine compounds but in the 'locations' near the great cities are the victims of the South African social system to be found. Some hundreds of thousands of detribalised natives, neither under direct nor indirect rule, live in neglected poverty in such suburban slums as Sophiatown near Johannesburg, with no municipal amenities or social services. Rarely are they visited by any white men except bands of police enforcing the pass-laws, and by missionaries of the Churches who provide the sole civilising influence. The Anglican Community of the Resurrection has distinguished itself in this field. These urban slums house the misfits of the segregation system, spoiled by industrialism for tribal life, beyond the stage where a healthy revival of indirect rule could rehabilitate them, even if there were land enough for them in the Reserves.

It would be unjust to conclude upon this gloomy note without one countervailing argument. The curse of Africa is poverty, no less in provinces that seem more innocent than in the sophisticated plural community of the Transvaal. Though South Africa is not a rich country, it is richer than Nigeria and the Gold Coast, if only because it has attracted £500 millions of external capital. Though the South African government appears to do little for the natives it does more than the Nigerians can do for themselves. Low as is the rate of literacy among the South African natives it is higher than in other African territories, and Fort Hare in Cape Colony was until 1946 the only native institution in Africa with the status of a university college. A danger is that explosive political doctrines may spread more rapidly among the deracinated urban natives than literacy or technical competence.

To adjust the rights and duties of the several segregated communities is a task of no uncommon difficulty which the white South Africans have boldly tackled. The development of state-controlled industry is more remarkable than in socialist Australia. The Iron and Steel Corporation (ISCOR), established in 1927 as a financial company in which the Union government holds a controlling interest, is already a mighty producer of steel from the ores of the western Transvaal, and of many by-products. Much may also be expected in other industries from the Industrial Development Corporation, a similar organisation set up in 1940. A balanced economy with such resources as these will be better able to support a segregated and plural society than the old unstable equilibrium of gold and cheap labour.

Native policy in the Union depends upon a reinforcement of labour from outside, and largely from the three protectorates which the Colonial Office rules through a High Commissioner. The three differ profoundly from one another.

Basutoland, an enclave in Union territory, is the home of a proud intelligent people whom the great chief Moshesh made into a nation with the help of French Protestant missionaries. They value their traditions, their liberty, and their land. The Basutos have not forgotten that their white neighbours drove them back into the mountains eighty years ago, depriving them of the rich grazing land which they still call the Conquered Territory. On the other hand their health-giving highlands include all the sources of the Orange River, a catchment area for water that the farmers of the Union covet. The grievance is mutual and is maintained with good humour on both sides. Basutoland, like many other parts of South Africa, is much eroded by overstocking so that land-shortage obliges a large proportion of the young men to seek work in the mines. Tribal life is well-developed and the standard of literacy high for Africa. For many years the protectorate has been managed without grants-in-aid from the Colonial Office.

Bechuanaland is an immense formless area of semi-desert with patches of low-grade pasture, thinly peopled by tribes among whom the Bamangwato are pre-eminent. They too owe their nationhood to a great chief, Khama. Though poor and backward they do not go to the mines in great numbers. In most years they have required a grant-in-aid from the Colonial Office.

Swaziland was saved from dismemberment after the South African War and declared a British protectorate in 1903. Its royal house enjoys great prestige in Africa where the tradition of *les rois thaumaturges* is still strong. Though indirect rule is practised here also, the position of the people is weaker since the land had been largely alienated before the Colonial Office took hold. In 1936 a population of 140,000 Swazis occupied 1,700,000 acres while 2700 white settlers occupied 2,400,000 acres. The Swazis cultivate their own land or work for white farmers and are not numerous at the mines.

South-West Africa was captured from the Germans in 1915 and allotted to the Union in 1920, under mandate from the League of Nations. Since 1925 it has been administered as if it were an integral part of the Union. About 11,000 German settlers elected to remain as South African citizens and the white population has increased to about 30,000 by immigration from the Union. The native population, always scanty, had been much reduced by thirty years of German misrule during which determined efforts had been made to expropriate and massacre the tribes. Those who survive are miserably poor and are credited with the lowest recorded literacy rate among the nations of the world.

4. THE RHODESIAS, NYASALAND

THE original charter of the British South Africa Company expired in 1914 after twenty-five years during which no dividend had been paid upon the shares. It was provisionally renewed by the Crown for a further period of ten years during which protracted discussions were held about the future of Rhodesia. The Company asserted that £7,000,000 had been spent on administration and claimed as compensation sovereign rights over all unappropriated land. Their claim was based upon concessions granted by King Lobengula to the Company, or bought by the Company from other grantees. Eventually the claim was referred to the Privy Council where Lord Sumner gave a classic decision, 29 July 1918, against the Chartered Company. He adjudicated that the military conquest of 1893 nullified all concessions made by Lobengula, which had thereby lapsed to the Queen. She had thus been 'an unseen and uninvited member of Jameson's little army'. All land to which no private title could be proved thus became Crown property, and thus the Crown could intervene to protect native rights. This great prerogative was vested in the High Commissioner for South Africa and some areas were scheduled as native reserves in 1920. The adjustment of claims between the Crown, the Company, the settlers, and the natives was not completed for many years.

A constitutional settlement was made in 1923. Rhodesia south of the Zambezi, where there were 34,000[1] British settlers residing with their families (among twenty times as many natives), was offered responsible government either as a province of the Union or as an autonomous British colony. South Africa just then was in a Nationalist, that is Afrikaner, mood which repelled the loyalist Rhodesians. By 8774 votes to 5988 they decided to become a self-governing British colony. It was a disappointment to many in the Union that Rhodesia should stand aside, for Rhodes had designed his province as a northward extension of white South Africa. The 'Imperial factor' which Rhodes had tried to exclude was here again to be reckoned with in the north.

But no sooner was Southern Rhodesia established as a self-governing state than its rulers adopted the same native policy as

[1] 82,000 white settlers in 1946.

the Union. They would not allow the Colonial Office to assert the paramount rights of the natives. Since they made a clean start and had no lack of land, they introduced the policy of segregation more generously, but with the same clear-cut racial distinction. At the final allotment of land in 1936, nearly half the total area of the country, 47 million acres, was provided for white settlement; 21 millions were reserved for native use, and a further 7 millions scheduled as available for native purchase; 2 millions for a national park; and 17 million acres were left unassigned. At this time Southern Rhodesia contained about 50,000 whites and about a million natives. As in the Union, so in Rhodesia the high standard of life for the white population was maintained at the expense of a low standard for the natives. Half the exports of the country came from the mines, where the same system of controlling labour prevailed as on the Rand. In 1936, 24,000 Rhodesian natives and 60,000 native immigrants from neighbouring territories were working there by contract. Neither in the towns nor in the Reserves, however, of Rhodesia were the natives so impoverished as in the Union.

The Chartered Company had received a sum of £3,250,000 in compensation for the loss of its territories, and had been allowed to retain mineral rights throughout the country. It sold these rights to the Southern Rhodesian government for £2,000,000, in 1933. Though gold and other metals have hitherto brought the largest returns it may yet prove that coal is the true wealth of Southern Rhodesia. English miners would be astonished at the sight of the forty-foot seam which outcrops almost to the surface at Wankies, a sample of coal-measures that are almost unlimited.

While Southern Rhodesia was admitted to be white settlers' country, Northern Rhodesia beyond the Zambezi, where the Colonial Office assumed control in 1923, was in another category. Here, the Chartered Company, deprived of its administrative function, could play a useful part as a mining and land-development company. The mines of the copper belt were worked, in the only way they could be worked, by white technicians employing British capital and native labourers. Elsewhere the country was reserved for the natives; Barotseland, the largest subdivision, which had been tribal territory since Lewanika's first treaty with the Crown in 1890, was placed under indirect rule on the Nigerian model in 1937. Nevertheless there were (1946) in Northern Rhodesia 11,000 white men and 10,000 white women whose inclinations tended towards union with the south.

The situation in Nyasaland, Livingstone's country, is a variant from either South African or West African style. As elsewhere in Africa progress required revenue, revenue meant direct taxation, and the obligation to pay taxes forced the natives to work for wages. The problem in Nyasaland was not racial discrimination but poverty of resources. It was long before a profitable crop was raised or exported. In the early days, such bodies as the African Lakes Corporation and even the missionary societies had acquired blocks of land for plantation crops so that Nyasaland is neither a settlers' country like Rhodesia, nor a peasants' country like the Gold Coast, but a planters' country like Malaya. Yet some crops have not responded to these methods. Cotton, once a plantation crop in Nyasaland, is now chiefly grown by the peasants on their own land while the planters' companies have turned to new crops such as tea. There was no prosperity in Nyasaland until communications were improved, but ninety years of Christian education and fifty of plantation agriculture had carried the natives past the profitable stage for indirect rule. Exports from Nyasaland were formerly limited by the awkward-ness of carriage down the Shiré River into the Zambezi and over the bar at the river-mouth. In 1904 the first stage of a railway was begun from Lake Nyasa to the north bank of the Zambezi. In 1919 the colony was able to raise a loan of £1,200,000 at 6% for extending the railway from the south bank through Portuguese territory to Beira. The third stage, the replacement of a ferry by the great Zambezi bridge, was completed in 1937 with the help of a loan from the Colonial Office—£3,000,000 on easy terms. The colony also bought out the interest of the African Lakes Corporation and the British Central Africa Company in their fleets of river-steamers.

5. TANGANYIKA AND KENYA

THE clash of politics in Africa took place in the uplands which had been divided by an arbitrary frontier, in 1890, into the colonies of German and British East Africa (Tanganyika and Kenya). When 'German East' was allotted to Great Britain in 1919 under mandate from the League of Nations the dream of Cecil Rhodes was accomplished. The British zone of influence ran from the Cape to Cairo. It was now the Afrikaner Smuts who could envisage the extension of a white dominion along 'the broad backbone of Africa' from the highlands of the Transvaal to the highlands of Mount Kenya.

But imperial policy was on the other tack. The Colonial Office, which no longer ruled the Dominions, was now chiefly concerned with the powers and the property it held in trust for the native races. Its successes on the West Coast warranted the extension of indirect rule, which appeared on the East Coast when Sir Donald Cameron was made Governor of Tanganyika in 1925. He introduced the Nigerian method of indirect rule on the grounds that it best fulfilled the terms of the mandate.[1] In Kenya there was direct conflict between the two policies.

All the early travellers in Kenya concurred in two opinions; they described the highlands as fertile temperate country suitable for European settlement, and they described it as almost empty country. The few inhabitants were roving bands of Masai, a pastoral people, mighty hunters and reputed the most ferocious tribe in Africa. No doubt, if the Masai did not hunt them out of it, the Kikuyu, a peaceable race of cultivators, would have been the occupiers but, before the white men came, they did not venture far into this desirable but perilous land. Throughout Africa the

---

[1] Tanganyika has also been selected as the site for the first experiments in large-scale production of ground-nuts for the British market. It was a new turn in British colonial policy to develop a country primarily in the interest of the consumer overseas. Two distinct corporations were founded and authorised to borrow £165,000,000: the Colonial Development Corporation, under direction of the Colonial Office, was concerned with the organisation in the colonies; the Overseas Food Corporation, under direction of the Ministry of Food, with the supply to the British consumer. The scheme was launched in 1946, by the United Africa Company, which obliged the government by undertaking the preliminary work.

1880's were a period of disruption in which the scanty population was still further reduced by plagues and tribal wars.

The opening of the Uganda Railway (1902) made white settlement practicable. Sir Charles Eliot, High Commissioner for British East Africa from 1900 to 1904, was an active coloniser. A strict man, he detested the barbarous habits of the Masai, particularly their sexual licence before marriage; he was horrified to discover that another tribe, the Kavirondo, wore no clothes at all. It was his duty to instil Christian morals, to clothe the naked, and to create habits of industry by bringing in settlers who would give an example of civilised life. 'We are not destroying any old or interesting system,' he said, 'we are simply introducing order into blank, uninteresting, brutal barbarism.'

In 1902 Joseph Chamberlain himself took a trip up the railway, whereupon Eliot launched his campaign. He issued an ordinance offering small freehold grants of land, on the Canadian homestead principle, to genuine white settlers. At first very few came but among the first was Hugh Cholmondeley 3rd Lord Delamere (1870–1931), a sporting peer whose ancestral estates in Cheshire neither provided money for his needs nor scope for his energies. He had made several earlier hunting-trips in north-east Africa before arriving at Nairobi to settle in January 1903. It was then a railway construction camp for Indian coolies and had just been burned to the ground as a sanitary precaution against an outbreak of bubonic plague. It began to rise from the ashes as the capital city of Eliot's projected colony.

For nearly thirty years Delamere dominated Kenya and it was perhaps to him that it owed its reputation as a sort of Bohemia in high life. A little, strong-featured, ginger-haired man with a rakish appearance, he was as unselfconscious as only an aristocrat can be, always odd and never affected. In any company he said exactly what he thought and behaved just as he chose. He 'ragged' like a scholboy, and enjoyed life hugely. It was his passion to make Kenya a *White Man's Country*, and his biography, written under that title by Elspeth Huxley, is the most comprehensive history of the settlement.

Delamere insisted from the first that white settlers would not want small-holdings, but large farms with grazing-rights over several thousand acres as in South Africa. Declining an offer from his friend Eliot to enter government service, he took up experimental farming and eventually organised the model Kenya estate, 'Equator Ranch'. He imported shorthorns from Cheshire to cross with native breeds of cattle, brought sheep and shepherds from New Zealand, sank thousands of pounds in planting every kind of crop and trying every form of processing, lost money royally, borrowed, and plagued the government for land, until he eventually leased 100,000 acres, to the scandal of those who opposed white settlement. He was an agricultural institution, a sample of systematic colonisation, not a profiteer. When Kenya was handed over to the Colonial Office (1904) and equipped with a normal administration (1907), Delamere was nominated to the Legislative Council; when an elective element was introduced he was at once elected by the settlers' vote. In both capacities he regarded himself as a constitutional leader of opposition, but embarrassed his colleagues by a total indifference to forms and conventions. He would horrify the flunkeys by suddenly deciding to lead a party of fellows from the club, in their shirt-sleeves, to Government House so that they could give His Majesty's Representative a piece of their mind, and very useful advice they gave him.

The first few hundred settlers had been largely drawn from South Africa, with the help of a subsidiary land-company launched by the British South Africa Company. The flow of immigrants then declined to a trickle until the method of land tenure was agreed. A system of issuing perpetual leases to white settlers in the highlands was not fully authorised until 1915. Meanwhile there had been many hesitations and reversals of policy.

A strange episode was the projected Zionist settlement of 1903, a by-product of Chamberlain's visit. World-wide indignation against anti-Jewish pogroms in Russian Poland induced Balfour's government to offer land in the Kenya highlands as a Jewish colony. Delamere and the settlers vigorously protested against the disposal of a British colony to aliens; but their protest had less effect than objections raised by the Zionists. Though the committee of the International Congress at Basle accepted the offer, a violent emotional reaction against a Jewish home anywhere but in Palestine arose among the rank and file of Zionists; and Palestine, in the days of Abdul Hamid, was quite out of the question. In November 1903 a Zionist delegation visited Kenya and after being confronted with a Masai war-dance, decided to

proceed no further. The benevolent interest of the Conservative
Party in the Zionist movement was to reappear some years later.

As settlers multiplied in the highlands, the nomadic habits of
the Masai became intolerable. They altogether refused to move
with the times. In 1904 it was a great effort of diplomacy to
induce them to settle in two vast reservations where they became
the richest pastoral tribe in Africa, with an average of sixty head
of cattle and 300 sheep to each family. Only eight years later the
pressure of white settlement brought about a further change which
is less easy to defend on grounds of equity. Half of the Masai
were arbitrarily removed to another area which, though it was
larger and just as fertile, was not where they wished to be. They
still took their own line. Characteristically they boycotted the
1914 War, since their idea of manly conduct was to hunt lions
with spears, not to carry burdens, go for route-marches, or make
cannon-fodder. The other tribes were more easily placed on
reservations.

In 1910 there were about 3000 white settlers in Kenya; by
1926 more than 12,000. A planned emigration of ex-soldiers in
1919 had greater success than most similar experiments at that
time. Of 1031 settlers who were placed on farms, more than three-
quarters were still in possession seven years later, a high proportion, since, here as elsewhere, no solid assistance was given to the
settlers beyond transport and leases of land. By 1920 Kenya had
reached the stage of constitutional progress where the demand
for responsible government was raised, with Delamere as protagonist. The first political issue was the status of the Indian
residents, whose cause was hotly debated between the Colonial
Office and the India Office in London as well as between British
and Indians in Kenya. Three Secretaries of State (Milner,
Churchill, and Devonshire) reigned at the Colonial Office
between 1920 and 1923, with three distinct policies, which did not
ease the solution of the problem.

The Indians in Kenya had a good case; they were the first-
comers. Long before the days of British rule the trade of East
Africa had been in the hands of Indian merchants (banians)
and, when British rule began, its first step had been the import
of Indian coolies to build the Uganda Railway. Frere and Kirk
had favoured the Indian community, though Livingstone had
not. In 1919 an Indian National Congress even petitioned the

League of Nations to place East Africa under mandate of British India, an agitation which Gandhi for tactical reasons discouraged.

If Kenya was to remain a British Crown Colony the Indians claimed, as British citizens, equality of status with the white emigrants. Having been deprived of this status in South Africa on the grounds that a self-governing Dominion must decide such questions for itself, they protested bitterly at similar treatment in colonial territory. Five ex-Viceroys supported their cause in the House of Lords. The objections raised by the white settlers were of necessity invidious and were stated very bluntly. They regarded Indian immigration as a demoralising influence in a country assigned for white settlement. They asserted that Indian moneylenders and coolies would have a corrupting rather than a civilising effect on the natives, that their low social standards would be distasteful to white colonists, that the Kenya Indians had a bad record in the 1914 War, and that the sympathy of the Congress leaders concealed the fact that the low-caste or no-caste Indians of Kenya were already treated with more consideration than that accorded by Congress members to low-caste Indians in their own country.

A preliminary agreement between the Under-Secretaries for the Colonies and India (Mr E. S. Wood[1] and Lord Winterton), giving the two races common electoral rights, produced a threat of rebellion among the white settlers which simmered from 1921 to 1923. They formed a vigilance committee and prepared a plan for seizing control of the government at Nairobi, if the final decision should be given against them. Deputations led respectively by Lord Delamere and Mr Sastri met at Downing Street in 1923, with the result that a compromise, known as the Kenya White Paper, was declared by the Duke of Devonshire. It delivered a sharp blow at both immigrant communities. The highlands were indeed reserved for white settlers, and the Indian representation in the Legislative Council was to be by communal voting, not on a single voter's roll. But no hope was held out of responsible government, and segregation was not to be the rule outside the white highlands. In this colony it was the whites, not the blacks, who were to be segregated in a reservation, since

[1] The Hon. Edward Wood (b. 1881) appears in chapter XVIII, 3, page 948, as Lord Irwin, Viceroy of India and later succeeded to his father's title as Lord Halifax.

'Kenya is an African territory and the interests of the African natives must be paramount, and if the interests of the immigrant races should conflict..., the former should prevail. In the administration of Kenya, H.M. Government regard themselves as exercising a trust on behalf of the African population, and they are unable to delegate or share this trust.'

With this compromise the agitation on either side died away. For the next few years the white settlers concentrated upon strengthening their own position under the rule of tactful and well-disposed Governors. Commission after commission came to South Africa to report, criticise, and suggest improvement, but without altering the general line of Kenya's development. It was rich settlers' country, drawing labour from native reserves which, though vast in area, were overstocked and underdeveloped. The estimated population in 1937 was 20,894 Europeans, 48,369 Indians, 14,077 Arabs and 3,280,000 African natives. The social system, as in Rhodesia, tended to assimilate to the South African model with a wide gulf between the wage-levels of white and black labour. A pass-law had been instituted in 1915. Critics of the white settlement policy—and they are numerous— complain that the Kikuyu and Kavirondo Reserves are over-crowded, to which the correct reply is that the population has vastly increased under British rule. Champions of the Kikuyu claim, twenty years after the event, that the tribe was expropriated by the early settlers, a charge that was not substantiated by the Morris-Carter Commission on Kenya Land in 1934. There was, however, something cynical about the encroachment upon the Kavirondo Reserve in 1932 when gold was found there. 'Land covered by mining lease was temporarily excluded.' The white reserves were finally gazetted in 1939 as covering about 16,000 square miles of the highlands, that is to say something less than 10% of the whole colony, excluding the northern deserts.

Politics in Kenya between 1924 and 1939 were largely concerned with the plan first proposed by Mr L. S. Amery for uniting the East African colonies into a single dominion. The reunion of Tanganyika with Kenya seemed a plain geographical necessity. At first Lord Delamere urged on the plan, organising a series of conferences between the white settlers of Kenya, Tanganyika, and Northern Rhodesia. Another Royal Commission led by Sir Hilton Young produced a draft which failed to please the settlers since it postponed the grant of responsible government. Closer union was to be achieved by granting great powers to a governor-general who would chiefly be concerned with protecting the paramount interest of the natives. When Lord Passfield was at the Colonial Office in 1930, he reaffirmed the policy of the White Paper of 1923 in stronger terms, warning the settlers not to expect a further instalment of self-government. The Kenya settlers thereupon withdrew their support from 'Closer Union', which has not yet come to pass. The four East African Territories (Kenya, Tanganyika, Uganda, Zanzibar) different as they are in political organisation, have drawn together in social and economic progress. All four territories, for example, send pupils to the college at Makerere, in Uganda, the nucleus of an East African University.

'I go back to Africa', said Livingstone in 1857 speaking in the accents of the purest philanthropy, 'to open a path for commerce and Christianity.' Rhodes, whose almost whimsical fancy loved to mock his own dream, was in his way a philanthropist too; his motto, he said, was 'philanthropy plus five per cent'. To the men of the 1930's their purpose in Africa seemed more complex, something to which Lugard had given the name of the Dual Mandate. Europe had a duty towards Africa, and Africa a duty towards Europe. Resources were given by nature to be developed, land to be improved; and some land was best cultivated by European capitalist methods, some by African peasants. The Dual Mandate showed signs of being reinterpreted in terms of geography, a new partition of Africa between blacks and whites. There was white man's and there was black man's country, but who was to delimit the frontier? The segregation policy of the Union had defined large areas in which white interests were declared paramount. These areas had been settled, cultivated, civilised, and permanently appropriated by the white race, just as the American prairie had been appropriated. Parts of Rhodesia and of Kenya were rather less securely reserved for the whites. Elsewhere, Africa south of the Sahara belonged to the Africans. Solved in this way the land problem was not intractable. The danger lay in labour not in land. Where the zones overlapped the native workers could not be expected to work at low wages for ever.

XX

SOME EXPERIMENTS IN SELF-GOVERNMENT

Argument: While constitutional progress was rapid in the Dominions it was sluggish or even retrograde in the colonies. Newfoundland, again in financial trouble, relapsed from Dominion Status to direct rule. Malta forfeited its constitution after a party deadlock. Only three of the West Indian colonies enjoyed any large measure of self-government between the Wars. At the conclusion of the second World War large grants of self-government were made to many colonies. Other forms of social progress were encouraged by the Colonial Welfare and Development Fund.

1. NEWFOUNDLAND, 1905–49[1]

A SINGLE year, 1933, showed the flexibility of the British imperial system when the Irish Free State untwisted the strands of political association, when Newfoundland surrendered its right of self-government, and when the constitution of Malta was suspended by the Crown.

The triumphant recognition of Dominion Status tended rather to emphasise the gap between dominions and colonies. In principle the Empire was a ladder up which the British dependencies were to move successively from direct, or indirect, administration by the Colonial Office to representative government, to responsible government, and finally to Dominion Status; in fact, the rate of constitutional as apart from administrative progress was, for many years, imperceptible except for those colonies which were already on the topmost rungs. Next after the five Dominions came Newfoundland, which was named as a Dominion in the Statute of Westminster though soon to be reduced to a lower level; Southern Rhodesia, where the 'Office' still reserved some authority over native questions; Kenya

---

[1] The figures quoted in this chapter are for the most part derived from the Chatham House Survey published under the name of *Newfoundland*, edited by H. Mackay (Oxford, 1946).

where responsible government was denied in the interest of
the natives; then a number of island colonies, Ceylon, Malta,
Cyprus, Mauritius, originally annexed for strategic reasons and
still controlled from Downing Street, with an eye to strategic
considerations. In the West and East Indies, West and Central
Africa, and in the western Pacific no colony had attained to
responsible government though in several there was an elective
majority in the legislative council.[1] Newfoundland, Malta,
and Ceylon present distinctive features which draw attention to
their political history between the wars.

A new era began in Newfoundland when, in 1905, Alfred Harms-
worth (afterwards Lord Northcliffe) obtained a concession for a
large area of unexplored forest land on the Exploits River, a part
of the island then almost unknown. Water-power was developed
and a town built at Grand Falls. Wood-pulp for cheap paper
rose in importance, from providing 1% by value of the island's
exports in the years 1897–1900 to 48% in the years 1937–40.
Northcliffe's Anglo-Newfoundland Development Company at
first provided the whole of this new commerce but in the 1920's
two American companies obtained similar concessions. In 1940
wood-pulp to the value of about $12,000,000 was exported, half
to the United Kingdom and half to the United States. Lumbering
is a seasonal trade for which some labour can be found between
the fishing seasons. It is not supposed by investigators that it is
capable of much further expansion. The third important industry
in Newfoundland is the production and treatment of metallic
ores, which are principally exported to Canada—516,000 tons of
iron ore worth $1,300,000 were exported in 1940. It seems
unlikely that this figure will be much exceeded in the future.

The fisheries have remained the principal means of employment in Newfoundland. Of those shown as 'gainfully employed'
in the census of 1935, 47% were fishermen or workers dependent
on the fisheries. This industry alone in Newfoundland is capable
of indefinite expansion and development. For the present its
economic return is meagre and, though the volume of export is

---

[1] A short sketch of the constitutional development of every colony is to be
found in the annual Colonial Office List. A full critical account of affairs in
Newfoundland, Malta, and Ceylon is given in Professor Hancock's *Survey of
British Commonwealth Affairs*.

maintained, the value has shrunk to 24% of the whole exports of the island. Throughout the nineteenth century the great bulk of exports were in the form of dried cod to the Mediterranean and the Latin countries. So recently as 1926–30, 60% of the fish went to these markets, which were destroyed by civil war in Spain, 'sanctions' against Italy, and the second German War. A much larger proportion[1] is now exported to the West Indies and Brazil, a factor which tends to draw Newfoundland away from the European into the American economy. The fishermen still live in isolated villages where primitive ways of life survive as in the west of Ireland. More than 800 out of the 1100 schools in Newfoundland are of one room only. The standard of educational proficiency is accordingly low, though it has improved since the foundation, in 1925, of Memorial University College at St John's. Even more serious is the high death-rate largely caused by preventible disease. The infant death-rate has never been less than ninety-two per thousand. Until recently, public health services (and many other social services too) reached the outlying regions on either side of the Strait of Belle Isle only through the agency of the International Grenfell Association.

Sir Wilfrid Grenfell (1865–1940) went to Labrador as a medical missionary in 1892. At first supported by the National Mission to Deep-sea Fishermen, and by private patrons in England and America, he obtained a subsidy from the Newfoundland government in 1900. His organisation, which by that time included hospitals and hospital ships, co-operative stores and farms, schools and orphanages, was incorporated as an International Association in 1912.

The fishermen of Newfoundland, a brave, loyal, hardy and industrious race, still retain, alone among the English-speaking peoples, a high birth-rate, which averaged over twenty-four per thousand in the 1930's. The population of the island at the census of 1935 was 290,000, almost all of English or Irish descent, about two-fifths of them being Roman Catholics.

The great depression in world trade in 1929–32 plunged Newfoundland into financial chaos from which she was quite unable to recover without external assistance. Between the wars overspending had been habitual, the average expenditure being

---

[1] Exports of fish, 1936–40: 36% to southern Europe, 19% to Brazil, 40% to the West Indies.

about 20% greater than the average revenue. This financial optimism was exposed when the market for all primary products collapsed. In February 1933 the Newfoundland government capitulated and asked for the Royal Commission which they had refused to accept in 1895 (see chapter x, 6, page 584). The Commissioners, over whom Lord Amulree presided, after criticising the Newfoundland regime sharply for financial optimism, inept leadership, sectarian politics, and in consequence a 'spoils system', recommended that the United Kingdom should resume the direct government of the colony in order to avoid a default in the payments on the internal debt of $101,000,000. Newfoundland accordingly forfeited her right of self-government on 16 February 1934. A Governing Commission of six members, three British and three Newfoundlanders, who were to be responsible to the Secretary of State for the Dominions, was nominated by His Majesty's Government. The House of Commons accepted this responsibility glumly; the Labour Party, then in opposition, opposed it on the grounds of expense; and in fact the Newfoundland Commission cost the British tax-payer £3,800,000.

Beyond reforming the administration and extending municipal institutions, which were woefully lacking, it cannot be said that the Commissioners were able to contribute much in the way of positive benefits. The first five years of the delegated government (1934–9) continued to be years of adversity, largely, as has been said above, owing to the breakdown of trade with Latin countries. In the year 1938 the exports were valued at $34,000,000 and the imports at $24,000,000 while, for the fiscal year 1938–9, the revenue ($11,000,000) still fell short of the expenditure by $3,000,000. The direction of trade, both in respect of imports and exports, was increasingly towards the New World rather than the Old.

The war of 1939, like all the other great European wars,

Imports to Newfoundland by value :	1857–60 (%)	1897–1900 (%)	1937–40 (%)
From the U.K.	40	31	23
From Canada	16	33	37
From U.S.A.	27	30	33
From elsewhere	17	6	7
	100	100	100

instantly produced a boom in Newfoundland. The revenue showed large surpluses amounting in all to $23,000,000. The national debt was reduced from $101,000,000 to $61,000,000 and the interest-rate converted from 5% to 3%. War loans raised in London to the extent of $12,000,000 were paid off and a free gift of $500,000 was made by the Newfoundland government to the Royal Air Force. It remains to be seen whether the islanders can maintain their higher standard of life and their national prosperity in the post-war world.

The commercial attraction towards the New World was much strengthened by the strategic attraction when the defence of Newfoundland was seen to have become a vital matter for Canada and the United States. In the summer of 1940 Canada made itself responsible for the land defence of the island. In August the United States and Canada set up a permanent joint board for the 'defence of the northern half of the western hemisphere'. Four temporary Canadian air bases were established at Torbay, Gander, Botwood, and Goose Bay in Labrador. In September 1940 proposals were made for the lease of bases in the British Empire to the United States. As a result of the agreement of March 1941,[1] three American air bases were formed in Newfoundland at Quidi Vidi, Argentina, and Stephenville. Goose Bay and Gander became the staging posts for the North Atlantic ferry services. Finally in October 1944 the Dominion of Canada acquired from Newfoundland a lease for ninety-nine years over the Goose Bay air base 'for the defence of Canada, Newfoundland, and Labrador'.

At the end of the second World War an elected convention considered the political future of the island, and recommended the restoration of self-government. The issue of confederation with Canada, twice rejected in earlier days, was raised again and now won some approval, especially in the industrial areas. Although provision had been made in the British North America Act (1867) for a procedure by which Newfoundland might join the Dominion, and although this provision had been safeguarded in the Statute of Westminster (1931), the British North America Act was not invoked. A decision was taken by the British Govern-

---

[1] Air bases were also leased to the United States in Bermuda, Jamaica, St Lucia, Antigua, Trinidad, the Bahamas, and British Guiana. The international Alaska Highway was constructed as a further consequence of these negotiations.

ment to place the problem directly before the electorate of New-foundland. At a referendum held on 3 June 1948, the electors recorded 22,000 votes for a continuance of government by com-mission, 63,000 votes for confederation with Canada, and 69,000 votes for the restoration of responsible self-government. As this was inconclusive, a second referendum was held, after six weeks of intense party activity. The alternative of government by com-mission was now dropped. In a straight contest on 22 July, 78,000 citizens voted for confederation, 71,000 for responsible government. Newfoundland was incorporated into the Dominion of Canada in March 1949, in spite of protests from the minority against being overruled, on so vital a matter, by so narrow a margin of votes. It appears that the minority voters were drawn largely from the older (liberal) fishing communities. At the Canadian election of June 1949, the Newfoundland electors re-turned five liberals and two conservatives to the parliament at Ottawa.

2. MALTA AND CYPRUS

MALTA, a rocky island about as large as the Isle of Wight, cannot provide food or even a sure water-supply for its 250,000 inhabitants, an enterprising race of travellers and merchants. Many serve in the Royal Navy and the merchant service, and many emigrate; the Maltese colony in Egypt numbers more than 20,000. Their language and their racial origin, like that of the Sicilians, is thought to be largely Saracenic and, since the six-teenth century, they have never been the subjects of any of the foreign dynasties that partitioned Italy. Yet they have been strongly influenced by Italian culture through the old nobility which has Italian connexions, and through the Church, for Malta is as ultramontane as Eire or Quebec. Italian liberal nationalism, a hundred years ago, had its echoes in Malta and none the less because the British Navy, which brought prosperity to the island, was the beneficent arm of a power that favoured the Italian liberators. The Anglo-Italian alliance in the first World War gave satisfaction to Maltese patriots so that the demand for democratic self-government which swept the world in 1919 did not take the form of an anti-British movement in Malta.

After the appearance of an enthusiastic national assembly, a constitution was granted to the island in August 1919 with imperial reservations of defence, religion, and the civil list. The problems of politics in Malta turned on the proper limits of clerical authority in political matters and on the language of government. The British, since the early days of their administration, had recognised the Roman Church as established; and regarding the Maltese language as a mere *patois*, they had introduced Italian as the language of the lawcourts. Under the new constitution English was the language of administration, Italian of the law, and Maltese was accepted as the 'language of popular intercourse.'

At the election of 1927 the 'constitutional' party was returned to power, led by Sir Gerald Strickland, an Anglo-Maltese Catholic nobleman. Party strife was violent, not to say scurrilous, and Strickland had to live down a whispering campaign of scandal. It was spread abroad, quite falsely, that he was a freemason. Having been opposed by the Maltese clergy, Strickland appealed to the Pope for protection against clerical intervention in party politics. The Pope responded by sending an apostolic delegate, that is an official of the highest status, who deepened the cleavage by issuing a terrific denunciation of Strickland (July 1929) as *persona non grata* to the Vatican. At this point the British government mildly expostulated, but without effect.

When the next election fell due, in May 1930, the bishops enjoined Maltese Catholics, on their conscience, to vote against Strickland, whereupon he suspended proceedings for an election, and the Colonial Office cut the knot in June by suspending a constitution that had become unworkable. The usual remedy, a Royal Commission, was applied in 1931.[1] The real strength of the Roman Church was backed by the pretentious influence of the Fascists, then at the height of their power. It suited them to demonstrate the effectiveness of their Concordat with the Vatican, and to inflate the domestic crisis of Maltese party politics into an international demonstration against British power in what the Fascists called *mare nostrum*. The more volatile elements in Maltese society were swept by a wave of fickle enthusiasm for Italianism; the Fascists loudly proclaimed Malta a lost Italian province that should be italianised like Sicily, where also Saracenic influence obscured the tradition of Rome.

[1] Lord Askwith's Commission (1931). Cmd. 3993.

The Commission of 1931 struck a blow at this superficial enthusiasm by deposing the Italian language from its privileged place in the lawcourts and by elevating the Maltese language to an equal status. With this and other changes designed to gratify Maltese sentiments, the constitution was restored. Nevertheless the electorate returned a two-thirds majority of nationalists (that is Italianists) who brought about another deadlock. The constitution was again suspended, in November 1933 (a few months after the surrender of the constitution of Newfoundland).

No further compromise was attempted for some years as no risks could be run in Malta when war with Italy was threatening. The Italian language was altogether displaced from official use in 1934, and partial self-government was restored in February 1939.

Malta's experiences in the second World War, when the island was almost continuously besieged from June 1940 to April 1943, cured the island politicians of their taste for Italian irredentism. Immediately after the expulsion of the Germans from North Africa preparations were made to restore full political liberty to the island which had won the admiration of the world. A constitution with full responsible government (except for the reserved subjects of defence and foreign policy) was prepared in 1945, and endowed with a free gift of £30 million for reconstruction from the British tax-payers. The nationalists, however, refused to co-operate and it was not until November 1947 that the new constitution could be formally promulgated.

The beautiful mountainous island of Cyprus, about as large as the peninsula of Devon and Cornwall, was declared a British protectorate in 1914, and in 1925 was given the status of a Crown Colony, with an elective majority in the legislative council. It is not surprising that a political agitation, fostered by the Greek Orthodox Church, should have grown up demanding the union (*enosis*) of Cyprus with Greece. After riots in 1931 and the destruction of the Governor's house by an irresponsible mob, the constitution was suspended. The island was not attacked by the enemy in the second World War. A constituent assembly was convened by the Colonial Office in 1947.

3. THE WEST INDIES, 1880–1947

THE West Indian sugar trade was always subject to violent fluctuations. The market was saved more than once by the continuous rise in the world-demand for sugar thoughout the nineteenth century. In the 'eighties it was hit hard by an enormous increase in the production of beet-sugar, grown for home consumption and protected by heavy bounties, in France, Germany, and the United States. Between 1882 and 1891 British imports of beet-sugar rose from 400,000 to a million tons, while imports of West Indian cane-sugar fell from 200,000 to 50,000 tons. The price too fell by half, bringing down the British West Indies into the deepest gulfs of depression. From this Joseph Chamberlain attempted to rescue them. A strong Royal Commission in 1897 prescribed as a remedy closer settlement of the land and peasant cultivation of other crops. This was not new and not final. Lord Rodney had said something like it in 1782 and Lord Moyne's Commission was to say it again in 1939. Lack of capital or lack of scientific method or lack of initiative on the part of the West Indian negroes had kept peasant cultivation in the realm of aspiration rather than fact. However some progress was now made, and bananas, citrus fruits, cocoa, coffee, spices, coconuts, and sea-island cotton were planted. The Imperial Department of Agriculture was founded to foster these experiments, in 1898. Chamberlain had so much faith in them as to send his own son Neville planting sisal in the Bahamas, though without success. Whereas all the islands had lived by sugar-planting, their natural diversity distinguished them as they turned to other crops. Jamaica, where there had long been a tradition of peasant life, turned to the banana trade, a good crop for small-holders and accordingly for the United Fruit Company of Boston that bought and shipped the crop; Trinidad and Grenada specialised in cocoa for the same reason. In some of the smaller islands sugar-planting was altogether replaced by some new staple; in Trinidad and Jamaica sugar fell to the second place; in Barbados, the Leeward Islands, and British Guiana it held its lead. It even drew ahead when Chamberlain persuaded the other powers to forgo their bounties on beet-sugar at the Brussels Convention of 1903, his last achievement. From 1904 to 1914 the West Indian sugar

64-2

estates were prosperous again, and opulent during the first World War. Then came another slump and, hardest blow of all, an actual discrimination against the West Indies by Great Britain itself. In 1921 the British established a beet-sugar industry at home under protection of a bounty. Though West Indian cane-sugar was covered by a preferential tariff, this had no effect in keeping up the world price. Another royal commission was followed by another international sugar agreement (1922). All exporting countries agreed upon a quota to which they would restrict their output of cane-sugar, and within the limits of the quota the West Indian planters held their own. But overproduc-tion was not confined to sugar-cane; all tropical products met with heavy competition. West Indian cocoa could not prevail against West African cocoa, nor West Indian against Jaffa oranges. Other crops were blighted by new diseases, notably the banana with 'leaf-spot' which can be overcome only by difficult and costly spraying.

Like all countries producing raw commodities the West Indies suffered severely in the world depression of the early 'thirties, and all the more because of the backwardness of their social services. The consequent unrest took a more positive form than the mere blind protests against misery that had been made in earlier times of bad trade. There were repeated outbreaks of rioting (in Trinidad, 1934; in St Kitts, Jamaica, St Vincent, and British Guiana, 1935; in Trinidad and Barbados, 1937; in Jamaica and British Guiana, 1938), and there were also signs of more positive thinking, a demand for a constructive policy. The unrest was perhaps aggravated by the closing of the frontiers. In earlier times the surplus population had drifted away for spells of employment in Central America or the United States. Between the wars all countries closed their ports to casual immigration so that West Indians who had seen better standards of living abroad felt all the more frustrated when condemned to stay in poverty on their overcrowded islands.

The East Indians (42% of the population in Trinidad, 34% in British Guiana, and some smaller groups elsewhere) are now also isolated in the West Indies since immigration from India ended in 1917. They need to be brought forward into the active life of the community.

Again the whole economy of the West Indies was investigated

by a Royal Commission under Lord Moyne in 1939. Their full and comprehensive report[1] emphasised the human factor in the problem, the wrongs that could not be righted by stabilising the export market. Since emancipation, the West Indian negroes had been land-hungry but not land-wise. While there were self-supporting peasants in Jamaica, Grenada, and Nevis, elsewhere the allotments could not support the cultivators who were obliged to supplement their crop by casual wage-earning at very low rates for piece-work. The sugar estate, managed by a white man and owned by a London company, was still the predominant economic unit, on which the peasant, in most islands, was in part parasitic. The Commissioners reported that the estates, on the whole, were very efficiently run. Like the sugar-planters, the peasant-cultivators tended to speculate on one cash-crop only, for export, instead of providing a living for themselves and their neighbours by mixed farming. For this reason among others, diseases of malnutrition were rampant.

Wage-labour was intermittent, poorly paid, and unprotected by codes of industrial legislation. Except at the sugar-estates or the docks there was small chance of employment. Two of the colonies surpassed the others in financial stability because they had some industrial development. Asphalt from the pitch lake of Trinidad and petroleum from the oilfields brought in money but did not find employment for many hands. Similarly the Bauxite Development Company, a subsidiary of the Aluminum Company of Canada, was valuable to British Guiana but employed no more than 1300 men. Canada has many links with the West Indies which have been strengthened since the R.M.S.P Company gave up the West Indian mail contracts, in 1915. Canadian shipping lines carry the mails, export the tropical products, and import foodstuffs including fish from Newfoundland, for the West Indians have no sea-fisheries.

Poverty and malnutrition among the West Indians are aggravated by the instability of their domestic life. Part of the heritage of slavery is an indifference to family ties, since the slave-owners, in the old days, discouraged wedlock. More than 60% of West Indian children are born illegitimate and all accounts declare that no moral improvement is apparent. On the contrary, the

[1] *The West Indies Royal Commission Report*, 1939 (Cmd. 6607) was not published until 1945.

customary 'faithful concubinage' is said to be giving way to promiscuity. Accordingly the birth-rate is everywhere very high while the infant death-rate, which was also shockingly high, is declining with the gradual growth of medical services. Between 1896 and 1936 the aggregate population of the British West Indies rose from 1,700,000 to 2,500,000 at a low estimate, and now increases at the rate of nearly 2% annually. A lack of moral restraint and family discipline may be ascribed to bad housing. Modern sanitation hardly exists. Medical services have been quite inadequate.

By the irony of history liberty for the slaves, in the days of the *laissez-faire* economists, meant social neglect. Freedom and education which were to have elevated them from barbarism were not enough. Such social services as the West Indians have enjoyed have been provided by the Churches. It was not until the present generation that these services were conceived to be the obligation of the state. All the islands have schools, though they are wretchedly equipped and staffed, because of their poverty. A co-ordinated system of state education for the whole group of colonies was one of the strongest recommendations of the Commission.

The chief effects of the Moyne Report were in the field of social services. Under pressure from the Colonial Office codes of protection for labour were introduced in every colony with recognition, and even encouragement, of trade unions. The immediate weakness of trade was relieved by an increase in the quota of sugar for export. Provision was also made for a re-organisation, or rather an organisation, of the services for health and education. Such paper promises would have meant little had not a suggestion by the Commissioners for a general welfare fund been taken up by the Colonial Office on a gigantic scale. Instead of a regional fund for the West Indies they instituted a fund for the whole colonial empire. By an act of 1940 the small Colonial Development Fund, an economic reserve, was reconstituted as the Colonial Development and Welfare Fund with a first allotment of £5,000,000, increased in 1945 to an annual allotment of about £10,000,000.

The Commissioners of 1939 were not of the opinion that an immediate grant of total democracy would be of practical assist-

ance to the West Indies. Since 1865 the tide of self-government had been setting back and, as recently as 1928, the powers
of the Governor in one colony, British Guiana, were increased. In 1939, only three of the older West Indian colonies
(Bermuda,[1] Barbados, and the Bahamas) retained their ancient
constitutions, with a large elective element in the legislature,
but there and elsewhere the franchise was limited. There is
no colour-line in the British West Indies as it is understood
in the Transvaal or Louisiana, but, none the less, the view
prevails that the white man is boss. The Governor and the high
officers are white men from England; the proprietors of the
sugar-estates are Englishmen, often resident in England. For
all his traditional pride and loyalty, the West Indian, who is a
free man as no negro is in the United States, cannot escape the
class distinction. In politics the elective element in the legislatures, always a ready-made opposition in every Crown Colony,
must be sensitive to the colour-feeling, must react against white
domination.

The progress of the last few years has taken the form of
broadening the base of government rather than changing its
character. Universal suffrage was introduced in Jamaica in 1945,
and in Trinidad in 1946. Elsewhere the franchise was extended
but full responsible government was not granted in the advanced
Jamaica Constitution of 1945.

The federation of the British West Indies is a complicated
administrative problem. How to combine the overcrowded
island of Barbados with the almost empty continental region
of British Guiana, the peasant colony of Jamaica with oil- and
asphalt-producing Trinidad, the small but proud old governments in the Leewards with their great parvenu rivals, is no easy
task, when some have easier communications with England than
with one another, and some have closer contacts with the United
States. The recommendations of the Commission were that the
impetus towards closer union should come from the islands themselves, not from the Colonial Office, that a beginning might be
made by combining the existing federations of the Leeward and
Windward Islands into one, but that unification of public services
was a more urgent question.

[1] Bermuda is not usually classed as a West Indian colony, though historically
associated with the West Indies.

Strategic and other considerations must tend to draw the Caribbean colonies into the North American Zone. A significant event was the formation, in 1942, of the Anglo-American Caribbean Commission 'for strengthening social and economic cooperation between the United States, its bases and possessions, and the British colonies in the Caribbean'.

XXI

A NOTE ON COMMONWEALTH RELATIONS (1932–49), AND SOME REFLEXIONS

Argument: The formula known as the Balfour Declaration is no longer adequate to the Commonwealth, which is now (1949) passing into a new epoch. At this turning-point we look back to survey the achievement of three hundred years.

The partition of the world by the Western powers is a complete phase of history. In this phase British power and influence, based upon a liberal philosophy, were supreme from about 1846 to about 1931. The political history of British India is a detached episode, to be distinguished from the colonial development in Africa and South-East Asia.

During the nineteenth century the new social sciences began to change the attitude of Europeans towards primitive races.

There were five modes of British expansion: the empire of settlement, the empire of trade, the empire of finance, the empire of conquest, the empire of ideas. Of these the first and last, made and maintained by the moral stability of the British people, are the most enduring. The legal conception of Empire as a Trust derives from British habits of mind. Reliance upon 'loyalty' as a bond of empire is misleading since the word is variously interpreted. Whatever else, the Crown has been the symbol of peace.

1. A NOTE ON COMMONWEALTH RELATIONS, 1932–49

In the short period of comparative calm between the Ottawa agreements and the second World War, the British Commonwealth enjoyed a greater degree of security and progress than any European power, perhaps greater even than the United States, where the depression of 1931 had shaken the basis of society. Since the Statute of Westminster the Commonwealth could hardly be described as a sovereign state. Economically, it was no longer united by dependence on the Free Trade and sterling-currency area of Great Britain but by a casual series of bilateral commercial treaties. Even the periodical imperial conferences seemed to have outlived their utility in an age when statesmen could fly round the world, in a few days, to confer on particular problems as they arose. Yet the moral unity of the Commonwealth was sure, as the events of the years 1939 to 1945 were to prove. The four original Dominions and Newfoundland ranged themselves beside Great Britain, in the war which threatened to overwhelm her, no less willingly than they had done in the previous generation, prodigal of their blood and their treasure as she with her own. Britain's finest hour was no less theirs. It was not Britain that fought alone for liberty in 1940, it was the British Commonwealth. The Commonwealth survived, with its legal and financial links weaker than before, its moral links stronger than ever. Southern Ireland, however, abstained—or rather Mr De Valera abstained, while uncounted thousands of Irishmen fought for liberty in the armies of Britain and the Dominions.

But in the course of the war, the difference between the 'white' Dominions and the other dependencies of the Crown had become more marked. The protection formerly extended to so many Islamic states in the Middle East seemed hardly feasible in the new age. Saddest to relate of all episodes in recent British history was the tale of cross-purposes which cost the British the goodwill of the Jews in Palestine, since the British alone among the nations had aided and befriended them. In India the attempt to build up a federal dominion had failed. Asiatic nations, grasping at their promised liberty, after the stresses of war, threatened to secede from the Commonwealth. Impatient democrats in every Crown Colony demanded that the speed of constitutional progress should be increased.

The promise of Dominion Status, and the realisation that Dominion Status meant virtual independence, beckoned the progressives in every backward community. It was now seen that this status from which the four original Dominions had emerged to full nationhood was, like responsible government, another temporary stage in political development. For the Commonwealth is moving into a new phase which lies beyond the scope of this book. Whatever it may become, it is no longer an extension of the British race overseas, no longer the Greater Britain which Dilke and Seeley applauded. Common citizenship, which in the days of white domination effectively meant common citizenship for white men, can no longer be maintained when Southern Ireland has seceded, and when India has been admitted to equality of status with South Africa. Nor can the Crown be regarded any longer as 'the keystone which binds up the arch of the Commonwealth'—the formula which Mr Massey of New Zealand adapted from Strafford—when the Commonwealth includes at least one state with a republican constitution.

It was to be expected that the period of reconstruction after a shattering war would bring unforeseen changes in so flexible, so protean, an organism. Here it will be sufficient to indicate some of the sign-posts that point to the future. An account has already been given of the progress along the beaten path of self-government made, between 1946 and 1949, by Newfoundland, Malta, Nigeria, Malaya, Jamaica, and several other colonies. Elsewhere, the right of secession from the Commonwealth has been an issue of practical politics. In principle, it was admitted in Mr Attlee's (rejected) offer to the Indian Congress, of 16 May 1946. Four eastern Dominions which acquired full self-government in 1947 considered secession as a possibility. Burma seceded, whereas Ceylon accepted Dominion Status. India and Pakistan, provisionally established as Dominions while they equipped themselves with constitutions, found advantages in retaining that status.

A Commonwealth Conference was held in October 1948, to consider these new problems. The premiers of India, Pakistan, and Ceylon attended, but no representative of Southern Ireland. After the conference it was announced that co-operation, under several heads, would be urged forward; and the world remarked that the word 'British' was scrupulously omitted from the announcement. Since the new Commonwealth was to include three Asiatic nations, which far outnumbered the older Dominions in population, there was some justification for the change. Mr Nehru then returned to India to convince his party that membership of the Commonwealth was compatible with the republicanism to which they were committed, a compromise requiring a new formula to replace the Balfour Declaration. Early in 1949 India and Southern Ireland adopted republican forms. The new Irish president, Mr Costello, cut the last link with the Commonwealth by an Act passed on 18 April 1949. The ruling principle of *sinn fein*, 'ourselves alone', was carried to such logical extremity that Southern Ireland also stood aside from the North Atlantic Pact, which the other democratic nations of the West signed in the same month. On the other hand, the government of the Indian Republic concurred with the Commonwealth Group (no longer to be described as the Dominions of the Crown) in declaring (27 April 1949) that they remained 'united as free and equal members of the Commonwealth of Nations', that they recognised the King as 'the symbol of the free association of the independent member nations and as head of the Commonwealth'.

There we leave them, and conclude by looking back over the long process that has brought them to this consummation.

2. SOME REFLEXIONS

FOR those who favour a cyclical or periodical view of history, the 450 years from the discovery of America to the present catastrophic decade present a useful range of evidence. The rise, the flowering, and the decay of a culture can be described in terms of the same chronological scheme, whether we consider the moral or the physical aspects of the human race in that epoch. Here, to take a simple instance, can be plainly stated Lord Acton's classic proposition,[1] Renaissance–Reformation–Revolution, the triumph of the liberal ideal, brought to such great intensity and extensity as almost to have restored the Golden Age, but perverted in the last forty years by the sheer wickedness of great men. Or here the student may observe the rise of the capitalist system motivated by the blind law of accumulation so as to produce plenty in the midst of poverty; he may discover exploitation, monopoly, and war, with the antithetical stirrings of those who are to enter upon the inheritance. But plainer still, evident to all who glance at an atlas and more relevant to our purpose, are the quantitative effects of forces set to work, no matter how, at the end of the fifteenth century.

Since the decade when Columbus crossed the Atlantic and Vasco Da Gama rounded the Cape, the empire of the world has

[1] 'This constancy of progress, of progress in the direction of organised and assured freedom, is the characteristic fact of Modern History, and its tribute to the theory of Providence.' (Inaugural Lecture, 1895.)

been won and lost by five small nations from the western fringes of Europe. In the eye of the cosmic historian, a thousand years hence, the five nations will seem to have been very much alike and to have acted on a common impulse. All were Christians of the Latin tradition, speaking cognate languages, deriving their information from the same scientific books, plotting their course on the same charts; all were emerging, though at different rates of progress, from a feudal to a commercial economy. None of the five was as rich or populous, or as well-supplied with comforts and luxuries, as the distant kingdoms that it overthrew.

The conquest falls into two phases. First came the expansion of the Spaniards and Portuguese, impelled by the motives that were called chivalrous—the desire to win glory and to extend the bounds of Christendom, motives which obliged them to gain military power, and to grasp the treasures that were the sinews of power. This process reached its climax early in the seventeenth century leaving behind, when the impulse faded, the new world of Latin America, a group of nations more prosperous and hardly less civilised than their mother countries. Before the first phase ended, the second was already well begun. A new wave of expansion overseas had set in motion the French, Dutch and English empire-builders by an impulse in which commercial factors were more conspicuous, though chivalrous, even quixotic, factors were not absent. But the three nations of the second phase dissipated their strength in contests with one another, and with the Spaniards and Portuguese, though the New World lay open before them, offering space for all. At the end of these wars, which fill out so large a part of the conventional histories of the seventeenth and eighteenth centuries, the Latin-American group of states stood firm and independent, united in culture though not in political organisation, while, on the North Atlantic coast, another group of thirteen English colonies had also survived the dissolution of Empires. Binding themselves in a political federation they announced, by the promulgation of the Monroe Doctrine in 1823, that they had cast loose from the Old World and assumed the leading place among the nations of the New. Another hundred years passed, however, before they achieved real independence. Throughout the nineteenth century American progress depended upon European (largely upon British) immigrants, capital loans, manufactured goods, arts and sciences.

It might have seemed, in 1823, that the age of imperialism was over. Spain and Portugal had retired from the field; France and Holland had been checked and diverted by the outcome of the wars; Britain had turned her attention again from dominion to trade. She had won so long a lead in manufacture and shipping, and increased that lead so rapidly in the succeeding age of steamers and deep-sea cables, that new territory was neither valued nor desired by the English governing class. Her empire was taking shape as a system of coaling-stations, strung together with telegraph wire, and guarded by the cruisers of the Royal Navy.

But in that age of expansion nothing grew more rapidly than the population. The complex and various causes of emigration: opportunity abroad and frustration at home, the flight from famine, love of adventure, treasure-seeking, atavistic tendencies towards nomadism, easier methods of transportation, all combined to urge the surplus of population overseas. New nations springing up abroad provided new markets for European manufactures, and for the intermittent overflow of capital investment. The waves of emigration mounted higher and spread wider as the numbers of the whole human race increased, a folk-wandering more extensive than that of the fifth century. Modern descendants of the Picts and Scots were on the move again, followed by successive waves of Germans, Scandinavians, and Slavs. Nor was the great emigration confined to Northern Europe, for Greeks and Italians flocked to the Americas, while Asia began to pour out her labouring masses, Chinese to South-East Asia, Indians to the Islands and the African coast.

All the unknown regions were penetrated and explored in this restless century, all the weaker kingdoms were brought into the spheres of influence of the Western powers. And instead of seizing fortresses and treaty-ports, these colonising nations now turned their attention to annexing territory, until formal sovereignty over almost the whole surface of the globe was claimed by one or other of them. The condition on which non-European powers were allowed to survive was that they should assimilate themselves to the European model. The empty spaces of Australia, North America, and Northern Asia were monopolised by British, Americans, and Russians; Central Africa was allotted by diplomatic agreements to Britain, France, Portugal, and Belgium;

South-East Asia fell ripe, or over-ripe, into the grasp of Britain, France, and Holland. (Germany, Italy, and Japan, coming late into the field, could not make their claims good.) In all these territories the colonial powers were confronted with similar problems of organisation; they must choose between a plantation and a peasant economy, between direct and indirect rule, as the vehicles of Western civilisation. By one means or the other they pacified all savage tribes, except in the remotest jungles, administered in all countries some modicum of Western law, extended the conventions of diplomacy to all states, and gave the world a brief era of justifiable optimism. Liberalism seemed to have triumphed, and the principle of continuous social progress to have been established. Disraeli's peace with honour was broken, between 1878 and 1914, only by wars of limited objective fought far away from the main centres of civilisation.

Since that time there has been continuous retrogression, though the liberal empires survived the shock of the first World War. The retreat from imperialism, again, may be regarded either as a failure of the liberal ideal or as the inevitable collapse of a vicious economic system. The decline of the West, however regarded, is an undeniable fact. The five nations of the Atlantic seaboard have sunk into the second rank, have lost their manufacturing superiority, have ceased to export men and money. The former 'Powers of Europe', who so recently dominated the world, now seem to be satellites, swinging into the orbits of the two great nations of the twentieth century. There is nothing new or astonishing in this development which was plainly foretold by Seeley more than sixty years ago.[1] 'Russia in Europe', he said, 'has already a population of near eighty millions on a territory of more than two millions of square miles, and the United States will have by the end of the [nineteenth] century a population as large upon a territory of four millions of square miles....At a time which many here present may live to see, Russia and the United States will surpass in power the states now called great as much as the great country-states of the sixteenth century surpassed Florence. Is not this a serious consideration...for a state like England, which has at the present moment the choice in its hands between two courses of action, the one of which may set it in that future age on a level with the greatest of these great

[1] *The Expansion of England.* Lecture VIII, 1883.

states of the future, while the other will reduce it to the level of a purely European Power looking back, as Spain does now, to the great days when she pretended to be a world-state.'

In 1883 England had by no means reached the climax of her greatness. Taking Seeley's advice she thought imperially, increasing her resources and improving her colonial system during the ensuing generation. The zenith of her career may be assigned to the Jubilee year, 1897, the moment of Joseph Chamberlain's triumph; or to 1913, the last year of world-peace, mass-emigration, and the open-door policy; or to 1921 when the territories of the Crown reached their greatest extent; but not much later, for the old liberal system did not survive the slump of 1931.

Of the five original colonising nations the British, on all counts, achieved the most: their empire endured the longest, spread the widest, commanded the greatest force, produced the most wealth, begot the most numerous population, had the most stimulating influence upon its neighbours. The British ruled more subject peoples than Charles V of whom it was first said that the sun never set upon his dominions; they were lords of more land than Genghiz Khan whose writ ran from Hungary to China; they multiplied so fast as to outnumber the seed of Abraham; they spread their language and culture farther than Alexander who carried Hellenism to India. The Dutch and English for some generations were close rivals; both were commercial Protestant nations with similar histories. The difference between them lies in an obscure region of sociology which cannot be investigated, for lack of evidence. Throughout the nineteenth century the British multiplied at an astounding rate, and the Dutch did not. The British flocked overseas, singly and collectively, the Dutch no more than maintained with men the empire they possessed.

Britain's century, when she led the world as surely as Spain in the sixteenth or France in the seventeenth, can be conveniently fixed as the period of prosperity between two great depressions; it runs from the hungry 1840's to the hungry 1930's, three generations of moral and physical progress such as the world can never have seen before, since only in that century did all the branches of the human race first become aware of one another. Then for the first time could they, and did they, agree upon some fundamentals: that peace was preferable to war, that all nations should be on diplomatic relations with one another, that foreign trade and travel ought to be encouraged, that laws should protect all classes of inhabitants impartially, that there should be no slavery, that the devices of science ought to be employed to relieve and to enrich suffering mankind. The boundary between the civilised and the savage world was obliterated. No longer was the culture of the leading nation a spot of light contrasting with the dark shadow of the surrounding barbarism. Western civilisation irradiated and dominated the whole world, with its optimistic addiction to liberty, law, and the idea of progress. It is strange to reflect that, a hundred years ago, these conceptions were condemned as reprehensible by many statesmen and philosophers, sad to reflect how nearly they became the universal principles of action before the nations reverted to state-worship, violence, and materialism.

The year 1846 is notable in British history for the conversion of the moderates of all parties to the principle of Free Trade, exemplified in the repeal of the Corn Laws. The occasion of repeal was a crop failure that led to famine in Ireland and hardly less in England and Scotland, swelling a tide of emigration that fluctuated but never ceased for nearly ninety years. It was in 1846 also that the Whigs made the first grants of full self-government in the colonies. Britain was never so great as in the first flush of the Free Trade economy, proclaiming to a world sunk in dynastic jealousies and barren political dogmas that freedom was the secret of power and wealth. She threw open the door at the Great Exhibition, inviting all peoples to partake of the blessings conferred by freedom, with a gesture of hostility only to the champions of restriction, exclusiveness, and slavery. Welcoming the produce of all nations, she invited them in turn to open the door to British manufactures.

Though the concept was too ingenuous, Free Trade won astonishing successes for thirty or forty years, and held its own for as long again in a protectionist world. The terms of trade were persistently favourable to the British after about the year 1860, since the price of imported foodstuffs tended to fall throughout the period. Thus, though money wages remained low in Britain, real wages, on the whole, tended to rise. The Free Trade economy survived the bad times of the 1880's and 1890's, partially survived the first World War, until the British Commonwealth and Empire reached a new consummation in 1931. Politically, the

Statute of Westminster was a fulfilment of the promise of 1846, not, as some critics supposed, an admission of failure. And 1931, like 1846, was a landmark in other fields of activity. The Government that proposed the statute was a coalition formed, in the trough of depression, to confront a total breakdown in trade. At Ottawa a few months later, the nations of the Commonwealth announced the failure of the open-door policy, abandoned the Free Trade dream, turned to a new system of restrictive quotas and bilateral agreements. This policy of salvage preserved the Commonwealth from immediate ruin but was none the less a makeshift, a second-best. Though there was recovery in trade, Britain did not again export a surplus of money or men. Since the gross reproduction rate for Great Britain had fallen below parity (after 1926, according to Kuczynski), the supposed surplus of population had come to an end. The birth-rate had also fallen sharply in the Dominions.

Imperialism had fulfilled its purpose and was in retreat. The new nations of the Commonwealth had attained maturity and the old nations of the Orient had awoken. The tide of Western culture which had for centuries been flowing eastward was ebbing back from Asia. A portent was the rise of Japan, which the Western nations at first encouraged but later resisted. The chaotic but dynamic forces emerging in China are part of the same phenomenon. But in India and South-East Asia the policy of Britain, like her policy in the Dominions, has been to go half-way to meet these movements by a steady, patient and often thankless effort to establish liberal principles of government, while leaving social progress to move at its own pace, fostered by beneficent commerce. There was if anything too little government rather than too much in these autocracies.

The British-Indian Empire was a political organism without parallel. So casually won, so coolly governed, so firmly distinguished by its ruling class of *sahibs* from the main stream of English social life, it was not legally described nor generally regarded as a part of the British colonial empire but as a separate kingdom. The story of British India is a detached episode in history; this was the empire made 'in a fit of absence of mind', and never consciously rooted in the life of the British masses. Three distinct sets of British people, and three only, frequented British India: the officials, a silent service drawn exclusively from the gentry, who were not conspicuous in the colonies; the merchants and planters who lived in India, as they would have lived in China or Brazil, a life apart, almost ignoring the community of Asiatics around them; the private soldiers recruited from the rootless poor. The *sahibs* indignantly repudiated the name of 'colonials' which was not an accurate description of their status. Service in India was a vocation, a duty, a livelihood, or a term of exile, but always an impermanent way of life.

It is not true to say that Indian economic interests were subordinated to British commercial requirements. Political India stood apart from commerce, and pressure-groups in London urged only an open door for trade in India as in China or the Argentine. Trade with India did not grow out of the political connexion and was not dependent on it.

The British Colonial Empire was subtly different in character, without the air of aristocratic *insouciance*. It was consciously formed on the assumption, hardly questioned in the nineteenth century, of the moral superiority of Western civilisation. It was the burden laid as a duty upon the shoulders of the white man to tame the savage, by means of Christianity and beneficent commerce; and the duty was most effectively done among primitive peoples. This was the spirit in which Central Africa and South-East Asia were partitioned in the 1880's and 1890's. Since that time a change has come in the attitude of the civilised man towards the savage, a change that calls for a digression.

It was characteristic of nineteenth-century liberalism that it could not remain self-satisfied. The free-thinking habit of mind could not refrain from questioning even the superiority of its own over other cultures. Among the many signs of intellectual activity in that age was the emergence of new sciences (or proto-sciences) based upon comparative sociology, which treated all nations, peoples and tongues as equally worthy of rational enquiry. Though wise men—at least since Herodotus—have defied the vulgar prejudice against the ways of foreigners, yet the scientists of the nineteenth century were the first to take up systematically the proper study of mankind. The social sciences, in particular, are based upon the new statistical method introduced by Bentham, applied to anthropology by Francis Galton (1822–1911) and developed by Karl Pearson (1857–1936) and his school.

Investigating and measuring types of men was a new approach to the age-old problem of man's place in nature. The materialist view of man as one of the animals, though not new in philosophy, was popularised by Huxley (*Man's Place in Nature*, 1863) and Darwin (*The Descent of Man*, 1871). To compare the habits and functions of men in different ages and regions, though it had often been a subject for general discussion in earlier times on intuitive or merely fanciful grounds, was now made the subject of precise and regular study. Three distinct lines of inquiry contributed to the new synthesis, the examination of prehistoric sites and relics in Western Europe, the excavation of buried cities in the Near East, and the reports of travellers on tribes still living under supposedly primitive conditions; in each line conjectures and tales of wonder gave way to scrupulous measurement and record.

Modern field archaeology may conveniently be dated from 1841, when M. Boucher de Perthes reported the discovery of worked flint implements in the gravel of the Somme valley at a depth which proved their extreme antiquity. The study of prehistoric implements revealed their resemblance to those used by contemporary savages, and so to that branch of the social sciences which has usurped the name of anthropology. The first popular comprehensive treatise published in England was Tylor's *Primitive Culture* (1871). Winwood Reade's *Martyrdom of Man* (1872), a treatise on world history, though deeply pessimistic, inspired many Victorian readers with a sense of the upward struggle from barbarism. The book was derived from the author's West African experiences. Travellers' tales which had been received with incredulity in the works of Herodotus and Marco Polo, even in those of James Bruce and Charles Waterton, were given a new credence when sent home, in the age of penny postage and the electric telegraph, by such men as Darwin, Galton, Huxley, Wallace and Bates. In particular the habits and the traditions of barbarian tribes began to get attention. Raffles in his *History of Java* (1817), Grey in his *Folk-lore of the Polynesians* (1855), and Burton in his recondite works on Africa and Arabia were prominent in throwing a new light upon savage customs which to earlier generations had seemed merely grotesque and repellent. They now began to appear as designs in a pattern of unwritten history which could be correlated with the discoveries of the archaeologists.

Even more striking was the revelation by Layard (*Discoveries at Nineveh*, 1853), Schliemann (*Troy and its Remains*, 1875), Evans (*Palace at Knossos*, 1900), and others, that the legends of classical antiquity were something less than the truth. Homer re-appeared as a historian and Herodotus as a geographer. Gradually the bloody rites of Dahomey and the Polynesian taboos were seen to have a cultural relation with the tale of the minotaur and the folk-lore embedded in the Old Testament. At the end of the century a new conception of myth and ritual provided a clue to the labyrinth of social habits and beliefs in the highest as in the lowest stages of culture. Myths might derive their validity from human nature itself, responding variously to environment but tending to assume a universal shape. One mythological pattern, observed in ancient Italy and in a contemporary Sudanese kingdom, was elaborately traced through classical history, European folk-lore, semitic legend, and modern travellers' tales by Sir James Frazer in *The Golden Bough* (1890–1915), a book that has pro-foundly changed the social outlook of our age.

The material study of human beings, their artefacts and their rules of conduct, was reinforced by a parallel study of language and literature leading to a similar conclusion. Something has already been said (see page 142) of Sir William Jones's Asiatic researches which initiated the modern science of comparative philology. The comparative study of literatures followed. When Max Müller published his gigantic series of the *Sacred Books of the East* (1875–98), Chinese, Indian and Persian literatures first became available to Western students in a compendious edition. Macaulay's arrogant assumption that all useful learning was derived from Graeco-Roman sources, and that other sources were fantastic nonsense, could then no longer be maintained. Theology itself was forced to abandon its Graeco-Roman ex-clusiveness after William James had published the *Varieties of Religious Experience* (1902), another formidably effective book. Those who had learned from Frazer that the rites and ceremonies of all religious cults are variants from a norm; and from William James that the response of the soul to the Divine Presence produces the same psychological phenomena whether the believer professes himself a Catholic or a Protestant, a Christian, a Buddhist or a Moslem; those who had discovered in the *Sacred Books of the East* systems as rational and as sophisticated as in the Christian Fathers;

they, at least, could no longer dismiss the larger part of mankind as heathens who in their blindness 'bow down to wood and stone'. But these advances in Western philosophy brought no comfort to the materialists. They were part of the reaction from rationalism, emphasising the irrational element in human nature which was partly revealed by the new psychology of the unconscious.

Fifty years earlier, in the complacent age of British expansion, it would have been hard to find an American, an Englishman, a Frenchman, or a German who questioned the inherent superiority of Europe over Asia, of modern civilisation over primitive barbarism. The idea of continuous progress was so firmly rooted that the few who doubted it were ridiculed. Comparative sociology at the end of the nineteenth century found a chink in the armour of self-sufficiency. Asia—even Darkest Africa—had social merits; and perhaps the White Man's Burden should be an obligation to protect the black man from too much civilisation. Hence arose the 'Zoological Gardens Policy' which in some colonial territories was designed to isolate the aborigines, allowing them to maintain their ancient ways. More widespread was the reversion to indirect rule, which implied the preservation of all that could conveniently be preserved of the aboriginal system under white supervision. Among its champions was Mary Kingsley (1862–1900),[1] as vehement an imperialist as her uncle, Charles. Her travels in West Africa, alone in spite of the Victorian conventions, taught her that there was much to be said in favour of savages, traders, and missionaries. All had their virtues and all could contribute to a new synthesis.

But more remarkable than the respect which civilised men began to pay to savages was the realisation in Asia that the character of ancient nations cannot be suddenly changed. They acquired the physical force of the West without losing the moral force derived from their own traditions. Thus in the twentieth century, as we have seen the resurgence of Asia, we may yet see, in Africa too, the rise of indigenous societies equipped with the resources of Western science.

During the three generations of British supremacy there were five modes of expansion: by settlement, by trade, by finance, by

---

[1] It was characteristic of her courage and unconventionality that she offered to nurse enemy prisoners when the South African War broke out, and died in a camp hospital, of typhoid fever.

conquest, and by the spreading of ideas. All had reached fulfilment by 1931.

The empire of settlement derived inevitably from the increase of population at a time when explorers had revealed new worlds, and steam transport made it possible to populate them. It began in a mood of land-hunger and ended when the supply of land-hungry peasants gave out. Industrial society ceased to produce rural pioneers though it could still export technicians. Greed for the possession of land, a farm of one's own, was replaced by greed for cash profit, so that rarely, in the new countries, does land-hunger turn into land-love. Wild Nature, when first encountered, is not a partner to be cherished, but an enemy to be subdued and robbed. So deforestation and over-cropping turn fertile valleys into dust-bowls. The pride of the new countries was not in their bold peasantry but in the speed at which they could become complex industrial societies, with the same economic stresses that afflicted the capitalist Old World. The British Dominions that reached full autonomy in 1931 were not many years behind the United States in urban development. In the 1930's they no longer relied upon Great Britain for supplies of men and money or even, beyond the limits of fair bargaining, for markets. Goodwill and a certain sense of moral unity were all that was left of obligation to the mother-country.

In the eyes of the British governing class the empire of trade had always meant more than the empire of settlement. The colonies were valued because they raised up nations of customers. In the British Century it was felt (though only stated by extreme radicals) that Free Trade would eventually break down national barriers, whereupon colonial status would be merged into the liberal, almost anarchic, world-state. This somewhat naive conception was falsified by the simple rule that customers became competitors.

The strength of British trade was magnified by the export of capital, the third mode of expansion. In public as in private life, loans are always gratefully accepted and bond-holders always unpopular. British experience in the nineteenth century suggests that political loans are disappointing; they rarely remunerate the lenders or enrich the borrowers. Overseas investment produced the best results when it stimulated a balanced flow of men and goods which could combine for the creation of a new society, as

Wakefield demonstrated a hundred years ago. Foreign lending pays both parties when the loan takes the form of a credit for the purchase of capital goods which are to be paid for in consumer goods. Thus it was that Britain financed the railways and founded the industries of half the world. After three generations, when the railways had established the industries, the continued flow of interest-payments to London was resented as a sort of tribute, in Australia hardly less than in the Argentine.

Conquest and annexation was the least characteristic mode of expansion. Rarely between 1760 and 1870 was the acquisition of territory conceived as a thing desirable in itself. Only in the history of British India did policy, at that time, dictate aggressive wars, and even then annexations were reluctantly made, as a last resort, after every form of alliance, protectorate, and indirect rule had been attempted. But the history of British India is a strange and transient phase in world affairs, as unprecedented in its end as in its beginning.

The great partitions of Africa and Asia were also episodic, a by-product of diplomatic rivalries in Europe. Loudly condemned by large sections of the politically conscious, the partitions were approved by the majority whom the expansion of trade, settlement, and finance had inspired with a short-lived enthusiasm for empire. The pressure of surplus capital seeking an outlet, in spite of the classic thesis of Hobson and his pupil, Lenin, is a quite inadequate explanation, if only because the partition took place in the lull (1884–1904) between two phases of copious investment overseas, not at the apex but at the trough of the curve.

Another mode of expansion may yet prove more lasting than trade, finance, or annexation. 'There is an Empire', said Macaulay in 1833, 'exempt from all natural causes of decay, the imperishable empire of our arts and our morals, our literature and our laws.' At every trading-station in the world the British commercial colony became, more or less consciously, a centre of British culture, not because there was an intention to propagate it, but because all other nations wanted to share the benefits of British industrial supremacy. Macaulay's minute on education would have been written in vain if the *babus* of Bengal had not been determined to learn the language of the masters of India. In a more debased form even than babu-English the language of the nation of shop-keepers spread along the shipping-routes until, in all the ports of the Old World from Sierra Leone to Tientsin, pidgin-English became the *lingua franca*. Britain really ruled the waves when half the world's sea-going trade sailed under the Red Ensign and the other half was equally dependent on British cable-stations, British coaling-stations, and the use of a few corrupted words from the English language.

Industrial civilisation is highly infectious. All nations, from the polished Chinese to the primitive Central Africans, agreed in recognising it as an advantage which the white men from the West should not be allowed to monopolise. The simplest savage, having once seen the technical accomplishments of the trader, can soon discover that the secret of the white man's magic lies in book-learning. And the same age that brought the trader brought the missionary; in many instances the latter came first and penetrated farthest. Whatever else they achieved, one thing is certain; the Protestant missionaries everywhere founded schools at which some instruction was given in reading the English Bible. For many millions of the most intelligent boys and girls of half the world, the mission school was, and is, the first means of approach to Western civilisation. There only can they learn English, the first step for the few who can aspire to technical, scientific, or political progress. In this respect the English-speaking mission-aries, in the nineteenth century, staked out a claim for British ideals over the most populous regions in the world. The English language is spreading more rapidly than ever before and may in time become, perhaps in some rationalised form, the universal means of communication, carrying with it some notions that are implicit in its vocabulary.

The British national economy that expanded by the five simultaneous processes of settlement, trade, finance, annexation and linguistic influence was not the creation of political planners, but the outcome of a national unity of purpose. Colonial reformers, exporting merchants, bankers, investors, planters, technicians, governors, naval and military officers, teachers, missionaries, all alike were members of one body, with no hierarchical organisation, but the closest contexture of habits, customs, morals, virtues, prejudices. Wherever they went, and they went everywhere, the British maintained their integrity, carrying with them certain firm habits of mind; a high standard of commercial morality, a distrust of absolute or totalitarian doctrine, an addiction to law and order without militarism, to comfort rather than luxury, to utility rather than art. Throughout the Great Century the secret of British power was the solidarity of this admirable governing class, an aristocracy that never refused admission to talent, that combined the most audacious independence in action with the strictest adherence to old English manners and morals, that never lost confidence in itself, never (and this marks the change that has taken place in our own generation) lost faith in its duty to lead the world.

But leadership did not imply the imposition upon other races of British social formulas. Unlike the melting-pot of the American Republic where immigrants of all nations were assimilated into a new nationality, the British Commonwealth was a diversity, a mosaic of plural societies which could preserve their own formulas, as did *canadiens*, Afrikaners, Maltese, Sinhalese, Malays, without losing the advantage of membership in the greater polity. In this sense the plural Dominions, Canada and South Africa, are intermediate between the settlement colonies and the colonies by conquest. The genius of the Empire worked to build up groups of small units into larger states and confederations, by means of a great variety of constitutional devices. The sovereignty of the Crown (which, without intending disrespect, I describe as the most fertile and admirable of all legal fictions) thus renewed its value, generation after generation, in innumerable combinations of circumstance; and hardly less valuable has been the Law of Trust.

Sir Ernest Barker has pointed out[1] a distinction at law, between two types of colony, that is at least as old as Blackstone. In the colonies by settlement, the colonists were presumed by the lawyers to 'carry the common law with them' and to enjoy all its privileges, including some form of representative government. In the colonies by conquest or cession, the 'despotic power of legislation' nominally exercised by the Crown meant in legal practice that the colonies were protected by the rules of equity. Officials who went to the colonies of this order carried the law of trust with them 'as part of the stock-in-trade of their minds'. And the principle of trusteeship, an essentially temporary status, suggested an eventual relinquishing of the trust when the wards of court should reach maturity.

We are now in a position to survey the British Commonwealth and Empire which may be imagined as a system of three con-

[1] *Ideas and Ideals of Empire*, 1941.

centric rings. The inner ring, the colonies of settlement, are mature communities with formed characters, as stable a group of nations as any in the unstable twentieth century. The second ring, the colonies by conquest or cession, are, one and all, in a period of rapid, evolutionary change. Their former status of wardship to a British trustee is everywhere being modified. Like adolescents demanding a latch-key, the politically conscious in every colony call for the final dissolution of the trusts; the guardian power responds with the prudent deliberation imposed by a sense of duty. Changes of status may carry several more of these colonial dependencies outside the second ring, beyond British political control but hardly beyond the outermost third ring, the indefinable zone pervaded by the British tradition, the empire of linguistic influence. Wherever the tongue of Milton and Shakespeare is understood, voices will bear witness for individualism, even for eccentricity, for a belief in the efficacy of tolerance and compromise, for a sense of liberty based on common-law rights, above all for the untranslatable spirit of fair play which is so different from abstract justice. Here is an Empire which still has great benefits to offer freely to the world.

We have long been accustomed to think that the Empire was united by something called 'loyalty' and, at a time when the function of the Crown is being modified, it may be worth while to examine this concept more precisely. For loyalty has been much misunderstood; it is a word rich in overtones. To the conservative Englishman it smacks of historic associations, the last enchantments of the Middle Ages, mutual duties in a stratified society, the Crown in its feudal setting of nobility and gentry, pomp and circumstance, the Court of St James, the College of Heralds, the Horse Guards in their panoply. In the Dominions the radical has no natural fondness but rather a lurking, perhaps unconscious, sense of hostility for these relics, which belong to Old England but not to him. Returning from a visit to London, a little ashamed at the romantic stirrings in his heart, he reacts against all that affectation. The paradox never yet understood by the English governing class was the combination of colonial loyalty with colonial democracy, since loyalty has a different connotation for the British overseas. 'Many native-born Australians', says a recent writer,[1] 'combine intense nostalgia for one of

[1] *Times Literary Supplement*, 1 January 1948.

the three kingdoms, and pride in British values, with abhorrence of the British class and industrial structure and intense suspicion of the machinations of the British Government.' The Crown has been a symbol of unity not because of its feudal traditions but because it escaped from them. Long before English radicals admitted it, radicals in the Dominions knew that the Crown would preserve the unity of the Commonwealth, although its accessories were obstacles to that unity.

Men are ruled by myths and may be judged by the nobility or baseness of the myths they create or accept. The British myth accreted round the legend of the Great White Queen who dispensed impartial justice, in the last resort, to so many nations during the sixty years of her reign. A cynic might object that the myth survived only because the actual interventions of the Crown (through the Secretary of State) were so rare as not to have much effect. But the power of the myth was, and is, an unchallengeable fact which endures because the myth enshrines a truth. The Crown, presiding with Olympian calm and unforgetting patience over Radicals and Tories, whites and blacks, governors and governed, intervening only to check some grave abuse, was the focal centre of the system and a wholly beneficent force. Without it the governing class might have deteriorated, and become as rapacious as the Senate of Rome. Above all the Crown was the symbol of peace.

The imposition of peace and the rule of law bring benefits that are easily overlooked. When possessed, these blessings are enjoyed unconsciously like the air we breathe; when lost, a generation too corrupt to regret the loss must soon arise. Let it be recorded that, for several generations, the British imposed the rule of law, by the authority of the Crown, upon one-quarter of mankind, while they used its mighty influence for peaceful commerce among all nations.

C. E. C.

November 1949

Patet quod genus humanum in quiete sive tranquillitate pacis ad proprium suum opus, quod fere divinum est, liberrime atque facillime se habet. Unde manifestum est, quod pax universalis est optimum eorum, quae ad nostrum beatitudinem ordinantur. Hinc est quod pastoribus de sursum sonuit, non divitiae, non voluptates, non honores, non longitudo vitae, non sanitas, non robur, non pulchritudo; sed PAX.

APPENDIX I

RULERS OF THE COLONIES

DATE	PRIME MINISTER	SECRETARY OF STATE	PERMANENT UNDER-SECRETARY
₆8	Duke of Grafton	Lord Hillsborough	
70	North		
72		Lord Dartmouth ⎱ for the American	
75–82		Lord G. Germain ⎰ Department	
		(afterwards Lord Sackville)	
₇82 Feb.	Rockingham	(American Department abolished by Burke. Until 1801, colonial affairs were usually referred to the Secretary of State for the Home Department)	
82 July	Shelburne		
₇83 Feb.	Portland (Coalition of Fox and North)		
83 Dec.	Pitt		
₀1	Addington (Tory)	Lord Hobart	S. of S. for War and the Colonies
₈04	Pitt (Tory)	Lord Camden	,,
₈05		Lord Castlereagh	,,
₈06	Grenville (Coalition)	W. Windham	,,
₈07	Portland (Tory)	Lord Castlereagh	,,
₈09	Perceval (Tory)	Lord Liverpool	,,
₁12	Liverpool (Tory)	Lord Bathurst	,,
₈27	Canning (Liberal Tory)	F. Robinson (later Viscount Goderich)	,, 1825 R. W. Hay
₈27	Goderich (Liberal Tory)	W. Huskisson	,,
₈28	Wellington (Tory)	Sir G. Murray	,,
₈30	2nd Earl Grey (Whig)	Viscount Goderich	,,
₈33		E. Stanley (later 14th Earl of Derby)	,,
₈34 July	Melbourne (Whig)	T. Spring-Rice	,,
₈34 Dec.	Peel (Conservative)	Lord Aberdeen	,,
₈35	Melbourne (Whig)	Lord Glenelg	,,
₈39		Lord Normanby	,, 1836 (Sir) J. Stephen
₈39		Lord John Russell	,,
₈41	Peel (Conservative)	Lord Stanley (later 14th Earl of Derby)	,,
₈45		W. E. Gladstone	,,
₈46	Russell (Whig)	Henry 3rd Earl Grey	,,
₈52 Feb.	Derby, 14th Earl of (Conservative)	Sir J. Pakington	,, 1847 H. Merivale
₈52 Dec.	Aberdeen (Coalition)	Duke of Newcastle	,,
		(1854 War Office separated from Colonial Office)	
₈54	Aberdeen (Coalition)	Sir G. Grey of Fallodon	H. Merivale
₈55 Feb.	Palmerston (Whig)	Sydney Herbert	
₈55 May		Lord J. Russell	
₈55 July		Sir W. Molesworth	
₈55 Nov.		H. Labouchere	

DATE	PRIME MINISTER	SECRETARY OF STATE	PERMANENT UNDER-SECRETARY
1858 Feb.	14th Earl of Derby (Conservative)	Lord Stanley (later 15th Earl of Derby)	
1858 May		Sir E. B. Lytton (later Lord Lytton)	
1859	Palmerston (Coalition)	Duke of Newcastle	1859 Sir F. Rogers (Lord Blachford)
1864		E. Cardwell	
1865	Russell (Liberal)	E. Cardwell	
1866	14th Earl of Derby (Conservative)	Lord Carnarvon	
1867		Duke of Buckingham	
1868 Feb.	Disraeli (Conservative)	Duke of Buckingham	
1868 Dec.	Gladstone (Liberal)	Lord Granville	
1870		Lord Kimberley	
			1871 Sir R. Herbert
1874	Disraeli (Conservative)	Lord Carnarvon	
1878		Sir M. Hicks-Beach	
1880	Gladstone (Liberal)	Lord Kimberley	
1882		15th Earl of Derby	
1885	Salisbury (Conservative)	F. A. Stanley (afterwards 16th Earl of Derby)	
1886 Feb.	Gladstone (Liberal)	Lord Granville	
1886 Aug.	Salisbury (Conservative)	E. Stanhope	
1887		Lord Knutsford	
1892	Gladstone (Liberal)	Lord Ripon	1892 Sir R. Meade
1894	Rosebery (Liberal)	Lord Ripon	
1895	Salisbury (Unionist)	J. Chamberlain	
			1897 Sir E. Wingfield
			1900 Sir M. Ommanney
1902	Balfour (Unionist)	J. Chamberlain	
1903		A. Lyttelton	
1906	Campbell-Bannerman (Liberal)	Lord Elgin	
			1907 Sir F. Hopwood
1908	Asquith (Liberal)	Lord Crewe	
1910		L. Harcourt	
			1911 Sir J. Anderson
1915	Asquith (Coalition)	Bonar Law	
1916	Lloyd George (Coalition)	Walter Long	1916 Sir G. Fiddes
1919		Lord Milner	
1921		Winston Churchill	1921 Sir J. Masterton-Smith
1922	Bonar Law (Conservative)	Duke of Devonshire	
1922	Baldwin (Conservative)		
1924 Jan.	MacDonald (Socialist)	J. H. Thomas	
1924 Nov.	Baldwin (Conservative)	L. S. Amery	
			1925 Sir S. Wilson
(1925 Dominions Office founded)			
1929	MacDonald (Socialist)	Lord Passfield	
1931 Aug.		J. H. Thomas	
1931 Nov.	MacDonald (Coalition)	Sir P. Cunliffe-Lister	
		(J. H. Thomas, Dominions S. of S.)	
			1933 Sir J. Maffey
1935 June	Baldwin (Coalition)	M. MacDonald	
1935 Nov.	Baldwin (Conservative)	J. H. Thomas	
1936 May	N. Chamberlain (Conservative)	W. Ormsby-Gore (Lord Harlech)	

DATE	PRIME MINISTER	SECRETARY OF STATE	PERMANENT UNDER-SECRETARY
			1937 Sir C. Parkinson
1938 May		M. MacDonald	
			1939 Sir G. Gater
			1940 Sir C. Parkinson
1940	Churchill (Coalition)	1940 Lord Lloyd	
		1941 Feb. Lord Moyne	
		1942 Feb. Lord Cranborne	
		1942 Nov. Oliver Stanley[1]	1942 Sir G. Gater
1945	Attlee (Socialist)	1945 Aug. G. H. Hall	
		1946 Oct. A. Creech-Jones	
		1950 James Griffiths	

[1] E. G. S. Stanley, 14th Earl of Derby was Colonial Secretary in the Whig Government of 1833 and again in the Tory Government of 1841. Later he was twice Prime Minister. His son, E. H. S. Stanley, the 15th Earl was Colonial Secretary in his father's second Conservative administration of 1858. He joined the Liberals in 1879 and was Colonial Secretary again in Gladstone's second administration, 1882–5. He handed over the seals to his conservative brother and heir. Mr Oliver Stanley is a grandson of the 16th Earl.

APPENDIX II *a*

EXPORTS, 1854–1934

Annual exports from the United Kingdom, from 1854 to 1934, estimated in thousands of pounds sterling. Gold and silver bullion and coin are excluded. Graph A shows exports to British countries, Graph B to all countries. (Based upon statistical abstracts issued by the Board of Trade.)

N.B. The figures for 1919–20 were inflated by the sudden removal of war-time controls.

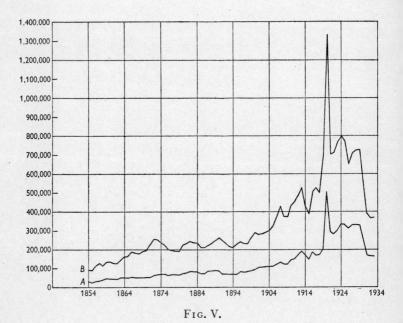

F IG . V.

APPENDIX II*b*

IMPORTS, 1854–1934

Annual imports into the United Kingdom, from 1854 to 1934, presented on the same scale as the exports (Appendix II*a*). Graph A shows imports from British countries, Graph B imports from all countries.

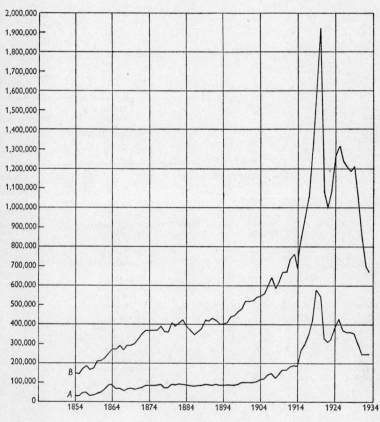

FIG. VI.

APPENDIX III

A GOVERNING-CLASS PEDIGREE

In a hundred years, the families of Bruce, Lambton, Grey, and Baring produced four Viceroys of India, three Governors-General of Canada, and three Secretaries of State for the Colonies.

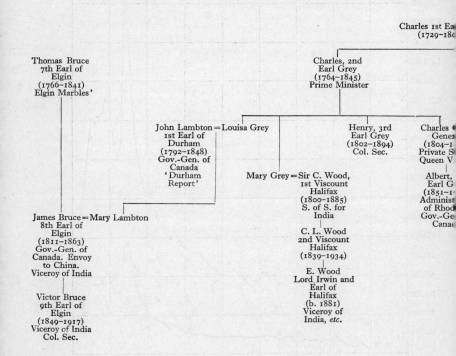

Charles 1st Ea
(1729–18(

Thomas Bruce
7th Earl of
Elgin
(1766–1841)
Elgin Marbles'

Charles, 2nd
Earl Grey
(1764–1845)
Prime Minister

John Lambton = Louisa Grey
1st Earl of
Durham
(1792–1848)
Gov.-Gen. of
Canada
'Durham
Report'

Henry, 3rd
Earl Grey
(1802–1894)
Col. Sec.

Charles
Gener
(1804–1
Private S
Queen V

Mary Grey = Sir C. Wood,
1st Viscount
Halifax
(1800–1885)
S. of S. for
India

Albert,
Earl G
(1851–1
Administ
of Rhod
Gov.-Ge
Canad

C. L. Wood
2nd Viscount
Halifax
(1839–1934)

James Bruce = Mary Lambton
8th Earl of
Elgin
(1811–1863)
Gov.-Gen. of
Canada. Envoy
to China.
Viceroy of India

E. Wood
Lord Irwin and
Earl of
Halifax
(b. 1881)
Viceroy of
India, etc.

Victor Bruce
9th Earl of
Elgin
(1849–1917)
Viceroy of India
Col. Sec.

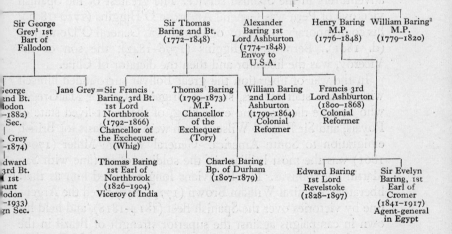

Franz Baring of Bremen
Lutheran Minister
|
Johann Baring
(1697–1748)
came to England 1717
|
Sir Francis Baring
1st Bart. (1740–1810)
founder of Baring Bros. and Co.

Sir George Grey[1] 1st Bart of Fallodon

Sir Thomas Baring 2nd Bt. (1772–1848)

Alexander Baring 1st Lord Ashburton (1774–1848) Envoy to U.S.A.

Henry Baring M.P. (1776–1848)

William Baring[2] M.P. (1779–1820)

George 2nd Bt. lodon —1882) Sec.

. Grey —1874)

dward 3rd Bt. 1st unt lodon —1933) gn Sec.

Jane Grey = Sir Francis Baring, 3rd Bt. 1st Lord Northbrook (1792–1866) Chancellor of the Exchequer (Whig)

Thomas Baring (1799–1873) M.P. Chancellor of the Exchequer (Tory)

William Baring 2nd Lord Ashburton (1799–1864) Colonial Reformer

Francis 3rd Lord Ashburton (1800–1868) Colonial Reformer

Thomas Baring 1st Earl of Northbrook (1826–1904) Viceroy of India

Charles Baring Bp. of Durham (1807–1879)

Edward Baring 1st Lord Revelstoke (1828–1897)

Sir Evelyn Baring, 1st Earl of Cromer (1841–1917) Agent-general in Egypt

eorge Grey, K.C.M.G. (1812–1898), the colonial governor, was of another family.
m Baring married Frances, sister of C. Poulett-Thompson, Lord Sydenham, Governor-General of Canada, 1839–41.

APPENDIX IV

THE BRITISH IN SOUTH AMERICA

THE following notes are mostly drawn from *The English in South America*, written and published in the Argentine in 1878, by M. G. Mulhall, the editor of an English newspaper at Buenos Ayres. He gives particulars of more than 1300 persons of British origin who distinguished themselves in South American affairs, beginning with Sebastian Cabot who, he alleges, named the River Plate in 1525. After describing the exploits of the buccaneers, the author discusses at length the careers of the Irish and Scottish adventurers in the Spanish service. The greatest of the Spanish viceroys of Peru was General Ambrose O'Higgins (1720–1801); his contemporary as viceroy of Mexico was General O'Donoghue (d. 1801). Bernard O'Higgins (1776–1842), the son of the Viceroy, was the liberator and then the dictator of Chile.

In the war of liberation the great Bolivar surrounded himself with British staff officers, such as Brigadier Gregor MacGregor who became dictator, and even king, of the short-lived state of Poyais, and Sir Belford Wilson; both were enthusiasts for British emigration to South America. General William Miller (1795–1861) was the most brilliant of the soldiers of fortune with San Martin and Bolivar. The Peruvians long regarded him as their liberator. Admiral William Brown (1777–1857) freed the Argentine by victories over the Spanish fleet (1814–1818), and held his own in campaigns against the superior strength of Brazil in the war of 1826. Sir T. Cochrane's exploits on the Pacific Coast, in co-operation with General Miller, set Chile free. After fighting for Peru and Brazil, and quarrelling with all his employers, Cochrane transferred his sword to the cause of the Greek patriots for a consideration of £37,000 paid in advance (see p. 474).

The ill-fated expeditions to Buenos Ayres in 1807 (see p. 246) turned the attention of many soldiers of fortune to South America. MacGregor volunteered to serve with Bolivar as early as 1813 and, after Waterloo, five distinct bodies of British volunteers, amounting to at least 5000 soldiers—many of them

Peninsular veterans—sailed to South America (1817–19). Very many died and few returned to Europe.

Long before that time Englishmen had settled in the Spanish and Portuguese colonies in spite of the laws designed to exclude them. Mulhall names several west-country merchants established in Brazil in the sixteenth century. In the eighteenth they managed gold-mines and diamond-mines. One of the first Jesuits to go to Paraguay (1586) was the Scottish Father Fields. The most eminent explorer among the Paraguayan Jesuits was Father Falkner (*fl.* 1740).

By the eighteen-twenties a flourishing British colony existed at the River Plate. Mulhall ascribes its origin to survivors from the crew of a buccaneer named Macnamara whose ship was lost in 1765. The Irish names of Sarsfield and Carrol, long known in Buenos Ayres, may date from that time. At least there were enough British merchants to found a Chamber of Commerce in 1811, a Bank in 1822, a packet-service to England in 1824, a chaplaincy in 1825, a newspaper in 1826, and a school in 1827. The Buenos Ayres *Guide* (1829) lists 49 British (or American) commercial houses and about 100 other tradesmen or professional men.

In 1825 Mr J. P. Robertson planted a colony of 300 Scottish settlers at Monte Grande, fifteen miles from Buenos Ayres. Though the settlement was dispersed in the wars, the Scots remained in the country and multiplied until their numbers were estimated in 1878 to be 2000 in Buenos Ayres alone. The first Scottish Church dates from 1838. Irish emigrants began to come in about 1830. Peter Sheridan, an Irish gentleman, and J. P. Robertson were the founders of the sheep-farming industry in the Argentine. The most distinguished Irishman in the country was the saintly Father Fahy (1804–71), founder of schools, libraries and convents. The British in the Argentine, according to Mulhall, numbered 30,000 in 1878. The excellent relations between Great Britain and the Argentine (occasionally marred by the unresolved dispute over the Falkland Islands) date from Woodbine Parish's treaty of 1825, which granted to Great Britain special advantages for a mail-packet service and declared a general agreement of friendship, commerce and navigation, with free trade and religious toleration for British merchants.

Similar British settlements were made around Montevideo in Uruguay where many of the largest *estancias*, such as the celebrated Fray Bentos estate, were owned by English and Scottish sheep-farmers in the eighteen-twenties. The greatest of them was Samuel Lafone, a Jerseyman, who began the development of the Falkland Islands. He claimed to have brought the first steamship to the River Plate in 1824. Chile too had its English pioneers. J. Waddington (d. 1876) made Valparaiso into a modern commercial port. Augustine Edwards (b. 1816), the son of Dr George Edwards, who settled in Chile in 1805, was the founder of an influential banking house.

Many attempts were made in the age of colonisation to plant colonies in South America by means of Land Companies. Among the few which succeeded was the Welsh colony at Chubut in Patagonia.

The first impetus came from the Rev. M. D. Jones of Bala Theological College who deplored the fact that Welshmen in America and the colonies lost their native tongue. After sites in Canada, Australia and New Zealand had been rejected, apparently because the colonial governments would not grant autonomy, Patagonia was selected as an empty, unoccupied land. The site was chosen after a reconnaissance, in 1862, by Sir L. J. Parry of Madryn Castle, David Williams of Carnarvon, and others, with the help of Dr William Rawson the President of the Argentine, who was of North American origin and whose name was given to the principal settlement. He agreed to allow fifty square miles of territory in the undeveloped southern plains for every 200 Welsh families introduced, and to provide them with maintenance during the early stages. It was supposed that their task would be to wage war against the fierce Araucanian Indians, but the Welsh succeeded in coming to friendly terms with them. Like all other colonial projectors the founders of Chubut much over-estimated their capabilities. The first batch of colonists, numbering 132, with the Rev. Lewis Humphreys as chaplain and with William Davis as 'president', sailed from Liverpool in 1865 and landed on an open beach which they called Madryn. They developed a new province in virgin territory fifty miles inland and were particularly successful at irrigation, but by 1878 their numbers were no more than 690. They were treated liberally by the Government of the Argentine. When A. F. Tschiffely (*This Way Southward*) visited the Chubut Valley in 1933, he found four hundred Welsh homesteads and half a million acres of irrigated wheatland. The settlers still spoke Welsh, while English, their second language, was giving way to Spanish.

Other colonising schemes, such as the Alexandra Company in the Gran Chaco (1870), the Paraguayan Colony of Robinson and Fleming (1872), and William Lane's communist experiment (see p. 599), failed miserably. The Land and Emigration Commission in England was largely concerned with dissuading emigrants from supporting such bubble schemes as these, and with diverting them to Australia.

Mulhall mentions more than a hundred British explorers and scientific investigators in South America, among whom the names of Charles Darwin, Charles Waterton, A. R. Wallace, H. W. Bates, and W. H. Hudson are the most familiar. J. and M. Clark who surveyed the route for the Trans-Andine railway, and Captain L. B. Wyse who surveyed the route for the Panama Canal may also be worthy of remembrance. The part played by British engineers, contractors, and projectors in South American mines, harbour works, roads, railways, and other public utilities is far too large for discussion here. At least four distinct parties of Cornish miners, in addition to Robert Stephenson's, were taken to the Andes between 1818 and 1826. But the two great constructional engineers in the age of steam were North Americans by birth, William Wheelwright (1798–1873) and Henry Meiggs. The mountain railways of Peru were designed by Meiggs in 1870–2 and built with money lent (and lost) in London. Wheelwright comes more directly into the story, since he frequently visited England and died there. All his schemes were financed in England and were carried out by English contractors. His was the first steamer to reach Valparaiso, in 1840, and he and Brassey built the trunk railways of the Argentine between 1863 and 1870. He founded the (British) Pacific Steam Navigation Company.

According to Mulhall's estimate, imports from Great Britain to South America in 1875 were worth £15,200,000; exports to Great Britain were worth £18,580,000. British capital investments in South America amounted to £130,000,000 of which £36,000,000 was held at the River Plate, £35,000,000 in Peru, £31,000,000 in Brazil, and £12,000,000 in Chile.

MAPS

Gall's Projection

MAP I   1053

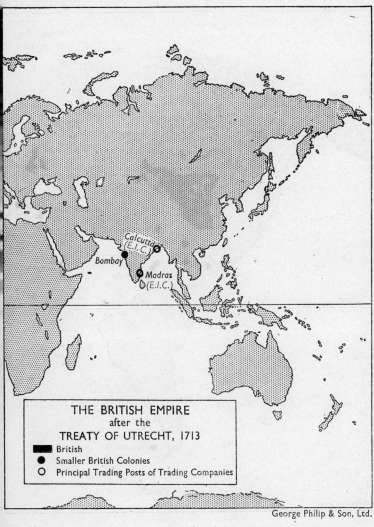

THE BRITISH EMPIRE
after the
TREATY OF UTRECHT, 1713

■ British
● Smaller British Colonies
○ Principal Trading Posts of Trading Companies

Calcutta
(E.I.C.)

Bombay

Madras
(E.I.C.)

George Philip & Son, Ltd.

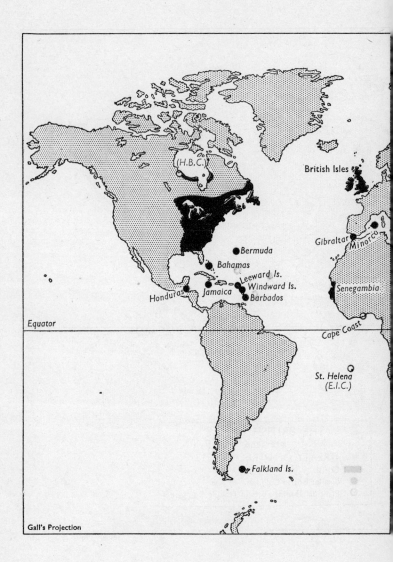

MAP II   1055

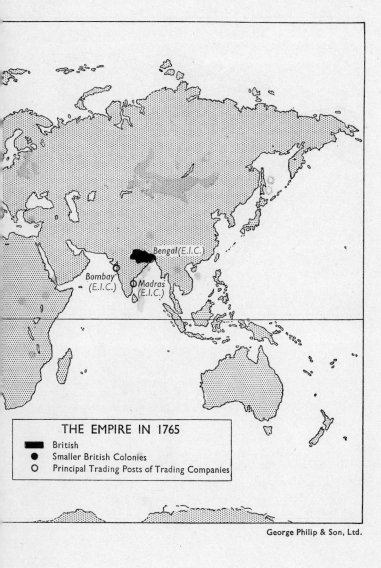

Bengal (E.I.C.)

Bombay
(E.I.C.)

Madras
(E.I.C.)

THE EMPIRE IN 1765

British
Smaller British Colonies
Principal Trading Posts of Trading Companies

George Philip & Son, Ltd.

Gall's Projection

MAP III 1057

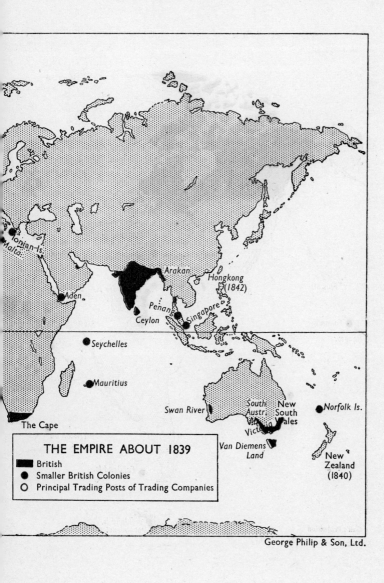

Ionian Is.
Malta

Aden

Arakan

Hongkong
(1842)

Penang
Singapore

Ceylon

Seychelles

Mauritius

Swan River

South
Austr.
Victoria
New
South
Wales

Norfolk Is.

The Cape

Van Diemens
Land

New
Zealand
(1840)

THE EMPIRE ABOUT 1839

British
Smaller British Colonies
Principal Trading Posts of Trading Companies

George Philip & Son, Ltd.

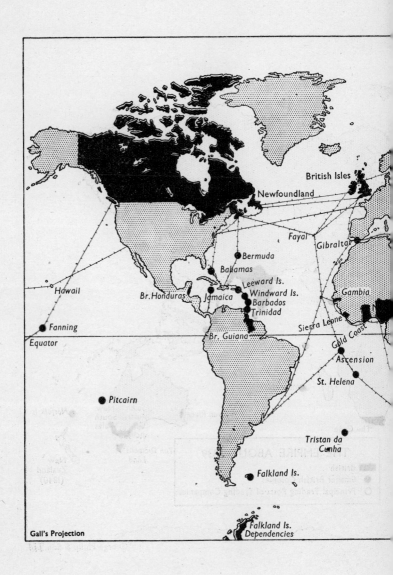

British Isles

Newfoundland

Fayal

Gibraltar

Bermuda

Bahamas

Leeward Is.

Hawaii

Br.Honduras   Jamaica

Windward Is.

Barbados

Trinidad

Gambia

Fanning

Sierra Leone

Br. Guiana

Gold Coast

Equator

Ascension

St. Helena

Pitcairn

Tristan da Cunha

Falkland Is.

Gall's Projection

Falkland Is.
Dependencies

MAP IV   1059

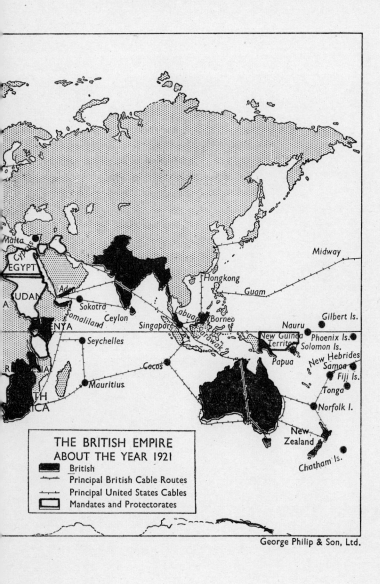

THE BRITISH EMPIRE
ABOUT THE YEAR 1921
British
Principal British Cable Routes
Principal United States Cables
Mandates and Protectorates

George Philip & Son, Ltd.

INDEX

Figures in bold type after personal names denote a main entry